IJCAI-91

Proceedings of the Twelfth International Conference on Artificial Intelligence

Volume 1

Darling Harbour, Sydney, Australia

24–30 August 1991

Sponsored by the
International Joint Conferences on Artificial Intelligence, Inc. (IJCAII)
Co-sponsored and hosted by the
National Committee on Artificial Intelligence and Expert Systems (NCAIES) of the Australian Computer Society (ACS)
With support and cooperation from the
Australian Government and Other Australian Corporations and Institutions

Edited by John Mylopoulos and Ray Reiter.

Distributed by Morgan Kaufmann Publishers, Inc.
2929 Campus Drive, Suite 260
San Mateo, California 94403 USA

Printed in Singapore

BRIEF CONTENTS

VOLUME 1

VOLUME 2

ORDERING INFORMATION

The following is a list of proceedings of IJCAI conferences available from Morgan Kaufmann Publishers. To place an order or receive information regarding these and other Morgan Kaufmann publications, please use the following address:

Morgan Kaufmann Publishers, Inc.
2929 Campus Drive, Suite 260
San Mateo, California 94403 USA
Telephone: (415) 578-9911; FAX (415) 578-0672

To order, please send a US$ check or money order, or provide credit card debit authorization for Visa, MasterCard, or American Express (include name on card, card number, expiry date, etc.) Shipping and Handling: US & Canada—for surface post, include $3.50 for the first volume and $2.50 for each additional volume; for international surface post, include $6.50 for the first volume and $2.50 for each additional volume. California residents, add appropriate tax. Be sure to provide your full shipping address.

Lower price listed below available to IJCAI conference registrants and members of national/regional AI societies only.

IJCAI-89
Detroit, Michigan
2 volumes, ISBN 1-55860-094-9
$75/$56.25

IJCAI-87
Milan, Italy
2 volumes; ISBN 0-934613-43-5
$65/$48.75

IJCAI-85
Los Angeles, California
2 volumes; ISBN 0-934613-02-8
$65/$48.75

IJCAI-83
Karlsruhe, West Germany
2 volumes; ISBN 0-934613-043-4
$65/$48.75

IJCAI-81
Vancouver, British Columbia
2 volumes; ISBN 0-934613-044-2
$65/$48.75

IJCAI-79
Tokyo, Japan
2 volumes; ISBN 0-934613-47-8
$65/$48.75

IJCAI-77
Cambridge, Massachusetts
2 volumes; ISBN 0-934613-48-6
$65/$48.75

IJCAI-75
Tbilisi, Georgia USSR
ISBN 0-934613-20-6
$65/$48.75

IJCAI-73
Stanford, California
ISBN 0-934613-58-3
$65/$48.75

IJCAI-71
London, England
ISBN 0-934613-34-6
$65/$48.75

IJCAI-69
Washington, D.C.
ISBN 0-934613-21-4
$65/$48.75

IJCAI 11-Year Set
1969–1989
14 volumes; ISBN 1-55860-139-2
$550/$412.50

IJCAI-89 and -91 VIDEOTAPE PROGRAMS: Short video programs selected by the video committee give an excellent overview of current applications involving AI technology in robotics, vision, language, planning, modeling, design, control, computer-aided instruction, expert systems, and diagnosis. The tapes are 2-hours in running time. NTSC-VHS or PAL-VHS, 1/2-inch formats available. Shipping in US/Canada: $3.50 per tape; international: $10.00.

1991 Video: ISBN 1-55860-183-X; $66.50/$49.88

1989 Video: ISBN 1-55860-097-3; $66.50/$49.88

European and Australian/New Zealand customers preferring to order locally may do so. Contact the following Morgan Kaufmann offices. (Prices may vary from above; please inquire as to pricing, availability, and shipping requirements)

UK/EUROPE: Morgan Kaufmann-UK, Afterhurst, Ltd., 27 Palmeira Mansions, Church Road, Hove, East Sussex BN3 2FA, UK; Telephone: (0273) 207 259; FAX: (0273) 205 612

AUSTRALASIA: Morgan Kaufmann-Australia: Astam Books Pty, Ltd. 162-168 Parramatta Road, Stanmore, NSW 2048 Australia, Telephone: (02) 550 3855; FAX: (02) 550 3860

FOREWORD

Chairing the IJCAI-91 program committee did have its rewards, one of which was seeing these proceedings through to their completion. The generous contributions of hundreds of AI researchers—authors, reviewers as well as program committee members—made it all possible. We can all take pride in the community effort leading up to this collection of papers, which represents the best of contemporary AI research worldwide.

Another reward that came with the responsibilities of the program committee chair was a privileged, bird's eye view of AI around the world. Based on our experiences over the past two years, we are convinced that today more than ever before, AI has extremely high research standards. Statistics speak eloquently on this point. This year, out of more than 970 submitted papers, only 185 were accepted by the IJCAI-91 program committee. This translates to a success ratio of 19.1%, the lowest in recent IJCAI history. The authors of papers in these proceedings can be justifiably proud of their achievement.

Over the years, international participation in IJCAI has been a source of much of its vitality. This year, we are pleased to note a very broad geographic representation in the conference program, with a total of 23 countries represented.

As one would expect, interests within the AI community have been shifting, not always in a predictable fashion. Current foci of research interests in the field are reflected in the following table, which provides a breakdown by area of the papers in the proceedings:

Area	Number of Papers
Architectures and Languages	14
Automated Reasoning	36
Cognitive Modeling	6
Knowledge Representation	25
Learning and Knowledge Acquisition	37
Logic Programming	9
Natural Language	19
Philosophical Foundations	6
Principles of AI Applications	4
Qualitative Reasoning	16
Robotics	5
Vision	8

This year, the program committee made a special effort to increase participation from research areas that have been drifting away from IJCAI to more specialized conferences. We hope that our successors will continue these efforts. AI started as a coherent discipline; it should be discouraged from becoming a collection of isolated research areas.

We can't begin to personally thank everyone who contributed to the conference program, but we do wish to single out a few for special mention. Barbara Grosz, the conference chair, was a joy to work with. We could always count on her for sound advice, cheerfully given. Don Walker, IJCAII's secretary-treasurer and all-around corporate memory, had all the right answers at all the right times. Michael McRobbie, the boundlessly energetic chair of the Australian National Committee, made good use of that energy in attending to the logistics of putting on a conference of this size and scope.

A sizeable part of the IJCAI-91 program was the responsibility of the program subchairs. Our thanks for a job well done to Joe Katz, who handled IJCAI workshops; Peter Patel-Schneider, for putting together an excellent set of panels; Martha Pollack, the tutorial chair; and Alain Rappaport, for the conference video program. We are especially grateful that their heroic efforts were largely transparent to the program co-chairs.

Closer to home, Veronica Archibald and Marina Haloulos were always ready and willing to help out in a crunch. They saved the day for us more often than we can remember. Perhaps the greatest burden of all those working to put together the conference program fell on Kim Smith in her role as administrative assistant to the program committee. More than anyone else, she had the responsibility of putting it all together—maintaining contact with the program committee members, the authors, the publishers, the conference chair, the trustees, the program subchairs, the IJCAI advisory committee—it hardly seems possible in retrospect. She did a marvelous job, and we thank her for it.

Finally, John Mylopoulos thanks Ray Reiter, and Ray Reiter thanks John Mylopoulos for a 50% reduction in workload and blood pressure, and a 100% increase in good humor during the two years leading up to this conference.

John Mylopoulos

Ray Reiter

IJCAI-91 CONFERENCE ORGANIZATION

Conference Committee

Conference Chair
Barbara Grosz
Aiken Computation Lab 20
Harvard University
33 Oxford Street
Cambridge, MA 02138 USA

Australian National Committee Chair
Michael McRobbie
Centre for Information Science Research
Australian National University
I Block (Old Admin. area), GPO Box 4
Acton, Canberra ACT 2601 AUSTRALIA

Program Co-Chair
John Mylopoulos
Department of Computer Science
10 King's College Rd.
University of Toronto
Toronto, Ontario M5S 1A4 CANADA

Program Co-Chair
Ray Reiter
Department of Computer Science
10 King's College Rd.
University of Toronto
Toronto, Ontario M5S 1A4 CANADA

Secretary-Treasurer
Donald E. Walker
Bellcore, MRE 2A379
445 South Street, Box 1910
Morristown, NJ 07960-1910 USA

Advisory Committee

Daniel Bobrow, Xerox Palo Alto Research Center (USA); Mike Brady, Oxford University (England);
Francisco J. Cantu-Ortiz, ITESM (Mexico); Luigia Carlucci-Aiello, Universita di Roma (Italy);
Koichi Furukawa, ICOT (Japan); Henry Kautz, AT&T Bell Laboratories (USA); Margaret King, ISSCO (Switzerland);
Tomas Lozano-Perez, MIT (USA); Rolf Nossum, Agder College (Norway);
S. Ramani, National Centre for Software Technology (India); Lu Ruqian, Academia Sinica (PRC);
Enn Tyugu, Estonian Academy of Sciences (Estonia)

Programme Committee

Panel Chair: Peter Patel-Schneider, AT&T Bell Labs (USA)

Workshop Chair: Joe Katz, MITRE Corporation (USA)

Tutorial Chair: Martha Pollack, SRI International (USA)

Video Chair: Alain Rappaport, Neuron Data (USA)

Harlyn Baker, SRI International (USA); Francesco Bergadano, University of Torino (Italy);
Margaret Boden, University of Sussex (England); Rod Brooks, Massachusetts Institute of Technology (USA);
Dan Corkill, University of Massachusetts (USA); Rina Dechter, University of California at Los Angeles (USA);
Norman Foo, University of Sydney (Australia); Michael Georgeff, Australian AI Institute (Australia);
Barbara Hayes-Roth, Stanford University (USA); Peter de Jong, IBM, Cambridge Scientific Center (USA);
Yves Kodratoff, Université de Paris-Sud (France); Benjamin Kuipers, University of Texas at Austin (USA);
John Laird, University of Michigan (USA); Kurt Van Lehn, LRDC (USA);
Vladimir Lifschitz, University of Texas at Austin (USA); Yuji Matsumoto, Kyoto University (Japan);
Gordon McCalla, University of Saskatchewan (Canada); Jack Minker, University of Maryland (USA);
Jack Mostow, Rutgers University (USA); Makato Nagao, Kyoto University (Japan); Bernhard Nebel, DFKI (Germany);
Henri Prade, Université Paul Sabatier (France); Richard Rosenberg, University of British Columbia (Canada);
Pierre Siegel, Université de Provence—Centre Saint Charles (France); N.S. Sridharan, FMC Corporation (USA);
Mark Steedman, University of Pennsylvania (USA); Luc Steels, Vrije Universiteit Brussel (Belgium);
David Touretzky, Carnegie Mellon University (USA); John Tsotsos, University of Toronto (Canada);
Marc Vilain, MITRE Corporation (USA); Wolfgang Wahlster, Universität des Saarlandes (Germany)

Australian National Committee

Robin Stanton (Deputy Chair), Australian National University
John Davidson, Digital Equipment Corporation; John Debenham, University of Technology, Sydney;
Robin Erskine, Australian National University; Norman Foo, University of Sydney; Peter Gerrand, Telecom Australia;
Michael McRobbie, Australian National University; Helen Meredith, The Australian; Kevin Morris, IBM Australia;
John O'Callaghan, CSIRO; Paul Purnell, Andersen Consulting; Amy Rankin, IBM Australia;
Peter Slezak, The University of NSW; Len Spencer, Sydney; Noel Teede, Telecom Australia;
David Watson, Dept. of Industry, Technology & Commerce; Brian Wilson, Andersen Consulting

IJCAII ORGANIZATION

CORPORATE SPONSORSHIP

Principal Corporate Sponsor

IBM Australia Ltd.

Major Corporate Sponsors

Andersen Consulting

Commonwealth Department of Industry, Technology and Commerce

Telecom Australia

Corporate Sponsors

Australian Computing and Communications Institute

Australian National University

Commonwealth Bank

Digital Equipment Corporation (Australia) Pty Ltd.

Commonwealth Scientific and Industrial Research Organization (CSIRO),
Division of Information Technology

Defence Science and Technology Organization, Information Technology Division

NSW State Government

IJCAI-91 AWARDS

The IJCAI Award for Research Excellence
Marvin Minsky, MIT

The Computers and Thought Awards
Rodney Brooks, MIT
Martha Pollack, SRI International

IJCAI Distinguished Service Award
Woodrow Bledsoe, University of Texas at Austin

IJCAI-91 Outstanding Paper Prize
To be announced

INVITED SPEAKERS AND PANELS

Invited Speakers

Takeo Kanade, Carnegie Mellon University
Depth, Shape and Motion in Computer Vision: Old Problems and New Results

Robert A. Kowalski, Imperial College of Science, Technology and Medicine
Logic Programming in Artificial Intelligence

John Ross Quinlan, University of Sydney
Recent Research in Data-Driven Learning

Shigeru Sato, Fujitsu Laboratories, Ltd.
The Commercial and Industrial Impacts of Artificial Intelligence Internationally

Panels

The Role of Chess in Artificial Intelligence Research
Robert Levinson (Chair), University of California at Santa Cruz
Jonathan Schaeffer, University of Alberta
Feng-hsiung Hsu, IBM T.J. Watson Research Center
T. Anthony Marsland, University of Alberta
David E. Wilkins, SRI International

Multiple Approaches to Multiple Agent Problem Solving
James A. Hendler (Chair), University of Maryland
Danny Bobrow, Xerox Palo Alto Research Centers
Les Gasser, University of Southern California
Carl Hewitt, Massachusetts Institute of Technology
Marvin Minsky, Massachusetts Institute of Technology

AI in Telecommunications
Andrew Jennings (Chair), Telecom Australia Research Laboratories
Akira Kurematsu, ATR Interpreting Telephone Laboratories
Adam Irgon, Bell Communications Research
Greg Vessonder, AT&T Bell Laboratories
Jon R. Wright, AT&T Bell Laboratories

Massively Parallel Artificial Intelligence
Hiroaki Kitano (Chair), Carnegie Mellon University
Tetsuya Higuchi, Electrotechnical Laboratory, Japan
Dan Moldovan, University of Southern California
David Waltz, Thinking Machines Corporation
James Hendler, University of Maryland

AI and Design
Saul Amarel (Chair), Rutgers University
Louis Steinberg, Rutgers University
Alvin Despain, University of Southern California
Penny Nii, Stanford University
Marty Tenenbaum, Enterprise Integration Technologies Co., and Stanford University
Peter Will, Hewlett Packard Laboratories

IJCAI-91 REVIEWERS

Aarts, Emile H. L.
Abramson, Harvey
Acock, Malcolm
Addis, Tom R.
Adelson, Beth
Agha, Gul
Aiba, Akira
Aida, Hitoshi
Aloimonos, Yiannis
Anderson, John S.
Anjaneyulu, K.S.R.
Ashley, Kevin
Attardi, Giuseppe
Ayache, Nicholas
Baader, Franz
Bacchus, Fahiem
Backofen, Rolf
Badler, Norman
Bagchi, A.
Baldwin, James
Bareiss, Ray
Barnett, Jeff
Barth, Gerhard
Barto, Andrew G.
Bates, Madeline
Bauer, Matthias
Beldiceanu, N.
Bell, John
ben Eliahu, Rachel
Berenji, Hamid
Berleant, Daniel
Berstein, Jared
Berwick, Bob
Besnard, Philippe
Biederman, Irving
Birnbaum, Lawrence
Bisiani, Roberta
Blake, Andrew
Blicher, Peter
Bobick, Aaron
Bobrow, Daniel
Bobrow, Robert
Boddy, Mark
Bolles, Robert
Boose, John
Botta, Marco
Bowyer, Kevin
Boy, Guy
Bratko, Ivan
Brazdil, Pavel
Breucker, Joost
Brewka, Gerd
Brisset, P.
Brown, Chris
Brown, David C.
Bundy, Alan
Burchert, Hans-Jurgen
Burstein, Mark
Busch, Douglas
Buxton, Bernard
Caferra, Ricardo
Castaing, J.
Chandrasekar, Mickey
Chapman, David
Chien, Andrew A.
Cholvy, Laurence
Christian, Jim
Church, Ken
Clark, Andy
Clark, James
Clarke, Michael
Cohen, Paul
Cohen, Phil
Cohen, Robin
Collaviza, Heléne
Collin, Zeev
Collins, Gregg
Colmerauer, Alain
Connell, Jon
Conry, Susan
Console, Luca
Cooper, Gregory
Cottrell, Gary
Crawford, James
Crowley, Jim
Cuyper, Jo de
D'Ambrosio, Bruce
da Victoria Lobo, Niels
Dahl, Deborah
Dahl, Veronica
Dalal, Mukesh
Davidor, Yuval
Daviol, Jean-Marc
Davis, Ernst
De Jong, Kenneth A.
de Mantaras, Lopes
Dekleer, Johann
del Cerro, Luis Farinas
Delahaye, J.P.
Dengel, Andreas
Derthick, Mark
Dickmanns, Ernst
Dincbas, Mehmet
Dodhiawala, R.
Doerry, Eck
Dolan, Charles
Donald, Bruce
Doyle, Jon
Doyle, Richard
Drescher, Gary
Driankov, Dimiter
Drummond, Mark
du Boulay, Ben
Dubois, Didier
Durfee, Ed
Dvorak, Daniel L.
Dyer, Michael
Eklund, Peter
Eklundh, Jan-Olof
Elkan, Charles
Ellman, Thomas
Elsom-Cook, Mark
Erman, Lee D.
Esposito, Floriana
Etzioni, Oren
Fagin, Ronald
Fahlman, Scott E.
Falkenhainer, Brian
Faltings, Boi
Farquhar, Adam
Faugeras, Olivier
Fayyad, Usama
Feather, Martin
Fehling, Michael
Fehrer, D.
Feldman, Jerome A.
Feldman, Yishai
Fickas, Steve
Fikes, Richard
Finger, Susan
Finin, Tim
Firby, Jim
Fisher, Robert
Forbus, Ken
Forstner, Wolfgang
Franke, David
Franova, Marta
Freitag, Harmut
Freuder, Gene
Friedland, Peter
Friedman, Batya
Friedrich, Gerhard
Fuhrmann, Andre
Gaines, Brian R.
Gallinari, Patrick
Ganascia, Jean Gabriel
Gasser, Les
Geffner, Hector
Gelfond, Michael
Gelsey, Andrew
Ghallab, Malik
Gilmore, John F.
Giordana, Attilio
Goddard, Nigel
Golmard, Jean-Louis
Goodman, Brad
Goodwin, Scott
Gottlob, Georg
Greer, Jim
Grefenstette, John J.
Gregory, Steve
Greiner, Russel
Grégoire, Eric
Grimson, Eric
Guesgen, Hans Werner
Gupta, Anoop
Habel, Christopher
Hajicová, Eva
Hammond, Kristian J.
Hamscher, Walter
Hanson, Allen
Hanson, S.J.
Harris, Nomi
Hart, Peter
Havens, Bill
Hawley, David
Hayes, Caroline
Hayes, Patrick
Hecking, Matthias
Heeger, David
Heinsohn, Jochen
Helm, B. Robert
Hendler, James
Hermann, Mike
Hester, T.
Hewitt, Carl
Hidaka, Tohru
Hildreth, Ellen
Hinton, Geoffrey E.
Hirsh, Hyam
Hirst, Graeme
Hobbs, Jerry
Holluver, Benhard
Holte, Rob

Holtzblatt, Lester
Horn, Werner
Horvitz, Eric
Howe, Adele
Höppner, Wolfgang
Huang, S.R.
Huhns, Michael N.
Hunter, Lawrence
Hutchinson, Seth
Huttenlocher, Dan
Ichiyoshi, Noboyuki
Imaz, Escalada
Ingrand, Felix
Irani, Keki
Isard, Stephen
Ishida, Toru
Iwasaki, Yumi
Jackson, Peter
Jacky, Jonathan
Jaffar, Joxan
Jain, Ramesh
Jenkin, Michael
Jenzarli, Ali
Jepson, Allan
Jones, Marlene
Jordan, Michael
Joshi, Aravind
Joskowicz, Leo
Jouannaud, J.P.
Junker, Ulrich
Kaelbling, Leslie
Kahn, Ken
Kak, Avi
Kanamori, Tadashi
Kanatani, Ken-ichi
Kant, Elaine
Kasif, Simon
Katsuno, Hirofumi
Kautz, Henry
Kedar, Smadar
Keller, Rich
Key, C.
Kibler, Dennis
Kifer, Michael
King, Margaret
Kinoshita, Yoshiki
Kirchner, Claude
Kittredge, Richard
Klavans, Judith
Klir, George J.
Kolodner, Janet
Koomen, Johannes A.
Korf, Rich
Kowalski, Robert
Kramer, Glenn A.
Krulwich, Bruce
Kruse, Rudolf
Kumar, Vipin
Kuper, Gabriel
Kurematsu, Akira
Ladkin, Peter
Laface, Piero
Lakemeyer, Gerhard
Lang, Jerome
Laubsch, Joachim
Laurent, Jean-Pierre
Lauritzen, Steffen L.
Lehman, Jill Fain
Lehnert, Wendy
Leitch, Roy
Lescanne, Pierre
Lesser, Victor
Levy, Francois
Linden, Ted
Lindstrom, Gary
Litman, Diane
Little, Jim
Liu, Xiaohui
Lopez de Mantaras, Ramón
Lowry, Michael
Lozano-Perez, Tomas
Lozinskii, Eliezer
Luck, Kai V.
Lugier, Denis
MacGregor, Robert
Mackworth, Alan K.
Maes, Pattie
Mahadevan, Sridhar
Mahanti, A.
Maher, Michael
Makinson, David
Malerba, Donato
Malik, Jitendra
Manderinck, Bernard
Manning, Carl
Marburger, Heinz
Marche, Claude
Marcus, Mitch
Marek, Wiktor
Marimont, David
Mataric, Maja
Matwin, Stan
Mauri, Giancarlo
Mays, Eric
Mazer, Murray S.
McAllester, Dave
McAllester, David
McCarty, Thorne
McCoy, Kathy
McDermott, Drew
Mcdermott, John
McDonald, David
Medioni, Gerard
Meiri, Itay
Mercuri, Rebecca T.
Milios, Evangelos
Miller, Craig
Millican, Peter
Mizoguchi, Fumio
Moinard, Yves
Montgomery, Tom
Mooney, Ray
Moral, Serafin
Morgenstern, Leora
Morik, Katharina
Morley, David
Morris, Paul
Mozer, Michael
Mozetic, Igor
Mugleton, Steven
Nakashima, Hideyuki
Nalwa, Vishvit
Narayanan, Srinivas
Neiberg, Maurine
Nicolas, Jacques
Niemann, Heinrich
Nii, H. Penny
Nirenburg, Sergei
Nitta, Katsumi
Nonnengart, Andreas
Nutt, Werner
Odile Cordier, Marie
Ohlbach H.J.
Ohlsson, Stellan
Ohta, Yuichi
Ohwada, Hayato
Okada, Naoyuki
Oxusoff, Laurent
Paaa, Gerhard
Padgham, Lin
Paillet, Jean Luc
Palmer, Martha
Passoneau, Rebecca
Pastre, Dominique
Patel-Schneider, Peter
Pazzani, Michael
Pearl, Judea
Pednault, Edwin
Pelavin, Rich
Peltason, Christof
Pereira, Fernando
Perlis, Donald
Perrault, Ray
Petrie, Charles
Pfeifer, Rolf
Phelps, Bob
Piazza, Rich
Pickering, C.
Pierre, Laurence
Pingali, Sarma
Pitrat, Jacques
Plasa, Enrique
Plate, Tony
Poggio, Tomaso
Pollack, Jordan
Ponce, Jean
Poole, David
Popowich, Fred
Porter, Bruce
Porto, Antonia
Pösio, Massimo
Präkelein, Axel
Prager, John M.
Prieditis, Armand
Protasi, Marco
Provan, Greg
Przymusinska, Halina
Przymusinska, Teodor
Pullman, Steve
Pustejovsky, James
Quek, Francis
Rademakers, Philip
Raiman, Oliver
Rajamoney , Shankar
Ram, Ashwin
Ramakrishnan, Raghu
Ramani, S.
Rao, Anand S.
Reggia, James A.
Reiser, Brian
Retz-Schmidt, Gudula
Rice, James
Rich, Charles
Richter, Michael M.
Ridoux, R.
Riesbeck, Chris
Ringwood, Graem
Riseman, Edward
Ritchie, Graeme
Rosenbloom, Paul
Rosenschein, Jeff
Rosenschein, Stan
Rossi, Francesca
Roth, Yuval
Rott, Hans
Rouveirol, Céline
Rumelhart, David E.
Rusinowitch, Michael
Ruspini, Enrique H.
Russell, Stuart
Rychener, Michael
Sacks, Elisha
Saint-Dizier, Patrick
Saitta, Lorenza

Sakama, Chiaki
Sakane, Kiyokazu
Sallantin, Jean
Sandewall, Erik
Sato, Taisuke
Satoh, Ken
Schlechta, Karl
Schmiedel, Albrecht
Schoppers, Marcel
Schrager, Jeff
Schrobe, Howard
Schubert, Len
Schuler, Doug
Schwarz, Grigorii
Schwind, Camille
Segre, Alberto
Seifert, Colleen
Self, John
Selman,Bart
Semeraro, Giovanni
Serra, Roberto
Setliff, Dorothy
Shachter, Ross
Shafer, Steven
Sharma, D.D.
Shastri, Lokendra
Shavlik, Jude
Shenoy, Prakash
Shirai, Yoshiaki
Shirley, Mark
Sidner, Candace L.
Siekmann, Gerd
Simi, Maria
Sloman, Aaron
Smets, Philippe
Smith, David
Smith, Douglas
Smith, Grahame
Solina, Franc
Soloway, Elliot
Sonenberg, Elizabeth A.
Sparck Jones, Karen
Spiegelhalter, David J.
Spies, Marcus
Spohrer, James
Sproat, Richard
Staples, John
Steier, David
Steinberg, Louis
Stiehl, Siegfried
Struss, Peter
Subrahmanian, V.S.
Sugihara, Kochiki
Sullivan, Joseph W.
Surtserland, Luesti
Sutton, Rich
Swartout, William
Sycara, Katia
Szeliski, Richard
Szolovits, Peter
Takeuchi, Akikazu
Taki, Kazuo
Tanaka, Hozumi
Tecuci, Gheorghe
Tenenbaum, Marty
Tenenberg, Josh
Thomason, Rich
Thompson, Henry
Tomita, Marasu
Tong, Chris
Topor, Rodney W.
Torasso, Pietro
Trilling, Laurent
Trusczcynski, Miroslaw
Turini, Franco
Uszkoreit, Hans
Van de Velde, Walter
Van Someren, Maarten W.
van Beek, Peter
Van, Kelly
Venipaty, Nageshwara Rao
Verber, Manfred
Verri, Alessandro
Vrain, Christel
Wald, Joe
Waltz, David L.
Warren, D.H.D.
Warren, David S.
Washington, Richard
Waters, Richard C.
Webber, Bonnie
Weber, Jay
Weischedel, Ralph
Weld, Daniel
Wellman, Michael
Werner, Eric
Whitehair, Bob
Wielinga, Bob
Wile, David
Wilensky, Robert
Wilson, Stewart W.
Winograd, Terry
Winslett, Marianne
Wobcke, Wayne
Wong, S.K.M.
Woodham, Robert
Woolf, Beverley
Yager, Ronald R.
Yamamoto, Masanobu
Yan, Qiang
Yang, Rong
Yeh, Alexander
Yen, John
Yonezawa, Aki
Yonezawa, Akinori
Zadrozny, Wlodek
Zhang, Jianping
Zhang, Ying
Zippel, Richard
Zucker, Steven
Zweben, Monte

IJCAI-91 PROGRAMME SCHEDULE

SUNDAY AUGUST 25

Evening
Opening Ceremonies
Presentation of the IJCAI Distinguished Service Award and the IJCAI-91 Outstanding Paper Prize

MONDAY AUGUST 26

9:00 A.M.–10:00 A.M.
Invited Speaker: Takeo Kanade

10:30 A.M.–12:30 P.M.
ML: Explanation-based Learning
NL: NL Processing
KR: Nonmonotonic Reasoning—Modal Logics
AR: Theorem Proving I
Arch: Knowledge Base Management

2:00 P.M.–3:30 P.M.
Panel 1—AI in Telecommunications
ML: Classifiers/Genetic Algorithms
KR: Belief
LP: Logic Programming I
Phil: Philosophical Foundations I

4:00 P.M.–5:30 P.M.
AI On Line
ML: Inductive Learning I
AR: Search
LP: Logic Programming II
KR: Reasoning with Inconsistency
Rob: Architectures

Evening
Computers & Thought Awards
Martha Pollack
Rod Brooks

TUESDAY AUGUST 27

9:00 A.M.–10:00 A.M.
Invited Speaker: Shigeru Sato

10:30 A.M.–12:30 P.M.
ML: Inductive Learning II
AR: Planning I
NL: Pragmatics
QR: Diagnosis
Vis: Object Recognition

2:00 P.M.–3:30 P.M.
Panel 2—Multiple Approaches to Multiple Agent Problem Solving
ML: Inductive Logic Programming
KR: Nonmonotonic Reasoning—Conditional Logics
AR: Search II
CM: Cognitive Modeling 1

4:00 P.M.–5:30 P.M.
AI On Line
ML: Concept Formation
KR: Concept Languages
AR: Theorem Proving II
Phil: Philosophical Foundations II
QR: Qualitative Modelling

WEDNESDAY AUGUST 28

9:00 A.M.–10:00 A.M.
IJCAI Research Excellence Award and Lecture: Marvin Minsky

10:30 A.M.–12:30 P.M.
KR: Topics in Knowledge Representation
AR: Planning II
NL: NL Systems
QR: Qualitative Modeling, Temporal Reasoning
Vis: Interpretation

2:00 P.M.–5:30 P.M.
Computer Chess Afternoon
Panel 3—The Role of Chess in Artificial Intelligence Research
Chess Match

THURSDAY AUGUST 29

9:00 A.M.–10:00 A.M.
Invited Speaker: Robert A. Kowalski

10:30 A.M.–12:30 P.M.
ML: Inductive Learning III
AR: Reason Maintenance
NL: Representation and Semantics
LP: Logic Programming III
Appl: Intelligent Tutoring Systems

2:00 P.M.–3:30 P.M.
Panel 4—AI and Design
ML: Case-based Learning
KR: Nonmonotonic Reasoning—Circumscription
AR: Theorem Proving III
Arch: Distributed AI I

4:00 P.M.–5:30 P.M.
AI On Line
ML: Classification & Generalization
KR: Concept Languages, Inheritance Reasoning
AR: Constraint Satisfaction
QR: Reasoning under Uncertainty I
Rob: Navigation

5:30 P.M.–6:30 P.M.
IJCAI General Meeting—All registrants welcome

FRIDAY AUGUST 30

9:00 A.M.–10:00 A.M.
Invited Speaker: J. Ross Quinlan

10:30 A.M.–12:30 P.M.
AR: Planning III
NL: Parsing and Morphology
Arch: Connectionist & Parallel Rule Systems
Summary Session: IJCAI-91, Learning & Knowledge Acquisition
Summary Session: KR-91, International Conference on Principles of Knowledge Representation and Reasoning

2:00 P.M.–3:30 P.M.
Panel 5—Massively Parallel Artificial Intelligence
ML: Knowledge Acquisition
CM: Cognitive Modeling 2
Summary Session: IJCAI-91, Automated Reasoning
Summary Session: 1990 International Symposium on AI & Mathematics

4:00 P.M.–5:30 P.M.
ML: Connectionist Models
Arch: Distributed AI II
QR: Reasoning under Uncertainty II
Summary Session: IJCAI-91, Natural Language
Summary Session: 1990 International Conference on Automated Deduction

LEGEND:
Appl: Principles of AI Applications
AR: Automated Reasoning
Arch: Architectures & Languages
CM: Cognitive Modeling
KR: Knowledge Representation
LP: Logic Programming
ML: Machine Learning
NL: Natural Language
Phil: Philosophical Foundations
QR: Qualitative Reasoning
Rob: Robotics
Vis: Vision

VOLUME 1

Architectures & Languages

Knowledge Base Management

Connectionist & Parallel Rule Systems

Distributed AI I

Distributed AI II

Automated Reasoning

Theorem Proving I

Theorem Proving II

Theorem Proving III

Search I

VOLUME 2

Learning & Knowledge Acquisition

ARCHITECTURES & LANGUAGES

Knowledge Base Management

A Methodology for Systematic Verification of OPS5-Based AI Applications

G.Ravi Prakash[1], E.Subrahmanian[2], and H.N.Mahabala[1]

[1]Dept. of Computer Science and Engineering
Indian Institute of Technology, Madras - 600036, India
e-mail : ravi@shiva.ernet.in

[2]Engineering Design Research Centre
Carnegie Mellon University, Pittsburgh, PA 15213, USA
e-mail : sub@edrc.cmu.edu

Abstract

One of the critical problems in putting AI applications into use in the real world is the lack of sufficient formal theories and practical tools that aid the process of reliability assessment. Adhoc testing, which is widely used as a means of verification, serves limited purpose. A need for systematic verification by compile-time analysis exists. In this article, we focus our attention on OPS5-based AI applications and present a methodology for verification which is based on compile-time analysis. The methodology is based on the principle of converting the antecedent and action-parts of productions into a linear system of inequalities and equalities and testing them for a feasible solution. The implemented system, called SVEPOA, supports interactive and incremental analysis.

1 Introduction

Reliability assessment of artificial intelligence (AI) applications is an important problem. One of the bottlenecks in taking AI applications to the end-user sites is the lack of sufficient formal theories and practical tools that aid the process of reliability assessment. AI applications attempt to automate (to higher degrees) intelligent decision making activities of humans. The consequences of errors in AI applications are likely to be more serious or costlier than those in conventional computer applications. Adhoc testing, which is widely used as means of verification, serves limited purpose. It, however large in volume, can only reveal the presence of errors but does not ensure their absence. A need for systematic verification of AI applications exists.

We present in this paper a methodology for systematic verification of OPS5-based AI applications. We have focused our attention on production systems [Newell72] in general and OPS5-like languages [Forgy81] in particular for reasons that production system model of reasoning is one of the earliest and widely used models by the AI researchers and many interesting prototype applications [e.g. McDermott82] have been developed using OPS5-like languages. We present here a methodology that is based on compile-time analysis. Through compile-time analysis, we discover certain properties and relations of productions and illustrate through discussions that the presence and absence of these properties and relations reveal errors, if any, in the design of the antecedent and action-parts of productions.

2 Production System Model and OPS5 Language

A Production System, Z, can be characterized by three components : Z = (D, P, C) where,

D is a Fact-base : a set of facts;

P is a Production-base : a set of productions;

C is a Control strategy : a set of search procedures.

Production systems can be classified based on

* the scheme of representation used for the objects, attributes, relationships, and states in the fact-base;

* the nature of the actions in the productions, i.e. monotonic (ignorable) or nonmonotonic (revocable or irrevocable) actions;

* the techniques used for control strategy (e.g. weak search methods or heuristic search methods).

Based on this classification, the OPS5 language and its underlying production system model can be characterized as :

1. OPS5 represents fact-base as a set of instantiated objects having values to (some of) their attributes;

2. antecedent-parts of productions in OPS5 are expressed as a conjunction of clauses (*positive* and *negated* clauses) where each clause is represented as a conjunction of one or more ordinal predicates involving attributes and constants/variables;

3. actions in productions of OPS5 are nonmonotonic; the actions are mainly two types : *make* to add new instantiations of objects to the fact-base and *remove* to delete existing ones (*modify* action can be treated as a combination of *make* and *remove*).

4. OPS5 offers MEA and LEX control strategies and *data-driven* (forward) reasoning.

This characterization of OPS5 is used in course of discussions in the rest of this paper.

3 Related Research Work

The research work reported earlier in [Nguyen85, Mahabala87, Ginsberg88 etc.] on the issue of consistency checking of production (or rule-based) systems are all related to monotonic production systems that use propositional formulae to represent fact-base and productions. The definitions and the techniques used in the verification by the above referenced work are found to be unsuitable for verification of OPS5-like production systems for two principal reasons : one is that the actions in OPS5 are nonmonotonic and the other is that the antecedent-parts in OPS5 productions can use predicates involving existential (in positive clauses) and universal (in negated clauses) quantifiers. Verification of OPS5-based applications by compile-time analysis requires entirely new techniques.

4 Sources of Errors in the Design of Productions

The process of designing an AI application using production system model involves translating domain knowledge into fact-base declarations and productions. During this process, often (excluding toy problems) the knowledge-engineer makes assumptions about what knowledge is to be stated explicitly (called qualification and ramification problems). As the fact-base and production-base are enlarged and refined, the knowledge-engineer needs to maintain the consistency of assumptions. Otherwise the production system is prone to contain errors. This is one source of errors. There are other sources of errors too, like the text-editing mistakes, the knowledge being often incomplete, etc.

5 Verification by Compile-time Analysis

We have manually analyzed toy and prototype AI application systems developed using OPS5. We have found that discovering the following relations and properties of productions by compile-time analysis helps the knowledge engineer to detect errors in the antecedent and action-parts of productions :

[1] conflict relations
[2] likely-to-activate relations
[3] dead-end productions
[4] impossible productions

In this section, we formally define these relations and properties and discuss their usefulness in the process of verification. Before we do so, we introduce certain terms which we use in defining the above listed relations and properties.

Activating and Resultant Sets :

The set of all valid fact-base states of a given OPS5-based AI application is called its state-space. Each production in the application system can be viewed as a state transformational operator (the term 'state' implies 'valid fact-base state'). Every production specifies a set of conditions (antecedent-part), which when satisfied, makes the production eligible for execution. The number of states that can satisfy the antecedent-part of a production is *zero* or *more* depending upon the logical and semantic consistency and specificity of conditions in the antecedent-part. We introduce here two terms, Activating-Set and Resultant-Set of a production.

Activating-Set (A_p) of a production, p :

$A_p \equiv \{ s_i \mid s_i$ is a state in state-space AND s_i satisfies the antecedent-part of the production, p $\}$

Activating-Set of a production, p, is the set of all states in the state-space that satisfy the antecedent-part of p.

Resultant-Set (R_p) of a production, p :

$R_p \equiv \{ s_j \mid s_j$ is a state in state-space AND s_j is obtained by applying the actions of the production, p, on some state $s_i \in A_p \}$

Resultant-Set of a production, p, is the set of all states in state-space, each of which results from applying the actions of production p onto some state s_i belonging to the Activating-Set of p.

Using the definitions for Activating-Set and Resultant-Set of a production, the relations and properties of a production as listed earlier in this section are defined below.

Conflict Relation :

A conflict relation is said to exist between two distinct productions p and q iff,

$(A_p \cap A_q) \not\equiv \phi$)

Discussion : Conflict relation exists between two distinct productions, p and q, (denoted as 'p.conflict.q') iff, the Activating-Sets A_p and A_q have common elements. In other words, there exist one or more fact-base states that can satisfy the antecedent-parts of both p and q. When solving AI problems using OPS5, the conflict-set (the set of productions that are satisfied by the current fact-base) often contains more than one production. So conflict relations between productions is a natural phenomenon in OPS5-based applications. But, while designing productions, the knowledge engineer may *over* or *under* specify the conditions in the antecedent-parts (because of qualification problem or incomplete knowledge). This gives rise to the possibility that the OPS5-based application system contains certain invalid conflict relations or does not contain certain valid conflict relations. To illustrate this point, consider the two productions given in example.1 (these productions are selected from the solution to the monkey and banana problem given in Appendix-One of [Brownston85] for easy readability). Consider that the contents of the fact-base are described by the test data given in example.2.

Example.1

```
(p  Holds::Object-NotCeil:On
   (goal ^status active ^type holds
                        ^object-name <o1>)
   (phys-object ^name <o1> ^weight light
                ^at <p> ^on <> ceiling)
   (monkey ^at <p> ^on <> floor)
-->
```

```
    (make goal ^status active ^type on
                ^object-name floor) )
(p  Holds::Object:Holds
    (goal ^status active ^type holds
                    ^object-name <o1>)
    (phys-object ^name <o1> ^weight light
                              ^at <p>)
    (monkey ^at <p> ^holds {<>nil <> <o1>})
-->
    (make  goal ^status active ^type holds
               ^object-name nil) )
```

Example.2

```
(make phys-object ^name banana ^weight light
              ^on ceiling ^at 3-3)
(make phys-object ^name ladder ^weight light
              ^on floor ^at 1-1)
(make monkey ^on ladder ^holds blanket
              ^at 1-1)
(make phys-object ^name blanket ^weight light
              ^at 1-1)
(make goal ^status active ^type holds
              ^object-name ladder)
```

The fact-base describes that there exists a goal for the monkey to hold the ladder; the ladder is on the floor at position 1-1; the monkey is at position 1-1, on the ladder and holding the blanket. Both the productions of example.1 are satisfied by the fact-base of example.2. So, a conflict relation exists between these two productions. Though the authors of Appendix-One of [Brownston85] very clearly state that there are no conflicting productions to either of these productions, we could find a conflict relation between them using our systematic compile-time analysis. Similarly, one can find that the production 'Holds::Object:Satisfied' has a conflict relation with the production 'Holds::Object-NotCeil:On' (both productions from Appendix-One of [Brownston85]), which the authors stated as impossible. What conflict relations are valid, and what are not, is a domain dependent feature. It is not possible to determine invalid conflict relations domain independently for (nonmonotonic) production systems built using OPS5-like languages (this is in contrast to monotonic production systems using propositional formulae, in which it is possible to define and identify conflicting productions domain-independently ('if p then q' and 'if p then NOT q') through syntactic analysis). Besides the presence of invalid conflict relations, the absence of valid conflict relations is also a cause of major concern to the knowledge engineer debugging a production system. We define a production system to be in error if it contains invalid conflict relations or does not contain valid conflict relations. Our contention is that if there are errors in a toy system (solution to the monkey and banana problem) of around 24 productions, the likelihood of errors in any real-world system of 2500 productions or more is much higher. Hence, a systematic compile-time analysis is much in place.

Likely-to-activate Relation :

A likely-to-activate relation is said to exist from a production, p to a production, q (q not necessarily different from p), iff,

$((R_p \cap A_q) \not\equiv \phi)$

Discussion : Likely-to-activate relation exists from a production, p to a production, q iff, the Resultant-Set of p, Rp, and the Activating-Set of q, Aq, have common elements. In other words, the execution of p can result in a fact-base state, such that, that fact-base state satisfies the antecedent-part of q. This relation is denoted by 'p.lta.q' (lta as an acronym for likely-to-activate). The process of finding a solution to a problem using production system model involves finding a path (the ordered set of likely-to-activate relations) from the initial fact-base state to the desired goal fact-base state. One of the major concerns of a knowledge engineer during the process of debugging is to find the invalid paths (or invalid likely-to- activate relations) taken by the system. Since adhoc testing cannot reveal the presence of all the invalid likely-to-activate relations, a systematic compile-time analysis is required. As with the conflict relations, what likely-to-activate relations are valid and what are not is a domain dependent feature. Besides the presence of invalid likely-to-activate relations, the absence of valid likely-to-activate relations also reflect errors. We define a production system to be in error if it contains invalid likely-to-activate relations or does not contain valid likely-to-activate relations.

Dead-end Productions :

A production, p, is said to be a dead-end production, iff

(1) $\forall$ (q $\in$ production-base) (p.lta.q is false) AND

(2) the action-part of p does not include an 'halt' action;

Discussion : A production, p is said to be a dead-end production iff, p does not have an lta relation to any other production, q, in the production-base and the action-part of p does not include an 'halt' action. While testing OPS5 applications, the knowledge engineer sometimes comes across a situation in which the execution of a production causes the conflict-set to be empty in the next cycle. Such situations are termed as dead-end situations and the productions that cause such situations are called dead-end productions. Since adhoc testing may not reveal all the dead-end situations, a compile-time analysis is needed.

The above definition of dead-end production is a weak definition. Productions satisfying the above definition are definitely dead-end productions. A production, p, not satisfying that definition can also be dead-end productions, if there are one or more states in R_p not belonging to A_q, for any other production, q.

We can define a production to be a pseudo-dead end production if its action-part includes an 'halt' action and it has atleast one lta relation to another production.

Impossible Productions :

A production, p, is said to be an impossible production, iff

(1) $(A_p \equiv \phi)$ OR

(2) $(A_p \cap S_{ini} \equiv \phi \wedge \neg\exists$ q (q.lta.p))

where S_{ini} is the set of all possible initial states.

Discussion : A production, p, is said to be an impossible production, iff 'the Activating-Set of p is empty' or 'p is not a start production and no other production in the production-base has an lta relation with p'. The Activating-Set of any production will be empty when the set of conditions in the antecedent-part of p are either logically or semantically inconsistent. Impossible productions never get instantiated into the conflict-set and are difficult to be detected by an adhoc testing method.

6 Computational Feasibility

The computational feasibility of finding the relations and the properties (described in Section 5) of a production depends on the nature of predicates that can be used in the antecedent and action-parts of productions. From a study of the BNF description of the syntax of OPS5 language given in [Brownston85], we have the following information. Predicates that can be used in the antecedent-part are of two types : (X_i.R.k) or (X_i.R.X_j) where X_i, X_j are attributes of objects declared by 'literalize' commands; R is one of the ordinal relations; $R \in \{ =, <>, <, \leq, >, \geq \}$; k is a constant (string, integer or real depending on X_i).

Predicates that can be used in the action-part are of three types : ($X_i = k$) , ($X_i = X_j$) , or (X_i = exp) where X_i, X_j, and k are the same as above and exp is any arithmetic expression.

Assumptions :

We make an assumption that the arithmetic expressions that can appear in the predicates of action-part are linear arithmetic expressions (that is, they do not involve non-linear expressions like (X_i*X_i) or (X_i*X_j*X_k) etc.). This assumption is fairly reasonable for two reasons : [i] many AI applications involve mostly symbolic reasoning rather than evaluating non-linear arithmetic expressions; [ii] through this assumption, the divide and conquer principle is used and the systems that involve predicates with only linear expressions are given an effective procedure for compile-time analysis. We also assume that for each attribute of every object declared by the literalize command, the range of values the attribute can take are finite. This assumption is realistic for many real world problems. We also like to note here that

* boolean constants, "true" and "false" can be encoded as integers 1 and 0 respectively;

* symbolic constants can be sorted in lexicographic order and mapped onto the natural numbers; and

* boolean/symbolic variables can be treated as integer variables.

Based on the above assumptions, the problem of finding the relations and the properties of productions reduces to the problem of finding whether there exists a feasible solution to a system of linear inequalities and equalities with integer variables. This is a known and solvable problem. We use the algorithm given in [Biswas87] that exploits the simplicity of the predicates. [Biswas87] offers a polynomial-time algorithm to find the feasibility if all the inequalities and equalities are 'simple' (please refer to [Biswas87] for the definition of 'simple' inequalities and equalities). We have observed in analyzing prototype applications that most often the antecedent and action-parts of productions contain 'simple' inequalities and equalities.

7 Implementation of SVEPOA

We have implemented our methodology in common LISP on MicroVaxII workstation. This program, called SVEPOA (stands for Systematic VErification Program for OPS5-based Applications) has the following two main features :

[1] Interactive Analysis Facility
[2] Incremental Analysis Facility

Interactive Analysis Facility : We observe that knowledge engineers often try to structure and segment an OPS5-based application and hence it may not be required to compare roductions in one segment with productions in other segments exhaustively. The Interactive Facility offers the knowledge engineer a method of choosing which properties (or relations) to discover in (or across) what segments of productions.

Incremental Analysis Facility : When SVEPOA is initially run, it stores the set of relations and properties discovered. In the subsequent analysis, SVEPOA uses and updates the set of relations and properties pertaining to an application.

The main subprograms of SVEPOA are find-conflict-relation, find-lta-relation, find-if-dead-end, find-if-impossible and find-feasibility. The functions of SVEPOA and its subprograms are described in the following procedures. A trace of the procedures for an example is given in Appendix-A.

procedure SVEPOA;

1. Ascertain the objects, their attributes and the range(s) of values for each attribute;

2. Sort the symbolic constants in lexicographic order and map them onto the natural numbers;

3. Ascertain the production(s) and the property or relation to be discovered; call the appropriate subprocedure;

4. Repeat step 3 until no more analysis is required;

subprocedure find-conflict-relation(p,q);

1. Find Cc, the conjunction of the antecedent-parts of p (Cp) and q (Cq); i.e Cc = (Cp) $\wedge$ (Cq);

2. Call subprocedure find-feasibility(Cc) to find out if there exists a feasible solution to Cc;

3. If Cc has a feasible solution then (p.conflict.q) is true else not;

subprocedure find-lta-relation(p,q);

Let Cp, Dp and Cq be the antecedent-part of p, action-part of p and antecedent-part of q respectively;

1. Convert each *modify* action in Dp into an equivalent combination of *remove* and *make* actions;

2. For each *remove* action, r, in Dp, delete the clause referenced by r from Cp;

3. For each *make* action, m, in Dp, add a clause containing the '=' predicates of m to Cp;

4. Cc = (Cp) $\wedge$ (Cq);

5. Call subprocedure find-feasibility(Cc);
6. If Cc has a feasible solution then (p.lta.q) is true else not;

subprocedure find-if-dead-end(p);
1. Find if the action-part of p (Dp) contains an 'halt' action;
2. If 'halt' action is not included in Dp then find out if there is atleast one other production, q, such that (p.lta.q) is true;
3. If 'halt' action is included in Dp then find out whether p is a pseudo-dead-end production; this is done by finding out if there is atleast one other production, q, such that (p.lta.q) is true;

subprocedure find-if-impossible(p);
1. Find out whether ($A_p \equiv \phi$) or not by testing if the antecedent-part of p (Cp) has a feasible solution;
2. If ($A_p \not\equiv \phi$) then find out whether (($A_p \cap S_{ini}$) $\equiv \phi$) or not; S_{ini} is expressed as a conjunction of input predicates describing the possible initial values of the attributes of the objects; the attributes not appearing in S_{ini}) can take any value from their ranges;
3. If (($A_p \cap S_{ini}$) $\equiv \phi$) then find out if there is atleast one other production such that (q.lta.p) is true;

subprocedure find-feasibility(Cc);
1. Conver the conditions in the clauses of Cc into the form (object.attribute R constant) or (object.attribute R variable) where R is the ordinal relation;
2. Each distinct object.attribute is treated as a variable while using Biswas algorithm; All symbolic constants are replaced by the corresponding natural numbers;
3. Apply DeMorgan's law onto each negated clause in Cc; for example, a negated clause of the form
¬((phys-object.on = <o1>)∧(phys-object.weight = heavy))
is converted to :
((phys-object.on <> <o1>) ∨ (phys-object.weight <> heavy))
4. Each '<>' condition in Cc is expressed as a disjunction of '<' , '>' relations;
5. Cc is converted into an equivalent disjunctive normal form expression; each disjunct, t, and the range of values of the unresolved variables (variables equated to constants are resolved variables) are passed onto the Biswas algorithm to find if t has a feasible solution;

8 Conclusions

Since adhoc testing cannot reveal all errors, a compile-time analysis to systematically verify AI applications is very much needed. We presented here a methodology that analyzes OPS5-based applications at compile-time and detects certain relations and properties of productions. Discovering the presence and absence of these relations and properties helps the knowledge engineer to find errors in the antecedent and action-parts of productions. Our methodology and the tool have the advantages as well as the disadvantages of a domain-independent analysis. Being domain-independent, our tool does not require formal specifications of the application. Asking for formal specifications of AI applications is often not only difficult but also limits the applicability of a tool to some specific classes of problems. Our tool, being domain-independent, can be used for analyzing any OPS5-based AI application. However, it has the limitation of being able to only point out *possible* errors but not *definite* errors. Also, we don't claim that the analysis done by our tool is complete. There may be other relations and properties of productions, detecting which will be useful during verification.

Acknowledgments : We express our sincere thanks to Richard Christie, Petter Stoa, Prof.S.N.Talukdar and Prof.C.R.Muthukrishnan for the useful discussions with them.

Appendix-A

We show the trace of the important steps of SVEPOA to find the conflict relation between productions of Example.1 of Section 5.

```
procedure :  SVEPOA
  1. Objects are goal, phys-object and
monkey; these objects are denoted by O1, O2
and O3 respectively; the range(s) of values of
the attributes of these objects are obtained;
for example,
  range( O2.name ) = [bananas, blanket, couch,
ladder];
  range( O3.at ) = [1-1, 1-2, .  .  .  10-10];
  2.  All the symbolic constants are sorted
and mapped onto the natural numbers; for
example, 1-1 → 1; 1-2 → 2; 10-10 → 100;
active → 101; etc.
  3.  Let the two productions
'Holds::Object:Not Ceil:On' (ref.  to as p)
and 'Holds::Object:Holds' (ref.  to as q) are
accepted;
  find-conflict-relation( p,q );

subprocedure :  find-conflict-relation(p,q);
  1.  Cc = ( Cp ) ∧ ( Cq );
  find-feasibility( Cc );

subprocedure :  find-feasibility(Cc);
  1.  The conditions in Cc are expressed in
the forms (object.attribute R constant) or
(object.attribute R variable); for example,
the first clause in Cc is expressed as
  ((goal.status = active) ∧  (goal.type =
holds) ∧  (goal.  object-name = <o1>));
  2.  Each distinct object.attribute in Cc is
treated is a variable; let the variables be
denoted as Z11 (for goal.status), Z12 (for
goal.type), Z13, etc.  in the order
respectively; all symbolic constants are
replaced by their corresponding natural
numbers; for example (monkey.on  <>  floor)
will now appear in Cc as (Z32  <>  107) as
"floor" is mapped onto 107 in this domain; now
Cc is :
```

Cc ≡ ((Z11 = 101) ∧ (Z12 = 109) ∧ (Z13 = <01>) ∧ (Z21 = <01>) ∧ (Z22 = 111) ∧ (Z23 = <p>) ∧ (Z24 <> 105) ∧ (Z31 = <p>) ∧ (Z32 <> 107) ∧ (Z33 <> 113) ∧ (Z33 <> <01>));

3. There are no negated clauses in Cc;

4. Each '<>' condition in Cc is expressed as a disjunction of '<', '>' relations; for example, (Z32 <> 107) is expressed as ((Z32 < 107) ∨ (Z32 > 107));

5. Cc is converted into an equivalent disjunctive normal form expression; each disjunct (there are 16 of them in this case) along with the range of values of the unresolved variables is passed onto the Biswas algorithm; one of the disjuncts of the dnf expression is :

t ≡ ((Z11 = 101) ∧ (Z12 = 109) ∧ (Z13 = <01>) ∧ (Z21 = <01>) ∧ (Z22 = 111) ∧ (Z23 = <p>) ∧ (Z24 > 105) ∧ (Z31 = <p>) ∧ (Z32 > 107) ∧ (Z33 < 113) ∧ (Z33 < <01>));

The unresolved variables are Z13, Z21, Z23, Z24, Z31, Z32, Z33; all these inequalities are 'simple' and Biswas algorithm returns the following solution :

Z13 = 110; Z21 = 110; Z23 = 1-1; Z24 = 107; Z31 = 1-1; Z32 = 110; Z33 = 104;

Interpretation :

```
goal.status = active;
goal.type = holds;
goal.object-name = ladder;
phys-object.name = ladder;
phys-object.weight = light;
phys-object.at = 1-1;
phys-object.on = floor;
monkey.at = 1-1; monkey.on = ladder;
monkey.holds = blanket;
So, (p.conflict.q) is true;
```

References :

[Biswas87] : Biswas,S. and Rajaraman,V. , 'An Algorithm to Decide Feasibility of Linear Integer Constraints Occurring in Decision Tables', IEEE Tran. on Software Engg., vol SE-13:1340-1347, Dec.,1987

[Brownston85] : Brownston,L., Farrell,R., Kant,E., Martin,N., 'Programming Expert Systems in OPS5', Addison-Wesley Pub., 1985

[Forgy81] : Forgy,C.L., 'OPS5 User's Manual', Carnegie-Mellon Univ., CMU-CS-81-135, July 1981

[Ginsberg88] : Ginsberg,A., 'Knowledge-Base Reduction : A new Approach to Checking Knowledge Bases for Inconsistency Redundancy', Proc. of AAAI Conf.,:585-589, August, 1988, St Paul, Minnasota, USA

[Mahabala87] : Mahabala,H.N., Ravi Prakash,G., et al, 'Expert System for Selection of Drill : A Case Study for use of Metaknowledge and Consistency Checks', Proc. of the II Int. conf. on Appln. of AI in Engg.', Boston, pp 371-386, 1987

[McDermott82] : McDermott,J., 'R1 : A Rule-based Configurer of Computer Systems', AI Journal, vol.19, Sept.,1982

[Newell72] : Newell,A. and Simon,H.A., 'Human Problem Solving', Prentice-Hall Inc., 1972

[Nguyen85] : Nguyen, T. et. al., 'Checking Expert System Knowledge Base for Consistency and Completeness', Proc. of IJCAI-85 : 375-378, 1985

Intelligent Assistance through Collaborative Manipulation[1]

Loren G. Terveen **David A. Wroblewski** **Steven N. Tighe**

AT&T Bell Laboratories
600 Mountain Ave.
Murray Hill, NJ 07974
terveen@research.att.com

US West
4001 Discovery Dr.
Boulder, CO 80303
davew@uswest.com

MCC
3500 W. Balcones Center Dr.
Austin, TX 78759
tighe@mcc.com

Abstract

This paper introduces, motivates, and illustrates an approach to the construction of intelligent assistance systems that we call *collaborative manipulation*. We show how a system can offer effective assistance through collaborative manipulation of objects in a shared workspace. We have developed this approach through experience with an intelligent knowledge editing tool, the HITS Knowledge Editor. We illustrate its effectiveness using scenarios taken from a user study.

1 Intelligent Assistance

Intelligent assistance is an active research field within AI [Chin, 1988; Lochbaum *et al*., 1990; Lemke and Fischer, 1990; Miller *et al*., 1990]. This research is motivated by several factors, including (1) the importance of collaboration in intelligent activity, (2) the scarcity of totally formalizable domains, and (3) people's need for help with increasingly complex computer applications.

Two key issues in the design of an intelligent assistance system are – *what is the role of the system in the interaction?* and *how is the system-user interaction managed*? Our work in building an intelligent assistant for the task of *knowledge editing* has led us to three design principles that address these issues. We call the approach characterized by these principles *collaborative manipulation*.

2 Collaborative Manipulation

We carry out our research within the paradigm of *cooperative problem solving systems* [Lemke and Fischer, 1990]. This approach begins from the premise that people and computers have vastly different strengths and weaknesses and that effective cooperation needs a division of responsibility based on the strengths of each party. Our contribution is to base system assistance on collaborative manipulation of objects in a shared workspace. The approach has three key aspects.

1. *Provide a workspace for joint user-system problem solving*. People at everyday tasks construct personalized work contexts that include task-relevant materials and *partial specifications of solutions* – think of a kitchen while someone is cooking or your workstation and desk while you debug a program or write a paper. In this paper, we focus on two properties of a workspace that are useful for an intelligent assistant: first, it provides access to users' *partial solutions*, enabling the assistant to compute advice in a timely manner, and second, the assistant can deliver significant aspects of its advice by manipulating objects in the shared workspace. We call the latter process *advertisement* [Wroblewski *et al*., 1991].

2. *An effective role for an intelligent assistance system is that of a design critic* [Fischer *et al*., 1990]. In design, a person constructs an artifact meeting certain constraints – in knowledge editing, users construct knowledge structures that encode their understanding of a domain and fit in with the constraints of a knowledge representation system. A critic "looks over the shoulder" of users as they perform a task and offers advice occasionally. In our system, critics propose completions of unfinished objects, detect problems, and suggest additional issues.

3. *The user-system interaction must be managed according to conventions that are appropriate to the abilities and roles of each party*. For example, a system should (1) avoid taking the initiative from users and forcing them to deal with advice at the convenience of the system, and (2) avoid imposing a fixed order of work on users. In our system, interaction is organized in terms of propose-critique-refine interchanges, in which the user always has the final say.

3 The HITS Knowledge Editor

Knowledge editing involves the entry, viewing, access, and maintenance of information in a knowledge base. Many systems make strong assumptions about the type and use of knowledge being entered [e.g. Kahn *et al*., 1987; Musen *et al*, 1987] in order to guide users. Our approach, however, along with Murray and Porter [1990] is to assist users in the knowledge editing task without making such assumptions.

Representing knowledge in a knowledge base is a difficult task. People must articulate knowledge to a higher degree of precision than is required for everyday communication and must encode the new knowledge in harmony with existing knowledge and representational conventions. The HITS Knowledge Editor (HKE) assists users in this task. HKE is a browsing/entry interface to CYC [Lenat and Guha, 1990]. HKE embodies an analysis of knowledge editing into six sub-activities [Terveen, 1991].

[1]This work was done while all three authors were at the MCC Human Interface Lab.

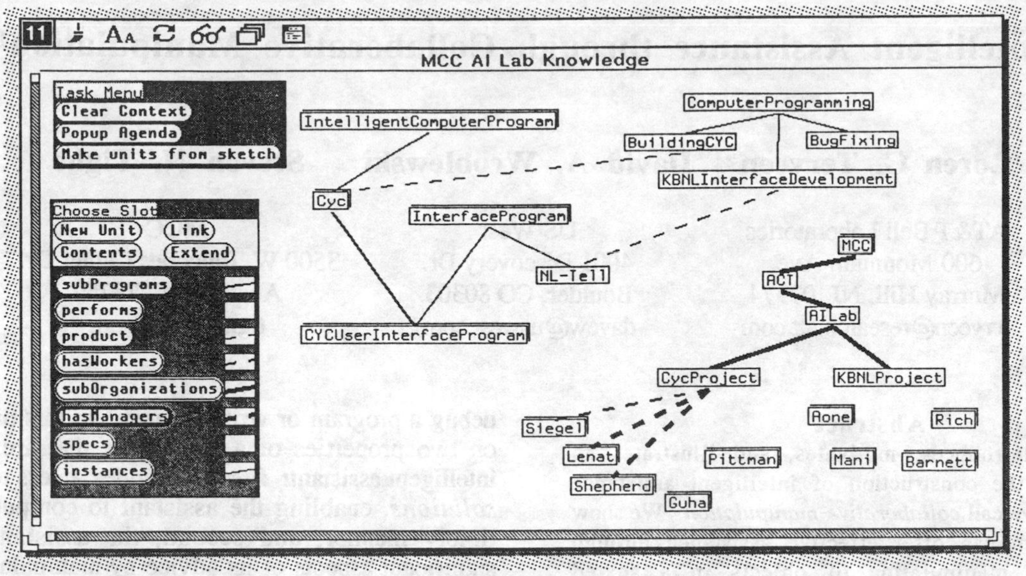

Double lines around an icon indicate that an object by this name exists in the knowledge base, e.g., MCC exists but ACT does not. The same convention is used for slot buttons in the Choose Slot menu: e.g., `performs` exists in the KB but `product` does not. The Choose Slot menu also functions like the legend of a map. Each slot has an associated line pattern, e.g., `subOrganizations` is represented by a thick solid line. The icons for two objects related by one of these slots are linked by the appropriate line pattern, e.g., MCC and ACT are related by the `subOrganizations` slot, so their icons are linked by a thick solid line.

Figure 1 – A sketch

We focus here on three activities that comprise knowledge *entry*, since this where HKE offers the most assistance.

- During *specification*, users sketch out new knowledge via a direct manipulation interface.
- During *incorporation*, the system merges the specification into the knowledge base and detects problems and issues.
- During *repair*, the system presents the problems and issues it has detected and works with the users to resolve them.

We illustrate how HKE assists in these three activities with a scenario taken from a user study [Terveen, 1991]. Pairs of subjects were asked to represent knowledge about the structure of their organization (the Artificial Intelligence or Human Interface Laboratory at MCC), such as researchers and their areas of expertise, projects, and software systems.

Some CYC terminology is necessary to understand the illustration. Objects in CYC are called ***units***. We use typewriter font to indicate units, e.g., `MCC`, `Terveen`, `Worker`. Slots are first class units. The domain of a slot is recorded on its `makesSenseFor` slot and the range of a slot is recorded on its `entryIsA` slot. By convention, slot names begin with lowercase letters, e.g., `hasWorkers` and `instanceOf`. We use predicate argument form to refer to assertions in the knowledge base, e.g., `hasWorkers(MCC, Terveen)` means that `Terveen` is a filler of the `hasWorkers` slot of `MCC`. We use the notation `unit.slot` to refer to the value or values of a particular slot of a particular unit, e.g., `MCC.hasWorkers` represents the set of workers at MCC.

3.1 Specification

Our user studies have shown that knowledge representation typically begins with a small group of people sketching out key objects and relationships on a piece of paper or a whiteboard. In HKE, users specify new knowledge by sketching a graph of objects and their relationships using a direct manipulation interface. Users can sketch only those objects and relationships that are of most immediate interest to them – they do not have to satisfy CYC's requirements for well-formed units immediately.

While sketching out new information, users often need to explore the knowledge base for existing information that is relevant to their task. HKE provides browsing methods to do this. Relevant objects can be collected in the sketch; thus, users can create a context for solving their problem as part of the problem solving process [Suchman, 1983]. Figure 1 shows an intermediate point in the specification activity of one pair of subjects.

3.2 Incorporation

When users are satisfied with their specification, they request HKE to incorporate it into the knowledge base. While doing so, HKE applies rules to each assertion that (1) *infer* additional assertions, (2) discover *constraints* between objects and (3) detect *troubles* or *suggestions* that apply to an object.

3.2.1 Inferences and Constraints

HKE infers required information that users have not specified based on how objects are used in the sketch. For example, in figure 1 the users introduced a new slot, `product`, without specifying either its domain and range. However, they did state that `Cyc` was a `product` of `BuildingCYC`, and `Cyc` already is known to be an instance of `IntelligentComputerProgram`. Therefore, the system inferred that the range of `product` was `IntelligentComputerProgram`.

Sometimes inferences can be made only on the basis of non-local information in the sketch, i.e., a value inferred on the basis of one assertion may affect an object in another assertion. HKE supports this by using *constraints*. For example, suppose HKE processes the assertions

- product(KBNLInterfaceDevelopment,NL-Tell) and
- product(BuildingCYC, Cyc),

in that order. When the system processes the first assertion, it does not know anything about the objects product, NL-Tell, and KBNLInterfaceDevelopment. However, based on this assertion it creates two constraints:

- product.makesSenseFor ∈ KBNLInterfaceDevelopment. instanceOf: the domain of product must a class which KBNLInterfaceDevelopment is a member of.
- product.entryIsA ∈ NL-Tell.instanceOf: the range of product must be a class which NL-Tell is a member of.

When HKE processes product(BuildingCYC, Cyc) and infers

entryIsA(product, IntelligentComputerProgram),

maintaining the second constraint enables HKE to infer that NL-Tell is an instance of IntelligentComputerProgram. When HKE determines that KBNLInterfaceDevelopment is an instance of ComputerProgramming, the first constraint will be maintained with similar results. Figure 2 summarizes part of the inference process just described.

HKE records the justification for each inference that it makes. Users can access the justification during the repair activity as a resource in deciding whether to accept or modify the system's inference (see figure 4). For example, they might decide that the range of product should be a more general class than IntelligentComputerProgram.

There are several reasons why the type of inferencing that HKE does is particularly useful. First, it reduces what users have to know and decide. For example, novice users may not know that they have to specify the domain and range of a slot, but HKE can make consistent guesses about this information based on how they have used the slot in their sketch. Second, no options are taken away from users: they are still free to modify the values that the system has inferred. In fact, arguably the most important feature of system inference is that it can draw users' attention to issues that they had not considered. Furthermore, the justification for an inference is available to users as they decide whether to accept it, and, if they decide to seek an alternative answer, the system provides follow-up options that guide users in exploring the space of alternatives. This also facilitates a kind of learning: users can become aware of both new issues and ways to resolve the issues.

3.2.2 Troubles

Every assertion stated by the users is examined to see if it is inconsistent with information already in the knowledge base – this is a *trouble*. Some troubles are relatively simple and localized. For example, the most common trouble encountered in the user studies was that users asserted a relationship between two objects, and the objects did not satisfy the domain or range constraints on the relationship. In figure 1 the users asserted hasManagers(CycProject, Lenat). However, the range of hasManagers is Manager and Lenat is not an instance of Manager, so HKE detects a trouble with this assertion.

Other troubles result from inconsistencies with inherited or inferred information. For example, in figure 1 the users asserted that CYCUserInterfaceProgram was an instance of InterfaceProgram. Through inheritance, this would have the effect of making CYCUserInterfaceProgram an instance of the class IndividualObject. However, CYCUserInterfaceProgram already is known to be a derived instance of Collection, and Collection and IndividualObject are declared to be *mutually disjoint*, i.e., no object can be an instance of both classes. Therefore, HKE detects a trouble with the users' assertion (figure 5).

When the system detects a trouble with an assertion from the users' specification, it does not attempt to add that assertion to the knowledge base nor does it immediately engage users in a dialogue to repair the trouble. Instead, it creates a resource for repairing the trouble, associates it with the assertion, and advertises the trouble through objects in the work context (see next section for discussion).

There are a number of reasons why HKE does not attempt to repair troubles automatically. First, HKE often knows alternative repair methods that it has no means of selecting among. Second, there may be repair methods that HKE does not know about – for example, radical changes to the class hierarchy can drastically change the set of legal assertions – and if users are skilled enough to think of such actions and perform them, they should be able to. Finally, sometimes the repairs that HKE offers are "dangerous" – they could have large ripple effects throughout the knowledge base – and should be done only after careful consideration. Therefore, all troubles are advertised to users, and the system assists in deciding how to repair troubles but does not do so automatically.

3.2.3 Suggestions

Suggestions are issues that deserve possible investigation, but do not prevent any part of the users' specification from being incorporated into the knowledge base. In figure 1, for example, the users defined a new class, ComputerProgramming, with three instances BugFixing, BuildingCYC, and KBNLInterfaceDevelopment. They later used the slot performs to relate different people to the three instances, e.g., performs (Lenat, BuildingCYC). The range constraint on performs let the system infer that the three objects were instances of the class PerformingAnAction. Rather than each of these objects being instances of both ComputerProgramming and PerformingAnAction, it might be preferable to make ComputerProgramming a subclass of PerformingAnAction. HKE therefore creates a suggestion that users consider this issue (see figure 4).

During incorporation, the system constructs a context (figure 2 shows selected parts) that includes the assertions from the users' specification and those inferred by the system. All the assertions concerning an individual object are organized into a checklist [Terveen and Wroblewski, 1990]. The context is annotated with other information including troubles, suggestions, and constraints. Since the context includes many items that must be acted on, (e.g., troubles must be resolved, suggestions should be deliberated, and inferences can be verified or modified), it is essential that the system's representation of the context is shared with the users. This is the topic of the next section.

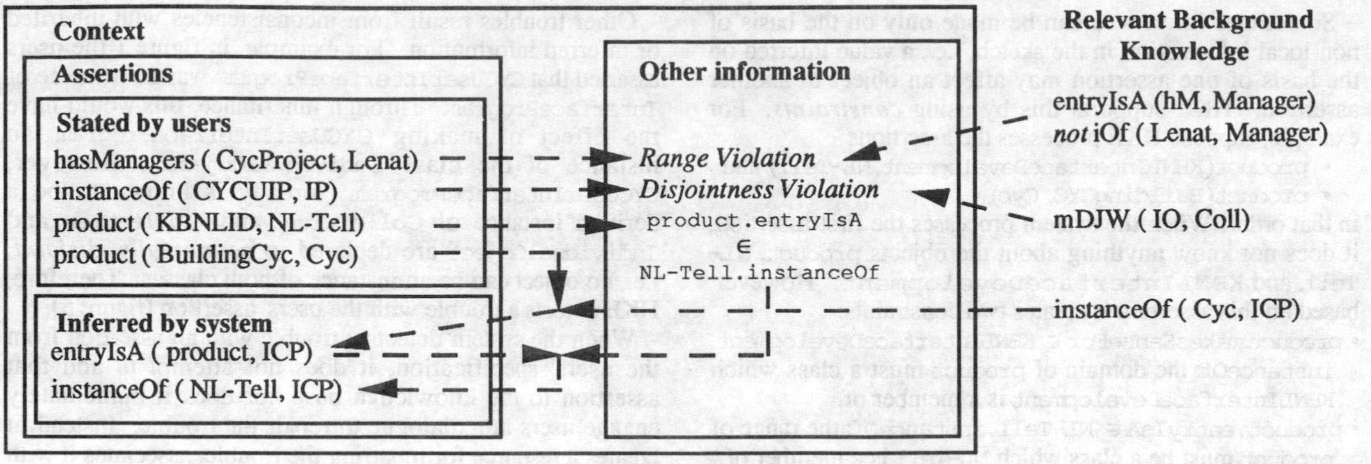

Abbreviations: CYCUIP – CYCUserInterfaceProgram, KBNLID – KBNLInterfaceDevelopment, hM – hasManagers
ICP – IntelligentComputerProgram, mDJW – mutuallyDisjointWith

Figure 2: Part of the context built by the system during incorporation

3.3 Repair

During repair, user and system jointly explore the consequences of the issues raised by the system during incorporation. In responding to system recommendations, users refine their initial conceptions of their domain based on the interaction between new and existing information.

The sketch and checklists serve as media for the system's recommendations. After incorporating a sketch, if the system detects troubles with an object, it displays that object in reverse video, and, if the system has suggestions about an object, it grays that object (see figure 3). Thus, the system uses the materials of the work context to advertise those objects that require further user attention.

Users repair an object by interacting with its checklist. The checklist advertises aspects of the object that require more attention. Figures 4 and 5 show the checklists for `ComputerProgramming` and `CYCUserInterfaceProgram` and an assistance resource accessible from each checklist.

Conventions used in checklists include the following. Reverse video indicates a trouble – e.g., the object `InterfaceProgram` on the `instanceOf` slot of `CYCUserInterfaceProgram` (figure 5). Italics indicate an inferred value – e.g., the object `Collection` on the `instanceOf` slot of `ComputerProgramming` (figure 4). A box around an object indicates that the object is incompletely specified – e.g., the object `product` on the `canHaveSlots` slot of `ComputerProgramming` (figure 4). A balloon icon with text indicates a suggestion (figure 4).

An assistance resource is associated with each object that requires user attention. The suggestion associated with `ComputerProgramming` and the trouble associated with `CYCUserInterfaceProgram` discussed in the previous section are shown in figure 4 and 5, respectively. Since the resources that explain troubles or suggestions or inferences are made persistent through association with objects in the workspace, users can interact with them, turn their attention elsewhere, then revisit them later.

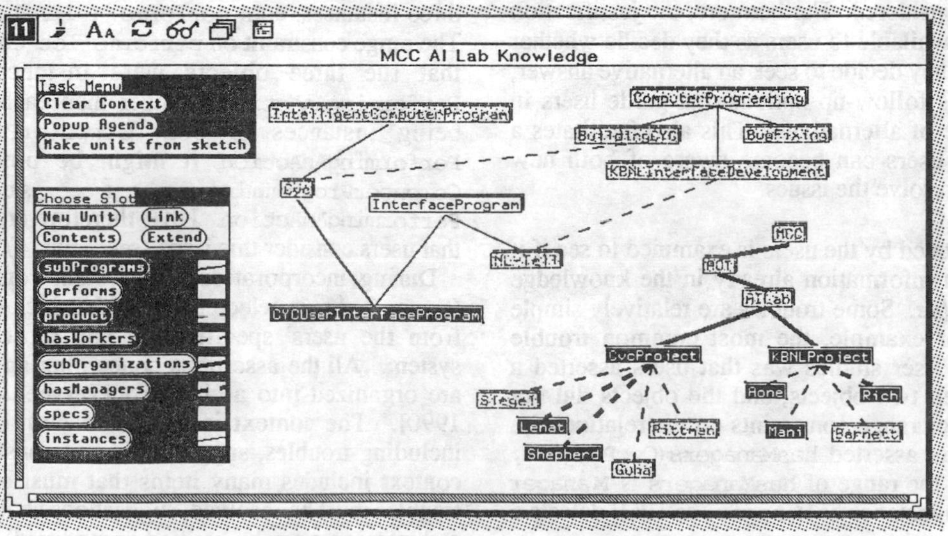

Figure 3: The sketch after incorporation

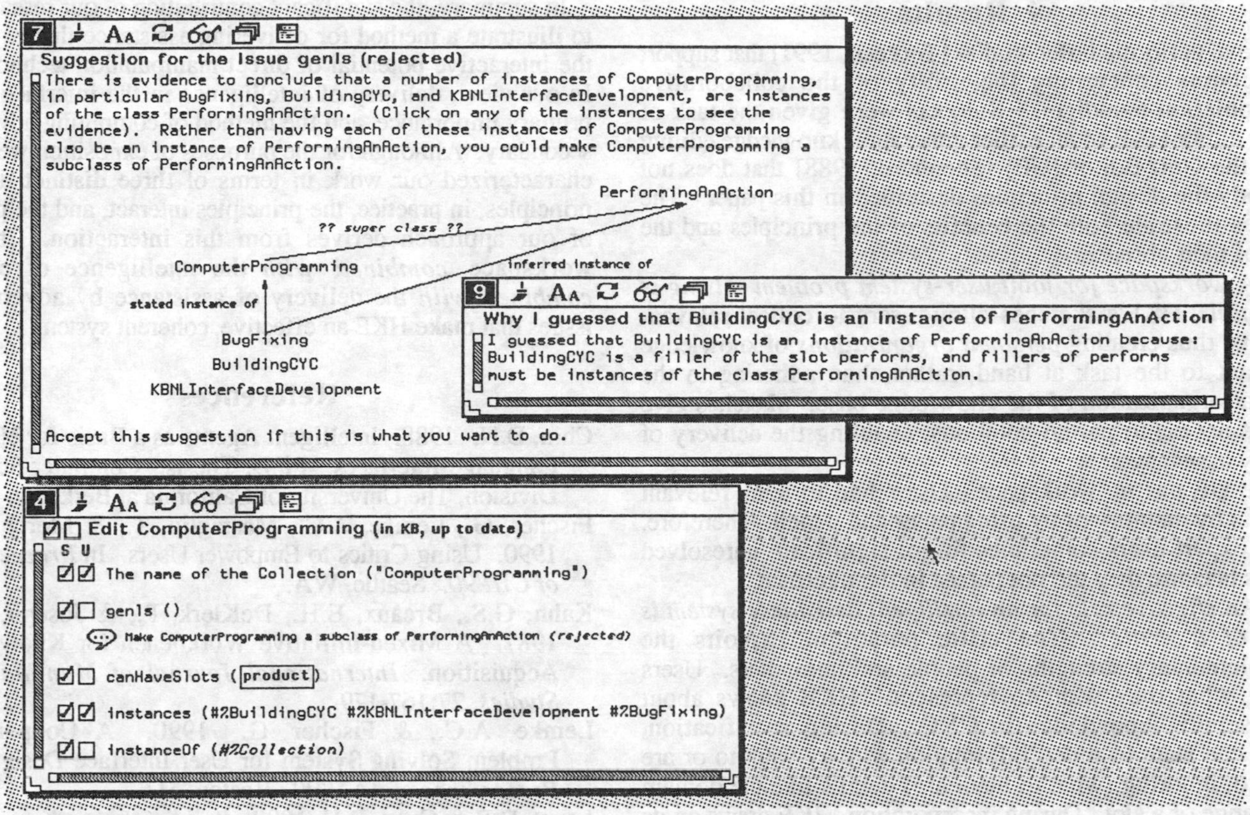

Figure 4: Checklist for ComputerProgramming, with an associated suggestion

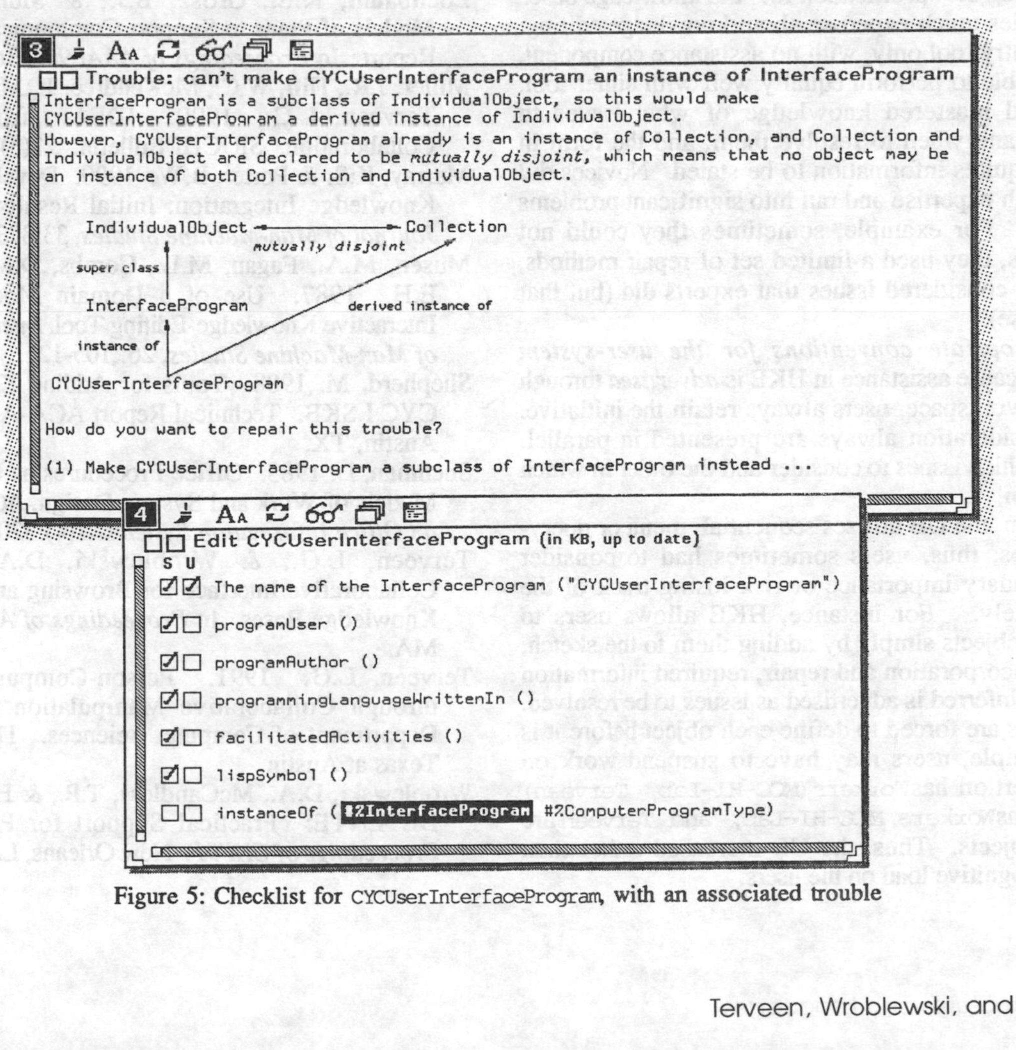

Figure 5: Checklist for CYCUserInterfaceProgram, with an associated trouble

4 Results

We have performed user studies [Terveen, 1991] that support our claims concerning the utility of the collaborative manipulation paradigm. Subjects were given the task of using either HKE or an earlier generation knowledge editing tool, the Unit Editor (UE) [Shepherd, 1988] that does not embody the design principles described in this paper. The studies illustrate both the benefits of the principles and the cost of their absence.

1. *A workspace for joint user-system problem solving is essential.* HKE's sketches allow users to collect relevant objects, thus creating *personal organizations* of knowledge relevant to the task at hand, rather than adhering to the logical organization of the knowledge base. Sketches give critics access to partial solutions, enabling the delivery of timely assistance.

The UE has no workspace. Users had to track relevant objects by memory or by using paper and pencil. Therefore, even expert users sometimes forgot significant unresolved issues because they did not persist in the interface.

2. *An effective role for an intelligent assistance system is that of a critic.* The critic paradigm exploits the complementary strengths of people and computers. Users know what they want to represent. HKE knows about representing knowledge in CYC. During specification, users can state as much information as they want to or are able to, ignoring (what to them are) details like the domain and range of a slot. During incorporation, HKE draws on its expertise about knowledge editing to detect issues that are raised by merging the specification into the knowledge base.

HKE embodies much expertise about knowledge editing; the UE is an entry tool only, with no assistance component. Experts were able to perform equally well with either tool, since they had mastered knowledge of what issues to consider, how and when to resolve them, and the form in which CYC requires information to be stated. Novices did not possess such expertise and ran into significant problems using the UE. For example, sometimes they could not repair problems, they used a limited set of repair methods, and they never considered issues that experts did (but that HKE would raise).

3. *Use appropriate conventions for the user-system interaction.* Because assistance in HKE is *advertised* through objects in the workspace, users always retain the initiative. Issues for consideration always are presented in parallel. Users choose which issues to consider and the order in which to consider them.

In comparison, the UE utilizes sequential menu or query-based dialogues; thus, users sometimes had to consider issues of secondary importance or risk losing track of the issues completely. For instance, HKE allows users to introduce new objects simply by adding them to the sketch. Later, during incorporation and repair, required information not supplied or inferred is advertised as issues to be resolved. In the UE, users are forced to define each object before it is used. For example, users may have to suspend work on stating the assertion has`Workers(MCC-HI-Lab, Terveen)` to ensure that has`Workers`, `MCC-HI-Lab`, and `Terveen` are well-formed objects. Thus, the UE increased rather than decreased the cognitive load on the users.

In summary, the significant contribution of our research is to illustrate a method for delivering assistance that exploits the interactive potential of direct manipulation technology. In our view, delivery of intelligence in the interface is of primary importance, and the method of computing advice is secondary. Although for the purposes of exposition we have characterized our work in terms of three distinct design principles, in practice, the principles interact, and the power of our approach derives from this interaction. It is a workspace *combined with* the intelligence of critics *combined with* the delivery of assistance by advertising issues that make HKE an effective, coherent system.

References

Chin, D.N. 1988. Intelligent Agents as a Basis for Natural Language Interfaces. Ph.D. Thesis. Computer Science Division, The University of California at Berkeley.

Fischer, G., Lemke, A.C., Mastaglio, T., & Morch, A.I. 1990. Using Critics to Empower Users. In *Proceedings of CHI'90*. Seattle, WA.

Kahn, G.S., Breaux, E.H., DeKlerk, P., & Joseph, R.L. 1987. A Mixed-Initiative Workbench for Knowledge Acquisition. *International Journal of Man-Machine Studies*, 27:167-179.

Lemke, A.C., & Fischer, G. 1990. A Cooperative Problem Solving System for User Interface Design. In *Proceedings of AAAI'90*. Boston, MA.

Lenat, D.B & Guha, R.V. 1990. *Building Large Knowledge Based Systems*. Reading, MA: Addison-Wesley.

Lochbaum, K.E., Grosz, B.J., & Sidner, C.L. 1990. Models of Plans to Support Communication: An Initial Report. In *Proceedings of AAAI'90*. Boston, MA.

Miller, J.R., Hill, W.C., McKendree, J., McCandless, T., & Terveen, L.G. 1990. IDEA: from Advising to Collaboration. SIGCHI Bulletin. 21(3): 53-58.

Murray, K.S. & Porter, B.W. 1990. Developing a Tool for Knowledge Integration: Initial Results. *International Journal of Man-Machine Studies*, 33:373-383.

Musen, M.A., Fagan, M.L., Combs, D.M., & Shortliffe, E.H. 1987. Use of a Domain Model to Drive an Interactive Knowledge-Editing Tool. *International Journal of Man-Machine Studies*, 26: 105-121.

Shepherd, M. 1988. Tools for Adding Knowledge to the CYC LSKB. Technical Report ACA-AI-068-88. MCC. Austin, TX.

Suchman, L. 1983. Office Procedures as Practical Action: Models of Work and System Design. *ACM Transactions on Office Information Systems*. 1(4):320-328.

Terveen, L.G., & Wroblewski, D.A. 1990. A Collaborative Interface for Browsing and Editing Large Knowledge Bases. In *Proceedings of AAAI'90*. Boston, MA.

Terveen, L.G. 1991. Person-Computer Cooperation through Collaborative Manipulation. Ph.D. Thesis. Department of Computer Sciences. The University of Texas at Austin.

Wroblewski, D.A., McCandless, T.P., & Hill, W.C. 1991. DETENTE: Practical Support for Practical Action. *Proceedings of CHI'91*. New Orleans, LA.

Effects of Parallelism on Blackboard System Scheduling

Keith Decker, Alan Garvey, Marty Humphrey and Victor Lesser *
Department of Computer and Information Science
University of Massachusetts
Amherst, MA 01003

Abstract

This paper investigates the effects of parallelism on blackboard system scheduling. A parallel blackboard system is described that allows multiple knowledge source instantiations to execute in parallel using a shared-memory blackboard approach. New classes of control knowledge are defined that use information about the relationships between system goals to schedule tasks — this control knowledge is implemented in the DVMT application on a Sequent multiprocessor using BB1-style control heuristics. The usefulness of the heuristics is examined by comparing the effectiveness of problem-solving with and without the heuristics (as a group and individually). Problem solving with the new control knowledge results in increased processor utilization and decreased total execution time.

1 Introduction

From the beginning the blackboard paradigm has been developed with parallelism in mind [Lesser *et al.*, 1975]. The idea of independent Knowledge Sources (KSs) that communicate only through a shared blackboard is a model that inherently encourages parallel execution. Many researchers have looked at making blackboard systems execute in parallel [Corkill, 1989, Fennell and Lesser, 1977, Rice *et al.*, 1989].

In particular the execution of multiple Knowledge Source Instantiations (KSI) in parallel (known as knowledge source parallelism) is discussed in several places in the literature. The Advanced Architectures Project at Stanford University [Rice, 1989, Rice *et al.*, 1989] has investigated blackboard parallelism at several levels of granularity. Their Cage architecture takes the existing AGE blackboard architecture and extends it to execute concurrently at several granularities, including knowledge source parallelism [Nii *et al.*, 1989]. Another project that investigated knowledge source parallelism is the work by [Fennell and Lesser, 1977] to study the effects of parallelism on the Hearsay II speech understanding system [Erman *et al.*, 1980]. One major contribution of that project is a detailed study of blackboard locking mechanisms. An alternative method for enforcing data consistency is the use of transactions as described by [Ensor and Gabbe, 1985].

One distinguishing feature of these studies of parallelism in blackboard systems is that they used simulated parallelism. Concurrently executing processes and interprocess communication were simulated using complex models of parallel environments. This was the case primarily because of the primitive nature of existing parallel hardware and the lack of sophisticated software development environments. Only recently have hardware and software capabilities come together to allow the actual implementation of parallel blackboard systems [Bisiani and Forin, 1989]. Useful parallel programming environments now exist, including implementations of Lisp. The work described in this paper was done on a Sequent multiprocessor using Top Level Common Lisp[1] (a version of Lisp that supports concurrent processing) and a special version of GBB 2.0[2] that was modified to allow parallel read access to the blackboard and to allow locking only part of the blackboard on write accesses.

Along with our actual use of parallel hardware, a major difference between our work and previous research is our focus on how control knowledge needs to change in a parallel environment. Previous work was more interested in investigating specific parallel models, while we are interested in what new control knowledge is useful. As we show, it is not enough to just add locks to a sequential blackboard system and execute the top n KSIs as rated by sequential control heuristics on n parallel processors. New heuristics need to be added that are sensitive to the requirements for effective parallel execution. Earlier work on Partial Global Planning[Durfee and Lesser, 1987] showed that constructing schedules using a high-level view of the solution space (derived by distributed agents from goal relationships) improved the utilization of distributed processors. This leads to the intuition that using goal relationships in scheduling may be helpful in

*The authors are listed in alphabetical order. This work was partly supported by the Office of Naval Research under a University Research Initiative grant number N00014-86-K-0764, NSF contract CDA 8922572, ONR contract N00014-89-J-1877, and a gift from Texas Instruments.

[1] Top Level Common Lisp is a trademark of Top Level, Inc.

[2] GBB 2.0 is a trademark of Blackboard Technologies, Inc.

a single agent, parallel-processing situation.

The next section discusses the details of our parallel architecture. Section 2.3 describes the new kinds of control knowledge that are useful in a parallel environment and identifies the kinds of data that are required to implement those new kinds of knowledge. Section 3 briefly introduces the Distributed Vehicle Monitoring Testbed, the application that motivates this work, and describes the new heuristics that were added for parallelism. Section 3.1 presents and discusses the results of the experiments we performed on the system, including the performance of the implementation and the effect of the added control heuristics. The final section summarizes the work and describes future research directions.

2 Architecture

The architecture is a straightforward extension to the BB1-style uniprocessor blackboard architecture described in [Decker *et al.*, 1989, Decker *et al.*, 1990]. In that architecture the processor takes the currently top rated KSI from the executable agenda. It executes the KSI action, which creates and modifies blackboard hypotheses. These hypotheses in turn stimulate goals, which trigger new KSs for execution. A scheduler orders the executable agenda and the loop begins again. This low-level control loop is highly parameterized; the parameters are set by control knowledge sources.

In our parallel system, several processors execute the low-level control loop concurrently. All of the hypotheses, goals, agendas, KSs, and control parameters are posted on shared global domain and control blackboards that are accessible to each processor. This basic architecture is very similar to the Cage simulations with KS-level parallelism and asynchronous control [Rice *et al.*, 1989].

Besides executing the low-level control loop in parallel, three major modifications to the existing system are made to allow effective use of parallelism. Locking mechanisms are provided to prevent conflicting blackboard accesses; the control knowledge sources are run sequentially, but the actions of many control KSs are broken up and run in parallel; and new classes of control knowledge are identified and implemented. The next three sections describe each of these modifications in more detail.

2.1 Blackboard Locking

Various schemes for blackboard locking appear in the literature. The most detailed is that described by Fennell and Lesser, who describe a method for locking blackboards that assures data integrity [Fennell and Lesser, 1977].

We have found that a much simpler locking mechanism is sufficient for our system. The only locking mechanism we provide is atomic read/write locks for blackboard writes. This mechanism is invoked when a blackboard write is done. It executes a read to see if the object to be written already exists. If it does, then the new object is merged with the existing object, otherwise the new object is written. Knowledge sources are designed so that they create hypotheses one at a time. Since only one lock is ever acquired at a time, deadlock is impossible. The operating system scheduler prevents starvation.

This simple mechanism is sufficient because the system can build several, possibly conflicting, partial solutions to a problem [Lesser and Corkill, 1981]. It does not require exactly one consistent working solution, so it does not return to and delete objects that cause inconsistencies. Because hypotheses are never deleted, the structure of the hypotheses on the blackboard never changes; only the beliefs in existing hypotheses may change. Changes in belief can be recognized and propagated by a separate knowledge source. If new hypotheses are created that would produce different results, then their creation will trigger new knowledge source instantiations that may be scheduled. We believe that other systems that share this characteristic will find that simple locking mechanisms are adequate. For example, the AGORA system uses "write-once" memory management where a blackboard element cannot be updated in place, but rather a copy is made [Bisiani and Forin, 1989].

Several types of locks were used in the implementation. Each blackboard level (space) is divided into a set of *buckets*. A blackboard data unit is stored in a small number of buckets based on its characteristics. Each bucket is given its own lock. Thus two KSIs can always write to different blackboard levels in parallel but one might block if they both write to the same bucket. Locks also control access to the KSI agenda and other internal data structures associated with the low-level control loop.

2.2 Executing the Control Knowledge Sources

Control knowledge sources change parameters that allow control over mechanisms such as filtering hypotheses or goals, merging hypotheses or goals, mapping from hypotheses to goals or goals to KSs, and the agenda rating mechanism. Control knowledge triggers on events on both the domain and control blackboards. In our current system control knowledge sources are run sequentially (meaning only one control KSI is executing at a time), however the actions of many of the control KSIs divide up the work and execute it in parallel on several processors. In the future we would like to investigate executing the control knowledge in parallel as well.

2.3 New Classes of Control Knowledge for Parallelism

Normal control knowledge (as used in a sequential environment) rates KSIs based on knowledge such as the belief of their input data, the potential belief in the output data, the significance of the output data given the current system goals, and their efficiency or reliability. In addition to these kinds of control knowledge there are several general classes of control knowledge that can be added to more effectively execute KSs in parallel. These general classes of control knowledge include:

Access Collisions: To avoid excessive conflicts for blackboard access, do not schedule two KSIs to work in the same part of the search space at the same time. For example, if KSI A and KSI B both write to a particular level of the blackboard, then they should not be scheduled for execution at the same time, because one of them will have to wait for the other to relinquish blackboard locks.

Task Ordering: Tasks may have absolute, unchangeable orderings (meaning they cannot be scheduled to execute in parallel at all), or there may be interdependence among tasks that lead to ordering preferences (one task provides data that will significantly affect the speed or quality of the result of another task.) For example, Task A may produce a result that makes the performance of Task B much faster. If so, Task A should be scheduled before Task B.

Task Bottlenecking: Performing certain tasks earlier in problem-solving may reduce future sequential bottlenecks. In general it is preferable to execute tasks that will allow more parallel options later. For example, there may be an absolute task ordering that requires that Task A be performed before Tasks B, C, and D, which can then be performed in parallel. Task A should be performed as soon as possible, because it will allow more parallelism later.

Task Invalidation: This is based on the "Competition Principle" in Hearsay-II [Hayes-Roth and Lesser, 1977]: the results of some tasks may completely remove the need to execute other tasks. Thus, when currently executing tasks are taken into account (assumed to complete), some pending tasks will be obviated. For example, Task A and Task B may perform the same operation, and produce the same result, in different ways. If Task A has been scheduled, then Task B should not be immediately scheduled, because it will be obviated if Task A completes successfully.

To take these general classes of control knowledge into account the system requires particular kinds of knowledge about the domain KSIs. In particular, avoiding *access collisions* requires knowledge about the input/output characteristics of a KSI (i.e., what parts of the blackboard it accesses and modifies.) *Task ordering* requires knowledge about task interactions. Often this knowledge is best captured through relationships among the goals of particular tasks. Avoiding *task bottlenecking* requires knowledge about the probable outcomes of tasks, again often expressed through goal relationships. *Task invalidation* uses knowledge about supergoal and subgoal relationships to understand the effect of KSI executions on other KSIs' goals.

There are four general categories of goal relationships that can be used (via KSI rating heuristic functions) to schedule domain KSs [Decker and Lesser, 1990]:

Domain Relations: This set of relations is generic in that they apply to multiple domains and domain dependent in that they can be evaluated only with respect to a particular domain, e.g., inhibits, cancels, constrains, predicts, causes, enables, and supergoal/subgoal (from which many useful graph relations can be computed, as shown below). These relations provide *task ordering* constraints, represented by temporal relations on the goals (see below).

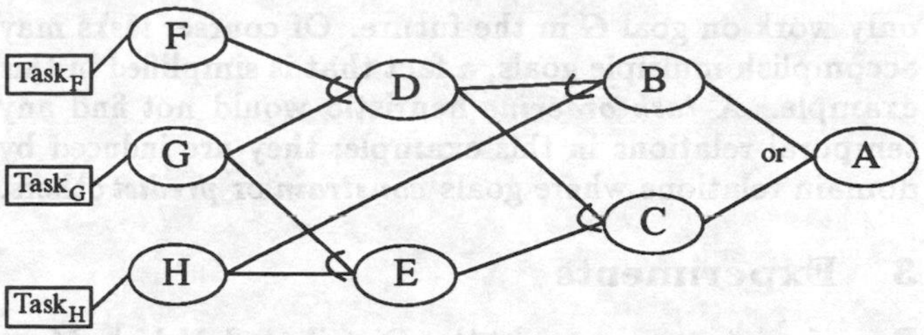

Figure 1: An abstracted goal relation graph

Graph Relations: Some generic goal relations can be derived from the supergoal/subgoal graphical structure of goals and subgoals, e.g., overlaps, necessary, sufficient, extends, subsumes, competes. The *competes* relation is used to produce *task invalidation* constraints. These relations also produce *task bottlenecking* information.

Temporal Relations: From Allen [Allen, 1984], these include before, equal, meets, overlaps, during, starts, finishes, and their inverses. They can arise from domain relations, or depend on the scheduled timing of goals — their start and finish times, estimates of these, and real and estimated durations.

Non-computational Resource Constraints: A final type of relation is the use of physical, non-computational resources. Two tasks that both use a single exclusive resource cannot execute in parallel. For example, if two tasks require that a single sensor be aimed or tuned differently, they cannot execute in parallel.

For example, examine the goal structure in Figure 1 (abstracted from an actual domain goal relation graph). Assume that task $Task_F$ is currently executing on a processor. The arcs in the graph represent the *goal/subgoal* domain relation on the goals[3]. From only this one domain relation, we can tell for example that F and G are *necessary* for D, D is *necessary* for B and C, and B is *sufficient* for A. F and G *extend*[4] one another, as do D and H. Goal B *competes* with C.

Thus a *task invalidation* heuristic might avoid scheduling a task that achieves goal B in parallel with one that achieves goal C. In the given situation (with $Task_F$ executing, and G and H available for processing), a *task bottleneck* heuristic might prefer to schedule a task to satisfy G, which will allow work on goals D and H in the future[5], over a task to satisfy H, which would allow

[3]While it looks similar, this is different from a typical data dependency diagram both in granularity and in the fact that it would be constructed dynamically during problem solving. At the present time we constructed one by hand to develop possible parallel heuristics for our domain.

[4]Goal 1 *extends* goal 2 if there exists a supergoal, goal 3, such that goals 1 and 2 are in the same AND conjunct.

[5]Goal D would become open, since its necessary subgoals F and G would be completed; goal H already was open.

only work on goal *G* in the future. Of course, tasks may accomplish multiple goals, a fact that is simplified in this example. A *task ordering* heuristic would not find any temporal relations in this example; they are induced by domain relations where goals *constrain* or *predict* others.

3 Experiments

Experiments were run on the Distributed Vehicle Monitoring Testbed (DVMT)[Lesser and Corkill, 1983], a knowledge-based signal interpretation system. The input to the DVMT is acoustic signals generated by moving vehicles and detected by acoustic sensors. The goal of the DVMT is to identify, locate and track patterns of vehicles moving through a two-dimensional space. The four main blackboard levels are: *signal* (for processing of signal data), *group* (for collections of signals attributed to a single vehicle), *vehicle* (for collections of groups that correspond to a single vehicle), and *pattern* (for collections of vehicles acting in a coordinated manner).

For our purposes, DVMT domain KSs can be divided into two main classes: synthesis and track extension. Synthesis KSs combine one or more related hypotheses at one level of the blackboard into a new hypothesis at the next higher level. Track extension KSs output track hypotheses, where a track is a list of sequential pieces of time-location data that identify the movements of a vehicle. The control KSs of the system can also be divided into two main classes: those that implement a goal-directed strategy and those that extend that strategy for parallel execution.

For these experiments, the DVMT processes the input data in three distinct phases. In the first phase (*find initial vehicles*), an initial set of control KSs execute, configuring the DVMT to perform a thorough analysis of all data at time 1. The purpose of this phase is to roughly identify the type and position of all vehicles that will be tracked in the experiment[6]. The data file we used contained 12 vehicles, and we defined four possible vehicle types with some signals and groups of signals shared by multiple vehicles. After these control KSs execute, and the domain KSs process all time 1 data, more control KSs are triggered and execute, configuring the DVMT for the second phase of processing. In the second phase (*approximate short tracks*), the DVMT performs quick, approximate processing to determine the likely identity and patterns of the vehicles being tracked. This phase ends when control KSs recognize that the DVMT has established a pattern (or explanation) for all the vehicles, though the patterns may be uncertain. For these experiments, we defined a short track to contain at least four time-location data points–thus, this phase ended after processing the time 4 data. Again, control KSs assign new values to system parameters, and the third phase (*perform pattern-directed processing*) commences. The DVMT devotes most of its processing in this phase to tracking vehicles involved in primary patterns, while performing cursory processing on vehicles involved in secondary patterns. This phase continues until all data in the input file has been processed. In these experiments, we included data until time 9.

[6]We have restricted these experiments such that every vehicle appears in the first set of acoustic samples, in order to simplify processing.

3.1 Examining the Basic Parallel Architecture

The first set of experiments involved collecting statistics on the basic parallel architecture without any added heuristics to take advantage of the parallelism. These experiments demonstrate that the locking system works, that the basic architecture provides for a good utilization of processors, and that the domain and our problem-solving method provide inherent parallelism.

Data for runs of the environment on 1 processor with no special parallel heuristics are summarized in Table 1. This table shows the time the single processor uses in each phase (and between phases) and the percent of the total time spent in each phase (and between phases). This data is used in comparisons to the other experiments described later. In this and all later experiments, data was collected with the locking and metering mechanisms enabled. The locking mechanism itself had almost no overhead, and as much of the metering as possible is done on a separate processor, completely outside of the processors being used for the experiment. The data collected by the metering processor did not involve locking any of the target processors. All of the experiments were conducted on a 16 processor Sequent Symmetry, and all of the experiments used less than 16 available processors (so no tasks were swapped off a processor).

Table 2 shows the speedup resulting from 5 processors and no parallel heuristics. Phase 1 parallelism arises mostly from being able to process all the data from the sensors in parallel. The tasks in phases 1 and 2 all must be executed, which also causes a high degree of inherent parallelism.

Centralizing the meta-controller that is implemented by control KSs proved not to be a bottleneck in processing; when not changing phases the meta-controller is almost dormant (simply checking for the end of a phase), and most of the work involved in changing phases (setting up new hypothesis and goal filters and running the hypotheses through them) is done in parallel. By running the low-level control loop (hyp to goal to KS mapping) in parallel we avoided the control bottleneck observed by Rice *et al.* in their first Cage experiment, where a set of KSs was executed synchronously by the controller [Rice *et al.*, 1989]. The only time that the system ever has to synchronize is at the beginning of a phase change, as the agenda from the last phase is empty and that of the next phase is still being generated. We have already begun work to eliminate this bottleneck as well, using a *channelized* architecture that gives us the ability to have different pieces of data at different phases of processing simultaneously.

3.2 Examining the Parallel Heuristics

By simply allowing KSIs to run in parallel, we achieved a significant improvement in the DVMT performance. However, it is clear from the discussion in Section 2.3 that we should be able to do better than just taking the top (single processor) rated KSI off of the agenda.

	Phase 1	1–2	Phase 2	2–3	Phase 3	Total
Real Time (seconds)	5224	1066	2118	1796	5656	15860
Percent of total time	33.0	6.7	13.3	11.3	35.7	100

Table 1: Summary of results of basic system with 1 processor and without parallel heuristics

	Phase 1	1–2	Phase 2	2–3	Phase 3	Total
Real Time (seconds)	1453	314	481	462	1433	4143
Speedup over 1 processor	3.6	3.4	4.4	3.9	3.9	3.8

Table 2: Summary of results of basic system with 5 processors and without parallel heuristics

Four new heuristics were added to incorporate knowledge about how parallelism affects scheduling. The BB1-style controller [Hayes-Roth, 1985] rates each KSI against each heuristic of each active focus. The architecture supports two types of heuristics — numeric and pass/fail. Numeric heuristics are summed to produce a rating; pass/fail heuristics must pass a KSI or it will not be executed. Either type of heuristic can also decide not to rate a KSI — the effect is of a rating of 0 or 'pass' but it is recorded differently. All the previous non-parallel domain heuristics were numeric but some of the new parallel heuristics are pass/fail.

1. *Pass Non-obviated Outputs.* Schedule KSIs that will not produce output that will be obviated if the currently executing KSIs complete successfully. This heuristic implements the *task invalidation* criteria described in Section 2.3. The usefulness of this heuristic is tied to the success rate of the KSIs in question — if the KSI currently executing is likely to finish successfully, then the heuristic will be likely to avoid duplicate work. This is a pass/fail heuristic — if there are no tasks available that will not be obviated by existing tasks, then the processor will wait. This heuristic is not needed in the single processor case because when a KSI completes its action, all KSIs that it obviates are removed from the agenda before the next KSI is chosen.

2. *Pass Primary Patterns.* This heuristic, which was a numeric rating heuristic in the single-processor system, was changed to a pass/fail heuristic. It is an example of a *task ordering* heuristic as described in Section 2.3. An implicit assumption of this heuristic is that KSs are not interruptible; so, when low priority KSIs are started, later arriving higher priority KSIs may not get a processor. When running an existing blackboard system in parallel, one should carefully examine the existing control heuristics to see if they will have the desired effect with multiple processors. While a high rating is sufficient in a single processor system to indicate that the KSs involved in a task are important to execute, in the multiprocessor case a decision must be made as to whether a processor should execute a KSI from a useful, but less important, task or wait idle for known important future tasks.

3. *Prefer Outputs on Different Regions.* Schedule KSIs that do not access the same blackboard regions as the currently executing KSIs. This heuristic implements the general *access collision* control knowledge described in Section 2.3. In our case, only blackboard write operations need to be locked. This heuristic will be more applicable in systems such as those described by [Fennell and Lesser, 1977] that do more elaborate locking. This is a numeric preference heuristic. Obviously this heuristic is not needed in the single processor case because only one KSI is being executed, so there cannot be any blackboard access collisions.

4. *Prefer Many Output Hyps.* Schedule KSIs that expect to produce many output hyps before those that expect to produce fewer output hyps. This heuristic implements the *task bottleneck* avoidance class of heuristics described above. By preferring to produce many outputs, more possible tasks may be enabled in the future. This is a weak numeric preference heuristic. This heuristic is not needed in the single processor case (in the DVMT domain) because the single processor will still have to execute all of the (non-obviated) KSIs, no matter how long the agenda is. The purpose of this heuristic is merely to get the queue to a long length quickly, improving multiple processor performance.

Table 3 is a comparison of the system with the four heuristics and 5 processors with the 1 processor system and the 5 processor system. We did not get as much speedup over the experiment without parallel heuristics as we had hoped. A primary reason for this is that the parallel version without heuristics was developed to run as fast and as efficiently as possible with 1 or more processors; we did not handicap it in any way. Our parameterized low-level control loop allows very few KSIs through that should not be executed (i.e., very little search). This hampers the heuristics especially in phases 1 and 2, which have very tight and precise control plans.

For example, the task obviation heuristic finds very few tasks to obviate. This is because we try to identify and filter out or merge hypotheses and goals that might create redundant tasks as early as possible (before they trigger KSs to form KSIs). However, this may not always be the best course to take — even our own system is being expanded to include multiple methods of achieving the same result by trading off some of the

	Phase 1	1–2	Phase 2	2–3	Phase 3	Total
Real Time (seconds)	1425	313	476	445	1181	3840
Speedup over 1 processor	3.7	3.4	4.5	4.0	4.8	4.1
Percent faster than 5 processors without heuristics	2.0	0.3	1.1	3.8	21.3	7.9

Table 3: Summary of results with 5 processors and parallel heuristics

	Phase 1	1–2	Phase 2	2–3	Phase 3	Total
Real Time Without Heuristic (seconds)	1474	555	755	455	1504	4743
Real Time With Heuristic (seconds)	1348	557	587	459	1436	4387
Percent Faster	8.5	0.0	22.2	-0.8	4.5	7.5

Table 4: Summary of results with and without the Task Obviation heuristic on 5 processors running a modified system

characteristics (such as precision and certainty) for time [Decker *et al.*, 1990]. This may result in more potentially obviatable tasks on the agenda. We test this hypothesis in Section 3.2.1.

The access collision heuristic is also relatively weak. This is because, as we have previously stated, KSIs seldom block on writing to the same area of a blackboard level, and may read in parallel. Access collision avoidance may be more important in systems that must lock objects for a long time to modify them. We tested this hypothesis in Section 3.2.2. Another problem stems from the *prefer many output hyps* heuristic; the DVMT tends to already work this way as a side effect of the domain heuristics, therefore the heuristic will not show an appreciable improvement when present.

As stated previously, the agendas in phases 1 and 2 were tightly regulated — the execution of a KSI on the agenda was necessary for overall problem solving progress. KSIs were not likely to be obviated by other KSIs, and most KSIs were involved in "good" work. However, this was not the case in phase 3. KSIs were created whose output would often be subsumed by the output of another KSI if this other KSI were given an opportunity to run (the first KSI is a candidate for obviation), and a fair number of secondary pattern KSIs existed on the agenda at any point in time. Given these characteristics of the agenda in phase 3, 21.3% speedup over the 5 processor system to 4.8 times speedup over 1 processor was achieved. The parallel heuristics allowed processors to make intelligent decisions regarding the next KSI to execute. As a result of the parallel heuristics, more KSIs were obviated, and processors often delayed executing the next KSI if none of the KSIs on the agenda appeared particularly appealing. It is also important to note that utilization was down somewhat in phase 3 because of the parallel heuristics, but the overall end-to-end processing time was reduced.

3.2.1 Testing the Task Obviation Heuristic

In order to test the *task obviation* parallel heuristic, we modified the basic parallel system by disabling the *KSI-merging* feature. This results in many KSIs, triggered by different data but intending to satisfy identical or similar goals, being placed on the agenda[7]. The scenario was run once with five processors without any parallel heuristics, and then again with the addition of the single task obviation heuristic. The results are shown in Table 4. Speedup was achieved particularly in phase two, when the addition of the task obviation heuristic caused a sufficient number of KSIs to be obviated, because KSIs were executed in a data-directed manner and thus tended to obviate others upon completion.

3.2.2 Testing the Access Collision Heuristic

In order to test the *access collision* parallel heuristic, we configured the DVMT to allow higher potential contention for system locks, without otherwise handicapping the system. Specifically, we modified the basic parallel system by disabling the *KSI-merging* feature and by artificially lengthening the time processors spend in the blackboard bucket locks. The first modification forces the creation of a separate KSI for each output goal (rather than merging similar goals). Since KSIs that perform essentially the same activities tend to get rated approximately the same, a processor will select a KSI for execution that will create results that one or more other KSIs running at the same time might produce. The effect of not allowing similar KSIs to merge will produce a high amount of contention for blackboard regions, because similar KSIs will be executing at the same time. The second modification simulates a system that requires a larger context for KSI execution — one that keeps more of the blackboard locked for longer times. The larger the context, the higher the probability of contention. The scenario was run once without any parallel heuristics, and then again with the addition of the single access collision heuristic. Both runs were with five processors.

Adding the heuristic to avoid regions that other processors are utilizing resulted in a significantly decreased

[7] A similar effect might have been achieved by activating multiple approximate processing methods, in addition to the normal precise methods, for each goal.

amount of time spent in locks. A processor in the run without the access collision heuristic spent an average of 18.4% of its time in locks, while the addition of the access collision heuristic reduced this time to 11.0%.

4 Conclusions

We investigated the effects of parallelism on blackboard scheduling. We have shown that we are able to get a speed-up for the DVMT application. We also showed that at least some of the speed-up was produced by our new heuristics that take parallel knowledge into account. It is our hypothesis that as the amount of search and interaction among search paths increases the heuristics will become more important. We are working to test this hypothesis.

As mentioned briefly in Section 3.1, we are currently investigating a *channelized* architecture that allows different vehicles to be in different phases of problem-solving simultaneously. That is, data for different vehicles can be processed using different filters, rated using different heuristics, and even use different approximate processing problem-solving methods all concurrently. We believe this has the potential to significantly increase parallelism, both because it removes the phase-changing bottleneck and because it clearly and simply divides up the work for parallel execution.

Acknowledgments

The authors would like to thank Kevin Q. Gallagher for his work in creating a shared memory parallel processing version of GBB 2.0.

References

[Allen, 1984] James F. Allen. Towards a general theory of action and time. *Artificial Intelligence*, 23:123–154, 1984.

[Bisiani and Forin, 1989] Roberto Bisiani and A. Forin. Parallelization of blackboard architectures and the Agora system. In V. Jagannathan, Rajendra Dodhiawala, and Lawrence S. Baum, editors, *Blackboard Architectures and Applications.* Academic Press, 1989.

[Corkill, 1989] Daniel D. Corkill. Design alternatives for parallel and distributed blackboard systems. In V. Jagannathan, Rajendra Dodhiawala, and Lawrence S. Baum, editors, *Blackboard Architectures and Applications.* Academic Press, 1989.

[Decker and Lesser, 1990] Keith Decker and Victor Lesser. Extending the partial global planning framework for cooperative distributed problem solving network control. In *Proceedings of the Workshop on Innovative Approaches to Planning, Scheduling and Control*, pages 396–408, San Diego, November 1990. Morgan Kaufmann. Also COINS TR-90-81.

[Decker *et al.*, 1989] Keith S. Decker, Marty A. Humphrey, and Victor R. Lesser. Experimenting with control in the DVMT. In *Proceedings of the Third Annual AAAI Workshop on Blackboard Systems*, Detroit, August 1989. Also COINS TR-89-85.

[Decker *et al.*, 1990] Keith S. Decker, Victor R. Lesser, and Robert C. Whitehair. Extending a blackboard architecture for approximate processing. *The Journal of Real-Time Systems*, 2(1/2):47–79, 1990. Also COINS TR-89-115.

[Durfee and Lesser, 1987] Edmund H. Durfee and Victor R. Lesser. Using partial global plans to coordinate distributed problem solvers. In *Proceedings of the Tenth International Joint Conference on Artificial Intelligence*, August 1987.

[Ensor and Gabbe, 1985] J. Robert Ensor and John D. Gabbe. Transactional blackboards. In *Proceedings of the Ninth International Joint Conference on Artificial Intelligence*, pages 340–344, August 1985. Also published in Readings in Distributed Artificial Intelligence, Alan H. Bond and Les Gasser, editors, p. 557-561, Morgan Kaufman, 1988.

[Erman *et al.*, 1980] L. D. Erman, F. Hayes-Roth, V. R. Lesser, and D. R. Reddy. The Hearsay-II speech-understanding system: Integrating knowledge to resolve uncertainty. *Computing Surveys*, 12(2):213–253, June 1980.

[Fennell and Lesser, 1977] R. D Fennell and V. R. Lesser. Parallelism in AI problem solving: A case study of Hearsay-II. *IEEE Transactions on Computers*, C-26(2):198–111, February 1977.

[Hayes-Roth and Lesser, 1977] Frederick Hayes-Roth and Victor R. Lesser. Focus of attention in the Hearsay-II speech understanding system. In *Proceedings of the Fifth International Joint Conference on Artificial Intelligence*, pages 27–35, August 1977.

[Hayes-Roth, 1985] Barbara Hayes-Roth. A blackboard architecture for control. *Artificial Intelligence*, 26:251–321, 1985.

[Lesser and Corkill, 1981] Victor R. Lesser and Daniel D. Corkill. Functionally accurate, cooperative distributed systems. *IEEE Transactions on Systems, Man, and Cybernetics*, SMC-11(1):81–96, January 1981.

[Lesser and Corkill, 1983] Victor R. Lesser and Daniel D. Corkill. The distributed vehicle monitoring testbed. *AI Magazine*, 4(3):63–109, Fall 1983.

[Lesser *et al.*, 1975] V. R. Lesser, R. D. Fennell, L. D. Erman, and D. R. Reddy. Organization of the Hearsay-II speech understanding system. *IEEE Transactions on Acoustics, Speech, and Signal Processing*, ASSP-23:11–23, February 1975.

[Nii *et al.*, 1989] H. Penny Nii, Nelleke Aiello, and James Rice. Experiments on Cage and Poligon: Measuring the performance of parallel blackboard systems. In M. N. Huhns and L. Gasser, editors, *Distributed Artificial Intelligence, Vol. II.* Morgan Kaufman Publishers, Inc., 1989.

[Rice *et al.*, 1989] James Rice, Nelleke Aiello, and H. Penny Nii. See how they run... the architecture and performance of two concurrent blackboard systems. In V. Jagannathan, Rajendra Dodhiawala, and Lawrence S. Baum, editors, *Blackboard Architectures and Applications.* Academic Press, 1989.

[Rice, 1989] James Rice. The Advanced Architectures Project. Technical report KSL-88-71, Knowledge Systems Laboratory, Stanford University, 1989.

The Automated Analysis of Rule-based Systems, Based on their Procedural Semantics.

Rick Evertsz
Scientia Ltd,
150 Brompton Road,
London, SW3 1HX,
United Kingdom.

Abstract

This paper describes a method of analysing rule-based systems, which models the *procedural semantics* of such languages. Through a process of 'abstract interpretation', the program, AbsPS, derives a description of the mapping between a rule base's inputs and outputs. In contrast to earlier approaches, AbsPS can analyse the effects of: conflict resolution, closed-world negation and the retraction of facts. This considerably reduces the size of the search space because, in the abstract domain, AbsPS takes advantage of the very same control information which guides the inference engine in the concrete domain. AbsPS can detect redundancies which would be missed if the procedural semantics were ignored. Furthermore, the abstract description of a rule base's input-output mapping can be used to prove that the rule base meets its specification.

1. Introduction

Much effort has been devoted to the problems of analysing forward-chaining rule-based systems with regard to improving their reliability and efficiency [cf. Suwa *et al.*, 1982; Nguyen *et al.*, 1985; Beauvieux, 1990]. To the extent that a rule-based system is a piece of software, it too can embody unintentional errors. Some of these errors merely reduce the efficiency of the rule base, whilst others may result in erroneous inferences. An example of the latter is the problem of contradictory rule subsets where, given an initial set of facts, two (possibly intersecting) groups of rules lead to contradictory conclusions (e.g. $P \wedge \neg P$). Examples of efficiency-reducing features include:

- redundant rules - where one or more rules are equivalent in terms of the states which match their antecedents, and the conclusions drawn in their consequents;
- subsumed rules - where a rule's antecedent matches a subset of those states matched by another, and the two rules have equivalent consequents;
- unreachable rules - where none of the initial states can ever lead to the invocation of a particular rule (this can reduce efficiency by wasting computational effort on processing the rule's antecedent);
- dead-end rules - these are rules whose consequents do not affect the other rules in the system, and so have no part to play in generating a solution.

The program, CHECK [Nguyen *et al.*, 1985], tackles these problems by examining the antecedents of pairs of rules, but can also apply a more complex analysis based on the dependencies between the consequents and antecedents of rules. For example, if one of the clauses in the antecedent of a rule is not matched by any of the consequent clauses of the rule base, nor by any of the facts entered by the user, then it can never be instantiated. Though this pairwise analysis of rules is 'incomplete' in the sense that it cannot find *all* inconsistencies and redundancies, it is still of practical use - the very restrictions which preclude completeness greatly improve the tractability of the analysis. Another approach, embodied in KB-reducer [Ginsberg, 1988], performs a full analysis of the knowledge base using ATMS techniques - this method is 'complete'. In the worst case, this is computationally intractable, however, experience with typical knowledge bases suggests that this does not happen in practice.

To date, those approaches which are 'complete' have embodied a number of assumptions which preclude their use in an important class of forward-chaining production system interpreters (or at least limit their effectiveness). They all assume monotonicity, i.e. the addition of new facts to the knowledge base does not invalidate previously deduced conclusions, and assertions can never be retracted. Secondly, the inference engine does not perform any conflict resolution - in KB-Reducer for example, each instantiated rule is fired exactly once, with no rules taking precedence over others [cf. also: Rousset, 1988; Meseguer, 1990]. CHECK too does not reason about the role played by conflict resolution.

The work described thusfar models the 'declarative semantics' of their respective inference engines. The trouble is that for many rule-based systems, the declarative semantics of the language are not equivalent to the procedural semantics. In order to reason effectively about knowledge bases expressed in such languages, one must accurately model their procedural semantics. For example, though one can spot some unreachable rules by virtue of the fact that no consequent clauses match the unreachable rule's antecedent, there may be rules whose antecedent clauses are matched, but which can never fire by virtue of the conflict resolution strategy employed. A complete analysis of such rule bases is only possible if one considers the inference engine's *control strategy*. In figure 1, if the conflict resolution strategy is based on rule specificity, then an analysis which is only based on the declarative semantics of the language would miss the fact that the rule R1 may not get a chance to fire when the assertion NO-WINGS(x) is present. If, as a result of conflict resolution, other rules in the rule base take over once R2 has fired, then R1 will be an unreachable rule for that class of inputs.

R1: if BIRD(x) then FLIES(x).
R2: if BIRD(x) & NO-WINGS(x) then RUNS(x).

Figure 1 – Specificity.

This paper describes a general-purpose method of reasoning about non-monotonic, forward-chaining rule bases which rely on *deterministic* conflict resolution for flow of control. This class of language is important, encompassing as it does a large proportion of the forward-chaining rule interpreters in use today (e.g. OPS5, ART, KEE). Our approach is based on the notion of 'abstract interpretation', where computation is performed in an abstract domain rather than the normal concrete one. Our implementation, AbsPS, operates on abstract data (i.e. data containing uninstantiated variables) and thereby accurately models the behaviour of the rule base on the set of concrete data subsumed by the abstract domain. An exhaustive search of the rule base, using abstract data, yields a complete and sound description of the space of possible behaviours of that rule base, provided that there are no cycles.

We have used AbsPS to find examples of redundant rules, dead-end rules and unreachable rules which would have been missed had AbsPS not reasoned about the role of conflict resolution and the effects of retracted assertions. More importantly, AbsPS has been used to prove that a rule base meets its specification. This is accomplished by comparing the results of AbsPS' analysis with a formal specification of the mapping between the rule base's inputs and outputs. In the final section of this paper, we outline further uses to which AbsPS can be put.

2. The Abstract Interpretation of Production Systems

A rule base plus its inference engine can be viewed as a partial function. The 'domain' of this function is the set of possible inputs which the rule base is defined to accept. The 'range' is the set of final databases which the rule base can generate from the input domain. In order to characterise this partial function we have developed a method which, given an abstract description of the input domain, generates a description of the set of final databases which can be generated, and refer to this as the rule base's 'I/O mapping' (input-output mapping). In generating the I/O mapping, a full analysis is made of all possible routes through the rule base, and this enables us to identify, for example, rules which do not contribute to the output of the rule base.

AbsPS was originally developed as part of PG, a program which takes pairs of rule bases and generates inputs which discriminate between them. The algorithm is described in detail in Evertsz [1990] and is complete for rule bases which do not contain cycles. AbsPS is given a rule base and an abstract specification of the set of inputs which the rule base is designed to handle. This specification differs from normal initial fact bases in that *ground* elements which can vary are replaced with uninstantiated variables. Each variable is associated with a domain description which represents the set of permissible values for that variable. Figure 2 shows an example of an input specification together with two concrete instances, one of which satisfies the specification, the other of which does not because the integer, 27, is out of range.

Input Specification:
GOAL(ASSESS_WEIGHT(x)), HEIGHT(x,h).
c:PRIMATE(x) ∧ c:INTEGER(h) ∧ h>50 ∧ h<100.
Positive Instance:
GOAL(ASSESS_WEIGHT(CHIMP)),
HEIGHT(CHIMP,76).
Negative Instance:
GOAL(ASSESS_WEIGHT(MANDRILL)),
HEIGHT(MANDRILL,27).

Figure 2 – An input specification.

The input specification contains two facts (predicates: GOAL and HEIGHT); in addition there is a set of constraints on the variables which define the variables' domains (in these examples constraints are prefixed with "c:" or are either ">" or "<").

Because Working Memory (WM) contains abstract descriptions of facts, the rules are matched using unification rather than the one-way pattern matching of normal forward-chaining PSs. The actions of AbsPS mirror those of a PS working on concrete data, however, all paths are explored. As each rule is unified and executed down a given path, new constraints on the variables are generated as a side-effect of unification. This environment is carried down the path from cycle to cycle and is *local* to that path. When a path is exhausted, the local environment constitutes a description of the set of final databases which can be generated down that path. For example, after applying the rule base to the input specification of figure 2, the description in figure 3 might have been produced.

Output Description:
WEIGHT(x,h/2),
where c:PRIMATE(x) ∧ c:INTEGER(h) ∧ h>75 ∧ h<85.

Figure 3 – One possible final database.

The description of **h**'s domain has been refined as a result of the rules applied down this path. Figure 4 shows a single rule which would have this effect.

if GOAL(ASSESS_WEIGHT(x)) & HEIGHT(x,h)
& c:PRIMATE(x) & c:INTEGER(h) & h>75 & h<85
then WEIGHT(x,h/2) & retract(GOAL(ASSESS_WEIGHT(x))
& retract(HEIGHT(x,h)).

Figure 4 – The rule R3.

The process of unifying the antecedent of this rule with WM generates the extra constraints on **h**. Note that because AbsPS maintains an abstract description of WM, it is also able to model the effects of retraction.

During abstract interpretation, invalid paths are pruned from the search space. For example, a rule whose antecedent contains the constraint h=75 would not be instantiated down a path in which the rule, R3, has already fired. This is because the firing of R3 constrains the value of **h**, in that local environment, to be between 75 and 85 exclusive. Such pruning of instantiations, whose domain variables do not intersect with the environment collected down the current path, drastically reduces the size of the search space, and is vital if one is to reduce the combinatorial explosion which can result when executing a rule base on abstract rather than concrete data.

The scheme described thusfar does not handle conflict resolution and so will generate many invalid I/O mappings. The paths which lead to these invalid mappings can be pruned early on by considering the effects of conflict resolution. Ignoring conflict resolution not only generates invalid I/O mappings, it also greatly increases the size of the search space because the rule base normally *relies* on conflict resolution for flow of control. We now describe a general method of characterising the role played by conflict resolution.

2.1. Abstract Conflict Resolution

An inference engine which employs conflict resolution will have an ordered set of conflict resolution principles which are applied one at a time until the conflicting set of instantiations is reduced to a singleton. These same principles can be used to filter the set of abstract instantiations generated on each cycle. However, during abstract interpretation it does not suffice to choose one instantiation for expansion and follow that path only; this is because each instantiation is likely to cover different subsets of the abstract domain. AbsPS must characterise these subsets and expand those instantiations with non-empty domains.

The key to characterising these domain subsets lies in generating *exclusion clauses* which describe the conditions under which those instantiations which appear to lose out during conflict resolution would actually be able to fire. Given a winning instantiation of the rule R_i, the other instantiations can only fire if R_i is not instantiated - i.e. if one of the constraints generated during the process of unifying R_i with WM is violated. If the constraints on R_i are $(C_1 \wedge ... \wedge C_n)$ and those on a losing rule, R_j, are $(C_1 \wedge C_2 \wedge C_4)$, then the exclusion clause which characterises the conditions under which it could not be instantiated is as shown in figure 5.

$$\neg((C_1 \wedge ... \wedge C_n) - (C_1 \wedge C_2 \wedge C_4))$$

gives: $\neg(C_3 \wedge C_5 \wedge ... \wedge C_n)$

which is: $\neg C_3 \vee \neg C_5 \vee ... \vee \neg C_n$

Figure 5 – Generating an exclusion clause.

This exclusion clause is added to the environments of the remaining instantiations. For some instantiations this will lead to a contradiction - such instantiations are discarded from the analysis because, down this path, there are no concrete instances which would enable them to be instantiated when R_i is not. The process of generating the exclusion clause is repeated on the remaining instantiations until no instantiations remain. Each instantiation, together with its associated exclusion clause, forms a new path emanating from the current state.

The simple example in figure 6 illustrates how conflict resolution should be handled in an abstract domain. If the inference engine incorporates a preference for rules which are more specific, then in the concrete domain R5 will be preferred in situations where both it and R4 are instantiated. However, there will be instances of **x** which enable R4 to fire, because R5 is not satisfied by that value of **x**. The exclusion clause, generated by negating the extra constraint in R5 describes this set of instances: x∉{PENGUIN,OSTRICH}.

R4: if BIRD(x) then FLIES(x).
R5: if BIRD(x) & x∈{PENGUIN,OSTRICH} then WALKS(x).

Figure 6 – R5 is more specific than R4.

The environment carried down the path emanating from R4 would include this extra constraint; as a result any rules which refer to the fact **BIRD(x)** would not be instantiated if they include constraints which exclude all of the members of **x**'s domain. For example, the rule R6 (figure 7) when unified with **BIRD(x)**, would fail to be instantiated because this would conflict with **x**'s current environment, x∉{PENGUIN,OSTRICH}.

R6: if BIRD(PENGUIN) then SWIMS(PENGUIN).

Figure 7 – Cannot be instantiated after R4.

We now conclude this section on the modelling of the procedural semantics of rule bases, by describing the special handling of negation.

2.2. Negation and the Closed-world Assumption

The class of inference engine which allows the retraction of assertions and employs conflict resolution, normally embodies another non-monotonic feature: the 'closed-world assumption' - if a fact is not known to be true, then it is assumed to be false. Current approaches to the analysis of rule bases do not incorporate this assumption - an assertion is only false if it is explicitly negated. In languages such as OPS5, a rule containing a negated antecedent clause can only be instantiated if there are no matching WM elements. These semantics are modelled in the abstract domain by building what is in effect an exclusion clause for negated elements; this specifies the *minimal* conditions which have to be satisfied for the negated clause to *fail* to unify with any elements in WM. This would be u≠a for R7 unified with the WM shown in figure 8.

R7: if PARENT(x,y) & PARENT(y,z) & ¬MALE(x) then GRANDMOTHER(x,z).
WM: PARENT(u,v), PARENT(v,w), MALE(a).
Exclusion Clause: u≠a.

Figure 8 – Building an exclusion clause.

2.3. Maintaining Environmental Consistency

During abstract interpretation, many paths are excluded because their environments are inconsistent. An inconsistent environment can be found during unification, when generating an exclusion clause and when dealing with negated patterns. Some of these environments are rejected by the unification algorithm even before they are generated, but the others need further analysis. The goal of this analysis is to spot environments which contain a contradiction - such environments can never be satisfied by any combination of concrete domain values and so should be discarded so as to avoid wasted computational effort.

This goal suggests that a refutation-based theorem prover would be well suited to the job. AbsPS incorporates a resolution theorem prover because this is one type of refutation system. It also employs the set of support strategy (this divides the current set of clauses into those that derive from the negated theorem, termed the 'set of support', and those that do not). The set of support strategy requires that every resolution involve at least one clause from the set of support, and thereby improves performance by restricting the set of potentially resolvable clause pairs. Now, if we know that some subset of the negated theorem is true, then that subset can be added to the set of axioms. This reduction, in the number of clauses in the negated theorem, further improves the beneficial effects of the set of support strategy. The incremental nature of PG's theorem-proving tasks, allows it to take advantage of just such a negated-theorem-dividing strategy. As each Abstract Instantiation fires, the set of constraints either gets larger, or stays the same size. So, if the set of constraints is currently, C_i, then on the next cycle, j, it will be C_j, where $C_j = C_i \cup C_{new}$ (C_{new} being the new constraints, local to the fired instantiation). On the face of it, C_j should form the negated theorem, to be passed to the theorem prover. However, we already know that C_i is consistent, as it was checked on the previous cycle. Thus, the clauses in C_i can be viewed as axioms. The negated theorem need only consist of the clauses in C_{new}; those in C_i can legitimately be added to the set of axioms.

This augmentation, of the algorithm is only worthwhile if one is using a theorem prover which incorporates the set of support refinement (or at least a similar division between axioms and potentially false clause sets).

2.4. Summary

In practice, the symbolic constraints on the domains of variables, generated as a side effect of modelling the procedural semantics of the language, yield a large reduction in the number of paths which must be explored. This is because the rule base will inevitably have been designed with this procedural model in mind; i.e. it uses the procedural semantics to *control* the deductive process, and AbsPS makes use of this very same control information to guide its analysis of the rule base.

3. Applications of Abstract Interpretation

Abstract interpretation is not needed to identify 'redundant rules' - the pairwise comparison of Nguyen *et al.* [1985] suffices even for languages with differing procedural and declarative semantics. Subsumed rules can be detected without performing abstract interpretation, however, they cannot be removed without further analysis. Many unreachable and dead-end rules can only be detected on the basis of the procedural semantics of the language.

3.1. Rule Base Redundancy

Perhaps surprisingly, 'subsumed rules' cannot be removed without doing full abstract interpretation. This is because of the role of conflict resolution. The more specific (i.e. subsumed) rule, though apparently redundant, may only be there to ensure that its behaviour is executed in cases where another more specific rule might have seized control from the *subsuming* rule. Therefore, it cannot be dispensed with without altering the behaviour of the rule base. AbsPS correctly identifies such instances, only flagging subsumed rules which are truly redundant (i.e. their increased specificity has no effect on the choice of path during conflict resolution).

AbsPS is also able to locate 'unreachable rules'. These are rules which did not fire during the abstract interpretation of the rule base. Some of these unreachable rules would have been missed by systems which ignore conflict resolution, and can be very hard to detect by eye because of the subtle interactions between these rules, conflict resolution and the other rules in the conflict set.

If some subset of the rule base is only involved in paths which do not contribute to a solution, then all of the rules in that subset can be safely removed. Again, there are many instances where such dead-end subsets can only be detected by considering conflict resolution, because an analysis based only on the declarative dependencies between rules will erroneously conclude that the subset contributes to a solution.

AbsPS does not automatically remove redundant rules but highlights the problems for the user to inspect. This is because the result may be a side effect of a 'bug' in the rule base. Conflict resolution can introduce subtle bugs which are hard for the user to detect. To illustrate, a rule R_i may never get a chance to fire because, for all possible initial fact bases, some other rule R_j always takes precedence. This might well be a bug; for example, the user may have omitted to include an extra clause in R_i's antecedent which ensures that R_i over-rules R_j under certain circumstances.

3.2. The Verification of Rule Bases

As rule-based systems are increasingly being considered for safety-critical applications, it has become important that one be able to verify that the system is 'correct' with respect to its specification. Because of the procedural semantics of many inference engines, this is not an easy task.

For a given input specification, AbsPS generates a description of the set of final databases computed by the rule base. This can be compared with the formal specification of the rule base. In AbsPS, this is not done automatically, rather, we compare the I/O mapping with the formal specification by hand to see if they concur. This is relatively easy because the I/O mapping has abstracted out all of the difficult-to-reason-about aspects of the rule base (i.e. pattern matching, conflict resolution and flow of control) and represents a declarative statement of what the rule base computes. Figure 9 shows a subset of the I/O mapping for the rule base from which R3 (figure 4) was derived.

Input Specification:
GOAL(ASSESS_WEIGHT(x)), HEIGHT(x,h).
c:INTEGER(h) $\wedge$ h>50 $\wedge$ h<100.

Output Description:
WEIGHT(x,h/2),
where c:INTEGER(h) $\wedge$ h>75 $\wedge$ h<85.
WEIGHT(x,h/3),
where c:INTEGER(h) $\wedge$ h<76.
WEIGHT(x,h*2),
where $\neg$c:PRIMATE(x) $\wedge$ c:INTEGER(h)
$\wedge$ h>50 $\wedge$ h<100.

Figure 9 – Subset of an I/O mapping.

Given the simple declarative nature of AbsPS' I/O mappings, we are confident that the process of comparing it with a formal specification can be automated.

3.3. Rule Base Chunking

Abstract interpretation can be used to analyse a rule base into useful groups. For example, if the rules within some subset of the rule base are only used in sequence without any other rules interrupting, then that sequence of rules can be collapsed into a single rule. Abstract interpretation yields the required information and could form the basis of a rule-chunking mechanism which improves efficiency.

Large, flat rule bases can be difficult to maintain and debug [cf. R1/XCON, McDermott, 1981]. One remedy is to group rules automatically into functional sub-groups. These modules can be viewed as self-contained wholes which communicate with other modules via restricted channels. Jacob and Froscher [1988] have developed a rule-clustering algorithm to tackle this problem. The algorithm endeavours to cluster rules so as to minimise inter-group coupling and maximise intra-group cohesiveness by examining the dependencies between the rules. Though applied to OPS5, this algorithm ignores the procedural semantics of the language and so may generate some 'loose' groupings. We are now applying AbsPS to this problem [Evertsz and Motta, 1991], however, it is too early to tell whether the increased precision is worthwhile.

4. Cyclical Rule Bases

Current approaches to analysing rule-based systems assume that there are no cycles. AbsPS is able to identify cycles, but is not able to reason about what they compute. During abstract interpretation, there are three major problems to be solved in analysing loops:

- Identifying the group of rules which forms the loop;
- Computing what changes on each loop iteration and deriving the termination condition for the loop;
- Representing the abstract behaviour of the loop so that other rules in the ruleset can manipulate the abstract sequence of WM changes effected by the loop.

Each of these problems is non-trivial, although identifying a loop is easier than the other two tasks. In most programming languages, identifying *explicit* loops is an easy problem. High-level languages provide structured looping constructs which are used to express iteration (e.g. Pascal's WHILE loop); thus, loops are made explicit by the language. Production systems do not incorporate syntactic conventions for flagging loops, rather, iteration occurs as a side-effect of the temporal aspects of the data in WM which force a particular control flow.

Abstract interpretation enables one to identify loops by modelling the temporal flow of concrete data items in terms of abstract ones. AbsPS does this by recording the fired instantiations as it goes along. If, down a given path, AbsPS is about to fire an instantiation of a rule which it fired earlier in the path, then the sequence of rules between those two points constitutes a loop. Note that this instantiation must be the one chosen for firing; merely being in the conflict set is not enough to constitute a loop.

Our definition of a loop is quite general. One can, however, think of other more restrictive definitions. For example, one could restrict our definition so that a repeating sequence of rules is only considered to be a loop if it processes items which it has produced on previous cycles. We argue that our chosen definition of 'loop' needs to be this general if we are to capture more obscure types of loop. For example, consider a rule, R_i, which on each cycle processes one of a sequence of elements in WM. This is equivalent to *generating* and processing them one at a time. It is unnecessarily restrictive to regard only the latter as a loop just because it processes values generated by itself on earlier cycles. R_i is just as cyclical, but processes the whole sequence *after* that sequence has been generated, rather than generating and processing the items one at a time.

Having identified a cyclical sequence of rules, beginning with R_i, it is not difficult to identify the termination condition of the loop - it terminates when one of the constraints of the rule is violated. AbsPS can already synthesise an expression which describes this condition - it does so when building an 'exclusion clause' during conflict resolution. The exclusion clause specifies the conditions under which a given rule could over-ride another which would otherwise have been selected during conflict resolution. The loop termination problem is a subset of the exclusion clause generation one. Rather than build a clause which expresses the conditions under which a rule would be prevented by another from firing, AbsPS builds a clause which expresses the conditions under which a rule could not fire, regardless of the other rules in the rule base - this is the termination condition.

Once the cycle has been identified and its termination condition generated, its output must be represented in such a way so as to enable the other rules to manipulate it. This temporal sequence of outputs could be represented as an aggregate data object, in the manner of Waters [1979]. This would enable AbsPS to manipulate it as a single entity. This functionality is still being developed and has yet to be implemented.

5. Tractability Issues

AbsPS' performance depends to a large extent on the characteristics of the rule base it is analysing. Because it explores all paths, it is the number and length of the paths which is the crucial feature, rather than the number of rules in the rule base. The number and length of paths is dependent, at least in part, on the size of the rule base, therefore rule base size is a rough guide to performance.

AbsPS has been used to analyse rule bases containing up to 50 rules. It takes on average 8 CPU minutes to analyse 20 rules and 45 CPU minutes to analyse 50 (Symbolics 3630). However, these timings are misleading because the program is implemented in a very naive fashion; the complete set of instantiations is recomputed on each cycle, for example. Many of the implementation techniques used in rule-based systems could be applied to abstract interpretation with little modification, including: the saving of instantiated rules and antecedent clauses from cycle to cycle (as in the Rete match algorithm, [Forgy, 1982]); the sharing of unification effort amongst equivalent antecedent clauses; and more efficient variable lookup [cf. Warren, 1977].

AbsPS' mean computational complexity is O(N*R*P), where N is the number of terms in the input specification, R the number of rules in the rule base and P the number of paths which can be followed for each term in the input specification. By implementing a more efficient abstract interpreter this performance could be improved to O(N*log(R)*P).

Though in the worst case the number of paths is combinatorially related to rule base size, AbsPS' performance is much better in practice. This is because it prunes paths a priori by taking advantage of the control information in the rule base. Indeed, rule base size is less of a problem if one partitions a rule base into self-contained modules with well-defined information flow between them; it would then be possible to analyse each module individually. Once a module had been analysed, it could be treated as a 'black box' and not analysed again until the user alters its contents. This methodology would be particularly valuable when incrementally developing a rule-based system - only those modules which have changed would have to be reanalysed. This is another compelling reason to develop an automatic rule-grouping algorithm.

6. Conclusions

We began by highlighting the problems which the procedural semantics of forward-chaining production systems cause for analysis. Previous approaches to the problem of analysing rule bases have only considered the language's declarative semantics - this is adequate so long as the procedural semantics are not an issue. We then described an algorithm for the abstract interpretation of production systems which models the effects of conflict resolution, closed-world negation and retraction.

This algorithm derives the I/O mapping for a rule base and can be used to identify common errors such as unreachable rules and dead-end paths. Because the algorithm abstracts out the intermediate procedural aspects of the rule base, its I/O mappings are well suited to formal verification. Though AbsPS cannot accurately reason about rule cycles, it can identify cycles and compute their termination conditions.

Abstract interpretation is a combinatorial problem, however, in practice it is tractable precisely because of its ability to make use of the control information which is implicit in the rule base. Grouping rules into self-contained functional units offers the prospect of interactive use of AbsPS if each group is small in size (of the order of 20 rules). Interestingly, abstract interpretation itself may offer a means by which such rule groups could be generated automatically.

Acknowledgements

Many thanks to Ian Assersohn and Stuart Watt for reading and commenting on earlier drafts, and to Enrico Motta for provocative discussions of this work. I am deeply indebted to Mark Elsom-Cook for his valuable input throughout this research.

References

[Beauvieux, 1990] A. Beauvieux. *A General Consistency (Checking and Restoring) Engine for Knowledge Bases.* ECAI90, Stockholm, pp77-82.

[Evertsz, 1990] R. Evertsz. *The Role of the Crucial Experiment in Student Modelling.* Doctoral Dissertation (and forthcoming CITE Report), IET, The Open University, U.K.

[Evertsz and Motta, 1990] R. Evertsz and E. Motta. – Work in Progress.

[Forgy, 1982] C.L. Forgy. *Rete: A Fast Algorithm for the Many Pattern/Many Object Pattern Match Problem.* Artificial Intelligence, 19, 1, pp17-38.

[Ginsberg, 1988] A. Ginsberg. *Knowledge Base Reduction: A New Approach to Checking Knowledge Bases for Inconsistency and Redundancy.* AAAI88, St Paul.

[Jacob and Froscher, 1988] R.J.K. Jacob and J.N. Froscher. *Facilitating Change in Rule-based Systems.* in Hendler, J.A. (ed.), Expert Systems: The User Interface Ablex Publishing Corp., pp249-284.

[McDermott, 1981] J. McDermott. *R1: The formative years.* AI Magazine, pp21-29.

[Meseguer, 1990] P. Meseguer. *A New Method to Checking Rule Bases for Inconsistency: A Petri Net Approach.* ECAI90, Stockholm, pp437-442.

[Nguyen *et al.*, 1985] T.A. Nguyen, W.A. Perkins, T.J. Laffey, and D. Pecora. *Checking an expert system knowledge base for consistency and completeness.* Proceedings of 9th IJCAI, pp375-378.

[Rousset, 1988] M.C. Rousset. *On the Consistency of Knowledge Bases: COVADIS System.* ECAI88, Munich.

[Suwa *et al.*, 1982] M. Suwa, A.C. Scott and E.H. Shortliffe. *An approach to verifying completeness and consistency in a rule-based expert system.* AI Magazine, Fall, pp16-21.

[Warren, 1977] D.H.D. Warren. *Logic programming and compiler writing.* DAI Research Report 44, University of Edinburgh.

[Waters, 1979] R.A. Waters. *A Method for Analyzing Loop Programs.* IEEE Transactions on Software Engineering, SE-5:3, May.

ARCHITECTURES & LANGUAGES

Connectionist & Parallel Rule Systems

Holographic Reduced Representations: Convolution Algebra for Compositional Distributed Representations

Tony Plate
Department of Computer Science
University of Toronto
Toronto, Ontario, Canada, M5S 1A4
tap@ai.utoronto.ca

Abstract

A solution to the problem of representing compositional structure using distributed representations is described. The method uses circular convolution to associate items, which are represented by vectors. Arbitrary variable bindings, short sequences of various lengths, frames, and reduced representations can be compressed into a fixed width vector. These representations are items in their own right, and can be used in constructing compositional structures. The noisy reconstructions given by convolution memories can be cleaned up by using a separate associative memory that has good reconstructive properties.

1 Introduction

Distributed representations [Hinton, 1984] are attractive for a number of reasons. They offer the possibility of representing concepts in a continuous space, they degrade gracefully with noise, and they can be processed in a parallel network of simple processing elements. However, the problem of representing compositional structure in distributed representations has been for some time a prominent concern of both followers and critics of the connectionist faith [Fodor and Pylyshyn, 1988; Hinton, 1990] .

Using connectionist networks, e.g., back propagation nets, Hopfield nets, Boltzmann machines, or Willshaw nets, it is easy to represent associations of a fixed number of items. The difficulty with representing compositional structure in all of these networks is that items and associations are represented in different spaces. Hinton [1990] discusses this problem and proposes a framework in which "reduced descriptions" are used. This framework requires that a number of vectors be compressed (reduced) into a single vector of the same size as each of the original vectors. This vector acts as a reduced description of the set of vectors and itself can be a member of another set of vectors. The reduction must be reversible so that one can move in both directions in a part-whole hierarchy. In this way, compositional structure is represented. However, Hinton does not suggest any concrete way of performing this reducing mapping.

Some researchers have built models or designed frameworks in which some some compositional structure is present in distributed representations. For some examples see the papers of Touretzky, Pollack, or Smolensky in [AIJ, 1990].

In this paper I propose a new method for representing compositional structure in distributed representations. Circular convolution is used to construct associations of vectors. The representation of an association is a vector of the same dimensionality as the vectors which are associated. This allows the construction of representations of objects with compositional structure. I call these *Holographic Reduced Representations* (HRRs), since convolution and correlation based memories are closely related to holographic storage, and they provide an implementation of Hinton's [1990] reduced descriptions. I describe how HRRs and error correcting associative item memories can be used to build distributed connectionist systems which manipulate complex structures. The item memories are necessary to clean up the noisy items extracted from the convolution representations.

2 Associative memories

Associative memories are used to store associations between items which are represented is a distributed fashion as vectors. Nearly all work on associative memory has been concerned with storing items or pairs of items.

Convolution-correlation memories (sometimes refered to as holographic-like) and matrix memories have been regarded as alternate methods for implementing associative memory [Willshaw, 1981; Murdock, 1983; Pike, 1984; Schönemann, 1987]. Matrix memories have received more interest, probably due to their relative simplicity and their higher capacity in terms of the number of elements in the items being associated.

The properties of matrix memories are well understood. Two of the best known matrix memories are "Willshaw" networks [Willshaw, 1981] and Hopfield networks.[Hopfield, 1982] Matrix memories can be used to construct auto-associative (or "content addressable") memories for pattern correction and completion. They can also be used to represent associations between two vectors. After two vectors are associated one can be used as a cue to retrieve the other.

There are three operations used in associative memories: encoding, decoding, and trace composition. The encoding operation takes two item vectors and produces a memory trace (a vector or a matrix). The decoding operation takes a memory trace and a single item (the cue), and produces a noisy version of the item that was originally associated with the cue. Memory traces can be composed (by addition or superposition) and the decoding operation will work with this sum of individual traces, but the retrieved item will be noisier. In some models encoding and decoding are linear, e.g., Murdock [1983], in others decoding is non-linear, e.g., Hopfield [1982], in others all the operations are non-linear, e.g., Willshaw [1981].

To illustrate this, let $\mathbf{I}$ be the space of vectors representing items [1], and $\mathbf{T}$ be the space of vectors or matrices representing memory traces. Let $\boxtimes : \mathbf{I} \times \mathbf{I} \to \mathbf{T}$ be the encoding operation, $\triangleright: \mathbf{I} \times \mathbf{T} \to \mathbf{I}$ be the decoding operation, and $\boxplus : \mathbf{T} \times \mathbf{T} \to \mathbf{T}$ be the trace composition operation. Let $\mathbf{a}$, $\mathbf{b}$, $\mathbf{c}$, $\mathbf{d}$, $\mathbf{e}$, and $\mathbf{f}$ be item vectors, and let T_i be memory traces.

The association of two items $\mathbf{a}$ and $\mathbf{b}$ is represented by the trace $T_1 = \mathbf{a} \boxtimes \mathbf{b}$. We can recover $\mathbf{a}$ from T_1 by using the decoding operation on T_1 and the cue $\mathbf{b}$: $\mathbf{b} \triangleright T_1$ is a degraded, or noisy, version of $\mathbf{a}$. Noisy versions of $\mathbf{b}$ can also be used as cues. Depending on the properties of the particular scheme, the retrieved vector will be more or less similar to $\mathbf{a}$.

A trace can represent a number of associations, e.g., $T_2 = (\mathbf{a} \boxtimes \mathbf{b}) \boxplus (\mathbf{c} \boxtimes \mathbf{d}) \boxplus (\mathbf{e} \boxtimes \mathbf{f})$. An item from any pair can be used as a cue to recover the other item of the pair, e.g., $\mathbf{c} \triangleright T_2$ gives a noisy version of $\mathbf{d}$. The noisiness of the recovered vector increases with the number of associations stored in a single memory trace. The number of associations that can be represented usefully in a single trace is usually referred to as the *capacity* of the memory model.

In matrix memories the encoding operation is the outer product, and in convolution memories the encoding operation is convolution. Addition and superposition have both been used as the trace composition operation in matrix and convolution memories.

2.1 Convolution-correlation memories

In nearly all convolution memory models the aperiodic convolution operation has been used to form associations.[2] The aperiodic convolution of two vectors with n elements each results in a vector with $2n-1$ elements. This result can be convolved with another vector (recursive convolution); and if that vector has n elements, the result has $3n-2$ elements. Thus the resulting vectors grow with recursive convolution. This same growing property is exhibited in a much more dramatic form by both matrix memories and Smolensky's [1990] tensor product representations.

Researchers have used three solutions to this problem of growth with recursive associations - (a) limit the depth of composition (Smolensky [1990]), (b) discard elements

outside the n central ones (Metcalfe [1982]), and (c) use infinite vectors (Murdock [1982]).

The growth problem can be avoided entirely by the use of circular convolution, an operation well known in signal processing. The result of the circular convolution of two vectors of n elements has just n elements. Since circular convolution does not have the growth property, it can be used recursively in connectionist systems with fixed width vectors.

There is a close relationship between matrix and convolution memories. A convolution of two vectors (whether circular or aperiodic) can be regarded as a compression of the outer product of those two vectors. The compression is achieved by summing along the transdiagonals of the outer product.

Circular convolution, denoted by the symbol $\circledast$, is illustrated in Figure 1. Each of the small circles represents the product of a pair of elements from $\mathbf{a}$ and $\mathbf{b}$, and these are summed along the indicated diagonals. While the circular convolution operation is straightforward, what is remarkable is that circular correlation, $\circledplus$, (illustrated in Figure 2) is its approximate inverse.[3] If a pair of vectors is convolved together to give a "memory trace", then one of the pair, the "cue", can be used to retrieve the other from the trace. Suppose we have a trace which is the convolution of the cue with another vector, $\mathbf{t} = \mathbf{c} \circledast \mathbf{x}$. Then correlation allows the reconstruction of a noisy version of $\mathbf{x}$ from $\mathbf{t}$ and $\mathbf{c}$: $\mathbf{y} = \mathbf{c} \circledplus \mathbf{t}$ where $\mathbf{y} \approx \mathbf{x}$. The correlation operation also has aperiodic and circular versions.

Circular convolution is defined as: $\circledast : \mathbf{R}^n \times \mathbf{R}^n \to \mathbf{R}^n$, such that $\mathbf{t} = \mathbf{c} \circledast \mathbf{x}$ where $t_i = \sum_{j=0}^{n-1} c_j x_{i-j}$. Subscripts are interpreted modulo n, which gives the operation its circular nature.

$$t_0 = c_0 x_0 + c_2 x_1 + c_1 x_2$$
$$t_1 = c_1 x_0 + c_0 x_1 + c_2 x_2$$
$$t_2 = c_2 x_0 + c_1 x_1 + c_0 x_2$$

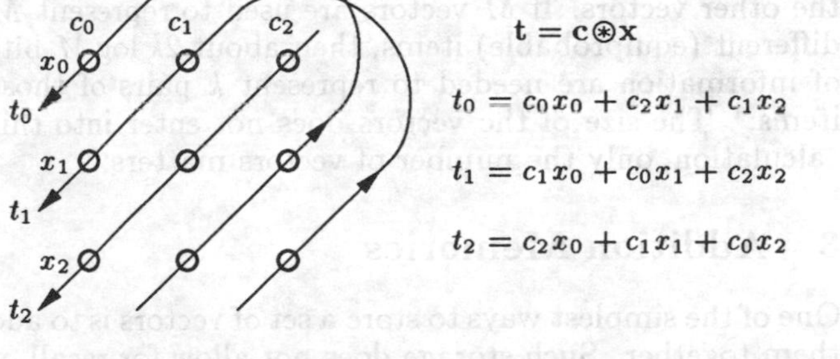

Figure 1: Circular convolution represented as a compressed outer product.

Circular correlation is defined as: $\circledplus : \mathbf{R}^n \times \mathbf{R}^n \to \mathbf{R}^n$, such that $\mathbf{y} = \mathbf{c} \circledplus \mathbf{t}$ where $y_i = \sum_{j=0}^{n-1} c_j t_{j+i}$.

Convolution can be computed in $O(n \log n)$ time using Fast Fourier Transforms (FFTs). The method is simple and well known: $\mathbf{a} \circledast \mathbf{b} = f^{-1}(f\mathbf{a} \odot f\mathbf{b})$, where f is a discrete Fourier transform (its range is a vector of complex numbers), f^{-1} is its inverse, and $\odot$ is the componentwise multiplication of two vectors.

---

[1] There are usually distributional constraints on the elements of the vectors, e.g., the elements should be drawn from independent distributions.

[2] The exception is the non-linear correlograph of Willshaw [1981], first published in 1969.

---

[3] Under certain conditions on the distribution of elements in the vectors.

$$y = c \circledast t$$
$$y_0 = c_0 t_0 + c_1 t_1 + c_2 t_2$$
$$y_1 = c_2 t_0 + c_0 t_1 + c_1 t_2$$
$$y_2 = c_1 t_0 + c_2 t_1 + c_0 t_2$$

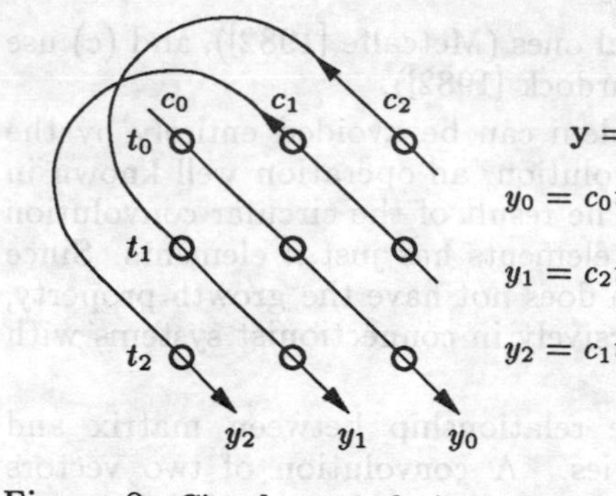

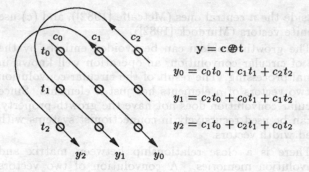

Figure 2: Circular correlation represented as a compressed outer product.

2.2 Distributional constraints on vectors

For correlation to decode convolution the elements of each vector must be independently distributed with mean zero and variance $1/n$ so that the euclidean length of each vector has a mean of one. Examples of suitable distributions are the normal distribution and the discrete distribution with values equiprobably $\pm 1/\sqrt{n}$. The analysis of signal strength and capacity depends on elements of vectors being independently distributed.

The tension between these constraints and the need for vectors to have meaningful features is discussed in Plate [1991].

2.3 How much information is stored

Since a convolution trace only has n numbers in it, it may seem strange that several pairs of vectors can be stored "in" it, since each of those vectors also has n numbers. The reason is that the vectors are stored with very poor fidelity; to successfully store a vector we only need to store enough information to discriminate it from the other vectors. If M vectors are used to represent M different (equiprobable) items, then about $2k \log M$ bits of information are needed to represent k pairs of those items.[4] The size of the vectors does not enter into this calculation, only the number of vectors matters.

3 Addition Memories

One of the simplest ways to store a set of vectors is to add them together. Such storage does not allow for recall or reconstruction of the stored items, but it does allow for recognition, i.e., determining whether a particular item has been stored or not.

The principle of addition memory can be stated as "adding together two high dimensional vectors gives something which is similar to each and not very similar to anything else."[5] This principle underlies both convolution and matrix memories and the same sort of analysis can be applied to the linear versions of each. Addition memories are discussed at greater length in Plate [1991]

---

[4]Slightly less than $2k \log M$ bits are required since the pairs are unordered

[5]This applies to the degree that the elements of the vectors are randomly and independently distributed.

4 The need for reconstructive item memories

If a system using convolution representations is to do some sort of recall (as opposed to recognition), then it must have an additional error correcting associative item memory. This is needed to clean up the noisy vectors retrieved from the convolution traces. This reconstructive memory must store all the items that the system could produce. When given as input a noisy version of one of those items it must either output the closest item or indicate that the input is not close enough to any of the stored items.

For example, suppose the system is to store pairs of letters, and suppose each one of the 26 letters is represented by the random vectors $\mathbf{a}, \mathbf{b}, ..., \mathbf{z}$. The item memory must store these 26 vectors and must be able to output the closest item for any input vector (the "clean" operation). Such a system is shown in Figure 3. The trace is a sum of convolved pairs, e.g., $\mathbf{t} = \mathbf{a} \circledast \mathbf{b} + \mathbf{c} \circledast \mathbf{d} + \mathbf{e} \circledast \mathbf{f}$. When the system is given one item as an input cue its task is to output the item that cue was associated with in the trace. It should also output a scalar value (the strength) which is high when the input cue was a member of a pair, and low when the input cue was not a member of a pair. When given $\mathbf{a}$ as a cue it should produce $\mathbf{b}$ and a high strength. When given $\mathbf{g}$ as a cue it should give a low strength. The item it outputs is unimportant when the strength is low.

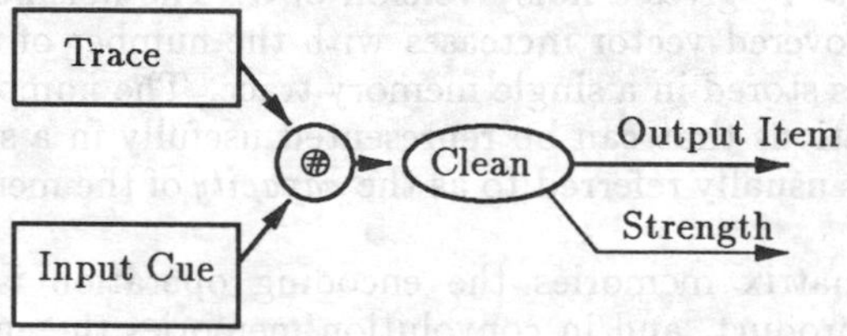

Figure 3: A hetero-associator machine.

The convolution trace stores only a few associations or items, and the item memory stores many items. The item memory acts as an auto-associator to clean up the noisy items retrieved from the convolution trace.

The exact method of implementation of the item memory is unimportant. Hopfield networks are probably not a good candidate because of their low capacity. Kanerva networks [Kanerva, 1988] have sufficient capacity, but can only store binary vectors.[6] For experiments I have been using a nearest neighbor matching memory.

5 Representing more complex structure

Pairs of items are easy to represent in any type of associative memory, but convolution memory is also suited to the representation of more complex structure.

5.1 Sequences

Sequences can be represented in a number of ways using convolution encoding. An entire sequence can be repre-

---

[6]Although most of this paper assumes items are represented as real vectors, convolution memories also work with binary vectors [Willshaw, 1981].

sented in one memory trace (providing the soft capacity limits are not exceeded), or chunking can be used to represent a sequence of any length in a number of memory traces.

Murdock [1983; 1987] proposes a chaining method of representing sequences in a single memory trace, and models a large number of psychological phenomena with it. The technique used stores both item and pair information in the memory trace, for example, if the sequence of vectors to be stored is **abc**, then the trace is

$$\alpha_1\mathbf{a} + \beta_1\mathbf{a}\circledast\mathbf{b} + \alpha_2\mathbf{b} + \beta_2\mathbf{b}\circledast\mathbf{c} + \alpha_3\mathbf{c},$$

where α_i and β_i are suitable weighting constants less than 1, generated from a two or three underlying parameters, with $\alpha_i > \alpha_{i+1}$. The retrieval of the sequence begins with retrieving the strongest component of the trace, which will be **a**. From there the retrieval is by chaining — correlating the trace with the current item to retrieve the next item. The end of the sequence is detected when the correlation of the trace with the current item is not similar to any item in the item memory.

Another way to represent sequences is to use the entire previous sequence as context rather than just the previous item [Murdock, 1987]. This makes it possible to store sequences with repetitions of items. To store **abc**, the trace is: $\mathbf{a} + \mathbf{a}\circledast\mathbf{b} + \mathbf{a}\circledast\mathbf{b}\circledast\mathbf{c}$. This type of sequence can be retrieved in a similar way to the previous, except that the retrieval cue must be built up using convolutions.

The retrieval of later items in both these representations could be improved by subtracting off prefix components as the items in the sequence are retrieved.

Yet another way to represent sequences is to use a fixed cue for each position of the sequence, so to store **abc**, the trace is: $\mathbf{p}_1\circledast\mathbf{a} + \mathbf{p}_2\circledast\mathbf{b} + \mathbf{p}_3\circledast\mathbf{c}$. The retrieval (and storage) cues $\mathbf{p}_i$ can be arbitrary or generated in some manner from a single vector, e.g., $\mathbf{p}_i = (\mathbf{p})^i$.

5.2 Chunking of sequences

All of the above methods have soft limits on the length of sequences that can be stored. As the sequences get longer the noise in the retrieved items increases until the items are impossible to identify. This limit can be overcome by chunking — creating new "non terminal" items representing subsequences [Murdock, 1987].

The second sequence representation method is the most suitable one to do chunking with. Suppose we want to represent the sequence **abcdefgh**. We can create three new items representing subsequences:

$$\begin{aligned}\mathbf{s}_{abc} &= \mathbf{a} + \mathbf{a}\circledast\mathbf{b} + \mathbf{a}\circledast\mathbf{b}\circledast\mathbf{c}\\ \mathbf{s}_{de} &= \mathbf{d} + \mathbf{d}\circledast\mathbf{e}\\ \mathbf{s}_{fgh} &= \mathbf{f} + \mathbf{f}\circledast\mathbf{g} + \mathbf{f}\circledast\mathbf{g}\circledast\mathbf{h}\end{aligned}$$

These new items must be added to the item memory and marked in some way as non-terminals. The representation for the whole sequence is:

$$\mathbf{s}_{abc} + \mathbf{s}_{abc}\circledast\mathbf{s}_{de} + \mathbf{s}_{abc}\circledast\mathbf{s}_{de}\circledast\mathbf{s}_{fgh}.$$

Decoding this chunked sequence is slightly more difficult, requiring the use of a stack and decisions on whether an item is a non terminal that should be further decoded. A machine to decode such representations is described in section 7.2.

5.3 Variable binding

It is simple to implement variable binding with convolution: convolve the variable representation with the value representation. If it is desired that the representation of a variable binding should be somewhat similar to both the variable and the value, the vectors for those can be added in. This gives $\alpha\mathbf{x}\circledast\mathbf{a} + \beta\mathbf{x} + \gamma\mathbf{a}$ as the representation of a variable binding.

This type of variable binding can also be implemented in other types of associative memory, e.g., the triple-space of BoltzCONS [Touretzky and Hinton, 1985], or the outer product of roles and fillers in DUCS [Touretzky and Geva, 1987]. However, in those systems the variable and value objects were of a different dimension than the binding object. Thus it was not possible add components of the variable and the value to the representation of the binding, nor use the binding itself as an item in another association.

5.4 Frame-slot representations

Frames can be represented using convolution encoding in an analogous manner to cross products of roles and fillers in [Hinton, 1981] or the frames of DUCS [Touretzky and Geva, 1987]. A frame consists of a frame label and a set of roles, each represented by a vector. An instantiated frame is the sum of the frame label and the roles (slots) convolved with their respective fillers. For example, suppose we have a (very simplified) frame for "seeing". The vector for the frame label is $\mathbf{l}_{see}$ and the vectors for the roles are $\mathbf{r}_{agent}$ and $\mathbf{r}_{object}$. This frame could be instantiated with the fillers $\mathbf{f}_{jane}$ and $\mathbf{f}_{spot}$, to represent "Jane saw Spot":

$$\mathbf{t}_{seeing} = \mathbf{l}_{see} + \mathbf{r}_{agent}\circledast\mathbf{f}_{jane} + \mathbf{r}_{object}\circledast\mathbf{f}_{spot}$$

Fillers (or roles) can be retrieved from the instantiated frame by correlating with the role (or filler). The vectors representing roles could be frame specific, i.e., $\mathbf{r}_{agent-see}$ could be different from $\mathbf{r}_{agent-run}$, or they could be the same (or just similar). Uninstantiated frames can also be stored as the sums of the vectors representing their components, e.g., $\mathbf{u}_{seeing} = \mathbf{l}_{see} + \mathbf{r}_{agent} + \mathbf{r}_{object}$. Section 7.1 describes one way of manipulating uninstantiated frames and selecting appropriate roles to fill.

The frame representation can be made similar to any vector by adding some of that vector to it. For example, we could add $\alpha\mathbf{f}_{jane}$ to the above instantiated frame to make the representation for Jane doing something have some similarity to the representation for Jane.

6 Reduced Representations

Using the types of representations described in the last section, it is a trivial step to building reduced representations which can represent complex hierarchical structure in a fixed width vector. We can use an instantiated frame[7] as a filler instead of $\mathbf{f}_{spot}$ in the frame built in the previous section. For example, "Spot ran.":

$$\mathbf{t}_{running} = \mathbf{l}_{run} + \mathbf{r}_{agent}\circledast\mathbf{f}_{spot}$$

[7] Normalization of lengths of vectors becomes an issue, but I do not consider this for lack of space.

could be used in a "seeing" frame "Dick saw Spot run.":

$$\begin{aligned}\mathbf{t}_{seeing} &= \mathbf{l}_{see} + \mathbf{r}_{agent}\circledast\mathbf{f}_{dick} + \mathbf{r}_{object}\circledast\mathbf{t}_{running} \\ &= \mathbf{l}_{see} + \mathbf{r}_{agent}\circledast\mathbf{f}_{dick} \\ &\quad + \mathbf{r}_{object}\circledast(\mathbf{l}_{run} + \mathbf{r}_{agent}\circledast\mathbf{f}_{spot})\end{aligned}$$

This representation can be manipulated with or without chunking. Without chunking, we could extract the agent of the object by correlating with $\mathbf{r}_{object} \circledast \mathbf{r}_{agent}$. Using chunking, we could extract the object by correlating with $\mathbf{r}_{object}$, clean it up, and then extract its agent, giving a less noisy vector than without chunking.

This implements Hinton's idea [1990] of a system being able to focus attention on constituents as well as being able to have the whole meaning present at once. It also suggests the possibility of sacrificing accuracy for speed — if chunks are not cleaned up the retrievals are less accurate.

7 Simple Machines that use HRRs

In this section two simple machines that operate on complex convolution representations are described. Both of these machines have been successfully simulated on a convolution calculator using vectors with 1024 elements.

7.1 Role/filler selector

To manipulate frames with roles and fillers one must be able to select the appropriate roles and fillers before convolving them. I describe here a way of extracting the most appropriate role from an uninstantiated frame. The most appropriate role for a particular filler might be either the "first" role in the frame, or the role that combines best with the given filler. Both of these selection criteria can be combined in a single mechanism. An uninstantiated frame is stored as the sum of the roles and a frame label. Each role and filler also must be stored separately in item memory.

Let the uninstantiated frame be $\beta\mathbf{l}+\alpha_1\mathbf{r}_1+\alpha_2\mathbf{r}_2+\alpha_3\mathbf{r}_3$. The task is to select the role that combines best with $\mathbf{f}$, the filler. Suppose there is some item $\mathbf{r}_2\circledast\mathbf{f}'$ in the item memory, such that $\mathbf{f}'$ is quite similar to $\mathbf{f}$. The presence of a similar binding in the item memory defines $\mathbf{r}_2$ as the "best fitting" role for $\mathbf{f}$.[8]

If the roles in the frame should be selected according to best fit, then the α_i should be approximately equal, but if $\mathbf{r}_1$ should be selected first, then α_1 should be greater.

The selection of the role is done by convolving the uninstantiated frame with the potential filler, i.e., $\mathbf{f}\circledast(\beta\mathbf{l} + \alpha_1\mathbf{r}_1 + \alpha_2\mathbf{r}_2 + \alpha_3\mathbf{r}_3)$. This is cleaned up in item memory to give $\mathbf{r}_2\circledast\mathbf{f}'$, which is then correlated with $\mathbf{f}$ to give a vector which can be written as $\gamma\mathbf{r}_2 + \mathbf{v}_{noise}$ where γ and the noise depend on the similarity of $\mathbf{f}$ to $\mathbf{f}'$.

This result is added to the uninstantiated frame to give $\beta\mathbf{l}+\alpha_1\mathbf{r}_1+(\alpha_2+\gamma)\mathbf{r}_2+\alpha_3\mathbf{r}_3+\mathbf{v}_{noise}$. The strongest role can be selected by cleaning up in item memory. Which is strongest will depend on the relative strengths of α_1, $(\alpha_2 + \gamma)$, and α_3, and the value of γ in turn depends on the similarity of $\mathbf{f}'$ to $\mathbf{f}$.

[8]This form of generalization by similarity can be used extensively.

The machine that accomplishes this operation is shown in Figure 4.

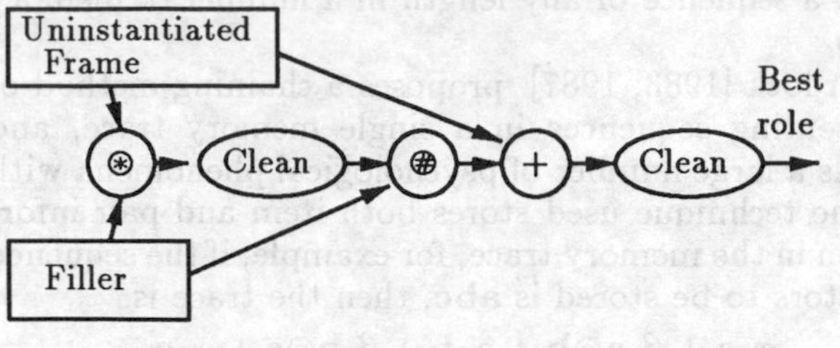

Figure 4: A role selection mechanism

7.2 Chunked sequence readout machine

A machine that reads out the chunked sequences described in section 5.2 can be built using two buffers, a stack, a classifier, a correlator, a clean up memory, and three gating paths. The classifier tells whether the item most prominent in the trace is a terminal, a non-terminal (chunk) or nothing. At each iteration the machine executes one of three action sequences depending on the output of the classifier. The stack could be implemented in any of a number of ways; including the way suggested in [Plate, 1991], or in a network with fast weights. The machine is shown in Figure 5.

The control loop for the chunked sequence readout machine is:

Loop: (until stack gives END signal)

Clean up the trace to recover most prominent item: $\mathbf{x} = \text{Clean}(\mathbf{t})$.

Classify $\mathbf{x}$ as a terminal, non-terminal, or nothing (in which case "pop" is the appropriate action) and do the appropriate of the following action sequences.

Terminal:

1 Item $\mathbf{x}$ is on output. T1 gates path to replace trace by its follower: $\mathbf{t} \leftarrow \mathbf{x}\circledast(\mathbf{t} - \mathbf{x})$.

Non-terminal:

1 Signal N1 tells stack to push the follower of the non terminal: $\mathbf{s} \leftarrow \text{push}(\mathbf{s}, \mathbf{x}\circledast(\mathbf{t} - \mathbf{x}))$.

2 Signal N2 gates path to replace trace by the non-terminal: $\mathbf{t} \leftarrow \mathbf{x}$.

Pop:

1 Signal P1 gates path to replace trace by top of stack: $\mathbf{t} \leftarrow \text{top}(\mathbf{s})$.

2 Signal P2 tells stack to discard top of stack: $\mathbf{s} \leftarrow \text{pop}(\mathbf{s})$. Stack gives END signal if empty.

This machine is an example of a system that can have the whole meaning present and that can also focus attention on constituents.

8 Mathematical properties

Mathematical properties of circular convolution and correlation are discussed in Plate [1991], including: algebraic properties; the reason convolution is an approximate inverse for correlation; the existence and usefulness of exact inverses of convolutions; and the variances of dot products of various convolution products.

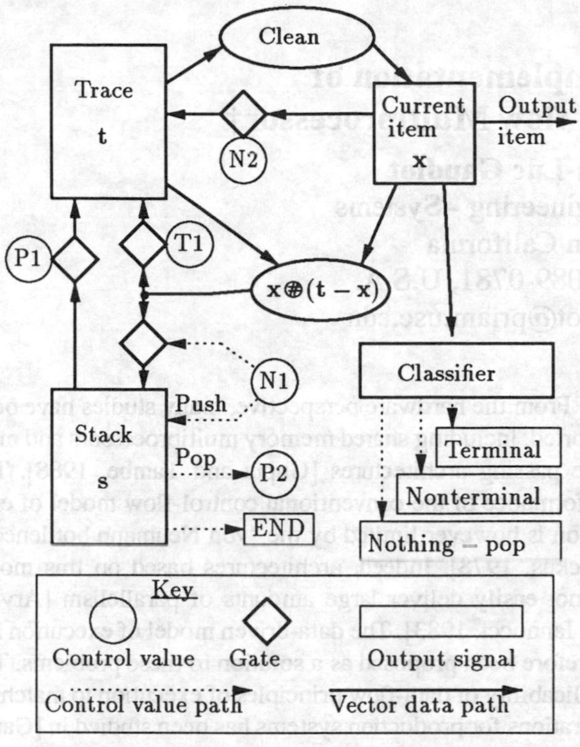

Figure 5: A chunked sequence readout machine.

9 Discussion

Circular convolution is a bilinear operation, and one consequence of the linearity is low storage efficiency. However, the storage efficiency is high enough to be usable and scales linearly. Convolution is endowed with several positive features by virtue of its linear properties. One is that it can be computed very quickly using FFTs. Another is that analysis of the capacity, scaling, and generalization properties is straightforward. Another is that there is a possibility that a system using HRRs could retain ambiguity while processing ambiguous input.

Convolution could be used as a fixed mapping in a connectionist network to replace one or more of the usual weight-matrix by vector mappings. Activations could be propagated forward very quickly using FFTs, and gradients could be propagated backward very quickly using FFTs as well. Such a network could learn to take advantage of the convolution mapping and could learn distributed representations for its inputs.

Memory models using circular convolution provide a way of representing compositional structure in distributed representations. The operations involved are linear and the properties of the scheme are relatively easy to analyze. There is no learning involved and the scheme works with a wide range of vectors. Systems employing this representation need to have an error-correcting auto-associative memory.

Acknowledgements

Conversations with Jordan Pollack, Janet Metcalfe, and Geoff Hinton have been essential to the development of the ideas expressed in this paper. This research has been supported in part by the Canadian Natural Sciences and Engineering Research Council.

References

[AIJ, 1990] Special issue on connectionist symbol processing. *Artificial Intelligence*, 46(1-2), 1990.

[Fodor and Pylyshyn, 1988] J. A. Fodor and Z. W. Pylyshyn. Connectionism and cognitive architecture: A critical analysis. *Cognition*, 28:3–71, 1988.

[Hinton, 1981] G. E. Hinton. Implementing semantic networks in parallel hardware. In *Parallel Models of Associative Memory.* Hillsdale, NJ: Erlbaum, 1981.

[Hinton, 1984] G. E. Hinton. Distributed representations. Technical Report CMU-CS-84-157, Carnegie-Mellon University, Pittsburgh PA, 1984.

[Hinton, 1990] G. E. Hinton. Mapping part-whole heirarchies into connectionist networks. *Artificial Intelligence*, 46(1-2):47–76, 1990.

[Hopfield, 1982] J. J. Hopfield. Neural networks and physical systems with emergent collective computational abilities. *Proceedings of the National Academy of Sciences U.S.A.*, 79:2554–2558, 1982.

[Kanerva, 1988] P. Kanerva. *Sparse Distributed Memory.* MIT Press, Cambridge, MA, 1988.

[Metcalfe Eich, 1982] Janet Metcalfe Eich. A composite holographic associative recall model. *Psychological Review*, 89:627–661, 1982.

[Murdock, 1982] Bennet B. Murdock. A theory for the storage and retrieval of item and associative information. *Psychological Review*, 89(6):316–338, 1982.

[Murdock, 1983] B. B. Murdock. A distributed memory model for serial-order information. *Psychological Review*, 90(4):316–338, 1983.

[Murdock, 1987] Bennet B. Murdock. Serial-order effects in a distributed-memory model. In David S. Gorfein and Robert R. Hoffman, editors, *MEMORY AND LEARNING: The Ebbinghaus Centennial Conference*, pages 277–310. Lawrence Erlbaum Associates, 1987.

[Pike, 1984] Ray Pike. Comparison of convolution and matrix distributed memory systems for associative recall and recognition. *Psychological Review*, 91(3):281–294, 1984.

[Plate, 1991] T. A. Plate. Holographic reduced representations: Convolution algebra for compositional distributed representations. Technical Report CRG-TR-91-1, University of Toronto, 1991.

[Schönemann, 1987] P. H. Schönemann. Some algebraic relations between involutions, convolutions, and correlations, with applications to holographic memories. *Biological Cybernetics*, 56:367–374, 1987.

[Smolensky, 1990] P. Smolensky. Tensor product variable binding and the representation of symbolic structures in connectionist systems. *Artificial Intelligence*, 46(1-2):159–216, 1990.

[Touretzky and Geva, 1987] D. S. Touretzky and S. Geva. A distributed connectionist representation for concept structures. In *Proceedings of the Ninth Annual Cognitive Science Society Conference.* Cognitive Science Society, 1987.

[Touretzky and Hinton, 1985] D. S. Touretzky and G. E. Hinton. Symbols among the neurons: Details of a connectionist inference architecture. In *IJCAI 9*, pages 238–243, 1985.

[Willshaw, 1981] D. Willshaw. Holography, associative memory, and inductive generalization. In *Parallel models of associative memory.* Erlbaum, Hillsdale, NJ, 1981.

A Macro Actor/Token Implementation of Production Systems on a Data-flow Multiprocessor†

Andrew Sohn and Jean-Luc Gaudiot
Department of Electrical Engineering - Systems
University of Southern California
Los Angeles, California 90089-0781, U.S.A.
sohn@priam.usc.edu, gaudiot@priam.usc.edu

Abstract

The importance of production systems in artificial intelligence has been repeatedly demonstrated by a number of expert systems. Much effort has therefore been expended on finding an efficient processing mechanism to process production systems. While data-flow principles of execution offer the promise of high programmability for numerical computations, we study here variable resolution actors, called *macro actors*, a processing mechanism for production systems. Characteristics of the production system paradigm are identified, based on which we introduce the concept of *macro tokens* as a companion to macro actors. A set of guidelines is identified in the context of production systems to derive well-formed macro actors from primitive micro actors. Parallel pattern matching is written in macro actors/tokens to be executed on our Macro Data-flow simulator. Simulation results demonstrate that the macro approach can be an efficient implementation of production systems.

1. Introduction

A major obstacle in the processing of artificial intelligence applications lies in the large search/match time. In rule-based production systems, for example, it is often the case that the rules and the database needed to represent a particular production system in a certain problem domain would be on the order of hundreds to thousands of rules and assertions. It is thus known that simply applying software techniques to the matching process would yield intolerable delays. Indeed, as it has been pointed out [Forgy, 1982], the time taken to match patterns over a set of rules can reach 90% of the total computation time spent in the processing of expert systems. This need for faster execution of production systems has spurred research in both the software and hardware domains.

From the software perspective, not only the matching step, but also the parallel firing of many productions have been studied. The Rete match algorithm has been developed to utilize the temporal redundancy in production systems [Forgy, 1982]. Further optimization of the Rete algorithm has been studied in the TREAT algorithm [Miranker, 1989], which supports the conflict set. Parallelization of the Rete algorithm has been reported to suit the multiprocessor environment [Tenorio and Moldovan, 1985].

† This work is supported in part by the U.S. Department of Energy, under Grant No. DE-FG03-87ER25043

From the hardware perspective, many studies have been reported, including shared memory multiprocessors and message passing architectures [Gupta and Tambe, 1988]. The performance of the conventional control-flow model of execution is however limited by the "von Neumann bottleneck" [Backus, 1978]. Indeed, architectures based on this model cannot easily deliver large amounts of parallelism [Arvind and Iannucci, 1983]. The data-driven model of execution has therefore been proposed as a solution to these problems. The applicability of data-flow principles of execution to matching operations for production systems has been studied in [Gaudiot and Sohn, 1990; Gaudiot and Bic, 1991].

In this paper, we further explore the applicability of data-flow principles of execution to production systems. It has been our observation that AI problems exhibit a behavior characteristically different from conventional numeric computations. We demonstrate in this paper that a macro actor/token approach will best match these characteristics. We shall start our discussion in section 2 by introducing two fundamental approaches to AI processing. Section 3 describes those characteristics of production systems from the parallel processing perspective, which we optimize by the utilization of macro data-flow principles. A brief analysis is presented to show *why* medium grain macro actors are preferred to fine grain micro actors. Section 4 discusses several strategies about *how* to derive well-formed macro actors from micro actors for production systems. Section 5 gives simulation results based on our execution model, the macro data-flow simulator. Performance evaluation is also discussed in the section. Conclusions as well as future research issues are offered in the last section.

2. Parallel Processing of Production Systems

A production system (PS) consists of a Production Memory (PM), a Working Memory (WM), and an Inference Engine (IE). PM (or rulebase) is composed of productions (or rules), each of which performs predefined actions (right-hand side, RHS) if all the necessary conditions (left-hand side, LHS) are satisfied. The productions operate on WM which is a database of assertions, called Working Memory Elements (WMEs). The inference engine repeatedly executes an inference cycle which consists of three steps: pattern matching, conflict resolution, followed by rule firing. The inference engine halts either when no rules can be satisfied or when the solution is found.

From the parallel processing perspective the PS paradigm can be viewed as a composition of *local-* and *global latencies*. The local latency, *t*, is the processing time of an inference cycle in the PS paradigm. Each step in the production cycle is considered a local latency, as shown in Fig.1(a). The global latency, *T*, depicted in Fig.1(a), is the processing time incurred for searching the state space. Given an initial state, the inference engine finds the next state by executing an inference cycle. Based on some heuristic control strategies, the system decides which state in the search tree should be explored. The global latency *T* is thus linearly proportional to the number of states *n* to be explored in the search tree.

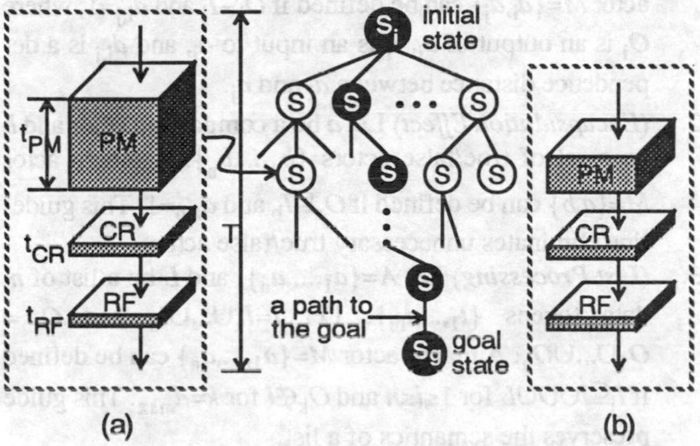

Fig.1: A search tree consisting of inference cycles. (a) an inference cycle before parallel processing, (b) after parallel processing. PM, CR, and RF stand respectively for pattern matching, conflict resolution, and rule firing

Techniques to reduce the global latency *T* in the PS paradigm can be basically classified into two categories: (1) *hardware/software parallel processing*, (2) *adaptive/ heuristic processing* [Wah *et al.*, 1989]. A straightforward technique would be to use as many Processing Elements (PEs) as needed. This would allow all branches to be explored in parallel as the search tree grows. This simple hardware approach with an infinite number of PEs can eliminate problems associated with backtracking and would hopefully find a solution in a finite amount of time. However, this technique is clearly impractical and too costly since for most AI problems the number of possible states in the search tree would be exponential even for modestly sized problems.

A way of reducing *T* from the adaptive/heuristic perspective is to prune unpromising branches in the search tree by deriving *heuristics* at compile time (or learning them at run time) and applying them. This second approach has been investigated by implementing neural network production systems [Sohn and Gaudiot, 1990a; 1990b] and will not be considered here since it is beyond the scope of this paper.

Our approach is centered around the data-flow principles of execution, more specifically, the *macro* data-flow principles [Gaudiot and Ercegovac, 1985]. As we shall see below, PSs exhibit distinctive characteristics. Indeed, one of the characteristics found in pattern matching is a list processing from which medium grain parallelism can be extracted.

3. Macro Data-flow Principles

A macro actor is a collection of scalar instructions. The objective behind lumping instructions into one larger unit is to improve performance by exploiting locality within these larger units. Similarly, a macro token is a collection of primitive data tokens. Consider an assertion IS(X Y). This assertion, when implemented, can be represented as a list of three elements (IS X Y). If we break it into three elements and form three data tokens (IS), (X), and (Y) as basic elements to operate on, each of these three tokens carry little useful information.

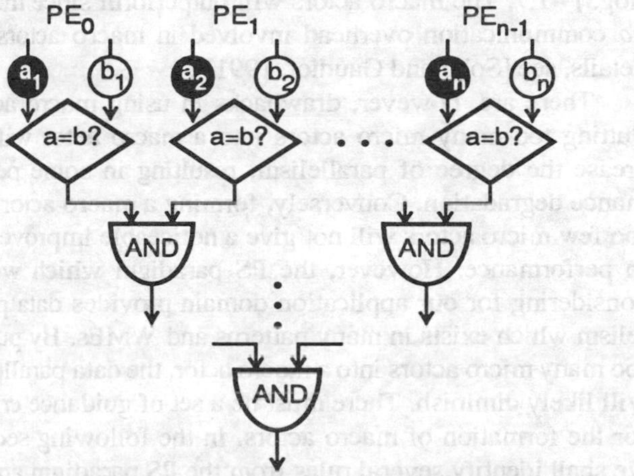

Fig.2: A data-flow graph in *micro* actors for the comparison of two lists $(a_1,...,a_n)$ and $(b_1,...,b_n)$. There are $n/2$ comparison actors to obtain a *maximum* parallelism.

When viewed from the architectural perspective, macro actors will substantially reduce the overhead in matching tags of data tokens. When using dynamic data-flow principles [Arvind and Iannucci, 1983], tokens carry tags which consist of the context, code block, or instance of a loop to which the token belongs. If the fact (IS X Y) is split into three data tokens and is compared with another three data tokens (IS), (X), and (Z), the tag matching time for three pairs of six data tokens is no less than three time units. However, when the two facts are compared in two lists, the tag matching time is *only* 1!

Consider a typical match operation, shown in Fig.2, which compares two lists, $(a_1,...,a_n)$ and $(b_1,...,b_n)$. To achieve the maximum parallelism existing in the fine grain micro approach, the *n*-pairs can be simultaneously compared in *n* PEs, each of which is connected through a (log *n*)-dim hypercube. Assume that two neighboring PEs must communicate through three facilities (two communication nodes and a link) and that each PE consists of four facilities connected in a pipeline fashion. If each facility take τ to execute, the total time to process *n* comparisons on *n* PEs would be

$$t_{\text{micro},n} = t_c + \lceil \log_2 n \rceil t_a + \lceil \log_2 n \rceil t_r$$

$= 4(1+\lceil \log_2 n\tau \rceil)\tau + 3\lceil \log_2 n \rceil \tau = (4+7\lceil \log_2 n \rceil)\tau$

where t_c=comparison time, t_a=addition time, and t_r=routing time. Note that in this simple calculation, it is assumed that no token waits in the matching/store unit of each PE. Furthermore, all the comparison actors are *ideally* allocated to neighboring PEs (which may not be realizable). The total time to compare 2 lists on 1 PE for the macro approach becomes

$t_{macro,1} = nt_c+(n-1)t_a = 4(2n-1)\tau$.

The ratio of the time taken for macro actors with 1 PE to micro actors with n PEs is

$R = t_{macro,1}/t_{micro,n} = 4(2n-1)/(4+7\lceil \log_2 n \rceil) = O(n/\log_2 n)$.

Note that in the micro-actor approach, we assumed that the token routing would be done in 1 step, i.e., 3τ. In general, such one-step routing is impractical for a 6-dim hypercube topology. Considering that the average number of elements in a list is five for production systems, the ratio becomes $R \approx 5/(\log 5) \approx 1.7$. The macro actors will outperform since there is *no* communication overhead involved in macro actors (for details, see [Sohn and Gaudiot, 1991]).

There are, however, drawbacks in using macro actors. Putting too many micro actors into a macro actor will decrease the degree of parallelism, resulting in some performance degradation. Conversely, forming a macro actor with too few micro actors will not give a noticeable improvement in performance. However, the PS paradigm which we are considering for our application domain provides data parallelism which exists in many patterns and WMEs. By putting too many micro actors into a macro actor, the data parallelism will likely diminish. There must be a set of guidance criteria for the formation of macro actors. In the following section, we shall identify several rules from the PS paradigm and establish criteria to guide the grouping process, thereby producing efficient and well-formed macro actors.

4. Formation of Macro Actors

4.1. Guidelines for well-formed macro actors

Let A be a set of micro (or primitive) actors, $\{a_1,...,a_n\}$, and T_A be a set of data tokens, $\{t_1,...,t_m\}$, manipulated by A. Let B be a macro actor derived from A such that $B \subseteq A$. Let t_1 be the time taken to process a micro actor on a PE. Let t_n be the time taken to process A on n PEs. Let T_1 be the time taken to process a macro actor on a PE. Let r be a ratio of T_1 to t_n, i.e., $r=T_1/t_n$. A macro actor B is said to be *well-formed* if $r<\varepsilon$, $\varepsilon \le 2$.

An objective behind setting such a ratio is in the fact that if the processing time of the macro actor is not more than twice of the processing time for the corresponding micro actors in an ideal environment, we shall form a macro actor from micro actors. The ideal environment refers to the ideal allocation of micro actors on n PEs and ideal routing policy on data tokens. As we discussed earlier in section 3, achieving such an ideal environment would be impractical. The macro actors would outperform because of no data token routing, no waiting for the mating data token (for two operand instructions), etc. In this paper, we simply set ε to 2 for macro actor formation. We now briefly describe the formation of well-formed macro actors (*wfms*).

Let I_i be a set of tokens input to a_i and O_i be a set of tokens output from actor a_i. We denote the dependence relation for $a_i,a_j \in A$ as follows: If $O_i \subseteq I_j$ such that $i \neq j$, $a_i \angle a_j$ for all i and j, where $\angle$ is a dependence operator which implies that a_i must be executed before a_j. By applying the dependence relation $a_i \angle a_j$ to A, we obtain an ordered set of actors, $B=\{b_1,...,b_m\}$, where $b_i=\{a \mid a_i \angle a_j \text{ is not true}\}$. The dependence distance for $b_i,b_j \in B$ is defined as $d(b_i,b_j)=d_{i,j}=i-j$. The maximum dependency distance d_{max} for B is m-1.

We list below five guidelines for the formation of *wfms* (the proof of correctness can be found in [Sohn and Gaudiot, 1991]):

1. (*Flow Dependency*) Let a_i and a_j be two actors. A macro actor $M=\{a_i,a_j\}$ can be defined if $O_i \subseteq I_j$ and $d_{i,j}$=1, where O_i is an output of a_i, I_j is an input to a_j, and $d_{i,j}$ is a dependence distance between a_i and a_j.
2. (*Encapsulation Effect*) Let a be a comparison actor and b be a set of true/false actors $\{b_1,...,b_n\}$. A macro actor $M=\{a,b\}$ can be defined if $O_a \subseteq I_b$ and $d_{a,b}$=1. This guideline eliminates unnecessary true/false actors.
3. (*List Processing*) Let $A=\{a_1,...,a_n\}$, and L be a list of m data tokens $\{t_1,...,t_m\}$. Let $I=I_1 \cup ... \cup I_n$ and $O = O_1 \cup ... \cup O_n$. A macro actor $M=\{a_1,...,a_n\}$ can be defined if $I_i \subseteq I \cup O \cup L$ for $1 \le i \le n$ and $O_k \notin I$ for $k=d_{max}$. This guide preserves the semantics of a list.
4. (*Array Operations*) Let $A=\{a_1,...,a_n\}$ and B = { Append, Select, Create, Copy}. If $A \cap B \neq \emptyset$, a macro actor M can be formed on $A-B$. Separating array operations from the macro actors removes the potential bottleneck in array operations.
5. (*Interconnection Topology*) Let $A=\{a_1,...,a_n\}$ such that d_{max} = Max$\{d_{i,j}\}$ =1 for all $a_i,a_j \in A$. Let m be a dimension of hypercube interconnection network. If $m \le n$, a set of macro actors $\{M_1,...,M_k\}$ is defined where $M_i=\{a_1,...,a_m\}$, $k=\lceil n/m \rceil$, and $1 \le i \le k$.

4.2. An example on the conversion process

Using these five guidelines, we shall now write several macro actors to implement a simple rule. The functionality of the rule that are important to implement production systems will be taken into account. Consider the following OPS5-like rule:

```
Rule: [A (Y Z)]                  ;;Condition Element 1
      [B (c X) (d Y)]            ;;Condition Element 2
      [C (p 1) (q 2) (r X)]      ;;Condition Element 3
      →
      [Modify B (c Y) (d X)]     ;;Action Element 1
```

Suppose that we have a Rete condition-dependency network constructed for the above rule [Gaudiot and Sohn, 1990]. Fig.3 shows a conversion process for the *first* condition element. A micro data-flow graph for the comparison operations on two elements, [A (Y Z)] and [A (B C)], is depicted in Fig.3(a) and the corresponding macro actor in Fig.3(b).

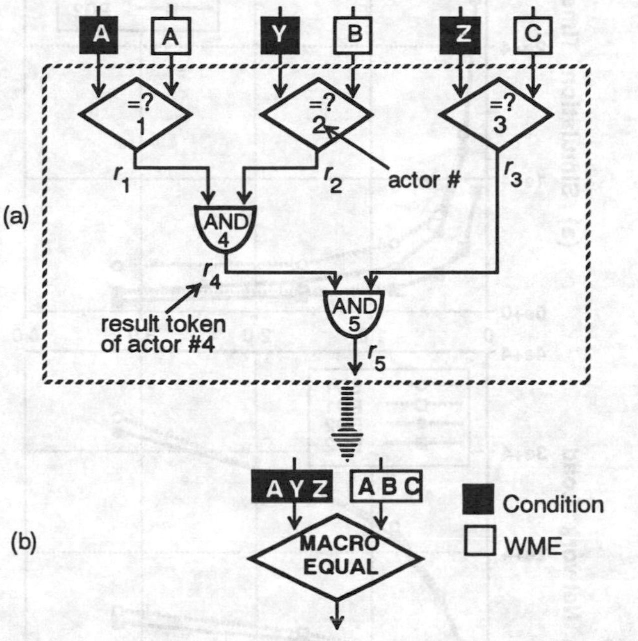

Fig.3: A conversion process. (a) a data-flow graph in micro actors, (b) a macro actor.

Rule *Guide3* is applied to this conversion process as follows: Let A be a set of five actors $\{a_1,...,a_5\}$ (three comparison actors and two AND actors), and L be a list of six data tokens $\{A,Y,Z,A,B,C\}$. Let r_i be the output token of an actor a_i. Applying a dependency distance to the set A, we partition A into three sets A_1, A_2, and A_3, where $A_1=\{a_1,a_2,a_3\}$, $A_2=\{a_4\}$, and $A_3=\{a_5\}$. We then find $d_{max}=2$ because $\text{Max}\{d_{A1,A2}, d_{A1,A3}, d_{A2,A3}\} = \text{Max}\{1,2,1\} = 2$. We also observe that

$$I=I_1\cup...\cup I_5=\{L,r_1,...,r_5\},\ O=O_1\cup...\cup O_5=\{r_1,...,r_5\} \quad (1)$$

From (1), we have $I_i\subseteq I\cup O$ for $1\le i\le 5$, and $O_{A3}=r_5\notin I$. Therefore, *Guide3* is satisfied and a macro actor $M = \{a_1,...,a_5\}$ can be formed. After *Guide5* is applied to the data-flow graph for the first condition element of the above rule, we obtain a graph shown in Fig.4. Note that for the sake of simplicity, five comparison micro actors of Fig.3(a) have been replaced by a single actor #1, *comp*, in Fig.4(a).

In Fig.4(a), there are 2 actors related to array operations: 'append' and 'select.' *Guide5* states that if there exists an actor a_i in A such that $a_i\in$\{append,select,...\}, then a macro actor M is considered on the set $A-a_i$. Applying the *Guide5* to the graph partitions it into 3 sets of micro actors A_1, A_2, and A_3, where $A_1=\{a_1,...,a_{12}\}$, $A_2=\{a_{13}\}$, and $A_3=\{a_{14}\}$. In the first step of the conversion process, the set of actors $\{a_1,...,a_5\}$ however is converted to a macro actor M_1. We therefore treat M_1 as a micro actor in the following discussion. Partitioning the graph into three graphs is shown in Fig.4(a).

The last rule we apply to the data-flow graph stems from the fact that there are six true/false actors in A_1 (see Fig.4(a)). *Guide1* states that if there is a comparison actor A which immediately affects a set of true/false actors B such that $O_A\subseteq I_B$ and $d_{A,B}=1$, then we should form a macro actor $M=\{A,B\}$.

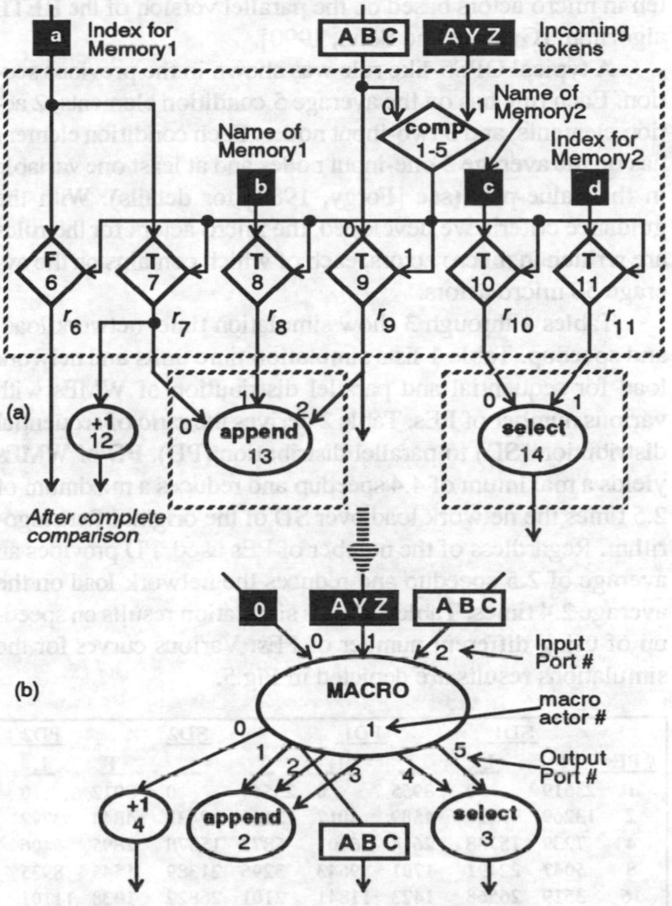

Fig.4: Converting (a) micro-actors to (b) a macro actor.

Let A be a macro comparison actor M_1 defined in the second step and B be a set of true/false actors, $\{a_6,...,a_{11}\}$. We observe from the graph that

$$O_A=\{r_5\} \text{ and } I_B=\{a,b,c,d,(A,Y,Z),r_5\} \quad (2)$$

From (2), we have $O_A\subseteq I_B$ and $d_{A,B}=1$. Therefore, *Guide1* is satisfied and a macro actor $M = \{A,B\} = \{M_1,a_6,...,a_{11}\} = \{a_1,...,a_{11}\}$ can be formed. The data-flow graph shown in Fig.4(a) is now completely converted into three macro actors $\{M_1,M_2,M_3\}$ and one micro actor a_{11}, where $M_1=\{a_1,...,a_{10}\}$, $M_2=\{a_{12}\}$, and $M_3=\{a_{12}\}$. The three macro actors are shown in Fig.4(b). The conversion process we have demonstrated thus far is for the first condition element. However, the same argument discussed above applies to other condition elements and we shall not discuss it any further. The set of guidelines described above is by no means a complete set. It can, however, serve as a starting point for the formation of *wfms* for other applications.

5. Simulation and Performance Evaluation

A simulation has been performed on the *Macro Data-Flow Multiprocessor* (MDFM) [Yoo and Gaudiot, 1989]. The machine contains 64 PEs interconnected by a 6-dim hypercube network. The target production system, which we call a 'generic production system,' has 15 rules, all of which are written in micro actors based on the parallel version of the RETE algorithm [Gaudiot and Sohn, 1990].

A typical OPS5-like rule was shown in the previous section. Each rule has on the average 5 condition elements, 2 action elements, and 3 two-input nodes. Each condition element has on the average 3 one-input nodes and at least one variable in the value-part (see [Forgy, 1982] for details). With the guidance criteria we developed, the micro actors for the rules are written in macro actors, each of which contains on the average 50 micro actors.

Tables 1 through 3 show simulation time, network load, and speedup. Table 1 lists simulation time units and network load for sequential and parallel distribution of WMEs with various number of PEs. Table 2 derives the ratio of sequential distribution (SD) to parallel distribution (PD). PD of WMEs yields a maximum of 4.4 speedup and reduces a maximum of 2.5 times the network load over SD of the original Rete algorithm. Regardless of the number of PEs used, PD provides an average of 2.5 speedup and reduces the network load on the average 2.4 times. Table 3 shows simulation results on speedup of using different number of PEs. Various curves for the simulations results are depicted in Fig.5.

# PEs	SD1		PD1		SD2		PD2	
	T	L	T	L	T	L	T	L
1	23619	0	8955	0	23544	0	8912	0
2	13269	9510	4589	4017	12161	9432	4840	3792
4	7239	15738	2614	6901	5873	15078	2895	6406
8	5047	22491	1701	9643	3296	21389	1545	8935
16	3519	26568	1423	11841	2101	26822	1038	11101
32	3336	33364	1314	14157	1434	31991	763	12874

Table 1: Simulation time(T) and network load(L) for a generic production system executed on MDFM.

# PEs	SD1/PD1		SD1/PD2		SD2/PD1		SD2/PD2	
	T	L	T	L	T	L	T	L
1	2.6	N/A	2.7	N/A	2.6	N/A	2.6	N/A
2	2.9	2.4	2.7	2.5	2.7	2.3	2.5	2.5
4	2.8	2.3	2.5	2.5	2.2	2.2	2.0	2.4
8	3.0	2.3	3.3	2.5	1.9	2.2	2.1	2.4
16	2.5	2.2	3.4	2.4	1.5	2.3	2.0	2.4
32	2.5	2.4	4.4	2.6	1.1	2.3	1.9	2.5

Table 2: Ratio of SD to PD.

No. of PEs	SD1	PD1	SD2	PD2
1	1.00	1.00	1.00	1.00
2	1.78	1.95	1.94	1.84
4	3.26	3.43	4.00	3.08
8	4.68	5.26	7.14	5.77
16	6.71	6.29	11.21	8.59
32	7.08	6.82	16.42	11.68

Table 3: Speedup, $S=T_1/T_n$, of a generic production system executed on Macro data-flow simulator.

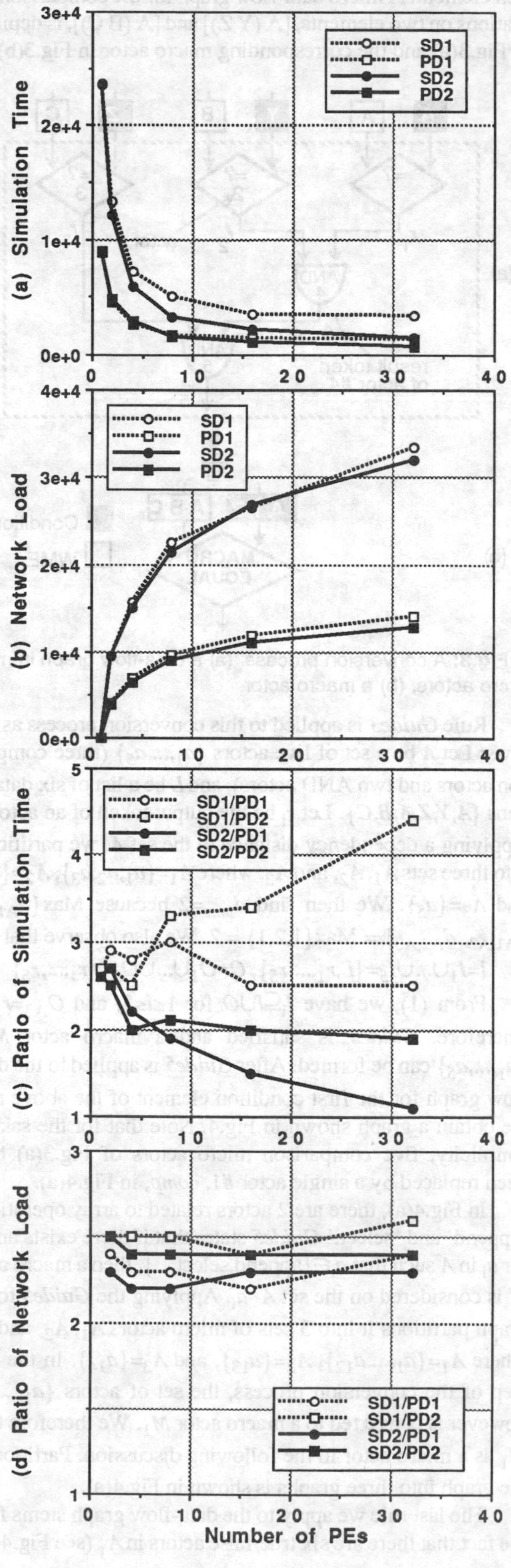

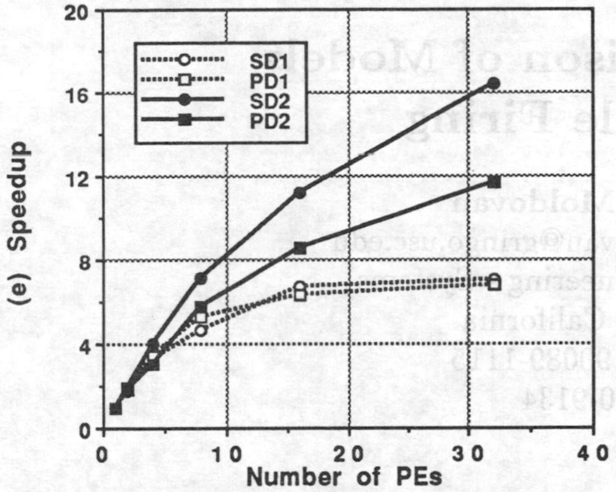

Fig.5: Simulation results on a generic production system with 15 rules. (a) Simulation time, (b) network load, (c) Ratio of SD to PD for simulation time, (d) Ratio of SD to PD for network load, and (e) Speedup. The maximum speedup we achieved by using data-driven principles of execution reached about **17** out of 32 PEs.

From the simulation results, we verify that: *First*, our parallel network with multiple root nodes reported in [Gaudiot and Sohn, 1990] gives an impressive improvement over the original sequential RETE network: the number of groups we had among condition elements of our generic production system is 3. The simulation time of the sequential RETE network, regardless of the number of PEs used, is almost always three times that of our parallel network, as seen from Table 1 and Fig.5(c). *Second*, the data-flow principles of execution can, not only efficiently perform the symbolic computation, but also yield an impressive performance over the conventional von Neumann model of execution for production system processing. From the speedup curve of Fig.5(e), we find that the data-flow principles of execution can indeed yield a 17-fold speedup when 32 PEs are used, regardless of the type of matching algorithms.

6. Conclusions

In this paper, a macro actor approach for AI problems, specifically production systems, has been demonstrated as an efficient implementation tool. Characteristics of production systems from parallel processing have been discussed to suit the macro data-flow multiprocessor environment. A simple example on comparison operations has been explained in detail from the macro perspective. Several guidelines have been demonstrated to form *wfms*. A condition element of a rule in PS is converted to macro actors. The results of a deterministic simulation with 15 rules with more than 100 condition and action elements on the macro data-flow simulator have revealed that the macro approach is an efficient implementation for the AI production systems. Indeed, the macro approach gives a 17-fold speedup on 32 PEs. Furthermore, our parallel matching algorithm with multiple root nodes gives an additional speedup of 3, regardless of the machine used. Assessments of the data-flow systems on productions systems have proven effective and we are currently investigating issues related to parallel firing of multiple rules toward true parallel production systems.

References

[Arvind and Iannucci, 1983] Arvind, R. A. Iannucci, "Two fundamental issues in multiprocessing: the dataflow solutions" MIT Laboratory for Computer Science, TM-241, September 1983.

[Backus, 1978] J. Backus, "Can programming be liberated from the von Neumann style? A functional style and its algebra of programs" *C. of ACM*, 21(8):613-641, Aug. 1978.

[Forgy, 1982] C.L. Forgy, "Rete: A Fast Algorithm for the Many Pattern/Many Object Pattern Match Problem," in *Artificial Intelligence*, 19:17-37, September 1982.

[Gaudiot and Bic, 1991] J.-L. Gaudiot and L. Bic, "Advanced Topics in Data-flow Computing," Prentice Hall, Englewood Cliffs, New Jersey, 1991.

[Gaudiot and Ercegovac, 1985] J.-L. Gaudiot and M.D. Ercegovac, "Performance evaluation of a simulated dataflow computer with low-resolution actors," *J. of Parallel Distributed Computing*, pages 321-351, Academic Press 1985.

[Gaudiot and Sohn, 1990] J.-L. Gaudiot and A. Sohn, "Data-Driven Parallel Production Systems," *IEEE Transactions on Software Engineering*, 16(3):281-293, March 1990.

[Gupta, 1987] A. Gupta, "Parallelism in Production Systems," Morgan Kaufmann Publishers, Inc., 1987.

[Gupta and Tambe, 1988] A. Gupta and M. Tambe, "Suitability of Message Passing Computers for Implementing Production Systems," in *Proc. National Conference on AI*, pages 687-692, August 1988.

[Miranker, 1989] D.P. Miranker, "TREAT: A New and Efficient Match Algorithm for AI Production Systems," Morgan Kaufmann Publishers, Inc., 1989.

[Sohn and Gaudiot, 1990a], A. Sohn and J.-L. Gaudiot, "Connectionist Production Systems in Local Representation," in *Proc. International Joint Conference onNeural Networks*, Washington, D.C., January 1990.

[Sohn and Gaudiot, 1990b], A. Sohn and J.-L. Gaudiot, "Representation and Processing Production Systems in Connectionist Architectures," *Int'l Journal of Pattern Recognition and Artificial Intelligence*, 4(2):199-214, June 1990.

[Sohn and Gaudiot, 1991], A. Sohn and J.-L. Gaudiot, "Processing of Production Systems on a Macro Data-flow Multiprocessor," USC, Dept. of EE-Systems, CE:TR-91.

[Tenorio and Moldovan, 1985] M.F.M. Tenorio and D.I. Moldovan, "Mapping Production Systems into Multiprocessors," in *Proc. International Conference on Parallel Processing*, pages 56-62, August 1985.

[Yoo and Gaudiot, 1989] N. Yoo and J.-L. Gaudiot, "A Macro Data-flow Simulator," USC, Dept. of E.E.-Systems, CE:TR-89-27.

[Wah *et al.*, 1989] B.W. Wah, M.B. Lowrie, and G.-J. Li, "Computers for Symbolic Processing," *Proceedings of the IEEE*, 77(4):509-540, April 1989..

Performance Comparison of Models for Multiple Rule Firing

Steve Kuo and Dan Moldovan
skuo@gringo.usc.edu and moldovan@gringo.usc.edu
Department of Electrical Engineering - Systems
University of Southern California
Los Angeles, California 90089-1115
DRB-363, (213) 740-9134

Abstract

The performance of production programs can be improved by firing multiple rules in a production cycle. Although considerable amount of research has been done on parallel processing of production programs, the problem of multiple rule firing has not been thoroughly investigated yet. In this paper, we begin by identifying the problems associated with multiple rule firing systems: the *compatibility problem* and the *convergence problem* and present three multiple rule firing models which address them. The *rule dependence model (RDM)* addresses the compatibility problem using inter-rule data dependence analysis. The *single-context-multiple-rules (SCMR) model* and the *multiple-contexts-multiple-rules (MCMR) model* address both the compatibility and the convergence problems. A production program executed under the SCMR and the MCMR models is guaranteed to reach a solution which is equivalent to the sequential execution. These three multiple rule firing models have been simulated on the RUBIC simulator, and the MCMR model, which has the highest performance, has been implemented on the Intel iPSC/2 hypercube. The simulation and implementation results are reported.

1 Introduction

Multiple rule firing production systems increase the available parallelism over parallel match systems by parallelizing not only the match phase, but all phases of the inference cycle. To speedup the derivation of correct solutions by firing multiple rules in a production cycle, two multiple rule firing problems – the *compatibility* and *convergence* problems – need to be addressed. The compatibility problem arises from the interferences between production rules. If a set of rules does not have inter-rule data dependence among themselves, they are said to be *compatible* and are allowed to execute concurrently. The convergence problem arises from the need to follow the problem solving strategy used in a production program. If the problem solving strategy is ignored in a multiple rule firing system, then two tasks may be executed out of sequence or two actions for the same task may be executed in the wrong order resulting in an incorrect solution.

There are three approaches to address the compatibility and convergence problems. The first approach considers only the compatibility problem and resolves it by data dependence analysis [6] [9] [11]. Both synchronous and asynchronous execution models have been proposed. In these models, rules which are compatible are fired concurrently in a production cycle. Because the convergence problem is not addressed in these models, the problem solving strategy for a production program may be violated when multiple rules are fired simultaneously. The second approach addresses the compatibility and convergence problems by developing parallel production languages. CREL [9] and Swarm [4] are two such languages. Production programs written in these languages do not use control flow or conflict resolution to ensure that the right rules are fired. Instead, production rules are fired as soon as they are matched. The correctness of these parallel production programs is guaranteed by showing that for any arbitrary execution sequence the correct solutions are always obtained [2]. A potential hurdle for CREL and Swarm is the possible difficulty to prove the correctness of a large production program. In addition, to be able to fire production rules as soon as they are matched may not be the same as being able to fire multiple rules concurrently. These questions will be answered when the benchmark production programs have been translated into CREL and Swarm programs and their performance measured.

The multiple rule firing models presented in this paper represents the third approach. They address the compatibility problem by data dependence analysis and the convergence problem by analyzing the control flow in a production program to maintain the correct task ordering. In a production program, a complex problem can be solved by dividing it into smaller tasks until they are easily solved. These tasks are called *contexts* and each context is solved by a set of *context rules*. The multiple rule firing models improve the performance of a production program by activating multiple contexts and firing multiple rules concurrently. They guarantee the correctness of the solution by determining the conditions under which multiple contexts and multiple rules can be activated and fired. The multiple rule firing models have been simulated on the RUBIC simulator and implemented on the Intel iPSC/2 hypercube. The results indicate that these models have successfully addressed the problems associated with multiple rule firing.

2 Resolving the Compatibility and Convergence Problems

To resolve the compatibility and convergence problems successfully, one needs to understand how problems are solved in production programs. A useful method in general problem solving is the method of stepwise refinement, which resolves a complex problem by dividing it into smaller and smaller subproblems (or tasks) until they are easily solved. If other subproblems need to be solved before solving a subproblem, the program control is transferred from one subproblem to another. Production programs also employ the method of stepwise refinement to solve complex problems. First, the production rules in a production program are divided into subsets of rules, one subset for each subproblem. A subset of rules is called a *context* and each individual rule in the subset is called a *context rule*. Every context rule in the same context has a special *context WME*. Rules in different contexts have different context WMEs. A programmer can control which context is active by adding and removing the context WMEs. Context rules are divided into *domain rules* and *control rules*. Domain rules address the subproblem associated with the context and conflict resolution is used to select the right rule to fire. If other subproblems need to be solved before solving a subproblem, the control rules transfer the program control to the appropriate contexts by modifying the context WMEs. By analyzing the control rules, the control flow between different contexts can be determined. The problem solving strategy and the control flow diagram for an example production program is shown in Figure 1.

In this paper, we present three multiple rule firing models: the *rule dependence (RDM) model*, the *single-context-multiple-rules (SCMR) model*, the *multiple-contexts-multiple-rules (MCMR) model*. They resolve the compatibility and convergence problems at two

$C_1 \rightarrow C_3$ signifies that the program control is transferred from C_1 to C_3

Context	Reachable set	Context	Reachable set
C_0	$\{C_0 C_1 C_2 C_3 C_4 C_5\}$	C_3	$\{C_3\}$
C_1	$\{C_1 C_3 C_4 C_5\}$	C_4	$\{C_4 C_5\}$
C_2	$\{C_2 C_5\}$	C_5	$\{C_5\}$

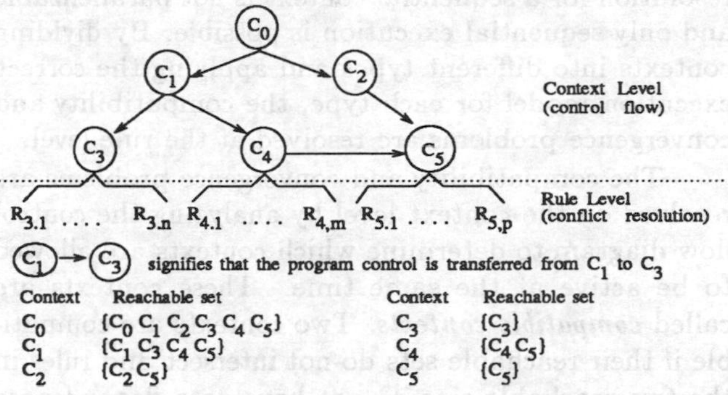

Figure 1: Control in Production Program

levels: the *rule* level and the *context* level. At the rule level, the compatibility problem is resolved by data dependence analysis. A set of rules is allowed to fire concurrently and are said to be *compatible* if executing them either sequentially or concurrently, the same state is reached. This is the case if there are no data dependences among rules in the set. The data dependence analysis is performed at compile time to construct a parallelism matrix $P = [p_{ij}]$ and a communication matrix $C = [c_{ij}]$. Rules R_i and R_j are compatible if $p_{ij} = 0$; they are incompatible if $p_{ij} = 1$. The communication matrix C is used for communication purpose when production rules are partitioned and mapped onto different processing nodes in a message-passing multiprocessor. Rules R_i and R_j need to exchange messages to update the database if $c_{ij} = 1$; they do not need to if $c_{ij} = 0$.

The convergence problem is resolved at the rule level by dividing contexts in a production program into three different types: (1) *converging* contexts, (2) *parallel nonconverging* contexts and (3) *nonconverging* or *sequential* contexts. A context C is a converging context if starting at a state satisfying the initial condition INIT for that context, all execution sequences result in states satisfying the post condition POST for that context [2] [4]. Otherwise context C is a nonconverging context. The conflict resolution can be eliminated for a converging context because all execution sequences converge to the correct solution. Compatible rules can be fired simultaneously within a converging context without error. This is because firing a set of compatible rules concurrently is equivalent to executing them in some sequential order and all execution sequences reach the correct solution for a converging context (for proof, see [8]). For a nonconverging context, conflict resolution must be used to reach the correct solution. The performance of a nonconverging context can be improved by parallelizing its conflict resolution. A parallel nonconverging context is a nonconverging context whose conflict resolution is parallelizable and as a result multiple rules may be selected. The conflict resolution for a sequential context is not parallelizable and only sequential execution is possible. By dividing contexts into different types and applying the correct execution model for each type, the compatibility and convergence problems are resolved at the rule level.

The compatibility and convergence problems are resolved on the context level by analyzing the control flow diagram to determine which contexts are allowed to be active at the same time. These contexts are called *compatible contexts*. Two contexts are compatible if their reachable sets do not intersect and rules in the two reachable sets do not have data dependences (for proof, see [7]). The reachable set for a context C_i is the set of contexts which are reachable by following the directed arcs in the control flow diagram starting from C_i. Context C_i is included in its own reachable set. The reachable set for context C_1 for the example production program in Figure 1 is $\{C_1, C_3, C_4, C_5\}$.

The production rules are analyzed at compile time to generate the compatibility context matrix $CC = [cc_{ij}]$. Two contexts C_i and C_j are compatible and are allowed to be active at the same time if $cc_{ij} = 0$; they are incompatible if $cc_{ij} = 1$. The programmer then consults the CC matrix and modifies the production rules if needed so that only the compatible contexts will be activated concurrently in production program execution. In this way, the compatibility and the convergence problems are resolved on the context level.

3 Multiple Rule Firing Models

In this section, we present three multiple rule firing models which incorporate the solutions presented in Section 2 in varying degrees. The RDM model resolves the compatibility problem by data dependence analysis. It does not address the convergence problem. The SCMR and MCMR models address both the compatibility and convergence problems. The difference between the two models is that only one context is active at a time for the SCMR model but multiple contexts may be active simultaneously for the MCMR model. A new parallel inference cycle, shown in figure 2, is needed for the RDM, SCMR and MCMR models. It consists of four phases: the *match* phase, the *conflict resolution (CR)* phase, the *compatibility determination (CD)* phase, and the *act* phase. The RDM, SCMR, and MCMR models follow this new parallel cycle with some modifications, depending on how each handles contexts.

3.1 Data Dependence Model

The rule dependence (RDM) model addresses only the compatibility problem, not the convergence problem.

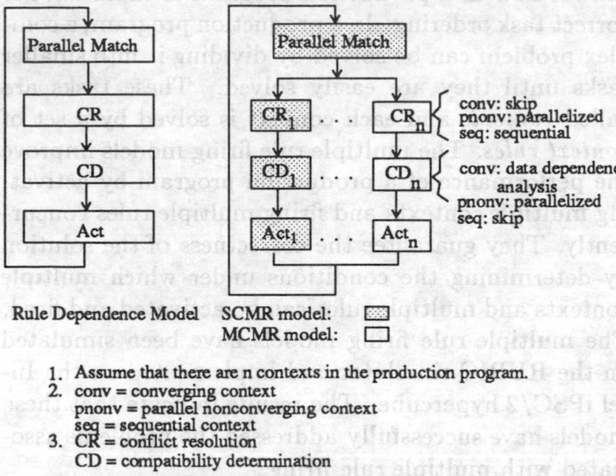

Figure 2: New Parallel Inference Cycle

The data dependence analysis is performed at compile time to construct the parallelism matrix $P = [p_{ij}]$ and the communication matrix $C = [c_{ij}]$. To capture the maximum parallelism, all four phases of the new parallel inference cycle are parallelized. For the match phase, either parallel shared-memory match algorithm [5] or parallel message-passing algorithm [1] is used, depending on the underlying architecture. At the conflict resolution phase, a dominant rule R_d is selected according to the conflict resolution strategy or at random. At the compatibility determination phase, a compatible set is chosen. Initially the compatible set contains only R_d. For each eligible rule R_i, if R_i is compatible with all rules in the compatible set according to the parallelism matrix P, it is added to the compatible set. This step is repeated until every eligible rule is checked. At the act phase, all the rules in the compatible set are fired concurrently. The data dependence model is similar to the models proposed by Ishida [6], Miranker [9] and Schmolze [11].

Because the RDM model fires rules from different contexts concurrently, it may activate incompatible contexts or fire multiple rules simultaneously for sequential contexts. If all contexts are converging contexts and are compatible with each other, the RDM model would reach the correct solution and obtain high performance because it captures all the parallelism there is in each cycle. If this is not the case, the RDM model fails.

3.2 SCMR and MCMR Models

The SCMR and MCMR models extend the RDM model and address the convergence problem by dividing contexts into converging and nonconverging contexts and analyzing whether two contexts can be activated concurrently. For the match phase, the same technology used for the RDM model is used for the

SCMR and MCMR models. But unlike the RDM model which performs the conflict resolution, compatibility determination and act phases for all rules globally, the SCMR and MCMR models execute these phase for each context individually. In addition, different actions are performed for different types of contexts during the conflict resolution, compatibility determination and act phases.

For a converging context, the conflict resolution phase is skipped. For a parallel nonconverging context, the conflict resolution is parallelized by a special algorithm. For a sequential context, the conflict resolution is retained. During the compatibility determination phase, compatible rules are determined by data dependence analysis and fired concurrently for a converging context. For a parallel nonconverging context, a special algorithm is used to determine the set of compatible rules. For a sequential context, the compatibility determination phase is skipped. During the act phase, converging and parallel nonconverging contexts execute the set of compatible rules concurrently, and the sequential contexts fire the dominant rule selected by the conflict resolution. By allowing compatible contexts to be executed independently, the SCMR and MCMR models avoid unnecessary synchronizations and improve the available parallelism. The main difference between the SCMR model and the MCMR model is that only one context is active for the SCMR model, but multiple contexts may be active for the MCMR model.

4 Results

Six production programs developed at USC, CMU and Columbia have been simulated on the RUBIC simulator using four models: the sequential, RDM, SCMR and MCMR models. The RUBIC simulator is written in LISP and currently running on the Sun Sparc workstation. By analyzing the simulation results, we can determine the validity of the RDM, SCMR and MCMR models and measure their performance.

Table 4.1 lists and describes the six test programs simulated on the RUBIC simulator. The test programs were first simulated under the sequential model and the sequential simulation results are summarized in Table 4.2. The test programs were then simulated under the RDM model, in which all compatible rules were fired in a production cycle. The RDM simulation results are summarized in Table 4.3. Under the RDM model, production programs Toru-Waltz16, Cafeteria, Snap-2d and Snap-TA reached the correct solutions but Tournament and Hotel failed. The reason that Toru-Waltz16, Cafeteria, Snap-2d and Snap-TA were successful was because they contained only converging contexts. Tournament and Hotel failed because they contained nonconverging contexts and firing multiple rules concurrently violating the problem solving strategies. If the SCMR and MCMR models work, then by using a special algorithm to parallelize the nonconverging context in Tournament and executing the nonconverging context in Hotel sequentially, the two test programs should reach the correct solutions. In this way, the validity of the SCMR and MCMR models can be verified.

Table 4.1 Test Production System

Program	Description
A	Tournament: scheduling bridge tournaments
B	Toru-Waltz16: implementing the Waltz's edge labelling algorithm
C	Cafeteria: setting up cafeteria
D	Snap-2d[1]: a two-dimensional semantic network
E	Snap-TA: verifying the eligibility of TA candidates
F	Hotel: modeling hotel operations

Table 4.2 Sequential Simulation Results

	Production Programs					
Measurements	A	B	C	D	E	F
# of rules	26	48	94	574	574	832
# of sequential cycles = α	528	207	493	590	1175	5115

The test programs have been simulated under the SCMR model and the simulation results are summarized in Table 4.4. All six production programs reached the correct solutions under the SCMR model as expected. By using a special algorithm for the nonconverging context in Tournament, multiple rules were fired concurrently without error and a speedup of 6.21-folds was achieved. By firing rules sequentially for the sequential context and concurrently for the converging contexts for Hotel, a speedup of 8.77-folds was obtained. For Toru-Waltz16, Cafeteria, Snap-2d, and Snap-TA, speedups of 3.06 to 8.94-folds have been obtained. The simulation results indicate that the SCMR model was able to capture a significant amount of available parallelism in production programs and we expected that the MCMR model would give even better performances.

The simulation results for the test programs under the MCMR model are summarized in Table 4.5. Like the SCMR model, all six production programs reached the correct solutions under the MCMR model as expected. For Tournament, Toru-Waltz16 and Snap-2d, only one context can be activated at at time. As a result, their MCMR performances were the same

[1]Snap is a simulator for semantic network array processor under development at USC [10].

Table 4.3 Simulation Results for Rule Dependence Model

	Production Programs					
Measurements	A	B	C	D	E	F
Are RDM solutions correct	no	yes	yes	yes	yes	no
# RDM cycles = β	165	65	78	66	126	254
$Speedup_{\alpha/\beta} = \alpha/\beta$	N/A[2]	3.18	6.13	8.94	9.40	N/A

Table 4.4 SCMR Simulation Results

	Production Programs					
Measurements	A	B	C	D	E	F
Are SCMR solutions correct	yes	yes	yes	yes	yes	yes
Max # rules fired per SCMR cycle	120	14	10	15	100	40
Max # contexts activated per cycle	1	1	1	1	1	1
Ave # contexts activated per cycle	1	1	1	1	1	1
# SCMR cycles = γ	85	65	156	66	158	475
$Speedup_{\alpha/\gamma} = \alpha/\gamma$	6.21	3.18	3.06	8.94	7.46	8.77

Table 4.5 MCMR Simulation Results

	Production Programs					
Measurements	A	B	C	D	E	F
Are MCMR solutions correct	yes	yes	yes	yes	yes	yes
Max # rules fired per MCMR cycle	120	14	14	15	106	77
Max # of contexts activated per cycle	1	1	5	1	4	7
Ave # of contexts activated per cycle	1	1	2.00	1	1.21	2.33
# MCMR cycles = δ	85	65	78	66	125	247
$Speedup_{\alpha/\delta} = \alpha/\delta$	6.21	3.18	6.13	8.94	9.40	20.38
$Speedup_{\gamma/\delta} = \gamma/\delta$	1.00	1.00	2.00	1.00	1.26	2.32

as their SCMR performances. For Cafeteria, Snap-TA and Hotel, multiple contexts were activated concurrently and they achieved speedups of 6.13, 9.40 and 20.38-folds or 2.00, 1.26 and 2.32-folds better than their SCMR speedups. This indicates that the MCMR model does capture more parallelism than the SCMR model, but the additional speedups obtainable using the MCMR model over the SCMR model depend on the nature of the production programs. To compare the MCMR speedups and the RDM speedups for production programs Toru-Waltz, Cafeteria, Snap-2d and Snap-TA is instructive. We see that for these programs, their MCMR and RDM speedups were the same. This is not surprising since the RDM model also activates multiple contexts and fires multiple rules concurrently like the MCMR model does. The problem is that sometimes it erroneously activates incompatible contexts and fires multiple rules concurrently for sequential context.

[2] N/A = Non-applicable

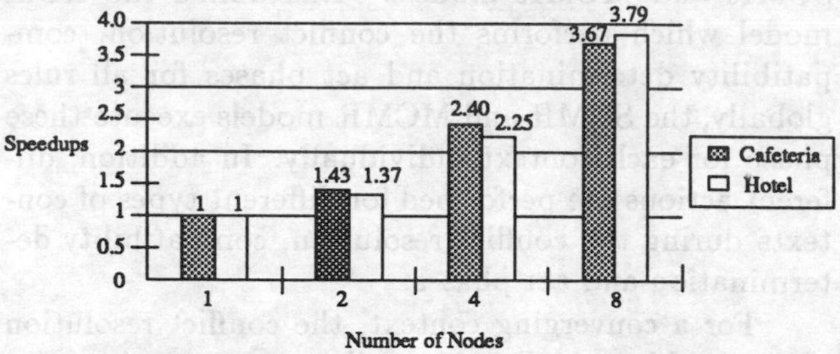

Figure 3: Performance for Partition-by-Context

4.1 Hypercube Performance Results

The MCMR model has been implemented on the Intel iPSC/2 hypercube because it provides the highest performance. Only eight nodes can be run concurrently due to the large memory requirement of LISP program. We have run two test programs, Cafeteria and Hotel, using two static partitioning schemes: partitioning-by-context and round-robin partitioning. When rules are partitioned by context, all rules in the same context are mapped to the same processing node. In round-robin partitioning, rules are allocated to the processing nodes in a circular fashion regardless of the contexts.

Cafeteria and Hotel were able to achieve good speedups when rules are partitioned by contexts. Their performance is shown in Figure 3. Due to the timing limitations of LISP on iPSC/2 only the real time was measured. The simulated speedup for Cafeteria is 6.13 and it achieved a speedup of 3.67 for 8 nodes. The simulated speedup for Hotel is 8 (only 8 nodes are available) and it achieved a speedup of 3.79. Since only eight nodes were available, the upward bound for speedup is eight. For this reason, the performances for Cafeteria and Hotel were quite close. But if more nodes were available, we expect the performance of Hotel to continue to increase with the number of the nodes while the performance of Cafeteria would stay the same.

The performance of Cafeteria using the round-robin partitioning, shown in Figure 4, is disappointing. However it is important to understand the cause in order to prevent it. The speedups dropped as more processing nodes were added. When rules in the same context are mapped to different nodes, they need to communicate with each other to perform the conflict resolution, the compatibility determination and the RHS actions. As the number of nodes increase, the number of messages increases. This is exactly what happened in the round-robin partitioning. As more nodes were used, the number of messages increased. In fact, the number of messages proliferated and the reduction in computation time was outweighed by the message communication time.

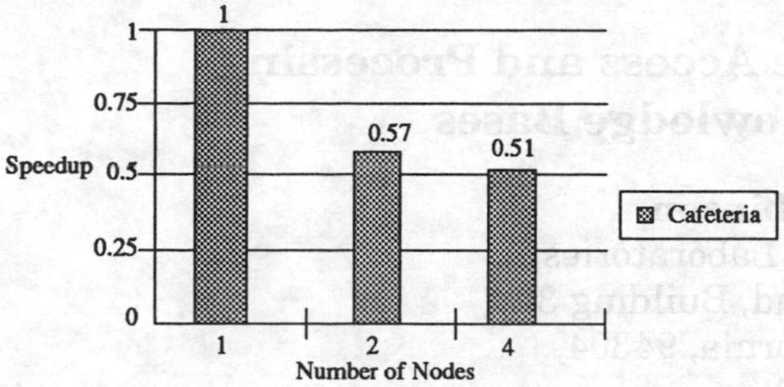

Figure 4: Performance for the Round-Robin Partitioning

Even though good speedups were obtained by allocating rules from a context to the same node, it is not clear whether this is the best partitioning. We intend to study the partitioning problem by developing an allocation algorithm based on simulated annealing. The allocation algorithm will read in the run-time information and use parallelism and communication matrices to estimate the computational and the communication costs for each partitioning. To accomplish this goal, we will also extend the timing functions to provide better run-time information.

5 Conclusion

In this paper, we have present three multiple rule firing models. The RDM model failed because it viewed a production program only as a collection of rules and did not consider the effect of multiple rule firing has on the problem solving strategy. On the other hand, the SCMR and MCMR models were successful because they addressed the multiple rule firing problems at both levels. Speedups of 3.18 to 8.94-folds were obtained for the test programs under the SCMR model. Speedups of 3.18 to 20.38-folds have been obtained for the MCMR model. The large speedups achieved under the SCMR and the MCMR models indicate that there is considerable amount parallelism in many production programs.

The execution of production programs on real parallel machines forces us to address the allocation and message communication problems. Production programs Cafeteria and Hotel have been executed on the Intel iPSC/2 hypercube using two partitioning schemes. When Cafeteria and Hotel are allocated by context, good speedups were obtained, but when Cafeteria was allocated in a round-robin fashion, the performance dropped as more nodes were added. We intend to use run-time traces and a simulated annealing method to further study partitioning. The run-time traces will be used to estimate the computation and the communication costs for different partitions. By comparing the simulated performance with the iPSC/2 performance for different allocations, the partitioning problem will be better understood.

References

[1] Acharya, A., Tambe, M. *"Production Systems on Message Passing Computers: Simulation Results and Analysis."* Proceeding of International Conference on Parallel Processing, 1989.

[2] Chandy, K. M., Misra, J. *"Parallel Program Design: A foundation."* Addison Wesley, Reading, Massachusetts, 1988.

[3] Cunningham, H.C., Roman, G.-C. *"A UNITY-Style Programming Logic for Shared Dataspace Programs."* IEEE Transactions on Parallel And Distribued Systems, July 1990.

[4] Gamble, R. *"Transforming Rule-based Programs: form the sequential to the parallel."* Third Int'l Conference on Industrial and Engineering Applications of AI and Expert Systems, July 1990.

[5] Gupta, A., Forgy, C., Kalp, D., Newell, A., Tambe, M.S. *"Parallel OPS5 on the Encore Multimax"*. In proceedings of the International Conference on Parallel Processing. August, 1988.

[6] Ishida, T. el at *"Towards the Parallel Execution of Rules in Production System Programs"*. International Conference on Parallel Processing, 1985, 568-575.

[7] Kuo, S., Moldovan, D., Cha, S. *"Control in Production Systems with Multiple Rule Firings."* Technical Report No. 90-10. Parallel Knowledge Processing Laboratory, USC.

[8] Kuo, S., Moldovan, D., Cha, S. *"A Multiple Rule Firing Modele - The MCMR Model."* Technical Report. Parallel Knowledge Processing Laboratory, USC.

[9] Miranker, D.P., Kuo, C., Browne, J.C. *"Parallelizing Transformations for A Concurrent Rule Execution Language."* In Proceeding of the International Conference on Parallel Processing, 1990.

[10] Moldovan, D., Lee, W., Lin, C. *"SNAP: A Marker-Propagation Architecture for Knowledge Processing."* Technical Report No. 90-1. Parallel Knowledge Processing Laboratory, USC.

[11] Schmolze, J. *"A Parallel Asynchronous Distributred Production System."* Proceeding of Eight National Conference on Artificial Intelligence. AAAI90. Page 65-71.

On Supporting Associative Access and Processing over Dynamic Knowledge Bases

Ian N. Robinson
Hewlett Packard Laboratories,
1501 Page Mill Road, Building 3L,
Palo Alto, California, 94304,
U.S.A.

Abstract

Dynamic knowledge bases are a fact of life in many artificial intelligence applications. Using current techniques, however, it is not always possible to provide the desired level of associative access to them whilst meeting real-time, or even near-real-time, performance criteria. This paper argues the case for a hardware associative storage system that uses symbolic pattern matching as its access mechanism. A working prototype of such a system, designed as a co-processor for a workstation host, is then described. The co-processor is based on an array of custom designed VLSI 'smart memory' chips. These combine storage and search/processing logic on the same die. Parallelism is exploited both on chip and between chips to yield a high system performance. The paper concludes with some examples of how this hardware can be used to support real applications.

1 Associative Pattern Matching

Associative operations based on pattern matching are fundamental to many artificial intelligence applications. This paper concentrates on the broad category of knowledge-base systems. In such systems rules are activated based on pattern matching as the ordering information - found in procedural (or compiled) systems - is not present. When, and how, a particular fact or rule is to be applied is typically not known until run-time.

A major contributor to this uncertainty lies in the application's interaction with the everyday world. There is also the interaction between rules and, in more complex architectures, between component reasoning systems. In fact it is seen as an advantage to maintain associative access within such complex systems, rather than 'hard-wired' connections, since it facilitates modularization of the component parts [Reece and Shafer, 1990].

In general, however, this lack of predictability imposes a limit on how many of these associative operations can be optimized away at compile-time. Thus the run-time component will still contain significant use of associative access to the data structures encoding the knowledge base. Unfortunately such associative operations are computationally expensive. To mitigate this, various compile-time techniques have been developed to translate the knowledge-base data structures into code sequences. These use indexing operations, commonly based on hashing, to handle the associative lookup, e.g. Rete for OPS5 [Forgy, 1982], WAM code for Prolog [Warren, 1977], HiPER for embedded knowledge-base systems [Highland and Iwaskiw, 1989].

As applications and their rules and queries become more complex, so too can the indexing schemes necessary to support the associative access. With simple data structures, finding one or two keywords to index on is fairly straightforward. As the structures and queries become more complex - possibly including the use of variables ('don't cares'), and with any of their elements being potential keywords - then correspondingly complex indexing structures are required (e.g. discrimination nets [Charniak *et al.*, 1980]). Otherwise a performance hit is taken every time a query does not conform to the chosen indexing scheme. Since the alternative is usually exhaustive linear search, such penalties can be costly.

These indexing schemes have acceptable performance when the database is reasonably static. However the more dynamic the knowledge base used by the application the greater the frequency of index table updates. Furthermore, the more complex the indexing scheme the greater the overhead involved in performing each individual update. Even relatively simple indexing schemes can be rendered impractical when the update rate of the entry indexed upon is too high. In [Stormon, 1989] the example is given of applying complex queries to the value entries of a stocks and commodities database. With this value being updated hundreds of times a second it is not practical to index on it, and so answering such queries requires a sequential scan of the database records.

With the intricate indexing schemes necessary to efficiently access complex knowledge bases, even less dynamism can be tolerated. Examples of such applications include intelligent control or monitoring systems such as in computer integrated manufacturing (CIM), medical and process monitoring, and autonomous vehicle and robot control systems. Typically such applications are required to reason about complex time varying systems - including themselves (e.g. dynamic resource allocation) - and face real-time constraints on the utility of their actions or decisions. The overhead involved in maintaining associative access in such dynamic applications severely impedes the ability of the system to meet its performance goals.

Even in systems where there is little pressure from outside events the internal dynamics can be considerable. Consider a system that reasons via hypothesis generation and test, or via constructing possible world scenarios. This involves adding new rules to the knowledge base at run-time, and employing them to test their efficacy. These rules may then be modified, or deleted and new ones added in their place. Maintaining an indexing scheme over such transitory data can entail considerable overhead.

In summary, these characteristics of unpredictability and dynamism move the onus of associative computation squarely back into the run-time system, where the associated overhead severely impacts system performance. The problem then is to support associative knowledge retrieval when the data structures encoding that knowledge can be quite complex and dynamic, with minimal overhead devoted to casting the structures into an efficiently accessible form.

2 Hardware: The Cache Analogy

Run-time being the domain of special purpose hardware, a solution is proposed based on associative memory techniques [Yau and Fung, 1977]. Software indexing schemes and their upkeep are by-passed altogether, and associative hardware is used to implement a rapid exhaustive search. The advantage of this approach is that the data structures are dealt with directly, with minimal to no encoding. Such use of associative hardware is not without precedent: consider the ubiquitous *cache memory.* The same characteristics of unpredictability and dynamism, though in this case of data and its location, gives rise to the requirement for run-time hardware to associatively match on addresses and return the associated data (or a signal that the data is not present - a 'miss').

This paper describes a cache-like system designed to operate with data structured in the form of symbolic *expressions.* Whilst a conventional cache supports rapid access based simply on memory addresses; this system has to support complex, non-predetermined, access to expressions of various lengths and structural complexity. By allowing control over access and modification of cached expressions some measure of associative processing can be supported. These additional capabilities lead the system to be configured as a co-processor rather than as a part of the host's memory system. Thus associative operations are off-loaded from the host CPU, just as graphics and floating-point co-processors off-load their particular tasks.

A significant body of work exists relating to hardware associative memories for such applications. Such hardware has typically been based on the traditional content-addressable memory (CAM) [Kogge *et al.*, 1989; Stormon, 1989; Wade and Sodini, 1989]. By comparison these suffer from restrictions on expression format, in some cases forcing entire stored expressions to be encoded into fixed length fields. Such approaches also tend to rely on comparators alone for the matching function, which presents problems when trying to capture the full syntax of symbolic expressions - both stored and used as queries. Lastly the storage organization used in the co-processor described here permits a significantly increased capacity over CAM-based architectures.

3 The Chameleon Board

Figure 1 shows a photograph of a wire-wrap prototype of this associative co-processor. Called the 'Chameleon board' (named after that creature's ability to pattern match with its environment) it is designed to be compatible with commercially available workstations, plugging in to the system's backplane.

Figure 1. Chameleon Board

The computational heart of the system is the array of custom 'smart memory' chips called *pattern addressable memories* (PAM's). These combine memory for symbol storage with parallel and distributed processing logic. This logic is in the form of processing elements (PE's) replicated through the on-chip storage. The array of PAM chips acts as one combined storage system. All the PE's operate in a SIMD fashion on their respective areas of memory. The op-code and any data for the operation, e.g. match query, are broadcast by a central array controller (located in the center of the board in the photograph).

This 'logic in memory', or 'smart memory', approach has the advantage of not requiring data to be transferred from storage to a remote - i.e. off-chip - processing site; and thus avoids the ensuing bandwidth limitations. Moreover, since the processing logic is replicated throughout the memory, the resultant parallelism gives rise to a very large effective processor bandwidth (*each* of the current PAM chips has an effective bandwidth in excess of 10Gb/s). This facilitates the rapid search of the chip's contents.

The array controller is responsible for maintaining the interface with the host system. It converts instructions from the host to the necessary op-code sequences, mediates data traffic between the array and the host, and controls the PEs' progress over its portion of storage.

A library of C-routines completes the implementation providing a high-level interface to the Chameleon hardware. For example, the instruction `insert(expression)` takes the expression pointed to by its argument and inserts it into the PAM array. Other instructions are provided for debugging purposes and allow access to the PAM chips', and the controller's, state.

4 Expression Syntax and Storage Format

Before outlining the various functions the Chameleon supports, the nature of the expressions stored and matched upon is first described. The symbols that go together to make up expressions are stored as 32-bit words. The most significant four bits denote a particular *type*, the remaining 28 a *name*. With the exception of integers, which are passed on unencoded, this name is a unique ID generated and maintained by the application running on the host. The name field can also be used to hold an integer *range*. This is encoded using bit-wise don't-cares [Wade and Sodini, 1989] so that, for instance, the quantity '<16' is represented as '0000000000xxxx'. Each '0', '1' or 'x' requires 2 name bits to encode it.

@event (Monday October 14 ?time ?appt)

header *constant* *integer* *variable*

@event (Monday ?month ?date 4-6 (group_mtg Room_303))

list-variable *integer-range* *parenthesis*

@event (&rest Room_303 &rest)

Figure 2. Symbol types

The symbol types identified by the type tag bits are illustrated in the example expressions of Figure 2 (taken from a simple day-planner database). The syntax is similar to that of Prolog for clauses - consisting essentially of constants, variables and substructure. This covers the requirements of most applications in the domains of interest. If the pattern match operation requires the internal components of sub-structure to be considered in the same pass, rather than just pointer comparisons, then that substructure must be expanded out in place. For example the list (group_mtg Room_303) in Figure 2 is represented by the actual sequence of symbols rather than by a pointer. The 'header' symbol indicates the start of a new expression - somewhat like a functor, though its use is predominantly structural. The *list-variable* is a special case of the normal variable, the difference being in what they pattern match with (the pattern matching rules will be described in the next section). Lastly it should be noted that expressions can be of arbitrary length.

The storage within each PAM chip is managed as a stack of symbol-wide *slots*. This management is internal to the PAM chip which possesses no address pins in the usual sense, since all access is associative. Expressions are stored one after another as sequences of symbols in the format described. Insertion is performed by the controller enabling a particular chip and then supplying the expression to be input a symbol at a time, each time along with a 'stack_push' op-code. Included in this on-chip storage management is support for a garbage-collect process which is used to compact deleted expressions out of the stack. Garbage collection takes place in parallel over the array of PAM chips.

5 Chameleon functions

Given a database of expressions stored in the PAM chips the Chameleon board supports the following basic operations: insertion (covered above), pattern match, modification, output and deletion. Pattern matching is the primary mechanism for selecting expressions, or specific slots within them, for subsequent operations.

The pattern match is computed on the fly as the query expression is broadcast, as a stream of symbols, to the PAM chips. For each query symbol entered, every PE scans its portion of memory for a match. The progress of this matching during the entry of the query expression is kept track of via 'match tokens' - storage for which is provided alongside every slot. A match token is only generated at a matching slot when the slot before it was itself marked previously; the only exception being the initial match on the header symbol. If the slot does not match, the token disappears. Thus when the query input terminates the only surviving match tokens will flag the ends of responders. This process is illustrated in Figure 3.

The rules for the pattern matching of expressions are illustrated in Figure 4 which shows how the three expressions of Figure 2 pattern match with each other. It should be emphasized that one of the strengths of this hardware system is that query and stored expressions can both use the full syntax, so any one of the expressions in Figure 4 could serve as the query. Briefly the pattern matching rules are as

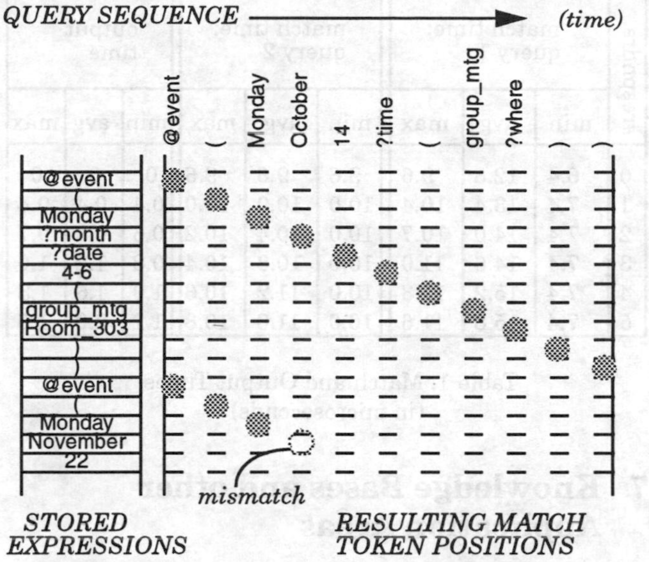

Figure 3. Pattern Matching

follows (using the labels from Figure 4): equal symbols match each other (=). A normal variable will match a constant or another variable (*a*), or a piece of sub-structure enclosed by parentheses (*b*). A list-variable on the other hand will match any sequence of non-header symbols, including none at all (*c*). The list-variable can be used to represent the *cdr* of a list. It can also simply be used as a 'don't-care' that stands in for multiple symbols, as in Figure 4.

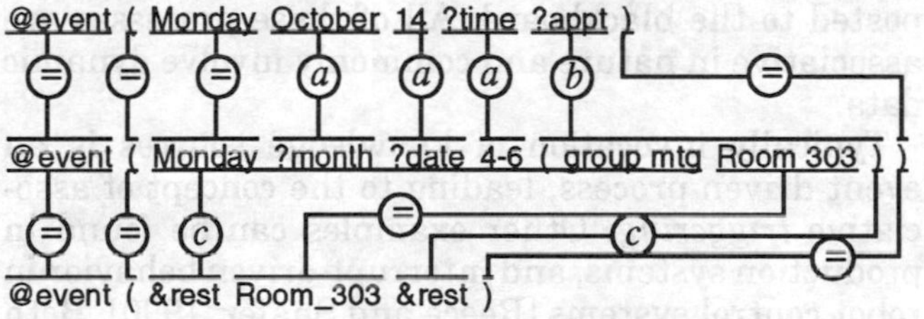

Figure 4. Pattern Matching Rules

Once a set of symbols or expressions has been selected by pattern matching, one possible subsequent action is to output them to the host. Output is guided by the match tokens: storage is scanned for flagged symbols, or the whole expressions in which they lie. Alternatively flagged symbols can be overwritten (modified) either on a case by case basis, via a read-modify-write sequence (such as in incrementing a value), or all together in parallel. The latter is particularly useful as it allows all responders to be recorded within the PAM. If all the expressions are stored with an extra *tag* word at the end (matched by a variable in the query) then all the responders' tags can be subsequently overwritten with some value denoting their new state.

Finally flagged expressions can be deleted by overwriting them with a special 'empty' symbol. When necessary the physical space that these deleted expressions occupy can be reclaimed via garbage collection.

The bulk of the logic required to support this functionality is contained in the PE's, one of which is illustrated in Figure 5. The comparator and attached logic ('L' in the diagram) handle most of the pattern matching rules. The 'jump wire' and its associated control logic ('J') is there to handle, for example, variable ↔ sub-structure matches (case (*b*) in Figure 4). In that case the match token must be effectively jumped from the beginning of a stored sub-structure to its end. This same mechanism is used for scanning the chip for responders during output. Query input and data i/o are handled over the global data bus.

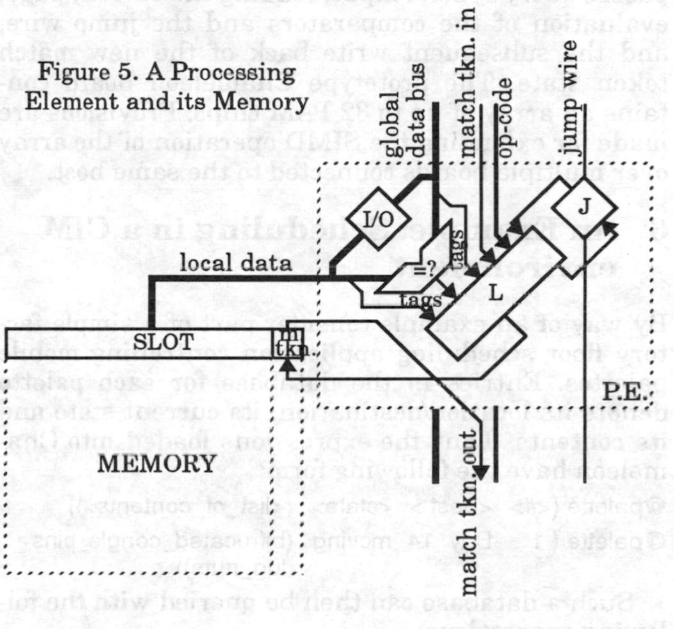

Figure 5. A Processing Element and its Memory

Figure 5 shows only the current slot connected to the PE, as briefly described at the outset each PE actually deals with a small portion of memory. This multiplexing offsets the area penalty due to the complexity of the PE. The current prototype is roughly 50% logic, 50% memory[1]. A consequence of this organization is that the PAM's memory array is divided into *pages*, the number of pages being equal to the number of slots attached to a PE. During matching, pages are discarded when they cease to contain match tokens. This reduces the performance impact of multiplexing the PE logic over the memory.

One final hardware mechanism is responsible for generating a cache-like 'miss' signal when the page being processed contains no match tokens. As well as facilitating the page pruning scheme above, this also permits an early response in cases where there are no responders to a query. Conversely, in Section 7 it will also be shown how this signal is used to alert the system to the presence of a responder.

[1]It is interesting to compare this with commercial RAM's, which are roughly only 60% memory.

In the last three sections a hardware system has been presented that meets the stated requirements. The system supports inserting, deleting, modifying and associative matching on and with complex symbolic expressions, using parallelism to achieve high system performance. The current prototype PAM chip contains 1024 32-bit-symbol-plus-2-bit-status slots and 64 PE's, dividing the storage into 16 pages. The chip has been designed and fabricated using a 1.2μ scalable design rule CMOS process, and has a die size of just 5.4mm x 4.9mm (approximately 140mils x 120mils). Using commercial design rules and die sizes, a PAM with a capacity of 1Mb and 128 PE's is quite practical.

The current PE cycle time is 200ns, this encompasses query symbol input, reading the current page, evaluation of the comparators and the jump wire, and the subsequent write back of the new match token state. The prototype Chameleon board contains an array of up to 32 PAM chips. Provisions are made for extending the SIMD operation of the array over multiple boards connected to the same host.

6 An Example: Scheduling in a CIM environment

By way of an example consider part of a simple factory floor scheduling application controlling mobile palettes. Entries in the database for each palette denote its location/destination, its current state and its contents. Thus the expressions loaded into Chameleon have the following form:

```
@palette (<#>  <dest.>  <state>  (<list_of_contents>))
@palette ( 1   Bay_14  moving  (bifrucated_congle_pins
                                 lug_nuts))
```

Such a database can then be queried with the following expressions:

```
@palette ( ?#  ?where  idle      ())
```

...find an empty palette.

```
@palette ( ?#  Bay_17  ?state   ( & lug_nuts & ))
```

...any lug nuts coming to, or currently at, Bay 17?

Times for the match and read out functions will depend on the number and distribution of partial and full responders through the chips and pages of PAM storage (the palette database is assumed to completely fill the Chameleon board, corresponding to roughly three to four thousand palettes). Table 1 lists the match and read-out times as a function of the number of responders for these two queries.

Although this is a fairly trivial example it should be noted that the @palette's and the slot values within them can be subject to constant insertion, deletion and modification via simple read/write operations on the PAM's storage. Also the complexity of the query, in terms of variables used, has little affect on the match performance. Using the results above such a scheduling system would be able to sustain interleaved update and query rates of 40,000 expressions per second each.

#respndrs.	match time: query 1			match time: query 2			output time		
	min	avg	max	min	avg	max	min	avg	max
0	6.4	12.8	9.6	9.6	9.6	9.6	0	0	0
1	7.4	13.4	10.4	10.0	10.0	10.0	0.4	0.4	0.4
2	7.4	14.0	10.7	10.0	10.4	10.2	0.6	0.8	0.7
3	7.4	14.6	11.0	10.0	10.8	10.4	0.8	1.2	1.0
4	7.4	15.2	11.3	10.0	11.2	10.6	1.0	1.6	1.3
5	7.4	15.8	11.6	10.0	11.6	10.8	1.2	2.0	1.6

Table 1. Match and Output Times (in microseconds)

7 Knowledge Bases and other Application Areas

The above example considered some application querying a dynamic database of facts or events. By adding rules to create a true knowledge base, the foundations are established for a hardware *blackboard system*. Blackboard systems [Hayes-Roth, 1985] are popular mechanisms for supporting the intelligent control systems described in Section 1. The blackboard provides a central knowledge base shared, transparently, by a number of knowledge sources. It serves to establish the context for knowledge processing actions, provide a repository for hypotheses and control the problem solving process. Knowledge sources are scheduled based on events posted to the blackboard. All of these processes are associative in nature and commonly involve dynamic data.

Typically invocation of knowledge sources is an event-driven process, leading to the concept of associative *triggering*. Other examples can be found in production systems, and interrupt-driven behavior in robot control systems [Reece and Shafer, 1990]. Both require actions to be triggered on complex combinations of events. From the pattern matching system's point of view these triggers form the database against which external events are matched. The match is signalled by the absence of the 'miss' signal. So, for example, "@temperature >400" supports range checking on a temperature value or, referring back to the simple palette example, a trigger could be entered to await a palette becoming empty at a certain location. It is also possible to look for conjunctions of events posted in any order. The mechanism to support this uses the tag words described earlier. Every sub-clause of the conjunction ends in a tag denoting its state - 'satisfied' or 'not_ satisfied'. This symbol is modified appropriately after each event expression is broadcast. A short sequence of instructions can then be run to test for conditions that do not contain any 'not_satisfied' symbols. By implementing these triggers in the PAM new conditions can be entered at run-time, and existing ones modified or deleted, all with no associated re-compilation. Full blown Rete-style systems can be implemented by replacing the 'satisfied' tag with an associative pointer to the corresponding beta node, where the join operation is also supported in the PAM (a scheme similar to Kogge *et al.* [1989]).

Other Chameleon applications include direct support for declarative languages such as Prolog, where pattern matching constitutes a large part of the fundamental execution mechanism [Kogge *et al.*, 1989; Robinson, 1986]. Although compilers exist for such languages, the Chameleon system again provides the capability to handle dynamically created clauses.

Lastly there are fields such as memory-based reasoning [Stanfill and Waltz, 1986] and genetic algorithms [Davis, 1987] in which systems attempt to reason or adapt themselves in the absence of rules. Such applications rely almost entirely on pattern matching and appear to be well suited to the capabilities of the Chameleon system.

It should be borne in mind when considering the capacity of Chameleon that, like a cache, it need only be of sufficient size to manage the transitory data in an application, not the entire database. Thus it could be viewed as filling the role of short term memory or as a support for a focus of attention. The end result is a system that allows complex applications to be run faster; or, as a corollary, real-time applications to be more complex.

8 Conclusions

In general, hardware has been perceived as an expensive and unpromising direction - much hoped for functionality being usurped by new compilation techniques. However, as long as there are dynamic and unpredictable environments then associative hardware, such as the Chameleon system, will have a role in meeting system performance needs. The PAM architecture is also poised to take advantage of the trend towards application-specific memories. Yesterday's off-the-shelf memories are beginning to be replaced by libraries of off-the-shelf RAM blocks for semi-custom ASIC's.

This paper has described, and demonstrated the applications of, an associative co-processor which in prototype form contains 1Mb of storage. The subsystem plugs into the backplanes of Hewlett Packard 9000/300 or 400 series workstations and acts as a hardware accelerator for a variety of symbolic pattern matching functions. Currently a PCB version of the board is being constructed so that these prototypes can be evaluated in a number of applications. As an alternative, a simulator is being completed which will maintain a log file describing execution times given the actual hardware.

Lastly, it is interesting to consider the potential of such a system using the 1Mb chips proposed earlier. Coupled with denser (SIMM-style) packaging the same 8" x 11" Chameleon board could have a capacity of 16M bytes and contain 16k PE's. Such a system would have an aggregate processor bandwidth of 5×10^{12} bits per second (per board).

References

[Charniak *et al.*, 1980] E. Charniak, C. K. Riesbeck. and D. V. McDermott. *Artificial Intelligence Programming*. Lawrence Erlbaum Associates, 1980.

[Davis, 1987] L. Davis, editor. *Genetic Algorithms and Simulated Annealing*. Morgan Kaufmann, 1987.

[Forgy, 1982] C. L. Forgy. RETE: A Fast Algorithm for the Many Pattern/Many Object Pattern Match Problem. *Artificial Intelligence*, 19:17-37, 1982

[Hayes-Roth, 1985] B. Hayes-Roth. A Blackboard Architecture for Control. *Journal of Artificial Intelligence*, 26: 251-321, 1985.

[Highland and Iwaskiw, 1989] F. D. Highland and C. T. Iwaskiw. Knowledge Base Compilation. In *Proceedings of the 11th International Joint Conference on Artificial Intelligence*, pages 227-232, August 1989.

[Kogge *et al.*, 1989] P. Kogge, J. Oldfield, M. Brule and C. Stormon. VLSI and Rule-Based Systems. In *VLSI for Artificial Intelligence*, pages 95-108, 1989. Kluwer Academic

[Reece and Shafer, 1990] D. A. Reece and S. Shafer. The Impact of Domain Dynamics on Intelligent Robot Design. Computer Science report CMU-CS-90-130, Carnegie Mellon University, May 1990.

[Robinson, 1986] I. Robinson. A Prolog Processor Based on a Pattern Matching Memory Device. In *Proceedings of the Third International. Conference on Logic Programming*, E. Shapiro editor, pages 172-179, 1986. Springer-Verlag.

[Stanfill and Waltz, 1986] C. Stanfill and D. Waltz. Toward Memory-Based Reasoning. *Communications of the ACM*, 29(12):1213-1228, December 1986.

[Stormon, 1989] C. Stormon. The Coherent Processor - A Content Addressable Memory for AI and Databases. In *Wescon'89: Conference Record*, pages 240-244, November 1989.

[Wade and Sodini, 1989] J. P. Wade and C. G. Sodini. A Ternary Content Addressable Search Engine. *IEEE Journal of Solid-State Circuits*, 24(4):1003-1013, August 1989.

[Warren, 1977] D. H. D. Warren. Implementing Prolog. Technical Report 39, Edinburgh University, 1977.

[Yau and Fung, 1977] S. S. Yau and H. S. Fung. Associative Processor Architecture - A Survey. *Computing Surveys*, 9(1):3-28, March 1977.

ARCHITECTURES & LANGUAGES

Distributed AI 1

Negotiations Over Time in a Multi-Agent Environment: Preliminary Report

Sarit Kraus*
Graduate School for Library Studies and
Dept. of Computer Science
Hebrew University, Jerusalem 91904 Israel
sarit@cs.huji.ac.il

Jonathan Wilkenfeld
Dept. of Government and Politics
University of Maryland
College Park, MD 20742
wilkenfeld@umd2.umd.edu

Abstract

One of the major foci of research in distributed artificial intelligence (DAI) is the design of automated agents which can interact effectively in order to cooperate in problem-solving. Negotiation is recognized as an important means by which inter-agent cooperation is achieved. In this paper we suggest a strategic model of negotiation for N agents ($N \geq 3$), that takes the passage of time during the negotiation process itself into consideration. Changes in the agent's preferences over time will change their strategies in the negotiation and, as a result, the agreements they are willing to reach. We will show that in this model the delay in reaching such agreements can be shortened and in some cases avoided altogether.

1 Introduction

One of the major foci of research in distributed artificial intelligence (DAI) is the design of automated agents which can interact effectively in order to cooperate in problem-solving. Negotiation is recognized as an important means by which inter-agent cooperation is achieved. That is, DAI is concerned with the design of agents which are able to communicate in such a way as to enhance the possibility of reaching mutually beneficial agreements concerning problems such as a division of labor or resources among the agents.

Negotiation has always been a central theme in DAI research [Davis and Smith, 1983; Georgeff, 1983; Malone *et al.*, 1988; Durfee, 1988; Durfee and Lesser, 1989; Rosenschein and Genesereth, 1985; Sathi and Fox, 1989; Conry *et al.*, 1988; Zlotkin and Rosenschein, 1990]. This research has focused on strategies for designing agents capable of reaching mutually beneficial agreements. Sycara ([Sycara, 1987]), using case-based reasoning, and Kraus et al. ([Kraus *et al.*, 1991]) modeled negotiations from a cognitive standpoint.

Yet it is also recognized that although negotiations are necessary for reaching such agreements, the negotiation process is both costly and time-consuming, and thus may increase the overhead of the operation in question (see [Bond and Gasser, 1988]). In negotiations on such issues as job-sharing or resource allocation, it is important to minimize the amount of time spent on negotiating mutually beneficial agreements so as not to detract from time spent on the task itself. Thus, in the presence of time constraints, negotiation time should be taken into consideration.

In [Kraus and Wilkenfeld, 1991a] we propose a strategic model of negotiation that takes the passage of time during the negotiation process itself into consideration. That study focused exclusively on a two-agent model. The present study generalizes this process by considering the N-agent environment.

Following [Rosenschein and Genesereth, 1985; Zlotkin and Rosenschein, 1990; Kraus and Wilkenfeld, 1990; Kraus and Wilkenfeld, 1991a] we examine negotiation using game theory techniques with appropriate modifications to fit artificial intelligence situations. We will focus primarily on works in game theory and economics that have studied the effect of time preferences on the negotiation process, following the classic paper by Rubinstein ([Rubinstein, 1982]). Unlike the work of Zlotkin and Rosenchein, [Zlotkin and Rosenschein, 1990] we investigate multi-agent environments (more than two agents) and our approach makes no assumptions about the protocol for negotiations. Also, our model takes the passage of time during the negotiation process itself into consideration. Furthermore, by taking the passage of time during the negotiation process into consideration, our approach is able to influence the outcome of the negotiation so as to avoid delays in reaching agreements.

2 Initial Setting

N autonomous agents A_1, A_2,...,A_N have a common goal they want to satisfy as soon as possible. In order to satisfy a goal, costly actions must be taken and an agent cannot satisfy the goal without reaching an agreement with one of the other agents. Each of the agents wants to minimize its costs, i.e., prefers to do as little as possible, if it can assume that the goal will be fulfilled properly without additional effort on its part. We note that

*This work was partially completed while the first author was at the Institute for Advanced Computer Studies and Dept. of Computer Science, University of Maryland, College Park.

even though the agents have the same goal (under our simplified assumptions), there is actually a conflict of interests. The agents have different preferences concerning goal satisfaction and for the different possible agreements which can be reached.

We make the following assumptions:

1. Full information - each agent knows all relevant information including the other agents' preferences for the different outcomes over time.

2. The agents are rational - they will behave according to their preferences.

3. Commitments are enforced - if an agreement is reached both sides are forced to follow it.

4. Assumptions (1)-(3) are common knowledge.

We demonstrate the cases we are interested in with the following example.

Example 2.1 *Three robots, A, B and C, stationed on a satellite, are instructed to move an expensive telescope from one location to another as soon as possible. Delay in moving the telescope will reduce the number of pictures sent back to scientists on earth. Any two of the robots can move the telescope, but the tools essential to perform the task are distributed among the three agents. Any of the agents can opt out of the negotiation, choosing not to satisfy the goal. If that occurs, the remaining two cannot achieve the goal (since critical tools will be missing).*

3 The Structure of Negotiations

Our strategic model of negotiations is a model of Alternative Offers.[1]

For reasons of simplification and clarity, we will concentrate on the case of three agents, but our results can be easily extended to N agents where an agent can satisfy a goal by reaching an agreement with another agent[2]. So, in our case, three agents, A, B and C have a common goal they want to satisfy as soon as possible. Each of them has a set of capabilities, P_A, P_B and P_C and a set of tools T_A, T_B and T_C respectively. The agents' capabilities influence their ability and their ways of satisfying the goal, and all the tools are needed to satisfy the goal. We now present formal definitions of agreements and strategies.

3.1 Agreements and Strategies

We first define the set of possible agreements. We assume that there exists a set of possible agreements between any two agents. We denote by $\mathcal{A}$ the set of agents.

Definition 3.1 Agreement:
Let Act be the set of actions required to satisfy a goal. An agreement is a pair (s_i, s_j), where $i, j \in \mathcal{A}$, $i \neq j$; $s_i \cup s_j = Act$. s_i is agent i's portion of the work[3]. *We assume that the set S_{ij} $i, j \in \mathcal{A}, i \neq j$ includes all the possible agreements between agents i and j. We also assume that $S_{ij} = S_{ji}$. Let $S \stackrel{\text{def}}{=} \cup_{ij} S_{ij}$ $i, j \in \mathcal{A}$ $i \neq j$, i.e., S is the set of all possible agreements.*

The negotiation procedure is as follows. The agents can take actions only at certain times in the set $\mathcal{T} = \{0, 1, 2...\}$. In each period $t \in \mathcal{T}$ one of the agents, say i, proposes an agreement to one of the other agents. The other agent (j) either accepts the offer (chooses Y) or rejects it (chooses N), or opts out of the negotiation (chooses O). Also, the third agent may opt out of the negotiation (chooses O), or it can choose not to do anything (chooses Nop). If the offer is accepted, without the third agent opting out, then the negotiation ends and the agreement is implemented (i.e., each of the agents that reached the agreement, does its part of the job and the other agent is obliged to contribute its tools). Also, opting out by one of the agents ends the negotiations since all the tools are required to satisfy the goal. After a rejection, another agent must make a counter offer, and so on.

There are no rules which bind the agents to any previous offers and there is no limit on the number of periods. The only requirement we make is that the length of a single period be fixed and the agents always make offers in the same order, i.e., agent i makes offers in time periods $t, t+3, t+6...$, agent j makes offers on periods $t+1$, $t+4...$, and similarly to the last agent. If an agreement is never reached, and none of the agents opts out, we assume the outcome to be D (Disagreement). We do not make any assumption about who begins the negotiations, i.e., who makes the first offer and who is the second agent to make an offer. So, without loss of generality we assume that $i, j, l \in \mathcal{A}, i \neq j \neq l$ are the first, the second and the third agents, respectively.

Definition 3.2 Negotiation Strategies:
A strategy is a sequence of functions. The domain of the ith element of a strategy is a sequence of agreements of length i and its range is the set $\{Y, N, O, Nop\} \cup S$. We first define a strategy f for an agent i who is the first agent to give an offer.

Let $f = \{f^t\}_{t=0}^{\infty}$, where $f^0 \in \{S_{ij} \cup S_{il}\}$, for $t = 3n, n \in \mathcal{T}$ $f^t : S^t \rightarrow \{S_{ij} \cup S_{il}\}$, and for $t = 3n+1$, $n \in \mathcal{T}$ $f^t : S^t \times \{S_{ji} \cup S_{jl}\} \rightarrow \{Y, N, O, Nop\}$ where if $s^{t+1} \in S_{ji}$, $f^t(s^0, s^1, ..., s^{t+1}) \in \{Y, N, O\}$, and if $s^{t+1} \in S_{jl}$, $f^t(s^0, s^1, ..., s^{t+1}) \in \{O, Nop\}$, ($S^t$ is the set of all sequences of length t of elements in S). For $t = 3n+2$, $n \in \mathcal{T}$ $f^t : S^t \times \{S_{li} \cup S_{lj}\} \rightarrow \{Y, N, O, Nop\}$ where if $s^{t+1} \in S_{li}$, $f^t(s^0, s^1, ..., s^{t+1}) \in \{Y, N, O\}$, and if $s^{t+1} \in S_{lj}$, $f^t(s^0, s^1, ..., s^{t+1}) \in \{O, Nop\}$. We denote by F the set of all strategies of the agent who starts the bargaining.

Similarly, we denote by G the set of all strategies of the agent j who is the second to make offers and we denote by H the set of all strategies of agent l who is the third

---

[1]See [Osborne and Rubinstein, 1990] for a detailed review of the bargaining game of Alternating Offers.

[2]In the case in which the agents may divide the labor between all of them, i.e., agreement may be reached only among all the agents, the model of Alternative Offers is usually disappointing (see [Osborne and Rubinstein, 1990]). It is still useful when the agents have specific types of utility functions (see [Stahl, 1977]).

[3]A similar definition can be given concerning a division of resources.

to make offers[4].

Let $\sigma(f,g,h)$ be a sequence of offers possibly ending with O in which agent i (who can be either A, B or C) starts the bargaining and adopts $f \in F$, agent j adopts $g \in G$ and agent l adopts $h \in H$. Let $T(f,g,h)$ be the length of $\sigma(f,g,h)$ (may be ∞). Let $La(f,g,h)$ be the last element of $\sigma(f,g,h)$ (if there is such an element). $La(f,g,h)$ may be either in S or O which denotes that one of the agents opted out without the agents reaching an agreement.

Definition 3.3 Outcome of the negotiation: *The outcome function of the game is defined by*

$$P(f,g,h) = \begin{cases} D & \text{if } T(f,g,h) = \infty \\ (La(f,g,h), T(f,g,h) - 1) & \text{otherwise} \end{cases}$$

Thus, the outcome (s,t) where $s \in S$ is interpreted as the reaching of an agreement s in period t. The agreement can be between any two agents. (O,t) is interpreted as one of the agents opting out of the negotiations, and the symbol D indicates a perpetual disagreement without any agent opting out.

3.2 Agents' Preferences Over Possible Outcomes

The last component of the model is the preferences of the agents on the set of outcomes. Each agent has preferences for agreements reached at various points in time, and for opting out at various points in time. The time preferences and the preferences between agreements and opting out are the driving force of the model.

Formally, we assume that any agent $i \in \mathcal{A}$ has a preference relation $\succeq_i$ on the set $\{S \times \mathcal{T}\} \cup \{\{O\} \times \mathcal{T}\} \cup \{D\}$, where $\mathcal{T}$ is the set of time periods.

We note here that by defining an outcome to be either a pair (s,t) or (O,t) or D, we have made a restrictive assumption about the agent's preferences. We assume that agents care only about the nature of the agreement or opting out, and the time at which the outcome is reached, and not about the sequence of offers and counteroffers that leads to the agreement. In particular, no agent regrets either having made an offer that was rejected or rejecting an offer (see, for example, the discussion of "decision-regret" in [Raiffa, 1982]).

We make some assumptions about the agents preferences. First we assume that the least-preferred outcome is disagreement (D).

(A0) For every $s \in S$ and $t \in \mathcal{T}$, $(s,t) \succ_i D$ and $(O,t) \succ_i D$ (Disagreement is the worst outcome).

The next two conditions (A1), (A2) concern the behavior of $\succ_i$ on $S_{ij} \times \mathcal{T}$, i.e., concerning agreements reached with another agent in different time periods. We will assume that the agents have no preference among the actions in Act , i.e., all actions are equally difficult. Condition (A1) requires that among agreements reached in the same period with the same agent, agent i prefers fewer numbers of actions s_i.

(A1) For $i \in \mathcal{A}$, $t \in \mathcal{T}$ and $s, r \in S_{ij}$, $j \in \mathcal{A}, j \neq i$, if $|r_i| < |s_i|$, then $(r,t) \succ_i (s,t)$.

[4]The full definitions of the j and l's strategies can be found in [Kraus and Wilkenfeld, 1991b].

We note that this condition does not hold for comparisons among agreements between different agents, i.e., beside the amount of work the agents should do it has other considerations that depend on the other agent's capacity to do its part of the job (P_j).

The next assumption greatly simplifies the structure of preferences among the agreements between any two agents. It requires that preferences between (s_1,t_1) and (s_2,t_2) where $s_i \in S_{ij}$, depend only on s_1, s_2 and the differences between t_1 and t_2.

(A2) For all $r, s \in S_{ij}$, $t_1, t_2, \delta \in \mathcal{T}$ and $i \in \mathcal{A}$, $(r,t_1) \succeq_i (s, t_1+\delta)$ iff $(r,t_2) \succeq_i (s,t_2+\delta)$ (Stationarity).

We note that assumption (A2) does not hold for O and for comparisons among agreements between different agents[5].

Example 3.1 *In the situation from Example 2.1, agents B and C believe that the safest way to move the telescope is by joint action of A and C. In such a case the only possible agreement is one in which agent A will do most of the work. On the other hand agent A prefers to reach an agreement with agent B. In such a case it will need to take fewer actions, and it prefers this despite the cost in safety of the move. It is not safe at all for agents B and C to move the telescope and none of the agents prefers such an agreement.*

When analyzing the model, the main question is whether a possibility exists that the agents will reach an agreement. An important feature of the model that strongly influences the outcome of the game is the preference of a player between an agreement and opting out. We need the following definition in order to compare between agreements and opting out.

Definition 3.4 *For every $t \in \mathcal{T}$ and $i \in \mathcal{A}$ we define* $\bar{S^i}^t_{jl} = \{s | s \in S_{jl}, (s,t) \succ_i (O,t), i,j,l \in \mathcal{A}, j \neq l\}$. *Let* $\bar{S^i}^t = \bar{S^i}^t_{ij} \cup \bar{S^i}^t_{il} \cup \bar{S^i}^t_{jl}$ *where* $i,j,l \in \mathcal{A}, i \neq j \neq l$. *If* $\bar{S^i}^t \neq \emptyset$, *we denote* $\hat{s}^{i,t} = \min_{\prec_i} \bar{S^i}^t$, *i.e.,* $\hat{s}^{i,t}$ *is the worst agreement that can be reached in period t which is still better to agent i than opting out. In case such an agreement does not exist, we define* $\hat{s}^{i,t} = -1$.

We would like now to introduce an additional assumption that will ensure that if all agents prefer some agreements over opting out, an agreement can be reached.

(A3) For any $t \in \mathcal{T}$, if for every $i \in \mathcal{A}$, $\hat{s}^{i,t} \neq -1$, then $\bar{S^i}^t \cap \bar{S^j}^t \cap \bar{S^l}^t \neq \emptyset$, where $i,j,l \in \mathcal{A}, i \neq j \neq l$.

3.3 Perfect Equilibrium

The main question is how a rational agent chooses his strategy for the negotiation. A useful notion is the Nash Equlibrium ([Nash, 1950; Luce and Raiffa, 1957]). A triplets of strategies (σ, τ, ϕ) is a Nash Equilibrium if, given τ and ϕ, no strategy of agent A can result in an outcome that agent A prefers to the outcome generated by (σ, τ, ϕ) and, similarly, to agent B given σ and ϕ and to agent C given σ and τ (assuming that A, B and C

[5]An example of a utility function which satisfies the above assumptions concerning agreements is the following: $U_i(s,t) = C_j + |Act - s_i| + t * c_i$ where $s \in S_{ij}$.

are the first, second and third agents to make an offer, respectively). If there is a unique equilibrium, and if it is known that an agent is designed to use this strategy, no agent will prefer to use a strategy other than these. However, the use of Nash Equilibrium is not an effective way of analyzing the outcomes of the models of Alternating Offers since it puts few restrictions on the outcome and yields too many equilibria points (see the proof in [Rubinstein, 1982]). Therefore, we will use the stronger notion of **(subgame) perfect equilibrium** (P.E.) (see [Selten, 1975]) which requires that the agents' strategies induce an equilibrium in any stage of the negotiation, i.e., in each stage of the negotiation, assuming that an agent follows the P.E. strategy, the other agent does not have a better strategy then to follow its own P.E. strategy. So, if there is a unique perfect equilibrium, and if it is known that an agent is designed to use this strategy, no agent will prefer to use a strategy other than this one in each stage of the negotiation.

4 All Agents Lose Over Time

Suppose all agents are losing over time. We assume that all agents prefer to reach a given agreement sooner rather than later, and that all agents prefer to opt out sooner rather than later. We also assume that if a player prefers an agreement over opting out in some period t, then it prefers the same agreement in time period t' prior to t over opting out in t'. Formally:

(A4) For any $i \in \mathcal{A}$ and $t, t_1, t_2 \in \mathcal{T}$, if $t_1 < t_2$ then $(O, t_1) \succ_i (O, t_2)$, and for any $s \in S$, $(s, t_1) \succ_i (s, t_2)$. If $(s, t) \succ_i (O, t)$, then for any $t' \in \mathcal{T}$ such that $t' < t$, $(s, t') \succ_i (O, t')$. If $(s, t) \succ_i (O, t+1)$, then for any $t' \in \mathcal{T}$ such that $t' < t$, $(s, t') \succ_i (O, t'+1)$.

We also assume that all agents prefer to take part in satisfying the goal. Formally:

(A5) For any agent $i \in \mathcal{A}$, $t \in \mathcal{T}$ and for agreements $s \in \{S_{ij} \cup S_{il}\}$ and $s' \in S_{jl}$, $j, l \in \mathcal{A}, j \neq l \neq i$, $(s, t) \succ_i (s', t)$.

The first case we consider is that there is a period in which one of the agents prefers opting out of the negotiation over any agreement. We also assume that in such a case the other agents still prefer at least one agreement over opting out in this period. We will now prove that in such a case if the game has not ended in prior periods, then an agreement will be reached in the prior period, or two periods prior, to the period in which one of the agents prefers opting out over any agreement. We will use additional notation. $\hat{S}^j_t = \{s | s \in S_{jl} \cup S_{ji}, (s, t) \succ_j (O, t+1)\}$ where $t \in \mathcal{T}, i, j, l \in \mathcal{A}, i \neq j \neq l$. $\hat{S}^j_t$ includes the offers agent j can make on time period t which are better than opting out in the next time period.

Lemma 1 *Let $(\hat{f}, \hat{g}, \hat{h})$ be a Perfect Equilibrium (P.E.) of a model satisfying A0-A5. Suppose there exists $T \in \mathcal{T}$ such that $T > 1$ and for any $t \in \mathcal{T}$, and for any $i \in \mathcal{A}$ if $t < T$ then $\hat{s}^{i,t} \neq -1$ and there exists $i \in \mathcal{A}$ such that $\hat{s}^{i,T+1} = -1$. Suppose it is j's turn, $j \in \mathcal{A}$, to make an offer in time period T. If $\hat{S}^j_T \cap \bar{S^l}^T \cap \bar{S^i}^T \neq \emptyset$, where $i, l \in \mathcal{A}, i \neq j \neq l$, then let $s^j = max_{\prec_j}\{\hat{S}^j_T \cap \bar{S^l}^T \cap \bar{S^i}^T\}$. Let $s^j \in S_{jk}$, $k = i$ or $k = l$, then using its perfect equilibrium strategy, j will offer k s^j and k will accept the offer.*

If $\hat{S}^j_T \cap \bar{S^l}^T \cap \bar{S^i}^T = \emptyset$ then suppose, without loss of generality, that it is i's turn to give an offer in time period $T-1$ then let $s^i = max_{\prec_i} \hat{S}^i_{T-1} \cap \bar{S^l}^{T-1} \cap \bar{S^j}^{T-1}$. Let $s^i \in S_{ik}$, $k = j$ or $k = l$, then using its perfect equilibrium strategy, i will offer k, in time period $T-1$, s^i and k will accept the offer.

In the first case we denote s^j by $\hat{s}$ and T by $\hat{T}$ and in the second case we denote s^i by $\hat{s}$ and $T-1$ by $\hat{T}$.

Proof: The proof of this lemma and the following lemmas and theorems can be found in [Kraus and Wilkenfeld, 1991b].

We will show that under certain conditions, in any period there will be an agreement that will be accepted.

Lemma 2 *Let $(\hat{f}, \hat{g}, \hat{h})$ be a Perfect Equilibrium (P.E.) of a model satisfying A0-A5 and let $\hat{s}$ and $\hat{T}$ be defined as in Lemma 1. Suppose $T < \hat{T}$ such that it is i's turn to make an offer. If for $j \in \mathcal{A}, j \neq i$ there exists $x^T_{ij} \in S_{ij}$ satisfies the following conditions:*

1. *$(x^T_{ij}, T) \succ_k (O, T)$ where $k \in \mathcal{A}$ and $i \neq k$, and $(x^T_{ij}, T) \succ_i (O, T+1)$.*
2. *$(x^T_{ij}, T) \succ_k (\hat{s}, \hat{T})$, where $k = i$ or $k = j$.*
3. *If exist $t \in \mathcal{T}, T < t < \hat{T}$ and $s \in S$, such that $(s, t) \succ_j (x^T_{ij}, T)$ then $(O, T+1) \succ_k (s, t)$ where $k \in \mathcal{A}, k \neq j$.*

then if agent i offers agent j x^T_{ij} in period T, then j using its P.E. strategy, will accept the offer. We denote the set of all the x^T_{ij}'s satisfying the above conditions by X^T_{ij}.

We will show now that in some cases, the negotiations are concluded in the first period. In other cases, some delay in reaching an agreement may occur. In the worst case, agreement will be reached only in period $\hat{T}$.

Theorem 1 *Let $(\hat{f}, \hat{g}, \hat{h})$ be a Perfect Equilibrium (P.E.) of a model satisfying A0-A5 and let X^T_{ij} be defined as in Lemma 2. Suppose for any $i, j \in \mathcal{A}, i \neq j$, $X^{\hat{T}-1}_{ij} \neq \emptyset$. If for all X^t_{ij} such that $i, j \in \mathcal{A}$, $i \neq j$, $t \in \mathcal{T}$ and $t < \hat{T}$, if $x \in X^t_{ij}$ then if there is $s \in S$, such that $(s, t) \succ_j (x, t-1)$ then $(O, t) \succ_k (s, t)$, for any $k \in \mathcal{A}, k \neq j$, then when the agents use their P.E. strategies, agreement will be reached in the first, second or the third periods.*

5 Time is Valuable Only to Some Agents

Suppose one of the agents does not lose over time and even gains at least in the early stages of the negotiation. For example, in the robots in Example 2.1, suppose agent A controls the telescope and uses it for his purposes until an agreement is reached. In this case we will assume that agent A prefers any agreement over opting out. As in example 3.1 we will assume that the set of agreements between B and C is empty and that there is only one possible agreement between C and A. Furthermore, we assume that both B and C prefer the agreement between

A and C over any agreement between A and B[6]. In this case we show that even when one of the agents gains over time but prefers not to opt out, if the other two agents, which lose over time, have the same preferences they can force the first agent to meet their conditions.

Formally we will make the following assumptions.

(A6) $S_{CB} = \{\emptyset\}$[7], and $S_{AC} = \{s_{AC}\}$. (The size of the set of possible agreements is limited).

(A7) For every $t \in T$ and for every $s \in S_{AB}$, $(s_{AC}, t) \succ_i (s, t)$, $i \in \{B, C\}$ and $(s, t) \succ_A (s_{AC}, t)$. (Agents B and C have contradictory preferences to agent A).

(A8) For any $t_1, t_2 \in T$ such that $t_1 < t_2$ and for any $s \in S$, $(s, t_2) \succ_A (s, t_1)$, $(O, t_2) \succ_A (O, t_1)$ and for $i \in \{B, C\}$, $(s, t_1) \succ_i (s, t_2)$, $(O, t_1) \succ_i (O, t_2)$. (Agent A gains over time and agents B and C lose over time).

(A9) For any $t \in T$ and for any $s \in S$, $(s, t) \succ_A (O, t)$. (Agent A prefers agreements over opting out).

(A10) If for any $t, t' \in T$ and for any $s \in S_{AC} \cup S_{AB}$, if $(s, t) \succ_B (O, t')$ then $(s, t) \succ_C (O, t')$ and if $(s, t) \succ_i (O, t)$, where $i \in B, C$ and $t' < t$ then $(s, t') \succ_i (O, t')$.

We will show now that if there is a period where agent B prefer opting out over any agreement then negotiations will be concluded before that period even though agent A gains over time.

Lemma 3 *Let $(\hat{f}, \hat{g}, \hat{h})$ be a Perfect Equilibrium (P.E.) of a model satisfying A0-A2 and A6-A10. If there exist $t_1, t_2 \in T$ such that $t_1 < t_2$, for any $s \in S_{AB}$, $(O, t_1) \succ_B (s, t_1)$, $(s_{AC}, t_2 - 1) \succ_B (O, t_2 - 1)$ and $(O, t_2) \succ_B (s_{AC}, t_2)$, then $P(\hat{f}^{t_1}, \hat{g}^{t_1}, \hat{h}^{t_1}) = (s_{AC}, \hat{t})$[8] $\hat{t} \in T$ where $\hat{t}$ is the maximal t such that it is either A or C's turn to make an offer, $t_1 \leq \hat{t} < t_2$ and $(s_{AC}, \hat{t}) \succ_B (O, t_1)$.*

The next theorem describes the behavior of the agents.

Theorem 2 *Let $(\hat{f}, \hat{g}, \hat{h})$ be a Perfect Equilibrium (P.E.) of a model satisfying A0-A2 and A6-A10. If there exist $t_1, t_2 \in T$ such that $t_1 < t_2$, for any $s \in S_{AB}$, $(O, t_1) \succ_B (s, t_1)$, $(s_{AC}, t_2 - 1) \succ_B (O, t_2 - 1)$ and $(O, t_2) \succ_B (s_{AC}, t_2)$, then if there is no $t < \hat{t}$ ($\hat{t}$ is defined in lemma 3) such that $(O, t) \succ_B (s_{AC}, \hat{t})$ and there is no $t < \hat{t}$ and $s \in S_{AB}$ such that $(s, t) \succ_B (s_{AC}, \hat{t})$ and $(s, t) \succ_A (s_{AC}, \hat{t})$ then $P(\hat{f}, \hat{g}, \hat{h}) = (s_{AC}, \hat{t})$.*

We will demonstrate the above results with the robots from Examples 2.1 and 3.1.

Example 5.1 *In the situation in examples 2.1 and 3.1, suppose the robots satisfy A0-A2 and A6-A10 and suppose $\forall s \in S_{AB}$, $(O, 2) \succ_B (s, 2)$ and $\forall t \in \mathcal{T}, t < 2$ there exists $s^t \in S_{AB}$ such that $(s^t, t) \succ_B (O, t)$, and $(O, 10) \succ_B (s_{AC}, 10)$ and $(s_{AC}, 9) \succ_B (O, 9)$. Suppose also that $(s_{AC}, 3) \succ_B (O, 0)$ and for any $s \in S_{AB}$, $(s_{AC}, 3) \succ_B (s, 0)$ but $\forall t \in \mathcal{T}, t > 3, (O, 2) \succ_B (s_{AC}, t)$. Suppose, A, B and C are the first, second and third agents to make an offer, respectively. In period 3 A will offer C to move the telescope together and C will agree.*

We will examine now the case where there is a time period smaller than $\hat{t}$ and an agreement between A and B that both agents prefer to reach in this time period over s_{AC} in period $\hat{t}$. We will need some additional notations for dealing with this case.

Definition 5.1 *Let $\hat{X} \stackrel{\text{def}}{=} \{(s, t) | s \in S_{AB}, (s, t) \succ_i (s_{AC}, \hat{t})$, where $i \in \{A, B\}, t \in T$ and $t < \hat{t}\}$ ($\hat{t}$ is defined in lemma 3). Let $\hat{x}^i \stackrel{\text{def}}{=} max_{\succ_i} \hat{X}, i \in \{A, B\}$.*

Theorem 3 *Let $(\hat{f}, \hat{g}, \hat{h})$ be a Perfect Equilibrium (P.E.) of a model satisfying A0-A2 and A6-A10. If there exist $t_1, t_2 \in T$ such that $t_1 < t_2$, for any $s \in S_{AB}$, $(O, t_1) \succ_B (s, t_1)$, $(s_{AC}, t_2 - 1) \succ_B (O, t_2 - 1)$ and $(O, t_2) \succ_B (s_{AC}, t_2)$, then if there is no $t < \hat{t}$ ($\hat{t}$ is defined in lemma 3), such that $(O, t) \succ_B (s_{AC}, \hat{t})$ and if $\hat{x}^A = (s', t') = \hat{x}^B$ then $P(\hat{f}, \hat{g}, \hat{h}) = (s', t')$.*

6 The Application of the Theory in Building Autonomous Agents

One of the main questions is how one can use the above theoretical results in building agents capable of acting and negotiating under time constraints.

We note that in each of the cases we have investigated, either in this paper or in [Kraus and Wilkenfeld, 1991a], where we presented a strategic model of negotiations for only two agents, the perfect-equilibrium strategies are determined by parameters of the situation.

So, one can supply agents with the appropriate strategies for each of the cases we have dealt with. When an agent participates in one of those situations, it will need to recognize which type of situation it is in. Assuming the agent is given the appropriate arguments about the situation it is involved in it can construct the exact strategy for its specific case and use it in the negotiations. Since we provide the agents with unique perfect equilibrium strategies, if we announce it to the other agents in the environment, the other agents can not do better than to use their similar strategies.

7 Conclusion and Future Work

In this paper we demonstrate how the incorporation of time into the negotiation procedure contributes to a more efficient negotiation process where there are at least three agents in the environment. We show that in different cases this model, together with the assumption that the agents' strategies induce an equilibrium in any stage of the negotiation, may result in the agent being able to use negotiation strategies that will end the negotiation with only a small delay. We suggest that these results are useful in particular in situations with time constraints. We are in the process of using this model in developing agents that will participate in crisis situations where time is an important issue.

The most obvious outstanding question concerns the relaxation of the assumption of complete information.

[6] Other examples where such situations occurred can be found in [Kraus and Wilkenfeld, 1991a; Kraus and Wilkenfeld, 1990].

[7] $\emptyset$ denotes the empty agreement.

[8] Let $s^0 ... s^T \in S$ define $f | s^0 ... s^T$ to be the strategy dervied from f after the offers $s^0, ..., s^T$ have been announced and already rejected. If $f^T(s_0, ..., s_{T-1})$ does not depend on $s_0, ... s_{T-1}$ we denote the result by f^T. Similarly for g and h.

In many situations the agents do not have full information concerning the other agents. Several works in game theory and economics have considered different versions of the model of Alternative Offers with incomplete information (see for example, [Rubinstein, 1985; Osborne and Rubinstein, 1990; Chatterjee and Samuelson, 1987]). We are in the process of modifying those results for use in DAI environments.

8 Acknowledgement

We would like to thank K. Arrow, R. Aumann, B. Bueno de Mesquita, J. Oppenheimer, A. Rubinstein and P. Young for helpful suggestions about game theory and negotiation. We would also like to thank J. Hendler and D. Perlis for helpful discussions.

References

[Bond and Gasser, 1988] A. H. Bond and L. Gasser. An analysis of problems and research in DAI. In A. H. Bond and L. Gasser, editors, *Readings in Distributed Artificial Intelligence*, pages 3–35. Morgan Kaufmann Publishers, Inc., San Mateo, California, 1988.

[Chatterjee and Samuelson, 1987] K. Chatterjee and L. Samuelson. Bargaining with two-sided incomplete information: An infinite horizon model with alternating offers. *Review of Economic Studies*, 54:175–192, 1987.

[Conry *et al.*, 1988] S. E. Conry, R. A. Meyer, and V. R. Lesser. Multistage negotiation in distributed planning. In A. H. Bond and L. Gasser, editors, *Readings in Distributed Artificial Intelligence*, pages 367–384. Morgan Kaufmann Publishers, Inc., San Mateo, California, 1988.

[Davis and Smith, 1983] R. Davis and R.G. Smith. Negotiation as a metaphor for distributed problem solving. *Artificial Intelligence*, 20:63–109, 1983.

[Durfee and Lesser, 1989] E. H. Durfee and Victor R. Lesser. Negotiating Task Decomposition and Allocation Using Partial Global Planning. In L. Gasser and M. N. Huhns, editors, *Distributed Artificial Intelligence, Volume II*, pages 229–244. Pitman/Morgan Kaufmann, London, 1989.

[Durfee, 1988] E. H. Durfee. *Coordination of Distributed Problem Solvers*. Kluwer Academic Publishers, Boston, 1988.

[Georgeff, 1983] M. Georgeff. Communication and interaction in multi-agent planning. In *Proc. of the National Conference on Artificial Intelligence*, pages 125–129, Washington, D.C., 1983.

[Kraus and Wilkenfeld, 1990] S. Kraus and J. Wilkenfeld. An automated strategic model of negotiation. In *AAAI-90 Workshop on Reasoning in Adversarial Domains*, Boston, 1990.

[Kraus and Wilkenfeld, 1991a] S. Kraus and J. Wilkenfeld. The function of time in cooperative negotiations. In *Proc. of AAAI-91*, California, 1991. To appear.

[Kraus and Wilkenfeld, 1991b] S. Kraus and J. Wilkenfeld. Negotiations over time in a multi agent environment. Technical Report UMIACS TR 91-51 CS TR 2649, Institute for Advanced Computer Studies, University of Maryland, 1991.

[Kraus *et al.*, 1991] S. Kraus, E. Ephrati, and D. Lehmann. Negotiation in a non-cooperative environment. *Journal of Experimental and Theoretical Artificial Intelligence*, 1991. Accepted for publication.

[Luce and Raiffa, 1957] R. D. Luce and H. Raiffa. *Games and Decisions*. John Wiley and Sons, 1957.

[Malone *et al.*, 1988] T. W. Malone, R. E. Fikes, and M. T. Howard. Enterprise: A marketlike task schedule for distributed computing environments. In B. A. Huberman, editor, *The Ecology of Computation*. North Holland, 1988.

[Nash, 1950] J. F. Nash. The bargaining problem. *Econometrica*, 18:155–162, 1950.

[Osborne and Rubinstein, 1990] M. J. Osborne and A. Rubinstein. *Bargaining and Markets*. Academic Press Inc., San Diego, California, 1990.

[Raiffa, 1982] H. Raiffa. *The Art and Science of Negotiation*. Harvard University Press, 1982.

[Rosenschein and Genesereth, 1985] J. Rosenschein and M.R. Genesereth. Deals among rational agents. In *Proc. of the Ninth International Joint Conference on Artificial Intelligence*, pages 91–99, Los Angeles, California, 1985.

[Rubinstein, 1982] A. Rubinstein. Perfect equilibrium in a bargaining model. *Econometrica*, 50(1):97–109, 1982.

[Rubinstein, 1985] A. Rubinstein. A bargaining model with incomplete information about preferences. *Econometrica*, 53(5):1151–1172, 1985.

[Sathi and Fox, 1989] A. Sathi and M.S. Fox. Constraint-directed negotiation of resource reallocations. In L. Gasser and M. N. Huhns, editors, *Distributed Artificial Intelligence, Volume II*, pages 163–194. Pitman/Morgan Kaufmann, London, 1989.

[Selten, 1975] R. Selten. Re-examination of the perfectness concept for equilibrium points in extensive games. *International Journal of Game Theory*, 4:25–55, 1975.

[Stahl, 1977] I. Stahl. An n-person bargaining game in an extensive form. In R. Henn and O. Moeschlin, editors, *Mathematical Economics and Game Theory*, Lecture Notes in Economics and Mathematical Systems No. 141. Berlin:Springer-Verlag, 1977.

[Sycara, 1987] K.P. Sycara. *Resolving Adversarial Conflicts: An Approach to Integrating Case-Based and Analytic Methods*. PhD thesis, School of Information and Computer Science, Georgia Institute of Technology, 1987.

[Zlotkin and Rosenschein, 1990] G. Zlotkin and J. Rosenschein. Negotiation and conflict resolution in non-cooperative domains. In *Proceedings of AAAI-90*, pages 100–105, Boston,MA, 1990.

A Decision-Theoretic Approach to Coordinating Multiagent Interactions

Piotr J. Gmytrasiewicz*, Edmund H. Durfee†, and David K. Wehe*
*Department of Nuclear Engineering
†Department of Electrical Engineering and Computer Science
University of Michigan
Ann Arbor, Michigan 48109

Abstract

We describe a decision-theoretic method that an autonomous agent can use to model multiagent situations and behave rationally based on its model. Our approach, which we call the Recursive Modeling Method, explicitly accounts for the recursive nature of multiagent reasoning. Our method lets an agent recursively model another agent's decisions based on probabilistic views of how that agent perceives the multiagent situation, which in turn are derived from hypothesizing how that other agent perceives the initial agent's possible decisions, and so on. Further, we show how the possibility of multiple interactions can affect the decisions of agents, allowing cooperative behavior to emerge as a rational choice of selfish agents that otherwise might behave uncooperatively.

Introduction

A central issue in distributed artificial intelligence (DAI) is how to get autonomous intelligent agents, each of whom has its own goals and preferences, to model each other and coordinate their activities for their mutual benefit. This paper describes a recursive method that agents can use to model each other in order to estimate expected utilities more completely in multiagent situations, and thus to make rational and coordinated decisions. Our method works by letting agents explicitly reason about how the collective actions of agents can affect the utilities of individual actions. Thus, to choose an action that maximizes its individual utility, an agent should predict the actions of others. The fact that other agents are likely to take the same approach gives rise to the recursive nesting of models.

Our Recursive Modeling Method (RMM) represents this recursion explicitly to allow an agent to arrive, within the bounds of its processing, on the most rational decision in the multiagent environment. RMM considers all of the available information an agent might have about others and summarizes the possible uncertainties as a set of probability distributions. This representation can reflect the uncertainty as to the other agents' intentions, abilities, long-term goals, and sensing capabilities. Furthermore, on a deeper level of the recursion, the agents may have information on how other agents are likely to view them, how they themselves think they are viewed, and so on.

Our work, thus, extends other work [Rosenschein and Breese, 1989] that uses a game theoretic approach to coordinating interactions without communication. That work unrealistically assumes that agents have full information about each other's choices, preferences, and perceptions. Other research efforts in DAI use similar formalisms to our work, but avoid the recursive issues that we are studying by allowing agents to communicate about their beliefs, goals, and preferences, in order to make explicit deals [Werner, 1989; Zlotkin and Rosenschein, 1989; Zlotkin and Rosenschein, 1990].

Research in cooperation indicates that agents can converge on cooperative strategies during repeated interactions without ever explicitly communicating [Axelrod, 1984]. The most well-known example is the Prisoner's Dilemma game, where a rational "one-shot" strategy is to defect, but where a "Tit-for-Tat" strategy is best for repeated interactions. Following the methodology of metagames [Howard, 1966; Reagade, 1987], the goal of our work is to develop a formal, algorithmic model that captures how cooperative strategies can be derived by self-interested, rational agents.

In the remainder of this paper, we begin by outlining the basic concept of a payoff matrix from decision and game theories, and then we define the RMM and illustrate it with an example. Subsequently, we show how the possibility of multiple interactions changes the character of games, and illustrate this using the Prisoner's Dilemma problem. We revisit the earlier example and apply the multiple interactions concept within RMM. We conclude by summarizing our results and current research directions.

Establishing Payoffs

A decision-theoretic approach to multiagent interaction requires that an agent view its encounters with other agents in terms of possible joint actions and their utilities, usually assembled in the form of a payoff matrix. We have developed a system, called the Rational Rea-

[0]This research was supported, in part, by the Department of Energy under contract DG-FG-86NE37969, and by the NSF under Coordination Theory and Collaboration Technology Initiative grant IRI-9015423.

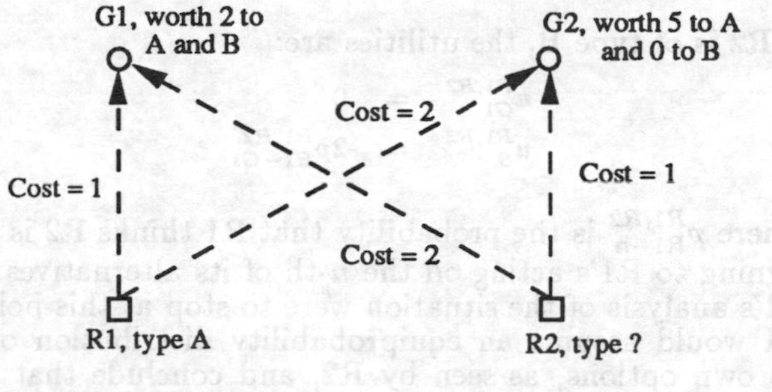

Figure 1: Example Scenario of Interacting Agents

soning System (RRS) [Gmytrasiewicz *et al.*, 1991a] that determines plans' utilities [Jackobs and Kiefer, 1973] to automatically generate the information for a payoff matrix. For brevity, we will not describe the details of RRS, beyond saying that it combines decision-theoretic techniques with hierarchical planning to generate alternative decisions (plans of action), and uses time-dependent calculations of utility to generate the expected payoffs. These calculations involve formal notions of agents' preferences and the ways specific tasks in the environment impact these preferences.

The Recursive Modeling Method

The Recursive Modeling Method (RMM) seeks to include all the information an agent might have about the other agents and can be viewed essentially as an extension of case analysis [Luce and Raiffa, 1957] to situations in which other players' payoffs and alternatives are uncertain. This technique attempts to put oneself in the shoes of the other player and to guess what he will prefer to do. Our approach thus follows, and extends to deeper levels of recursion, the main idea of a hypergame method [Bennett and Huxham, 1982; Vane and Lehner, 1990]. Our principal contribution is a complete and rigorous formalism that, unlike similar work [Cohen and Levesque, 1990; Rosenschein, 1988], directly relates the recursive levels of the agents' knowledge to the utilities of their actions and thus to the intentions of rational agents [Dennett, 1986].

Example Multigent Interaction

To put our description in concrete terms, consider the example scenario of two interacting agents (Figure 1). The environment has agents of type A and B. Agents of type A can perceive all of the goals in the environment, while B agents can only see goals of type G1. Moreover, A agents are aware of the two types of agents, A and B, while B agents are aware only of their type. Further, A agents can perform all of the types of goals, while B agents are equipped only for G1 goals. The utility of a G1 goal is equal to 2 for both types of agents, while the utility of a G2 goal is 5 for A agents and 0 for B agents. The cost of an attempt by either agent to achieve the farther goal is 2, and the cost of attempting the closer goal is 1. For simplicity, we assume that the agents can achieve only one goal.

Let us focus our attention on R1, which is of type A. We see R1 as having three options: pursue G1, pursue G2, or do something (including nothing) else (G1, G2 and S, for short). Using the above information, R1's payoffs are computed as the difference between the total worth of all the performed goals and the cost of achieving its own goal. For example, if R1 pursues G2 and R2 pursues G1, then the payoff for R1 is the total worth of the achieved goals minus its own cost: (2+5) - 2 = 5. These payoffs are assembled in the following payoff matrix:

		R2		
		G1	G2	S
	G1	1	6	1
R1	G2	5	3	3
	S	2	5	0

This matrix represents R1's utilities for its possible decisions (G1, G2, or S) depending on R2's decisions (G1, G2, or S). These utilities are described as the payoffs of R1 given the joint moves of both agents.

R1 may reasonably assume that R2 is trying to maximize its own payoff (see also [Dennett, 1986]), but the difficulty in predicting R2's actions is that R1 is uncertain as to R2's type. R1 thus does not know whether R2 will see, value, or pursue G2. In RMM, these uncertainties are represented in terms of probability distributions. Furthermore, R2's actions are likely to depend on how R2 views R1. R1 will thus form alternative models of itself corresponding to how it thinks R2 might perceive it.

We will now proceed to introduce the general form of RMM that captures the intuitions mentioned above. We will come back to the example scenario depicted in Figure 1 and solve it subsequently.

The General Form of RMM

To generalize over an arbitrary number of agents, let us assume that R1 is dealing with (N-1) other agents, R2, ..., RN. The utility of the m-th element of R1's set of alternative actions can be evaluated as:

$$u_m^{R1} = \sum_k \cdots \sum_l \{p_{R2-k}^{R1} \cdots p_{RN-l}^{R1} u_{m,k,\ldots,l}^{R1}\} \qquad (1)$$

where p_{Ri-k}^{R1} represents the probability R1 assigns to Ri's choosing to act on the k-th element of Ri's set of options, which we will refer to as an intentional probability. $u_{m,k,\ldots,l}^{R1}$ is R1's payoff (utility) as an element of the N-dimensional game matrix.

What makes the situation recursive is the fact that R1 may attempt to determine the intentional probabilities p_{Ri-k}^{R1} by guessing how the game looks from Ri's point of view. R1 models agent Ri using probability distributions p_{Pi}^{R1}, p_{Ai}^{R1}, and p_{Wi}^{R1}, which we will call modeling probabilities. p_{Pi}^{R1} summarizes R1's knowledge about Ri's preferences (the goals it will value). p_{Ai}^{R1} summarizes R1's knowledge about Ri's abilities, given its preferences. p_{Wi}^{R1} summarizes R1's knowledge about how Ri sees the world (content of Ri's world model), given its abilities. In every case of Ri having various preferences, abilities and world models, R1 can assume that Ri is rational (assumption of intentionality, see also [Dennett, 1986; Rosenschein, 1988]) and consider the probability that the k-th element of Ri's set of options is of the highest utility to Ri. R1 can then use the modeling probabilities to compute p^{R1}_{Ri-k} as the following probabilistic mixture:

$$p^{R1}_{Ri-k} = \sum_{Pi} \sum_{Ai} \sum_{Wi} \{p^{R1}_{Pi} p^{R1}_{Ai} p^{R1}_{Wi} \times Prob(Max_{k'}(u^{R1,Ri}_{k'}) = u^{R1,Ri}_{k})\} \quad (2)$$

where $u^{R1,Ri}_{k'}$ is the utility R1 estimates that Ri will assign to its option k', and is computed as

$$u^{R1,Ri}_{k'} = \sum_{r} \ldots \sum_{s} \{p^{R1,Ri}_{R1-r} \ldots p^{R1,Ri}_{RN-s} u^{R1,Ri}_{k',r,\ldots,s}\} \quad (3)$$

The $u^{R1,Ri}_{k',r,\ldots,s}$ is how R1 sees Ri's payoffs in the N-dimensional game matrix. The probabilities R1 thinks Ri assigns to agent Rn acting on its o-th option $p^{R1,Ri}_{Rn-o}$, can in turn be expressed in terms of $p^{R1,Ri,Rn}_{Rv-w}$ and $u^{R1,Ri,Rn}_{o',w,\ldots}$ and so on.

Solving the Example Interaction

Given the payoff matrix computed before, R1 can compute the expected utilities of each of its alternatives based on equation (1) as follows:

$$\begin{aligned} u^{R1}_{G1} &= p^{R1}_{R2-G1} + 6p^{R1}_{R2-G2} + p^{R1}_{R2-S} \\ u^{R1}_{G2} &= 5p^{R1}_{R2-G1} + 3p^{R1}_{R2-G2} + 3p^{R1}_{R2-S} \\ u^{R1}_{S} &= 2p^{R1}_{R2-G1} + 5p^{R1}_{R2-G2} \end{aligned} \quad (4)$$

where p^{R1}_{R2-k} denotes the probability that R1 assigns to R2's intending to act on its k-th option. R1 can stop the computation without recursion, in which case it assumes an equiprobable intentional probability distribution $p^{R1}_{R2} = (p^{R1}_{R2-G1}, p^{R1}_{R2-G2}, p^{R1}_{R2-S}) = (1/3, 1/3, 1/3)$ (following the entropy maximization principle [Neapolitan, 1990]). Based on this distribution with zero levels of recursion, R1 would choose G2, which we can summarize as:

Decision 0: $R1^0 \rightarrow G2$.

Alternatively, R1 could determine the values of p^{R1}_{R2-k} using equations (2) and (3). Plunging deeper into the recursion, R1 has to look at the game from R2's point of view. R2 can be either type A or B, and the corresponding payoff matrices are:

		R1		
		G1	G2	S
R2(A)	G1	0	5	0
	G2	6	4	4
	S	2	5	0

		R1	
		G1	S
R2(B)	G1	0	0
	S	2	0

The utilities of R2's options, if it is of type A, are:

$$\begin{aligned} u^{R1,R2}_{G1} &= 5p^{R1,R2}_{R1-G2} \\ u^{R1,R2}_{G2} &= 6p^{R1,R2}_{R1-G1} + 4p^{R1,R2}_{R1-G2} + 4p^{R1,R2}_{R1-S} \\ u^{R1,R2}_{S} &= 2p^{R1,R2}_{R1-G1} + 5p^{R1,R2}_{R1-G2} \end{aligned} \quad (5)$$

If R2 is of type B, the utilities are:

$$\begin{aligned} u^{R1,R2}_{G1} &= 0 \\ u^{R1,R2}_{S} &= 2p^{R1,R2}_{R1-G1} \end{aligned} \quad (6)$$

where $p^{R1,R2}_{R1-n}$ is the probability that R1 thinks R2 is assigning to R1's acting on the n-th of its alternatives. If R1's analysis of the situation were to stop at this point, R1 would assume an equiprobability distribution over its own options, as seen by R2, and conclude that R2 will pursue G2 if it is A, and S if it is B. Let us assume that R1 does not know whether R2 is A or B and thus assigns the probability $p^{R1}_{R2(A)} = 0.5$ to the possibility that R2 is of type A. Here, the probability $p^{R1}_{R2(A)}$ encapsulates all of the modeling probabilities regarding R2's preferences, abilities and world model. R1 can now use equation (2) to estimate the intentional probability distribution over R2's options G1, G2 and S, as $p^{R1}_{R2} = 0.5(0,1,0) + 0.5(0,0,1) = (0, .5, .5)$. In this case, R1 would estimate the expected utility of its own choices from equation (4) as:

$$\begin{aligned} u^{R1}_{G1} &= 3.5, \\ u^{R1}_{G2} &= 3 \\ u^{R1}_{S} &= 2.5. \end{aligned} \quad (7)$$

We see that R1 will opt for G1 at this first stage of the recursion. Let us summarize this as:

Decision 1: $R1^1 \rightarrow G1$.

We now go on to the next step of the recursion and consider how R1 would see itself through R2's eyes, and how that would influence R1's decision.

If R2 is A, it will form two possible views of the game from R1's perspective, corresponding to R1 being A or B, respectively:

		R2		
		G1	G2	S
R1(A)	G1	1	6	1
	G2	5	3	3
	S	2	5	0

		R2	
		G1	S
R1(B)	G1	1	1
	S	2	0

At this point, using an equiprobability distribution over R2's options, R1 would think that R2 would conclude that R1 will pursue G2 if it is A, and equally likely G1 or S if it is B. Assuming that R2 would treat R1's being A or B as equiprobable ($p^{R1,R2}_{R1(A)} = 0.5$), the resulting intentional distribution over R1's options G1, G2 and S, would be $p^{R1,R2}_{R1} = 0.5(0,1,0) + 0.5(.5,0,.5) = (.25, .5, .25)$. The expected payoffs of R2, as seen by R1, can then be computed from equation (5) as:

$$\begin{aligned} u^{R1,R2}_{G1} &= 5p^{R1,R2}_{R1-G2} = 2.5 \\ u^{R1,R2}_{G2} &= 6p^{R1,R2}_{R1-G1} + 4p^{R1,R2}_{R1-G2} + 4p^{R1,R2}_{R1-S} = 4.5 \\ u^{R1,R2}_{S} &= 2p^{R1,R2}_{R1-G1} + 5p^{R1,R2}_{R1-G2} = 3 \end{aligned} \quad (8)$$

If R2 is B, its view of R1 would consist of a single view, since it could only see R1 as type B. R1's payoff matrix in this case is:

		R2	
		G1	S
R1(B)	G1	1	1
	S	2	0

In this case, using an equiprobability distribution over R2's choices does not give R2 a clue about R1's choice. It will use the equiprobability distribution over R1's options in equation (6) and compute as follows:

$$\begin{aligned} u_{G1}^{R1,R2} &= 0 \\ u_S^{R1,R2} = 2p_{R1-G1}^{R1,R2} &= 1 \end{aligned} \quad (9)$$

Thus, R1 will find that R2 will choose G2, if it is A, and S, if it is B, to give $p_{R2}^{R1} = (0, .5, .5)$. Using equation (4) again, the expected utilities of R1 are:

$$\begin{aligned} u_{G1}^{R1} &= 3.5 \\ u_{G2}^{R1} &= 3 \\ u_S^{R1} &= 2.5 \end{aligned} \quad (10)$$

Thus, at the second stage of the recursion, R1's conclusion as to its best option is:

Decision 2: $R1^2 \rightarrow G1$.

Let us have a look at the conclusions R1 would reach at the stages of the recursion considered so far:

Decision 0: $R1^0 \rightarrow G2$.

Decision 1: $R1^1 \rightarrow G1$.

Decision 2: $R1^2 \rightarrow G1$.

Thus, if R1 were to treat R2 as a complete unknown, as in the zeroth stage, it would decide for G2. Going deeper and considering how R2 may view the situation, R1's best option changes to G1. Going even deeper and seeing himself being analyzed by R2, R1's best option remains G1, despite R1 being aware that, if R2 were A, it would incorrectly think that, if R1 were A, R1 would pursue G2! This has a stabilizing effect on the deeper levels of recursion, and G1 remains R1's best option (assuming that R1 treats the modeling probabilities of the agents' types on deeper levels of the recursion as equiprobable as well).

The payoff matrices of both players considered in the above example can be depicted as in Figure 2. The recursion can, in principle, be continued indefinitely, but usually, for a given problem, going below certain level does not contribute anything new to the analysis. This level is the one at which the game starts looking the same from the perspective of the either player. Consider probabilities $p_{R2(A)}^{R1}$ and $p_{R2(A)}^{R1,R2,R1}$ in Figure 2. If they are equal (R1 sees R2 in the same way as R1 thinks R2 thinks it is being seen by R1), no new information would be contributed beyond the 4-th level of the recursion (assuming that $p_{R1(A)}^{R1,R2}$ and $p_{R1(A)}^{R1,R2,R1,R2}$ are in turn equal, and so on).

Non-Converging Example Interaction

The fact that the stages of the recursion start looking very similar from stage to stage does not mean that a unique probability distribution over the other agents' options can be reached in every case. A variation of the example interaction illustrates this. Imagine that R1, being A and quite sure that it looks like A, estimates the probability of R2's (if it is A) correctly identifying R1 as A as being high, say $p_{R1(A)}^{R1,R2} = 0.9$. The resulting intentional distribution over R1's options G1, G2 and S, as seen by R2 if it is A, would be $p_{R1}^{R1,R2} = (.05, .9, .05)$. The calculations in equations (8) and (9) then result in S being the best option of R2, if it is of either type ($p_{R2}^{R1} = (0, 0, 1)$). This, in turn, would result in the following expected utilities for R1:

$$\begin{aligned} u_{G1}^{R1} &= 1 \\ u_{G2}^{R1} &= 3 \\ u_S^{R1} &= 0 \end{aligned}$$

R1, in this case, would thus arrive at

Decision 2: $R1^2 \rightarrow G2$.

Were R1 to consider the next level, it would come up with the probability distribution over R2's options $p_{R2}^{R1} = (0, .5, .5)$ and

Decision 3: $R1^3 \rightarrow G1$.

This instability continues at the deeper levels of recursion with RMM unable to decide whether R2 makes its choices according to probability distribution (0, .5, .5) or (0, 0, 1). Our approach to resolving this situation is to apply the principle of indifference to the probability distributions over R2's choices. In the above case, the distributions (0, .5, .5) and (0, 0, 1) are merged with 0.5 weighting factor each, resulting in $p_{R2}^{R1} = (0, .25, .75)$. The calculation of the expected utilities of R1's options using this merged distribution over R2's options results in G2 being R1's best option, which we regard as a solution in this case. Let us note, that R1's decision to pursue G2 can also be called an uncooperative option, in a sense that it treats R2 as if it were not there, and that R2 would prefer that R1 choose G1, if it were either type A or B. We will come back to this point in the next section.

Our preliminary investigation of the general convergence properties of RMM suggests that, if the method does not yield a unique intentional probability distribution over the other agents' options (as in the previous example), it will converge on a *finite* set of alternative distributions, which can then be combined. The finiteness of this set is essentially due to the finite knowledge base of the agents, and, in particular, to the fact that they cannot have explicitly given knowledge about what other agents think about others thinking about others thinking ..., to infinite levels. It is, in fact, likely that the recursive hierarchy of payoff matrices will start becoming uniform down from level 4 or 5. That, in turn, permits agents to determine the finite set of intentional probability distributions of the others at relatively high levels of the hierarchy.

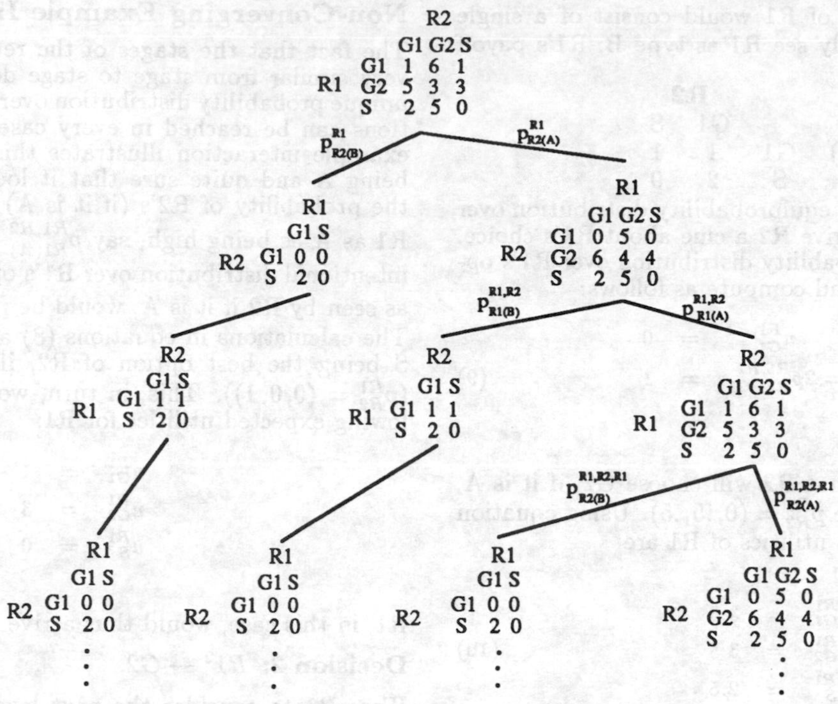

Figure 2: Example of the Recursive Hierarchy

The assumption of intentionality, as formalized in equation (2), can give rise to various probability distributions over agents' options, depending on how strongly they are assumed to be coupled to the probabilities of others' options. In the examples above, we followed the most straightforward, and possibly the most risky, path of assigning an equal, nonzero probability to the options with the highest expected payoff, and zero to all of the rest. Another cautious extreme would be to assign a probability of zero to all of the dominated options, and use the equiprobability assumption for the rest. The influence of these and other ways of interpreting equation (2) are under study.

Multiple Interactions

As shown in the previous section, selfish, rational agents employing RMM may fail to exhibit cooperative behaviors in one-time encounters. In this section, we present a methodology based on metagame analysis [Howard, 1966] that, when integrated with the RMM, makes agents more cooperative when they might interact repeatedly.

To introduce our methodology, we temporarily abandon our scenario of Figure 1. Instead, we use the Prisoner's Dilemma game, as a well known, and very simple example of a game in which repeated interactions lead to cooperation. We then revisit the example of Figure 1.

Repeated Prisoner's Dilemma

Most realistic problem domains involve a finite number of agents that periodically interact, so agents that have interacted in the past could encounter each other repeatedly. A strategy that is rational for one interaction might be counterproductive in repetitive situations where agents can consider their prior experiences in deciding on their actions.

The simplest illustration is the Prisoner's Dilemma (PD), with this payoff matrix:

		II	
		c	d
I	C	3\3	0\5
	D	5\0	1\1

If player I can be sure that he will never play with player II again, he would note that the payoffs of his D move dominate the payoffs of C. That is, no matter what player II does, player I is better off with D. Since the game is symmetric, both players choose to defect and a joint move D/d, with a payoff of 1 to each player, results. The paradox of PD is that, if both players were irrational, they could cooperate and each receive a payoff of 3. Thus, in a one-time interaction, a paradoxical, noncooperative solution results.

It has been previously demonstrated that, for repeated Prisoner's Dilemma, the one-time strategy is a poor choice [Axelrod, 1984; Smith, 1984]. In a population of alternative strategies that compete with each other over multiple generations, Axelrod experimentally discovered that a "Tit-for-Tat" strategy, in which a player is predisposed to cooperate but will defect against a player who defected in their previous encounter, is the "fittest" for PD.

We derive this result more rigorously using metagame theory [Howard, 1966; Reagade, 1987]. Let us define a strategy, or a metamove, of player I as an initial move to be made complemented by a mapping from the set

					II				
		S1	S2	S3	S4	S5	S6	S7	S8
	S1	4\4	4\4	16\1	16\1	8\3	8\3	20\0	20\0
	S2	4\4	4\4	12\7	9\9	7\7	10\10	14\9	9\9
	S3	1\16	7\12	10\10	4\14	5\15	11\11	14\9	8\13
I	S4	1\16	9\9	14\4	8\8	6\11	9\9	20\0	20\0
	S5	3\8	7\7	15\5	11\6	6\6	10\5	18\3	14\4
	S6	3\8	10\10	11\11	9\9	5\10	12\12	12\12	9\9
	S7	0\20	9\14	9\14	0\20	3\18	12\12	12\12	3\18
	S8	0\20	9\9	13\8	0\20	4\14	9\9	18\3	8\8

Figure 3: Metagame Matrix for Prisoner's Dilemma

of moves of his opponent {c, d}, to the set of moves of player I {C, D}. A strategy will be understood as a response of player I to the previous move of player II, following the specified first move. The strategies of player I, S1 through S8, as generated by RRS, are:

S1: (D (D (c d)) C)

S2: (D (C (c)) (D (d)))

S3: (D (C (c d)) D)

S4: (D (D (c)) (C (d)))

S5: (C (D (c d)) C)

S6: (C (C (c)) (D (d)))

S7: (C (C (c d)) D)

S8: (C (D (c)) (C (d)))

The first strategy, for instance, instructs the player to start with D and then play D no matter what the opponent did in their most recent encounter. The sixth strategy, which is the "Tit-for-Tat" strategy, calls for an opening with C and responding with C to c and with D to d.

The strategies of the other player are defined symmetrically. The payoffs of the players exercising these strategies in the PD game played four times can be depicted in the meta-PD matrix shown in Figure 3. Using standard game-theoretic techniques it can be determined that strategy S6 ("Tit-for-Tat"), is a dominant, equilibrium strategy for each of the players in the meta-PD in this case.

The metagame approach can be applied in RMM by replacing the original payoff matrix by a metamatrix with strategies instead of individual moves, and with payoffs reflecting the accumulation of the outcomes over the expected number of interactions. For the case of the meta-PD game matrix above (and for other meta-PD games with the expected number of interactions over four), RMM chooses "Tit-for-Tat" strategy as a rational one.

Repetition in Example Interaction

Unlike the pure metagame approach, however, RMM can deal with more realistic situations in which options and payoffs of other players are uncertain. Returning to our robotic example of a one-time interaction (Figure 1), recall that we introduced a variation in which R1 thinks that R2 will correctly identify R1 as type A with a probability 0.9. Unlike the equiprobable case where R1 decides to pursue G1, this skewed probability leads it to choose G2. As we mentioned, it can also be called an uncooperative option, in the sense that it treats R2 as if it were not there, and that R2 would prefer that R1 choose G1, if it were either type A or B. Of course, R1 would then welcome reciprocation by R2's choice of G2, if it happens to be type A.

We have applied the metagame approach for the repeated case of the above interaction using RMM. The hierarchy of matrices depicting the accumulated payoffs for all of the possible strategies in the above example is too large to include here, so we just report our end result. The best strategy of R1, as RMM finds, is: (G1 (G2 (G1 S)) (G1 (G2)) S). This strategy directs R1 to choose G1 initially, rather than the uncooperative choice of G2. In the subsequent interactions R1 will reciprocate with G1 in response to G2, the cooperative alternative of R2. R2's uncooperative choices, G1 and S, will cause R1 to pursue G2. R1 will never choose S.

RMM reaches this result as a stable outcome for an expected number of interactions over three. For 2 or 3 interactions, RMM stabilizes and gives equal preference to three strategies (G1 (G1 (G1 G2)) (G2 (S)) S), (G1 (G2 (G1 S)) (G1 (G2)) S), and (G1 (S (G1)) (G1 (G2)) (G2 (S))). For a one time interaction, the result mirrors the one obtained previously, directing R1 to pursue G2.

The result of RMM applied to R2 in the above scenario also provides the cooperative strategy for it, if it is of type A. Its behavior for one-time interaction was to choose S. For multiple interactions, the choice strategy for R2 is a cooperative strategy of starting with G2 and always responding with G2 to R1's G1. That means that R1 will not be disappointed when counting on R2 to pursue G2 and cooperation between the two agents will result.

Conclusions and Further Research

We have presented a powerful method, called the Recursive Modeling Method, that we believe rational, autonomous agents should use to interact with other agents. RMM uses all of the available information the agents may have about each other and themselves, modeling the uncertainties as probability distributions. It explicitly accounts for the recursive nesting of beliefs evident in agents' encounters, in which their decisions depend on what they expect others to do. RMM can also easily be extended to account for the possibility of repetitive interactions. We have shown how this fact influences the agents' willingness to exhibit cooperative behaviors toward each other.

There are a number of issues regarding RMM and its extension to repetitive interactions that remain to be investigated. They include the choice of the level of the elaboration of plans that are to be included as options in the scheme and its cost and benefit characteristics. For repetitive interactions, the influence of previous encounters on predictions for the future has to be addressed more rigorously. The potential computational burden of examining all of the possible strategies, particularly as the number of agents grows larger, may become an obstacle in applying our method, and ways to remedy this problem that involve the concept of "bounded rationality" in the agents are being investigated. We believe that RMM also offers an excellent tool for studying communication [Gmytrasiewicz *et al.*, 1991b]. Finally, our method uses an intentional approach normatively assuming that other agents will do what seems to be rational for them. To deal with realistic situations where agents can update models of each other through observation and plan recognition, we will complement RMM with an empirical method [Gmytrasiewicz, 1991].

References

[Axelrod, 1984] Robert Axelrod. *The Evolution of Cooperation.* Basic Books, 1984.

[Bennett and Huxham, 1982] P. G. Bennett and C. S. Huxham. Hypergames and what they do: A 'soft OR' approach. *Journal of Operational Research Society*, 33:41–50, 1982.

[Cohen and Levesque, 1990] P. R. Cohen and H. J. Levesque. Rational interaction as the basis for communication. In P. R. Cohen, J. Morgan, and M. E. Pollack, editors, *Intentions in Communication.* MIT Press, 1990.

[Dennett, 1986] D. Dennett. Intentional systems. In D. Dennett, editor, *Brainstorms.* MIT Press, 1986.

[Gmytrasiewicz *et al.*, 1991a] Piotr J. Gmytrasiewicz, Edmund H. Durfee, and David K. Wehe. Combining decision theory and hierarchical planning for a time-dependent robotic application. In *Proceedings of the Seventh IEEE Conference on AI Applications*, pages 282–288, February 1991.

[Gmytrasiewicz *et al.*, 1991b] Piotr J. Gmytrasiewicz, Edmund H. Durfee, and David K. Wehe. The utility of communication in coordinating intelligent agents. In *Proceedings of the National Conference on Artificial Intelligence*, July 1991.

[Gmytrasiewicz, 1991] Piotr J. Gmytrasiewicz. Rational reasoning system: Application of decision theory in autonomous robotics. Technical report, University of Michigan, In preparation 1991.

[Howard, 1966] N. Howard. The theory of metagames. *General Systems*, 11:167–200, 1966.

[Jackobs and Kiefer, 1973] W. Jackobs and M. Kiefer. Robot decisions based on maximizing utility. In *Proceedings of the Third International Joint Conference on Artificial Intelligence*, pages 402–411, August 1973.

[Luce and Raiffa, 1957] R. D. Luce and H. Raiffa. *Games and Decisions.* John Wiley and Sons, 1957.

[Neapolitan, 1990] Richard E. Neapolitan. *Probabilistic Reasoning in Expert Systems.* John Wiley and Sons, 1990.

[Reagade, 1987] Rammohan K. Reagade. Metagames and metasystems. In John P. van Gigch, editor, *Decisionmaking about Decisionmaking.* Abacus Press, 1987.

[Rosenschein and Breese, 1989] Jeffrey S. Rosenschein and John S. Breese. Communication-free interactions among rational agents: A probablistic approach. In Les Gasser and Michael N. Huhns, editors, *Distributed Artificial Intelligence*, volume 2 of *Research Notes in Artificial Intelligence*, pages 99–118. Pitman, 1989.

[Rosenschein, 1988] Jeffrey S. Rosenschein. The role of knowledge in logic-based rational interactions. In *Proceedings of the Seventh Phoenix Conference on Computers and Communications*, pages 497–504, Scottsdale, AZ, February 1988.

[Smith, 1984] J. M. Smith. The evolution of animal intelligence. In C. Hookway, editor, *Minds, Machines and Evolution.* Cambridge University Press, 1984.

[Vane and Lehner, 1990] R. R. Vane and P. E. Lehner. Hypergames and AI in automated adversarial planning. In *Proceedings of the 1990 DARPA Planning Workshop*, pages 198–206, November 1990.

[Werner, 1989] Eric Werner. Cooperating agents: A unified theory of communication and social structure. In Les Gasser and Michael N. Huhns, editors, *Distributed Artificial Intelligence*, volume 2 of *Research Notes in Artificial Intelligence.* Pitman, 1989.

[Zlotkin and Rosenschein, 1989] Gilad Zlotkin and Jeffrey S. Rosenschein. Negotiation and task sharing among autonomous agents in cooperative domains. In *Proceedings of the Eleventh International Joint Conference on Artificial Intelligence*, pages 912–917, August 1989.

[Zlotkin and Rosenschein, 1990] Gilad Zlotkin and Jeffrey S. Rosenschein. Negotiation and conflict resolution in noncooperative domains. In *Proceedings of the National Conference on Artificial Intelligence*, pages 100–105, July 1990.

Towards a Formal Theory of Communication for Multiagent Systems

Munindar P. Singh*

Dept of Computer Sciences and Artificial Intelligence Lab
University of Texas — MCC
Austin, TX 78712-1188 — Austin, TX 78759
USA — USA

Abstract

Agents in multiagent systems interact to a large extent by communicating. Such communication may be fruitfully studied from the point of view of speech act theory. In order for multiagent systems to be formally and rigorously designed and analyzed, a semantics of speech acts that gives their objective model-theoretic conditions of satisfaction is needed. However, most research into multiagent systems that deals with communication provides only informal descriptions of the different message types used. And this problem is not addressed at all by traditional speech act theory or by AI research into discourse understanding. I provide a formal semantics for the major kinds of speech acts at a level that has not been considered before. The resulting theory applies uniformly to a wide range of multiagent systems. Some applications of this theory are outlined, and some of its theorems listed.

1 Introduction

Multiagent systems are ubiquitous in Artificial Intelligence. Even in the simplest such systems, the epithet is justified only if the agents involved interact with each other in different ways. One of the most natural ways in which intelligent interaction may occur is through communication, especially communication about action. Agents may command, request, advise, or permit each other to do certain actions. They may also promise actions of their own, or prohibit those of others. When complex multiagent systems are to be designed or analyzed a formal theory of the kinds of communication that may take place among agents would be crucial. Unfortunately, no theory is currently available that provides the *objective semantics* of the messages exchanged. This paper describes research that has been done to fill this void. This research uses ideas about the ability and intentions of situated agents that were motivated and developed on independent grounds, albeit with a view to their final application to this problem [Singh, 1991; Singh, 1990a; Singh, 1990b]. This connection to other theories is reason to be reassured that this theory is not *ad hoc*, and will coherently fit in a bigger picture. The theory presented in this paper has ramifications in several subareas of AI, notably, multiagent planning and action, autonomous agents, and cooperative work [Gasser and Huhns, 1989; Huhns, 1987].

Traditionally, speech act theory classifies communications or messages into several kinds of *illocutionary acts* [Searle, 1969; Searle and Vanderveken, 1985]. These include *assertives, directives, commisives, permissives* and *prohibitives*. Briefly, assertives are statements of fact; directives are commands, requests or advice; commisives (e.g., promises) commit the speaker to a course of action; permissives issue permissions; and prohibitives take them away. Classical logic applies only to the case of assertives and considers only their truth and falsity. Therefore, it is inappropriate for other kinds of speech acts (Hamblin describes and criticizes several nonclassical logics for commands [Hamblin, 1987, pp. 97–136], so I do not consider them here). Research in speech act theory, on the other hand, concentrates on describing the conditions under which a particular speech act (of whatever form) may be said to have occurred [Grice, 1969; Searle, 1975]. The AI literature in this area too is concerned with the linguistic or discourse-related aspects of this problem (e.g., for identifying the illocutionary force of indirect speech acts [Allen and Perrault, 1980], or defining their effects on the mutual beliefs of agents [Cohen and Levesque, 1988]).

Of interest here is the orthogonal problem of formally describing the conditions of satisfaction for the different kinds of speech acts. I take the view that communication occurs because agents need to interact effectively and to influence each others' actions. While the illocutionary force of a speech act can be trivially determined from the syntax (in an artificial language that our agents would use), the objective conditions of the satisfaction of a speech act are a part of the semantics. A formal semantics is important because (1) as designers and analyzers, we need a rigorous understanding of communication in the systems we design; and (2) we would often like to embed a version of the semantics in the agents themselves so they can use it in their reasoning about their

*This research was partially supported by the Microelectronics and Computer Technology Corporation, and by the National Science Foundation (through grant # IRI-8945845 to the Center for Cognitive Science, University of Texas).

own (and others') speech acts.

The main original contributions of this paper are the following: (1) It argues that there is a level of formal semantics of speech acts that is distinct from both (a) what is traditionally considered their semantics, namely, the conditions under which they may be said to have occurred; and (b) their pragmatics, namely, the effects they may or ought to have on the speaker's and hearer's cognitive states. I.e., the proposed semantics differs from both the illocutionary and the perlocutionary aspects of speech acts. (2) This paper argues that the semantics of speech acts roughly corresponds to the conditions under which we would affirm that the given speech act had been satisfied. (3) It is proposed that this semantics can be captured in the usual model-theoretic framework by introducing different operators that distinguish the satisfaction of a speech act from its mere occurrence. (4) The actual definitions are to be given in terms of the intentions and know-how of the participants and the state of the world (at some salient time or times).

A problem not addressed here concerns the effects a speech act has on the hearer. These depend on issues like the social relationship of the agents or on matters of performance—these are not easy to describe, and are connected to processes of deliberation and belief revision [Perrault, 1987], rather than to the semantics of communication *per se*. Perrault provides some postulates for such revision using default logic. His focus is on the pragmatics of speech acts in natural language understanding, rather than the semantics as considered here. In any case, a semantics would help clarify our intuitions even about the pragmatic aspects of speech acts. As a clarification of my goals, note that the role of the proposed semantics is akin to that of classical semantics for assertives. Classical semantics only tells us when an assertive is objectively satisfied—it makes no claims about when an assertive should actually be uttered or believed.

Therefore, the focus here is on satisfaction conditions. The conditions of satisfaction for most kinds of speech acts differ significantly from those of assertives that are ordinarily considered in logic. Assertives, being claims of fact, are true or false; other speech acts call for a more complex framework in which their felicity or success can be described. In the context of imperatives, Hamblin distinguishes between what he calls *extensional* and *whole-hearted* satisfaction [Hamblin, 1987, pp. 153–157]. Briefly, the former notion admits accidental success, while the latter does not. Hamblin realized that these were useful things that may be said of a speech act; however, his aim was simply to be able state prescriptive conditions on when what kind of imperatives ought to be issued, and the philosophical problems that arise when one is in a "quandary." Thus his focus seems to have been pragmatic. I take advantage of some of his ideas, but make a finer distinction and extend it to other important kinds of speech acts here, formally relating them to intentions and know-how in the process. In §4.2, I address the problem of what kind of prescriptive constraints on communication may be stated, but see that as essentially supervenient on the semantics.

In §2, I discuss three different senses of satisfaction for the five kinds of speech acts considered in this paper. In §3, I describe a theory of intentions and know-how, and a formal model which I then use to formalize the different notions of satisfaction. In §4, I show how this theory may be used in the design of multiagent systems, and list some useful theorems.

2 Shades of Satisfaction

As remarked above, communication among agents in a multiagent system can be best understood by appealing to speech act theory [Austin, 1962; Searle, 1969]. In speech act theory an "illocution" (which I identify with a message) is seen to have two parts: an *illocutionary force* and a *proposition*. The illocutionary force distinguishes, e.g., a command from a promise; the proposition describes the state of the world that is, respectively, commanded or promised. This suggests a simple syntax for messages in an artificial language. A message, m, is a pair $\langle i, p\rangle$, where i identifies the illocutionary force, and p the proposition. Here i is an atomic symbol from the set {directive, commisive, permissive, prohibitive, assertive}; and p is a logical formula.

This much is quite standard even in the AI literature that deals with communication among agents [Huhns *et al.*, 1990; Thomas *et al.*, 1990]. However, none of the AI papers so far give a rigorous formal semantics for messages of different illocutionary forces. This lacuna is filled by this paper. But before I come to the formalization, I must discuss the different senses of *satisfaction* of speech acts. The rest of this section extends the discussion in [Hamblin, 1987, pp. 153–157]. Note that these different senses agree for the case of assertives.

The propositional part of a message specifies the state of the world that the message is, in some sense, about. An assertive asserts of that state that it holds (i.e., currently, though the proposition could be temporally indexed); a directive asks the hearer to bring that state about; a commisive commits the speaker to bringing it about; and so on. Thus the satisfaction of a message depends both on its illocutionary force and its proposition. The different notions of satisfaction are motivated using directives; other speech acts are considered in §3.

In the simplest sense of satisfaction, called *extensional* satisfaction in [Hamblin, 1987, p. 153], a message is said to be satisfied (with only minor qualifications) just if its proposition turns out to hold. E.g., a directive is satisfied when the proposition becomes true. Extensional satisfaction looks only at the immediate state of the world—the proposition may have been made true accidentally, or for the "wrong reasons," but would still meet the requirements for extensional satisfaction. This notion of satisfaction meets weak behavioral specifications; e.g., if the success of a speech act is part of a plan, then when it succeeds the agent can legitimately proceed to the next stage of the plan. However, this notion is not acceptable for complex systems because fortuitous circumstances would not, in general, arise often in them. A system whose agents were designed on this basis would turn out to be not sufficiently robust—e.g., we would expect a guarantee that some directives would be satisfied in a variety of circumstances, rather than that they once were. Also, it is of not much help practically, since it yields no insights about how the individual agents in a multiagent system ought to be designed.

This motivates the next sense of satisfaction, *whole-hearted* satisfaction. The whole-hearted satisfaction of a directive requires not only that the specified proposition be made true, but be made true in a sure-fire manner. The concerned agent should not only bring about the right state of the world, but know how to bring it about and intend to bring it about (thus it would bring it about in a way that exploits its know-how). By using whole-hearted satisfaction, the designer can require that an agent not issue two commands, which cannot both be whole-heartedly satisfied (due to limited know-how), even if they can both be extensionally satisfied.

Even whole-hearted satisfaction admits cases where the relevant proposition was made true, but only because it was going to be made true anyway, irrespective of whether the given speech act was performed. I.e., the speech act was pointless and played no real role in its satisfaction. This happens when, for a directive, the hearer was going to do the desired actions anyway. Often, it is useful to eliminate these conditions, so that the given speech act is really necessary. This requires that not only must the proposition in the speech act be made true in a sure-fire way, it must be made true *because* of that speech act. This, *relevant* satisfaction, is the strongest notion of satisfaction that I consider here.

The taxonomy of speech acts of this paper is motivated by the fact that permissives, prohibitives and directives have different satisfaction conditions (*cf.* [Bach and Harnish, 1979, pp. 39–54] and [Searle and Vanderveken, 1985, ch. 9], where permissives and prohibitives are lumped together with directives). The more convention-oriented or culture-oriented illocutionary forces (e.g., christenings, greetings) are not considered here. Interrogatives are semantically quite like directives, but need special treatment to allow for answers; they are not included in this paper for reasons of space.

3 Formalization of Satisfaction Conditions

The different notions of satisfaction of speech acts depend on the definitions of know-how and intention. A formal rigorous theory of situated know-how and intentions has already been developed and reported. Here the same framework and technical definitions are used to give an account of the different sorts of satisfaction of several kinds of speech acts. This project has been inspired by that of C. L. Hamblin, who died while writing [Hamblin, 1987]. He argued that an account of imperatives must be built on top of a theory of abilities and intentions, especially, one which is "...not hidden in the mind, however, but expressed in action ..." [Hamblin, 1987, foreword by Belnap, p. viii]. He did not have such a formal theory of know-how and intentions, but I take this advice seriously, and try to give a semantics of several kinds of speech acts in terms of my earlier theory of intentions and know-how, where these concepts are defined in terms of the actions of agents situated in an objective model [Singh, 1990b; Singh, 1990a; Singh, 1991]. I briefly describe that theory, and then turn to the formal model.

3.1 Know-how and Intentions

This theory of know-how and intentions is meant to apply to both traditional plan-based architectures and modern situated ones. It uses the concept of *strategies* as abstract descriptions of the agents' behavior. Strategies correspond to plans in traditional systems and to the architectural structure of reactive agents, as instantiated at a given time. A strategy is simply the designer's description of the agent and the way in which it behaves. An agent knows how to achieve A, if it can achieve A whenever it so "intends." Let each agent have a strategy that it follows in the current situation. Intuitively, an agent knows how to achieve A relative to a strategy Y, iff it possesses the skills required to follow Y in such a way as to achieve A. Thus know-how is partitioned into two components: the "ability" to have satisfactory strategies, and the "ability" to follow them. Similarly, an agent intends to achieve A by performing a strategy Y, iff it currently has strategy Y and the successful performance of Y by it entails A; i.e., iff the agent is trying to perform Y to achieve A. Note that having an intention does not entail having the know-how to match it, and vice versa. Another important primitive is *can-prevent*, notated K_{prev}. This is related to know-how and applies when the given agent is able to perform actions so as to prevent the occurrence of the given condition. For reasons of space, the technical details of [Singh, 1991; Singh, 1990a; Singh, 1990b] are not included here. The presentation below is self-contained, however.

3.2 The Formal Model

The formal model here is based on possible worlds. Each possible *world* has a branching *history* of *times*. Agents influence the future by acting, but the outcome also depends on other events. A *scenario* at a given world and time is any linear branch of the future beginning there—this corresponds to a particular run or trace of the given system. A *subscenario* is a triple, $\langle S, t, t' \rangle$, which denotes a section of scenario S from time t to t'. The interpretation $[\![\,]\!]$ assigns sets of world-times pairs to predicates, for each possible tuple of their arguments; it assigns sets of subscenarios to each action, for each agent who might do it. Truth in the model, M, is defined relative to a world w and a time t: $M \models_{w,t} p$ denotes that p is true in M at w and t. Another useful notion is of truth relative to a scenario and a time in it (a scenario determines the world): $M \models_{S,t} p$ denotes that p is true in M on S at t. The formal language here is the predicate calculus, augmented with temporal logic (used in §4.3), and three predicates, 'K_{how},' 'intends' and 'K_{prev},' each applying to an agent, a strategy and a formula.

Speech acts are, first of all, actions. For simplicity, they are seen as the actions of just their speakers, and occur over subscenarios. Let 'says-to' be a parametrized speech act, to be used as 'says-to(y, m).' This action will be seen as an action done by agent x. $\langle t_s, t_h \rangle \in [\![\text{says-to}(y, m)]\!]^x$ means that agent x communicated message m to agent y in the time from t_s (the time of speaking) to t_h (the time of hearing). This just says that the message was successfully transmitted (it is possible to allow failed transmissions, but that is not useful here). Define a new predicate 'comm' that applies to two agents, and a message. 'Comm(x, y, m)' is true at w, t just if x said (or started to say) m to y then. A transmitted message may, of course, not be satisfiable. In order to be able to talk of the different kinds of satisfaction of messages, I introduce three operators: ESAT, WSAT and RSAT (collectively called SAT below) that apply on formulas of the form 'comm(x, y, m).' They respectively state that the given message is extensionally, whole-heartedly, and relevantly satisfied. Now the conditions of truth are given for each of these three operators and for each of the possible illocutionary forces, relative to a scenario and a time.

The definition of truth is standard for the classical and temporal parts of the logic (the reader may consult [Emerson, 1989] for details). For p not of the form SATq, $M \models_{S,t} p$ iff $M \models_{w,t} p$, where S is a scenario at w, t. For p of the form SATq, it is convenient to give these definitions relative to a scenario and time, rather than directly relative to a world and time. We would like to define $M \models_{w,t} p$ as $M \models_{S,t} p$, where S is restricted in some way. S has to be restricted because there is always (in practice) a scenario where SATq would fail. One natural restriction is to scenarios compatible with the speaker's current intentions (or strategy). This ensures SATq as long as the speaker's intentions do not change.

3.3 Extensional Satisfaction

Extensional satisfaction is defined relative to a scenario and a time in it (thus "future" means future within that scenario). A directive is satisfied at a scenario and time just if its proposition becomes true at a future time on that scenario. A commisive too is satisfied just if its proposition becomes true at some future time on the given scenario. An assertive is satisfied just at those times where its proposition is true. A permissive is satisfied on a scenario and time just if it is taken advantage of sometimes in the future of that time on that scenario. A prohibitive is satisfied just if it is never violated in the future of the given time on the given scenario. Thus the agents' intentions and know-how do not matter for extensional satisfaction.

1. $M \models_{S,t}$ ESAT(comm$(x, y, \langle$directive, $p\rangle)$) iff $(\exists t' \in S : t' \geq t \wedge M \models_{S,t'} p)$
2. $M \models_{S,t}$ ESAT(comm$(x, y, \langle$commisive, $p\rangle)$) iff $(\exists t' \in S : t' \geq t \wedge M \models_{S,t'} p)$
3. $M \models_{S,t}$ ESAT(comm$(x, y, \langle$permissive, $p\rangle)$) iff $(\exists t' \in S : t' \geq t \wedge M \models_{S,t'} p)$
4. $M \models_{S,t}$ ESAT(comm$(x, y, \langle$prohibitive, $p\rangle)$) iff $(\forall t' \in S : t' > t \rightarrow M \not\models_{S,t'} p)$
5. $M \models_{S,t}$ ESAT(comm$(x, y, \langle$assertive, $p\rangle)$) iff $M \models_{S,t} p$

3.4 Whole-hearted Satisfaction

Whole-hearted satisfaction too is defined relative to a scenario and a time. A directive is satisfied on a scenario and time just if its proposition becomes true at a future time in that scenario, and all along the scenario from the given time to then, the hearer has the know-how, as well as the intention to achieve it. I.e., if the hearer has a strategy (that it may be said to be following) relative to which it has the know-how and the intention to achieve p (as explained in §3.1). Similarly, a commisive is satisfied just when its proposition becomes true at some future time on the given scenario, and all along the scenario from the given time to then, the *speaker* has the know-how to achieve it and also intends it. The condition for assertives is unchanged.

A permissive is satisfied at a scenario and a time just if it is taken advantage of by the hearer at a future point on that scenario. But when a permissive is taken advantage of, it allows the hearer to do actions at certain times that it could not have done before because they might possibly lead to the condition becoming true. Thus a permissive is satisfied on a scenario on which the hearer does at least one action whose performance can lead to a situation where it is unable to prevent that condition from occurring (i.e., the hearer can now risk letting that condition hold). Similarly, a prohibitive is satisfied at a scenario and time just if none of the actions done by the hearer on that scenario (in the future), can lead to a situation where the hearer would be unable to prevent the condition from occurring (i.e., the hearer does not risk violating the prohibition).

1. $M \models_{S,t}$ WSAT(comm$(x, y, \langle$directive, $p\rangle)$) iff $(\exists t' \in S : t' \geq t \wedge M \models_{S,t'} p \wedge (\forall t'' : t \leq t'' < t' \rightarrow (\exists Y : M \models_{S,t''} K_{how}(y, Y, p) \wedge \text{intends}(y, Y, p))))$
2. $M \models_{S,t}$ WSAT(comm$(x, y, \langle$commisive, $p\rangle)$) iff $(\exists t' \in S : t' \geq t \wedge M \models_{S,t'} p \wedge (\forall t'' : t \leq t'' < t' \rightarrow (\exists Y : M \models_{S,t''} K_{how}(x, Y, p) \wedge \text{intends}(x, Y, p))))$
3. $M \models_{S,t}$ WSAT(comm$(x, y, \langle$permissive, $p\rangle)$) iff $(\exists t' \in S : t' \geq t \wedge (\forall a : (\exists t'' : \langle S, t', t''\rangle \in [\![a]\!]^y) \rightarrow (\exists S', t''' : t''' \in S' \wedge \langle S', t', t'''\rangle \in [\![a]\!]^y \wedge (\forall Y : M \not\models_{S',t'''} K_{prev}(y, Y, p)))))$
4. $M \models_{S,t}$ WSAT(comm$(x, y, \langle$prohibitive, $p\rangle)$) iff $(\forall t' \in S : t' > t \rightarrow (\forall a : (\exists t'' : \langle S, t', t''\rangle \in [\![a]\!]^y) \rightarrow (\forall S', t''' : t''' \in S' \wedge \langle S', t', t'''\rangle \in [\![a]\!]^y \rightarrow (\exists Y : M \models_{S',t'''} K_{prev}(y, Y, p)))))$

3.5 Relevant Satisfaction

Relevant satisfaction is also defined relative to a scenario and a time. It resembles the previous case, but differs in adding a requirement that roughly says that the given speech act is the true reason for its success. A directive is satisfied just when its proposition becomes true at a time in the future of the given time, and all along the scenario from the given time to then, the hearer has the know-how to achieve it, and furthermore that this know-how does not arise in at least one scenario that is a temporal alternative to the given one. The definition for commisives is analogous. The condition for assertives continues to be the same as before.

A permissive is satisfied at a scenario and a time just if it is taken advantage of by the hearer at a future time on the given scenario, with an additional requirement that

that there be an alternative scenario to the given one where it is not taken advantage of. As before, when a permissive is taken advantage of, it is WSAT. However, in this case, it must also be the case that on at least one other scenario, the permissive is not WSAT. Intuitively, this scenario is one of those where a stronger permission is not in force. The condition for prohibitives parallels that for permissives. Let $\mathbf{S}_{w,t}$ be the set of all scenarios beginning at w, t; below, let $S \in \mathbf{S}_{w,t}$.

1. $M \models_{S,t} \mathsf{RSAT}(\mathrm{comm}(x,y,m))$ iff $M \models_{S,t} \mathsf{WSAT}(\mathrm{comm}(x,y,m)) \wedge (\exists S' \in \mathbf{S}_{w,t} : M \not\models_{S',t} \mathsf{WSAT}(\mathrm{comm}(x,y,m)))$

This definition could have been strengthened by adding a notion of the "closeness" of scenarios to each other, so that we could say that S' above was not just any scenario but one of the ones closest to S. However, this idea is not pursued in this paper.

4 Applying the Theory

The two main motivations for developing this theory are to provide a rigorous foundation for the design of multiagent systems and to justify some prescriptive claims about how agents should communicate in them. This theory has given objective criteria to evaluate the correctness of different scenarios, or runs of a multiagent system. In design, the problem is to create a system which allows only correct scenarios to be actualized. Prescriptive claims for agents tell them what to do given their beliefs and intentions, so that correct scenarios emerge. I discuss these two problems below, and then some important formal consequences of this theory.

4.1 Designing Multiagent Systems

One extension needed is to distinguish between messages of the same major illocutionary force that are different in some important respects. E.g., commands differ from requests, since they presuppose authority on part of the speaker, and can cause a change in the hearer's intentions under a wider variety of circumstances than requests. A correct scenario with a command must WSAT it as a directive (assuming authority); one with a request must WSAT it too, but only if some other conditions on cooperation are met. The designer needs to constrain the issuing of directives, and/or increase know-how and constrain intentions so that the system actualizes only correct scenarios. E.g., requiring that agents persist with their strategies for sufficiently long considerably simplifies generating runs that on which directives and commisives are WSAT. Correctness must be ensured for all the message types that can occur in the system.

As an example, consider the contract net [Davis and Smith, 1983]. In its simplest form, a *manager* sends out a call for bids to all *contractors*—treat this as requesting the hearer to bid and to promise that it will do the task for a certain price (if it wants to bid). Contractors who bid thus promise that if requested to do the task and given their price, they will do it. The manager selects one contractor and requests it to do the task. In any correct design for this protocol, the contractors must have (at the appropriate times) (1) the know-how to answer correctly whether they will bid on a given task, and to promise as described above; and (2) the corresponding intentions. Thus the design goal reduces to ensuring conditions (1) and (2) for all the agents.

The different senses of SAT yield rigorous definitions for three kinds of correctness conditions for multiagent systems. A scenario can be defined to be correct in the sense of SAT if all the messages passed on it are satisfied in the same sense. In general terms, the designer's goal is to ensure that all runs that may be actualized are correct. This reduces to the goal that the intentions and know-hows of the agents are such that only correct scenarios are actualized. This is the sense of correctness that designers use in practice. They usually achieve this kind of correctness by, e.g., hard-wiring the intention to cooperate in their agents, or by setting up hierarchical structures such that some directives (commands) are always obeyed, and others (requests) obeyed whenever they do not conflict with the hearer's current intentions.

4.2 Normative Constraints on Communication

The objective criteria given above can be used to motivate some normative constraints on communication among the agents in a multiagent system. These constraints could be used by the designer, and possibly by the agents themselves to reason about the messages they exchange. Note that these are just meant as weak constraints, and may be easily overridden. If (some of) these constraints are obeyed, the scenarios that are actualized are not just correct but also "good." Imposing these constraints can simplify a design since certain good properties can then be taken for granted.

1. An agent should issue a directive only if its intentions are satisfied (i.e., its current strategies are performed successfully) on all scenarios on which the directive is WSAT. This is the converse of the definition for $M \models_{w,t} \mathsf{WSAT}q$ suggested in §3.2—this ensures that actions by the hearer will not render the speaker's own intentions impossible to achieve.
2. All messages sent must be RSAT, where the quantification over scenarios is restricted to scenarios compatible with the speaker's current intentions.
3. Agents ought to persist with their strategies (i.e., their strategy at a later time should be the appropriate "tail" of their strategy at an earlier time). This not only simplifies the WSAT and RSAT conditions for directives and commisives, but also simplifies the interactions among agents by, e.g., making it easy for an issuer of a directive to not take on a strategy that would interfere with its compliance.
4. All messages sent by one speaker must be mutually consistent in the sense of being jointly satisfiable on at least some scenarios. E.g., different directives should not clash with each other and prohibitives should not preclude the satisfaction of directives and other prohibitives. This prevents many unacceptable situations, but can cause problems if some redundant permissions are issued, i.e., those that might never be used on some scenarios where

the directives are met. So one should exclude (such) permissions from this constraint.

4.3 Some Theorems

A useful feature of the present theory is that it brings the different kinds of SAT within the fold of logic. In order to write some formal consequences of the preceding definitions, I will need to define some temporal operators. Here E means "in *some* scenario beginning at this time"; $A \equiv \neg E \neg$; pUq "q holds in the future and p holds until then"; P "at a past time up to the beginning of this scenario"; $Fp \equiv \mathsf{true}Up$ "eventually p"; and $Gp \equiv \neg F \neg p$ "always p" [Emerson, 1989]. E evaluated at a scenario is evaluated at the first point in that scenario.

1. RSAT entails WSAT; WSAT entails ESAT.
2. For a given scenario, $\mathsf{ESAT}(\mathrm{comm}(x, y, \langle i, p\rangle)) \equiv Fp$ for $i \neq$ prohibitive. For prohibitives, it $\equiv G\neg p$.
3. $\mathsf{RSAT}(\mathrm{comm}(x, y, \langle i, p\rangle)) \equiv \mathsf{WSAT}(\mathrm{comm}(x, y, \langle i, p\rangle)) \wedge E\neg\mathsf{WSAT}(\mathrm{comm}(x, y, \langle i, p\rangle))$

   This follows easily from the definition.
4. $\mathsf{WSAT}(\mathrm{comm}(x, y, \langle \mathrm{directive}, p\rangle)) \equiv \mathsf{ESAT}(\mathrm{comm}(x, y, \langle \mathrm{directive}, p\rangle)) \wedge (\exists Y : (K_{how}(y, Y, p) \wedge \mathrm{intends}(y, Y, p)))Up$

   A directive is WSAT iff it is ESAT and until it is, the hearer intends to and knows how to achieve it.
5. $\mathsf{WSAT}(\mathrm{comm}(x, y, \langle \mathrm{directive}, p\rangle)) \equiv \mathsf{ESAT}(\mathrm{comm}(x, y, \langle \mathrm{directive}, p\rangle)) \wedge \mathsf{ESAT}(\mathrm{comm}(x, y, \langle \mathrm{prohibitive}, \neg(\exists Y : K_{how}(y, Y, p) \wedge \mathrm{intends}(y, Y, p)) \wedge \neg Pp\rangle))$

   This is an important intuitive result since it shows that a directive interpreted in the WSAT sense has the force of a directive in the ESAT sense conjoined with a *prohibitive* in the ESAT sense.

5 Conclusions

None of the extant theories of communication address quite the same problem as I have addressed in this paper. The theory presented here refines and formalizes some intuitions about communication among agents. I started out with a set of obvious and well-known intuitions about the nature of communication derived from classical speech act theory. However, I motivated and approached an important problem that has not been addressed in the literature on speech act theory, or even in the AI literature. My commitment is stronger to the general claims than to the specifics. However, using definitions of the intentions and know-how of an agent, I was systematically able to give rigorous definitions of the conditions of satisfaction for speech acts of different of illocutionary forces. These definitions capture many of our intuitions about when, as speakers and hearers, we believe that a given speech act has been satisfied. This theory has applications in the design of multiagent systems, where constraints on the know-how and intentions of agents are derived from their desired communicative behavior. It can also yield some well-motivated normative constraints on communication among agents. An advantage of the formal approach is that this process can be guided by the several theorems that exist.

References

[Allen and Perrault, 1980] J. F. Allen and C. R. Perrault. Analyzing intention in utterances. *Artificial Intelligence*, 15:143–178, 1980.

[Austin, 1962] J. L. Austin. *How to do Things with Words.* Clarendon, Oxford, UK, 1962.

[Bach and Harnish, 1979] K. Bach and R. M. Harnish. *Linguistic Communication and Speech Acts.* MIT Press, Cambridge, MA, 1979.

[Cohen and Levesque, 1988] P. R. Cohen and H. J. Levesque. Rational interaction as the basis for communication. Tech. Rep. 433, SRI International, Menlo Park, CA, Apr. 1988.

[Davis and Smith, 1983] R. Davis and R. G. Smith. Negotiation as a metaphor for distributed problem solving. *Artificial Intelligence*, 20:63–109, 1983.

[Emerson, 1989] E. A. Emerson. Temporal and modal logic. In J. van Leeuwen, ed., *Handbook of Theoretical Computer Science.* North-Holland Publishing Company, Amsterdam, 1989.

[Gasser and Huhns, 1989] L. Gasser and M. N. Huhns, eds. *Distributed Artificial Intelligence, Volume II.* Pitman, London, 1989.

[Grice, 1969] P. Grice. Utterer's meaning and intentions. *Philosophical Review*, 1969.

[Hamblin, 1987] C. L. Hamblin. *Imperatives.* Basil Blackwell Ltd., Oxford, UK, 1987.

[Huhns, 1987] M. N. Huhns, ed. *Distributed Artificial Intelligence.* Pitman, London, 1987.

[Huhns *et al.*, 1990] M. N. Huhns, D. Bridgeland, and N. Arni. A DAI communication aide. Tech. Rep. ACT-RA-317-90, Microelectronics and Computer Technology Corp., Austin, TX, Oct. 1990.

[Perrault, 1987] R. Perrault. An application of default logic to speech act theory. Tech. Rep. 90, CSLI, Stanford, CA, Mar. 1987.

[Searle and Vanderveken, 1985] J. R. Searle and D. Vanderveken. *Foundations of Illocutionary Logic.* Cambridge University Press, Cambridge, UK, 1985.

[Searle, 1969] J. R. Searle. *Speech Acts.* Cambridge University Press, Cambridge, UK, 1969.

[Searle, 1975] J. R. Searle. Indirect speech acts. In P. Cole and J. L. Morgan, eds., *Syntax and Semantics, Volume 3.* Academic Press, New York, NY, 1975.

[Singh, 1990a] M. P. Singh. Group intentions. In *10th Workshop on Distributed AI*, Oct. 1990.

[Singh, 1990b] M. P. Singh. Towards a theory of situated know-how. In *ECAI*, Aug. 1990.

[Singh, 1991] M. P. Singh. A logic of situated know-how. In *AAAI*, July 1991.

[Thomas *et al.*, 1990] B. Thomas, Y. Shoham, and A. Schwartz. Modalities in agent-oriented programming. Computer Science Department, Stanford University, Feb. 1990.

ARCHITECTURES & LANGUAGES

Distributed AI II

Communication and Inference through Situations

Hideyuki Nakashima
Electrotechnical Laboratory
1-1-4 Umezono
Tsukuba Ibaraki 305
Japan
nakashim@etl.go.jp

Stanley Peters
CSLI
Ventura Hall
Stanford, CA 94305
USA
peters@csli.stanford.edu

Hinrich Schütze
CSLI
Ventura Hall
Stanford, CA 94305
USA
schuetze@csli.stanford.edu

Abstract

In this paper, we show how to use common knowledge computationally in solving problems involving cooperation of multiple agents, when common knowledge is available. We will explain why a procedural approach to common knowledge is better suited to solving multiple-agent problems than a static one.

We show, even if one can never prove that common knowledge has been attained ([Halpern and Moses, 1990]), that assuming it has been attained is often safe and efficacious. The ability to detect fairly reliably when certain conditions are not met suffices as a guideline for when to assume something is common knowledge. In principle, the problem of when one has individual knowledge is about as difficult.

We use the *situation oriented* programming language PROSIT. By combining reasoning *about* situations and *in* situations, PROSIT makes possible an especially intuitive and simple solution of hypothetical reasoning problems involving common knowledge ([Nakashima and Tutiya, 1991]).

1 Introduction

Treatment of common knowledge is important in connection with multi-agent systems. When several or many agents cooperate to solve a problem that cannot be solved by any single one, it is essential for them to have models of other agents and to communicate with one another. In treating such systems, we need abstractions of a higher level than individual knowledge/beliefs, namely the knowledge/belief of groups of agents. Indeed, [Levesque *et al.*, 1986] claims that the concept of joint intention is necessary to formalize problem solving by a group.

In this paper, we will show that

- common knowledge can be used algorithmically in solving problems cooperatively, and
- common knowledge is assumed rather than established.

To represent common knowledge, we use the framework of situation theory, which has been developed to provide a powerful logical foundation for analyzing information flow when partiality of information is crucial ([Barwise, 1989], [Devlin, 1991]), as it is in distinguishing between individual and common knowledge.

We will compare our model of common knowledge with Barwise's ([Barwise, 1989a]) and show why his model is not the best to make use of common knowledge in inference. We then apply our model to the three wisemen problem.

1.1 Situation Theory

Fundamental notions of situation theory include item of information (called an *infon*) and *situation* (a part of the world capable of making an infon a fact). A typical infon would be that a particular relation holds (alternatively, does not hold) of particular objects. For instance, the information that Pat, a card player, has the ace of clubs is the infon

```
(has Pat a_clubs).
```

An infon is a fact, if it is, by virtue of some part of the world making it so, i.e. some situation *supporting* (often written $\models$, but we write `!=`) the infon. For instance, a situation `g` in a card game in which Pat has the ace of clubs supports this infon, i.e.

```
(!= g (has Pat a_clubs)).
```

The knowledge that this is so will likely be included in Pat's individual knowledge – information which we can write as the two infons

```
(knows Pat pk)  (!= pk (has Pat a_clubs))
```

where `pk` is Pat's individual knowledge situation. If the information is possessed not only by Pat but is moreover common knowledge of Pat and Max, the other player in the game, we have the infons

```
(knows Pat ck)  (knows Max ck)
(!= ck (has Pat a_clubs))
```

for the common knowledge situation `ck`, which is a subsituation of both `pk` and Max's individual knowledge situation `mk`. That `ck` is common knowledge is itself common knowledge, i.e.

```
(!= ck (knows Pat ck))
(!= ck (knows Max ck)).
```

The last three of these propositions form the heart of Barwise's logical analysis of common knowledge [Barwise, 1989a].

Note crucially that different situations may be responsible for the facthood of different items of information, i.e. different situations may support different infons that are factual. The fact that Max actually has the ace of spades, i.e. `(!= g (has Max a_spades))`, might not be known to Pat

```
(no (!= pk (has Max a_spades)))
```

and therefore may not be common knowledge of Max and Pat.

```
(no (!= ck (has Max a_spades)))
```

But it can still be individual knowledge of Max's.

```
(!= mk (has Max a_spades))
```

Situations are often closed under constraints. For instance, the card game situation g respects the constraint that each card is held by at most one player; thus Pat having the three of clubs involves Max not having that card.

```
(<= (no (has Max 3_clubs)) (has Pat 3clubs))
```

Since g respects this constraint, if g is consistent and

```
(1) (!= g (has Max 3_clubs))
```

it is valid to infer

```
(2) (no (!= g (has Pat 3_clubs)).
```

If Max knows he has the three of clubs, i.e.

```
(3) (!= mk (has Max 3_clubs))
```

he will be aware of (1). If he also knows that g is a consistent situation respecting the constraint under consideration, Max can infer (2). From this he can go on to conclude

```
(!= g (no (has Pat 3_clubs)))
```

using the definiteness of g with regard to who holds which cards. In consequence of the second fact above it can thus come to be that

```
(!= mk (no (has Pat 3_clubs))).
```

We will turn soon to a specific problem mixing individual and common knowledge of agents in a more challenging way, showing how to formalize the problem in terms of situation theory and how this helps in solving it computationally. But let us first introduce the programming language we use for implementing our proposal.

2 PROSIT

In this section we give a short introduction to PROSIT, the programming language we use, and the reasons why it is especially suitable for human-like reasoning.

PROSIT (PROgramming in SItuation Theory) is a programming language implemented in CommonLisp that has many features of Situation Theory built into it ([Nakashima *et al.*, 1988]). In particular, a program can build up and navigate within situation structures; infons can be asserted in situations; and constraints hold between different situations in the situation structure. The inference engine is similar to a Prolog interpreter.

The numbers in the following description of the main constructs of PROSIT refer to Figure 3.

- Variables are marked with a `*`.
- (1): `<=` is a constraint (implemented as a backward chaining rule): `(white *x)` holds if the infons in (2) - (12) are true.
- (2): `(me *x)` binds `*x` to the current situation (reflection).
- (8): `!` asserts its argument into the current situation.
- (8): `[_` is the subchunk relation. The first argument is part of the second (both arguments are situations). Example: After the assertion (8), whenever `(rel a b)` holds in `c-channel`, `(!= c-channel (rel a b))` holds in `*y`. No inheritance relation holds between the two situations.
- (9): `@<` is the inheritance relation (or subsituation relation). Any infon holding in the first situation will also hold in the second.

The following properties make PROSIT especially suitable for writing programs doing human-like reasoning:

Inconsistencies. Reasoning is different from applications like numerical or accounting programs in that inconsistencies can occur. Moreover, inconsistencies play an active role; they are used to get at new information.

PROSIT's situation structure facilitates using contradictions for this purpose: contradictions can be kept local, preventing them from generating unsound inferences; and they can be reflected upon in a situation that the contradictory one is a subchunk of.

Direct programming. PROSIT allows navigation in the situation tree, i.e. the situation tree is not only a data structure, but also a *programming structure*. One can, therefore, always program from the point of view of the person whose reasoning has to be modelled. Instead of programming from an abstract level ("A thinks that B believes that C knows ...") reasoning can be *directly* translated into PROSIT code. This results in easy-to-write and well-structured programs.

Situated programming. In PROSIT we can state constraints in a general form that will be used differently in different situations by picking up the particular information available in a situation. This "lean" programming is possible because situations contain only the information pertinent to them; computations can be made local and efficient, ignoring what is happening "further up" (cf. [Nakashima and Tutiya, 1991]).

An example of how a general constraint picks up information from a situation is the special predicate `(me *x)` that binds its variable to the current situation.

3 Two Computational Approaches

to Common Knowledge

In this section, we investigate two different approaches to handling common knowledge in computation: a static and a procedural one.

3.1 The Static Model

The static representation consists essentially of the three following lines ([Barwise, 1989a]):

```
(1) (!= ck σ)
(2) (!= ck (knows Pat ck))
(3) (!= ck (knows Max ck))
```

σ is the "nucleus" of the common knowledge, the infon that the persons Pat and Max both know. What makes this situation common knowledge, as opposed to merely shared knowledge, is the fact that Pat and Max know of each other's knowledge *and are aware of this*.

We can translate this straightforwardly into PROSIT as follows:

- We need not use the fact that Pat and Max know `pk` and `mk` respectively. We simply express that Pat knows the fact σ as `(!= pk σ)`. (Recall that `pk` and `mk` stand for the knowledge of Pat and Max.)
- With this simplification, (2) and (3) are equivalent to `(!= ck (!= pk ck))` and `(!= ck (!= mk ck))`, respectively. This is precisely the definition of the subchunk relation, which we therefore use for the representation of (2) and (3).
- We incorporate the fact that what is common knowledge is also individual knowledge of each member of the group by making `ck` a subsituation of `pk` and `mk`.

The program, then, is the one shown in Figure 1. Any of the queries in Figure 2 will be answered **yes**. Notice that Pat and Max know not only everything about each other's knowledge but are also well informed about what is common knowledge.

We now come to to the crucial test for the usefulness of this representation: the integration of private and common knowledge. We try to apply the static approach to the Conway paradox:

> During a card game both Max and Pat have an ace. If asked whether they have any knowledge about the other person's cards they will answer no and this answer won't be different if the question is repeated; but if someone tells them "At least one of you has an ace", a fact they can infer from their own cards, the answer will be "No" for the first answering (Max) and "Yes, he/she has an ace" for the second of the two (Pat).

Pat reasons as follows to the conclusion. If Max didn't have an ace, he could infer that I have one because he knows that there is at least one ace. But then he wouldn't have answered "No" when he was asked whether I had an ace. Hence, the assumption that he doesn't have an ace is wrong.

How can we do Pat's reasoning within the data structures sketched above? The argument hinges on the assumption `(no (has Max ace))`. Where do we put this assumption? We're confronted with the following dilemma: If we put it in `ck` or `mk`, then `(no (has Max ace))` will become part of Max's knowledge, which is clearly inadequate. If we put it in `pk`, then `(!= pk (no (has Max ace)))` becomes part of Max's knowledge, since `pk` is a subchunk of `ck` and what holds in `ck` is inherited by `mk`. This is inadequate too: we don't want Pat's assumptions to influence Max's knowledge. If we put the assumption in a situation `s` outside of `ck`, our common knowledge representation cannot be used: If we want to do situated reasoning in `s`, the common knowledge facts are not available.

So we cannot prove the desired proposition using a proof by contradiction. We do not deny the obvious fact that, in principle, one can derive any valid proposition without resorting to a proof by contradiction. For every proof that makes an assumption that is then shown to lead to an inconsistency, there is a "positive" argument proving the same proposition.

To derive the fact that Max has an ace by using positive arguments exclusively, requires common knowledge to include all possible alternatives:

```
(or (and (has Max ace) (has Pat ace))
    (and (no (has Max ace)) (has Pat ace))
    (and (has Max ace) (no (has Pat ace))))
```

The reasoners have to have the necessary common knowledge "prior to" reasoning, instead of deriving it only when needed. This demand is too strong in general for intelligent agents.

We believe that proofs by contradiction model much human reasoning more closely than positive proofs. We will see that in the case of the wisemen problem the natural way to solve it is a proof by contradiction, not a positive argument.

3.2 The Procedural Model

Taking into account the lessons we have learned from the static approach we propose a model with the following three key features:

1. The "common knowledge" situation is flat and noncircular.
2. Whereas in the static approach there was just one situation for each person, in our model all instances of knowledge situations are different. E.g. Max's knowledge and beliefs and Pat's knowledge and beliefs of what Max knows will be realized by distinct situations.
3. The common knowledge feature in our model will be provided by explicitly asserting a link between each instance of a knowledge situation and the "common knowledge" situation so that its contents can flow into this instance.

Now the character of common knowledge is not represented by a static, circular "common knowledge" situation as in the static approach. The common knowledge situation here is a *communication channel* that contains all information that is known to be commonly accessible. The circularity of common knowledge is realized

```
(! ([_ ck ck))                          ; declare ck to be self-referential
(! (!= ck ([_ ck mk)))                  ; subchunk relations: the common knowledge is a
(! (!= ck ([_ ck pk)))                  ;  subchunk of both Max's and Pat's knowledge
(! (!= ck (@< ck mk)))                  ; subsituation relations: Max and Pat's knowledge
(! (!= ck (@< ck pk)))                  ;  inherit from the common knowledge situation
(! (!= ck (has Pat ace-of-clubs)))      ; let (has Pat ace-of-clubs) be our sigma
```

Figure 1: Implementation of the Static Model

```
(!= ck (!= pk (has Pat ace-of-clubs)))
(!= ck (!= mk (!= pk (!= mk (has Pat ace-of-clubs)))))
(!= ck (!= mk (!= ck (has Pat ace-of-clubs))))
(!= ck (!= pk (!= ck (!= ck (!= pk (has Pat ace-of-clubs))))))
```

Figure 2: Inferences in the Static Model

procedurally by explicitly giving each knowledge/belief situation access to the communication channel (3).

Feature (2) reflects our view that common knowledge is generally interesting only if combined with other non-common, i.e. personal knowledge. If we want to mix personal and common knowledge to actually make use of what is mutually believed, we have to provide a new situation for each additional piece of personal knowledge that is added. This prevents assumed or wrong information from getting where it might lead to unsound inferences.

In the next section we show how we use the procedural model to implement our solution to the wisemen problem.

4 The Three Wisemen Problem

> Three wisemen are sitting at a table, facing each other, each with a white hat on his head. Someone tells them that each of them has a white or red hat but that there is at least one white hat. Each wiseman can see the others' hats but not his own. If a fourth person asks them whether they know their own colour, then the first two wisemen will answer no, but, after that, the third one will answer yes.

Note the parallel with the Conway paradox:[1] The wisemen already know *individually* that there is at least one white hat; again individual knowledge by itself would be useless, only the combination of private and common knowledge yields the desired result.

We analyze the problem as follows:

- **common knowledge:**
  1. There are three agents A, B and C; all are wise, i.e. good reasoners and thoughtful; each wears either a red or a white hat; at most two hats are red.
  2. Each can see the others' colours.
  3. None can see his own colour.
  4. Each can hear and understand all utterances.
  5. All these facts are common knowledge.
- **individual knowledge:**

  For each agent:

  A: B is white. C is white.

  B: A is white. C is white.

  C: A is white. B is white.

The problem has the following features:

1. All agents have the same inference mechanism.
2. All agents know (1).
3. Knowledge of the facts is somewhat different for each agent.
4. These facts cannot be directly transferred among agents.
5. Information is collected by observing the others' behaviour.

Let us now examine how to implement this analysis in PROSIT. For lack of space, we will only consider the two central constraints which are shown in Figure 3.

Note that we use situations to represent one person's internal model of the others. Situations here are not necessarily actual situations in the world. They are rather abstract ones (see [Nakashima and Tutiya, 1991] for a justification of using abstract situations in reasoning). In Figure 3, the situation bound to `*y` is such a model. It is a situation internal to `*x` and has no necessary connection with the actual `*y` (which is another wiseman). `*x` knows that `*y` perceives the third wiseman `*z`. `*x`'s mental model of `*y` therefore has to contain all facts about `*z` that can be inferred from (in this case) seeing `*z`. `transfer_knowledge_about_third` makes sure that these perceivable facts are added to `*x`'s mental model of `*y`. Since we don't want to get into the intricacies of perception, we have written `(colour *colour)` into the procedure, colour being the only relevant perceivable property in this case.

Other parts of the program will take care of the individual knowledge and the right content of the common knowledge situation. Note that the common knowledge

[1] We use the Conway paradox, which is a kind of "Two Wisemen Problem," in order to make the argument against the static model easier to understand.

```
(<= (white *x)                      ; ( 1) try to deduce (white *x)
    (me *x)                         ; ( 2) -|
    (wiseman *y)                    ; ( 3)  | bind *x to the wiseman doing this
    (wiseman *z)                    ; ( 4)  | reasoning and *y and *z to
    (not (= *x *y))                 ; ( 5)  | the two other wisemen
    (not (= *z *x))                 ; ( 6)  |
    (not (= *z *y))                 ; ( 7) -|
    (! ([_ c_channel *y))           ; ( 8) make channel accessible to hypothetical
    (! (@< c_channel *y))           ; ( 9)   reasoning situation for *y
    (! (!= *y (red *x)))            ; (10) assert assumption (red *x) in *y
    (transfer_knowl_on_3rd *y *z)   ; (11) add in *y what *x and *y know about *z
    (inconsistent *y)               ; (12) if the assumption produces an inconsistency in *y,
    ))                              ; (13)   it is wrong, which proves its opposite: (white *x)

(<= (transfer_knowledge_about_third *y *z)
    (or
     (and
      (colour *colour)              ; choose a colour to bind *colour (example: red)
      (*colour *z)                  ; if e.g. (red *z) is true
      (! (!= *y (*colour *z)))      ; then assert that *y knows this fact
      )
     (true)                         ; don't do anything if there's nothing
     ))                             ;  to transfer
```

Figure 3: Implementation of the Procedural Model

situation is more like a communication channel here: it is non-circular. It contains all commonly known facts, including the above constraints (which we take to be the meaning of "being wise" in this setting).

Common knowledge is realized procedurally by making `c_channel` accessible to each new instance of a reasoning situation. It is important to point out that, in PROSIT, each time a situation is made a subchunk or a subsituation of a constant, a situation with that constant as name is created (if it did not exist before). So each assumption is made in a newly created situation. The implementation thus respects the properties of the problem we stated in our analysis.

The clauses of our program speak directly about what facts are supposed to be known by each person (i.e. to hold in his knowledge situation), making for a more natural and straightforward program than McCarthy's predicate logic formalization of the wisemen problem in terms of possible worlds ([McCarthy, 1990]). The partiality of information supported by situations obviates the need to specify what is not known, which he must do along with specifying what is known. This in turn allows us to avoid explicit statements about the passage of time. For the wisemen problem, asserting as common knowledge each response to a query suffices to make the wisemen's knowledge increase with time.

5 Discussion: Common Knowledge for Reasoning

Halpern and Moses prove in [Halpern and Moses, 1990] that it is impossible to attain common knowledge. The reason is that there is no safe communication or (what is basically the same) there are no perfect clocks, i.e. no truly simultaneous access to communication channels.

Yet it appears that humans use common knowledge frequently, from which it follows that we sometimes possess it. Considering the wisemen problem, for example, we see that wise men can reason through arbitrarily many iterations: A knows that B knows that C knows that .... The muddy children problem is an even better example; with *k* muddy children, solving the problem requires *k* iterations of: (⟨ some person⟩ *knows*). Using the shared (i.e. common knowledge) situation is required in order to reason about common knowledge. No bounded number of iterations on individual knowledge will suffice.

We need common knowledge to solve problems like the wisemen puzzle, but Halpern and Moses showed that it is unattainable. How can we resolve this tension?

Halpern and Moses formalized weaker versions of common knowledge which are attainable in practice, and may suffice for carrying out a number of actions. Here we take a different approach: our solution is to **assume** safe communication even though safety is not really guaranteed. In practice, people don't question the safe communication assumption when trying to solve the wisemen problem. No one objects, "You didn't tell me that A really heard B answer 'No'."[2]

Knowledge possessed in common by a group is nothing more than appropriately coordinated individual knowledge, viz. knowledge that each member of the group has and that each member knows all have. The latter characteristic means common knowledge requires individual knowledge about group members' knowledge. Establishing the required common knowledge involves the diffi-

[2] We made this assumption explicit in our computational solution.

culties that establishing individual knowledge generally involves. For example, how can you know whether I understand and believe something you tell me?

Despite the difficulty of establishing individual knowledge – including the coordinating knowledge that makes something common knowledge of a group of individuals – human agents often function quite successfully by assuming something to be known and acting on that basis while keeping an eye open for indications that the supposed knowledge is false after all.

In point of fact, human reasoning is not the only domain where common knowledge is relevant; it is equally necessary for human communication using natural language. Clark and Marshall [Clark and Marshall, 1986] show that some uses of the definite article (e.g. referring with "the card" to a card on a table seen by two people who are viewing each other) involves common knowledge under the following conditions.

- triple co-presence
- simultaneity assumption
- attention assumption
- rationality assumption

These are exactly the hypotheses that are **implicitly assumed by someone trying to solve the wisemen problem.**

We propose to deal in a heuristic way with the problem of common knowledge to support reasoning and logic. Just as communication normally succeeds because a person can ordinarily tell if one of the four necessary conditions fails to be met, so also a reasoning agent can safely assume that what appears to be common knowledge is in fact that – unless one of the necessary conditions for genuinely common knowledge fails.

We note the following parallel. Skeptics doubt people even have much individual knowledge. They argue that the connection between reality and human minds is tenuous at best. However, that need not keep logicians from developing mechanisms for reasoning with knowledge.

Someone who doubts the possibility of common knowledge is skeptical about the possibility of communication. Even though one can never be sure about the security of communication, that shouldn't keep one from working with common knowledge – because humans do in fact use it for reasoning.

6 Conclusion

We have shown how to use common knowledge computationally in solving problems involving cooperation of multiple agents, when common knowledge is available. Although the static, circular representation is theoretically beautiful, it is hard to use in actual problem solving because there is no room for bringing in individual (*non*-common) knowledge. The procedural representation of common knowledge we presented as an alternative applies readily to solving the three wisemen problem.

We have also shown, even if one can never prove common knowledge has been attained, that assuming it has been attained is often safe and efficacious. The ability to detect fairly reliably when, for instance, one of Clark and Marshall's four conditions enumerated in the preceding section is not met suffices as a guideline for when to assume something is common knowledge. In principle, the problem of when one has individual knowledge is about as difficult.

Acknowledgements

The authors are indebted to Joachim Laubsch and Amnon Ribak for helpful contributions to the solution of the wisemen problem presented here, to Michael Frank for his work on implementing PROSIT and to the anonymous IJCAI reviewers for comments and criticism.

We also thank the Center for the Study of Language and Information for support and for a most stimulating working environment. The research reported here was supported in part by a grant from the System Development Foundation to Stanford University.

References

[Barwise, 1989] Jon Barwise. *The Situation in Logic*. CSLI Lecture Notes No. 17, University of Chicago Press, 1989.

[Barwise, 1989a] Jon Barwise. 'On the model theory of common knowledge'. In [Barwise, 1989], pp. 201–220.

[Clark and Marshall, 1986] Herbert H. Clark and Catherine R. Marshall. 'Definite reference and mutual knowledge'. In [Joshi *et al.*, 1981].

[Devlin, 1991] Keith Devlin. *Logic and Information I: Infons and Situations*. Cambridge University Press, to appear 1991.

[Halpern and Moses, 1990] Joseph Y. Halpern and Yoram Moses. 'Knowledge and common knowledge in a distributed environment'. In *JACM*, **37**, 1990, pp. 549–558.

[Joshi *et al.*, 1981] Aravind K. Joshi, Bonnie L. Webber and Ivan A. Sag. *Elements of Discourse Understanding*. Cambridge University Press, 1981.

[Levesque *et al.*, 1986] Hector J. Levesque, Philip R. Cohen, and José H. T. Nunes. 'On acting together'. In *Proc. of AAAI-90*, pp. 94–99, 1990.

[McCarthy, 1990] John McCarthy. 'Formalization of Two Puzzles Involving Knowledge'. In Vladimir Lifschitz (Ed.). *Formalizing Common Sense*. Ablex Publishing Corporation, Norwood NJ, 1990.

[Nakashima *et al.*, 1988] Hideyuki Nakashima, Hiroyuki Suzuki, Per-Kristian Halvorsen and Stanley Peters. 'Towards a computational interpretation of situation theory'. In *Proceedings of the International Conference on Fifth Generation Computer Systems, FGCS-88*, Tokyo, 1988.

[Nakashima and Tutiya, 1991] Hideyuki Nakashima and Syun Tutiya. 'Inference *in* a situation *about* situations'. To appear in *Situation Theory and its Applications, 2*, 1991.

Commitment and Effectiveness of Situated Agents

David N. Kinny
Department of Computer Science
University of Melbourne
Parkville 3052, Australia

Michael P. Georgeff
Australian Artificial Intelligence Institute
1 Grattan Street
Carlton 3053, Australia

Abstract

Recent research in real-time Artificial Intelligence has focussed upon the design of situated agents and, in particular, how to achieve effective and robust behaviour with limited computational resources. A range of architectures and design principles has been proposed to solve this problem. This has led to the development of simulated worlds that can serve as testbeds in which the effectiveness of different agents can be evaluated. We report here an experimental program that aimed to investigate how commitment to goals contributes to effective behaviour and to compare the properties of different strategies for reacting to change. Our results demonstrate the feasibility of developing systems for empirical measurement of agent performance that are stable, sensitive, and capable of revealing the effect of "high-level" agent characteristics such as commitment.

1 Introduction

The crucial problem facing designers of *situated agents* – artificial systems capable of effective, rational behaviour in dynamic and unpredictable environments – is to ensure that the agent's responses to important changes in its environment are both appropriate and timely. These requirements appear to conflict, since the reasoning that seems to be needed to choose appropriate actions could require an arbitrarily large amount of time to perform. Somehow this reasoning must be limited and controlled – there must be a *rational balance* between reasoning and acting.

Designs and architectures that address this problem can be placed on a spectrum according to the amount of reasoning they perform. At one end are reactive systems [Agre and Chapman, 1987; Schoppers, 1987] that minimize the need for run-time computation by precompiling appropriate responses to situations into a form that can be utilized without reasoning. At the other extreme are *real-time reasoning systems* [Georgeff and Ingrand, 1989; Fehling and Wilber, 1989] that attempt to achieve rational balance by reasoning based upon explicit representations of their beliefs, goals, and intentions. Purely reactive systems are capable of effective behaviour in some dynamic environments, but cannot guarantee it in the unanticipated situations that are inevitable in real-world domains. Real-time reasoning systems can behave more robustly in such situations because of their ability to reason about multiple conflicting goals, how best to achieve them, their relative value and urgency, etc.

Recent theoretical work has clarified the role of goals, intentions, and commitment in constraining the reasoning that an agent performs [Cohen and Levesque, 1990; Rao and Georgeff, 1991] and has examined the trade-off between reaction and deliberation [Bratman *et al.*, 1988]. However, these theories are quite general, and say little about specific real-time reasoning strategies and their effect on agent behaviour. To evaluate the effect of such strategies, we require (in the absence of a comprehensive theory) a controlled environment in which we can conduct experiments, and appropriate measures of agent performance so that different strategies can be meaningfully compared. Such an environment, called a *simulated world*, should ideally capture the essential features of real-world domains while permitting flexible, accurate, and reproducible control of the world's characteristics. A number of such worlds have been developed [Cohen *et al.*, 1989; Pollack and Ringuette, 1990], but there have been few published reports of the results of experimental evaluation of agent performance.

This paper describes the experimental work we have been doing in this direction. The main aims of the work were to:

- Assess the feasibility of experimentally measuring agent effectiveness in a simulated environment.
- Investigate how commitment to goals contributes to effective agent behaviour.
- Compare the properties of different strategies for reacting to change.

The experimental system was based upon the PRS real-time reasoning system [Georgeff and Ingrand, 1989] operating within the Tileworld environment [Pollack and Ringuette, 1990]. In the next section we briefly review the essential features of the experimental system and introduce the terminology used in our analysis. We then present and analyze the results of several sequences of experiments.

2 The Experimental System

2.1 The Environment

The Tileworld [Pollack and Ringuette, 1990] is a comprehensive testbed for experimental evaluation of agent performance. The number of independent control parameters is large, and the problems an agent needs to solve in order to function effectively in this domain are nontrivial. However, such a testbed was considered too rich for the initial investigative experiments we had planned. Therefore, to reduce the complexity of the object-level reasoning required of our agent, we employed a simplified Tileworld with no tiles.

In essence, our Tileworld is a 2-dimensional grid on which an agent scores points by moving to targets, known as *holes*. When the agent reaches a hole, the hole is *filled*, and disappears. The task is complicated by the presence of fixed obstacles. The Tileworld is 4-connected; the agent can move horizontally or vertically, but not diagonally. A lower bound on the shortest path length between two points is thus given by the the Manhattan distance $(\Delta_x + \Delta_y)$.

Holes appear in randomly selected empty squares, and exist for a length of time known as their *life-expectancy*, unless they disappear prematurely due to the agent's actions. The actual time for which a hole exists is its *lifetime*. The interval between the appearance of one hole and the next is known as the *gestation period*. Each hole has a specific value, its *score*. Life-expectancies, gestation periods, and scores are taken from independent random distributions.

2.2 The Agent

We chose to use the PRS real-time reasoning system [Georgeff and Ingrand, 1989] to construct a simple but adequately competent agent in which the effects of different object-level and meta-level strategies could be quantified. Accordingly, we made a number of simplifying assumptions in its design:

- The agent has perfect, zero-cost knowledge of the current state of the world, but no knowledge of its future. We ignored issues of uncertainty.
- The agent forms only correct and complete plans. We did not attempt to explore partial planning, anytime algorithms [Dean and ael Boddy, 1988], etc.
- The agent plans only at a single level, forming plans consisting of a sequence of steps to a single hole, rather than multiple hole tours.

Our agent is based upon a simple plan/act cycle. In the planning phase, it uses a path planner to produce a (shortest path) plan for each current option (hole), and a *plan selection strategy* to select one of these plans. In the action phase, part or all of the chosen plan is executed. Various attributes of this process are parameterized, allowing a range of different agent behaviours to be produced. The time cost of planning, known as the *planning time*, is also a controlled parameter. (The actual computational cost of planning is immaterial.)

Plan selection strategies choose between plans on the basis of the distance, score, and age of the target hole. A utility function applied to these attributes produces an integer-valued measure of the value of the plan, and the plan with the maximum value is selected. We implemented a number of utility functions that selected among plans on the basis of different weightings of these attributes.

2.3 Degree of Commitment and Reactivity

One of the primary aims of our work was to investigate different aspects of agent commitment and its effect on performance. First, we wished to examine the effect of an agent's degree of commitment to its current plan, independent of events in the world. Pollack and Ringuette [1990] define a *bold* agent as one that never reconsiders its options before the current plan is executed in its entirety, and a *cautious* agent as one that reconsiders every new option. We use the same terminology here, but in a restricted sense.

Our agent is potentially faced with a new set of options after each step it takes, both because the world changes and because its plan utility function can be position sensitive. We implemented a crude parameterization of its degree of boldness by specifying the maximum number of plan steps that the agent executes before replanning. A value of 1 produces a cautious agent that replans after every step, while a sufficiently large value produces a bold agent.

Second, we wished to investigate how sensitivity to change could affect agent behaviour. Such change could potentially trigger replanning, but in dynamic domains replanning must be limited or action will not be sufficiently timely. The key is to decide cheaply using some simple estimate of utility whether an event warrants more expensive deliberation [Russell and Wefald, 1989]. PRS is particularly well-suited for the implementation of such *event filters* [Pollack and Ringuette, 1990] because of its reactive meta-level processing capability. By appropriately specifying the ***meta-level invocation criteria*** [Georgeff and Ingrand, 1989], a range of sensitivities to external change can be built into the agent's reflective strategies. In this way, we implemented several different *reaction strategies* to control what events would trigger replanning, and so explored a number of types of *rational* commitment, as opposed to the *blind* commitment of an agent that continues to execute its plans without regard to external events.

2.4 Performance Measurement

The Tileworld and our agent both measure time by an abstract clock. They execute synchronously, with the ratio of their clock rates set by a parameter γ called the *rate of world change*. This parameter allows the dynamism of the world, as perceived by the agent, to be varied over a wide range.

The natural notion of how well an agent performs in the Tileworld is its score, or rather the sum of the scores of the holes it has filled. Absolute score is of little use as a measure of effectiveness, as hole scores are taken from random distributions whose characteristics are parameterized, experiment lengths vary, and worlds can have different characteristics and speeds.

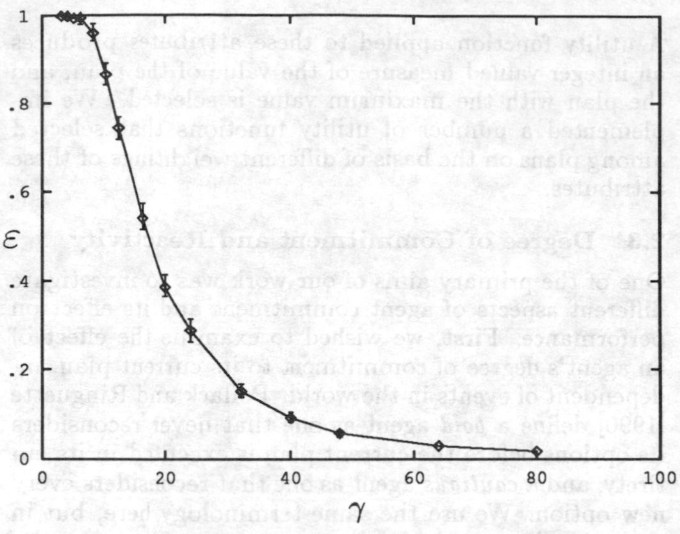

Figure 1: Effect of Rate of World Change

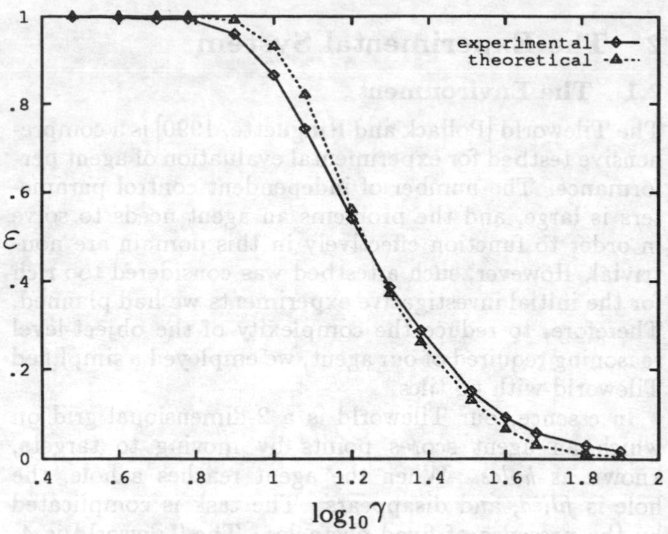

Figure 2: Effect of Rate of World Change (log x-scale)

Previous experimental results [Pollack and Ringuette, 1990] had revealed the undesirability of using performance measures based on CPU-time or elapsed time, and our abstract time unit was arbitrary. Accordingly, we defined an agent's effectiveness $\mathcal{E}$ to be its score divided by the maximum possible score[1] it could have achieved. This gave a measure of performance that was largely independent of game length, and proved to be stable and reproducible.

2.5 Experimental Procedures

During the course of a single Tileworld game, an agent's effectiveness fluctuates, due to random variations in hole scores and positions and the fact that the agent scores by increments rather than continuously. An individual game had to be sufficiently long for the agent's effectiveness to converge to a stable value. By plotting the effectiveness $\mathcal{E}$ as a function of game length, we could determine what this length should be.

Across different, but statistically similar games, we observed small variations in agent effectiveness whose magnitude declined as game length increased. This led us to define a *standard experiment* consisting of 5 games with identical initial configurations, but differing in the random seed that determined their evolution. The variation in effectiveness was recorded and served as a confidence limit on the mean effectiveness value. Each such experiment produced one point on a graph. A *characterization* of an agent consisted in running such an experiment at up to 15 points spanning a 2^5 range of values in γ. This produced a curve such as that shown in Figure 1. The error bars indicate the measured variation in $\mathcal{E}$. We will usually omit them for clarity. Their magnitude is typical of our standard experiments.

The stability of the results of such standard experiments was excellent. Each required about 30 minutes of CPU-time on a Sun Sparcstation, with a characterization taking up to 8 hours.

[1]The sum of the scores of all holes appearing in the trial.

3 Results and Analysis

In this section we present the results of several sequences of experiments aimed at investigating how agent effectiveness changes as some world or agent parameter is varied. The parameters selected for investigation were:

- Rate of world change
- Agent planning time
- Degree of commitment
- Reaction strategy

The results that follow all use a plan selection strategy that maximizes hole score divided by distance, which is arguably "rational" since this is a measure of the rate at which the agent can hope to score. It is similar to the ***subjective expected utility*** of Pollack and Ringuette [1990]. Experiments comparing different plan selection strategies are reported elsewhere [Kinny, 1990].

3.1 Rate of World Change

The experimental parameter that has the most fundamental influence upon agent effectiveness is the rate γ at which the world changes. Figure 1 shows the effectiveness $\mathcal{E}$ of a bold agent as a function of γ across 2 orders of magnitude.

At the baseline rate of world change ($\gamma = 1$) in our standard world, holes appear and disappear sufficiently slowly that any agent with a moderately effective strategy will successfully fill each hole soon after it appears and achieve a perfect score ($\mathcal{E} = 1$).

As γ increases, hole life-expectancies decrease reciprocally, as measured by the agent's clock. Eventually holes start to disappear before the agent has filled them, and $\mathcal{E}$ drops below 1. This decline in effectiveness has a sudden onset and is initially steep, with $\mathcal{E}$ falling from 0.9 to 0.5 for a factor of 2 increase in γ. As γ increases further the decline in $\mathcal{E}$ becomes more gradual and eventually asymptotically approaches zero.

The experimental performance curve in Figure 2 shows the same data plotted against $\log_{10}\gamma$. The log scale spreads the decline in $\mathcal{E}$ more uniformly, making comparison of curves easier. We refer to such a plot of $\mathcal{E}$ vs $\log_{10}\gamma$ as an effectiveness or performance curve. Families of such curves provide a means for comparing the effect of change in other experimental parameters, and are the standard method of presenting such results in subsequent sections.

An explanation of the shape of these effectiveness curves can be obtained by considering the equilibrium between hole appearance and the agent's hole filling activities. A given hole's life-expectancy l and gestation period g are taken from independent uniform distributions. At the baseline rate of world change, these are:

Parameter	Minimum	Average	Maximum
Gestation g	60	150	240
Life-expectancy l	240	600	960

Were it not for the activities of the agent, a hole's lifetime would be equal to its life-expectancy, and the expected number of holes in the world h_{ave} would be given by $h_{\text{ave}} = l_{\text{ave}}/g_{\text{ave}} = 4$.

The total time f the agent takes to fill a hole is determined by the time spent planning, moving, and replanning. For an agent that reconsiders its options every k steps, this is given by $f = d(p/k + m)$, where p is the planning time, d is the distance to the hole (or more precisely the path length of the plan), and m is the time to move a single step (henceforth always 1). Setting $k = d$ gives a bold agent that commits to executing its entire plan, while setting $k = 1$ gives a cautious agent that replans after every step. For the curve in Figure 2, the average filling time f_{ave} is approximately 15.

When this time is smaller than the minimum hole gestation period g_{min}, as is the case when $\gamma < 4$, then h_{ave} will be less than 1. The agent will spend only a fraction of its time actually filling holes or planning; the rest of the time it will be waiting for a hole to appear. As γ increases this idle time will decrease to zero, and h_{ave} will rise above 1.

For $g_{\text{min}} < f < 2g_{\text{min}}$, usually at most one new hole will appear while the agent is filling a prior one, so despite the fact that $h_{\text{ave}} > 1$, a bold agent rarely has to choose which hole to fill next. Note, however, that often the ***task timelimit*** (the time left for the agent to fill a selected hole) will be less than the hole's life-expectancy, because of the delay between a hole's appearance and the agent's targeting it. For $2g_{\text{min}} < f < g_{\text{ave}}$, the agent will more often have to choose between possible targets, but nonetheless will still be able, on average, to fill holes faster than they appear. Sometimes it will miss a hole, so $\mathcal{E}$ begins to drop below 1. At this point, the agent's plan selection strategy becomes important.

When $f > g_{\text{ave}}$, holes are appearing faster than the agent can fill them, so necessarily the population h_{ave} will rise. The average time between a hole appearing and the agent trying to fill it will increase, leading to shorter task timelimits. Thus the probability that a hole will disappear before being filled will increase and $\mathcal{E}$ will decline. To begin with, this decline will be rapid. Ultimately, the rise in h_{ave} will be limited by the upper bound of the holes' natural life-expectancies l and the

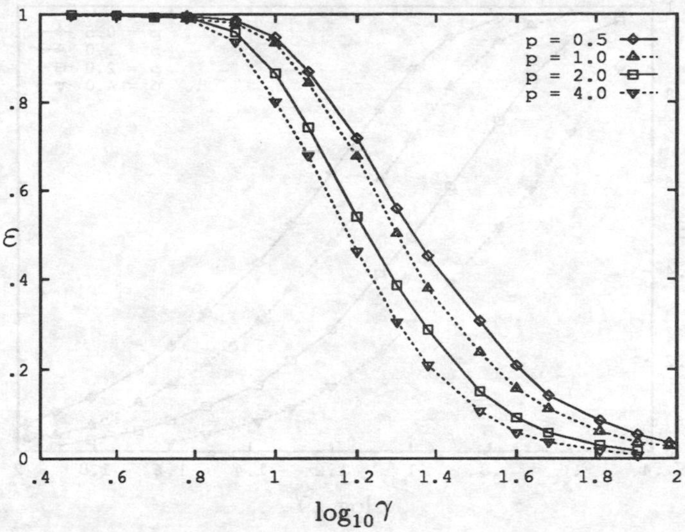

Figure 3: Effect of Planning Time (bold agent)

decline in $\mathcal{E}$ becomes less steep. The agent succeeds in filling those holes whose life-expectancies are sufficiently long or that are targeted sufficiently promptly. Even in highly dynamic worlds, there will be some holes that meet these criteria – hence the asymptotic behaviour. Note that the agent may successfully fill only some small fraction of the holes, but by judicious choice of targets may achieve a significantly higher value of $\mathcal{E}$.

We can put this informal explanation of the shape of an agent's performance curve onto a mathematical footing by calculating the distribution of path lengths in this domain. Ignoring the effect of the agent's plan selection strategy on the distribution of selected path lengths, we can approximate $\mathcal{E}$ by finding what fraction of these paths result in f being smaller than the average task deadline, which can be calculated[2] from the average hole population and life-expectancy. This leads to the theoretical performance curve in Figure 2. The agreement between the curves is good, the noticeable difference being that the decline in the experimental curve begins earlier but is less steep. This is partly due to our ignoring the fact that the hole life-expectancies come from a distribution.

3.2 Agent Planning Time

The planning time p is the agent parameter that determines the cost of forming a plan. If it is small, the agent can afford to replan often. If it is large, frequent replanning is not effective.

Figure 3 shows the performance curves for a bold agent with p equal to 0.5, 1, 2, and 4. These performance curves are near-identical, differing only by an x-axis offset. Since a given level of effectiveness is associated with a given ratio of hole life-expectancy l to filling time f, and $l \propto 1/\gamma$, the effect on $\mathcal{E}$ of varying p, and hence multiplying f by some constant c, is equivalent to multiplying γ by c, i.e. scaling the x-axis. Since the x-axis is a log scale this appears as a constant offset.

[2]For details see [Kinny, 1991]

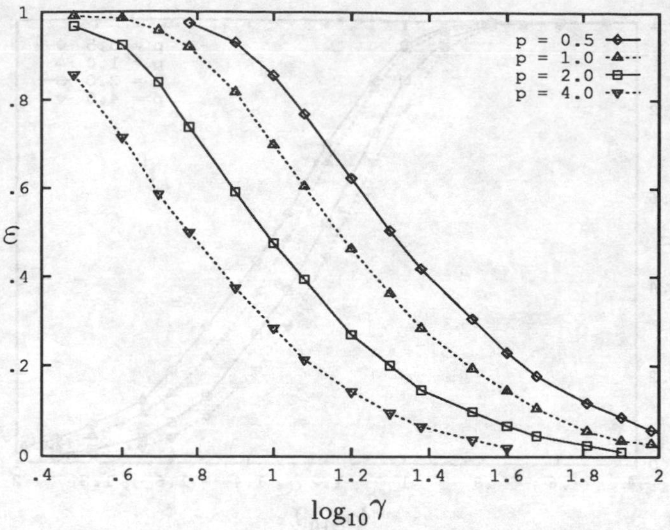

Figure 4: Effect of Planning Time (cautious agent)

Figure 4 shows the performance curves for a cautious agent with p equal to 0.5, 1, 2, and 4. Again we observe a family of similar curves differing by a scale factor, but the falloff in performance as p rises is far more pronounced, with the curves being more widely separated. The filling time f is more sensitive to p, since replanning occurs after every step. The other noticeable difference is the reduced rate of decline in $\mathcal{E}$ as γ increases. This is attributable to the fact that, all other things being equal, f is higher for a cautious agent than a bold agent, hence the point at which $\mathcal{E}$ begins to decline occurs earlier. The decline is slower, however, because the proportion of f contributed by p is independent of distance, whereas for a bold agent it increases for shorter path lengths. Another contributing factor is the ability of the cautious agent to be opportunistic. This is discussed in the next section.

3.3 Degree of Boldness

We have seen differences between bold and cautious agents as planning time is varied. In this section we consider in more detail the effect of boldness on performance, also examining agents that are intermediate in boldness in that they commit to executing several steps of a plan before reconsidering their options.

Figure 5 shows the performance curves of 3 agents differing only in the length of the plans to which they commit. The cautious agent replans after 1 step, the "normal" agent after 4, and the bold agent after the entire plan has been executed. All have planning time $p = 4$. In this case the bold agent is superior to the normal agent, which is superior to the cautious agent. The performance curves exhibit the differing slopes that were noted in section 3.2, the normal agent being intermediate between the other two.

An interesting phenomenon appears as we continue to make this comparison while decreasing the planning time p (Figures 6 and 7). As p decreases two things happen: the gap between the cautious and the bolder agents becomes narrower, and the normal agent becomes

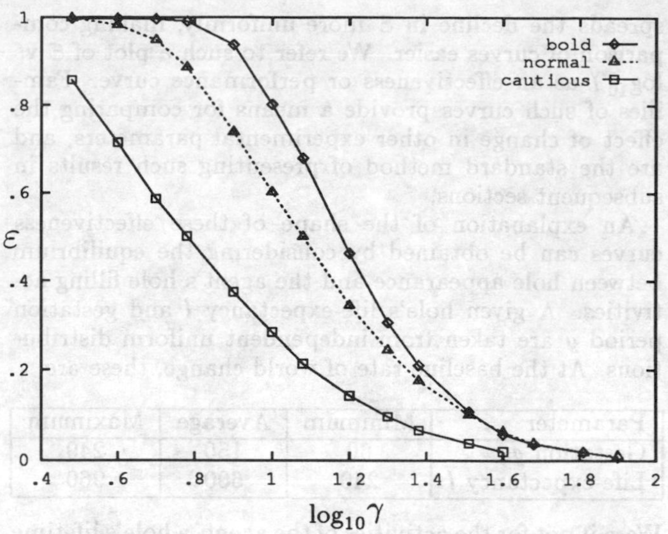

Figure 5: Effect of Degree of Boldness ($p = 4$)

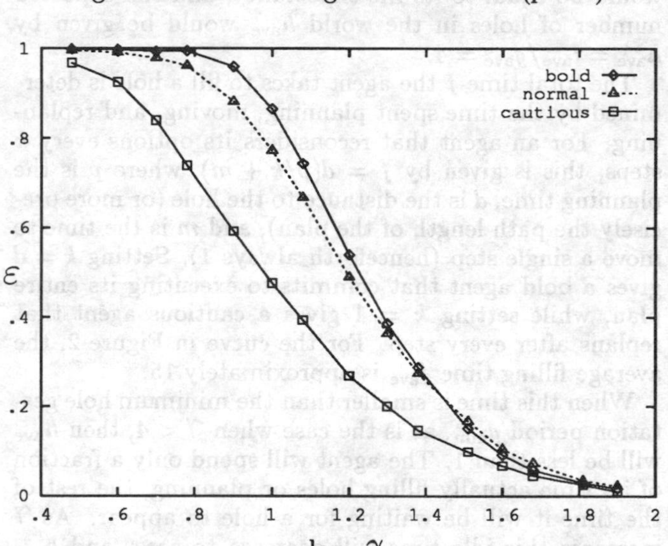

Figure 6: Effect of Degree of Boldness ($p = 2$)

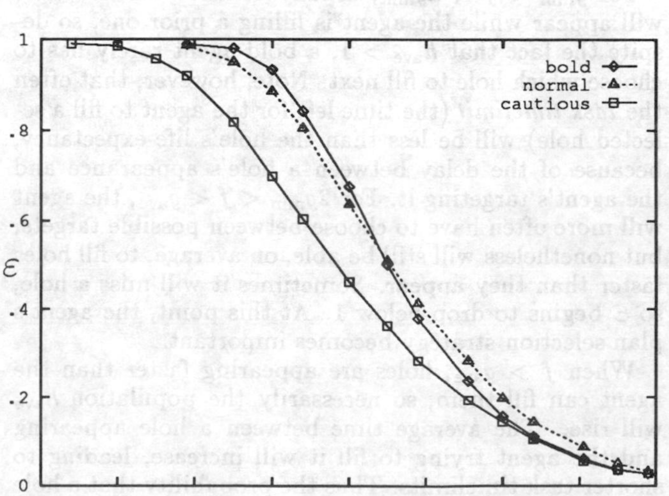

Figure 7: Effect of Degree of Boldness ($p = 1$)

superior to the bold agent in more dynamic worlds. In the final graph the cautious agent is as effective as the bold agent at high rates of change.

We can explain this behaviour fairly naturally by considering the tradeoff between the costs and benefits of replanning. In a world where things change slowly, frequent replanning is not advantageous. On the contrary, the increased time spent planning may be an onerous burden. As the degree of dynamism increases, however, boldness becomes a less successful strategy, as it continues to pursue vanished targets or fails to notice better opportunities that have arisen. More cautious agents can be opportunistic and take advantage of serendipitous change, as well as dropping plans that have become futile. In highly dynamic worlds only a small fraction of the agent's plans are successful, and the advantages of opportunism and plan execution monitoring outweigh those of commitment, provided that p is not too great.

3.4 Reaction Strategies

Until now, all committed agents that we have been considering have been blind in their commitment, in that they ignore changes in the world that occur during plan execution. As we saw above, this brings disadvantages as the dynamism of the world increases. Different strategies for reacting to change in the world can improve upon this blind or fanatical commitment.

The appropriate response to an event is sometimes to ignore it and other times to deliberate, depending on the agent's current plans, the nature of the event, and the state of the world. The key to effective control of deliberation is to have a reaction strategy that is sensitive to the right environmental cues, producing rational commitment.

We implemented and assessed a range of reaction strategies, including replanning

- when the target disappears,
- when the target disappears or any hole appears, and
- when the target disappears or a nearer hole appears.

The performance curves for these strategies, for a bold agent with $p = 2$, appear in Figure 8. We observe that reacting to the disappearance of the target improves performance significantly. Combining this with replanning when a nearer hole appears is better still. On the other hand, reacting to any new hole is worse than blind commitment, except for high values of γ. In Figure 9 we see a similar set of results for a bold agent with $p = 1$. As may have been anticipated, the strategy of reacting to every new hole has improved relative to blind commitment, due to the decreased cost of planning.

In the previous section we saw that a more cautious agent was superior to a bold agent in highly dynamic worlds. We investigated whether this still held for more rational types of commitment. In Figure 10 we see the effect of degree of boldness for an agent that replans whenever its target disappears. Comparing these results with Figure 7, it is seen that the simple change in commitment from blind to reactive results in the bold agent being everywhere superior to the more cautious ones.

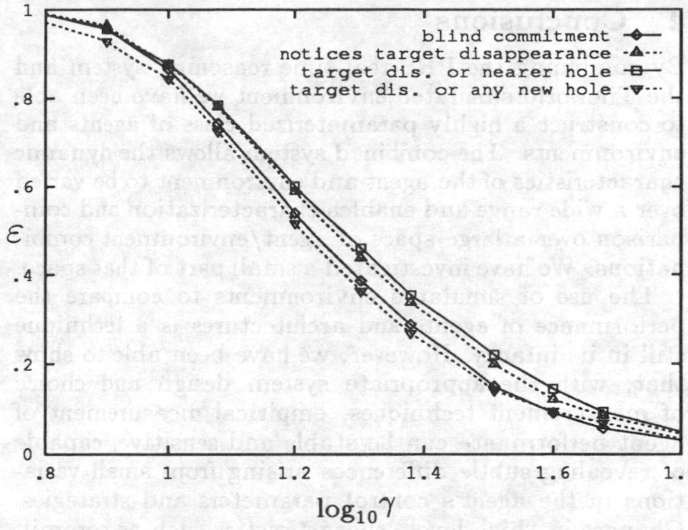

Figure 8: Effect of Reaction Strategy ($p = 2$)

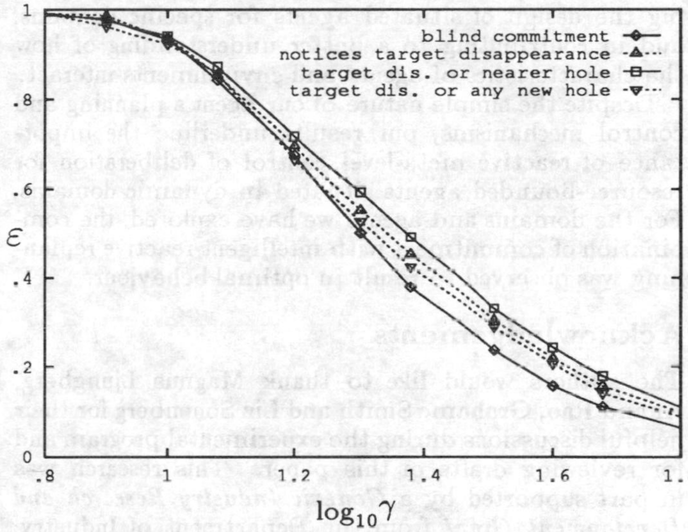

Figure 9: Effect of Reaction Strategy ($p = 1$)

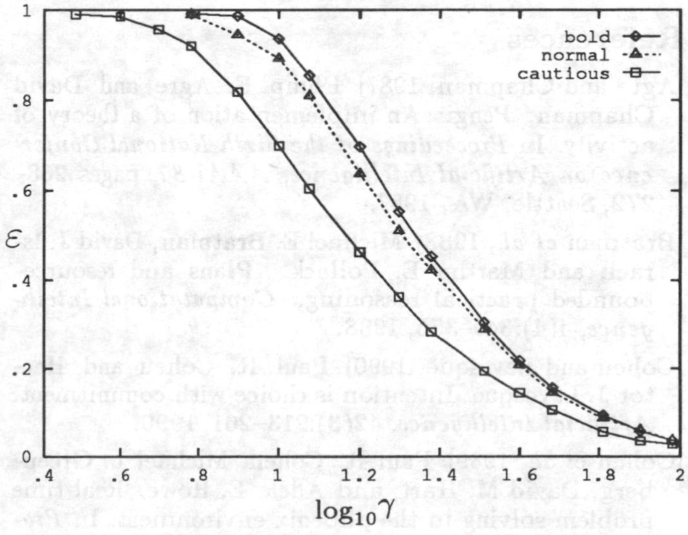

Figure 10: Effect of Boldness (reactive agent, $p = 1$)

4 Conclusions

By combining the PRS real-time reasoning system and the Tileworld simulated environment we have been able to construct a highly parameterized class of agents and environments. The combined system allows the dynamic characteristics of the agent and environment to be varied over a wide range and enables characterization and comparison over a large space of agent/environment combinations. We have investigated a small part of that space.

The use of simulated environments to compare the performance of agents and architectures is a technique still in its infancy. However, we have been able to show that, with the appropriate system design and choice of measurement techniques, empirical measurement of agent performance can be stable and sensitive, capable of revealing subtle differences arising from small variations in the agent's control parameters and strategies. Changes in "high-level" characteristics such as commitment have clearly visible effects. These experimental systems are likely to have an increasing role to play in guiding the design of situated agents for specific domains, and in contributing to a better understanding of how the characteristics of agents and environments interact.

Despite the simple nature of our agent's planning and control mechanisms, our results underline the importance of reactive meta-level control of deliberation for resource-bounded agents situated in dynamic domains. For the domains and agents we have explored, the combination of commitment with intelligent reactive replanning was observed to result in optimal behaviour.

Acknowledgements

The authors would like to thank Magnus Ljungberg, Anand Rao, Grahame Smith and Liz Sonenberg for their helpful discussions during the experimental program and for reviewing drafts of this paper. This research was in part supported by a *Generic Industry Research and Development Grant* from the Department of Industry, Technology and Commerce, Australia and in part by the Australian Civil Aviation Authority.

References

[Agre and Chapman, 1987] Philip E. Agre and David Chapman. Pengi: An implementation of a theory of activity. In *Proceedings of the Sixth National Conference on Artificial Intelligence, AAAI-87*, pages 268–272, Seattle, WA, 1987.

[Bratman *et al.*, 1988] Michael E. Bratman, David J. Israel, and Martha E. Pollack. Plans and resource-bounded practical reasoning. *Computational Intelligence*, 4(4):349–355, 1988.

[Cohen and Levesque, 1990] Paul R. Cohen and Hector J. Levesque. Intention is choice with commitment. *Artificial Intelligence*, 42(3):213–261, 1990.

[Cohen *et al.*, 1989] Paul R. Cohen, Michael L. Greenberg, David M. Hart, and Adele E. Howe. Real-time problem solving in the phoenix environment. In *Proceedings of the Workshop on Real-Time Artificial Intelligence Problems at IJCAI-89*, 1989.

[Dean and ael Boddy, 1988] Thomas Dean and Mich ael Boddy. An analysis of time-dependent planning. In *Proceedings of the Seventh National Conference on Artificial Intelligence, AAAI-88*, pages 49–54, Saint Paul, MA, 1988.

[Fehling and Wilber, 1989] M. R. Fehling and B. M. Wilber. Schemer-II: An architecture for reflective, resource-bounded problem solving. Technical Report 837-89-30, Rockwell International Science Center, Palo Alto Laboratory, Palo Alto, CA, 1989.

[Georgeff and Ingrand, 1989] Michael P. Georgeff and Felix Ingrand. Decision-making in an embedded reasoning system. In *Proceedings of the Eleventh International Joint Conference on Artificial Intelligence, IJCAI-89*, pages 972–978, Detroit, MI, 1989.

[Kinny, 1990] David N. Kinny. Measuring the effectiveness of situated agents. Technical Report 11, Australian AI Institute, Carlton, Australia, 1990.

[Kinny, 1991] David N. Kinny. Achieving rational balance. Technical Report 19, Australian AI Institute, Carlton, Australia, 1991.

[Pollack and Ringuette, 1990] Martha E. Pollack and Marc Ringuette. Introducing the Tileworld: Experimentally evaluating agent architectures. In *Proceedings of the Eighth National Conference on Artificial Intelligence, AAAI-90*, pages 183–189, Boston, MA, 1990.

[Rao and Georgeff, 1991] Anand S. Rao and Michael P. Georgeff. Modeling rational agents within a BDI-architecture. In *Proceedings of the Second International Conference on Principles of Knowledge Representation and Reasoning*, Boston, MA, 1991.

[Russell and Wefald, 1989] Stuart Russell and Eric Wefald. Principles of metareasoning. In *Proceedings of the First International Conference on Principles of Knowledge Representation and Reasoning*, pages 400–411, Toronto, 1989.

[Schoppers, 1987] Marcel J. Schoppers. Universal plans for reactive robots in unpredictable environments. In *Proceedings of the Tenth International Joint Conference on Artificial Intelligence, IJCAI-87*, pages 852–859, Milan, Italy, 1987.

Generating Integrated Interpretation of Partial Information Based on Distributed Qualitative Reasoning

Takashi Nishiyama
Artificial Intelligence Group
Information System Center
Matsushita Electric Works, Ltd.
1048, Kadoma, Osaka 571
JAPAN

Osamu Katai
Sosuke Iwai
Tetsuo Sawaragi
Dept. of Precision Mechanics
Faculty of Engineering
Kyoto University
Yoshida Honmachi, Sakyo-ku
Kyoto 606-01
JAPAN

Hiroshi Masuichi
FUJI XEROX®
3-3-5, Akasaka, Minato-ku
Tokyo 107
JAPAN

Abstract

Situation assessment (SA) is regarded as a problem solving process that involves the acquiring and integrating of partial information sensed from the world in order to produce a global interpretation. A new approach to SA called distributed sensor network (DSN) has recently been proposed. DSN consists of sensor nodes, each of which has its own knowledge or model to generate a partial interpretation by matching the sensed information with the model. These nodes exchange and share their interpretations with other nodes to integrate them into a consistent global interpretation. In this paper, a qualitative model of the world is introduced to each sensor node, since the sensor information is local and partial from the spatial and temporal point of view. Each node can generate a partial interpretation which can predict a future evolution after the observed event, by the state transition on the qualitative model. The partial interpretation thus generated is represented as an envisioning tree. In order to integrate the several partial interpretations into a global one, an integration node is introduced which connects the envisioning trees by pruning inconsistent branches under global perspectives, to achieve a spatial and temporal interpolation between the sensed information.

1 Introduction

Situation assessment (SA), important for developing an intelligent autonomous system, is regarded as a problem solving process that involves the acquiring and integrating of partial information sensed from the world in order to produce a global interpretation. A notable new approach called distributed sensor network (DSN) has recently been developed. DSN consists of a number of "sensor nodes", each of which has its own knowledge or model to produce a partial interpretation by matching the obtained information with its model. These nodes also exchange their partial interpretations with other nodes in order to integrate them into a consistent global interpretation. Researchers have tried to establish a DSN by integrating the current sensing technology with artificial intelligence methodology [Wesson *et al.*, 1981].

In this study, we introduce a **qualitative model** [de Kleer, 1977] on the world into each sensor node as shown in Figure1(a). Since, in spatial and temporal terms, the sensor information obtained is local and partial for any occurring event, a qualitative model by which unknown portion of such events can be inferred should be employed; that is, it should enable spatial and temporal interpolation to be done. Furthermore, since the sensor information involves a certain degree of uncertainty due to noise, the inference method should be robust. Taking these requirements into consideration, we will introduce a

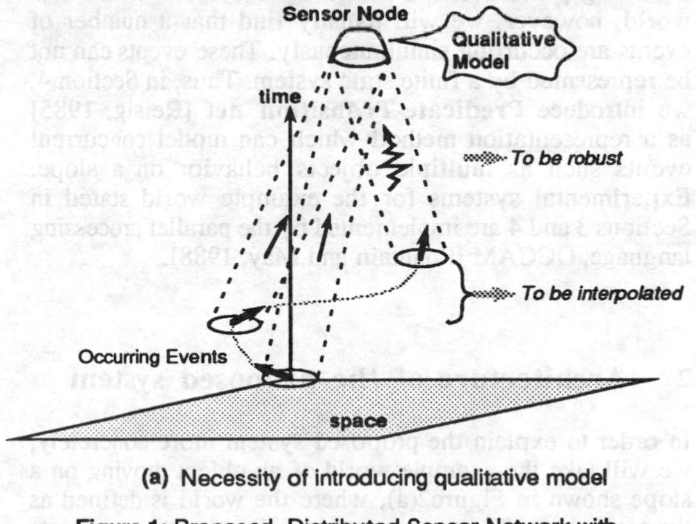

(a) Necessity of introducing qualitative model

Figure 1: Proposed Distributed Sensor Network with qualitative model on the world qualitative model which consists of qualitative constraints derived from common sense knowledge about the structure and behavior of the world in question.

Figure1(b) shows an overview of the proposed DSN system having the qualitative model. The system consists of two types of nodes, a sensor node and an integration node. Since each piece of sensor information is local and partial, we can regard the **Total World** as consisting of a certain number of **Partial Worlds**. To each Partial World, a sensor node is attached which obtains partial information concerning an event in that world, and matches the information with the model to produce a partial interpretation. In this case, the interpretation is an a posteriori evolution of that event. Due to lack of information, however, the evolution produces numerous vestigial branches. The integration node thus functions to receive the various partial interpretations from the sensor nodes and integrate them into a global interpretation. That is, since it knows the temporal and spatial relationships that hold among the obtained information, the node can prune the inconsistent branchings to generate a consistent interpretation from among numerous possible interpretations.

In the system shown in Figure1(b), the individual sensor nodes are **distributed on task load** to reduce the whole load of the system, since these nodes share the same tasks and can execute their tasks in parallel. By contrast, the sensor node and the integration node are **distributed on function**, because these two types of nodes have different tasks and execute their tasks in parallel.

In Section 2, we explain an architecture of the proposed DSN system, taking an object moving on a slope as an example world. In Section 3, we discuss events occurring sequentially in the world, and represent the occurring processes as a **finite state system**. In the real world, however, we will usually find that a number of events are occurring simultaneously. These events can not be represented by a finite state system. Thus, in Section 4, we introduce **Predicate-Transition net** [Reisig, 1985] as a representation method which can model concurrent events such as multiple objects behavior on a slope. Experimental systems for the example world stated in Sections 3 and 4 are implemented by the parallel processing language, OCCAM [Pountain and May, 1988].

2 Architecture of the proposed system

In order to explain the proposed system more concretely, we will take the example world of an object moving on a slope shown in Figure2(a), where the world is defined as the total slope. The sensors are initially set at some points on the world. To each sensor, a sensor node is attached as shown in Figure2(b). Based on sensor positions, we can

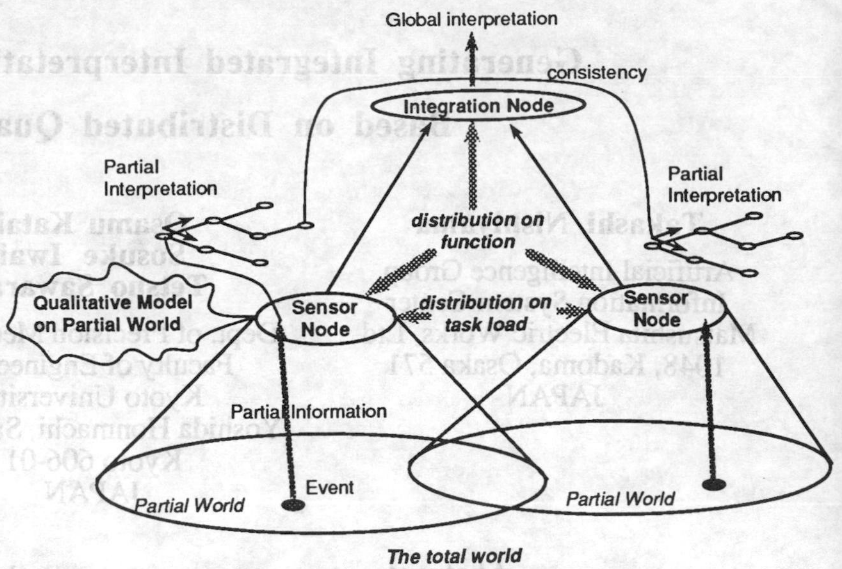

(b) An overview of the proposed system

Figure 1: Proposed Distributed Sensor Network with qualitative model on the world

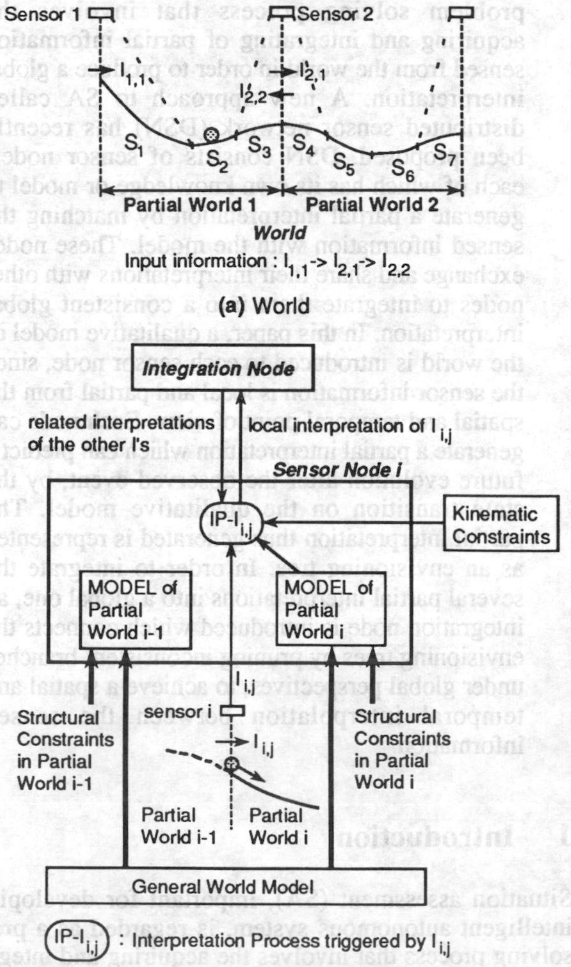

(a) World

(b) Generation of partial interpretation and Instantiation of MODEL of Partial World

Figure 2: Architecture of the proposed DSN system for an object moving on a slope divide the world into Partial Worlds 1, 2,... As shown in Figure2(b), each sensor monitors the boundary point between Partial World i-1 and i for some i. Thus when the sensor detects the partial information, $I_{i,j}$ (i; sensor number, j; information number), i.e., the object crossing to the right at that point, the attached sensor node activates an interpretation process of $I_{i,j}$ (IP-$I_{i,j}$). This process generates an evolution based on the qualitative model of object behavior on Partial World i (MODEL of Partial World i) to meet kinematic constraints, and sends the evolution, that is, the local interpretation of $I_{i,j}$, to the integration node.

MODEL of Partial World i is an instantiation of the General World Model mentioned in the next section, which represents the object behavior on slopes of any structure. If the structural constraints of Partial World, that is, the connective relationships among S_1, S_2,..., are given, a General World Model is compiled and a concrete MODEL of Partial World i is instantiated.

3 Generating Interpretations of Single Object Behavior on Slopes

3.1 Snapshot discretization of a single object's continuous behavior

We can regard the slopes of any structure as consisting of a number of primitive slopes shown in Figure3(a), if we divide that slope according to its flexion, maximum, or minimum points. An object's behavior on these primitive slopes can be described as representations, called snapshots, shown in Figure3(b). For example, snapshot A_L represents the object moving to the right from the left edge of slope A. Thus, an object moving on any slope can be represented as a connected series of these snapshots.

In connecting snapshots, we have to take into consideration the two constraints shown in Figure4: the connectivity among the primitive slopes and the continuity of the object behavior on the connected slopes. One constraint is that, for instance, slope A's right boundary can be connected to B or C's left boundary, but not to D's, as shown in Figure4(a). As an example of the other constraint, snapshot A_R can be connected to either snapshots B_R, C_L or B_L as shown in Figure4(b). Connections (ii) and (iii) are unique qualitative representations; that is, in the usual representation, the object behavior of changing direction can be described as a series of three events; "the event of moving to the left through the right edge of slope A" -> "the event of changing its direction on the slope" -> "the event of moving to the right through that edge of A". By contrast, the representations we propose simplify this series of events by not specifying the middle event. Namely, in our method, the middle event can be interpolated by the other events. This makes our behavioral representation simpler.

3.2 Finite state diagram representation for snapshot changes

When we regard a snapshot as a state and a snapshot change as a transition, we can obtain the finite state diagram shown in Figure5(a), which is the General World Model shown in Figure2(b). This is a structural representation for object behavior on any slope, and does not depend on the concrete structure of the instance slope in question.

3.3 Concrete model of single object behavior on an instance slope

If the connective relationships of the instance slope are given, the General World Model shown in Figure5(a) is compiled and a concrete model is instantiated. For example, the relationships of the slope of Partial World 1 in Figure2 are that slope S_1 is an A-type, which is connected on the right to a C-type slope S_2. Based on these relationships, an

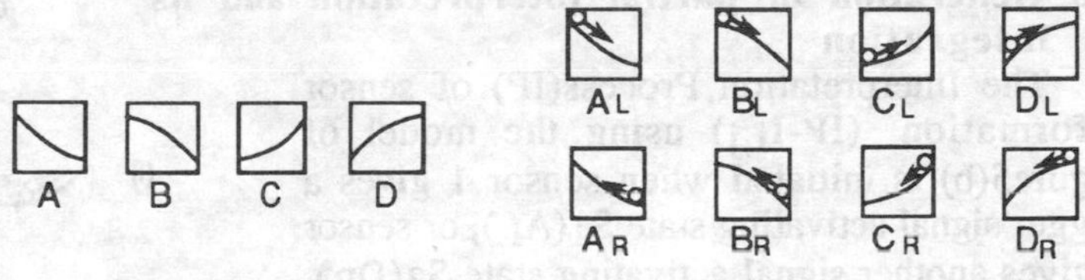

(a) Primitive slopes (b) Snapshots

Figure 3: Qualitative representation of an object's movement

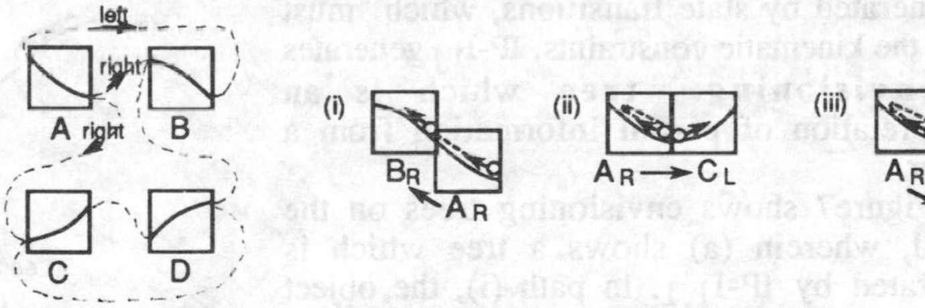

(a) Connective relationships (b) Continuity of behavior

Figure 4: Constraints on snapshots connection

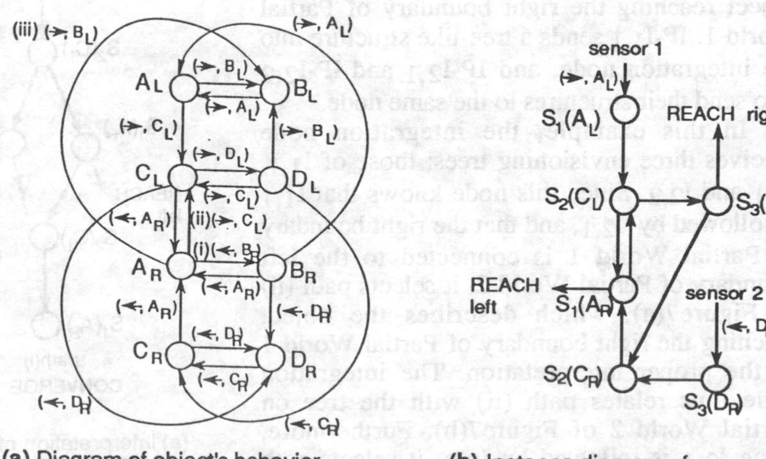

(a) Diagram of object's behavior on any slope (b) Instance diagram of Partial World 1 in Figure 2(a)

Figure 5: Finite state system

appropriate part of Figure5(a) is chosen and instantiated. Figure5(b) shows an instantiation diagram, which represents the object behavior on Partial World 1 of Figure2(a).

3.4 Kinematic constraints on single object behavior

We will now consider the following two constraints about object behavior.

Kinematic constraint 1:
On a slope consisting of slopes S_i and S_{i+1}, if any one of the transitions between the two snapshots shown in Figure6 (i), (ii), ..., (vi) occurs, then whenever the object comes back to slope S_i or S_{i+1} again, the same transition between snapshots will necessarily occur.

Kinematic constraint 2:
If the transitions of either (i) or (iv) occur, then the object will go back and forth around the connecting point between slopes S_i and S_{i+1}, and will "converge" on that boundary point.

3.5 Generation of partial interpretation and its integration

The Interpretation Process(IP) of sensor information (IP-$I_{i,j}$) using the model of Figure5(b) is initiated when sensor 1 gives a trigger signal activating state $S_1(A_L)$, or sensor 2 gives another signal activating state $S_3(D_R)$. After IP-$I_{i,j}$ is started, the qualitative behavior, which is the prediction after the trigger signal, is generated by state transitions, which must meet the kinematic constraints. IP-$I_{i,j}$ generates an **envisioning tree** which is an interpretation of partial information from a sensor.

Figure7 shows envisioning trees on the world, wherein (a) shows a tree which is generated by IP-$I_{1,1}$. In path (i), the object converges around the connecting point between slopes S_1 and S_2, since this path meets kinematic constraint 2. Path (ii) shows the object reaching the right boundary of Partial World 1. IP-$I_{1,1}$ sends a tree-like structure into the integration node, and IP-$I_{2,1}$ and IP-$I_{2,2}$ also send their structures to the same node.

In this example, the integration node receives three envisioning trees: those of $I_{1,1}$, $I_{2,1}$ and $I_{2,2}$. Since this node knows that $I_{1,1}$ is followed by $I_{2,1}$, and that the right boundary of Partial World 1 is connected to the left boundary of Partial World 2, it selects path (ii) in Figure7(a), which describes the object reaching the right boundary of Partial World 1 as the proper interpretation. The integration node thus relates path (ii) with the tree on Partial World 2 of Figure7(b). Furthermore, since $I_{2,1}$ is followed by $I_{2,2}$, it selects path (iii) in Figure7(b), which describes the object changing direction on slope S_6 and reaching the left boundary of Partial World 2. The integration node thus relates path (iii) with the tree of Figure7(c). In this example, since no other information is obtained after $I_{2,2}$, the integration node selects only those paths in the tree (Figure7(c)) which describe the object converging around the concave point in Partial World 1, i.e., the connecting point between slopes S_1 and S_2. The integration node thus generates an integrated tree-like structure consisting of path(ii) -> path(iii) -> path(iv) and so on, as the consistent interpretation of object behavior on the Total World.

4 Generating Interpretation of Multiple Objects Concurrent Behavior

4.1 General constraint about multiple objects concurrent behavior

Multiple objects behavior is regarded as an asynchronous and concurrent process subject to the following general constraint:

Two objects which are side by side move holding the relative relationships of position between them.

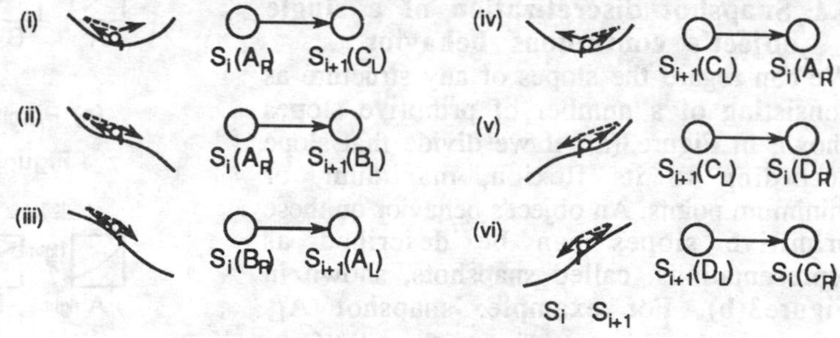

Figure 6: Kinematic constraints

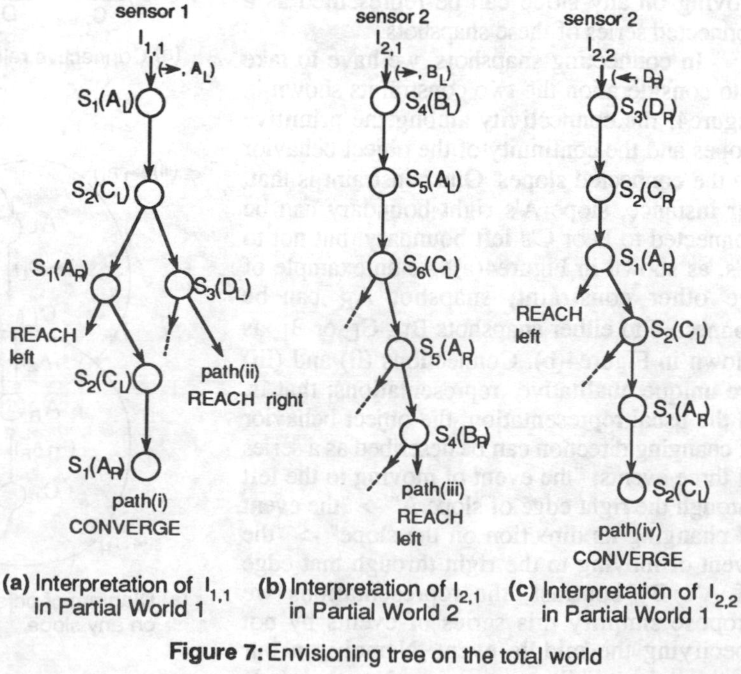

(a) Interpretation of $I_{1,1}$ in Partial World 1 (b) Interpretation of $I_{2,1}$ in Partial World 2 (c) Interpretation of $I_{2,2}$ in Partial World 1

Figure 7: Envisioning tree on the total world

In other words, an object on the right side can not "go through" an object on the left side.

4.2 Representation of the constraint by Predicate/Transition net

Since an asynchronous and concurrent process such as multiple objects behavior can not be represented by a finite state system, i.e. MODEL of Partial World in Figure5, we will introduce Predicate/Transition net (P/T-net) [Reisig, 1985], which can precisely represent the dependency and independency of that process. P/T-net is a high level Petri net, in which being true or not on a predicate denoted by a place depends on what "individual token" exists on that place. When the constraint on multiple objects behavior is described, each individual token denotes each object named "a", "b", and so on.

4.2.1 Predicate Place for representing the relative relationships between multiple objects

As shown in the left-hand side of Figure8(a), the left and right objects are moving on a slope consisting of S_i and S_{i+1}. The constraint on this slope is represented in the right-hand side of that figure. Two individual tokens, **a** and **b** on place $S_i(A_L)$, show that both the left object "b" and the right object "a" are moving to the right on slope S_i. Place "Left" is a predicate place, which represents that variable L is to the left of variable R when a coupled token <L,R> exists. In Figure8(a), since object "b" is to the left of object "a", constants "b" and "a" are substituted for variables L, R, respectively. This makes Place "Left" active as shown by the <b,a> token.

4.2.2 Transition with an inhibitor arc

As shown in Figure8(a), object "b" on slope S_i can not move to the right slope S_{i+1} without object "a" moving to slope S_{i+1}. Arc (---o) with variable <R> linking place $S_i(A_L)$ and transition t_1 is an inhibitor arc, which shows that a right object moving on slope S_i constrains a left object moving on that slope. That is, since predicate place "Left" is true and constant "a" is substituted for that variable R, transition t_1 is not allowed to fire. By contrast, transition t_2 is allowed to fire, thus token **a** can move to place $S_{i+1}(C_L)$.

4.2.3 Collision Transition

As shown on the left-hand side of Figure8(b), if objects "a" and "b" are moving toward one another, then the two objects will collide and move in opposite directions. This event is regarded as two changes of snapshots: change of object "b" from A_L to A_R, and change of object "a" from A_R to A_L. These two changes are represented as a transition called "collision transition" as shown on the right-hand side of Figure8(b).

4.2.4 Control of transitions by predicate place "Left"

As mentioned above, the constraint governing the relative relationships of position is explicitly represented as predicate place "Left". That is, if a sensor node acquires a piece of information concerning an object, then this node determines the name of that object, and substitutes the constant name for variables, that is, L or R of a coupled token located on that place. Thus, predicate place "Left" controls the firing of a transition with an inhibitor arc and a collision transition by substituting constants "b" or "a" for variables <L> or <R> associated with the arcs leading to those transitions.

Figure8 shows the constraint on multiple objects behavior on A-type primitive slope and a slope connected to its right side. There is also the constraint on B-, C-, and D-type primitive slopes and slopes connected to both their sides.

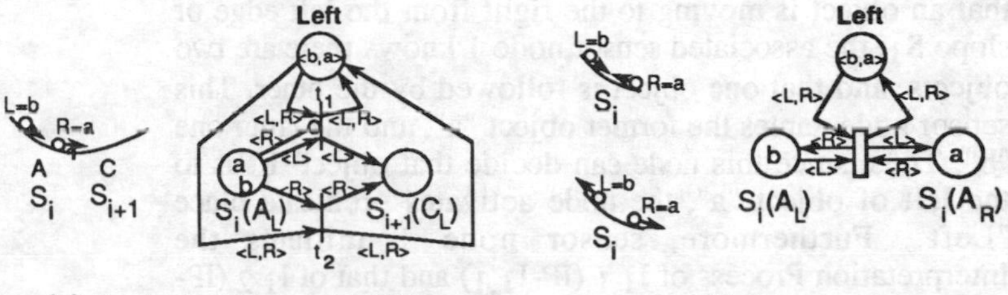

(a) Predicate place and inhibitor arc (b) collision transition

Figure 8: Representation of constraints on multiple objects concurrent behavior on A-type primitive slope

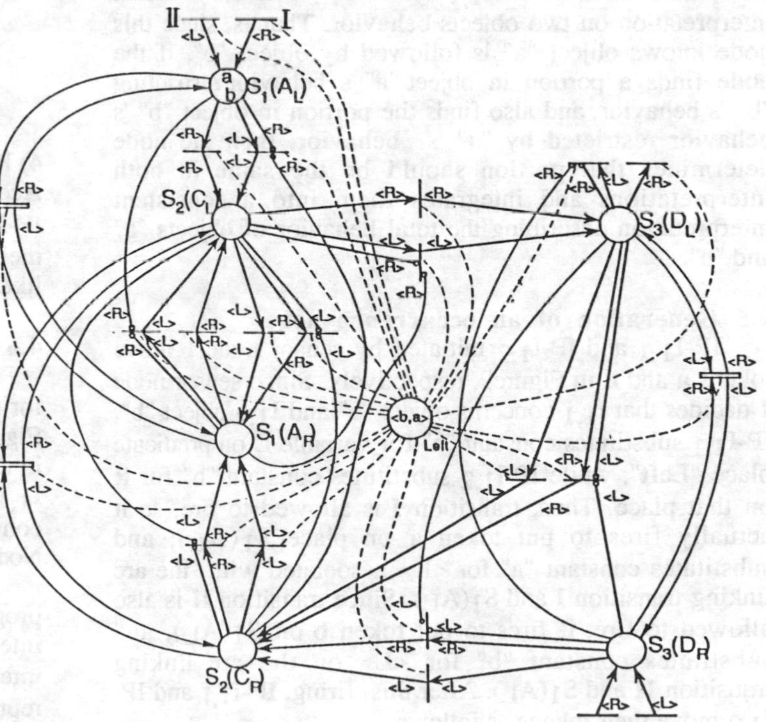

Figure 9: Predicate/transition-net modelling of Partial World 1 in Figure 2

4.3 Concrete model of multiple objects behavior

As stated in ***3.3***, the concrete model of single object behavior on an instance slope is generated to meet the connective relationships along that slope. A concrete model of multiple objects concurrent behavior is generated by adding the above mentioned constraint to the single object model. Thus, the multiple objects model is described as a P/T-net such as shown in Figure9, which shows two objects behavior on the slope of Partial World 1 in Figure2(a).

4.4 Generation of partial interpretation and its integration

When sensor 1 of Figure2(a) sequentially receives two pieces of information; $I_{1,1}$ and $I_{1,2}$, both of which mean that an object is moving to the right from the left edge of slope S_1, the associated sensor node 1 knows there are two objects, and that one object is followed by the other. This sensor node names the former object "a", and the latter one "b". Thus, since this node can decide that object "b" is to the left of object "a", the node activates predicate place "Left". Furthermore, sensor node 1 initiates the Interpretation Process of $I_{1,1}$ (IP-$I_{1,1}$) and that of $I_{1,2}$ (IP-$I_{1,2}$) ; the former generates a partial interpretation of object "a", and the latter generates that of "b". IP-$I_{1,1}$ and IP-$I_{1,2}$ execute state transition in parallel on the concrete model shown in Figure9 to meet the kinematic constraints.

The integration node integrates the partial interpretations from IP-$I_{1,1}$ and IP-$I_{1,2}$ into a consistent interpretation on two objects behavior. That is, since this node knows object "a" is followed by object "b", if the node finds a portion in object "a" 's behavior restricting "b" 's behavior, and also finds the portion in object "b" 's behavior restricted by "a" 's behavior, then the node determines that portion should be the same in both interpretations and integrates them into a consistent interpretation describing the total behavior of objects "a" and "b".

4.5 Generation of an occurrence net

IP-$I_{1,1}$ and IP-$I_{1,2}$ initiated by sensor node 1 move tokens **a** and **b** in Figure9, respectively. Since sensor node 1 decides that $I_{1,1}$ concerns object "a" and $I_{1,2}$ object "b", IP-$I_{1,1}$ substitutes constant "a" for variable L on predicate place "Left", while IP-$I_{1,2}$ substitutes constant "b" for R on that place. Thus, transition **I** is allowed to fire, so it actually fires to put token **a** on place $S_1(A_L)$, and substitutes constant "a" for <R> associated with the arc linking transition I and $S_1(A_L)$. Since transition **II** is also allowed to fire, it fires to put token **b** on $S_1(A_L)$, and substitutes constant "b" for <L> on the arc linking transition II and $S_1(A_L)$. After this firing, IP-$I_{1,1}$ and IP-$I_{1,2}$ move their tokens as follows:

1) If either of the two tokens exists or both of them exist on place $S_i(\bullet)$, the associated Interpretation Process (IP) selects one of the transitions, t_i , input place of which is $S_i(\bullet)$. (Snapshots shown in Figure3 exist in the parentheses.)
2) It is assumed that slope S_{i-1} is to the left of slope S_i, and slope S_{i+1} is to the right of slope S_i. If the output place of t_i is $S_{i+1}(\bullet)$, then IP attends variable <L> on the arc leading to t_i and substitutes the name of its associated token for that variable to meet predicate place "Left" supplying the constant for that variable L. On the other hand, if the output place of t_i is $S_{i-1}(\bullet)$, then IP attends variable <R> on the arc to t_i and substitutes the name of the token for the variable to meet predicate place "Left" supplying the constant for that variable R.
3) Whether t_i fires or not is determined as follows:
   3-1) t_i is a transition with an inhibitor arc (---o).
   Predicate place "Left" substitutes its constant for the variable with the inhibitor arc of t_i, and checks whether or not the token having that constant name is located on the input place of t_i. If not, since the normal arc to t_i is activated by a token located on the input place of t_i as mentioned in 2), t_i actually fires to move that token to the output place and substitutes the name of the token for the variable with the arc to the output place. When t_i is the output transition of place $S_3(D_L)$, the firing of that transition distinguishes the token.
   3-2) t_i is a collision transition.
   Predicate place "Left" checks whether or not the two tokens are located on the two input places as shown in Figure8(b). If one token is located on one input place linked by the input arc associated with the name of that token, and if the other token is also located on the other input place, then a collision transition fires to exchange the two tokens and to put them on the output places. Furthermore, the names of those tokens are substituted for variables with the output arcs, respectively.
4) Return to 1).

According to the above processing flow, both IP-$I_{1,1}$ and IP-$I_{1,2}$ generate their own occurrence nets, which describe their tokens movement. These nets correspond to the tree-like structure of state transition as shown in ***3.5***.

4.6 Implementation using OCCAM language

Figure10(a) illustrates an implementation by OCCAM for the inference process in the proposed system shown in Figure2. (Only the key structure of the program is shown in this figure.) PAR construction (i) declares that both IP-$I_{1,1}$ and IP-$I_{1,2}$ can be executed in parallel, and PAR construction (ii) also declares that PAR (i) and Integration Node process can be executed in parallel.

Figure10(b) shows the output of the OCCAM program, that is, the occurrence net describing a piece of interpretation of $I_{1,1}$ and $I_{1,2}$. In this figure, (i) is the interpretation of $I_{1,1}$ concerning Partial World 1, which represents object "a" reaching the right boundary of World 1: (ii) is the interpretation of $I_{1,2}$ representing object "b" reaching the right boundary of that world being restricted by object "a" 's behavior. Net (i) (object "a" 's behavior) is similar to the portion describing object "a" 's behavior restricting "b" 's behavior in net (ii). The integration node decides this portion to be the same among the two objects

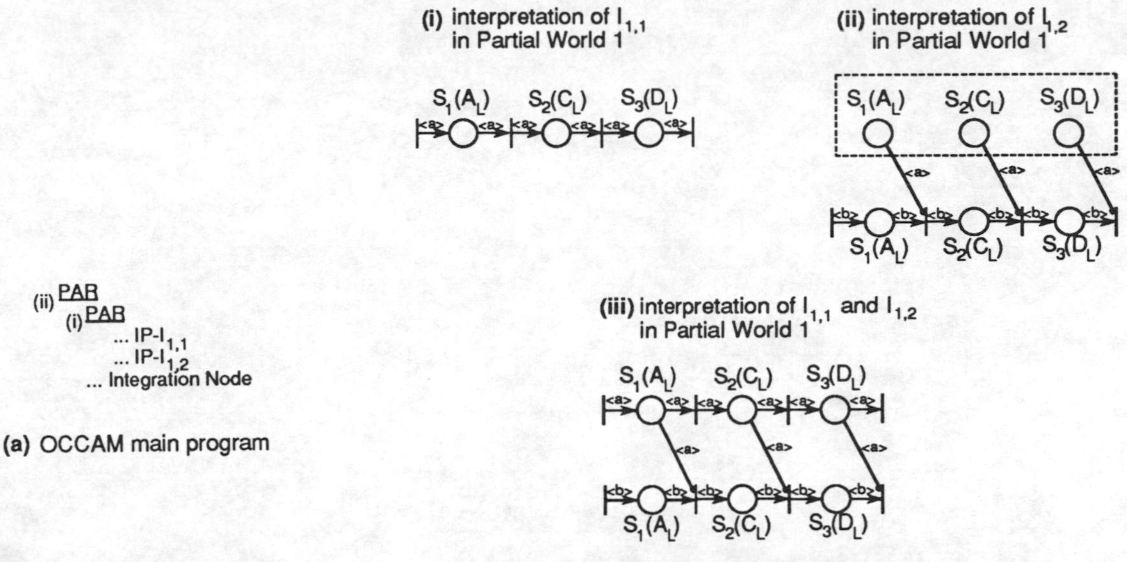

(b) Output of the OCCAM program
(The occurrence nets on Partial World1 of Figure 2)

Figure 10: Implementation using OCCAM language

behavior. Thus, that node integrates the two interpretations into a consistent global interpretation shown in (iii), which describes that object "a" reaches the right boundary followed by "b".

5 Conclusions

In this study, qualitative reasoning techniques are introduced into the interpretation of pieces of sensor information which are local and partial from the spatial and temporal point of view. This reasoning method interpolates these pieces of information to organize them into a consistent global one. That is, thanks to the qualitative models possessed by the sensor nodes, partial interpretations of acquired information can be extended and related to each other, by which the integration node can then select the proper interpretations to generate a consistent global interpretation.

In this paper, we have taken objects moving on a slope as an example world. The sequential behavior of a single object was represented as a finite state system, and the concurrent behavior of multiple objects was represented as a Predicate-Transition net. By the use of these qualitative models, the interpolative reasoning becomes robust and is easy to implement.

Acknowledgements

We are grateful to Dr. Junji Nomura, Senior Staff Researcher of Artificial Intelligence Group in Matsushita Electric Works, Ltd. for his valuable discussion and collaboration.

References

[Wesson *et al.*, 1981] Robert Wesson, Frederick Hayes-Roth, John W. Burge, Cathleen Stasz, and Carl A. Sunshine. Network Structures for Distributed Situation Assessment. *IEEE Transactions on System, Man, and Cybernetics*, SMC-11(1); 5-23, January 1981.

[de Kleer, 1977] Johan de Kleer. Multiple Representations of Knowledge in a Mechanics Problem-Solver. In *Proceedings of the Fifth International Joint Conference on Artificial Intelligence*, pages 299-304, Cambridge, Massachusetts, August 1977. International Joint Committee on Artificial Intelligence.

[Reisig, 1985] Wolfgang Reisig. *Petri Nets An Introduction*. Springer-Verlag Berlin Heidelberg New York Tokyo, 1985.

[Pountain and May, 1988] Dick Pountain and David May. *A Tutorial Introduction to OCCAM Programming*. Blackwell Scientific Publications Ltd, London, 1988.

AUTOMATED REASONING

Theorem Proving I

A Resolution Method for Temporal Logic

Michael Fisher*

Department of Computer Science
University of Manchester
Manchester, U.K.
(michael@cs.man.ac.uk)

Abstract

In this paper, a resolution method for propositional temporal logic is presented. Temporal formulae, incorporating both past-time and future-time temporal operators, are converted to *Separated Normal Form* (SNF), then both non-temporal and temporal resolution rules are applied. The resolution method is based on classical resolution, but incorporates a temporal resolution rule that can be implemented efficiently using a graph-theoretic approach.

1 Introduction

This report describes a resolution procedure for discrete, linear, propositional temporal logic. This logic incorporates both past-time and future-time temporal operators and its models consist of sequences of states, each sequence having finite past and infinite future.

A naive application of the classical resolution rule to temporal logics fails as two complementary literals may not represent a contradictory formula, depending on their temporal context. Because of such problems with resolution, the majority of the decision methods for temporal logics have been based either on tableaux or automata-theoretic techniques [Wolper, 1985; Vardi and Wolper, 1986]. Recently, however, interest has been rekindled in the use of resolution in such logics.

The resolution method described in this report relies on a translation of temporal formulae into a normal form. This normal form is derived from that developed for use in METATEM [Barringer *et al.*, 1989], an executable temporal logic, and the rewrite rules used to produce the normal form are derived from the work on the transformation and determinisation of METATEM programs [Fisher and Noel, 1990]. Several of these transformations are similar to those developed in [Sakuragawa, 1986].

Before developing the resolution procedure in detail, an outline of the temporal logic used, will be given.

2 A Linear Temporal Logic

In this section, a propositional temporal logic based on a linear and discrete model of time, with finite past and infinite future, is introduced. Temporal logic can be seen as classical logic extended with various modalities. Commonly, these are $\Diamond$, $\Box$, and $\bigcirc$. The intuitive meaning of these connectives is as follows: $\Diamond A$ is true now if A is true *sometime* in the future; $\Box A$ is true now if A is true *always* in the future; and $\bigcirc A$ is true now if A is true at the *next* moment in time. Similar connectives are introduced to enable reasoning about the *past*.

2.1 Syntax

Well-formed formulae (wff) are defined as follows.

- any element of PROP is a wff,
- if A and B are wff's, then the following are all wff's

$\neg A$	$A \vee B$	$A \wedge B$	$A \Rightarrow B$
$\Diamond A$	$\Box A$	$A \mathcal{U} B$	$A \mathcal{W} B$
$\blacklozenge A$	$\blacksquare A$	$A \mathcal{S} B$	$A \mathcal{Z} B$
$\bigcirc A$	$\odot A$	$\bullet A$	(A)

Further sub-classifications of temporal formulae are defined as follows. A *literal* is defined as either a proposition (i.e., an element of PROP), or the negation of a proposition. A *State-formula* is either a literal or a boolean combination of other state-formulae.

Future-time formulae (non-strict) are defined as follows

- if A is a state-formula, then A is a future-time formula,
- if A and B are future-time formulae, then $\neg A$, $A \wedge B$, $A \vee B$, $A \Rightarrow B$, $A \mathcal{U} B$, $A \mathcal{W} B$, $\bigcirc A$, $\Diamond A$, and $\Box B$ are all future-time formulae.

Strict past-time formulae are defined as follows

- if A and B are either state-formulae or strict past-time formulae, then $\odot A$, $\bullet B$, $A \mathcal{S} B$, $A \mathcal{Z} B$, $\blacklozenge A$, and $\blacksquare B$ are all strict past-time formulae,
- if A and B are strict past-time formulae, then $\neg A$, $A \wedge B$, $A \vee B$, and $A \Rightarrow B$ are all strict past-time formulae.

2.2 Semantics

The temporal logic used is based on a discrete, linear model, σ, having finite past and infinite future, i.e.

$$\sigma = s_0, s_1, s_2, s_3, \ldots$$

Here, each s_i is called a *state* and is a subset of PROP representing the propositions that are true at the ith moment in

*This work was supported by ESPRIT under Basic Research Action 3096 (SPEC).

time. An interpretation for this logic is defined as a pair (σ, i), where σ is the model and i the index of the state at which the temporal statement is to be interpreted.

A semantics for well-formed temporal formulae is defined as a relation between interpretations and formulae, and is defined inductively as follows, with the (infix) semantic relation being represented by $\models$. The semantics of a proposition is defined by the valuation given to it in the model:

$$(\sigma, i) \models p \quad \text{iff} \quad p \in s_i \qquad \text{for } p \in \text{PROP}.$$

The semantics of the standard propositional connectives are as in classical logic, for example

$$(\sigma, i) \models A \vee B \quad \text{iff} \quad (\sigma, i) \models A \quad \text{or} \quad (\sigma, i) \models B.$$

The semantics of the unary future-time temporal operators is defined as follows

$$(\sigma, i) \models \bigcirc A \quad \text{iff} \quad (\sigma, i+1) \models A$$
$$(\sigma, i) \models \Diamond A \quad \text{iff} \quad \text{there exists a } j \geq i \text{ s.t. } (\sigma, j) \models A$$
$$(\sigma, i) \models \Box A \quad \text{iff} \quad \text{for all } j \geq i \text{ then } (\sigma, j) \models A.$$

The two binary future-time temporal operators are interpreted as follows

$$(\sigma, i) \models A \mathcal{U} B \quad \text{iff} \quad \text{there exists a } k \geq i \text{ s.t. } (\sigma, k) \models B \text{ and for all } i \leq j < k \text{ then } (\sigma, j) \models A$$
$$(\sigma, i) \models A \mathcal{W} B \quad \text{iff} \quad (\sigma, i) \models A \mathcal{U} B \quad \text{or for all } j \geq i \text{ then } (\sigma, j) \models A$$

If past-time temporal formulae are interpreted at a particular state, s_i, then states with indices less than i are *in the past* of the state s_i. The semantics of unary past-time operators are given as follows:

$$(\sigma, i) \models \bullet A \text{ iff } i = 0 \quad \text{or} \quad (\sigma, i-1) \models A$$
$$(\sigma, i) \models \odot A \text{ iff } i > 0 \quad \text{and} \quad (\sigma, i-1) \models A$$
$$(\sigma, i) \models \blacklozenge A \text{ iff there exists a } j \text{ s.t. } 0 \leq j < i \text{ and } (\sigma, j) \models A$$
$$(\sigma, i) \models \blacksquare A \text{ iff for all } j \text{ s.t. } 0 \leq j < i \text{ then } (\sigma, j) \models A.$$

Note that, in contrast to the future-time operators, the $\blacklozenge$ ('sometime in the past') and $\blacksquare$ ('always in the past') operators are interpreted as being *strict*, i.e., the current index is not included in the definition. Also, as there is a unique start state, termed the *beginning of time*, two different last-time operators are used. The difference between $\odot$ and $\bullet$ is that for any formula A, $\odot A$ is false, while $\bullet A$ is true, when interpreted at the beginning of time. In particular, $\bullet$**false** is *only* true when interpreted at the beginning of time; otherwise it is false.

Apart from their strictness, the binary past-time operators are similar to their future-time counterparts; their semantics is defined as follows.

$$(\sigma, i) \models A \mathcal{S} B \text{ iff there exists a } k \text{ s.t. } 0 \leq k < i \text{ and } (\sigma, k) \models B \text{ and for all } j \text{ s.t. } k < j < i \text{ then } (\sigma, j) \models A$$
$$(\sigma, i) \models A \mathcal{Z} B \text{ iff for all } j \text{ such that } 0 \leq j < i \text{ then } (\sigma, j) \models A \quad \text{or} \quad (\sigma, i) \models A \mathcal{S} B$$

The $\Diamond$ and $\Box$ (and their past-time counterparts) can be derived from the $\mathcal{U}$ and $\mathcal{W}$ operators ($\mathcal{S}$ and $\mathcal{Z}$) respectively as follows:

$$\Diamond A \equiv \textbf{true}\, \mathcal{U} A$$
$$\Box A \equiv A \mathcal{W} \textbf{false}$$

As an interpretation consists of a model/state-index pair, we say that a wff is satisfied in a particular model, at a particular state. The terminology is often extended to include a wff being *satisfied in a model*. A formula is satisfied in a model if it is satisfied in that model, at the beginning of time.

3 A New Approach to Temporal Resolution

When developing proof methods for non-classical logics, such as modal and temporal logics, it is natural to investigate extending classical methods into these domains. As the classical resolution rule is of the form

$$\frac{\vdash A \vee p \qquad \vdash B \vee \neg p}{\vdash A \vee B}$$

one might ask whether such an inference rule can be used directly in temporal logics. Unfortunately, the use of such a rule in temporal logics has two main problems:

1. Can $\Box(A \vee p)$ and $\bigcirc(B \vee \neg p)$ be resolved? If so, what is the resolvent?
   This problem is characteristic of those found when resolution is required between complementary literals occurring in different temporal contexts.
2. An obvious temporal resolution rule, extended directly from the classical rule, would be

$$\frac{\vdash A \vee \Box p \qquad \vdash B \vee \Diamond \neg p}{\vdash A \vee B}$$

   However, sometimes the '$\Box$' is hidden, e.g.

$$p \wedge \Box(x \Rightarrow \bigcirc(p \wedge y)) \wedge x \wedge \Box(y \Rightarrow \bigcirc(p \wedge x))$$

   This formula actually implies $\Box p$, but it is difficult to apply the resolution rule directly. Also, the resolution rule given above can not be applied to $\mathcal{U}$ and $\mathcal{W}$ formulae.

In (2), the $\Box p$ must be recognised if temporal resolution is to be applied between this formula and $\Diamond \neg p$. One solution to this is to provide a variety of resolution rules that 'recognise' various formulations of $\Box$. However, as there are a large number of formulae in which '$\Box$-like' formulae can occur, this approach is impractical.

The difficulties in recognising $\Box$ is one of the problems caused by the interaction between the $\bigcirc$ and $\Box$ operators. This interaction involves induction and accounts for many of the problems relating to the production of proof techniques for temporal logics.

The approach outlined in this report is to rewrite arbitrary temporal formulae into *Separated Normal Form* (SNF). The method relies on the fact that, in SNF, the only future-time temporal operator that occurs is the *sometime* operator, '$\Diamond$'. For those literals that appear outside the scope of a $\Diamond$ operator, non-temporal resolution is applied; for those inside the scope of a $\Diamond$ operator, temporal resolution is applied.

The non-temporal resolution rule is only applied between non-temporal formulae that refer to the same state. Thus, the problem of applying classical resolution rules across temporal contexts is avoided. By the definition and derivation of SNF, any two (non-temporal) literals appearing in a formula refer to the same state.

Temporal resolution is applied to formulae containing the '$\Diamond$' operator, such as $\Diamond q$. In this case, the formula can be resolved with a set of formulae, S, which, when satisfied, imply that q will never be satisfied (i.e. $\Box\neg q$). As $\Diamond q$ guarantees that q must be satisfied at some stage in the future, the resolution rule derives the constraint that the formulae in S can never satisfied while $\Diamond q$ is outstanding. Thus, the second problem described above is partially solved in that once a hidden $\Box$-formulae is found it can be resolved with a complementary $\Diamond$-formula. The actual search for the formulae that represent the $\Box$-formula now becomes a search for formulae on which to apply the temporal resolution rule, and this search can be implemented using graph-theoretic techniques (see §8).

The process of applying temporal and non-temporal resolution rules to a set of formulae in SNF eventually terminates. On termination, either **false** has been derived, showing that the formula is unsatisfiable, or the formula is satisfiable. As in classical resolution, simplification and subsumption procedures are applied throughout the process.

4 Separated Normal Form

Gabbay has shown [Gabbay, 1989] that for a linear temporal logic of the form described above, arbitrary formulae can be *separated* into their past-time, present and future-time components. We use this result to develop our normal form, called *Separated Normal Form* (SNF).

A temporal formula in SNF is of the form

$$\Box \bigwedge_{i=1}^{n} (P_i \Rightarrow F_i).$$

Here, each P_i is a *strict* past-time temporal formula and each F_i is a (non-strict) future-time formula. Each of the '$P_i \Rightarrow F_i$' (called *rules*) is further restricted to be of one the following

$$\bullet\,\textbf{false} \Rightarrow \bigvee_{k=1}^{r} l_k \qquad \text{(an } \textit{initial } \Box\text{-rule)}$$

$$\circ \bigwedge_{j=1}^{m} l_j \Rightarrow \bigvee_{k=1}^{r} l_k \qquad \text{(a } \textit{global } \Box\text{-rule)}$$

$$\bullet\,\textbf{false} \Rightarrow \Diamond l \qquad \text{(an } \textit{initial } \Diamond\text{-rule)}$$

$$\circ \bigwedge_{j=1}^{m} l_j \Rightarrow \Diamond l \qquad \text{(a } \textit{global } \Diamond\text{-rule)}$$

where each l_j, l_k, or l is a literal.

Sets of rules in SNF incorporate the following restriction. For each literal, l, there are at most two rules with a single occurrence of l (i.e., not as part of a disjunction) as their future-time component. If there are two such rules, one must be initial, while the other must be global. This ensures that there is, at most, one rule defining the initial value of l and, at most, one rule constraining l after the beginning of time.

5 Rewriting Formulae into SNF

In this section, we show how any arbitrary formula of our temporal logic can be rewritten as an equivalent formula in SNF. Rather than give the full set of transformation rules used to translate a temporal formula in this way, a few selected transformations, together with an overview of the translation process, will be presented. (A more complete description of the transformation rules will be given in the full paper — see also [Fisher and Noel, 1990] for similar rules.)

The transformation rules are given as rewrite rules over sets of formulae. In this section, we only consider the translation of formulae such as

$$\Box \bigwedge_{i=1}^{n} (P_i \Rightarrow F_i),$$

where P_i is a (strict) past-time formula and F_i is a future-time formula, into SNF. The separation that was necessary to reach this form will not be considered here as it is described elsewhere [Gabbay, 1989; Barringer *et al.*, 1989].

The translation of the above form into SNF initially involves removing all past-time temporal operators (apart from one level of last-time operators) from the P_i and all future-time operators (apart from, at most, one '$\Diamond$' operator) from the F_i. After these operators have been removed, the remaining formulae must be rewritten to the correct conjunctive or disjunctive form (as described in §4).

The transformations are carried out in the context of a '$\Box$' operator, i.e., a rewrite rule such as

$$\{A \Rightarrow B\} \longrightarrow \left\{ \begin{array}{ccc} C & \Rightarrow & D \\ E & \Rightarrow & F \end{array} \right\}$$

is to be read as a translation from a formula such as $\Box(A \Rightarrow B)$ to $\Box((C \Rightarrow D) \wedge (E \Rightarrow F))$.

During the transformation process, characterised by the rewrite rules, new propositions may be introduced. These are propositions that have not previously appeared in the formula and are represented by the symbols x, y, z, etc.

5.1 Pushing Negations

Initially, some basic (simplifying) rewrites are applied. The first such set of rewrites removes $\Box$, $\blacklozenge$, and $\blacksquare$ operators and replaces them with their definitions in terms of $\mathcal{W}$, $\mathcal{S}$, and $\mathcal{Z}$, respectively. Next, rewrite rules that 'push' negation operators to the propositions, are applied. This ensures that all negations only appear when applied to propositions, and this translation is analogous to the translation into *Negation Normal Form* used in classical logics.

5.2 Removing Past-time Operators

Next, the removal of past-time operators such as $\mathcal{S}$ and $\mathcal{Z}$, and the removal of multiple last-time operators is considered. Three (simplified) rewrite rules that are used for this purpose are given as follows[1].

$$\{A\,\mathcal{S}\,B \Rightarrow F\} \longrightarrow \left\{ \begin{array}{lcl} \circ(B \vee (A \wedge x)) & \Leftrightarrow & x \\ \bullet\,\textbf{true} & \Rightarrow & \neg x \vee F \end{array} \right\}$$

$$\{A\,\mathcal{Z}\,B \Rightarrow F\} \longrightarrow \left\{ \begin{array}{lcl} \bullet(B \vee (A \wedge y)) & \Leftrightarrow & y \\ \bullet\,\textbf{true} & \Rightarrow & \neg y \vee F \end{array} \right\}$$

$$\{\mathcal{L}_1\mathcal{P}(\mathcal{L}_2 A) \Rightarrow F\} \longrightarrow \left\{ \begin{array}{ccc} \mathcal{L}_2 A & \Rightarrow & z \\ \mathcal{L}_1\mathcal{P}(z) & \Rightarrow & F \end{array} \right\}$$

[1]Here, $A \Leftrightarrow B$ is used as a shorthand for the two rules, $A \Rightarrow B$ and $(\neg A) \Rightarrow (\neg B)$.

In the first two rules, a new proposition is introduced to represent the formula being replaced and its value is linked to the fixpoint representing the formula. This is, effectively, the same process used in QPTL [Wolper, 1982] to represent fixpoint operations using quantifiers [Banieqbal and Barringer, 1989], but, because of the finite nature of the past, only one type of fixpoint is used. In the last rule, $\mathcal{L}_1$ and $\mathcal{L}_2$ represent arbitrary last-time operators.

5.3 Removing Future-time Operators

To remove the future-time operators, $\mathcal{U}$, $\mathcal{W}$, and $\bigcirc$, and to simplify $\Diamond$-formulae so that each $\Diamond$ operator is only applied to a literal, rather than a general temporal formula, the following rewrite rules are applied. Note that the $\mathcal{F}$ used here represents a general future-time temporal context.

$$\{P \Rightarrow \mathcal{F}(A \mathcal{W} B)\} \longrightarrow \left\{\begin{array}{lcl} P & \Rightarrow & \mathcal{F}(B \vee (A \wedge x)) \\ \boldsymbol{\circ} x & \Leftrightarrow & B \vee (A \wedge x) \end{array}\right\}$$

$$\{P \Rightarrow \mathcal{F}(A \mathcal{U} B)\} \longrightarrow \left\{\begin{array}{lcl} P & \Rightarrow & \mathcal{F}(B \vee (A \wedge y)) \\ \boldsymbol{\circ} y & \Leftrightarrow & B \vee (A \wedge y) \\ P & \Rightarrow & \mathcal{F}(\Diamond B) \end{array}\right\}$$

$$\{P \Rightarrow \mathcal{F}(\bigcirc A)\} \longrightarrow \left\{\begin{array}{lcl} \boldsymbol{\circ} z & \Leftrightarrow & A \\ P & \Rightarrow & \mathcal{F}(z) \end{array}\right\}$$

$$\{P \Rightarrow \mathcal{F}(\Diamond A)\} \longrightarrow \left\{\begin{array}{lcl} \bullet \mathbf{true} & \Rightarrow & A \vee \neg z \\ \bullet \mathbf{true} & \Rightarrow & \neg A \vee z \\ P & \Rightarrow & \mathcal{F}(\Diamond z) \end{array}\right\}$$

Again, the technique of introducing a new proposition symbol to represent a particular formula is used. As the $\Box$ operator represents a maximal fixpoint, the $\mathcal{W}$ operator (which is also a maximal fixpoint) can be translated directly into its fixpoint definition. However, a combination of a fixpoint definition and '$\Diamond$' operator must be used to represent the $\mathcal{U}$ operator, which is a minimal fixpoint. The third rule removes all occurrences of $\bigcirc$ operators, and the final transformation rule is used if a $\Diamond$ operator is not applied to a literal.

5.4 Rewriting Non-Temporal Formulae

Having removed all the operators that are not required in SNF, further rewrite rules can be used to translate the remaining rules into the appropriate form. This involves ensuring that all past-time components are either '$\bullet$ **false**' or '$\boldsymbol{\circ}$' applied to a conjunction of literals, and that all future-time components are either a disjunction of literals, or '$\Diamond l$', where l is a literal.

As examples, we give some of the transformation rules used to manipulate last-time formulae into the appropriate form. Notice that *weak* last-time operators ('$\bullet$') are removed except when applied to **false**.

$$\{\bullet A \Rightarrow F\} \longrightarrow \left\{\begin{array}{lcl} \boldsymbol{\circ} A & \Rightarrow & F \\ \bullet \mathbf{false} & \Rightarrow & F \end{array}\right\}$$

$$\left\{\begin{array}{lcl} \boldsymbol{\circ} A & \Rightarrow & F \\ \boldsymbol{\circ} B & \Rightarrow & F \end{array}\right\} \longrightarrow \{\boldsymbol{\circ}(A \vee B) \Rightarrow F\}$$

$$\{\boldsymbol{\circ} A \wedge \bullet B \Rightarrow F\} \longrightarrow \{\boldsymbol{\circ}(A \wedge B) \Rightarrow F\}$$

$$\{\boldsymbol{\circ} A \vee \bullet B \Rightarrow F\} \longrightarrow \{\bullet(A \vee B) \Rightarrow F\}$$

Similar rules are used to transform future-time components into the appropriate disjunctive form.

This concludes our brief overview of the rewrite rules used for translating formulae into SNF. There are, however, some obvious simplifications that can be carried out on the rules constructed using the above rewrites. Discussion of such simplifications will be deferred until §6.2.

Finally, note that any well-formed formula in our logic can be translated to an equivalent set of rules in SNF. As an arbitrary formula in the logic can be separated into past, present, and future components [Gabbay, 1989], the translations described above can each be shown to preserve satisfiability. Though the proof of this theorem is relatively straightforward, it does require the use of quantified propositional temporal logic [Wolper, 1982] as it must be shown that a formula in which a new proposition has been introduced is unsatisfiable if, and only if, the original formula is unsatisfiable.

6 The Resolution Procedure

Given a set of rules in SNF, both non-temporal and temporal resolution rules can be applied. Their application and effect is described in the following sections.

6.1 Non-Temporal Resolution

The non-temporal resolution rule is, essentially, the classical resolution rule and is only applied to $\Box$-rules; $\Diamond$-rules are processed using the temporal resolution rule described in §6.3.

The non-temporal resolution rule used here can again be expressed as a rewrite rule:

$$\left\{\begin{array}{lcl} P & \Rightarrow & B \vee a \\ Q & \Rightarrow & C \vee \neg a \end{array}\right\} \longrightarrow \{\, P \wedge Q \;\Rightarrow\; B \vee C \,\}$$

As with classical resolution, various strategies for the application of this rule can be employed, and simplification rules can be used during, and after, its application.

6.2 Simplification

The basic simplification rules are

$$\{\boldsymbol{\circ} \mathbf{false} \Rightarrow F\} \longrightarrow \{\}$$
$$\{P \Rightarrow \mathbf{true}\} \longrightarrow \{\}$$

The removal of such rules is obvious, since $\boldsymbol{\circ}$ **false** can never be satisfied, and $P \Rightarrow$ **true** is always satisfiable.

Similarly, subsumption rules may be applied. Along with the standard (classical) subsumption, the following rule for subsumption between SNF rules can be applied.

$$\left\{\begin{array}{lcl} P & \Rightarrow & F \\ Q & \Rightarrow & G \end{array}\right\} \xrightarrow{\vdash P \Rightarrow Q,\, \vdash G \Rightarrow F} \{Q \Rightarrow G\}$$

This rewrite rule can only be applied if the conditions, $\vdash P \Rightarrow Q$ and $\vdash G \Rightarrow F$ are satisfied.

If, after simplification, a formula of the form

$$\boldsymbol{\circ} R \Rightarrow \mathbf{false}$$

has been derived, then the following rewrite rule can be invoked.

$$\{\boldsymbol{\circ} R \Rightarrow \mathbf{false}\} \longrightarrow \{\bullet \mathbf{true} \Rightarrow \neg R\}$$

If this rule is used, the new constraint must be rewritten into SNF and non-temporal resolution re-applied. The process is repeated until either all $\Box$-rules containing complementary literals have been processed, or one of the following rules has been derived.

$$\begin{array}{lrcl} a) & \bullet\,\textbf{false} & \Rightarrow & \textbf{false} \\ b) & \bullet\,\textbf{true} & \Rightarrow & \textbf{false} \\ c) & \bigcirc\,\textbf{true} & \Rightarrow & \textbf{false} \end{array}$$

If any of these formulae occur, then the original formula is unsatisfiable and the resolution process terminates.

6.3 Temporal Resolution

If the non-temporal resolution procedure described in §6.1 terminates, without **false** having been derived, temporal resolution can be applied.

Before applying temporal resolution, the following rewrite rule is applied to all global $\Box$-rules. (Note that this transformation is not strictly necessary, but simplifies the presentation of the temporal resolution rule.)

$$\left\{ \begin{array}{lcl} \bigcirc P & \Rightarrow & F \\ \bigcirc Q & \Rightarrow & G \end{array} \right\} \longrightarrow \{\bigcirc(P \wedge Q) \Rightarrow (F \wedge G)\} \qquad (\dagger)$$

The temporal resolution rule applies to one $\Diamond$-rule, such as $P \Rightarrow \Diamond\neg l$ and a set of global $\Box$-rules. Here, if P is satisfied, then the rule is satisfiable unless the set of $\Box$-rules force l to always be true. Thus, our approach is to, for every such set of rules, ensure that these, and P, are never satisfied at the same time.

The temporal resolution rule is characterised as follows.

$$\left\{ \begin{array}{lcl} \bigcirc A_0 & \Rightarrow & B_0 \\ \ldots & & \ldots \\ \bigcirc A_n & \Rightarrow & B_n \\ \mathcal{L}P & \Rightarrow & \Diamond\neg l \end{array} \right\}$$

$$\begin{array}{lr} \text{for all } 0 \le i \le n.\ \vdash B_i \Rightarrow l & \text{and} \\ \vdash B_i \Rightarrow \bigvee_{j=0}^{n} A_j & \text{and} \\ \vdash (A_i \wedge l) \Rightarrow \bigvee_{k=0}^{n} B_k & \end{array}$$

$$\downarrow$$

$$\left\{ \begin{array}{lcl} \bullet\,\textbf{true} & \Rightarrow & \neg P \vee \bigwedge_{i=0}^{n} \neg A_i \\ \mathcal{L}P & \Rightarrow & (\bigwedge_{i=0}^{n} \neg A_i)\, \mathcal{W} \neg l \end{array} \right\}$$

A set of rules that, together, imply that l is always true, is termed a *loop* in l. The side conditions on the resolution rule ensure that the the set of rules $\{ \bigcirc A_i \Rightarrow B_i \mid 1 \le i \le n\}$ form a loop in l. Note that even this rule is a simplification — the full rule is quite complex and does not require the application of rewrite ($\dagger$) beforehand.

If a loop in l can be found, and there is a rule such as $\mathcal{L}P \Rightarrow \Diamond\neg l$, then the following new rules are added:

1. $\bullet\,\textbf{true} \Rightarrow \neg P \vee \bigwedge_{i=0}^{n} \neg A_i$
   This rule expresses the constraint that none of the conditions for entering a loop in l must be allowed to occur at the same time as P occurs.
2. $\mathcal{L}P \Rightarrow (\bigwedge_{i=0}^{n} \neg A_i)\, \mathcal{W} \neg l$
   This rule expresses the constraint that once P has occurred, none of the conditions for entering a loop must be allowed to occur until the eventuality initiated by P has been satisfied.

6.3.1 Example

As an example, consider the set of rules representing the conjunction of the formulae described earlier, i.e.

$$p \wedge \Box(x \Rightarrow \bigcirc(p \wedge y)) \wedge x \wedge \Box(y \Rightarrow \bigcirc(p \wedge x))$$

and $\Diamond\neg p$. Once the formulae have been rewritten into SNF and non-temporal resolution has been attempted (none occurs), the set of rules is as follows.

$$\begin{array}{rlcl} 1. & \bullet\,\textbf{false} & \Rightarrow & x \\ 2. & \bullet\,\textbf{false} & \Rightarrow & p \\ 3. & \bullet\,\textbf{false} & \Rightarrow & \Diamond\neg p \\ 4. & \bigcirc x & \Rightarrow & p \wedge y \\ 5. & \bigcirc y & \Rightarrow & p \wedge x \end{array}$$

Temporal resolution can be applied to rules 3, 4, and 5, as rules 4 and 5 form a loop in p. This generates the new constraint

$$\bullet\,\textbf{false} \Rightarrow (\neg x \wedge \neg y)\, \mathcal{W} \neg p$$

which is rewritten in SNF as:

$$\begin{array}{rlcl} 6. & \bullet\,\textbf{false} & \Rightarrow & \neg p \vee \neg x \\ 7. & \bullet\,\textbf{false} & \Rightarrow & \neg p \vee \neg y \\ 8. & \bullet\,\textbf{false} & \Rightarrow & \neg p \vee z \\ 9. & \bigcirc z & \Rightarrow & \neg p \vee \neg x \\ 10. & \bigcirc z & \Rightarrow & \neg p \vee \neg y \\ 11. & \bigcirc z & \Rightarrow & \neg p \vee z \end{array}$$

Applying non-temporal resolution on rules 6, 1, and 2, generates a contradiction.

7 Correctness of the Resolution Procedure

The soundness, completeness and termination of the resolution procedure have been established. Proofs will be given in the full paper.

8 Implementation

Though the temporal resolution rule is complete, its use introduces various practical problems. A naive search of all the possible subsets of rules that match the preconditions of the resolution rule would be prohibitively expensive, consequently we have developed a procedure for finding loops in a particular literal within sets of rules. Lack of space prevents us from giving a full exposition of the approach, but we will give a brief outline below.

For every rule of the form $P \Rightarrow \Diamond\neg l$, all rules that imply l are collected together. This set of rules is then represented directly as an AND/OR graph, with each rule representing a set of edges, or as a standard state-graph. In either case, loops in l correspond to terminal strongly connected components (SCCs) of the graph structure. These can be found through the use of a suitable version of Tarjan's algorithm. Using either representation, the complexity of the operation is exponential in the number of rules in the original set.

Once all the terminal SCCs of the graph have been found, temporal resolution can be applied to all the rules in these SCCs, with any new rules generated are added to the original set of rules. If no terminal SCC is found, the procedure moves on to processing the next $\Diamond$-rule.

9 Related Work

A great variety of resolution-based proof methods for modal logics have been developed [del Cerro, 1984; Gabbay, 1987; Ohlbach, 1988; Enjalbert and del Cerro, 1989], yet few of these can be used for temporal logics that incorporate the '*next*' operator. Several resolution methods specific to temporal logics hove been developed. Venkatesh, [Venkatesh, 1986], develops a resolution method for a future-time fragment of propositional temporal logic using customised resolution and unwinding rules. Sakuragawa, [Sakuragawa, 1986] uses transformations similar to those described in this report to generate a normal form for temporal formulae, but does not develop specific proof rules. In [Abadi and Manna, 1990], a resolution method, based on non-clausal resolution, is developed and applied to both propositional and first-order temporal logics.

10 Further Work

A prototype system based on the approach described in this report has been implemented and initial results are encouraging. Investigations into heuristics for the application of both temporal and non-temporal resolution rules are under way, as are investigations into alternate graph-theoretic techniques for implementing temporal resolution.

We can extend the method described in this report to first-order temporal logics that have unvarying domains and that satisfy the separation property. This is current work and will form part of a future report. One point to note is that not all temporal logics allow separation, though most linear temporal logics do [Gabbay, 1989].

Finally, the resolution method described in this paper can be used as part of a *backward-chaining* execution mechanism that complements the forward-chaining that is standard in METATEM, a framework for executable temporal logics [Barringer *et al.*, 1989].

References

[Abadi and Manna, 1990] M. Abadi and Z. Manna. Non-clausal Deduction in First-Order Temporal Logic. *ACM Journal*, 37(2):279–317, April 1990.

[Banieqbal and Barringer, 1989] B. Banieqbal and H. Barringer. Temporal Logic with Fixed Points. In *Proceedings of the Colloquium on Temporal Logic and Specification (LNCS Vol. 398)*, pages 62–74, Altrincham, U.K., 1989. Springer-Verlag.

[Barringer *et al.*, 1989] H. Barringer, M. Fisher, D. Gabbay, G. Gough, and R. Owens. METATEM: A Framework for Programming in Temporal Logic. In *REX Workshop on Stepwise Refinement of Distributed Systems: Models, Formalisms, Correctness (LNCS Volume 430)*, pages 94–129, Mook, Netherlands, June 1989. Springer Verlag.

[del Cerro, 1984] Luis Fariñas del Cerro. Resolution Modal Logics. In *Proceedings of Advanced NATO Study Institute on Logics and Models for Verification and Specification of Concurrent Systems*, pages 46–78, La Colle-sur-Loup, France, October 1984.

[Enjalbert and del Cerro, 1989] P. Enjalbert and L. Farinas del Cerro. Modal Resolution in Clausal Form. *Theoretical Computer Science*, 65:1–33, 1989.

[Fisher and Noel, 1990] Michael D. Fisher and Philippe A. Noel. Transformation Rules for METATEM Programs. METATEM project report, Department of Computer Science, University of Manchester, May 1990. (Draft).

[Gabbay, 1987] D. Gabbay. Modal and Temporal Logic Programming. In A. Galton, editor, *Temporal Logics and their Applications*, pages 121–168. Academic Press, 1987.

[Gabbay, 1989] D. Gabbay. Declarative Past and Imperative Future: Executable Temporal Logic for Interactive Systems. In B. Banieqbal, H. Barringer, and A. Pnueli, editors, *Proceedings of Colloquium on Temporal Logic in Specification (LNCS Volume 398)*, pages 402–450, Altrincham, U.K., 1989. Springer-Verlag.

[Ohlbach, 1988] Hans-Jürgen Ohlbach. A Resolution Calculus for Modal Logics. *Lecture Notes in Computer Science*, 310:500–516, May 1988.

[Sakuragawa, 1986] T. Sakuragawa. Temporal Prolog. Technical report, Research Institute for Mathematical Sciences, Kyoto University, 1986. to appear in Computer Software.

[Vardi and Wolper, 1986] Moshe Y. Vardi and Pierre Wolper. Automata-theoretic Techniques for Modal Logics of Programs. *Journal of Computer and System Sciences*, 32(2):183–219, April 1986.

[Venkatesh, 1986] G. Venkatesh. A Decision Method for Temporal Logic based on Resolution. *Lecture Notes in Computer Science*, 206:272–289, 1986.

[Wolper, 1982] P. Wolper. *Synthesis of Communicating Processes from Temporal Logic Specifications.* PhD thesis, Stanford University, 1982.

[Wolper, 1985] Pierre Wolper. The Tableau Method for Temporal Logic: An overview. *Logique et Analyse*, 110–111:119–136, June-Sept 1985.

FORMALIZING AND USING PERSISTENCY

Thomas Guckenbiehl
Fraunhofer-Institute of Information and Data Processing (IITB)
Fraunhoferstr. 1
D-7500 Karlsruhe
FRG
guc@iitb.fhg.de

Abstract

In many formalizations of a changing world things do not change all the time but are persistent thoughout a time interval. Often this persistency is represented by facts refering to intervals int which are still valid if int is replaced by any subinterval int'. Approaches like episode propagation or Penberthy's temporal unification try to employ this property for efficient reasoning. However these approaches lack formality. In this paper their way of reasoning about persistency is reconstructed as inference rules that combine appropriate time-boxes with standard resolution. In many cases Bürckert's Constrained Resolution may be used. More complex examples may be handled by a new inference rule, called Persistency Resolution. An analysis of this rule leads to a more general notion of persistency.

1 Introduction

During the last decade temporal reasoning has turned out to be crucial for intelligent systems acting in the real world. This resulted in a lot of work on how to represent temporal knowledge and how to reason with it. With respect to reasoning one may distinguish at least four levels on which work has been done:

- *Reasoning about the temporal structure* is concerned with the handling of constraints between time points or intervals by so called *time-boxes* (e. g. [Allen, 1983; van Beek, 1989]).
- *Temporal Data Base Management* explores efficient techniques for storage of facts like "She was at home between 2 and 4 o'clock" and answering questions like "Was she at home between 3 and 3.30?" (e. g. [Kahn and Gorry, 1977]; Dean and McDermott, 1987]).
- *Temporal Elaboration* tries to infer monotonically new facts by applying general knowledge about a domain to facts from a temporal data base (e. g. [Decker 88]).
- *Temporal Extension* uses additional heuristics like the Closed World Assumption or the Persistency-by-default Assumption to infer facts that are not implied monotonically by the knowledge base (e. g. [Dean and McDermott, 1987; Shoham, 1987], traditional discrete-event simulation).

This paper is concerned with temporal elaboration of statements that incorporate something like $\mathrm{TRUE}(\Phi, \mathrm{int})$ to express that some property Φ holds throughout some time interval int. I will use $\mathrm{TRUE}(\Phi, t_0)$, if int is the single element set $\{t_0\}$. The semantics of such *facts*, which have been popular in AI since the work of McDermott [1982] and Allen [1983], has been clarified e. g. by [Galton, 1990]. To distinguish them from general facts in a knowledge base they will be called *persistence facts* in the sequel.

Although this representation is adequate and intuitive in many domains, it cannot be handled efficiently by standard inference procedures. The combination of a time-box and resolution is more adequate, as demonstrated in the next section.

2 Problems with Persistent Facts

Consider e. g. the following rule from the description of an AND-gate:

(1) $\mathrm{TRUE}(\mathrm{in}_1 = 1, T) \land \mathrm{TRUE}(\mathrm{in}_2 = 1, T) \Rightarrow \mathrm{TRUE}(\mathrm{out} = 1, T)$

If we know the persistence facts

(2) $\mathrm{TRUE}(\mathrm{in}_1 = 1, [0, 100])$

(3) $\mathrm{TRUE}(\mathrm{in}_2 = 1, [50, 200])$

about the inputs, we would like to infer

(4) $\mathrm{TRUE}(\mathrm{out} = 1, [50, 100])$.

Hyperresolution using standard unification does not work, since the matchers $\{T \leftarrow [0, 100]\}$ and $\{T \leftarrow [50, 200]\}$ arising from matching the two conditions to (2) and (3) resp. are inconsistent.

A first order approach might handle the problem representing persistency by some axiom

(PA) $\mathrm{int}' \subseteq \mathrm{int} \land \mathrm{TRUE}(\Phi, \mathrm{int}) \Rightarrow \mathrm{TRUE}(\Phi, \mathrm{int}')$.

Then knowledge about set-inclusion may be used to apply this axiom to (2) and (3), infering TRUE(in_1 = 1, [50, 100]) and TRUE(in_2=1, [50, 100]). Finally the reasoning system may apply (1) to these new facts to infer (4). But how does it get to know that int' in (PA) should be instantiated to [50, 100] and not to some other interval? In particular, there is an infinite set of possible instantiations which satisfy both conditions of (1).

It is not clear to us if Time Map Management System like that of Dean can handle such problems. Following the examples given in [Dean and McDermott, 1987], Dean's TMM seems to proceed as follows: while matching the first condition to (2), it unifies T with [0, 100]. Then it looks for a fact that satisfies the second condition throughout this interval. Hence it would not be able to use (3) and infer (4).

There have been more informal approaches capable to do the desired reasoning, e. g. Episode Propagation (c. f. [Williams, 1986; Decker, 1988]) and Temporal Unification (c. f. [Penberthy, 1987]).

An episode propagator is a constraint propagator where the values of constraint variables are interpreted as sets of episodes from the history of an attribute. An attribute α is a function on time points, and an episode may be represented as a persistence fact TRUE(α = V, int). Single episodes are propagated between histories and constraints which, like (1), relate different episode patterns.

[Penberthy, 1987] proposed *Temporal Unification*, a special purpose unification procedure for atoms containing intervals as arguments. If the atom is persistent with respect to this argument, Penberthy calls it a fact interval and the atom a fact. Otherwise it is called an event interval and the atom an event. Temporal Unification of intervals int_1 and int_2 yields their intersection if both are fact intervals or the same event interval. If only one of them, say int_1, is a fact interval and $int_2 \subseteq int_1$, the unifier is int_2. In all other cases the intervals are ununifiable.

This paper extracts the key ideas behind these ad hoc approaches and casts them into formal inference rules that combine standard resolution with appropriate constraint reasoners. For instance Constrained Resolution [Bürckert, 1990] may be used in the first example. More complex examples may be handled by a new inference rule called Persistency Resolution. A closer look at this rule reveals that it is not restricted to persistence facts but may also be used with statements about processes like "The car is moving" and even nontemporal statements like "It rained throughout the country".

After giving some notation, section 4 presents a special formalization of Persistence facts, on which sections 5 and 6 base Constrained Resolution and Persistency Resolution. A discussion of a more general notion of persistency closes the paper.

3 Notation

In contrast to tense logical languages (c. f. [Rescher and Urquhart, 1971]), which contain modal operators like 'G' or 'H', variable and constant symbols will be used to denote time-points and intervals as well as functions and relations on them explicitly. Only such interpretations are allowed that give these symbols their natural extension. As syntactical variables for expressions of our language 'trm' represents an arbitrary term, symbols starting with capital letters denote variables, while constants start with lower case letters. In particular 'T' denotes a time-point, 'X' may denote an interval or a time-point, 't' symbolizes a time-point constant and 'int' an interval constant. Small greek letters ξ_i are used for atoms with a nontemporal topsymbol and large greek letters for arbitrary formulae. Small greek letters σ represent substitutions. expr[$X_1, \ldots, X_n$] symbolizes that expr contains at most the pairwise different temporal variables $X_1, \ldots, X_n$ (though there may be other nontemporal ones). All variables are assumed to be universally quantified, and renaming of variables will be avoided if possible.

4 Qualified Formulae

A closer look at the example from section 2 reveals that standard inference techniques are inefficient because standard unification is unable to process the information implicit in statements TRUE(Φ, int): that Φ holds in all time points T contained in int and therefore TRUE(Φ, int') is also true for every subinterval int' of int. Matching the first condition of (1) to (2) constrains the valid assignments to T to elements of [0, 100], while matching the second condition to (3) further constrains them to elements of [50, 200]. Our informal reasoning joins both constraints to derive (4).

Therefore I propose to make the information implicit in TRUE(Φ', trm) explicit by formalizing this expression as

(5) $\forall T: (T \in trm \Rightarrow \Phi[T])$, if trm denotes an interval

(6) $\{T \leftarrow trm\}\ \Phi[T]$, if trm denotes a time point

where T is a new variable and Φ modifies Φ' to mirror its dependency on time (e. g. by additional temporal arguments).

For instance we may formalize our example from section 2 as

(1') $\neg(in_1(T)=1) \lor \neg(in_2(T)=1) \lor (out(T)=1)$

(2') $T' \in [0, 100] \Rightarrow in_1(T')=1.$

(3') $T' \in [50, 200] \Rightarrow in_2(T')=1.$

More generally, trm may be characterized as the solution-set of a constraint $\Psi_C[T]$, e. g. $(T \in int_1 \wedge T \in int_2)$ or $(T = lb(int))$ where lb denotes the greatest lower bound. Furthermore we are not restricted to a single temporal variable. Hence (5) is an instance of

(7) $\Psi_C[X_1, \ldots, X_n] \quad \Rightarrow \quad \Phi[X_1, \ldots, X_m]$, with $m \leq n$.

In the sequel a formula that contains the TRUE-operator will be called a *persistence formula*. Furthermore a formula like (7) will be called a *qualified formula* (or *q-formula*) with *qualification* Ψ_C and *kernel* Φ. A *negative q-formula* is a formula $\neg(\Psi_C \Rightarrow \Phi)$ and a *qualified literal* (or *q-literal*) is either a positive or a negative q-formula. If the kernel is an atom we talk about *qualified atoms* (or *q-atoms*). If it does not contain any nontemporal variables, it will be called a *qualified fact* or *q-fact*.

Although in modified form, qualified facts have been around in AI for quite some time. For instance the propositions in an ATMS (c. f. [deKleer, 1986]) may be viewed as qualified by their label, i. e. a disjunction of sets of assumptions. Another example are clauses of Constraint Logic Programs (c. f. [Jaffar and Lassez, 1986]). Recently they have been generalized by [Bürckert, 1990] in the form of Constrained Clauses, which correspond to positive q-formulae.

5 Constrained Resolution

Seemingly, previous work has only dealt with positive q-formulae $\Psi_C \Rightarrow \Phi$. One reason is probably that such formulae can be rewritten as $\neg\Psi_C \vee \Phi$. This expression may be regarded as a single clause, if Φ is in clause-form and inference is done using combinations of special purpose reasoners for the qualification and general techniques for the kernel. [Hrycej, 1988] for instance integrates a time box for Allen's interval calculus with Prolog along these lines. [Bürckert, 1990] has generalized such combinations by an inference rule called *Constrained Resolution*:

(CR)
$$\begin{array}{lcl} \Psi_C & \Rightarrow & [\ \xi \quad \vee \ \Phi\ ] \\ \Psi_C' & \Rightarrow & [\neg \xi' \ \vee \ \Phi'\ ] \end{array}$$

if $\sigma(\Psi_C \wedge \Psi_C' \wedge trm_1 = trm_1' \wedge \ldots \wedge trm_n = trm_n')$ is satisfiable:

$$\sigma(\Psi_C \wedge \Psi_C' \wedge trm_1 = trm_1' \wedge \ldots \wedge trm_n = trm_n') \Rightarrow \sigma[\Phi \vee \Phi'],$$

where σ is the most general unifier of ξ and ξ' and trm_i, trm_i' are corresponding temporal terms in ξ and ξ'.

Bürckert proves that, given some appropriate constraint theory, this rule is sound and complete.

One easily checks that applying this rule to (1'), (2') and (3') yields

(4') $\quad (T \in [0, 100]) \wedge \quad (T \in [50, 200]) \quad \Rightarrow out(T) = 1$.

Final simplification of the qualification by the constraint reasoner results in the desired q-fact

(4'') $\quad (T \in [50, 100]) \quad \Rightarrow \quad out(T) = 1$

In many situations Constrained Resolution is a good formalization of reasoning about persistency. For instance if we include some delay of 30 ns into our model of the AND-gate, replacing (1) by

(8) $\quad TRUE(in_1 = 1, T) \wedge TRUE(in_2 = 1, T) \Rightarrow TRUE(out = 1, T+30)$,

Constrained Resolution still works.

However it fails for persistence formulae whose clause-form contains some negated persistence atom $\neg TRUE(\Phi, int)$. Consider e. g. the set-up times for data inputs to a flip/flop. This is the minimal time span prior to a clock pulse for which an input has to stay constant. It prevents spurious changes of the inputs during a clock pulse from influencing the output. Formulating this for a D-flip/flop with 200 ns set-up time and 50 ns delay yields

(9) $\quad TRUE(d = V, [T-200, T]) \wedge TRUE(pulse = occuring, T) \Rightarrow TRUE(q = V, T+50)$

with the clause-form

(9') $\quad \neg TRUE(d = V, [T-200, T]) \vee \neg TRUE(pulse = occuring, T) \vee TRUE(q = V, T+50)$.

Considering this rule and the facts

(10) $\quad TRUE(d = 0, [0, 400])$

(11) $\quad TRUE(pulse = occuring, 100)$

(12) $\quad TRUE(pulse = occuring, 300)$

we should be able to derive that the rule is not applicable to (10) and (11) but to (10) and (12), yielding

(13) $\quad TRUE(q = 0, 350)$.

The problems come in as we try to change these formulas into constrained clauses by introducing explicit qualifications:

(9'') $\quad \neg\ \forall T_1 : (T_1 \in [T-200, T] \Rightarrow d(T_1) = V) \vee \neg(pulse(T) = occuring) \vee q(T+50) = V$

(10') $\quad T' \in [0, 400] \Rightarrow d(T') = 0$

(11') $\quad pulse(100) = occuring$

(12') $\quad pulse(300) = occuring$.

Obviously, the first disjunct of (9''), which resulted from the first negated persistence literal in (9'), corresponds to two clauses. To apply Constrained Resolution, we have to introduce the new skolem-function f and transform (9'') into clause-form. This results in two constrained clauses

(9''a) $\quad f(T, V) \in [T-200, T] \vee \neg(pulse(T) = occuring) \vee q(T+50) = V$

(9''b) $\neg (d(f(T,V))=V)$
$\lor \quad \neg (\text{pulse}(T)=\text{occuring}) \quad \lor \quad q(T+50)=V.$

Applying (CR) to (9''b) and (10') yields

(14) $f(T,0) \in [0,400]$
$\Rightarrow [\neg (\text{pulse}(T)=\text{occuring}) \quad \lor \quad q(T+50)=0].$

Further application of (CR) to (14) and (12') gives after simplification by the time-box:

(15) $f(300,0) \in [0,400] \quad \Rightarrow \quad [q(350)=0].$

On the other hand applying (CR) to (9''a) and (12') results in

(16) $\neg (f(300,V) \in [100,300]) \Rightarrow \quad [q(350)=V].$

To derive $q(350)=0$, as we intuitively did, we have to combine the qualifications of (15) and the instance of (16) under $\{V \leftarrow 0\}$ and recognize that every interpretation of $f(300,0)$ satisfies at least one of them. However this is beyond the scope of Constrained Resolution.

To handle such examples we have to look for another inference rule.

6 Qualified Resolution and Persistency Resolution

The problem in applying (CR) to our last example arises because the splitting of (9'') results in spreading the constraints relevant to our informal reasoning over the two clauses (15) and (16). The reason for splitting (9'') was that Constrained Resolution resolves standard literals in constrained clauses, but cannot deal with negative qualified literals. So the basic idea for a more suited inference rule is to allow for the resolution of such negative q-literals to positive ones. This leads to *Qualified Resolution*:

$$\textbf{(QR)} \quad \neg \; (\Psi_C \Rightarrow \xi) \quad \lor \quad \Phi$$
$$(\Psi_C' \Rightarrow \xi')$$

---

if $\neg\sigma[(\Psi_C \Rightarrow \Psi_C') \land trm_1=trm_1' \land \ldots \land trm_n=trm_n']$ is satisfiable:

$$\sigma[(\Psi_C \Rightarrow \Psi_C') \land trm_1=trm_1' \land \ldots \land trm_n=trm_n'] \Rightarrow \sigma\Phi,$$

where σ is a most general unifier of ξ and ξ' and trm_i, trm_i' are the corresponding temporal terms of ξ and ξ', resp. (A correctness proof for this inference rule may be found in [Guckenbiehl, 1990].)

Since the residuum constraint does neither correspond to a single clause nor to a q-literal, it cannot be handled by standard or Qualified Resolution. Hence like Constrained Resolution this inference rule requires an additional constraint reasoner. I do not know yet under which conditions provision of a (semi-) decision algorithm for constraints guarantees (refutation-) completeness of the whole inference rule.

Persistency Resolution

Even if constraint-satisfiability is decidable, it will in general be computationally expensive, since the residuum constraint is not atomic and therefore the constraint resulting from multiple applications of (QR) is not a single clause. Fortunately there is a specialization of Qualified Resolution, which I call *Persistency Resolution*, that yields such a residuum. In the first place it requires that q-literals have the form

$$[T_1 \in trm[X_1,\ldots,X_n] \land \ldots \land T_m \in trm[X_1,\ldots,X_n] \Rightarrow \xi[T_1,\ldots,T_m],$$

where $T_1,\ldots,T_m$ do not appear outside the q-literal. We may restrict the discussion to $m=1$, since the generalization to $m>1$ is just a combination of the methods explored in the sequel. Then we have:

$$\textbf{(PR)} \quad \neg\,(T_1 \in trm[X_1,\ldots,X_n] \quad \Rightarrow \quad \xi[T_1]) \quad \lor \; \Phi[X_1,\ldots,X_n]$$
$$(T_1' \in trm' \quad \Rightarrow \quad \xi'[T_1'])$$

---

if $\sigma[(trm[X_1,\ldots,X_n] \subseteq trm') \land trm_1=trm_1' \land \ldots \land trm_n=trm_n']$ is satisfiable:

$$\sigma[(trm[X_1,\ldots,X_n] \subseteq trm') \land trm_1=trm_1' \land \ldots \land trm_n=trm_n'] \Rightarrow \sigma\Phi[X_1,\ldots,X_n],$$

where σ is a most general unifier of ξ and ξ' which unifies T_1 and T_1', and trm_i, trm_i' are the corresponding temporal terms of ξ and ξ', resp. The simple correctness proof is given in [Guckenbiehl, 1990], but as with the general case I have no completeness results.

Persistency Resolution in the examples

Since (1'), (2') and (3') from our first example may be transformed into the appropriate form, we may use Persistency Resolution instead of Constrained Resolution to derive (4). In the second example we use (PR) to resolve the first q-literal of (9'') and (10'):

(17) $\neg([T-200,T] \subseteq [0,400])$
$\lor \quad \neg((T_2 \in \{T\}) \quad \Rightarrow \quad (\text{pulse}(T_2)=\text{occuring}))$
$\lor \quad ((T_3 \in \{T+50\}) \quad \Rightarrow \quad q(T_3)=0)$

Further application of (PR) to (17) and (11') together with syntactic transformation gives

(18) $[([T-200,T] \subseteq [0,400]) \land (\{T\} \subseteq \{100\}) \land (T_3 \in \{T+50\})]$
$\Rightarrow q(T_3)=0,$

while application to (17) and (12') results in

(19) $[([T-200,T] \subseteq [0,400]) \land (\{T\} \subseteq \{300\})$
$\land \quad (T_3 \in \{T+50\})] \quad \Rightarrow \quad q(T_3)=0.$

As in Constraint Logical Programming appropriate constraint handlers may now simplify the qualifications to false and $(T_3 = 350)$, resp.

7 Generalizing Persistency

Up to now propositions were related to time points which had been collected into intervals. However consider the following sentences:

- "The car is moving all the time."

(Notice that a predicate like moving basically refers to intervals instead of time-points and hence corresponds to a process instead of a persistence fact. The reason is that we cannot decide a proposition like "The car is moving" by observation of the world at a single time point, e. g. represented by a photography. We have to look at a film, that represents the world during a time interval. We may however define predicates like in-a-move refering to time points and derive $\text{in-a-move}(car, t_0)$ from $\text{moving}(car, int)$ and $t_0 \in int$.)

- "We always go swimming on mondays." (such propositions have been studied by [Ladkin, 1986])
- "It rains throughout the country".
- "Birds are studied by ornithologists.".

By analyzing these examples and comparing them to a persistence fact like $\mathrm{TRUE}(\Phi, int)$, we may recognize the following similarities:

Firstly, all of them talk about collections of entities: e. g. intervals (viewed as sets of time-points or collection of their subintervals), sets of days, areas (viewed as sets of their subareas), classes (viewed as sets of their subclasses).

Secondly, all propositions remain true, if this collection is replaced by a subcollection: if we always go swimming on mondays, we always go swimming on every first monday of a month; if it rains throughout the country, it also rains throughout the north or south of the country; if ornithologists study birds, they also study robins (although perhaps not every particular one).

And finally, if the propositions are true for two collections, then they are also true for their union.

Notice that we only talked about the concept of membership in the collection, but not about any other properties, like order, density or whatever. And looking at (PR) we see that Persistency Resolution as well only requires the concepts membership and subset. It is the time box that needs additional knowledge about the structure of time to decide on the satisfiability of constraints. Hence we may use (PR) for reasoning about areas in space, about classes or about other kinds of collections, if we can provide for an appropriate constraint reasoner. This leads to the following definitions:

A *persistency structure* $\mathbf{S}$ is a triple ((POS ∪ COL), PFUNC, ({⊆, ∈} ∪ PREL)), with

- POS is a set of objects, called **positions**;
- COL is a set of objects, called **collections**, containing elements $c_\varnothing$ (the empty collection) and c_{POS} (the collection of all positions).
- PFUNC is a set of n-ary functions on (POS ∪ COL);
- '∈' is a relation on POS x COL with $p \in c_{POS}$ for all positions p and $p \in c_\varnothing$ for no position p.
- '⊆' is the subset relation on POS x POS, induced by '∈'.
- PREL is a set of n-ary relations on (POS ∪ COL);

Notice that we do not require POS and COL to be disjoint. Hence every interval may be used as a collection of its subintervals.

As with time we include the symbols of $\mathbf{S}$ into our logical language, together with Variable symbols C for collections and P for positions. Therefore we may define *Generalized Persistency Resolution* as

$$\textbf{(GPR)}\quad \neg (P_1 \in trm[X_1, \ldots, X_n] \Rightarrow \xi[P_1]) \vee \Phi[X_1, \ldots, X_n]$$
$$(P_1' \in trm' \Rightarrow \xi'[P_1'])$$

---

if $[(trm[X_1, \ldots, X_n] \subseteq trm') \wedge trm_1 = trm_1' \wedge \ldots \wedge trm_n = trm_n']$ is satisfiable:

$$\sigma[(trm[X_1, \ldots, X_n] \subseteq trm') \wedge trm_1 = trm_1' \wedge \ldots \wedge trm_n = trm_n'] \Rightarrow \sigma\Phi[X_1, \ldots, X_n],$$

where σ is a most general unifier of ξ and ξ' which unifies P_1 and P_1', provided that P_1 does not appear in $\Phi[X_1, \ldots, X_n]$, and trm_i, trm_i' are those corresponding terms of ξ and ξ', resp., that are interpreted over $\mathbf{S}$.

To decide on the satisfiability of the resolution residuum, (GPR) needs special inference procedures that can handle constraints on the particular persistency structure.

8 Conclusion

Reasoning with persistence facts like $\mathrm{TRUE}(\Phi, int)$ is crucial for temporal reasoning, but difficult for standard first order inference procedures. The problem is that they do not account for the implicit information about subintervals of int. Williams' episode propagation and Penberthy's Temporal unification attempt to implement our intuitive style of reasoning about persistency. They use special inference procedures whose integration with more general techniques appears rather ad hoc. To analyze the prerequisites and potential of these approaches a more formal discussion of how to combine time-boxes with general resolution is necessary.

It turned out that for many examples of informal reasoning about persistency Bürckert's Constrained Resolution is an adequate model. However if some formula contains multiple literals $\mathrm{TRUE}(\Phi, trm)$, of which at least one is negative and refers to an interval, Constrained Resolution breaks down. Such formulae can be resolved by a new inference rule, called Persistency Resolution. Analysis of the basic elements of this rule finally led to a more general notion of persistency that is not restricted to time-points and intervals.

[Guckenbiehl, 1990] characterizes the functionality of a constraint reasoner which enables the integration of Persistency Resolution into a forward chaining production system. Furthermore, it describes the implementation of this functionality for certain forms of constraints on points and open, closed and halfopen intervals on the reals. This constraint-reasoner has been used in the Extended Episode Propagator (c. f. [Guckenbiehl, 1991]).

I am not aware of any other formal treatment of how to combine temporal and general inference techniques for efficient elaboration of persistence facts, although a lot is currently done on the more ambitious task of using additional assumptions like persistency-by-default or Closed-world. Furthermore ther is some work on exploiting theory unification for temporal reasoning (e. g. [Ohlbach, 1989] that may be important for reasoning with persistence facts.

Persistency Resolution is just a first step towards formal reasoning with persistence facts, and as always much remains to be done. On the formal level the properties of Qualification and Persistency Resolution, particularly completeness, have to be elaborated in more detail. On the conceptual level other interpretations of persistency, e. g. persistency in space, should be explored. On the implementational level this requires the design of appropriate constraint-reasoners.

Acknowledgements

I would like to thank my colleagues at IITB and fellow researchers from SFB 314 for valuable comments on an earlier draft of this paper. in particular I have benefited from discussions with Gisela Schäfer-Richter, Andreas Nonnengart and Hans-Jürgen Bürckert. This work has been supported by the Deutsche Forschungs Gemeinschaft (DFG) in its Special Collaboration Program on AI and Knowledge Based Systems (SFB 314), project X2.

References

[Allen, 1983] J. F. Allen: "Maintaining Knowledge about Temporal Intervals", *Comm. ACM*, 26, No. 11 (November 1983), pp. 832 - 843.

[Allen, 1984] J. F. Allen: "Towards a general theory of Action and Time", *Artificial Intelligence*, 23 (1984), pp. 123-154.

[Bürckert, 1990] H. - J. Bürckert: "A resolution principle for clauses with constraints", *Proc. 10. International Conference on Automated Deduction*, Springer LNAI 449, pp. 187-192, 1990.

[Dean and McDermott, 1987] T. L. Dean and D. McDermott: "Temporal Data Base Management", *Artificial Intelligence*, 32 (1987), pp. 1-55.

[Decker, 1988] R. Decker: "Modelling the temporal behavior of technical systems", *Proc. German Workshop on Artificial Intelligence GWAI*, 1988, pp. 41 - 50.

[deKleer, 1986] J. deKleer: "An Assumption Based Truth Maintenance System", *Artificial Intelligence*, 28 (1986), pp. 127-162.

[Galton, 1990] A. Galton: "A critical examination of Allen's Theory of Action and Time", *Artificial Intelligence*, 42 (1990), pp. 159-188.

[Guckenbiehl, 1990] T. Guckenbiehl: *Reasoning with persistent facts*, internal report, FhG-IITB, 1990.

[Guckenbiehl, 1991] T. Guckenbiehl: *The Extended Episode Propagator*, Internal Report, FhG-IITB, in preparation.

[Hrycej, 1988] T. Hrycej: "Temporal Prolog", *Proc. European Conference on Artificial Intelligence*, Munich, 1988, pp. 296-301.

[Kahn and Gorry, 1977] K. Kahn and A. Gorry: "Mechanizing Temporal Knowledge", *Artificial Intelligence* 9 (1977), pp. 87-108.

[Ladkin, 1986] P. Ladkin: "Time Representation: A Taxomony of interval relations", *Proc. AAAI National Conference on Artificial Intelligence*, 1986, pp. 360-366.

[McDermott, 1982] D. McDermott: "A temporal logic for Reasoning about Processes and Plans", *Cognitive Science*, 6 (1982), pp. 101 - 155.

[Ohlbach, 1989] H.-J. Ohlbach: *Context Logic*, Universität Kaiserslautern, SEKI-report SR-89-08, 1989.

[Penberthy, 1987] J. S. Penberthy: "Temporal Unification and the Temporal Partial Order", *Proc. 5th IEEE-Conf. on AI applications*, San Diego, 1987, pp. 223 - 228.

[Rescher and Urquhart, 1971] N. Rescher and A. Urquhart: *Temporal Logic*, Berlin, 1971.

[Shoham, 1987] Y. Shoham: *Reasoning about Change: Time and Causation from the Standpoint of Artificial Intelligence*, Ph. D. Thesis, Yale University, Comp Sc. Dept., May 1987.

[van Beek, 1989] P. van Beek: "Approximation Algorithms for Temporal Reasoning", *Proc. International Joint Conference on Artificial Intelligence*, 1989, pp. 1291-1296.

[Williams, 1986] B. Williams: "Doing Time: Putting Qualitative Reasoning on firmer ground", *Proc. AAAI National Conference on Artificial Intelligence*, 1986, pp. 105 - 112.

Reflective reasoning with and between a declarative metatheory and the implementation code

Fausto Giunchiglia[1,2] and **Paolo Traverso**[1]
[1]IRST - Istituto per la Ricerca Scientifica e Tecnologica
38050 Povo, Trento, Italy
[2]DIST, University of Genoa, Via Opera Pia 11A, Genova, Italy
fausto@irst.it leaf@irst.it

Abstract

The goal of this paper is to present a theorem prover where the underlying code has been written to behave as the **procedural metalevel** of the object logic. We have then defined a logical **declarative metatheory MT** which can be put in a one-to-one relation with the code and automatically generated from it. MT is proved correct and complete in the sense that, for any object level deduction, the wff representing it is a theorem of MT, and viceversa. Such theorems can be translated back in the underlying code. This opens up the possibility of deriving control strategies automatically by metatheoretic theorem proving, of mapping them into the code and thus of extending and modifying the system itself. This seems a first step towards "really" self-reflective systems, *ie.* systems able to reason deductively about and modify their underlying computation mechanisms. We show that the usual logical reflection rules (so called reflection up and down) are derived inference rules of the system.

1 Introduction

Reflective and metatheoretic reasoning are well known techniques applied in knowledge representation and automated deduction (see for instance [Bundy, 1988], [Constable *et al.*, 1986], [Bowen and Kowalski, 1982], [Smith, 1983], [Gordon *et al.*, 1979]). Roughly speaking, in the past, metareasoning has been performed according to two different paradigms. In the first, from now on called **procedural**, the metalevel consists of a programming language and metareasoning is performed by *computation* in it. One example in AI is [Smith, 1983], another in theorem proving is LCF and its metalanguage ML [Gordon *et al.*, 1979]. In LCF the user can write control strategies as programs (usually called *tactics*) in ML to guide the search for a proof of a theorem. In the second paradigm, from now on called **declarative**, the metalevel is a logical metatheory and metareasoning is performed by *deduction* on metalevel statements. One example in AI is [Weyhrauch, 1980], one in theorem proving is [Howe, 1988]. Both approaches are sometimes incorporated and alternatively used; thus, for instance, in NuPrl [Constable *et al.*, 1986] and Isabelle [Paulson, 1989] both ML and a declarative logical metatheory can be used to build derived inference rules. In logic programming, metainterpreters [Bowen and Kowalski, 1982] can be seen both procedurally and declaratively.

In this paper, we present a system (called GETFOL [1]) with both a procedural and a declarative metalevel. In this respect GETFOL is similar to NuPrl and Isabelle; on the other hand GETFOL has features which make it very different from any other system proposed so far:

(1) the metalevel programming language is the same as the underlying implementation language and the code implementing the object logic has been written to be its procedural metalevel.

(2) the logical declarative metatheory **MT** can be put in a one-to-one relation with the code and automatically generated from it (and viceversa).

(3) MT is correct and complete in the sense that, for any object level deduction (performed by running the code implementing the object level logic), the wff representing it is a theorem of MT[2]. Such theorems, possibly proved automatically by metatheoretic theorem proving, can be "mapped back" into the underlying code as new reasoning modules. These modules, if executed, will produce the proof represented by the theorem they have been translated from.

As a consequence of these three facts, it is possible to generate (parts of) MT automatically from the implementation language, to prove in MT "certain" theorems and then to "transform" them into new code. The result is an extension or, possibly, a modification of the system itself. The GETFOL underlying code is not a "black box", fixed once and for all at the time of the development, but can change over time. This seems a first step towards "really" self-reflective systems, *ie.* systems able to reason deductively about and thus, possibly, modify, their

[1]GETFOL is a reimplementation/ extension of the FOL system [Weyhrauch, 1980]. GETFOL has, with minor variations, all the functionalities of FOL plus extensions, some of which described here, to allow metatheoretic theorem proving.

[2]The notions of correctness and completeness here involved are sometimes called adequacy and faithfulness, respectively.

underlying reasoning strategies. As a side effect of this "reflective" relation existing between computation and deduction, the usual logical reflection rules (reflection up and reflection down) [Giunchiglia and Smaill, 1989] can be proved to be (a form of) derived inference rules.

The paper is structured as follows. Section 2 describes how the implementation has been constructed to behave as the procedural metalevel of the system. Section 3 describes MT and how it can be automatically generated from the implementation code. In section 4, it is proved that MT represents all the object level deductions and that deduction in MT is the analogous operation of writing tactics in the implementation language. This is the fundamental property that allows the interpretation of theorems of MT in terms of the underlying code (section 5) via the use of reflection up and down. Finally, section 6 gives some conclusions and a short discussion of the related work.

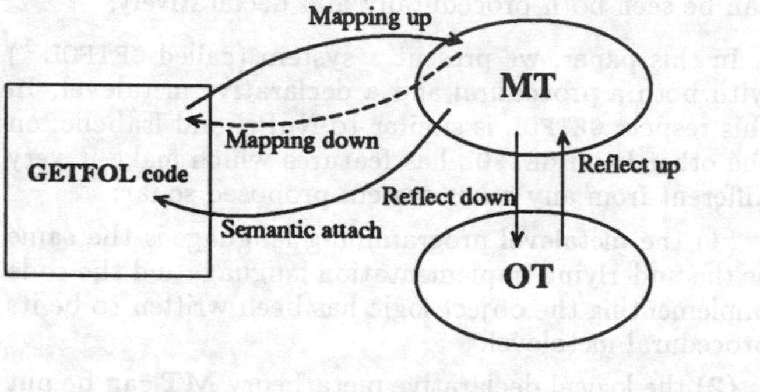

Figure 1: The GETFOL system.

2 The system code as the procedural metalevel

GETFOL allows the definition of multiple distinct theories. Each theory is formally defined as a triple ⟨Language, Axioms, Set of inference rules⟩. To simplify things we consider here the case where we have only one object theory OT=$\langle \mathcal{L}, \mathcal{A}x, \mathcal{R}\rangle$ and one metatheory MT=$\langle \mathcal{ML}, \mathcal{MA}x, \mathcal{R}\rangle$ (see figure 1). MT and OT use a first order classical sequent logic. By ***sequent*** we mean here a pair (Γ, A), written also $\Gamma \vdash A$, where A is a formula and Γ a set of formulas. For simplicity, in this paper we suppose MT and OT use the same set of inference rules $\mathcal{R}$. The inference rules, which are a sequent version of Prawitz' natural deduction (ND) calculus [Weyhrauch, 1980], allow introduction and elimination only in the post-sequent A. In the following, to simplify notation, when not relevant, we write A for $\Gamma \vdash A$. Thus, for instance

$$\wedge\text{E}\ \frac{A \wedge B}{A} \quad \forall\text{I}\ x_1\ x_2\ \frac{A(x_2)}{\forall x_1 A(x_1)} \quad \forall\text{E}\ x\ t\ \frac{\forall x A(x)}{A(t)}$$

are respectively one of the two conjunction elimination rules ($\wedge E$) and the universal quantifier introduction and elimination rules ($\forall I$,$\forall E$). The functions in the underlying GETFOL code implementing these inference rules are given in figure 2. Thus, for instance, when applicable, (alli-fun $A(x_2)$ x_1 x_2) returns $\forall x_1 A(x_1)$ which is then added (by proof-add-theorem) to the current proof. Notice that, even if the underlying code has been written to treat errors (*eg.* the application of ($\wedge E$) to a disjunction), this issue is not dealt with in this paper.

```
(DEFLAM ande (X)
 (IF (AND (IS-A-THEOREM X) (CONJ X))
  THEN (proof-add-theorem (ande-fun X))))

(DEFLAM alli (X1 X2 X3)
 (IF (AND (AND (IS-A-THEOREM X1)
        (AND (IS-A-VAR X2) (IS-A-VAR X3)))
        (NO-FREE X3 X1))
  THEN (proof-add-theorem (alli-fun X1 X2 X3))))

(DEFLAM alle (X1 X2 X3)
 (IF (AND (AND (IS-A-THEOREM X1)
        (AND (IS-A-VAR X2) (IS-A-TERM X3)))
        (FORALL X1))
  THEN (proof-add-theorem (alle-fun X1 X2 X3))))
```

where IS-A-VAR and IS-A-TERM evaluate to TRUE if the argument is a variable or a term of the object logic, IS-A-THEOREM evaluates to TRUE if the argument is an asserted theorem in the proof and proof-add-theorem adds its argument to the proof.

Figure 2: GETFOL implementation of $\wedge E$, $\forall I$ and $\forall E$.

Strategies and derived inference rules can be defined in a metalevel functional language, GET, which is a subset of the implementation language of GETFOL. To preserve correctness, the development environment is such that the user can write tactics which fail but that never assert a non-theorem. For instance, considering the code in figure 2, proof-add-theorem, ande-fun, alli-fun and alle-fun are not available to the user. In this respect, GET is similar to ML as used in LCF, Nuprl or Isabelle. For instance, the GET code implementing the (simple) derived inference rule that corresponds to the deduction

$$\forall I \frac{\wedge E \dfrac{\forall E \dfrac{\forall x(A(x) \wedge B(x))}{A(x) \wedge B(x)}}{A(x)}}{\forall x A(x)}$$

is:

```
(DEFLAM all-distr-con (x1 x2 x3)
 (alli (ande (alle x1 x2 x3)) x2 x3))
```

Strategies can be defined by using conditionals and iterations:

```
(DEFLAM strategy1 (x1 x2 x3)
 (IF (AND (FORALL x1) (CONJ (alle x1 x2 x3)))
  THEN (all-distr-con x1 x2 x3)
  ELSE (repeat 'tactic2 x1 x2 x3)))
```

where FORALL and CONJ are built-in GETFOL predicates which evaluate to TRUE when their argument is, respectively, a universally quantified formula and a conjunction, (repeat 'tactic args) iterates the application of tactic over args as many times as possible. strategy1 can be described as: "if x1 is a universally quantified conjunction, then derive the first conjunct of `x1`, otherwise exhaustively apply `tactic2`", where `tactic2` is a previously defined tactic.

What has been described so far suggests that GET can be used as the procedural metalevel of GETFOL, analogously to what happens with ML in LCF, NuPrl or Isabelle, or even with metainterpreters in Prolog. This is, in fact, the case when writing tactics. The difference comes from the fact that (exploiting that GET is also GETFOL's implementation language), the built-in GET functions to perform logic inference are exactly those used to implement the basic inference rules, *eg.* those in figure 2. More generally, *all the GETFOL code has been carefully written to allow the identification of the procedural metalanguage with the implementation language.* Thus, for instance, the implementation provides GET with all the syntax manipulation routines (such as `FORALL`, `CONJ`, `ande`), with all the proof manipulation routines (such as `IS-A-THEOREM`), with all the theory manipulation routines and so on. Not only must the code produce extensionally the right behaviour (satisfying the usual correctness criteria), but it must also be written to be at the same time the *procedural metalevel of the logic it implements.* In other words, it must have the right function and predicate symbols, the internal structure of the function and predicate definitions must be such that they can be put in a one-to-one relation with the axioms describing their behavior (all of this is described in section 3), and far harder, it must be such that computation can be directly mapped into the metathereotic "representation" of the deduction it produces (described in section 4).

We call the production of code satisfying the requirements above, "**the mechanization** of the logic" (to distinguish it from the process of producing an implementation of the logic). Mechanizing a logic is far harder than implementing it. On the other hand, as the rest of the paper will show, the mechanization of the logic can be exploited to build really self-reflective systems, *ie.* systems able to reason deductively about and modify their computation mechanisms. In fact it becomes then possible to generate automatically a logical metatheory MT from the code and, viceversa, to compile certain theorems of MT as system implementation code. Modification of the system's underlying computation mechanism is achieved by re-writing already existing (parts of) procedures. Note that this is not done in any of the existing theorem provers or metainterpreters. From this perspective, the work which most closely resembles ours is Brian Smith's [Smith, 1983]. The fundamental difference is that our metalanguage is a logical metatheory; this allows us to generate *provably correct* computation procedures *automatically* by metatheoretic theorem proving.

3 The declarative metatheory MT

MT's set of inference rules is fixed, being $\mathcal{R}$. We need to define MT's language $\mathcal{ML}$ and axioms $\mathcal{MA}x$. $\mathcal{ML}$, has names for the elements of OT (axioms and assumptions s, formulas w, variables x and so on); this is achieved by having for any such element an individual constant ("s", "w", "x" and so on) as part of $\mathcal{ML}$. These constants are the "quotation mark names" [Giunchiglia and Traverso, 1990] of the objects of OT.

```
[(DEFLAM <fun> (X1 ... Xn) <body>] =
   ∀ [X1] ... ∀ [Xn] ([<body>])
[(IF <t1> THEN <t2>)] = [<t1>] → [<t2>]
[(IF <t1> THEN <t2> ELSE <t3>)] =
   if [<t1>] then [<t2>] else [<t3>]
[(AND <t1> <t2>)] = [<t1>] ∧ [<t2>]
[(IS-A-THEOREM <t>)] = T([<t>])
[(proof-add-theorem <t>)] = T([<t>])
[(CONJ X1)] = Conj([X1])
[(FORALL X1)] = Forall([X1])
[(NO-FREE X1 X2)] = NoFree([X1],[X2])
[(IS-VAR X1)] = Var([X1])
[(IS-TERM X1)] = Term([X1])
[(ande-fun X1)] = ande([X1])
[(alli-fun X1 X2 X3)] = alli([X1],[X2],[X3])
[(alle-fun X1 X2 X3)] = alle([X1],[X2],[X3])
...
[X1] = x1
...
[Xn] = xn
...
```

where functions and predicates in $\mathcal{ML}$ (for instance *Forall*, *NoFree*, *Var*, *Term*, *ande*, *alli*, *alle* and so on) intuitively represent the computational operations performed by the code they are mapped from. The T predicate indicates "theoremhood".

Figure 3: m_{up} - mapping from the code to the metatheory.

Each inference rule of OT gets "mapped up" to a distinct axiom of $\mathcal{MA}x$. This mapping, called "m_{up}", performs a one-to-one translation from the code into elements of MT (see figure 3, $m_{up}(x)$ is written as $[x]$) Thus, for instance, the axioms generated by applying m_{up} to the GET code implementing $\wedge E$, $\forall I$ and $\forall E$ (see figure 2) are listed in figure 4. A complete definition of m_{up} and the code over which it can operate is outside the goals of this paper. The important point to notice is the fact that m_{up} (and its inverse) can be implemented to do the translation in either direction automatically.

$$\begin{array}{ll} (\mathcal{A}_{\wedge\mathcal{E}l}): & \forall x(T(x) \wedge Conj(x) \rightarrow T(ande(x))) \\ (\mathcal{A}_{\forall\mathcal{I}}): & \forall x_1 \forall x_2 \forall x_3 (T(x_1) \wedge Var(x_2) \wedge Var(x_3) \\ & \wedge NoFree(x_3, x_1) \rightarrow T(alli(x_1, x_2, x_3))) \\ (\mathcal{A}_{\forall E}): & \forall x_1 \forall x_2 \forall x_3 (T(x_1) \wedge Var(x_2) \wedge Term(x_3) \\ & \wedge Forall(x_1) \rightarrow T(alle(x_1, x_2, x_3))) \end{array}$$

Figure 4: Metatheoretic axioms mapped from the code.

We can observe in figure 3 that the two GET operations of testing if something is a theorem already asserted in the object theory (performed by `IS-A-THEOREM`) and of asserting a proved theorem (performed by `proof-add-theorem`) are translated into the same metatheoretic predicate T[3]. This is because OT, as

[3]Notice that this seems to contradict our previous state-

represented in MT, is the minimal set closed under the application of the inference rules to the axioms. Therefore, because MT is a metatheory of the transitive closure of OT, the procedural difference between a wff "being asserted" as a theorem and a wff "to-be asserted" as a theorem is lost.

The assertion of the axioms generated by m_{up} requires adding function and predicate symbols to $\mathcal{ML}$: for each inference rule of OT we have a function symbol in $\mathcal{ML}$ with the appropriate arity, for instance *ande*, *alli* and *alle* for $\wedge E$, $\forall I$ and $\forall E$ respectively. $\mathcal{ML}$'s predicates are $Conj$, $Forall$, $Nofree$, Var, $Term$ and so on.

MT's logic allows the use of the construct *if p then t_1 else t_2*, where p is a wff and t_1, t_2 are terms. The *if* construct, very important in order to make the MT's axiomatization mirror very closely the underlying code, is actually not first order. On the other hand it can be easily proved that *if* can be defined in a conservative extension of classical ND. GETFOL allows the use of the *if* construct and has an introduction and an elimination inference rule for it.

4 Deduction in MT versus program definition

The goal of this section is to prove that, given a mapping between wffs in MT and deductions in OT, *for any object level deduction (performed by running the code implementing the object level logic), the corresponding wff is a theorem of the metatheory and viceversa.* To do this we need to define how object level proofs are represented in the metatheory. This is achieved by defining a mapping **w** from sequent trees Π in OT to wffs of MT. Sequent trees are trees of sequents, each labeled by an inference rule. Sequent tree leaves are axioms or assumptions (sequents of the form $A \vdash A$). Sequent trees are not necessarily deductions as the rule labelling a sequent may not be applicable. We say that Π is a sequent tree of s if s is the endsequent of Π. The endsequent is the "root" of the sequent tree. The formulae mapped from sequent trees are called **sequent tree formulas** (in short **twffs**) and are of the form $\mathcal{P} \rightarrow T(t)$, where $\mathcal{P}$ are the **preconditions** and t the **sequent tree term** of the twff. $\mathcal{P}$ and t are inductively defined over the complexity of Π as follows:

Base: if $\Pi = s$, then $\mathbf{w}(\Pi) = T(\text{"}s\text{"})$;

Step: as examples, let us consider the cases of $\wedge E$ and $\forall I \xi \eta$. Let $\mathbf{w}(\Pi_1) = \mathcal{P}_1 \rightarrow T(t_1)$ be a twff. If Π is a sequent tree built from Π_1 by adding the rule label $\wedge E$, then $\mathbf{w}(\Pi) = \mathcal{P}_1 \wedge Conj(t_1) \rightarrow T(ande(t_1))$. If the added label is $\forall I \xi \eta$, then $\mathbf{w}(\Pi) = \mathcal{P}_1 \wedge Var(\text{"}\xi\text{"}) \wedge Var(\text{"}\eta\text{"}) \wedge NoFree(t_1, \text{"}\eta\text{"}) \rightarrow T(alli(t_1, \text{"}\xi\text{"}, \text{"}\eta\text{"}))$.

Notice that there is an isomorphism between twffs and the sequent trees they represent. In particular the sequent tree term records the tree of applications of inference rules while the preconditions record precisely the

ment that the m_{up} is one-to-one. In certain cases (T is one of these) m_{up} and its inverse distinguish between occurrences (in this case, corresponding either to IS-A-THEOREM or to proof-add-theorem).

tests which allow the applications of inference rules.

Now we concentrate on showing that MT (which can be proved consistent) has the desired properties[4]:

Theorem 1 (MT correct and complete for OT) : *Let Π be any sequent tree of s in OT. Let t be the sequent tree term of the twff $\mathbf{w}(\Pi)$. Then $\vdash_{MT} T(t) \iff \Pi$ is a proof of s.*

Proof [Hinted]: ($\Leftarrow$): corollary of theorems 2 and 3 below.

($\Rightarrow$): similar to the proof of theorem 3. Q.E.D.

Theorem 1, guarantees that, for any provable $T(t)$, there is a proof of a theorem in the object theory and viceversa[5]. As a consequence, given a GET program that succeeds in building an OT proof, theoremhood applied to a term corresponding to the proof itself can be proved in MT. Notice that theorem 1 considers only derived inference rules. This result can be generalized to deal with an extension of MT, expressive enough to represent tactics, written as programs with conditionals, iterations, failure detection and so on. This non-trivial issue, which assures a complete translation of GET into MT and viceversa is not discussed here.

Theorem 1 does not tell us anything about how to prove $T(t)$, in other words, about how to construct in MT the derived inference rules. A possible technique is suggested by the following two theorems.

Theorem 2 (Twff provability) *For any sequent tree formula $\mathcal{P} \rightarrow T(t)$, $\vdash_{MT} \mathcal{P} \rightarrow T(t)$.*

Proof[hinted]: The proof is performed by induction over the complexity of Π. As an example of step case, let us consider $\wedge E$. Let us suppose that the induction hypothesis is $\mathcal{P} \rightarrow T(t)$. From it we can derive that $\mathcal{P} \vdash T(t)$. From the instantiation of axiom $(\mathcal{A}_{\wedge \mathcal{E} \mathcal{I}})$ in figure 4 we obtain $T(t) \wedge Conj(t) \rightarrow T(ande(t))$, from which we can then derive (also considering the induction hypothesis) $\mathcal{P} \vdash Conj(t) \rightarrow T(ande(t))$. For the deduction theorem we derive thus $\mathcal{P} \rightarrow (Conj(t) \rightarrow T(ande(t)))$ which is equivalent to $\mathcal{P} \wedge Conj(t) \rightarrow T(ande(t))$. Q.E.D.

The proof suggests how twffs can be deduced in the metatheory: basic twffs can be obtained directly as instantiations of the axioms in figure 4; complex twffs can then be composed out of simpler ones following the steps hinted in the proof. This is not the only way to build twffs, [Giunchiglia and Traverso, 1990] describes some examples in detail.

The fact that **all** the twffs are provable in MT is exactly what we should have expected. In fact, any twff corresponds to a program that can be defined by the user in the system code. To say that any twff can be derived in the metatheory is equivalent to say that any strategy can be written in the code. *Derivation of a theorem in MT is the analogous operation of writing code in the implementation language.* Notice that this suggests a new way to develop tactics: instead of coding them in

[4] For lack of space, only proof outlines are given.

[5] If not desiderable, completeness can be easily dropped by generating MT only partially; for instance, we may not have the names of all the objects in OT.

the procedural metalanguage the user can theorem prove them in MT. The user can thus write the hardest steps and, interactively, generate tactics by theorem proving. This amounts to giving the user the possibility to derive not only the object level proofs but also the tactics (this idea has some resemblance with the work on proof planning [Bundy, 1988], see [Giunchiglia and Traverso, 1990] for a more in depth discussion).

A different matter is whether the strategy is successful. In the programming language, a defined strategy may generate an object level proof or fail. Similarly, the sequent tree may or may not be a proof. For instance, a twff whose sequent tree term is $ande(\text{“}A \wedge B\text{”})$ corresponds to a proof, but that whose term is $ande(\text{“}A \vee B\text{”})$ does not. In metalevel programming languages (like ML [Gordon *et al.*, 1979]), given two simple tactics corresponding to the ones above, they need to be executed in order to know that the former succeeds whereas the latter fails. In MT, ***the derivability of preconditions determines whether twffs correspond to proofs:***

Theorem 3 (Preconditions) : *Let Π be any sequent tree of s in OT. Let $\mathcal{P}$ be the preconditions of the twff* $\mathbf{w}(\Pi)$. *Then $\vdash_{MT} \mathcal{P} \Longleftrightarrow \Pi$ is a proof of s.*

Proof[hinted]. The proof is performed over the complexity of Π. As an example of the step case let us consider $\wedge E$. Let Π be:

$$\wedge E \ \frac{\begin{array}{c}\Pi_1\\ s_1\end{array}}{s}$$

Let $\mathbf{w}(\Pi_1)$ be $\mathcal{P}_1 \rightarrow T(t_1)$.

($\Rightarrow$) If Π is a proof then $\wedge E$ is applicable and the wff of s_1 is a conjunction. This implies $\vdash_{MT} Conj(t_1)$. By the induction hypothesis we conclude $\vdash_{MT} \mathcal{P}_1$. Then as $\mathcal{P}$ is $\mathcal{P}_1 \wedge Conj(t_1)$ we have $\vdash_{MT} \mathcal{P}$.

($\Leftarrow$) If $\vdash_{MT} \mathcal{P}_1 \wedge Conj(t_1)$, then by induction hypotheses we prove Π_1 is a proof. We prove that $\vdash_{MT} Conj(t_1)$ implies that s_1 is a conjunction. Then the $\wedge E$ rule is applicable and Π is a proof. Q.E.D.

Notice that, because of theorem 3, the success of tactics can be stated without executing them.

5 Metatheory interpretation as system code execution

Theorem 1 guarantees that, for any successful GET strategy, the corresponding twff can be deduced. The idea is to map any twff into GET code and use it to prove the goal. This idea of mapping back can be seen in two ways:

(1) The inverse of m_{up} can be defined and used to **compile** twffs back in the code (the "mapping down" arrow in figure 1). For any twff, the result is a strategy available to the user.

(2) Twffs can be **interpreted** in terms of the GET code. The result is the assertion of the sequent as a theorem in OT.

In the remainder of the paper we concentrate on the interpretation of twffs. In $\mathbf{w}(\Pi) = \mathcal{P} \rightarrow T(t)$ we can distinguish three parts: the preconditions $\mathcal{P}$, the predicate T and the sequent tree term t. The assertion of the theorem in OT can be seen as the sequence of three steps: **(i)** prove $\mathcal{P}$ and obtain $T(t)$ (subsection 5.1), **(ii)** from t generate the name of the endsequent s of Π, "s" (not described as very similar, in principle, to step (i)), finally **(iii)**, from $T(\text{“}s\text{”})$ assert s in OT (subsection 5.2).

5.1 Proving $\mathcal{P}$

Theorem 3 tells us that the preconditions of any twff representing an object level proof can be proved by theorem proving in MT. This is the "usual" approach taken so far in theorem proving. A problem with this approach may be the size of the search space in MT which, even dropping the completeness requirement, can explode when complex metareasoning is required. The correspondence existing between MT and the GET code provides us with an alternative technique for proving in MT facts about OT. The idea is to avoid the explicit axiomatization of parts of OT and to perform computation instead of deduction. As shown above, having a mechanization of the logic gives us a one-to-one mapping between elements of the signature of MT and GET functions (section 3, figure 3) and opens up the possibility to see deductions in MT in terms of computation in GET (section 4, theorems 1,2). For how twffs are defined, their syntactic structure explicitly resembles the structure of the computation tree they represent. As a consequence we can compute in GET following the syntax of the twff. Let us consider, as an example, the case where one of the conjuncts of $\mathcal{P}$ is $Conj(\text{“}A \wedge B\text{”})$. $Conj$ has been mapped up from the code function CONJ and "$A \wedge B$" is the metatheoretic constant which denotes the theorem $A \wedge B$. Executing (CONJ $A \wedge B$) gives TRUE, this means that the metatheoretic sentence $Conj(\text{“}A \wedge B\text{”})$ is true and can be rewritten to the constant for truth, $True$.

Notice that, in order to implement the machinery described above, GETFOL must keep track of the link between the functions and predicates of the signature of MT and the GET functions they have been mapped from (by m_{up}). It must also remember which elements of OT the constants in $\mathcal{ML}$ are names of. GETFOL has in its code a data structure where it memorizes the pairs $\langle \text{“}o\text{”}, o \rangle$, where "$o$" is an MT constant, name of o, a syntactic object in OT. The possibility to create pairs $\langle$ name, object $\rangle$ is implemented by the *semantic attachment* functionality [Weyhrauch, 1980] shown in figure 1.

Let us give the formal definition of the interpreter implemented in GETFOL, $\mathcal{I}$, which maps twffs into computation. Let us restrict ourselves to terms and atomic wffs. Let us suppose that, for any object in OT, o, "o" is a constant in MT. Then $\mathcal{I}$ can be defined as follows [6]:

$$\mathcal{I}(\text{“}o\text{”}) = o$$
$$\mathcal{I}(g(o_1, ..., o_p)) = \mathcal{I}(g)(\mathcal{I}(o_1), ..., \mathcal{I}(o_p))$$
$$\mathcal{I}((h_m \diamond ... \diamond h_1)(o_1 ... o_p)) = (\mathcal{I}(h_m) \diamond ... \diamond \mathcal{I}(h_1))(\mathcal{I}(o_1), ..., \mathcal{I}(o_p))$$

[6] "$\diamond$" means function composition. The notation should be made precise, by explaining how to denote function composition with functions with more than one argument. Since not relevant in this context, this issue is not faced.

Thus, for instance, instead of proving infinitely many metatheoretic theorems of the form $Conj(``A_i \wedge B_i")$, we can apply $\mathcal{I}$ to $Conj(``A_i \wedge B_i")$ to obtain $\mathcal{I}(Conj(``A_i \wedge B_i")) = \mathcal{I}(Conj)(\mathcal{I}(``A_i \wedge B_i")) = \mathcal{I}(Conj)(A_i \wedge B_i) =$ (CONJ $A_i \wedge B_i$)[7].

Notice that for any atomic wff or term wt, $\mathcal{I}(wt)$ is the execution of the code c such that $m_{up}(c) = wt$.

Supposing that, for any n-ary function and predicate symbol fp, fp computes the right extension (with n-ary function symbols, the $(n+1)$-element of their set theoretic definition; with predicate symbols, either TRUE or FALSE) then $\mathcal{I}$ performs exactly the interpretation of terms and atomic wffs in a first order model. This result can be generalized to twffs and, more in general, to any sentence in MT. Thus the correctness and completeness of this translation of deduction into computation can be proved from the correctness and completeness results for first order logic[8].

What said above amounts to saying that OT is the standard model for MT. This is, we think, a correct way to see things and very much in agreement with Tarski's original definition of interpretation [Tarski, 1956]. More on seeing interpretation, from a computational point of view (in terms of the recursive definition of $\mathcal{I}$), as the process of extracting objects from (quotation-mark and structural- descriptive) names is in section 4 of [Giunchiglia and Traverso, 1990]).

5.2 MT-OT interaction via reflection

We can prove the following lemma:

Lemma 1 (Name equality) *Let Π be any sequent tree of s in OT. Let "s" be the quotation mark name of s. Let t be the sequent tree term of the twff* $\mathbf{w}(\Pi)$. *Then* $\vdash_{MT} t = ``s" \iff \Pi$ *is a proof of* s.

A sequent tree term t, when corresponding to a proof Π in OT, can be proved equal to the quotation mark name of the theorem proved by Π and viceversa. From theorem 1 and lemma 1 we can thus derive the following result:

Corollary 1 (Reflection) *: Let Π be any sequent tree of s in OT. Let "s" be the quotation mark name of s. Then* $\vdash_{MT} T(``s") \iff \Pi$ *is a proof of* s.

In other words $\vdash_{MT} T(``s") \iff \vdash_{OT} s$. Then the reflection rules [Giunchiglia and Smaill, 1989]

$$R_{down}\frac{\vdash_{MT} \; T(``s")}{\vdash_{OT} \; s} \qquad R_{up}\frac{\vdash_{OT} \; s}{\vdash_{MT} \; T(``s")}$$

are (a sort of) derived inference rules between theories in the multitheory system MT- OT. Notice that the procedural distinction between "being an already asserted theorem" and " being a theorem to be asserted", lost by m_{up}, is brought back by the reflection rules. In fact, R_{up} can be executed only on theorems already asserted in OT, while, viceversa, R_{down} can be executed to assert new theorems in OT. Occurrences of T that in the compilation down from MT to GET would be translated into IS-A-THEOREM correspond to applying R_{up}; viceversa, the occurrences of T that would be compiled down into proof-add-theorem correspond to applying R_{down}. The use of reflection up and down allows us to give a declarative explanation of the interaction between reasoning in OT and reasoning in MT and, in particular, of how (and why) it is possible to assert theorems in OT as a result of deduction in MT.

5.3 Deducing in OT via reasoning in MT

In this section we show how a twff can be interpreted to prove a theorem in OT. As a prototypical example, let us consider the following twff:

$$\begin{aligned} &T(``s") \wedge Forall(``s") \wedge Conj(alle(``s", ``x", ``x")) \wedge \\ &NoFree(``x", ande(alle(``s", ``x", ``x"))) \\ &\rightarrow T(alli(ande(alle(``s", ``x", ``x")), ``x", ``x")) \end{aligned}$$

Let us take s as a shorthand for $\forall x(A(x) \wedge B(x))$. In this case the above twff is a theorem in MT and "represents" the proof implemented by the program (all-distr-conj s x x) (see section 2). Given the sequent s asserted in OT we can apply R_{up} to obtain $T(``s")$ in MT. $T(``s")$ can be used to derive

$$\begin{aligned} &Forall(``s") \wedge Conj(alle(``s", ``x", ``x")) \wedge \\ &NoFree(``x", ande(alle\ (``s", ``x", ``x"))) \\ &\rightarrow T(alli(ande(alle(``s", ``x", ``x")), ``x", ``x")) \end{aligned}$$

The interpretation of $Forall(``s")$ leads to the execution of (FORALL $s$) which evaluates to TRUE. The same happens with all the other conjuncts. Thus, by simple propositional reasoning, it is possible to derive $T(alli(ande(alle\ (``s", ``x", ``x")), ``x", ``x"))$.

The interpretation of $alle(``s", ``x", ``x")$ leads to the execution of (alle-fun s x x) which evaluates to $A(x) \wedge B(x)$. The result of the interpretation of the whole term is then $\forall x A(x)$. Reflection down can thus be used to assert the new theorem in OT:

$$R_{down}\frac{\vdash_{MT} \; T(``\forall x A(x)")}{\vdash_{OT} \; \forall x A(x)}$$

The code performing the above steps is implemented in GETFOL and can be run by the command REFLECT [Giunchiglia and Smaill, 1989]. *Notice that running the code compiled by the "mapping down" would give the same result as running* REFLECT. The inverse of m_{up} is to REFLECT exactly what compilation is to interpretation: execution of code generated by the inverse of m_{up} produces the same results as interpreting metalevel theorems via REFLECT.

6 Conclusions and related work

In this paper we have presented a theorem prover, GETFOL, where the underlying code has been written to

[7] By (CONJ $A_i \wedge B_i$) we mean the result of the application of the GET function CONJ to its arguments.

[8] Note that truth is tested in the standard model. It is well known that the set of wffs true in a model is larger than the set of valid wffs. On the other hand it can be proved that, the interpretation in GETFOL restricted to atomic ground wffs (the elements of $\mathcal{P}$) returns TRUE iff the wff is valid in all models of MT and thus provable in MT.

behave as the procedural metalevel of the logic it implements. This approach seems a first step towards the development of systems able to modify deductively and automatically their underlying computation machinery. In fact:

(a) a logical metatheory MT can be automatically generated from the code;

(b) (some of) the theorems of MT represent object level computations;

(c) these theorems can be automatically compiled back in the system code to extend or to modify it (modification is achieved by redefining GET function symbols);

(d) these theorems can be automatically interpreted to assert object level theorems. In this case, as a side effect, we have a proven correct way to mix, *at run time*, object and metalevel theorem proving via the use of reflection up and down. More on this issue can be found in [Giunchiglia and Traverso, 1990] which also has a long section on the related work, in particular with [Bundy, 1988; Weyhrauch, 1980].

As far as we know, this approach is new and has never been proposed before. However, some comparisons with existing systems can nevertheless be made.

The idea of a metatheory mapped directly from the system code is somehow similar to the idea underlying the work on metafunctions [Boyer and Moore, 1981] (in the Boyer and Moore theorem prover the code *is* the metatheory). In [Boyer and Moore, 1981], user defined term-rewriting functions can be checked to verify whether they preserve the "meaning" of terms. Aside from the technical differences, a fundamental difference is that we provide a metatheory in which we can perform automatic deduction to *build* correct control strategies, while Boyer and Moore *verify* the correctness of the user defined strategies.

Besides Boyer and Moore's work [Boyer and Moore, 1981], none of the existing theorem provers, has the possibility of using the results of deduction in the metatheory to produce modifications of the underlying system code. This is, for instance, the case also in NuPrl [Constable *et al.*, 1986; Howe, 1988], even if in NuPrl the synthesis of new tactics can be obtained by metatheoretic theorem proving (via the "propositions-as-types" paradigm). Analogously, metainterpreters can control the Prolog search strategy but cannot modify it. That is, the user can write a metainterpreter for any desired search strategy, however the metainterpreter will be executed by using the Prolog built-in search strategy.

For what concerns the issue of self-modification, the work which most closely resembles ours is Brian Smith's [Smith, 1983]. The substantial difference is that, in GETFOL, metatheoretic statements are generated by metalevel deduction and not by computation and that the tactics derived are provably correct. No non-theorems can be proved.

Aknowledgments

The authors thank the Mechanized Reasoning Group at IRST and the Mathematical Reasoning Group in Edinburgh, in particular Alan Bundy, David Basin, Alessandro Cimatti, Luciano Serafini, Alex Simpson and Alan Smaill. Vanni Criscuolo, Bob Kowalski, Carolyn Talcott, Frank VanHarmelem and Richard Weyhrauch are also thanked.

References

[Bowen and Kowalski, 1982] K.A. Bowen and R.A. Kowalski. Amalgamating language and meta-language in logic programming. In S. Tarlund, editor, *Logic Programming*, pages 153–173, New York, 1982. Academic Press.

[Boyer and Moore, 1981] R.S. Boyer and J.S. Moore. Metafunctions: proving them correct and using them efficiently as new proof procedures. In R.S. Boyer and J.S. Moore, editors, *The correctness problem in computer science*, pages 103–184. Academic Press, 1981.

[Bundy, 1988] A. Bundy. The Use of Explicit Plans to Guide Inductive Proofs. In R. Luck and R. Overbeek, editors, *CADE9*. Springer-Verlag, 1988. Longer version available as DAI Research Paper No. 349, Dept. of Artificial Intelligence, Edinburgh.

[Constable *et al.*, 1986] R.L. Constable, S.F. Allen, H.M. Bromley, et al. *Implementing Mathematics with the NuPRL Proof Development System*. Prentice Hall, 1986.

[Giunchiglia and Smaill, 1989] F. Giunchiglia and A. Smaill. Reflection in constructive and non-constructive automated reasoning. In J. Lloyd, editor, *Proc. Workshop on Meta-Programming in Logic Programming*. MIT Press, 1989. IRST Technical Report 8902-04. Also available as DAI Research Paper 375, Dept. of Artificial Intelligence, Edinburgh.

[Giunchiglia and Traverso, 1990] F. Giunchiglia and P. Traverso. Plan formation and execution in a uniform architecture of declarative metatheories. In M. Bruynooghe, editor, *Proc. Workshop on Meta-Programming in Logic*. MIT Press, 1990. Also available as IRST Technical Report 9003-12.

[Gordon *et al.*, 1979] M.J. Gordon, A.J. Milner, and C.P. Wadsworth. *Edinburgh LCF - A mechanised logic of computation*, volume 78 of *Lecture Notes in Computer Science*. Springer Verlag, 1979.

[Howe, 1988] D. J. Howe. Computational metatheory in Nuprl. In R. Lusk and R. Overbeek, editors, *CADE9*, 1988.

[Paulson, 1989] L. Paulson. The fundation of a generic theorem prover. *Journal of Automated Reasoning*, 5:363–396, 1989.

[Smith, 1983] B.C. Smith. Reflection and Sematincs in LISP. In *Proc. 11th ACM POPL*, pages 23–35, 1983.

[Tarski, 1956] A. Tarski. *Logic, Semantics, Metamathematics*. Oxford University Press, 1956.

[Weyhrauch, 1980] R.W. Weyhrauch. Prolegomena to a theory of Mechanized Formal Reasoning. *Artificial Intelligence. Special Issue on Non-monotonic Logic*, 13(1), 1980.

Ordering-Based Strategies for Horn Clauses*

Nachum Dershowitz
Department of Computer Science
University of Illinois at Urbana-Champaign
1304 West Springfield Avenue
Urbana, IL 61801, U.S.A.
email: nachum@cs.uiuc.edu

Abstract

Two new theorem-proving procedures for equational Horn clauses are presented. The largest literal is selected for paramodulation in both strategies, except that one method treats positive literals as larger than negative ones and results in a unit strategy. Both use term orderings to restrict paramodulation to potentially maximal sides of equations and to increase the amount of allowable simplification (demodulation). Completeness is shown using proof orderings.

1 Introduction

The completeness of positive-unit resolution for sets of Horn clauses $p_1 \wedge \cdots \wedge p_n \Rightarrow p_{n+1}$ is well-known. An advantage of a unit strategy is that the number of literals in clauses never grows; it suffers from the disadvantage of being a bottom-up method. Ordered resolution, in which the literals of each clause are arranged in a linear order $>$ and only the largest literal may serve as a resolvent, is also complete for Horn clauses [Boyer, 1971]. The purpose here is to design Horn clause strategies that make more comprehensive use of orderings in controlling inference.

A *conditional equation* is a universally-quantified Horn clause in which the only predicate symbol is equality ($\simeq$). Conditional equations are important for specifying abstract data types and expressing logic programs with equations. We write such a clause in the form $e_1 \wedge \cdots \wedge e_n \Rightarrow s \simeq t$ $(n \geq 0)$, meaning that the equality $s \simeq t$ holds whenever all the equations e_i, called *conditions*, hold. If $n = 0$, then the (positive unit) clause, $s \simeq t$, will be called an *unconditional equation*. Horn clauses with both equality and non-equality literals can be expressed as conditional equations with equality literals only by turning each nonequality atom l into a Boolean equation $l \simeq T$, for the truth constant T. A conditional equation $e_1 \wedge \cdots \wedge e_n \Rightarrow s \simeq t$ is valid for E iff $s \simeq t$ is valid for $E \cup \{e_1, \ldots, e_n\}$; hence, proving validity of conditional equations reduces to proving validity of unconditional ones.

*This research supported in part by the National Science Foundation under Grant CCR-9007195.

Positive-unit resolution, or any other complete variation of resolution, could be used to prove theorems in equational Horn theories (the equality axioms, including functional reflexivity, are Horn), but the cost of treating equality axioms like any other clause is prohibitive. For this reason, special inference mechanisms for equality, notably paramodulation [Robinson and Wos, 1969], have been devised. In the Horn case, a unit strategy can be combined with paramodulation [Henschen and Wos, 1974; Furbach, 1987].

In this paper, we describe two complete theorem-proving methods for equational Horn theories. As in [Hsiang and Rusinowitch, 1986; Kounalis and Rusinowitch, 1987; Zhang and Kapur, 1988; Rusinowitch, 1989; Bachmair and Ganzinger, 1990; Nieuwenhuis and Orejas, 1990], our goal is to minimize the amount of paramodulation, while maximizing the amount of simplification—without threatening completeness. Orderings, described in detail in Section 2, are used to choose which literals participate in a paramodulation step, and which side of an equality literal to use. They utilize orderings of terms and atoms to restrict inferences, and are generalizations of *ordered completion* [Bachmair *et al.*, 1986; Hsiang and Rusinowitch, 1987], an "unfailing" extension of the "completion procedure" in [Knuth and Bendix, 1970] for unconditional equational inference. Completion operates on asymmetrical equations, that is, on *rewrite rules*, and has as its goal the production of confluent (Church-Rosser) systems of rules that can be used to decide validity. To achieve this, the larger sides of rules are overlapped on (non-variable) subterms of each other, producing equations that are called "critical pairs". Brown [1975] and Lankford [1975] first suggested combining completion for oriented unconditional equations, with paramodulation for unorientable ones and resolution for non-equality atoms. Paul [1986] studied the application of completion to sets of Horn clauses with equality.

Completion was extended to conditional equations by Kaplan [1987], who turns equations into rules only if they satisfy a certain "decreasingness" condition. The problem is that the critical pair of two decreasing rules can easily be nondecreasing. Like standard completion, both these methods may fail on account of inability to form new rules. Kounalis and Rusinowitch [1987] suggested narrowing conditions to achieve completeness.

Recently, several restrictions of paramodulation based on term orderings have been proposed for the full first-order case, including [Zhang and Kapur, 1988; Rusinowitch, 1989; Bachmair and Ganzinger, 1990]. For a survey of rewriting, see [Dershowitz and Jouannaud, 1990].

Section 3 presents a set of inference rules that severely restricts resolution with paramodulation by incorporating an ordering on (atoms and) terms. Limiting inference partially controls growth; keeping clauses fully simplified stunts growth even further. Such restrictions are of paramount importance in any practical theorem prover, but their (refutational) completeness has been difficult to establish. For our completeness proofs, sketched in Section 4, we adapt the proof-ordering method of [Bachmair *et al.*, 1986] to conditional proofs. Section 4.1 demonstrates the completeness of a unit strategy (suggested in [Dershowitz, 1990]) and Section 4.2 considers a strategy based on conditional completion of decreasing rules. Proof orderings allow us to limit narrowing to negative literals in the unit strategy, something that appears impossible with the recent transfinite-tree proof method used in [Hsiang and Rusinowitch, 1987]. The crux of our proof normalization argument is the observation that any conditional equational proof not in "normal form" must either have a "peak", that is, two applications of equations such that the middle term is the largest of all those involved and all subproofs are in normal form, or a "drop", that is, an application of an equation (or reflexivity of equals) to an instance of a condition in which all subproofs are in normal form. The strategies are designed to eliminate peaks and drops, thereby reducing the complexity assigned to the proof.

Section 5 concludes with a short discussion.

2 Simplification Orderings

Let $\mathcal{T}$ be a set of (first-order) terms, with variables taken from a set $\mathcal{X}$, and $\mathcal{G}$ be its subset of *ground* (variable-free) terms. If t is a term in $\mathcal{T}$, by $t|_\pi$ we signify the subterm of t rooted at position π; by $t[s]_\pi$, we denote the term t with its subterm $t|_\pi$ replaced by some term s.

Term orderings are of central importance in the proposed methods. A total ordering $>$ on ground terms $\mathcal{G}$ is called a *complete simplification ordering* [Hsiang and Rusinowitch, 1987] if it has (a) the "replacement property", $s > t$ implies that any term $u[s]_\pi$, with subterm s located at some position π, is greater under $>$ than the term $u[t]_\pi$ with that occurrence of s replaced by t, and (b) the "subterm property", $t \geq t|_\pi$ for all subterms $t|_\pi$ of t. Such a ground-term ordering must be a well-ordering (see [Dershowitz, 1987]). A *completable simplification ordering* on all terms $\mathcal{T}$ is a *partial* ordering $\succ$ (c) that can be extended to a complete simplification ordering $>$ on ground terms, such that (d) $s \succ t$ implies that $s\sigma > t\sigma$ for all ground substitutions σ. Furthermore, we will assume (e) that the constant T is minimal in $\succ$.

Imagine a total ordering of atoms and with no equations, per se. The method of Section 4.1, then, is just selected positive-unit resolution, in which the largest negative literal is chosen. The appropriate inference rule would be expressed as:

$$\frac{E \cup \left\{ \begin{array}{rcl} q \wedge s \simeq T & \Rightarrow & u \simeq T, \\ & & l \simeq T \end{array} \right\}}{E \cup \left\{ \begin{array}{rcl} q \wedge s \simeq T & \Rightarrow & u \simeq T, \\ & & l \simeq T, \\ q\sigma & \Rightarrow & u\sigma \simeq T \end{array} \right\}}$$

where σ is the most general unifier (*mgu*) of l and s. Here, the positive unit clause $l \simeq T$ is resolved with the negative literal $s \simeq T$ in the clause $q \wedge s \simeq T \Rightarrow u \simeq T$, and produces a new Horn clause $q\sigma \Rightarrow u\sigma \simeq T$. The new clause is a logical consequence of the two given clauses, since $s\sigma = l\tau\sigma$, where τ renames variables in l so that it shares none with s. The clause would be generated *only* when $s > q$, by which we mean that s is the largest negative literal in its clause.

A total simplification ordering on non-ground literals is not actually possible (which is why the ordering of the parent clause is inherited in ordered resolution), but can be approximated by a partial ordering. If only a partial ordering $\succ$ is given, we resolve negative literals that are potentially maximal. That is, we apply the above rule if $s\sigma \not\prec q\sigma$, or, in other words, if the instance $s\sigma$ of s created by resolution is not necessarily smaller than the other instantiated negative literals. Since some of the rules we consider delete or simplify antecedent clauses, the above format for inference rules, with the equations that participated in the inference also appearing as part of the consequent, is advantageous.

Suppose E is a set of Horn clauses in conditional equation form. To handle equality literals $l \simeq r$, we need to unify at subterms of conditions, not just at the literal level. Note that whenever we refer to equations in a set, we mean that it, or the symmetric equation (with l and r exchanged), or a variant with variables renamed uniformly, actually appears in the set. With that in mind, if l unifies with a non-variable subterm $s|_\pi$ of a maximal term s in a condition $s \simeq t$ of a conditional equation $q \wedge s \simeq t \Rightarrow u \simeq v$, then a new Horn clause is created by applying the most general unifying substitution σ to the conditional equation, and then replacing $l\sigma$ with $r\sigma$, as per the unit clause $l \simeq r$. The conditions ensure that $s\sigma$ is the (potentially) larger side of the condition that is being paramodulated into and that the replacement yields a (potentially) smaller condition.

3 Inference Rules

We formulate our theorem-proving procedure as an inference system operating on a set of conditional equations, and parameterized by a completable ordering $\succ$. We define a symmetric binary relation $\leftrightarrow$, for a particular set of conditional equations E, as the smallest relation satisfying $t[l\sigma]_\pi \leftrightarrow t[r\sigma]_\pi$ for all $u_1 \simeq v_1 \wedge \cdots \wedge u_n \simeq v_n \Rightarrow l \simeq r$ in E such that $u_i\sigma \leftrightarrow^* v_i\sigma$ for each i, where $\leftrightarrow^*$ is the reflexive-transitive closure of $\leftrightarrow$. This relation corresponds to "substitution of equals" according to the axioms in E. We also define a *decreasing rewrite* relation $\rightarrow_E$ on terms $\mathcal{T}$. An instance $p\sigma \Rightarrow u\sigma \simeq v\sigma$ of a conditional equation is "decreasing" if $u\sigma \succ v\sigma$ in the completable ordering and the proofs of the conditions only involve terms smaller than $u\sigma$. We write $u \rightarrow_e v$ (with respect to a partial ordering $\succ$), if $u \leftrightarrow_e v$ using a decreasing instance of e. For unit equation e, $\rightarrow_e$ is just the intersection of $\leftrightarrow_e$ and $\succ$. Decreasingness is essentially the same condition as imposed on conditional rewrite rules by the completion-like procedures of [Kaplan, 1987; Ganzinger, 1987]. In these methods, superposition is used when the left-hand side is larger than the conditions; narrowing, when a condition dominates the left-hand side. As theorem provers, however, they are refutationally *in*complete, since they make no provision for "unorientable" equations $s \simeq t$ such that $s \not\succ t$ and $t \not\succ s$.

The inference rules we present may be classified into three "expansion" rules and four "contraction" rules. Contraction rules significantly reduce space requirements, but make proofs of completeness much more subtle.

Superpose:
$$\frac{E \cup \left\{ \begin{array}{l} p \Rightarrow l \simeq r, \\ q \Rightarrow u \simeq v \end{array} \right\}}{E \cup \left\{ \begin{array}{l} p \Rightarrow l \simeq r, \\ q \Rightarrow u \simeq v, \\ p\mu \wedge q\mu \Rightarrow u\mu[r\mu]_\pi \simeq v\mu \end{array} \right\}}$$
$$\text{if } \left\{ \begin{array}{l} u|_\pi \notin \mathcal{X} \\ \mu = mgu(u|_\pi, l) \\ u\mu \not\preceq p\mu, q\mu, v\mu, u\mu[r\mu]_\pi \end{array} \right.$$

Superposition (i.e. oriented paramodulation of positive equational literals) is performed only at non-variable positions ($u|_\pi \notin \mathcal{X}$). Only positive equations are used in this rule, and only in a decreasing direction ($u\mu \not\preceq p\mu, q\mu$). Either side of an equation may be used for superposition, but only if, in the context of the paramodulation, it is potentially the largest term involved ($u\mu \not\preceq v\mu, u\mu[r\mu]_\pi$). Note that the two conditional equations may actually be the same (except for renaming). Here and later, when a rule refers to a clause of the form $q \Rightarrow u \simeq v$, an unconditional equation ($u \simeq v$) is also intended. When both participating equations are unconditional, an unconditional "ordered" critical pair is generated.

We need, additionally, a rule that paramodulates into maximal negative literals:

Narrow:
$$\frac{E \cup \left\{ \begin{array}{lcl} p & \Rightarrow & l \simeq r, \\ q \wedge s \simeq t & \Rightarrow & u \simeq v \end{array} \right\}}{E \cup \left\{ \begin{array}{lcl} p & \Rightarrow & l \simeq r, \\ q \wedge s \simeq t & \Rightarrow & u \simeq v, \\ p\mu \wedge q\mu \wedge s\mu[r\mu]_\pi \simeq t\mu & \Rightarrow & u\mu \simeq v\mu \end{array} \right\}}$$
$$\text{if } \left\{ \begin{array}{l} s|_\pi \notin \mathcal{X} \\ \mu = mgu(s|_\pi, l) \\ s\mu \not\preceq p\mu, q\mu, t\mu, s\mu[r\mu]_\pi \end{array} \right.$$

Whenever this or subsequent rules refer to a conditional equation like $q \wedge s \simeq t \Rightarrow u \simeq v$, the intent is that $s \simeq t$ is any one of the conditions and u is either side of the implied equation.

The last expansion rule in effect resolves a maximal negative literal with reflexivity of equals ($x \simeq x$):

Reflect:
$$\frac{E \cup \{\, q \wedge s \simeq t \;\Rightarrow\; u \simeq v \,\}}{E \cup \left\{ \begin{array}{lcl} q \wedge s \simeq t & \Rightarrow & u \simeq v, \\ q\sigma & \Rightarrow & u\sigma \simeq v\sigma \end{array} \right\}}$$
$$\text{if } \left\{ \begin{array}{l} \sigma = mgu(s,t) \\ s\sigma \not\preceq q\sigma \end{array} \right.$$

The contraction rules all simplify the set of conditional equations. The first deletes trivial conditional equations:

Delete:
$$\frac{E \cup \{\, q \;\Rightarrow\; u \simeq u \,\}}{E}$$

The next rule allows for deletion of conditions that are trivially true:

Condense:
$$\frac{E \cup \{\, q \wedge s \simeq s \;\Rightarrow\; u \simeq v \,\}}{E \cup \{\, q \;\Rightarrow\; u \simeq v \,\}}$$

The last two contraction rules use decreasing instances to simplify other clauses. One rule simplifies conditions; the other applies to the equation part. In both cases, the original clause is *replaced* by a version that is logically equivalent, assuming the rest of E.

Simplify:
$$\frac{E \cup \{\, p \;\Rightarrow\; u \simeq v \,\}}{E \cup \{\, q \;\Rightarrow\; u \simeq v \,\}} \qquad \text{if } p \rightarrow_E q$$

Compose:
$$\frac{E \cup \{\, q \;\Rightarrow\; u \simeq v \,\}}{E \cup \{\, q \;\Rightarrow\; w \simeq v \,\}}$$
$$\text{if } \left\{ \begin{array}{l} u \rightarrow_{p \Rightarrow l \simeq r} w,\ p \Rightarrow l \simeq r \in E \\ v \succ u \vee (u \simeq v) \rhd (l \simeq r) \end{array} \right.$$

By $u \simeq v \rhd l \simeq r$ we mean that the larger of u and v, say u, is strictly greater than the larger side of $l \simeq r$, say l, in the *encompassment* ordering (wherein a term is larger than its proper subterms and smaller than its proper instances), or that $u = l$ but v is strictly greater than r under $\succ$. This allows the larger side of an equation to be simplified by a more general equation, and the smaller side to be rewritten in any case.

We use the notation $E \vdash E'$ to denote *one* inference step, applying any of the seven rules to a set E of conditional equations to obtain a new set E'. The inference rules are evidently sound, in that the class of provable theorems is unchanged by an inference step.

4 Strategies

Let $>$ be any complete simplification ordering extending the given partial ordering $\succ$. A *proof* of an equation $s \simeq t$ between *ground* terms (any variables in s and t may be treated as Skolem constants) is a "derivation"

$$s = t_1 \underset{e_1\sigma_1}{\overset{\pi_1}{\longleftrightarrow}} t_2 \underset{e_2\sigma_2}{\overset{\pi_2}{\longleftrightarrow}} \cdots \underset{e_m\sigma_m}{\overset{\pi_m}{\longleftrightarrow}} t_{m+1} = t$$
$$\qquad\quad P_1 \qquad\quad P_2 \qquad\qquad P_m$$

of $m+1$ terms ($m \geq 0$), each step $t_k \leftrightarrow t_{k+1}$ of which is either *trivial* ($t_{k+1} = t_k$), or else is justified by a conditional equation e_k in E, a position π_k in t_k, a substitution σ_k for variables in the equation, and subproofs P_k (of the same form) for each conditions $u_{k,j}\sigma_k \simeq v_{k,j}\sigma_k$ of the applied instance $e_k\sigma_k$. Steps employing an unconditional equation do not have subproofs as part of their justification. (By the completeness of positive-unit resolution for Horn clauses, any equation $s \simeq t$ that is valid for a set E of conditional equations is amenable to such an equational proof.)

We use $\leftarrow$ for the inverse of $\rightarrow$, and $\rightarrow^*$ and $\leftarrow^*$ for the reflexive-transitive closures of $\rightarrow$ and $\leftarrow$, respectively. By a *peak*, we mean a proof segment of the form $s \leftarrow u \rightarrow t$; by a *valley*, we mean a proof segment of the form $u \rightarrow^* w \leftarrow^* t$; by a *drop*, we mean a step $s \rightarrow t$ with valley subproofs; a *plateau* is a trivial subproof of form $s \leftrightarrow s$. The *depth* of a proof is the maximum nesting of subproofs; it is one more than the maximum depth of its subproofs.

4.1 Unit Stratgey

The inference rules of the previous section are designed to allow any equational proof to be transformed into normal form. A strategy based on these rules is complete if we can show that, with enough inferences, any theorem has a normal-form proof. For the unit strategy, a *normal-form* proof is a valley proof of depth 0. That is the same as saying that a normal-form proof has no peaks, no drops, and no plateaus. Normal-form proofs may be thought of as "direct" proofs; in a refutational framework the existence of such a proof for $s \simeq t$ means that demodulation of s and t using positive unit equations suffices to derive a contradiction between the Skolemized negation $s' \not\simeq t'$ of the given theorem and $x \simeq x$.

We must demonstrate that for any proof $s \leftrightarrow^* t$ of $s \simeq t$ in E_0, there eventually exists an unconditional valley proof $s \rightarrow^* w \leftarrow^* t$. In the unit strategy, only expansions involving an unconditional equation are necessary. Specifically, both equations used by **superpose** are unconditional and the positive literal used in **narrow** is a unit. Were it not for contraction rules, it would be relatively easy to show that **narrow** and **reflect** eventually provide an unconditional proof of $s \simeq t$, and that **superpose** eventually turns that into a valley.

We call an inference "fair" if all persistent superpositions of *unit* clauses, narrowings via unit clauses, and reflections have been considered:

Unit Strategy: An inference sequence $E_0 \vdash E_1 \vdash \ldots$ is *fair* with respect to the unit strategy if

$$\mathbf{exp}^1(E_\infty) \subseteq \bigcup_{i \geq 0} E_i,$$

where E_∞ is the set $\liminf_j E_j = \cup_{i\geq 0} \cap_{j \geq i} E_j$ of *persisting* conditional equations and $\mathbf{exp}^1(E_\infty)$ is the set of conditional equations that may be inferred from persisting equations by one application of **superpose** with p and q empty, **narrow** with p empty, or **reflect**.

Theorem 1. *If an inference sequence $E_0 \vdash E_1 \vdash \ldots$ is fair for the unit strategy, then for any proof of $s \simeq t$ in E_0, there is a normal-form proof of $s \simeq t$ in E_∞.*

This is shown by transfinite induction on proofs. The term ordering $>$ is extended to the transitive closure of it and the proper subterm ordering. This in turn is extended to equations by considering the equation as a multiset of two terms, and using the multiset extension of this ordering. (In the multiset ordering [Dershowitz and Manna, 1979], a multiset is decreased by replacing an element with any finite number of smaller elements.) An equation is greater than a term if and only if one of its sides is. Conjunctions of equations are compared as multisets of these multisets, and a conjunction is larger than a term if one of its conjuncts is. Proofs are measured in the following way: Consider a step

$$s = w[l\sigma]_\pi \underset{e\sigma}{\overset{\pi}{\longleftrightarrow}} w[r\sigma]_\pi = t$$

in a ground proof or its subproofs, where e is the conditional equation $q \Rightarrow l \simeq r$ justifying the step, σ is the substitution, and s is the larger of s and t (in the complete simplification ordering $>$ extending $\succ$). To each such step, we assign the weight

$$(\{q\sigma, s, l\sigma\}, e)$$

Steps are compared in the lexicographic ordering of these pairs. The first components of pairs are compared in the multiset extension of the ordering on conjunctions and terms described above. (Note that s is always greater or equal to $l\sigma$, and that for decreasing instances it is also greater than $q\sigma$.) Second components are compared using the extension $\rhd$ of the encompassment ordering described earlier. Proofs are compared in the well-founded multiset extension of the lexicographic ordering on steps. We use $\gg$ to denote this proof ordering. It can be shown by standard arguments (see, e.g., [Dershowitz and Jouannaud, 1990]) that $\gg$ is well-founded.

Note that if $s \rightarrow_e t$, then the cost of this step is always greater than the cost of the steps in its subproofs. Also, if $s \rightarrow t \rightarrow u$, then the cost of the first step is larger than that of the second.

We need to show that inferences never increase the complexity of proofs and, furthermore, that there are always inferences that can decrease the complexity of non-normal proofs. Then, by induction with respect to $\gg$, the eventual existence of a normal-form proof follows.

Lemma 1. *If $E \vdash E'$, then for any proof P in E of an equation $s \simeq t$, there exists a proof P' in E' of $s \simeq t$, such that $P \gg P'$ or $P = P'$.*

This is established by consideration of the effects of each contracting inference rule that deletes or replaces equations, since for expansion rules, $E \subseteq E'$, and we can take $P' = P$. The conditions imposed on **compose** are essential for showing a decrease in $\gg$. (A more general contraction rule would simply allow deletion of any equation that admits a smaller proof vis-a-vis $\gg$.)

Lemma 2. *If P is a non-normal-form proof in E, then there exists a proof P' in $E \cup \mathbf{exp}^1(E)$ such that $P \gg P'$.*

The argument depends on a distinction between "non-critical" subproofs, for which there is a proof P' in E

itself, and "critical" subproofs, for which equations in $\mathbf{exp}^1(E)$ are needed. A peak

$$t' \leftarrow^{\pi}_{p\sigma\Rightarrow l\sigma\simeq r\sigma} t \rightarrow^{\rho}_{q\tau\Rightarrow u\tau\simeq v\tau} t''$$

where $t = w[l\sigma]_\pi[u\tau]_\rho$, is *critical* if the position π is at or below the position ρ in w at which $u \simeq v$ is applied, but not at or below a position corresponding to any variable in u, or (symmetrically) if ρ falls within the non-variable part of the occurrence of l in w. Similarly, a drop $t \rightarrow^{\pi}_{q\sigma\Rightarrow e\sigma} t''$ is *critical* if the first or last step of one of the subproofs for $q\sigma$ takes place within the non-variable part of the condition q.

Since any proof must have at least one subproof of depth 0, any non-normal proof must have a plateau, an *unconditional* peak, or a drop of depth 1 with (unconditional) valley subproofs. Thus, we need not worry about peaks involving a conditional rule, nor drops in which the proof of some condition is not unconditional. All plateaus can be spliced out. Critical unconditional peaks, critical drops with non-empty unconditional valley subproofs, and drops with empty proofs of conditions can each be replaced by a smaller proof, using the conditional equation generated by a required application of **superpose**, **narrow**, or **reflect** inference, respectively. Narrowing can be restricted to the maximal side of the maximal condition, since a drop with non-empty subproofs must have a step emanating from the larger side of its largest condition.

Non-critical unconditional peaks $t' \leftarrow t \rightarrow t''$ have alternative, smaller proofs $t' \rightarrow^* t \leftarrow^* t''$ in E by the version of the Critical Pair Lemma in [Lankford, 1975]. Consider a non-critical drop $w[u\sigma] \leftrightarrow_{q\sigma\Rightarrow u\sigma\simeq v\sigma} w[v\sigma]$, with unconditional subproof $p\sigma \rightarrow p' \rightarrow^* p'' \leftarrow^* p'''$, where $p\sigma$ is no smaller than any other term in the subproof $q\sigma$. Suppose p has a variable x at position π and the first step applies within the variable part $p|_\pi$. That is, $p\sigma = p\sigma[x\sigma]_\pi \rightarrow p\sigma[r]_\pi = p'$. Let τ be the same substitution as σ except that $\tau : x \mapsto r$. There is a smaller proof (smaller, vis-a-vis $\gg$) in E: $w[u\sigma] \leftarrow^* w[u\tau] \leftrightarrow_{q\sigma\Rightarrow u\sigma\simeq v\sigma} w[v\tau] \rightarrow^* w[v\sigma]$. Any rewrites $x\sigma \rightarrow r$ that need to be added to turn a proof of $q\sigma$ into a proof of $q\tau$ are also smaller.

Theorem 1 follows: If $s \simeq t$ is provable in E_0, then (by Lemma 1) it has a proof P in the limit E_∞. If P is non-normal, then (by Lemma 2) it admits a smaller proof P' using (in addition to E_∞) a finite number of equations in $\mathbf{exp}^1(E_\infty)$. By fairness, each of those equations appeared at least once along the way. Subsequent inferences (by Lemma 1) can only decrease the complexity of the proof of such an equation once it appears in a set E_i (and has a one-step proof). Thus, each equation needed in P' has a proof of no greater complexity in E_∞ itself, and hence (by the multiset nature of the proof measure), there is a proof of $s \simeq t$ in E_∞ that is strictly smaller than P. Since the ordering on proofs is well-founded, by induction there must be a normal proof in E_∞.

4.2 Decreasing Strategy

In the above method, only unconditional equations are used for superposition and narrowing. An alternative is to design an inference system that distinguishes between decreasing and nondecreasing non-unit clauses. We give here a method based on the incomplete completion method in [Ganzinger, 1987]. The required inferences (using **superpose** and **narrow**) are again a stringent restriction of paramodulation.

For the decreasing method, we redefine a normal-form proof of $s \simeq t$ to be a valley proof in which each subproof is also in normal form and each term in a subproof is smaller than the larger of s and t; see [Dershowitz and Okada, 1988]. Any non-normal-form proof has a peak made from decreasing instances with normal-form subproofs, or has a nondecreasing step with normal-form subproofs, or has a trivial step. The Critical Pair Lemma of [Kaplan, 1987] for decreasing systems can be adapted to ground confluence of decreasing systems. Superposition is needed between decreasing conditional rules. As before, we must perform enough expansions with persistent conditional equations for there to always be a normal-form proof in the limit.

Decreasing Strategy: An inference sequence $E_0 \vdash E_1 \vdash \cdots$ is *fair* with respect to the decreasing strategy if

$$\mathbf{exp}(E_\infty) \subseteq \bigcup_{i\geq 0} E_i,$$

where $\mathbf{exp}(E_\infty)$ is the set of conditional equations that may be inferred from persisting equations by one application of an expansion rule **superpose**, **narrow**, or **reflect**.

Theorem 2. *If an inference sequence is fair for the decreasing strategy, then for any proof of $s \simeq t$ in the initial set E_0 of conditional equations, there is a normal-form proof of $s \simeq t$ in the limit E_∞.*

5 Discussion

We presented two complete theorem-proving strategies based on the use of term-orderings. Both strategies provide for simplification (demodulation) by what we called "decreasing" equations.

Our unit strategy is the first to combine a restriction to paramodulation with unit equations with a strategy based on maximal terms. It limited inferences in the following ways: (1) The functional reflexive axioms are not needed and, at the same time, paramodulation into variables is avoided (as for some versions of paramodulation); (2) for all (resolution and paramodulation) inferences, at least one of the equations must be unconditional (as in positive unit resolution and positive unit paramodulation); (3) unless an equation is unconditional only its conditional part is used for paramodulation (analogous to positive-unit resolution); (4) only maximal terms (with respect to a given ordering) are used (analogous to ordered resolution). Unlike [Kounalis and Rusinowitch, 1987], we use only unit clauses when paramodulating into conditions; unlike [Bachmair *et al.*, 1989], all inferences use only the maximal side of an equation.

The second strategy prefers paramodulation between positive literals. It requires less paramodulation and offers more simplification than [Kounalis and Rusinowitch, 1987], for example. In essence, it treats decreasing equations like unit clauses of the first strategy. When the ordering supplied to the prover is empty (the empty ordering is completable), the method reduces to "special" paramodulation, in which the functional-reflexive axioms are not needed and paramodulation into variables is not performed (see [Lankford, 1975]). The limitations on paramodulation are like those in [Bertling, 1990], but we give a specific, practical strategy for simplification.

The strength of these methods, both in minimizing possible inferences and maximizing potential simplifications, is brought to bear by employing more complete orderings than the empty one. A nonempty ordering eliminates many potential paramodulations and allows conditional equations that are simplifiable to be replaced without compromising (refutation) completeness. In practice, any efficiently computable ordering should be better than uncontrolled paramodulation. The polynomial and path orderings commonly used in rewrite-based theorem provers [Dershowitz, 1987] are completable. In particular, the recursive path orderings have decidability properties [Jouannaud and Okada, 1991] that make it ideal for this purpose. Choosing an ordering that takes the goal (theorem) into account can impart a top-down flavor to an otherwise bottom-up procedure.

We used the same ordering for simplification as for choosing the maximal literal. In fact, a different selection strategy can be used for choosing the literal to narrow, as in [Bertling and Ganzinger, 1989], but then the term ordering must be used to choose the larger side of the equality.

References

[Bachmair and Ganzinger, 1990] Leo Bachmair and Harald Ganzinger. Completion of first-order clauses with equality. In M. Okada, editor, *Proceedings of the Second International Workshop on Conditional and Typed Rewriting Systems*, Montreal, Canada, June 1990. *Lecture Notes in Computer Science*, Springer, Berlin, to appear.

[Bachmair *et al.*, 1986] Leo Bachmair, Nachum Dershowitz, and Jieh Hsiang. Orderings for equational proofs. In *Proceedings of the IEEE Symposium on Logic in Computer Science*, pages 346–357, Cambridge, MA, June 1986.

[Bachmair *et al.*, 1989] Leo Bachmair, Nachum Dershowitz, and David A. Plaisted. Completion without failure. In H. Aït-Kaci and M. Nivat, editors, *Resolution of Equations in Algebraic Structures 2: Rewriting Techniques*, chapter 1, pages 1–30. Academic Press, New York, 1989.

[Bertling and Ganzinger, 1989] Hubert Bertling and Harald Ganzinger. Completion-time optimization of rewrite-time goal solving. In N. Dershowitz, editor, *Proceedings of the Third International Conference on Rewriting Techniques and Applications*, pages 45–58, Chapel Hill, NC, April 1989. Vol. 355 of *Lecture Notes in Computer Science*, Springer, Berlin.

[Bertling, 1990] Hubert Bertling. Knuth-Bendix completion of Horn clause programs for restricted linear resolution and paramodulation. In S. Kaplan and M. Okada, editors, *Extended Abstracts of the Second International Workshop on Conditional and Typed Rewriting Systems*, pages 89–95, Montreal, Canada, June 1990. Revised version to appear in *Lecture Notes in Computer Science*, Springer, Berlin.

[Boyer, 1971] Robert S. Boyer. *Locking: A restriction of resolution*. Ph.d., University of Texas at Austin, Austin, TX, 1971.

[Brown, 1975] Thomas Carl Brown, Jr. *A Structured Design-Method for Specialized Proof Procedures*. PhD thesis, California Institute of Technology, Pasadena, CA, 1975.

[Dershowitz and Jouannaud, 1990] Nachum Dershowitz and Jean-Pierre Jouannaud. Rewrite systems. In J. van Leeuwen, editor, *Handbook of Theoretical Computer Science B: Formal Methods and Semantics*, chapter 6, pages 243 320. North-Holland, Amsterdam, 1990.

[Dershowitz and Manna, 1979] Nachum Dershowitz and Zohar Manna. Proving termination with multiset orderings. *Communications of the ACM*, 22(8):465–476, August 1979.

[Dershowitz and Okada, 1988] Nachum Dershowitz and Mitsuhiro Okada. Proof-theoretic techniques and the theory of rewriting. In *Proceedings of the Third IEEE Symposium on Logic in Computer Science*, pages 104–111, Edinburgh, Scotland, July 1988.

[Dershowitz, 1987] Nachum Dershowitz. Termination of rewriting. *J. of Symbolic Computation*, 3(1&2):69–115, February/April 1987. Corrigendum: *4*, 3 (December 1987), 409–410.

[Dershowitz, 1990] Nachum Dershowitz. A maximal-literal unit strategy for Horn clauses. In S. Kaplan and M. Okada, editors, *Extended Abstracts of the Second International Workshop on Conditional and Typed Rewriting Systems*, pages 21–27, Montreal, Canada, June 1990. Concordia University. Revised version to appear in *Lecture Notes in Computer Science*, Springer, Berlin.

[Furbach, 1987] Ulrich Furbach. Oldy but goody: Paramodulation revisited. In Morik, editor, *Proceedings of the GI Workshop on Artificial Intelligence*, pages 195–200, 1987. Vol. 152 of *Informatik Fachberichte*.

[Ganzinger, 1987] Harald Ganzinger. A completion procedure for conditional equations. In S. Kaplan and J.-P. Jouannaud, editors, *Proceedings of the First International Workshop on Conditional Term Rewriting Systems*, pages 62–83, Orsay, France, July 1987. Vol. 308 of *Lecture Notes in Computer Science*, Springer, Berlin (1988).

[Henschen and Wos, 1974] L. Henschen and L. Wos. Unit refutations and Horn sets. *J. of the Association for Computing Machinery*, 21:590–605, 1974.

[Hsiang and Rusinowitch, 1986] Jieh Hsiang and Michaël Rusinowitch. A new method for establishing refutational completeness in theorem proving. In

J. H. Siekmann, editor, *Proceedings of the Eighth International Conference on Automated Deduction*, pages 141–152, Oxford, England, July 1986. Vol. 230 of *Lecture Notes in Computer Science*, Springer, Berlin.

[Hsiang and Rusinowitch, 1987] Jieh Hsiang and Michaël Rusinowitch. On word problems in equational theories. In T. Ottmann, editor, *Proceedings of the Fourteenth EATCS International Conference on Automata, Languages and Programming*, pages 54–71, Karlsruhe, West Germany, July 1987. Vol. 267 of *Lecture Notes in Computer Science*, Springer, Berlin.

[Jouannaud and Okada, 1991] Jean-Pierre Jouannaud and Mitsuhiro Okada. Satisfiability of systems of ordinal notations with the subterm property is decidable. In *Proceedings of the Eighteenth EATCS Colloquium on Automata, Languages and Programming*, Madrid, Spain, July 1991. To appear.

[Kaplan, 1987] Stéphane Kaplan. Simplifying conditional term rewriting systems: Unification, termination and confluence. *J. Symbolic Computation*, 4(3):295–334, December 1987.

[Knuth and Bendix, 1970] Donald E. Knuth and P. B. Bendix. Simple word problems in universal algebras. In J. Leech, editor, *Computational Problems in Abstract Algebra*, pages 263–297. Pergamon Press, Oxford, U. K., 1970. Reprinted in *Automation of Reasoning 2*, Springer, Berlin, pp. 342–376 (1983).

[Kounalis and Rusinowitch, 1987] Emmanuel Kounalis and Michaël Rusinowitch. On word problems in Horn theories. In S. Kaplan and J.-P. Jouannaud, editors, *Proceedings of the First International Workshop on Conditional Term Rewriting Systems*, pages 144–160, Orsay, France, July 1987. Vol. 308 of *Lecture Notes in Computer Science*, Springer, Berlin (1988).

[Lankford, 1975] Dallas S. Lankford. Canonical inference. Memo ATP-32, Automatic Theorem Proving Project, University of Texas, Austin, TX, December 1975.

[Nieuwenhuis and Orejas, 1990] Robert Nieuwenhuis and Fernando Orejas. Clausal rewriting. In S. Kaplan and M. Okada, editors, *Extended Abstracts of the Second International Workshop on Conditional and Typed Rewriting Systems*, pages 81–88, Montreal, Canada, June 1990. Concordia University. Revised version to appear in *Lecture Notes in Computer Science*, Springer, Berlin.

[Paul, 1986] Etienne Paul. On solving the equality problem in theories defined by Horn clauses. *Theoretical Computer Science*, 44(2):127–153, 1986.

[Robinson and Wos, 1969] G. Robinson and L. Wos. Paramodulation and theorem-proving in first order theories with equality. In B. Meltzer and D. Michie, editors, *Machine Intelligence 4*, pages 135–150. Edinburgh University Press, Edinburgh, Scotland, 1969.

[Rusinowitch, 1989] Michaël Rusinowitch. *Démonstration Automatique: Techniques de réécriture*. InterEditions, Paris, France, 1989.

[Zhang and Kapur, 1988] Hantao Zhang and Deepak Kapur. First-order theorem proving using conditional equations. In E. Lusk and R. Overbeek, editors, *Proceedings of the Ninth International Conference on Automated Deduction*, pages 1–20, Argonne, Illinois, May 1988. Vol. 310 of *Lecture Notes in Computer Science*, Springer, Berlin.

AUTOMATED REASONING

Theorem Proving II

A Model Elimination Calculus for Generalized Clauses

Toni Bollinger
IBM Deutschland GmbH - Wissenschaftliches Zentrum
Institut für Wissensbasierte Systeme
Schloßstr.70
D-7000 Stuttgart 1, Germany
e-mail: bollinge@ds0lilog.bitnet

Abstract

Generalized clauses differ from (ordinary) clauses by allowing conjunctions of literals in the role of (ordinary) literals, i.e. they are disjunctions of conjunctions of simple literals. An advantage of this clausal form is that implications with conjunctive conclusions or disjunctive premises are not split into multiple clauses. An extension of Loveland's model elimination calculus [Loveland, 1969a, Loveland, 1978] is presented able to deal with such generalized clauses. Furthermore we describe a method for generating lemmas that correspond to valid instances of conjunctive conclusions. Using these lemmas it is possible to avoid multiple proofs of the premises of implications with conjunctive conclusions.

1 Introduction

Several extensions of the resolution rule and its refinements have been proposed able to deal with quantifier free first order logic formulas (e.g. see [Muray, 1982] for an extension of the resolution rule and [Stickel, 1982] for a modification of the connection-graph procedure). These proof procedures have the advantage that it is not necessary to build a clausal normal from, i.e., despite from establishing a prenex normal form and skolemizing existentially quantified variables no normalization operations are necessary. This enhances the readability and understandability of proofs and can also lead to shorter deductions.

However, these modifications do not necessarily exploit the control structure implicit in logical formulas. In particular, although an implication $a \rightarrow b \wedge c$ is not broken into two clauses $\neg a \vee b$ and $\neg a \vee c$, it is not excluded that a has to be proven twice in a proof of $b \wedge c$. This happens when, for instance the proof search performs a kind of backward chaining.

In this paper we present an extension of the model elimination calculus [Loveland, 1969a, Loveland, 1978] which overcomes this drawback. It works on so called *generalized clauses* which are disjunctions of *complex literals* being conjunctions of (simple) literals. For example, the implication $(a \vee b) \rightarrow (c \wedge d)$ is equivalent to the generalized clause $(\neg a \wedge \neg b) \vee (c \wedge d)$ where $\neg a \wedge \neg b$ and $c \wedge d$ are complex literals.

This restriction to generalized clauses is mainly motivated by pragmatic considerations, as we use the extended model elimination calculus for processing the predicate logic part of the knowledge representation language $\mathrm{L_{LILOG}}$ [Pletat and v. Luck, 1990, Bollinger and Pletat, 1991] in the LEU/2[1] text understanding and question answering system [Geurts, 1990]. Items of a knowledge base need to be easily comprehensible. This is the case for Prolog like rules and facts, but not for arbitrary logical formulas. Even if they are quite simple they can be misinterpreted, e.g., for seeing that the formulae $a \rightarrow (b \rightarrow c)$ and $(a \rightarrow b) \rightarrow c$ are not equivalent one needs at least some basic knowledge in logic. On the other hand by using definite or indefinite clauses, knowledge cannot be expressed in a compact way. Generalized clauses are therefore a good compromise. Rules with a conjuntive conclusion or a disjunctive premise are not torn apart. Equivalences between conjunctions of literals can be represented by two generalized clauses.

In the next section we explain how Loveland's weak model elimination calculus can be adapted to generalized clauses. Compared to Loveland's calculus, deductions in this calculus require in general less inference steps as well as less computations. We then describe a method for generating lemmas. Using these lemmas, we show that redundant proofs of the premises of rules with a conjunctive conclusion can be avoided. We conclude with a discussion of the calculus.

2 Extending Model Elimination to Generalized Clauses

2.1 Model Elimination for Ordinary Clauses

Model Elimination[2] can be considered as a refinement of linear resolution where resolution steps are restricted to input clauses. Resolution steps with predecessor clauses in the proof tree are simulated by the reduction rule. For this it is necessary to mark resolved literals instead of deleting them.

[1] LEU is the acronym for "LILOG Experimentierumgebung" - LILOG experimental environment.

[2] To be more precise it is Loveland's *weak* model elimination method [Loveland, 1978] that we will present in the following.

More precisely, instead of clauses, we have *chains* which are ordered sequences of ordinary literals, called *O-literals*, and resolved literals, *R-literals*. R-literals are enclosed in brackets ([L]) for distinguishing them from O-literals. Chains containing only O-literals are *elementary* chains. *Unit* chains consist of only one literal. We call the universal closure of the disjunction of its O-literals the *clausal interpretation* of a chain. A chain is called *admissible* if the right-most literal is an O-literal[3]. The *contraction-operation* transforms a chain into an admissible one by removing all R-literals to the right of the right-most O-literal.

The model elimination method consists of two inference operations:

- the *extension rule* corresponding to the resolution rule and
- the *reduction rule.*

For defining them we use the notion of *complementarity of literals*:

Definition 1 (Complementarity of literals) *Two literals L_1 and L_2 can be made complementary with a most general unifier Θ iff L_1 and the complement of L_2 are unifiable with a most general unifier Θ.*

The two model elimination rules are defined as follows:

Definition 2 (ME extension) *Let $c_1 = c_1' L_1$ and $c_2 = c_2' L_2 c_2''$ be two admissible chains, L_1 and L_2 be O-literals and α be a renaming of the variables in c_2 such that c_1 and $c_2\alpha$ have no variables in common. If L_1 and $L_2\alpha$ can be made complementary with a most general unifier Θ, then the contraction of $(c_1'[L_1]c_2'\alpha c_2''\alpha)\Theta$ is called the* ME extension *of c_1 with c_2.*

Definition 3 (ME reduction) *Let $c = c'[L_1]c''L_2$ be an admissible chain. If L_1 and L_2 can be made complementary with a most general unifier Θ then the contraction of $(c'[L_1]c'')\Theta$ is a result of the* ME reduction *of c.*

The rationale behind the reduction rule is that in a chain $c'[L]c''$ the subchain $c'L$ is always an instance of a chain used for an extension step. Hence the reduction of a chain corresponds to an extension step eventually followed by a factorization.

For completing the presentation of model elimination we have to introduce the notions of model elimination (ME) deduction and model elimination (ME) refutation:

Definition 4 (ME deduction) *Given a set S of elementary chains, an* ME deduction *of a chain c from S is a finite sequence of chains $c_1, \ldots, c_n$ with*

- $c_1 \in S$,
- *for i=2,...,n c_i is obtained by ME extension of c_{i-1} with an (auxiliary) chain from S or by ME reduction of c_{i-1},*
- $c = c_n$.

[3] Loveland's definition in [Loveland, 1978] contains 3 supplementary conditions for the admissibility of chains. But it is easy to see and has already been stated in [Casanova *et al.*, 1989] that their removal neither affects soundness nor completeness of (weak) model elimination.

Definition 5 (ME refutation) *A refutation of a set S of elementary chains is a deduction from S of the empty chain $\Box$.*

Example 1 *We will use the following example throughout this paper for illustrating our modifications of the standard model elimination calculus.*
Given the following axioms:
ax_1: $\forall x G(x) \lor Y(x) \rightarrow C(x) \land S(x)$,
ax_2: $G(p) \lor Y(p)$,
where G(x) may stand for "x is a gourmet", Y(x) for "x is a yuppy", C(x) for "x likes to drink champaign", S(x) for "x likes to eat snails" and p can be interpreted as "Peter", one likes to prove the goal
g: $\exists x C(x) \land S(x)$.
After having built a clausal normal form of the axioms and the negated goal we get the following refutation of the resulting set of chains:

(a_{11})	$\neg G(x)C(x)$	
(a_{12})	$\neg G(x)S(x)$	
(a_{13})	$\neg Y(x)C(x)$	
(a_{14})	$\neg Y(x)S(x)$	
(a_2)	$G(p)Y(p)$	
(1)	$\neg C(x)\neg S(x)$	negated goal
(2)	$\neg C(x)[\neg S(x)]\neg G(x)$	ext. with a_{12}
(3)	$\neg C(p)[\neg S(p)][\neg G(p)]Y(p)$	ext. with a_2
(4)	$\neg C(p)[\neg S(p)][\neg G(p)][Y(p)]S(p)$	ext. with a_{14}
(5)	$\neg C(p)$	reduction
(6)	$[\neg C(p)]\neg G(p)$	ext. with a_{11}
(7)	$[\neg C(p)][\neg G(p)]Y(p)$	ext. with a_2
(8)	$[\neg C(p)][\neg G(p)][Y(p)]C(p)$	ext. with a_{13}
(9)	$\Box$	reduction

Extension and reduction are sound inference rules. Further they form a (refutationally) complete calculus. The following two theorems state this in a more formal way:

Theorem 1 (Soundness of ME) *If a chain c is the result of an ME deduction from a set S of elementary chains, then the clausal interpretation of c is a logical consequence from S.*

Theorem 2 (Completeness of ME) *If a set S of elementary chains is minimally unsatisfiable, i.e., if every proper subset of S is satisfiable, then for any chain $c \in S$ there is a ME refutation of S starting with c.*

2.2 Resolution for Generalized Clauses

First we formally define the notion of complex literal and generalized clause.

Definition 6 (Complex literal) *A* complex literal *is a conjunction of (simple) literals.*

Definition 7 (Generalized clause) *A* generalized *clause is a disjunction of complex literals.*

When resolving two arbitrary quantifier free formulas (see [Murray, 1982]) first the polarities of all atomic subformulas have to be determined. If they contain two unifiable atomic subformulas with opposite polarity, the unifying substitution is applied to the two formulas. Then all occurences of the atom with positive polarity are replaced by F, representing *false*, and all occurrences of the negative atom in the other formula by T, standing for *true*. The disjunction of these two modified formulas represents the resolvent, which is further simplified by exploiting properties of logical connectives like $a \wedge F \leftrightarrow F$ or $a \vee F \leftrightarrow a$.

Adapting this resolution rule to generalized clauses is straightforward. In generalized clauses the sign of the simple literals indicates the polarity of their atomic formulas. During the resolution operation the positive literal is replaced by F, such that the complex literals it appears in can be reduced to F (complex literals are conjunctions). Hence they can be removed from the resolvent. The same happens with the complex literals where the negative (simple) literal occurrs in, as its atomic formula is replaced by T which is equivalent to replacing the literal by F. Therefore resolving two generalized clauses C_{G1} and C_{G2} consists of unifying a simple literal L_1 of C_{G1} with the complement of a simple literal L_2 from C_{G2}, applying the unifying substitution Θ to $C_{G1} \vee C_{G2}$ and discarding from the resulting generalized clause all complex literals with occurrences of $L_1\Theta$ or $L_2\Theta$.

2.3 Model Elimination for Generalized Clauses

The notions introduced in Section 2.1 can easily be adapted to generalized clauses. Now we have *complex O- and R-literals* and *generalized chains* consisting of complex O- and R-literals. Complex literals are noted as conjunctions of simple literals. If a complex O-literal consists of more than one simple literal it is enclosed in (round) parentheses. As before, R-literals are marked by (square) brackets. The chain $P(a)[Q(b)][P(b) \wedge R(a)](Q(c) \wedge P(c))$, for instance, consists of two complex O- and R-literals.

The definition of admissibility and the contraction operation have to be modified accordingly.

When resolving two generalized clauses only simple literals are compared. This also holds when two complex literals are made complementary. We can therefore define the *complementarity of complex literals* in the following way:

Definition 8 (Complementarity of compl. literals) *Let $\mathcal{L}_1 = L_{11} \wedge \ldots \wedge L_{1m}$ and $\mathcal{L}_2 = L_{21} \wedge \ldots \wedge L_{2n}$ be two complex literals. $\mathcal{L}_1$ and $\mathcal{L}_2$ can be made* complementary, *with a* most general unifier Θ, *iff a simple literal L_{1i} from $\mathcal{L}_1$ and the complement of a simple literal L_{2j} from $\mathcal{L}_2$ are unifiable with most general unifier Θ.*

There may be more than one possible most general unifier for making two complex literals complementary; e.g. for $P(a) \wedge P(b)$ and $\neg P(x)$ we have two most general unifiers: $\Theta_1 = \{a/x\}$ and $\Theta_2 = \{b/x\}$. But all the most general unifiers can be computed since the number of all simple literal pairs from two complex literals is finite.

When resolving two generalized clauses, all complex literals containing the resolved simple literals are discarded. Deleting or bracketing these literals during an extension step may lead to complications, for complex literals standing left of an R-literal may be deleted or transformed to an R-literal. It is therefore possible that the left subchain relative to an R-literal is no longer an instance of a predecessor chain in a deduction. But this is a condition for the correctness of the reduction rule.

Fortunately, it suffices to bracket resp. delete only the complex literals that are made complementary. We can therefore define *generalized model elimination (MGE) extension* and *reduction* rule in the following way:

Definition 9 (GME extension) *Let $\mathcal{C}_1 = \mathcal{C}_1'\mathcal{L}_1$ and $\mathcal{C}_2 = \mathcal{C}_2'\mathcal{L}_2\mathcal{C}_2''$ be two admissible generalized chains, $\mathcal{L}_1$ and $\mathcal{L}_2$ be complex O-literals and α be a renaming of the variables in $\mathcal{C}_2$ such that $\mathcal{C}_1$ and $\mathcal{C}_2\alpha$ have no variables in common. If $\mathcal{L}_1$ and $\mathcal{L}_2\alpha$ can be made complementary with a most general unifier Θ, then the contraction of $(\mathcal{C}_1'[\mathcal{L}_1]\mathcal{C}_2'\alpha\mathcal{C}_2''\alpha)\Theta$ is called the* GME extension *of $\mathcal{C}_1$ with $\mathcal{C}_2$.*

Definition 10 (GME reduction) *Let $\mathcal{C} = \mathcal{C}'[\mathcal{L}_1]\mathcal{C}''\mathcal{L}_2$ be an admissible generalized chain. If the complex literals $\mathcal{L}_1$ and $\mathcal{L}_2$ can be made complementary with a most general unifier Θ then the contraction of $(\mathcal{C}'[\mathcal{L}_1]\mathcal{C}'')\Theta$ is a result of the* GME reduction *of $\mathcal{C}$.*

GME deduction and GME refutation can be defined analogously to ME deduction and ME refutation. One has only to replace in Definition 4 and 5 "chain" by "generalized chain" and "ME" by "GME".

Example 2 *Having built generalized chains for the axioms and the negated goal of Example 1 we get the following GME-refutation:*

(a_1)	$(\neg G(x) \wedge \neg Y(x))(C(x) \wedge S(x))$	
(a_2)	$G(p)Y(p)$	
(1)	$\neg C(x)\neg S(x)$	*neg. goal*
(2)	$\neg C(x)[\neg S(x)](\neg G(x) \wedge \neg Y(x))$	*ext.* (a_1)
(3)	$\neg C(p)[\neg S(p)][\neg G(p) \wedge \neg Y(p)]G(p)$	*ext.* (a_2)
(4)	$\neg C(p)$	*reduction*
(5)	$[\neg C(p)](\neg G(p) \wedge \neg Y(p))$	*ext.* (a_1)
(6)	$[\neg C(p)][\neg G(p) \wedge \neg Y(p)]G(p)$	*ext.* (a_2)
(7)	$\square$	*reduction*

GME extension and GME reduction are sound inference rules. The soundness of GME extension follows from the soundness of resolution for quantifier free formulas. A GME reduction can be simulated by an extension step with a predecessor clause in the deduction such that the clausal interpretations of the resulting chains are equivalent. Hence the GME reduction rule is sound too.

We get therefore the following theorem that can be proven by induction on the length of the concerning deduction:

Theorem 3 (Soundness of GME) *If a generalized chain $\mathcal{C}$ is the result of a GME deduction from a set S of elementary generalized chains, then the clausal interpretation of $\mathcal{C}$ is a logical consequence of S.*

The proof of the completeness of generalized model elimination is based on the following lemma, where the function *coc* produces a kind of conjunctive normal form of a generalized chain.

Lemma 1 *Let $\mathcal{S}$ be a set of generalized elementary chains and let coc ("contained ordinary chains") be a mapping from generalized chains to sets of ordinary chains that is defined as follows:*
$coc(\mathcal{C}) = \{L_{1i_1} L_{2i_2} \ldots L_{ni_n} \| \ j_i = 1,\ldots,m_j, j = 1,\ldots,n\}$ *with* $\mathcal{C} = \mathcal{L}_1\mathcal{L}_2\ldots\mathcal{L}_n$, *where* $\mathcal{L}_j = L_{j1} \wedge \ldots \wedge L_{jm_j}$ *is either a complex O- or an R-literal and L_{ji} inherites the literal type from $\mathcal{L}_j$. Furthermore let $S = \bigcup_{\mathcal{C} \in \mathcal{S}} coc(\mathcal{C})$. If there is a ME-deduction of a chain c from S then there is also a GME-deduction of a generalized chain $\mathcal{C}$ from $\mathcal{S}$ with $c \in coc(\mathcal{C})$.*

Given an ME-deduction of a chain c from S, the proof of this lemma consists essentially of constructing from $\mathcal{S}$ an isomorphic GME-deduction of a generalized chain $\mathcal{C}$ containing c. Being technical it is omitted here and can be found in an extended version of this paper [Bollinger, 1991].

Theorem 4 (Completeness of GME) *If a set $\mathcal{S}$ of generalized elementary chains is minimally unsatisfiable, i.e., if every proper subset of $\mathcal{S}$ is satisfiable, then for any chain $\mathcal{C} \in \mathcal{S}$ there is a refutation of $\mathcal{S}$ starting with $\mathcal{C}$.*

Proof: *As $\mathcal{S}$ is unsatisfiable, $S = \bigcup_{\mathcal{C} \in \mathcal{S}} coc(\mathcal{C})$ is unsatisfiable too. Let $S' \subseteq S$ be a minimally unsatisfiable subset of S. For any $\mathcal{C} \in \mathcal{S}$ we have $coc(\mathcal{C}) \cap S' \neq \emptyset$. If that would not be the case, $\mathcal{S}\backslash\{\mathcal{C}\}$ would be unsatisfiable (due to $coc(\mathcal{S}\backslash\{\mathcal{C}\}) \supseteq S'$), which contradicts the assumption that $\mathcal{S}$ is minimally unsatisfiable.*
Let $c \in coc(\mathcal{C}) \cap S'$. Due to the completeness of model elimination there is a ME deduction of $\Box$ starting with c. As $c \in coc(\mathcal{C})$ Lemma 1 can be applied and we obtain that there is also a GME deduction of $\Box$ from $\mathcal{S}$ starting with $\mathcal{C}$. $\Box$

3 Generating Lemmas

Although GME-refutations in general are shorter than the corresponding ME-refutations, we still have the problem of redundant proofs of premises, whose rules have conjunctive conclusions. In Example 2 we saw that the chain a_1 was applied twice, whereas one application should suffice. In chain (2) the "premise" literal $\neg G(x) \wedge \neg Y(x)$ of a_1 stands to the right of the resolved literal. If this literal is proven one can deduce the conclusion. This is done by the two subsequent inference steps, i.e. at that moment $C(p) \wedge S(p)$ should have been deduced as a lemma. How can we achieve this?

We introduce a third type of literals called *lemma candidates* or *L-literals*. When extending a chain $\mathcal{C}$ with an auxiliary chain $\mathcal{C}_a$ the resolved literal in $\mathcal{C}_a$ is declared as a lemma candidate and is put beside the bracketed literal, the resolved (complex) literal of $\mathcal{C}$ in the resulting chain. Lemma candidates are put into braces, such that in Example 2 above, the extension step of chain (1) with chain a_1 yields:

(2') $\neg C(x)[\neg S(x)]\{C(x) \wedge S(x)\}(\neg G(x) \wedge \neg Y(x))$

If it is possible to deduce the empty chain from the subchain to the right of an L-literal, the corresponding instantiation of the L-literal becomes a valid lemma.

More formally we have:
If $\mathcal{C}_a^1 \neq \Box$ or $\mathcal{C}_a^2 \neq \Box$, an extension step of $\mathcal{C}_1 = \mathcal{C}_1^1\mathcal{L}_1$ with $\mathcal{C}_a = \mathcal{C}_a^1\mathcal{L}_2\mathcal{C}_a^2$ yields,
$\mathcal{C}_2 = (\mathcal{C}_1^1[\mathcal{L}_1]\{\mathcal{L}_2\}\mathcal{C}_a^1\mathcal{C}_a^2)\Theta$.
If there is a deduction of $\Box$ starting with $(\mathcal{C}_a^1\mathcal{C}_a^2)\Theta$ and if Φ is the composition of the most general unifiers in that deduction, then we also have a deduction of $\mathcal{L}_2\Theta\Phi$ starting with $(\mathcal{L}_2\mathcal{C}_a^1\mathcal{C}_a^2)\Theta$.

The refutation of $(\mathcal{C}_a^1\mathcal{C}_a^2)\Theta$ has to be performed when trying to refute $\mathcal{C}_2$. Since chains represent disjunctions of literals, it cannot be taken for granted that a refutation of $\mathcal{C}_2$ contains also a refutation of $(\mathcal{C}_a^1\mathcal{C}_a^2)\Theta$. For this no literal of $\mathcal{C}_1^1[\mathcal{L}_1]$ has to be involved in any extension or reduction step when, during the refutation of $\mathcal{C}_2$, $(\mathcal{C}_a^1\mathcal{C}_a^2)\Theta$ is processed. This is certainly the case if the literals in $(\mathcal{C}_a^1\mathcal{C}_a^2)\Theta$ are eliminated by extension steps. The situation is different for reduction steps. A reduction performed with an R-literal from $\mathcal{C}_1^1[\mathcal{L}_1]$ during the refutation of $\mathcal{C}_2$ can't be transferred to a refutation of $(\mathcal{C}_a^1\mathcal{C}_a^2)\Theta$. For that the R-literal has to stand to the right of $[\mathcal{L}_1]$ in $\mathcal{C}_2$ or a chain deduced from $\mathcal{C}_2$.

We take into account this restriction in the following way: Let us suppose that a reduction step can be applied to $\mathcal{C} = \mathcal{C}^1[\mathcal{L}_2]\mathcal{C}^2\mathcal{L}_1$ by making complementary the literals $\mathcal{L}_1$ and $\mathcal{L}_2$. The lemma candidates in $\mathcal{C}^1$ are not affected by this as the involved O- and R-literal are on the right of $\mathcal{C}^1$. However, for the lemma candidates in $\mathcal{C}^2$ the R-literal $[\mathcal{L}_2]$ stands to the left. Therefore these lemma candidates become invalid and have to be eliminated.

The modifications of the contraction operation, of the GME extension and the GME reduction rule are clear now. The contraction operation also deletes rightmost L-literals, that become valid lemmas. The extension rule may introduce a new L-literal being the "resolved" literal of the auxiliary chain. L-literals standing between the R- and O-literal involved in a reduction operation are deleted.

Example 3 *The refutation of Example 2 is modified as follows if lemmas are generated:*

(a_1)	$(\neg G(x) \wedge \neg Y(x))(C(x) \wedge S(x))$
(a_2)	$G(p)Y(p)$
negated goal:	
(1)	$\neg C(x)\neg S(x)$
extension with (a_1):	
(2)	$\neg C(x)[\neg S(x)]\{C(x) \wedge S(x)\}(\neg G(x) \wedge \neg Y(x))$
extension with (a_2):	
(3)	$\neg C(p)[\neg S(p)]\{C(p) \wedge S(p)\}[\neg G(p) \wedge \neg Y(p)]G(p)$
reduction and generation of lemma (l) $C(p) \wedge S(p)$:	
(4)	$\neg C(p)$
extension with (l):	
(5)	$\Box$

Loveland also proposes a method for generating lemmas. In [Loveland, 1969b], he introduces the notion of *scope* associated with R-literals. It is initialized to 0 and updated when the R-literal is involved in a reduction step. In that case, it is set to the maximum of its actual scope and the number of R-literals standing to the right of it. If due to subsequent reduction and extension steps the scope exceeds the number N of R-literals to the right it is set to N. The subchain in the scope of an R-literal L_R with scope N is the subchain from L_R to the N-th R-literal to the right.

Lemmas can be formed when an R-literal L_R is removed by the contraction operation. The maximal subchain in the scope of an R-literal is taken in which L_R occurs (as the last literal). The lemma is generated by leaving the O-literals unchanged and turning the negation of the R-literals into O-literals.

Example 4 *We show a part of a deduction where lemmas are generated. The indices of the R-literals indicate their scope.*

(i) $P(a)[Q(x)]_0[P(y)]_0\neg Q(a)[R(z)]_0\neg P(a)$

reduction without contraction:

(i+1) $P(a)[Q(x)]_0[P(a)]_1\neg Q(a)[R(z)]_0$

contraction and gen. of lemma $\neg P(a)\neg Q(a)\neg R(z)$*:*

(i+1') $P(a)[Q(x)]_0[P(a)]_1\neg Q(a)$

reduction without contraction:

(i+2) $P(a)[Q(a)]_1[P(a)]_0$

contraction and generation of lemma $\neg Q(a)\neg P(a)$*:*

(i+2') $P(a)$

Specializing our method for lemma generation to ordinary chains we see that it corresponds exactly to the case where Loveland's method is restricted to the generation of unit lemma chains. Lemma candidates are not explicitely recorded since for simple literals they are identical to the negation of the corresponding R-literal. For complex literals this is necessary, as we do not have $\mathcal{L}_1\Theta = \neg\mathcal{L}_2\Theta$ in general when they are complementary.

The removal of lemma candidates after a reduction step has its counterpart in the fact that, according to Loveland's method, the generation of lemmas is based on the maximal subchain in the scope of an R-literal yielding up to the rightmost R-literal. This has the effect that lemmas for R-literals within this subchain (except the leftmost one) are not created.

It is easy to generalize Loveland's method to generalized chains. In this way it is possible to generate lemmas being the instance of disjunctive conclusions. However, from a practical point of view, non-unit lemmas are less useful in general.

4 Discussion

Generalized clauses and chains are interesting extensions of their standard versions. Any quantifier free logical formula can be represented by one such clause or chain. This facilitates especially the processing of disjunctive goals. In contrast to ordinary chains (and clauses) a negated goal can always be transformed to exactly one generalized chain. Moreover, having a set of ordinary chains representing the negated goal, a refutation may succeed with only one of them as the starting chain. Hence for ordinary chains we have the problem of choosing the right chain steming from the negated goal. This problem does not occur for generalized chains, as we have only one goal chain, and from Lemma 1 we know, that its refutation succeeds if it succeeds for one of the ordinary goal chains.

From an implementational viewpoint, generalized model elimination (GME) constitutes only a slight modification of the model elimination method (ME). In contrast to resolution for arbitrary quantifier free formulas, not a lot of supplementary computation has to be performed. The polarity of the literals has already been determined, only simple literals are compared when two complex literals are made complementary. The only real difference to ME consists in the fact that several simple literals are deleted or bracketed during an extension and reduction operation. Of course, if lemmas should be generated, additional computations have to be performed concerning the L-literals. But compared with Loveland's method for lemma generation their complexity is not higher. The computational overhead of GME with respect to ME is therefore low.

However, as GME refutations are generally shorter than ME refutations, (cf. Example 1 compared to Example 2) the overall amount for computing a refutation is lower for GME. This effect is enhanced if lemmas are generated, since the really interesting lemmas are those generated for rules with conjunctive conclusions.

Looking at the search space, one realizes that the number of potential extension and reduction steps is greater for GME than for ME, since complex literals may consist of several simple literals. We know also from the proof of Lemma 1 that for every ME-deduction of a chain c there is an isomorphic GME-deduction of a generalized chain containing c. Hence the search space explored for finding GME-refutations contains more redundancies, i.e., paths leading to identical solutions. This is not critical, if one solution is looked for, as GME-refutations can be shorter. In such a case a depth oriented search strategy is appropriate. If all solutions are looked for, it is necessary to employ a strategy that avoids exploring redundant paths. The development of such strategies is one of the points that need to be investigated further.

GME may perform better than ME if the ressources for the search are restricted. E.g., if the search depth is limited, with GME more solutions can be found, as GME-refutations are shorter.

The generation of lemma should be restricted to the useful ones, since the addition of every new lemma increases the search space. Certainly, creating a lemma candidate when performing an extension step with a unit chain is superfluous, as the deduced lemma is an instance of the used auxiliary unit chain. Simple L-literals are in general less interesting than complex L-literals. Therefore it may be reasonable to generate lemma candidates only if the resolved literal in the auxiliary chain is a real complex literal.

However even the most useful lemmas introduce new redundancies into the search space, i.e., the same solution can be found by using a lemma and by performing the extension and reduction steps that led to the deduction of the lemma. These new redundancies can be neglected, when only one solution is looked for, since it suffices to apply the lemmas first, before trying extension steps with non-unit chains.

When looking for all solutions, we have again the problem of avoiding paths leading to identical solutions. The situation becomes even more complex since the knowledge base changes dynamically with the addition of lemmas. It may also happen that for finding all solutions, lemmas computed at another branch of the proof tree have to be used. Controling the generation and the use of lemmas is therefore another point that will be investigated further.

One pragmatical solution would be to leave it to the user to decide when to apply a rule that lead to the introduction of a lemma. Like with the *cut* in Prolog, the user would be able to prune a part of the search space. The user has then the responsability for taking care that no solutions are lost.

In the LILOG project the knowledge engineers asked for such a feature. It happens often that a conjunction of literals should be treated as one literal. Introducing a new predicate symbol was not possible due to constraints imposed by the text understanding application. In such a case the solutions found by the use of lemmas were sufficient.

5 Conclusion

GME is a useful extension of ME. We have established some of its advantages and have pointed out areas of further investigation. Since GME applied to ordinary chains behaves exactly like ME, one has the flexibility to switch between GME and ME. The normalization procedure has only to produce ordinary chains, and the computational overhead for processing ME with the generalized method is low.

An order sorted version of this calculus with lemma generation has been implemented in Quintus Prolog[4] for the LEU/2 text understanding system. GME has proven to be very useful, given the nature of the application domain, in which a majority of the rules written in the knowledge representation language L_{LILOG} had conjunctive conclusions.

Control issues have to be investigated further. The major problem is how to avoid investigating paths in the search space that lead to redundant solutions. The generation of lemmas can be considered as a kind of rote learning. One may also think of storing certain lemmas permanently or of applying machine learning techniques like "explanation based generalization" for creating more general lemmas. However, for avoiding the classical machine learning problem: "the more you know the slower you go", good strategies need to be developed for controling the generation, the use and eventually the permanent storage of lemmas.

Acknowledgements

I would like to thank Zuzana Dobeš, Karl Hans Bläsius and Udo Pletat for helpful comments on this paper.

References

[Bollinger and Pletat, 1991] Toni Bollinger and Udo Pletat. Knowledge in operation. IWBS-Report, IBM Deutschland, Scientific Center, 1991.

[Bollinger, 1991] Toni Bollinger. A model elimination calculus for generalized clauses. IWBS-Report, IBM Deutschland, Scientific Center, 1991.

[4] Quintus Prolog is a trademark of Quintus Computer Systems, Inc.

[Casanova *et al.*, 1989] M.A. Casanova, R. Guerreiro, and A. Silva. Logic programming with general clauses and defaults based on model elimination. In *Proceedings of the 11th International Joint Conference on Artificial Intelligence*, pages 395–400, Detroit, MI, 1989.

[Geurts, 1990] Bart Geurts. Natural language understanding in LILOG: An intermediate overview. IWBS-Report 137, IBM Deutschland, Scientific Center, 1990.

[Loveland, 1969a] D. Loveland. A simplified format for the model elimination theorem-proving procedure. *Journal of the Association for Computing Machinery*, 16(3):349–363, 1969. Also published in [Siekmann and Wrightson, 1983, pages 233-248].

[Loveland, 1969b] D. Loveland. Theorem-provers combining model elimination and resolution. In B. Meltzer and D. Michie, editors, *Maschine Intelligence 4*, pages 73–86. Edinburgh University Press, Edinburgh, 1969. Also published in [Siekmann and Wrightson, 1983, pages 249-263].

[Loveland, 1978] D. Loveland. *Automated Theorem Proving: A Logical Basis*, volume 6 of *Fundamental Studies in Computer Science*. North-Holland, New York, 1978.

[Muray, 1982] N.V. Muray. Completely non-clausal theorem proving. *Artificial Intelligence*, 18(1):67–85, 1982.

[Pletat and v. Luck, 1990] U. Pletat and K. v. Luck. Knowledge representation in LILOG. In K. H. Bläsius, U. Hedtstück, and C.-R. Rollinger, editors, *Sorts and Types for Artificial Intelligence*, volume 449 of *Lecture Notes in Artificial Intelligence*. Springer-Verlag, Berlin, Germany, 1990.

[Siekmann and Wrightson, 1983] Jörg Siekmann and Graham Wrightson, editors. *Automation of Reasoning 2*. Springer-Verlag, Berlin, Germany, 1983.

[Stickel, 1982]
Mark E. Stickel. A nonclausal connection-graph resolution theorem-proving program. In *Proceedings of the 2nd National Conference of the American Association for Artificial Intelligence*, pages 229–233, Pittsburgh, Pa., 1982.

Consolution and its Relation with Resolution*

Elmar Eder
Fachbereich Mathematik/Informatik
Universität Marburg
D-3550 Marburg
Germany

Abstract

In this paper the method of consolution for clause form theorem proving is introduced. Consolution is based on the connection method. This means that in a consolution derivation the paths through the input formula are checked for complementarity. In contrast to resolution this checking can be done in a systematic way as in any connection calculus. It is proved that the consolution calculus presented here is sound and complete and that it can simulate resolution step by step and is a generalization of resolution. It combines the advantages of the connection method such as the directedness of search with the advantages of resolution such as the possibility of the use of lemmata.

1 Introduction

In the field of automated theorem proving, there are a number of calculi that have been proposed and implemented for deducing the validity or, equivalently, the unsatisfiability of a formula of first order predicate logic. The best known such calculus is resolution [Robinson, 1965] which is (usually) restricted to formulas in clause form. Another major method for automated deduction is the connection method (see [Bibel, 1987]). We have to distinguish between the concepts of a calculus and a method. A *calculus* has fixed rules which are given once and for all. On the other hand, a *method* for deduction is a design philosophy for designing calculi. A method determines a class of calculi by providing means and concepts for the specification of calculi, and, usually, theorems which are useful for proving the adequacy of calculi specified with these means. Resolution is a calculus whereas the connection method is a method. A number of calculi, called connection calculi, have been developed on the basis of the connection method.

There has been a long discussion on the advantages and disadvantages of the connection method versus resolution. Some clear advantages of the connection method are the greater directedness of its proof search and the fact that its calculi do not disrupt the structure of the input formula as resolution does. This means it provides more information that can be used by strategies for directing the proof search. On the other hand, the connection calculi developed so far lack an important feature that is present in resolution, namely the use of lemmata. In resolution, a clause that has been derived can be reused for resolution an arbitrary number of times. The lack of this feature makes a derivation in these connection calculi for some classes of formulas considerably longer than in resolution (see [Eder, 1989]).

In this paper we introduce the method of consolution which is based on the connection method. We also specify a particular consolution calculus as a basic calculus which may still be enhanced. Consolution has a very close relationship to resolution. In fact, resolution is a restriction of consolution in the sense that a strategy can be imposed upon the consolution calculus to make it identical to resolution. Thus consolution provides a bridge between the connection method and resolution. It allows to combine the directedness of the proof search present in the connection method with the powerful tool of the use of lemmata present in resolution.

2 The connection method

We give here only a brief description of those concepts underlying the connection method which are relevant for consolution. As in resolution, a formula in normal form is represented by a set of clauses in the connection method.[1] But since the connection method is formulated as a method for proving validity rather than unsatisfiability of formulas, we consider here the disjunctive normal form rather than the conjunctive normal form. So, a clause represents the existential closure of the conjunction of its literals, and a set of clauses represents the disjunction of the formulas represented by its clauses. A set of clauses is also called a *matrix*. A clause is usually

*Most of the research and work leading to this paper was done during a stay at ICOT in Tokyo. I want to thank Wolfgang Bibel for his help in the formulation of the method and for valuable hints and discussions.

[1] Actually, the connection method is not restricted to formulas in clause form. Since, however, any arbitrary formula can be transformed to clause form by a fast structure-preserving transformation (see [Greenbaum *et al.*, 1982; Eder, 1985; Plaisted and Greenbaum, 1986]), we shall for simplicity restrict ourselves to clause form formulas in this paper.

depicted as a vertical column consisting of its literals. A matrix is depicted in two-dimensional representation as the columns depicting its clauses, written next to each other. For example, the formula

$$(P \wedge Q) \vee (\neg P \wedge Q) \vee \neg Q$$

is represented by the matrix

$$\{\{P, Q\}, \{\neg P, Q\}, \{\neg Q\}\}$$

which is depicted as

$$\begin{matrix} P & \neg P & \neg Q \\ Q & Q & \end{matrix}$$

A *path through* a matrix is a set of literals, exactly one taken from each clause. In our example there are four paths through the matrix, and $\{P, \neg P, \neg Q\}$ is one of them. Two literals are *complementary* if one of them is the negation of the other. A *connection* in a set of clauses is a pair of literals which can be made complementary by instantiation, ie., by application of substitutions. A path is *complementary* if it contains two complementary literals. The connection method is based on the following theorem.

A formula in disjunctive normal form is valid if and only if there is a finite set of instances of its clauses through which each path is complementary.

A theorem prover implementing the connection method takes the clauses of the input formula and checks all paths through this set of clauses systematically for complementarity. At each step, a connection is chosen in a path that has not yet been checked for complementarity. If necessary, this connection has to be made complementary by unification, thus instantiating the involved clauses in the proper way. Moreover, it may be necessary to take into account more than one instance of a clause. In this case a new variant of the involved clause has to be considered. A detailed introduction to the connection method can be found in [Bibel, 1987].

3 Basic definitions

By a *path in* a matrix we mean a subset of a path through a matrix. Thus, a path in a matrix is a set of literals, at most one chosen from each clause. We shall also use the term *partial path* for a path in a matrix. An *extension* of a path p in a matrix M is a path q in M such that $p \subseteq q$. If c is a clause, p and q are finite sets of literals and $\mathcal{P}$ and $\mathcal{Q}$ are finite sets of finite sets of literals then we define

$$\mathcal{P}_c := \{\{L\} \mid L \in c\}.$$
$$pq := p \cup q.$$
$$\mathcal{PQ} := \{pq \mid p \in \mathcal{P} \text{ and } q \in \mathcal{Q}\}.$$

$\mathcal{P}_c$ is the set of (one-element) paths through the (one-clause) matrix $\{c\}$. If M and N are disjoint matrices, ie., disjoint finite sets of clauses, then pq is a path in $M \cup N$ for every path p in M and for every path q in N. Similarly, $\mathcal{PQ}$ is a set of paths in $M \cup N$ for every set $\mathcal{P}$ of paths in M and for every set $\mathcal{Q}$ of paths in N. We call the set $\mathcal{PQ}$ the ***product*** of the sets $\mathcal{P}$ and $\mathcal{Q}$.

4 Consolution in propositional logic

The idea behind consolution is the following. In order to prove the validity of a given formula using the connection method, all paths through its matrix have to be checked for complementarity. At each stage of a connection proof a certain set of paths has already been checked for complementarity whereas all the remaining paths still have to be processed this way. In consolution at each stage of a proof process, this remaining set of paths yet to be checked for complementarity is represented. It would be inefficient, however, to explicitly represent each path of this set since the number of paths in general increases exponentially with the number of clause instances. Instead, this set of paths is coded in the form of a set of partial paths. Each partial path encodes the set of all its extensions through the whole matrix. So one partial path may encode many paths through the matrix. Let us consider an example which for simplicity is taken from propositional logic.

Suppose we want to prove the validity of the formula

$$(P \wedge Q) \vee (\neg P \wedge Q) \vee \neg Q.$$

The following tree is a proof tree of this formula by consolution.

$\{\{P\}, \{Q\}\}$ $\{\{\neg P\}, \{Q\}\}$

$\{\{P, Q\}, \{Q, \neg P\}, \{Q\}\}$ $\{\{\neg Q\}\}$

$\{\}$

Each node of the tree is marked with a set of (partial) paths in the matrix M

$$\begin{matrix} P & \neg P & \neg Q \\ Q & Q & \end{matrix}$$

representing the given formula. A leaf of the proof tree is marked with the set $\mathcal{P}_c$ of all one-element paths through some clause c of the formula, ie. $\mathcal{P}_c = \{\{L\} \mid L \in c\}$. Since every path through the given matrix M is an extension of a path through c for every $c \in M$, the set $\mathcal{P}_c$ encodes the set of all paths through M. Thus the marks $\mathcal{P}_c$ of the leaves reflect the fact that at the beginning of the proof process all paths through M still have to be checked for complementarity.

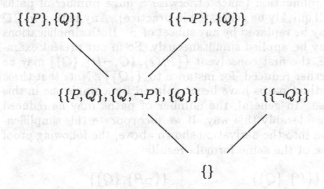

The inference rule, also called *consolution*, takes the set of partial paths from each premise and combines these sets into a new set, called the *consolvent*. This combination can be regarded to consist of two parts. The first part consists of building the product $\mathcal{P}\mathcal{Q}$ of $\mathcal{P}$ and $\mathcal{Q}$. For example, if $\mathcal{P} = \{\{P\},\{Q\}\}$ and $\mathcal{Q} = \{\{\neg P\},\{Q\}\}$ then $\mathcal{P}\mathcal{Q} = \{\{P,\neg P\},\{P,Q\},\{Q,\neg P\},\{Q\}\}$. The second part of the inference rule consists in simplifications of $\mathcal{P}\mathcal{Q}$. One such simplification is the elimination of complementary paths. To continue the illustration of our example, this means that the complementary path $\{P,\neg P\}$ is removed from $\mathcal{P}\mathcal{Q}$. Actually, both parts are to be seen as a single operation, a remark which bears its relevance on the efficiency of implementation. But for the ease of the reader's understanding we will continue to make the distinction.

The proof in our example is completed by applying consolution once again to the result of the previously illustrated step and the remaining leaf $\{\{\neg Q\}\}$. The resulting empty set is the criterion of a successful derivation (as in resolution). To summarize, for a formula F in disjunctive normal form, a *proof* of F is a derivation of the empty set from the sets $\mathcal{P}_c$ $(c \in M)$ with the consolution rule, where M is the set of clauses of F.

While this explains the essentials of the calculus, the following additional details complete its description. Above we have used a single simplification which is elimination of complementary paths. This is all needed for completeness and soundness of the calculus. For efficiency, it is necessary to incorporate at least the following simplification (since otherwise a huge number of paths will quickly be generated in practice). Any path p in $\mathcal{P}\mathcal{Q}$ may be replaced by any subset of p. Both simplifications may be applied simultaneously. So in our present example, the first consolvent $\{\{P,Q\},\{Q,\neg P\},\{Q\}\}$ may be further reduced, for instance to $\{\{Q\}\}$. Note that three distinct paths have been replaced by a single one in this case. In general, the number of paths may be reduced considerably this way. If we incorporate this simplification into the derivation shown above, the following proof tree of the same formula results.

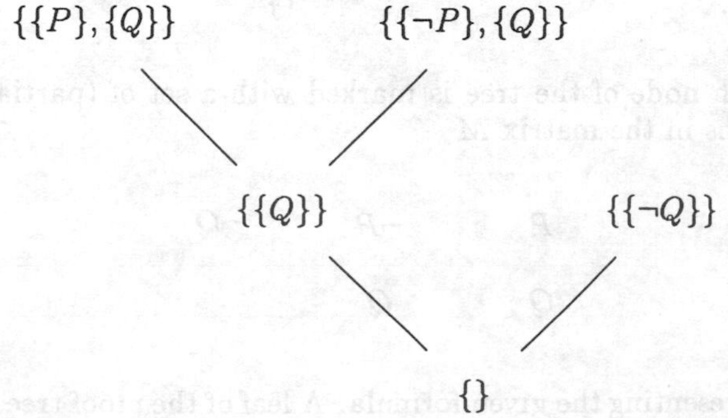

In summary, any consolution calculus must, among its simplifications within the consolution rule, include the elimination of complementary paths. While it is not absolutely necessary, the shortening of paths is understood to be always included in consolution. As an aside we mention that such an inclusion amounts to an extension of the basic calculus. A further extension of consolution might include Prawitz' matrix reduction, but no investigation has been made yet into this possibility.

Note that consolution allows a systematic checking of paths. If we enumerate the paths through a matrix in any given order then a consolution derivation can check them one after the other in this order. A suitable application of shortening of paths will make this systematic checking more efficient by allowing to check more than one path in one step. Systematic checking of paths is not possible with resolution since there at each step the paths are shortened to length 1.

5 Consolution in first oder logic

The lifting of consolution to first order logic is done in much the same way as it is done for resolution. In this section we give a formal description of consolution for full first order logic.

By a *path set* we mean a finite set of finite sets of literals. We shall use this term even if these sets of literals are not paths in some particular matrix.

Definition 5.1
A path set $\mathcal{Q}$ is obtained from a path set $\mathcal{P}$ by *elimination of complementary paths* if there is a set of connections in elements of $\mathcal{P}$ and a most general unifier σ of this set of connections such that $\mathcal{Q}$ is the set of noncomplementary elements of $\mathcal{P}\sigma$.

Definition 5.2
A path set $\mathcal{Q}$ is obtained from a path set $\mathcal{P}$ by *shortening of paths* if there is a surjective mapping $f : \mathcal{P} \to \mathcal{Q}$ such that $f(p) \subseteq p$ holds for all $p \in \mathcal{P}$.

Definition 5.3
A path set $\mathcal{R}$ is obtained from a path set $\mathcal{P}$ by *simplification* if there is a path set $\mathcal{Q}$ such that $\mathcal{Q}$ is obtained from $\mathcal{P}$ by elimination of complementary paths and such that $\mathcal{R}$ is obtained from $\mathcal{Q}$ by shortening of paths.

The inference rule

$$\frac{\mathcal{P} \qquad \mathcal{Q}}{\mathcal{R}}$$

if there exists a variant $\mathcal{Q}'$ of $\mathcal{Q}$ which does not have any variables in common with $\mathcal{P}$ such that $\mathcal{R}$ is obtained from the product $\mathcal{P}\mathcal{Q}'$ by simplification.

We say then that the path set $\mathcal{R}$ is a *consolvent* of the path sets $\mathcal{P}$ and $\mathcal{Q}$.

Definition 5.4
A *derivation* of a matrix M is a finite sequence $(\mathcal{P}_0, \ldots, \mathcal{P}_n)$ of path sets such that the following conditions hold.

1. For all $k = 1, \ldots, n$, the set $\mathcal{P}_k$ equals $\mathcal{P}_c$ for some $c \in M$, or $\mathcal{P}_k$ is a consolvent of $\mathcal{P}_i$ and $\mathcal{P}_j$ for some $i, j < k$.
2. $\mathcal{P}_n = \emptyset$.

Theorem 5.1
A formula in disjunctive normal form is valid if and only if there is a derivation of its matrix by consolution.

Proof: In order to prove correctness, let us assume that F is a formula and M its matrix. Further assume that $(\mathcal{P}_0, \ldots, \mathcal{P}_n)$ is a derivation of M by consolution. To each finite set p of literals we attribute a formula F_p as follows. Let F_p be the disjunction of all literals of p. To each path set $\mathcal{P}$ we attribute a formula $F_\mathcal{P}$ as follows. Let $F_\mathcal{P}$ be the existential closure of the conjunction of all F_p with $p \in \mathcal{P}$. It then holds that $\{\neg F_\mathcal{P}, \neg F_\mathcal{Q}\} \models \neg F_\mathcal{R}$ if $\mathcal{R}$ is a consolvent of $\mathcal{P}$ and $\mathcal{Q}$ (The proof is exactly the same as the proof for the soundness of the resolution rule). Moreover, $\mathcal{P}_c \models F$ for all $c \in M$. By induction on j it follows that $F_{\mathcal{P}_j} \models F$ for all $j = 0, \ldots, n$. In particular for $j = n$, the set $\mathcal{P}_j$ is the empty set and therefore $F_{\mathcal{P}_j}$ is the empty conjunction, ie., the verum $\top$. So $\top \models F$ which means that F is valid.

For the proof of completeness we shall see in the next section that every set of clauses for which there is a resolution refutation, also has a consolution derivation. From the completeness of resolution it then follows that also consolution is complete.

q.e.d.

In the completeness proof note the duality between proving validity of a formula in disjunctive normal form and proving unsatisfiability of a formula in conjunctive normal form. On the level of clauses and matrices there is no difference between affirmative and refutational proving. In fact any refutational calculus can just as well be formulated in an affirmative way and vice versa, and it would not even make a difference in the codes of implementations.

6 Relations to resolution

If we look at the last proof tree shown in Section 4 then we see that its path sets contain only one-element paths. If we replace each path with the single literal which it contains then we obtain the tree

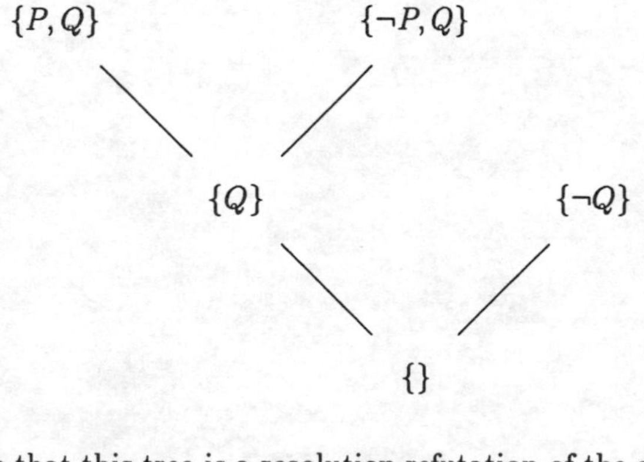

Note that this tree is a resolution refutation of the given clause set. In this way any resolution refutation of a set of clauses can be obtained by consolution. To be more specific, the following holds.

Theorem 6.1
Let M be a matrix and let $(c_0, \ldots, c_n)$ be a resolution refutation of M. Then $(\mathcal{P}_{c_0}, \ldots, \mathcal{P}_{c_n})$ is a consolution derivation of M.

Proof: The only non-trivial part of the proof is to show that $\mathcal{P}_e$ is a consolvent of $\mathcal{P}_c$ and $\mathcal{P}_d$ if e is a resolvent of c and d. So let e be a resolvent of c and d and let $c_0 \cup d_0$ be the set of literals resolved upon where $c_0 \subseteq c$ and $d_0 \subseteq d$.[2]. Let d' be the clause obtained from d by seperating apart the variables of c and d. So, d' is a variant of d. Let d'_0 be the corresponding variant of d_0. Then $\mathcal{P}_{d'}$ is a variant of $\mathcal{P}_d$, and $\mathcal{P}_c\mathcal{P}_{d'}$ is the set of all $\{I, J\}$ such that $I \in c$ and $J \in d'$. Let K be the set of all pairs (I, J) such that $I \in c_0$ and $J \in d'_0$. Then the set $\mathcal{Q}$ defined as

$$\{\{I\sigma, J\sigma\} \mid I \in c \text{ and } J \in d' \text{ and not } (I, J) \in K\}$$

is obtained from $\mathcal{P}_c\mathcal{P}_{d'}$ by elimination of complementary paths (choosing as connections the elements of K). For each path $\{I, J\} \in \mathcal{Q}$ we define

$$f(\{I, J\}) := \begin{cases} \{I\} & \text{if } I \notin c_0 \\ \{J\} & \text{otherwise} \end{cases}$$

Then the range of f is $\mathcal{P}_e$. So $\mathcal{P}_e$ is obtained from $\mathcal{Q}$ by shortening of paths. Thus $\mathcal{P}_e$ is a consolvent of $\mathcal{P}_c$ and $\mathcal{P}_d$.

q.e.d.

From this theorem it follows that consolution can simulate resolution step by step (and therefore consolution is complete as indicated in the last section). On the other hand, consolution is much more general than resolution because it can handle paths of arbitrary lengths. In fact, resolution can be seen as one consolution strategy where all paths are shortened to length 1 in a certain way at each step. Other strategies of consolution are given by the connection calculi that have been developed so far. They involve paths of arbitrary lengths.

As a further remark we point out that the sets resulting by consolution from paths in a given matrix are not always paths in the matrix as in the example shown above. Rather they may also be the union of such paths even in propositional logic. For illustration, the reader may also think of paths in a matrix that has multiple occurrences of clauses.

7 Conclusion

Consolution is a method for clause form theorem proving. We have proved that the consolution calculus presented here is complete and sound and that it can simulate resolution step by step. It is more general than resolution because resolution allows only paths of length 1 whereas consolution allows paths of arbitrary length. This advantage becomes most apparent from the fact that consolution allows a systematic checking of paths as any connection calculus does. Such a systematic checking of paths is not possible in resolution since there the paths are shortened to length 1 in every step. On the other hand, consolution provides the powerful tool of the use of lemmata which is present in resolution but lacking in previous connection calculi. A consolvent that has once been derived can be used as a parent in any number of further consolution steps.

[2] We assume that factorization is included in the resolution rule as in [Robinson, 1965]

References

[Bibel, 1987] Wolfgang Bibel. *Automated Theorem Proving*. Artificial Intelligence. Vieweg, Braunschweig/Wiesbaden, second edition, 1987.

[Eder, 1985] Elmar Eder. An implementation of a theorem prover based on the connection method. In W. Bibel and B. Petkoff, editors, *Artificial Intelligence, Methodology, Systems, Applications (AIMSA'84)*, pages 121–128, Amsterdam, New York, Oxford, 1985. European Coordinating Committee for Artificial Intelligence, North-Holland.

[Eder, 1989] Elmar Eder. A comparison of the resolution calculus and the connection method, and a new calculus generalizing both methods. In E. Börger, H. Kleine Büning, and M. M. Richter, editors, *CSL'88, 2nd Workshop on Computer Science Logic, Duisburg, FRG, October 1988, Proceedings, Lecture Notes in Computer Science 385*, pages 80–98, Berlin, Heidelberg, New York, 1989. Springer-Verlag.

[Greenbaum *et al.*, 1982] S. Greenbaum, A. Nagasaka, P. O'Rorke, and D. A. Plaisted. Comparison of natural deduction and locking resolution implementations. In D. Loveland, editor, *Proceedings of the 6th Conference of Automated Deduction*, pages 159–171. Springer Lecture Notes in Computer Science 138, 1982.

[Plaisted and Greenbaum, 1986] David Plaisted and Steven Greenbaum. A structure-preserving clause form translation. *Journal of Symbolic Computation*, 2:293–304, 1986.

[Robinson, 1965] J. A. Robinson. A machine-oriented logic based on the resolution principle. *Journal of the ACM*, 12:23–41, 1965.

How to Prove Higher Order Theorems in First Order Logic

Manfred Kerber
Fachbereich Informatik, Universität Kaiserslautern
D-6750 Kaiserslautern, Germany
kerber@informatik.uni-kl.de

Abstract

In this paper we are interested in using a first order theorem prover to prove theorems that are formulated in some higher order logic. To this end we present translations of higher order logics into first order logic with flat sorts and equality and give a sufficient criterion for the soundness of these translations. In addition translations are introduced that are sound and complete with respect to L. Henkin's general model semantics. Our higher order logics are based on a restricted type structure in the sense of A. Church, they have typed function symbols and predicate symbols, but no sorts.

Keywords: higher order logic, second order logic, translation, morphism, soundness, completeness

> Die Grenzen meiner Spache bedeuten die Grenzen meiner Welt.
> *Ludwig Wittgenstein,*
> *Tractatus logico-philosophicus 5.6*

1 Introduction

First order logic is a powerful tool for expressing and proving mathematical facts. Nevertheless higher order expressions are often better suited for the representation of mathematics and in fact almost all mathematical text books rely on some higher order fragments for expressiveness. In order to prove such theorems mechanically there are two options: either to have a theorem prover for higher order logic such as TPS [Andrews *et al.*, 1990] or to translate the higher order constructs into corresponding first order expressions and to use a first order theorem prover. As important as the first development is – which may be the way of the future – we follow the second approach because strong first order theorem provers are available today.

The Limitations of First Order Logic

First order logic and the set theories of ZERMELO-FRAENKEL or VON NEUMANN-GÖDEL-BERNAYS have been developed for the formalization of mathematical concepts and for reasoning about them. Other approaches are RUSSEL'S ramified theory of types and CHURCH'S simple theory of types which formalize higher order logic. Mathematicians use a (compared to the formal approaches) informal technical language that is much closer to higher order logic augmented by "naïve" set theory than to first order logic. They know about the antinomies and avoid them, for example by the omission of expressions like "$\{x|x \notin x\}$". They also know that there is a (hopefully) clean foundation of set theory, how this is done in detail is in general however not of much interest to a working mathematician (if he is not working on the foundations of mathematics like logic or set theory).

Formal set theory is of course a very strong tool, especially when higher concepts are introduced by abbreviations. Beginning with the binary relation "$\in$" one can (and this is really done by N. BOURBAKI) define the concepts subset, intersection, union, function, relation, power set, and so on. The definition of a function as a left-total, right-unique relation is rather complex and remote from the construct of a function symbol that is provided originally in logic in order to express functions. The representation of concepts using functions is more adequate in a higher order language. For instance in higher order logic it is possible to write:

$\forall +\ \textit{commutative}(+) \iff \forall x, y\ x + y \equiv y + x$ or
$\forall P\ \textit{symmetric}(P) \iff (\forall x, y\ P(x, y) \Longrightarrow P(y, x))$

Here P is a predicate variable, and *symmetric* is a predicate constant, which expects a predicate term as its argument. This cannot be written immediately in first order logic, because we quantify over P, so P would have to be a variable. On the other hand it must be a predicate because of the expression $P(x, y)$, hence a predicate variable, and this is excluded in first order logic. Nevertheless this definition is expressable in first order logic. Many concepts cannot be axiomatized in first order logic at all, for example the set $\mathbb{N}$ of natural numbers is not first order characterizable: the induction axiom is second order. Another example of the inadequacy of first order logic comes from the theorem of LÖWENHEIM-SKOLEM: For instance every first order axiomatization of the real numbers $\mathbb{R}$ has a countable model.

Why and How Translation

Representing knowledge in an adequate way – adequate with respect to the naturalness of the representation of the object – is one thing, the other thing is to have an adequate and strong form of reasoning. If one uses higher order logic there are two possibilities: either to build strong higher order theorem provers or to translate into first order logic. We shall follow the second approach in this paper.

1.1 Example: A common translation of our formula above in a first order logic is:

$\forall P$ *symmetric*$(P) \iff$
$(\forall x, y$ *apply*$(P, x, y) \implies$ *apply*$(P, y, x))$

apply is a predicate; it is interpreted freely, although it is intended that it is true exactly when P holds for the other arguments.

The following problems occur:

- Under what conditions can such a translation be correct? That is, if we translate a formula and we obtain a tautology, when is the original formula a tautology too?
- In what sense can such a translation be complete? That is, if we translate a tautology, do we always obtain a tautology?

For general considerations concerning the expressiveness of higher order logic, it is obvious that if we find a translation from higher order to first order logic, it cannot be complete in the general sense, especially since the theorem of LÖWENHEIM-SKOLEM must hold and because of GÖDEL'S incompleteness result. In principle such a translation must be equivalent to some set theoretical formulation as stated in MOSTOWSKI'S isomorphism theorem [Mostowski, 1949].

Related Work

J. VAN BENTHEM and K. DOETS [1983] give a translation of a restricted higher order logic without function symbols and without higher order constants and identities to a standard first order logic. They introduce the general idea of a translation, and its soundness and completeness. The translation to standard first order logic leads to more complicated formulae than the translation to a sorted version, because it is necessary to relativize quantification with respect to the corresponding type.

Of great influence for the present paper are the translation techniques of H. J. OHLBACH [1989], who translates modal logics and other non-classical logics to a context logic, where contexts are restricted higher order expressions. These contexts are translated to an order sorted first order logic.

Here a translation of (almost) full higher order logic with function symbols to a many sorted first order logic with equality is given. We do not need a general order sorted logic as long as we do not use a sorted higher order source logic.

2 Higher Order Logic

In this section we define formally a higher order logic based on CHURCH'S simple theory of types, much of the notation is taken from [Andrews, 1986]. However, we shall write the types in a different way. For example if P is a binary predicate symbol on individuals, we write its type as $(\iota \times \iota \to o)$ instead of $(o\iota\iota)$ for better readability. Apologies to all who are familiar with CHURCH'S original notation.

The Syntax

Let us introduce type symbols first, then define terms and formulae for the logics $\mathcal{L}^\omega$. The n-th order predicate logics $\mathcal{L}^n$ are then defined as subsets of $\mathcal{L}^\omega$.

2.1 Definition (Types of $\mathcal{L}^\omega$): ι is a type of order 0 that denotes the type of the individuals. o is a type of order 1 and denotes the type of the truth values. If $\tau_1, \ldots, \tau_m$, and σ are type symbols not equal to o (with $m \geq 1$) then $(\tau_1 \times \cdots \times \tau_m \to \sigma)$ is a type of order 1 + maximum of the orders of $\tau_1, \ldots, \tau_m, \sigma$. It denotes the type of m-ary functions with arguments of types $\tau_1, \ldots, \tau_m$, respectively, and value of type σ. If $\tau_1, \ldots, \tau_m$ are type symbols not equal to o (with $m \geq 1$) then $(\tau_1 \times \cdots \times \tau_m \to o)$ is a type of order 1 + maximum of the orders of $\tau_1, \ldots, \tau_m$. It denotes the type of m-ary predicates with arguments of types $\tau_1, \ldots, \tau_m$, respectively.

2.2 Definition (Signature of $\mathcal{L}^\omega$): The signature of a logic in $\mathcal{L}^\omega$ is a set $\mathcal{S} = \bigcup_\tau \mathcal{S}_\tau^{const} \cup \bigcup_\tau \mathcal{S}_\tau^{var}$ where each set $\mathcal{S}_\tau^{const}$ is a (possibly empty) set of constant symbols of type τ and $\mathcal{S}_\tau^{var}$ a countable infinite set of variable symbols of type τ. We assume that the sets $\mathcal{S}_\tau$ are all disjoint, in addition we sometimes mark the elements of a set $\mathcal{S}_\tau$ by its type τ as index. A logic in $\mathcal{L}^\omega$ is defined by its signature $\mathcal{S}$ and is denoted $\mathcal{L}^\omega(\mathcal{S})$. If there is only one signature we often write $\mathcal{L}^\omega$ instead of $\mathcal{L}^\omega(\mathcal{S})$.

2.3 Definition (Terms of $\mathcal{L}^\omega$):

1. Every variable or constant of a type τ is a term.
2. If $f_{(\tau_1 \times \cdots \times \tau_m \to \sigma)}, t_{\tau_1}, \ldots, t_{\tau_m}$ are terms of the types indicated by their subscripts, then we get a term of type σ by $f_{(\tau_1 \times \cdots \times \tau_m \to \sigma)}(t_{\tau_1}, \ldots, t_{\tau_m})$.

2.4 Definition (Formulae of $\mathcal{L}^\omega$):

1. Every term of type o is a formula.
2. If φ and ψ are formulae and x is a variable of any type, then $(\neg\varphi)$, $(\varphi \wedge \psi)$, and $(\forall x \varphi)$ are formulae.

2.5 Definition ($\mathcal{L}^n$, for $n \geq 1$): $\mathcal{L}^{2n}$ is a subset of $\mathcal{L}^\omega$ so that every variable and every constant is of order less or equal to n, $\mathcal{L}^{2n-1}$ is a subset of $\mathcal{L}^{2n}$ such that no variable of order n is quantified.

The Semantics

The standard semantics is due to TARSKI and has been extended by HENKIN [1950] to the general model semantics, we shall follow these concepts.

We use the following notation: Let $A_1, \ldots, A_m$, and B be sets, then $\mathcal{F}(A_1, \ldots, A_m; B)$ denotes the set of all functions from $A_1 \times \cdots \times A_m$ to B.

2.6 Definition:

- A *frame* is a collection $\{\mathcal{D}_\tau\}_\tau$ of nonempty sets $\mathcal{D}_\tau$, one for each type τ, such that $\mathcal{D}_o = \{\mathtt{T}, \mathtt{F}\}$ and $\mathcal{D}_{(\tau_1 \times \cdots \times \tau_m \to \sigma)} \subseteq \mathcal{F}(\mathcal{D}_{\tau_1}, \ldots, \mathcal{D}_{\tau_m}; \mathcal{D}_\sigma)$. The members of $\mathcal{D}_o$ are called ***truth values*** and the members of $\mathcal{D}_\iota$ are called ***individuals***.
- An *interpretation* $\langle \{\mathcal{D}_\tau\}_\tau, \mathcal{J} \rangle$ of $\mathcal{L}^\omega$ consists of a frame and a function $\mathcal{J}$ that maps each constant of type τ of $\mathcal{L}^\omega$ to an element of $\mathcal{D}_\tau$.

- An *assignment* into a frame $\{\mathcal{D}_\tau\}_\tau$ is a function ξ that maps each variable of type τ of $\mathcal{L}^\omega$ to an element of $\mathcal{D}_\tau$. Given an assignment ξ, a variable x_τ, and an element $d \in \mathcal{D}_\tau$, $\xi[x_\tau \leftarrow d]$ is defined as ξ except for x_τ where it is d.

2.7 Definition (Interpretation): An interpretation $\mathcal{M} = \langle\{\mathcal{D}_\tau\}_\tau, \mathcal{J}\rangle$ is a weak interpretation (weak model, general model) for $\mathcal{L}^\omega$ iff there is a binary function $\mathcal{V}^\mathcal{M}$ so that for every assignment ξ and term t of type τ, $\mathcal{V}_\xi^\mathcal{M} t \in \mathcal{D}_\tau$ and the following conditions hold:

1. for all variables x_τ, $\mathcal{V}_\xi^\mathcal{M} x_\tau = \xi x_\tau$
2. for all constants c_τ, $\mathcal{V}_\xi^\mathcal{M} c_\tau = \mathcal{J} c_\tau$
3. for composed terms $\mathcal{V}_\xi^\mathcal{M}(f_{(\tau_1\times\cdots\times\tau_n\to\sigma)}(t_{\tau_1},\ldots,t_{\tau_m})) = \mathcal{V}_\xi^\mathcal{M}(f_{(\tau_1\times\cdots\times\tau_n\to\sigma)})(\mathcal{V}_\xi^\mathcal{M} t_{\tau_1},\ldots,\mathcal{V}_\xi^\mathcal{M} t_{\tau_m})$
4. $\mathcal{V}_\xi^\mathcal{M}(\varphi \wedge \psi) = \mathcal{V}_\xi^\mathcal{M}\varphi \wedge \mathcal{V}_\xi^\mathcal{M}\psi$ *
5. $\mathcal{V}_\xi^\mathcal{M}(\neg\varphi) = \neg\mathcal{V}_\xi^\mathcal{M}\varphi$
6. $\mathcal{V}_\xi^\mathcal{M}(\forall x_\tau \varphi) = \forall d \in \mathcal{D}_\tau \mathcal{V}_{\xi[x_\tau\leftarrow d]}^\mathcal{M}\varphi$

It is a strong interpretation (strong model, standard model), if $\mathcal{D}_\tau = \mathcal{F}(\mathcal{D}_{\tau_1},\ldots,\mathcal{D}_{\tau_m};\mathcal{D}_\sigma)$ for all occurring types τ with $\tau = (\tau_1 \times \cdots \times \tau_m \to \sigma)$.

2.8 Remark: It is easy to see that in $\mathcal{L}^1$ for every weak model of a formula set there is a strong model with the same interpretation function $\mathcal{J}$.

Sorted Logics

Now we introduce our target language, a standard many-sorted first order logic with equality predicates on all sorts. Let Σ be a (finite) set of sorts. We define the signature $\mathcal{S}_\Sigma$ of a logic in $\mathcal{L}^1_{sort}$ as a union of possibly empty sets $\mathcal{S}^{(s_1,\ldots,s_m):s}$ (m-ary function constants), $\mathcal{S}^{(s_1,\ldots,s_m)}$ (m-ary predicate constants), $\mathcal{S}^s_{const}$ (object constants), and the infinite countable sets $\mathcal{S}^s_{var}$ (object variables), where $s_1,\ldots,s_m,s \in \Sigma$. In each $\mathcal{S}^{(s,s)}$ we have the binary predicate symbol $\equiv^{(s,s)}$. We index the elements of $\mathcal{S}_\Sigma$ sometimes by their sorts. For instance a function symbol f of sort $(s_1,\ldots,s_m):s$ is written as $f^{(s_1,\ldots,s_m):s}$. Sorted terms and formulae can be defined as usual and we underly the usual semantics. For details see [Kerber, 1990].

The order sorted logic covers this simple situation and therefore the input language of a theorem prover like the Markgraf Karl Refutation Procedure [MKRP, 1984] is well-suited for dealing with the defined logic.

3 Logic Morphisms

Now we shall define those concepts that are necessary to describe the relation between formalizations in different logics. The important concepts are: logic, morphism, quasi-homomorphism, and soundness and completeness of a morphism.

3.1 Definition (Morphism of Logics): Let $\mathcal{F}^1$ and $\mathcal{F}^2$ be two logical systems ($\mathcal{L}^\omega$, $\mathcal{L}^n$, or $\mathcal{L}^1_{sort}$), then a morphism Θ is a mapping that maps the signature $\mathcal{S}$ of a logic $\mathcal{F}^1(\mathcal{S})$ in $\mathcal{F}^1$ to a signature of a logic $\mathcal{F}^2(\Theta(\mathcal{S}))$ in $\mathcal{F}^2$ and that maps every formula set in $\mathcal{F}^1(\mathcal{S})$ to a formula set in $\mathcal{F}^2(\Theta(\mathcal{S}))$.*

3.2 Definition (Soundness): Let Θ be a morphism from $\mathcal{F}^1$ to $\mathcal{F}^2$. Θ is called strongly (weakly) sound iff the following condition holds for every formula set Γ in $\mathcal{F}^1$: if Γ has a strong (weak) model in $\mathcal{F}^1$ then there is a strong (weak) model of $\Theta(\Gamma)$ in $\mathcal{F}^2$.

3.3 Definition (Completeness): Let Θ be a morphism from $\mathcal{F}^1$ to $\mathcal{F}^2$. Θ is called strongly (weakly) complete iff the following condition holds for every formula set Γ in $\mathcal{F}^1$: if $\Theta(\Gamma)$ has a strong (weak) model in $\mathcal{F}^2$ then there is a strong (weak) model of Γ in $\mathcal{F}^1$.

3.4 Definition (Quasi-Homomorphism): Let $\mathcal{F}^1(\mathcal{S}_1)$ and $\mathcal{F}^2(\mathcal{S}_2)$ be two logics. A mapping Θ that maps every formula and every term of $\mathcal{F}^1(\mathcal{S}_1)$ to a formula respectively to a term of $\mathcal{F}^2(\mathcal{S}_2)$ is called a quasi-homomorphism iff the following conditions are satisfied:

1. For all terms:
   - 1.1 if x is a variable of $\mathcal{F}^1(\mathcal{S}_1)$ then $\Theta(x)$ is a variable of $\mathcal{F}^2(\mathcal{S}_2)$.
   - 1.2 if c is a constant of $\mathcal{F}^1(\mathcal{S}_1)$ then $\Theta(c)$ is a constant of $\mathcal{F}^2(\mathcal{S}_2)$.
   - 1.3 if $f(t_1,\ldots,t_m)$ is a term of $\mathcal{F}^1(\mathcal{S}_1)$ then $\Theta(f(t_1,\ldots,t_m)) = \vartheta(\Theta(f),\Theta(t_1),\ldots,\Theta(t_m))$ with $\vartheta(a,a_1,\ldots,a_m) = \begin{cases} a(a_1,\ldots a_m) & \text{or} \\ \alpha_a(a,a_1,\ldots a_m) \end{cases}$ The constants α have to be chosen appropriately out of $\mathcal{S}_2$, especially they have to be *new*, that is, there must be no element $\alpha' \in \mathcal{S}_1$ so that $\alpha_a = \Theta(\alpha')$. The case which is chosen can depend only on the a, not on the $a_1,\ldots,a_m$. (α stands for *apply*.)
2. For all formulae φ_1, φ_2 and for all variables x:
   - 2.1 $\Theta(\varphi_1 \wedge \varphi_2) = \Theta(\varphi_1) \wedge \Theta(\varphi_2)$
   - 2.2 $\Theta(\neg\varphi) = \neg\Theta(\varphi)$
   - 2.3 $\Theta(\forall x\varphi) = \forall\Theta(x)\Theta(\varphi)$
3. All terms that are not formulae of $\mathcal{F}^1(\mathcal{S}_1)$ are mapped to terms that are not formulae of $\mathcal{F}^2(\mathcal{S}_2)$.

4 A Sufficient Criterion for Soundness

In this section we give a sufficient criterion for the soundness of translations of formulae of $\mathcal{L}^n$ onto formulae of $\mathcal{L}^1_{sort}$, which is strong enough to cover most requirements.

4.1 Theorem: If Θ is an injective quasi-homomorphism from $\mathcal{L}^n(\mathcal{S})$ to $\mathcal{L}^1_{sort}(\mathcal{S}_\Sigma)$, then Θ is weakly sound.

Proof: Let $\mathcal{M}$ be a weak model of a formula set Γ, $\mathcal{M} = \langle\{\mathcal{D}_\tau\}_\tau, \mathcal{J}\rangle$ is a weak model for any φ out of Γ, that is, $\mathcal{V}_\xi^\mathcal{M}\varphi = \mathtt{T}$ for every assignment ξ. We are going to construct a model $\hat{\mathcal{M}} = \langle\{\hat{\mathcal{D}}^{``\tau"}\}_{``\tau"}, \hat{\mathcal{J}}\rangle$ of

*We use the connectives and quantifiers in a naïve way at the meta-level.

*A formula is regarded as a formula set with one element. Especially we write $\Theta(\varphi)$ instead of $\Theta(\{\varphi\})$.

$\Theta(\varphi)$, where "τ"* denotes the sort upon which the type τ is mapped. We define the sets $\hat{\mathcal{D}}^{"\tau"} := \mathcal{D}_\tau$. $\hat{\mathcal{J}}$ is defined as $\hat{\mathcal{J}}(\Theta(c)) := \mathcal{J}(c)$ for all constants c in $\mathcal{S}$. (Here and in the sequel we make use of the injectivity of Θ. Additionally we use the fact that constants are mapped onto constants.) The assignments $\hat{\xi}$ are defined by $\hat{\xi}(\Theta(x)) := \xi(x)$. Because of $\hat{\mathcal{D}}^{"\tau"} = \mathcal{D}_\tau$ we get all assignments in this way. Recall that we have no function or predicate variables in $\mathcal{L}^1_{sort}$. We also use the fact that variables are mapped onto variables. For the functions $\alpha_a^{"\tau"}$ with $\tau = (\tau_1 \times \cdots \times \tau_m \to \sigma)$ we can define the interpretation so that it takes the interpretation of the first argument, which is a function, and applies it to the other arguments. We can do this, because these functions are new. Formally this interpretation can be written: for all $f \in \mathcal{D}^{"\tau"}$, for all $x_1 \in \mathcal{D}^{"\tau_1"}, \ldots, x_m \in \mathcal{D}^{"\tau_m"}$ $\mathcal{V}_{\hat{\xi}}^{\hat{\mathcal{M}}}(\alpha_f^{"\tau"})(f, x_1, \ldots, x_m) := f(x_1, \ldots, x_m)$. Note that $f \in \mathcal{D}^{"\tau"} = \mathcal{D}_\tau$ is a function and hence applicable. Analogously we define the interpretation for the predicates $\alpha_p^{"\tau"}$.

Now $\hat{\mathcal{M}}$ is a model of $\Theta(\varphi)$, which is proved by showing inductively that for all terms and formulae $\mathcal{V}_{\hat{\xi}}^{\hat{\mathcal{M}}} \circ \Theta = \mathcal{V}_{\xi}^{\mathcal{M}}$. The proof is straightforward and can be found in [Kerber, 1990]. ■

4.2 Theorem: If Θ is an injective quasi-homomorphism from $\mathcal{L}^n(\mathcal{S})$ to $\mathcal{L}^1_{sort}(\mathcal{S}_\Sigma)$, then Θ is strongly sound.
Proof: If there is a strong model of a formula set Γ in $\mathcal{L}^n(\mathcal{S})$, then this model is also a weak model. By the previous theorem there is hence a weak model of $\Theta(\Gamma)$ in $\mathcal{L}^1_{sort}(\mathcal{S}_\Sigma)$. By a sorted version of remark 2.8 there is also a strong model of $\Theta(\Gamma)$. ■

By the theorems above it follows directly that the translation used in example 1.1 is weakly and strongly sound.

4.3 Remark: Note that the formulae that are obtained by these translations are not essentially more difficult than the original ones and that the structure of the formulae (number and position of quantifiers or junctors) is respected. In the image the terms are never more nested than in the original. The only thing that can change, is that the number of arguments in a term is increased by one.

5 A Complete Translation

Now we want to define morphisms $\hat{\Theta}_n$ from $\mathcal{L}^n$ to $\mathcal{L}^1_{sort}$ which are not only sound but also complete. We define the morphisms for odd n, for even n they are obtained as the restrictions of the next higher odd n, that is $\hat{\Theta}_{2n} := \hat{\Theta}_{2n+1}|_{\mathcal{L}^{2n}}$. The morphisms $\hat{\Theta}$ are defined as $\hat{\Theta}(\varphi) = \hat{\Theta}'(\varphi) \cup EXT$, where $\hat{\Theta}'$ is a quasi-homomorphism and EXT is the set of extensionality axioms which depends only on the signature. In the following we drop the index n. Again we abbreviate *apply* as α.

*By "τ" we mean the string after expanding the abbreviation for τ, for instance, if $\tau = (\iota \times \iota \to o)$ then "τ" is "$(\iota \times \iota \to o)$".

5.1 Definition (Standard Translation $\hat{\Theta}_{2n-1}$): Let $\mathcal{S}^{2n-1} = \bigcup_\tau \mathcal{S}_\tau$ be the signature of a logic in $\mathcal{L}^{2n-1}$. We define a signature $\mathcal{S}_\Sigma$ of a logic in $\mathcal{L}^1_{sort}$ by assigning to each predicate constant of order n, arity m, and type $\tau = (\tau_1 \times \cdots \times \tau_m \to o)$ a predicate constant of order 1, arity m (that is, of type $(\iota \times \cdots \times \iota \to o)$)* and sort $("\tau_1", \ldots, "\tau_m")$. All constants and variables of order less than n and of a type σ are mapped onto constants and variables of type ι and sort "σ". Because we assumed all members in $\mathcal{S}^{2n-1}$ to be disjoint, we can use the same names for the images.
Additionally we have in $\mathcal{S}_\Sigma$ for each type τ of order less than n with $\tau = (\tau_1 \times \cdots \times \tau_m \to o)$ a new $(m+1)$-ary predicate constant $\alpha^{"\tau"}$ of sort $("\tau", "\tau_1", \ldots, "\tau_m")$ and for each type τ of order less than n with $\tau = (\tau_1 \times \cdots \times \tau_m \to \sigma)$, $\sigma \neq o$ a new $(m+1)$-ary function constant $\alpha^{"\tau"}$ of sort $("\tau", "\tau_1", \ldots, "\tau_m") : "\sigma"$.
Now we are going to define a quasi-homomorphism $\hat{\Theta}'$. For terms it is defined inductively by:

- T1 for all variables x_τ, $\hat{\Theta}'(x_\tau) = x^{"\tau"}$
- T2 for all constants c_τ of order equal n with $\tau = (\tau_1 \times \cdots \times \tau_m \to o)$, $\hat{\Theta}'(c_\tau) = c^{("\tau_1", \ldots, "\tau_m")}$
- T3 for all constants c_τ of order less than n, $\hat{\Theta}'(c_\tau) = c^{"\tau"}$
- T4 For a term with an m-ary function term f of type τ as top expression we define $\hat{\Theta}'(f(t_1, \ldots, t_m)) = \alpha^{"\tau"}(\hat{\Theta}'(f), \hat{\Theta}'(t_1), \ldots, \hat{\Theta}'(t_m))$

For formulae we define $\hat{\Theta}'$ inductively by:

- F1 For an atomic formula with predicate constant p of order n as top expression we define $\hat{\Theta}'(p(t_1, \ldots, t_m)) = \hat{\Theta}'(p)(\hat{\Theta}'(t_1), \ldots, \hat{\Theta}'(t_m))$
- F2 For a term with an m-ary predicate term p of type τ and order less than n as top expression we define $\hat{\Theta}'(p(t_1, \ldots, t_m)) = \alpha^{"\tau"}(\hat{\Theta}'(p), \hat{\Theta}'(t_1), \ldots, \hat{\Theta}'(t_m))$
- F3 For all other formulae we define $\hat{\Theta}'$ as the homomorphic extension.

EXT is the set of the following $\mathcal{L}^1_{sort}$-formulae:

- A1 For every function constant $\alpha^{"\tau"}$ with $\tau = (\tau_1 \times \cdots \times \tau_m \to \sigma)$: $\forall f^{"\tau"} \forall g^{"\tau"} (\forall x_1^{"\tau_1"}, \ldots, \forall x_m^{"\tau_m"}$ $\alpha^{"\tau"}(f, x_1, \ldots, x_m) \equiv^{("\sigma", "\sigma")} \alpha^{"\tau"}(g, x_1, \ldots, x_m))$ $\Longrightarrow f \equiv^{("\tau", "\tau")} g$
- A2 For every predicate constant $\alpha^{"\tau"}$ with $\tau = (\tau_1 \times \cdots \times \tau_m \to o)$: $\forall p^{"\tau"} \forall q^{"\tau"} (\forall x_1^{"\tau_1"}, \ldots, \forall x_m^{"\tau_m"}$ $\alpha^{"\tau"}(p, x_1, \ldots, x_m) \iff \alpha^{"\tau"}(q, x_1, \ldots, x_m))$ $\Longrightarrow p \equiv^{("\tau", "\tau")} q$

Now we can define $\hat{\Theta}(\varphi) = \hat{\Theta}'(\varphi) \cup EXT$.

5.2 Remark: It should become obvious now, why we excluded types like $(o \to o)$: For instance let P be a predicate of this type, Q be a predicate of type $(\iota \to o)$,

*Recall: In $\mathcal{L}^{2n-1}$ there is no function constant of order n.

and c be a constant of type ι. Then the translation of $P(Q(c)) \wedge Q(c)$ can be only the apply-construct $\alpha^{"(o\to o)"}(P, \alpha^{"(\iota\to o)"}(Q,c)) \wedge \alpha^{"(\iota\to o)"}(Q,c)$ or the direct translation $P(\alpha^{"(\iota\to o)"}(Q,c)) \wedge \alpha^{"(\iota\to o)"}(Q,c)$. But both formulae are not well formed, because $\alpha^{"(\iota\to o)"}(Q,c)$ has to be a formula and a term at once. Even worse in general a *uniform* (quasi-homomorphic) translation is not possible, because $Q(c)$ must be translated in the first case to a term and in the second to a formula, what is not allowed in first order logic. I think that this example is also a counterexample for the correctness of the translation given by BENTHEM and DOETS [1983] for a language without function symbols. A possible translation of the unrestricted typed higher order logic has also to provide a translation of formulae of the kind $P(Q(c)) \wedge Q(c)$. This is possible by having as functional symbols only the $\alpha^{"\tau"}$; all other symbols are object variables or object constants. Especially the junctor "$\wedge$" has also to be translated to a constant.

5.3 Theorem: $\hat{\Theta}$ is weakly and strongly sound. (For a proof see [Kerber, 1990].)

5.4 Theorem: $\hat{\Theta}$ is weakly complete.
Proof: Let Γ be a formula set in $\mathcal{L}^{2n-1}(\mathcal{S})$. Let $\mathcal{M}$ be a weak model of $\hat{\Theta}(\Gamma)$. Then $\mathcal{M}$ is a model of $\hat{\Theta}(\varphi)$ for every formula φ in Γ. Let $\mathcal{M}$ be $\langle\{\mathcal{D}^s\}_s, \mathcal{J}\rangle$ and ξ be an arbitrary assignment. Then we have $\mathcal{V}_\xi^{\mathcal{M}}(\hat{\Theta}(\varphi)) = \mathtt{T}$. We want to construct a model $\check{\mathcal{M}}$ of φ, so that for all assignments $\check{\xi}$ we have $\mathcal{V}_{\check{\xi}}^{\check{\mathcal{M}}}(\varphi) = \mathtt{T}$. Therefore we define $\check{\mathcal{D}}_\iota := \mathcal{D}^{"\iota"}$ and $\check{\mathcal{D}}_o := \{\mathtt{T},\mathtt{F}\}$. For all other types τ with $\tau = (\tau_1 \times \cdots \times \tau_m \to \sigma)$ we have to define $\check{\mathcal{D}}_\tau \subseteq \mathcal{F}(\check{\mathcal{D}}_{\tau_1}, \ldots, \check{\mathcal{D}}_{\tau_m}; \check{\mathcal{D}}_\sigma)$. We do it by inductively defining injective functions $\natural_\tau$ from $\mathcal{D}^{"(\tau_1\times\cdots\times\tau_m\to\sigma)"}$ to $\mathcal{F}(\check{\mathcal{D}}_{\tau_1}, \ldots, \check{\mathcal{D}}_{\tau_m}; \check{\mathcal{D}}_\sigma)$ and setting $\check{\mathcal{D}}_\tau := \natural_\tau(\mathcal{D}^{"\tau"})$. Hence $\natural_\tau$ is a bijective function from $\mathcal{D}^{"\tau"}$ to $\check{\mathcal{D}}_\tau$.*
We define $\natural_\tau$ inductively:
$\natural_\iota : \mathcal{D}^{"\iota"} \to \check{\mathcal{D}}_\iota$ is the identity mapping. (This function is obviously bijective.)
Let $\natural_{\tau_i}$ and $\natural_\sigma$ be defined for $\mathcal{D}^{"\tau_1"}, \ldots, \mathcal{D}^{"\tau_m"}$ and $\mathcal{D}^{"\sigma"}$. We are going to define a function $\natural_\tau$ with $\tau = (\tau_1 \times \cdots \times \tau_m \to \sigma)$, $\sigma \neq o$, for $\mathcal{D}^{"\tau"}$. For all $x \in \mathcal{D}^{"\tau"}$ $\natural_\tau(x)$ is defined as the function $\natural_\tau(x)(\check{x}_1, \ldots, \check{x}_m) := \natural_\sigma(\mathcal{V}_\xi^{\mathcal{M}}(\alpha^{"\tau"})(x, \natural_{\tau_1}^{-1}(\check{x}_1), \ldots, \natural_{\tau_m}^{-1}(\check{x}_m)))$ for all $\check{x}_1 \in \check{\mathcal{D}}_{\tau_1}$, $\ldots$, $\check{x}_m \in \check{\mathcal{D}}_{\tau_m}$.
The following diagram may help to see the involved mappings at a glance:

$$\begin{array}{cccccccc}
\mathcal{V}_\xi^{\mathcal{M}}(\alpha^{"\tau"}) : \mathcal{D}^{"\tau"} & \times & \mathcal{D}^{"\tau_1"} & \times\cdots\times & \mathcal{D}^{"\tau_m"} & \longrightarrow & \mathcal{D}^{"\sigma"} \\
!\downarrow \natural_\tau & & \uparrow \natural_{\tau_1}^{-1} & & \uparrow \natural_{\tau_m}^{-1} & & \downarrow \natural_\sigma \\
\check{\mathcal{D}}_\tau \hookrightarrow \mathcal{F}(& & \check{\mathcal{D}}_{\tau_1} & ,\ldots, & \check{\mathcal{D}}_{\tau_m} & ; & \check{\mathcal{D}}_\sigma)
\end{array}$$

By the corresponding extensionality axiom in EXT it can be shown that $\natural_\tau$ is bijective (see [Kerber, 1990]).
For $\sigma = o$ and for order of τ is equal to n we define $\natural_\tau(p)(\check{x}_1, \ldots, \check{x}_m) := p(\natural_{\tau_1}^{-1}(\check{x}_1), \ldots, \natural_{\tau_m}^{-1}(\check{x}_m))$, and for order of τ less than n, $\natural_\tau(x)(\check{x}_1, \ldots, \check{x}_m) := \mathcal{V}_\xi^{\mathcal{M}}(\alpha^{"\tau"})(x, \natural_{\tau_1}^{-1}(\check{x}_1), \ldots, \natural_{\tau_m}^{-1}(\check{x}_m))$ for all $\check{x}_1 \in \check{\mathcal{D}}_{\tau_1}, \ldots$, $\check{x}_m \in \check{\mathcal{D}}_{\tau_m}$. The bijectivity is shown analogously with help of the extensionality axioms.
$\natural$ is the polymorphic mapping defined by all the individual $\natural_\tau$. Now we are going to show that if $\mathcal{M}$ is a model of $\hat{\Theta}(\varphi)$, that is, for all assignments ξ we have $\mathcal{V}_\xi^{\mathcal{M}}(\hat{\Theta}(\varphi)) = \mathtt{T}$, we have $\check{\mathcal{M}}$ is a model of φ, that is, for all assignments $\check{\xi}$ we have $\mathcal{V}_{\check{\xi}}^{\check{\mathcal{M}}}(\varphi) = \mathtt{T}$ with $\check{\mathcal{M}} = \langle\{\check{\mathcal{D}}_\tau\}_\tau, \check{\mathcal{J}}\rangle$. $\check{\mathcal{J}}$ is defined as $\natural \circ \mathcal{J} \circ \hat{\Theta}'$. The assignments $\check{\xi}$ are defined as $\natural \circ \xi \circ \hat{\Theta}'$. Because $\natural$ and $\hat{\Theta}'$ are bijective, we get all assignments this way.
By induction on the construction of terms it can be proved, that for all terms: $\mathcal{V}_{\check{\xi}}^{\check{\mathcal{M}}} = \natural \circ \mathcal{V}_\xi^{\mathcal{M}} \circ \hat{\Theta}'$ and for all formulae: $\mathcal{V}_{\check{\xi}}^{\check{\mathcal{M}}} = \mathcal{V}_\xi^{\mathcal{M}} \circ \hat{\Theta}'$. The proof can be found in [Kerber, 1990]. Summarizing we have: if $\mathcal{V}_\xi^{\mathcal{M}}(\hat{\Theta}(\varphi)) = \mathtt{T}$ then $\mathcal{V}_\xi^{\mathcal{M}}(\hat{\Theta}'(\varphi)) = \mathtt{T}$ then $\mathcal{V}_{\check{\xi}}^{\check{\mathcal{M}}}(\varphi) = \mathtt{T}$. ■

5.5 Remark: Because $\hat{\Theta}'$ is an injective quasi-homomorphism, $\hat{\Theta}'^{-1}$ provides a calculus for $\mathcal{L}^n$. If we add rules that enforce that function symbols and predicate symbols are equal if they agree in all arguments, we can transform every sound and complete first order calculus of $\mathcal{L}^1_{sort}$ by $\hat{\Theta}$ to a sound and weakly complete calculus for $\mathcal{L}^n$. We can execute the proof in $\mathcal{L}^1_{sort}$ and then lift it to a proof in $\mathcal{L}^n$.

5.6 Remark: One might wonder why we proposed a sufficient criterion for the soundness of translations, when we have a translation that is sound and complete and hence could be used always. However in a concrete situation it can be better not to translate into the full sound and complete formulae, because the search space may become too big. It would not be a good idea to add the extensionality axioms if they are not really needed. In addition we can prevent instantiation if we translate certain constants not by an *apply* or if we use different *apply* functions or predicates although we could use the same. On the other hand the completeness result guarantees that we can find a translation at all. Which one we choose may be very important for the theorem prover to find a proof. Whereas the extensionality axioms are relatively harmless, for ***really higher order*** theorems it is necessary to add so-called comprehension axioms (compare [Andrews, 1986, p.156]) in order to approximate weak semantics to strong semantics. For many theorems these axioms are not necessary, for the others one must choose the axioms very carefully, otherwise the first order theorem prover will get a search space that is too big. It is the advantage of higher order theorem proving compared to our approach, that there one does not need these axioms (for the prize of the undecidability of unification). In the appendix we give an example of a theorem, where a comprehension axiom is necessary.

6 Summary and Open Problems

In the sections above we introduced the basic machinery for translating higher order formulae to first order logic.

*In order to get strong completeness it would be necessary to achieve bijectivity from $\mathcal{D}^{"\tau"}$ to $\mathcal{F}(\check{\mathcal{D}}_{\tau_1}, \ldots, \check{\mathcal{D}}_{\tau_m}; \check{\mathcal{D}}_\sigma)$. For $n > 1$ this is impossible because of Gödel's incompleteness theorem.

We introduced a sufficient criterion for the soundness of such a translation, namely that it has to be an injective quasi-homomorphism. Then we gave a complete translation for the restricted higher order language.

In the full version of the paper [Kerber, 1990] we generalized the results to logics with equality. An interesting and useful generalization would be to a higher order *sorted* logic. Then the first order logic should have a sort structure at least as powerful as that of the higher order source logic. The results should be transferable although the formal treatment can become strenuous.

Acknowledgement

I like to thank AXEL PRÄCKLEIN for many discussions and thorough reading of a draft and JÖRG SIEKMANN for his advice that resulted in numerous improvements.

References

[Andrews *et al.*, 1990] Peter B. Andrews, Sunil Issar, Dan Nesmith, and Frank Pfenning. The TPS theorem proving system. In M.E. Stickel, editor, *Proc. of the 10th CADE*, pages 641–642, Kaiserslautern, Germany, July 1990. Springer Verlag, Berlin, Germany. LNAI 449.

[Andrews, 1986] Peter B. Andrews. *An Introduction to Mathematical Logic and Type Theory: To Truth through Proof.* Academic Press, Orlando, Florida, USA, 1986.

[Benthem and Doets, 1983] Johan van Benthem and Kees Doets. *Higher Order Logic*, volume I: Elements of Classical Logic of *Handbook of Philosophical Logic, D. Gabbay, F. Guenthner, Edts.*, chapter I.4, pages 275–329. D.Reidel Publishing Company, Dodrecht, Netherlands, 1983.

[Henkin, 1950] Leon Henkin. Completeness in the theory of types. *Journal of Symbolic Logic*, 15:81–91, 1950.

[Kerber, 1990] Manfred Kerber. How to prove higher order theorems in first order logic. SEKI Report SR-90-19, Fachbereich Informatik, Universität Kaiserslautern, Kaiserslautern, Germany, 1990.

[MKRP, 1984] Karl Mark G Raph. The Markgraf Karl Refutation Procedure. Technical Report Memo-SEKI-MK-84-01, Fachbereich Informatik, Universität Kaiserslautern, Kaiserslautern, Germany, January 1984.

[Mostowski, 1949] Andrzej Mostowski. An undecidable arithmetical statement. *Fundamenta Mathematicae*, **36**:143–164, 1949.

[Ohlbach, 1989] Hans Jürgen Ohlbach. Context logic. SEKI Report SR-89-08, Fachbereich Informatik, Universität Kaiserslautern, Kaiserslautern, Germany, 1989.

Appendix

We present an MKRP-proof of CANTOR's theorem that the power set of a set has greater cardinality than the set itself. We use the formulation of [Andrews, 1986, p.184]. A comprehension axiom is necessary. We write ι as I, o as O, $\rightarrow$ as T, $\alpha^{\text{"}(\iota\rightarrow(\iota\rightarrow o))\text{"}}$ as A[IT[ITO]], and so on.

```
Formulae given to the editor
Axioms:
* SORT DECLARATIONS *
SORT I,ITO,IT[ITO]:ANY
* TERM DECLARATIONS *
TYPE A[ITO](ITO I)
TYPE A[IT[ITO]](IT[ITO] I):ITO
TYPE SUBSET(ITO ITO)
* DEFINITION SUBSET *
ALL A,B:ITO SUBSET(A B) EQV
            (ALL X:I A[ITO](A X) IMPL A[ITO](B X))
* COMPREHENSION AXIOM *
ALL S:ITO ALL G:IT[ITO] EX P:ITO
(ALL X:I A[ITO](P X) EQV
 (A[ITO](S X) AND (NOT A[ITO](A[IT[ITO]](G X) X))))

Theorems:
ALL S:ITO (NOT EX G:IT[ITO] ALL F:ITO
SUBSET (F S) IMPL (EX J:I A[ITO](S J) AND
                          A[IT[ITO]](G J) = F))
Refutation:
A1: All x:Any + =(x x)
A2: All x:I y:It[ito] z:Ito - A[ITO](f_1(z y) x)
                              + A[ITO](z x)
A3: All x:I y:It[ito] z:Ito - A[ITO](f_1(z y) x)
                              - A[ITO](a[it[ito]](y x) x)
A4: All x:I y:It[ito] z:Ito + A[ITO](f_1(z y) x)
              - A[ITO](z x)   + A[ITO](a[it[ito]](y x) x)
T5: All x:Ito + A[ITO](x f_2(x))  + A[ITO](c_1 f_3(x))
T6: All x:Ito + A[ITO](x f_2(x))
              + =(a[it[ito]](c_2 f_3(x)) x)
T7: All x:Ito - A[ITO](c_1 f_2(x))  + A[ITO](c_1 f_3(x))
T8: All x:Ito - A[ITO](c_1 f_2(x))
              + =(a[it[ito]](c_2 f_3(x)) x)

T5,1 & A2,1  -> R8:  All x:It[ito] y:Ito
                     + A[ITO](c_1 f_3(f_1(y x)))
                     + A[ITO](y f_2(f_1(y x)))
R8,2 & T7,1  -> R9:  All x:It[ito]
                     + A[ITO](c_1 f_3(f_1(c_1 x)))
                     + A[ITO](c_1 f_3(f_1(c_1 x)))
R9 1=2       -> D10: All x:It[ito]
                     + A[ITO](c_1 f_3(f_1(c_1 x)))
T6,1 & A2,1  -> R12: All x:It[ito] y:Ito
                     + =(a[it[ito]](c_2 f_3(f_1(y x)))
                        f_1(y x))
                     + A[ITO](y f_2(f_1(y x)))
R12,2 & T8,1 -> R13: All x:It[ito]
                     + =(a[it[ito]](c_2 f_3(f_1(c_1 x)))
                        f_1(c_1 x))
                     + =(a[it[ito]](c_2 f_3(f_1(c_1 x)))
                        f_1(c_1 x))
R13 1=2      -> D14: All x:It[ito]
                     + =(a[it[ito]](c_2 f_3(f_1(c_1 x)))
                        f_1(c_1 x))
D14,1 & A3,2 -> P15: All x:Ito y:It[ito]
                     - A[ITO](f_1(c_1 y) f_3(f_1(c_1 y)))
                     - A[ITO](f_1(x c_2) f_3(f_1(c_1 y)))
P15 (factor) -> F16: - A[ITO](f_1(c_1 c_2)
                              f_3(f_1(c_1 c_2)))
A4,1 & F16,1 -> R17: - A[ITO](c_1 f_3(f_1(c_1 c_2)))
                     + A[ITO](a[it[ito]](c_2
                                    f_3(f_1(c_1 c_2)))
                              f_3(f_1(c_1 c_2)))
R17,2 & D14  -> RW18:- A[ITO](c_1 f_3(f_1(c_1 c_2)))
                     + A[ITO](f_1(c_1 c_2)
                              f_3(f_1(c_1 c_2)))
RW18,2 & P15,2-> R19:- A[ITO](c_1 f_3(f_1(c_1 c_2)))
                     - A[ITO](f_1(c_1 c_2)
                              f_3(f_1(c_1 c_2)))
R19,2 & RW18,2-> R20:- A[ITO](c_1 f_3(f_1(c_1 c_2)))
                     - A[ITO](c_1 f_3(f_1(c_1 c_2)))
R20 1=2      -> D21: - A[ITO](c_1 f_3(f_1(c_1 c_2)))
D21,1 & D10,1-> R22: []
```

Reasoning of Geometric Concepts based on Algebraic Constraint-directed Method

Hitoshi IBA*
Machine Inference Section,
Electrotechnical Laboratory
1-1-4 Umezono, Tsukuba-city,
Ibaraki, 305, Japan, iba@etl.go.jp

Hirochika INOUE
Dept. of Mechanical Eng.,
Faculty of Eng., Univ. of Tokyo
7-3-1 Hongou, Bunkyou-ward,
Tokyo, 113, Japan

Abstract

We present an algebraic approach to geometric reasoning and learning. The purpose of this research is to avoid the usual difficulties in symbolic handling of geometric concepts. Our system **GREW** is grounded on a reasoning scheme that integrate the symbolic reasoning and algebraic reasoning of Wu's method. The basic principle of this scheme is to describe mathematical knowledge in terms of symbolic logic and to execute the subsidiary reasoning for Wu's method. The validity of our approach and **GREW** is shown by experiments, such as applying to learning-by-example of computer vision heuristics or solving locus problems.

1 Introduction

This paper presents a new approach for learning or reasoning of geometric concepts based on algebraic constraint-directed methods.

Geometric reasoning is available for many applications, such as robotics, CAD and computer vision. However, most previous reasoning systems, which are based on predicate logic, have difficulties in handling geometric notions. This is because the usual symbolic approach fails to grasp the essential characteristics of geometry, and cannot solve complicated problems, such as those which require auxiliary lines.

As a result, handling geometric concepts causes great trouble in many applications of reasoning. For instance, consider the heuristics called *skewed symmetry* in computer vision [Kanade81]. This is a famous geometric constraint which claims that a two-dimensional skewed symmetry is a projected image of a genuine three-dimensional symmetry (Fig.1). Because of transformation-invariant characteristics such as shear transformation, it is very difficult to represent this constraint by usual predicate logic, still more to establish the reasoning system. In order to solve these difficulties, we select Wu's method as algebraic approach, and construct a geometric reasoning system (**GREW**: Geometric REasoning based on Wu's method). This system is based on the integrated scheme of symbolic reasoning and algebraic method. We show its validity by experiments, such as learning computer-vision heuristics and solutions to locus problems.

*I wish to thank members in FAI-WG (Foundation of Artificial Intelligence) and CLP-WG (Constraint Logic Programming) of ICOT for useful comments and discussion on earlier drafts of this work.

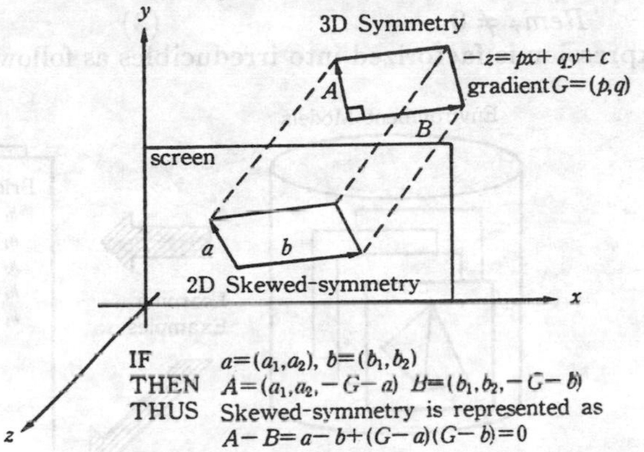

Fig.1 Skewed symmetry

2 Geometric reasoning based on algebraic method

2.1 Wu's Method

In general, the hypotheses of a geometrical theorem can be represented in triangular forms of algebraic expressions. That is,

$$tri_1(u_1,\cdots u_d, x_1,\cdots x_{r-1}, x_r) = 0$$
$$tri_2(u_1,\cdots u_d, x_1,\cdots x_{r-1}) = 0$$
$$\cdots\cdots\cdots\cdots$$
$$tri_r(u_1,\cdots u_d, x_1) = 0 \qquad (1)$$

Where $u_1,\cdots u_d$ are independent variables and $x_1,\cdots x_{r-1}, x_r$ dependent. Under these hypotheses, the conclusion is represented as follows.

$$Conc(u_1,\cdots u_d, x_1,\cdots x_{r-1}, x_r) = 0 \qquad (2)$$

With these preparations, the geometric proof is equivalent to deciding whether the expression (2) is equal to zero under the equality system of the condition (1). Wu's theorem gives a deterministic procedure for this decision [Wu78]. That is,

(2) is equal to zero under (1) ;
i.e. the conclusion of the theorem is valid
$\iff Rem_r = 0$

Rem_r (called (final) remainder term) is calculated as follows.

$Rem_0 = Conc$

$Rem_{i+1} =($ the remainder of Rem_i divided by tri_{i+1} under $x_{r-i})$

The above procedure is called Wu's method [Chou84]. We have constructed an algebraic theorem proving system based on Wu's method. This system uses strategies for the efficient triangulation, such as decomposition of reducible cases, simplification of expressions, and conflict resolution of auxiliary or degenerate conditions. We have experimented in many examples to confirm that the efficient process is achieved [Iba90].

2.2 Algebraic constraint-directed method for geometric reasoning

We realized geometric reasoning based on the algebraic. method. In this section, we explain the constraint-directed principle with Wu's method.

Consider the case that the final remainder of Wu's method is not zero;

$$Rem_r \neq 0 \qquad (3)$$

This expression is factorized into irreducibles as follows,

$$Rem_r = f_1^{e1} f_2^{e2} \cdots f_k^{ek}$$

If we make a new set of hypotheses such as;

$$tri_1, \cdots .tri_r \cup f_j (j = 1, \cdots k) \qquad (4)$$

and retry Wu's method under this new hypotheses, then the new remainder generally equals to zero. Thus each f_j is regarded as new algebraic constraints for validating the conclusion under the old hypotheses. These f_j's are derived heuristics or candidates of geometrical descriptions. Therefore we apply Wu's method to geometric reasoning with the following fundamental principle;

CASE I: Conclusion is given beforehand.
In this case, each derived f_j works like a candidate of newly-found heuristics that validates the original conclusion under the hypotheses tri_j.

CASE II: Conclusion is not given.
In this case we apply Wu's method by choosing one tri_j as *Conc*.The independent variables u_i regulate the resultant remainder description. That is, the final remainder Rem_r is represented on the basis of independent variables. Therefore it is necessary to choose appropriate independent variables for fi-

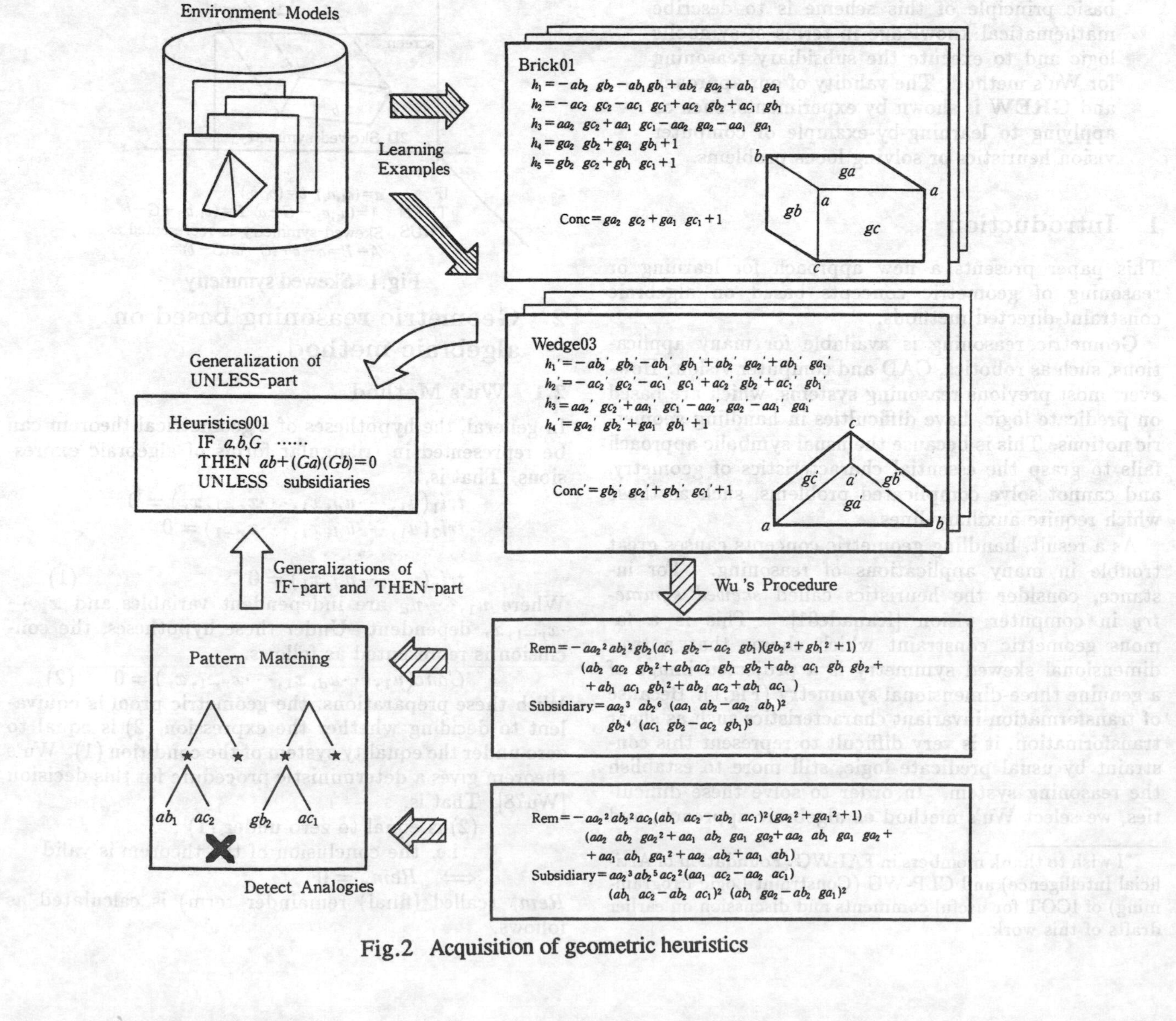

Fig.2 Acquisition of geometric heuristics

nal expressions, and f_j is regarded as the geometric representation on the basis of u_i.

We call the above principle as the constraint-directed reasoning, which is justified alge-geometrically as follows. The final remainder (3) forms a subset of algebraic variety of hypotheses and the conclusion. Thus the desired geometric information is represented, though partially, as algebraic constraints of remainder terms.

To illustrate this algebraic constraint-directed approach, we show its application to learning-by-example of geometric heuristics in computer vision. We alge-geometrically represent heuristics or relations in computer vision as follows.

IF $\underline{condition_1}$ (constraints on variables)
THEN $\underline{conclusion}\ f(x_1, \cdots, x_r) = 0$
UNLESS $\underline{condition_2}$

Conclusion f corresponds to the part of expressions that may occur in the final remainder term of Wu's method. *Condition*$_1$ describes constraints on variables in f. Learning of heuristics is realized by deriving *condition*$_1$ and conclusion part from common terms in the final remainder of Wu's method. This strategy is based on the above claim in CASE I.

Fig.2 shows the learning process of Kanade's heuristics, in which the skewed-symmetry heuristic (Fig.1) is learned from exemplar bricks and wedges. In this case, hypotheses and the conclusion consist of six expressions with bricks, and five with wedges. These expressions are after [Swain86]. For instance, $h_1, \cdots h_6$ represent a brick as a whole (Fig.3). Here, $h_1, \cdots h_3$ correspond to Mackworth constraints or parallel-line heuristics [Kanade81]. More precisely, h_1 shows that the vector $(\vec{GB} - \vec{GA})$ is vertical with the vector ab, and this is equivalent to the fact that upper and lower lines of face **B** (projected to parallel segments in two-dimensions) are also parallel in three-dimensions. And $h_4, \cdots h_6$ mean that faces **A**,**B**,**C** are vertical with each other in three-dimensions because the normal vector of face **A** is $(ga_1, ga_2, 1)$ and so on (Fig.1). The whole system of $h_1, \cdots h_6$ together gives a complete description of two-dimensional visibility and three-dimensional model of bricks and their relations.

The remainder resulting from Wu's method is shown as *Rem* in Fig.2. Though omitted in the figure, learning examples are actually taken from six types of bricks and five types of wedges. The reasoning process is executed such as pattern-matching, eliminating trivial cases (aa_2), and storing analogous patterns of terms $(ab_2ac_2gb_{22} + \cdots)$ and $(aa_2ab_2ga_{22} + \cdots)$. The matching of $(ac_1gb_2 - ac_2gb_1)$ and $(ab_1ac_2 - ab_2ac_1)$ failed because the dimensions of gb, ab, ac are different (gb is gradient, and ab, ac are metric). After necessary generalizations, the following representation is obtained as a heuristic.

IF $\vec{a}, \vec{b}, \vec{G}$: two-dimensional vectors
THEN $(\vec{a}, \vec{b}) + (\vec{G}, \vec{a}) * (\vec{G}, \vec{b}) = 0$
UNLESS auxiliary conditions of $\vec{a}, \vec{b}, \vec{G}$

Where $\vec{G}$ is a x,y coordinate of three-dimensional gradient of the parallelogram formed by vector $\vec{a}$ and $\vec{b}$. $(\vec{a}, \vec{b})$ means an inner product of vectors. **UNLESS** part represents a subsidiary premise which makes this heuristic applicable [Swain86]. Through the use of this **UNLESS** knowledge, we have established the appropriate maintenance and modification of constraint-directed models for robotics [Iba88].

The above representation is equivalent to the one in [Kanade81], which shows the validity of our approach. In the same way, other kinds of geometric heuristics in computer vision can be learned from examples; for example, parallel-line heuristics and Mackworth constraints [Iba90].

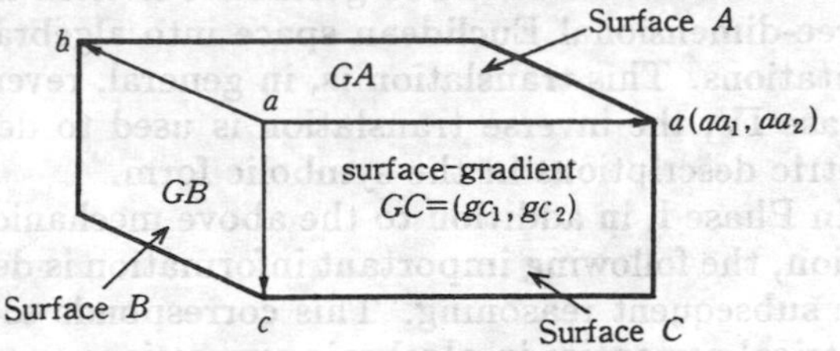

Fig.3 Line drawing of brick

3 Geometric reasoning system: GREW

Algebraic method elaborately solves reasoning problems with auxiliary lines or ad-hoc heuristics. However, at the same time, this approach is accompanied by computational problems such as the selection of independent variables or the derivation of geometric information from algebraic expressions. These kinds of problems are difficult to solve only within algebraic domains of polynomials (called syntax of expressions). Rather, reasoning with symbolic descriptions (called semantics of expressions) is required.

In order to realize an effective handling of geometric notions, we have constructed an integrated reasoning scheme; integration both of symbolic reasoning and algebraic reasoning of Wu's method (Fig.4). The basic principle of this scheme is to describe mathematical knowledge in terms of symbolic logic and to execute subsidiary reasoning for Wu's method. Thus, our system establishes appropriate handling of geometric semantics.

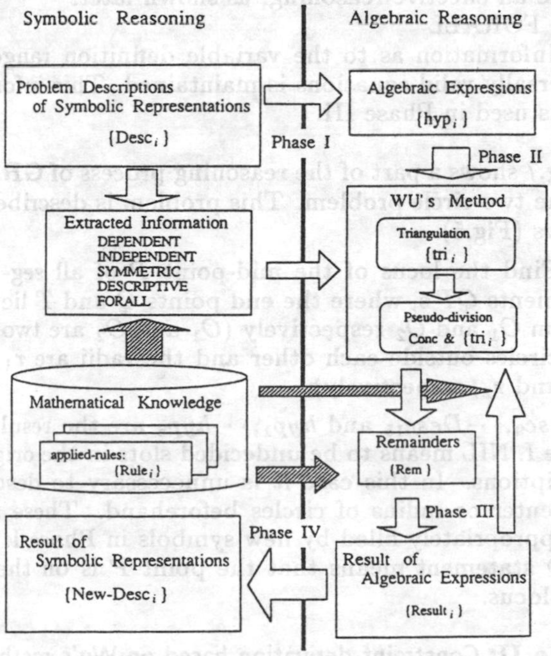

Fig.4 Symbolic and algebraic reasoning

Our system **GREW** consists of four fundamental phases as follows.

Phase I: Translation of symbolic representations into algebraic representations

Input expressions $Desc_i$ for **GREW** are represented by symbols. In Phase I, these descriptions are translated into algebraic representations hyp_i. We realized the translation of about 20 geometric notions in two- or three-dimensional Euclidean space into algebraic representations. This translation is, in general, reversible. In Phase IV, the inverse translation is used to derive geometric descriptions in the symbolic form.

In Phase I, in addition to the above mechanical translation, the following important information is derived for the subsequent reasoning. This corresponds to the geometrical semantics in algebraic expressions.

(1) DESCRIPTIVE
The information as to which variables exist in the original problem description. This is used in Phase IV.

(2) INDEPENDENT
This maintains important information of dependent variables used in the triangular derivation (Phase II). In locus problems (Fig.5,6), variables in the FIND statement are independent because they are designated to lie in the desired locus. On the other hand, added variables are generally candidates for dependents.

(3) DEPENDENTS
This represents a set of dependent variables, which can be derived from problem descriptions by judging whether to lie on the same figure or geometric relations. It is difficult, in general, to determine INDEPENDENT and DEPENDENTS completely. Thus some sorts of heuristics are essential. These two kinds of information are used for the triangular derivation in Phase II.

(4) SYMMETRIC
The information as to the symmetry of descriptions. Symmetries are ubiquitous in geometric problems and enable an effective reasoning, as shown later.

(5) FORALL
The information as to the variable definition range for universally valid equations is maintained. This information is used in Phase III.

Fig.7 shows a part of the reasoning process of **GREW** for the two-circle problem. This problem is described as follows (Fig.5).

> Find the locus of the mid-point P of all segments QT's, where the end points Q and T lie on O_1 and O_2 respectively (O_1 and O_2 are two circles outside each other and the radii are r_1 and r_2, respectively).

$Desc_9, \cdots Desc_{15}$ and $hyp_1, \cdots hyp_8$ are the results of Phase I. NIL means to be undecided slots in the original descriptions. In this case it is unnecessary to describe the center or radius of circles beforehand. These slots are appropriately filled by new symbols in Phase I. The FIND statement means that the point P is on the desired locus.

Phase II: Constraint-derivation based on Wu's method

This phase is the core of our reasoning system **GREW**, which deduces algebraic constraints with Wu's method. Here the triangular form is derived with the following principles of selecting dependents; that is, selecting as many variables that belong to the same set in DEPENDENTS as possible, and avoiding the selection of variables in INDEPENDENT and FORALL. These principles work as heuristics for Phase IV.

Phase III: Algebraic reasoning based on mathematical knowledge

The reasoning is executed on the final remainder terms. Mathematical knowledge is maintained for this execution as follows.

(1) Manipulations of algebraic expressions
Simplify the final remainder terms by factorizing or transforming. This is effective when focused variables are given beforehand, such as locus problems. In locus problems those variables are designated by FIND statements (Fig.7,8).

(2) Reasoning as to universally valid equations
In order to derive the condition for making the final remainder term zero, the reasoning about universally valid equations is executed with FORALL descriptions.

$$\text{Eg. } At + Bs = 0 \text{ (for all } t, s) \iff A = B = 0$$
$$Axy + Bx^2 + Cy^2 + D = 0 \text{ (for all } x, y) \iff A = B = C = D = 0$$

(3) Reasoning as to trigonometric functions
Reasoning about trigonometric functions are essential for describing circles.

$$\text{Eg.} Acos(t) + Bsin(t) + C = 0 \ (0 \leq t \leq 2\pi) \implies A^2 + B^2 \geq C^2$$

(4) Solving inequalities
Try to solve simple inequalities.

(5) Manipulations on vectors or matrices
Components of vectors or matrices are manipulated in connection with its geometric representation.

Eg. Vectors $\vec{a} = (a_1, a_2), \vec{b} = (b_1, b_2)$ are given;
$\vec{a}$ is vertical with $\vec{b} \iff a_1b_1 + a_2b_2 = 0$
$2 \mid a_1b_2 - a_2b_1 \mid =$ the area of the parallelogram formed by $\vec{a}$ and $\vec{b}$

(6) Reasoning by pattern matching between expressions
Reasoning is executed based on symmetry or analogy of derived algebraic expressions. Geometric semantics are essential for this. We illustrated the learning experiment in this reasoning (Fig.2).

Phase IV: Inverse translation into symbolic representations

Translate algebraic expressions into symbolic representations inversely. The basic strategy is to make pattern-matching with the template of deduced algebraic expressions in Phase I. DESCRIPTIVE information is used so as to derive symbolic expressions as general as possible (the least number of variables newly introduced).

4 Experimental Results

We have confirmed the validity of **GREW** and our algebraic constraint-directed reasoning scheme by many experiments such as locus problems (Fig.5,6) and construction problems [Iba90]

Fig.7 shows a part of the reasoning process of **GREW** for the two-circle problem. The constraint-directed reasoning is executed based on inequality relations of trigonometry and quadratic inequalities (type (1)(3)(4) in Phase III). $New - Dec_5$ is finally derived and shows that the point P is in the range which is outside a circle (the center is a mid-point of centers of circle O_1 and circle O_2, and the radius is $\frac{|r_1-r_2|}{2}$), and which is inside a circle (the center is the same, and the radius is $\frac{(r_1+r_2)}{2}$).

As another example, Fig.8 shows the solution to 3D skew-line problem . This problem is described as follows.

> Two lines XX' and YY' are given. These lines are not in the same two-dimensional plane, and are vertical with each other. Find a locus of the mid point M of all segments KL's, where the end points K and L are on lines XX' and YY' respectively, and the distance of KL is constant p (Fig.6).

In phase I, new variables are generated for directional vectors of lines, and algebraic expressions are derived with these parameter variables. The reasoning as to universally valid equations is executed in Phase III, and the algebraic constraints are derived as follows.

$$(1) a_1(x_1 - y_1) + a_0(x_0 - y_0) = 0$$
$$(2) y_2 - x_2 = 0$$
$$(3) 4(\alpha - y_2)^2 + 4(\beta - x_1)^2 + 4(\gamma - x_0)^2 - p^2 = 0$$

Because of the symmetrical relation (SYMMETRIC in Phase I), the following equation is added.

$$(4) 4(\alpha - x_2)^2 + 4(\beta - y_1)^2 + 4(\gamma - y_0)^2 - p^2 = 0$$

In Phase III, from (1) and (2), it is deduced that two vectors (a_0, a_1, a_2) and $(x_0 - y_0, x_1 - y_1, x_2 - y_2)$ are vertical with each other. It is also deduced that (b_0, b_1, b_2) is vertical with $(x_0 - y_0, x_1 - y_1, x_2 - y_2)$, because (b_0, b_1, b_2) and (a_0, a_1, a_2) are vertical with each other (hyp_1,Fig.8(a)).

$$(a_0, a_1, a_2) \perp (x_0 - y_0, x_1 - y_1, x_2 - y_2)$$
$$(b_0, b_1, b_2) \perp (x_0 - y_0, x_1 - y_1, x_2 - y_2) \quad (\#)$$

Thus points of the locus are the intersection of two spheres (each center is (x_0, x_1, x_2) and (y_0, y_1, y_2) respectively, and radius is $\frac{p}{2}$, where (x_0, x_1, x_2) and (y_0, y_1, y_2) satisfy (#)). Furthermore, in checking sufficient conditions for the locus, it is also deduced that this intersection lies on the same plane, which is omitted here. As a result, $New - Desc$ descriptions are derived in Phase IV, where !- means a vector subtraction operator.

5 Future research

Our reasoning scheme has an advantage in handling of geometric notions, and we mean to make applications of this method to more practical domains; such as path-planning problems or environment model managements of intelligent robots [Iba88]. For this purpose, we now research on further extensions in the algebraic reasoning. This is to cope with the failure in Phase IV, that is, the failure to derive appropriate geometrical information from algebraic representations. This failure is caused by the lack of primitives to make inverse translations from algebraic expressions, or by the inappropriate algebraic reasoning in phase III. From the more practical viewpoint, we think it important to calculate approximated solutions based on the final remainder terms by using numeric methods or simulations. A program called TLA embodies this kind of methodology for mechanical simulations [Kramer90]. On the other hand, mathematical expert systems seem to us promising, in which formal handling of geometric semantics could be realized by the knowledge or meta-knowledge in mathematics. Thus our future research of concern is to further extend our method in this direction to realize the appropriate control of reasoning in algebraic domains, and to formalize its algorithm with both domains; symbolic and algebraic.

6 Conclusion

Reasoning about geometric notions is difficult to execute only by the usual symbolic method. This paper presents a new scheme for geometric reasoning with algebraic constraint-directed method. Although our algebraic approach avoids the complicated problem of reasoning in auxiliary lines or handling of heuristics, at the same time it encounters computational difficulty in selecting independent variables. To solve this, we have tried to derive geometric semantics of algebraic expressions from the original problem description, and to establish the constraint-directed reasoning based on these semantics. Finally, the validity of our system **GREW** has been shown by experiments.

References

[Chou, 1984] Chou,S. Proving elementary geometry theorems using Wu's algorithm. *Contemporary mathematics*, 29, American Mathematical Society, 1984

[Iba *et al.*, 1988] Iba,H. Matsubara,H. and Inoue,H. View and visibility for managing incomplete environment models. In *Proc. of IEEE International Workshop on intelligent robots and systems*, 1988

[Iba, 1990] Iba,H. Reasoning of geometric concepts based on algebraic method. Ph.D Thesis, University of Tokyo, 1990

[Kanade, 1981] Kanade,T. Reconstruction of the three-dimensional shape of an object from a single view. *Artificial intelligence*, 17, 1981

[Kramer, 1990] Kramer,G.A. Solving geometric constraint systems. In *Proc. of the Eighth AAAI*, 1990

[Swain *et al.*, 1986] Swain,M.J. and Mundy,J.L. Experiments in using a theorem to prove and develop geometrical theorems in computer vision. In *Proc. of IEEE, Robotics and Automation*, 1986

[Wu, 1978] Wu,W. On the decision problem and the mechanization of theorem-proving in elementary geometry. *Scientia Sinica*, 21, 1978

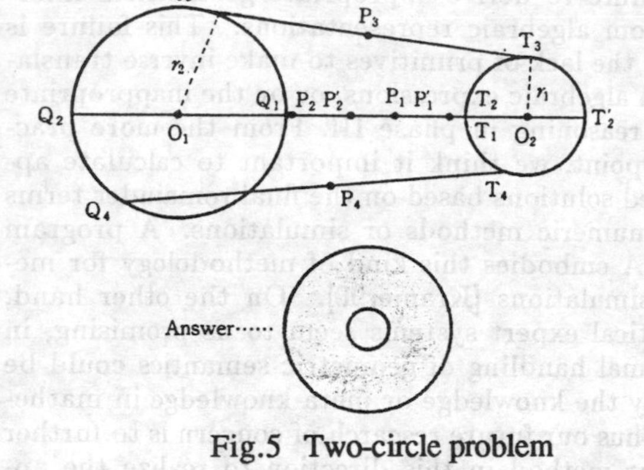

Fig.5 Two-circle problem

PHASE I : Translation into algebraic expressions

Desc$_1$: (ON \$Q \$O$_1$)
Desc$_2$: (ON \$T \$O$_2$)
Desc$_3$: (IS − CIRCLE \$(O$_1$ 2) NIL r$_1$)
Desc$_4$: (IS − CIRCLE \$(O$_2$ 2) NIL r$_2$)
Desc$_5$: (IS − POINT \$(Q 2) NIL)
Desc$_6$: (IS − POINT \$(T 2) NIL)
Desc$_7$: (IS − POINT \$(P 2) (MID − POINT \$Q \$T))
Desc$_8$: (FIND \$P)

⇓

Desc$_9$: (IS − CIRCLE \$(O$_1$ 2) \$A r$_1$)
Desc$_{10}$: (IS − CIRCLE \$(O$_2$ 2) \$B r$_2$)
Desc$_{11}$: (IS − POINT \$(Q 2) (q$_1$ q$_2$))
Desc$_{12}$: (IS − POINT \$(T 2) (t$_1$ t$_2$))
Desc$_{13}$: (IS − POINT \$(A 2) (a$_1$ a$_2$))
Desc$_{14}$: (IS − POINT \$(B 2) (b$_1$ b$_2$))
Desc$_{15}$: (IS − POINT \$(P 2) (p$_1$ p$_2$))

$hyp_1 = -r_1 s_1 + q_1 - a_1$
$hyp_2 = -c_1 r_1 + q_2 - a_2$
$hyp_3 = s_1^2 + c_1^2 - 1$
$hyp_4 = t_1 - r_2 s_2 - b_1$
$hyp_5 = t_2 - c_2 r_2 - b_2$
$hyp_6 = -t_1 - q_1 + 2p_1$
$hyp_7 = -t_2 - q_2 + 2p_2$
$hyp_8 = s_2^2 + c_2^2 - 1$

DESCRIPTIVE
$\{O_1, O_2, r_1, r_2, Q, T, P\}$
INDEPENDENT
$\{p_1, p_2\}$
DEPENDENTS
$\{a_1, a_2, r_1, q_1, q_2\} \cup \{b_1, b_2, r_2, t_1, t_2\}$
$\cup \{p_1, p_2, t_1, t_2, q_1, q_2\} \cup \{c_1, s_1\} \cup \{c_2, s_2\}$
SYMMETRIC
$\{(O_1, O_2), ((a_1, a_2, r_1, q_1, q_2)(b_1, b_2, r_2, t_1, t_2))\}$
FORALL
(trigonometric c1 s1) ∧ (trigonometric c2 s2)

PHASE II : Wu's method

$$\begin{aligned} Rem_7 = & -(4p_1r_1s_1 - 2b_1r_1s_1 - 2a_1r_1s_1 + r_2^2 - r_1^2 \\ & +4c_1p_2r_1 - 2b_2c_1r_1 - 2a_2c_1r_1 - 4p_2^2 + 4b_2p_2 \\ & +4a_2p_2 - 4p_1^2 + 4b_1p_1 + 4a_1p_1 - b_2^2 \\ & -2a_2b_2 - b_1^2 - 2a_1b_1 - a_2^2 - a_1^2) \end{aligned}$$

with Conc = hyp$_8$
$x_1 = c_1, x_2 = q_1, x_3 = q_2, x_4 = t_1,$
$x_5 = t_2, x_6 = s_2, x_7 = c_2$

PHASE III : Algebraic reasoning

Applied − rule$_1$: $\mathbf{A}cos\theta + \mathbf{B}sin\theta + \mathbf{C} \equiv 0 \ (0 \le \forall\theta \le 2\pi)$
$\Longrightarrow \mathbf{A}^2 + \mathbf{B}^2 \ge \mathbf{C}^2$
where $cos\theta = c_1 \ sin\theta = s_1$
⇓ $(FORALL - condition)$ *in* Rem_7

Result$_1$:

$$\begin{aligned} & -r_2^4 + (2r_1^2 + 8p_2^2 + (-8b_2 - 8a_2)p_2 + 8p_1^2 + (-8b_1 - 8a_1)p_1 + 2b_2^2 \\ & + 4a_2b_2 + 2b_1^2 + 4a_1b_1 + 2a_2^2 + 2a_1^2)r_2^2 - r_1^4 + (8p_2^2 + (-8b_2 - 8a_2)p_2 \\ & + 8p_1^2 + (-8b_1 - 8a_1)p_1 + 2b_2^2 + 4a_2b_2 + 2b_1^2 + 4a_1b_1 + 2a_2^2 + 2a_1^2)r_1^2 \\ & - 16p_2^4 + (32b_2 + 32a_2)p_2^3 + (-32p_1^2 + (32b_1 + 32a_1)p_1 - 24b_2^2 - 48a_2b_2 \\ & - 8b_1^2 - 16a_1b_1 - 24a_2^2 - 8a_1^2)p_2^2 + ((32b_2 + 32a_2)p_1^2 + ((-32b_1 - 32a_1)b_2 \\ & - 32a_2b_1 - 32a_1a_2)p_1 + 8b_2^3 + 24a_2b_2^2 + (8b_1^2 + 16a_1b_1 + 24a_2^2 + 8a_1^2)b_2 \\ & + 8a_2b_1^2 + 16a_1a_2b_1 + 8a_2^3 + 8a_1^2a_2)p_2 - 16p_1^4 + (32b_1 + 32a_1)p_1^3 - a_2^4 \\ & + (-8b_2^2 - 16a_2b_2 - 24b_1^2 - 48a_1b_1 - 8a_2^2 - 24a_1^2)p_1^2 + ((8b_1 + 8a_1)b_2^2 - a_1^4 \\ & + (16a_2b_1 + 16a_1a_2)b_2 + 8b_1^3 + 24a_1b_1^2 + (8a_2^2 + 24a_1^2)b_1 + (-4a_1a_2^2 - 4a_1^3)b_1 \\ & + 8a_1a_2^2 + 8a_1^3)p_1 - b_2^4 - 4a_2b_2^3 + (-2b_1^2 - 4a_1b_1 - 6a_2^2 - 2a_1^2)b_2^2 - 2a_1^2a_2^2 \\ & + (-4a_2b_1^2 - 8a_1a_2b_1 - 4a_2^3 - 4a_1^2a_2)b_2 - b_1^4 - 4a_1b_1^3 + (-2a_2^2 - 6a_1^2)b_1^2 \ge 0 \end{aligned}$$

Applied − rule$_2$: *factorize and factorsum*
⇓

Result$_2$: **LHS** $\Longrightarrow$

$$\begin{aligned} & -(r_2^2 - 2r_1r_2 + r_1^2 - 4p_2^2 + 4b_2p_2 + 4a_2p_2 - 4p_1^2 \\ & +4b_1p_1 + 4a_1p_1 - b_2^2 - 2a_2b_2 - b_1^2 - 2a_1b_1 - a_2^2 - a_1^2) \\ & (r_2^2 + 2r_1r_2 + r_1^2 - 4p_2^2 + 4b_2p_2 + 4a_2p_2 - 4p_1^2 + 4b_1p_1 \\ & +4a_1p_1 - b_2^2 - 2a_2b_2 - b_1^2 - 2a_1b_1 - a_2^2 - a_1^2) \end{aligned}$$

$$\Longrightarrow$$

$$\begin{aligned} & -\{(r_2 - r_1)^2 - 4(p_2 - \tfrac{a_2+b_2}{2})^2 - 4(p_1 - \tfrac{a_1+b_1}{2})^2\} \\ & \{(r_2 + r_1)^2 - 4(p_2 - \tfrac{a_2+b_2}{2})^2 - 4(p_1 - \tfrac{a_1+b_1}{2})^2\} \end{aligned}$$

Applied − rule$_3$: $(x - a)(x - b) \le 0 \ (a \le b) \iff a \le x \le b$
where $x = (p_1 - \frac{a_1+b_1}{2})^2 + (p_2 - \frac{a_2+b_2}{2})^2$
⇓

Result$_3$: $(p_1 - \frac{a_1+b_1}{2})^2 + (p_2 - \frac{a_2+b_2}{2})^2 - (\frac{r_1+r_2}{2})^2 \le 0$
Result$_4$: $(p_1 - \frac{a_1+b_1}{2})^2 + (p_2 - \frac{a_2+b_2}{2})^2 - (\frac{r_1-r_2}{2})^2 \ge 0$

PHASE IV : Translation into symbolic representations

New − Desc$_1$: (ON \$P (DOMAIN
(IN − SIDE \$O$_3$)
(OUT − SIDE \$O$_4$)))

New − Desc$_2$: (IS − CIRCLE \$(O$_3$ 2)
\$PP
(times $\frac{1}{2}$ (plus r$_1$ r$_2$)))

New − Desc$_3$: (IS − CIRCLE \$(O$_4$ 2)
\$PP
(times $\frac{1}{2}$ (abs (minus r$_1$ r$_2$))))

New − Desc$_4$: (IS − POINT \$(PP 2)
(MID − POINT \$A \$B))

⇓

New − Desc$_5$: (ON \$P
(DOMAIN
(IN − SIDE
(CIRCLE
(MID − POINT (CENTER − OF \$O$_1$)
(CENTER − OF \$O$_2$))
(times $\frac{1}{2}$ (plus r$_1$ r$_2$))))
(OUT − SIDE
(CIRCLE
(MID − POINT (CENTER − OF \$O$_1$)
(CENTER − OF \$O$_2$))
(times $\frac{1}{2}$ (abs (minus r$_1$ r$_2$)))))))

Fig.7 Solution to locus problem (1)

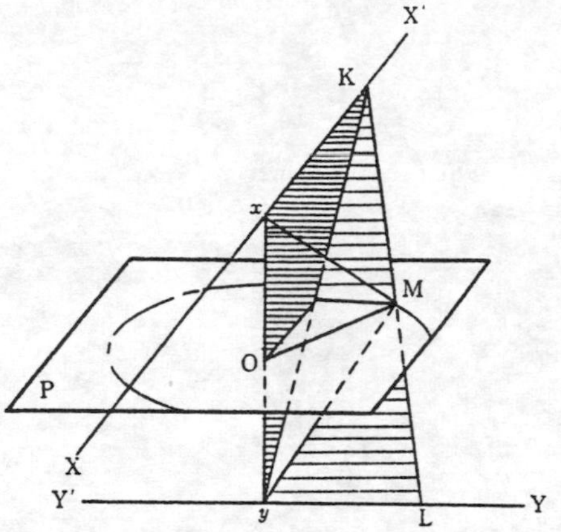

Fig.6 Skew-line problem

PHASE I : Translation into algebraic expressions

```
Desc1  : (ON $K $XX')
Desc2  : (ON $L $YY')
Desc3  : (IS – LINE $(XX' 3) NIL NIL)
Desc4  : (IS – LINE $(YY' 3) NIL NIL)
Desc5  : (IS – POINT $(K 3) NIL)
Desc6  : (IS – POINT $(L 3) NIL)
Desc7  : (IS – POINT $(M 3) (MID – POINT $K $L))
Desc8  : (IS – PERPENDICULAR $XX' $YY')
Desc9  : (EVAL (eq (DISTANT $K $L) p))
Desc10 : (FIND $M)
```

⇓

```
Desc11 : (IS – LINE $(XX' 3) $X $A))
Desc12 : (IS – LINE $(YY' 3) $Y $B))
Desc13 : (IS – POINT $(K 3) (k0, k1, k2))
Desc14 : (IS – POINT $(L 3) (l0, l1, l2))
Desc15 : (IS – POINT $(M 3) (α, β, γ))
Desc16 : (IS – POINT $(X 3) (x0, x1, x2))
Desc17 : (IS – POINT $(Y 3) (y0, y1, y2))
Desc18 : (IS – VECTOR $(A 3) (a0, a1, a2))
Desc19 : (IS – VECTOR $(B 3) (b0, b1, b2))
```

$$\begin{aligned}
\mathrm{hyp}_1 &= a_2b_2 + a_1b_1 + a_0b_0\\
\mathrm{hyp}_2 &= -x_0 - a_0t_0 + k_0\\
\mathrm{hyp}_3 &= -x_1 - a_1t_0 + k_1\\
\mathrm{hyp}_4 &= -x_2 - a_2t_0 + k_2\\
\mathrm{hyp}_5 &= -y_0 - b_0t_1 + l_0\\
\mathrm{hyp}_6 &= -y_1 - b_1t_1 + l_1\\
\mathrm{hyp}_7 &= -y_2 - b_2t_1 + l_2\\
\mathrm{hyp}_8 &= -l_0 - k_0 + 2\alpha\\
\mathrm{hyp}_9 &= -l_1 - k_1 + 2\beta\\
\mathrm{hyp}_{10} &= -l_2 - k_2 + 2\gamma\\
\mathrm{hyp}_{11} &= p^2 - (k_2 - l_2)^2 - (k_1 - l_1)^2 - (k_0 - l_0)^2
\end{aligned}$$

DESCRIPTIVE
$\{XX', YY', p, K, L, M\}$
INDEPENDENT
$\{t_0, t_1, \alpha, \beta, \gamma\}$
DEPENDENTS
$\{k_0, k_1, k_2, l_0, l_1, l_2\} \cup \{a_2, b_2, a_1, b_1, a_0, b_0\}$
SYMMETRIC
$\{ (XX', YY'),$
$((a_0, a1, a_2, k_0, k_1, k_2, x_0, x_1, x_2, t_0)$
$(b_0, b1, b_2, l_0, l_1, l_2, y_0, y_1, y_2, t_1))\}$
FORALL
(real – number t_0 t_1)

PHASE II : Wu's method

$$\begin{aligned}
\mathrm{Rem}_{10} = \; & -a_0^2(4y_2^2 + 4b_2t_1y_2 - 8\gamma y_2 - 4a_1t_0y_1\\
& -4a_0t_0y_0 - 4b_2t_1x_2 + 4x_1^2 + 4a_1t_0x_1\\
& -8\beta x_1 + 4x_0^2 + 4a_0t_0x_0 - 8\alpha x_0\\
& -p^2 + 4\gamma^2 + 4\beta^2 + 4\alpha^2)
\end{aligned}$$

with Conc = hyp_{11}
$x_1 = a_2, x_2 = a_1, x_3 = b_1, x_4 = b_0, x_5 = l_0,$
$x_6 = k_2, x_7 = l_1, x_9 = k_1, x_{10} = l_2, x_{11}k_0$

PHASE III : Algebraic reasoning

Applied – rule$_1$: $\mathbf{A}t + \mathbf{B}s + \mathbf{C} \equiv 0$ $(\forall\ s\ t\ \in\ \Re)$
$\Longrightarrow\ \mathbf{A} = \mathbf{B} = \mathbf{C} \equiv 0$
where $t = t_0$ $s = t_1$
(FORALL – condition) in Rem_{10}

⇓

$$\begin{aligned}
\mathit{Result}_1 &: 4\gamma^2 - 8y_2\gamma + 4y_2^2 + 4x_1^2 + 4x_0^2 - 8\alpha x_0\\
&\quad -p^2 + 4\beta^2 + 4\alpha^2 - 8\beta x_1 \equiv 0\\
\mathit{Result}_2 &: 4a_1(x_1 - y_1) + 4a_0(x_0 - y_0) \equiv 0\\
\mathit{Result}_3 &: 4b_2y_2 - 4b_2x_2 \equiv 0
\end{aligned}$$

Applied – rule$_2$: *Additional reasoning*
using SYMMETRIC
where $XX' \iff YY'$

⇓

$$\begin{aligned}
\mathit{Result}_4 &: 4\gamma^2 - 8x_2\gamma + 4x_2^2 + 4y_1^2 + 4y_0^2 - 8\alpha y_0\\
&\quad -p^2 + 4\beta^2 + 4\alpha^2 - 8\beta y_1 \equiv 0\\
\mathit{Result}_5 &: 4b_1(y_1 - x_1) + 4b_0(y_0 - x_0) \equiv 0\\
\mathit{Result}_6 &: 4a_2x_2 - 4a_2y_2 \equiv 0
\end{aligned}$$

Applied – rule$_3$: **Judging perpendicular** $\vec{V_1} \cdot \vec{V_2} = 0$
$\iff \vec{V_1} \perp \vec{V_2}$

⇓

$$\mathit{Result}_7 : \begin{pmatrix} a_0\\ a_1\\ a_2 \end{pmatrix} \perp \begin{pmatrix} x_0 - y_0\\ x_1 - y_1\\ x_2 - y_2 \end{pmatrix}$$

$$\mathit{Result}_8 : \begin{pmatrix} b_0\\ b_1\\ b_2 \end{pmatrix} \perp \begin{pmatrix} x_0 - y_0\\ x_1 - y_1\\ x_2 - y_2 \end{pmatrix}$$

PHASE IV : Translation into symbolic representations

```
New – Desc1 : (ON $M (AND
                  (SPHERE   $X   p/2)
                  (SPHERE   $Y   p/2))
New – Desc2 : (ON $X $XX')
New – Desc3 : (ON $Y $YY')
New – Desc4 : (IS – PERPENDICULAR
                  (! – $X $Y) $XX')
New – Desc5 : (IS – PERPENDICULAR
                  (! – $X $Y) $YY')
```

Fig.8 Solution to locus problem (2)

AUTOMATED REASONING

Theorem Proving III

An Inference Rule for Hypothesis Generation
*

Robert Demolombe
ONERA/CERT
2 avenue E.Belin B.P. 4025
31055 Toulouse, France

Luis Fariñas del Cerro
IRIT
Université Paul Sabatier
118 route de Narbonne
31052 Toulouse, France

Abstract

There are many new application fields for automated deduction where we have to apply abductive reasoning. In these applications we have to generate consequences of a given theory having some appropriate properties. In particular we consider the case where we have to generate the clauses containing instances of a given literal L. The negation of the other literals in such clauses are hypothesis allowing to derive L.

In this paper we present an inference rule, called L-inference, which was designed in order to derive those clauses, and a L-strategy. The L-inference rule is a sort of Input Hyperresolution. The main result of the paper is the proof of the soundness and completeness of the L-inference rule. The L-strategy associated to the L-inference rule, is a saturation by level with deletion of the tautologies and of the subsumed clauses. We show that the L-strategy is also complete.

1 Introduction

Traditionally automated deduction systems are devoted to prove if a given formula is a theorem; their applications , as is well knwon, have been very succesful in many domains of Computer Science. Gradually this traditional functionality has been extended.

For example in Logic Programming, or in Deductive Databases, it is not enough to know if a closed formula is a theorem, indeed we want to know the set of substitutions used in the proof of a formula.

Recently applications, like ATMS, automated diagnosis, generation of "why not" explanations, conditional answering in Deductive Databases, partial deduction, all of them involving some kind of abductive reasoning, have emphasized the need of new functionalities. For every of these new applications it is necessary to produce, for a given formula, the set of hypothesis we have to add to a given theory to prove this formula. This shows that we are now expecting from an automated deduction method more information than an answer of the form : "yes", or "no", or a set of substitutions.

For these new aplications (see [7, 9, 11, 1, 5], and Inoue [4] for hypothesis generation) the expected information is, for a given Database DB, and a given query Q which is not derivable from DB, the set of hypothesis X such that $X \rightarrow Q$ is derivable from DB, and X is as general as possible. Such X are called the *minimal supports* for Q by Reiter and de Kleer in [14].

In order to mechanize the production of hypothesis some new algorithms have been defined. For example, in the frame of Propositional Calculus, by Siegel [13], Cayrol and Tayrac [10], Oxusoff and Rauzy [12], and Kean and Tsiknis [6], and in the frame of First Order Calculus, by Cholvy [2], and Inoue [4].

The objective of this paper is to present a new inference rule, and its associated strategy, which have been designed in order to efficiently compute the minimal support for a query.

We shall assume the reader is familiar with traditional theorem proving techniques as they are presented in [3].

2 General definition of the generation hypothesis problem

In all the paper we consider a First Order Language where formulas are in clausal form.

Let S be a set of consistent clauses, a query adressed to S is represented by a literal L.

It is not restrictive to have only query represented by a

*This work has been partially supported by the CEC, in the context of the Basic Research Action, called MEDLAR.

single literal. Indeed, if the query is a first order formula F we can introduce a new atomic formula Q, and we can add to S the clauses generated by the clausal form of : $Q \leftrightarrow F$. Then the answer to the query Q provides the minimal support for Q.

The answer to the query L, relative to S, is a set of clauses containing instances of L, defined by :

ans(L,S) = { L'∨X | S ⊢ L'∨X, where L' is an instance of L, and L'∨X is not a tautology, and there is no clause c derivable from S such that c strictly subsumes L'∨X [1] }

According to this definition the clauses in ans(L,S) are minimal with regard to the subsumption.

If L' ∨ X is in ans(L,S), the negation of X is an hypothesis which allows to infer L' in the context of S.

It is worth noting some consequences of the condition of minimality. If L' ∨ X is minimal we have :

- L' is not derivable from S. That means that if L'∨X is in the answer, **we need additional hypothesis to derive L'**.
- X is not derivable from S. Therefore the corresponding **hypothesis to infer L' is consistent with S**.
- there exists no clause L' ∨ X' derivable from S such that L' ∨ X' subsumes L' ∨ X. Since the condition L' ∨ X' subsumes L' ∨ X implies X' subsumes X, **there is no weaker hypothesis than X** to infer L' in the context of S.

A consequence of L'∨X not being a tautology is that X is not the trivial hypothesis ¬L'.

Example1 :

S = {P(x,y) ∨ ¬Q(x,y) ∨ S(x,y), Q(a,b), ¬S(a,c), Q(b,d)}

Let L=P(a,x) be the query, the answer is :

ans(L,S) = {P(a,x) ∨ ¬Q(a,x) ∨ S(a,x), P(a,b) ∨ S(a,b), P(a,c) ∨ ¬Q(a,c)}

3 Definition of the Inference Rule

Definition 1. Let L be a literal. A clause C is an **L-clause** iff there is a literal L' in C such that L is an instance of L'.

[1] We say that c "strictly subsumes" c' if c subsumes c' and c' does not subsumes c

Definition 2. Let L be a literal and let $M_i \vee e_i$, $1 \leq i \leq p$, be a set E of clauses, called electrons, such that each M_i is a literal, and each e_i is an L-clause. Let n be the clause : $N_1 \vee N_2 \vee \ldots \vee N_p \vee n'$, where the N_i's are literals, which is called the nucleus. A finite sequence of L-clauses $R_0, \ldots, R_p$ is an **L-inference** iff :

- R_0 is n,
- each R_{i+1} is a resolvent obtained (by the Resolution principle) from R_i and $M_i \vee e_i$, where the literal M_i is resolved against the instance of the literal N_j, which is in R_i, $1 \leq j \leq p$.

R_p is called the **L-resolvent** of E and n, and the R_i, for $1 \leq i \leq p-1$, are called the **intermediate resolvents**. The L-inference will be represented by : $\frac{E \quad n}{R_p}$

Definition 3. Let S be a set of clauses. A **L-deduction** of C_n from S is a finite sequence $C_0 \ldots C_n$ of clauses such that : each C_i is either a clause in S or there are $C_{i_1}, \ldots C_{i_k}$ in the L-deduction, with each $i_j < i$, such that C_i is the L-resolvent of $C_{i_1}, \ldots C_{i_k}$, by an L-inference whose nucleus is in S.

Definition 4. A **R-deduction** of C_n from S is a finite sequence $C_0 \ldots C_n$ of clauses such that : each C_i is either in S or there are C_{i_1}, C_{i_2} in the R-deduction, with each $i_j < i$, such that C_i is the resolvent (by the Resolution Principle) of C_{i_1} and C_{i_2}.

Theorem 1. (R.C.T. Lee [8]) Let S be a set of clauses, if c is a clause derivable from S, there is a clause c', subsuming c, such that c' is derivable from S by a R-deduction.

Theorem 2. Let S be a set of clauses and L a given literal. If there is a R-deduction of L ∨ C, then there is a L-deduction of L ∨ C.

Proof. The proof is by induction on the number n of inferences in the R-deduction of L ∨ C from S.

For n=1, L ∨ C is the resolvent of two clauses C_1 and C_2 in S. Then either C_1 or C_2 (say C_1) is of the form M∨e, where e is a L-clause, and M is the resolved literal. Therefore the R-inference is a L-inference.

For the induction step we assume we have a R-deduction of L ∨ C from S using n inferences. Let's consider in this R-deduction some clause C_0 which is the resolvent of two clauses C_1 and C_2 which are in S.

Then there is a R-deduction of L ∨ C from S and C_0 using n-1 inferences.

We distinguish the following two cases:

Case 1. C_0 is a L-clause. For the same reason as in the base induction step $\frac{C_1 \quad C_2}{C_0}$ is an L-inference. Then by induction hypothesis the R-deduction of L ∨ C from S and C_0 there exists a L-deduction D of L ∨ C from S and C_0. If we add the L-inference : $\frac{C_1 \quad C_2}{C_0}$ before the first occurence of C_0 in D, we get a L-deduction of L ∨ C from S.

Case 2. C_0 is not a L-clause. Then by induction hypothesis there exists a L-deduction D of L ∨ C from S and C_0. Assume the L-inference using C_0, in D, is of the form $\frac{E \quad C_0}{C_3}$, where E is a set of electrons and C_0 is the nucleus .We define a partition of the set E into two sets E_1 and E_2 as follows : a clause e in E is in E_1 if and only if the literal in e which is resolved in the inference $\frac{E \quad C_0}{C_3}$ is provided by the clause C_1.

Then we transform the proof d : $\frac{E \quad \frac{C_1 \quad C_2}{C_0}}{C_3}$,
where $\frac{E \quad C_0}{C_3}$ is an L-inference, and $\frac{C_1 \quad C_2}{C_0}$ is an R-inference,

into d' : $\frac{\frac{E_1 \quad C_1}{C_4} \quad \frac{E_2 \quad C_2}{C_5}}{C_6}$.

The inferences $\frac{E_1 \quad C_1}{C_4}$ and $\frac{E_2 \quad C_2}{C_5}$ are L-inferences, because $\frac{E \quad C_0}{C_3}$ is a L-inference, i.e. each intermediate resolvent in the L-inference is an L-clause, and the resolved literals in E_1 (resp. E_2) and C_1 (resp. C_2) are the same literals as the literals resolved in E and C_0. Then C_4 and C_5 are L-clauses, and in the inference : $\frac{C_4 \quad C_5}{C_6}$, the resolved literals are the same as in the inference : $\frac{C_1 \quad C_2}{C_0}$; moreover these literals are not the literals which make C_4 and C_5 be L-clauses, then $\frac{C_4 \quad C_5}{C_6}$ is an L-inference. So C_6 is an L-clause, and the transformed proof d' is an L-deduction.

The set of literals which must be unified, and resolved, in the proof d and in the proof d' are the same, then the two sets of equations defining the most general unifiers in d and d' are the same. Then the substitution applied to the literals of E, C_1 and C_2, whose instances are in C_3, is the same as the substitution applied to the literals of E_1, E_2, C_1 and C_2 whose instances are in C_6. Therefore C_6 is identical to C_3. Finally if we replace in D the proof d by d' we get an L-deduction of L ∨ C from S.

In the case where there are several occurences of C_0 in the proof D, and C_0 is involved in several L-inferences of the form $\frac{E' \quad C_0}{C'_3}$, we remove each C_0 occurence with a similar transformation. Notice that each transformation decreases by one the number of C_0 occurences. Then after a finite number of tranformation of the L-deduction D we obtain a L-deduction of L ∨ C from S. Q.E.D.

The following completeness theorem is a trivial consequence of Theorem 1 and Theorem 2.

Theorem 3. Let S be a set of clauses, if L ∨ c is a clause derivable from S, there exists a clause L′ ∨ c′, subsuming L ∨ c, which is derivable from S by an L-deduction.

Proposition Since every L-inference is a sequence of application of Resolution principle, the L-inference rule is sound.

One could notice that an L-deduction is very close to an OL-deduction, or an SL-deduction (see [8]) with top clause ¬L. However OL-resolution has been proved to be complete to generate the empty clause, but it fails to be complete for clause generation. Inoue, in [4], modified the standard OL-resolution, by adding a new rule, called "Skip", that allows to reach completeness. The complexity of the proof of Theorem 1 clearly suggests that there is no evidence that a strategy which is complete to generate the empty clause is also complete for the generation of clauses. That is why the proof of Theorems 2 and 3 is, in our view, the main contribution of our work.

4 Definition of the L-strategy

A saturation algorithm is considered in order to define an effective procedure to compute the L-clauses. This algorithm could be improved using more sofisticated strategies like ordering.

The L-strategy computes the answer to a query into two steps. In the first step is computed a set of clauses, called extended answer, containing more clauses than the clauses in the answer. Namely answers may contain hypothesis which are inconsistent with S. In the second step we have to remove all the clauses L′ ∨ X in the extended answer such that X is derivable from S. In this second step the clause X is known, then testing if X is derivable from S can be done by any standard theorem proving strategy. For this reason this second step is not described in this paper, and we shall present only the first step.

Definition 5. We call **extended answer** the following set of clauses :

eans(L,S) = {L′∨X | S ⊢ L′∨X, where L' is an instance of L, and L′∨X is not a tautology, and there is no clause c in eans(L,S) such that c strictly subsumes L′ ∨ X }

Note that this definition is weaker than the previous one. Indeed, if $L' \vee X \in ans(L,S)$, X is not derivable from S, while if $L' \vee X \in eans(L,S)$, X may be derivable from S.

Notation : We denote [S] a set of clauses where all the subsumed clauses have been removed.

Definition 6. Let S be a set of clauses, and let L be a query, the **L-strategy** computes the sets $S_0, \ldots, S_{i+1}, \ldots$, inductively as follows :

$S_0 = [\{(L' \vee X)\sigma \mid L' \vee X \in S$ and σ is the most general unifier of L and $L'\}]$

...

$S_{i+1} = [S_i \cup \{L' \vee X \mid$ there exists a set of electrons E in S_i, and a nucleus n in S, such that $L' \vee X$ is the L'-resolvent of E and n$\}]$

...

For the purpose of the next definition we consider deductions as proof-trees instead of proof-sequences.

Definition We call **depth of a deduction** the number of inference steps in the longest path of the proof-tree corresponding to this deduction.

Theorem 4. If $L' \vee X$ is in eans(L,S), where L' is an instance of L, then there exists some i, and a clause c, such that c is in S_i, and c is equivalent to $L' \vee X$

Proof : The proof is by induction on the depth j of the L'-deduction of $L' \vee X$ from S.

For the base case (j=0) the proof is trivial.

For the induction step, assume there is an L'-deduction, of depth $j+1$, of $L' \vee X$ from S, where the last L'-inference is of the form $\frac{E \quad n}{L' \vee X}$.

First we show that tautologies can be removed.

If a $L' \vee X$ proof uses a tautology, then we can show by induction that this tautology is either n or an electron of E. In that case we can also show that it is possible to transform the last two inferences in a proof whithout tautology.

Now we show that subsumed clauses can be removed.

Let $e = M \vee e'$ be an electron in E, where M is the resolved literal. If e does not belong to eans(L,S), there is an L-clause c in eans(L,S) subsuming e. We distinguish the following two cases :

Case1 : c susbsumes e'. Then c subsumes the instance of e' which is in $L' \vee X$. That contradicts the fact that $L' \vee X$ is in eans(L,S).

Case2 : c does not subsumes e'. Then c is of the form $M' \vee c'$, where M' is an instance of M. In this case we can transform the inference $\frac{E \quad n}{L' \vee X}$ by replacing e in E by c. Then the new L'-resolvent subsumes $L' \vee X$ because c' subsumes e' . That contradicts the fact that $L' \vee X$ is in eans(L,S).

Therefore e belongs to eans(L,S). Since the depth of the L'-deduction is equal to j, by induction hypothesis e is in S_j.

The same conclusion holds for any electron in E, so from the definition of S_{j+1} in function of S_j we can conclude that $L' \vee X$ is in S_{j+1}.

5 Some typical examples

In this section we present two examples showing the main features of our approach.

Example2 is a very simple example illustrating the interest of the L-strategy for automated diagnosis.

Let's consider a very simple system l, with components : b, b_1, b_2, and c, whose correct working is defined by the following rules and facts :

$l - works \leftarrow b - works \wedge c - works$
$b - works \leftarrow b_1 - works \wedge b_2 - works$
$b_1 - works$

If we respectively denote by : L, B, B_1, B_2 and C, the propositions : l-works, b-works, b_1-works, b_2-works and c-works, we have :

$S = \{ L \vee \neg B \vee \neg C,\ B \vee \neg B_1 \vee \neg B_2,\ B_1 \}$

Query : L

$S_0 = \{L \vee \neg B \vee \neg C \}$

$S_1 = \{L \vee \neg B \vee \neg C,\ L \vee \neg B_1 \vee \neg B_2 \vee \neg C \}$

$S_2 = \{L \vee \neg B \vee \neg C,\ L \vee \neg B_2 \vee \neg C \}$

The answer : $L \vee \neg B_2 \vee \neg C$ can be interpreted as : "l-works if b_2-works and c-works", or as well as : " a possible explanation that l does not work is that b_2 or c does not work".

Example3, which is in Propositional Calculus, is interesting because it shows that the standard Input resolution strategy is not complete. Indeed with this strategy we cannot infer $L \vee A$, while $L \vee A$ is derivable with the L-strategy. Here we can see that the reason why the L-strategy is complete, although it is an Input strategy, is that the L-strategy is also an Hyperresolution.

$S = \{ L \vee M \vee N,\ \neg M \vee N,\ M \vee \neg N,\ \neg M \vee \neg N \vee A \}$

Query : L.

$S_0 = \{L \vee M \vee N\}$

$S_1 = \{L \vee M,\ L \vee N\}$

The clauses : $L \vee N \vee \neg N \vee A$, and $L \vee M \vee \neg M \vee A$ are not in S_1 because they are tautologies, and $L \vee M \vee N$ is not in S_1 because it is subsumed by $L \vee M$.

$S_2 = \{L \vee M,\ L \vee N,\ L \vee A\}$

$L \vee A$ is generated by an L-inference where the two electrons are : $L \vee M$ and $L \vee N$, and the nucleus is : $\neg M \vee \neg N \vee A$. The clauses $L \vee \neg M \vee A$ and $L \vee \neg N \vee A$ are not in S_2 because they are subsumed by $L \vee A$.

Example4 shows how we can get infinite answers. The intuitive meaning of the query is : *What conditions implies that x is an ancestor of y ?"*. Since the query does not refer to a specific set of persons, there is an infinite set of conditions which guarantee that x is an ancestor of y; each condition correponds to a different level in the ancestor's hierarchy.

$S = \{L(x,y) \vee \neg Ancestor(x,y),\ \ Ancestor(x,y) \vee \neg Father(x,y),$
$Ancestor(x,y) \vee \neg Ancestor(x,z) \vee \neg Father(z,y)\ \}$

Query : L(x,y).

$S_0 = \{L(x,y) \vee \neg Ancestor(x,y)\ \}$

$S_1 = \{L(x,y) \vee \neg Ancestor(x,y),\ \ L(x,y) \vee \neg Father(x,y),$
$L(x,y) \vee \neg Ancestor(x,z_1) \vee \neg Father(z_1,y)\ \}$

$S_2 = \{L(x,y) \vee \neg Ancestor(x,y),\ \ L(x,y) \vee \neg Father(x,y),$
$L(x,y) \vee \neg Father(x,z_1) \vee \neg Father(z_1,y),$
$L(x,y) \vee \neg Ancestor(x,z_2) \vee \neg Father(z_2,z_1) \vee \neg Father(z_1,y)\}$

...

$S_i = \{L(x,y) \vee \neg Ancestor(x,y),\ \ L(x,y) \vee \neg Father(x,y),$
$L(x,y) \vee \neg Father(x,z_1) \vee \neg Father(z_1,y),$
$L(x,y) \vee \neg Ancestor(x,z_2) \vee \neg Father(z_2,z_1) \vee \neg Father(z_1,y),$
...
$L(x,y) \vee \neg Ancestor(x,z_i) \vee \neg Father(z_i,z_{i-1}) \vee \ldots \vee \neg Father(z_2,z_1) \vee \neg Father(z_1,y)\}$

6 Conclusion

We have defined an inference rule and a strategy to generate the most general hypothesis allowing to infer a formula, represented by a single literal L, in the context of a given theory. This strategy is efficient in the sense that it generates only L-clauses. Then the only useless generated closes are those ones which are not minimal with regard to the subsumption. Moreover we have the feeling that this second step cannot take advantage of the work done in the first step, and they can be executed into two independent steps without waste of efficiency.

Nevertheless many refinements of the strategy should be investigated in the future. One of them is to make use of an order on the predicate symbols.

An important issue we want to investigate in the future is the case of infinite answers. A first approach is to find a finite representation of those infinite sets, having some desirable properties. For example to be easy to understand. Another approach is to provide only partial answers, and to cut the computation in a "clean" state. The right approach certainly depends on the application field.

Our method can be considered as a step in order to supply new functionalities for automated deduction methods.

Acknowledgements :

Thanks to reviewers for their constructive and valuable comments.

References

[1] J.M. Boi, E. Innocente, A. Rauzy, and P. Siegel. Production fields : A new approach to deduction problems and twoalgorithms for propositional calculus. In *To appear*, 1991.

[2] F. Bry. Intensional Updates : abduction via deduction. In *Proc. 7th Int. Conf. on Logic Programming.* MIT Press, 1990.

[3] L. Cholvy. Answering queries adressed to a rule base. *Revue d'Intelligence Artificielle*, 4(1), 1990.

[4] R.C.T. Lee C.L. Chang. *Symbolic Logic and Mechanical Theorem Proving.* Academic Press, 1973.

[5] K. Inoue. Consequence-Finding Based on Oredered Linear Resolution. Technical report, ICOT-Research Center, 1990.

[6] A.C. Kakas and P. Mancarella. Database updates through abduction. In *Proc. of VLDB-90*, 1990.

[7] A. Kean and G. Tsiknis. An incremental method for generating prime implicants/implicates. *Journal of Symbolic Computation*, 9:185–206, 1990.

[8] R. Kowalski. *Problems and Promises of Computational Logic.* Springer-Verlag, Brussels, 1990.

[9] R.C.T. Lee. *A completeness theorem and a computer programm for finding theorems derivable from given axioms.* PhD thesis, Univ. of California at Berkley, 1967.

[10] H.J. Levesque. A knowledge-level account of abduction (preliminary version). In *Proc. of IJCAI-89*, 1989.

[11] M.Cayrol and P.Tayrac. Arc : un atms basé sur la résolution cat-correcte. *Revue d'Intelligence Artificielle*, 3(3), 1990.

[12] E. Mmicozzi and R.Reiter. A note on linear resolutio strategies in consequence-finding. *Artificial Intelligence*, 3:175–180, 1972.

[13] Oxusoff and Rauzy. *Evaluation sémantique en Calcul Propositionnel.* PhD thesis, Université Aix-Marseille, 1989.

[14] R. Reiter and de Kleer. Foundations of assumption-based truth maintenance system. In *AAAI-87*, 1987.

Consequence-Finding Based on Ordered Linear Resolution

Katsumi Inoue
ICOT Research Center
Institute for New Generation Computer Technology
1-4-28 Mita, Minato-ku, Tokyo 108
Japan

Abstract

Since linear resolution with clause ordering is incomplete for consequence-finding, it has been used mainly for proof-finding. In this paper, we re-evaluate consequence-finding. Firstly, consequence-finding is generalized to the problem in which only interesting clauses having a certain property (called characteristic clauses) should be found. Then, we show how adding a skip rule to ordered linear resolution makes it complete for consequence-finding in this general sense. Compared with set-of-support resolution, the proposed method generates fewer clauses to find such a subset of consequences. In the propositional case, this is an elegant tool for computing the prime implicants/implicates. The importance of the results lies in their applicability to a wide class of AI problems including procedures for nonmonotonic and abductive reasoning and truth maintenance systems.

1 Introduction

It is well known in automated deduction that while resolution [Robinson, 1965] is complete for proof-finding (called *refutation* complete), that is, it can deduce *false* from every unsatisfiable set of formulas, it is not deductively complete for finding every logical consequence of a satisfiable set of formulas. Lee [1967] addresses himself to this problem and defines the *consequence-finding* problem, which is expressed in the following form:

> Given a set of formulas T and a resolution procedure P, for any logical consequence D of T, can P derive a logical consequence C of T such that C subsumes D?

If a resolution procedure is complete for consequence-finding, then it is useful in spite of lacking deductive completeness because in general the logical consequences not deducible from the theory are neither interesting nor useful. Namely, such a formula is subsumed by some formula deducible from the theory and thus it is weak.

Historically, consequence-finding had been investigated intensively since the resolution principle [Robinson, 1965] was invented for proof-finding. Lee's [1967] completeness theorem was proved for the original resolution principle. Slagle, Chang and Lee [1969] extended the result to various kinds of semantic resolution. However, after Minicozzi and Reiter [1972] extended these results to various linear resolution strategies in the early 70s, consequence-finding was once abandoned in research of automated theorem proving and attention has been directed towards only proof-finding [1]. It appears that there are three reasons for this discouragement:

1. The results presented by [Minicozzi and Reiter, 1972] are in some sense negative. Linear resolution involving C-ordering [Loveland, 1978; Reiter, 1971; Kowalski and Kuhner, 1971; Chang and Lee, 1973; Shostak, 1976] (literals are ordered in each clause in the theory), which is the most familiar and efficient class of resolution procedures, is incomplete for consequence-finding. Thus, the completeness result that we would most like to obtain does not hold.
2. It is neither practical nor useful to find all of the consequences in general. However, there has not been an intellectual method which directly searches interesting formulas, instead of getting all theorems and then filtering them by some criteria.
3. As opposed to proof-finding, consequence-finding has lacked useful applications in AI.

In this paper, we re-evaluate consequence-finding and give new perspectives. The proposals are motivated and justified by the following solutions to the above three problems:

1. Recently, Finger [1987] gave a complete procedure based on set-of-support deduction for generating formulas (called *ramification*) derivable from a theory and a newly added formula as an initial set of support. We provide a complete procedure for consequence-finding, which contains more restriction strategies than Finger's, by adding one rule called *skip* operation to C-ordered linear resolution.
2. Bossu and Siegel [1985] give a complete algorithm for finding the set of positive clauses derivable from a groundable theory (called *characteristic clauses*).

[1] One can see that textbooks of resolution-based theorem proving, such as [Chang and Lee, 1973; Loveland, 1978], have no sections for consequence-finding.

Recently, Siegel [1987] redefined the notion of characteristic clauses for propositional theories and proposed a complete algorithm for finding them. We show how our results can both improve the efficiency of Bossu and Siegel's algorithm and lift Siegel's for the general case. Moreover, easy modifications of the proposed procedure can be shown to be applied to more efficient variations of consequence-finding.

3. Przymusinski [1989] defines MILO-resolution to be used in his query answering procedure for *circumscription* of ground theories. MILO-resolution can be characterized as C-ordered linear resolution with skip operation [Inoue and Helft, 1990]. On the other hand, most procedures for *abduction* [Pople, 1973; Cox and Pietrzykowski, 1986; Finger, 1987; Poole, 1989; Stickel, 1990] can utilize consequence-finding procedures to generate explanations [Inoue, 1990]. We show how the proposed procedure can be applied to generate such interesting formulas for nonmonotonic and abductive reasoning. In the propositional case, the technique can be viewed as an elegant algorithm to compute *prime implicants/implicates*, and thus can be utilized for the *clause management system* [Reiter and de Kleer, 1987] that is a generalization of the ATMS [de Kleer, 1986].

The importance of the results presented lies in their applicability to a wide class of AI problems. In other words, the methods shed some light on better understanding and implementation of many AI techniques.

The present paper is organized as follows. The next section characterizes consequence-finding in a general way, and shows how various AI problems can be well defined by using this notion of characteristic clauses. Section 3 presents the basic procedure, which is sound and complete for characteristic-clause-finding, based on C-ordered linear resolution. Efficient but incomplete variations of the basic procedure and their properties are provided in Section 4. Because of space limitation, proofs of propositions are given in the full paper.

2 Characterizing Consequence-Finding

We define a *theory* as a set of clauses, which can be identified with a *conjunctive normal form (CNF) formula.* A *clause* is a disjunction (possibly written as a set) of *literals,* each of which is a possibly negated atomic formula. Each variable in a clause is assumed to be universally quantified. For a method converting a formula to this form of theory, see [Loveland, 1978]. If S is a set of clauses, by $\overline{S}$ we mean the set formed by taking the negation of each clause in S. The empty clause is denoted by $\Box$. A clause C is said to *subsume* a clause D if there is a substitution θ such that $C\theta \subseteq D$ and C has no more literals than D [2]. For a set of clauses Σ, by $\mu\Sigma$ or $\mu[\Sigma]$ we mean the set of clauses of Σ not subsumed by any other clause of Σ. A clause C is a *theorem*, or a *(logical) consequence* of Σ if $\Sigma \models C$. The set of theorems of Σ is denoted by $Th(\Sigma)$.

[2] This definition of subsumption is called *θ-subsumption* in [Loveland, 1978]. Unlike in the propositional case, the second condition is necessary because a clause implies its factor.

2.1 Characteristic Clauses

We use the notion of *characteristic clauses,* which is a generalized notion of logical consequences and helps to analyze computational aspects of many of AI problems. The idea of characteristic clauses was introduced by Bossu and Siegel [1985] for evaluating a kind of closed-world reasoning and was later redefined by Siegel [1987] for propositional logic. The description below is more general than [Bossu and Siegel, 1985; Siegel, 1987; Inoue, 1990] in the sense that the notion is not limited to some special purposes and that it deals with the general case instead of just the propositional cases. Also, these notions are independent of implementation; we do not assume any particular resolution procedure in this section. Informally speaking, characteristic clauses are intended to represent "interesting" clauses to solve a certain problem, and are constructed over a sub-vocabulary of the representation language.

Definition 2.1 (1) We denote by $\mathcal{R}$ the set of all predicate symbols in the language. For $R \subseteq \mathcal{R}$, we denote by R^+ (R^-) the positive (negative) occurrences of predicates from R in the language. The set of all atomic formulas is denoted as $\mathcal{A} = \mathcal{R}^+$, and the set of literals is denoted $\mathcal{L} = \mathcal{A} \cup \overline{\mathcal{A}} = \mathcal{R}^+ \cup \mathcal{R}^-$.
(2) A *production field* $\mathcal{P}$ is a pair, $\langle L_{\mathcal{P}}, Cond \rangle$, where $L_{\mathcal{P}}$ (called the *characteristic literals*) is a subset of $\mathcal{L}$, and $Cond$ is a certain condition to be satisfied. When $Cond$ is not specified, $\mathcal{P}$ is just denoted as $\langle L_{\mathcal{P}} \rangle$. The production field $\langle \mathcal{L} \rangle$ is denoted $\mathcal{P}_{\mathcal{L}}$.
(3) A clause C *belongs to a production field* $\mathcal{P} = \langle L_{\mathcal{P}}, Cond \rangle$ if every literal in C belongs to $L_{\mathcal{P}}$ and C satisfies $Cond$. The set of theorems of Σ belonging to $\mathcal{P}$ is denoted by $Th_{\mathcal{P}}(\Sigma)$.
(4) A production field $\mathcal{P}$ is *stable* if for any two clauses C and D such that C subsumes D, it holds that if D belongs to $\mathcal{P}$, then C also belongs to $\mathcal{P}$.

Example 2.2 Examples of stable production fields.
(1) $\mathcal{P}_1 = \mathcal{P}_{\mathcal{L}}$: $Th_{\mathcal{P}_1}(\Sigma)$ is equivalent to $Th(\Sigma)$.
(2) $\mathcal{P}_2 = \langle \mathcal{A} \rangle$:
$Th_{\mathcal{P}_2}(\Sigma)$ is the set of positive clauses implied by Σ.
(3) $\mathcal{P}_3 = \langle \overline{A},\ \textit{size is less than } k \rangle$ where $A \subseteq \mathcal{A}$:
$Th_{\mathcal{P}_3}(\Sigma)$ is the set of negative clauses implied by Σ containing less than k literals all of which belong to $\overline{A}$.

Example 2.3 $\mathcal{P}_4 = \langle \mathcal{A},\ \textit{size is more than } k \rangle$ is not stable. For example, if $k = 2$ and $p(a), q(b), r(c) \in \mathcal{A}$, then $D_1 = p(a) \vee q(b)$ subsumes $D_2 = p(a) \vee q(b) \vee r(c)$, and D_2 belongs to $\mathcal{P}_4$ while D_1 does not.

Definition 2.4 (Characteristic Clauses) Let Σ be a set of clauses, and $\mathcal{P}$ a production field. The *characteristic clauses of* Σ *with respect to* $\mathcal{P}$ are:

$$Carc(\Sigma, \mathcal{P}) = \mu\, Th_{\mathcal{P}}(\Sigma).$$

$Carc(\Sigma, \mathcal{P})$ contains all the unsubsumed theorems of Σ belonging to a production field $\mathcal{P}$. To see why this notion is a generalization of consequence-finding, let $\mathcal{P}$ be $\mathcal{P}_{\mathcal{L}}$. From the definition of consequence-finding, for any clause $D \in Th(\Sigma)$, a complete procedure P can derive a clause $C \in Th(\Sigma)$ such that C subsumes D. Therefore, P can derive every clause $C' \in \mu Th(\Sigma)$ because

C' is not subsumed by any other theorem of Σ. Hence, $Carc(\Sigma, \mathcal{P}_{\mathcal{L}}) = \mu Th(\Sigma)$ must be contained in the theorems derivable from Σ by using P. Note also that the empty clause belongs to every stable production field $\mathcal{P}$, and that if Σ is unsatisfiable, then $Carc(\Sigma, \mathcal{P})$ contains only $\Box$. This means that proof-finding is a special case of consequence-finding. Next is a summarizing proposition.

Proposition 2.5 Let Σ be a theory, $\mathcal{P}$ a stable production field. A clause D is a theorem of Σ belonging to $\mathcal{P}$ if and only if there is a clause C in $Carc(\Sigma, \mathcal{P})$ such that C subsumes D. In particular, Σ is unsatisfiable if and only if $Carc(\Sigma, \mathcal{P}) = \{\Box\}$.

As we will see later, when new information is added to the theory, it is often necessary to compute newly derivable consequences caused by this new information. For this purpose, consequence-finding is extended to look for such a ramification of new information.

Definition 2.6 (New Characteristic Clauses) Let Σ be a set of clauses, $\mathcal{P}$ a production field, and F a formula. The *new characteristic clauses of F with respect to Σ and $\mathcal{P}$* are:

$$Newcarc(\Sigma, F, \mathcal{P}) = \mu\,[Th_{\mathcal{P}}(\Sigma \cup \{F\}) - Th(\Sigma)]\,.$$

In other words, $C \in Newcarc(\Sigma, F, \mathcal{P})$ if: (i) $\Sigma \cup \{F\} \models C$, (ii) C belongs to $\mathcal{P}$, (iii) $\Sigma \not\models C$, and (iv) no other clause subsuming C satisfies (i)–(iii).

The next three propositions show the connections between the characteristic clauses and the new characteristic clauses. Firstly, $Newcarc(\Sigma, F, \mathcal{P})$ can be represented by the set difference of two sets of characteristic clauses.

Proposition 2.7

$$Newcarc(\Sigma, F, \mathcal{P}) = Carc(\,\Sigma \cup \{F\}, \mathcal{P}) - Carc(\Sigma, \mathcal{P})\,.$$

When F is a CNF formula, $Newcarc(\Sigma, F, \mathcal{P})$ can be decomposed into a series of *primitive Newcarc operations* each of whose added formula is just a single clause.

Proposition 2.8 Let $F = C_1 \wedge \cdots \wedge C_m$ be a CNF formula. Then,

$$Newcarc(\Sigma, F, \mathcal{P}) = \mu\,[\,\bigcup_{i=1}^{m} Newcarc(\Sigma_i, C_i, \mathcal{P})\,]$$

where $\Sigma_1 = \Sigma$, and $\Sigma_{i+1} = \Sigma_i \cup \{C_i\}$, for $i = 1, \ldots, m-1$.

Finally, the characteristic clauses $Carc(\Sigma, \mathcal{P})$ can be expressed by constructively using primitive *Newcarc* operations. Notice that for any atomic formula p, if $\Sigma \not\models p$, $\Sigma \not\models \neg p$, and $p \vee \neg p$ belongs to some stable production field $\mathcal{P}$, then $p \vee \neg p$ belongs to $Carc(\Sigma, \mathcal{P})$.

Proposition 2.9 Let $\Sigma_m = \{C_1, \cdots, C_m\}$. Then,

$$Carc(\emptyset, \mathcal{P}) = \{\, p \vee \neg p \mid p \in \mathcal{A} \text{ and } p \vee \neg p \text{ belongs to } \mathcal{P}\,\},$$

$$Carc(\Sigma_{i+1}, \mathcal{P}) = \mu\,[Carc(\Sigma_i, \mathcal{P}) \cup Newcarc(\Sigma_i, C_i, \mathcal{P})],$$

where $\Sigma_1 = \emptyset$, and $\Sigma_{i+1} = \Sigma_i \cup \{C_i\}$, for $i = 1, \ldots, m-1$.

2.2 Applications

We illustrate how the use of the (new) characteristic clauses enables elegant definition and precise understanding of many AI problems.

2.2.1 Propositional Case

In the propositional case, $\mathcal{A}$ is reduced to the set of propositional symbols in the language. The subsumption relation is now very simple: a clause C subsumes D if $C \subseteq D$. A theorem of Σ is called an *implicate* of Σ, and the *prime implicates* [Kean and Tsiknis, 1990] of Σ are:

$$PI(\Sigma) = \mu Th(\Sigma)\,.$$

The characteristic clauses of Σ with respect to $\mathcal{P}$ are the prime implicates of Σ belonging to $\mathcal{P}$. When $\mathcal{P} = \mathcal{P}_{\mathcal{L}}$, it holds that $Carc(\Sigma, \mathcal{P}) = PI(\Sigma)$ [3].

Computing prime implicates is an essential task in the ATMS [de Kleer, 1986] and in its generalization called the *clause management system* (CMS) [Reiter and de Kleer, 1987]. The CMS is responsible for finding minimal supports for the queries:

Definition 2.10 [Reiter and de Kleer, 1987] Let Σ be a set of clauses and C a clause. A clause S is a *support for C with respect to* Σ if: (i) $\Sigma \models S \cup C$, and (ii) $\Sigma \not\models S$. A support S for C with respect to Σ is *minimal* if no other support S' for C subsumes S. The set of minimal supports for C with respect to Σ is written $MS(\Sigma, C)$.

The above definition can be easily extended to handle any formula instead of a clause as a query. Setting the production field to $\mathcal{P}_{\mathcal{L}}$ we see that:

Proposition 2.11 [Inoue, 1990] Let F be any formula.

$$MS(\Sigma, F) = Newcarc(\Sigma, \neg F, \mathcal{P}_{\mathcal{L}}).$$

When we choose the primitive *Newcarc* operation as a basic computational task, the above proposition does not require computation of $PI(\Sigma)$. On the other hand, the *compiled* approach [Reiter and de Kleer, 1987] takes $PI(\Sigma)$ as input to find $MS(\Sigma, C)$ for any clause C easily:

$$MS(\Sigma, C) = \mu\,\{\, P - C \mid P \in PI(\Sigma) \text{ and } P \cap C \neq \emptyset\}\,.$$

In the ATMS [de Kleer, 1986], there is a distinguished set of *assumptions* $A \subseteq \mathcal{L}$. An ATMS can be defined as a system responsible for finding the negations of all minimal supports for the queries consisting of only literals from $\overline{A}$ [Reiter and de Kleer, 1987; Inoue, 1990]. Therefore, the ATMS *label* of a formula F relative to a given theory Σ and A is characterized as

$$L(F, A, \Sigma) = \overline{Newcarc(\Sigma, \neg F, \mathcal{P})}, \quad \text{where } \mathcal{P} = \langle \overline{A} \rangle.$$

Inoue [1990] gives various sound and complete methods for both generating and updating the labels of queries relative to a non-Horn theory and literal assumptions.

2.2.2 Abductive and Nonmonotonic Reasoning

The task of the CMS/ATMS can be viewed as propositional *abduction* [Reiter and de Kleer, 1987; Levesque, 1989; Inoue, 1990]. For general cases, there are many proposals for a logical account of abduction [Pople, 1973; Cox and Pietrzykowski, 1986; Finger, 1987; Poole, 1989; Stickel, 1990], whose task is defined as generation of explanations of a query.

[3] The *prime implicants* of a disjunctive normal form formula can be defined in the same manner if the duality of $\wedge$ and $\vee$ is taken into account.

Definition 2.12 Let Σ be a theory, $H \subseteq \mathcal{L}$ (called the *hypotheses*), and G a closed formula. A conjunction E of ground instances of H is an *explanation of G from (Σ, H)* if: (i) $\Sigma \cup \{E\} \models G$ and (ii) $\Sigma \cup \{E\}$ is satisfiable[4].
An explanation E of G is *minimal* if no proper subconjunction E' of E satisfies $\Sigma \cup \{E'\} \models G$.
An *extension of* (Σ, H) is the set of logical consequences of $T \cup \{M\}$ where M is a maximal conjunction of ground instances of H such that $T \cup \{M\}$ is satisfiable.

Abduction can be characterized as follows:

Proposition 2.13 [Inoue and Helft, 1990] The set of all minimal explanations of G from (Σ, H) is

$$\overline{Newcarc(\Sigma, \neg G, \mathcal{P})}, \text{ where } \mathcal{P} = \langle \overline{H} \rangle .$$

There is an extension of (Σ, H) in which G holds iff

$$Newcarc(\Sigma, \neg G, \mathcal{P}) \neq \emptyset, \text{ where } \mathcal{P} = \langle \overline{H} \rangle .$$

Another important problem is to predict formulas that hold in all extensions. This problem is known to be equivalent to *circumscription* under the unique-names and domain-closure assumptions. Proving a formula holds in a circumscriptive theory [Przymusinski, 1989; Ginsberg, 1989], as well as other proof methods for non-monotonic reasoning formalisms (including explanation-based argument systems [Poole, 1989] and variations of closed-world assumptions [Bossu and Siegel, 1985; Minker and Rajasekar, 1990]), are based on finding explanations of the query, and showing that these explanations cannot be refuted:

Proposition 2.14 [Inoue and Helft, 1990] Suppose that $L_{\mathcal{P}} = P^{+} \cup Q^{+} \cup Q^{-}$, where P is the minimized predicates and Q is the fixed predicates in circumscription policy and that $\mathcal{P} = \langle L_{\mathcal{P}} \rangle$. Every circumscriptive minimal model satisfies a formula F if and only if there is a conjunction G of clauses from $Th_{\mathcal{P}}(\Sigma \cup \{\neg F\})$ such that $Newcarc(\Sigma, \neg G, \mathcal{P}) = \emptyset$.

Since we have characterized the prime implicates, the CMS/ATMS, abduction and circumscription [5], any application area of these techniques can be directly characterized by using the notion of the (new) characteristic clauses: for instance, diagnosis, synthesis [Finger, 1987] (plan recognition, prediction, design), and natural language understanding [Stickel, 1990].

3 Ordered-Linear Resolution for Consequence-Finding

We now present the basic procedure for implementing the primitive *Newcarc* operation. The important feature of the procedure is that it is *direct*, namely it is both sensitive to the given added clause to the theory and restricted to searching only characteristic clauses.

3.1 Basic Procedure

Given a theory Σ, a stable production field $\mathcal{P}$ and a clause C, we show how $Newcarc(\Sigma, C, \mathcal{P})$ can be computed by extending *C-ordered linear resolution* [6]. As seen in Propositions 2.8 and 2.9, both $Newcarc(\Sigma, F, \mathcal{P})$ for a CNF-formula F and $Carc(\Sigma, \mathcal{P})$ can be computed by using this primitive *Newcarc* operation. There are two reasons why C-ordered linear resolution is useful for computing the new characteristic clauses:

1. A newly added single clause C can be treated as the *top clause* of a linear deduction. This is a desirable feature for consequence-finding since the procedure can directly derive the theorems relevant to the added information.
2. It is easy to achieve the requirement that the procedure should focus on producing only those theorems that belong to $\mathcal{P}$. This is implemented by allowing the procedure to *skip* the selected literals belonging to $\mathcal{P}$. The computational superiority of the proposed technique compared to set-of-support resolution that is used by Finger's resolution residue [Finger, 1987], apart from the fact that C-ordered linear resolution contains more restriction strategies in natural ways, comes from this relevancy notion of directing search to $\mathcal{P}$.

Some procedures are known to perform this computation for restricted theories [7]. For propositional theories, Siegel [1987] proposes a complete algorithm by extending SL-resolution [Kowalski and Kuhner, 1971]. Inoue and Helft [1990] point out that MILO-resolution [Przymusinski, 1989], an extension of OL-resolution [Chang and Lee, 1973], can be viewed as C-ordered linear resolution with skip operation for ground theories with a particular production field for circumscription (see Proposition 2.14).

The following proposed procedure called *SOL (Skipping Ordered Linear) resolution* is a kind of generalization of [Przymusinski, 1989; Siegel, 1987]. An *ordered* clause is a sequence of literals possibly containing *framed literals* [Chang and Lee, 1973] which represents literals that have been resolved upon: from a clause C an ordered clause $\vec{C}$ is obtained just by ordering the elements of C; conversely, from an ordered clause $\vec{C}$ a clause C is obtained by removing the framed literals and converting the remainder to the set. A *structured* clause $\langle P, \vec{Q} \rangle$ is a pair of a clause P and an ordered clause $\vec{Q}$, whose clausal meaning is $P \cup Q$.

[4] This definition is based on [Poole, 1989] and deals with *ground* explanations. To get universally quantified explanations, we need to apply the *reverse Skolemization* algorithm [Cox and Pietrzykowski, 1986].

[5] When a query in abduction or circumscription contains existentially quantified variables, it is sometimes desirable to know for what values of these variables the query holds. This *answer extraction* problem is considered in [Helft *et al.*, 1991].

[6] By the term C-ordered linear resolution, we mean the family of linear resolution using ordered clauses and the information of literals resolved upon. Examples of C-ordered linear resolution are Model Elimination [Loveland, 1978], m.c.l. resolution [Reiter, 1971], SL-resolution [Kowalski and Kuhner, 1971], OL-resolution [Chang and Lee, 1973], and the GC procedure [Shostak, 1976]. This family is one of the most familiar and efficient classes of resolution for non-Horn theories because it contains several restriction strategies.

[7] Bossu and Siegel's [1985] saturation procedure finds $Carc(\Sigma, \mathcal{P})$ where $L_{\mathcal{P}}$ are fixed to ground atoms. However, it does not use C-ordering, but A-ordering (a total ordering of all the ground atomic formulas).

Definition 3.1 Given a theory Σ, a clause C, and a production field $\mathcal{P}$, an *SOL-deduction of a clause S from $\Sigma + C$ and $\mathcal{P}$* consists of a sequence of structured clauses $D_0, D_1, \ldots, D_n$, such that:

1. $D_0 = \langle \Box, \vec{C} \rangle$.
2. $D_n = \langle S, \Box \rangle$.
3. For each $D_i = \langle P_i, \vec{Q_i} \rangle$, $P_i \cup Q_i$ is not a tautology.
4. For each $D_i = \langle P_i, \vec{Q_i} \rangle$, $P_i \cup Q_i$ is not subsumed by any $P_j \cup Q_j$, where $D_j = \langle P_j, \vec{Q_j} \rangle$ is a previous structured clause, $j < i$. This rule is not applied if D_i is generated from D_{i-1} by applying 5(a)i.
5. $D_{i+1} = \langle P_{i+1}, \vec{Q_{i+1}} \rangle$ is generated from $D_i = \langle P_i, \vec{Q_i} \rangle$ according to the following steps:
   (a) Let l be the *left-most* literal of $\vec{Q_i}$. P_{i+1} and $\vec{R_{i+1}}$ are obtained by applying either of the rules:
      i. **(Skip)** If $P_i \cup \{l\}$ belongs to $\mathcal{P}$, then $P_{i+1} = P_i \cup \{l\}$ and $\vec{R_{i+1}}$ is the ordered clause obtained by removing l from $\vec{Q_i}$.
      ii. **(Resolve)** If there is a clause B_i in Σ such that $\neg k \in B_i$ and l and k are unifiable with mgu θ, then $P_{i+1} = P_i\theta$ and $\vec{R_{i+1}}$ is an ordered clause obtained by concatenating $\vec{B_i}\theta$ and $\vec{Q_i}\theta$, framing $l\theta$, and removing $\neg k\theta$.
      iii. **(Reduce)** If either
         A. P_i or $\vec{Q_i}$ contains an unframed literal k different from l (*factoring*), or
         B. $\vec{Q_i}$ contains a framed literal $\boxed{\neg k}$ (*ancestry*),

         and l and k are unifiable with mgu θ, then $P_{i+1} = P_i\theta$ and $\vec{R_{i+1}}$ is obtained from $\vec{Q_i}\theta$ by deleting $l\theta$.
   (b) $\vec{Q_{i+1}}$ is obtained from $\vec{R_{i+1}}$ by deleting every framed literal not preceded by an unframed literal in the remainder (*truncation*).

Remarks. (1) At Rule 5a, we can choose the *selected literal* l with more liberty like SL-resolution or SLI-resolution [Minker and Rajasekar, 1990].

(2) Rule 4 is included for efficiency. This is overlooked in OL-deduction (and so is in MILO-resolution), but is present in Model Elimination [Loveland, 1978].

(3) When $\mathcal{P}$ is in the form of $\langle L_{\mathcal{P}} \rangle$, factoring (5(a)iiiA) can be omitted in intermediate deduction steps like Weak Model Elimination [Loveland, 1978]. In this case, Rules 3 and 4 are omitted, and factoring is performed at the final step, namely it is taken into account only for P_i in a structured clause of the form $\langle P_i, \Box \rangle$.

(4) The selection of rules 5(a)i, 5(a)ii and 5(a)iii must be non-deterministic; for $l \in L_{\mathcal{P}}$ any rule may be applied. This is not a straightforward generalization of MILO-resolution or Siegel's algorithm, because they do not deal with **Reduce** as an alternative choice of other two rules, but make $\vec{Q_{i+1}}$ as the reduced ordered clause of the ordered factor of $\vec{R_{i+1}}$ that is obtained by **Skip** or **Resolve**. Both Przymusinski and Siegel claim that the lifting lemma should work for their procedures. Unfortunately, this simpler treatment violates the completeness described below. Furthermore, even for proof-finding, OL-resolution, which also handles the ancestry rule as a subsequent rule of **Resolve**, is incomplete. For example, when the theory is given as

$$\Sigma = \{ \quad p(a) \vee p(x) \vee \neg q(x), \quad (1)$$
$$\neg p(b), \quad (2)$$
$$q(b) \quad (3) \quad \},$$

it is easy to see that $\Sigma \models p(a)$. However, there is no OL-refutation from $\Sigma + \neg p(a)$:

(4)	$\underline{\neg p(a)}$	given top clause
(5)	$\underline{p(x)} \vee \neg q(x) \vee \boxed{\neg p(a)}$	resolution with (1)
(6)	$\underline{\neg q(a)} \vee \boxed{\neg p(a)}$	reduction

Here, each underlined literal denotes a selected literal in the next step. The clause (6) is the dead-end of the OL-deduction. Hence, the reduction rule must be an alternative rule. Model Elimination and SL-resolution deal with the reduction rule as an alternative.

The **Skip** rule (5(a)i) reflects the following operational interpretation of a *stable* production field $\mathcal{P}$: by Definition 2.1 (4), if a clause C does not belong to $\mathcal{P}$ and a clause D is subsumed by C, then D does not belong to $\mathcal{P}$ either. That is why we can prune a deduction sequence if no rule can be applied for a structured clause D_i; if **Skip** was applied nevertheless, any resultant sequence would not succeed, thus making unnecessary computation.

Theorem 3.2 (Soundness and Completeness) (1) If a clause S is derived using an SOL-deduction from $\Sigma + C$ and $\mathcal{P}$, then S belongs to $Th_{\mathcal{P}}(\Sigma \cup \{C\})$.
(2) If a clause T *does not belong to $Th_{\mathcal{P}}(\Sigma)$, but* belongs to $Th_{\mathcal{P}}(\Sigma \cup \{C\})$, then there is an SOL-deduction of a clause S from $\Sigma + C$ and $\mathcal{P}$ such that S subsumes T.

Recall that C-ordered linear resolution is refutation-complete as shown, for example, by [Loveland, 1978], but is incomplete for consequence-finding [Minicozzi and Reiter, 1972]. Theorem 3.2 (2) says that SOL-resolution is complete for characteristic-clause-finding, and thus complete for consequence-finding when $\mathcal{P}$ is $\mathcal{P}_{\mathcal{L}}$.

Example 3.3 Consider the theory Σ and the clause C:

$$\Sigma = \{ \quad \neg c \vee \neg a \quad (1),$$
$$\neg c \vee \neg b \quad (2) \quad \},$$
$$C = \quad a \vee b\,.$$

There is no OL-deduction of $\neg c$ from $\Sigma + C$, but $\neg c$ is derived using an SOL-deduction from $\Sigma + C$ and $\mathcal{P}_{\mathcal{L}}$ as:

(3)	$\langle \Box, \ \underline{a} \vee b \rangle$,	given top clause
(4)	$\langle \Box, \ \underline{\neg c} \vee \boxed{a} \vee b \rangle$,	resolution with (1)
(5)	$\langle \neg c, \ \boxed{\not a} \vee \underline{b} \rangle$,	skip and truncation
(6)	$\langle \neg c, \ \underline{\neg c} \vee \boxed{b} \rangle$,	resolution with (2)
(7)	$\langle \neg c, \ \boxed{\not b} \rangle$.	factoring and truncation

Note that an OL-deduction stops at (4).

Definition 3.4 Let $\Delta(\Sigma, C, \mathcal{P})$ be the set of clauses derived using all SOL-deductions from $\Sigma + C$ and $\mathcal{P}$. The *production from $\Sigma + C$ and $\mathcal{P}$* is:

$$Prod(\Sigma, C, \mathcal{P}) = \mu\, \Delta(\Sigma, C, \mathcal{P}).$$

Theorem 3.5 Let C be a clause.

$$Newcarc(\Sigma, C, \mathcal{P}) = Prod(\Sigma, C, \mathcal{P}) - Th_{\mathcal{P}}(\Sigma).$$

Theorem 3.5 says the primitive $Newcarc(\Sigma, C, \mathcal{P})$ is contained in the production from $\Sigma + C$ and $\mathcal{P}$. To remove the clauses in the production derivable from Σ, we can use proof-finding: $\Sigma \models S$ iff there is an SOL-deduction of $\Box$ from $\Sigma + \neg S$ and $\langle \emptyset \rangle$. However, when the characteristic literals $L_{\mathcal{P}}$ is small compared with the whole literals $\mathcal{L}$, the computation of $Carc(\Sigma, \mathcal{P})$ can be performed better as the search focuses on $\mathcal{P}$. Then, the check can be reduced to subsumption tests on $Carc(\Sigma, \mathcal{P})$ by Proposition 2.5. The role of $Carc(\Sigma, \mathcal{P})$ in this case is similar to the minimal *nogoods* in the ATMS [de Kleer, 1986]. This checking can be embedded into an SOL-deduction by adding the following rule:

4a. For each $D_i = \langle P_i, \vec{Q_i} \rangle$, P_i is not subsumed by any clause of $Carc(\Sigma, \mathcal{P})$.

Proposition 3.6 If Rule 4a is incorporated into SOL-deduction, then $Prod(\Sigma, C, \mathcal{P}) = Newcarc(\Sigma, C, \mathcal{P})$.

3.2 Computing Prime Implicates

If the given theory is propositional, the prime implicates can be constructed using every clause as a top clause:

Proposition 3.7 [Inoue, 1990] Given $PI(\Sigma)$ and a clause C, $PI(\Sigma \cup \{C\})$ can be found incrementally:

$$\begin{aligned} PI(\emptyset) &= \{ p \vee \neg p \mid p \in \mathcal{A} \}, \text{ and} \\ PI(\Sigma \cup \{C\}) &= \mu [PI(\Sigma) \cup Prod(PI(\Sigma), C, \mathcal{P}_{\mathcal{L}})] . \end{aligned}$$

Notice that, in practice, no tautology will take part in any deduction; tautologies decrease monotonically. The computation of all prime implicates of Σ by Proposition 3.7 is much more efficient than the brute-force way of resolution proposed in [Reiter and de Kleer, 1987]. Also, ours uses C-ordered linear resolution and thus naturally has more restriction strategies than set-of-support resolution that is used in Kean and Tsiknis's [1990] extension of the consensus method.

This difference becomes larger when there are some distinguished literals representing assumptions in ATMS cases. The most important difference lies in the fact that the formulations by [Reiter and de Kleer, 1987; Kean and Tsiknis, 1990] require the computation of all prime implicates whereas ours only needs characteristic clauses that are a subset of the prime implicates [Inoue, 1990].

4 Variations

In Step 5a of an SOL-deduction (Definition 3.1), we treat two rules **Skip** (Rule 5(a)i) and **Resolve** (Rule 5(a)ii) as alternatives in order to guarantee the completeness of SOL-resolution. In this section, we violate this requirement, and show efficient variations of SOL-resolution and their applications to AI problems. Note that **Reduce** (Rule 5(a)iii) still remains as an alternative choice of other two rules (see Remark (3) of Definition 3.1).

4.1 Preferring Resolution

The first variation, called *SOL-R deduction*, makes **Resolve** precede **Skip**, namely **Skip** is tried to be applied only when **Resolve** cannot be applied. In a special case of SOL-R deductions, where the production field is fixed to $\mathcal{P}_{\mathcal{L}}$, **Skip** is always applied whenever **Resolve** cannot be applied for any selected literal in a deduction. In abduction, the resultant procedure in this case "hypothesizes whatever cannot be proven". This is also called *dead-end abduction*, which is first proposed by Pople [1973] in his abductive procedure based on SL-resolution [Kowalski and Kuhner, 1971] [8]. The criterion is also used by Cox and Pietrzykowski [1986].

4.2 Preferring Skip

The next variation, called *SOL-S deduction*, places **Skip** and **Resolve** in the reverse order of SOL-R deductions. That is, when the selected literal belongs to $L_{\mathcal{P}}$, only **Skip** is applied by ignoring the possibility of **Resolve**.

This skip-preference has the following nice properties. Firstly, this enables the procedure to prune the branch of the search tree that would have resulted from the literal being resolved upon. Secondly, SOL-S deductions are correct model-theoretically. Let us divide the set of clauses Δ produced by using SOL-deductions from $\Sigma + C$ and $\mathcal{P}$ into two sets, say Δ_1 and Δ_2, such that

$$\Delta = \Delta_1 \cup \Delta_2 \text{ and } \Sigma \cup \Delta_1 \models \Delta_2 .$$

Note that $Prod(\Sigma, C, \mathcal{P}) = \mu\Delta$. Then adding Δ_2 to Δ_1 does not change the models of $\Sigma \cup \Delta_1$:

$$Mod(\Sigma \cup \Delta_1) = Mod(\Sigma \cup \Delta) = Mod(\Sigma \cup Prod(\Sigma, C, \mathcal{P})),$$

where $Mod(T)$ is the models of T. Thus only Δ_1 needs to be computed model-theoretically. The next theorem shows SOL-S deductions produce precisely such a Δ_1.

Theorem 4.1 If a clause T is derived by an SOL-deduction from $\Sigma + C$ and $\mathcal{P}$, then there is an SOL-S deduction of a clause S from $\Sigma + C$ and $\mathcal{P}$ such that $\Sigma \cup \{S\} \models T$.

In abduction, recall that for a clause $S \in \Delta$ and $H = L_{\mathcal{P}}$, $\neg S$ is an explanation of $\neg C$ from (Σ, H) if $\Sigma \not\models S$. Thus, an explanation in $\overline{\Delta_1}$ is the weakest in the sense that for any clause $S_2 \in \Delta_2$, there exists a clause $S_1 \in \Delta_1$ such that $\Sigma \cup \{\neg S_2\} \models \neg S_1$ holds [9].

In circumscription, this is particularly desirable since we want to answer whether a query holds in every minimal model or not; the purpose of using explanation-based procedures is purely model-theoretic. One of advantages of Przymusinski's [1989] procedure lies in the fact that MILO-resolution performs a kind of SOL-S deductions [Inoue and Helft, 1990].

4.3 Between Skipping and Resolving

One further generalization of this kind of preference would lead us to *best-first* abduction. Stickel [1990] uses the minimal-cost proof where we can choose each operation whose expected computational cost is minimum, but it is difficult to apply the idea to non-Horn theories.

[8] Pople's ***synthesis*** operation performs "factor-and-skip".

[9] An explanation E_1 is said to be ***less-presumptive than*** E_2 if $\Sigma \cup \{E_2\} \models E_1$ [Poole, 1989]. Therefore, an explanation in $\overline{\Delta_1}$ is a least-presumptive explanation of $\neg C$ from (Σ, H).

5 Conclusion

We have revealed the importance of consequence-finding in AI techniques. Most advanced reasoning mechanisms such as abduction and default reasoning require global search in their proof procedures. This global character is strongly dependent on consequence-finding, in particular those theorems of the theory belonging to production fields. That is why we need some complete procedure for consequence-finding. For this purpose, we have proposed SOL-resolution, an extension of C-ordered linear resolution augmented by the skip rule. The procedure is sound and complete for finding the (new) characteristic clauses. The significant innovation of the results presented is that the procedure is direct relative to the given production field. We have also presented incomplete, but efficient variations of the basic procedures with nice properties.

Acknowledgment

I especially wish to thank Mark Stickel for his valuable comments on SOL-resolution and Nicolas Helft for discussion on earlier work. I would also like to thank Ray Reiter, Ryuzo Hasegawa, Koichi Furukawa and Wolfgang Bibel for helpful suggestions on this topic, and Kazuhiro Fuchi for giving me the opportunity to do this work.

References

[Bossu and Siegel, 1985] Genevieve Bossu and Pierre Siegel. Saturation, nonmonotonic reasoning, and the closed-world assumption. *Artificial Intelligence*, 25: 23–67, 1985.

[Chang and Lee, 1973] Chin-Liang Chang and Richard Char-Tung Lee. *Symbolic Logic and Mechanical Theorem Proving*. Academic Press, New York, 1973.

[Cox and Pietrzykowski, 1986] P.T. Cox and T. Pietrzykowski. Causes for events: their computation and applications. In *Proceedings of the Eighth International Conference on Automated Deduction*, Lecture Notes in Computer Science 230, pages 608–621, Springer-Verlag, 1986.

[de Kleer, 1986] Johan de Kleer. An assumption-based TMS. *Artificial Intelligence*, 28: 127–162, 1986.

[Finger, 1987] Joseph J. Finger. Exploiting constraints in design synthesis. Technical Report STAN-CS-88-1204, Department of Computer Science, Stanford University, Stanford, CA, April 1987.

[Ginsberg, 1989] Matthew L. Ginsberg. A circumscriptive theorem prover. *Artificial Intelligence*, 39: 209–230, 1989.

[Helft *et al.*, 1991] Nicolas Helft, Katsumi Inoue and David Poole. Query answering in circumscription. In *Proc. of the 12th IJCAI*, Sydney, Australia, 1991.

[Inoue, 1990] Katsumi Inoue. An abductive procedure for the CMS/ATMS. In: J.P. Martins and M. Reinfrank, editors, *Proceedings of the 1990 Workshop on Truth Maintenance Systems*, Lecture Notes in Artificial Intelligence, Springer-Verlag, 1991.

[Inoue and Helft, 1990] Katsumi Inoue and Nicolas Helft. On theorem provers for circumscription. In *Proceedings of the Eighth Biennial Conference of the Canadian Society for Computational Studies of Intelligence*, pages 212–219, Ottawa, Ontario, May 1990.

[Kean and Tsiknis, 1990] Alex Kean and George Tsiknis. An incremental method for generating prime implicants/implicates. *J. Symbolic Computation*, 9: 185–206, 1990.

[Kowalski and Kuhner, 1971] Robert Kowalski and Donald Kuhner. Linear resolution with selection function. *Artificial Intelligence*, 2: 227–260, 1971.

[Lee, 1967] Richard Char-Tung Lee. A completeness theorem and computer program for finding theorems derivable from given axioms. Ph.D. thesis, University of California, Berkeley, CA, 1967.

[Levesque, 1989] Hector J. Levesque. A knowledge-level account of abduction (preliminary version). In *Proc. of the 11th IJCAI*, pages 1061–1067, Detroit, MI, 1989.

[Loveland, 1978] Donald W. Loveland. *Automated Theorem Proving: A Logical Basis*. North-Holland, Amsterdam, 1978.

[Minicozzi and Reiter, 1972] Eliana Minicozzi and Raymond Reiter. A note on linear resolution strategies in consequence-finding. *Artificial Intelligence*, 3: 175–180, 1972.

[Minker and Rajasekar, 1990] Jack Minker and Arcot Rajasekar. A fixpoint semantics for disjunctive logic programs. *J. Logic Programming*, 9: 45–74, 1990.

[Poole, 1989] David Poole. Explanation and prediction: an architecture for default and abductive reasoning. *Computational Intelligence*, 5: 97–110, 1989.

[Pople, 1973] Harry E. Pople, Jr. On the mechanization of abductive logic. In *Proc. of the 3rd IJCAI*, pages 147–152, Stanford, CA, 1973.

[Przymusinski, 1989] Teodor C. Przymusinski. An algorithm to compute circumscription. *Artificial Intelligence*, 38: 49–73, 1989.

[Reiter, 1971] Raymond Reiter. Two results on ordering for resolution with merging and linear format. *J. ACM*, 18: 630–646, 1971.

[Reiter and de Kleer, 1987] Raymond Reiter and Johan de Kleer. Foundations of assumption-based truth maintenance systems: preliminary report. In *Proc. of the 6th AAAI*, pages 183–187, Seattle, WA, 1987.

[Robinson, 1965] J.A. Robinson. A machine-oriented logic based on the resolution principle. *J. ACM*, 12: 23–41, 1965.

[Shostak, 1976] Robert E. Shostak. Refutation Graphs. *Artificial Intelligence*, 7: 51–64, 1976.

[Siegel, 1987] Pierre Siegel. Représentation et utilisation de la connaissance en calcul propositionnel. Thèse d'État. Université d'Aix-Marseille II, Luminy, 1987.

[Slagle *et al.*, 1969] J.R. Slagle, C.L. Chang and R.C.T. Lee. Completeness theorems for semantic resolution in consequence-finding. In *Proc. of the IJCAI*, pages 281–285, Washington, D.C., 1969.

[Stickel, 1990] Mark E. Stickel. Rationale and methods for abductive reasoning in natural-language interpretation. In: R. Studer, editor, *Natural Language and Logic, Proceedings of the International Scientific Symposium*, pages 233–252, Lecture Notes in Artificial Intelligence 459, Springer-Verlag, 1990.

Proof Transformation with Built-in Equality Predicate

Christoph Lingenfelder
IBM Deutschland GmbH
Institute for Knowledge Based Systems
P.O. Box 103068
D-6900 Heidelberg
phone: 49 6221 404 359
email: LINGENF@DHDIBM1.bitnet

Axel Präcklein*
Fachbereich Informatik
Universität Kaiserslautern
Postfach 3049
D-6750 Kaiserslautern
phone: 49 631 205 3344
email: prckln@informatik.uni-kl.de

Abstract

One of the main reasons why computer generated proofs are not widely accepted is often their complexity and incomprehensibility. Especially proofs of mathematical theorems with equations are normally presented in an inadequate and not intuitive way. This is even more of a problem for the presentation of inferences drawn by automated reasoning components in other AI systems. For first order logic, proof transformation procedures have been designed in order to structure proofs and state them in a formalism that is more familiar to human mathematicians. In this report we generalize these approaches, so that proofs involving equational reasoning can also be handled. To this end extended refutation graphs are introduced to represent combined resolution and paramodulation proofs. In the process of transforming these proofs into natural deduction proofs with equality, the inherent structure can also be extracted by exploiting topological properties of refutation graphs.

1 Introduction

With the increasing strength of Automated Deduction Systems the length and complexity of computer generated proofs has reached a degree where they have become almost impossible to understand even for the expert. This has led to a state where only specialists are capable to understand and check a proof found by an automated deduction system.

But whenever human beings are addressed, the need for easily understandable and clearly structured arguments is apparent. Therefore it is necessary to be able to present proofs in a better structured way. Ideally one would like the proof to be given in natural language, with a large variety of inference rules. As a preliminary step in this direction it is useful to transform the computer generated proof into natural deduction which, although still a system of formal logic, has been devised to approximate as much as possible an intuitive form of reasoning.

The transformation of proofs into a natural deduction formulation has solved some of the problems, see [Andrews, 1980; Miller, 1983; Lingenfelder, 1986], but by and large the increasing length and complexity of the transformed proofs adds to their incomprehensibility rather than to reduce it. It is therefore paramount to be able to state the proofs in a hierarchically structured way, as mathematicians do, formulating subgoals and lemmata. There has been some success in structuring computer generated proofs, cf. [Lingenfelder, 1989; Pfenning and Nesmith, 1990; Huang, 1991], but all of these approaches are restricted to logics without equality.

We feel, however, that this is a severe restriction, as equality is essential for any natural coding of mathematical problems and of AI problems in general. Therefore, we generalize Lingenfelder's approach, so that proofs involving equational reasoning can also be structured automatically.

In section 2 the different calculi and proof representations are introduced. Section 3 extends the basic system of proof transformation so that equality reasoning is also covered. This fits well into the transformation approach, if equational reasoning is not dominating. Here equality is seen as a specific theory (in the sense of theory resolution [Stickel, 1985]) so that a further generalization to arbitrary theories can be envisaged.

The task of finding the underlying proof structure is presented in section 4. This can be accomplished by the elegant expedient of exploiting topological properties of the refutation graphs in order to come up with a well-organized proof. Structure can be imposed upon the proofs by introducing lemmata, both to avoid duplication of parts of the proof and to arrange a larger proof in a sequence of subgoals easier to understand. Another means of structuring a proof is its division into several disjoint parts by employing the method of case analysis. This constitutes very often the only possibility to use a conditional equation without having to fall back on a proof by contradiction.

2 Proof Formats

In this section we will describe the logical calculi used in this paper. Everything is standard first order predicate logic with equality, and we need resolution (with paramodulation) and a natural deduction system based on Gerhard Gentzen's calculus NK [Gentzen, 1935]. There are no differences from the usual way of defining these concepts as done for instance in [Gallier, 1986] or [Loveland, 1978].

Additionally, as our actual starting point of the proof transformation will not be a resolution proof, but rather the result of a graph-based theorem prover, we must introduce the representation of proofs as graphs.

* Supported by the Deutsche Forschungsgemeinschaft, SFB 314

2.1 Clause and Refutation Graphs with Equality

Definition: A *clause graph* consists of a set of literal nodes, that are partitioned into clause nodes. Each literal node is labeled with a literal; the distinction between the literal nodes and the literals themselves is needed because the same literal may be attached to several literal nodes. Finally the links of the clause graph connect disjoint sets of literal nodes, such that for all links the following conditions hold:

(π_1) The literal nodes in a link are labeled with literals with unifiable atoms.

(π_2) A link must connect at least one positive and one negative literal.

Definition: A clause graph is said to *represent* a clause set S if every clause node C has the form $[-A(s)\ s{\neq}t\ A(t)]$ or there is a *parent clause* $C' \in S$ and a ground substitution γ such that the restriction of the literal labeling to C is a bijection between its literal nodes and the literals of $\gamma C'$. Clause nodes of the form $[-A(s)\ s{\neq}t\ A(t)]$ are called *equality clause nodes.*

Definition: A *deduction graph* is a non-empty, ground, and acyclic clause graph. A *cycle* is a sequence of clause nodes and links $C_1,\Pi_1,C_2,\ldots C_n,\Pi_n,C_1$, such that all the Π_i are different and they contain literal nodes with opposite sign in their respective neighbour clause nodes. A *refutation graph* is a deduction graph where all literal nodes belong to a link.

Definition: For a formula F and a clause graph Γ representing C(F), a relation Δ between the literal nodes of Γ and the atom occurrences in F is a *clause graph relation* if it is compatible with the relation established by the normalization process, by which the clause form is constructed from the formula. It is obvious from this definition that the literal nodes of equality clause nodes are never related to atom occurrences of F.

2.2 Natural Deduction Proofs with Equality

In 1933, Gerhard Gentzen developed a formal system for mathematical proofs with the intention to describe as closely as possible the actual logical inferences used in mathematical proofs. To quote from [Gentzen, 1935]: *"der möglichst genau das richtige logische Schließen bei mathematischen Beweisen wiedergibt"*

The actual form of the proof lines is taken from Andrews [Andrews, 1980], but they differ only in their syntax from Gentzen's rule system NK in [Gentzen, 1935].

Definition: A natural deduction proof line consists of a finite set of formulae, called the *assumptions*, a single formula, called *conclusion*, and a *justification*, written $\{\mathcal{A} \vdash F \text{ Rule } \mathfrak{R}\}$. A finite sequence S of proof lines is a *natural deduction derivation* of a formula F from assumptions $\mathcal{A}$, if F is the conclusion of the last line of S, $\mathcal{A}$ is the set of assumptions of this last line, and every line in S is correctly justified by one of the rules of the calculus.

A proof line $\lambda = \{\mathcal{A} \vdash F \text{ Rule } \mathfrak{R}\}$ within a sequence of proof lines is correctly justified iff $\mathcal{A} \vdash F$ matches the lower part of Rule $\mathfrak{R}$ and there are proof lines before λ in the sequence matching the upper part of Rule $\mathfrak{R}$.

A finite sequence S of proof lines is a *natural deduction proof* of a formula F if it is a natural deduction derivation of F from an empty set of assumptions.

Now we list some rules of the natural deduction calculus, the letters F, G, and H represent formulae and $\mathcal{A}$ represents a finite set of formulae.

<u>Assumption Rule (Ass):</u>
$$\frac{}{\mathcal{A}, F \vdash F}$$

This rule introduces a new assumption. The following rules are introduction and elimination rules for the various logical connectives. Only the rule of contradiction does not fit into this scheme.

<u>Deduction Rule (⇒I):</u>
$$\frac{\mathcal{A}, F \vdash G}{\mathcal{A} \vdash F \Rightarrow G}$$

<u>AND-Elimination (∧E):</u>
$$\frac{\mathcal{A} \vdash F \wedge G}{\mathcal{A} \vdash F} \quad \text{and} \quad \frac{\mathcal{A} \vdash F \wedge G}{\mathcal{A} \vdash G}$$

<u>Rule of Contradiction (Contra):</u>
$$\frac{\mathcal{A} \vdash F \qquad \mathcal{B} \vdash \neg F}{\mathcal{A}, \mathcal{B} \vdash \bot}$$

<u>Rule of Cases (∨E):</u>
$$\frac{\mathcal{A} \vdash F \vee G \qquad \mathcal{B}, F \vdash H \qquad \mathcal{C}, G \vdash H}{\mathcal{A}, \mathcal{B}, \mathcal{C} \vdash H}$$

<u>Universal Generalization (∀I):</u>
$$\frac{\mathcal{A} \vdash F_c}{\mathcal{A} \vdash \forall x\ Fx}$$

provided that c does not occur in $\mathcal{A}$, and $Fc = \{x \mapsto c\}Fx$.

<u>Universal Instantiation (∀E):</u>
$$\frac{\mathcal{A} \vdash \forall x\ Fx}{\mathcal{A} \vdash Ft}$$

where $Ft = \{x \mapsto t\}Fx$.

In addition to the rules for Gentzen's calculus NK we add the following rules to handle the equality predicate:

<u>Rule of Reflexivity (Ref):</u>
$$\frac{}{\mathcal{A} \vdash t=t}$$

<u>Rule of Equality (=):</u>
$$\frac{\mathcal{A} \vdash F(s) \qquad \mathcal{B} \vdash s=t}{\mathcal{A}, \mathcal{B} \vdash F(t)} \quad \text{and} \quad \frac{\mathcal{A} \vdash F(t) \qquad \mathcal{B} \vdash s=t}{\mathcal{A}, \mathcal{B} \vdash F(s)}$$

3 Proof Transformation

The construction of natural deduction proofs (NDPs), by humans and computers alike, is conducted in single steps. To prove any valid formula F one always starts with a line $\{\vdash F\}$. Such a line is obviously no proof, because it is not correctly justified. Now the proof is constructed by deriving subgoals until it is completed. In the intermediate states one may find completed subproofs, but also others that are not yet done. To formalize the procedure of the search for such a natural deduction proof, we use Generalized Natural Deduction Proofs as defined in [Lingenfelder, 1990].

3.1 General Procedure

Definition: A finite sequence S of proof lines is called a *Generalized Natural Deduction Proof (GNDP)* of a formula F, if F is the conclusion of the last line of S, the last line of S has no assumptions, and every line is either justified by a rule of the calculus, or it is justified by a proof (possibly in a different calculus) of its conclusion from its assumptions.

This allows lines not correctly justified within the calculus, but it is assumed that these lines are "sound", in the sense that $(\bigwedge \text{assumptions} \Rightarrow \text{conclusion})$ is a valid formula. Such lines are called *external* lines, lines justified within the calculus are called *internal*. When no external lines are present in a GNDP, it is a normal NDP.

Definition: Given a refutation graph Γ justifying an external line of a GNDP with assumptions F_i and conclusion G, and a clause graph relation Δ, relating all the literal nodes of Γ to atom occurrences in $F_1 \wedge F_2 \wedge \ldots \wedge F_n \Rightarrow G$. Then a clause node is *negatively polarized* if any of its literal nodes is related to an atom occurrence in the theorem formula G. Otherwise the clause node represents an axiom and is said to be *positively polarized.* In particular equality clause nodes are positively polarized.

3.2 Transformation Rules

The transformation rules are to be read as follows: the lines before the arrow (⟶) are replaced by those following it in the next generalized NDP of the sequence. Some of the rules add a new internal line which is simply written below its parent lines. In the description, $\mathcal{A}$ is a list of assumption formulae, capital letters indicate single formulae, α, β, γ, ... are used as labels for the lines, the justification Rule ℜ stands for an arbitrary rule of the natural deduction calculus, and the justifications π, π', π_1, and π_2 represent proofs of the respective lines. For all these rules one must make sure that the proofs π', π_1, or π_2 can be constructed from π. If the proof is given in form of a refutation graph this can be accomplished automatically.

The rules can be divided into three classes. Internal rules introduce new internal lines without any relation to current external lines, this corresponds to forward reasoning. External rules try to reduce a current external line, this realizes backward reasoning. Mixed rules depend on both, external and internal lines, reducing an external line in the light of previously derived formulae.

I∀: To add for an arbitrary term t.

(α)	$\mathcal{A}$	⊢	∀xFx	Rule ℜ
(β)	$\mathcal{A}$	⊢	Ft	∀E(α)

M-Cases:

(α)	$\mathcal{A}$	⊢	A∨B	ℜ
(ζ)	$\mathcal{A}$	⊢	F	π

⟶

(α)	$\mathcal{A}$	⊢	A∨B	ℜ
We consider separately the cases of (α)				
Case 1:				
(β)	$\mathcal{A}$, A	⊢	A	Hyp
(γ)	$\mathcal{A}$, A	⊢	F	π_1
Case 2:				
(δ)	$\mathcal{A}$, B	⊢	B	Hyp
(ε)	$\mathcal{A}$, B	⊢	F	π_2
End of cases (1, 2) of (α)				
(ζ)	$\mathcal{A}$	⊢	F	Cas(α,γ,ε)

As we are mainly concerned with the effect of equality reasoning in a proof, we will now state the rules handling the application of an equation.

E-=⊥:

(γ)	$\mathcal{A}$	⊢	⊥	π

⟶

(α)		⊢	s = s	Ref
(β)	$\mathcal{A}$	⊢	s ≠ s	π'
(γ)	$\mathcal{A}$	⊢	⊥	Contra

E-=:

(α)	$\mathcal{A}$	⊢	s = t	Rule ℜ
(γ)	$\mathcal{A}$	⊢	F(t)	π

⟶

(α)	$\mathcal{A}$	⊢	s = t	Rule ℜ
(β)	$\mathcal{A}$	⊢	F(s)	π'
(γ)	$\mathcal{A}$	⊢	F(t)	=(β,α)

This is not the complete set of transition rules; all the other rules necessary to describe a complete system for proof transformation can be found in [Lingenfelder, 1990].

3.3 Proof Transformation System with Equality

The complete set of transformation rules constitutes a proof system for natural deduction proofs. This means that for any valid formula F, there is a finite sequence of GNDPs starting with { ⊢ F } and ending with an NDP for F. Every element in this sequence can be constructed from its predecessor by application of one of the transition rules.

The transformation rules are selected according to appropriate heuristics, making use of the information in a given proof, for instance a previously computed refutation graph. In [Lingenfelder, 1990] it is shown how a proof represented as a refutation graph without equality can guide the "search" for a natural deduction proof. In this context, search means to transform the given, graph-represented proof into the natural deduction calculus, rather than to find an original proof.

After an application of rule E-= replacing t by s in a goal formula F a refutation graph for F(s) can be constructed by removing the equality clause node [–L(s) s≠t L(t)] and the equation clause node [s = t] unless used elsewhere. Then in all the literal nodes adjacent to L(t) t is substituted by s. Now the link at –L(s) is combined with that at L(t), thus closing the gap resulting from the removal of the equality clause node. The resulting graph proves the formula F(s).

Similarly, when E-=⊥ is applied, the polarization of the clause node [s≠s] is changed from positive to negative. Note that the refutation graph has no negatively polarized part when a proof by contradiction is represented. The structure of the graph remains unchanged.

Example: In this example we show a refutation graph for F(t), which equals Pt ∧ (A∨B), and the resulting graph proving F(s): Ps ∧ (A∨B). The negatively polarized clause nodes are drawn with double boxes.

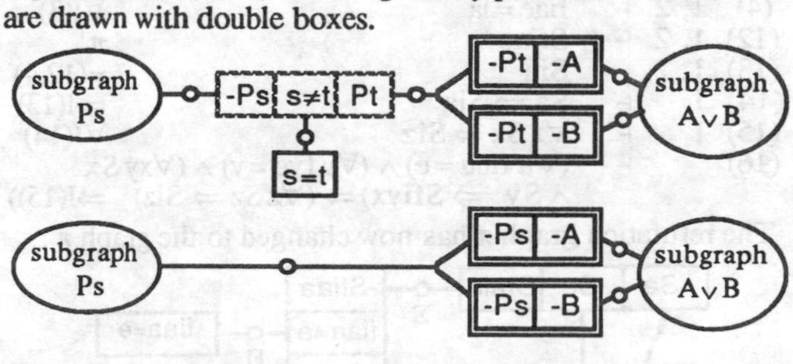

3.4 Application of Transition Rules

As an example of the proof transformation procedure, we use a part of the subgroup criterion. The formula F to prove is

$$(\forall u\, fiuu = e) \wedge (\forall v\, fve = v) \wedge (\forall xy\, Sx \wedge Sy \Rightarrow Sfiyx) \Rightarrow (\forall z\, Sz \Rightarrow Siz).$$

The refutation graph, the clause graph relation, and the

ground substitution have been automatically generated by the theorem prover MKRP, see [Ohlbach and Siekmann, 1989; Lehr, 1988]. Below the refutation graph is shown; theory clause nodes are indicated by dashed lines.

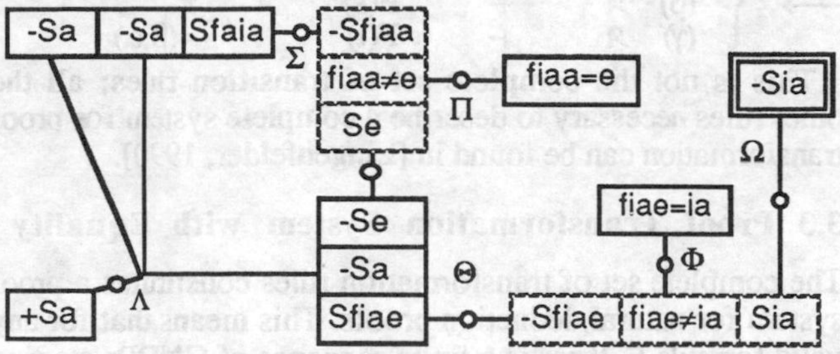

The transformation process is started with the "trivial" GNDP for F

(16)	$\vdash$	$(\forall u\ fiuu=e) \wedge (\forall v\ fve=v) \wedge (\forall xy\ Sx \wedge Sy \Rightarrow Sfiyx) \Rightarrow (\forall z\ Sz \Rightarrow Siz)$	Graph

After some transformation steps not involving equality, the following GNDP is constructed:

(1)	1	$\vdash$	$(\forall u\ fiuu=e) \wedge (\forall v\ fve=v) \wedge (\forall xy\ Sx \wedge Sy \Rightarrow Sfiyx)$	Ass
Let a be an arbitrary constant				
(2)	2	$\vdash$	Sa	Ass
(13)	1, 2	$\vdash$	Sia	π
(14)	1	$\vdash$	$Sa \Rightarrow Sia$	$\Rightarrow$I(13)
(15)	1	$\vdash$	$\forall z\ Sz \Rightarrow Siz$	$\forall$I(14)
(16)		$\vdash$	$(\forall u\ fiuu=e) \wedge (\forall v\ fve=v) \wedge (\forall xy\ Sx \wedge Sy \Rightarrow Sfiyx) \Rightarrow (\forall z\ Sz \Rightarrow Siz)$	$\Rightarrow$I(15)

At this point the external line 13 cannot further be processed by external rules. A consultation of the refutation graph tells us that the literal node corresponding to Sia is only connected to a theory clause node. Therefore Sia must be derived using the rule of equality. As a preliminary operation we must isolate the equation fiae = ia, using internal rules, then E-= can be applied. Now the GNDP takes on the form shown below:

(1)	1	$\vdash$	$(\forall u\ fiuu=e) \wedge (\forall v\ fve=v) \wedge (\forall xy\ Sx \wedge Sy \Rightarrow Sfiyx)$	Ass
Let a be an arbitrary constant				
(2)	2	$\vdash$	Sa	Ass
(3)	1	$\vdash$	$\forall v\ fve=v$	$\wedge$E(1)
(4)	1, 2	$\vdash$	fiae = ia	$\forall$I(3)
(12)	1, 2	$\vdash$	Sfiae	π'
(13)	1, 2	$\vdash$	Sia	=(12,4)
(14)	1	$\vdash$	$Sa \Rightarrow Sia$	$\Rightarrow$I(13)
(15)	1	$\vdash$	$\forall z\ Sz \Rightarrow Siz$	$\forall$I(14)
(16)		$\vdash$	$(\forall u\ fiuu=e) \wedge (\forall v\ fve=v) \wedge (\forall xy\ Sx \wedge Sy \Rightarrow Sfiyx) \Rightarrow (\forall z\ Sz \Rightarrow Siz)$	$\Rightarrow$I(15))

The refutation graph π has now changed to the graph π':

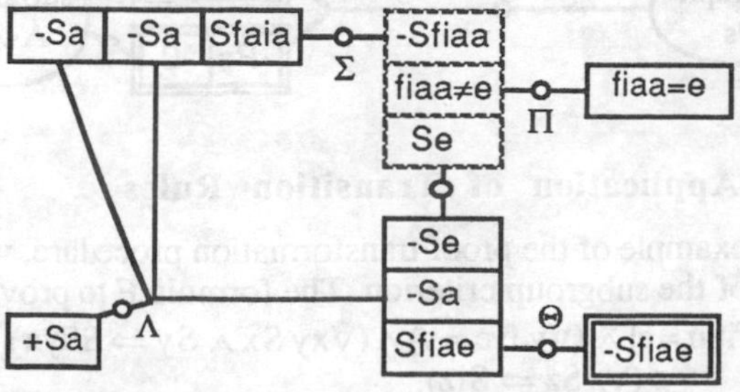

Now the transformation process continues as in the first order case, with one more application of an equality rule to produce the final natural deduction proof.

4 Structuring the Proof

4.1 General Procedure

An initial "trivial" generalized natural deduction proof (GNDP) is constructed to start a transformation process as described in section 3. Now some of the transformation rules, E$\wedge$ for instance, lead to additional external lines, and as a consequence to a division of the refutation graph according to the splitting theorem [Lingenfelder, 1990]. In the simplest case the refutation graph proving $F \wedge G$ is "cut" through the clause [–F –G], such that the two resulting components are refutation graphs for F and G, respectively. In general, however, the two components may have a non-empty intersection, and this is similarly the case for the other rules leading to a division of the refutation graph. The splitting theorem does not take this into account, so that these shared subgraphs are always duplicated and therefore processed more than once.

This does not matter if the intersection is comparatively small, when it may easily be copied and later used several times in the resulting subproofs. If it is relatively large and complex, however, it may be sensible to prove a lemma first and then use it in all the proof parts. In order to formalize such a procedure, the transformation rule E-Lemma is introduced.

E-Lemma					
	(β_1)	$\mathcal{A}_1$	$\vdash$	F_1	π_1
	$\vdots$			$\vdots$	
	(β_n)	$\mathcal{A}_n$	$\vdash$	F_n	π_n
$\longrightarrow$	(α)	$\bigcap \mathcal{A}_i$	$\vdash$	G	π_0
	(β_1)	$\mathcal{A}_1$	$\vdash$	F_1	π_1'
	$\vdots$			$\vdots$	
	(β_n)	$\mathcal{A}_n$	$\vdash$	F_n	π_n'

This rule must of course be used with discretion, i.e. only when specifically called for by a heuristic. In [Lingenfelder, 1990] it is explained in detail how topological properties of the graph induce lemmata. If paramodulation steps are represented using equality clause nodes in the refutation graph the search algorithm in [Lingenfelder, 1990] can be used unchanged.

Another way to structure proofs is the division into the cases of a disjunction. This is formalized by the rule M-Cases. The most important case for its application in pure first order logic comes up, when an existentially quantified formula cannot be proven constructively. With built-in equality there is one additional reason for a case analysis. As the natural deduction calculus only allows the application of unit equations, special considerations are needed for conditional equations. One solution of this problem could be the division of the proof into cases such that the equation is assumed to hold in one of them.

4.2 Equality Clause Nodes

Paramodulation steps of the computer generated proof are represented in the refutation graph using special "equality" clause nodes. For example the combination of a paramodulation step Pa to Pb via a=b and a resolution step between Pb and some literal –Pb is simulated as a sequence of three resolution steps of the unit clauses [Pa], [a=b], and [–Pb] with the equality clause node [–Pa a≠b Pb]. This clause node denotes the trivial fact that $Pa \wedge a{=}b \Rightarrow Pb$. The symmetry of the equality predicate is incorporated into the unification algorithm and hence this additional property must not be considered in the graph. In the natural deduction calculus this fact is reflected by the existence of two symmetric rules for the application of an equation. Alternatively one might have chosen a rule axiomatizing the symmetry explicitly, viz.

$$\frac{\mathcal{A} \vdash s=t}{\mathcal{A} \vdash t=s}$$

But this does not comply with intuitive mathematical reasoning, where equations are rarely oriented and therefore such a symmetry rule never needs to be used explicitly.

Conditional equations, that is, equational literals in non unit clauses, need no special handling, because the only difference is that the negated equation in the equality clause node is connected to a non unit clause node and therefore to a deduction graph. However, the formulation of the proof can be more difficult because the equation is not always true. One can either prove the equality as a lemma or divide the proof into cases, in one of which the equality holds.

The decision between these possibilities depends on general considerations, as for example the complexity of resulting lemmata or the position of negatively polarized clause nodes in the graph. Yet there is one heuristic depending on equality. Case analysis is most profitable if the condition for an equation is itself an equation used for paramodulation. Then both obstructing conditions are removed in parallel.

Usually mathematicians employ case analysis only when the disjunction is an axiom or has been previously derived. Equality clause nodes, however, represent implications and therefore are unattractive for this purpose. But if –Pa or a≠b is first derived from the contrapositive of $Pa \wedge a{=}b \Rightarrow Pb$, a case analysis may be the best choice.

Often several equations are successively applied to a formula leading to chains of equality clause nodes. If any of the chain links are separating, and therefore candidates for lemmata, only the links joining the chain to the rest of the graph should be selected. Otherwise the equality argument would be torn asunder.

A more syntactical criterion is the distinction between completion and rewriting steps, which can be made if the underlying paramodulation rule discriminates these steps according to the Knuth-Bendix algorithm. Completion steps are more important and substantial while rewriting steps can usually be considered a calculation rather than a proof.

The structuring procedure can be generalized to theory resolution with arbitrary theories. A resolution step between two literals that are complementary in the given theory is represented with a clause node containing the residue and a syntactically complementary literal for each resolution literal.

It is clear that this method can only handle proofs with a relatively small number of paramodulation steps. Otherwise a large number of equality clause nodes would obscure the structure of the proof. This is especially the case when paramodulation steps are performed into other equations. Therefore purely or even substantially equational proofs need special considerations due to their inherent internal structure.

4.3 Example

As an example we chose one of Pelletier's problems [Pelletier, 1986], which is among the simpler standard examples in equality theorem proving:

There are x and y such that any z equals x or y. If two distinct constants a and b have a property P then the property P holds universally. In first order notation with equality this is represented by the following formula:

$$\exists x,y\ \forall z\ (z=x \vee z=y) \wedge (a \neq b) \wedge Pa \wedge Pb \ \Rightarrow \forall w\ Pw$$

The resolution and paramodulation proof is first translated into a refutation graph. The clause nodes I1 and I2 in the upper graph are both instances of the deduction graph below; a complete refutation graph can be obtained by inserting two copies of the deduction graph for I1 and I2. x and y, as well as w become Skolem constants in clause form, and therefore also in the refutation graph. They are named 1, 2, and 3 in the sequel.

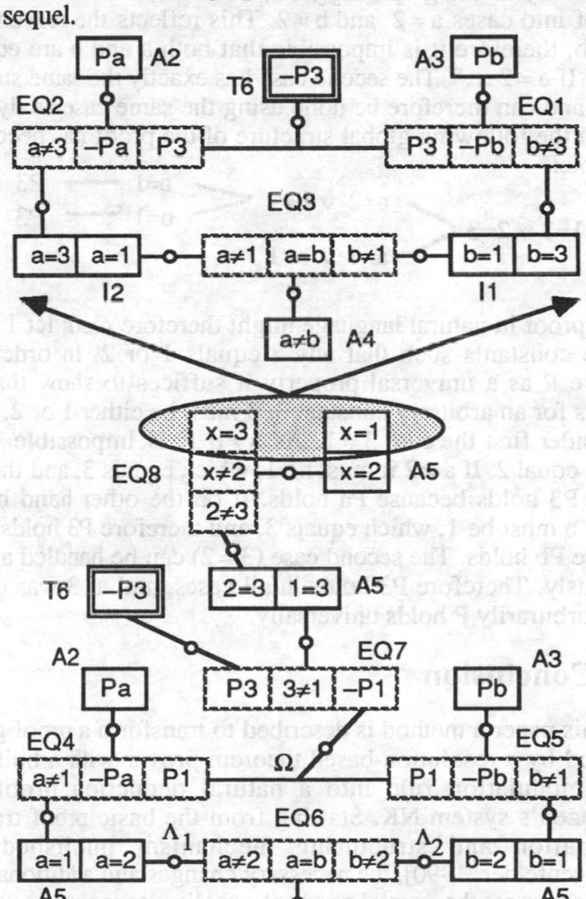

The first operations performed in the transformation process are automatic applications of rules introducing the Skolem constants in the theorem. The other Skolem constants are introduced by need, whenever they appear in a subgraph that is currently worked with. Of course it may be necessary to isolate the existentially quantified formula first.

Now we know all the prerequisites for the structuring of this proof. At first we consider the subgraph which is used in two different copies in the refutation graph. Here the disjunction of free literal nodes $(x=1 \vee x=3)$ cannot immediately be used as a lemma because the deduction graph contains a negatively polarized clause node (T6). One heuristic to obtain a lemma in this case would be to use a maximal positively polarized subgraph of this deduction graph instead. This corresponds to a lemma $P3 \vee \forall x\,(x=1 \vee x=3)$. Note that the variable situation allows the introduction of a universally quantified lemma.

Alternatively, we can split the proof into cases as the situation meets the conditions explained above. The instance $1=3 \vee 2=3$ of axiom A5 is used, so that only a very small overlap remains in one of the resulting cases. Actually this overlap corresponds only to a trivial rewrite step.

It remains to be checked whether the two cases of the proof should be further structured. The links Λ_1 and Λ_2 are found to be separating in case 1, indicating a proof by analyzing the cases $a=2$ and $a \neq 2$ or, alternatively, $b=2$ and $b \neq 2$. The symmetry of the graph suggests, however, a division of the proof into cases $a \neq 2$ and $b \neq 2$. This reflects the reasoning "$a \neq b$, therefore it is impossible that both a and b are equal to 2. If $a \neq 2$ ...". The second case has exactly the same structure and can therefore be done using the same case analysis. Then the following global structure of the proof has become visible:

```
                                 a=1 ——— P3
              a≠2 ∨ b≠2   <
                                 b=1 ——— P3
1=3 ∨ 2=3  <
              a≠1 ∨ b≠1         ...
```

A proof in natural language might therefore read: let 1 and 2 be constants such that any z equals 1 or 2. In order to prove P as a universal property it suffices to show that it holds for an arbitrary constant 3. 3 must be either 1 or 2. We consider first the case $3=1$. As $a \neq b$ it is impossible that both equal 2. If $a \neq 2$ it must be 1, which equals 3, and therefore P3 holds because Pa holds. If on the other hand $b \neq 2$ then b must be 1, which equals 3, and therefore P3 holds because Pb holds. The second case $(3=2)$ can be handled analogously. Therefore P3 holds in all cases, and as 3 was chosen arbitrarily P holds universally.

5 Conclusion

In this paper a method is described to transform a proof generated by a resolution-based theorem prover with a built-in paramodulation rule into a natural deduction proof in Gentzen's system NK. Starting from the basic proof transformation and structuring mechanism published in [Lingenfelder, 1990], the necessary changes and additions are made to meet the special needs of equality reasoning.

Paramodulation steps are represented in the refutation graph by equality clause nodes and additional links for each application of an equation. The extension of this mechanism to arbitrary theory resolution appears to be straightforward. The most remarkable result is the fact that this basis allows to employ the structuring algorithm essentially unchanged. The only extensions were to handle conditional equations by case analysis or as a lemma and some specialized heuristics for the consideration of equational steps.

An open question with respect to the structuring of proofs is the presentation of proofs based only or mainly on the equality predicate. The representation of pure unconditional equality proofs in equality graphs, as in [Bläsius, 1986], seems to be a promising starting point to construct a procedure analogous to the algorithm described here.

References

[Andrews, 1980] Peter B. Andrews. *Transforming Matings into Natural Deduction Proofs*. Proc of 5th CADE, pages 281-292, Springer-Verlag, 1980.

[Bläsius, 1986] Karl-Hans Bläsius. *Equality Reasoning Based on Graphs*. PhD Thesis, Uni Kaiserslautern, SEKI-Report SR-87-01, 1986.

[Gallier, 1986] Jean H. Gallier. *Logic for Computer Science, – Foundations of Automatic Theorem Proving*. Harper & Row, Publishers, New York, 1986.

[Gentzen, 1935] Gerhard Gentzen. *Untersuchungen über das logische Schließen I*. Math. Zeitschrift 39:176-210, 1935.

[Eisinger, 1988] Norbert Eisinger. *Completeness, Confluence, and Related Properties of Clause Graph Resolution*. PhD Thesis, Uni Kaiserslautern, Report SR-88-07, 1988.

[Huang, 1991] Xiaorong Huang. *On a Natural Calculus for Argument Presentation*. to appear as SEKI-Report, Uni Kaiserslautern, 1991.

[Lehr, 1988] Siegfried Lehr. *Transformation von Resolutionsbeweisen des MKRP*. Studienarbeit, Uni Kaiserslautern, 1988.

[Lingenfelder, 1986] Christoph Lingenfelder. *Transformation of Refutation Graphs into Natural Deduction Proofs*. Report SR-86-10, Uni Kaiserslautern, 1986.

[Lingenfelder, 1989] Christoph Lingenfelder. *Structuring Computer Generated Proofs*. Proc of 11th IJCAI, Detroit, 1991.

[Lingenfelder, 1990] Christoph Lingenfelder. *Structuring Computer Generated Proofs*. PhD Thesis, Uni Kaiserslautern, 1990.

[Loveland, 1978] Donald W. Loveland. *Automated Theorem Proving: A Logical Basis*. North Holland, 1978.

[Miller, 1983] Dale Miller. *Proofs in Higher Order Logic*. Ph.D. Thesis, Carnegie Mellon University, Tech Report MS-CIS-83-87, University of Pennsylvania, 1983.

[Ohlbach and Siekmann, 1989] Hans J. Ohlbach and Jörg H. Siekmann. *The Markgraf Karl Refutation Procedure*. Report SR-89-19, Uni Kaiserslautern, 1989.

[Pfenning and Nesmith, 1990] Frank Pfenning and Daniel Nesmith. *Presenting Intuitive Deductions via Symmetric Simplification.*, Proc of 10th CADE, pages 336-350, Springer-Verlag, 1990.

[Pelletier, 1986] Francis Jeffrey Pelletier. *Seventy-Five Problems for Testing Automatic Theorem Provers*. Journal of Automated Reasoning, 2(2):191-216, 1986.

[Stickel, 1985] Mark E. Stickel. *Automated Deduction by Theory Resolution*. Journal of Automated Reasoning, 1(4):333-356, 1985.

AUTOMATED REASONING

Search I

AN EXPECTED-COST ANALYSIS OF BACKTRACKING AND NON-BACKTRACKING ALGORITHMS

C.J.H. McDiarmid
Department of Statistics
University of Oxford
Oxford England OX1 3TG
email: MCD@vax.oxford.ac.uk

G.M.A. Provan
Department of Computer and Information Science
University of Pennsylvania
Philadelphia PA 19104-6389 USA
email: provan@cis.upenn.edu

Abstract

Consider an infinite binary search tree in which the branches have independent random costs. Suppose that we must find an optimal (cheapest) or nearly optimal path from the root to a node at depth n. Karp and Pearl [1983] show that a bounded-lookahead backtracking algorithm A2 usually finds a nearly optimal path in linear expected time (when the costs take only the values 0 or 1). From this successful performance one might conclude that similar heuristics should be of more general use. But we find here equal success for a simpler *non-backtracking* bounded-lookahead algorithm, so the search model cannot support this conclusion. If, however, the search tree is generated by a branching process so that there is a possibility of nodes having no sons (or branches having prohibitive costs), then the non-backtracking algorithm is hopeless while the backtracking algorithm still performs very well. These results suggest the general guideline that backtracking becomes attractive when there is the possibility of "dead-ends" or prohibitively costly outcomes.

1 INTRODUCTION

Many algorithms considered in operations research, computer science and artificial intelligence may be represented as searches or partial searches through rooted trees. Such algorithms typically involve backtracking but try to minimize the time spent doing so (e.g. [Bitner and Reingold, 1975; Brown and P. W. Purdom, 1981; Brown and P. W. Purdom, 1982; Dechter, 1990; Haralick and Elliott, 1980; Karp, 1976; Knuth, 1975; Nudel, 1983; P. W. Purdom, 1983; Stone and Stone, 1986]). Indeed for some problems it may be best to avoid backtracking [de Kleer, 1984].

The paper extends work of [Karp and Pearl, 1983], and gives a probabilistic analysis of backtracking and non-backtracking search algorithms in certain trees with random branch costs. We thus cast some light on the question of when to backtrack: it seems that backtracking is valuable just for problems with "dead-ends" (or outcomes with prohibitively high costs).

Let us review briefly the model and results of Karp and Pearl [1983]. They consider an infinite search tree in which each node has exactly two sons. The branches have independent (0, 1)-valued random costs X, with $p = P(X = 0)$.[1] The problem is to find an optimal (cheapest) or nearly optimal path from the root to a node at depth n.

The problem changes nature depending on whether the expected number $2p$ of zero-cost branches leaving a node is $> 1, = 1$ or < 1. When $2p > 1$ a simple uniform cost breadth-first search algorithm $A1$ finds an optimal solution in expected time $O(n)$; and when $2p = 1$ this algorithm takes expected time $O(n^2)$. When $2p < 1$ any algorithm that is guaranteed to find a solution within a constant factor of optimal must take exponential expected time. However, in this case a "bounded-lookahead plus partial backtrack" algorithm $A2$ usually finds a solution close to optimal in linear expected time. This successful performance of the backtracking algorithm $A2$ for the difficult case when $2p < 1$ seems to suggest that similar backtrack-based heuristics should be of more general use for attacking NP-hard problems.

This paper shows that a simple *non-backtracking* bounded-lookahead algorithm $A3$ performs as successfully as the backtracking algorithm $A2$, on the basis of this search model. Similar comments hold if we allow more general finite random costs on the branches.

However, there is a qualitative difference if we allow nodes to have no sons (or allow branches to have infinite costs) so that there are "dead-ends". We extend Karp and Pearl's work by considering search in random trees generated by a branching process, where the branches have independent random finite costs X. (This model includes the case of infinite costs—nodes would just produce fewer sons). In this extended model, let m be the mean number of sons of a node, let p_0 be the probability that a node has no sons, and as before let $p = P(X = 0)$.

Our results concerning algorithms $A1$ and $A2$ are natural extensions of Karp and Pearl's results. Thus the uniform cost algorithm $A1$ finds an optimal solution in linear expected time if $mp > 1$ and in quadratic expected time if $mp = 1$. If $mp < 1$ then any algorithm with a constant performance guarantee must take exponential

[1] We have swapped p and $1 - p$ from the original paper.

expected time, but the backtracking algorithm $A2$ finds a nearly optimal solution in linear expected time.

However, the performance of the non-backtracking algorithm $A3$ depends critically on the parameter p_0. Suppose that $mp < 1$, so that optimal search is hard. If $p_0 = 0$, so that as in the Karp and Pearl model there are no dead-ends, then algorithm $A3$ usually finds a nearly optimal solution in linear expected time; that is, it performs as successfully as the backtracking algorithm $A2$. However, if $p_0 > 0$ then algorithm $A2$ usually fails to find a solution. Thus our model suggests that backtracking becomes attractive when there is the possibility of dead-ends.

In the next section we give details concerning the search model and the algorithms $A1, A2$ and $A3$, and then in section 3 we present our results. Section 4 briefly discusses the effect of noise on the algorithmic performance. In section 5 we make a few comments on proofs.

2 MODEL AND ALGORITHMS

We suppose that the search tree is the family tree of a branching process. For an introduction to the theory of such processes see for example [Harris, 1963; Athreya and Ney, 1972; Karp and Pearl, 1983]. Thus the search tree has a root node, at depth 0. Each node at depth n independently produces and is joined to a random number Z of sons at depth $(n+1)$. We shall assume that the mean number m of sons produced satisfies $1 < m < \infty$. Thus the expected number of nodes at depth n is m^n and grows exponentially with n.

The Karp and Pearl model is the special case when each node always has exactly two sons. On the other hand our search model here is a special case of the more complicated model considered in [McDiarmid, 1990], namely an age-dependent branching process of Crump-Mode type [Crump and Mode, 1968]. For such a model the implications concerning backtracking are just the same.

Let q denote the extinction probability for the branching process, that is the probability that the search tree is finite. Since $m > 1$ it follows that $q < 1$. Let p_0 be the probability a node has no sons. Clearly $q > 0$ if and only if $p_0 > 0$, and these conditions correspond to the existence of "dead-ends" in the search tree.

We suppose that the branches have independent non-negative random costs X with finite mean. A simple translation allows us to assume without loss of generality that small costs can occur; that is, for any $\delta > 0$ we have $P(X < \delta) > 0$. The distinction between zero and non-zero costs turns out to be important. We let $p = P(X = 0) \geq 0$.

The cost of a path is the sum of its branch costs. We want to find an optimal (cheapest) or nearly optimal path from the root to a node at depth n, for large n. Let C_n^* denote the random optimal cost of such a path, where $C_n^* = \infty$ if there is no such path. Thus $P(C_n^* = \infty) \to q$ as $n \to \infty$. The interesting case is when the search tree is infinite, and we shall usually condition on this happening, so that almost surely C_n^* is finite.

We shall discuss the performance of three algorithms, $A1, A2$ and $A3$, the first two of which are taken from [Karp and Pearl, 1983]. Algorithm $A1$ is a uniform cost breadth-first search algorithm and will be analyzed for the cases $mp > 1$ and $mp = 1$, when there are many zero-cost branches and search is easy. Algorithm $A2$ is a hybrid of local and global depth-first search strategies and will be analyzed for $mp < 1$. Algorithm $A3$ consists of repeated local optimal searches, and will be analyzed also for $mp < 1$. Note that $A1$ is an exact algorithm, whereas $A2$ and $A3$ are approximation algorithms.

For each algorithm Aj, we let the random cost of the solution found be C_n^{Aj} ($= \infty$ if no solution is found), and the random time taken be T_n^{Aj}. We measure time by the number of nodes of the search tree encountered.

The three algorithms are as follows:

Algorithm A1: At each step, expand the leftmost node among those frontiers nodes of minimum cost. The algorithm halts when it tries to expand a node at depth n. That node then corresponds to an optimal solution.

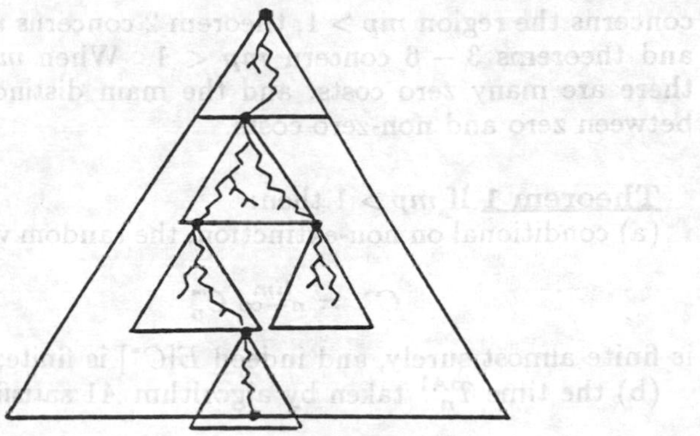

Figure 1: Operation of algorithm $A2$: The triangles represent local depth-first searches for (α, L)-sons.

Algorithm A2: Algorithm $A2$ has three parameters: d, L, and α. An (α, L)-regular path is a path which consist of segments each of length L and cost at most αL (except that the last segment may have length $< L$). $A2$ conducts a depth-first search to find an (α, L)-regular path from a depth d node to a depth n node. In other words, $A2$ is a depth-first strategy which stops at regular intervals of L levels to appraise its progress. If the cost increase from the last appraisal is at most αL, the search continues; if that cost increase is above αL, the current node is irrevocably pruned, the program backtracks to a higher level, and the search resumes. If it succeeds in reaching depth n, $A2$ returns the corresponding path as a solution: if it fails, the search is repeated from another depth d node. If all the nodes at depth d fail to root an (α, L)-regular path to a depth n node, $A2$ terminates with failure.

Algorithm A3: The simple bounded-lookahead or "horizon" heuristic is a staged-search algorithm which avoids backtracking. It has one parameter L. Starting at the root it finds an optimal path to a node at depth L, makes that node the new starting point and repeats. If L is a constant clearly $A3$ takes linear expected time.

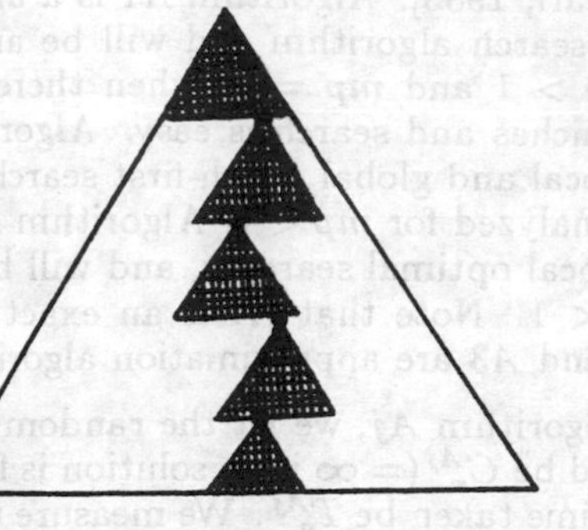

Figure 2: Operation of algorithm $A3$: The triangles represent local complete-enumeration searches for a least-cost path.

3 RESULTS

We summarize our results in six theorems. Theorem 1 concerns the region $mp > 1$, theorem 2 concerns $mp = 1$ and theorems $3 - 6$ concern $mp < 1$. When $mp \geq 1$, there are many zero costs, and the main distinction is between zero and non-zero costs.

<u>**Theorem 1**</u> If $mp > 1$ then:
(a) conditional on non-extinction, the random variable

$$C^* = \lim_{n \to \infty} C_n^*$$

is finite almost surely, and indeed $E[C^*]$ is finite; and
(b) the time T_n^{A1} taken by algorithm $A1$ satisfies

$$E[T_n^{A1}] = O(n).$$

Thus, if the search tree is infinite, the optimal cost C_n^* remains bounded as $n \to \infty$, and algorithm $A1$ finds an optimal path in linear expected time.

By restricting ourselves to 0,1 costs and uniform r-ary trees (so that each node has r sons) we may obtain a tighter result than in part (a) above, namely

$$P(C_n^* > k) < \left[\frac{r(1-p)}{r-1}\right]^{r^{(k+1)}} \quad (1)$$

The case $r = 2$ is a slight improvement on theorem 3.1 of Karp and Pearl [1983], and our proof (given below) is simpler and easier to generalise.

Next we consider the critical case $mp = 1$. It is convenient to make some simplifying assumptions on the typical random family size Z and cost X. We assume roughly that Z is not too big, and that the cost 0, which occurs with probability p, is "isolated", i.e. for some $\epsilon > 0$, $P(X < \epsilon) = 0$.

<u>**Theorem 2**</u> Let $mp = 1$:
(a) If $E[Z^{2+\delta}] < \infty$ for some $\delta > 0$,

$$P(0 < X < 1) = 0$$
$$\text{and} \quad P(X = 1) > 0,$$

then, conditional on non-extinction

$$\frac{C_n^*}{\log_2 \log_2 n} \to 1 \text{ almost surely as } n \to \infty.$$

(b) If $E[Z^2] < \infty$ then the time T_n^{A1} taken by algorithm $A1$ satisfies

$$E[T_n^{A1}] = O(n^2).$$

Part (a) shows that if the optimal cost C_n^* is finite then it is usually close to $\log_2 \log_2 n$. This result is a special case of theorem 2 of [Bramson, 1978]: see also theorem 3.2 of [Karp and Pearl, 1983]. Part (b) states that the algorithm $A1$ finds an optimal solution in quadratic expected time.

Our main interest is in the case $mp < 1$, when we cannot quickly find optimal solutions and thus it is of interest to analyze heuristic approximation methods.

<u>**Theorem 3**</u> If $mp < 1$, then any algorithm that is guaranteed to find a solution within a constant factor of optimal must take exponential average time.

<u>**Theorem 4**</u> Let $mp < 1$. For $\alpha \geq 0$ let

$$\rho(\alpha) = \inf_{t \geq 0} E[\exp t(\alpha - X)].$$

Then there is a unique solution α^* to the equation $\rho(\alpha) = 1/m$; $\alpha^* > 0$ and conditional on non-extinction,

$$\frac{C_n^*}{n} \to \alpha_* \text{ as } n \to \infty$$

almost surely and in mean.

Thus if the optimal cost C_n^* is finite then it is usually close to $\alpha^* n$. For discussion concerning this result see [Hammersley, 1974; Kingman, 1975].

<u>**Theorem 5**</u> Let $mp < 1$, and consider the random cost C_n^{A2} yielded by the "bounded lookahead plus partial backtrack" algorithm $A2$. For any $\epsilon > 0$ there are parameters d, α, L such that algorithm $A2$ runs in linear expected time, and almost surely

$$C_n^{A2} \leq (1 + \epsilon) C_n^* \quad \text{for } n \text{ sufficiently large.}$$

Thus algorithm $A2$ usually finds a nearly optimal solution (whether dead-ends can occur or not). This seems to be very successful performance, but in one sense it is not. For given any sensible parameters there will be a positive probability of failing to produce a solution (even when $p_0 = 0$ so that there are no dead-ends), and thus of course $E[C_n^{A2}] = \infty$.

However, returning "failure" (as in Karp and Pearl's algorithm $A2$) rather than a path of greater than near-optimal cost may possibly be too extreme. Failure of $A2$ to find a near-optimal solution can be easily avoided by adding a suitable "second phase" if the present algorithm fails. A possible second phase could be a depth-first search for a root-leaf path (ignoring costs).

Theorem 6 Let $mp < 1$, and consider the random cost C_n^{A3} yielded by the bounded lookahead but non-backtracking algorithm $A3$:

(a) If $p_0 = 0$ then for any $\epsilon > 0$ there is a (constant) parameter L such that the algorithm $A3$ runs in linear expected time; and almost surely

$$C_n^{A3} \leq (1+\epsilon)C_n^* \text{ for } n \text{ sufficiently large,}$$

and further

$$E[C_n^{A3}] \leq (1+\epsilon)C_n^* \text{ for } n \text{ sufficiently large.}$$

(b) If $p_0 > 0$, and if the lookahead parameter $L = o(n)$ (as is only reasonable) then almost surely

$$C_n^{A3} = \infty \text{ for } n \text{ sufficiently large.}$$

Part (a) above shows that if no dead-ends can occur then the simple non-backtracking heuristic $A3$ usually finds a nearly optimal solution and does so quickly. Part (b) show that $A3$ is hopeless if dead-ends can occur. Further, suppose that $L = O(\log n)$ so that each stage can be performed in polynomial average time. Then even if we consider a polynomial number of different starting points as with algorithm $A2$, still almost surely each search will fail if n is sufficiently large. This will follow from the proof of theorem 6.

4 EFFECTS OF READING ERRORS

In this section we discuss briefly the interesting effect of noise (i.e. reading errors) in the basic Karp and Pearl model. Suppose that the algorithm $A1$ may make occasional independent random reading errors. Thus, for the case of (0, 1)-costs, there is a probability $\delta_0 \geq 0$ that a 0-cost is read as a 1, and a probability $\delta_1 \geq 0$ that a 1-cost is read as a 0; and so the probability that a 0 is read is:

$$\tilde{p} = p(1-\delta_0) + (1-p)\delta_1.$$

It is easy to see that if δ_0 and δ_1 are small then there will be a correspondingly small change in $\frac{1}{n}$ times the expected solution value obtained by an error-prone algorithm $A1$ (compared with the value obtained by an error-free algorithm $A1$).

However, near the critical value $p = \frac{1}{2}$ there may be a dramatic change in the expected running time. If p is just greater than $\frac{1}{2}$, small reading errors could make $\tilde{p} < \frac{1}{2}$.[2] Then although an error-free algorithm ($A1$) runs in linear expected time, an error-prone version takes exponential expected time. Conversely, if p is just less than $\frac{1}{2}$, small reading errors could make $\tilde{p} > \frac{1}{2}$. Then although an error-free algorithm $A1$ takes exponential expected time, an error-prone algorithm $A1$ runs in linear expected time. Thus although the optimal value is robust with respect to reading errors, the time taken by algorithm A1 to compute the optimal cost is certainly not robust when p is near $\frac{1}{2}$.

[2] Recall that p is the probability that a random cost equals 0.

5 COMMENT ON PROOFS

This section presents the following two proofs: (1) inequality 1, which has appeared before only in [Provan, 1985]; and (2) theorem 6, a proof of the performance of the simple bounded-lookahead algorithm $A3$—this theorem is not like anything from [Karp and Pearl, 1983], and it is also quick and easy to prove. Theorems 1-6 can be deduced from the corresponding results in [McDiarmid, 1990] by specialising to the model discussed here and using standard truncation arguments. The proofs of theorems 1—5 can follow roughly similar lines to the proofs of the corresponding results in Karp and Pearl [1983].

Proof of inequality 1: Consider a branching process in which the number of sons of an individual has the binomial distribution with parameters r and p. Let q be the extinction probability. Then

$$P(C_n^* > k) < q^{r^k},$$

since if $C_n^* > k$ then each of the r^k subtrees rooted at the nodes at depth k must fail to have an infinite path of zero-cost branches. We shall show that (for $rp > 1$) we have

$$q < x^r \quad \text{where } x = \frac{r(1-p)}{(r-1)},$$

and then inequality 1 will follow. Using standard branching processes theory, q is the least positive root s of $f(s) = s$, where the generating function $f(s) = (1-p+ps)^r$. Since f is convex it suffices to demonstrate that

$$\begin{array}{rcl} f(x^r) & < & x^r, \\ \text{that is } 1-p+px^r & < & x. \end{array}$$

But

$$x = 1 - p + \frac{x}{r},$$

and so this is equivalent to showing that

$$rpx^{(r-1)} < 1.$$

To do this, introduce

$$\begin{array}{llcll} & g(y) & = & (r-(r-1)y)y^{(r-1)} & \text{for } 0 \leq y \leq 1. \\ \text{But} & g(1) & = & 1, & \\ \text{and} & g'(y) & = & r(r-1)(1-y)y^{(r-2)} & \text{for } 0 < y < 1, \\ \text{so} & g(y) & < & 1 & \text{for } 0 < y < 1. \end{array}$$

Finally, put $y = x$ to obtain, as required,

$$1 > (r-(r-1)x)x^{(r-1)} = rpx^{(r-1)}. \square$$

Proof Of Theorem 6

(a) We have already noted that for any constant lookahead L the algorithm $A3$ runs in linear expected time. By theorem 5,

$$\frac{1}{n}E[C_n^*] \to \alpha^* > 0 \quad \text{as } n \to \infty.$$

Let $\epsilon > 0$ and choose L so that

$$\frac{1}{L}E[C_L^*] < (1+\epsilon)\alpha^*.$$

Now C_n^{A3} is at most the sum of $\lceil \frac{n}{L} \rceil$ independent random variables each distributed like C_L^*. Hence, by the strong law of large numbers, almost surely

$$\frac{C_n^{A3}}{n} < (1+2\epsilon)\alpha^* \quad \text{for } n \text{ sufficiently large.}$$

But again by theorem 4, almost surely:

$$\frac{C_n^*}{n} > (1-\epsilon)\alpha^* \quad \text{for } n \text{ sufficiently large,}$$

and part (a) of theorem 6 now follows.[3]

(b) To prove part (b) we need only observe that

$$P(C_n^* = \infty) \geq 1 - (1-p_0)^{n/L} \rightarrow 1 \text{ as } n \rightarrow \infty \text{ if } L = o(n).\square$$

6 CONCLUSIONS

This paper has studied the performance of both backtracking and non-backtracking tree search algorithms in finding a least-cost root-leaf path in random trees with random non-negative costs. The investigations extend the work of Karp and Pearl in several ways, but in particular through the introduction of dead-ends. This analysis suggests the following conclusions:

1. When the possibility of "catastrophe" (dead ends or prohibitive costs) can be ignored then backtracking methods do not seem attractive, and a far simpler approach like that of the "horizon heuristic" *A3* is preferable.
2. When catastrophe looms then a backtracking method like Karp and Pearl's bounded-lookahead plus partial backtrack algorithm A2 does seem an attractive option.

This conclusion lends some mathematical support to certain empirical studies which show that, under given conditions, backtracking algorithms do not perform as well as non-backtracking algorithms. Examples are the empirical analysis of [Dechter and Meiri, 1989; Haralick and Elliott, 1980] in binary constraint satisfaction problems, and the analysis of [de Kleer, 1984] in reason maintenance systems.

References

[Athreya and Ney, 1972] K.B. Athreya and P.E. Ney. *Branching Processes.* Springer-Verlag, Berlin, 1972.

[Bitner and Reingold, 1975] J. R. Bitner and E. M. Reingold. Backtrack programming techniques. *Communications of the ACM*, 18:651–655, 1975.

[Bramson, 1978] M. D. Bramson. Minimal displacement of branching random walk. *Z. Wahrsch. Varw. Gabiete*, 45:89–108, 1978.

[3]It is also easy to prove a weaker version of this result using only an easy part of theorem 4 and the subadditivity of the sequence $E[C_n^*]$.

[Brown and P. W. Purdom, 1981] C. A. Brown and P. W. Purdom, Jr. . An average case analysis of backtracking. *SIAM J. Computing*, 10 (3):583–593, 1981.

[Brown and P. W. Purdom, 1982] C. A. Brown and P. W. Purdom, Jr.. An empirical comparison of backtracking algorithms. *IEEE Trans. PAMI*, 4, 1982.

[Crump and Mode, 1968] K.S. Crump and C.J. Mode. A general age-dependent branching process. *Journal of Mathematical Analysis and Applications*, 24, 1968.

[de Kleer, 1984] J. de Kleer. Choices without backtracking. *Proc. AAAI*, 79–85, 1984.

[Dechter, 1990] R. Dechter. Enhancement Schemes for Constraint Processing: Backjumping, Learning and Cutset Decomposition. *Artificial Intelligence*, 41(3):273–312, 1990.

[Dechter and Meiri, 1989] R. Dechter and I. Meiri. Experimental Evaluation of Preprocessing Techniques in Constraint Satisfaction. In *Proc. IJCAI*, 271–276, 1989.

[Hammersley, 1974] J. M. Hammersley. Postulates for subadditive processes. *Annals of Probability*, 2:652–680, 1974.

[Haralick and Elliott, 1980] R. M. Haralick and G. L. Elliott. Increasing tree search efficiency for constraint satisfaction problems. *Artificial Intelligence*, 14:263–313, 1980.

[Harris, 1963] T. E. Harris. *The Theory of Branching Processes.* Springer-Verlag, Berlin, 1963.

[Karp, 1976] R. M. Karp. The probabilistic analysis of some combinatorial search algorithms. In J. F. Traub, editor, *Algorithms and Complexity*, pages 1–19, Academic Press, 1976.

[Karp and Pearl, 1983] R. M. Karp and J. Pearl. Searching for an optimal path in a tree with random costs. *Artificial Intelligence*, 21:99–116, 1983.

[Kingman, 1975] J.F.C. Kingman. The First Birth Problem for an Age-Dependent Branching Process. *Annals of Probability*, 3:790–801, 1975.

[Knuth, 1975] D. E. Knuth. Estimating the efficiency of backtrack programs. *Mathematics of Computation*, 29:121–136, 1975.

[McDiarmid, 1990] C.J.H. McDiarmid. Probabilistic Analysis of Tree Search. In G.R. Gummett and D.J.A. Welsh, editors, *Disorder in Physical Systems*, pages 249–260, Oxford Science Publications, 1990.

[Nudel, 1983] B. Nudel. Consistent labeling problems and their algorithms: expected complexities and theory-based heuristics. *Artificial Intelligence*, 21:135–178, 1983.

[Provan, 1985] G. M. Provan. A Probabilistic Analysis of Search Algorithms in Uniform Trees. Mathematical Institute, University of Oxford, Unpublished D. Phil. qualifying dissertation, 1985.

[P. W. Purdom, 1983] Jr. P. W. Purdom. Search rearrangement backtracking and polynomial average time. *Artificial Intelligence*, 21:117–133, 1983.

[Stone and Stone, 1986] H. Stone and J. Stone. *Efficient Search Techniques: An Empirical Study of the N-Queens Problem.* Technical Report TR TC 12057 (#54343), IBM T.J. Watson Research Center, 1986.

Admissible Search Methods for Minimum Penalty Sequencing of Jobs with Setup Times on One and Two Machines

Anup K. Sen, A. Bagchi and Bani K. Sinha
Indian Institute of Management Calcutta
Joka, Diamond Harbour Road
P.O. Box 16757, Calcutta - 700 027, India

Abstract

Many efficient implementations of AI search algorithms have been realized in recent years. In an effort to widen the area of application of search methods to problems that arise in industry, this paper examines the role that search can play in solving certain types of hard optimization problems that involve the proper sequencing of jobs in one-machine job-shops and two-machine flow-shops. The problems studied here have the following general form: The completion of a job at time f induces a penalty G(f), where G(.) is a given penalty function which can be different for different jobs; the jobs must be so sequenced that the total penalty summed over all jobs is minimized. The objective is to improve upon current methods and to show that problems earlier considered formidable can at least be attempted, if not resolved satisfactorily, using admissible search algorithms. The crucial aspect is the derivation of good admissible heuristics that can direct the search narrowly to a goal. The search graph is not necessarily a tree. Algorithm A* has been run on randomly generated data using the derived heuristic estimates to solve a variety of penalty minimization problems; some indicative experimental results are provided.

1 Introduction

Recent years have witnessed a renewed spurt of interest in the theory and implementation of best-first search techniques [Pearl, 1984]. This interest is yet to be adequately reflected, however, in the application of AI search methods to optimization problems that arise in industry, many of which cannot be solved conveniently by any of the known algorithms. Viswanathan and Bagchi [1988] describe a successful attempt at applying search methods to rectangular cutting stock problems, but such examples are few. In this context, an area that appears to hold great promise is *sequencing and scheduling*, where most problems of practical importance require the use of branch-and-bound or dynamic programming methods [French, 1982; Lawler *et al.*, 1982]. Now that efficient implementations of best-first search algorithms such as A*, IDA* [Korf, 1985], and MREC [Sen and Bagchi, 1989] have been realized, search could prove superior to other methods in cases where reasonably tight lower bounds can be derived.

This paper investigates the role that best-first search can play in solving certain types of one-machine and two-machine job sequencing problems that arise in job-shops and flow-shops. The major objective is to enlarge the sphere of application of best-first search, and at the same time to illustrate how good admissible heuristics can be defined for practical problems. A typical problem studied by us has the following form. Jobs J_i, $1 \leq i \leq n$, with processing times a_i, $1 \leq i \leq n$, have been submitted to a one-machine job-shop at time $t = 0$. The jobs are to be processed on the given machine one at a time. Let the processing of job J_i be completed at time f_i. *Penalty functions* $G_i(.)$, $1 \leq i \leq n$, are supplied, such that the penalty associated with completing job J_i at time f_i is $G_i(f_i)$. An example of a penalty function is $G_i(f_i) = c_i f_i^2$, where the c_i's are given constants, the penalty associated with a job being proportional to the square of the finish time of the job. The jobs must be sequenced on the machine in such a way that the total penalty

$$F = \sum \{ G_i(f_i) \mid 1 \leq i \leq n \}$$

is minimized. The penalty functions are non-decreasing, and in general non-linear. Moreover, a job has a *setup time* that is independent of its position in the processing sequence; we say that the setup times are *separable*. In a more general formulation, the setup times can be *sequence-dependent*, i.e. the setup time of a job can depend on the job that immediately precedes it in the processing sequence. Problems of this type have obvious relevance to industry, but are known to be very hard to solve satisfactorily in their full generality, the number of job sequences being exponential in the number of jobs. No efficient general methods of solution have been reported. Schild and Fredman [1963] proposed a scheme for non-linear penalty functions that ignored setup times but nevertheless required a great deal of computation; improvements were subsequently suggested by Townsend [1978] and Bagga and Kalra [1980], but these were specific to quadratic penalty functions. Another special case has been studied by Rinnooy Kan *et al.* [1975]. As for two-machine flowshop situations, work has been confined to the determination of minimum length schedules in the presence of setup times (see, for example, [Gupta and Darrow, 1985; Sule, 1982; Corwin and Esogbue, 1974]); penalty functions have not yet been considered by anyone in any detail.

This paper, which is in the nature of a preliminary report, describes how best-first search techniques can be used to determine minimal penalty job sequences for one and two machines when the setup times are separable. A* is the search algorithm used. Each case involves the computation of a reasonably tight lower bound that can serve to guide the search fairly narrowly to a goal. Search graphs have been implemented as graphs and not as trees whenever it has been found possible to do so; this tends to speed up the execution. In the two-machine case the search methods given below are not always *order preserving* [Pearl, 1984, p. 102], and unless the search graph is a tree the solution may not be optimal. The programs have been run on random data that try to simulate real-life situations. The results we have obtained are most encouraging; our main contribution lies in showing how useful best first search can be in attacking job sequencing problems traditionally regarded as very difficult, such as the determination of a minimum penalty job sequence for a two-machine flow-shop however simple the penalty function, or for a single machine when the penalty for a job is proportional to a non-integral power of the finish time of the job.

2 One Machine Job Sequencing Problems

2.1 Problem Description

For the one-machine problem with sequence-dependent setup times we define the following notation :

n	number of jobs
J_i	ith job
a_i	processing time (> 0) for job J_i
$s_{i,j}$	setup time for job J_j when it immediately follows job J_i in the processing sequence
f_i	completion time of job J_i
d_i	deadline for job J_i
$G_i(.)$	penalty function for job J_i
c_i	penalty coefficient for job J_i
F	total penalty for a given sequence

If J_i is the first job in the sequence, then $s_{0,i}$ represents its setup time. After the last job in the sequence is completed, the machine need not be brought back to any specific state. A penalty of $G_i(f_i - d_i)$ is incurred for job J_i when $f_i > d_i$; if $f_i \leq d_i$ then no penalty is incurred for J_i. The formulation can be generalized to include the cost of carrying in inventory those jobs that get completed before their respective deadlines. In order to simplify the problem it is frequently assumed that all deadlines are zero; we make this assumption in the paper.

When the setup times are separable as in [Sule, 1982], we have the following alternative notation :

p_i	initialization time for job J_i
q_i	cleanup time for job J_i
A_i	$p_i + a_i + q_i$

Initialization time refers to the time needed to initialize the machine settings before job J_i can be processed, while cleanup time refers to the time needed to clean the machine and bring it back to a specified state after the processing of job J_i has been completed. When job J_j follows job J_i in the sequence, the total setup time (q_i + p_j) can be viewed as corresponding to $s_{i,j}$ in the general case; again, if J_i is the first job in the sequence, then p_i corresponds to $s_{0,i}$ in the general case. Let the jobs be processed in the sequence

$$J_{j(1)},\ J_{j(2)},\ \ldots,\ J_{j(n)}$$

and let the completion time of job $J_{j(k)}$ be $f_{j(k)}$. Then for $1 \leq k \leq n$, $\quad f_{j(k)} = \sum \{ A_{j(i)} \mid 1 \leq i \leq k \} - q_{j(k)}$.
Note that the finish time of a job does not include the cleanup time for the job; the cleanup time gets added when the finish times of the jobs that follow in the sequence are computed. For one-machine problems, there is no loss of generality if the initialization time of a job is included in the processing time and not considered separately. As an illustration of the kind of problem we are trying to solve, consider the following example:

Example: Penalty for a job J_i proportional to its finish time f_i; separable setup times.

Here, $G_i(f_i) = c_i f_i$, where the c_i's are constants, c_i being the penalty coefficient for job J_i. Thus

$$F = \sum \{ c_{j(k)} f_{j(k)} \mid 1 \leq k \leq n \}$$
$$= \sum_k c_{j(k)} \sum \{ A_{j(i)} \mid 1 \leq i \leq k \} - \sum_k c_k q_k$$

To minimize F we just need to arrange the jobs in the order [French, 1982]:

$$A_{j(1)}/c_{j(1)} \leq A_{j(2)}/c_{j(2)} \leq \ldots \leq A_{j(n)}/c_{j(n)},$$

since the last sum in the expression for F is a constant. Here we do not need to take help of search methods. □

In more complex situations we are forced to take recourse to AI search methods. Algorithm A* is implemented in the standard manner [Nilsson, 1980; Pearl, 1984]. OPEN is maintained as a priority queue. Nodes generally correspond to unordered subsets of jobs; the root node is the empty set. When a node corresponding to a subset of k jobs gets selected from OPEN and expanded, it generates (n-k) sons, each son being a subset of (k+1) jobs. A problem gets solved when a complete set of n jobs gets selected from OPEN. For two-machine problems, a node sometimes corresponds to an ordered sequence of jobs. The following additional notation is used in the specifications of the problems:

N	current node (either an unordered subset of jobs or an ordered partial sequence of jobs)
$g(N)$	cost of minimal cost path currently known from the root node to node N
$h(N)$	heuristic estimate at node N
$h^*(N)$	cost of minimal cost path from node N to a goal node
P	set of jobs already processed at node N
Q	set of jobs remaining to be processed at node N
T	time at which all jobs in P get completed
q_{last}	cleanup time of last job in P
m	number of jobs in Q

2.2 Non-Linear Penalty Functions

Case I Penalty for a job proportional to square of its completion time; all initialization and cleanup times are zero.

Here $G_i(f_i) = c_i f_i^2$. Townsend [1978] proposed a new method for computing lower bounds in a best-first branch-and-bound algorithm to solve this problem; certain improvements were subsequently suggested by Bagga and Kalra [1982]. We compute the heuristic estimate h(N) at the current node N as follows :

Order the processing times of the m jobs in Q in the non-decreasing order

$$a_{j(1)} \leq a_{j(2)} \leq \ldots \leq a_{j(m)}$$

Also order the penalty coefficients of the jobs in Q *independently* in the non-increasing order

$$c_{i(1)} \geq c_{i(2)} \geq \cdot \cdot \geq c_{i(m)}.$$

Take the heuristic estimate as

$$h(N) = \sum \{ c_{i(k)} f_{j(k)}^2 \mid 1 \leq k \leq m \}$$

where $f_{j(k)} = T + \sum \{ a_{j(u)} \mid 1 \leq u \leq k \}$,

and $T = \sum \{ a_k \mid J_k \text{ is in } P \}$.

Our computation ensures that h(N) is a lower bound on h*(N), the cost of the optimal path from N to a goal, since the penalty functions strictly dominate each other and have no crossover points. The sorting of the processing times and the penalty coefficients is done only once at start. Thereafter, we just have to keep track of which jobs are in Q, and when computing the heuristic estimate we simply skip over those terms in the sorted lists that correspond to jobs in P.

The method can be generalized to handle penalty functions for job J_i that are proportional to $(f_i)^k$ or to $\exp(kf_i)$, where k is a real constant independent of i. Such functional forms have not been considered by Townsend [1978] or Bagga and Kalra [1980].

In our experiments, programs were written in C and run on the SUN 3/60 workstation. The search graph was a graph and not a tree. The heuristic is *monotone* [Nilsson, 1980], so that a node is expanded at most once. But it is still advantageous to use a graph representation because this allows the g-values of unexpanded nodes to get updated in OPEN. A tree representation causes an explosion in the number of nodes generated and expanded. To implement graphs efficiently, we need to be able to find out quickly whether a newly generated successor is already present in the graph. This can be achieved by the use of a *hashing scheme*. A node N corresponds to a subset of jobs; the bit representation of N is viewed as a binary number which is then hashed using the modulo method. All particulars about a node are stored in the hash table; entries in the priority queue are pointers to the hash table. Two different penalty functions of the form $G_i(f_i) = c_i(f_i)^k$ were considered, with k = 2.0 and k = 1.5. Processing times (a_i) of jobs were integers and were chosen randomly in the range 1 to 99 from a uniform distribution. Penalty coefficients (c_i) were also integers and were generated in the range 1 to 9 in the same way. For each set of jobs, the execution time, the total number of nodes generated, and the total number of nodes expanded were averaged over 25 runs. Results are given in Table I. It was found experimentally that for k = 2, Townsend's algorithm runs slightly faster than ours, but these results are not shown in the table.

TABLE I

	k = 2.0			k = 1.5		
Number of Jobs	Exec Time (sec)	Nodes Gen	Nodes Exp	Exec Time (sec)	Nodes Gen	Nodes Exp
12	0.83	2118	855	2.39	1799	669
13	1.63	3980	1478	4.63	3266	1092
14	3.29	7561	2871	9.36	6130	2098
15	7.43	14123	5519	19.28	11322	3953

For k = 1.5, computations were done using real numbers, and so the execution times are larger. The heuristic is quite tight: For 14 jobs, only 7561 nodes are generated when k = 2.0, while there are 14! job sequences.

Case II Penalty for a job proportional to square of its completion time; separable setup times.

No algorithm has yet been proposed for this problem. We determine the heuristic estimate h(N) as follows. Let

$$q = \min \{ q_k \mid J_k \text{ is in } Q \}$$

Order the jobs in Q according to the conditions

$$(p_{j(1)} + a_{j(1)}) \leq (p_{j(2)} + a_{j(2)}) \leq \ldots \leq (p_{j(m)} + a_{j(m)}),$$

and order the penalty coefficients as in Case I. The expression for h(N) is the same as in Case I, but here take

$$f_{j(k)} = T + q_{last} + \sum \{ (p_{j(u)} + a_{j(u)}) \mid 1 \leq u \leq k \} + (k - 1)q$$

and $T = \sum \{ A_k \mid J_k \text{ is in } P \} - q_{last}$.

As in Case I, h(N) ≤ h*(N), and h is monotone. Again, the method can be extended to powers other than two and to exponentials. A* was run with the above heuristics. Data was generated as in Case I; the initialization and cleanup times were also generated randomly, but in the range 1 to 9 to keep them smaller than the processing times. Nodes still correspond to unordered subsets of jobs. Results are shown in Table II for the case k = 2. A depth-first branch-and-bound implementation was also tried out, but was found to be much slower in execution.

TABLE II

Number of Jobs	Exec Time (sec)	Nodes Gen	Nodes Exp
10	0.18	535	191
12	0.75	1910	676
14	2.93	6647	2246

Case III General non-linear penalty functions; separable setup times.

This generalizes Case II. Here we consider penalty functions G_i that have the non-negative integers as domain and the non-negative real numbers as range; each G_i is non-decreasing and possibly non-linear, and the G_i's do not necessarily have identical functional forms [Schild and Fredman, 1963]. Let q, T and $f_{j(k)}$ be defined as in Case II, and let

$$G(x) = \min \{ G_i(x) \mid J_i \text{ is in } Q \}.$$

When computing the heuristic estimate arrange the jobs as in Case II and then use G and q instead of the G_i's and the q_i's, but when computing g(N) use the actual G_i and q_i values. Close bounds are hard to obtain when the G_i's have different functional forms.

Claim: $h(N) \le h^*(N)$.

Proof: Express $h^*(N)$ as a function of T, and of the parameters G_i, p_i, a_i and q_i of the jobs J_i in Q. Replace each occurrence of G_i and q_i in the expression for $h^*(N)$ by G and q respectively; this gives a value $h_0(N) \le h^*(N)$. But when G and q are used for computing the heuristic estimate, h(N) is the smallest estimate we can get, so that we must have $h(N) \le h_0(N)$. □

Some experimental results are given in Table III. As before, nodes correspond to unordered sets of jobs and the heuristic is monotone. The penalty functions were chosen to have the form $G_i(f_i) = c_i f_i + c_{i'}(f_i)^2$. The coefficients c_i and $c_{i'}$ were both randomly generated in the range 1 to 9.

Table III

Number of Jobs	Exec Time (sec)	Nodes Gen	Nodes Exp
10	1.51	1011	775
11	3.54	2019	1624
12	8.25	4091	3400

3 Two-Machine Flow-Shop Problems

In the two-machine flow-shop problem, each job must be processed twice; it must be processed on the first machine before it is processed on the second machine. The completion time of a job is the time at which its processing on the second machine is finished. The classic algorithm of Johnson [1954] finds a minimum length schedule. Our objective is to minimize the total penalty. This problem has been generally considered to be intractable, and there are very few references on the topic. Search methods can be applied here with advantage. We use the notation introduced earlier with the following additions and modifications:

- M_1 — machine 1
- M_2 — machine 2
- p_i, a_i, q_i — initialization, processing and cleanup times of J_i on M_1
- r_i, b_i, s_i — initialization, processing and cleanup times of J_i on M_2
- A_i — $p_i + a_i + q_i$
- B_i — $r_i + b_i + s_i$
- T_1 — completion time on M_1 of all jobs in P
- T_2 — completion time on M_2 of all jobs in P
- q_{last} — cleanup time on M_1 of the last job in P
- s_{last} — cleanup time on M_2 of the last job in P

A well known theorem (see French [1982], Theorem 5.1, p. 67) states that in the absence of setup times, there is an optimal schedule in which jobs are sequenced in the same order on the two machines. This theorem remains valid when the setup times are separable, but not when they are sequence-dependent [Gupta and Darrow, 1985]. Since our study is confined to separable setup times, we can restrict ourselves to job sequences which are identical for the two machines.

Case I Penalty for a job equal to its completion time; all initialization and cleanup times are zero.

Here g(N) is the sum of the finish times of the jobs in P. To determine h(N), order the processing times on M_1 of the m jobs in Q as follows:

$$a_{i(1)} \le a_{i(2)} \le \ldots \le a_{i(m)}$$

Order the processing times on M_2 of the jobs in Q *independently* as follows:

$$b_{j(1)} \le b_{j(2)} \le \ldots \le b_{j(m)}$$

Let $X = mT_1 + \sum \{(m + 1 - k)\, a_{i(k)} + b_k \mid 1 \le k \le m \}$

$Y = mT_3 + \sum \{(m + 1 - k)\, b_{j(k)} \mid 1 \le k \le m \}$

where $T_3 = \max \{ T_1 + a_{i(1)}, T_2 \}$,

and take $h(N) = \max \{ X, Y \}$.

Claim $h(N) \le h^*(N)$.

Proof We have to show that $X \le h^*(N)$ *and* $Y \le h^*(N)$. The jobs in Q have been so ordered that the finish time on M_1 of the kth job in Q is the earliest possible; moreover, each of the jobs in Q must be processed on M_2, and the processing on M_2 of the kth job in Q cannot begin until the processing on M_1 of the kth job is over. This proves that $X \le h^*(N)$. Again, the processing of any job in Q cannot commence on M_2 before T_3, so $Y \le h^*(N)$. □

Sequencing problems of up to 12 jobs can be readily solved using a tree representation for the search graph, where a node corresponds to an ordered sequence of jobs. Such a formulation is essentially equivalent to a best-first branch and bound procedure. If we represent a node as an unordered subset of jobs we find that the search is faster but no longer order preserving, because when the jobs in P are permuted, not only g(N) but also T_2, and therefore T_3, get altered. This has the unusual consequence that with a graph representation, non-optimal solutions are outputted even when the heuristics are admissible. It was found experimentally, however, that the solutions are close to optimal, so that the method can still be useful in practice. Experimental results are given in Table IV. Data was generated

TABLE IV

	Tree				Graph			
No of Jobs	Exec Time (sec)	Nodes Gen	Nodes Exp	Opt Cost	Exec Time (sec)	Nodes Gen	Nodes Exp	Cost Obtd
10	0.29	1192	210	2652	0.28	268	68	2660
11	0.86	3343	563	3212	0.72	441	103	3226
12	4.59	15741	2622	3723	2.56	834	204	3734

independently and randomly for the jobs on the two machines. It is interesting to observe that if we change the expressions for X and Y to

$$X = T_1 + \sum \{ a_k \mid 1 \le k \le m \} + b_{j(1)}$$
$$Y = T_3 + \sum \{ b_k \mid 1 \le k \le m \}$$

and set g(N) = 0 and h(N) = max { X, Y }, we get a minimum length schedule. This gives us an alternative to Johnson's algorithm, but the latter runs much faster.

Case II Penalty for a job proportional to its completion time; separable setup times.

This generalizes Case I. Here $G_i(f_i) = c_i f_i$, where the c_i's are the penalty coefficients as before. Let g(N) be the weighted sum of the finish times of the jobs in P. To compute h(N) order the processing times on M_1 of the m jobs in Q as follows:

$$A_{i(1)}/c_{i(1)} \le A_{i(2)}/c_{i(2)} \le \ldots \le A_{i(m)}/c_{i(m)}$$

Independently order the processing times on M_2 of the jobs in Q:

$$B_{j(1)}/c_{j(1)} \le B_{j(2)}/c_{j(2)} \le \ldots \le B_{j(m)}/c_{j(m)}$$

Also, let D be the inner product, for the jobs in Q, of the m-element b-vector with the corresponding c-vector, where the b_i's in the b-vector are arranged in non-decreasing order while the c_i's in the c-vector are arranged in non-increasing order. Now take

$$X = \sum_{k=1}^{m} (T_1 + q_{last} + \sum \{ A_{i(u)} \mid 1 \le u \le k \})\, c_{i(k)} + D - \sum \{ q_k c_k \mid J_k \text{ is in } Q \}$$
$$Y = \sum_{k=1}^{m} (T_3 + \sum \{ B_{j(u)} \mid 1 \le u \le k \})\, c_{j(k)} - \sum \{ s_k c_k \mid J_k \text{ is in } Q \}$$

where $T_3 = \max \{ T_1 + q_{last} + p_{i(1)} + a_{i(1)} - r_{max},\ T_2 + s_{last} \}$

$r_{max} = \max \{ r_k \mid J_k \text{ is in } Q \}$.

Let h(N) = max { X, Y }. Experimental results are given in Table V. Here, too, h(N) is a lower bound on h*(N). If we can redefine X and Y as follows

$$X = T_1 + q_{last} + \sum \{ A_k \mid 1 \le k \le m \} + b_{j(1)} - q_{max}$$
$$Y = T_3 + \sum \{ B_k \mid 1 \le k \le m \} - s_{max}$$

where $q_{max} = \max \{ q_k \mid J_k \text{ is in } Q \}$, and $s_{max} = \max \{ s_k \mid J_k \text{ is in } Q \}$

and set g(N) = 0 and h(N) = max { X, Y }, we get an alternative to Sule's [1982] method for finding a minimum length schedule when setup times are separable.

TABLE V

Number of Jobs	Exec Time (sec)	Nodes Gen	Nodes Exp
10	0.34	1140	208
11	0.83	2670	439
12	4.15	12241	1926

Case III Penalty for a job proportional to square of its completion time; all initialization and cleanup times are zero.

The penalty functions are as in Case II of Section 2.2. Compute g(N) by summing, over the jobs in P, the squares of the finish times multiplied by the appropriate penalty coefficients. Order as in Case I the processing times on M_1 of the jobs in Q, and independently the processing times on M_2 of the jobs in Q. Also order the corresponding penalty coefficients c_i in non-increasing order:

$$c_{k(1)} \ge c_{k(2)} \ge \ldots \ge c_{k(m)}$$

Let $X = \sum_{u=1}^{m} c_{k(u)} [(T_1 + \sum \{ a_{i(w)} \mid 1 \le w \le u \})^2 + (b_{j(u)})^2]$

$$Y = \sum_{u=1}^{m} c_{k(u)} (T_3 + \sum \{ b_{j(w)} \mid 1 \le w \le u \})^2$$
$$Z = \sum_{u=1}^{m} c_{k(u)} (T_1 + \sum \{ a_{i(w)} \mid 1 \le w \le u \} + b_{j(1)})^2,$$

where T_1 and T_3 are as in Case I, and take h(N) = max { X, Y, Z }.

We again have h(N) ≤ h*(N). This case, as well as the next, can be generalized to powers other than two and to exponentials. Experimental results for the square penalty function are given in Table VI.

TABLE VI

Number of Jobs	Exec Time (sec)	Nodes Gen	Nodes Exp
8	0.57	1730	453
9	1.81	4965	1181
10	13.90	33750	7828

Case IV Penalty for a job proportional to square of its completion time; separable setup times.

In this case let $q = \min \{ q_k \mid J_k \text{ is in } Q \}$

$s = \min \{ s_k \mid J_k \text{ is in } Q \}$

Order the processing times on M_1 and M_2 of the jobs in Q independently as follows:

$$(p_{i(1)} + a_{i(1)}) \le (p_{i(2)} + a_{i(2)}) \le \ldots \le (p_{i(m)} + a_{i(m)})$$
$$(r_{j(1)} + b_{j(1)}) \le (r_{j(2)} + b_{j(2)}) \le \ldots \le (r_{j(m)} + b_{j(m)})$$

Let the penalty coefficients be arranged in non-increasing order as in Case III. Arrange the m-element b-vector in non-decreasing order, square each element, and let D be the inner product of the resulting vector with the corresponding m-element c-vector arranged as above.

TABLE VII

Number of Jobs	Exec Time (sec)	Nodes Gen	Nodes Exp
8	0.46	1084	260
9	3.25	6917	1632

Now let b_{Qmin} be the smallest b_i in Q, and let

$$X = \sum_{u=1}^{m} c_{k(u)} [T_1 + q_{last} + \sum \{ (p_{i(w)} + a_{i(w)}) \mid 1 \le w \le u \} + (u-1)q]^2 + D$$
$$Y = \sum_{u=1}^{m} c_{k(u)} [T_3 + \sum \{ (r_{j(w)} + b_{j(w)}) \mid 1 \le w \le u \} + (u-1)s]^2$$
$$Z = \sum_{u=1}^{m} c_{k(u)} [T_1 + q_{last} + \sum \{ (q_{i(w)} + a_{i(w)}) \mid 1 \le w \le u \} + (u-1)q + b_{Qmin}]^2$$

and take $h(N) = \max \{ X, Y, Z \}$

Experimental results are given in Table VII.

4 Conclusion

The major aim of this paper has been to open a new area of application for AI search methods, and to illustrate how good admissible heuristics can be derived for some practical problems. It has been shown that certain types of difficult but practical one-machine and two-machine job sequencing problems, for which efficient algorithms are not currently known, can be tackled in a reasonably satisfactory way by admissible search schemes. The work reported here can be extended in many directions. Even before any extension in scope is attempted, more intensive experimental testing needs to be undertaken of the admissible heuristics derived here on real life data gathered from job-shops and flow-shops. The following additional issues and questions could be taken up for closer examination and study:

i) Is it possible to modify the methods described here to solve sequencing problems involving sequence-dependent setup times? In the one-machine case, this problem has some similarities with the travelling salesman problem. In the two-machine case, an optimal schedule can sequence jobs in different orders on the two machines; this greatly complicates the situation, and perhaps a totally new approach is necessary.

ii) When there are more than two machines in a flow-shop, an optimal schedule can order jobs in different orders on the machines. One way out of the difficulty is to restrict oneself to *permutation schedules* only [Lageweg *et al.*, 1978], in which jobs are sequenced in the same order on all machines, but this has the obvious limitation that optimal schedules may not be realized. Can search methods be used to determine good permutation schedules ?

iii) In a real life problem, a job normally has a deadline by which the processing must be completed; no penalty accrues for a job that gets completed within its deadline. Is it possible to modify the heuristic estimate functions to take care of deadlines ? A positive answer will greatly increase the worth of this approach.

References

[Bagga and Kalra, 1980] P. C. Bagga and K. R. Kalra, A Node Elimination Procedure for Townsend's Algorithm for Solving the Single Machine Quadratic Penalty Function Scheduling Problem, *Management Science*, vol 26, no 6, 1980, pp 633-636.

[Cheng'en, 1989] Y. Cheng'en, A Dynamic Programming Algorithm for the Travelling Repairman Problem, *Asia-Pacific Journal of Operational Research*, vol 6, no 2, 1989, pp 192-206.

[Corwin and Esogbue, 1974] Corwin, B. D. and Esogbue, A. O., Two-Machine Flow-Shop Scheduling Problems with Sequence Dependent Setup Times : A Dynamic Programming Approach, *Naval Research Logistics Quarterly*, vol 21, 1974, pp 515-524.

[French, 1982] S. French, *Sequencing and Scheduling: An Introduction to the Mathematics of the Job-Shop*, Ellis Horwood Ltd, 1982.

[Gupta and Darrow, 1985] J. N. D. Gupta and W. P. Darrow, Approximate Schedules for Two-Machine Flow-Shop With Sequence Dependent Setup Times, *Indian Journal of Management and Systems*, vol 1, no 1, 1985, pp 6-11.

[Johnson, 1954] S. M. Johnson, Optimal Two-and-Three-Stage Production Schedules With Setup Times Included, *Naval Research Logistics Quarterly*, vol 1, 1954, pp 61-68.

[Korf, 1985] R. E. Korf, Depth-First Iterative Deepening: An Optimal Admissible Search, *Artificial Intelligence*, vol 27, no 1, 1985, pp 97-109.

[Lageweg *et al.*, 1978] B. J. Lageweg, J. K. Lenstra and A. H. G. Rinnooy Kan, A General Bounding Scheme for the Permutation Flow-Shop Problem, *Operations Research*, vol 26, no 1, 1978, pp 53-67.

[Lawler *et al.*, 1982] E. L. Lawler, J. K. Lenstra and A. H. G. Rinnooy Kan, Recent Developments in Deterministic Sequencing and Scheduling: A Survey, in *Deterministic and Stochastic Scheduling* (Eds. M. A. H. Dempster, J. K. Lenstra and A. H. G. Rinnooy Kan), D Reidel Publishing Co., 1982.

[Nilsson, 1980] N. J. Nilsson, *Principles of Artificial Intelligence*, Tioga-Springer Verlag, 1980.

[Pearl, 1984] J. Pearl, *Heuristics*, Addison-Wesley, 1984.

[Rinnooy Kan *et al.*, 1975] A. H. G. Rinnooy Kan, B. J. Lageweg and J. K. Lenstra, Minimizing Total Costs in One Machine Scheduling, *Operations Research*, vol 23, no 5, 1975, pp 908-927.

[Schild and Fredman, 1963] A. Schild and I. J. Fredman, Scheduling Tasks with Deadlines and Non-linear Loss Functions, *Management Science*, vol 9, 1963, pp 73-81.

[Sen and Bagchi, 1989] Anup K. Sen and A. Bagchi, Fast Recursive Formulations for Best-First Search That Allow Controlled Use of Memory, *Proc. IJCAI-89*, International Joint Conference on Artificial Intelligence, Detroit, U.S.A., 1989, pp 297-302.

[Sule, 1982] Sule, D. R., Sequencing n Jobs on Two Machines with Setup, Processing and Removal Times, *Naval Research Logistics Quarterly*, vol 29, no 3, 1982, pp 517-519.

[Townsend, 1978] W. Townsend, The Single Machine Problem With Quadratic Penalty Function of Completion Times : A Branch and Bound Solution, *Management Science*, vol 24, no 5, pp 530-534.

[Viswanathan and Bagchi, 1988] K. V. Viswanathan and A. Bagchi, An Exact Best-First Search Procedure for the Constrained Rectangular Guillotine Knapsack Problem, *Proc. AAAI-88*, American Association for Artificial Intelligence, St. Paul, U.S.A., 1988, pp 145-149.

Learning Admissible Heuristics while Solving Problems

Anna Bramanti-Gregor and Henry W. Davis
Department of Computer Science
Wright State University, Dayton Ohio 45435

Abstract

A method is presented that causes A^* to return high quality solutions while solving a set of problems using a non-admissible heuristic. The heuristic guiding the search changes as new information is learned during the search, and it converges to an admissible heuristic which 'contains the insight' of the original non-admissible one. After a finite number of problems, A^* returns only optimal solutions.

Experiments on sliding tile problems suggest that learning occurs very fast. Beginning with hundreds of randomly generated problems and an overestimating heuristic, the system learned sufficiently fast that only the first problem was solved non-optimally. As an application we show how one may construct heuristics for finding high quality solutions at lower cost than those returned by A^* using available admissible heuristics.

1 Introduction

A problem with A^* is that it often gives low quality solutions when its heuristic overestimates[1]. Optimal or near-optimal solutions are often desired and a strong underestimating heuristic is not always available. In [Davis et *al.*, 1989] we describe how an admissible heuristic h_M can be derived from a non-admissible heuristic h. The potential savings in node expansions when A^* uses $g+h_M$ as an evaluator (denoted $A^*(h_M)$) is shown to be considerable when compared to previously suggested methods that attempt to find optimal solutions with non-admissible heuristics.

In this paper we extend the definition of h_M to an admissible heuristic which includes the 'collective insight' of one or more available heuristics. Using the h_M concept, we describe a method whereby, while solving a set of problems, the quality of the solutions returned by A^* can be made to steadily improve. As more problems are solved, a dynamically changing approximation to h_M, denoted Γh_M, is learned. As it is learned, Γh_M is also used to guide the search. We prove that, in a probabilistic sense, Γh_M converges to h_M, causing $A^*(\Gamma h_M)$ to be admissible after a finite number of problems have been solved.

Variations of the learning technique are described. These are chosen based on the amount of computation per problem the user wishes to invest in improving solution quality. In *constant learning* the overhead per problem is very low: a single relatively small computation. A user who is continuously using A^* in some domain may keep this type of learning active indefinitely. His system will evolve, at low cost, but slowly, towards the finding of optimal solutions. *Quadratic learning* requires more computation per problem than constant learning but Γh_M converges to h_M after solving fewer problems.

In many applications high quality satisficing solutions are more desirable than optimal ones if they can be found with low time-overhead. We propose using quadratic learning to address this problem, by turning off the learning early so that the heuristic developed can be used before it evolves any further. This technique of turning off the learning early in the problem session is called here *early learning*. The purpose is to create a heuristic which (1) causes A^* to find high quality solutions, and (2) causes A^* to expand a relatively small number of nodes.

Experiments were performed in the *8*-puzzle domain to get some empirical insight into the technique's effectiveness. We tested two available non-admissible heuristics, sometimes in combination with an admissible one. We used quadratic learning on samples of *1998* and *605* randomly generated problems. The results of two groups of experiments are described in this paper. In one group we gauged the speed of learning. It was fast: The preponderance of information learned is acquired within eight randomly chosen problems. In all but the first problem, during which much of the learning occurs, A^* always returned optimal solutions.

In the second group of experiments we attempted to measure the effectiveness of using the early learning method to build heuristics. We combined non-admissible heuristics with an admissible one; our goal was to learn a composite heuristic which would cause A^* to return high-quality solutions while expanding fewer nodes than when using the admissible heuristic alone. In one of the experiments reported below, the learned heuristic returned solution quality within 6% of optimal while reducing by half the number of nodes expanded by A^*. In another experiment the system learned a heuristic which always returned optimal solutions at a *15%* reduction in node expansion; however we cannot guarantee that the solutions returned will always be optimal. We conclude

[1] A solution has 'high quality' when the ratio of its length to the optimal solution length is close to one.

that the proposed method of building composite heuristics through learning shows promise of being useful.

2 Notation and Preliminaries

We use the following notation:

R^+	Non-negative real numbers.
G	Locally finite directed graph with arc length bounded below by a positive number.
problem	An element $(s,t) \in G x G$. s is viewed as the start and t as the goal.
$k(m,n)$	Length in G of minimum length path from m to n; ∞ if there is none.
$h^*(n)$	$k(n,t)$ where the goal t is implicit.
$H(m,n)$	heuristic estimate of $k(m,n)$. Assume $H(m,n) \in R^+$ and $H(n,n) = 0$ for all $n \in G$.
$h^t(n)$, $h(n)$	$H(n,t)$; when t is implicit we write $h(n)$. We think of t as a goal.
$g(n)$	Shortest distance yet found by A^* from start state to n.
$A^*(h^t)$, $A^*(h)$	A^* algorithm using $g + h^t$ as an evaluation function; when t is implicit, we write $A^*(h)$.
X	Number of nodes expanded by A^* on some problem.
SQ	Solution quality: ratio of length of solution returned by A^* to the optimal length.
admissible	Either $h \leq h^*$ or, equivalently, $H \leq k$. An algorithm is *admissible* if it returns optimal solutions when given solvable problems.

An example used later is the *8*-puzzle, a sliding tile problem (see, *eg.*, [Pearl, 1984] or [Nilsson, 1980]). A common admissible heuristic for it is the 'Manhattan distance': $H(m,n)$ denotes the sum over all tiles of the vertical and horizontal distance of each tile in m from its position in n. The problem of finding an optimal path connecting two *8*-puzzle states is part of a family of *NP*-hard problems [Ratner *et al.*, 1986].

If H is a heuristic, define for all $x \in R^+$:

(2.1) $MAXH(x) = \max\{H(m,n): (m,n) \in GxG, k(m,n) \leq x\}$.

For example, a simple enhancement of the Manhattan distance is obtained by adding to it a 'sequence score' term (see [Nilsson, 1980, p. 85]). Denote the enhancement H_3. $MAXH_3$ is shown in Figure 2.1. In general, $MAXH$ is a non-decreasing function. If G is finite, then it is a step function whose value at any jump-point is the higher of the two alternatives.[2]

h_M is defined in [Davis et al., 1989] and redefined here. Let H be a heuristic estimate (admissible or not) and let $h^t(n) = H(n,t)$. For all $n \in G$ define

(2.2) $h^t_M(n) = \min\{x: h^t(n) \leq MAXH(x), x \in R^+\}$.

We write $h_M(n)$, instead of $h^t_M(n)$, when context allows. Definition (2.2) and the reason why h^t_M is admissible are best understood with a picture: In Figure 2.2 we let H, and its associated h, be the enhanced Manhattan distance, discussed above. Suppose, for example, $h^t(n) = 35$. (2.2) says that, to find $h^t_M(n)$ on the x axis, project horizontally to $MAXH$ from 35 on the y-axis and then vertically to the x-axis. The resulting value, 4, is defined to be $h^t_M(n)$. $h^t_M(n) \leq h^*(n)$ because, if $h^*(n)$ were less than 4, say x_1, then there would be an $x_1 < 4$ with $MAXH(x_1) \geq 35$, contrary to the way we obtain $h^t_M(n)$. Thus h^t_M is admissible.

A note on the case when the H we start with is admissible: In this event $MAXH$ never rises above the diagonal of Figure 2.2, whence, $h^t_M \geq h^t$; *ie.*, h_M is at least as informed as h. This suggests a superiority of h_M over h because more informed admissible heuristics cause less node expansion [Nilsson, 1980]. However, usually $h_M = h$ because it is common for $MAXH(x)$ to lie on the diagonal when h is admissible. (For example, $h_M = h$ when h is the Manhattan distance.)

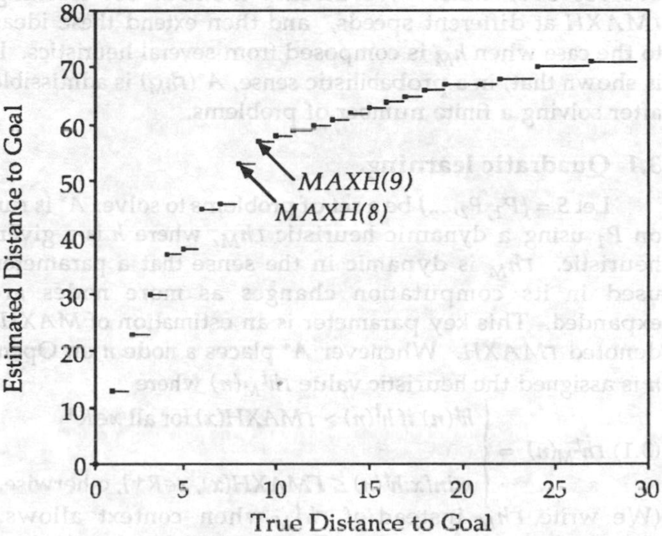

Figure 2.1. $MAXH_3$ where H_3 is the enhanced Manhattan distance. Its value at jump points is the highest of the two alternatives.

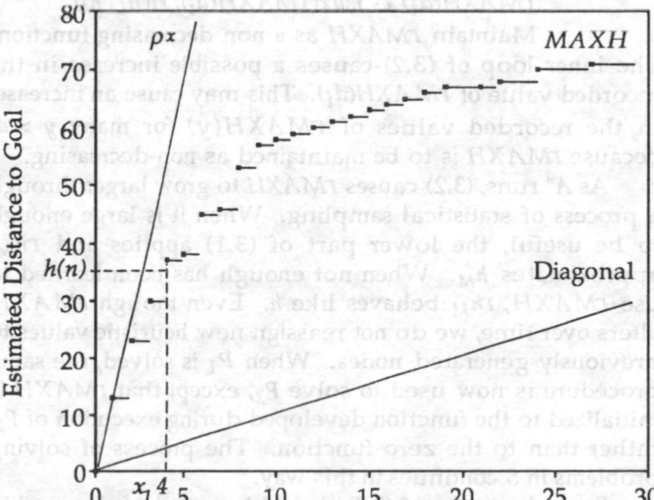

Figure 2.2. Interpretation of (2.2). See text for discussion.

[2] If G is infinite, then the 'max' operator in (2.1) and the 'min' operator in (2.2), below, should be thought of as 'supremum' and 'infimum', respectively.

Finally, we wish to extend definition (2.2) to an admissible heuristic which 'captures the insight' of several given heuristic $h_1,...,h_p$ (admissible or not). Define a heuristic $h_{(1,...,p)M}$, composed from $h_1,...,h_p$, as follows: Let h^t_{iM} be given by (2.2) and let

(2.3) $h^t_{(1,...,p)M}(n) = \max\{h^t_{1M}(n),..., h^t_{pM}(n)\}$.

$h^t_{(1,...,p)M}$ is admissible and is at least as informed as h^t_{iM}.

3 Learning and its Convergence

The critical question one asks when using h_M in (2.2) is 'how do we compute $MAXH$?' In the learning technique, statistics are collected as A^* runs enabling an approximation to $MAXH$, called $rMAXH$, to be built. This enables A^* to use an approximation to h_M, called rh_M. rh_M evolves over time. We discuss methods for learning $rMAXH$ at different speeds, and then extend these ideas to the case when h_M is composed from several heuristics. It is shown that, in a probabilistic sense, $A^*(rh_M)$ is admissible after solving a finite number of problems.

3.1 Quadratic learning.

Let $S = \{P_1, P_2, ...\}$ be a set of problems to solve. A^* is run on P_1 using a dynamic heuristic rh_M, where h is a given heuristic. rh_M is dynamic in the sense that a parameter used in its computation changes as more nodes are expanded. This key parameter is an estimation of $MAXH$, denoted $rMAXH$. Whenever A^* places a node n on Open, n is assigned the heuristic value $rh^t_M(n)$ where

$$(3.1)\quad rh^t_M(n) = \begin{cases} h^t(n) \text{ if } h^t(n) > rMAXH(x) \text{ for all } x\in R^+ \\ \min\{x: h^t(n) \leq rMAXH(x),\ x\in R^+\}, \text{ otherwise.} \end{cases}$$

(We write rh_M instead of rh^t_M when context allows.) $rMAXH$ is a non-decreasing function initialized to the zero function. It is updated as follows: suppose node n has just been selected from Open by A^* and let $s= n_o, n_1, ..., n_{j+1}=n$ be the search tree path from s to n . Execute

(3.2) *For* $i = 0, 1, ..., j$ DO

$d_i \leftarrow g(n) - g(n_i)$

$rMAXH(d_i) \leftarrow max(rMAXH(d_i), H(n_i , n))$

Maintain $rMAXH$ as a non-decreasing function

The inner loop of (3.2) causes a possible increase in the recorded value of $rMAXH(d_i)$. This may cause an increase in the recorded values of $rMAXH(y)$ for many $y > d_i$ because $rMAXH$ is to be maintained as non-decreasing.

As A^* runs, (3.2) causes $rMAXH$ to grow larger through a process of statistical sampling. When it is large enough to be useful, the lower part of (3.1) applies and rh_M approximates h_M. When not enough has been learned to use $rMAXH$, rh_M behaves like h. Even though $rMAXH$ alters over time, we do not reassign new heuristic values to previously generated nodes. When P_1 is solved, the same procedure is now used to solve P_2, except that $rMAXH$ is initialized to the function developed during execution of P_1, rather than to the zero function. The process of solving problems in S continues in this way.

Several aspects of (3.2) should be noted. It is possible that $d_i > k(n_i,n)$ because the search tree path to n may not be optimal. Also $H(n_i,n)$ may not equal its maximum value for nodes separated by optimal paths of length $k(n_i,n)$. Both of these events contribute to make

(3.3) $rMAXH(x) \leq MAXH(x)$ for all $x\in R^+$

This, in turn, causes

(3.4) $rh^t_M(n) \geq h^t_M(n)$ for all $n, t \in G$,

when $rMAXH$ has grown sufficiently large that the lower part of (3.1) is applicable.

The idea of the technique is that, as more is learned during problem solving, $rMAXH$ increases to $MAXH$, rh_M decreases to h_M, and $A^*(rh_M)$ returns solutions of increasingly better quality while rh_M converges to an admissible heuristic. The number of nodes expanded by $A^*(rh_M)$ on the other hand increases when compared with those expanded by A* using the unacceptable heuristic h. (This is because admissible heuristics, such as h_M, force more breadth into the search.) One could turn off this learning process when the time-quality tradeoff is acceptable, and hold the current $rMAXH$ fixed. The turn-off point is determined by pragmatics because we cannot say with certainty how close the algorithm is to convergence at any time.[3]

Let X be the number of nodes expanded by $A^*(rh_M)$ in some problem. We call the procedure of (3.2) *quadratic learning* because the amount of time per problem directly spent in learning $rMAXH$ is $O(X^2)$. To see this, notice that (3.2) is executed $X + 1$ times and, at each execution, $rMAXH$ is updated at most X times (*ie.*, $j \leq X$). The space needs of learning are small: an array whose size approximates the diameter of G to hold $rMAXH$ when arc lengths are unit.

3.2 Reducing the time overhead of learning.

Linear learning differs from quadratic learning in that it takes fewer statistics per problem to learn $rMAXH$: When a node n is selected from Open we do not sample the search tree path to n, as in (3.2), but instead take a single sample:

(3.5) $rMAXH(g(n)) \leftarrow \max(rMAXH(g(n), H(s,n))$

maintain $rMAXH$ as a non-decreasing function

This is called 'linear' because the direct overhead of learning is $O(X)$ per problem. It has the virtue that it may be kept active over a long period with substantially less time overhead than in the quadratic case.

The advantage of linear learning is accentuated by *constant learning*. In this only one statistic per problem is taken while learning $rMAXH$: Namely, (3.5) is performed only if n is a goal. The direct time overhead of learning on each problem is now a constant which is independent of the problem size. This kind of learning may be kept active indefinitely with only a very low time overhead.[4]

3.3 Learning a composite of several heuristics.

Suppose, for example, we are given h_1, h_2 and we wish

[3] Several experiments with this 'early learning' technique are described in Section 4.3.

[4] In practice, constant learning should be preceded by several runs using quadratic learning. Otherwise it may be a long time before $rMAXH(x)$ is non-zero for low values of x. Learning credible values for these low x at an early time greatly enhances performance.

to form the approximation $rh_{(1,2)M}$ which should converge to $h_{(1,2)M}$. A direct way to proceed is as follows: In the gathering of statistics (as described in (3.2) or (3.5)), both $rMAXH_i$, $i = 1, 2$, are updated; use the $rMAXH_i$ so obtained to define rh^t_{iM} by (3.1); finally, in analogy with (2.3), set

(3.6) $\quad rh^t_{(1,2)M}(n) = \max\{rh^t_{1M}(n), rh^t_{2M}(n)\}$, for all $n \in G$.

In analogy with (3.4), one has, when both $rMAXH_i$ have grown sufficiently, that

$$rh^t_{(1,2)M}(n) \geq h^t_{(1,2)M}(n) \quad \text{for all } n,t \in G.$$

The technique extends to more than two heuristics in an obvious way.

If one of the h_i, say h_1, is already admissible, one could use a variant of (3.6) obtained by replacing rh^t_{1M} with h^t_1. As pointed out in Section 2, this substitution is equivalent to using h^t_{1M} when $MAXH_1$ has its values on the 'diagonal'. Convergence of A^* to an admissible algorithm is faster in this case.[5]

3.4 A probabilistic Learning Theorem.

Will the learning described above eventually cause only optimal solutions to be found? The theorem below shows that, in a probabilistic sense, the answer is 'yes'. Proof is in the appendix.

Theorem 3.1 (Probabilistic Learning Theorem). Assume G is finite and that $P_1, P_2, \ldots$ are randomly, and independently, generated problems from $G \times G$. Assume $A^*(rh_M)$ is using any one of the learning techniques described above. With probability 1, there exists i such that after $P_1, \ldots, P_i$ are solved we have: $\quad rh^t_M = h^t_M \quad$ for all $t \in G$.

Hence, $A^*(rh_M)$ is admissible from some point on.

4. Experiments with Quadratic Learning

The effectiveness of learning may vary with the problem domain. To get some idea of what to expect, we conducted experiments in the *8*-puzzle using the quadratic learning method. We used the Manhattan distance, h_2, along with two non-admissible heuristics: h_3, the enhanced Manhattan distance, and h_4. Briefly, h_4 adds to h_2 weighted row-column and diagonal terms: the former counts the number of interchanged tile pairs which are in the proper row or column; the latter counts the number of tiles that are diagonally displaced and are blocked by in-place tiles. While h_3 almost always overestimates and seldom finds optimal solutions, h_4 normally under-estimates and usually, but not always, finds optimal solutions.[6]

Our experiments were with rh_{3M}, rh_{4M}, $rh_{(2,3)M}$ and $rh_{(2,4)M}$. We had two sample sets: the first consisted of *1998* randomly generated problems, and the second consisted of the initial *605* problems of the first. We sometimes reordered them to study how this affected experimental results.

4.1 Speed of Learning

We cannot know when the true $MAXH$ has been learned because we do not know its value. However we can get an assesment of learning speed in the following way: Generate a large sample of random problems and record $rMAXH$ when $A^*(rh_M)$ is through solving the set of problems; now compare this $rMAXH$ with the $rMAXH$ which was learned at various 'snapshot points' during the problem solving session. This will show us how quickly the learning procedure acquired its final version of $rMAXH$.

In the *8*-puzzle, learning occurs quickly. For example, Figure 4.1 shows snapshots of how much $A^*(rh_{3M})$ learns while solving a set of *1998* randomly generated problems. After one problem $rMAXH$ has been learned for distances *1* to *8* and after *8* problems through distance *17*. Furthermore, at this point its knowledge of $rMAXH$ for the remaining distances is within *6%* of its final values. It acquired no more knowledge after executing *1331* problems.

The pattern of Figure 4.1 was consistently observed: When the problems are randomly sorted, the vast amount of learning occurs within *8* problems. One could speed the learning process up by putting hard problems (*ie.*, large start-goal distances) at the beginning and slow it down by putting easy ones first.[7]

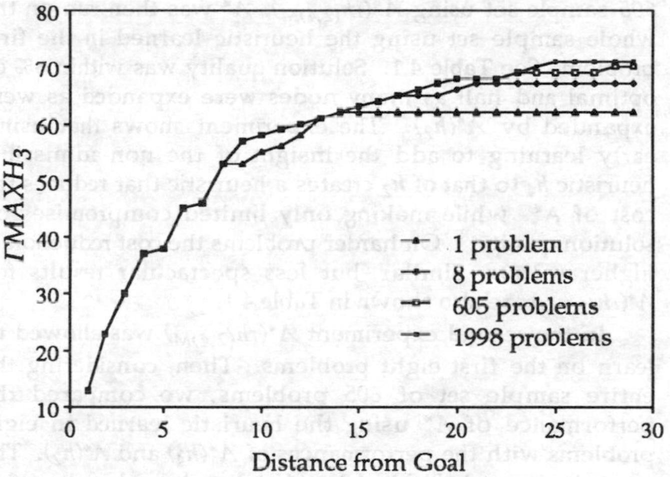

Figure 4.1. Extent to which $rMAXH_3$ is learned after *1*, *8*, *605*, and *1998* problems. Most information is learned after *8* problems. Quadratic learning is being performed during searches by $A^*(rh_{3M})$.

4.2 Solution Quality while Learning: Observation and Theory

We observed high solution quality while learning on randomly sorted problems sets: In our experiments A^* returned an optimal solution in all but the first problem. This could not be guaranteed and surprised us. When the problems are arranged with the easy ones first, we observed that A^* returned several non-optimal solutions.

In the proof of the learning theorem (see appendix) it is brought out that we may expect $MAXH(x)$ to be learned

[5] If $MAXH_1$ is not diagonal, then the heuristic converged to, while admissible, is not the same as $h_{(1,2)M}$ and may be weaker. See discussion in Section 2.

[6] h_4 is a variation of a heuristic discovered semi-automatically by Politowski [1986].

[7] In the experiments reported here the problems are randomly sorted and the first has start-goal distance of *19*. This is considered a relatively easy problem because in the *8*-puzzle the mean optimal distance between states is 22.

first for low values of x and then for higher values. This is the pattern shown in Figure 4.1 by the four successive snapshots of the knowledge acquired. Of course we don't know with certainty whether or not the true $MAXH(x)$ is learned. When it is learned for all $x \leq x_o$, say, then, according to the appendix, $A^*(rh_M)$ returns optimal solutions for all problems whose start-goal distance is less or equal to x_o. The observed behavior of $A^*(rh_M)$ suggests that the learned $MAXH$ may, in fact, be correct.

4.3 Early learning to build a composite heuristic

Suppose that, during a problem solving session with $A^*(rh_M)$, we stop the learning before all problems are solved. The heuristic which has evolved up to this turn-off point is said to have been acquired by *early learning*. Experiments were conducted to see how effectively early learning could be used to build a composite heuristic from two others. Our general finding is that, by early learning, the composite heuristic acquired is often one which produces high quality solutions at low cost. Cost is measured as number of nodes expanded per problem. We give two examples below.

Learning was allowed on only the first problem of the *605* sample set using $A^*(rh_{(2,4)M})$. A^* was then run on the whole sample set using the heuristic learned in the first problem. See Table 4.1. Solution quality was within 6% of optimal and half as many nodes were expanded as were expanded by $A^*(h_2)$. The experiment shows that using early learning to add the insight of the non-admissible heuristic h_4 to that of h_2 creates a heuristic that reduces the cost of A* while making only limited compromises on solution quality.[8] On harder problems the cost reduction is higher (72%). Similar, but less spectacular results for $A^*(rh_{(2,3)M})$ are also shown in Table 4.1.

In the second experiment $A^*(rh_{(2,4)M})$ was allowed to learn on the first eight problems. Then, considering the entire sample set of 605 problems, we compared the performance of A^* using the heuristic learned in eight problems with the performances of $A^*(h_4)$ and $A^*(h_2)$. The result is shown in Table 4.2. $A^*(rh_{(2,4)M})$ produced perfect solution quality and expanded substantially fewer nodes then did the other algorithms: *15%* fewer than $A^*(h_2)$ and *48%* fewer than $A^*(h_4)$, with even better performance on the hard problems.[9]

Once the learning process is turned off, the use of $rh_{(2,4)M}$ requires only a little more time per node then the sum of that required to evaluate both h_2 and h_4; the extra time is for lookups into two tables of size bounded by the diameter of the graph, and a miximizing process. The resulting heuristic causes high quality solutions and relatively low node expansion count. In a general setting, the use of a composite heuristic like $rh_{(2,4)M}$ is justified if the computational time for evaluating both h_2 and h_4 is sufficiently low.

No. of problems		average performance $A^*(rh_{(2,3)M})$ SQ	X	$\%X_2$	$A^*(rh_{(2,4)M})$ SQ	X	$\%X_2$
easy (1-20)	187	1.02	170	96	1.03	152	86
med (21-25)	346	1.05	645	79	1.07	496	61
hard (26-29)	72	1.04	1236	51	1.07	679	28
All (1-29)	605	1.04	569	70	1.06	411	51

Table 4.1 Performance comparison of $A^*(rh_{(2,3)M})$ and $A^*(rh_{(2,4)M})$ with $A^*(h_2)$. Early learning has occurred on one randomly chosen problem. Its start goal distance was *19*. X denotes number of nodes expanded. *SQ* is solution quality (defined in Section 2) and is *1.00* for $A^*(h_2)$.

No. of problems		average performance $A^*(r_8h_{(2,4)M})$ SQ	X	$\%X_2$	X_4
easy (1-20)	187	1.00	154	87	56
med (21-25)	346	1.00	704	86	54
hard (26-29)	72	1.00	2012	83	48
All (1-29)	605	(*)1.00	690	85	52

Table 4.2 Performance comparison of $A^*(r_8h_{(2,4)M})$ with $A^*(h_2)$ and $A^*(h_4)$. Note (*): All solutions found were optimal but there is no guarantee that this will always happen. Early learning has pccurred on *8* problems.

No. of problems		average performance $A^*(h_2)$ SQ	X2	$A^*(h_3)$ SQ	X3	$A^*(h_4)$ SQ	X4
easy (1-20)	187	1.00	178	1.22	104	1.00	277
med (21-25)	346	1.00	818	1.24	166	1.00	1312
hard (26-29)	72	1.00	2427	1.20	208	1.00	4187
All (1-29)	605	1.00	812	1.22	152	(*)1.00	1334

Table 4.3. Performances of $A^*(h_2)$, $A^*(h_3)$ and $A^*(h_4)$ are given for comparison with previous data. h4 causes strong solution quality but poor time complexity. The opposite is true of h3. The text assumes that the solution quality of $A^*(h_3)$ is unacceptable. Note (*): All but *10* solutions were optimal; *1.00* results from averaging to two decimal places.

5. Conclusion

It is possible to find optimal solutions with a non-admissible heuristic h by letting A^* use $g + h_M$ as an evaluator, where h_M is an admissible heuristic associated with h; h_M contains much of the 'insight' that h has. There is a difficulty in calculating h_M because it is based on an upper bound function for h which is hard to access.

We have described a technique for solving a set of problems using $A^*(rh_M)$, where rh_M is a dynamically changing approximation of h_M. As problems are solved, statistics are gathered enabling rh_M to evolve from h to h_M. In the process, A^* returns solutions of increasingly better quality. We proved that, in a probabilistic sense, rh_M converges to h_M, causing $A^*(rh_M)$ to be admissible after a finite number of problems have been solved.

The above ideas extend to the case in which, instead of

[8] A^* using h_4 alone expands many more nodes than does $A^*(h_2)$. See Table 4.3.

[9] As h_4 is usually optimistic it is tempting to combine h_2 and h_4 by forming the heuristic $h_{24} = max(h_2, h_4)$. One could then compare the performance of A^* using h_{24} with that of $A^*(rh_{(2,4)M})$. But it turns out that one always has $h_4 \geq h_2$ so $h_{24} = h_4$. Thus there is no need to consider $A^*(h_{24})$.

a single heuristic h, one starts with a finite set of heuristics, say $h_1,...,h_p$. The admissible heuristic, h_M, to which we now have convergence, is a composite of $h_1,...,h_p$ (and contains their 'collective insight').

To gain some empirical understanding of this type of learning we performed experiments in the 8-puzzle domain using a variation of our technique called 'quadratic learning'. Learned information was acquired surprisingly quickly. The preponderance of information acquired in many hundreds of random problems was actually learned after solving only eight of them. Although we always started with an overestimating heuristic, the system learned so fast that all but the first problem were solved optimally.

In another experiment, we used 'early learning' to combine an admissible heuristic with a non-admissible one. The goal was to create a heuristic which caused A^* to expand significantly fewer nodes than when it used the admissible heuristic alone; but nevertheless we wanted A^* to yield high quality satisficing solutions. We were able to achieve this. In one case, for example, we obtained a reduction in node count of nearly half while only losing 6% in solution quality.

Our results show that it can be fruitful, while solving problems, to learn the statistical properties of the heuristic guiding the search. Knowledge of these properties may then be used to alter the heuristic itself, bestowing it with traits suitable to the application need. Moreover altering the heuristic can be done while the search is ongoing.

Appendix. Proof of Theorem 3.1

We give the argument for constant learning. This implies the linear and quadratic case because these learn at least as much in each problem as constant learning. For notational simplicity we do not consider the combined heuristic case of Section 3.3. The argument in that case is similar.

Let $[a,b]$, $[a,b)$ denote $\{x: x \in R^+, a \le x \le b\}$ and $\{x: x \in R^+, a \le x < b\}$ respectively. The theorem follows from the two lemmas below. We omit the proof of Lemma A.1, as it is clear.

Lemma A.1. Suppose $u > 0$ and that at the end of some initial finite sequence of problems we have $rMAXH(x)= MAXH(x)$ for all $x \in [0, u]$. Then in any future problem (s,t) we have

$$rh^t_M(n) = h^t_M(n) \qquad \text{whenever } n \in G \text{ and } k(n,t) \le u.$$

Lemma A.2. Let $w_1 < w_2 < ... < w_p$ be the discontinuity points of $MAXH$. Let $w_o=0$ and let $w_{p+1} \ge w_p$ be the length of the largest optimal path in G. Then given any $j \in \{0,1,...,p+1\}$ there exists, with probability 1, some i such that after $P_1,...,P_i$ are solved by $A^*(rh_M)$ we have for all future problems that

(A.1) $rMAXH(x) = MAXH(x)$ whenever $x \in [0,w_j]$

Proof: Figure A.1 illustrates the situation. We use induction on j. If $j = 0$, then (A.1) is clear. Assume (A.1) is true for $j = k-1$. We must show it is true for $j = k$. Suppose the truth of (A.1) in the $j = k-1$ case occurs after $P_1,...,P_{i1}$ have been solved.

If $u > w_{k-1}$ and $MAXH(u) = MAXH(w_{k-1})$ then (A.1) holds with w_j replaced by u; this is because both $rMAXH$ and $MAXH$ are non-decreasing, they agree at w_{k-1}, and $rMAXH \le MAXH$. If $k-1 = p$ and w_{p+1} is not a discontinuity point (it is not in Figure A.1), then we are done. Assume that w_k is a discontinuity point. Then, after solving $P_1,...,P_{i1}$,we have that for all future problems

(1) $rMAXH(x) = MAXH(x)$ *for all* $x \in [0,w_k)$

We must show that, after solving more problems, the truth of (1) extends to w_k.

Let $(s,t) \in GxG$ satisfy $k(s,t) = w_k$ and be such that $H(s,t)$ is the largest number in $\{H(m,n): m, n \in G, k(m,n) = w_k\}$. As the problems P_j are chosen randomly and independently from GxG, the probability of (s,t) never being chosen after $P_1,...,P_{i1}$ is zero. Thus, with probability 1, there is some $i > i_1$ such that $P_i = (s,t)$. We shall show that after solving P_i we have

(2) $rMAXH(x) = MAXH(x)$ for all $x \in [0,w_k]$.

This will complete the induction and establish the lemma.

Let $s= n_o,n_1,...,n_q = t$ be an optimal path for P_i. In lemma A.1 set $u = k(n_1,t)$ to conclude that rh^t_M is optimistic on all the nodes $n_1,...,n_q$ during the solution of P_i, because of (1). After the first iteration of $A^*(rh^t_M)$, when n_o is removed from Open, there will be a least r, $1 \le r \le q$, such that $n_r \in$ Open. For this node, $g(n_r)+rh^t(n_r) \le w_k$, since $n_o,...,n_q$ is an optimal path. It follows that $A^*(rh^t_M)$, selects from Open, upon halting, an optimal goal for P_i; that is, one whose g-value is w_k. At this point, the constant learning procedure correctly updates $rMAXH(w_k)$ so that (2) holds. Δ

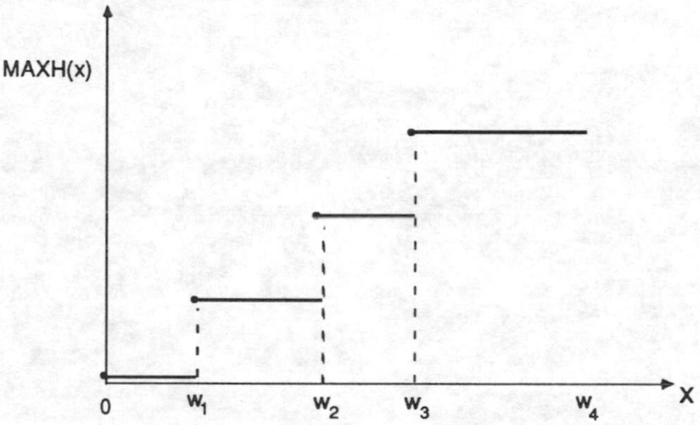

Figure A.1. Possible graph of $MAXH$: $p = 3$, $w_4 > w_3$. In this case w_4 is not a discontinuity point but, in general, it might be.

References

[Davis *et al.*, 1989] Davis H.W., Bramanti-Gregor A., and Chen X., Towards finding optimal solutions with non-admissible heuristics: a new technique, *Proceedings of the 11th International Joint Conference on Artificial Intelligence*, 303-308, 1989.

[Nilsson, 1980] Nilsson N.J., *Principle of Artificial Intelligence*, Tioga Publishing Co., Palo Alto, Ca., 1980.

[Politowski, 1986] Politowski G., *On the Construction of Heuristic Functions*, Ph.D. Thesis, University of California, Santa Barbara, 1986.

[Ratner *et al.*, 1986] Ratner D. and Warmuth M., Finding a shortest solution for the NxN extension of the 15-puzzle is intractable, *Proceedings of the 5th National Conference on AI* (1986) 168-172.

AUTOMATED REASONING

Search II

Using Aspiration Windows for Minimax Algorithms

Reza Shams *
Alcatel-ELIN
Forschungszentrum
Ruthnerg. 1-7, A–1210 Wien
Austria

Hermann Kaindl
SIEMENS AG Österreich
Gudrunstraße 11
A–1101 Wien
Austria

Helmut Horacek
Universität Bielefeld
Postfach 8640
D-4800 Bielefeld 1
Germany

Abstract

This paper is based on investigations of several algorithms for computing exact minimax values of game trees (utilizing backward pruning). Especially, the focus is on trees with an ordering similar to that we have actually found in game playing practice. We compare the algorithms using two different distributions of the static values, the uniform distribution and a distribution estimated from practical data. Moreover, this is the first systematic comparison of using aspiration windows for all of the usual minimax algorithms. We analyse the effects of aspiration windows of varying size and position.

The use of an *aspiration window* not only makes *alpha-beta search* competitive, but there also exists previously unpublished dependencies of its effects upon certain properties of the trees. In general, the more recently developed algorithms with exponential space complexity are not to be recommended for game-playing practice, since their advantage in having to visit fewer nodes is more than outweighed under practical conditions by their enormous space requirements. Finally, we propose a method for an analytic determination of estimates of the *optimal window size*, presupposing evidence about some characteristic properties of the domain of application. In summary, we discovered and found empirical evidence for several effects unpredicted by theoretical studies.

1. Introduction and Background

For long, the only known method for computing the exact *minimax value* of a *game tree* without generating this tree in its entirety was the so-called *alpha-beta algorithm* (for a description and historical review see for instance [Knuth & Moore 75]). In the meantime, several other pruning algorithms have been found. A short review and references will be given in Section 2, and more elaborate descriptions can be found for instance in [Kaindl 90] and in the cited references.

Naturally the question arises which is the most efficient algorithm (more precisely, under which conditions). For some of these algorithms there exists exact formulae for the expected number of terminal positions on certain game trees (random trees with uniform branching degree and distinct terminal values) [Pearl 84]. These render alpha-beta (in its pure form) clearly less efficient than its competitors. However, for trees of the kind occurring in real games the situation is not this clear: [Marsland & Campbell 82] defined *strongly ordered* trees, in which 70% of the time the first branch from each node is best. [Campbell & Marsland 83] and [Marsland *et al.* 87] investigated different tree ordering types using a form of Monte Carlo simulation.

With respect to issues of relative efficiency, such criteria seem to be a promising attempt to model the actual conditions occurring in computer game playing. Therefore, we actually gathered such data (among others) with the chess program MERLIN[1]. The statistics compiled from 438 move decisions (most of them under tournament conditions) showed a mean value of 90.3% (with a standard deviation of 8.2%) for the relative frequency of the first branch from each node being "best" (more such statistics can be found in [Kaindl 88]). Since we were mainly interested in a comparison using parameters which reflect best the practical conditions occurring in real game playing, we choose to investigate very strongly ordered trees.

Comprehensive experiments under such conditions showed some interesting results (see [Kaindl *et al.* 89]). As a main result, alpha-beta (in its pure form) is also less efficient than its competitors on ordered trees, although it profits most from an increased ordering of the trees. In practice, however, many enhancements to alpha-beta are used (see [Schaeffer 86, 89] for a comprehensive set of experiments comparing their performance in the domain

* The contribution of this author was performed as "Diplomarbeit" supervised by the second author (comparable to a Master's thesis) before joining Alcatel-ELIN Forschungszentrum. It was supported by SIEMENS AG Österreich, especially in providing facilities.

[1] MERLIN is a collaborate effort of the second and the third author together with Marcus Wagner. It played some major computer tournaments, for instance it tied for 10th out of 22 participants at the World Computer Chess Championship in 1983, and for 6th out of 24 participants at the World Computer Chess Championship in 1989.

of computer chess). While most of these enhancements just serve the purpose of achieving improved ordering, it is also common practice to use an *aspiration window* for alpha-beta, but to our best knowledge there is no published account of the effects of varying window size. Note, that alpha-beta was only compared in its pure form (in particular without such windows) in the previous theoretical studies. Our comparisons gave a strong indication of its improvements using such a window, which made it fully competitive to the newer algorithms. While this enhancement is often used for improving alpha-beta, we are not aware of a published comparison of the effects of using windows for the other algorithms. Hence, we found it interesting to compare "all" the minimax search algorithms using such a window.

Moreover, we had serious doubt that in practice all the possible values are equally likely resulting from the static evaluator, as usually assumed in theoretical studies. Therefore, we became interested in the effects of using a distribution of the values estimated from practical data, compared to having them equally distributed. The question is, how the simplifying assumption of uniform distribution affects the results.

Since using an aspiration window always bears the danger of having to repeat the search (*re-search*), in case the minimax value is outside the window, the effort for computing it may even become greater than that when using no window at all. While the techniques of estimating the positioning of such a window are quite developed, its *size* is only determined by experienced guessing. Hence, we present the first method for an analytic determination of estimates of the optimal window size.

2. Algorithms Compared

Like alpha-beta (AB), the newer algorithms SCOUT [Pearl 80] and *palphabeta* [Fishburn & Finkel 80] have linear space requirements. These have similar average performance [Musczycka & Shinghal 85]. In our experiments, we actually used a slightly improved variant called *negascout* (NS) [Reinefeld 83]. SSS* [Stockman 79] and DUAL* [Marsland *et al.* 87] are *best-first* search algorithms and consequently have exponential space requirements.

Enhancements to NS have led to INS (*informed* NS), which saves information for the case that subtrees must be re-searched [Marsland *et al.* 87]. Hence, INS has storage requirements comparable to SSS* or DUAL* (see also [Schaeffer 86]). These enhancements have similar effects as the use of the usual hash tables in game playing programs.

AB is normally used in practice in its refined version *aspiration alpha-beta* (AAB). Usually, game playing programs can estimate the minimax value quite accurately to lie within a certain range, even before the search is done. (This ability is strongly related to the use of *iterative deepening* in most programs: searching the tree successively deeper and deeper, see e.g. [Korf 85].) This range is usually called the *aspiration window*, and its bounds are used as an (artificial) initialisation of the parameters α and β at the root. Quite similarly to NS, a re-search with modified parameters is necessary, when the actual minimax value is not inside this window.

More precisely, a slightly modified version of the alpha-beta algorithm is used in this context today which was proposed by [Fishburn & Finkel 80]. In case the minimax value is outside the original window, it can provide tighter bounds for the re-search. Hence, they called it "Fail-soft Alpha-Beta" (abbreviated here by FAB). More details on this can be found in [Marsland & Campbell 82]. However, we could not find any quantitative data on the savings compared to the original version of aspiration alpha-beta which is *not* utilizing the advantages of FAB. (This version we call OLDAAB here.)

In the following we generalize the method of using a window for all the given algorithms. The use of an aspiration window for NS and INS is analogous to that for AB. We call these algorithms ANS and AINS. However, for the corresponding versions of SSS* and DUAL*, ASSS* and ADUAL*, the window is useful only from *one* side, by initialising their internal bound with the upper or the lower bound of the window, respectively. When the minimax value is inside the window, this is obvious from their way of handling their internal bound. Of course, when the value of the second bound of the window is reached or exceeded, stopping the search is possible according to [Campbell & Marsland 83] and [Reinefeld 89]. However, when the exact minimax value has to be determined this is not to be recommended. A re-search with the new bound would have to be done, in effect wasting resources by searching again parts of the tree whose results would be available when continuing the stopped search. Therefore, ASSS* and ADUAL* cannot utilize their second bound, and they should not be hindered by it. A pseudo-code formulation of the key part of ASSS* looks like the following:

```
Value := SSS*(Position, b);
if Value = b then
    Value := SSS*(Position, +∞);
end if;
```

Analogously, the key part of ADUAL* can be formulated as follows:

```
Value := DUAL*(Position, a);
if Value = a then
    Value := DUAL*(Position, -∞);
end if;
```

3. Experiment Design

As usual for mathematical analysis as well as simulation studies, the standard model of a *uniform* game tree of width w and depth d has been used. In our experiments, we kept w fixed ($w = 5$) while varying d from 3 to 9.

Since the approach of generating such trees proposed and used by [Schaeffer 86] requires only $O(wd)$

storage, we have also adopted it for our experiments. It works on the principle of deriving the value of a subtree from information available at its parent node. A minimax value is chosen and used with the specified ordering criteria to build a tree from the root down. The ordering parameters can be specified here in the form of w weights reflecting the chance that each of the w moves from any node will lead to a subtree having the minimax value of this node. A more detailed description can also be found in [Marsland *et al.* 87].

While we have made some few experiments with *random* trees (*independent and identically distributed*, see [Pearl 84]), our emphasis was on *very* strongly ordered trees. For the chance of the first branch being best we chose the values 70%, 80%, and 90%. Since the effect of the ordering of the remaining moves appears to be largely negligible [Kaindl *et al.* 89], we assumed them to have equal chance of being best.

Let the distribution function $F_X(x) = P(X \leq x)$ characterise the random variable X ranging over the same interval as the static evaluation function $f(n)$. The probability $p = P(X = x)$ for node n is the probability of the event that $f(n)$ returns x. $F_X(x)$ has been assumed to be uniform (as usual) and alternatively estimated from practical data of a chess program. The compiled statistics revealed that the static values around 0 occured very frequently. For this reason, a normal distribution could not fit these data well (according to statistical tests). Hence, we defined a distribution function $F_{X_1}(x)$ approximating our data as an estimate of $F_X(x)$ (see [Shams 90]). It seems that the exact shape of the distribution function is not really important for the results of the simulation runs, only the values around 0 must have a significantly higher probability.

Several different *window sizes* were chosen in our experiments: 1, 79, 159, 239, 319, 399, 479, and 639 values *inside* the window, out of the range −999...999. (This corresponds to 0.05%, 4%, 8%, 12%, 16%, 20%, 24% and 32% of the total value range.) The window containing 1 value has been called *narrow window* by [Marsland *et al.* 87] and is of special interest, because it is the smallest window possible for a successful search. The *window position* has been chosen uniformly over the whole range. In case the minimax value is outside the window, we have performed additional experiments, in which it was more likely that the window position is "closer" to the minimax value (a more realistic assumption).

In these experiments, 20 simulations were done for the case, that the minimax value MM is inside the window (a, b), and 20 in case it is outside. This means 10 simulations with $MM \leq a$, and 10 with $MM \geq b$. In both of these cases AAB, ANS and AINS perform a re-search in the sense of "failing low" and "failing high", respectively. However, ASSS* only re-searches if $MM \geq b$ and ADUAL* does so if $MM \leq a$. The overall performance figure is gained by weighting the data according to the frequency observed in practice (see below).

Generally, every stochastic event has been simulated by a call to a *pseudo-random number generator*, parameterized independently of the relative frequencies achieved earlier in the tree generation process. While the *seed* for the random number generator was different for each of the generated trees, each of the algorithms searched the same trees, of course. As a measure of performance we selected the *number of bottom positions* (NBP), as usual. It is known, that some of the algorithms (SSS* and DUAL*) have more overhead than others (AB, NS and INS) [Marsland *et al.* 87]. However, whether this is significant (in the sense of running time) depends strongly on the cost of going from one node to another and evaluating terminal nodes in the domain of application, as well as the encodings. In particular, the running times of SSS* and DUAL* in the simulations are significantly larger than those of AB, NS and INS. The situation is atypical, however, since in the simulations just calls to a random number generator are performed instead of real operations, which are usually more expensive.

The empirical data have been prepared in illustrative figures. Of course, only a very limited selection of these can be presented here. A comprehensive set is available, however, in [Shams 90].

4. Results of Using Aspiration Windows

Specific results regarding AB and AAB should be noted. Many of the published comparisons of minimax algorithms as well as our experiments show that AB (in its pure form) is less effective than its newer competitors. Some investigations of its improvement through an *aspiration window* indicate savings on the order of 20% (according to our experience with MERLIN and [Gillogly 78, Baudet 78, Marsland 83]), which make the alpha-beta algorithm competitive. This is also supported by our results with AAB. They showed even a slight superiority of AAB in case of using a window of realistic size.

The deeper the search, the more can be saved in absolute terms of NBP using AAB instead of AB. Compared to the algorithms which do not use a window, AAB shows the least degradation in performance (relative to the minimal tree) when the search depth is increased. From our empirical data it seems that the use of an aspiration window leads to a certain reduction in branching factor, depending on the window size.

So the question arises, whether the other algorithms can utilize a window just as well. Based on experiments with chess programs, we could conjecture that NS and its variants only marginally improve by use of an aspiration window. In fact, these algorithms use a similar idea internally. As described above, ASSS* and ADUAL* can use windows only from one side. Actually, the results of our experiments provide empirical evidence that AB profits most from using an aspiration window.

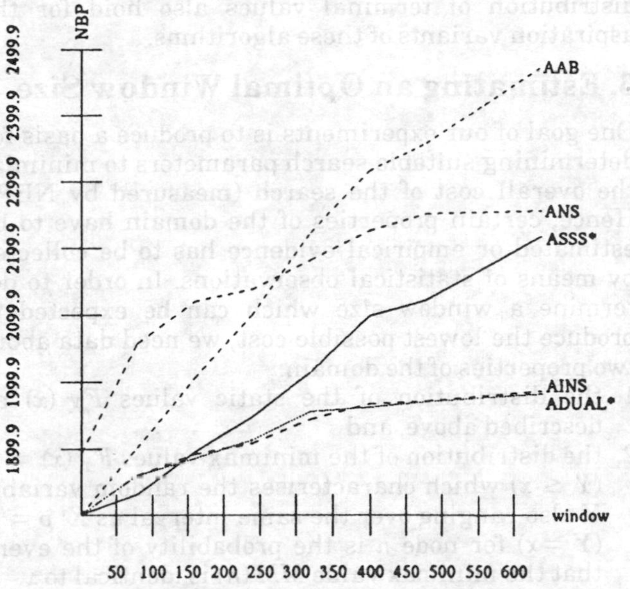

Fig. 1. Comparison of algorithms with varying window size to minimal tree – NBP, averaged over depths 3 to 9, distribution of terminal nodes' values according to $F_{X_1}(x)$, width = 5.

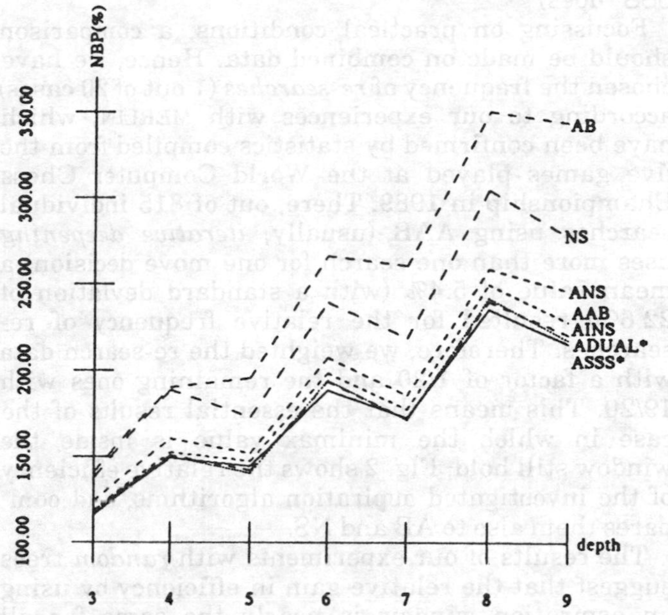

Fig. 2. Comparison of algorithms to minimal tree – NBP(%), one re-search (in case of aspiration algorithms), window containing 79 values, 80% first-move-best, distribution of terminal nodes' values according to $F_{X_1}(x)$, width = 5.

Now let us have a more detailed look at these results. First we consider the case that the minimax value is *inside* the window. When using small windows like those in practice, ANS is the worst of the algorithms compared here, although NS is clearly better than AB. In the average, the gain in efficiency by decreasing window size is approximately "linear", though with a different slope for the various algorithms (see Fig. 1). Moreover, we observed some exceptional cases, when a larger window results in a more efficient search than a smaller one. This is particularly remarkable for AAB, but it is only possible here when both bounds of one window differ from the bounds of the other. An example and a proof sketch for this phenomenon can be found in [Shams 90].

In *very* strongly ordered trees, the differences caused by various window sizes are small. There may be the hint for practice to avoid too small windows, since the risk of having to re-search may be greater than the savings. The method for estimating the window size presented below takes this into account implicitly.

If the first search fails, a re-search has to be done with an opened window. In these cases, ASSS* is the most efficient algorithm. With increasing ordering of the trees, AINS becomes nearly as efficient as ASSS*. ANS is here better than AAB, just as NS is better than AB, while without "failing" and when using smaller windows AAB is more efficient than ANS.

Again, there is an approximately linear behavior according to the window size, though with different slopes and more pronounced differences among the algorithms. Moreover, there is a different reason here for exceptions: An initially larger window may well cause a more costly first search, but this may result in a better bound for the second one, in effect reducing the overall effort. These exceptional cases are more frequent than those occurring when the minimax value is *inside* the window.

There is also an interesting phenomenon when the minimax value is identical to one of the bounds. Each of the two searches may visit fewer bottom nodes than the minimal tree contains, while the sum must of course be at least as large.

In general, our results showed that "failing low" is more expensive than "failing high". This observation coincides with the results of experiments with the minimal window as reported by [Marsland *et al.* 87].

As described above, ASSS* and ADUAL* can use only one of the window bounds. Hence in our experiments, re-searches are performed only in 10 instead of 20 cases, in which the minimax value is outside the window. Taking the results of all 20 simulation runs into consideration, these algorithms are the most efficient ones, ASSS* being the best. However, concentrating on the re-search cases only, ADUAL* is surprisingly inefficient, while ASSS* is still the best. Plausible reasons for this phenomenon are that ADUAL* visits comparably many nodes in the initial failing search, and it "fails low", which we have observed to be more costly than "failing high" (as SSS* does).

Focussing on practical conditions, a comparison should be made on combined data. Hence, we have chosen the frequency of *re-searches* (1 out of 20 cases) according to our experiences with MERLIN, which have been confirmed by statistics compiled from the five games played at the World Computer Chess Championship in 1989. There, out of 815 individual searches using AAB (usually, *iterative deepening* uses more than one search for one move decision) a mean value of 5.4% (with a standard deviation of 22.6%) resulted for the relative frequency of re-searches. Therefore, we weighted the re-search data with a factor of 1/20 and the remaining ones with 19/20. This means that the essential results of the case in which the minimax value is inside the window still hold. Fig. 2 shows the relative efficiency of the investigated aspiration algorithms, and compares them also to AB and NS.

The results of our experiments with *random* trees suggest that the relative gain in efficiency by using an aspiration window is nearly the same for all investigated algorithms, except that AB and NS (the ones with linear storage requirements) profit more. However, their aspiration versions are still less efficient than those of the others.

Our comparison of AAB with OLDAAB revealed a previously unknown property of FAB. With increasing search depth their efficiency becomes more and more the same. Empirical data showing this phenomenon are illustrated in [Shams 90, Figs. 90–101]. As we found out, the main reason is that with increasing depth it is more likely that FAB returns the same value as the original AB, namely the alpha or beta bound. Hence, it appears that the advantage of FAB over the original alpha-beta algorithm is only marginal. However, since it cannot be worse and its overhead is negligible, FAB is still to be preferred.

5. Effects of Different Distributions

All the algorithms are more efficient on trees with uniform distribution of terminal values than on those having terminal values distributed according to F_{X_1}. A plausible reason for this effect is as follows. As usual in practice, the minimax value lies more likely near the mean of the distribution of all the values. In contrast, when using the uniform distribution, more often large values (positive and negative) outside the window occur, which result more frequently in cutoffs.

Especially AB shows more gain in efficiency from a better ordering on trees with terminal values distributed according to F_{X_1}, presumably because there is simply more to gain. In the average, DUAL* is most efficient on trees with both distributions, but using F_{X_1} the performance of INS becomes essentially the same (see [Shams 90, Figs. 9–11]). On trees with uniform distribution of the terminal values, SSS* is even slightly more efficient than DUAL* when searching to even depths, while it is clearly worse for odd depths. F_{X_1} makes SSS*'s performance slightly worse. In general, the results of dependencies on the distribution of terminal values also hold for the aspiration variants of these algorithms.

6. Estimating an Optimal Window Size

One goal of our experiments is to produce a basis for determining suitable search parameters to minimize the overall cost of the search (measured by NBP). Hence, certain properties of the domain have to be estimated or empirical evidence has to be collected by means of statistical observations. In order to determine a window size which can be expected to produce the lowest possible cost, we need data about two properties of the domain:

1. the distribution of the static values $F_X(x)$ as described above, and
2. the distribution of the minimax values $F_Y(x) = P(Y \leq x)$ which characterises the random variable Y also ranging over the same interval as X; $p = P(Y = x)$ for node n is the probability of the event that the minimax value $MM(n)$ is identical to x.

The function $F_Y(x)$ is used to estimate the probability of avoiding a re-search, depending on the window size. Of course, $F_X(x)$ and $F_Y(x)$ are related to the static evaluation function used.

The cost of a search depends on whether the minimax value is inside (C_{in}) or outside (C_{out}) the pregiven window, and consequently in the average case on the frequency of each of these occurrences. C_{in} and C_{out} depend on $F_X(x)$ and on the window size s. As slight simplifications which seem to be justified in most practical cases of interest we assume s to be odd, and a window centered around 0 (the data collected have been shifted appropriately). The total cost can be computed according to the formula

$$C_{total} = C_{in}(F_X(x), s) \cdot \int_{-(s-1)/2}^{(s-1)/2} F_Y'(x)\,dx + C_{out}(F_X(x), s) \cdot \left(1 - \int_{-(s-1)/2}^{(s-1)/2} F_Y'(x)\,dx\right)$$

If the functions can be formulated analytically, the derivation of C_{total} with respect to s can be computed to get the extreme values, the minimum of which is the optimal window size. For our purpose, $F_Y(x)$ is based on statistics compiled from the tournament games of the chess program MERLIN at the World Championship in 1989. Unfortunately, the usual continuous distributions for estimating $F_Y(x)$ could not fit these data well (according to statistical tests). Therefore, we had to use the discrete values of our

TABLE 1. s_{opt} is the calculated value for the estimate of the optimal window size based on our data from practice. The value in parantheses is scaled in "pawn units", the usual measure in computer chess practice. C_{total} is the total cost in NBP for this minimum window size based on the simulation results.

	AAB	ANS	AINS	ASSS*	ADUAL*
s_{opt}	81 (1.23)	53 (0.83)	135 (2.11)	81 (1.27)	123 (1.92)
C_{total}	1997.59	2102.85	1914.82	1881.82	1898.33

statistics. As for the functions C_{in} and C_{out} we have applied interpolation between the data obtained from the simulation runs. The results are summarized in Table 1.

Although the optimal window size is significantly different for each of the algorithms, their absolute differences of cost are within a margin of about 5 percent for "reasonable" choices of the window size (about 50 to 150). Nevertheless, a correlation between total cost and optimal window size can be observed. The difference between AINS and ADUAL* manifests in larger cost of re-searches for AINS. Hence, a larger window for AINS is plausible despite its larger cost. The estimate of an optimal window size for SSS* is due to its comparably low value for C_{in} at a specific window size (79). In other regions, its cost is always slightly higher than that of DUAL*.

7. Conclusion

The main results can be summarized as follows:

- Pure alpha-beta search is the least effective backward-pruning algorithm also on very strongly ordered trees. However, using an *aspiration window* can make it competitive since it profits most from using such a window. Under realistic conditions AAB is fully competitive (see Fig. 2), which is also supported by experience with computer chess. Moreover, we have observed previously unpublished dependencies of using such a window upon certain properties of the trees.
- While ASSS* and ADUAL* visit slightly fewer nodes than their counterparts, we would suggest that they should not be used especially in domains where good ordering can be achieved, because this minor advantage is more than outweighed by their exponential space complexity. Achieving such an ordering should be feasible in most structured domains, using methods like the *history heuristic* of [Schaeffer 86, 89]. Moreover, even though these algorithms visit fewer nodes, they are likely to be slower in practice due to their overhead in managing the list of "open" nodes.
- Regarding the algorithms with linear space complexity, NS can only slightly be improved by using an aspiration window (ANS). Using smaller windows, AAB has been found to be more efficient than ANS, and only the variant of NS with exponential space complexity, AINS, is comparably better (see Fig. 2).
- Our comparison between the variants of aspiration AB using FAB in contrast to the original version of alpha-beta search revealed that the deeper the search the more likely FAB returns one of the bounds as its result.
- The assumption of uniform distribution of terminal values must be handled with care, since it affects the results.
- Presupposing evidence about some characteristic properties of the domain of application, we found a method for an analytic determination of estimates of the optimal window size for each of the algorithms compared.

Purely theoretical studies did not provide us with these results, since realistic modelling of the conditions in practice makes the analysis at least very difficult. More and more simplifications often lead to the loss of important conditions. For instance, alphabeta search under realistic conditions is by far not as inefficient as suggested by theoretical analysis. Purely empirical studies in specific domains, on the other hand, always leave doubt on the generality of their results. Our experience with computer chess is consistent with the results of the simulation studies (as far as they are comparable). We hope that our approach of less rigid modelling and the use of simulation studies can help to bridge the gap between theory and practice.

Acknowledgments

We would like to thank Jonathan Schaeffer for giving us a very good basis for our experiments, in providing us especially with the C code of his tree generation algorithm. Wolfgang Ginzel's effort in writing software for plotting the figures is greatly acknowledged.

References

Campbell, M.S., and Marsland, T.A., A Comparison of Minimax Tree Search Algorithms, *Artificial Intelligence* **20** (4), 1983, 347-367.

Fishburn, J., and Finkel, R.A., *Parallel Alpha-Beta Search on Arachne*. Tech. Report #394, Department of Computer Science, University of Wisconsin, Madison, Wis., July, 1980.

Kaindl, H., Useful Statistics from Tournament Programs, *ICCA Journal* **11** (4), 1988, 156-159.

Kaindl, H., Tree Searching Algorithms, in *Computers, Chess, and Cognition*, T. A. Marsland and J. Schaeffer, Eds., New York: Springer-Verlag, 1990, 133-158.

Kaindl, H., Wagner, M., and Horacek, H., Comparing Various Pruning Algorithms on Very Strongly Ordered Game Trees, *Proc. New Directions in Game-Tree Search Workshop*, Edmonton, Canada, May, 1989, 111-120. A comprehensive version is available as Tech. Report #50, Department of Statistics and Computer Science, University of Vienna, Austria, January, 1988.

Knuth, D.E., and Moore, R.W., An Analysis of Alpha-Beta Pruning, *Artificial Intelligence* **6** (4), 1975, 293-326.

Korf, R.E., Depth-First Iterative-Deepening: An Optimal Admissible Tree Search, *Artificial Intelligence* **27** (1), 1985, 97-109.

Marsland, T.A., and Campbell, M.S., Parallel search of strongly ordered game trees, *ACM Comput. Surv.* **14** (4), 1982, 533-552.

Marsland, T.A., Reinefeld, A., and Schaeffer, J., Low Overhead Alternatives to SSS*, *Artificial Intelligence* **31** (2), 1987, 185-199.

Musczycka, A., and Shinghal, R., An empirical comparison of pruning strategies in game trees, *IEEE Trans. Syst. Man Cybern.* **15** (3), 1985, 389-399.

Pearl, J., Asymptotic Properties of Minimax Trees and Game-Searching Procedures, *Artificial Intelligence* **14** (2), 1980, 113-138.

Pearl, J., *Heuristics: Intelligent Search Strategies for Computer Problem Solving*. Reading, Mass: Addison-Wesley Publ. Co., 1984.

Reinefeld, A., An Improvement of the Scout Tree Search Algorithm, *Journal of the International Computer Chess Association* **6** (4), 1983, 4-14.

Reinefeld, A., *Spielbaum-Suchverfahren*. Berlin: Springer-Verlag, 1989.

Schaeffer, J., *Experiments in Search and Knowledge*. Ph.D. Thesis, University of Waterloo, Ontario, May, 1986.

Schaeffer, J., The History Heuristic and Alpha-Beta Search Enhancements in Practice, *IEEE Trans. Pattern Anal. Mach. Intell.* **PAMI-11** (11), 1989, 1203-1212.

Shams, R., Ein experimenteller Vergleich ausgewählter Suchverfahren. Diplomarbeit, Institut für Praktische Informatik, Technische Universität Wien, 1990.

Stockman, G.C., A Minimax Algorithm Better than Alpha-Beta?, *Artificial Intelligence* **12** (2), 1979, 179-196.

HIGH-PERFORMANCE A* SEARCH USING RAPIDLY GROWING HEURISTICS

Stephen V. Chenoweth
Research & Development
NCR Corporation-WHQ5E
Dayton, OH 45479

Henry W. Davis
Wright State University
Dept. of Computer Science
Dayton, OH 45435

Abstract

In high-performance A* searching to solve satisficing problems, there is a critical need to design heuristics which cause low time-complexity. In order for humans or machines to do this effectively, there must be an understanding of the domain-independent properties that such heuristics have. We show that, contrary to common belief, accuracy is not critical; the key issue is whether or not heuristic values are concentrated closely near a rapidly growing "central function." As an application, we show that, by "multiplying" heuristics, it is possible to reduce exponential average time-complexity to polynomial. This is contrary to conclusions drawn from previous studies. Experimental and theoretical examples are given.

1 Introduction

Two groups of studies, [Bagchi and Sen, 1988; Pearl, 1984, Chapter 7], have appeared in which heuristics are modeled as random variables (RV's); the model is used to determine what properties heuristics must have if A* is to have average polynomial, versus exponential, asymptotic time-complexity. The state space graph is assumed to be a uniform, b-ary tree, with start at the root, bi-directional arcs each of unit cost, and a single goal N units from start.[1]

Let $h^*(n)$, $h(n)$, respectively, return true and estimated distance to goal from node n. The studies assume that the errors, $h^*(n) - h(n)$, suitably normalized, are independent and identically distributed RV's. We call this the "IID model" of heuristics. In the IID model, attaining average polynomial A* complexity is essentially equivalent to requiring that the values of $h(n)$ be clustered near $h^*(n)$; the allowed deviation is a logarithmic function of $h^*(n)$ itself.[2] See Figure 1.

As a result of studies using the IID model, the impression has been given that high-performance A* search requires accurate heuristics. In this paper we describe a model which is more realistic than the IID model because it places no constraints on errors, or on h; we call it the "NC model." Conclusions from the NC model are not in agreement with those of the IID model: They predict polynomial A* complexity whenever the values of $h(n)$ are logarithmically clustered near $h^*(n) + \eta(h^*(n))$, where η is an arbitrary, non-negative, non-decreasing function. See Figure 2. Heuristics whose values grow slower than distance to goal cause exponential complexity. See Figure 3. If we think of clustering as a kind of "precision" and clustering near h* as "accuracy," then the difference is this: The IID model favors heuristics with logarithmic accuracy and the NC model favors those which are rapidly growing and have logarithmic precision.

Sections 2, 3 state our results more precisely. Proofs are in an appendix. In Section 4 we apply the NC model to the phenomenon of "multiplying": That is, replacing a heuristic h with zh for some $z \geq 0$. Studies with the IID model predict that multiplying is of no value in eliminating exponential complexity. The NC model, however, shows that multiplying can often change exponential A* complexity to polynomial. Experimental and theoretical examples are given.

1.1 Motivation for the Mathematical Modeling of Heuristics

John Gaschnig's 1979 dissertation [Gaschnig, 1979] gave the first thorough experimental results on the correlation between the mathematical properties of heuristics and A* performance. His opening sentence states that the work is "based on the premise that in the future more of the subject matter of artificial intelligence (AI) research will be understood mathematically than at present." We agree with Gaschnig's view that establishing such foundations is a challenging, long-term AI objective.

Gaschnig proposed a mathematical model to explain his data, but recognized that in large part it failed to do so [Gaschnig, 1979, Section 3.5.1]. Our motivation is based on the view that heuristics are central to AI, and that we cannot claim to understand them until we have mathematical models which explain experimental results obtained by using them.

Two other reasons for studying the mathematical properties of heuristics and how they affect search are as follows:

(1) Intractability results [Garey and Johnson, 1979] indicate that many problems require a prohibitive amount of time to solve in the worst case. Compromises must be made. One type of compromise is to accept *average* polynomial time complexity. Heuristic search provides a mechanism for this, but we need a theory which tells us precisely when a heuristic provides such payoff.

(2) As our interest in increasingly hard problems grows, our need for good heuristics also grows. Several studies have been made about how humans and machines

[1] In [Bagchi and Sen, 1988] the primary interest is in multiple goals. However, we discuss their results only for the single-goal problem, as that is our interest here.

[2] Confer Theorems 3.1, 3.2 in [Bagchi and Sen, 1988] or Theorem 1 in [Pearl, 1984, Chapter 7].

may design such heuristics [Rendell, 1983; Pearl, 1984, Chapter 4; Christensen and Korf, 1986; Politowski, 1986; Mostow and Prieditis, 1989; Bramanti-Gregor and Davis, 1991]. We believe that such research requires a predictive mathematical model of heuristics. That is, there are domain-independent mathematical properties which a "good" heuristic has, and these must be understood if humans or machines are going to design them.

The A* algorithm is a sensible place to begin because (a) it is a very widely used heuristic search algorithm, and (b) although formally simple, it is not yet well understood how its performance relates to the mathematical properties of the heuristic it uses. Predictive models for A* should enable us to build better mathematical models for game-tree searching, IDA*, AO*, and more sophisticated production control strategies. One ultimate goal is that the search component in AI systems be based more on scientific theory and less on *ad hoc* discoveries of the designer.

1.2 Model Assumptions: Significance and Tradeoffs

A heuristic h is a function which returns a number when evaluated on a node n. What is the advantage in viewing $h(n)$ as a RV? It is that we may view our complexity conclusions as reflecting the aggregate properties of A* performance when A* is run over many problem instances. A possible disadvantage is that constraints made on the $h(n)$ in order to make the mathematics tractable may not reflect the aggregate behavior of real heuristics. The resulting conclusions about A* performance may be of limited use. This is a problem with the IID model. An appeal of the NC model is that no constraints are placed on the $h(n)$.

The assumption that the state space graph is a b-ary tree is useful in providing potential for exponential explosion. The assumption of a single goal is made here to simplify the mathematics. [Bagchi and Sen, 1988] have studied the multi-goal case in the IID model. This, plus the introduction of cycles, is interesting because it allows the possibility of compromising on solution quality when working on worst case intractable problems.[1]

2 Notation and Basic Relations

The graph, G, is an infinite uniform b-ary tree with bi-directional edges of unit cost. See Figure 4. The start node, n_1, is at the root and a unique solution path $n_1, \ldots, n_{N+1}$ leads to the goal, n_{N+1}, which is N units away. The

[1] "Solution quality" refers to the extent to which the solution found is not optimal. It is not an issue when there is a single goal and the state space graph is a tree (as is assumed in this paper).

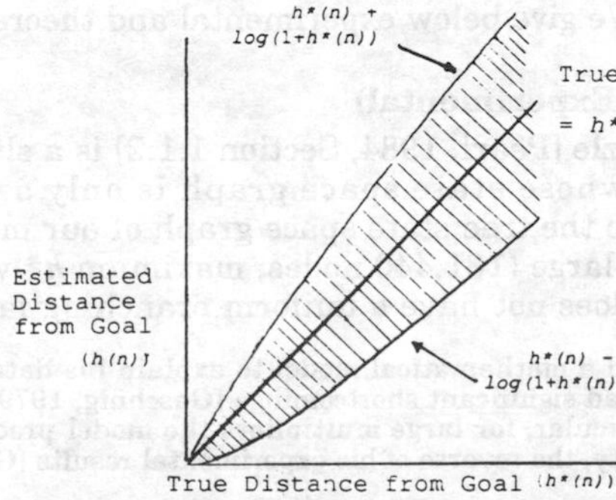

Figure 1. In the IID model, polynomial A* complexity is essentially equivalent to requiring that the heuristic of A* have its values "clustered" as in the shaded region.

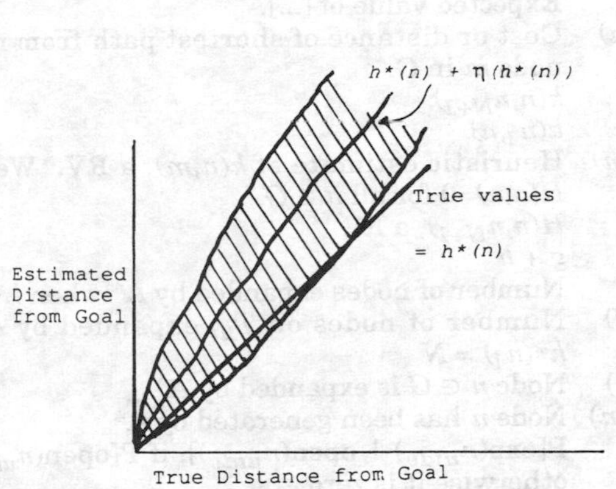

Figure 2. Assume the logarithmic cluster of Figure 1 is now centered on $h^*(n)+\eta(h^*(n))$ instead of on $h^*(n)$. The NC model predicts polynomial complexity; the IID model predicts exponential complexity (unless η is itself a logarithmic function).

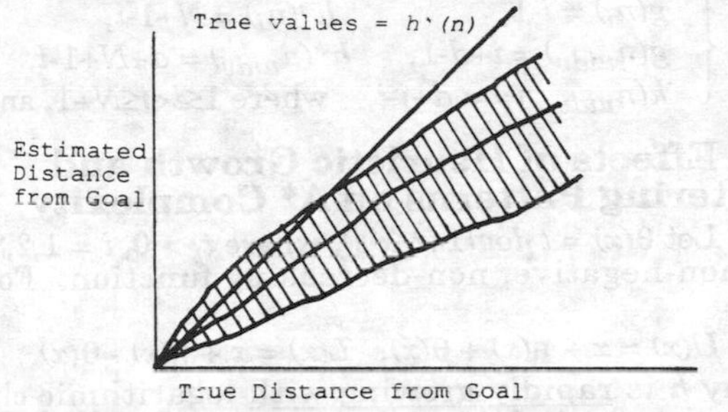

Figure 3. Heuristics whose values increase slower than those of h^* cause exponential A* complexity (Theorem 2).

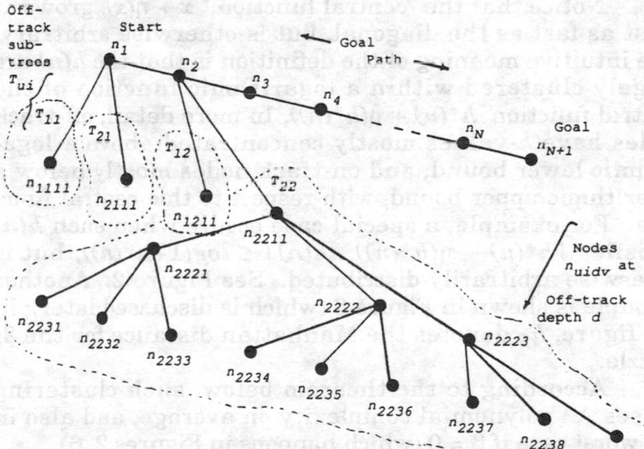

Figure 4. State space graph G with $b = 3$.

nodes $n_1, \ldots, n_N$ (excluding n_{N+1}) are called on-track. Off-track nodes are all other nodes, excluding n_{N+1} and its descendants. The b-1 off-track children of n_i form the roots of the off-track subtree T_{ui}, $1 \le u \le b\text{-}1$, $1 \le i \le N$.

Off-track nodes are denoted n_{uidv}, where T_{ui} denotes the off-track subtree containing n_{uidv}, $d \ge 1$ indicates its depth, and $v \in \{1, \ldots, b^{d-1}\}$ references a particular node on level d within T_{ui}.

We use the following symbolism:

P[...]	Probability of [...].
E[...]	Expected value of [...].
$k(n,m)$	Cost or distance of shortest path from node n to node m in G.
$h^*(n)$	$k(n,n_{N+1})$
$g(n)$	$k(n_1,n)$
$H(n,m)$	Heuristic estimate of $k(n,m)$, a RV. We assume $H(n,n)=0$ for all $n \in G$.
$h(n)$	$H(n,n_{N+1})$, a RV
f	$g + h$
$Z(N)$	Number of nodes expanded by A* when $h^*(n_1) = N$
$Z_{ui}(N)$	Number of nodes on T_{ui} expanded by A* when $h^*(n_1) = N$
exp(n)	Node $n \in G$ is expanded by A*
open(n)	Node n has been generated by A*
q_{uidv}	P[exp(n_{uidv}) ∣ open(n_{uidv})], if P[open(n_{uidv})] > 0; otherwise it is zero.
L^N_i	$\max \{f(n_j): i+1 \leq j \leq N+1\}$.
$\psi(i)$	$\max \{j : f(n_j) = L^N_i, i+1 \leq j \leq N+1\}$, a RV.
n_c	If $n = n_i$ or n_{uidv}, then $n_c = n_{\psi(i)}$. Here $1 \leq i \leq N$.

The following formulas are used in the sequel:

$$\textbf{(2.1)} \quad \begin{cases} g(n_i) = i\text{-}1, & h^*(n_i) = N+1-i, \\ g(n_{uidv}) = i+d-1, & h^*(n_{uidv}) = d+N+1-i, \\ k(n_{uidv}, n_j) = d+j-i, & \text{where } 1 \leq i < j \leq N+1, \text{ and } d \geq 1. \end{cases}$$

3 Effects of Heuristic Growth and Clustering Patterns on A* Complexity

Let $\theta(x) = t_1 log(1+t_2 x^{t_3})$, where $t_i > 0$, $i = 1,2,3$. Let η be a non-negative, non-decreasing function. For $x \geq 0$, define

(3.1) $U(x) = x + \eta(x) + \theta(x)$, $L(x) = x + \eta(x) - \theta(x)$.

We say h is <u>rapidly</u> <u>growing</u> <u>with</u> <u>logarithmic</u> <u>cluster</u> if there exists $\beta \in [0,1)$ such that

(3.2) For all off-track $n = n_{uidv}$ we have
$P[(h(n) \geq L(h^*(n))) \wedge (h(n_c) \leq U(h^*(n_c)))] \geq 1 - (\beta/b)^d$.

Notice that the "central function," $x + \eta(x)$, grows at least as fast as the diagonal, but is otherwise arbitrary. The intuitive meaning of the definition is that the $h(n)$ are largely clustered within a logarithmic function of the central function $h^*(n) + \eta(h^*(n))$. In more detail, off-track nodes have h-values mostly concentrated above a logarithmic lower bound, and on-track nodes mostly below a logarithmic upper bound, with respect to this central function. For example, a special case occurs when each $h(n)$ satisfies $|h^*(n) + \eta(h^*(n)) - h(n)| \leq log(1+h^*(n))$, but is otherwise arbitrarily distributed. See Figure 2. Another example is shown in Figure 6 (which is discussed later); in the figure, h_2 denotes the Manhattan distance for the 8-Puzzle.

According to the theorem below, such clustering causes A* polynomial complexity on average, and also in the worst case if $\beta = 0$ (which happens in Figures 2, 6).

<u>Theorem</u> <u>1</u> **(Logarithmic Cluster Complexity Theorem). If h is rapidly growing with logarithmic cluster then E[$Z(N)$] is polynomial in N; also, $Z(N)$ is polynomial if $\beta = 0$ in (3.2).**

As an example, we ran A* on the graph of Figure 4 with N up to 20 and $b = 2$. The heuristic h had values as in Figure 2 (logarithmic cluster) with $\eta(x) = x^2$. Within these constraints h was designed to be as misleading as possible, returning the maximum allowed number on-track and the minimum allowed number off-track. A* expanded N nodes; i.e., it had linear complexity. The high-performance of A* using this heuristic is surprising because the traditional view, based on the IID model, is that good heuristics need to be accurate.

In contrast to Theorem 1, the theorem and corollary below show that slowly growing heuristics cause exponential complexity. The corollary says to expect exponential complexity if the maximum of $h(n)$-values eventually grows slower than does $h^*(n)$. This is shown in Figure 3. The theorem has a more delicate interpretation: If $h(n)$ for open off-track nodes is likely to be growing slower than $h^*(n)$ eventually, then we may expect exponential complexity.

<u>Theorem</u> <u>2</u> **(Slowly Growing Heuristic Complexity Theorem). Suppose there exists a differentiable function w such that for some $\varepsilon \in (0,1)$,**

$$\lim_{x \to \infty} w'(x) < 1 - \varepsilon,$$

and for some $\alpha \in (1,b]$, some N_1 a positive integer, we have that node n off-track and $h^*(n) > N_1$ imply

$$P[h(n) \leq w(h^*(n)) \mid \text{open}(n)] \geq \alpha/b \quad \text{whenever} \quad P[\text{open}(n)] > 0.$$

Then E[$Z(N)$] is exponential in N.

<u>Corollary</u>. **Let w be as in Theorem 2. If there exists integer $N_1>0$ such that P[$h(n) \leq w(h^*(n))$] = 1 for all n satisfying $h^*(n) > N_1$. then E[$Z(N)$] is exponential.**

4 Multiplying Heuristics to Reduce A* Complexity

If h is a heuristic function one might hope to lower A* complexity by using, instead of h, the <u>multiplied</u> <u>heuristic</u>, zh, where $z \geq 0$ is a real number. We call z a <u>multiplier</u>. [Gaschnig, 1979] first demonstrated via compelling statistical evidence that the use of multipliers with heuristics can substantially reduce A* complexity.[1] Two other attempts have been made to explain with a mathematical model the effects of multiplying. Both use the IID model. [Pearl, 1984, see especially pp. 206, 209] concludes that multiplying cannot turn exponential growth rate into sub-exponential. [Bagchi and Sen, 1988, page 158] conclude that search with multiplied heuristics, "in its average performance, appears to enjoy no clear advantage over ordinary heuristic search."[2]

The NC model provides a simple rationale for expecting multiplications to reduce exponential search complexity to sub-exponential in many cases; it also suggests a good multiplier: Suppose the maximum values of a heuristic h are growing slower than h^* but that overall the heuristic values show a logarithmic cluster around some "central function." Choose $z > 0$ such that the central function, multiplied by z, grows faster than the diagonal, if such is possible. According to Theorems 1 and 2, above, replacing h by zh reduces A* complexity from exponential to polynomial. We give below experimental and theoretical examples of this.

4.1 Example 1 (Experimental)

The 8-Puzzle [Pearl, 1984, Section 1.1.2] is a sliding block problem whose state space graph is only a first approximation to the tree state space graph of our model. While relatively large (181,440 nodes, maximum h^*-value 30), it is finite, does not have a uniform branching factor,

[1]Gaschnig proposed a mathematical model to explain his data, but recognized that it had significant shortcomings [Gaschnig, 1979, Section 3.5.1]. In particular, for large multipliers the model predicted increasing complexity, the reverse of his experimental results [Gaschnig, 1979, p. 112].

[2]The problem with using the IID model to study multiplied heuristics is that multiplying an IID-model heuristic may throw it out of the IID model. An example of this is given in [Chenoweth, 1990, Chapter 5]. This reference also contains a more detailed analysis than is given here of the effects of multiplying heuristics.

and contains cycles. However, most cycles are quite long, making the state space graph rather "tree-like"; search trees built by A* on 8-Puzzle problems have average branching factors close to 1.4. We would hope that, to a first approximation, our model is applicable to this domain.

We use as a heuristic for A* the Manhattan distance, h_2: This is the sum over all tiles of the horizontal and vertical distance of the tile from its goal position. Figure 5 shows the observed values of h_2 from a sample of 1998 randomly generated problems. From the *maxh* plot and Theorem 2 we expect exponential complexity when A* uses $g + h_2$ as its evaluation function. Figure 7, taken from a sample of 605 randomly generated problems, shows that this indeed occurs ($z = 1$ curve: Notice that the ordinate has a logarithmic scale).

Consider the *avgh* curve of Figure 5 as a "central function" around which h_2-values cluster. We multiply h_2 by 4 so that $4 \cdot avgh$ increases at least as fast as the diagonal, a requirement of Theorem 1. Figure 6 shows the result, and also that the values of $4h_2$ are concentrated within a logarithmic envelope of $4 \cdot avgh$. According to Theorem 1 we may expect polynomial complexity when A* uses $g + 4h_2$. The pattern of data observed in Figure 7 corroborates this expectation. It turns out that increasing the multiplier above 4 causes relatively little improvement in A* performance.

4.2 Example 2 (Theoretical)

There are many theoretical examples of heuristics for which multiplication transforms A* complexity from exponential to polynomial. For instance, let $R(x) = (x + \log(1+x))/2$, $S(x) = x/2$, and let each $h(n)$ be distributed arbitrarily between $S(h^*(n))$ and $R(h^*(n))$, as is shown in Figure 8. By Theorem 2, A* search is exponential when using h. By Theorem 1, it is polynomial when using zh, for any $z \geq 2$.

5 Conclusions

In high-performance A* searching to solve satisficing problems, there is a critical need to design heuristics which cause low time-complexity. In order for humans or machines to do this effectively, there must be an understanding of the domain-independent properties that such heuristics have. We have shown that, contrary to previous belief, accuracy is not critical; the key issue is whether or not

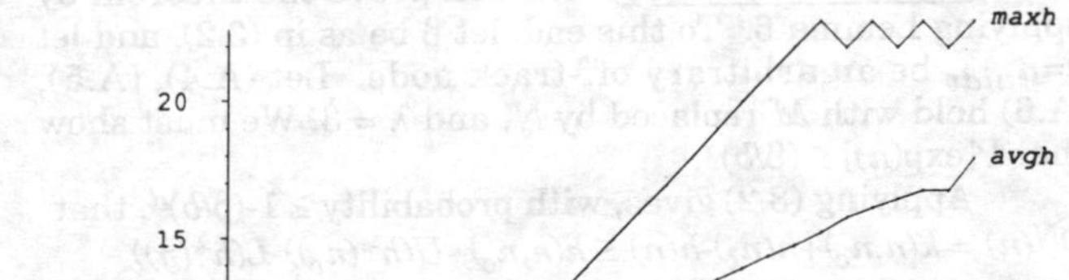

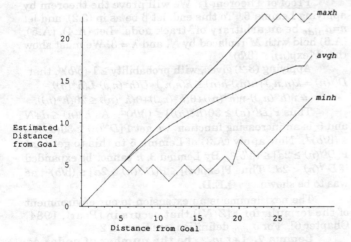

Figure 5. Observed values of h_2 [Chen, 1989]. *avgh, maxh, minh,* respectively, denote average, maximum, and minimum values returned by $h_2(n)$ for various values of $h^*(n)$.

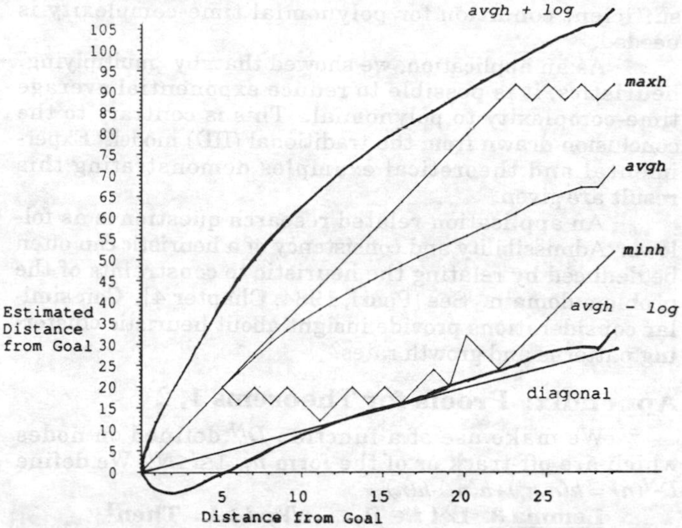

Figure 6. Observed values of $4h_2(n)$ lie between the functions $avgh(x) \pm 11.35\log(1+x)$, where $x = h^*(n)$. This is denoted *avgh*±log in the Figure.

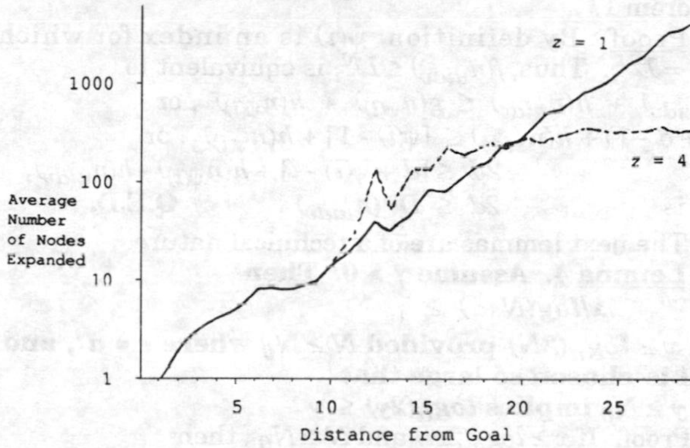

Figure 7. Number of nodes expanded by A* versus distance to goal when using heuristic zh_2, $z = 1, 4$. Data from [Chen, 1989].

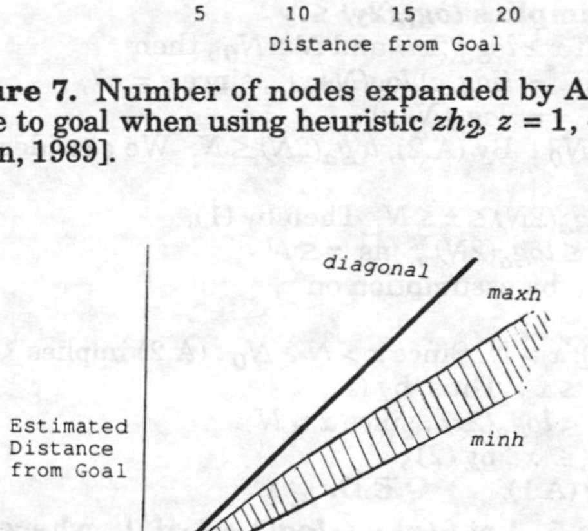

Figure 8. Values assumed by h in Example 2: *maxh, minh* are determined by the functions R, S described there. The state space graph is as in Figure 4.

heuristic values are concentrated closely near a rapidly growing "central function."

An open question is how much concentration, or clustering, is needed to assure polynomial time-complexity. We have shown that logarithmic clustering is adequate. Results reported in [Chenoweth, 1990; Chenoweth and Davis, 1990] show that the clustering can be polynomial when heuristic values grow fast enough. A necessary and sufficient condition for polynomial time-complexity is needed.

As an application, we showed that, by "multiplying" heuristics, it is possible to reduce exponential average time-complexity to polynomial. This is contrary to the conclusion drawn from the traditional (IID) model. Experimental and theoretical examples demonstrating this result are given.

An application-related research question is as follows: Admissibility and consistency of a heuristic can often be deduced by relating the heuristic to constraints of the problem domain. See [Pearl, 1984, Chapter 4]. Can similar considerations provide insight about heuristic clustering patterns and growth rates?

Appendix: Proofs for Theorems 1, 2

We make use of a function D^N defined on nodes which are off-track or of the form n_i, $1 \le i \le N$: We define $D^N(n) = k(n,n_c)+h(n_c)-h(n)$.

Lemma 3. Let $i \in \{1, \dots, N\}$, $d \ge 1$. Then[1]

$$f(n_{uidv}) \le L^N_i \text{ iff } D^N(n_{uidv}) \ge 2d.$$

Lemma 3 is important because a node n_{uidv} cannot be expanded if $f(n_{uidv}) > L^N_i$. This fact is used in the proof of Theorem 1.

Proof. By definition $\psi(i)$ is an index for which $f(n_{\psi(i)}) = L^N_i$. Thus, $f(n_{uidv}) \le L^N_i$ is equivalent to

$$g(n_{uidv}) + h(n_{uidv}) \le g(n_{\psi(i)}) + h(n_{\psi(i)}), \text{ or}$$
$$(i + d - 1) + h(n_{uidv}) \le [\psi(i) - 1] + h(n_{\psi(i)}), \text{ or}$$
$$2d \le [d + \psi(i) - i] + h(n_{\psi(i)}) - h(n_{uidv}),$$

which is $2d \le D^N(n_{uidv})$. **Q.E.D.**

The next lemmas are of a technical nature.

Lemma 4. Assume $\gamma > 0$. Then

(A.1) $x/log(N+x) \ge \gamma$

for all $x \ge log_a(2N)$ provided $N \ge N_0$ where $e = a^\gamma$, and $N_0 \ge 1$ is chosen so large that

(A.2) **$y \ge N_0$ implies $log_a(2y) \le y$.**

Proof. If $x \ge log_a(2N)$ and $N \ge N_0$, then

(1) $\gamma\, log(N+x) = (log_a e)\, log(N+x)$, since $e = a^\gamma$,
$= log_a(N+x)$.

Take any $N \ge N_0$. By (A.2), $log_a(2N) \le N$. We consider two cases:

Case (1): $log_a(2N) \le x \le N$. Then by (1),
$\gamma\, log(N+x) \le log_a(2N)$, as $x \le N$
$\le x$, by assumption on x,
which is (A.1).

Case (2): $x > N$. Since $x > N \ge N_0$, (A.2) implies

(2) $log_a(2x) \le x$. Thus, by (1),
$\gamma\, log(N+x) < log_a(2x)$, since $x > N$
$\le x$, by (2),
again yielding (A.1). **Q.E.D.**

Lemma 5. Let $\theta(x) = t_1 log(1 + t_2 x^{t_3})$, where $t_i > 0$, $i = 1,2,3$. Let $\lambda > 0$, and suppose M is a positive integer. Then

(A.3) **$2d/\theta(d+M) \ge \lambda$ whenever**

(A.4) $\begin{cases} d \ge log_a(2M), \text{ and} \\ a = exp(1/\lambda c t_1 t_3); \text{ where} \end{cases}$

(A.5) $\begin{cases} c = \log 3 / \log 2; \text{ and where } M \text{ satisfies} \\ M \ge max\{ (2/t_2)^{1/t_3}, (1/2)\, a^{\lambda c t_1 log\, t_2}, N_1 \}, \end{cases}$

(A.6) **where $y \ge N_1$ implies $log_a(2y) \le y$.**

Proof. First note that our choice of c in (A.5) gives $c\, log(v) \ge log(1+v)$ for all $v \ge 2$, which is easily checked.

[1] When one relation involving RV's is derived from another using simple algebraic transformations, we omit stating the "with probability 1" constraint.

(A.3) is true provided

(1) $d/[c\, log(t_2[d+M]^{t_3})] \ge \lambda t_1/2$

because of (A.5) and the first part of (A.6). But (1) is true provided $d/\{log\, t_2 + t_3 log[d+M]\} \ge \lambda c t/2$, or

(2) $(log\, t_2)/d + (t_3 log(d+M))/d \le 2/[\lambda c t_1]$.

By Lemma 4 (with $x=d$, $\gamma=\lambda c t_1 t_3$, and $N_0=N_1$),

$$[t_3 log(d+M)]/d \le 1/[\lambda c t_1]$$

provided (A.4) holds and $M \ge N_1$. For such d the left side of (2) is $\le [log\, t_2]/[log_a(2M)] + 1/[\lambda c t_1] \le 2/[\lambda c t_1]$ provided $[log\, t_2]/[log_a(2M)] \le 1/[\lambda c t_1]$; that is,

(3) $log_a(2M) \ge \lambda c t_1 log(t_2)$,

which is included in (A.6). This proves (A.3). **Q.E.D.**

Lemma 6. Let θ be as in Lemma 5. Set $\lambda = 3$ and $M = N$ (= $h^*(n_1)$) in (A.4), (A.5), and (A.6). Assume there exist $\beta \in [0,1)$ such that for all off- track nodes n_{uidv} we have $P[exp(n_{uidv})] \le (\beta/b)^d$ whenever (A.4), (A.5), and (A.6) hold. Then $E[Z(N)]$ is polynomial in N. If $\beta=0$, then $Z(N)$ is polynomial.

Proof.. Set $M = N$ in the statement of Lemma 5. Let $L(N) = log_a(2N)$, where a is as in (A.4). Consider any N greater than the right side of (A.6). Then, for any off-track sub-tree T_{ui}, we have

$$\text{(1)}\quad E[Z_{ui}(N)] = \sum_{d=1}^{\infty} \sum_{v=1}^{b^{d-1}} P[exp(n_{uidv})]$$

$$\le \sum_{d<L(N)} \sum_{v=1}^{b^{d-1}} 1 + \sum_{d \ge L(N)} \sum_{v=1}^{b^{d-1}} P[exp(n_{uidv})]$$

$$\le \sum_{d=1}^{L(N)} b^{d-1} + \sum_{d \ge L(N)} b^{d-1} (\beta/b)^d \quad \text{by hypothesis,}$$

$$\le \frac{b^{L(N)} - 1}{b - 1} + \frac{\beta^{L(N)}}{b(1 - \beta)} \le \frac{2}{1 - \beta} b^{L(N)}.$$

Therefore,

$$E[Z(N)] = N + \sum_{u=1}^{b-1} \sum_{i=1}^{N} E[Z_{ui}(N)]$$
$$\le N + [2Nb\, b^{L(N)}] / [1-\beta],$$

which is polynomial. If $\beta=0$, then, with probability 1, the left side of (1) may be replaced by $Z_{ui}(N)$ and the summation on the right side involves only $d < L(N)$. Thus, each $Z_{ui}(N)$, and hence $Z(N)$, is polynomial. **Q.E.D.**

Proof of Theorem 1. We will prove the theorem by applying Lemma 6. To this end, let β be as in (3.2), and let $n=n_{uidv}$ be an arbitrary off-track node. Let (A.4), (A.5), (A.6) hold with M replaced by N, and $\lambda = 3$. We must show that $P[exp(n)] \le (\beta/b)^d$.

Applying (3.2) gives, with probability $\ge 1-(\beta/b)^d$, that

$$D^N(n) = k(n,n_c)+h(n_c)-h(n) \le k(n,n_c)+U(h^*(n_c))-L(h^*(n))$$
$$= \eta(h^*(n_c))-\eta(h^*(n))+\theta(h^*(n_c))+\theta(h^*(n)) \le 2\theta(h^*(n)).$$

Thus $P[D^N(n) \ge 3\theta(h^*(n))] \le (\beta/b)^d$. As $h^*(n) \le d+N$ and θ is an increasing function, we get $P[D^N(n) \ge 3\theta(d+N)] \le (\beta/b)^d$. Now apply (A.3) of Lemma 5 to this to get that $P[D^N(n) \ge 2d] \le (\beta/b)^d$. By Lemma 3, n cannot be expanded if $D^N(n) < 2d$. Thus $P[exp(n)] \le P[D^N(n) \ge 2d] \le (\beta/b)^d$, as was to be shown. **Q.E.D.**

The next lemma is an extension to our environment of the formula for $E[Z(N)]$ that occurs in [Pearl, 1984, Chapter 6]. For q_{uidv} definition, see Section 2.

Lemma 7. Let w_{uid} be the number of nodes A* expands at level d of the off-track subtree T_{ui}. Then

$$\text{(A.7)}\quad E[w_{uid}] = \sum_{v=1}^{b^{d-1}} \prod_{m=1}^{d} q_{u,i,m,a(d,m,v)}$$

$$\text{(A.8)}\quad P[\exp(n_{uidv})] = \prod_{m=1}^{d} q_{u,i,m,a(d,m,v)}$$

where $a(d,d,v) = v$ and, in general, $n_{u,i,m,a(d,m,v)}$ is the level m ancestor in T_{ui} of n_{uidv}, $m = 1,2, \ldots, d$.

Proof. As A* finds a solution, n_i is expanded, so open(n_{ui11}) is certain. Consequently P[exp(n_{ui11})] = q_{ui11}. As T_{ui} contains only one node at level 1, q_{ui11} is also the expected number of expanded nodes at level 1. This proves the lemma when $d = 1$.

Assume the lemma is true for the $d - 1$ case. We must show it is true for the d case. Now, since open(n_{uidv}) if and only if exp($n_{u,i,d-1,a(d,d-1,v)}$),

$$P[\exp(n_{uidv})] = P[\exp(n_{uidv}) \wedge \exp(n_{u,i,d-1,a(d,d-1,v)})]$$
$$= 0 \text{ if } P[\exp(n_{u,i,d-1,a(d,d-1,v)})] = 0;$$

otherwise,

$$P[\exp(n_{uidv})] = P[\exp(n_{uidv}) \mid \exp(n_{u,i,d-1,a(d,d-1,v)})] \cdot P[\exp(n_{u,i,d-1,a(d,d-1,v)})],$$
$$= P[\exp(n_{uidv}) \mid \text{open}(n_{uidv})] \cdot P[\exp(n_{u,i,d-1,a(d,d-1,v)})].$$

Then, in either case,

$$P[\exp(n_{uidv})] = q_{uidv} \prod_{m=1}^{d-1} q_{u,i,m,a(d,m,v)}$$

by the induction hypothesis,

$$= \prod_{m=1}^{d} q_{u,i,m,a(d,m,v)}.$$

This establishes (A.8) for the inductive step, whence it is generally true. Now (A.7) follows for the inductive step by applying (A.8) : E[w_{uid}] is simply the sum over all level d nodes of the probability that each is expanded. **Q.E.D.**

Proof of Theorem 2 and the Corollary. Let $q = 1 - \varepsilon$. We first note that

(1) $w(x) \le q(x-t) + t$

for some $t \ge 1$ and all $x \ge t$. This is because for x sufficiently large, say, $x \ge t \ge 1$, $w(x)$ both lies below the diagonal and has slope $< q$. Thus, for all $x \ge t$, $w(x)$ lies below the line through (t, t) whose slope is q, that is, (1) holds. Let $\varphi(x) = (1-q)^2x/(1+q)$ and let $N_0 = max\{N_1+t, [(1+q)t-1]/q\}$. We first show that, if $n = n_{utdv}$, $N > N_0$ and $d \le \varphi(N-t)$, u and v are arbitrary, then

(2) P[exp(n) | open(n_{utdv})] $\ge \alpha/b$ whenever P[open(n)] > 0.

For all such N and d, $N > N_0 \ge [(1+q)t - 1]/q$, so $qN + N > (1+q)t - 1 + N$; that is,

$$N+1-2t > qt - t + N - qN = (1-q)(N-t)$$
$$= [(1+q)/(1-q)]\varphi(N-t) \ge [(1+q)/(1-q)]d.$$

Multiplying both sides by $1-q$ and separating N gives

(3) $N > q(N+1-2t+d)-1+2t+d = \{q[(N+d+1-t)-t]+t\}+\{d+t-1\}$
$\ge \{w(N+d+1-t)\} + \{d+t-1\}$ by (1),
$= w(h^*(n_{utdv})) + g(n_{utdv})$

Notice that $h^*(n_{utdv}) = N+d+1-t \ge (N_1+t)+d+1-t > N_1$. Thus, if P[open($n_{utdv}$)] > 0 then

$\alpha/b \le$ P[$h(n) \le w(h^*(n))$ | open(n)] by our hypothesis
= P[$f(n) \le w(h^*(n)) + g(n)$ | open(n)]
$\le$ P[$f(n) < N$ | open(n)], by (3)
$\le$ P[$f(n) < f(n_o)$ | open(n)], since $f(n_{N+1})=N$
$\le$ P[exp(n) | open(n)], which establishes (2).

To complete the proof of the theorem apply Lemma 7:

$$E[Z(N)] \ge E[Z_{ut}(N)], \text{ where } u \in \{1,\ldots,b-1\},$$
$$\ge \sum_{d=1}^{\varphi(N-t)} \sum_{v=1}^{b^{d-1}} \prod_{m=1}^{d} q_{u,t,m,a(d,m,v)}, \text{ by (A.7)}$$
$$\ge \sum_{d=1}^{\varphi(N-t)} b^{d-1}\left(\frac{\alpha}{b}\right)^{d}, \text{ by (2)},$$
$$\ge [\alpha^{\varphi(N-t)}] / \alpha b,$$

which is exponential in N. This proves Theorem 2.

The corollary follows from the theorem by noting that P[$h(n) \le w(h^*(n))$] = 1 implies that P[($h(n) \le w(h^*(n))$) $\wedge$ open(n)] = P[open(n)] and so P[$h(n) \le w(h^*(n))$ | open(n)] = 1. **Q.E.D.**

References

[Bagchi and Sen, 1988] Bagchi, A., and Sen, A. Average-case analysis of heuristic search in tree-Like networks. In *Search in Artificial Intelligence*, ed. by L. Kanal and V. Kumar, New York: Springer-Verlag, pages 131-165, 1988.

[Bramanti-Gregor and Davis, 1991] Bramanti-Gregor, A., and Davis, H.W. Learning admissible heuristics while solving problems. *Proceedings of the 12th International Joint Conference on Artificial Intelligence*, 1991.

[Chen, 1989] Chen, X. Generating and transforming heuristic functions to get desired properties. Master's Thesis, Wright State University, Department of Computer Science and Engineering, 1989.

[Chenoweth, 1990] Chenoweth, S.V. *An Analysis of the Asymptotic Performance of the A* Algorithm*. Ph.D. Dissertation, Wright State University, Department of Computer Science and Engineering, 1990. See also: New approaches for understanding the asymptotic complexity of A* tree searching, by S.V. Chenoweth and H.W. Davis and The mathematical modeling of heuristics, by H.W. Davis and S.V. Chenoweth, to appear in *Annals of Mathematics and Artificial Intelligence*, Volume F.

[Chenoweth and Davis, 1990] Chenwoeth, S.V., and Davis, H.W. Heuristics with polynomial growth patterns and the complexity of A*. In *Methodologies for Intelligent Systems, Selected Papers*, ed. by M.L. Emrich, *et al*, International Center for Application Technology, Knoxville, TN, pages 49-62, 1990.

[Christensen and Korf, 1986] Christensen, J., and Korf, R.E. A united theory of heuristic evaluation functions and its application to learning. *Proceedings of the AAAI*, pages 148-152, 1986.

[Garey and Johnson, 1979] Garey, M.R., and Johnson, D.S. *Computers and Intractability, a Guide to the Theory of NP-Completeness*. New York: W.H. Freeman and Company, 1979.

[Gaschnig, 1979] Gaschnig, J. *Performance Measurement and Analysis of Certain Search Algorithms*. Ph.D. Dissertation, Carnegie-Mellon University, 1979.

[Mostow and Prieditis, 1989] Mostow, J., and Prieditis, A.E. Discovering admissible heuristics by abstracting and optimizing: A transformational approach. *Proceedings of the 11th International Joint Conference on Artificial Intelligence*, pp. 701-707, 1989.

[Pearl, 1984] Pearl, J. *Heuristics: Intelligent Search Strategies for Computer Problem Solving*. Reading, Massachusetts: Addison-Wesley Publishing Company, 1984.

[Politowski, 1986] Politowski, G. *On the Construction of Heuristic Functions*. Ph.D. Thesis, U. C. Santa Cruz, 1986.

[Rendell, 1983] Rendell, L. A new basis for state-space learning systems and a successful implementation. *Artificial Intelligence* 20, pp. 369-392, 1983.

Moving Target Search

Toru Ishida
NTT Communications and
Information Processing Laboratories
1-2356, Take, Yokosuka,
238-03, JAPAN
ishida%nttkb.ntt.jp@relay.cs.net

Richard E. Korf
Computer Science Department
University of California, Los Angeles
Los Angeles, Ca. 90024, U.S.A.
korf@lanai.cs.ucla.edu

Abstract

We consider the case of heuristic search where the location of the goal may change during the course of the search. For example, the goal may be a target that is actively avoiding the problem solver. We present a moving target search algorithm (MTS) to solve this problem. We prove that if the average speed of the target is slower than that of the problem solver, then the problem solver is guaranteed to eventually reach the target. An implementation with randomly positioned obstacles confirms that the MTS algorithm is highly effective in various situations.

1 Introduction

All existing heuristic search algorithms assume that the goal state is fixed and does not change over the course of the search. For example, in the problem of driving from the current location to a desired goal location along a network of roads, it is assumed that the goal location is fixed and does not change during the drive. In this paper, we relax the assumption of a fixed goal, and allow it to move over time. In the road navigation example, instead of driving to a particular address, the task may be to reach another vehicle which is in fact moving as well.

There is no assumption that the target will eventually stop, but the goal is achieved when the position of the problem solver and the position of the target coincide. In order to have any hope of success in this task, the problem solver must be able to move faster than the target. Otherwise, the target could evade the problem solver indefinitely, even in a finite problem space, merely by avoiding being trapped in a dead-end path.

Existing search algorithms can be divided into two classes: off-line and real-time. Off-line algorithms, such as A*[1], compute an entire solution path before executing the first step in the path. Real-time algorithms, such as Real-Time-A*[2], perform sufficient computation to determine a plausible next move of the problem solver, execute that move in the physical world, then perform further computations to determine the following move, etc., until the goal is reached. These algorithms do not find optimal solutions, but can commit to actions in constant time per move.

If one were to use an off-line algorithm such as A* for the moving goal problem, by the time an optimal path was found to the current position of the goal, and the path was executed, the goal would have moved to a new position. If one were then to repeat the algorithm with the new current state and the new goal position, one could follow the target. In fact, this approach would work if the time to perform the search was negligible. However, we assume that search takes time, and thus even if the problem solver could move faster than the target, if it has to stop periodically to plan a new path, its speed advantage over the target may be lost.

Therefore, we must consider real-time algorithms that can rapidly react to each move of the target, and always make the best move toward the current location of the target. The next section briefly reviews previous work on such algorithms for the case of a fixed goal location.

2 Previous Work: LRTA*

Learning-real-time-A*(LRTA*)[2] is a real-time search algorithm for fixed goal states. As such, it commits to individual moves in constant time, and interleaves the computation of moves with their execution. It builds and updates a table containing heuristic estimates of the distance from each state in the problem space to the fixed goal state. Initially, the entries in the table correspond to heuristic evaluations, or zero if none are available, and are assumed to be lower bounds on actual distance. Through repeated exploration of the space, however, more accurate values are learned until they eventually equal the exact distances to the goal.

The LRTA* algorithm repeats the following steps until the problem solver reaches a goal state. Let x be the current position of the problem solver.

1. Calculate $f(x') = h(x') + k(x, x')$ for each neighbor x' of the current state, where $h(x')$ is the current heuristic estimate of the distance from x' to a goal state, and $k(x, x')$ is the cost of the edge from x to x'.
2. Move to a neighbor with the minimum $f(x')$ value. Ties are broken randomly.
3. Update the value of $h(x)$ to this minimum $f(x')$ value.

The reason for updating the value of $h(x)$ is that since

the $f(x')$ values represent lower bounds on the actual distance to the goal through each of the neighbors, the actual distance from the given state must be at least as large as the smallest of these estimates.

In a finite problem space with positive edge costs, in which there exists a path from every node to a goal, LRTA* is *complete* in the sense that it will eventually reach a goal. Furthermore, if the initial heuristic values are lower bounds on the actual values, then over repeated problem-solving trials, the values learned by LRTA* will eventually converge to their exact values along every optimal path to the goal. LRTA*, however, requires that the position of the goal state be fixed.

3 Problem Formulation

In this section we give a precise characterization of the moving target search problem. We represent the problem space as a connected graph. The graph is undirected, allowing motion of either the problem solver or the target along any edge in either direction. To simplify the following discussions, we assume that all edges in the graph have unit cost. Given a graph with non-uniform but rational edge costs, we can convert it to a graph with unit edge costs, without changing the topology of the graph, by choosing the unit to be the lowest common denominator of the edge costs, and then inserting into any edge with a larger value enough intermediate nodes of degree two so that each edge has unit cost.

There is an initial position of the problem solver and an initial position of the target. We assume the problem solver and the target move alternately, and can traverse at most one edge in a single move. The problem solver has no control over the movements of the target. The task is accomplished when the problem solver and the goal occupy the same node. The problem is further characterized by the following constraints.

Speed of the problem solver and the target:
Given unit edge costs, we reduce the speed of the target by assuming that periodically the target will make no move, and remain at its current position. Thus, the target can move at the same speed as the problem solver for only so long before losing a step by skipping a turn to move. We will slightly relax this assumption in Section 7.

Available information about the target and problem space:
We start with the assumption that the problem solver always knows the target's position, but will generalize this later in Section 7. We do not assume that the problem solver knows the topology of the problem space in the vicinity of the target position, nor the topology in the vicinity of the problem solver, other than the locations of the immediate neighbors of the current location of the problem solver. In other words, the problem solver does not have a map of the problem space.

A heuristic static evaluation function:
Another assumption is that there also exists a heuristic static evaluation function that returns an estimate of the distance between any pair of states. The only constraint placed on the static evaluation function is that it be admissible, meaning it never overestimates the actual distance between any pair of points. For example, a function returning the Euclidean distance in the plane is admissible, but so is a heuristic function that returns zero for every pair of points. Thus, we do not assume that the heuristic static evaluation function provides any useful information.

4 Moving Target Search Algorithm

In this section, we present the algorithm, called *moving-target search* (MTS). It is a generalization of LRTA* to the case where the goal can move. MTS must acquire heuristic information for each goal location. Thus, MTS maintains a matrix of heuristic values, representing the function $h(x,y)$ for all pairs of states x and y. Conceptually, all heuristic values are read from this matrix, which is initialized to the values returned by the static evaluation function. Over the course of the search, these heuristic values are updated to improve their accuracy. In practice, we only store those values that differ from their static values. Thus, even though the complete matrix may be very large, it may be quite sparse, and sparse matrix techniques may be used for time and space efficiency.

There are two different events that occur in the algorithm: a move of the problem solver, and a move of the target, each of which may be accompanied by the updating of a heuristic value. The problem solver and target alternate moves, and heuristic values are updated as necessary, until the position of the problem solver and the target are equal. In the description below, x is the current position of the problem solver, and y is the current position of the target.

When it is the problem solver's turn to move, it calculates $f(x',y) = h(x',y) + 1$ for each of its neighbors x' of x, and chooses a neighbor w with the smallest f value to move to. Ties are broken randomly. If $f(w,y) > h(x,y)$, then $h(x,y)$ is updated to $f(w,y)$. The reason is that since any path from x to y must go through one of its neighbors x', the cost of the minimum path from x to y must be as large as the minimum cost path through any of its neighbors x'.

When it is the target's turn to move, the problem solver observes its move from y to its neighbor y', calculates $h(x,y')$, and compares it to $h(x,y)$, where x is the current state of the problem solver. If $h(x,y') > h(x,y) + 1$, then $h(x,y)$ is updated to $h(x,y') - 1$. The reason is that since the old and new positions of the target are at most one unit apart, the distance to the old position must be at least as large as the distance to the new position minus one unit.

The algorithm is described more succinctly below.

When the problem solver moves from x:

1. Calculate $f(x',y) = h(x',y)+1$ for each neighbor x' of x.

2. Move to the neighbor with the minimum $f(x', y)$. Ties are broken randomly.
3. Update the value of $h(x, y)$ as follows:

$$h(x,y) \longleftarrow max \left\{ \begin{array}{c} h(x,y) \\ min_{x'}\{h(x',y)+1\} \end{array} \right\}$$

When the target moves from y to y':

1. Calculate $h(x, y')$ for the target's new position y'.
2. Update the value of $h(x, y)$ as follows:

$$h(x,y) \longleftarrow max \left\{ \begin{array}{c} h(x,y) \\ h(x,y')-1 \end{array} \right\}$$

It should be emphasized that this is only one algorithm to solve this problem. In particular, it was designed to perform the minimum amount of computation necessary to guarantee success. Performance of the algorithm could be considerably improved by updating more heuristic values with each move. For example, the update of $h(x, y)$ performed with each move of the problem solver could also be similarly applied to $h(x, z)$ for values of z other than the target position y. The drawback of this is that such computation requires time and memory, and may not be of any use if the target never visits position z.

5 Completeness of Moving Target Search

In this section, we prove that a problem solver executing MTS is guaranteed to eventually reach the target, as long as the target periodically skips a move. We begin by showing that the updates preserve admissibility of the heuristic values. Then, we define a positive quantity called *heuristic disparity*, which is a combination of the difference between the current heuristic values and their exact values, and the current estimated heuristic distance from the problem solver to the target. We show that in any pair of moves of the problem solver and the target, this quantity can never increase, and decreases whenever the target does not move. Since it cannot be negative, and if it ever reaches zero the problem is solved, the algorithm must eventually terminate successfully.

Lemma:

Updating in MTS preserves admissibility of heuristic values.

Proof:

Assume that the current values are admissible. There are two types of updates, those occurring with moves of the problem solver, and those accompanying moves of the target.

In the case of problem solver moves, if $h(x, y)$ is updated, it is set equal to $h(w, y) + 1$, where $h(w, y)$ is the minimum of $h(x', y)$ for all neighbors x' of x. Since any path from x to y must go through one of its neighbors x', and each neighbor is one unit away, the cost of the minimum path from x to y must be one greater than the minimum cost path from any neighbor x' to y. If $h(x', y)$ is a lower bound on the cost from x' to y, then $h(w, y)$ is a lower bound on the cost from any neighbor x' to y, and hence $h(w, y) + 1$ must be a lower bound on the cost from x to y. Thus, this update preserves admissibility.

In the case of moves of the target, if $h(x, y)$ is updated, it is set equal to $h(x, y') - 1$, where y' is the new position of the target. Since y is at most one unit away from y', the distance from x to y can only differ from the distance from x to y' by at most one unit. Thus if y' is at least $h(x, y')$ units from x, then y must be at least $h(x, y') - 1$ units from x. Thus, this update preserves admissibility as well.

By induction on the total number of updates, updating preserves admissibility.

Theorem:

In a finite problem space, in which a path exists between every pair of nodes, starting with non-negative admissible initial heuristic values, a problem solver executing MTS will eventually reach the target, if the target periodically skips moves.

Proof:

Define the *heuristic error* at a given state of the computation as the sum over all pairs of states a and b of $h^*(a, b) - h(a, b)$ where $h^*(a, b)$ is the length of the shortest path between a and b, and $h(a, b)$ is the current heuristic value. Define the *heuristic distance* as $h(x, y)$, the current heuristic value between the current state of the problem solver, x, and the current state of the target, y. Define the *heuristic disparity* as the sum of the heuristic error and the heuristic difference.

First, consider a move of the problem solver from x to x'. If $h(x', y) < h(x, y)$, then no update occurs, and the heuristic distance from problem solver to target after the move, $h(x', y)$, is at least one unit less than the heuristic distance between them before the move, $h(x, y)$. Thus, the move causes the heuristic distance and hence the heuristic disparity to decrease by at least one unit. Conversely, if $h(x', y) \geq h(x, y)$, then $h(x, y)$ is increased to $h(x', y) + 1$. As a result, the total heuristic error decreases by $h(x', y) + 1 - h(x, y)$, while the heuristic distance increases by $h(x', y) - h(x, y)$, for a net decrease of one unit in the heuristic disparity. Thus, in either case, the heuristic disparity decreases by at least one unit.

Now consider a move of the target from y to y'. If $h(x, y') \leq h(x, y) + 1$, then there is no update and the heuristic difference and the heuristic disparity increase by at most one unit. Conversely, if $h(x, y') > h(x, y) + 1$, then $h(x, y)$ is increased to $h(x, y') - 1$. Thus, the total heuristic error decreases by $h(x, y') - 1 - h(x, y)$, but the heuristic difference increases by $h(x, y') - h(x, y)$, for a total increase in the heuristic disparity of one unit. In either case, the heuristic disparity increases by at most one unit.

Since a move by the problem solver always decreases the heuristic disparity by one unit, and a move by the target can only increase it by at most one unit, in a pair of moves by problem solver and target the heuristic disparity cannot increase. When the target eventually skips a move, the heuristic disparity will decrease by at least one unit. With repeated skipped moves by the target, heuristic disparity must continue to decrease over time.

Since there is a path between every pair of states, $h^*(a,b)$ is finite for all a and b, and since there are a finite number of states, total heuristic error is finite. Similarly, since all heuristic values are admissible and hence finite, heuristic difference is also finite. Therefore, heuristic disparity is finite. Since all heuristic values are admissible, total heuristic error is non-negative, and since heuristic values are non-negative, heuristic difference is non-negative. Thus, heuristic disparity is non-negative. Either the algorithm terminates successfully, or the heuristic disparity reaches zero, meaning that both total heuristic error and heuristic difference are zero. At that point, all heuristic values are exact, and the heuristic distance between problem solver and target is zero, meaning they are in the same location. This constitutes a successful termination.

6 Efficiency of Moving Target Search

6.1 Space Complexity

An upper bound on the space complexity of moving target search is N^2, where N is the number of states in the problem space. The reason is that in the worst case, heuristic values between every possible pair of states would have to be stored. In practice, however, the space complexity will usually be much lower. Since there exists a function which computes the static heuristic value between any pair of points, it is only necessary to store in memory those values that differ from the static values. When a heuristic value is needed, if it is not in the table, then it is computed by the function. Since at most only one update occurs per move of the problem solver or target, we never need more memory that the total number of moves of problem solver and target combined. In fact, we may need considerably less since an update does not necessarily occur with every move. Thus, the overall space complexity is the minimum of N^2 and the total number of moves of the problem solver and target.

6.2 Time Complexity

The worst-case time complexity of MTS is N^3, where N is the number of states in the problem space. This can be obtained by investigating the maximum heuristic disparity. The total heuristic error is upper bounded by N^3, because there are N^2 heuristic values between every possible pair of states, and the maximum heuristic value of each state is N. On the other hand, if no updates of heuristic values occur, then the maximum number moves of the problem solver to reach the target is N/S, where S is the fraction of moves that are skipped by the target. This is because the maximum heuristic difference is N, and it must decrease by at least one every time the target skips a move. Thus the overall time complexity, which is the sum of these two terms, is still N^3 in the worst case. The worst case assumes initial heuristic values of zero everywhere. In this case, the learning cost for correcting heuristic error is the major component of the time complexity of MTS.

6.3 Learning Over Multiple Trials

Over the course of a single problem solving episode, MTS gradually learns more accurate heuristic values, until the target is reached. If we choose new initial states for both the problem solver and the target, but start with the set of heuristic values left over from the previous problem solving episode, the knowledge learned from previous trials is immediately transferable to the new episode, with the result being better performance than if we started with the initial heuristic values. If we continue to preserve heuristic values from one episode to another, eventually the heuristic values will converge to their exact values for every pair of states. At that point, the problem solver will always make the best possible moves in pursuing the target, and the time complexity of an individual trial reduces to N/S. Of course, for complete learning, N^2 space is required to store all heuristic values.

7 Relaxing Some Constraints on MTS

7.1 Speed of the Problem Solver and the Target

In previous sections, we assumed that the problem solver can move faster than the target, but this is not strictly necessary. A weaker condition is that the target can move as fast as the problem solver, but occasionally makes errors in avoiding the problem solver. For this purpose, we define an apparently optimal move of the target to be one that increases the distance from the problem solver by at least one unit, according to the heuristic values. If the heuristic values are exact, then an apparently optimal move is in fact an optimal move. However, if there is error in the heuristic values, then an apparently optimal move may or may not be in fact optimal, and an optimal move may or may not appear to be optimal. In order for it to be possible for the problem solver to catch the target, we assume that the target periodically makes apparently suboptimal moves.

Even in this case, a problem solver executing MTS will sill eventually reach the target. This is because an apparently suboptimal move by the target is one that does not increase the heuristic difference. Thus, there is no update and the heuristic disparity does not increase. An apparently suboptimal move of the target, coupled with a move of the problem solver, decreases the heuristic disparity by at least one unit. Thus, the heuristic disparity continues to decrease over time.

7.2 Available Information about the Target

We previously assumed that the problem solver always knows the position of the target. This assumption can also be relaxed by only requiring that the problem solver know the position of the target at some point before the problem solver reaches the last known position of the target. This generalization allows the problem solver to

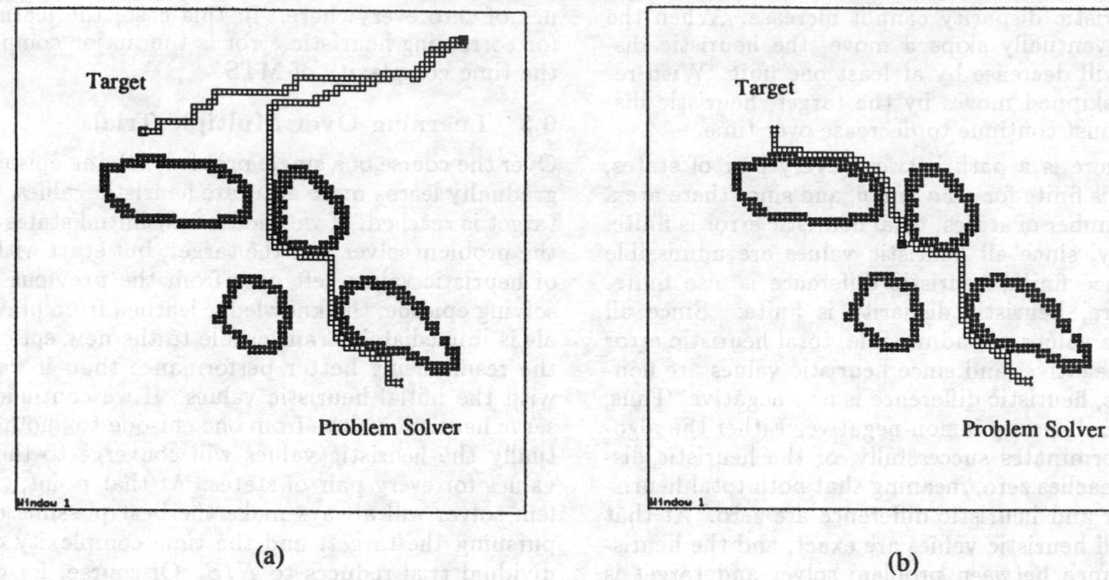

Figure 1: Sample Tracks of MTS

temporarily lose sight of the target, and thus may be more practical in real applications.

Suppose the problem solver and the target have moved at most t times between the target being observed at y and then at z. In this case, the updating of the heuristic values is generalized as follows.

1. Calculate $h(x,z)$ for the target's new position z.
2. Update the value of $h(x,y)$ as follows:

$$h(x,y) \longleftarrow max\left\{ \begin{array}{l} h(x,y) \\ h(x,z)-t \end{array} \right\}$$

The update is admissible, because y is at most t units away from z, and the distance between x and y can only differ from the distance between x and z by at most t units. Thus if z is at least $h(x,z)$ units from x, then y must be at least $h(x,z)-t$ units from x.

To prove the completeness of the generalized MTS, we must slightly modify the proof in Section 5. If $h(x,z) \leq h(x,y)+t$, then there is no update and the heuristic difference and the heuristic disparity increase by at most t units. Conversely, if $h(x,z) > h(x,y)+t$, then $h(x,y)$ is increased to $h(x,z)-t$. Thus, the total heuristic error decreases by $h(x,z)-t-h(x,y)$, but the heuristic difference increases by $h(x,z)-h(x,y)$, for a total increase in the heuristic disparity of t units. In either case, the heuristic disparity increases by at most t units. Since a move by the problem solver always decreases the heuristic disparity by at least one unit, the heuristic disparity decreases by t units in the period between when the target is observed at y and then at z. On the other hand, a move by the target from y to z can only increase it by at most t units. Thus, in the combined sequence of t moves by the problem solver and the target, the heuristic disparity cannot increase.

8 Experimental Evaluation

We have implemented MTS in a rectangular grid problem space (100×100) with randomly positioned obstacles. We allow motion along the horizontal and vertical dimensions, but not along the diagonal. Interesting target behavior was obtained by allowing a human user to indirectly control the motion of the target. The user moves a cursor around the screen using a mouse, and the target always moves toward the current position of the cursor, using static heuristic values for guidance. Figure 1 shows the experimental setup along with sample tracks of the target and problem solver with manually placed obstacles. In Figure 1(a), the user's task is to avoid the problem solver, which is executing MTS, for as long as possible, while in Figure 1(b), the task is to meet the problem solver as quickly as possible.

8.1 Experiments on Different Target Response Modes

Figure 2 illustrates the search cost represented by the total number of moves of the problem solver for various response strategies of the target. The response modes are: 1) the target actively avoids the problem solver *(Avoid)*, 2) the target moves randomly *(Random)*, 3) the target moves cooperatively to try to meet the problem solver *(Meet)*, and 4) the target remains stationary *(Stationary)*. In *Meet* and *Avoid*, the target also performs MTS: in *Meet*, the target moves to decrease the heuristic distance to the problem solver, while in *Avoid*, the target moves to increase the heuristic distance.

The speed of the target is set to 80% of the problem solver. In other words, it skips one of every five moves. To erase problem space boundaries, we formed a torus by connecting the opposite boundaries. The problem solver and the target are initially positioned as far apart

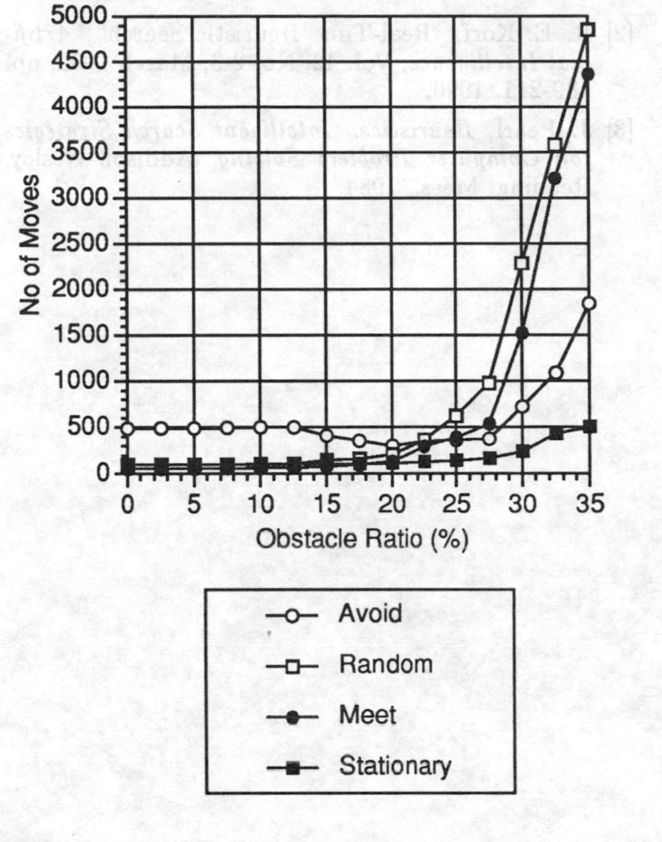

Figure 2: Performance with Different Target Response Modes

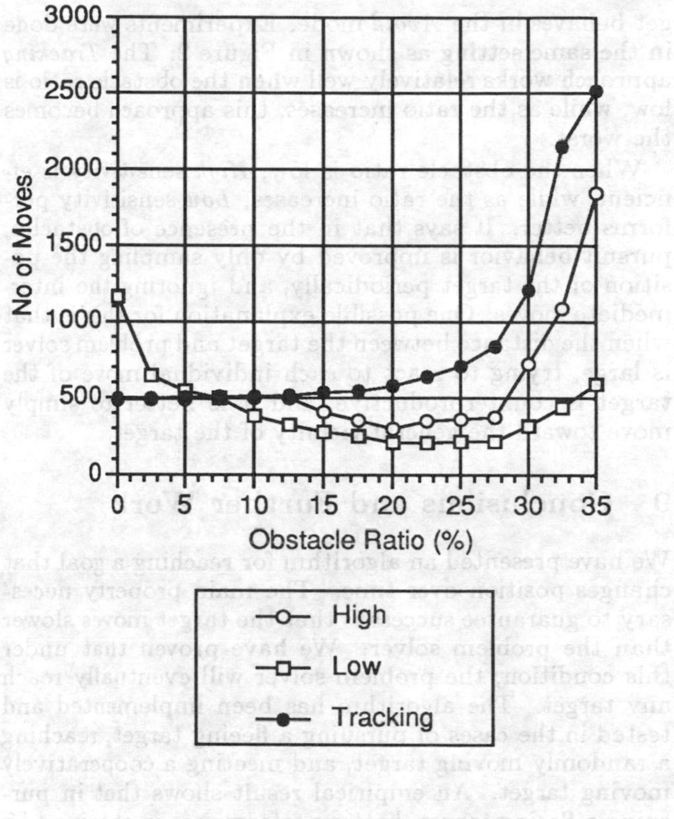

Figure 3: Performance with Various Problem Solver Sensitivities

as possible in the torus, i.e., 100 units in Manhattan distance. Obstacles are randomly positioned. For example, an obstacle ratio of 20% means 2000 junctions in the 100 × 100 grid are randomly replaced by obstacles. With high obstacle ratios (more than 20%), obstacles join up and form walls with various shapes. When the ratio reaches 40%, the obstacles tend to disconnect the problem space, separating the target from and the problem solver. Euclidean distance is used as the heuristic static evaluation function. The number of moves in the figures are obtained by averaging 100 trials.

8.2 Experiments on Different Target Response Modes

As shown in Figure 2, with relatively few obstacles, the target that is easiest to catch is one that is trying to *Meet* the problem solver, and the most difficult target to catch is one that is trying to *Avoid* the problem solver, as one would expect. When the obstacles become more numerous, however, it becomes harder to catch a target making *Random* moves and one that is trying to *Meet* the problem solver, than a target trying to *Avoid* the problem solver or a stationary target. At first, this result seems counterintuitive. If one is trying to avoid a faster pursuer as long as possible, however, the best strategy is not to run away, but to hide behind obstacles. Both *Meet* and *Random* approximate this strategy better than *Avoid*. The reason *Avoid* is more effective than remaining stationary is that *Avoid* makes the problem solver spend more time learning new heuristic values.

8.3 Experiments on the Problem Solver's Sensitivity

As discussed in Section 7.2, the generalized MTS algorithm allows the problem solver to temporarily lose sight of the target. In other words, even if the problem solver always knows the target's location, it can ignore some of this information. Can this improve the performance of the problem solver?

One possibility is for the problem solver to always keep track of the current position of the target, or *(High)* sensitivity. Another possibility is that the problem solver only observes the target position when it reaches the previous position of the target, or *(Low)* sensitivity. We also implemented a approach called *Tracking*, in which MTS is not utilized: the problem solver first moves to the initial position of the target, keeping track of all moves made by the target in the meantime, and once the initial state of the target is reached, the problem solver simply follows the target by repeating each of its moves. While this approach can be applied only when the problem solver always knows the target's position, it is worth comparing it to MTS.

Figure 3 shows the empirical results, in which the target behaves in the *Avoid* mode. Experiments were done in the same setting as shown in Figure 2. The *Tracking* approach works relatively well when the obstacle ratio is low, while as the ratio increases, this approach becomes the worst.

When the obstacle ratio is low, *High* sensitivity is efficient, while as the ratio increases, *Low* sensitivity performs better. It says that in the presence of obstacles, pursuit behavior is improved by only sampling the position of the target periodically, and ignoring the intermediate moves. One possible explanation for this is that when the distance between the target and problem solver is large, trying to react to each individual move of the target is counterproductive, and it is better to simply move toward the general vicinity of the target.

9 Conclusions and Further Work

We have presented an algorithm for reaching a goal that changes position over time. The main property necessary to guarantee success is that the target moves slower than the problem solver. We have proven that under this condition, the problem solver will eventually reach any target. The algorithm has been implemented and tested in the cases of pursuing a fleeing target, reaching a randomly moving target, and meeting a cooperatively moving target. An empirical result shows that in pursuing a fleeing target, better performance is obtained by ignoring some moves of the target and only sampling its position periodically.

More generally, this work can be viewed as a case study of problem solving in a dynamic and unpredictable environment. In this case, the unpredictability stems from the motion of the goal. However, additional uncertainty could be introduced without any modifications of the algorithm. For example, new obstacles could be dynamically added to the space during the course of the search. While this will cause performance to degrade initially, the existence of these new obstacles will eventually be reflected in the learned heuristic values.

Acknowledgment

The authors wish to thank Tsukasa Kawaoka and Ryohei Nakano for their support during this work at NTT Laboratories. This research benefitted from discussions with Kazuhiro Kuwabara, Yoshiyasu Nishibe, and Makoto Yokoo. The bulk of this research was performed while the second author was a visitor at, and supported by, NTT Laboratories. Additional support to the second author was provided by an NSF Presidential Young Investigator Award, NSF grant IRI-8801939, and a grant from Rockwell International.

References

[1] P. E. Hart, N. J. Nilsson and B. Raphael, "A formal basis for the heuristic determination of minimum cost paths", *IEEE Transactions on Systems Science and Cybernetics*, SSC-4, No. 2, pp.100-107, 1968.

[2] R. E. Korf, "Real-Time Heuristic Search", *Artificial Intelligence*, Vol. 42, No. 2-3, March 1990, pp. 189-211. 1990.

[3] J. Pearl, *Heuristics: Intelligent Search Strategies for Computer Problem Solving*, Addison-Wesley, Reading, Mass., 1984.

AUTOMATED REASONING

Planning I

Composing Real-Time Systems

Stuart J. Russell and **Shlomo Zilberstein**
Computer Science Division
University of California
Berkeley, California 94720 U.S.A.
russell@colditz.berkeley.edu shlomo@bastille.berkeley.edu

Abstract

We present a method to construct real-time systems using as components *anytime* algorithms whose quality of results degrades gracefully as computation time decreases. Introducing computation time as a degree of freedom defines a scheduling problem involving the activation and interruption of the anytime components. This scheduling problem is especially complicated when trying to construct *interruptible* algorithms, whose total run-time is unknown in advance. We introduce a framework to measure the performance of anytime algorithms and solve the problem of constructing interruptible algorithms by a mathematical reduction to the problem of constructing *contract* algorithms, which require the determination of the total run-time when activated. We show how the composition of anytime algorithms can be mechanized as part of a compiler for a LISP-like programming language for real-time systems. The result is a new approach to the construction of complex real-time systems that separates the arrangement of the performance components from the optimization of their scheduling, and automates the latter task.

1 Introduction

Our objective in this research has been to develop and automate a methodology for the construction of utility-driven, real-time agents. A real-time agent is an agent whose utility function depends on time. For example, a utility function defined as the number of widgets assembled per hour depends on time; a robot designed to maximize this utility function is a real-time agent. Similarly, problems such as chess-playing, reentry navigation for a space shuttle, financial planning and trading, and medical monitoring in an intensive care unit have utility functions that depend on time, and therefore require the construction of real-time systems. This approach generalizes the traditional view of real-time systems as systems that can guarantee a response after a fixed time has elapsed [Laffey *et al.*, 1988], in that deadlines can be expressed by a sharp drop in the utility function.

We show in this paper how to construct real-time systems using anytime algorithms[1] as basic blocks. Anytime algorithms are algorithms whose quality of results degrades gracefully as computation time decreases, hence they introduce a tradeoff between computation time and quality of results. The algorithm's *performance profile* (PP) gives a probabilistic description of the quality of results as a function of time (we define and generalize this notion in section 2). For example, consider a hierarchical diagnosis algorithm that recursively performs a test to identify the defective component of an assembly. This algorithm can be interrupted at any time to produce a partial diagnosis whose quality can be measured by the level of specificity. By translating the quality of results into a utility measure that takes into account the time needed to produce these results, we can compute the optimal amount of time that should be allocated to diagnosis, after which a complete defective component should be replaced rather than being further analyzed. A similar technique was used by Boddy and Dean [1989] for solving a real-time path planning problem and by Horvitz [1987] for real-time decision making in the health care domain.

An important distinction that has to some extent been ignored in the literature should be made between *interruptible* algorithms and *contract* algorithms. Interruptible algorithms produce results of the 'advertised quality' even when interrupted unexpectedly; whereas contract algorithms, although capable of producing results whose quality varies with time allocation, must be given a particular time allocation in advance. If a contract algorithm is interrupted at any time shorter than the contract time it may yield no useful results. An important result of this paper, given in section 2, shows that there is in fact a simple reduction from interruptible algorithms to contract algorithms.

In this work we extend the use of anytime algorithms to the construction of complex real-time systems. It is unlikely that a complex system will be developed by implementing one large anytime algorithm. Systems are normally built from components that are developed and tested separately. In standard algorithms, the quality of the output is fixed, so composition can be implemented

[1] Dean and Boddy [1988] coined the term "anytime algorithm" in their paper on time-dependent planning.

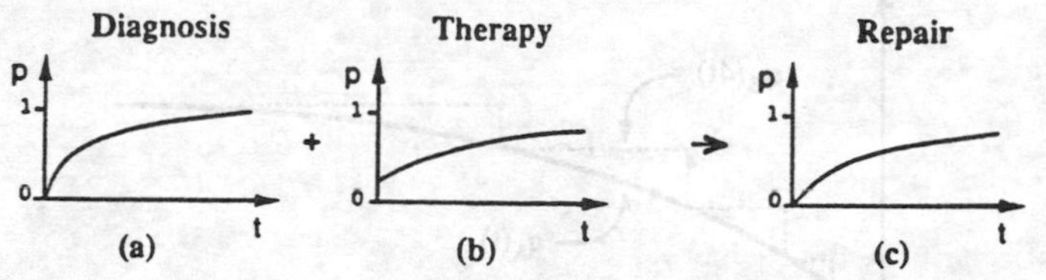

Figure 1: Composition of anytime algorithms

by a simple call-return mechanism. However, when algorithms have resource allocation as a degree of freedom, there arises the question of how to construct, for example, the optimal composition of two anytime algorithms, one of which feeds its output to the other. Consider making a repair system from a 'diagnosis' component and a 'therapy' component. The more time spent on diagnosis, the more likely the hypothesis is to be correct. The more time spent on therapy planning, the more likely the problem is to be fixed, *assuming the diagnosis is correct*. Given the performance profiles of the two subsystems (as shown in Figure 1ab), it is straightforward to construct the optimal apportionment of resources for a given total allocation, and hence to construct the optimal anytime algorithm for the whole problem (whose performance profile is shown in Figure 1c).

To summarize, in our approach the user specifies the structural decomposition of a complex problem into elementary performance components, each of which can be a traditional or an anytime algorithm. For example, the repair system might be specified as:

```
(defun repair (x)
  (apply-therapy x (diagnose x)))
```

Our system generates an anytime algorithm for the original problem by scheduling and monitoring the components in an optimal way (with respect to a given utility function). The rest of this paper describes this method in detail. In Section 2 we define the probabilistic description of the performance of anytime algorithms and examine their essential properties. In Section 3 we present a framework for evaluating anytime algorithms within the context of a given domain and a utility function. In Section 4 we explain and demonstrate the task of compiling anytime algorithms. Finally, Section 5 summarizes the benefits of our approach and discusses related work and further work to be undertaken.

2 Anytime algorithms

Anytime algorithms are characterized by their *performance profile* (PP), a probabilistic description of the quality of results as a function of time. The exact meaning and concrete representation of a PP is implementation dependent. In this section we define three types of PP and explain the basic properties of anytime algorithms.

2.1 Performance profiles

A PP maps computation time to a probabilistic description of the quality of the results. The main reason for the uncertainty concerning the quality of results (especially with deterministic algorithms) is the fact that the input to the algorithm is unknown. Therefore, a PP should always be interpreted with respect to a particular probability distribution of input.

Given an anytime algorithm $\mathcal{A}$, let $q_{\mathcal{A}}(x,t)$ be the quality of results produced by $\mathcal{A}$ with input x and computation time t; let $q_{\mathcal{A}}(t)$ be the expected quality of results with computation time t; and let $p_{\mathcal{A},t}(q)$ be the probability (density function in the continuous case) that $\mathcal{A}$ with computation time t produces results of quality q. A complete description of the performance of $\mathcal{A}$ is given by the following definition:

Definition 2.1 *The* **performance distribution profile (PDP)**, *of an algorithm $\mathcal{A}$ is a function $D_{\mathcal{A}} : \mathcal{R} \to Pr(\mathcal{R})$ that maps computation time to a probability distribution of the quality of the results.*

In some cases the summation over all possible inputs may produce too wide a range of qualities and the information provided by the PP may be too general. In that case we use conditional PPs by partitioning the input domain into classes and storing a separate PP for each class (this partitioning is done using any attribute of the input, such as size or a complexity measure).

Definition 2.2 *The* **expected performance profile (PEP)**, *of an algorithm $\mathcal{A}$ is a function $E_{\mathcal{A}} : \mathcal{R}^+ \to \mathcal{R}$ that maps computation time to the expected quality of the results.*

Note that $E_{\mathcal{A}}(t) = \sum_q p_{\mathcal{A},t}(q)q = \sum_x Pr(x)q_{\mathcal{A}}(x,t)$. This is exactly what Dean and Boddy [1988] used as a performance profile.

Definition 2.3 *The* **performance interval profile (PIP)**, *of an algorithm $\mathcal{A}$ is a function $I_{\mathcal{A}} : \mathcal{R}^+ \to \mathcal{R} \times \mathcal{R}$ that maps computation time to the upper and lower bounds of the quality of the results.*

Note that if $I_{\mathcal{A}}(t) = [L, U]$ then $\forall x : L \leq q_{\mathcal{A}}(x,t) \leq U$.

The quality of results described by a PP is measured in one of the following ways:

1. **Certainty** – Probability of correctness determines quality (e.g. randomized algorithms for primality testing).
2. **Accuracy** – Error bound determines quality (e.g. Newton's method).
3. **Specificity** – Amount of detail determines quality (e.g. hierarchical diagnosis).

While accuracy is typically used to measure quality in numerical domains, and specificity in symbolic domains, the former can be seen as a special case of the latter; an inaccurate numerical solution is very specific but incorrect, and could be mapped to an equally useful, correct statement that the solution lies within a certain interval. Anytime algorithms can also have multidimensional quality measures, for example PAC algorithms for inductive learning are characterized by an uncertainty measure δ and a precision measure ϵ.

2.2 Elementary anytime algorithms

Elementary anytime algorithms are already widely available, contrary to popular supposition. Many existing general programming and reasoning techniques produce useful anytime algorithms: search techniques such as iterative deepening; asymptotically correct inference algorithms such as approximate query answering [Elkan, 1990; Vrbsky *et al.*, 1990], bounded cutset conditioning (see [Horvitz, 1987]), and variable precision logic [Michalski and Winston, 1986]; various greedy algorithms (see [Boddy and Dean, 1989]); iterative methods such as Newton's method; adaptive algorithms such as PAC learning algorithms [Haussler, 1990] or neural networks; Monte Carlo algorithms for simulating probabilistic models; and the use of optimal meta-level control of computation [Russell and Wefald, 1989].

2.3 Interruptible vs contract algorithms

As mentioned in section 1, we distinguish between two types of anytime algorithms. *Interruptible* algorithms are those whose run-time need not be determined at the time of activation. They can be interrupted at any time to yield results whose quality is characterized by their PP. Many of the elementary anytime algorithms mentioned above, such as iterative deepening algorithms, are interruptible. *Contract* algorithms require a specific time allocation when activated. For example, Korf's RTA* [1988] performs a depth-first or best-first search within a predetermined search horizon that is computed from the time allocation provided, and can therefore modeled as a contract algorithm. Although this algorithm can produce results for any given time allocation, if it is interrupted before the expiration of the allocation it may yield no results.

Every interruptible algorithm is trivially a contract algorithm, however the converse is not true. In general, the greater freedom of design makes it easier to construct contract algorithms than interruptible ones. The following theorem is therefore essential for the compilation of interruptible algorithms.

Theorem 1 *For any contract algorithm $\mathcal{A}$, an interruptible algorithm $\mathcal{B}$ can be constructed such that* $q_{\mathcal{B}}(4t) \geq q_{\mathcal{A}}(t)$.

Proof: Construct $\mathcal{B}$ by running $\mathcal{A}$ repeatedly with exponentially increasing time limits. Let the sequence of run-time segments be $\tau, 2\tau, ..., 2^i\tau, ...$, and assume that the code required to control this loop can be ignored. Note also that $\sum_{i=0}^{i=n-1} 2^i = 2^n - 1$. The worst case occurs when $\mathcal{B}$ is interrupted after almost $(2^n - 1)\tau$ time units, just before the last iteration terminates and the returned result is based on the previous iteration with a run-time of $2^{n-2}\tau$ time units. Since $\frac{2^n-1}{2^{n-2}} < 4$, we get the factor of 4. If we replace the multiplier of time intervals by α we get a time ratio of: $\frac{\alpha^n-1}{\alpha^{n-1}-\alpha^{n-2}}$. The lower bound of this expression is 4, for $\alpha = 2$, hence the above sequence of run-times is optimal[2].

[2]This factor can obviously be reduced by scheduling the contract algorithm on multiple processors. The parallel scheduling options are non-trivial, and are not discussed in this paper.

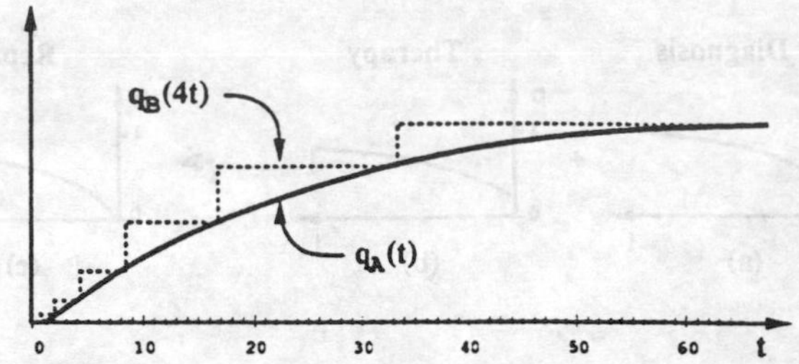

Figure 2: PP of the constructed interruptible algorithm

Note that τ may be arbitrarily small and should be in general the shortest run-time for which there is a significant improvement in the results of $\mathcal{A}$.

Figure 2 shows a typical performance profile for the contract algorithm $\mathcal{A}$, and the corresponding performance profile for the constructed interruptible algorithm $\mathcal{B}$, reduced along time axis by a factor of 4.

As an example, consider the application of this construction method to Korf's RTA*, a contract algorithm. As the time allocation is increased exponentially, the algorithm will increase its depth bound by a constant; the construction therefore generates an iterative deepening search automatically.

3 Evaluating anytime algorithms

Traditional algorithms are verified in the context of input and output predicates specified by the designer. Optimizing performance means simply reducing the execution time of a correct algorithm. The use of anytime algorithms in agents requires taking into account the real-time environment in which they operate and the utility function of the agent (or its designer). It is assumed that imprecise results have some value depending on their quality and the utility function of the system. The following framework, roughly analogous to that of [Horvitz, 1987], defines precisely what it means to be a better anytime algorithm; this depends not only on the PP of the algorithm but also on the domain and utility function (which are defined by the user).

A utility function is defined over the states of the domain: $U : \mathcal{S} \rightarrow \mathcal{R}$.

Given an algorithm $\mathcal{A}$, let $[S, q]$ denote the state of the domain that is reached by providing results of quality q when the domain is in state S. We can always view $\mathcal{A}$ as a decision making algorithm and the new state is simply the state resulting from performing the action recommended by the $\mathcal{A}$.

Now, given the current state S_0 and a certain time period t, we want to compute the comprehensive utility of the results produced by $\mathcal{A}$ with computation time t. The problem is that there is uncertainty concerning:

1. The quality of results of $\mathcal{A}$ at time t.
2. The state of the domain at time t.

The probabilistic description of the former is given by the PP of $\mathcal{A}$, and the probabilistic description of the latter is given by the model of the environment (we assume that the environment is not affected by which algorithm is running up until t; $p_t(S_i)$ is the probability that the state of the domain will be S_i at time t). Hence we get:

$$U_C(\mathcal{A},t) = \sum_i p_t(S_i) \sum_q p_{\mathcal{A},t}(q) U([S_i,q])$$

The value of an algorithm is then defined as the maximal utility achieved by optimal time allocation, that is:

$$V(\mathcal{A}) = \max_t \{U_C(\mathcal{A},t)\}.$$

Based on this definition we can define an order relation over anytime algorithms: we say that $\mathcal{A}_1 \succ \mathcal{A}_2$ if $V(\mathcal{A}_1) > V(\mathcal{A}_2)$. This relation replaces the traditional notion of correctness.

4 Compilation of anytime algorithms

The compilation of anytime algorithms is the process of constructing an optimal anytime algorithm using anytime algorithms as components. Creating interruptible algorithms directly is complicated, because the total time allocation is unknown in advance. We therefore start by considering only the construction of contract algorithms and then we extend the results to interruptible algorithms using Theorem 1.

The compilation methods that we describe in this section will be integrated into a programming language for anytime computation. Our goal is to develop a compiler for a language that might be in fact syntactically indistinguishable from simple LISP, but all of whose functions might in principle be anytime algorithms. We suggest LISP as the basic language since it is already widely used for AI applications, it allows the association of objects (such as PPs) with functions, and its functional nature is more suitable for the kind of composition of algorithms that we propose.

In our proposed language, the user simply specifies how the total real-time system is built by composing and sequencing simpler elements, and the compiler generates and inserts code for resource subdivision and scheduling given only the PPs of the most primitive routines. Furthermore, the flexibility of each function makes possible richer forms of composition than is normally available in programming languages; for example, a task can be solved by interleaving several solution methods until one produces the answer. The overall performance profile of the resulting system is computed by the compiler, allowing it to be used as a new building block for still more complex systems. The following in-flight aircraft monitoring system is an example of the kind of program that our compiler is eventually intended to handle:

```
(defun monitor ()
  (calibrate-instruments)
  (if (setq pl (passengers-missing))
      (mapc #'(lambda (p) (remove-from-plane
                (hunt-for-bags p))) pl))
  (wait-for-take-off-permission)
  (loop
    (if (setq co (collision-imminent))
        (alert-pilot (plan-avoidance)))
    (if (setq ep (engine-problems))
        (alert-pilot
          (plan-repair ep (diagnose ep))))
    (if (setq cp (off-course
          (determine-current-position)))
      (any (alert-pilot cp)
           (plan-course-adjustment cp)
           (effect-course-adjustment cp)))))
```

In this program fragment, the only algorithms that are not anytime are `remove-from-plane`, `alert-pilot`, and `off-course`. All others could consume arbitrary amounts of resources, depending on the accuracy and certainty produced, and hence need to be scheduled appropriately.

4.1 Choosing the right type of PP

Earlier we defined three types of performance profiles the most informative of which was the probability distribution profile (PDP). This representation is both expensive to maintain and complicated to compile, especially in the continuous case. The simplest representation, the expected performance profile (PEP) is not suitable for our compilation scheme as explained below. We use performance interval profiles (PIP) that keep the lower and upper bounds of the quality of results. Assuming that performance is monotonically increasing, we can compute the quality bounds of a complex algorithm using the quality bounds of its components.

4.2 Compiling contract algorithms

We analyze first several cases of compilation of contract algorithms — that is, the problem is to produce a contract algorithm from anytime components (which can be either interruptible or contract algorithms). The constructs we consider are certainly not an exhaustive collection, but serve to illustrate the issues involved in building the compiler.

4.2.1 Sequences

We first consider the optimal composition of two anytime algorithms, $\mathcal{A}_1$ and $\mathcal{A}_2$, one of which feeds its output to the other. The repair system that was described earlier illustrates this situation. Let q_1 and q_2 be the performance profiles of $\mathcal{A}_1$ and $\mathcal{A}_2$, and let $U^*(q_1,q_2)$ be the *quality combination function*, that is, the function that defines how the quality of the module depends on the quality of the components. For each allocation of time, t, $\mathcal{A}_1$ gets x time units and $\mathcal{A}_2$ gets the remaining $t-x$ time units, where x is chosen to maximize $U^*(q_1(x), q_2(t-x))$. The performance profile of the compound module is therefore

$$q^*(t) = \max_{0 \le x \le t} U^*(q_1(x), q_2(t-x))$$

Similarly, in the case of n steps we get:

$$q^*(t) = \max_{\sum x_i = t} U^*(q_1(x_1), \ldots, q_n(x_n))$$

Figure 3 shows a problem with two alternative anytime algorithms that can solve the entire problem (for example, two different bin-packing algorithms for the same van on a single trip). In this case the quality combination function is the maximum of the two components

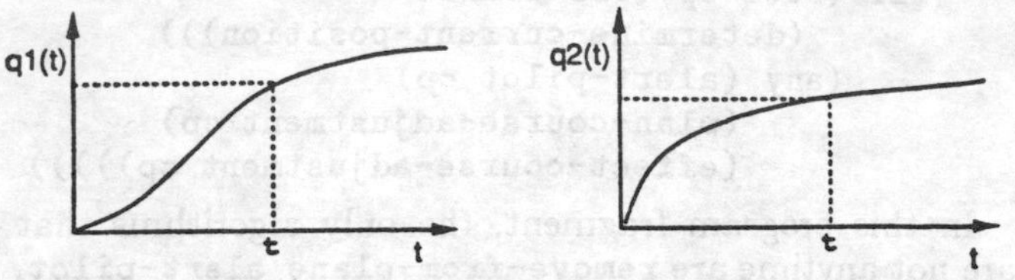

Figure 3: Compilation of a sequence

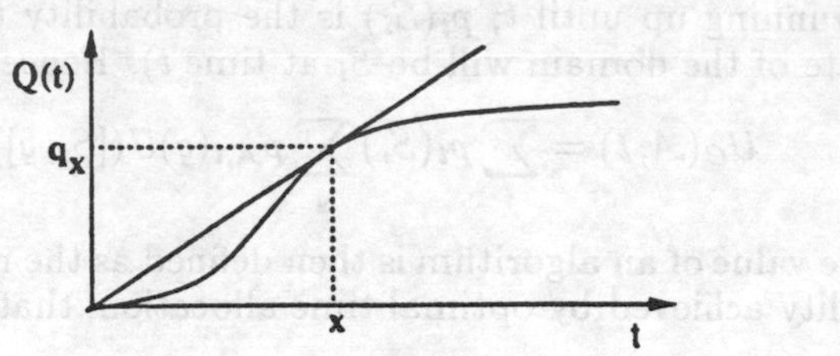

Figure 4: Compilation of a loop

(since we can use the best solution among the alternatives) and the given amount of time should be allocated to the component that has higher expected quality. This is essentially the case studied by Dean and Boddy [1988]. Rather than using a generalized sequence construct and a particular quality combination function, it might be appropriate to supply a special construct any for the case of multiple alternative methods.

4.2.2 Conditional statement

Consider a real-time currency trading program that uses one of two different trading strategies (A and B) depending on whether interest rate will rise (P). We would represent this by the conditional statement:

(if $\mathcal{P}$ then $\mathcal{A}$ else $\mathcal{B}$)

Conditional statements have several variations depending on whether the condition $\mathcal{P}$ is calculated by an anytime algorithm or whether there is a penalty, over and above the cost of time, for executing $\mathcal{A}$ when the condition is false. Here we analyze the compilation for the case in which $\mathcal{P}$ is a fixed-time algorithm that returns (after time $t_{\mathcal{P}}$) the probability (p) that the condition is true. We also assume that the overall quality is the quality of $\mathcal{A}$ when the condition is true and the quality of $\mathcal{B}$ when the condition is false. The optimal time allocation is given by:

$$\max_{0 \leq x \leq t - t_{\mathcal{P}}} \{pq_{\mathcal{A}}(x) + (1-p)q_{\mathcal{B}}(t - t_{\mathcal{P}} - x)\}$$

A partially evaluated version of this expression is inserted into the 'object code', to be evaluated at run-time when the value of p is known. A PP can be computed at compile time based on the *a priori* value of p.

4.2.3 Loops

Any system that repeatedly performs a complex task can be implemented using a loop through a sequential anytime process. Examples include operating systems, part-picking robots, and network communication servers. In these cases, an infinite loop is an adequate model:

(loop < *body* >)

The time allocation should maximize the utility gain per unit time, that is, at each iteration we choose x such that:

$$\max_{0 \leq x \leq t} \{Q_S(x)/x\}$$

where $Q_S(x)$ is the PP of the body of the loop. This amounts to stopping the sequence when it reaches the point of contact of the steepest tangent to the PP (figure 4). Loops with anytime termination tests offer more complex but very interesting optimization problems.

4.3 Compiling interruptible algorithms

With interruptible algorithms we cannot simply allocate a certain amount of time to each component since we do not know the total computation time in advance. For example, in the case of the repair system mentioned earlier, if we allocate a certain amount of time to 'diagnose' and the execution is interrupted before 'therapy' starts, then there will be no results to report. We therefore have to interleave the execution of all the components so that results are generated continuously.

The compilation of interruptible algorithms is solved by reduction to contract algorithms using Theorem 1. The idea is to create the best contract algorithm, using the compilation methods described above, and then create an interruptible version from the contract algorithm using the iterating construction described in the proof of the theorem.

5 Conclusion

We have presented a method for constructing real-time systems based on the use of elementary anytime algorithms together with a set of compilation methods to optimally compose these algorithms. Our method is a meta-level approach in which the meta-level problem is limited to scheduling of anytime algorithms. Laffey *et al* [1988] claim that "Currently, ad hoc techniques are used for making a system produce a response within a specified time interval". Our approach has several advantages over current techniques: it achieves optimal performance not just acceptable performance; it can handle situations in which resource availability is unknown at design time; it allows for a wide range of possible run-times and hence is more flexible; it provides machine independent real-time modules. Finally, our approach avoids a time-consuming hand-tuning process associated with the construction of real-time systems because the compilation methods are mechanized.

5.1 Related work

As mentioned above, there has been considerable work on designing and using individual anytime algorithms, both before and after Dean's coining of the term 'anytime'. There has, however, been very little work capitalizing on the additional degree of freedom offered by anytime algorithms — freedom in the very general sense that the algorithm offers to fulfill an entire spectrum of input-output specifications, over the full range of run-times, rather than just a single specification. This freedom is required by a user with a time-dependent utility function rather than a fixed output specification[3].

One exception is the Concord system, developed by Lin *et al.* [1987]. Concord is a programming language that supports approximate computations in which the run-time of the subroutine is controlled by the consumer of the results. The main design issues involve the run-time environment structures needed to support flexible procedure calls. Its development was motivated, like our compilation scheme, by the problem of optimizing performance given a limited supply of system resources. For each procedure, a supervisor is used to record values of the approximate results obtained to date, together with a set of error indicators. When a procedure is terminated, its supervisor returns the best result found. Intermediate results are handled by the caller using a mechanism similar to exception handling. The handlers for imprecise results determine whether a result is acceptable or not, this decision is local to the caller, rather than being made in the global utility context that we use. In this sense, Concord actually performs satisficing rather than optimization. Concord has several other disadvantages compared to our approach: it leaves to the programmer the decision of what quality of results is acceptable; it does not mechanize the scheduling process but only provides tools for the programmer to perform this task; and it does not provide for simple cumulative development of more complex anytime systems.

5.2 Further work

There is still much system work to be done in order to implement a complete set of compilation methods as an integral part of a programming language for anytime computation. We also need to understand how best to represent multidimensional, probabilistic and conditional performance profiles, and how to insert monitors to check the partial results obtained and update the PPs accordingly.

We are currently extending the framework to cover the generation and scheduling of *anytime actions* and *observation actions*, both of which are essential for the construction of autonomous agents. Anytime actions are actions whose outcome quality improves gradually over time. For example, moving toward a target in order to get a better view is an interruptible anytime action. Aiming a gun at a target is another example of an interruptible anytime action. In many cases anytime actions can be implemented by interleaving computation and action. Our ultimate goal in this project is to construct a real-time agent that acts by performing anytime actions and makes decisions using anytime computation.

[3] In fact, the notion of anytime applies much more broadly, for example to contracts among economic agents. A crude version is presented by the model ranges offered by car and computer manufacturers, where different allocations of money will obtain different quality of results. We are beginning to investigate the economics literature to see if similar generalizations have been proposed.

References

[Boddy and Dean, 1989] M. Boddy and T. Dean. Solving time-dependent planning problems. Technical Report CS-89-03, Department of Computer Science, Brown University, Providence, 1989.

[Dean and Boddy, 1988] T. Dean and M. Boddy. An analysis of time-dependent planning. In *Proceedings of the Seventh National Conference on Artificial Intelligence*, pages 49–54, Minneapolis, Minnesota, 1988.

[Elkan, 1990] C. Elkan. Incremental, approximate planning: abductive default reasoning. In *Proceedings of the AAAI Spring Symposium on Planning in Uncertain Environments*, Palo Alto, California, 1990.

[Haussler, 1990] D. Haussler. Probably approximately correct learning. In *Proceedings of the Eighth National Conference on Artificial Intelligence*, pages 1101–1108, Boston, Massachusetts, 1990.

[Horvitz, 1987] E. J. Horvitz. Reasoning about beliefs and actions under computational resource constraints. In *Proceedings of the 1987 Workshop on Uncertainty in Artificial Intelligence*, Seattle, Washington, 1987.

[Korf, 1988] R. Korf. Real-time heuristic search: new results. In *Proceedings of the Seventh National Conference on Artificial Intelligence*, pages 139–144, Minneapolis, Minnesota, 1988.

[Laffey *et al.*, 1988]
T. J. Laffey, P. A. Cox, J. L. Schmidt, S. M. Kao and J. Y. Read. Real-time knowledge based systems. *AI Magazine*, 9(1):27-45, Spring 1988.

[Lin *et al.*, 1987] K. J. Lin, S. Natarajan, J. W. S. Liu and T. Krauskopf. Concord: A system of imprecise computations. In *Proceedings of COMPSAC '87*, pages 75-81, Tokyo, Japan, October 1987.

[Michalski and Winston, 1986] R. S. Michalski and P. H. Winston. Variable precision logic. *Artificial Intelligence*, 29(2):121-146, 1986.

[Russell and Wefald, 1989] S. J. Russell and E. H. Wefald. Principles of metareasoning. In R.J. Brachman *et al.*, (Eds), *Proceedings of the First International Conference on Principles of Knowledge Representation and Reasoning*, Morgan Kaufmann, San Mateo, California, 1989.

[Vrbsky *et al.*, 1990] S. V. Vrbsky, J. W. S. Liu and K. P. Smith. An object-oriented query processor that returns monotonically improving approximate answers. Technical Report UIUCDCS-R-90-1568, University of Illinois at Urbana-Champaign, 1990.

[Zilberstein, 1990] S. Zilberstein. Compilation of anytime algorithms. Research Proposal, University of California, Berkeley, November 1990.

Bottleneck Identification Using Process Chronologies*

Eric Biefeld and Lynne Cooper
Jet Propulsion Laboratory
California Institute of Technology
4800 Oak Grove Drive
Pasadena, CA 91109-8099
U. S. A.

Abstract

We present a heuristics-based approach to deep space mission scheduling which is modeled on the approach used by expert human schedulers in producing schedules for planetary encounters. New chronological evaluation techniques are used to focus the search by using information gained during the scheduling process to locate, classify, and resolve regions of conflict. Our approach is based on the assumption that during the construction of a schedule there exist several disjunct temporal regions where the demand for one resource type or a single temporal constraint dominates (bottleneck regions). If the scheduler can identify these regions and classify them based on their dominant constraint, then the scheduler can select the scheduling heuristic.

1 Introduction

In a heuristics-based automated scheduling system, it is possible to construct a large set of scheduling heuristics such that each scheduling heuristic optimizes a different aspect of the schedule [Smith and Ow, 1985]. For example, one scheduling heuristic could temporally colocate steps that use the same resources, reducing set-up times. While a particular scheduling heuristic optimizes one aspect of the schedule, it can cause inefficiencies in the other aspects of the schedule. Thus, the scheduler must carefully choose which scheduling heuristic to run and limit the scope of its application.

This paper presents the results of research on developing a heuristics-based approach to automated scheduling. The approach is based on the assumption that during the construction of a schedule there exist several disjunct temporal regions of the schedule where the demand for one resource type or a single temporal constrain dominates (referred to as bottlenecks). If the scheduler can identify these regions, and choose the appropriate heuristics to optimize[1] for the dominant constraint within the regions, then the system can construct an efficient solution.

In this paper, we will provide the background and motivation for this approach, discuss the object representations necessary to support it, describe the mechanisms used for locating, classifying, and resolving bottlenecks, and describe the results achieved toward implementing this approach. Discussion of related work is also included.

2 Background

Mission scheduling is characterized by large numbers of science experiments which are considered mutually independent except for their competition for limited spacecraft resources [Biefeld and Cooper, 1989]. For missions such as the Voyager Grand-Tour of the planets, the requested tasking far exceeds the capability of the spacecraft resources. Most of the science requests will never be scheduled, so the problem is one of configuring a subset of the requested tasks in such a way as to optimize the total science return. While there is considerable flexibility in scheduling an individual task, producing schedules with the necessary science return density requires the interleaving of tasks in a manner which increases the total number of experiments that can be performed.

Due to the complexity and size [Dean, 1986] of the domain, mission scheduling is currently performed by teams of expert human schedulers. When constructing a mission schedule, the expert human schedulers work incrementally. They first lay out a rough draft of the schedule complete with large numbers of conflicts and high levels of over-subscription [Biefeld and Cooper, 1988]. They proceed by identifying problem areas, classifying these areas, and using the appropriate techniques to resolve any conflicts. As they cycle through the problem regions, they build up knowledge about this particular scheduling problem, e.g. where the major resource

*This research was done at the Jet Propulsion Laboratory, California Institute of Technology, and was sponsored by the U.S. Department of Defense through an agreement with the National Aeronautics and Space Administration. In addition to the authors, individuals participating in this project include David Atkinson, Len Charest, Richard Doyle, Loretta Falcone, Kirk Kandt, Raymond Lam, Gaius Martin, Elmain Martinez, and Harry Porta.

[1]Optimize is not used in the mathematical sense. Because of the intractability of the problem domain, a working definition is: to develop a schedule which an expert human scheduler cannot easily improve.

contentions are located, and which tasks have a high level of interaction or are difficult to place into the schedule. This information is then used to guide their future scheduling actions.

The approaches used in classical planning systems such as NONLIN [Tate, 1976], FORBIN [Dean *et al.*, 1987], and DEVISER [Vere, 1983], are fundamentally different from the approaches used by the human mission schedulers. The classical planning systems build a schedule sequentially, with each scheduling action resulting in either a conflict-free schedule ready to have additional tasks added to it, or an illegal schedule which requires backtracking to correct.

An alternative approach, presented in this paper, is modeled after expert human schedulers. The Operations Mission Planner (OMP) models the inherently cyclic nature of the human scheduling process and the types of information that the human schedulers develop as they are generating and refining a schedule.

3 Representations

OMP makes use of two primary object types: tasks and resources. A task is a request to the scheduler for the use of resources (e.g. a science experiment on Voyager). It includes all of the internal constraints such as time windows (e.g. when the red spot of Jupiter is visible to the spacecraft). A resource is a commodity on the spacecraft (e.g. cameras, downlink, power). It is modeled as a resource timeline representing the constraints on its use (e.g. capacity, direction, bandwidth). Detailed descriptions of how OMP implements tasks and resources are given in the following sections.

3.1 Tasks

Tasks are represented in OMP as data objects with parametrized slots and demons which ensure internal consistency for the task representation. A task is composed of a set of steps and the temporal constraints that exist between the steps. A task can have several different sets of steps which satisfy it. The template for a task request is shown below.

Name: A symbol representing the name of the task.

Description: A string providing background information on the task.

Windows: The list of temporal intervals in which the task can be scheduled.

Repetitions: The number of times to repeat the task during the schedule.

Priority: The priority of this task (relative to other tasks) for this schedule.

Scenarios: The order(s) in which to perform the task steps and their associated preference(s), this can include alternative ways in which to implement a given task breakdown.

Steps: A list of steps.

Step#: The step's identification number.

Duration: Minimum and maximum (desired) duration for the step.

Delay: The minimum and maximum time delay between this step and the previous step.

Resources: The resources requested by the step.

3.2 Steps and Activities

In OMP, a step is a temporal interval which consumes resources. Each step has specified duration constraints, temporal windowing constraints, and a list of the resources requested. A step object, S, specifies the start and end times of the step (Interval, I), and pairs representing the resource assigned, R, and the amount of resource assigned to the step (Usage, SU).

$$S = [I, (R_i, SU_i(I))] \text{ where } (R_i \in (R_1 ... R_N))$$

An activity is a set of steps and the associated constraints [Le Pape and Smith, 1987] which satisfy a request. There may be more than one activity that satisfies a task request (see SCENARIO slot above). While OMP actually schedules at the step level, demons attached to the activity ensure that the task is always consistent and that all task constraints are met. Therefore, the only constraint satisfaction that the scheduling engine (discussed below) must perform is to satisfy resource constraints.

3.3 Resources

There are four fundamental types of resources: capacity, consumable/renewable, state-continuous, and state-discrete [Starbird, 1987]. A capacity resource is basically a pooled resource. Tasks request and use the resource, then free it up for other tasks to use (e.g. spacecraft downlink). A consumable resource is one for which there is a limited supply, and once it is used by a task, it is no longer available (e.g. spacecraft fuel). A renewable is a special case of consumable, where the resource can be replenished (e.g. storage tape; it is used up during recording, and "replenished" during playback). A state resource represents a resource whose state (configuration, position, etc.) must be a certain value in order to support a task. A State-continuous resource is one in which the state of the resource can best be described by a continuous variable (e.g. the direction that an antenna is pointing). State-discrete resources, on the other hand, are represented by discrete values (e.g. on/off, low-gain/medium-gain/high-gain).

The OMP system has represented two of these types of resources: capacity and state-continuous. However, they were represented independently in two separate implementations of OMP. The following discussion assumes a capacity type resource. The Conflict Level function must be redefined for the other types of resources.

OMP resources are represented as timelines. Each timeline is a sequence of contiguous, discrete temporal intervals represented by the following parameters:

Interval (t_s, t_e): The start and end times of the interval.

Resource Capacity (CA): The maximum capacity of the resource, known *a priori*. Can be a function of time.

Step Assignments (SA): A list of steps requesting the resource during a given temporal region.

Resource Usage (RU): The average amount of the resource requested by the assigned steps during a given temporal region where:

$$RU(I) = \sum_{(S_i|S_i \in SA)} SU_i/\mathrm{dur}(I)$$

Conflict Level (CL): The average level of conflict (contention for resources) during a given temporal region where:

$$CL(I) = \mathcal{F}(RU(I), CA(I))$$

Each resource, RS, is represented by a temporal ordered list of tuples, where for each time tick, t,

$$RS(t) = [CA(t), SA(t), RU(t), CL(t)]$$

3.4 Regions

OMP adds a descriptive layer over the timelines called regions. A region is a variable-length, continuous time segment on a single resource. It is designated by a start time and end time and is defined dynamically by the scheduler. In addition to the general parameters associated with the resource timeline (RS), each region, RE_i, has special-purpose parameters.

$$RE = [I, F, CL, RU]$$

Interval (I): The temporal area bounded by the start and end times of the region.

Focus Level (F): The number of times a given time slot has been the FOCUS of the scheduler.

OMP defines several types of specialized regions:

Conflict Region (CR): A variable length, continuous time interval where the requested usage is greater than the theoretical capacity of the resource during that interval.

$$CL_{RS}(I) > \alpha$$

where α corresponds to the percent of over subscription allowed by the current scheduling phase.

Focus Region (FR): The conflict region which the scheduler has chosen to work on during the upcoming scheduling pass.

Effected Region (ER): Any region which is changed as a result of a scheduling action in a focus region.

Bottleneck Region (BNR): A *set* of regions (not necessarily continuous) which comprise a bottleneck.

4 Scheduling

The OMP approach to scheduling is based on the following assumptions:

1. The schedule can be decomposed into several disjunct temporal regions where a small set of constraints dominates (bottlenecks).
2. A parametrized scheduling heuristic instituting a specialized search can be used to optimize for the dominant constraint within the bottleneck.
3. The scheduler can merge the resulting partial schedules and complete any unspecified portions while maintaining the highly optimized sections.

OMP decomposes a scheduling problem by using chronologies to locate, classify, and resolve bottlenecks. An intuitive, working definition of a bottleneck is: A set of disjunctive temporal regions where:

1. A small set of resource constraints dominate;
2. The potential resource demand based on possible requests exceeds the available resource capacity.

4.1 Locate Bottlenecks

OMP's approach to locating bottlenecks is not based on a static evaluation of requests versus resource limits [see CORTES; Section 6]. Instead it is based on the observation that repeatedly applying a conflict-repair strategy to a schedule will cause the conflict level(s) within a region(s) to change. By tracking changes in the conflict levels in different regions, OMP is able to locate interdependent regions and merge them into a bottleneck. The chronology subsystem is responsible for capturing the information needed to locate the bottlenecks.

4.1.1 Chronograms and Chronology

After performing the initial expansion of the tasks into activities and making preliminary resource assignments, the scheduler focuses on the area of the schedule with the most conflicts. The scheduler performs a shallow search which lowers the number of conflicts in this area. Only the activities that are involved in the conflict are modified. The impact of these modifications on the resources is recorded in an object called a chronogram. The procedure is:

1. Select a FR from the various CR on the schedule using the appropriate selection criteria (e.g. select the CR with the maximum CL);
2. Move tasks out of the FR until the selection parameter (e.g. CL) is less than the threshold value set by scheduler;
3. Create a chronogram and add it to the chronology;
4. Repeat untill no conflicts exist or a bottleneck is identified.

The shallow search used by OMP is a simple hill climber whose utility function is composed of the conflict level within the focus region, the total conflict level of the schedule and the number of times an activity has been modified. While the search tries to minimize the total conflict level, it will at times increase the conflict level over the total schedule in order to lower the conflict level within the focus region.

A newly created conflict region will eventually become the focus of the scheduler. Solving this region may, in turn, cause other conflicts and so on, until the original conflict region is once again in conflict. As the search progresses through the oversubscribed resources, the level of conflict in these and other areas oscillate. The conflict areas that oscillate in this manner are classified as potential bottlenecks.

Each time the system focuses on a new region it creates an entry into the chronology called a chronogram. A chronogram includes the focus region, the change in conflict level of the focus region, and a list of any other resource regions whose conflict level changed (the effected regions), and the actual change in conflict ΔCL_{ER} for the effected regions.

$$\text{Chronogram}(C_i),\ C_i = [FR, F, CL, \Delta CL, (ERs, CL_{ER})],$$

and

$$\text{Chronology}(CY),\ CY = (C_i, i = 1, M)$$

for M scheduling passes

Eventually, the number of times the system has focused on the same region will reach a heuristic threshold. This signifies that the search is wandering around in circles and it is time to analyze the chronology to identify the bottlenecks.

4.1.2 Chronograph

The first step in processing the chronology is to build a graph for each chronogram. Each region in the chronogram is a node and an arc is placed between the focus region node and the effected region nodes in the chronogram. A pulse count of one is assigned to each of the newly created nodes indicating the number of times this region has changed its conflict level. The strength of the arc is the ratio of the change in conflict level of the region and the focus region.

Node (Ni): For $(R_i | R_i \in ERs)$, a node, N_i,is created with a

Pulse Count (PC): $PC(N_i) = 1$.

Arc (A_i): For every node, N_i, there exists an arc, A_i, which connects R_i and the FR, with an

Arc Strength (S_i): $S_i = |\Delta CL_{R_i} / \Delta CL_{FR}|$.

The next step in processing the chronology is to merge the individual chronographs. OMP combines any nodes that represent the same region. If any two regions on the same resource overlap temporally, the ratio of overlap duration to total temporal duration is used to determine if the regions should be combined. When two nodes are combined, the temporal extent of the resulting node is the union of the original two nodes' temporal extents and the pulse count is the sum of the original two nodes' pulse count. Any two arcs which link the same nodes are combined and the resulting strength is the sum of the strengths of the original two arcs. After all the graphs have been merged, any node whose pulse count is below a heuristic threshold is deleted from the graph and any arc whose strength is below a threshold is also deleted. The graph is then split into a set of connected graphs and a bottleneck is created for each of the connected graphs.

4.2 Classify and Resolve Bottlenecks

Once OMP has identified the bottlenecks, the next goal is to classify them.

OMP calculates a set of metrics for each bottleneck. These metrics evaluate the conflict level, temporal scope (number, size, and continuity of temporal intervals involved), and resource scope (number of different resources involved) of the individual bottlenecks. Once a bottleneck has been evaluated based on these metrics, appropriate strategies can be employed to resolve the bottleneck. The goal of the strategies is to either produce a conflict-free schedule within the bottleneck region or break-down the bottleneck into more manageable pieces.

If the metrics indicate that a bottleneck is massively oversubscribed (i.e. the requested usage within the bottlenecks is greater then 150% of the theoretical capacity of the bottleneck), OMP will employ strategies which delete the lower priority activities from the bottleneck until the requested demand is reduced to about 120% over the theoretical capacity. After the demand has been lowered OMP will once again search for bottlenecks.

The variance in the resource usage is a metric which checks for uniform usage throughout the bottleneck. If, for example the variance is high then a simple hill climber, which minimizes the square of the resource demand, is applied to the bottleneck to level out the resource usage. After this leveling strategy has completed then the system will apply a more specific strategy to reduce the total conflict within the bottleneck.

Another metric used to classify a bottleneck is the total temporal extent and the number of resources the bottleneck employs. If the bottleneck is temporally large in scope then a general purpose strategy is used which adds constraints to the activities in the bottleneck, causing the large bottleneck to split into several smaller bottlenecks. If the bottleneck is small in scope, then a strategy that optimizes for a specific type of resource is applied to the bottleneck. For example, if the resource tracks the pointing direction of an antenna and the direction changes frequently during the temporal extent of the bottleneck, a lot-sizing[2] strategy is applied which collects requests with similar direction requirements together. This strategy reduces the panning (setup time) of the antenna and thus frees up the antenna for additional requests.

5 Status

The current implementation of OMP has been tested on a Space Station Freedom (SSF) scenario consisting of 400 tasks (~1000 steps), using 17 different capacity resources. OMP generates a 7–day schedule. Using the approach presented in this paper, OMP is able to develop a schedule in approximately 15 minutes. Randomly reordering the input requests has a less than two percent impact on the number of tasks in the schedule. (Although the actual schedule that's produced is highly input dependent, the general characteristics of the schedule such as total number of tasks in schedule and profile with respect to task priority, vary only slightly).

OMP currently performs no preprocessing on the input tasking. It uses an extremely simple loading algorithm which randomly assigns the steps to the resources.

[2] Lot-sizing is a concept from manufacturing scheduling where several tasks of the same type are scheduled together as a lot in order to reduce equipment setup time.

Additional analysis is needed to identify the potential benefits which could be realized by incorporating a more intelligent loading scheme.

The chronology analysis techniques discussed in this paper center around the merging and separating of individual chronographs. We are currently investigating a more efficient methodology for building the chronographs which takes advantage of the fact that by careful selection of the next focus region, you can build up a chronograph incrementally with a high degree of confidence that all of the nodes of the graph are part of the same bottleneck region. We believe that this technique, chronological coherence, could eliminate the need for an in-depth analysis and reduction of the chronograph into a series of directed graphs and improve the overall efficiency of the scheduler.

The heuristic threshold values referred to throughout Section 4 are currently set manually and cannot be changed during the course of a scheduling session. A future goal for OMP is to incorporate learning capabilities which would enable OMP to dynamically set the values of those parameters during the production of a schedule.

OMP has proven itself capable of handling a complex, real-world domain. It produced realistic schedules in a reasonable amount of time for a large, detailed problem domain. The crux of OMP research up to this point has been to prove that an automated approach modeled after expert human schedulers could be developed. The possibility of producing such an automated scheduling system has been established. Future work will concentrate on the feasibility of this approach.

6 Related Work

Other work in mission scheduling done at JPL includes DEVISER, which was tested on Voyager's Uranus near-encounter sequence. While DEVISER was able to produce Voyager schedules for cruise mode operations, it was impractical to use for the highly packed encounter sequences [McLaughlin and Wolff, 1989]. In order to constrain the search, the expert human scheduler who built the knowledge base had to 1) divide the encounter tasks into several smaller groups; 2) modify the knowledge base for each set of tasks to limit the search; and 3) manually integrate the partial schedules into a complete schedule.

After the near-encounter test was finished, various techniques for heuristically limiting the search were investigated. These techniques included: 1) dynamic rule subsetting; 2) dynamic rule ordering; 3) pruning search paths; and 4) backtracking to check points instead of the previous state. While these mechanisms were technically possible to implement, the domain experts could not formulate domain-specific heuristics which used these mechanisms.

When attempting to limit the search of DEVISER, the expert would construct a schedule by hand and analyze the bottlenecks within this schedule. The expert was unable to use DEVISER to extract this type of information. This (and other observations of the human expert) led to the use of chronologies for identifying bottlenecks.

The FORBIN planner uses the Time Map Manager (TMM) [Dean and McDermontt, 1987] as a temporal truth maintenance database and incorporates many classical planning techniques. The TMM uses the constraints knowledge base to make temporal predictions on plan viability. However, since the TMM is not capable of detecting all of the steps' interactions, FORBIN has a scheduling module, Heuristic Task Scheduler (HST) [Miller, 1988], which searches the partially constructed plan for a totally specified schedule. If a viable schedule is found, FORBIN goes on to the next goal to be expanded while the particular parameters chosen by the scheduler will not be enforced, in keeping with a policy of least commitment.

One of the major heuristics used by HST for limiting the search space is *"generate only the feasible schedules"* [Miller, 1988]. Like HST, the TMM can only work with feasible schedules. OMP, on the other hand, does most of its processing on infeasible schedules. As Dean noted *"It is often convenient in debugging plans to determine what the repercussions are of modifying certain constraints ... What you want is a blow-by-blow account of what things might go wrong, so you can assess what might be done"* [Dean, 1985]. A basic premise of OMP's architecture is that a careful analysis of the implications of the infeasibility of a schedule allows the scheduler to tightly control the search and that the increase in search control more than compensates for the increase in the search space.

The Opportunistic Intelligent Scheduler (OPIS) [Smith *et al.*, 1986] is a job shop scheduler that grew out of ISIS [Fox and Smith, 1984]. OPIS implements multiple scheduling perspectives. It incorporates the order-based perspective used in ISIS and adds a resource-based perspective. The resource-based perspective is used to focus the search on the resource bottlenecks.

Like OMP, OPIS uses different strategies to resolve a bottleneck depending on the metrics of the bottleneck. However, OPIS uses a simple infinite capacity scheduler to find bottlenecks that is easily fallible under conditions other than its test domain [Ow and Smith, 1988]. The technique described in this paper for finding bottlenecks is more robust and allows the system to distinguish the structure of a bottleneck.

CORTES [Fox and Sycara, 1990] and RALPH [Johnson and Werntz, 1987] use a look ahead technique [Johnson and Roadifer, 1986; Muscettola and Smith, 1987; Sadeh and Fox, 1990] that is conceptually similar to the technique presented in this paper. This technique is based on first constructing a probabilistic model of the activities. If an activity can be scheduled in a large temporal window, then it has a non-zero probability distribution within this temporal window which depends inversely on the duration of the window and is proportional to the duration of the activity. The activity probability distribution is then weighted by its resource usage and the activity resource distribution is summed for all the activities. The resulting resource usage distribution is compared to the resource capacity to locate potential bottlenecks.

OMP uses a statistical technique to generate the same

information found in the resource usage distributions. Instead of calculating the probability of a resource usage level, OMP generates resource usage samples during its initial search. These samples are used to statistically calculate a resource usage distribution.

A significant advantage of the OMP approach is that not only are the bottleneck regions identified but the regions are collected into independent bottlenecks. With the probability approach mentioned above all the bottleneck regions are identified but there is no direct information on how these regions are connected.

While OMP is not a learning program there has been recent work [Eskey and Zweben, 1990] in extending Explanation-Based Learning of search control rules [Minton, 1988] to learn the general conditions under which chronic contention occurs. A chronic contention is similar to a bottleneck. However, instead of having to analyze the schedule to find the bottlenecks, the general conditions under which they will occur are learned.

The advantage of an EBL approach is that the system can quickly identify possible chronic conditions. However, the connection between the bottleneck regions depends on the particular set of tasking and the exact timing of the orbit of the spacecraft. Since this can radically vary from day to day it makes exact prediction of the bottleneck regions very hard without actually roughing out the schedule. While a good *a priori* guess of the chronic resources could speed up the initial processing of the schedule, OMP can produce its first rough set of bottlenecks in three to five minutes, so the potential time savings is small. Extending this concept to the learning of how to classify a bottleneck once it has been found does, however, offer substantial performance gains.

7 Summary

In this paper, we have presented a heuristics-based automated scheduling prototype, the Operations Mission Planner (OMP), modeled after the expert human schedulers who produce schedules for planetary encounters. OMP uses new chronological evaluation techniques to focus the search by using information gained incrementally during the scheduling process to locate, classify, and resolve bottlenecks. Our approach is based on the assumption that during the construction of a schedule there exist several disjunct temporal regions where the demand for one resource type or a single temporal constraint dominates (bottleneck regions). Using chronologies, the scheduling system builds a limited history of the scheduling process and then analyzes the information inherent in that history using a set of metrics. A rule-based system then classifies the bottlenecks based on the metrics and determines the appropriate scheduling actions to resolve the bottleneck. In order to implement the chronology system, OMP incorporates special data items in its representations of both tasking and resources. A special data type, the chronogram, is also used to record the effects of a scheduling pass. The chronograms are transformed into a graph representation and, using graph analysis techniques, the chronographs are merged into a set of connected graphs which represent the bottleneck regions.

References

[Biefeld and Cooper, 1988] Eric Biefeld and Lynne Cooper. Replanning and Iterative Refinement in Mission Scheduling. *Sixth Annual Intelligence Community AI Symposium,*, Washington, DC., October 1988.

[Biefeld and Cooper, 1989] Eric Biefeld and Lynne Cooper. Comparison of Mission and Job Shop Scheduling. *Proceedings of the Third International Conference on Expert Systems and the Leading Edge in Production Planning and Control*, pages 483–494, Hilton Head Island, South Carolina, May 1989.

[Dean, 1985] Thomas Dean,. An Approach to Reason about Time for Planning and Problem Solving. Technical Report 433, Yale University,1985.

[Dean, 1986] Thomas Dean,. Intractability and Time Dependent Planning. *Proceedings of Workshop on Planning and Reasoning About Action*, pages 143–164, June 1986.

[Dean and McDermontt, 1987] Thomas Dean and Drew McDermott. Temporal Data Base Management. *Artificial Intelligence Journal*, 32(1):1–55, 1987.

[Dean *et al.*, 1987] Thomas Dean, R. James Firby, and David Miller. Hierarchical Planning involving Deadlines, Travel Time, and Resources. *Computational Intelligence*, 4(4), November 1988.

[Eskey and Zweben, 1990] Megen Eskey and Monte Zweben. Learning Search Control for Constraint-Based Scheduling. Internal NASA Ames Research Document,1990.

[Fox and Sycara, 1990] Mark Fox and Katia Sycara. Overview of CORTES: A Constraint Based Approach to Production Planning, Scheduling and Control. *Proceedings of the Fourth International Conference on Expert Systems in Production and Operations Management*, pages 1–15, Hilton Head Island, South Carolina, May 1990.

[Fox and Smith, 1984] Mark Fox and Stephen Smith. ISIS: A Knowledge-Based System for Factory Scheduling. *Expert Systems*, 1(1):25–49, July 1984.

[Johnson and Roadifer, 1986] Craig Johnson and James Roadifer. A Look-Ahead Strategy for Heuristic Activity Scheduling. *Joint Conference of the Operations Research Society of America and the Institute of Management Sciences*, October 1986.

[Johnson and Werntz, 1987] Craig Johnson and David Werntz. Automation of the Resource Allocation and Planning System at NASA's Jet Propulsion Laboratory. *SPACE: Technology, Commerce and Communications*, Houston, Texas, November, 1987.

[Le Pape and Smith, 1987] Claude Le Pape and Stephen Smith. Management of Temporal Constraints for Factory Scheduling. *Proceedings of the Working Conference on Temporal Aspects in Information Systems*, May 1987.

[McLaughlin and Wolff, 1989] W. I. McLaughlin and D. M. Wolff. Automating the Uplink Process for Planetary Missions. *AIAA 27th Aerospace Science Meeting*, Reno, Nevada, January 1989.

[Miller, 1988] David Miller. A Task and Resource Scheduling System for Automated Planning. *Annals of Operations Research*, 12(1–4):69–198, February 1988.

[Minton, 1988] Steven Minton. Quantitative results Concerning the Utility of Explanation-Based Learning. *Proceedings of the Seventh National Conference on Artificial Intelligence*, pages 564–569, Saint Paul, Minnesota, August 1988.

[Muscettola and Smith, 1987] Nicola Muscettola and Stephen Smith. A Probabilistic Framework for Resource-Constrained Multi- Agent Planning. *Proceedings of the Tenth International Joint Conference On Artificial Intelligence*, page 1063–1066, Milan, August 1987.

[Ow and Smith, 1988] Peng Si Ow and Stephen Smith. Viewing Scheduling as an Opportunistic Problem-Solving Process. *Annals of Operations Research*,12(1-4):85–108, February 1988.

[Sadeh and Fox, 1990] Norman Sadeh and Mark Fox. Variable and Value Ordering Heuristics for Activity-Based Job-Shop Scheduling. *Proceedings of the Fourth International Conference on Expert Systems in Production and Operations Management*, pages 134–144, Hilton Head Island, South Carolina, May 1990.

[Smith *et al.*, 1986] Stephen Smith, Mark Fox, and Peng Si Ow. Constructing and Maintaining Detailed Production Plans: Investigations into the Development of Knowledge-Based Factory Scheduling Systems. *AI Magazine*, 7(4):45–61, 1986.

[Smith and Ow, 1985] Stephen Smith and Peng Si Ow. The Use of Multiple Problem Decompositions in Time Constrained Planning Tasks. *Proceedings of the Ninth International Joint Conference On Artificial Intelligence*, pages 10130–1015, Los Angeles, California, August 1985.

[Starbird, 1987] Tom Starbird. Space Flight Operations Center Sequence Subsystem (SEQ) Functional Requirements Document for Planning. JPL Internal Document D–4697; NASA, Jet Propulsion Laboratory, California Institute of Technology, Pasadena California, August 1987.

[Tate, 1976] Austin Tate, Project Planning Using a Hierarchical Non-linear Planner. Department of Artificial Intelligence Report No. 25, Edinburgh University, 1976.

[Vere, 1983] Steven Vere. Planning in Time: Windows and Durations for Activities and Goals. *IEEE Transactions on Machine Intelligence PAMI-5*, No. 3, pages 246–267, May 1983.

Incomplete Information and Deception in Multi-Agent Negotiation

Gilad Zlotkin
Jeffrey S. Rosenschein
Computer Science Department
Hebrew University
Givat Ram, Jerusalem, Israel
gilad@cs.huji.ac.il, jeff@cs.huji.ac.il

Abstract

Much distributed artificial intelligence research on negotiation assumes complete knowledge among the interacting agents and/or truthful agents. These assumptions in many domains will not be realistic, and this paper extends previous work to begin dealing with the case of inter-agent negotiation with incomplete information.

A discussion of our existing negotiation framework sets out the rules by which agents operate during this phase of their interaction. The concept of a "solution" within this framework is presented; the same solution concept serves for interactions between agents with incomplete information as it did for complete information interactions.

The possibility of incomplete information among agents opens up the possibility of deception as part of the negotiation strategy of an agent. Deception during negotiation among autonomous agents is thus analyzed in the constrained Blocks Domain, and it is shown that beneficial lies do exist in some scenarios. The three types of interactions, cooperative, compromise, and conflict, are examined. An analysis is made of how each affects the possibility of beneficial deception by a negotiating agent.

1 Introduction

The subject of negotiation has been of continuing interest in the distributed artificial intelligence (DAI) community [Smith, 1978; Rosenschein and Genesereth, 1985; Durfee, 1988; Malone *et al.*, 1988; Sycara, 1988; Kuwabara and Lesser, 1989; Conry *et al.*, 1988; Kreifelts and von Martial, 1990; Laasri *et al.*, 1990; Kraus and Wilkenfeld, 1991; Ephrati and Rosenschein, 1991]. Despite the large amount of research on this topic, there does not yet exist a universally accepted definition of what the word even means; as Gasser points out in [Gasser, 1991], "'negotiation' [is] a term that has been used in literally dozens of different ways in the DAI literature." Nevertheless, it is clear to the DAI community as a whole that the operation of intelligent autonomous agents would be greatly enhanced if they were able to communicate their respective desires and compromise to reach mutually beneficial agreements.

The work described in this paper follows the general direction of [Rosenschein and Genesereth, 1985; Zlotkin and Rosenschein, 1989] in treating negotiation in the spirit of game theory, while altering game theory assumptions that are irrelevant to DAI.

Much of the research on negotiation assumes complete knowledge among the interacting agents and/or truthful agents. These assumptions in many domains are not realistic, and this paper extends previous work [Zlotkin and Rosenschein, 1989; Zlotkin and Rosenschein, 1990b] to begin dealing with the case of inter-agent negotiation with incomplete information.

2 The Overall Negotiation Framework

Each agent i in the interaction is assumed to have a goal g_i, and wants to transform the world from an initial state s to a state that satisfies this goal. The set of all states satisfying g_i is denoted by G_i. A goal has an associated *worth* to the agent, which is also the maximum the agent is willing to pay in order to achieve that goal.

Because two agents co-existing within the same environment might interfere with actions of the other, there needs to be coordination of activity. At the same time, depending on the particular domain and goals involved, there may be the possibility that the agents will actually be able to help each other and achieve both goals with a lower overall cost.

A *deal* between agents is generally a joint plan, where agents share the work of transforming the world from the initial state to some final state. The plan is "joint" in the sense that the agents might probabilistically share the load, compromise over which agent does which actions, or even compromise over which agent gets its goal satisfied. In this final case, the deal is actually a probabilistic distribution over joint plans (what was called a "multi-plan deal" in [Zlotkin and Rosenschein, 1990c]).

In the broad sense, the utility for an agent of a deal is the difference between the worth of the agent's goal achieved through that deal, and the cost of that agent's part of the deal.

2.1 The Process of Negotiation

The interaction between agents occurs in two consecutive stages. First the agents negotiate, then they execute the entire joint plan upon which they had agreed. No divergence from the negotiated deal is allowed. The sharp separation of stages has consequences, in that it rules out certain negotiation tactics that might be used in an interleaved process. A more general negotiation framework that allowed concurrent negotiation and execution might, however, be approximated by concatenating several negotiation/execution processes together, provided that each agent remembers and uses information about the preceding negotiations.

We assume that negotiation is an iterative process: at each step, both agents simultaneously offer a deal. Our protocol specifies that at no point can an agent demand more than it did previously—in other words, each offer either repeats the previous offer or makes a concession to the opponent's position. The negotiation can end in one of two ways:

- Conflict: if neither agent makes a concession at some step, they have by default agreed on the (domain dependent) "conflict deal."
- Agreement: if at some step agent A offers agent B more than B himself asks for, they agree on A's offer, and if both agents overshoot the others' demands, then a coin toss breaks the symmetry.

The result of these rules is that the agents cannot "stand still" in the negotiation, nor can they backtrack. Thus the negotiation process is strongly monotonic and ensures convergence to a deal.

2.2 The Concept of a Solution

When we say that we are looking for a "solution" to the negotiation problem, we mean two things:

1. A precise definition of deals and utility, which may include probabilistic sharing of actions, probabilities associated with achieving final states, partial achievement of goals, and domain dependent attributes (e.g., the nature of the conflict deal). Previous work discussed ***pure deals***, ***mixed deals*** [Zlotkin and Rosenschein, 1989], ***semi-cooperative deals*** [Zlotkin and Rosenschein, 1990b], and ***multi-plan deals*** [Zlotkin and Rosenschein, 1990c].
2. A specification of how an agent should negotiate, given a well-defined negotiation environment.

How should one evaluate solutions? There are several ways of doing this, related to how we evaluate deals, how we evaluate agents, and how we evaluate interactions among the agents.

- **Deals:** Deals may have a variety of attributes that are considered desirable. Certain kinds of deals provide solutions to more general situations (e.g., semi-cooperative deals offer solutions to conflict resolution, whereas mixed deals do not), thus increasing the size of the ***negotiation set*** (the set of possible agreements). Deals may have other positive attributes, such as requiring less initial information.
- **Agents:** Agents are expected to be designed so that they are individual rational (meaning they agree on deals with positive utility).
- **Inter-agent interactions:** When two agents negotiate, it is desirable that they converge to a *pareto optimal* deal (meaning the only way the deal could be improved for one agent would be to worsen the deal for the other agent).

It is also highly desirable that an agent's negotiation strategy be in *equilibrium*—a strategy S is said to be in equilibrium if assuming that your opponent is using S, the best you can do is to also use S. Thus, no other agent will be able to take advantage of that agent by using a different negotiation strategy. Moreover, there is no need to exercise secrecy regarding the design of that agent—on the contrary, it is actually beneficial to broadcast its negotiation strategy, so that the other agent doesn't blunder and potentially cause both harm. Different types of deals may change the availability of strategies that are in equilibrium.

There is, in a sense, a meta-game going on between the designers of autonomous agents. Each one wants to design an agent that maximizes the designer's utility. There are strong motivations to design your agent so that it uses a negotiation strategy in equilibrium, in that it results in "best performance" in pair-wise competitions between your agent and any other given agent—conflicts will be avoided whenever possible, and deals that are reached will be pareto optimal.[1]

2.3 Negotiation with Incomplete Information

If agents negotiate without having full information regarding the other agent's goal, they need to take this lack of information into account in their negotiation strategy. There are several frameworks for dealing with this:

- In [Zlotkin and Rosenschein, 1989], we introduced the notion of a "−1 negotiation phase" in which agents simultaneously declare their goals before beginning the negotiation. The negotiation then proceeds as if the revealed information were true. There, we analyzed the strategy that an agent should adopt for playing the extended negotiation game, and in particular, whether the agent can benefit by declaring something other than his true goal.
- An alternative approach is for the agents to start the negotiation with incomplete information, increasing their knowledge as the negotiation process proceeds. Methods for increasing knowledge about another agent's goal we call "goal recognition" techniques.[2]

[1] However, there may be ecological motivations for designing agents that don't use equilibrium strategies, since multiple non-equilibrium agents might all benefit from their deviant strategies. For example, ecologically a group of agents that all play Cooperate in the Prisoners' Dilemma will do better than a group using the equilibrium strategy of Defect, even though a Defecting agent will win in a head-to-head competition with a Cooperating agent [Axelrod, 1984]. Nevertheless, we here concentrate on pair-wise equilibrium, and search for equilibrium negotiation strategies.

[2] The techniques used for goal recognition will depend on the form of the goal itself. For example, a goal comprised

2.4 Discoverable Lies vs. Undiscoverable Lies

We are unwilling to compel the designers of intelligent, autonomous agents not to design lying into their creations. In fact, the point of this research is to analyze whether or not such a design consideration has any advantages—maybe lies are helpful to societies of autonomous agents, and maybe they are not. While unwilling to outlaw lies, we *are* willing to consider what happens when a penalty mechanism is introduced, such that agents that are discovered lying would be punished. At times [Zlotkin and Rosenschein, 1989], we have considered infinite negative penalties when a lie was discovered. Even an infinite negative penalty, however, does not rule out a space of lies that could never be discovered, and agents might still benefit by using those lies.

We are also willing to assume that agents will keep their commitments; if an agent commits to some action as part of a deal, he will carry the action out.

2.5 Worth of a Goal and its Role in Lies

Throughout our research, we have assumed that agents associate a *worth* to the achievement of a particular goal. Sometimes, this worth is exactly equal to what it would cost the agent to achieve that goal by himself. At other times, we have analyzed what negotiation strategies are suitable when the worth of a goal to an agent exceeds the cost of the goal to that agent [Zlotkin and Rosenschein, 1990c]. The worth of a goal is the baseline for calculating the utility of a deal for an agent.

The worth of a goal is intimately connected with what specific deals agents will agree on. First, an agent will not agree on a deal that costs him more than his worth (he would have negative utility from such a deal). Second, since agents will agree on a deal that gives them both equal utility [Zlotkin and Rosenschein, 1989], if an agent has a lower worth, it will ultimately reduce the amount of work in his part of the deal. Thus, one might expect that if agent A wants to do less work, he will try to fool agent B into thinking that, for any particular goal, A's worth is lower than it really is. This strategy, in fact, often turns out to be beneficial, as seen below.

2.6 Lies in the Postmen Domain

The question of when it might benefit an agent to lie during negotiation was raised in [Zlotkin and Rosenschein, 1989]. The Postmen Domain (agents delivering letters over an undirected graph) was introduced, and several negotiation protocols were examined. When negotiating over *pure deals* (a redistribution of tasks among agents), there are situations where an agent can benefit by either hiding a goal or claiming to have a phantom goal that does not really exist. It was shown in [Zlotkin and Rosenschein, 1990a] that the availability of beneficial lies in the Postmen Domain is strongly related to the way the two agents' goals are coupled. When their goals are tightly coupled (i.e., delivery of one set of letters significantly reduces the cost of delivery of the second set), then beneficial lies are likely to be found. When the agents' goals are decoupled then a beneficial lie cannot be found.

solely of a conjunction of positive predicates could be deduced through a process of set intersection of positive examples.

By introducing the concept of an all-or-nothing *mixed deal* (a probabilistic redistribution of tasks among agents), beneficial lies were effectively eradicated.[3] Thus, in the Postmen Domain, the existence or non-existence of beneficial lies was sensitive to the negotiation protocol being used.

3 The Constrained Blocks Domain

We here quickly review the constrained Blocks Domain, first presented in [Zlotkin and Rosenschein, 1990b].

There is a table and a set of blocks. A block can be on the table or on some other block, and there is no limit to the height of a stack of blocks. However, on the table there are only a bounded number of slots into which blocks can be placed. There are two operations in this world: PickUp(i) — Pick up the top block in slot i (can be executed whenever slot i is not empty), and PutDown(i) — Put down the block that is currently being held into slot i. An agent can hold no more than one block at a time. Each operation costs 1.

An Example in the Blocks Domain:
The initial state can be seen at the left in Figure 1. g_A is "The Black block is on a Red block which is on the table at slot 2" and g_B is "The White block is on a Red block which is on the table at slot 1".

In order to achieve his goal alone, each agent has to execute four PickUp and four PutDown operations that cost (in total) 8. The two goals do not contradict each other, because there exists a state in the world that satisfies them both, as can be seen on the right side of Figure 1. There also exists a joint plan that moves the world from the initial state to a state that satisfies *both* goals with total cost of 8—one agent lifts the white block, while the other agent rearranges the other blocks suitably (by picking up and putting down each block once), whereupon the white block is put down. The agents will agree to split this joint plan with probability 0.5, leaving each with an expected utility of 4.

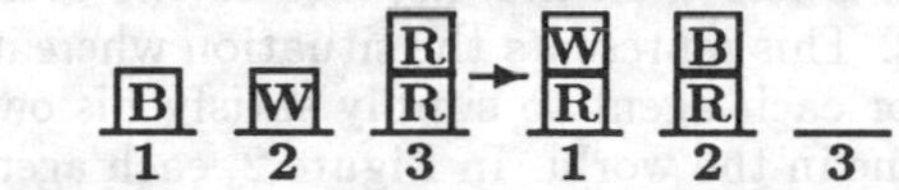

Figure 1: A Simple Cooperative Example

3.1 Types of Interactions — Cooperative, Compromise, Conflict

As presented in [Zlotkin and Rosenschein, 1990b], there are universally three types of possible interactions, from the point of view of an individual agent.

- A *cooperative* situation is one in which there exists a deal in the negotiation set that is preferred by an agent over achieving his goal alone. Here, an agent welcomes the existence of the other agents.

[3]The original result relied on the assumption that a phantom letter might be discovered in a probabilistic agreement. The result has been strengthened, and it has been shown that even if the phantom letter cannot be discovered (e.g., the phantom letter can be generated by the lying agent as needed), there are still no beneficial lies when the agents use all-or-nothing mixed deals.

- A *compromise* situation is one where there are individual rational deals for an agent. However, an agent would prefer to be alone in the world, and to accomplish his goal alone. Since he is forced to cope with the presence of other agents, he will agree on a deal. All of the deals in the negotiation set are better for the agent than leaving the world in its initial state s.
- A *conflict* situation is one in which the negotiation set is empty—no individual rational deals exist.

It is possible for different agents to have differing views of an interaction—it might be, for example, a cooperative situation for one and a compromise situation for the other. However, a conflict situation is always symmetric.

Given two agents' goals and an initial state, the type of interaction in which they find themselves is a function of the negotiation protocol they are about to use. Part of the reason for introducing new negotiation protocols is specifically to change conflict situations into non-conflict situations. By default, when we refer to the three terms above (cooperative, compromise, and conflict), we mean relative to agents negotiating over *mixed joint plans* that achieve both agents' goals.

Each of these situations can be visualized informally using diagrams. The cooperative situation can be seen in Figure 2, the compromise situation in Figure 3, and the conflict situation in Figure 4. A point on the plane represents a state of the world. Each oval represents a collection of world states that satisfies an agent's goal. s is the initial state of the world. The triple lines emanating from s represent a joint plan that moves the world to some other state; the agents share in carrying out the plan. The overlap between ovals represents final states that satisfy the goals of both agents A and B. Informally, the distance between s and either oval represents the cost associated with a single-agent plan that transforms the world to a state satisfying that agent's goal.

Note that in Figure 3, the distance from s to either agent's oval is less than the distance to the overlap between ovals. This represents the situation where it would be easier for each agent to simply satisfy his own goal, were he alone in the world. In Figure 2, each agent actually benefits from the existence of the other, since they will share the work of the joint plan.

In Figure 4, a semi-cooperative deal is pictured: the agents will carry out a joint plan to an intermediate state t, and then will flip a coin with probability q to decide whose goal will be individually satisfied [Zlotkin and Rosenschein, 1990b]; each single arrow represents a one-agent plan.

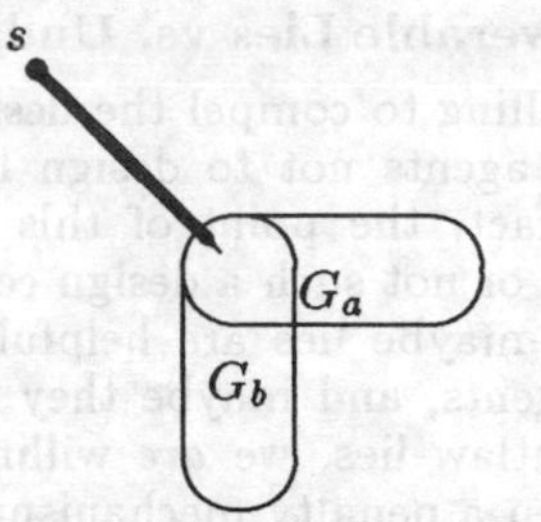

Figure 2: The Cooperative Situation

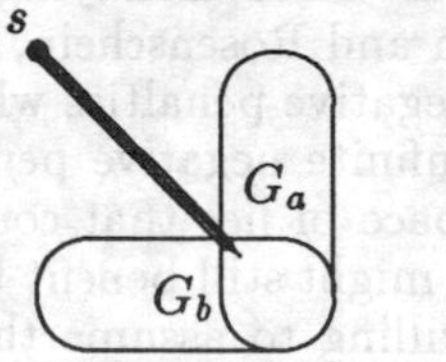

Figure 3: The Compromise Situation

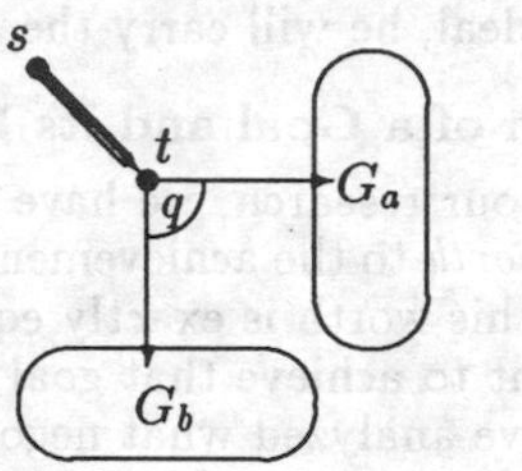

Figure 4: The Conflict Situation

3.2 Beneficial Lies in Non-Conflict Situations

Consider our Blocks World example above, drawn in Figure 1. Recall that the agents' true goals are as follows: g_A is "The Black block is on a Red block which is on the table at slot 2," and g_B is "The White block is on a Red block which is on the table at slot 1".

What if agent A lies about his true goal, claiming that he wants a Black block on *any* other block at slot 2? If A were alone in the world, he could apparently satisfy this relaxed goal at cost 2. Assuming that agent B reveals his true goal, the agents can only agree on one plan: A will lift a block (either the White or Black one), while B does all the rest of the work. The apparent utility for A is then 0 (still individual rational), while B has a utility of 2. In reality, A has an actual utility of 6. A's lie has benefited him.

This works because A is able to reduce the apparent cost of his carrying out his goal alone (which ultimately causes him to carry less of a burden in the final plan), while not compromising the ultimate achievement of his real goal. The reason his real goal is "accidentally" satisfied is because there is only one state that satisfies B's real goal and A's apparent goal, coincidentally the same state that satisfies both of their real goals.

The lie above is not A's only beneficial lie in this example. What if A claimed that his goal is "Slot 3 is empty and the Black block is clear"? Interestingly, this goal is quite different from his real goal. If A were alone in the world, he could apparently satisfy this variant goal at cost 4. The agents will then be forced again to agree on the deal above: A does two operations, with apparent utility of 2, and B does six operations, with utility of 2. Again, A's actual utility is 6.

There is a relation here between the two types of lies given above, and the "hiding letter" and "phantom letter" lies in the Postmen Domain. An agent in the Blocks World has the option of relaxing his true goal when he lies; the set of states that will satisfy his relaxed goal is then a superset of the set of states satisfying his true goal.[4] This is analogous to hiding a letter, and is what

[4] An agent will never benefit from pretending that the states satisfying his goals are a *subset* of the true goal states, since that would increase his apparent cost, and worsen his position in the negotiation.

agent A did when he said that any block under the Black block would be fine, even though he really wanted a Red block there. Consider Figure 5, where agent A's expanded apparent goal states are represented by the thicker oval and labeled G'_a.

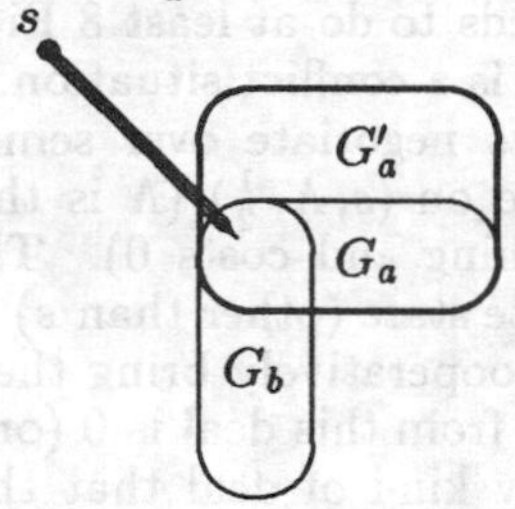

Figure 5: Expanding Apparent Goal States with a Lie

Note that the expansion of the goal states is toward the initial state s. This is the meaning of lowering one's apparent cost, and is necessary for a beneficial lie.

Alternatively, the agent can manufacture a totally different goal for the purposes of reducing his apparent cost, analogous to creating a phantom letter. Agent A did this when he said he wanted slot 3 empty and the Black block clear. Consider Figure 6, where agent A's altered apparent goal states are again represented by the thick outline and labeled G'_a. Note again, that the expansion of the goal states is toward the initial state s.

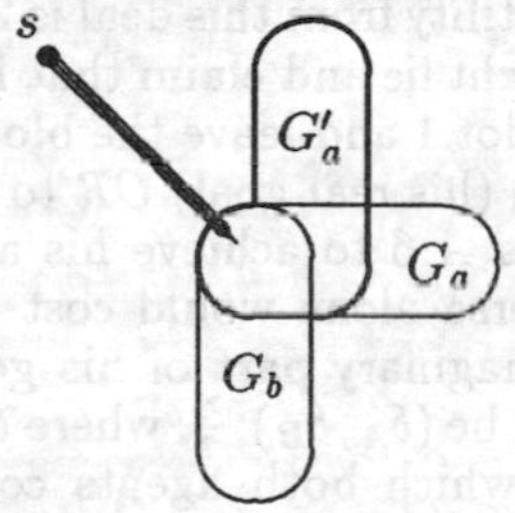

Figure 6: Altering Apparent Goal States with a Lie

The agent then needs to make sure that the intersection of his apparent goal states and his true goal states is not empty. Although this is a necessary precondition for a successful lie, it is of course not a sufficient precondition for a successful lie. Both of the lies in the above example will be useful to agent A regardless of the negotiation protocol that is being used: pure deal, mixed deal, semi-cooperative deal, or multi-plan deal.

Lying about the goal set (either expanding it or doing some other arbitrary alteration) is particularly useful when the domain causes tight coupling of the agents' goals. As was seen in the Postmen Domain, the likelihood of finding a beneficial lie grows with the coupling of the two agents' goals. With a phantom goal set, for example, things may have to be (usefully) changed in the real world in order to satisfy the phantom goals. At this point in our research, however, we have no insights regarding how an agent might discover either kind of beneficial lie systematically. For example, lowering the apparent cost of an agent's goal will not necessarily result in a beneficial lie—the agent must also ensure that the agreed-upon final state will both satisfy his own goal and not be too expensive (by creating an apparent conflict with the other agent's goal).

Another way of viewing this is that beneficial lies exist in the Blocks World because goals can be "accidentally" achieved, and a lying agent can take advantage of this fact. Accidental achievement may come about both because the agents might share the same goal, and because tight coupling in the domain may cause the goal to be satisfied when some unrelated action is carried out. This is not the case in the Postmen Domain—no one can accidentally deliver your letter. Hiding letters, therefore, rules out accidental achievement of those hidden goals, and therefore the lying agent must carry out those goals by himself, to his detriment. In the Blocks World, you can hide part of your goal, and still see it achieved unwittingly by the other agent.

3.3 Lies in Conflict Situations

It might seem that when agents are in a conflict situation, the potential for beneficial lies is reduced. After all, it might appear that the agents' conflict is related to their goals being decoupled, and according to our previous observation, coupled goals aid beneficial lying. In fact, beneficial lying *can* exist in conflict situations, because conflicting goals do not mean decoupled goals.

"Conflict" between agents' goals means that there does not exist a mixed joint plan that achieves both goals and is also individual rational. This is either because such a state does not exist, or because the joint plan is too costly to be individual rational. Even when conflict exists between goals, they may be tightly coupled, and therefore a beneficial lie may exist.

Taking Advantage of a Common Subgoal in a Conflict Situation: Let the initial state of the world be as in the left side of Figure 7. One agent wants the block currently in slot 1 to be in slot 2; the other agent wants it to be in slot 3. In addition, both agents share the goal of swapping the two blocks currently in slot 4 (i.e., reverse the stack's order). Formally, the goals are $g_A = \{\text{At}(R,2), \text{At}(W,4), \text{On}(B,W)\}$ and $g_B = \{\text{At}(R,3), \text{At}(W,4), \text{On}(B,W)\}$.

The cost for an agent of achieving his goal alone is 10. Negotiating over the true goals would lead the agents to agree to do the swap cooperatively (at cost of 2 each), achieving the state shown on the right of Figure 7, and *then* flip a coin, with a weighting of $\frac{1}{2}$, to decide whose goal will be individually satisfied. This deal brings them an overall expected utility of 2 (i.e., $\frac{1}{2}(10-2)-2$).

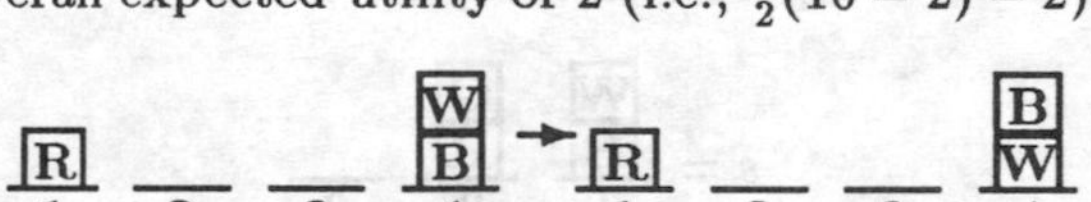

Figure 7: Taking Advantage of a Common Subgoal

What if agent A lies and tells B that his goal is $g'_A = \{\text{At}(R,2), \text{On}(B,W)\}$? Agent A thus "hides" the fact that his real goal has the stack of blocks at slot 4, and claims that he does not really care where the stack is. The cost for agent A of achieving his apparent goal is 6, because now he can supposedly build the reversed stack at slot 3 with a cost of 4. Assuming that agent B reveals his true goal, the agents will still agree to cooperatively bring the world to the same state shown on the right of Figure 7, but now the weighting of the coin will be $\frac{4}{7}$. This deal would give agent A an apparent utility of $1\frac{3}{7}$ (i.e., $\frac{4}{7}(8-2)-2$) which is also B's real utility (i.e., $\frac{3}{7}(10-2)-2$). A's real utility, however, is $2\frac{4}{7} = \frac{4}{7}(10-2)-2$. This lie is beneficial for A.

The situation is illustrated in Figure 8, where A's lie modifies his presumed goal states so that they are closer to the initial state, but the plan still ends up bringing the world to one of his *real* goal states.

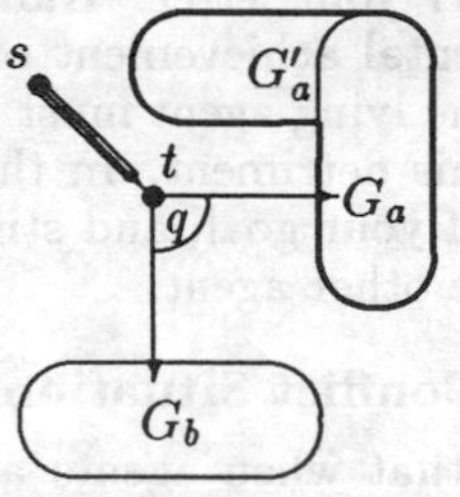

Figure 8: Lying in a Conflict Situation

In the example above, the existence of a common subgoal between the agents allowed one agent to exploit the coupled goals. The lying agent relaxes his true goal by claiming that the common subgoal is mainly its opponent's demand—as far as he is concerned (he claims), he would be satisfied with a much cheaper subgoal. If it is really necessary to achieve the expensive subgoal (he claims), more of the burden must fall on his opponent.

One might think that in the absence of such a common subgoal, there would be no opportunity for one agent to beneficially lie to the other. This is only partially true. When the goals are decoupled and the agents are negotiating over semi-cooperative deals, then there does not exist an intermediate state t to which the agents would agree to cooperatively bring the world. All the deals that the agents can agree on will have $t = s$, and will look like Figure 9. In this case, the utility for both agents of any deal (i.e., any value of q) will be 0.[5]

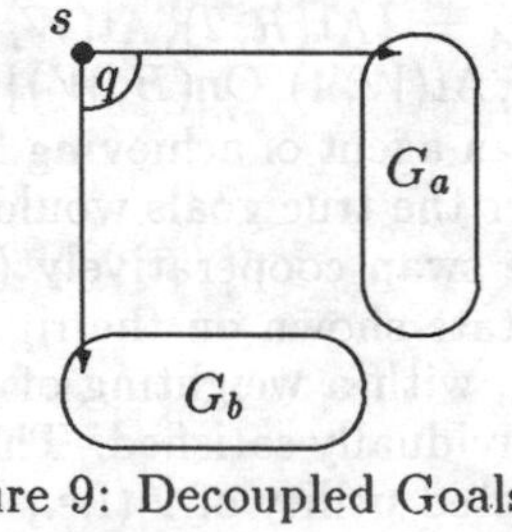

Figure 9: Decoupled Goals

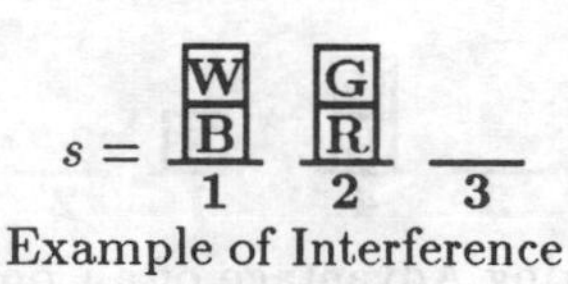

Figure 10: Example of Interference Decoy Lie

Another Example of Beneficial Lying in a Conflict Situation: The initial state s can be seen in Figure 10. A's goal is to reverse the blocks in slot 1, and to leave the blocks in slot 2 in their initial position. B's goal is to reverse the blocks in slot 2, and to leave the blocks in slot 1 in their initial position. To achieve his goal alone, each agent needs to do at least 8 PickUp/PutDown operations. This is a conflict situation.

If the agents negotiate over semi-cooperative deals, they will agree on $(s, \Lambda, \frac{1}{2})$ (Λ is the empty joint plan that does nothing and costs 0). There does not exist an intermediate state (other than s) to which the agents will agree to cooperatively bring the world. The utility for each agent from this deal is 0 (or $\frac{1}{2}\epsilon$). However, this is not the only kind of deal that the agents can agree on in this situation. If the agents are using multi-plan deals, then they can agree on a better deal.

Definition 1 *A* multi-plan deal *is (δ_A, δ_B, q), where the δ_i are mixed joint plans, and $0 \leq q \leq 1 \in \mathbb{R}$ is the probability that the agents will perform δ_A (they will perform δ_B with probability $1-q$).*

Negotiation over multi-plan deals will cause the agents to agree on (δ_A, δ_B): $\frac{1}{2}$, where δ_i is the mixed joint plan in which both agents cooperatively achieve i's goal. The best joint plan for doing the reverse in either one of the slots costs 2 PickUp/PutDown operations for each agent. Each agent's utility from this deal is $2 = (\frac{1}{2}(8-2)-\frac{1}{2}(2))$.

Agent A might lie and claim that his goal is to reverse the blocks in slot 1 and leave the blocks in slot 2 in their initial position (his real goal) *OR* to have W be alone in slot 2. It costs A 6 to achieve his apparent goal alone; to do the reverse alone would cost him 8, and thus to achieve the imaginary part of his goal is cheaper. The agreement will be (δ_A, δ_B): $\frac{4}{7}$, where δ_i is again the mixed joint plan in which both agents cooperatively achieve i's goal. It turns out to be cheaper for both agents to cooperatively carry out A's real goal than it is to cope with A's imaginary alternative. A's apparent utility will be $1\frac{3}{7} = \frac{4}{7}(6-2) - \frac{3}{7}(2)$; this is also B's utility. A's actual utility, however, will be $2\frac{4}{7} = \frac{4}{7}(8-2) - \frac{3}{7}(2)$, which is greater than the unvarnished utility of 2 that A would get without lying. So even without a common subgoal, A had a beneficial lie, but only because of the multi-plan deal protocol. Here we have been introduced to a new type of lie, a kind of "interference decoy," that can be used even when the agents' goals are decoupled.

4 Conclusions

Incomplete information between negotiating agents does not require a new concept of "solution." We can continue to use the concept of solution associated with complete information negotiation.

The existence of beneficial lies during negotiation can be sensitive both to the domain, as well as to the type of negotiation protocol used. In the Postmen Domain, for example, beneficial lies exist when agents negotiate over pure deals, but are eliminated when a more general deal type (i.e., all-or-nothing mixed deals) is used. In the Blocks Domain, however, the lies that are facilitated by tightly coupled goals are not eliminated by using a more general type of deal. Moreover, using an extremely

[5]This is a borderline situation in which the agents are indifferent between achieving their goals and leaving the world in its initial state. It still seems reasonable to assume that an agent would prefer to achieve his goal even though technically his utility is 0. To overcome this problem, we can assume that the worth of a goal to an agent is equal to the cost of this goal plus ϵ (an infinitesimally small number that is the same for all agents). An agent would prefer to achieve his goal in this case because his utility would be ϵ instead of 0, and q will always be equal to $\frac{1}{2}$.

general negotiation over multi-plan deals actually opens up the space of lies; the new "interference decoy" kind of lie can be used with multi-plan deals even when the agents' goals are decoupled.

Using goal recognition techniques will not eliminate lying by agents. The best we can hope for from any such approach is to enable the agents to reach pareto optimal deals (exactly the same deals that they would have reached with complete information). Therefore, regardless of the protocol being used, an agent could always negotiate as if he had a different goal. If a beneficial lie exists, he can still benefit from the deception, even if it is an "implicit" as opposed to explicit deception. Since, however, it may be computationally difficult to find beneficial lies (or even impossible given symmetric incomplete information between the agents), our negotiation protocols may still be usable in real-world situations. Beneficial lies may exist, but be difficult or impossible to find.

5 Acknowledgments

This research has been partially supported by the Leibniz Center for Research in Computer Science, by the Israel National Council for Research and Development (Grant 032-8284), and by the Center for Science Absorption, Office of Aliya Absorption, the State of Israel.

References

[Axelrod, 1984] Robert Axelrod. *The Evolution of Cooperation.* Basic Books, Inc., New York, 1984.

[Conry *et al.*, 1988] Susan E. Conry, Robert A. Meyer, and Victor R. Lesser. Multistage negotiation in distributed planning. In Alan H. Bond and Les Gasser, editors, *Readings in Distributed Artificial Intelligence*, pages 367–384. Morgan Kaufmann Publishers, Inc., San Mateo, California, 1988.

[Durfee, 1988] Edmund H. Durfee. *Coordination of Distributed Problem Solvers.* Kluwer Academic Publishers, Boston, 1988.

[Ephrati and Rosenschein, 1991] Eithan Ephrati and Jeffrey S. Rosenschein. The Clarke Tax as a consensus mechanism among automated agents. In *Proceedings of the Ninth National Conference on Artificial Intelligence*, Anaheim, California, July 1991.

[Gasser, 1991] Les Gasser. Social conceptions of knowledge and action: DAI foundations and open systems semantics. *Artificial Intelligence*, 47(1–3):107–138, 1991.

[Kraus and Wilkenfeld, 1991] Sarit Kraus and Jonathan Wilkenfeld. Negotiations over time in a multi agent environment: Preliminary report. In *Proceedings of the Twelfth International Joint Conference on Artificial Intelligence*, Sydney, Australia, August 1991.

[Kreifelts and von Martial, 1990] Thomas Kreifelts and Frank von Martial. A negotiation framework for autonomous agents. In *Proceedings of the Second European Workshop on Modeling Autonomous Agents and Multi-Agent Worlds*, pages 169–182, Saint-Quentin en Yvelines, France, August 1990.

[Kuwabara and Lesser, 1989] Kazuhiro Kuwabara and Victor R. Lesser. Extended protocol for multistage negotiation. In *Proceedings of the Ninth Workshop on Distributed Artificial Intelligence*, pages 129–161, Rosario, Washington, September 1989.

[Laasri *et al.*, 1990] B. Laasri, H. Laasri, and V. R. Lesser. Negotiation and its role in cooperative distributed problem problem solving. In *Proceedings of the Tenth International Workshop on Distributed Artificial Intelligence*, Bandera, Texas, October 1990.

[Malone *et al.*, 1988] T. Malone, R. Fikes, and M. Howard. Enterprise: A market-like task scheduler for distributed computing environments. In B. A. Huberman, editor, *The Ecology of Computation.* North-Holland Publishing Company, Amsterdam, 1988.

[Rosenschein and Genesereth, 1985] Jeffrey S. Rosenschein and Michael R. Genesereth. Deals among rational agents. In *Proceedings of the Ninth International Joint Conference on Artificial Intelligence*, pages 91–99, Los Angeles, California, August 1985.

[Smith, 1978] Reid G. Smith. *A Framework for Problem Solving in a Distributed Processing Environment.* PhD thesis, Stanford University, 1978.

[Sycara, 1988] Katia P. Sycara. Resolving goal conflicts via negotiation. In *Proceedings of the Seventh National Conference on Artificial Intelligence*, pages 245–250, St. Paul, Minnesota, August 1988.

[Zlotkin and Rosenschein, 1989] Gilad Zlotkin and Jeffrey S. Rosenschein. Negotiation and task sharing among autonomous agents in cooperative domains. In *Proceedings of the Eleventh International Joint Conference on Artificial Intelligence*, pages 912–917, Detroit, Michigan, August 1989.

[Zlotkin and Rosenschein, 1990a] Gilad Zlotkin and Jeffrey S. Rosenschein. Blocks, lies, and postal freight: The nature of deception in negotiation. In *Proceedings of the Tenth International Workshop on Distributed Artificial Intelligence*, Bandera, Texas, October 1990.

[Zlotkin and Rosenschein, 1990b] Gilad Zlotkin and Jeffrey S. Rosenschein. Negotiation and conflict resolution in non-cooperative domains. In *Proceedings of the Eighth National Conference on Artificial Intelligence*, pages 100–105, Boston, Massachusetts, July 1990.

[Zlotkin and Rosenschein, 1990c] Gilad Zlotkin and Jeffrey S. Rosenschein. Negotiation and goal relaxation. In *Proceedings of The Workshop on Modelling Autonomous Agents in a Multi-Agent World*, pages 115–132, Saint-Quentin en Yvelines, France, August 1990.

Solving "How to Clear a Block" with *CONSTRUCTIVE MATCHING* methodology

Marta Fraňová, Yves Kodratoff

CNRS & Université Paris Sud,

LRI, Bât. 490, 91405 Orsay, France

Abstract[1]

Constructive Matching is a methodology for proving by induction **Specifications Theorems** (ST), i.e., theorems of the form ∀x ∃z (P(x) ⇒ Q(x,z)). ST formalize the problem of constructing a program specified by *given an input vector x, an input condition P, find an output vector z verifying Q(x,z), whenever P(x) holds.*

Till now, we have applied our method to the so-called *Constructible Domains*, for which one disposes of a unique way of building any input and output data. The goal of this paper is to enlarge our methodology to well-founded domains which are not constructible. As a simple example, Manna and Waldinger's "How to Clear a Block" problem[2] is solved. As opposed to theirs, our method **does** consider strategic aspects of program derivation from a formal specification.

1 Introduction

In [Franova, 85] we have developed a methodology, called *Constructive Matching* (*CM*), for proving by induction Specification Theorems, i.e., theorems of the form ∀x ∃z (P(x) ⇒ Q(x,z)). These theorems formalize program synthesis as follows. Given input vector x verifying the input condition P(x), find an output vector z such that the input-output relation Q(x,z) holds. Practical reasons, such as the availability of examples and implementation limitations, led us to restrict our method to particular inductively constructed sets, called *Constructible Domains* (CD). These are specified by their constructors, enabling new elements to be built from old ones and, possibly, from elements of an already defined domain. In CD each element has a unique representation in terms of constructors. This amounts to saying that we do not allow relations among constructors.

E.g., the set of natural numbers (*NAT*) can be considered as a CD with constructors **0** and **s**. This gives us the domain *NAT* = {**0**, **s**(**0**),**s**(**s**(**0**)), ...} which may be identified with the familiar sequence of integers { 0, 1, 2, ... }. Each element x of *NAT* is either **0** or can be written as **s**(y), where y is an element of *NAT*. In the following, we shall call **s**(y), a representative of x, and y a subrepresentative of x.

More generally, we call y a **subrepresentative** of x if it has the form x = Constructor(y).

[1] This research has been partly supported by the *Programme de Recherches Coordonées en Intelligence Artificielle* from the French *Ministère de la Recherche et de la Technologie*. It is a shortened version of [Franova and Kodratoff, 91a].

[2] Using this problem, Manna and Waldinger show the interest of the deductive approach for the synthesis of imperative programs that may alter data structures or produce other side effects, and illustrate how program synthesis can be carried over to the planning domain. Our goal is the same as theirs, i.e., illustrating that our methodology can be also carried over to planning.

Moreover, in CD, we have considered mainly recursive[3] definitions given with respect to constructors.

For instance, the basic form of such a recursive definitions for a function f defined on the natural numbers, is

$$f(z) = \begin{cases} z_0, & \text{if } z = 0 \\ g(a,f(a)), & \text{if } z = \mathbf{s}(a)\ \&\ H(a) \end{cases}$$

where z_0 is a constant, g is a suitable recursive function and H is a suitable recursive predicate. Note that this definition introduces an existentially quantified variable 'a', which is a subrepresentative of z. Therefore, no actual new variable has been introduced.

Another typical feature of CD is that definitions do not allow the introduction of existentially quantified variables (EQV) other than subrepresentatives of others. As we illustrate in section 4, the introduction of new EQV is typical of non CD.

For instance, let us consider a predicate P, the recursive case of which is defined by the axiom **P(f(u,v),y), if P(u,y)&Q(v)**, where f is not a constructor. Then, this kind of axiom is not admissible in CD, since it contains EQV[4] u and v. Note that the *put-table-clear* axiom (section 4.3) is of this form.

In order to stress the difference between EQV met in the theorem, and those met in definitions, we shall call the latter ones **unspecified variables** (because they are indeed "unspecified" in the definition).

In general, our method is able to prove a given theorem only if the well-founded order necessary for proving this theorem is expressed in the axioms.

For instance, let us define the addition of two natural numbers by:

$$u+v = \begin{cases} u, & \text{if } v = 0 \\ \mathbf{s}(u+p(v)), & \text{if } v > 0 \end{cases}$$

This definition calls recursively the predecessor (p) of given number v. Therefore, the well-founded order determined by this definition allows us to perform only proofs that require one-step induction, i.e., in order to prove, say, ∀x F(x), we have to prove F(0) and F(p(n)) ⇒ F(n). If ∀x F(x) requires other kinds of well-founded orderings, for instance, with respect to the quotient of n when divided by a number m such that **s**(0) < m < n, and if in the theory none of the functions or predicates call such an element, then our current method fails (see details in [Franova, 91a]).

Moreover, if a recursive definition is of the form

$$f(x) = h(x,f(t))$$

we assume that there is a well-founded ordering in which t is smaller than x. We have not yet studied the problem of finding such a well-founded ordering. Presently, we propose that the user uses the results of Boyer and Moore [79] in order to check that his definitions are correct.

[3] D. Barstow made available to us an example for which we were unable to find a recursive definition of one of the predicates involved in ST. Our method cannot be applied to that kind of problem.

[4] In fact, the axiom P(f(u,v),y), if P(u,y) & Q(v) should correctly be written as P(x,y), if ∃u ∃v (x=f(u,v) & P(u,y) & Q(v)).

In this paper we enlarge our methodology to well-founded domains (WFD) that are not necessarily constructed with a help of constructors, and which may introduce EQV in the definitions. We explain in [Franova, 88a] that finding a strategy for a proof of an atomic formula is one of basic problems of mechanizing inductive proofs. We therefore limit ourselves here only to this particular problem, even if the simple example we solve here (Manna&Waldinger's "How to Clear a Block" problem [87]), illustrates our overall methodology.

2 *CM*-methodology

One of the main differences of our method, in comparison with other approaches in inductive theorem proving [Boyer and Moore, 79; Bundy *et al.*, 90] is actually very deep since it takes place in the basic step of any theorem proving methodology, viz. in the way atomic formulae are proven. In [Franova, 88a] we have shown the consequences of the choices done at such a low level on the way subproblems are generated during the course of a complete proof.

Classical methods for proving by induction atomic formula can be classified as simplification[5] (or rewrite) methods, i.e., they attempt to transform the atomic formula into simpler and simpler form, until the formula TRUE is reached.

Our method for proving atomic formulae can rather be qualified as a "complication" method, stressing so that we rather progressively build more and more large sets of constraints describing the condition at which the formula is TRUE. The proof is completed when these conditions are proven to be implied by those of the problem.

We call our way of proving an atomic formula a *Constructive Matching* **formula construction**, or *CM*-**formula construction.**

Let us give a brief motivation for this name. *If F is an n-place predicate symbol and t_1, ..., t_n are terms, then F(t_1, ..., t_n) is an atomic formula.* This definition of an atomic formula shows that an atomic formula is "constructed", or "build up", from a predicate name and terms in the following manner: We take an n-place symbol F providing the syntactical scheme F(_ , _ , ..., _), where "_" represent empty positions (or arguments) to be filled up by concrete terms, so that finally F(t_1, ..., t_n) is obtained. In classical thinking, this process of "filling up" empty argument places is mentally performed in one step, i.e., we start from F(_ , ...,) and reach immediately F(t_1, ..., t_n).

As opposed to this one step operation, we consider a piece-wise construction of an atomic formula. We start with the syntactical scheme F(_ , ..., _). We then take the first term t_1 and we fill up the first empty argument of our scheme by this term, so we have F(t_1, _ , ..., _). Then, we fill up the first empty argument in the last scheme by t_2, obtaining F(t_1, t_2, ..., _), etc.

We thus construct (purely syntactically) in n steps the formula F(t_1, ..., t_n). However, in theorem proving, we need to speak of the validity of a given formula in a theory *T* made from the axioms. This is why we will consider axioms defining the predicate F. These axioms allow us to change the above syntactical construction into a construction which, if successfully performed, provides a proof for F(t_1, ..., t_n).

[5] [Boyer and Moore, 79] is an example of a simplification method.

Let us show briefly how axioms are involved in the process of our construction of an atomic formula F(t_1,t_2), created from a predicate F and two terms t_1 and t_2, i.e., n = 2. The order of filling up arguments depends now on given definitions. For simplicity, we suppose here that definitions involved indicate that t_1 has to be filled up first. The *CM*-formula construction can then be briefly described as follows.

We start by building an abstract formula F(t_1,ξ) with an abstract argument ξ, i.e., instead of considering an empty argument place, we take a variable which has a special character since it does not occur in F(t_1,t_2), and moreover it represents (or, equivalently, is an abstraction of) all terms which can fill up the empty argument of the scheme F(t_1,_) in order to obtain an atomic formula. Therefore, we call it an **abstract argument** in order to avoid confusing it with the quantified variables of the theorem.

Let us give a very simple example which shows also a difference with the simplification approach, by proving the formula **s(s(0))** < **s(s(s(s(0))))** (written 2<4, for brevity), and using the following recursive definition of the predicate <:

(1) **0** < n, if n = **s**(b)
(2) **s**(m) < n, if n = **s**(b) & m < b

The definition of "<" is recursive with respect to the first argument. This is why, in the formula 2<4, the second argument (i.e., non-recursive) is replaced by an abstract argument ξ. Up to now, we have constructed purely syntactically the formula 2<ξ, without considering yet the validity of this formula.

Now, the definition of F provides conditions for the validity of the formula F(t_1,ξ). Let us denote by *C* the set of all ξ for which F(t_1,ξ) is true, i.e., *C* = {ξ | F(t_1,ξ) is true}.

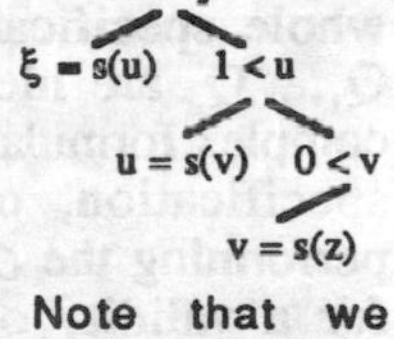

Using the definition of the predicate "<" we see that any ξ that satisfies the formula 2<ξ must be of the form ξ=**s**(u), where 1<u, therefore, u must be of the form **s**(v) with 0<v, and therefore, using (1), v must be of the form **s**(z). This yields the final form of ξ and so the class of all ξ that satisfy the formula 2<ξ is *C* = { ξ / there exists z such that ξ = **s(s(s(**z**)))**}. Note that we obtain *C* by unfolding [Burstall and Darlington, 77] the formulae 2<ξ , 1<u, 0<v. For each of them we obtain conditions, that are collected and combined. The final step is the withdrawal of the new "abstract arguments" u, v which are recognized as being useless. This leaves ξ expressed in relation with a new variable-argument z.

In other words, we solve our problem in a top-down manner, pick up the final leaf (v=**s**(z)), carry this bottom leaf up to the root of the tree. During this last step, the final leaf is applied to all other leaves of the tree. The solution obtained (in case of success) is given by the set of independent leaves in which the final leaf has been applied.

In our example, final leaf is v=**s**(z). It is applied successively to u=**s**(v) yielding u=**s**(**s**(z)), then to ξ=**s**(u), yielding ξ=**s**(**s**(**s**(z))). Therefore we have that the solution of our problem 2<ξ is ξ=**s**(**s**(**s**(z))).

We are then left with checking if the replacement of ξ by t_2 preserves the validity of F(t_1,ξ), i.e., we have to check whether t_2 ∈ *C*.

In our example, we have to check whether 4 belongs to *C*. In fact, it does, since 4 = **s**(**s**(**s**(**s**(0)))), i.e., z = **s**(0).

The same problem is tackled by the simplification approach in a different manner:

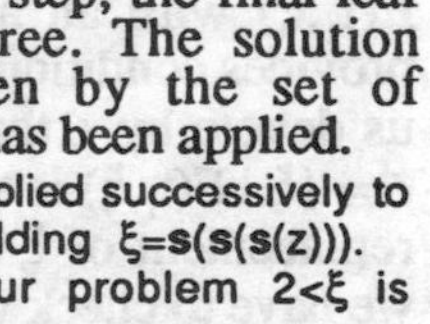

Applying (2) to 2<4 leads to two subproblems. Firstly, it is necessary to show that there is an element b such that 4=**s**(b). Here, we succeed since b=3. Then it is necessary to prove 1<3. In this step, our original problem, proving the formula 2<4 is replaced by another equivalent problem: Prove 1<3. One therefore "forgets" the original problem. Applying (2) to 1<3 leads again to two similar subproblems. Firstly, it is necessary to show that there is an element b such that 3=s(b). Here, we succeed since b=2. Then it is necessary to prove 0<2. Here, once again we "forget" the formula 1<3 and we concentrate our effort to the formula 0<2. Using (1) this simplifies to TRUE, because there is an element b (b=1) such that 2=s(b). This proves our original formula.

This simplification approach proves the formula in a top-down manner, but the final leaf is TRUE in the case of success. Therefore, as opposed to our method, there are no final bottom-up steps in the simplification approach.

It may seem that our "constructive" method makes the proof more complicated (as compared to the simplification methods) without anything to gain. Recall, however, that simplification procedures have been developed for theorems without EQV. Therefore, our method which is suitable for specification theorems, is more powerful, even if it may seem more awkward and non-useful for theorems with universally quantified variables only. As compared to classical simplification thinking, it may seem also more artificial, because, by our method, we may generate an existentially quantified lemma when proving a universally quantified theorem. The simplification methods are built in such a manner that all the subproblems generated are universally quantified, while this restriction is not necessary to our *CM*-methodology.

Program synthesis methodologies ([Manna and Waldinger, 80; Kodratoff and Picard, 83; Bibel and Hörnig, 84; Dershowitz, 85; Smith, 85; Perdrix, 86; Biundo, 88]) do not consider the problem of strategy for proving an atomic formula as the main problem. In fact, these methods take the whole specification, say $Q_1(x,z)$ & ... & $Q_n(x,z)$, where $Q_1,...,Q_n$ are literals, and perform transformations on this complex formula[6]. As opposed to such a treatment of a given specification, our method deals firstly[7] with $Q_1(x,z)$, performing the *CM*-formula construction it finds conditions for a validity of this formula. After this step has been completed, and assuming the conditions obtained, our method starts taking care of $Q_2(x,z)$, and so on, until the last literal $Q_n(x,z)$ is treated.

Thus, as a summary, let us state that, in order to prove an atomic formula $F(t_1,t_2)$, created from a predicate F and two terms t_1 and t_2, we start by building an abstract formula $F(t_1,\xi)$ with an abstract argument ξ. The definition of F provides conditions for the validity of the formula $F(t_1,\xi)$. Let us denote by C the set of all ξ for which $F(t_1,\xi)$ is true, i.e., $C = \{\xi \mid F(t_1,\xi) \text{ is true}\}$. We are then left with checking if the replacement of ξ by t_2 preserves the validity of $F(t_1,\xi)$, i.e., we have to check whether $t_2 \in C$.

3 *CM*-formula construction for WFD

In the previous section we pointed out that the main reason for performing the *CM*-formula construction is its suitability for proving specification theorems. We also described the way to proceed when a given specification is a conjunction of atomic formulae. Therefore, in this section, we shall concentrate on a specification theorem[8] $\forall x\, \exists z\, Q(x,z)$, where Q(x,z) is an atomic formula.

Let us denote by ST_0 this theorem and by σ_p the substitution $\{x \leftarrow p\}$, where p is smaller than x. Using the general induction principle and x being the induction variable, we have to prove $\{ \sigma_p(\exists z\, Q(x,z)) \} \Rightarrow \exists z\, Q(x,z)$.

For this general induction principle scheme, we do not have a division into a base step and an induction step. From the computational point of view, however, it is interesting to "simulate" a base step for ST_0, since we then obtain the non-recursive parts of the desired programs.

3.1 Base step (a general outline)

One way to simulate a base step is done by using the tautology $Q(x,t) \Rightarrow Q(x,t)$ as explained and exemplified in [Franova and Kodratoff, 91a].

Let us consider now the induction step, i.e., we try to find out recursive parts of the program.

3.2 Induction step solutions (a general outline)

During this step we shall perform the *CM*-formula construction presented in an intuitive way in section 2. For simplicity, and in order to keep the notation of section 2, Q(x,z) will be called $F(t_1,t_2)$[9]. We suppose that F is defined in *T* recursively (at least) with respect to the first argument.

As pointed out in section 2, we start by building an abstract formula $F(t_1,\xi)$ with an abstract argument ξ. Then

Step 1: We ***evaluate*** the term t_1, i.e., we apply to t_1 axioms defining functions occurring in t_1 until no further axioms can be applied. For brevity, we suppose here that t_1 is already evaluated, and that the evaluations yielded no condition.
Step 2: We ***evaluate*** $F(t_1,\xi)$ in order to ***find conditions for the validity*** of the formula $F(t_1,\xi)$.

With respect to the recursive definition of F this step gives a composition of the recursive call and some formula, say G.

We have $F(t_1,\xi)$ **if** comp(G,F(t,ξ)).

Here, it may happen that t in the recursive call is expressed in terms of new EQV[10] that do not appear in ST_0. For instance, later we show that constructing the formula Clear(ξ,b) (using the *put-table-clear* axiom from section 4.2) leads to

Clear(ξ,b) if ξ = put'(w,x,table) & On(w,x,b) & Clear(w,x).

This formula says that Clear(ξ,b) is valid only if there is a state w and a block x such that ξ can be written as put'(w,x,table) and moreover if On(w,x,b) & Clear(w,x) holds. Thus, x and w are existentially quantified, i.e., x and w are unspecified variables. The presence of such variables in a proof is not admissible, because it makes the proof to be a nonconstructive one. Therefore, during an actual proof we have to express unspecified variables in terms of variables given in ST_0. Whenever we express a variable in terms of variables given in ST_0, we say that we **concretize** this variable, or, equivalently, we say that we try to **make** this variable **more explicit**. The following step is necessary only when such unspecified variables appear.

Step 2*: We try to ***concretize*** unspecified variables until the recursive call formula contains variables of ST_0 so that the application of the induction hypothesis is possible.

We will try to concretize unspecified variables in F(t,ξ) exploring where the atomic formulae of comp(G,F(t,ξ)) may come from. Thus, we apply our *CM*-formula construction to

[6] See [Franova, 91c] for more details about differences between our method and the other program synthesis methods.

[7] There are heuristics which suitably order literals in a given specification. For instance, if x is an input and z is an output, then the specification ordered(z) & permut(x,z) is reordered to permut(x,z) & ordered(z). Moreover, in such a reordered specification, $Q_1(x,z)$ must be an atomic formula.

[8] For simplicity, we assume here that the input condition P(x) is TRUE.

[9] Thus, we assume here that Q(x,z) is created from a binary predicate F and the terms t_1 and t_2.

[10] Remember that we call such EQV "unspecified variables" and that such variables are not possible for CD.

the atomic formulae of comp(G,F(t,ξ)). Clearly, in general, heuristics have to be developed here to choose the order in which the formulae from comp(G,F(t,ξ)) are examined. In section 4 we will follow one possible heuristic: The priority of formulae with a larger number of variables of ST_0.

This concretization of unspecified variables changes F(t,ξ) to a new formula, say F(t',ξ).

Step 3: We now try to ***apply induction*** hypotheses in order to ***concretize***[11] ξ.

Recall that $\sigma_p = \{ x \leftarrow p \}$, where p is smaller than x. The generic form of induction hypotheses (IH) is

$$\forall u\ \sigma_p F(t_1(x,u),t_2(x,u)).$$

The quantification here is due to a possible presence of universally quantified variables other than x in ST_0. Thus, if ST_0 contains no other universally quantified variables, the form of IH is $\sigma_p F(t_1(x),t_2(x))$. Attempting to apply IH leads to a comparison between F(t',ξ) and $\forall u\ \sigma_p F(t_1(x,u),t_2(x,u))$, which, in general, yields the transformational problem represented by the equations

$$\exists u\ (\ t' = \sigma_p t_1(x,u)\ )\ \&\ (\ \xi = \sigma_p t_2(x,u)\ ).$$

The solution of this problem allows the replacement of ξ by the more concrete element $\sigma_p t_2(x,u)$. Let us denote this element by α. Therefore, the elements of the class for which the theorem is true, *C*, are represented by α.

Step 4: Our goal is now to verify if t_2 belongs to *C*, i.e., we have to check if we can **replace** α by t_2.

This is equivalent to performing a unification of α and t_2 modulo the theory *T*. Our *CM*-term construction performs this operation (see [Franova, 88b]).

Step 5: We have to perform final simplifications.

The reader can now see that our formula construction is an algorithm which mechanizes a proof of an atomic formula, because a successfully completed construction provides a proof. On the other hand, this construction is an algorithm, because we know what we want to obtain and **how to obtain it.**

- Clearly, in order to find conditions for the validity of $F(t_1,\xi)$ we **evaluate** $F(t_1,\xi)$ using the definition of F in the same way as the unfold operation [Burstall and Darlington, 77].
- We know then that we have to apply induction hypotheses, so we **generate equations comparing IH and the previously obtained expansion.**
- The success of the last equation solving problem allows the concretization of ξ by a more concrete α and allows at least the most trivial simplification, which is here **eliminating recursion formulae from the obtained expansion.**
- We have then to replace α by t_2, so we **generate an equation between α and t_2.**

4 Example: How to Clear a Block (HCB)

Here, a plan for the problem[12] is specified as follows. The problem is to clear a given block, where we are not told whether the block is already clear or, if it is known not to be clear, how many blocks are above it. We adopt here the plan theory developed by Manna and Waldinger [87] (further referred to as the **mw-plan** theory) for describing situational logic events in terms of classical logics, and their notation.

4.1 Notations

For a given blocks a, u and v

clear(a) is true if the block a is clear
on(u,v) is true if the block u is on the object v
hat(a) is the block directly on a, if it exists
put(u,v) is the action which places block u on top of v

In situational logic we have to consider the value of a function or a predicate with respect to a state, i.e., we have to introduce an explicit state argument w for them. For example, for the predicate clear and the function hat we have

Clear(w,a) is true if the block a is clear in state w
hat'(w,a) is the block on top of the block a in state w

Actions are represented as functions that yield states; for example put'(w,u,v) is the state obtained from state w by putting block u on object v.

4.2 Axioms for mw-plan theory

THE FUNCTION ":"

If s is a state and e an object, then s:e denotes the object designated by e in state s.

To any n-ary function symbol f a new n+1-ary symbol f' is associated with the property

w:f(u₁,...,uₙ) = f'(w,w:u₁, ..., w:uₙ) *(object linkage)*

for example, a fixed block w:hat(u) can be expressed equivalently by hat'(w,w:u).

THE RELATION "::"

This relation is analogous to ":", but the relation :: is for predicates. If s is a state and e is a proposition, then s::e is a proposition denoting the truth-value designated by e in state s. E.g., s::clear(d) is true if the block s:d is clear in state s.

Analogously to the *object linkage*, the *propositional linkage* linkage axiom is introduced. To any n-ary predicate symbol r a new n+1-ary symbol R is associated with the property

$$w::r(u_1,...,u_n) \equiv R(w,w:u_1,...,w:u_n) \quad \textit{(propositional linkage)}$$

for example, s::clear(d) ≡ Clear(s,s:d), i.e., s::clear(d) is true if the block s:d is clear in state s.

THE EXECUTION FUNCTION ";"

If s is a state and p a plan, s;p denotes the state obtained by executing plan p in state s. E.g., s;put(a,d) is the state obtained by putting block a on object d in state s.

Analogously to the above *linkage* axioms, the *plan linkage* linkage axiom is introduced. To any n-ary plan symbol g a new n+1-ary symbol g' is associated with the property

$$w;g(u_1,...,u_n) = g'(w,w:u_1, ..., w:u_n) \quad \textit{(plan linkage)}$$

for example, w;put(u,v) = put'(w,w:u,w:v).

The *empty plan* Λ is taken to be a right *identity* under the execution function. This is formalized by the axiom.

$$w;\Lambda = w \quad \textit{(empty plan)}$$

There are objects that do not depend on states considered. For instance, the constant table always denotes the same object. These objects are called rigid designators, i.e., an object u is a *rigid designator*, if for all states w

$$w:u = u \quad \textit{(rigid designator)}$$

THE PLAN COMPOSITION FUNCTION ";;"

This notion of composing plans is introduced in the following way. If p_1 and p_2 are plans, $p_1;;p_2$ is the composition of p_1 and p_2 where it is understood that p_1 is executed first and then only p_2 is executed. This is expressed by the *plan composition* axiom

$$w;(p_1;;p_2) = (w;p_1);p_2 \quad \textit{(plan composition)}$$

[11] Thus, in this step we try to concretize the abstract argument by expressing it in terms of variables of the theorem under consideration and/or of induction hypotheses corresponding to this theorem. It may happen that a given theory allows a direct replacement of ξ by something more explicit provided some condition C is verified. If C is TRUE and we succeed in performing steps 4 and 5 of our procedure, then it means that the given theorem is provable without the use of induction. If C is not TRUE, then we obtain a conditional solution which, in the case of specification theorems, provides non-recursive parts of programs (as illustrated in section 4).

[12] It is assumed that we are in a world of blocks in which objects are a table and blocks. These blocks are all the same size, so that only one block can fit directly on top of another. It is also assumed that the robot arm may lift only one block at a time.

for all states w and plans p_1 and p_2. For simplicity, the distinction between the composition function ;; and the execution function ; is ignored. We will write ; for both and rely on context to make the meaning clear.
This composition is assumed to be associative.

$(p_1;p_2);p_3 = p_1;(p_2;p_3)$ *(associativity)*

The *empty plan* Λ is taken to be the *identity* under composition, i.e., for all plans p

Λ;p = p;Λ = p *(identity)*

4.3 Axioms for the blocks world

Facts about the block world and effects of actions are expressed as plan theory axioms. For simplicity, sort conditions such as state(w) are omitted. Variables are understood to be universally quantified.

if not Clear(w,y) then On(w,hat'(w,y),y) *(hat)*

The *hat* axiom describes the following situation: If (in the state w) the block y is not clear then there is a block directly on y.

if Clear(w,x)
then On(put'(w,x,table),x,table) *(put-table-on)*

The *put-table-on* axiom allows to put a block x (in the state w) on the table whenever x is a clear block, i.e., if there is no block directly on x.

if On(w,x,y) & Clear(w,x)
then Clear(put'(w,x,table),y) *(put-table-clear)*

The *put-table-clear* axiom describes the following situation: If (in the state w) the block x is directly on the block y and if x is a clear block, then y becomes a clear block when we put x on the table.

Even if the given axioms could suggest that we might define constructors **hat** (for objects) and **put** (for actions), the given domain is nonconstructible, because the given axioms introduce new EQV (see section 1), such as *w* and *x*.

4.4 Specification Theorem for HCB

The problem to clear a given block is expressed as:

$$\forall s_0 \forall b\, \exists z_1\, \text{Clear}(s_0;z_1,b).$$

As in [Manna and Waldinger, 87], we denote the Skolem function corresponding to this ST by makeclear, i.e., we try to find a function makeclear such that z_1 = makeclear(s_0,b).

4.4.1 Choice of induction variable

The variable b is chosen as the induction variable.

4.4.2 Generating IH

Using the general induction principle scheme, we generate the induction hypothesis in the state s_0

if u ∠ b then there is z such that
Clear(s_0;z,(s_0;z):u) (IH)

Here ∠ is an unspecified yet well-founded ordering. During the actual proof, we shall need to assert that the objects are indeed in such a relation, thus defining the well-founded ordering, on the fly, so to speak. If the recursive functions we start from are really computable, they should be associated to an existing well-founded ordering, which is exactly the one we are thus discovering.

Now, we will follow the algorithm described in section 3. To F in the scheme corresponds Clear, to t_1 corresponds b, to t_2 corresponds $s_0;z_1$.

4.4.3 *CM*-construction of Clear(s_0;z_1,b)

4.4.3.1 Base step solutions

This means that we try to construct the formula Clear(s_0;z_1,b) (i.e., find a value z_1 for which the last formula is true) using the tautology Clear(ξ,b)⇒Clear(ξ,b). The part of code we extract in this step [Franova and Kodratoff, 91a] is

makeclear(s_0,b) = Λ, if Clear(s_0,b).

4.4.3.2 Induction step solutions

We try to construct the formula Clear(s_0;z_1,b) (i.e., find a value z_1 for which the last formula is true) using IH.

<u>Step 1:</u> The term b is already evaluated.

<u>Step 2:</u> **The definition of Clear gives conditions for the validity of the formula**

Clear(ξ,b) (1)

The only axiom which leads to a formula of the form Clear(...) is *put-table-clear*. In order to be able to apply it, we have to compare (1) and Clear(put'(w,x,table),y), where w, x, y are universally quantified. Comparing (1) and Clear(put'(w,x,table),y) leads to the equation solving

ξ = put'(w,x,table), b = y.

Let us denote by PrecondAx the precondition of the *put-table-clear* axiom in which the variable y is replaced by b, i.e., the formula

On(w,x,b)&Clear(w,x). (2)

Thus, using the *put-table-clear* axiom, the class of all ξ for which Clear(ξ,b) holds is determined by

C={ ξ | ξ = put'(w,x,table) & PrecondAx}. (3)

This reads: Any element ξ satisfying the formula Clear(ξ,b) must have the form put'(w,x,table), for any w and x satisfying (2). Nevertheless, variables w, x are still unspecified. Next steps will deal with that.

<u>Step 2*:</u> Let us consider PrecondAx, i.e., formula (2). As we have explained in section 3, we will try to concretize w and x in (2) exploring where the atomic formulae of PrecondAx may come from. Thus, we have to apply our *CM*-formula construction to (some of) the atomic formulae of (2). The formula On(w,x,b) contains a known value, namely b, this is why this formula is first examined. The application of *put-table-on* is not possible, if we suppose that we cannot identify the table and an object, which is here the element b. The only axiom we can apply is therefore the *hat* axiom. The application of this axiom requires comparing On(w,x,b) and On(v,hat'(v,q),q). The solution we obtain is

v ← w, q ← b, x ← hat'(w,b).

The precondition of the *hat* axiom reads then not(Clear(w,b)). (3) changes here to

C={ ξ | ξ = put'(w,hat'(w,b),table) & Clear(w,hat'(w,b)) & not(Clear(w,b))}. (4)

Next step will concretize w.

<u>Step 3:</u> As we have mentioned already in footnote 11, this step consists of two subproblems:

Step 3.1: Trivial Transformations

In [Franova and Kodratoff, 91a] we explain in detail that this step succeeds to find the following conditional non-recursive part of the program we want to synthesize:

makeclear(s_0,b) = put(hat(b),table)
if Clear(s_0,hat'(s_0,b)) & not(Clear(s_0,b))

Step 3.2: Non - trivial Transformations

We try to apply induction hypotheses to (4). Comparing IH and formulae in (4) we can see that IH (with z = makeclear(s_0,u)) can be compared to the formula Clear(w,hat'(w,b)). This leads to the equations

w = s_0;makeclear(s_0,u), u = hat(b)

However, the application of IH is justified only if we are able to prove that hat(b)∠b.[13] Let us assume that we have means to confirm this relation. This leads to

[13] Some complementary knowledge is necessary to establish this relation. Presently, when we check that such a relation holds during the application of the induction hypothesis, we assume *a priori* that this relation holds, in order to avoid interrupting the theorem proving process. The validity of such an assumption can be verified by the user. We are planning to automatize this process. This problem is

$w \leftarrow s_0;\text{makeclear}(s_0,\text{hat}(b))$.

Using *plan linkage*, we have put'(w,hat'(w,b),table) = w;put(hat(b),table). Finally, the class C changes to

$$C = \{ \xi \mid \xi = s_0;\text{makeclear}(s_0,\text{hat}(b));\text{put}(\text{hat}(b),\text{table}) \ \& \ \text{not}(\text{Clear}(s_0;\text{makeclear}(s_0,\text{hat}(b)),b))\}, \quad (5)$$

i.e., we can replace the abstract argument ξ by the more concrete one

$s_0;\text{makeclear}(s_0,\text{hat}(b));\text{put}(\text{hat}(b),\text{table})$.

We denote it, as in the general scheme, by α.

Step 4: Our goal is now to verify if $s_0;z_1$ belongs to C in (5), i.e., we have to check if we can **replace** α by $s_0;z_1$. Trivially, we obtain

$z_1 \leftarrow \text{makeclear}(s_0,\text{hat}(b));\text{put}(\text{hat}(b),\text{table})$.

Step 5: No simplifications are necessary.

In conclusion, we have the program

makeclear(s_0,b) =
Λ, if Clear(s_0,b)
put(hat(b),table), if Clear(s_0,hat'(s_0,b))&not(Clear(s_0,b))
makeclear(s_0,hat(b));put(hat(b),table).

5 Conclusion

In all our previous work we presented the *CM*-construction of atomic formulae as a method which helps to solve strategic aspects of inductive theorem proving applied to program synthesis. This paper shows that our *Constructive Matching* methodology can be applied and adapted to other well-founded theories, not only to CD, even though the present implementation works only for CD.

Summarizing, we have illustrated in this paper the following characteristic features of our *CM* methodology:

- It provides a couple (what has to be achieved; what it has to be achieved from) at any step of an inductive proof. This is the main characteristic. Note that this feature reduces the search space of a proof, the last is the main problem of deductive approach to program synthesis.
- For the induction step, it uses the general induction scheme and a kind of "forced" application of this scheme (more details are given in section 4).
- If necessary, it applies the *CM*-formula construction to formulae obtained as conditions for the validity of F (see step 2*).

CM methodology can be compared to the notion of a plan in Bundy's reconstruction [Bundy, 88] of Boyer&Moore methodology. Our methodology could create one of the most general plans in Bundy's reconstruction, because it comprises most of Bundy's "reconstructed" tactics[14]. A deep analogy between Bundy's approach and our methodology is illustrated by the importance of universally quantified induction hypotheses acknowledged by both approaches [Franova, 85; Bundy *et al.*, 90].

similar to verifying the correctness of the given axioms. Besides, the relation hat(b) < b seems to be a reasonable well-founded relation for induction proofs in blocks world problems. However, analogously to constructible domains, for particular problems, how the well-founded relation looks, depends always on the given axioms (or the given theory). In other words, we cannot know in advance the well-founded relation which is to be used in blocks world problems, since it depends on the available definitions.

[14] For instance, all examples presented in [Bundy *et al.*, 90] are successfully solved by our methodology. This shows that our way of constructing a formula provides a solution for the problem of making possible the application of induction hypotheses, this problem being the topic of Bundy's "rippling-out" tactics. Since we prove also theorems containing existential quantifiers, our approach is clearly more general than Bundy's.

Moreover, a "rational reconstruction" of our methodology would allow the introduction of existential quantifiers into Bundy's improved system, thus recognizing program synthesis as an inductive theorem proving problem, or, in other words, bringing program synthesis back where it belongs classically - inductive theorem proving.

In [Franova, 91c] we describe in detail the strengths and weaknesses of our methodology viewed as a program synthesis methodology.

Acknowledgments

We express our thanks to an anonymous referee for many constructive critics.

References

[Bibel and Hörnig, 84] W. Bibel, K. M. Hörnig: LOPS - A System Based on a Strategical Approach to Program Synthesis; in A. Biermann, G. Guiho,Y. Kodratoff (ed): *Automatic Program Construction Techniques*; Macmillan Publishing Company, London, 1984, 69-91.

[Biundo, 88] S. Biundo: Automated synthesis of recursive algorithms as a theorem proving tool; in [Kodratoff, 88], 553-558.

[Boyer and Moore, 79] R. S. Boyer, J S. Moore: *A Computational Logic*; Academic Press, 1979.

[Bundy, 88] A. Bundy: The use of Explicit Plans to Guide Inductive Proofs; in E. Lusk, R. Overbeek, (ed): *9th International Conference on Automated Deduction*; LNCS 310, Springer-Verlag, Berlin, 1988, 111-120.

[Bundy *et al.*, 90] A. Bundy, F. van Harmelen, A. Smaill, A. Ireland: Extensions to the Rippling-Out Tactic for Guiding Inductive Proofs; in M. E. Stickel, (ed.): *10th International Conference on Automated Deduction*; Proceedings, Lecture Notes in Artificial Intelligence No. 449, Springer-Verlag, 1990, 132-146.

[Burstall and Darlington, 77] R. M. Burstall, J.Darlington: A transformation system for developing recursive programs; *J. ACM* 24, 1, January, 1977, 44-67.

[Dershowitz, 85] N. Dershowitz: Synthesis by Completion; in [Joshi, 85], 208-214.

[Franova and Kodratoff, 91a] M. Franova, Y. Kodratoff: Solving "How to Clear a Block" with CONSTRUCTIVE MATCHING methodology; extended version of this paper, Rapport de Recherche L.R.I., July, 1991.

[Franova and Kodratoff, 91b] M. Franova, Y. Kodratoff: Program Synthesis is Theorem Proving; Rapport de Recherche L.R.I., July, 1991.

[Franova, 85] M. Franova: CM-strategy : A Methodology for Inductive Theorem Proving or Constructive Well-Generalized Proofs; in [Joshi, 85], 1214-1220.

[Franova, 88a] M. Franova: Fundamentals for a new methodology for inductive theorem proving: CM-construction of atomic formulae; in [Kodratoff,88], 137-141.

[Franova, 88b] M. Franova: Fundamentals of a new methodology for Program Synthesis from Formal Specifications: CM-construction of atomic formulae; Thesis, Université Paris-Sud, November, Orsay, France, 1988.

[Franova, 91a] M. Franova: Generating induction hypotheses by Constructive Matching methodology for Inductive Theorem Proving and Program Synthesis revisited; Rapport de Recherche No.647, L.R.I., Université de Paris-Sud, Orsay, France, February, 1991.

[Franova, 91b] M. Franova: Failure analysis in Constructive Matching methodology; Rapport de Recherche L.R.I., July, 1991.

[Franova, 91c] M. Franova: Constructive Matching methodology for Inductive Theorem Proving and Program Synthesis revisited; RR L.R.I., July, 1991.

[Joshi, 85] A. K. Joshi, (ed): *Proceedings of the Ninth International Joint Conference on Artificial Intelligence*; August, Los Angeles, 1985.

[Kodratoff and Picard, 83] Y. Kodratoff, M. Picard: Complétion de systèmes de réécriture et synthèse de programmes à partir de leurs spécifications; Bigre No.35, October, 1983.

[Kodratoff, 88] Y. Kodratoff, (ed): *Proceedings of the 8th European Conference on Artificial Intelligence*; August 1-5, Pitman, London, United Kingdom, 1988.

[Manna and Waldinger, 80] Z. Manna, R.Waldinger: A Deductive Approach to Program Synthesis; *ACM Transactions on Programming Languages and Systems*, Vol. 2., No.1, January, 1980, 90-121.

[Manna and Waldinger, 87] Z. Manna, R. Waldinger: How to Clear a Block: A Theory of Plans; *Journal of Automated Reasoning* 3, 1987, 343-377.

[Perdrix, 86] H. Perdrix: Program synthesis from specifications; in *ESPRIT'85, Status Report of Continuing Work*, North-Holland, 1986, 371-385.

[Smith, 85] D. R. Smith: Top-Down Synthesis of Simple Divide and Conquer Algorithm; *Artificial Intelligence*, vol. 27, no. 1, 1985, 43-96.

AUTOMATED REASONING

Planning II

Generalizing Nonlinear Planning to Handle Complex Goals and Actions with Context-Dependent Effects

Edwin P.D. Pednault
AT&T Bell Laboratories
Crawfords Corner Road
Holmdel, NJ 07733

Abstract

This paper presents a general, mathematically rigorous approach to nonlinear planning that handles both complex goals and actions with context-dependent effects. A goal can be any arbitrary well-formed formula containing conjunctions, disjunctions, negations, and quantifiers. Actions are likewise not constrained and can have an unrestricted number of complex, situation-dependent effects. The approach presented here can thus be used to solve a wider range of problems than previous approaches to nonlinear planning. The approach is based on previous work by the author on linear planning. The same mathematical framework is used with the results extended to nonlinear plans.

1. Introduction

Efforts have been made over the past several years to place automatic planning on a firm mathematical foundation. These efforts have focused on two types of planning techniques: *linear planning*, in which plans are represented as (linear) sequences of actions [Pednault 1985, 1986, 1987, 1988, 1989], and *nonlinear planning*, in which partially-ordered networks (i.e., directed acyclic graphs) are used to represent plans [Chapman 1985, 1987; Christensen 1990a, 1990b; McAllester and Rosenblitt 1991; Yang and Tenenberg 1990].

Work on the theory of linear planning has resulted in a general planning method capable of handling both arbitrarily complex goals involving conjunctions, disjunctions, negations, quantifiers, etc., as well as arbitrarily complex actions whose effects can change according to the situations in which they are performed [Pednault 1986, 1988]. A planner that incorporates some of these results has recently been implemented by McDermott [McDermott 1991]. McDermott's work provides independent confirmation of the theory and it begins to address some of the implementation issues that the theory entails.

In contrast, work on the theory of nonlinear planning has focused on a simplified version of the STRIPS framework [Fikes and Nilsson 1971] in which goals are constrained to be conjunctions of literals, and actions are constrained to those representable by means of simple add and delete lists. Several planning systems have been implemented that incorporate these results [Chapman 1985, 1987; Christensen 1990b; McAllester and Rosenblitt 1991; Yang and Tenenberg 1990]. However, because of the limited representation employed for goals and actions, the range of problems that these systems can solve is quite restricted. This is particularly true in comparison to the range of problems that can be solved by the linear planning techniques cited above. Clearly, a gap exists in the generality of the formal results obtained to date for linear and nonlinear planning methodologies.

The purpose of this paper is to bridge this gap by presenting a general approach to nonlinear planning capable of handling arbitrarily complex goals and actions. This approach is an extension of the linear planning methods previously developed by the author. The extensions preserve the range of problems that can be solved while taking advantage of the ability of partial orders to represent several possible sequences of actions simultaneously. This ability can potentially make the nonlinear approach more attractive than the linear method upon which it is based.

2. Mathematical Considerations

In all mathematical approaches to planning that have been developed to date, planning algorithms are constructed from theorems that define the kinds of actions a plan must contain in order to achieve one's goals. Chapman and others calls these theorems *truth criteria*. I prefer the term *causality theorems* because these theorems establish causal connections between the goals to be achieved, and the actions and subgoals that must appear in the plan.

General causality theorems exist that can be used as the basis for constructing linear planners [Pednault 1985, 1986, 1988]. They will likewise be used in this paper for the purpose of nonlinear planning. The main causality theorem can be stated informally as follows:

Theorem 1 (*Main Causality Theorem*): A condition φ will be true at a point p during the execution of a plan if and only if one of the following holds:

(1) An action a is executed prior to point p such that a causes φ to become true and φ remains true thereafter until at least point p.

(2) φ is true in the initial state and remains true until at least point p.

Formal statements and proofs of this theorem have been previously reported [Pednault 1985, 1986, 1988]. The important thing to note for our current purposes is that Theorem 1 is stated with respect the to sequence in which the actions of a plan are executed. A linear plan defines a single execution sequence; a nonlinear plan defines several possible sequences. Thus, in applying this theorem to nonlinear planning, we will in effect be applying it to each of the execution sequences defined by a nonlinear plan.

To apply Theorem 1, one must have the ability to assert that a particular action causes a particular goal to become true, and to assert that a particular action preserves the truth of a particular goal once it has been achieved. In many planners, such as the one considered by Chapman [Chapman 1985, 1987], these kinds of assertions are quite straightforward to make because the representations employed limit themselves to actions with context-independent effects. Such actions will either cause a particular goal to become true in all circumstances, cause the goal to become false in all circumstances, or leave the truth value of the goal unaltered in all circumstances. To assert that a particular action achieves a particular goal, one need only verify that the action does in fact achieve the goal and eliminate from consideration any action that fails to do so. To assert that a particular goal is to be preserved between two points in a plan, one need only verify that all intervening action either achieve the goal or leave its truth value unaltered, and eliminate from consideration any plan (or execution sequence of a nonlinear plan) that violates this protection constraint. Thus, except for keeping track of the intervals during which certain goals are to be preserved, the other assertions that particular actions must achieve particular goals or preserve particular goals need not be represented explicitly in a plan. They need only be embodied implicitly in the procedures by which a plan is constructed. Note that this is only true for actions with context-independent effects.

In the general case, the effect of an action can depend on the situation in which it is performed. Asserting that such an action achieves or preserves a goal then amounts to asserting that the action is performed in a situation in which is has this effect. These kinds of assertions cannot be made implicitly; they must be represented explicitly. In the linear planning approach previously developed by the author, these assertions are made by introducing additional preconditions to the actions in a plan. These additional preconditions, which are collectively called *secondary preconditions*, define the conditions under which the actions have their desired effects. Two types of secondary preconditions are used: *causation preconditions*, which define the contexts in which actions achieve desired goals, and *preservation preconditions*, which define the contexts in which actions preserve the truth of goals. Causation and preservation preconditions can be defined in terms of regression operators [Waldinger 1977] in a very general way [Pednault 1986, 1988]. Remarkably, a causality theorem exists that is essentially equivalent to Theorem 1 except that it is expressed in terms of achieving the appropriate secondary preconditions. In the statement of this theorem which follows, Σ_φ^a is used to denote the causation precondition for action a to achieve φ, while Π_φ^a denotes the preservation precondition for action a to preserve φ.

Theorem 2 (*Causality Theorem for Secondary Preconditions*): A condition φ will be true at a point p during the execution of a plan if and only if one of the following holds:

(1) An action a is executed prior to point p such that

(a) Σ_φ^a is true immediately before executing a.

(b) Π_φ^b is true immediately before the execution of each action b between a and point p.

(2) φ is true in the initial state and Π_φ^a is true immediately before the execution of each action a prior to point p.

An example of causation and preservation preconditions are the so-called "codesignation constraints" (i.e., equality constraints) employed in Chapman's TWEAK program. When inserting a new action or using an existing action to achieve a goal, TWEAK introduces codesignation constraints as needed to ensure that the goal unifies with one of the formulas in the add list of the action. These equality constraints satisfy the definition of causation preconditions [Pednault 1986, 1988] and are effectively used as such in TWEAK. TWEAK also has the option of introducing noncodesignation constraints (inequalities) to prevent a goal from unifying with one of the formulas in the delete list of a potential "clobbering" action. These inequality constraints satisfy the definition of preservation preconditions and are clearly used as such in TWEAK. Causation and preservation preconditions, however, are not limited to equality formulas. In general, they can be arbitrarily complex formulas whose complexity is a function of the degree to which an action's effects are context dependent.

In the author's previous work, Theorem 2 plays the same role in constructing a linear planner that Chapman's "modal truth criterion" [Chapman 1985, 1987] plays in constructing a nonlinear planner. Theorem 2, however, applies to all actions that can be represented in terms of state transitions, whereas the modal truth criterion is limited to actions representable in a limited STRIPS framework. In addition, goals can be arbitrarily complex formulas involving conjunctions, disjunctions, negations, and quantifiers—φ in Theorems 1 and 2 is not restricted to atomic formulas and their negations as is the case for the modal truth criterion.

To synthesize linear plans, Theorem 2 can be converted into a nondeterministic procedure in much the same way that Horn clauses are converted into procedures in PROLOG. The procedure is nondeterministic in the sense that the clauses of Theorem 2 define alternate ways of achieving a goal, but it is impossible to determine beforehand which will lead to a solution. Search is therefore required to explore the possibilities.

In the first clause of Theorem 2, action a might already appear in the plan constructed thus far, or it might have to be added. Hence, this clause defines two alternatives: one in which a new action is inserted into the plan to achieve a goal, the other in which an existing action is used for this purpose. The second clause defines only one alternative, which is to prevent the goal from becoming false if it is true in the initial state. In each case, the appropriate secondary preconditions are introduced as subgoals to actions as per Theorem 2. These three alternative ways of achieving a goal in a linear plan are discussed in detail elsewhere [Pednault 1986, 1988]. We will now consider how these alternatives generalize when constructing nonlinear plans.

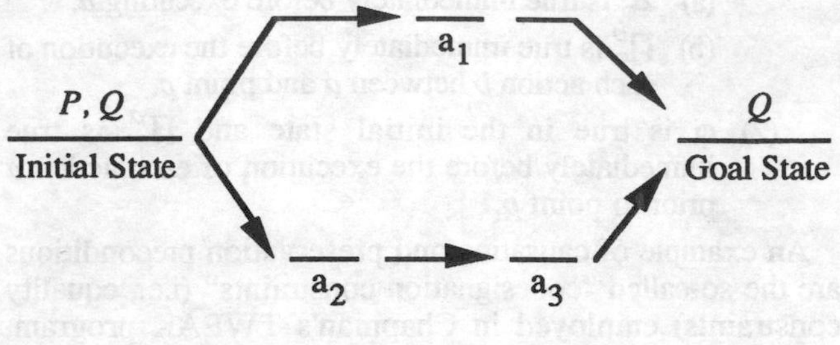

Figure 1: A Sample Nonlinear Plan.

3. Using Theorem 2 in Nonlinear Planning

The first thing to note about Theorem 2 is that it cannot be applied to nonlinear planning in the same manner it is applied to linear planning. The reason is that when dealing with actions that have context-dependent effects, it is possible for a goal to be achieved by a certain action in one execution sequence of a nonlinear plan, a different action in another sequence, and to be preserved by all actions in a third sequence. Therefore, it is impossible in the general case for a single set of secondary preconditions to cover all possible execution sequences of a nonlinear plans. A single set of subgoals, however, is the sort of thing one would want when building a planner.

To illustrate why a single set of secondary preconditions is not sufficient in the general case, consider the three actions, a_1, a_2, and a_3, shown in Figure 1. Action a_1 causes Q to become true if it is not already true, and it causes P to become false if it is not already false. Actions a_2 and a_3 both have the same effect, which is to toggle the truth value of Q whenever P holds. In other words, a_2 and a_3 cause Q to become false if both P and Q are presently true, and they cause Q to become true if P is true and Q is false. The plan in Figure 1 defines three possible orders of execution: $a_1 a_2 a_3$, $a_2 a_1 a_3$, and $a_2 a_3 a_1$. Each each execution sequence

results in Q being true in the goal state. However, in the first sequence, Q is true by virtue of the fact that it never becomes false (i.e., all three actions preserve the truth of Q); in the second sequence a_1 causes Q to become true after a_2 makes it false; and in the third execution sequence a_2 is the action that finally achieves Q. Because Q is achieved in different ways in each execution sequence, a different set of secondary preconditions must be satisfied in each case as dictated by Theorem 2. The secondary preconditions for each execution sequence are shown in Figure 2.

Figure 2 also illustrates why Chapman's modal truth criterion does not hold for actions with context-dependent effects. His criterion requires that, for every action in the plan capable of negating a goal before the point at which the goal must be true, there is an intervening action in the plan that re-achieves the goal. However, in the first two orderings of the plan shown in Figure 2 (i.e., $a_1 a_2 a_3$ and $a_2 a_1 a_3$), action a_3 is capable of negating Q yet there are no actions that follow a_3 that re-achieve Q. Nevertheless, Q is true in the final state. The reason is that while a_3 is capable of negating Q, it can only do so when P is true at the time the action is performed. Such context-dependent behavior is not accounted for in Chapman's criterion.

We are now faced with a dilemma. On the one hand, when constructing a nonlinear planner, it is desirable to introduce a single set of secondary preconditions that apply to every execution sequence defined by a plan. On the other hand, Theorem 2 tells us that in general a different set of secondary preconditions will be needed for different execution sequences. We could try to maintain these different sets explicitly for each execution sequence; however, we would then be doing a rather convoluted form of linear planning. By representing each execution sequence explicitly, we would defeat the purpose of nonlinear representations altogether, which is to represent multiple execution sequences implicitly. How then can we use Theorem 2 to construct nonlinear plans in the general case?

$$P, Q \text{ (Initial State)} \xrightarrow{\Pi_Q^{a_1}} a_1 \; \begin{array}{c} \neg P \\ Q \end{array} \xrightarrow{\Pi_Q^{a_2}} a_2 \; \begin{array}{c} \neg P \\ Q \end{array} \xrightarrow{\Pi_Q^{a_3}} a_3 \; \begin{array}{c} \neg P \\ Q \end{array} \xrightarrow{} Q \text{ (Goal State)} \qquad \Pi_Q^{a_1} = True$$

$$\Pi_Q^{a_2} = \neg P$$

$$P, Q \text{ (Initial State)} \xrightarrow{} a_2 \; \begin{array}{c} P \\ \neg Q \end{array} \xrightarrow{\Sigma_Q^{a_1}} a_1 \; \begin{array}{c} \neg P \\ Q \end{array} \xrightarrow{\Pi_Q^{a_3}} a_3 \; \begin{array}{c} \neg P \\ Q \end{array} \xrightarrow{} Q \text{ (Goal State)} \qquad \Pi_Q^{a_3} = \neg P$$

$$\Sigma_Q^{a_1} = True$$

$$P, Q \text{ (Initial State)} \xrightarrow{} a_2 \; \begin{array}{c} P \\ \neg Q \end{array} \xrightarrow{\Sigma_Q^{a_3}} a_3 \; \begin{array}{c} P \\ Q \end{array} \xrightarrow{\Pi_Q^{a_1}} a_1 \; \begin{array}{c} \neg P \\ Q \end{array} \xrightarrow{} Q \text{ (Goal State)} \qquad \Sigma_Q^{a_3} = P \wedge \neg Q$$

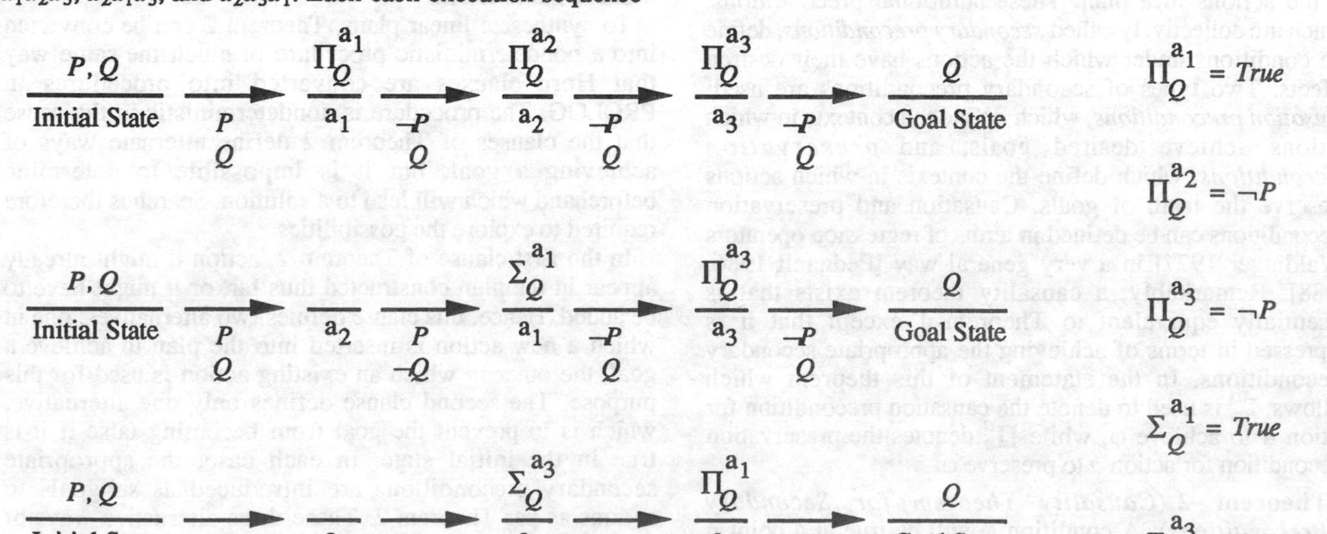

Figure 2: Q is achieved in different ways in different execution sequences

The answer is to recognize that the main role of nonlinear representations is to reduce the size of the search space by allowing several execution sequences to be represented and manipulated simultaneously. In generalizing nonlinear planning, we need only maintain the partial order as long as this is advantageous. At any point, we are at liberty to decompose a nonlinear plan into several alternate plans by introducing additional ordering constraints. Specifically, if actions *a* and *b* are mutually unordered in a nonlinear plan (i.e., if the plan does not specify which action is to be executed first), then we are at liberty to force an ordering. However, when doing so, we must consider all possibilities (in this case, *a* before *b* and *b* before *a*). If all possibilities are not considered, a solution to the planning problem could inadvertently be eliminated from the search space through this oversight. The decision to force an ordering among two or more actions therefore gives rise to a set of alternate plans that covers the set of possible execution sequences defined by the original plan. To maintain completeness, each of these alternate plans must be introduced into the search space as a possible decomposition of the original plan.

This principle of decomposing a plan by forcing an ordering among actions can be used to resolve the dilemma of needing multiple sets of secondary preconditions for a nonlinear plan. If a decomposition is chosen so that for each resulting plan the same secondary preconditions apply to every execution sequence of that plans, then the problem of having multiple sets of secondary preconditions would disappear. Each nonlinear plan in the decomposition would have a different set of secondary preconditions; however, the secondary preconditions of each plan would apply to all the execution sequences of that plan. By taking this approach, Theorem 2 can be applied in much the same manner as for linear planning, except that nonlinear plans might have to be decomposed in the process.

In the following discussion, the necessary plan decompositions are described procedurally. A mathematical analysis of these decompositions and their proofs of correctness are presented in a forthcoming paper [Pednault forthcoming]. They are not present presented here due to space limitations.

Consider what must be done to carry out the fewest number of decompositions necessary to satisfy the constraints described above. Three cases need to be considered, one for each of the three ways of achieving a goal implicit in Theorem 2 (i.e, protecting the goal from the initial state, inserting a new action that achieves it, and using an existing action for this purpose). As will soon become apparent, decompositions will only need to be performed as a result of protecting a goal from one point in a plan to another. Therefore, it is useful to begin the analysis by considering the case of achieving a goal by protecting it from the initial state.

According to Theorem 2, if a goal is protected from the initial state, the appropriate preservation preconditions must hold for every action that is between the initial state and the point at which the goal is to be achieved when the plan is executed. Thus, if we were to achieve a goal by protecting it from the initial state, we would certainly have to introduce preservation preconditions as subgoals for every action necessarily constrained to lie between these two points in the plan constructed thus far. However, what about the actions that lie between the initial state and the point at which the goal is to be achieved in some execution sequences but not in others? Clearly, some of these actions might have no effect on the goal, in which case their preservation preconditions would be the formula *TRUE*. Since *TRUE* is always satisfied, the plan need not be altered on the basis of these actions. Other actions, however, might always have the effect of negating the goal, in which case their preservation preconditions would be the formula *FALSE*. It is inconsistent for such actions to lie between the initial state and the point at which the goal is to be achieved given that we are trying to prevent the goal from becoming false in this interval. Therefore, ordering constraints must be introduced into the plan to assert that actions whose preservation preconditions are *FALSE* necessarily follow the point at which the goal is to be achieved. The introduction of these ordering constraints is essentially a special case of the *linking out* procedure first introduced in Tate's NONLIN program [Tate 1977].

The final group of actions that could potentially lie between the initial state and the point at which the goal is to be achieved are those that are capable of preserving the goal, but only in certain circumstances. These circumstances are described by the preservation preconditions for those actions. If the preservation preconditions are not satisfied, the actions could potentially negate the goal. Therefore, in accordance with Theorem 2, each preservation precondition must be achieved as a subgoal to the corresponding action in every execution sequence in which that action lies between the initial state and the point at which the goal is to be achieved. In all other execution sequences, the action follows the point at which the goal is to be achieved. Its preservation precondition is superfluous in this case and need not be achieved. Therefore, to avoid multiple sets of secondary preconditions, the plan constructed thus far must be decomposed into two or more alternate plans that effectively group the various execution sequences according to whether or not preservation preconditions must be introduced for the various actions. Note that each alternative then becomes part of the search space, since the alternate plans define different sets of potential solutions.

The decomposition can be accomplished as follows. If only one action is affected, two alternative plans are produced. In one plan, the action is linked out by introducing an ordering constraint to assert that the action necessarily follows the point at which the goal is to be achieved. In the other plan, the appropriate preservation precondition is introduced as a subgoal to the action, and the action is *linked in* [Tate 1977] by introducing an ordering constraint to assert that the action necessarily precedes the point at which the goal is to be achieved. The first plan defines all execution sequences of the original plan in which the preservation precondition need not be introduced. The second plan defines the remaining sequences in which the preservation precondition must be introduced. The combined execution sequences of the two plans are thus the same as the execution sequences of the original plan. If several actions potentially require preservation preconditions, this decomposition process must be repeated for each of these actions in turn, with each successive decomposition applied to the results of the preceding one. The net result is several alternate plans that then become part of the search space.

A similar process of introducing preservation preconditions and ordering constraints must be followed when achieving a goal by introducing a new action, or when using an existing action for this purpose. In general, when protecting a goal from one point in a plan to another, preservation preconditions must be introduced as subgoals to all actions that necessarily lie between these two points. Every action that could possibly lie in this interval whose preservation precondition reduces to the formula *FALSE* must be excluded from the interval by introducing ordering constraints so that the action either necessarily follows the interval or necessarily precedes the interval. This is Tate's general linking out procedure [Tate 1977] . Note that all possible linking-out combinations must be considered for all actions that are affected. In addition, every action that could possibly lie in the interval but whose preservation precondition reduces to neither *TRUE* nor *FALSE* must either be excluded from the interval in the manner just described, or be constrained to lie within the interval and have the appropriate preservation precondition introduced as a subgoal. As before, actions whose preservation preconditions reduce to the the formula *TRUE* need not be considered in this process.

A second way in which a goal can be achieved is by introducing a new action into the plan that makes the goal true and then protecting the goal up to the point at which it is to be achieved. The insertion process is straightforward enough: Ordering constraints are introduced to assert that the new action necessarily follows the initial state and necessarily precedes the point at which the goal is to be achieved. The appropriate causation precondition is then introduced as a subgoal to the new action (as per Theorem 2), together with the preconditions that are normally introduced by planning programs to ensure the action will be executable. Once the action has been inserted, the goal must be protected from the new action up to the point at which it is to be achieved. This is done as described in the preceding paragraph. Finally, since the action could potentially interfere with existing goals that have previously been protected in the plan, the new action must be evaluated with respect to the existing protections, with further plan decompositions performed to either exclude the new action from a protected interval, or constrain it to lie within the protected interval with the appropriate preservation precondition added as a subgoal.

The final way in which a goal can be achieved is by using an existing action. If the existing action is not already constrained to precede the point at which the goal is to be achieved, then an ordering constraint must be added to the plan to establish this relationship (linking in). Once the ordering constraint has been established, the appropriate causation precondition is added as a subgoal to the existing action and the goal is protected from the existing action to the point it is to be achieved in the manner described previously. Unlike the case in which a new action is introduced, there is no need to compare the existing action to goals already protected in the plan, since this analysis would have already been performed at an earlier stage in the planning process. The preconditions for the execution of the existing action would likewise have been introduced at a earlier stage.

The three ways of modifying a nonlinear plan to achieve a goal that have just been described can be embodied in a plan transformation rule much as was done in my previous work on linear planning [Pednault 1986]. The resulting rule generalizes the corresponding rule for linear plans and is used to generate a search tree of possible solutions. When implementing a planning system, the nonlinear rule rule can be combined with the other rules discussed in the author's dissertation to take advantage of formal objects and to decompose complex goals into simpler ones. This is discussed in detail in a forthcoming paper [Pednault forthcoming]

4. The Homeowner's Problem

The following example illustrates the approach to nonlinear planning described above. The example is presented informally. The problem, however, can be formalized by representing the actions in my ADL language [Pednault 1985, 1986, 1989]. The appropriate secondary preconditions can then be derived from this representation. This is discussed in detail in [Pednault forthcoming], but not here because of space limitations.

Suppose you have just closed on a house that you agreed to buy "as is." You arrive at your new "pride and joy" to find that the water has been turned off and a number of sizable holes have been punched into the walls. This situation is not to your liking, so you decide to rectify the problem by turning the water on and fixing the walls (Figure 3a). After experimenting with the water main a bit (Figure 3b), you discover that the reason there are holes in the walls is that the plumbing behind the walls leaks profusely. Fixing the walls can be accomplished only if the plumbing is fixed or the water main is kept off. This condition is therefore introduced as a causation precondition to fixing the walls (Figure 3c). Turning the water on after fixing the walls will create new holes unless the plumbing is fixed. This condition is therefore introduced as a preservation precondition to the parallel action of turning the water on (Figure 3c). This is done so as not to negate the protected goal of having the walls fixed.

Realizing that there is no way to avoid fixing the plumbing, you decide to incorporate this step into your plan (Figure 3d). Fixing the plumbing after patching the walls would merely require that new holes be torn open to gain access. A preservation precondition cannot be introduced to avoid this interaction, since in this case the precondition simplifies to the formula *FALSE* (i.e., one cannot avoid having holes in the wall when fixing the plumbing). The only option is to fix the plumbing before patching the walls (Figure 3d). At this point, either of the two execution sequences defined by the plan will achieve the original goals of turning the water on and fixing the walls.

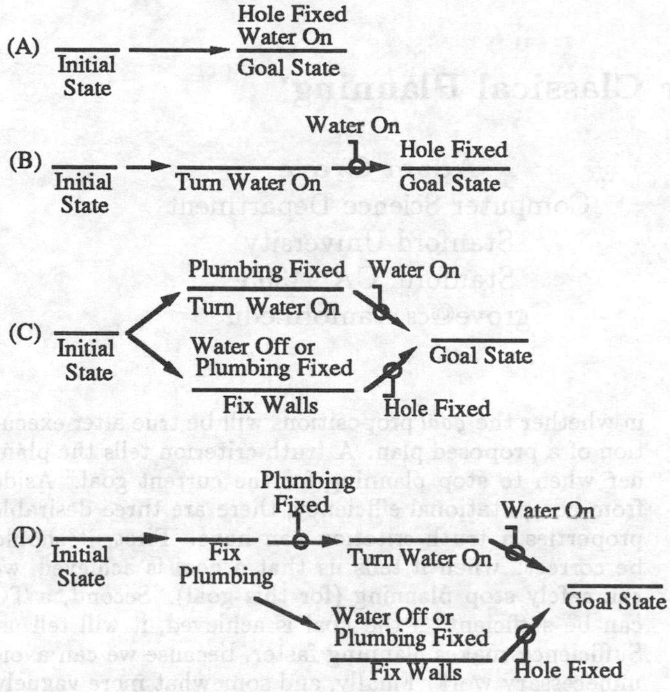

Figure 3: Steps in the Solution of the Homeowner's Problem

This example illustrates the two ways of preventing protected goals from being negated by parallel actions. In Figure 3c, the preservation precondition of fixing the plumbing was introduced as a subgoal to turning the water on so as not to negate the protected goal of having the walls fixed. This method could not be used with regard to the action of fixing the plumbing in Figure 3d, so this action was excluded from the protected interval by introducing an ordering constraint.

5. Discussion and Conclusions

In comparing the nonlinear planning approach presented in this paper to the linear planning approaches previously presented by the author, several things can be observed. The first is that, when viewed at the level of the execution sequences, there is essentially no difference in the way in which the plans are being constructed. Both approaches rely on Theorem 2 in the same way. Both generate the same space of potential solutions at the execution level. The only real difference is that partial orders enable several execution sequences to be represented simultaneously in the nonlinear planning approach. This can potentially have the effect of cutting down the branching factor and, hence, the size of the search space. This last statement may at first seem paradoxical given the kind of plan decompositions that are performed when goals are protected. However, keep in mind that these alternatives also appear in the search space of the linear planner. Thus, in the worst case, the nonlinear planning approach will have no worst a search space than the linear approach.

In the best case, the nonlinear approach should be far superior. In cases where the actions unconditionally preserve the goals on parallel branches of a plan, the preservation preconditions for those action simplify to the formula *TRUE*. Thus, the plan need not be decomposed, and preservation preconditions need not be introduced on parallel branches. The result is a tremendous reduction in the size of the search space. This case typically arises when the actions on parallel branches affect disjoint parts of the world. Nonlinear planning achieves its highest level of efficiency for problems in which this special case occurs.

References

Chapman, D. (1985). *Planning for Conjunctive Goals*. Technical Report 802, M.I.T. AI Lab.

Chapman, D. (1987). "Planning for Conjunctive Goals." *Artificial Intelligence*. **32**: 333-377.

Christensen, J. (1990a). *Automatic Abstraction in Planning*. Ph.D. Thesis, Computer Science Department, Stanford University, Stanford, California.

Christensen, J. (1990b). "A Heirarchical Planner that Generates its Own Hierarchies." *Proc. AAAI-90*, Boston, Massachusetts, pp 1004-1009.

Fikes, R. E. and N. J. Nilsson. (1971). "STRIPS: A New Approach to the Application of Theorem Proving to Problem Solving." *Artificial Intelligence*. **2**: 189–208.

McAllester, D. and D. Rosenblitt. (1991). "Systematic Nonlinear Planning." *Proc. AAAI-91 (submitted)*,

McDermott, D. (1991). "Regression Planning." *International Journal of Intelligent Systems*. : (in press).

Pednault, E. P. D. (1985). *Preliminary Report on A Theory of Plan Synthesis*. Technical Report 358, AI center, SRI International, Menlo Park, California.

Pednault, E. P. D. (1986). *Toward a Mathematical Theory of Plan Synthesis*. PHD Thesis, Dept. of Electrical Engineering, Stanford University, Stanford Ca.

Pednault, E. P. D. (1987). "Formulating Multiagent, Dynamic-World Problems in the Classical Planning Framework." In*Reasoning About Actions and Plans: Proceedings of the 1986 Workshop*, M. P. Georgeff and A. L. Lansky (ed). Los Altos, Ca., Morgan Kaufmann.

Pednault, E. P. D. (1988). "Synthesizing Plans that Contain Actions with Context-Dependent Effects." *Computational Intelligence*. **4**(4): 356-372.

Pednault, E. P. D. (1989). "ADL: Exploring the Middle Ground Between STRIPS and the Situation Calculus." *Proc. KR'89*, Toronto, Canada, pp 324.

Pednault, E. P. D. (forthcoming). "Generalizing Nonlinear Planning."

Tate, A. (1977). "Generating Project Networks." *Proc. IJCAI-77*, Massachusetts Institute of Technology, Cambridge, Mass, pp 888-893.

Waldinger, R. (1977). "Achieving Several Goals Simultaneously." In*Machine Intelligence 8*, E. Elcock and D. Michie (ed). Edinburgh, Scotland, Ellis Horwood.

Yang, Q. and J. D. Tenenberg. (1990). "ABTWEAK: Abstracting a Nonlinear, Least Commitment Planner." *Proc. AAAI-90*, Boston, Massachusetts, pp 204-209.

A Formal Model for Classical Planning*

Jens Christensen†
Computer Science Department
Stanford University
Stanford, CA 94305
jens@cs.stanford.edu

Adam Grove
Computer Science Department
Stanford University
Stanford, CA 94305
grove@cs.stanford.edu

Abstract

In this paper, we describe a formal semantic model that applies to many "classical" planning systems. This gives a unifying framework in which to study diverse planners, and motivates formal logics that can be used to study their properties. As an example of the model's utility, we present a general truth criterion which tests for the necessary truth of a proposition at arbitrary points in the planning process.

1 Introduction

In this paper we investigate a formal model for a broad class of A.I. planning systems. We define the range of applicability of our model later; here, we simply note that it is relevant to such well-known "classical" planners as STRIPS [Fikes and Nilsson, 1971], NOAH [Sacerdoti, 1977], NONLIN [Tate, 1977], TWEAK [Chapman, 1987] and SIPE [Wilkins, 1988]. Each of these planners has its own very distinctive features. But there are also many similarities, and we can define a useful *formal* model of the concept of "plan" used by all of them.

The model can be used to provide *semantics* for much of the planning process. That is, we can develop a logic which is interpreted as making assertions about plans. Relative to the model and the logic, claims about particular plans or planning systems can be proven true or false. Section 3 gives a concrete application of this: we develop a *truth criterion* for a broad class of planning systems. The concept of a truth criterion (TC) is due to Chapman [Chapman, 1987]. In fact, many of the ideas in this paper were inspired by Chapman's work and so we spend the rest of this introduction contrasting the goals of his work and ours.

In general, a planner's truth criterion is the test it uses to check whether a particular proposition holds at some point in a proposed plan. It is easy to see how important this test is. For example, we are always interested in whether the *goal* propositions will be true after execution of a proposed plan. A truth criterion tells the planner when to stop planning for the current goal. Aside from computational efficiency, there are three desirable properties a truth criterion can have. First, it should be correct: when it tells us that a goal is achieved, we can safely stop planning (for this goal). Second, a TC can be sufficient: if the goal is achieved, it will tell us. Sufficiency makes planning faster, because we can avoid unnecessary work. Finally, and somewhat more vaguely, a truth criterion may be informative. By this we mean that, when a proposition fails to hold, the TC gives us information about why it does not and we can use this to guide further planning steps.

Chapman presented a model for one particular planning system (his "TWEAK" formalism). Using this model, assertions about plans such as "proposition p necessarily holds after execution of action **a**" are given a precise meaning. Chapman gave an interesting test for the necessary truth of a proposition which is, relative to his model, provably correct and sufficient. Furthermore, this TC is informative; it is possible to "read off" all the useful modifications we might make to a plan to ensure the proposition's truth. Given any reasonable search strategy that explores the suggested possibilities, the resulting planner will be correct and complete.[1]

We also give a precise semantic model for planning, in Section 2. However, whereas Chapman discusses just one, quite restrictive, planning system, we discuss a general theory for all "classical" planners. This reflects our goal to develop a theory that is useful for comparing many different planners. In contrast, Chapman is able to develop a new, straightforward, and provably correct planner by taking advantage of features particular to the system he studies.

We discuss a logic for describing and reasoning about our models. The idea of using a logic was implicit in Chapman's work, but never developed; for although he attempts to give a version of his TC in "logical notation", the formula presented contains minor errors and so does not quite correspond to his criterion. This has no effect on his results, because the real criterion, its proof.

*The first author was partially supported by NASA Grant NCC2-494 and by Texas Instruments Contract No. 7554900. The second author is supported by an IBM Graduate Fellowship.

†Present address: Teknekron, 530 Lytton Ave, Palo Alto, CA 94301.

[1] That is, it always finds a working plan if this is possible, and never terminates with a plan that doesn't satisfy all goals.

and all discussion of its application, are in English. But in general, a well-defined formal language is useful because it can prevent ambiguity. Furthermore, we can use a formal logic to give syntactic proofs of assertions about the planner (such as the correctness of a proposed truth criterion). Theorem proving is much easier to automate than subtle semantic arguments like those used by Chapman.

2 The Model and Logic

Our model applies to planning systems that depend on a *single-agent* and *situation-based* world model and work by *refining nonlinear plans.* Before presenting the model itself, we look at these issues.

Plans are constructed for agents that operate in some well-defined environment. We only consider planners whose world model is like the situation calculus ([McCarthy, 1968]). More precisely, we suppose that a particular state of the world is described by a set of objects, often called *propositions*, which throughout we consider to come from some fixed set $\mathcal{P}$.[2] We say that a proposition holds at, or is true in, a state if it is a member of that state. We assume that basic operations in the world, the actions, are functions mapping one state to another resulting state (i.e., they are functions from subsets of $\mathcal{P}$ to subsets of $\mathcal{P}$). Of the class of all possible actions, $\mathcal{A}$, the agent we are planning for can presumably execute some known subset, say $\mathcal{R}$. If the agent executes a sequence of actions starting in state I, the final state must be what results from applying the composition of the actions to I.

The purpose of a planner is to find a sequence of actions in $\mathcal{R}$ which ensures that, when the world contains a given collection of *initial* propositions, then after execution it is certain that all of some given collection of *goal* propositions holds. We will call any sequence of actions, together with the set I, a *complete plan.* We are interested in planners that proceed by considering *sets* of complete plans, and slowly narrow the size of the sets until all the complete plans that remain guarantee the goals (i.e., this is the least-commitment approach to planning). Because it is never practical to manipulate arbitrary sets of plans, a planner always uses some compact representation system, which we will call the *plan representation language*, to describe such sets. Here, we make the assumption that the planners use a language which describes *nonlinear* plans. A nonlinear plan is given by:

- $I \subseteq \mathcal{P}$, which is the initial state.
- A fixed, finite collection P of *plan steps* $A_1, \ldots, A_n$. Each plan step is associated with a collection of actions in $\mathcal{R}$ (an *action-set*). Where there can be no confusion, we will blur the distinction between a plan step and its associated action-set.
- A partial order on plan steps, $\prec$.
- A set of constraints on the n plan steps. The constraints specify which combinations of actions in $A_1 \times A_2 \times \ldots \times A_n$ are actually permitted.

It is easy to see how a nonlinear plan describes a set of complete plans: it stands for all such plans obtainable by extending $\prec$ into a total order on the A_i, and then choosing (subject to the constraints) one action from each A_i. The term "nonlinear" is used because we need only give a partial order on the plan steps.

Virtually all the planners mentioned in Section 1 manipulate some form of nonlinear plan.[3] Within the framework described so far (which has just concerned itself with representations) planners differ in three main ways. First, many planners only allow certain special types of actions to occur in $\mathcal{R}$. A very common restriction on $\mathcal{R}$ is what we call the STRIPS assumption ([Fikes and Nilsson, 1971]). Under this assumption, an action $a \in \mathcal{R}$ must have a very simple structure: in any situation, a has the effect of first removing some fixed set of propositions (traditionally called the *delete list*) then adding all of some other fixed set (the *add list*).[4] Second, plan representation languages differ in how they describe the action-sets associated with a plan step in a partial plan. One common technique, used in Chapman's system among others, allows action "schemas" such as Puton(x,y) which stand for all actions obtained instantiating the *variables* x, y; we discuss such systems in somewhat more detail later. Finally, planners can differ significantly in their constraint schemes (for example, Chapman uses a simple language that constrains the values his variables can be instantiated to). Note that the constraint language and the action-set representation language are interrelated.

In our model, these differences are represented within a uniform framework. We first define a partial plan, which is a tuple $(I, P, \prec)$ (where each component is as described above). The structure of partial plans can be viewed as a plan representation language, but it is very weak because we make no provision for constraints. Our model is based on the observation that a nonlinear plan in a general language, possibly with constraints, can be

[2]Propositions are often thought of as being formulas in some formal logic. However, it is not always possible or useful to take this view.

[3]Some of these planners, such as NOAH, NONLIN, and SIPE, also make use of a hierarchical structure on actions. That is, there is a concept of "high level" actions and/or propositions, which can be expanded into a more detailed and more complex objects at a lower abstraction level. Our model does not capture this aspect of a plan representation system. This does not invalidate its usefulness however, because, as Wilkins [Wilkins, 1988] points out, all hierarchical planners operate on a series of *planning levels*, where on any one level the degree of abstraction never changes. Within one level our model is usually applicable. Nevertheless, giving a deeper theory for these concepts would probably be the most interesting extension to the model we are proposing here.

[4]In addition, we sometimes specify a set of *preconditions*, which are propositions that must be true before an action is regarded as being truly executable. Considerations of executability are ignored in the model we present (and, in effect, this is also true for Chapman's model). During planning, preconditions become (sub-)goals that must be achieved, and so typically only influence the goal selection component of the planner.

described using a collection of partial plans.

Definition: A *plan-structure* is a finite tree, where the nodes are partial plans. If $\mathbf{n}_i = (I_i, P_i, \prec_i)$ is an ancestor of, or equal to, $\mathbf{n}_j = (I_j, P_j, \prec_j)$, then we write $\mathbf{n}_i \rightarrow \mathbf{n}_j$ and say that $\mathbf{n}_j$ is a specialization of $\mathbf{n}_i$. Whenever this is the case, we insist that $\prec_i \subseteq \prec_j$, $I_i \subseteq I_j$, and $P_i = P_j$. However, although $P_i = P_j$, we do not assume that the action-sets associated with a particular plan step A_i are identical in the two partial plans, but we do require that the action-set for A_i in $\mathbf{n}_i$ is a superset of the corresponding action-set in $\mathbf{n}_j$, for all i. From this condition it follows that complete plans (i.e., partial plans that represent a single complete plan) must be leaf nodes in the tree. Conversely, we also require that every leaf must be complete.

From any $\mathbf{n}_i$ there are a large number of potential specializations (formed by constraining the partial order in some way, and restricting the action-sets associated with some of the plan steps). However, not all these possibilities can be considered by the planner. This is because the planner has a limited language for describing action-sets, so that not all possible subsets of $\mathcal{R}$ can be captured, and also because of constraints. This is perhaps the key point: the main differences between different planners' representations system can be captured by differences in how the specialization relation works.

We can define a formal language, which makes assertions about plan-structures. Because the model is so general, the language covers many planning systems. To shorten the presentation, we introduce our language informally. The key features are:

- The language is a based on a sorted first-order logic, with the usual connectives, and quantification for the two sorts *plan-steps* and *propositions*. At any node in the model, the domain of *plan-steps* is, of course, just the plan-steps at the node, and the domain of the sort *propositions* is $\mathcal{P}$.[5]
- The language has two primitive modal operators, $\Box_S$ and $\Box$. At a node in a plan, $\Box_S\phi$ is true just if ϕ is true in all nodes which are specializations of the first, and $\Box\phi$ is true if ϕ holds in all specializations which are complete plans. We read $\Box\phi$ as "ϕ is necessarily true". The "necessary" modality is the key to our logic; a necessary property of a nonlinear plan is true of all the complete plans it describes. The truth criterion we give later is of interest because it shows that, sometimes, we can discover whether a formula is necessarily true without considering all these complete plans individually.

  We sometimes use the duals of $\Box$ and $\Box_S$, written $\Diamond$ and $\Diamond_S$, which are defined in the usual way as $\Diamond = \neg\Box\neg$ and $\Diamond_S = \neg\Box_S\neg$ respectively.
- There is a binary predicate $\prec$ between plan steps. At $\mathbf{n}$, $a \prec b$ if in fact the plan step (denoted by) a precedes b.
- There is one unary predicate Initially on propositions. If p is a term denoting a proposition, Initially(p) is true at a node if the denotation of p is in I (for that node).
- There are three binary predicates, **Asserts**, **Denies** and **Holds** which relate propositions to plan steps. First suppose that $\mathbf{n}$ is a complete plan, say $(I, P, \prec)$, and that p denotes a proposition in $\mathcal{P}$. Then Holds(p, a) is true at $\mathbf{n}$ if the proposition denoted by p is true immediately prior to the plan step denoted by a. This is well defined because of the nature of complete plans, and because we know the initial state I. In a complete plan, Asserts(a, p) is true if Holds(p, a) is false but p holds immediately after a is executed. (Denies is defined similarly; p must be true before a but false afterwards.)

  When $\mathbf{n}$ is not complete, the denotations of Asserts, Denies and Holds can be defined arbitrarily.

There are several interesting formulas that are valid in all plan-structures. One of the most important is the following axiom, that captures the fundamental connection between Asserts, Denies, Holds, and Initially as we have defined them.

$$\begin{aligned}&\Box(\mathsf{Holds}(p,a) \equiv \\ &\quad (\neg\exists b(b \prec a) \land \mathsf{Initially}(p)) \lor \\ &\quad \exists c\,((c \prec a) \land \neg\exists d((c \prec d) \land (d \prec a)) \land \\ &\qquad (\mathsf{Asserts}(c,p) \lor (\mathsf{Holds}(p,c) \land \neg\mathsf{Denies}(c,p)))))\end{aligned}$$

Later, we will refer to this formula as the *Holds axiom.*

All nonlinear planning languages share some common weaknesses and our language can help make these precise. For example, it is a consequence of the use of partial orders on plansteps that formulas like the following are valid:

$$\begin{aligned}&\forall x,y,z\ \Box_S((x \prec z) \land (\neg((x \prec y) \land (y \prec z)))) \Rightarrow \\ &\qquad \Box_S(y \prec x) \lor \Box_S(z \prec y)\end{aligned}$$

That is, using partial orders does not allow us to impose a constraint that simply says "x must come immediately before z"; we must also commit to whether x and z are before or after every other action y.

There are also many formulas that are not valid in the general case, but are true of particular systems. If the STRIPS assumption about actions in $\mathcal{R}$ is assumed, then additional axioms like the following hold.

$$\begin{aligned}&\forall x,y,z\ \Diamond_S(x \prec y) \land \Diamond_S(\mathsf{Asserts}(z,p)) \Rightarrow \\ &\qquad \Diamond_S((x \prec y) \land (\mathsf{Asserts}(z,p) \lor \mathsf{Holds}(p,z))\end{aligned}$$

Such formulas say that the propositions asserted (or denied) by an action are essentially independent of the ordering imposed on plan-steps. This is a very strong property which simplifies planning enormously when it is reasonable. Most planners use STRIPS-like actions.

Another special axiom that is true in systems like Chapman's TWEAK is:

$$\begin{aligned}&\forall x_1, x_2, \ldots, x_n \\ &\quad \Box(\mathsf{Asserts}(x_1,p) \lor \ldots \lor \mathsf{Asserts}(x_n,p)) \Rightarrow \\ &\qquad (\Box\mathsf{Ensures}(x_1,p) \lor \ldots \lor \Box\mathsf{Ensures}(x_n,p))\end{aligned}$$

[5] Note that these domains are independent of the node in a plan-structure. In a presentation of the formal properties of the logic (for which we have insufficient space here) this observation has some important consequences (such as the truth of the "Barcan" axiom; see [Hughes and Cresswell, 1968]).

(In this axiom, Ensures(x,p) is simply an abbreviation for Asserts(x,p) $\vee$ Holds(p,x).) This axiom can be understood as showing that the constraint language in TWEAK is rather weak; it cannot be used to constrain a group of actions to assert p, except in the rather trivial case where one particular action is guaranteed to assert p anyway. We have insufficient space to explain in detail how such axioms arise in Chapman's system. In brief, Chapman's action-set language makes use of "propositions" with *variables*, which are essentially placeholders that are instantiated during planning. For example, in the "blocks world" a plan step might be associated with action schema Pickup(x), with add list Holding(x) (and perhaps some preconditions, such as Clear(x)). This stands for all actions in $\mathcal{R}$ obtainable by instantiating x to a real object.[6] It turns out to be very important for Chapman's TC that variables can be instantiated in infinitely many ways; and the reason for this is essentially to guarantee the truth of axioms like the above, although this can appear quite mysterious until Chapman's proof is read. In our language we express many of the important properties Chapman required without using planner specific features such as variables. It is not possible to reprove Chapman's TC exactly in our system, because his TC makes use of features specific to TWEAK. However, a TC which is very similar in spirit can be proven just by making assumptions, such as the formula just given, whose truth can be tested for any nonlinear planning system.

3 Truth Criterion

Chapman proved that his TWEAK truth criterion is correct and sufficient for his model. However, as he points out, this criterion fails for any planning system just somewhat more expressive than his. One basic shortcoming of Chapman's truth criterion is its requirement that, whenever a proposition necessarily holds at some point in the plan, it is necessarily asserted by one particular plan step. But in general, it is possible for multiple plan steps to act together to guarantee the truth of a proposition, even where no one step alone is enough.

In this section, we discuss a new truth criterion that is correct and sufficient for any planning system within the scope of our model.

3.1 Presentation

Intuitively our truth criterion can be read as follows. A proposition p is necessarily true immediately before plan step a iff, in all specializations of the plan, two conditions hold: (1) If a is necessarily the first plan step, then it is necessarily the case that p is initially true, and (2) whenever there is a plan step c that is necessarily immediately before a, then if c does not possibly assert p then p must hold at c and not possibly be denied by c.

In our logic this TC is given as:

$$\Box_S\ (\ (\neg\exists b\ \Diamond(b \prec a) \Rightarrow \Box\mathsf{Initially}(p)) \wedge \\ \forall c\ (\Box(c \prec a) \wedge \neg\exists d\ \Diamond((c \prec d) \wedge (d \prec a))) \Rightarrow \\ (\neg\Diamond\ \mathsf{Asserts}(c,p) \Rightarrow \\ \Box\mathsf{Holds}(p,c) \wedge \neg\Diamond\mathsf{Denies}(c,p))\ )$$

Using our logic, it is possible to give a (lengthy) syntactic proof showing that the TC holds if and only if $\Box$Holds(p,a) (see [Christensen, 1990]). In principle, this proof could be checked by an automatic theorem prover, and perhaps even generated by one. Here, we simply give a sketch of a semantic proof.

We first show that whenever $\Box$Holds(p,a) fails to hold, our TC is false also. So suppose $\neg\Box$Holds(p,a). Consider one of the completions where $\neg$Holds(p,a). There are two cases: either a is the first step of the plan or it is not. If the former, the Holds axiom shows that $\neg$Initially(p). But then our TC fails since this completion is a specialization where a is necessarily the first plan step and $\neg\Box$Initially(p).

If a is not the first plan step then there must be some other plan step, c, which is immediately before a; then the Holds axiom shows that $\neg$Asserts(c,p) and either $\neg$Holds(p,c) or Denies(c,p). It follows that $\neg\Diamond$Asserts(c,p) holds in this completion, but one of $\Box$Holds(p,c) and $\neg\Diamond$Denies(c,p) is false. Therefore our TC does not hold.

Next, we show if our TC does not hold, then neither does $\Box$Holds(p,a). Suppose the TC is false in a partial plan. Then there must be some specialization of the plan where either (1) a is necessarily the first plan step and $\neg\Box$Initially(p) or (2) there is some plan step c immediately before a with $\neg\Diamond$Asserts(c,p) and either $\Diamond$Denies(c,p) or $\neg\Box$Holds(p,c). If (1), there must be a completion where a is the first plan step and $\neg$Initially(p). Then, by the Holds axiom, $\neg$Holds(p,a) is true in this completion and therefore $\neg\Box$Holds(p,a) holds in our plan. If (2) there must be some completion where either (i) there is some plan step c immediately before a and $\neg$Asserts(c,p) and Denies(c,p) or (ii) there is some plan step c immediately before a and $\neg$Asserts(c,p) and $\neg$Holds(p,c). In either case, by the Holds axiom, $\neg$Holds(p,a), which implies that $\neg\Box$Holds(p,a).

3.2 Algorithm for Checking our Truth Criterion

The straightforward implementation of our TC involves examining every specialization of a plan. This is clearly not desirable. In fact, the most naive truth criterion, namely applying the Holds axiom to every completion of a partial plan, is no less efficient. However, the potential for efficiency improvements results from noticing two important properties. First, we only need to examine those specializations where the following holds:

$$\neg\exists b\ \Diamond(b \prec a) \vee \\ \exists c\ (\ \Box(c \prec a) \wedge \\ \neg\exists d\ \Diamond((c \prec d) \wedge (d \prec a)) \wedge \neg\Diamond\mathsf{Asserts}(c,p)\ )$$

In the following, we will refer to the expression inside the initial $\Box_S$ of our TC as CTC(p,a). It is easy to see

[6] Note that expressions like Holding(x) are part of the plan representation language, and are meaningless unless considered in the context of the planning process. This contrast with true propositions in $\mathcal{P}$, for example Holding(BLOCKA), which can be used to describe the state of the world. In languages like Chapman's, it is important to keep in mind that "variables" like x are just formal objects used by the planner, and do not connote any formal first-order quantification.

To test if $\Box$Holds(p, a):

For every weakest specialization such that there is a plan step c necessarily immediately before a which does not possibly assert p:

Check that c does not possibly deny p and necessarily Holds(p, c).

For any weakest specialization such that a is the first plan step:

Check that Initially(p) necessarily holds.

Figure 1: Algorithm for checking truth criterion.

that if the above expression does not hold in a specialization then CTC(p, a) must hold there.

Second, we only need to examine the *weakest* such specializations. A specialization is weaker than another if the latter is a specialization of the former. If CTC(p, a) does not hold in such a specialization we can stop, since in that case $\neg\Box_S$CTC(p, a). If CTC(p, a) does hold in such a specialization then it holds for all specializations of that specialization. For a proof of this, see [Christensen, 1990]. Using these two properties we arrive at the algorithm in figure 1.

The algorithm for checking the truth criterion requires time exponential in the length of the plan. Chapman proved that determining $\Box$Holds(p, a) in any system where the schema representation is sufficiently strong to include conditionals is NP-Hard.[7] It is therefore extremely unlikely that any polynomial time algorithm will ever be found for verifying the truth criteria of such systems. However, our algorithm will often be considerably more efficient than the application of the Holds axiom to all the completions of a plan, as we shall see shortly. Furthermore, as we discuss later, it represents a good starting point in the development of incomplete or unsound algorithms which might overcome the complexity barrier.

3.3 Restricted Ranges of Variables

Chapman gives an example of an extension to TWEAK that causes his TC to fail. Recall that TWEAK uses "variables", which are placeholders the planner uses to reason about groups of actions. If TWEAK is extended with a mechanism for restricting the range of variables, then Chapman's TC is no longer sufficient. For example, in TWEAK, if CLEAR(x) is denied by a TWEAK plan step, this step can be specialized into infinitely many actions which deny propositions that satisfy the CLEAR(x) schema, e.g. CLEAR(A), CLEAR(B), CLEAR(C), CLEAR$(Harry)$, etc., where A, B, C, and *Harry* are constants. Restricting the range of variables might be desirable to ensure that variables adhere to a certain type, e.g. we might wish to restrict variable x to the values {A, B, C}, thereby eliminating the possibility CLEAR$(Harry)$.

Suppose we have the plan in figure 2. In this example, Punch(Bob, John) necessarily holds in the final situation.

[7] Conditional actions, which can be modeled in our system, will be described later.

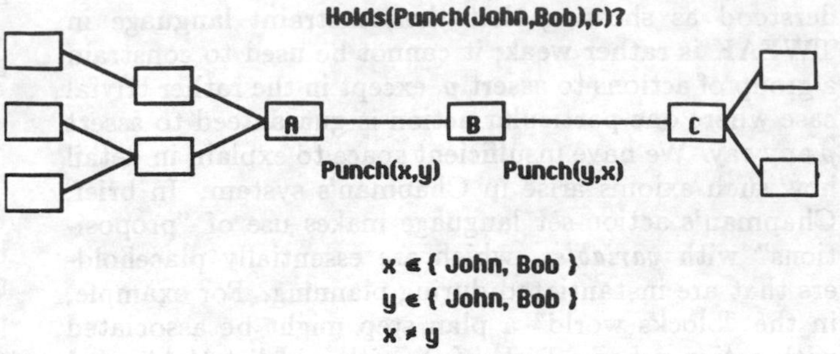

Figure 2: Example where Chapman's TC fails.

However, it is not necessarily asserted by any one step, and so fails Chapman's truth criterion.

On the other hand, our truth criterion succeeds. Furthermore, our truth criterion algorithm requires that only two specializations of the plan be checked. To see this let us step through the algorithm. We would begin by evaluating Holds(Punch(Bob, John),C). Clearly, there are no specializations where C is the first plan step. However, there are two distinct weakest specialization such that there is a plan step immediately before C and that plan step does not possibly assert Punch(Bob, John). These are simply the specializations where the constraints $y \neq$ Bob and $x \neq$ John have been respectively added. We will examine the former specialization. In this specialization plan step B must not possibly deny Punch(Bob, John). This is in fact so, since plan step B does not deny anything.

Furthermore, we want $\Box$Holds(Punch(Bob, John), B). This is checked with another application of the TC. There are no specializations where B is the first plan step. However, in this case there are no specializations where there is a plan step immediately before B that does not possibly assert Punch(Bob, John). To guarantee this would mean adding either $x \neq$ Bob or $y \neq$ John. If we add the former then both y and x must denote John, which is not allowed. If we add the latter then y can't possibly denote any object, which is also disallowed.

The evaluation of the other specialization proceeds in an analogous manner. As can be seen from stepping through the algorithm, it is somewhat reminiscent of resolution theorem proving, in that we continually attempt to disprove the proposition until a contradiction is found. It is different from resolution theorem proving in that it is guaranteed to terminate if a contradiction is not found in this manner.

3.4 Conditional Actions

Figure 3 shows a plan which, while simple, cannot be represented by TWEAK, or by most other classical planning systems. One exception is [Pednault, 1988], who presents a plan language that supports conditional actions and a method for synthesizing linear plans using these actions.

The actions in figure 3 might be described as being *conditional,* because their effect depends on the state of the world in which they are executed. In contrast.

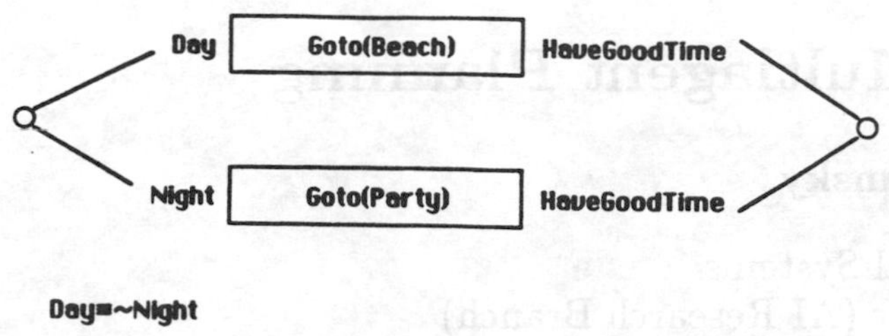

Figure 3: Example with conditional actions.

STRIPS-like actions have a constant effect (in any world where their preconditions are true).[8] In the figure, one can always go to the beach; there are no executability preconditions as such. However, nothing will be achieved at night. This is a very simple conditional action representation and nothing in our model precludes us from having arbitrarily complex conditional actions; our model allows any action that is a function mapping states to states.

The algorithm for determining our truth criterion would begin by considering one of the specializations where there is an action immediately before the final situation which does not possibly assert HaveGoodTime. Assume it considers Goto(Beach) first. We must constrain ¬day to be true, or else HaveGoodTime would possibly be asserted. Then, we verify that Goto(Beach) cannot deny HaveGoodTime and recurse on Holds(HaveGoodTime,Goto(Party)). However, there are no specializations with an action immediately before Goto(Party) where HaveGoodTime is not possibly asserted. If there were then both ¬night and ¬day must hold, which is impossible.

3.5 Conclusion and Further Work

In practical terms, one might argue, our truth criterion is not useful since the algorithm for verifying it appears to be inherently exponential. This contrasts with Chapman's truth criterion, which can be verified in polynomial time. However, the value of a polynomial time truth criterion is somewhat questionable, given that the planning process is still undecidable. Furthermore, TWEAK achieves efficiency in the truth criterion at the cost of limitations in expressive power.

As domains become more complex it becomes less and less likely that the TWEAK representation can be used to adequately model them. For example, TWEAK is unable to efficiently model HACKERS cubical blocks world, and completely unable to solve problems whose solution requires conditional actions.

There is an interesting tradeoff between expressivity of a planning language and the search process using that language. As expressivity is added to the language the number of choice points at each plan node in the search tree increases. Furthermore, efficient truth criteria such as Chapman's are less likely to exist. On the other hand, because of the finer resolution greater expressivity allows, over-commitment is more easily avoided, and so the amount of backtracking can be reduced. Also, the increased expressivity allows more knowledge to be encoded at each node, thereby allowing for possibly more informed choices. So it is far from clear what the optimal point along this spectrum of expressivity is. We note that much of planning research has concerned itself with developing planners which support powerful plan representations.

Of course, such planners are generally not based on provably correct truth criteria. Our truth criterion could in principle be used instead. However, for efficiency reasons, it is likely that the actual algorithm used would be tailored to take advantage of the planner's specific plan representation. It might even be the case that completeness, or even in some circumstances, correctness, is sacrificed in order to achieve efficiency gains. However, the designer of the truth criterion would have a sound and complete reference point from which to start, and would therefore be well aware of the corners that were cut to achieve efficiency. It remains to be seen what the appropriate tradeoff between efficiency, correctness, completeness, and expressive power of the plan representation is.

[8] The idea of modifying the STRIPS paradigm, to allow for "preconditions" which determine action's effects, can be found occasionally in the literature; for instance, these are Pednault's *secondary preconditions.*

References

[Chapman, 1987] Chapman, D., "Planning for Conjunctive Goals," *Artificial Intelligence*, **32** (July 1987) 333-378.

[Christensen, 1990] Christensen, J., "Automatic Abstraction in Planning," PhD Dissertation, Stanford University, 1990.

[Fikes and Nilsson, 1971] Fikes, R. E. and Nilsson, N. J., "STRIPS: A new Approach to the Application of Theorem Proving to Problem Solving," *Artificial Intelligence*, 2(3-4) (1971) 189-208.

[Hughes and Cresswell, 1968] Hughes, G.E. and Cresswell, M.J., "An Introduction to Modal Logic," Methuen and Co, London, England, 1968.

[McCarthy, 1968] McCarthy, J., "Programs with Common Sense," in: Minsky, M. (Ed.), *Semantic Information Processing*, MIT Press, Cambridge, MA, 1968.

[Pednault, 1988] Pednault, E., "Synthesizing Plans that Contain Actions with Context-Dependent Effects," *Computational Intelligence*, 4(4) (1988) 356-372.

[Sacerdoti, 1977] Sacerdoti, E., *A Structure for Plans and Behavior*, Elsevier, North-Holland, New York, 1977.

[Tate, 1977] Tate, A., "Generating Project Networks," *Proceedings IJCAI-77*, Cambridge, Massachusetts, (1977) 888-893.

[Wilkins, 1988] Wilkins, D. E., *Practical Planning*, Morgan Kaufman, San Mateo, California, 1988.

Localized Search for Multiagent Planning

Amy L. Lansky

Sterling Federal Systems
NASA Ames Research Center (AI Research Branch)
MS 244-17, Moffett Field, CA 94035 U.S.A

Abstract

This paper describes the localized search mechanism of the GEMPLAN multiagent planner. Both formal complexity results and empirical results are provided, demonstrating the benefits of localized search. A localized domain description is one that decomposes domain activities and requirements into a set of regions. This description is used to infer how domain requirements are semantically localized and, as a result, to enable the decomposition of the planning search space into a set of spaces, one for each domain region. Benefits of localization include a smaller and cheaper overall search space as well as heuristic guidance in controlling search. Such benefits are critical if current planning technologies and other types of reasoning are to be scaled up to large, complex domains.

1 Introduction

The focus of this paper is the use of *locality* — the inherent structural qualities of a domain — to control the explosive cost of planning and other forms of reasoning. The use of localized reasoning, while quite intuitive and natural, has not been a fundamental aspect of most AI systems. A localized domain description is one that is explicitly decomposed into a set of regions. Each region may be viewed as a subset of potential domain activity with an associated set of requirements or *"constraints"* that pertain only to the activities within that region. We refer to this delineation of constraint applicability as *constraint localization.* (Throughout this paper we use the term "constraint" very broadly to refer to *any* type of goal or domain property that the planner must fulfill.)

Localized planning is the process of creating a valid domain plan by searching a set of smaller, regional planning search spaces rather than a single large "global" space. Each GEMPLAN search space may be visualized as a plan-construction search tree, where each tree node is associated with a region plan and each arc is associated with a plan modification that transforms the preceding plan into a new plan in order to satisfy some region constraint. Localized search is a powerful technique for reducing the size and cost of the entire planning search space. Although this paper discusses localized search as applied to planning, the technique is generally applicable to any form of decomposable reasoning search.

This research has been made possible in part by the National Science Foundation, under Grant IRI-8715972.

In addition to GEMPLAN, a scheduler, an abduction-based planner, and an image understanding system have already incorporated aspects of GEMPLAN's localized search method.

The GEMPLAN domain representation allows for a myriad of decompositional strategies, including the use of regions that overlap, are disjoint, are organized hierarchically, or form any combination thereof. The allowance for overlap, in particular, renders our localized search method quite useful for realistic domains. Criteria for decomposition are usually suggested by the innate characteristics of a domain – e.g., its physical structure, its behavioral processes, its functional elements, and its abstraction hierarchies. A good decomposition typically reflects several such criteria. Consider, for example, a building-construction domain. Viewed globally, the domain may be described by a set of constraints, some of which describe the structure and requirements for a specific building, some that encode the characteristics of contractors and physical resources, and those that describe construction "rules of thumb." Clearly, most of these constraints apply only to a subset of the construction activities to be planned. One way to decompose the domain is according to the physical structure of the building – e.g., to utilize separate regions to model each room. Other regions could model the individual building processes – e.g., the contractors. In most cases, physically-motivated regions and process-based regions will overlap. Figure 1 depicts a possible decomposition for a small construction domain.

The primary goal of localization is to cluster activities into regions so that constraints are applied as narrowly as possible. The actual decomposition chosen will determine the exact scope of applicability of domain constraints – i.e., each region's constraints are assumed to apply only to the activities within that region. However, different localization decompositions will incur different planning costs. As we will show, there is a trade-off between increased decomposition and the resulting increased costs necessary for coping with regional overlap. While most of our empirical tests have utilized user-provided decompositions, we are currently developing a technique for automatically learning good decomposition strategies. This work bears some similarity to Knoblock's learning of domain abstractions [4]; however, Knoblock's abstractions must be strictly hierarchical.

The use of localized reasoning has several benefits. From a representational point of view, locality provides a solution to aspects of the frame problem; constraint localization may be viewed as a frame rule which limits interaction among domain actions and properties. Most importantly, locality provides a rationale for partitioning a potentially explosive global planning space into a set of smaller, localized planning spaces. This has three interrelated benefits: (1) The absolute *size* of the union of a set of localized planning spaces is usually smaller than that of a non-localized space; (2) At each node in the search space, expensive planning algorithms need be applied to much smaller regional plans. Thus, search *cost* is cheaper, even if search space size is unaffected; (3) Since a localized domain description provides information about how constraints and activities interact, it serves as a heuristic for constraint application. In particular, localized search enables the application of constraints only to relevant segments of the overall emerging plan and causes constraints to be applied only *when* then actually need to be. All of these factors facilitate scaling up to large domains.

The notion of localized search is related to several other research efforts. The consistency maintenance techniques used in localized search for dealing with regional overlap, for example, are similar to data consistency methods used by shared, distributed databases. Other planning researchers have looked at methods of problem decomposition in order to reduce search complexity [1, 5], but they have focused primarily on goal reduction and operator reformulation rather than search space decomposition. The goals of controlling the scope of constraint applicability and constraint triggering are shared by work in truth maintenance and constraint propagation. Our use of locality, however, generally produces a much coarser-grained connectivity than that found in a TMS or CSP net. GEMPLAN regions record constraint interrelatedness without the need for incremental update or truth checking; they are thus less expensive. Semantically, however, localization can provide significant information. For instance, even if a constraint syntactically appears relevant to a broader fragment of the overall plan, its inclusion within a region will limit its application to within that region. Localized search also imposes an explicit control over constraint application that is distinct from anything intrinsically provided by a TMS or CSP net. Recent work in discovering "textures" in CSP networks [3] to control constraint propagation bears some similarity to localization, although CSP constraints are usually extensional and propositional, whereas GEMPLAN constraints are broader in content and usually intensional. One interesting use of locality is deKleer's work on localizing or merging clauses in a TMS [2]. In deKleer's case, merging is done to gain completeness. In localized search, partitioning is done to gain efficiency, but with no loss of completeness.

The rest of this paper is organized as follows. Section 2 provides an overview of the GEMPLAN architecture and a description of the localized search algorithm. This

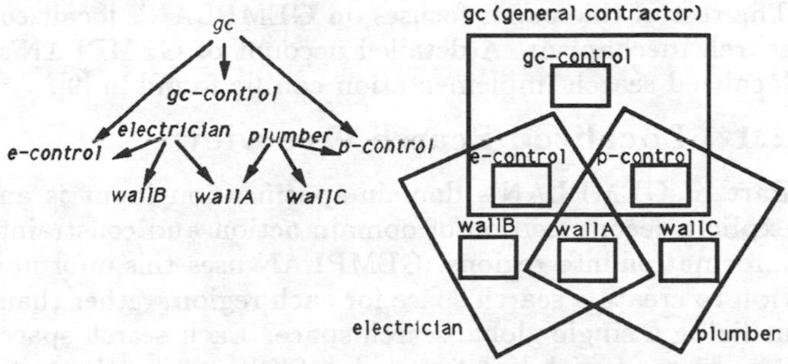

Figure 1: A Localized Construction Domain Description

discussion is made concrete in Section 3, which describes a simple planning scenario. Section 4 discusses various tradeoffs inherent in localized search, and then substantiates these intuitions with a complexity analysis. This is followed by the empirical results of Section 5.

2 The GEMPLAN Planner

GEMPLAN is a planner designed for multiagent domains that require complex coordination. It has been applied to multiagent blocks-world problems, the Tower of Hanoi, and several versions of a construction domain. The system includes an execution facility, and has the ability to apply constraints before or during execution. It may thus be viewed as a combined pre-planner/dynamic-planner. While the existing system is primarily designed for pre-planning, we have begun implementation of a next-generation GEMPLAN system, called COLLAGE, that will span the pre-planning/dynamic-planning spectrum in a more seamless fashion.

GEMPLAN differs from standard hierarchical planners in several ways. Besides its use of localized search, GEMPLAN has the ability to satisfy a broad range of domain "constraint forms," not simply the attainment and maintenance of state conditions. Note that we use the term "constraint" in a very broad sense – i.e., to refer to any sort of property that the planner knows how to test and make true. The system includes a set of general-purpose constraint satisfaction algorithms for a set of constraint forms, which may be further augmented by user-supplied constraint-satisfaction methods. The default constraint algorithms are fully general for partially-ordered plans and perform the task of plan construction by introducing actions, action interrelationships, and variable bindings. GEMPLAN's current constraint repertoire includes: (1) The attainment and maintenance of goal conditions and preconditions – i.e., the traditional planning algorithms used by STRIPS-based planners. Actions may have conditional effects, and established conditions are protected; (2) Action decomposition. GEMPLAN allows for reasoning about actions at mixed levels of detail, rather than confining itself to reasoning "one level at a time," as do some hierarchical planners [10]; (3) A variety of temporal and causal constraints; (4) Required patterns of behavior expressed as regular expressions; (5) CSP constraints on potential values of plan variables.

More details on GEMPLAN appear elsewhere [6, 7, 8]. The rest of this paper focuses on GEMPLAN's localized search mechanism. A detailed account of GEMPLAN's localized search implementation can be found in [9].

2.1 Localized Search Overview

Part of GEMPLAN's domain specification input is an explicit decomposition of domain action and constraint information into regions. GEMPLAN uses this information to create a search space for each region, rather than utilizing a single global search space. Each search space is concerned with building a plan for its region that satisfies all regional constraints. The planner may thus be viewed as a set of "mini-planners," tied together by the structural relationships between regions.

The localized search algorithm has two basic functions: (1) controlling the flow of constraint application – in particular, shifts between regional search spaces; and (2) maintaining the consistency of the overall search space. Besides assuring that all regions are searched at least once (to satisfy goal constraints), localized search typically shifts from one regional search space to the search space for a region R only if previous plan modifications have impacted R's plan. That is, search will flow only to those regions whose plans have been affected and whose constraints truly need to be checked. Planning for a region can impact the plan for another region only if they share a common portion of the overall plan (i.e., they overlap). And because the search spaces of overlapping regions reason about shared subplans, localized search must make sure that they share a consistent view of these subplans.

2.2 Region Description

Let us assume that a domain is specified as a set of regions. Each region R is defined by a *region description*: <*actions(R), subregions(R), constraints(R), tree(R)*>. The set *actions*(R) consists of action *types*, instances of which may occur directly within R (but not within a subregion of R). The set *subregions*(R) consists of subregions belonging to R. For each such subregion Q, we use the notation $Q \subset R$. The set *constraints*(R) includes constraints that pertain to activities within R and its subregions. Finally, each region is associated with a plan-construction search tree *tree*(R).

Consider the construction domain of Figure 1. It has been partitioned into regions corresponding to the activities of an electrician, plumber, and general contractor. These regions are further decomposed to include subregions that contain the activities of the electrician and plumber at various walls as well as their respective "control" activities (these might include communication actions between contractors). Each wall region would be associated with constraints that are relevant only to the actions taking place at that wall; e.g., wallA might include constraints relating to coordination the plumber and electrician. The electrician, plumber, and gc region constraints, which apply to all their subregions, describe more global requirements; e.g., the gc constraints might describe how the contractors communicate instructions.

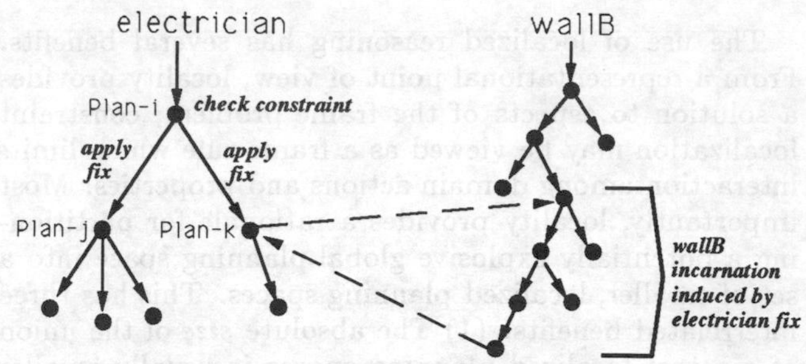

Figure 2: Region Search Trees

2.3 Plan Representation

The focus of regional search is to incrementally construct a *region plan*. Each region plan consists of a *local region plan* and a set of *subplans* (the region plans of its subregions). For example, if $R1 \subset R$ and $R2 \subset R$, the region plan for R will include a local region plan for R and region plans for $R1$ and $R2$. GEMPLAN associates all plan information with the smallest region that encompasses that information. This assures that plan information is visible to all relevant regions. The region plans of $R1$ and $R2$ will thus include all plan information that deals exclusively with $R1$ and $R2$, respectively. The local region plan of R will include plan information that deals specifically with activities in R or that pertains to relationships among R, $R1$, and $R2$ (and therefore cannot be associated strictly with $R1$ or $R2$).

2.4 Region Search Trees

Figure 2 depicts portions of planning search trees for the electrician and wallB regions of our sample domain. Each tree reflects search through a space of "plan construction" operations – i.e., it is a plan-construction search space (rather than a state search space). Each tree node is associated with the region plan constructed up to that point in the search, and each tree arc is associated with a plan modification or "fix" that transforms a region plan into a new region plan. Upon reaching a node, the planner must choose which region constraint to check next. (Thus, an implicit branching factor in the search space is the set of all relevant constraints at each node.) If the chosen constraint is not satisfied by the plan associated with that node, constraint satisfaction algorithms or "fixes" must be applied (there may be several fix algorithms for each constraint, as well as many possible solutions or "fixes" per fix algorithm), resulting in a set of new region plans at the next level down in the tree. A GEMPLAN fix typically adds new actions, relations, and variable bindings to a region plan, and may also generate new subregions. Deletion of plan information can only be accomplished by backtracking (this restriction will be lifted in the COLLAGE system). GEMPLAN uses, by default, a depth-first search strategy. It tries constraints in the order supplied by the domain specification, fixes in the order supplied by GEMPLAN's internal constraint mechanism, and backtracks only if all fixes fail for a particular constraint. However, since search should optimally be driven by domain-dependent information and the structure of the growing plan, GEMPLAN allows for flexible tuning of tree search. The order in which constraints and fixes are applied, as well as backtracking schemes, can be made context dependent.

2.5 Transfer Between Trees

In the current GEMPLAN system, transfer of control flow between regions occurs according to a fixed algorithm. Aside from assuring that each region is visited at least once to address goal constraints, transfer between regions generally occurs in response to information transmitted to the search mechanism by a fix. Suppose we are in *tree*(R). After applying a fix for one of R's constraints to R's region plan, the fix must return a subset of R's subregions, $R1, ..., Rm$, whose plans have been affected by the fix. The GEMPLAN search algorithm will then inhibit further search within *tree*(R) until *tree*($R1$)...*tree*(Rm) are all satisfactorily searched. As depicted in Figure 2, if electrician affects the subplan for region wallB via the introduction of new actions there, search within *tree*(electrician) cannot safely proceed until wallB's tree is searched and its constraints are rechecked and satisfied.

Notice how shifts between parent and child regions induce a partitioning on the child's search tree. We call these search fragments *incarnations* – search within the child is reinvoked or "reincarnated" each time the child's plan is modified in some way by a parental fix. Each time a child's tree is reincarnated, all of its affected constraints must be rechecked. One restriction on GEMPLAN's search control mechanism is that all search strategies (e.g., alternative backtracking schemes) must be applied within the confines of an individual incarnation. This greatly simplifies the problem of search consistency.

2.6 Global Correctness and Consistency

Two important challenges of localized search are making sure that all regional constraints are checked when they need to be (global correctness) and assuring that all regional search tree information is consistent (global consistency). This would be fairly straightforward if domain structure were strictly hierarchical. However, since we allow for regional overlap, added effort is required. For example, if a fix in *tree*(electrician) affects region wallA's plan, it is not enough to simply recheck wallA's constraints and return to *tree*(electrician). Region plumber's representation of wallA's subplan must also be updated within *tree*(plumber), and search must also eventually occur within *tree*(plumber) to recheck its constraints. We call this overall process *completion*.

Let us consider completion in more detail. When search within an incarnation for region R is terminated, all changes for that region must be reflected within the tree of every ancestor region A of R. This will involve update of subplans and other information relating to R at relevant nodes in *tree*(A). Assuming that the final plan for R's *preceding* incarnation was *Rplan*, the nodes to be updated will be precisely those that have information about *Rplan*. Next, some method must be used to ensure that A's search space is eventually reincarnated. This could be done via an auxiliary facility that keeps track of which regions must be checked. We are taking this approach in COLLAGE; the facility will fully control region incarnation and will also allow for parallel incarnation of regions.

In the current GEMPLAN system, the DAG formed by the inclusion relation $\subset$ must be completed by a spanning tree. This tree is then used as a guideline for controlling regional transfer. Each region, except some designated "top" region must have a parent via the $\subset$ relation or be artificially "assigned" a parent via the spanning tree. For example, gc, electrician, and plumber are not subregions of any enclosing region. Although they do not logically belong to another region as far as constraint applicability, we must make sure that each has a "parent" for search control purposes. We denote this pseudo-parental relationship by $\subset_p$ and choose gc as the "top" region, with electrician $\subset_p$ gc and plumber $\subset_p$ gc. Search initiates at the "top" region and transfers from parent to child only if $\subset$ or $\subset_p$ holds and if the child's region needs to be checked.

3 Example

We now clarify the preceding discussion with a simple planning scenario. Let us assume that the electrician, plumber, and wallA regions are associated with the following constraints:[1]

```
ELECTRICIAN CONSTRAINTS:
(1) action(install-socket(wallA,locA1))
(2) decompose(install-socket(W,L),
        {W.electprep(L) => W.insertsocket(L)})

PLUMBER CONSTRAINTS:
(1) action(install-pipe(wallA,locA1))
(2) decompose(install-pipe(W,L),
        {W.plumbprep(L) => W.insertpipe(L)})

WALLA CONSTRAINTS:
(1) (forall L)
    [(forall prep:{electprep(L),plumbprep(L)})
      pattern((prep)*=>)]
(2) fcfs([[electprep,insertsocket],
          [plumbprep,insertpipe]])
```

The first electrician constraint requires a socket to be installed in wallA. An action constraint simply results in the addition of an action to the plan.[2] The second constraint requires that each install-socket(W,L) action be decomposed into an electprep action followed

[1] This informal description is intended for didactic purposes only. A full GEMPLAN domain description requires specification of regional action types and domain structure, allows for specification and instantiation of region types, may include many more types of constraints, and may include various search heuristics. Capitalized tokens denote variables. Each variable has a scope limited to the constraint in which it is found. An action of form X.Y denotes an action Y occurring at location X.

[2] One way to introduce actions into the plan might have been via STRIPS-based goal conditions or preconditions. In this domain, it is more convenient to add the actions explicitly, since only one type of action is available for attaining the desired effect.

```
                    install-socket(wallA,locA1)
                                ∧
        electprep(locA1)   ⇒   insertsocket(locA1)
wallA:         ⇓                        ⇓
        plumbprep(locA1)   ⇒   insertpipe(locA1)
                                ∨
                    install-pipe(wallA,locA1)
```

Figure 3: A Construction Plan

by an **insertsocket** action at wall W, location L. The plumber constraints are similar. In this case, one pipe is to be installed in wallA. The two wallA constraints pertain to the coordination of the electrician and plumber actions at that wall. The first constraint states that all **electprep** and **plumbprep** actions at the same location must follow a certain pattern – they must be totally ordered by the temporal relation =>. The second constraint additionally requires that the electrician and plumber have access to the same locations of wallA on a first-come-first-serve basis. The constraint provides a set of action pairs and has the following semantics: any required execution ordering of the first actions in each pair (in this case, required orderings between **prep** actions) will determine the ultimate ordering of the second actions in each pair (the ordering of **insertsocket** and **insertpipe** actions). Since a total ordering is forced on all **prep** actions at the same location, this will force electricians and plumbers to insert their devices in common locations on a first-come-first-serve basis.

We now describe the construction of the plan in Figure 3. Reasoning begins at the "top" region gc, which, in this case, has no constraints of its own, but is responsible for invocation of the electrician and plumber search trees. In this case, electrician is invoked first and its first constraint adds the specified **install-socket** action into the electrician plan. Constraint 2 then decomposes this action into **electprep** and **insertsocket** actions at wallA, causing changes in the wallA subplan of electrician. Before search continues within *tree*(electrician), search within *tree*(wallA) must occur. Both wallA constraints are checked, but both are satisfied at this point. The newly completed incarnation of wallA therefore does not add any new information to the subplan for wallA associated with electrician, but the process of completion causes the new version of the wallA plan (that includes the changes made by electrician) to be inserted appropriately into nodes of *tree*(plumber).

All electrician constraints are now satisfied. Search returns to gc, which invokes search in *tree*(plumber). The plumber constraints cause the addition of the **install-pipe** action and its decomposition into the appropriate subactions at wallA. Search must now occur for the affected wallA region. This causes the actions **electprep(locA1)** and **plumbprep(locA1)** to be forced into some total order (**electprep(locA1) => plumbprep(locA1)** is chosen) and then, as a result of the second wallA constraint, a similar ordering is imposed on **insertsocket(locA1)** and **insertpipe(locA1)**. The new wallA plan is appropriately inserted into both

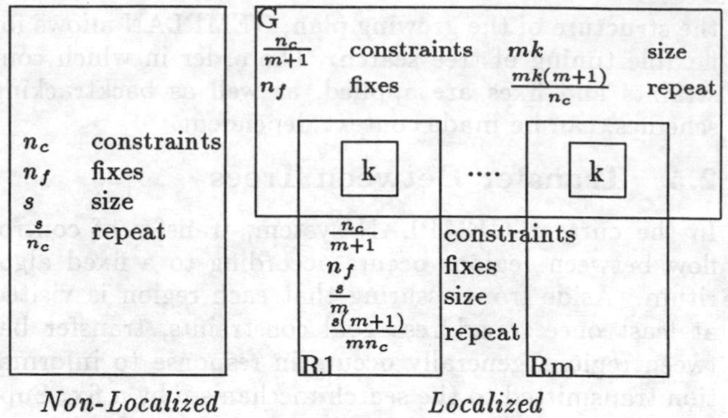

Figure 4: Non-localized and Localized Domains

tree(electrician) and *tree*(plumber) (due to completion). All plumber constraints are now satisfied and search returns to gc. The constraints within electrician are then rechecked (due to the changes at wallA), but they are still satisfied. Search then terminates successfully.

4 Complexity Analysis

It is clear that no general complexity result can be given for localized search – the size and complexity of the planning search trees for a particular problem will depend on the structure of the domain, the constraints associated within each region, the complexity of their satisfaction algorithms, the domain search heuristics, and the specific domain problem being solved. In order to provide some theoretical estimate of the benefits of localized search, however, we present a complexity analysis that compares search of a non-localized domain with search of a simple localized version of the same domain. We provide best- and worst-case search costs, assuming that constraint algorithms are either all constant, linear, quadratic, or exponential in cost (obviously, most domains will have a mixture of these).

Although our analysis is quite idealized, it is corroborated by the empirical results of Section 5 and jibes with our basic intuitions about the tradeoffs inherent in localized search. In particular, it is clear that the completion costs necessary for dealing with overlap are nontrivial. These include search-tree update of ancestral regions to maintain consistency, and possibly wasteful rechecking of affected regional search trees (for example, the rechecking of the electrician constraints at the end of the preceding scenario). The problem of needless rechecking of regional trees can be mitigated by maintaining tighter relevancy hooks between actions and constraints (which GEMPLAN optionally provides) to inhibit unnecessary constraint checking. However, the problem is impossible to avoid completely. On the other hand, needless rechecking would be worse in global search.

Our analysis is based on the non-localized and localized domain configurations depicted in Figure 4. For both domains, we assume a total of n_c constraints, n_f possible fixes for each constraint, and a final plan consisting of s actions. The cost of checking any constraint on a plan of size j is $c(j)$ and the cost of fixing a plan

complexity of c(i) and f(i)	*Non-Localized (best-case)*	*Localized (best-case)*	*Non-Localized (worst-case)*	*Localized (worst-case)*
constant (b)	$2bs$	$2b(s+mk)+C$	$b(n_c n_f)^s$	$b(m(\frac{n_c n_f}{m+1})^{\frac{s}{m}} + (\frac{n_c n_f}{m+1})^{mk}) + C$
linear (ib)	bs^2	$b(\frac{s^2}{m} + (mk)^2) + C$	$bs(n_c n_f)^s$	$b(s(\frac{n_c n_f}{m+1})^{\frac{s}{m}} + (\frac{n_c n_f}{m+1})^{mk}) + C$
quadratic (i^2)	$\frac{2}{3}s^3$	$\frac{2}{3}(\frac{s^3}{m^2} + (mk)^3) + C$	$s^2(n_c n_f)^s$	$\frac{s^2}{m}(\frac{n_c n_f}{m+1})^{\frac{s}{m}} + (mk)^2(\frac{n_c n_f}{m+1})^{mk} + C$
exponential (b^i)	$2b^s$	$2(mb^{\frac{s}{m}} + b^{mk}) + C$	$(bn_c n_f)^s$	$m(\frac{bn_c n_f}{m+1})^{\frac{s}{m}} + (\frac{bn_c n_f}{m+1})^{mk} + C$

Table 1: Complexity Results

of size j is $f(j)$. For the localized case, we assume the domain consists of m regions $R_1...R_m$ and a region G. The actions in the final plan are divided equally among the regions $R_1...R_m$, so that each builds a plan of size $\frac{s}{m}$. Each of the $R_1...R_m$ regions also contains a subregion consisting of k actions that overlaps with region G. Thus, G's region plan consists of mk actions. The n_c constraints of the original problem are evenly distributed among $G, R_1, ...R_m$ so that each region is associated with $\frac{n_c}{m+1}$ constraints. (Note that the "k" regions have no local constraints associated with them.)

Let us now consider the cost of a generic region search tree. For a region i, we assume there are n_{c_i} constraints, that each constraint has n_f fixes, and that the final size of the region plan is s_i. Because a constraint fix may violate previously satisfied constraints, constraints may need to be repeatedly checked and fixed. We call the number of times the search must cycle through the constraints the search "*repeat factor*." Assuming that a region i has a repeat factor of r_i, its tree depth is $r_i n_{c_i}$, with average depth to adding an action being $\frac{r_i n_{c_i}}{s_i}$. (Thus, we assume that at most one action is added per fix. In most domains, many actions may be added per fix.) We then assume an implicit search space that alternately branches due to choice of a constraint (the costs $c(j)$ accumulated due to constraint testing) and choice of a fix (the costs $f(j)$ accumulated due to constraint fixing). By "best-case search" we mean depth-first search without backtracking – i.e., the cost of one path from the root to the leaves of the search space. The cost of best-case search for region i is

$$\sum_{0 \le j \le s_i} \frac{r_i n_{c_i}}{s_i}(c(j) + f(j)).$$

In contrast, worst-case search cost measures the cost of searching the entire space:

$$\sum_{1 \le j \le r_i n_{c_i}} n_{c_i}^j n_f^{j-1} c((j-1) \ div \ \frac{r_i n_{c_i}}{s_i}) + n_{c_i}^j n_f^j f((j-1) \ div \ \frac{r_i n_{c_i}}{s_i}).$$

To compare the complexity of these formulae for the non-localized and localized cases, we must set the repeat factor r_i for each region. For this analysis, we let r_i be $\frac{s_i}{n_{c_i}}$ – that is, we assume that exactly one action is added per fix, that the size of the plan is larger than the number of constraints, and that the depth of the region tree is equal to the number of actions in the region plan. The complexities of all cases are summarized in Table 1. For all of the localized search cases, we must also add to the total cost of the search trees an additional completion cost C. Assuming that completion occurs each time an action is added within a region of overlap and that the cost of each completion operation is a function of the plan data structures that must be updated, C is $O(m^2k)$.

As can be seen, localized search is nearly always better than non-localized search – in most cases much better. The only exceptions are constant-complexity best-case search (when there is no reduction of search space size *nor* constraint algorithm cost) or when the cost of completion overshadows the cost of the search. The amount by which localized search wins over non-localized search is proportional to the amount by which s dominates both $\frac{s}{m}$ (the plan size of each of the subregions $R_1...R_m$) and mk (the plan size of G). Thus, increased decomposition is always worthwhile, except for the cost of increased overlap (reflected in the size of mk and the cost of completion C). The gains of localized search become exponential as the complexity of the constraint algorithms increases and the bushiness of the search space increases. These gains come from three sources:

1. The *size* of the search space. This size reduction become more significant as the bushiness of the search space (the amount of backtracking) increases.
2. The *cost* at each node. Even if the absolute size of the non-localized and localized search spaces are the same, expensive constraint algorithms need be applied to much smaller plans in the localized case.
3. The *search heuristics* provided by localization. Because of the semantic information provided by a localized domain description, the most relevant constraints tend to be applied at the right time, enabling a reduction in search space bushiness.

5 Empirical Results

All of our empirical experiences with GEMPLAN bear out the efficacy of localized search. Our largest application thus far is a building-construction domain which requires both resource allocation and temporal coordination. The application was used to test and compare a variety of localization configurations. In our study, all of the localized configurations were superior to the non-localized configuration. Even though planning for this domain manifested best-case search in both the localized and non-localized cases (there was no backtracking), GEMPLAN attains speedups of greater than 50% using the best decomposition. This speedup can be attributed to a reduction in the cost of the constraint algorithms rather than a decrease in search space size. Exponential speedups can be expected for domains with bushier search spaces and more complex constraint algorithms.

Test Case (49 actions)	*Number of regions*	*Overlap* <count,size>	*Weighted Sum* <total,overlap>	*Timing* total=constraints+search
non-localized	1	<0,0>	<8624,0>	110.08=77.38+32.70
localized(1)	24	<28,134>	<1544,104>	82.55=51.55+31.00
localized(2)	16	<5,32>	<2894,88>	76.55=58.40+18.15
localized(3)	19	<18,76>	<1834,88>	61.24=46.31+14.92
(97 actions)				
non-localized	1	<0,0>	<27354,0>	877.80=628.13+249.67
localized(1)	37	<52,236>	<4736,104>	503.02=354.65+148.37
localized(2)	28	<5,32>	<10602,88>	718.90=559.55+159.35
localized(3)	31	<35,102>	<5468,88>	435.30=345.27+90.03

Table 2: Empirical Results

Table 2 provides a variety of statistics about the tested decompositions (the system is written in Prolog and runs on a SPARC workstation). The "number of regions" column gives the total number of regions that have at least one constraint and one action in the final plan (this number corresponds to the $m+1$ factor in the complexity analysis). The "overlap" column gives two figures: an overlap *count* and an overlap *size*. The overlap count is the sum, over all regions of overlap, of how many parents each region of overlap has. To obtain overlap size, we additionally multiply the count for each region of overlap by the number of actions it contains. Overlap count and size provide good estimates of completion cost and are related to the mk factor in the complexity analsysis. The "weighted sum" column gives a pair of numbers: *total* and *overlap*. The total weighted sum is the sum, over each constraint check and fix that was performed, of the product of plan size and a constraint-difficulty weighting (ranging from 1 to 4). It thus gives a good measure of the constraint checking and fixing cost. The overlap weighted sum is the same sum over constraints belonging to regions of overlap. Finally, the "timing" column gives three numbers: the total CPU time in seconds, which is a sum of the time spent dealing with constraint application and the remaining time, spent mostly in search.

The table provides results for the creation of a 49-action construction plan and for a 97-action construction plan. Results are included for four domain decompositional strategies, with the 97-action plan simply having more walls, contractors, etc. The first strategy is non-localized. The localized(1) configuration is highly decomposed but also has significant amounts of overlap between regions. The localized(2) case has less localization and much less overlap. Case localized(3) has an intermediate level of both localization and overlap, and attains the best results in both cases.

As with our formal analytical results, these results show that increased localization provides increased benefit, except for the added expense due to regional overlap. However, notice that, in the 97-action case, localized(1) is faster than localized(2). This shows that, as plan size increases, the cost of dealing with overlap is overshadowed by search and constraint costs. Even though the size of the search space was not significantly different among the various decompositions (because there was no backtracking), search cost still increased with decreased localization. This is because the plan structures become unwieldy as plans become large and the search implementation is affected by the size of these structures.

6 Conclusion

This paper has described an algorithm for localized search, as well as complexity and empirical results that illustrate how localized search can provide substantial gains in performance. The idea is quite intuitive and natural, but has, surprisingly, not been a fundamental aspect of most AI systems. Its application to automated reasoning is vital if such systems are to meet the requirements of large, complex domains.

Acknowledgments

Lode Missiaen helped design and implement GEMPLAN's localized search algorithm and Anna Karlin assisted with the complexity results. John Bresina, Mark Drummond, Megan Eskey, Andrew Philpot, Monte Zweben, and the IJCAI reviewers provided useful comments.

References

[1] Bresina, J., Marsella, S. and C. Schmidt. "Predicting Subproblem Interactions," Technical Report LCSR-TR-92, LCSR, Rutgers University (February 1987).

[2] deKleer, J. "Exploiting Locality in a TMS," *AAAI-90*, Boston, Massachusetts, pp. 264-271 (1990).

[3] Fox, M.S., Sadeh, N., and C. Baykan. "Constrained Heuristic Search," *IJCAI-89*, Detroit, Michigan, pp. 309-315 (1989).

[4] Knoblock, C.A. "Learning Abstraction Hierarchies for Problem Solving," in *Seventh International Workshop on Machine Learning*, pp. 923-928 (1990).

[5] Korf, R.E. "Planning as Search: A Quantitative Approach," *Artificial Intelligence (33,1)*, pp. 65-88 (1987).

[6] Lansky, A.L. "Localized Representation and Planning," in *Readings in Planning*, J. Allen, J. Hendler, and A. Tate (editors), Morgan Kaufmann (1990).

[7] Lansky, A.L. "Localized Event-Based Reasoning for Multiagent Domains," *Computational Intelligence Journal, Special Issue on Planning (4,4)* (1988).

[8] Lansky, A.L. "A Representation of Parallel Activity Based on Events, Structure, and Causality," in *Reasoning About Actions and Plans*, M. Georgeff and A. Lansky (editors), Morgan Kaufmann, pp. 123-160 (1987).

[9] Missiaen, L. "Localized Search," Technical Note 476, AI Center, SRI International, Menlo Park, CA 94025 (1989).

[10] Wilkins, D.E. "Domain-independent Planning: Representation and Plan Generation," *Artificial Intelligence (22,3)* pp. 269-301 (1984).

Commitment Strategies in Planning: A Comparative Analysis

Steven Minton and **John Bresina** and **Mark Drummond**
Sterling Federal Systems
NASA Ames Research Center, Mail Stop 244-17
Moffett Field, CA 94035 U.S.A.

Abstract

In this paper we compare the utility of different commitment strategies in planning. Under a "least commitment strategy", plans are represented as partial orders and operators are ordered only when interactions are detected. We investigate claims of the inherent advantages of planning with partial orders, as compared to planning with total orders. By focusing our analysis on the issue of operator ordering commitment, we are able to carry out a rigorous comparative analysis of two planners. We show that partial-order planning *can* be more efficient than total-order planning, but we also show that this is not necessarily so.

1 Introduction

Since the introduction of non-linear planning over a decade ago (Sacerdoti, 1977), the superiority of non-linear planning over linear planning has been tacitly acknowledged by the planning community. However, there has been little analysis supporting this intuition. In this paper, we focus on one aspect of non-linear planning: the use of *partially ordered* plans rather than *totally ordered* plans. The idea has been that a partially ordered plan allows a planner to avoid premature commitment to an incorrect operator ordering, and thus improve efficiency. We analyze the costs and benefits of using partially ordered and totally ordered plans to implement different commitment strategies for operator ordering.

Why should we be concerned about an issue that is over a decade old? Since modern planners are not very different from early planners in their basic approach, the issue is still with us. In this paper, we address the issue by first considering a simple total-order planner, and from this planner we construct a partial-order planner which can have an exponentially smaller search space. Next, we show that a second, independent source of power is available to a partial-order planner, namely, the ability to make more informed planning decisions. The relationship between our two planners demonstrates the potential utility of a least commitment strategy. We also show that a partial-order planner based on Chapman's (1987) Tweak can be less efficient than our total-order planner, and we examine why this can happen.

2 Background

Planning can be characterized as search through a space of possible plans. A *total-order planner* searches through a space of totally ordered plans; a *partial order planner* is defined similarly. We introduce these definitions because the terms "linear" and "non-linear" are overloaded. For example, some authors have used the term "non-linearity" when focusing on the issue of *goal ordering.* That is, some "linear" planners, when solving a conjunctive goal, require that all subgoals of one conjunct be achieved before subgoals of the others; hence, planners that can arbitrarily interleave subgoals are often called "non-linear". This version of the linear/non-linear distinction is different than the partial-order/total-order distinction investigated here. The former distinction impacts planner completeness, whereas the total-order/partial-order distinction is orthogonal to this issue (Drummond & Currie, 1989).

We claim that the only significant difference between partial-order and total-order planners is planning efficiency. It might be argued that partial-order planning is preferable because a partially ordered plan can be more flexibly executed. However, this flexibility can also be achieved with a total-order planner and a post-processing step that removes unnecessary orderings from the totally ordered solution plan to yield a partial order. The polynomial time complexity of this post-processing is negligible compared to the search time for plan generation (Veloso *et al.*, 1990). Hence, we believe that execution flexibility is, at best, a weak justification for the supposed superiority of partial-order planning.

In order to analyze the relative efficiency of partial-order and total-order planning, we begin by considering a total-order planner and a partial-order planner that can be directly compared. By elucidating the key differences between these planning algorithms, we reveal some important principles that are of general relevance.

3 Terminology

A plan consists of an ordered set of *steps*, where each step is a unique operator instance. Plans can be *totally ordered*, in which case every step is ordered with respect to every other step; or *partially ordered*, in which case steps can be unordered with respect to each other. We assume that a library of operators is available, where each operator has preconditions, deleted conditions, and added conditions; each deleted condition must be a precondition. Each condition must be a non-negated propositional literal. Later, we consider how our results can be extended to more expressive languages.

A *linearization* of a partially ordered plan is a total order over the plan's steps consistent with the existing partial order. In a totally ordered plan, a precondition of a plan step is *true* if it is added by an earlier step and not deleted by any intervening step. In a partially ordered plan, a step's precondition is *possibly true* if there exists a linearization in which it is true, and a step's precondition is *necessarily true* if it is true in *all* linearizations. A step's precondition is *necessarily false* if it is not possibly true.

A *planning problem* is defined by a start state and goal state pair, where a *state* is a set of propositions. For convenience, we represent a problem as a two-step *initial plan*, where the first step adds the start state propositions and the preconditions of the final step are the goal state propositions. The planning process starts with this initial plan and searches through a space of possible plans. A successful search terminates with a *solution* plan, *i.e.*, a plan in which all steps' preconditions are necessarily true. The search space can be characterized as a tree, where each node corresponds to a plan and each arc corresponds to a plan transformation. Each transformation incrementally extends (*i.e.*, refines) a plan by adding additional steps or orderings. Thus, each leaf in the search tree corresponds either to a solution plan or a dead-end, and each intermediate node corresponds to an unfinished plan which can be further extended.

4 A Tale of Two Planners

In this section we define two simple planning algorithms. The first algorithm, shown in figure 1, is TO, a total-order planner motivated by Warren (1974), Tate (1974), and Waldinger (1975). TO accepts an unfinished plan, P, and a goal set, G, containing the preconditions of steps in P which are currently false. If the algorithm terminates successfully then it returns a totally-ordered solution plan. Note, there are two backtracking points in this procedure: operator and ordering selection. As used in step 4, the *last deleter* of a precondition c for a step O_{need} is a step O_{del} before O_{need} which deletes c, such that there is no other deleter of c between O_{del} and O_{need}. The first plan step is considered the last deleter if it does not add c and no other step before O_{need} deletes c.

Our purpose here is to characterize the search space of the TO planning algorithm, and the pseudo-code we give does this by defining a depth-first procedure for enumerating possible plans. All the algorithms described in this paper can also be implemented as breadth-first procedures in the obvious way, and in that case, all are provably complete (Minton *et al.*, 1991).

The second planner is UA, a partial-order planner, shown in figure 2. UA is similar to TO in that it uses the same procedures for goal selection and operator selection, and unlike TO in that its solution plans are partially ordered. Step 4 of UA orders steps based on "interactions". Two steps in a plan are said to *interact* if they

TO(P,G)

1. **Termination:** If G is empty, report success and stop.
2. **Goal selection:** Let c be a goal in G, and let O_{need} be the plan step for which c is a precondition.
3. **Operator selection:** Let O_{add} be an operator in the library that adds c. If there is no such O_{add}, then terminate and report failure. *Backtrack point: all such operators must be considered for completeness.*
4. **Ordering selection:** Let O_{del} be the last deleter of c. Insert O_{add} somewhere between O_{del} and O_{need}, call the resulting plan P'. *Backtrack point: all such positions must be considered for completeness.*
5. **Update goal set:** Let G' be the set of preconditions in P' that are not true.
6. **Recursive invocation:** TO(P', G').

Figure 1: The TO Planning Algorithm

are unordered with respect to each other and there exists a precondition c of one step that is added or deleted by the other.[1] The significant difference between UA and TO lies in step 4: TO orders the new step with respect to *all* others, whereas UA adds *only* those orderings that are required to eliminate interactions. It is in this sense that UA is *less committed* than TO.

Since UA orders all steps which interact, the plans that are generated have a special property: each precondition in a plan is either *necessarily* true or *necessarily* false. We call such plans *unambiguous*. This property yields a tight correspondence between the two planners' search spaces. Suppose UA is given the unambiguous plan P_{ua} and that TO is given P_{to}, one of its linearizations. P_{ua} and P_{to} have the same set of goals since, by definition, each goal in P_{ua} is necessarily false and if a precondition is necessarily false, it is false in every linearization.

Consider the relationship between the way that UA extends P_{ua} and TO extends P_{to}. Since the two plans have the same set of goals, and since both planners use the same goal selection method, both algorithms pick the same goal; therefore, O_{need} is the same for both. Similarly, both algorithms consider the same library operators to achieve this goal. Since P_{to} is a linearization of P_{ua}, and O_{need} is the same in both plans, both algorithms find the same last deleter as well.[2] When TO adds a step to a plan, it orders the new step with respect to all existing steps. When UA adds a step to a plan, it orders the new step *only* with respect to interacting steps. UA considers all possible combinations of orderings which eliminate interactions, so for any plan produced by TO, UA produces a corresponding plan that is less-ordered or equivalent. The following sections exploit this tight correspondence between the search spaces of UA and TO. In the next section we compare the entire search spaces of UA and TO, and later we compare the number of nodes actually visited under different search strategies.

[1] Note, a step that deletes c interacts with one that adds or deletes c according to this definition because a step's deleted conditions are required to be a subset of its preconditions.

[2] There is a unique last deleter in an unambiguous plan since two steps which delete the same condition interact, and thus, must be ordered.

UA(P,G)

1. **Termination:** If G is empty, report success and stop.
2. **Goal selection:** Let c be a goal in G, and let O_{need} be the plan step for which c is a precondition.
3. **Operator selection:** Let O_{add} be an operator in the library that adds c. If there is no such O_{add}, then terminate and report failure. *Backtrack point: all such operators must be considered for completeness.*
4. **Ordering selection:** Let O_{del} be the last deleter of c. Order O_{add} after O_{del} and before O_{need}. Repeat until there are no interactions:
   - o Select a step O_{int} that interacts with O_{add}.
   - o Order O_{int} either before or after O_{add}. *Backtrack point: both orderings must be considered for completeness.*

   Let P' be the resulting plan.
5. **Update goal set:** Let G' be the set of preconditions in P' that are necessarily false.
6. **Recursive invocation:** UA(P',G').

Figure 2: The UA Planning Algorithm

5 Search Space Comparison

Recall that a search space can be characterized as a tree. We denote the search space of TO by $tree_{to}$, and similarly the search space of UA by $tree_{ua}$. We show that for any given problem, $tree_{to}$ has at least as many nodes as $tree_{ua}$. This is done by proving the existence of a function $\mathcal{L}$ which maps nodes in $tree_{ua}$ to sets of nodes in $tree_{to}$ that satisfies the following two conditions.

1. For every node u in $tree_{ua}$, there exists a non-empty set $\{t_1, \ldots, t_m\}$ of nodes in $tree_{to}$ such that $\mathcal{L}(u) = \{t_1, \ldots, t_m\}$.
2. $\mathcal{L}$ maps distinct nodes in $tree_{ua}$ to disjoint sets of nodes in $tree_{to}$; that is, if $u_1, u_2 \in tree_{ua}$ and $u_1 \neq u_2$, then $\mathcal{L}(u_1) \cap \mathcal{L}(u_2) = \{\}$.

Let's examine why the existence of an $\mathcal{L}$ with these two properties is sufficient to prove that the size of UA's search tree is no greater than that of TO. Figure 3 provides a guide for the following discussion. Intuitively, we can use $\mathcal{L}$ to count nodes in the two search trees. For each node counted in $tree_{ua}$, we use $\mathcal{L}$ to count a non-empty set of nodes in $tree_{to}$. The first property of $\mathcal{L}$ means that every time we count a node in $tree_{ua}$, we count at least one node in $tree_{to}$; this implies that $\mid tree_{ua} \mid \leq \sum_{u \in tree_{ua}} \mid \mathcal{L}(u) \mid$. Of course, we must further show that each node counted in $tree_{to}$ is counted only once; this is guaranteed by the second property of $\mathcal{L}$, which implies that $\sum_{u \in tree_{ua}} \mid \mathcal{L}(u) \mid \leq \mid tree_{to} \mid$. Thus, the conjunction of the two properties implies that $\mid tree_{ua} \mid \leq \mid tree_{to} \mid$.

We can define a function $\mathcal{L}$ that has these two properties as follows. Let u be a node in $tree_{ua}$, let t be a node in $tree_{to}$, and let *parent* be a function from a node to its parent node. Then $t \in \mathcal{L}(u)$ if and only if the plan at t is a linearization of the plan at u and either both u and t are root nodes of their respective search trees, or $parent(t) \in \mathcal{L}(parent(u))$. Intuitively, $\mathcal{L}$ maps a node u in $tree_{ua}$ to all linearizations which share common derivation ancestry. This is illustrated in figure 3, where for each node in $tree_{ua}$ a dashed line is drawn to the corresponding set of nodes in $tree_{to}$.

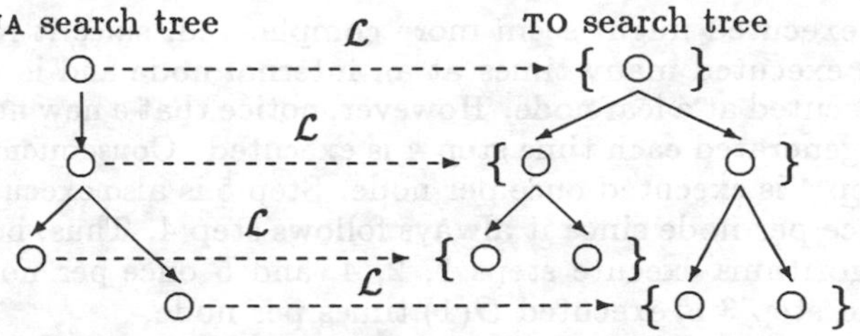

Figure 3: How $\mathcal{L}$ maps from $tree_{ua}$ to $tree_{to}$

We can show that $\mathcal{L}$ satisfies both of the properties by induction on the depth of the search trees. Detailed proofs are in the appendix. To prove the first property, we show that for every plan contained in $tree_{ua}$, all linearizations of that plan are contained in $tree_{to}$. This can be proved by examining the tight correspondence between the search trees of UA and TO. To prove the second property, we show that $\mathcal{L}$ maps nodes u_1 and u_2 at the same depth in $tree_{ua}$ to disjoint sets of nodes in $tree_{to}$: if u_1 and u_2 do not have the same parent, then the property holds; if they have the same parent, then the plans at u_1 and u_2 are distinct (by the definition of UA), in which case their linearizations are disjoint.

How much smaller is $tree_{ua}$ than $tree_{to}$? The mapping described above provides an answer. For each node u in $tree_{ua}$ there are $\mid \mathcal{L}(u) \mid$ distinct nodes in TO, where $\mid \mathcal{L}(u) \mid$ is the number of linearizations of the plan contained at node u. The exact number depends on how unordered the plan at node u is. A totally *unordered* plan has a factorial number of linearizations and a totally ordered plan has only a single linearization. Thus, the only time that the size of $tree_{ua}$ equals the size of $tree_{to}$ is when every plan in $tree_{ua}$ is totally ordered; otherwise, $tree_{ua}$ is strictly smaller than $tree_{to}$, and possibly exponentially smaller.

6 Time Cost Comparison

While the size of UA's search tree is possibly exponentially smaller than that of TO, it does not follow that UA is necessarily more efficient. Efficiency is determined by two factors: the time cost per node during search (discussed in this section) and the size of the subtree actually explored to find a plan (discussed below).

In this section we show that while UA can indeed take more time per node, the extra time is relatively small and grows only polynomially with the size of the plan. In our analysis, the size of the plan is simply the number of steps in the plan.[3] In comparing the relative efficiency of UA and TO, we first consider the number of times that each algorithm step is executed per node visited and then consider the time complexity of each step.

For both UA and TO, steps 1 and 2 are each executed once per node, and the number of executions of step 3 per node is bounded by a constant (the number of operators in the library). Analyzing the number of times step 4

[3] We disregard operator size and the number of conditions in any given "state", since we assume these are bounded by a constant for a given domain. An analysis that includes these factors does not affect our conclusion.

is executed might seem more complicated, since it may be executed many times at an internal node and is not executed at a leaf node. However, notice that a new node is generated each time step 4 is executed. Consequently, step 4 is executed once per node. Step 5 is also executed once per node since it always follows step 4. Thus, both algorithms execute steps 1, 2, 4, and 5 once per node, and step 3 is executed $O(1)$ times per node.

In examining the costs for each step, we first note that for both algorithms, steps 1, 2, and 3 can be accomplished in $O(1)$ time. The cost of step 4, the ordering step, is different for TO and UA. In TO, step 4 is accomplished by inserting the new operator, O_{add}, somewhere between O_{del} and O_{need}. If the possible insertion points are considered starting at O_{need} and working towards O_{del}, then step 4 takes constant time, since each insertion constitutes one execution of the step. On the other hand, step 4 in UA involves carrying out interaction detection and elimination. This step can be accomplished in $O(e)$ time, where e is the number of edges in the graph required to represent the partially ordered plan (Minton *et al.*, 1991). If n is the number of steps in the plan, then in the worst case, there may be $O(n^2)$ edges in the graph, and in the best case, $O(n)$ edges. To carry out step 5 may require examining the entire plan, and thus, for UA, takes $O(e)$ time and for TO, $O(n)$ time.

To summarize, UA pays the penalty of having a more complex ordering procedure (step 4), as well as the penalty for having a more expressive plan language (a partial order as compared to total order) which is reflected in the extra cost of step 5. Overall, UA requires $O(e)$ time per node, whereas TO only requires $O(n)$ time.

Step	Executions Per Node	TO Cost	UA Cost
1	1	$O(1)$	$O(1)$
2	1	$O(1)$	$O(1)$
3	$O(1)$	$O(1)$	$O(1)$
4	1	$O(1)$	$O(e)$
5	1	$O(n)$	$O(e)$

Table 1: Cost Per Node Comparisons

7 Overall Efficiency Comparison

The previous sections compared TO and UA in terms of relative search space size and relative time cost per node. The extra processing time required by UA for each node would appear to be justified since its search space may contain exponentially fewer nodes. To complete our analysis, we must consider the number of nodes actually visited by each algorithm under a given search strategy.

Consider a *breadth-first* search technique that explores the entire search tree up to the depth of the smallest solution plan. By the search tree correspondence established earlier, both algorithms find the first solution at the same depth. Thus, TO explores all linearizations of the plans explored by UA. We can formalize the overall efficiency comparison as follows. For a node u in $tree_{ua}$, we denote the number of steps in the plan at u by n_u, and the number of edges by e_u. Then for each node u that UA generates, UA incurs time cost $O(e_u)$; whereas, TO incurs time cost $O(n_u) \cdot \mid \mathcal{L}(u) \mid$, where $\mid \mathcal{L}(u) \mid$ is the number of linearizations of the plan at node u. Therefore, the ratio of the total time costs of TO and UA is as follows, where $bf(tree_{ua})$ denotes the subtree considered by UA under breadth-first search.

$$\frac{\text{cost}(\text{TO}_{bf})}{\text{cost}(\text{UA}_{bf})} = \frac{\sum_{u \in bf(tree_{ua})} O(n_u) \cdot \mid \mathcal{L}(u) \mid}{\sum_{u \in bf(tree_{ua})} O(e_u)}$$

The cost comparison is not so clear-cut for depth-first search, since TO does not necessarily explore all linearizations of the plans explored by UA. A node in a search tree is said to *succeed* if it is on a path to a solution, otherwise, it is said to *fail*. When a node in UA's search tree fails, all corresponding nodes for TO also fail. If a UA node succeeds, then some subset of the corresponding TO nodes succeed. If, under a depth-first strategy, UA and TO generate corresponding plans in the same order, then *(i)* for every failed node u that UA generates, TO generates all nodes in $\mathcal{L}(u)$ and *(ii)* for every UA node u that succeeds, TO generates at least one node in $\mathcal{L}(u)$. However, in actuality, UA and TO need not generate corresponding plans in the same order. In this case, while the search *spaces* correspond, there is no guarantee that the planners will explore corresponding subtrees. Nevertheless, the relative size of the subtree explored by TO under depth-first search can be *expected* to be proportional to the average size of $\mid \mathcal{L} \mid$, since the relative size of TO's full search space is proportional to this value.

This intuition is supported by empirical experimentation with depth-limited versions of UA and TO. In a blocksworld domain where *all* steps interact, UA tends to explore the same number of nodes as TO under depth-first search. On another version of the blocksworld, where the probability of two randomly selected steps interacting is approximately 0.5, UA tends to explore many fewer nodes. For example, on a representative problem, with a solution depth (and depth-bound) of eight, TO explored 8.0 times as many nodes as UA. This ratio tends to increase with solution depth; for a problem with solution depth of nine, TO explored 15.4 times as many nodes. Although UA required more time per node, in terms of total search time, UA ran 4.6 times faster than TO on the first problem and 9.0 times faster than TO on the second problem. The results under breadth-first search were also as expected: when all steps interact, UA and TO search exactly the same number of nodes, and when relatively few steps interact, UA explores many fewer nodes than TO. For example, in our low-interaction version of the blocksworld, on a problem where the first solution is found at depth seven, TO explored 4.8 times as many nodes as UA, and UA ran 2.8 times faster. We caution that this is a small-scale study, intended only to illustrate our theoretical results.

The performance of TO can be improved with the addition of dependency-directed backtracking. Although space does not permit analysis of this search strategy, we note that by using dependency-directed backtracking, TO will behave almost identically to UA. Specifically, when TO backtracks to a node, a dependency analysis can indicate whether or not the failure below was independent of the ordering decision at that node. Of course, this dependency analysis increases the cost per node.

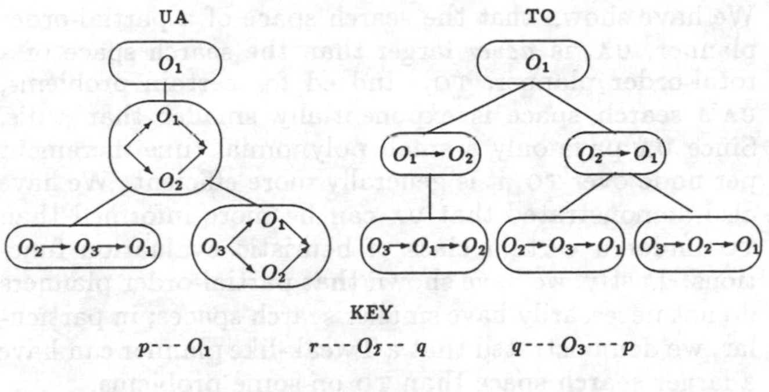

Figure 4: Comparison of UA and TO on an example.

8 Heuristic Advantages

It is often claimed that partial-order planners are more efficient due to their ability to make more informed ordering decisions. So far, we have shown that a partial-order planner can be more efficient simply because its search tree is smaller, independent of its ability to make more informed decisions. We now show that a partial-order planner does in fact have a "heuristic advantage" as well.

In the UA planning algorithm, step 4 arbitrarily orders interacting steps. Similarly, step 4 of TO arbitrarily chooses an insertion point for the new step. It is easy to see, however, that some orderings should be tried before others in a heuristic search. This is illustrated by figure 4, which compares UA and TO on a particular problem. The key in the figure describes the relevant conditions of the library operators, where preconditions are indicated to the left of an operator and added conditions are indicated to the right (there are no deletes). For brevity, the start step and final step are not shown. Consider the node in $tree_{ua}$ containing the plan with unordered steps O_1 and O_2. When UA introduces O_3 to achieve precondition p of O_1, step 4 of UA will order O_3 with respect to O_2, since these steps interact. However, it makes more sense to order O_2 before O_3, since O_2 achieves precondition q of O_3. This illustrates a simple planning heuristic: "prefer the orderings that yield the fewest false preconditions". This strategy is not guaranteed to produce the optimal search or plan, but tends to be effective and is commonly used.

Notice, however, that TO cannot exploit this heuristic as effectively as UA because it must prematurely commit to an ordering on O_1 and O_2. Due to this inability to postpone an ordering decision, TO must choose arbitrarily between the plans $O_1 \rightarrow O_2$ and $O_2 \rightarrow O_1$, before the impact of this decision can be evaluated.

In the general case, UA is more informed than TO by any heuristic h that satisfies the following property: for any UA node u and corresponding TO node t, $h(u) \succeq h(t)$; that is, a partially ordered plan must be rated at least as high as any of its linearizations. (Note that for unambiguous plans the heuristic function in our example satisfies this property.) When we say that UA is *more informed* than TO, we mean that under h, some child of u is rated at least as high as every child of t. This is true since every child of t is a linearization of some child of u, and therefore no child of t can be rated higher than a child of u. Furthermore, there may be a child of u such that none of its linearizations is a child of t, and therefore this child of u can be rated higher than every child of t. Assuming that h is a good heuristic, this means that UA can make a better choice than TO.

MT(P,G)

1. **Termination:** If G is empty, report success and stop.
2. **Goal selection:** Let c be a goal in G, and let O_{need} be the plan step for which c is a precondition.
3. **Operator selection:** Let O_{add} be either a plan step possibly before O_{need} that adds c or an operator in the library that adds c. If there is no such O_{add}, then terminate and report failure. *Backtrack point: all such operators must be considered for completeness.*
4. **Ordering selection:** Order O_{add} before O_{need}. Repeat until there are no steps possibly between O_{add} and O_{need} which delete c:
   Let O_{del} be such a step; choose one of the following ways to make c true for O_{need}
   - Order O_{del} before O_{add}.
   - Order O_{del} after O_{need}.
   - Choose a step O_{knight} that adds c that is possibly between O_{del} and O_{need}; order it after O_{del} and before O_{need}.

   Backtrack point: all alternatives must be considered for completeness.

   Let P' be the resulting plan.
5. **Update goal set:** Let G' be the set of preconditions in P' that are not necessarily true.
6. **Recursive invocation:** MT(P',G').

Figure 5: A Propositional Planner based on the MTC

9 A Less Committed Planner

We have shown that UA, a partial-order planner, has certain computational advantages over a total-order planner, TO, due to its ability to delay commitments. However, there are planners that are less committed than UA. In fact, there is a continuum of commitment strategies that we might consider. At the extreme liberal end of the spectrum is the strategy of maintaining a *totally unordered* set of steps during search, until there exists a linearization that is a solution plan.

Compared to many well-known planners, UA is conservative since it requires each plan to be unambiguous. This is not required by NOAH (Sacerdoti, 1977), NonLin (Tate, 1977), and Tweak (Chapman, 1987), for example. How do these less-committed planners compare to UA and TO? One might expect a less-committed planner to have the same advantages over UA that UA has over TO. However, this is not necessarily true. For example, we show in this section that Tweak's search tree is larger than TO's in some circumstances.[4] See figure 5 for a propositional planner, MT, based on Chapman's (1987) Modal Truth Criterion, the formal statement that characterizes Tweak's search space.

The proof that UA's search tree is no larger than TO's search tree rested on the two properties of $\mathcal{L}$ elaborated

[4] We use Tweak for this comparison because, like UA and TO, it is a formal construct rather than a realistic planner, and therefore more easily analyzed.

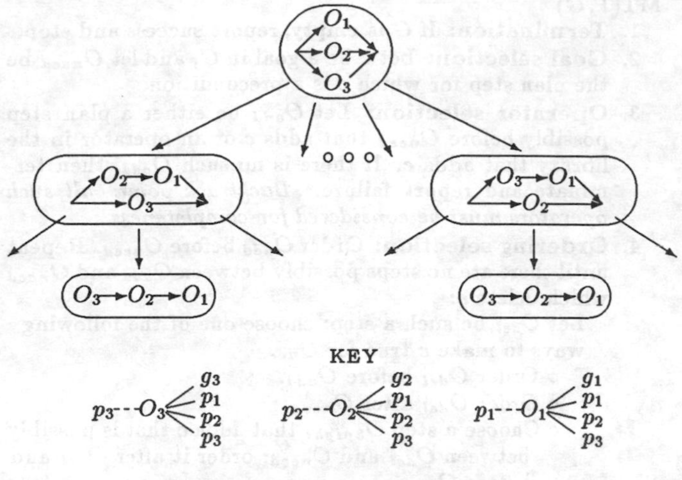

Figure 6: "Overlapping" plans.

in section 5. By investigating the relationship between MT and TO, we found that the second of these properties does not hold for MT, and its failure illustrates how MT can explore more nodes than TO (and consequently UA) on certain problems. The second property guarantees that UA does not generate "overlapping" plans. The example in figure 6 shows that MT fails to satisfy this property because it can generate plans that share common linearizations, leading to considerable redundancy in the search. The figure shows three steps, O_1, O_2, and O_3, where each O_i has precondition p_i, and added conditions g_i, p_1, p_2, and p_3. The final step has preconditions g_1, g_2, and g_3, but the start and final steps are not shown in the figure. The node at the top of the figure contains a plan constructed by MT where goals g_1, g_2, and g_3 have been achieved, but p_1, p_2, and p_3 remain to be achieved. Subsequently, in solving the precondition p_1, MT generates plans which share the linearization $O_3 \rightarrow O_2 \rightarrow O_1$ (among others). In comparison, both TO and UA only generate the plan $O_3 \rightarrow O_2 \rightarrow O_1$ once. In fact, it is simple to show that, under breadth-first search, MT generates many more nodes than TO on this example, due to redundancy (and also more than UA, by transitivity).

This example shows that although one planner may be less committed than another, it is not necessarily more efficient. In general, a partially ordered plan can represent a large set of linearizations, but of course, there can be many more partial orders over a set of steps than there are linearizations. A general lesson from this is that a search space should be defined so as to minimize redundancy whenever possible. In particular, partially ordered plans with linearization overlap should be avoided.

10 Concluding Remarks

By focusing our analysis on the single issue of operator ordering commitment, we were able to carry out a rigorous comparative analysis of two planners. In contrast, most previous work has focused on the definition of a single planner, and comparative analyses have been rare.[5]

[5] Soderland and Weld (1991) have very recently, and independently, carried out a comparative analysis of two planners, corroborating some of the results reported in Section 5.

We have shown that the search space of a partial-order planner, UA, is *never* larger than the search space of a total-order planner, TO. Indeed for certain problems, UA's search space is exponentially smaller than TO's. Since UA pays only a small polynomial time increment per node over TO, it is generally more efficient. We have also demonstrated that UA can be more informed than TO under a certain class of heuristic evaluation functions. Lastly, we have shown that partial-order planners do not necessarily have smaller search spaces; in particular, we demonstrated that a Tweak-like planner can have a larger search space than TO on some problems.

How general are these results? While our analysis has considered only two specific planners, the tradeoffs that we have examined are of general relevance. We believe these tradeoffs are manifested in other styles of planner, including temporal-projection planners (Drummond, 1989) and STRIPS-like planners such as Prodigy (Minton *et al.*, 1989). We conjecture that one can define a partial-order version of Prodigy, for instance, which corresponds to the original in the same way that UA corresponds to TO. The key difficulty in analyzing possible correspondences between such planners is establishing a mapping between the planners' search trees.

What about more expressive operator languages? We have defined TO and UA to use propositional operators, but many problems demand operators with variables, conditional effects, or conditional preconditions. UA and TO can be extended to use such operators so that the search space correspondence still holds. In such cases, the relative advantages of UA over TO will be preserved as long as the time cost of detecting possible interactions remains relatively small. For example, if library operators have variables, but are fully instantiated during the operator selection step, then our analysis holds without modification. The work required to demonstrate step interaction tends to increase with the expressiveness of the operator language used (Dean & Boddy, 1988; Hertzberg & Horz, 1989); nevertheless, we believe the cost of detecting interactions can often be kept low by using a conservative definition of step interaction.

The general lesson from this work is that partial-order planning *can* be better than total-order planning, but this isn't necessarily so. When designing a partial-order planner, one must understand the effect of plan representation on the planner's search space, the cost incurred per node, and sources of possible redundancy in the search space.

Acknowledgements: The TORPOR group thanks Mark Boddy for helping start this project, and Andy Philips, for implementing and helping design the algorithms. Thanks also to our various reviewers.

A Proof of Correspondence $\mathcal{L}$

Definition: A *plan* is a pair $< \theta, \prec >$, where θ is a set of steps, and $\prec$ is the "before" relation on θ, *i.e.* $\prec$ is a *strict partial order* on θ. Notationally, $O_1 \prec O_2$ if and only if $(O_1, O_2) \in \prec$.

Definition: A plan P' is a *1-step extension* of a plan P with respect to a planning algorithm, if P' can be produced from P in one invocation of the algorithm.

Property 1: For every node u in $tree_{ua}$, there exists a non-empty set $\{t_1, \ldots, t_m\}$ of nodes in $tree_{to}$ such that $\mathcal{L}(u) = \{t_1, \ldots, t_m\}$.

Proof: It suffices to show that if a plan P is contained in a node u at depth d in $tree_{ua}$, then each linearization of P is contained in some node t at depth d in $tree_{to}$, such that $t \in \mathcal{L}(u)$.
Base case: The statement trivially holds for depth 0.
Induction step: Under the hypothesis that the statement holds for depth n, we now prove, by contradiction, that the statement holds for depth $n+1$. Suppose that there exists a node u with plan $P_u = <\theta, \prec_u>$ at depth $n+1$ in $tree_{ua}$ such that $P_t = <\theta, \prec_t>$ is a linearization of P_u and there is no node t containing P_t at depth $n+1$ in $tree_{to}$ such that $t \in \mathcal{L}(u)$. Let $P'_u = <\theta', \prec'_u>$ be at node u', the parent of u; *i.e.*, P_u is a 1-step extension of P'_u with respect to UA. By the definition of UA, $\theta = \theta' \cup \{O_{add}\}$, where O_{add} added some c that is a precondition of some plan step O_{need} that is necessarily false in P'_u. Hence, $P'_t = <\theta', \prec'_t>$ is a linearization of P'_u, where $\prec'_t = \{(O_i, O_j) \mid (O_i, O_j) \in \prec_t \text{ and } O_i, O_j \neq O_{add}\}$; that is, P'_t is the result of removing O_{add} from P_t. Thus, by the induction hypothesis, there exists a node t' at depth n in $tree_{to}$ that contains P'_t, such that $t' \in \mathcal{L}(u')$.

For the supposition to hold, it must be the case that P_t is not a 1-step extension of P'_t with respect to TO. Since c is necessarily false in P'_u, it is false in P'_t, one of its linearizations. Likewise, since c is necessarily true in P_u, it is also true in P_t. Let O_{del} be the last deleter of c in P'_t. Then, since P'_t is a linearization of P'_u, O_{del} must be a last deleter of c in P'_u. Therefore, in P_u (by definition of UA), and hence in P_t (by definition of linearization), O_{del} is ordered before O_{add}, which is ordered before O_{need}. Hence, P_t is a 1-step extension of P'_t with respect to TO, which contradicts the supposition. Therefore, the statement holds for nodes at depth $n+1$. *Q.E.D.*

Property 2: $\mathcal{L}$ maps distinct nodes in $tree_{ua}$ to disjoint sets of nodes in $tree_{to}$; that is, if $u_1, u_2 \in tree_{ua}$ and $u_1 \neq u_2$, then $\mathcal{L}(u_1) \cap \mathcal{L}(u_2) = \{\}$.

Proof: By the definition of $\mathcal{L}$, if $t_1, t_2 \in \mathcal{L}(u)$, then t_1 and t_2 are at the same tree depth d in $tree_{to}$; furthermore, u is also at depth d in $tree_{ua}$. Hence, it suffices to prove that if nodes u_1 and u_2 are at depth d in $tree_{ua}$ and $u_1 \neq u_2$, then $\mathcal{L}(u_1) \cap \mathcal{L}(u_2) = \{\}$.
Base case: The statement vacuously holds for depth 0.
Induction step: Under the hypothesis that the statement holds for depth n, we prove, by contradiction, that the statement holds for nodes at depth $n+1$. Suppose that there exist two distinct nodes, u_1 and u_2, at depth $n+1$ in $tree_{ua}$ such that $t \in \mathcal{L}(u_1) \cap \mathcal{L}(u_2)$. Then (by definition of $\mathcal{L}$), $parent(t) \in \mathcal{L}(parent(u_1))$ and $parent(t) \in \mathcal{L}(parent(u_2))$. Since $parent(u_1) \neq parent(u_2)$ contradicts the induction hypothesis, suppose that u_1 and u_2 have the same parent u_0. Let $<\theta_1, \prec_1>$ be the plan at u_1, and let $<\theta_2, \prec_2>$ be the plan at u_2. These two plans are distinct 1-step extensions, with respect to UA, of the same (parent) plan. There are two cases to consider: either *(i)* $\theta_1 \neq \theta_2$ or *(ii)* $\theta_1 = \theta_2$ and $\prec_1 \neq \prec_2$. In the first case, since the two plans do not contain the same set of plan steps, they have disjoint linearizations, and hence, $\mathcal{L}(u_1) \cap \mathcal{L}(u_2) = \{\}$, which contradicts the supposition. In the second case, $\theta_1 = \theta_2$; hence, both plans resulted from adding plan step O_{add} to the parent plan. Since $\prec_1 \neq \prec_2$, there exists a plan step O_{int} that interacts with O_{add} such that in one plan O_{int} is ordered before O_{add} and in the other plan O_{add} is ordered before O_{int}. Thus, in either case, the linearizations of the two plans are disjoint, and hence, $\mathcal{L}(u_1) \cap \mathcal{L}(u_2) = \{\}$, which contradicts the supposition. Therefore, the statement holds for nodes at depth $n+1$. *Q.E.D.*

References

[Chapman, 1987] D. Chapman. Planning for Conjunctive Goals. *Artificial Intelligence*, Vol. 32.

[Dean & Boddy, 1988] T. Dean and M. Boddy. Reasoning About Partially Ordered Events. *Artificial Intelligence*, Vol. 36.

[Drummond & Currie, 1989] M. Drummond and K.W. Currie. Goal-ordering in Partially Ordered Plans. *Proceedings of IJCAI-89*, Detroit, MI.

[Drummond, 1989] M. Drummond. Situated Control Rules. *Proceedings of the Conference on Principles of Knowledge Representation and Reasoning*, Toronto, Canada.

[Hertzberg & Horz, 1989] J. Hertzberg and A. Horz. Towards a Theory of Conflict Detection and Resolution in Nonlinear Plans. *IJCAI-89*, Detroit, MI.

[Minton *et al.*, 1989] S. Minton, J.G. Carbonell, C.A. Knoblock, D.R. Kuokka, O. Etzioni and Y. Gil. Explanation-Based Learning: A Problem-Solving Perspective, *Artificial Intelligence*, Vol. 40.

[Minton *et al.*, 1991] S. Minton, J. Bresina, M. Drummond, and A. Philips. An Analysis of Commitment Strategies in Planning: The Details. Technical report 91-08, NASA Ames, AI Research Branch.

[Sacerdoti, 1977] E. Sacerdoti. *A Structure for Plans and Behavior*. American Elsevier, New York.

[Soderland & Weld, 1991] S. Soderland and D.S. Weld. Evaluating Nonlinear Planning. Technical report 91-02-03, Univ. of Washington, Computer Science Dept.

[Tate, 1974] A. Tate. Interplan: A Plan Generation System Which Can Deal With Interactions Between Goals. Univ. of Edinburgh, Machine Intelligence Research Unit Memo MIP-R-109.

[Tate, 1977] A. Tate. Generating Project Networks. In *Proceedings of IJCAI-77*, Boston, MA.

[Waldinger, 1975] R. Waldinger. Achieving Several Goals Simultaneously. SRI AI Center Technical Note 107, SRI, Menlo Park, CA.

[Veloso *et al.*, 1990] M.M. Veloso, M.A. Perez and J.G. Carbonell. Nonlinear Planning with Parallel Resource Allocation. In *Proceedings of the Workshop on Innovative Approaches to Planning, Scheduling and Control*, San Diego, CA.

[Warren, 1975] D. Warren. Warplan: A System for Generating Plans. Memo 76, Computational Logic Dept., School of AI, Univ. of Edinburgh.

AUTOMATED REASONING

Planning III

Parallel Non-Binary Planning in Polynomial Time

Christer Bäckström
Dept. of Computer Science,
Linköping University
S-581 83 Linköping, Sweden
email: cba@ida.liu.se

Inger Klein
Dept. of Electrical Engineering,
Linköping University
S-581 83 Linköping, Sweden
email: inger@isy.liu.se

Abstract

This paper formally presents a class of planning problems which allows non-binary state variables and parallel execution of actions. The class is proven to be tractable, and we provide a sound and complete polynomial time algorithm for planning within this class. This result means that we are getting closer to tackling realistic planning problems in sequential control, where a restricted problem representation is often sufficient, but where the size of the problems make tractability an important issue.

1 Introduction

A large proportion of earlier papers about planning focus either on implementation of planners, or on representation problems, using logic or otherwise, and do not address computational issues at all.

Among earlier work on planning complexity, Chapman [1987] has designed an algorithm, called TWEAK, which captures the essentials of constraint-posting nonlinear planners. TWEAK is proven correct, but does not always terminate. Chapman has proven that the class of problems TWEAK is designed for is undecidable. Dean and Boddy [1988] have investigated some classes of temporal projection problems with propositional state variables. They report that practically all but some trivial classes are NP. It should be noted, however, that they assume a non-deterministic domain where events actually occur only if their pre-conditions are fulfilled. Korf [1987] presents some complexity results for traditional search based planning. He shows how the complexity can be reduced for problems where subgoals are serializable or independent, and he also shows how macro-operators and abstract actions can reduce complexity under certain assumptions.

The majority of papers on temporal logics discuss representation of problems, and results about complexity and computability are almost non-existent. An implementation of a restricted version of one temporal logic, ETL, is reported by Hansson [1990]. His decision procedure solves temporal projection in exponential time, but is not guaranteed to terminate for planning. Recent work by van Beek [1990] presents some complexity results for some temporal ordering problems in a point algebra and a simplified interval algebra. These results are relevant, but not immediately applicable, to planning.

Chapman [1987] says: 'The restrictions on action representation make TWEAK almost useless as a real-world planner.' He also says: 'Any Turing machine with its input can be encoded in the TWEAK representation.' It seems that any useful class of planning problems is necessarily undecidable. However, we think that a planner that is capable of encoding a Turing machine has much more power than needed for most problems. It seems that TWEAK is too limited in some aspects, but overly expressive in other aspects. We think that finding classes of problems that balance such aspects against each other, so that they are decidable or even tractable, is an important and interesting research challenge. On the other hand, we should probably not have much hope of finding one single general planner with such properties. The research task is rather to find different classes of problems which are strong in different aspects, so as to be tuned to different kinds of application problems.

We have focussed our research on problems where the action representation is even more restricted than in TWEAK, but where we can prove interesting theoretical properties. Our intended applications are in the area of sequential control, a subfield of control theory, where a restricted problem representation is often sufficient, but where the size of the problems make tractability an important issue (see section 6).

In previous papers [Bäckström and Klein, 1990a, Bäckström and Klein, 1990b] we have presented a polynomial-time, $O(m^3)$ in the number of state variables, planning algorithm for a limited class of planning problems, the SAS-PUBS class. Compared to previous work on complexity of algorithms for knowledge-based or logic-based planning, our algorithm achieves computational tractability, but at the expense of only applying to a significantly more limited class of problems. Our general research strategy is to start with a restricted but tractable class of planning problems and to then gradually extend this class while establishing its properties after each such step. This is a very usual strategy in most disciplines of science, but is, unfortunately, not very common in AI. A similar strategy has been pursued by Brachman and Levesque [1984] who have studied the relationship between generality and tractability in knowledge representation languages.

The SAS-PUBS class constitutes the first step along the strategy just outlined, but this class is probably too simple to be of other than theoretical interest. However, even with very moderate extensions one would probably obtain problem classes that occur frequently in practice. This paper presents the *SAS-PUS* class, which is an extension of the SAS-PUBS class and which brings us closer to reality. We prove this class also to be tractable by presenting a sound and complete polynomial time planning algorithm for it. Furthermore, the algorithm only orders those actions that must necessarily be executed in sequence and allows for parallel execution of unordered actions.

2 Ontology of Worlds, Actions and Plans

This section defines our planning ontology with the main concepts being: world states, actions, and plans. Although presented in a slightly different way, the ontology is essentially as described by Sandewall and Rönnquist [1986]. For further explanation and intuition regarding action structures, the reader is referred to Sandewall and Rönnquists paper.

2.1 World Description

We assume that the world can be modelled by a finite number of *features*, or state variables, where each feature can take on values from some finite discrete domain, or the value *undefined*, *u*. For technical reasons, the contradictory value, *k*, is added. The combination of the values of all features is a *partial state*, and if no values are undefined the state is also a *total state*. If it is clear from the context, or if it does not matter whether a state is total or not, we simply call it a *state*. The order $\sqsubseteq$, reflecting information content, is defined on the feature values s.t. the undefined and contradictory values contain less and more information, respectively, than all the other values. These other values contain equal amount of information and are mutually incomparable.

Definition 2.1

1. $\mathcal{M}$ is a finite set of *feature indices*.
2. $\mathcal{S}_i$, where $i \in \mathcal{M}$, is the *domain* for the i:th feature. $\mathcal{S}_i$ must be finite. $\mathcal{S}_i^+ = \mathcal{S}_i \cup \{u, k\}$ where $i \in \mathcal{M}$ is the *i:th extended domain*. $\mathcal{S} = \prod_{i \in \mathcal{M}} \mathcal{S}_i$ is the *total state space* and $\mathcal{S}^+ = \prod_{i \in \mathcal{M}} \mathcal{S}_i^+$ is the *partial state space*.
3. $s[i]$ for $s \in \mathcal{S}^+$ and $i \in \mathcal{M}$ denotes the value of the i:th feature of s. The function $dim : \mathcal{S}^+ \rightarrow 2^{\mathcal{M}}$ is defined s.t. for $s \in \mathcal{S}^+$, $dim(s)$ is the set of all feature indices i s.t. $s[i] \neq u$. If $i \in \dim(s)$ then i is said to be *defined* for s. A state $s \in \mathcal{S}^+$ is said to be *consistent* if $s[i] \neq k$ for all $i \in \mathcal{M}$.
4. $\sqsubseteq$ is a reflexive partial order on $\mathcal{S}_i^+$ defined as
$$\forall x, x' \in \mathcal{S}_i^+ (x \sqsubseteq x' \leftrightarrow x = u \vee x = x' \vee x' = k)$$
$\langle \mathcal{S}_i^+, \sqsubseteq \rangle$ forms a flat lattice for each i.
5. $\sqsubseteq$ is a reflexive partial order over $\mathcal{S}^+$ defined as
$$\forall s, s' \in \mathcal{S}^+ (s \sqsubseteq s' \leftrightarrow \forall i \in \mathcal{M}(s[i] \sqsubseteq s'[i]))$$
so $\langle \mathcal{S}^+, \sqsubseteq \rangle$ forms a lattice. □

The lattice operations $\sqcup$, join, and $\sqcap$, meet, are defined as usual on the lattices $\langle \mathcal{S}_i^+, \sqsubseteq \rangle$ and $\langle \mathcal{S}^+, \sqsubseteq \rangle$.

2.2 Action Types and Actions

Plans are constituted by ***actions***, the atomic objects that will have some effect on the world when the plan is executed. Each action in a plan is a unique *occurrence*, or instantiation, of an *action type*, the latter being the specification of how the action 'behaves'. Two actions are of the same type iff they behave in exactly the same way. The 'behaviour' of an action type is defined by three partial state valued functions, the *pre-*, the *post-*, and the ***prevail-condition***. Given an action, the conditions of its type are interpreted as follows: the pre-condition states what must hold at the beginning of the action, the post-condition states what will hold at the end of the action, and the prevail-condition states what must hold during the action. One could think of the pre- and post-conditions as defining non-sharable resources and the prevail-condition as defining sharable resources, using operating systems terminology.

Every action type is subject to the following constraints: all conditions must be consistent, the pre- and post-conditions must define exactly the same features, the pre- and post-condition must not specify the same value for any of their defined features, and a feature defined in the pre-condition must not be defined in the prevail-condition. We also demand that two distinct action types must differ in at least one condition.

In order to distinguish actions of the same type we attach a unique *label* to each action. We also let an action 'inherit' the conditions from its associated action type.

Definition 2.2

1. $\mathcal{H}$ is a set of action types.
2. $b, e, f : \mathcal{H} \rightarrow \mathcal{S}^+$ are functions giving the pre-, post- and prevail-condition, respectively, of an action type.
3. $\mathcal{L}$ is an infinite set of *action labels*.
4. A set $\mathcal{A} \subseteq \mathcal{L} \times \mathcal{H}$ is a set of ***actions*** iff no two distinct elements in $\mathcal{A}$ have identical labels. □

2.3 Plans

An ordered set of actions is a ***plan*** from one total state to another total state iff, when starting in the first state, we end up in the second state after executing the actions of the plan in the specified order. The plan is ***linear*** if the set is totally ordered, and it is ***non-linear*** if it is partially ordered. In a non-linear plan, the order between two actions does not have to be specified if these actions can be executed in arbitrary order. The persistence handling essentially uses the STRIPS assumption [Fikes and Nilsson, 1971], and, since the formalism is very restricted, the frame problem [Hayes, 1981, Brown, 1987] is also avoided. The definition of plans is based on the relation $\longmapsto$ which defines how ordered sets of actions can transform one state into another.

Definition 2.3 The relation $\longmapsto \subseteq \mathcal{S} \times 2^{(\mathcal{L} \times \mathcal{H})} \times 2^{(\mathcal{L} \times \mathcal{H})^2} \times \mathcal{S}$ is defined s.t. if $s, s' \in \mathcal{S}$, Ψ is a set of actions, $a \in \Psi$, and σ is a total order on Ψ then $\longmapsto$ is defined as:

1. $s \overset{\emptyset,\emptyset}{\longmapsto} s$
2. $s \overset{\{a\},\emptyset}{\longmapsto} s'$ iff $b(a) \sqcup f(a) \sqsubseteq s$, $e(a) \sqcup f(a) \sqsubseteq s'$ and $s[i] = s'[i]$ for all $i \notin dim(b(a) \sqcup f(a))$
3. $s \overset{\Psi,\sigma}{\longmapsto} s'$ where $|\Psi| \geq 2$ iff $a_1, \ldots, a_n$ are the actions in Ψ in the order σ and there are states $s_1, \ldots, s_n \in \mathcal{S}$ s.t. $s = s_0$, $s' = s_n$ and $s_{k-1} \overset{\{a_k\},\emptyset}{\longmapsto} s_k$ for $1 \leq k \leq n$. □

Definition 2.4 A tuple $\langle \Psi, \rho \rangle$ is a *linear plan* from s_o to $s_\star$ iff Ψ is a set of actions and ρ is a total order on Ψ s.t. $s_o \overset{\Psi,\rho}{\longmapsto} s_\star$. Similarly, a tuple $\langle \Psi, \rho \rangle$ where ρ is a partial order on Ψ is a *non-linear plan* from s_o to $s_\star$ iff $\langle \Psi, \sigma \rangle$ is a linear plan for any total order σ on Ψ s.t. $\rho \subseteq \sigma$. □

A plan for a specific problem is *minimal* iff there is no other plan solving the same problem using fewer actions.

Definition 2.5 A plan $\langle \Psi, \rho \rangle$ from s_o to $s_\star$ is *minimal* iff there is no other plan $\langle \Phi, \sigma \rangle$ from s_o to $s_\star$ s.t. $|\Phi| < |\Psi|$. □

We say that two actions are *independent*, meaning they can be executed in parallel, iff any feature changed by one of the actions is undefined in all conditions of the other action and whenever both actions define the same feature in their prevail-conditions, they define the same value for this feature. We further say that a plan is a *parallel plan* if all its unordered actions are independent, and it is *maximally parallel* if no pair of independent actions is ordered.

Definition 2.6 Two actions a and a' are *independent* iff, for all $i \in \mathcal{M}$, all of the following conditions hold:

1. $b(a)[i] \neq u$ implies $b(a')[i] \sqcup f(a')[i] = u$
2. $b(a')[i] \neq u$ implies $b(a)[i] \sqcup f(a)[i] = u$
3. $f(a)[i] \sqsubseteq f(a')[i]$ or $f(a')[i] \sqsubseteq f(a)[i]$ □

Definition 2.7 A non-linear plan $\langle \Psi, \rho \rangle$ from s_o to $s_\star$ is a *parallel* plan iff all pairs of actions $a, a' \in \Psi$ s.t. neither $a\rho a'$ nor $a'\rho a$ are independent. □

Definition 2.8 A parallel plan $\langle \Psi, \rho \rangle$ is *maximally parallel* iff $\langle \Psi, \sigma \rangle$ is not parallel for any $\sigma \subset \rho$. □

3 Classes of Planning Problems

The class of planning problems according to our ontology so far is called the *SAS*, Simplified Action Structures, class.

We also want to talk about more restricted classes, so we define some useful properties that can be ascribed to problem classes. We say that a domain is *binary* if it has exactly two elements, $|\mathcal{S}_i| = 2$. The set of action types is *unary* if all action types change exactly one feature, *post-unique* if no two different action types can change a certain feature to the same value, and *single-valued* if no two action types have defined but different values of their prevail-conditions for the same feature.

The rest of this paper concentrates on the *SAS-PUS* class (PUS meaning post-unique, unary, and single-valued). The implications of these restriction are discussed in section 6. The SAS-PUS class is an extension of the previously presented SAS-PUBS class, which also requires the domains to be binary.

Definition 3.1 A planning problem is in the SAS-PUS class iff it is SAS and $\mathcal{H}$ is unary, post-unique and single-valued. □

4 SAS-PUS Planning

This section presents an algorithm for finding minimal plans for the SAS-PUS class and also states some theoretical results about the algorithm and the SAS-PUS class. The proofs are omitted because of the page limit, but they can be found in our report [Bäckström and Klein, 1991].

The definitions of most functions and procedures used in the algorithm should be obvious, but the following three might need some explanation.

FindActionPost(A,i,x) Searches the set A of actions for a member a s.t. $e(a)[i] = x[i]$ and which is returned if it exists. If such an a does not exist, the value **nil** is returned.

FindAndRemove(A,i,x) Like *FindActionPost* but also removes a from A.

Order(a,a',r) Adds ara' to the relation r.

Algorithm 4.1

Input: $\mathcal{M}$, a set of feature indices, $\mathcal{A}$, a set containing two actions of each type in $\mathcal{H}$, and s_o and $s_\star$, the initial and final states respectively.

Output: D, a set of actions, and r a relation on D.

Procedure *Plan*($s_o, s_\star$: *state*; $\mathcal{M}$: *set of*
  feature indices; $\mathcal{A}$: *set of actions*);
  var i : *feature index*; a, a' : *action*;
    D, P, T : *set of actions*; L : *list of actions*;
    r : *relation on* D;

Procedure *BuildChain*(s_F, s_T : *state*;)
  i : *featureindex*; A : *set of actions*; D, T : **in out**
  set of actions; r : **in out** *relation*);
  vars : *state*; a, a' : *action*; L : *list of actions*;
  begin{BuildChain}
    $L :=$ **nil**; $a' :=$ **nil**; $s := s_T$;
    while $s[i] \neq s_F[i]$ **do**
      $a :=$ *FindAndRemove*(A, i, s);
      if $a =$ **nil then fail**
      else
        Insert(a, D); *Insert*(a, T); *Concat*(a, L);
        if $a' \neq$ **nil then** *Order*(a, a', r)
        $a' := a$; $s := b(a)$;
    return L;
  end; {BuildChain}

  begin{Plan}
    $D := \emptyset$; $T := \emptyset$; $r := \emptyset$;
    for $i \in \mathcal{M}$ **do**

```
26        L := BuildChain(s_o, s_⋆, i, A, D, T, r);
27        P := Copy(D);
28        while T ≠ ∅ do
29            a := RemoveAnAction(T);
30            for i ∈ M do
31                if f(a)[i] ⋢ s_o[i] then
32                    a' := FindActionPost(D, i, f(a));
33                    if a' ≠ nil then Order(a', a, r)
34                    else
35                        L := BuildChain(s_o, f(a), i, A, D, T, r);
36                        Order(Last(L), a, r);
37                if f(a)[i] ⋢ s_⋆[i] then
38                    a' := FindActionPre(D, i, f(a));
39                    if a' ≠ nil then Order(a, a', r)
40                    else
41                        L := BuildChain(f(a), s_o, i, A, D, T, r);
42                        Order(a, First(L), r);
43                    a' := FindActionPre(P, i, s_o);
44                    if a' ≠ nil then Order(Last(L), a', r)
45            TransitiveClosure(r);
46        if "r is not antireflexive" then fail
47        return ⟨D, r⟩;
48    end; {Plan}
```

The main variables are D, T and r. D is a non-decreasing set of actions which will eventually be the set of actions in the plan, if the algorithm succeeds. Every action ever inserted into D is also inserted into T, and the use of this set will become clear later on. r is a relation on D, and it will eventually be the execution order of the plan.

The function *BuildChain* has the purpose of trying to find a, possibly empty, sequence of actions in A which, if executable, changes the i:th feature from $s_F[i]$ to $s_T[i]$. If such a sequence is found, it is removed from A and inserted into D and T. Otherwise, the algorithm fails.

The main body of the algorithm first calls *BuildChain* once for each feature i to find a sequence of action changing i from $s_o[i]$ to $s_⋆[i]$. D now contains all actions primarily needed to change s_o into $s_⋆$, but all of these actions do not necessarily have their prevail-conditions satisfied. The purpose of the while loop in the algorithm is to achieve that all actions have their prevail-conditions satisfied. Since all actions in T are eventually removed from T and processed by the body of the while loop, all actions in the final plan will have their prevail-conditions satisfied. For each action a in T, the body of the while loop tests, for each feature i, whether the prevail-condition of the current action is satisfied in s_o. Nothing need be done if this is the case, but, otherwise, the algorithm checks if there is already a sequence of actions in D that changes the i:th feature from s_o to $f(a)$. If there is such a sequence, it is ordered before a, and, otherwise, *BuildChain* is called to find such a sequence. Since the actions needed to satisfy the prevail-condition of a might interfere with the primary actions changing s_o into $s_⋆$, we must also assure that $f(a)[i]$ is changed into $s_⋆[i]$. This is done in the second half of the body of the while loop, and in a way analogous to the first part. The difference is that if *BuildChain* is called, it finds a sequence of actions changing $f(a)[i]$ into $s_o[i]$, not $s_⋆[i]$. The reason for this is that if $s_o[i] ≠ s_⋆[i]$, then there is

already a sequence of actions in D changing $s_o[i]$ into $s_⋆[i]$, and which is then ordered after the newly found sequence. After computing the transitive closure of r, it is tested for antireflexivity, and the algorithm fails if the order contains circularities. The algorithm is proven sound and complete.

Theorem 4.1 Given a SAS-PUS planning problem, if there is any plan solving the problem then algorithm 4.1 finds a minimal non-linear plan that solves the problem, otherwise it fails. □

The main reason that the algorithm can be so simple is that the set of action types is single-valued. This gives as a result that any action affecting a certain feature is either ordered before or after all actions defining this feature in their prevail-conditions. In other words, all actions defining a certain feature in their prevail-conditions can share action sequences achieving this value and assuring the final value. This is also the reason that no plan contains more than two actions of each type.

It can also be proven that the plan returned by the algorithm is maximally parallel.

Theorem 4.2 Algorithm 4.1 can be implemented to run in $O(m^3n^3)$ time using $O(m^2n^2)$ space where $m = |M|$ and $n = \max_{i∈M} |S_i|$. □

Both complexity figures can be reduced by more detailed analysis of the size of H, the difference in domain sizes, and other factors. It should also be noted that the only data structure requiring more than $O(mn)$ space is the output data, and that we are not likely to be interested in the transitive closure in practical applications.

The main explanation for the complexity result is that the set of action types is post-unique and single-valued. Post-uniqueness implies that there is never any choice of which action type to use. Single-valuedness implies, as was mentioned above, that no plan contains more than two actions of each type, which thus bounds the number of iterations of the main while loop.

5 Example

This section presents an example that fits in the SAS-PUS class. The example is a much simplified version of a LEGO[1] car factory which is used for undergraduate laborations in sequential control at Linköping University [Strömberg, 1990]. The task is to assemble a LEGO car from pre-assembled parts as shown in figure 1.

We represent the problem using three features defined as follows:

$s[1]$: 1: Chassis in chassis storage, 2: Chassis at workstation

$s[2]$: 1: Top in top storage, 2: Top at workstation, 3: Top on chassis

$s[3]$: 1: Wheels in wheel storage, 2: Wheels at workstation, 3: Wheels on chassis

Obviously, $M = \{1, 2, 3\}$ and states are written as $⟨s[1], s[2], s[3]⟩$. We assume that the set H consists of the

---

[1]LEGO is a trademark of the LEGO Group.

h	b(h)	e(h)	f(h)	Explanation
h_1	$\langle 1, u, u \rangle$	$\langle 2, u, u \rangle$	$\langle u, u, u \rangle$	Move chassis to workstation
h_2	$\langle 2, u, u \rangle$	$\langle 1, u, u \rangle$	$\langle u, u, u \rangle$	Move chassis to chassis storage
h_3	$\langle u, 1, u \rangle$	$\langle u, 2, u \rangle$	$\langle u, u, u \rangle$	Move top to work station
h_4	$\langle u, 2, u \rangle$	$\langle u, 3, u \rangle$	$\langle 2, u, u \rangle$	Mount top
h_5	$\langle u, u, 1 \rangle$	$\langle u, u, 2 \rangle$	$\langle u, u, u \rangle$	Move wheels to work station
h_6	$\langle u, u, 2 \rangle$	$\langle u, u, 3 \rangle$	$\langle 2, u, u \rangle$	Mount wheels

Table 1: Action types for the example

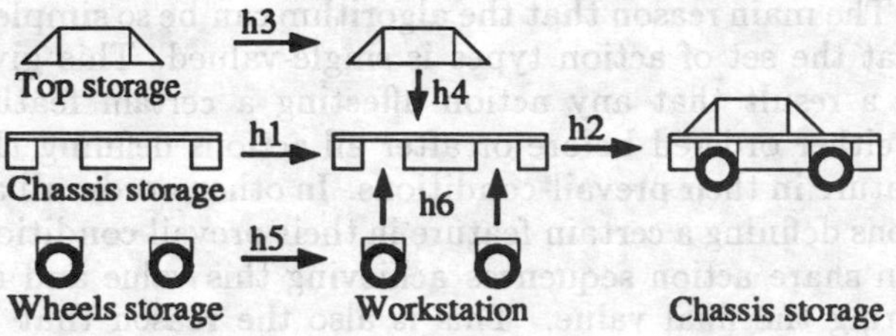

Figure 1: The LEGO car example

action types in table 1, and that the set $\mathcal{A}$ is $\{a_1, \ldots, a_{12}\}$ where a_i and a_{i+6} are of type h_i for $1 \leq i \leq 6$.

We also assume that the initial state is $s_o = \langle 1, 1, 1 \rangle$, all parts in storage, and the final state is $s_\star = \langle 1, 3, 3 \rangle$, an assembled car in the chassis storage.

The algorithm first calls *BuildChain* once for each $i \in \mathcal{M}$ to change $s_o[i]$ into $s_\star[i]$. *BuildChain* finds the empty sequence for feature 1, and the sequences a_3, a_4 and a_5, a_6 for features 2 and 3, respectively. Now, $\mathcal{A} = \{a_1, a_2, a_7, \ldots, a_{12}\}$, $D = T = \{a_3, a_4, a_5, a_6\}$ and r consists of $a_2 r a_4$ and $a_5 r a_6$.

The actions in T, plus those added to T during the following process, are removed one at a time and processed by the while loop. a_3 and a_5 fall straight through the loop body since their prevail-conditions are trivially satisfied. The prevail-condition of a_4 is not satisfied in the initial state, and there are no actions in D providing the prevail-condition of a_4. *BuildChain* is thus called, and it returns the action a_1 which changes the 1st feature to satisfy the prevail-condition of a_4. Similarly, *BuildChain* finds the action a_2 which assures the desired final value of this feature. Both these actions are inserted into D and T, and $a_1 r a_4$ and $a_4 r a_2$ are inserted into r. The action a_6 has the same prevail-condition as a_4, so there are already actions, namely a_1 and a_2, in D that provide its prevail-condition and assures the final value of the 1st feature. No actions are inserted into D, but r is extended with $a_1 r a_6$ and $a_6 r a_2$. The actions a_1 and a_2 are also removed from T, but their prevail-conditions are trivially satisfied.

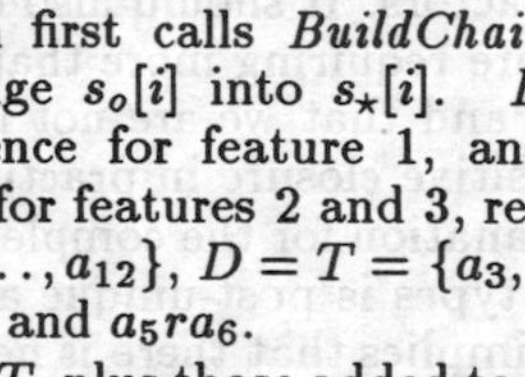

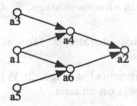

Figure 2: The plan for the example (transitive arcs omitted).

The algorithm then computes the transitive closure of r, and, since r is anti-reflexive, it succeeds and returns the plan $\langle D, r \rangle$, where D is $\{a_1, \ldots, a_6\}$ and r is as depicted in figure 2.

6 Discussion

The restriction that $\mathcal{H}$ be unary is serious for planning problems where two or more features can change simultaneously, but it is not always the same combinations of features that change simultaneously. Allowing non-binary domains does not help much in this case. Although one could represent several feature domains as one multi-valued feature, this would most likely violate the restrictions on action types in the SAS class. Post-uniqueness need not be a very limiting restriction for applications where there is little or no choice what plan to use, and where the size of the problem is the main difficulty when planning. However, for problems where $\mathcal{H}$ is non-unary or not single-valued, the major problem can be to choose between several different ways of achieving the goal. In this case, it will usually be impossible to make a post-unique formalization of the problem. The most serious restriction for the majority of practical applications is, in our opinion, the restriction that $\mathcal{H}$ is single-valued. As an example, requiring single-valuedness prevents us from modelling a problem where one action type requires a certain valve to be open and some other action type requires the same valve to be closed in their prevail-conditions.

The class one gets when relaxing the single-valuedness restriction is likely to be very interesting from a practical point of view. This class is conjectured sufficient for representing some interesting classes of real-world problems in *sequential control*, a subfield of *discrete event systems* within control theory. Examples of application areas are process plants and automated manufacturing. A particularly interesting problem here is to restart a process after a break-down or an emergency stop. After such an event, the process may be in anyone of a very large number of states, and it is not realistic to have precompiled plans for how to get the process back to normal again from any such state. Restarting is usually done manually and often by trial-and-error, and it is thus an application where automated planning is very relevant. It is interesting to note that such plans are complex because of their size, not because of complex actions. A process plant like a paper mill can have tens of thousands of sensors and actuators, so the number of features can be very large. It is easy to realize that the complexity issues are very important in this kind of applications.

Since single-valuedness seems to be the most serious restriction, it would be natural to try to eliminate that restriction first. Unfortunately, it can be shown that the resulting class of problems is intractable. However, this is because the plans themselves are of exponential size in the worst case, and such plans are unlikely to be of practical interest. We believe that it is possible to replace single-valuedness with other restrictions that are fulfilled for many practical problems, but which reduces the complexity drastically, and we are currently investigating such restrictions.

It would also be interesting to try to combine results along the line in this paper with the work on extended actions structures, allowing interdependent parallel actions or interval-valued features [Bäckström, 1988a, Bäckström, 1988b, Bäckström, 1988c].

7 Conclusion

We have identified a class of deterministic planning problems, the SAS-PUS class, which allows non-binary state variables and parallel actions. We have also presented a sound and complete polynomial time algorithm for finding minimal plans in this class. This result provides a kind of lower bound for planning; at least this class of problems is tractable. Since the SAS-PUS class is an extension of the previously presented SAS-PUBS class, we have managed to take a step upwards in expressibility while retaining tractability.

References

[Bäckström, 1988a] Christer Bäckström. Action structures with implicit coordination. In *Proceedings of the Third International Conference on Artificial Intelligence: Methodology, Systems, Applications (AIMSA-88)*, pages 103–110, Varna, Bulgaria, September 1988. North-Holland.

[Bäckström, 1988b] Christer Bäckström. Reasoning about interdependent actions. Licentiate Thesis 139, Department of Computer and Information Science, Linköping University, Linköping, Sweden, June 1988.

[Bäckström, 1988c] Christer Bäckström. A representation of coordinated actions characterized by interval valued conditions. In *Proceedings of the Third International Symposium on Methodologies for Intelligent systems (ISMIS-88)*, pages 220–229, Torino, Italy, October 1988. North-Holland.

[Bäckström and Klein, 1990a] Christer Bäckström and Inger Klein. Planning in polynomial time: The SAS-PUBS class. Research Report LiTH-IDA-R-90-16, Department of Computer and Information Science, Linköping University, Linköping, Sweden, August 1990.

[Bäckström and Klein, 1990b] Christer Bäckström and Inger Klein. Planning in polynomial time. In *Expert Systems in Engineering: Principles and Applications. International Workshop.*, pages 103–118, Vienna, Austria, September 1990. Springer.

[Bäckström and Klein, 1991] Christer Bäckström and Inger Klein. Parallel non-binary planning in polynomial time: The SAS-PUS class. Research Report LiTH-IDA-R-91-11, Department of Computer and Information Science, Linköping University, Linköping, Sweden, April 1991.

[van Beek, 1990] Peter van Beek. Reasoning about qualitative temporal information. In *Proceedings of the Eighth National Conference on Artificial Intelligence (AAAI-90)*, pages 728–734, Boston, Massachussettes, August 1990. MIT Press.

[Brachman and Levesque, 1984] Ronald J Brachman and Hector J Levesque. The tractability of subsumption in frame-based description languages. In *Proceedings of the Fourth National Conference on Artificial Intelligence (AAAI-84)*, pages 34–37, Austin, Texas, 1984.

[Brown, 1987] Frank Brown, editor. *The Frame Problem in Artificial Intelligence, Proceedings of the 1987 Workshop*, Lawrence, Kansas, April 1987. Morgan Kaufman.

[Chapman, 1987] David Chapman. Planning for conjunctive goals. *Artificial Intelligence*, 32:333–377, 1987.

[Dean and Boddy, 1988] Thomas Dean and Mark Boddy. Reasoning about partially ordered events. *Artificial Intelligence*, 36:375–399, 1988.

[Fikes and Nilsson, 1971] Richard E Fikes and Nils J Nilsson. Strips: A new approach to the application of theorem proving to problem solving. *Artificial Intelligence*, 2:189–208, 1971.

[Hansson, 1990] Christer Hansson. A prototype system for logical reasoning about time and action. Licentiate Thesis 203, Department of Computer and Information Science, Linköping University, Linköping, Sweden, January 1990.

[Hayes, 1981] Patrick J Hayes. The frame problem and related problems in artificial intelligence. In Bonnie Lynn Webber and Nils J. Nilsson, editors, *Readings in Artificial Intelligence*, pages 223–230. Morgan Kaufman, 1981.

[Korf, 1987] Richard E Korf. Planning as search: A quantitative approach. *Artificial Intelligence*, 33:65–88, 1987.

[Sandewall and Rönnquist, 1986] Erik Sandewall and Ralph Rönnquist. A representation of action structures. In *Proceedings of the Fifth National Conference on Artificial Intelligence (AAAI-86)*, pages 89–97, Philadelphia, Pennsylvania, August 1986. Morgan Kaufman.

[Strömberg, 1990] Jan-Erik Strömberg. Styrning av LEGO-bilfabrik. 2nd revised edition. Department of Electrical Engineering, Linköping University, February 1990.

Complexity Results for Planning

Tom Bylander
Laboratory for Artificial Intelligence Research
Department of Computer and Information Science
The Ohio State University
Columbus, OH 43210
U. S. A.

Abstract

I describe several computational complexity results for planning, some of which identify tractable planning problems. The model of planning, called "propositional planning," is simple—conditions within operators are literals with no variables allowed. The different planning problems are defined by different restrictions on the preconditions and postconditions of operators. The main results are: Propositional planning is PSPACE-complete, even if operators are restricted to two positive (non-negated) preconditions and two postconditions, or if operators are restricted to one postcondition (with any number of preconditions). It is NP-complete if operators are restricted to positive postconditions, even if operators are restricted to one precondition and one positive postcondition. It is tractable in a few restricted cases, one of which is if each operator is restricted to positive preconditions and one postcondition. The blocks-world problem, slightly modified, is a subproblem of this restricted planning problem.

1 Introduction

If the relationship between intelligence and computation is taken seriously, then intelligence cannot be explained by intractable theories because no intelligent creature has the time to perform intractable computations. Nor can intractable theories provide any guarantees about the performance of engineered systems. Presumably, robots don't have the time to perform intractable computations either.

Of course, heuristic theories are a valid approach if partial or approximate solutions are acceptable. However, my purpose is not to consider the relative merits of heuristic theories and tractable theories. Instead, I shall focus on formulating tractable planning problems.

Planning is the reasoning task of finding a sequence of operators that achieve a goal from a given initial state.

*This research has been supported in part by DARPA/AFOSR contract F49620-89-C-0110 and AFOSR grant 89-0250.

It is well-known that planning is intractable in general, and that several obstacles stand in the way [Chapman, 1987]. However, there are few results that provide clear dividing lines between tractable and intractable planning. Below, I clarify a few of these dividing lines by analyzing the computational complexity of a planning problem and a variety of restricted versions, some of which are tractable.

The model of planning, called "propositional planning," is impoverished compared to working planners. It is intended to be a tool for theoretical analysis rather than programming convenience. Preconditions and postconditions of operators are limited to being literals, i.e., letters or their negations. An initial state then can be represented as a finite set of letters, indicating that the corresponding conditions are initially true, and that all other relevant conditions are initially false. A goal is represented by two sets of conditions, i.e., the goal is to make the first set of conditions true and the other set false. For convenience, these are called positive and negative goals, respectively. Operators in this model do not have any variables or indirect side effects.

Different planning problems can be defined by different constraints on the number and kind of pre- and postconditions. Figure 1 illustrates the results, showing which planning problems are PSPACE-complete, NP-hard (but in PSPACE), NP-complete, and polynomial.[1] These results can be summarized as follows:

> Propositional planning is PSPACE-complete even if each operator is limited to one postcondition (with any number of preconditions).
>
> Propositional planning is PSPACE-complete even if each operator is limited to two positive (non-negated) preconditions and two postconditions.
>
> It is NP-hard if each operator is restricted to one positive precondition and two postconditions.
>
> It is NP-complete if operators are restricted to positive postconditions, even if operators are restricted to one precondition and one positive postcondition.

[1] A problem is in PSPACE if it can be solved in polynomial space. As is customary, it is assumed that PSPACE-complete problems are harder than NP-complete problems, which in turn are harder than polynomial problems. However, even $P \neq PSPACE$ is not yet proven.

It is polynomial if each operator is restricted to positive preconditions and one postcondition. The blocks-world problem, slightly modified, is a subclass of this restricted planning problem.

It is polynomial if each operator has one precondition and if the number of goals is bounded by a constant.

It is polynomial if each operator is restricted to no preconditions.

One additional box in the figure identifies a commonality between four of the problems.[2]

The remainder of this paper is organized as follows. First, I describe previous results on the complexity of planning. Then, propositional planning is defined. Next, I demonstrate the complexity results and show how the blocks world is covered by one of the results. Finally, I discuss the impact of these results on the search for tractable planning.

2 Previous Results

The literature on planning is voluminous, and no attempt to properly survey the planning literature is attempted here. Instead, the reader is referred to Allen et al. [1990] and Hendler et al. [1990]. Despite the large literature, results on computational complexity are sparse. In turn, I discuss previous results from Dean and Boddy [1987], Korf [1987], and Chapman [1987].

Dean and Boddy [1987] analyze the complexity of temporal projection—given a partial ordering of events and causal rules triggered by events, determine what conditions must be true after each event. Their formalization of temporal projection shares many features with planning, e.g., their causal rules contain antecedent conditions (preconditions) and added and deleted conditions (postconditions). In fact, the notation for propositional planning is mostly borrowed from Dean and Boddy. However, they only consider problems of prediction in which a partial ordering of events is given, whereas the equivalent planning problem would be to find some ordering of any set of events that achieves some set of conditions.

Korf (1987) considers how various global properties of planning problems (e.g., serializable subgoals, operator decomposability, abstraction) affect the complexity of using problem space search to find plans. In contrast, I focus exclusively on local properties of operators. However, except for Korf's own analysis of operator decomposability [Korf, 1985], neither he nor I describe the relationship from these properties of planning problems to the properties of operators. Clearly, this is a "gap" that future work should address.

[2]The following are other results not judged to be as interesting, but are included here for completeness. Propositional planning is NP-complete if each operator is restricted to positive preconditions and negative postconditions, even if restricted to one positive precondition and two negative postconditions. It is polynomial in the previous cases if the number of goals is bounded by a constant. It is polynomial if each operator is restricted to positive preconditions and positive postconditions.

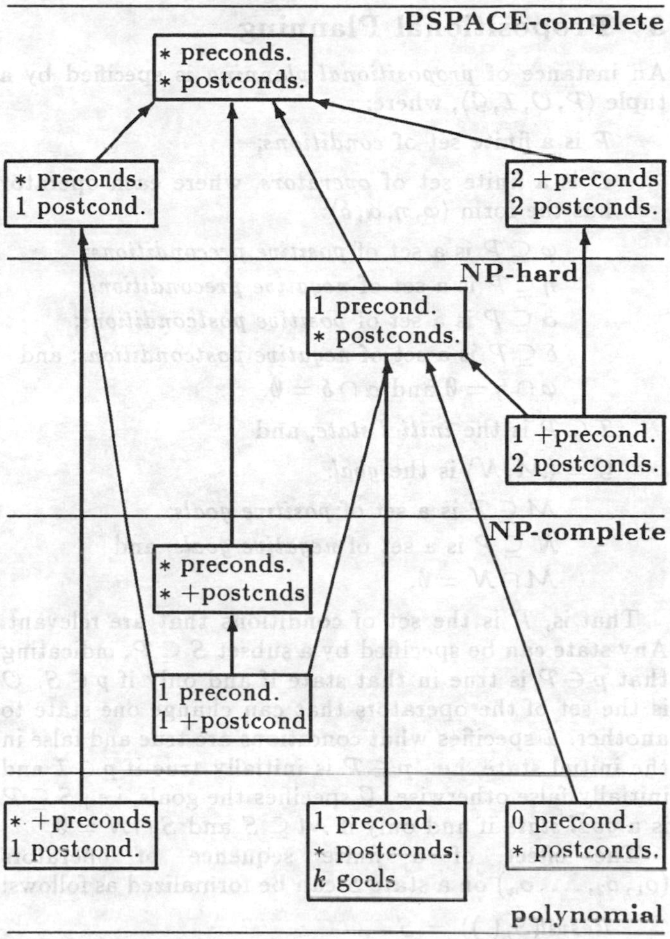

Figure 1: Complexity Results for Hierarchy of Propositional Planning Problems

Perhaps the most important complexity results for planning are due to Chapman's analysis of his planner TWEAK [Chapman, 1987]. Because virtually all other planners are as expressive as TWEAK, his results have wide applicability. TWEAK's representation includes the following features. The preconditions and postconditions of an operator schema are finite sets of "propositions." A proposition is represented by a tuple of elements, which may be constants or variables, and can be negated. A postcondition of an operator can contain variables not specified by any precondition of the operator, which in effect allows creation of new constants.

Chapman proved that planning is undecidable and so clearly demonstrated the difficulty of planning in general, but it is not obvious what features of TWEAK's representation are to blame for the complexity. What happens to the complexity, for example, if postconditions cannot introduce new variables? What happens if the size of states are bounded for any given instance of a planning problem? Are there any interesting restricted planning problems that are tractable? By considering a model of planning with considerably fewer features, the following analysis begins to address these questions.

3 Propositional Planning

An instance of *propositional planning* is specified by a tuple $\langle \mathcal{P}, \mathcal{O}, \mathcal{I}, \mathcal{G} \rangle$, where:

$\mathcal{P}$ is a finite set of *conditions*;

$\mathcal{O}$ is a finite set of *operators*, where each operator has the form $\langle \varphi, \eta, \alpha, \delta \rangle$:

- $\varphi \subseteq \mathcal{P}$ is a set of *positive preconditions*;
- $\eta \subseteq \mathcal{P}$ is a set of *negative preconditions*;
- $\alpha \subseteq \mathcal{P}$ is a set of *positive postconditions*;
- $\delta \subseteq \mathcal{P}$ is a set of *negative postconditions*; and
- $\varphi \cap \eta = \emptyset$ and $\alpha \cap \delta = \emptyset$.

$\mathcal{I} \subseteq \mathcal{P}$ is the *initial state*; and

$\mathcal{G} = \langle \mathcal{M}, \mathcal{N} \rangle$ is the *goal*:

- $\mathcal{M} \subseteq \mathcal{P}$ is a set of *positive goals*;
- $\mathcal{N} \subseteq \mathcal{P}$ is a set of *negative goals*; and
- $\mathcal{M} \cap \mathcal{N} = \emptyset$.

That is, $\mathcal{P}$ is the set of conditions that are relevant. Any state can be specified by a subset $S \subseteq \mathcal{P}$, indicating that $p \in \mathcal{P}$ is true in that state if and only if $p \in S$. $\mathcal{O}$ is the set of the operators that can change one state to another. $\mathcal{I}$ specifies what conditions are true and false in the initial state, i.e., $p \in \mathcal{P}$ is initially true if $p \in \mathcal{I}$ and initially false otherwise. $\mathcal{G}$ specifies the goals, i.e., $S \subseteq \mathcal{P}$ is a *goal state* if and only if $\mathcal{M} \subseteq S$ and $S \cap \mathcal{N} = \emptyset$.

The effect of a finite sequence of operators $(o_1, o_2, \ldots, o_n)$ on a state S can be formalized as follows:

$$Result(S, (\,)) = S$$

$$Result(S, (o)) = \begin{cases} (S \cup \alpha) \setminus \delta & \text{if } \varphi \subseteq S \wedge S \cap \eta = \emptyset \\ S & \text{otherwise} \end{cases}$$

$$\begin{aligned} &Result(S, (o_1, o_2, \ldots, o_n)) \\ &\quad = Result(Result(S, (o_1)), (o_2, \ldots, o_n)) \end{aligned}$$

In essence, any operator can be applied to a state, but only has an effect if its preconditions are satisfied. If its preconditions are satisfied, its positive postconditions are added and its negative postconditions are deleted, cf. [Fikes and Nilsson, 1971]. An operator can appear multiple times in a sequence of operators.

A finite sequence of operators $(o_1, o_2, \ldots, o_n)$ is a *solution* to an instance of propositional planning if $Result(\mathcal{I}, (o_1, o_2, \ldots, o_n))$ is a goal state.

An instance of a propositional planning problem is *satisfiable* if it has a solution. PLANSAT is defined as the decision problem of determining whether an instance of propositional planning is satisfiable. Below, the computational complexity of PLANSAT and restricted versions of PLANSAT are demonstrated.

To show how a planning instance can be modeled by propositional planning, consider the Sussman anomaly. In this blocks-world instance, there are three blocks A, B, and C. Initially C is on A, A is on the table, and B is on the table. The goal is to have A on B, B on C, and C on the table. Only one block at a time can be moved. The conditions, initial state, and goals can be represented as follows:

$$\begin{aligned} \mathcal{P} &= \{A\text{-on-}B, A\text{-on-}C, B\text{-on-}A, \\ &\qquad B\text{-on-}C, C\text{-on-}A, C\text{-on-}B\} \\ \mathcal{I} &= \{C\text{-on-}A\} \\ \mathcal{M} &= \{A\text{-on-}B, B\text{-on-}C\} \\ \mathcal{N} &= \{A\text{-on-}C, B\text{-on-}A, C\text{-on-}A, C\text{-on-}B\} \end{aligned}$$

The negative goals $\mathcal{N}$ exploit the fact that C is on the table if it is not on top of anything else.

The operator to unstack A can be represented as:

$$\begin{aligned} \varphi &= \emptyset \\ \eta &= \{B\text{-on-}A, C\text{-on-}A\} \\ \alpha &= \emptyset \\ \delta &= \{A\text{-on-}B, A\text{-on-}C\} \end{aligned}$$

That is, A can be moved to the table if nothing is on A. As a result, A will not be on top of any other block.

The operator to stack A on B can be represented as:

$$\begin{aligned} \varphi &= \emptyset \\ \eta &= \{B\text{-on-}A, C\text{-on-}A, A\text{-on-}B, C\text{-on-}B\} \\ \alpha &= \{A\text{-on-}B\} \\ \delta &= \{A\text{-on-}C\} \end{aligned}$$

That is, A can be stacked on B if nothing is on top of A or B. The result is that A will be on B and not on top of any other block.

Obviously, any blocks-world instance can be easily modeled as propositional planning. More generally, any TWEAK planning instance can be polynomially reduced to a propositional planning instance if the initial state is finite, if each variable in an operator schema is limited to a polynomial number of values, and if each operator schema is limited to a constant number of variables. An exponential number of values for a variable would lead to an exponential number of propositional planning conditions. A polynomial number of variables in an operator schema would lead to an exponential number of propositional planning operators.

4 Complexity Results

This section describes and demonstrates our complexity results for propositional planning. Due to space limitations, some of the proofs are overly abbreviated. As mentioned above, PLANSAT is the decision problem of determining whether an instance of propositional planning is satisfiable.

4.1 PSPACE-complete Propositional Planning

Theorem 1 *PLANSAT is PSPACE-complete.*

Proof: PLANSAT is in NPSPACE because a sequence of operators can be nondeterministically chosen, and the size of a state is bounded by the number of conditions. That is, if there are n conditions and there is a solution, then the length of the smallest solution path must be less than 2^n. Any solution of length 2^n or larger must have "loops," i.e., there must be some state that it visits twice. Such loops can be removed, resulting in a solution of length less than 2^n. Hence, no more than 2^n nondeterministic choices are required. Because NPSPACE = PSPACE, PLANSAT is also in PSPACE.

Turing machines whose space is polynomially bounded can be polynomially reduced to PLANSAT. The

PLANSAT conditions can be encoded (and roughly translated) as follows:

$in_{i,x}$	Symbol x is in tape position i.
$at_{i,q}$	The input tape head is at the ith position and the Turing machine is in state q.
$do_{i,q,x}$	Perform the transition at the ith position for state q on character x.
accept	The Turing machine accepts the input.

If q_0 is the initial state of the Turing machine, its input is $x_1x_2\ldots x_k$, and the space used by the Turing machine is bounded by n, then the the initial state and goals for propositional planning can be encoded as:

$$\mathcal{I} = \{at_{0,q_0}, in_{0,\#}, in_{1,x_1}, in_{2,x_2}, \ldots, in_{k,x_k}, in_{k+1,\#}, in_{k+2,\#}, \ldots, in_{n-1,\#}\}$$
$$\mathcal{M} = \{accept\}$$
$$\mathcal{N} = \emptyset$$

$\mathcal{I}$ is encoded so that that position 1 to position k contain the input and the remaining positions (position 0 and positions $k+1$ to $n-1$) contain a special symbol #.

Suppose that the Turing machine is in state q, the input tape is at the ith position, x is the character at the ith position, and the transition is to replace x with y, move to the right, and be in state q'. This can be encoded using three operators:

$$\begin{array}{lll} \varphi = \{at_{i,q}, in_{i,x}\} & \varphi = \{do_{i,q,x}, in_{i,x}\} & \varphi = \{do_{i,q,x}, in_{i,y}\} \\ \eta = \emptyset & \eta = \emptyset & \eta = \emptyset \\ \alpha = \{do_{i,q,x}\} & \alpha = \{in_{i,y}\} & \alpha = \{at_{i+1,q'}\} \\ \delta = \{at_{i,q}\} & \delta = \{in_{i,x}\} & \delta = \{do_{i,q,x}\} \end{array}$$

The first operator "packs" all the information about the current position into a single condition. The second operator changes the symbol. The third operator moves to the next position and the new state. To handle boundary conditions, encode no operators for $at_{-1,q}$ and $at_{n,q}$.

A Turing machine accepts an input if it is in an accepting state and no transition can be made from the current symbol. For each such case, an operator to add *accept* can be encoded.

Because there are a polynomial number of $\langle i, q, x\rangle$ combinations, there will be a polynomial number of conditions and operators. Thus, any PSPACE Turing machine with its input can be polynomially reduced to a propositional planning instance. □

Note that none of the above operators requires more than two positive preconditions and two postconditions. This leads to the following corollary.

Corollary 2 *PLANSAT with operators restricted to two positive preconditions and two postconditions is PSPACE-complete.*

Using the same conditions as encoded above, the following theorem can be demonstrated:

Theorem 3 *PLANSAT with operators restricted to one postcondition (allowing any number of preconditions) is PSPACE-complete.*

Proof: Let $Do_i = \{do_{u,v,w} \mid u = i\}$. That is, Do_i is the set of all *do* conditions whose first subscript is i. Then the Turing machine transition described above can be encoded using the following six operators:

$$\begin{array}{ll} \varphi = \{at_{i,q}, in_{i,x}\} & \varphi = \{at_{i,q}, in_{i,x}, do_{i,q,x}\} \\ \eta = Do_{i-1} \cup Do_{i+1} & \eta = \emptyset \\ \alpha = \{do_{i,q,x}\} & \alpha = \emptyset \\ \delta = \emptyset & \delta = \{at_{i,q}\} \end{array}$$

$$\begin{array}{ll} \varphi = \{do_{i,q,x}, in_{i,x}\} & \varphi = \{do_{i,q,x}, in_{i,x}, in_{i,y}\} \\ \eta = \{at_{i,q}\} & \eta = \emptyset \\ \alpha = \{in_{i,y}\} & \alpha = \emptyset \\ \delta = \emptyset & \delta = \{in_{i,x}\} \end{array}$$

$$\begin{array}{ll} \varphi = \{do_{i,q,x}, in_{i,y}\} & \varphi = \{do_{i,q,x}, in_{i,y}, at_{i+1,q'}\} \\ \eta = \{in_{i,x}\} & \eta = \emptyset \\ \alpha = \{at_{i+1,q'}\} & \alpha = \emptyset \\ \delta = \emptyset & \delta = \{do_{i,q,x}\} \end{array}$$

In essence, two operators replace each operator in the previous reduction. The structure of the operators ensures that they must be performed in sequence. The key part is the first operator, whose negative preconditions include all *do* conditions whose first subscript is $i-1$ or $i+1$. This ensures that the *do* condition associated with the previous transition has been removed (see the sixth operator) before the next Turing machine transition begins. This is why any number of preconditions may be necessary. □

4.2 NP-complete and NP-hard Propositional Planning

Let PLANSAT+ be PLANSAT with operators restricted to positive postconditions.

Theorem 4 *PLANSAT+ is NP-complete.*

Proof: PLANSAT+ operators can never negate a condition, so a previous state is always a subset of succeeding states. Also, operators within an operator sequence that have no effect can always be removed. Hence, if a solution exists, the length of the smallest solution can be no longer than the number of conditions. Thus, PLANSAT+ is in NP because only a linear number of nondeterministic choices is required.

3SAT can be polynomially reduced to PLANSAT+. 3SAT is the problem of satisfying a formula in propositional calculus in conjunctive normal form, in which each clause has at most three factors.

Let $\mathcal{F}$ be a formula in propositional calculus in 3SAT form. Let $U = \{u_1, u_2, \ldots, u_m\}$ be the variables used in $\mathcal{F}$. Let n be the number of clauses in $\mathcal{F}$. An equivalent PLANSAT+ instance can be constructed using the following types of conditions.

T_i	u_i = true is selected.
F_i	u_i = false is selected.
C_j	The jth clause is satisfied.

The initial state and goals can be specified as:

$$\mathcal{I} = \emptyset$$
$$\mathcal{M} = \{C_1, C_2, \ldots, C_n\}$$
$$\mathcal{N} = \emptyset$$

That is, the goal is to satisfy each of the clauses.

For each variable u_i, two operators are needed:

$$\begin{array}{ll} \varphi = \emptyset & \varphi = \emptyset \\ \eta = \{F_i\} & \eta = \{T_i\} \\ \alpha = \{T_i\} & \alpha = \{F_i\} \\ \delta = \emptyset & \delta = \emptyset \end{array}$$

That is, u_i = true can be selected only if u_i = false is not, and vice versa. In this fashion, only one of u_i = true and u_i = false can be selected.

For each case where a clause c_j contains a variable u_i, the first operator below is needed; for a negated variable $\overline{u_i}$, the second operator below is needed:

$$\begin{array}{ll} \varphi = \{T_i\} & \varphi = \{F_i\} \\ \eta = \emptyset & \eta = \emptyset \\ \alpha = \{C_j\} & \alpha = \{C_j\} \\ \delta = \emptyset & \delta = \emptyset \end{array}$$

Clearly, every C_j can be made true if and only if a satisfying assignment can be found. Thus PLANSAT+ is NP-hard. Since PLANSAT+ is also in NP, it follows that PLANSAT+ is NP-complete. □

Note that each operator above only requires one precondition and one positive postcondition. This leads to the following corollary.

Corollary 5 *PLANSAT+ with operators restricted to one precondition and one postcondition is NP-complete.*

There is one additional intractability result.

Theorem 6 *PLANSAT with operators restricted to one positive precondition and two postconditions is NP-hard.*

Proof: This can be shown by reduction from 3SAT, similar to that for Theorem 4. One additional type of condition is needed:

U_i The value of u_i is unknown.

The initial state is $\{U_1, \ldots, U_m\}$.

Now all that is needed are different operators for selecting an assignment.

$$\begin{array}{ll} \varphi = \{U_i\} & \varphi = \{U_i\} \\ \eta = \emptyset & \eta = \emptyset \\ \alpha = \{T_i\} & \alpha = \{F_i\} \\ \delta = \{U_i\} & \delta = \{U_i\} \end{array}$$

Again, both u_i = true and u_i = false cannot be selected.

The same operators for clauses as in the proof for Theorem 4 can be used. □

4.3 Polynomial Propositional Planning

Theorem 7 *PLANSAT with operators restricted to positive preconditions and one postcondition is polynomial.*

Proof Outline: The difficulty is that some negative goals might need to be temporarily true to make some positive goals true or some negative goals false. Fortunately, because of the restrictions on the operators, it can be shown that any plan can be transformed to another plan that first makes conditions true and then makes conditions false. Thus, if there is a solution, there is a state S that meets the following conditions:

- S can be reached from the initial state $\mathcal{I}$ via operators with positive postconditions;
- the positive goals $\mathcal{M}$ are a subset of S; and
- $S \setminus \mathcal{N}$, i.e., a state that satisfies the negative goals, can be reached from S via operators with negative postconditions.

Because each operator has only positive preconditions and affects only one condition, and because the positive goals are true of S, the only thing remaining is to make all the negative goals false, i.e., to achieve $S \setminus \mathcal{N}$. There is no reason to make other conditions false.

Let *Turnon* then be a subroutine that inputs a set of conditions X and returns the maximal state $S \subseteq \mathcal{P} \setminus X$ that can be reached from $\mathcal{I}$. Let *Turnoff* be another subroutine that inputs a set of conditions S and returns the maximal state $S' \subseteq S$ such that $S \setminus \mathcal{N}$ can be reached from S'. It can be shown that each subroutine is polynomial, and that each maximal state is unique.

The following algorithm determines if a solution exists by iterating between *Turnon* and *Turnoff*:

$X \leftarrow \emptyset$
loop
  $S \leftarrow$ *Turnon*(X)
  if $\mathcal{M} \not\subseteq S$ then reject
  $S' \leftarrow$ *Turnoff*(S)
  if $S = S'$ then accept
  $X \leftarrow X \cup (S \setminus S')$
  if $X \cap \mathcal{I} \neq \emptyset$ then reject
end loop

It can be shown that every condition added to X is a condition that, if true, prevents the goal state from being reached. Since X grows monotonically, the algorithm is polynomial. □

Theorem 8 *PLANSAT with k goals and operators restricted to one precondition is polynomial.*

Proof: This is the algorithm. Construct all possible combinations of k conditions. Mark those combinations true of the initial state. For each marked combination, mark any combinations that can be reached from that combination via an operator. After all possible combinations are marked, if the combination of conditions corresponding to the goal is marked then accept, otherwise reject.

This is why the algorithm works. Consider a solution plan and any one of the k goals. To reach this goal, there must be a "chain" of operators leading from one condition in the initial state through one condition at a time until the goal is reached. Consider now the k chains of operators for the k goals. Consider also any state reached during the execution of the solution plan. This state will correspond to k nodes on the k chains. Any state that satisfies the k conditions corresponding to those nodes can reach the goal state. Since this is true for all states reached by the solution plan, it must be the case that only k conditions at a time need to be considered to determine what combinations of k conditions can be reached. □

Note that if operators can have more than one precondition, then a conjunctive goal problem can be converted into a single goal problem by adding operators that map the original set of goals onto a single "supergoal."

Theorem 9 *PLANSAT with operators restricted to no preconditions is polynomial.*

Proof: It is possible to work backwards from the goals. First look for operators that do not clobber any of the goals. Goals that are achieved by these operators can be removed from consideration. These operators can also be removed from consideration. Then look for operators that do not clobber the remaining goals, and remove from consideration these operators and the goals they achieve. This can be repeated until the remaining goals are true of the initial state (accept) or until no more appropriate operators can be found (reject). □

4.4 The Blocks World

Theorem 7 can be used to show that the blocks-world problem is tractable.

Theorem 10 *The blocks-world problem can be solved using operators restricted to positive preconditions and one postcondition.*

Proof: Note that stacking one block on another can be accomplished by first moving the former block on the table and then moving it on top of the latter block. Thus, solving any blocks-world instance only requires operators to move a block to the table and to move a block from the table.

Let $\{B_1, B_2, \ldots, B_n\}$ be the blocks in an instance of the blocks-world problem. The conditions can be encoded as follows:

$off_{i,j}$ B_i is *not* on top of B_j.

If B_i is on the table, then all $off_{i,k}$ will be true. If B_i has a clear top, then all $off_{k,i}$ will be true. If B_i is on top of B_j, then all $off_{i,k}$ except for $off_{i,j}$ will be true.

For each B_i and B_j, $i \neq j$, the operator to move B_i from on top of B_j to the table can be encoded as:

$$\begin{aligned}\varphi &= \{off_{1,i}, off_{2,i}, \ldots, off_{n,i},\\ &\quad off_{1,j}, off_{2,j}, \ldots, off_{i-1,j}, off_{i+1,j}, \ldots, off_{n,j}\}\\ \eta &= \emptyset\\ \alpha &= \{off_{i,j}\}\\ \delta &= \emptyset\end{aligned}$$

That is, if nothing is on B_i and nothing is on B_j except possibly B_i, then when this operator is applied, the result is that B_i will not be on top of B_j.

For each B_i and B_j, $i \neq j$, the operator to move B_i from on the table to on top of B_j can be encoded as:

$$\begin{aligned}\varphi &= \{off_{1,i}, off_{2,i}, \ldots, off_{n,i},\\ &\quad off_{1,j}, off_{2,j}, \ldots, off_{n,j},\\ &\quad off_{i,1}, off_{i,2}, \ldots, off_{i,n}\}\\ \eta &= \emptyset\\ \alpha &= \emptyset\\ \delta &= \{off_{i,j}\}\end{aligned}$$

That is, if nothing is on B_i and B_j, and if B_i is not on top of any other block, then when this operator is applied, the result is that B_i will be on top of B_j.

Since there are only $O(n^2)$ $\langle i,j \rangle$ combinations, only $O(n^2)$ conditions and operators are needed to encode a blocks-world instance.

As required, all preconditions are positive and each operator has only one postcondition. Thus, Theorem 7, in a sense, explains why the blocks world is tractable.[3]

[3] The algorithm for Theorem 7 corresponds to the unimaginative, but robust, strategy of moving all the blocks to the table, which makes all the conditions positive, and then forming the stacks from the table on up.

5 Remarks

Planning is intractable even if the size of states are bounded and operators have no variables. Merely allowing two preconditions and two postconditions for operators gives rise to an extremely hard problem. However, operators must have preconditions, postconditions, and apparently many more "features" to implement any interesting domain [Chapman, 1987; Hendler *et al.*, 1990]. While additional features might be good for making a planner more useful as a programming tool, generality has its downside—tractability cannot be guaranteed unless there are sufficient restrictions on the operators.

Some restricted propositional planning problems are tractable. Restricting operators to positive preconditions and one postcondition explains the tractability of the blocks-world. Restricting operators to one precondition and limiting the number of goals is the only interesting case where restricting the number of goals leads to tractability. Restricting operators to no preconditions shows that planning is tractable if preconditions can be ignored, e.g., if preconditions of operators can be easily satisfied without clobbering already achieved goals.

However, many, if not most, planning domains violate these categories. Thus, these domains cannot be shown to be tractable based on restrictions on the local properties of operators. As mentioned in the section on previous research, Korf [1987] lists several global properties of planning problems that lead to efficient search for plans. Understanding how these properties are realized as restrictions on the set of operators as a whole is a promising research approach.

Unfortunately, the prospects for a single domain-independent planning algorithm are pessimistic. The three tractable problems above appear to require quite different algorithms, and many other tractable planning problems are yet to be discovered. This indicates that it will be more fruitful to adopt different algorithms for different types of planning problems.

References

[Allen *et al.*, 1990] Allen, J.; Hendler, J.; and Tate, A., editors 1990. *Readings in Planning.* Morgan Kaufmann, San Mateo, CA.

[Chapman, 1987] Chapman, D. 1987. Planning for conjunctive goals. *Artif. Intell.* 32(3):333–377.

[Dean and Boddy, 1987] Dean, T. and Boddy, M. 1987. Reasoning about partially ordered events. *Artif. Intell.* 36(3):375–399.

[Fikes and Nilsson, 1971] Fikes, R. E. and Nilsson, N. J. 1971. STRIPS: A new approach to the application of theorem proving to problem solving. *Artif. Intell.* 2(3/4):189–208.

[Hendler *et al.*, 1990] Hendler, J.; Tate, A.; and Drummond, M. 1990. AI planning: Systems and techniques. *AI Magazine* 11(2):61–77.

[Korf, 1985] Korf, R. E. 1985. Macro-operators: A weak method for learning. *Artif. Intell.* 26(1):35–77.

[Korf, 1987] Korf, R. E. 1987. Planning as search: A quantitative approach. *Artif. Intell.* 33(1):65–88.

A Message Passing Algorithm for Plan Recognition

Dekang Lin
Dept. of Advanced Computing & Engineering
Alberta Research Council
Calgary, Alberta, Canada T2E 7H7
dekang@noah.arc.ab.ca

Randy Goebel
Dept. of Computing Science
University of Alberta
Edmonton, Alberta, Canada T6G 2H1
goebel@cs.Ualberta.ca

Abstract

We present a general framework for plan recognition whose formulation is motivated by a general purpose algorithm for effective abduction. The knowledge representation is a restricted form of first order logic, which is made computationally explicit as a graph structure in which plans are manifest as a special kind of graph walk. Intuitively, plans are fabricated by searching an action description graph for relevant connections amongst instances of observed actions.

The class of plans for which our method is applicable is wider than those previously proposed, as both recursive and optional plan components can be represented. Despite the increased generality, the proposed message-passing algorithm has an asymptotic upper bound that is an improvement on previous related work.

1 Introduction

In cases where we have incomplete specifications of how agents act in environments, the motivation for plan recognition is to somehow attribute a plan to the agent's observed actions, in order to help create a less incomplete specification of behaviour. The extra information, regardless of how it is fabricated, is typically used to do things like explain actions already taken, or to predict actions to be taken. Applications of plan recognition have been found in discourse understanding [Litman and Allen, 1991], intelligent interfaces [Goodman and Litman, 1990], cooperative problem solving [Lochbaum *et al.*, 1990] and the analysis of goal-directed behavior in general.

Kautz [Kautz, 1987] proposed a formal theory of plan recognition. The advantages of Kautz's theory include its formal declarative semantics and expressive richness of its plan representation. Unfortunately, Kautz's plan recognition algorithm is exponential in the size of the knowledge base [Kautz, 1987, p.119] and thus may prove difficult to scale up. Vilain [Vilain, 1990] showed that, by imposing certain restrictions on plan representation, the plan recognition problem may be turned into a context free grammar parsing problem, which has well-known polynomial solutions. However, in order for Vilain's scheme to work, the plan components (steps) must be fully ordered and cannot be shared or interleaved. These conditions appear to be too restrictive in most applications.

Rather than restrict the plan representation formalism to suit parsing algorithms, we propose a new algorithm for plan recognition that is a generalization of a message passing algorithm for context-free grammar parsing [Lin and Goebel, 1990]. The plans libraries are represented by first order logic (FOL) formulas, as in [Kautz, 1987]. The solutions for the plan recognition problem are scenarios which, together with background knowledge (plan libraries), logically entail the observations. The complexity of our algorithm is linear in size (number of axioms) of the knowledge base. If the same set of restrictive assumptions are made as in [Vilain, 1990], the complexity of our algorithm becomes $O(|\mathcal{H}|n^3)$, where $|\mathcal{H}|$ is the size (number of nodes and links) of the plan hierarchy and n is the number of observations to be explained. In contrast, the complexity of Vilain's algorithm is $O(|\mathcal{H}|^2n^3)$.

Another contribution of this research is a formal, declarative treatment of specificity of explanations. Specificity has always been a confusing issue in plan recognition. Some have argued that the most specific explanation should be preferred because more specific information should preempt the more general. Alternatively, a more general statement about a plan instance is more likely to be true and therefore preferable. In [Kautz, 1987], specificity preference is not formally specified. Rather, it is dealt with by a `consider-spec` flag in the procedural description of the plan recognition algorithm. In Vilain's simplification this issue is totally ignored. We have taken the approach where preference is given to the *most general* of the scenarios that consist only of arguments that are the *most specific* with respect to the observations.

2 Plan Representation

Our plan representation scheme is similar to that of [Kautz, 1987], but is more general in that recursive and optional plan components can be represented. On the other hand, the constraints in Kautz's plan representation language can be any FOL formula that does not contain predicates representing plan types, here, the constraints have more restrictive patterns.

The motivation for the more restrictive patterns of constraints is a computational one. A major source of complexity in Kautz's algorithm is the fact that the explanation graphs in Kautz's algorithm are not able to contain local ambiguities. That is, two or more alternative explanations of a subset of observations from a plan type may combine with a similar set of alternatives for a different subset to produce an exponential growth in the number of global alternatives. However, local ambiguity may be globally irrelevant, in which case containment implies that local ambiguities are not multiplied. Our message passing algorithm is able to block the propagation of local ambiguities; a more restrictive form of constraints in our plan representation language guarantees that the global consistency is satisfied if the local constraints are satisfied.

We partition the domain of discourse into *plan instances* and *attribute values*, which are denoted by `PI` and `AV` respectively. *Attributes* are functions which maps plan instances `PI` to attribute values. For example, *time* is an attribute which maps a plan instance to the time interval representing its duration. The set of attributes is denoted by A.

A plan type is a unary predicate on `PI` (or equivalently, a subset of `PI`). We use the symbol P to denote the set of plan types. For example, **MkNdl** (Make Noodle) and **Boil** are two plan types. The relationships between a plan and its immediate components are represented by *features*, which are functions from `PI` to `PI`. For example, that **Boil** is an immediate component of **MkNdl** is represented by a feature f_1 which maps an instance of **MkNdl** into an instance of **Boil**. The set of features is denoted by F.

The symbol $\perp$ denotes the void element in `PI`. For an element $x \in \mathtt{PI}$, $f(x) = \perp$ means that x does not have an f-component. We defined $p(\perp)$ to be false and $f(\perp) = \perp$, for any $p \in P$, and $f \in F$.

Plans are axiomized by three sets of FOL formulas: Abstraction Axioms, Feature Restriction Axioms, Attribute Value Constraints.

Definition 2.1 (Abstraction Axioms) *An abstraction axiom is a formula of the form:* $\forall x.p_1(x) \rightarrow p_2(x)$, *where* $p_1, p_2 \in P$.

The following are two examples of abstraction axioms:

$$\forall x.\mathbf{MkSpagPesto}(x) \rightarrow \mathbf{MkPasta}(x)$$
$$\forall x.\mathbf{MkSpag}(x) \rightarrow \mathbf{MkNdl}(x)$$

Corresponding to each abstraction axiom $\forall x.p(x) \rightarrow q(x)$, there is a specialization function q_spec_p such that

$$q\_spec\_p(x) = \begin{cases} x & \text{if } p(x) \text{ is true} \\ \perp & \text{otherwise} \end{cases}$$

The specialization functions make the functional inverse of abstraction axioms explicit.

Definition 2.2 (Feature Restriction Axioms) *A feature restriction axiom is a formula of the form:*

$$\forall x.p(x) \wedge (f(x) \neq \perp) \rightarrow p'(f(x))$$

where $p, p' \in P$ *and* $f \in F$.

We write $p \xrightarrow{f} p'$ as a short hand for this axiom. Intuitively, each plan type p has an associated set of feature restriction axioms which define the possible components of each instance of p. The condition $f(x) \neq \perp$ ensures that the plan type of a component is specified only when a component exists. For example, suppose f_1 is a feature (function) that maps an instance of **MkNdl** to a component, say its second step, an instance of **Boil**. Then there is a feature restriction axiom $\forall x.\mathbf{MkNdl}(x) \wedge (f_1(x) \neq \perp) \rightarrow \mathbf{Boil}(f_1(x))$.

A feature $f \in F$ is said to be a *feature of a plan type* $p \in P$ provided that there exists a feature restriction axiom $\forall x.p(x) \wedge (f(x) \neq \perp) \rightarrow p'(f(x))$. For example, f_1 is a feature of **MkNdl**, because

$$\forall x.\mathbf{MkNdl}(x) \wedge (f_1(x) \neq \perp) \rightarrow \mathbf{Boil}(f_1(x))$$

is a feature restriction axiom.

If a plan instance x belongs to plan type p and f is a feature of p (or a superclass of p), then $f(x)$ is an *immediate component* of x. The *components of a plan instance* x are the plan instances that are either immediate components of x or, recursively, components of the immediate components of x.

Definition 2.3 (Attribute Value Constraints) *There are two types of attribute value constraints: local constraints and percolation constraints.*

A Local Constraint *specifies how the attributes of a plan instance are related, and is expressed by a formula of the form:*

$$\forall x.p(x) \rightarrow r(a_{i_1}(x), a_{i_2}(x) \ldots, a_{i_n}(x))$$

where $p \in P$, *r is a n-ary predicate over attribute values* (`AV`) $(n = 1, 2, \ldots)$.

A Percolation Constraint *specifies how the attributes of an plan instance are determined by the attributes of its immediate components and is a formula of the form:*

$$\forall x, v \;.\; p_1(x) \wedge p_2(f(x)) \wedge a'(f(x)) = v \;\longrightarrow\; a(x) = v$$

where $p_1, p_2 \in P$, f *is feature of* p_1 *and* $a, a' \in A$ *are attributes.*

Suppose *time*, *time_f₁*, and *time_f₄* are attributes and *before* is a binary predicate on `AV`, then

$$\forall x.\mathbf{MkSpag}(x) \rightarrow before(time\_f_4(x), time\_f_1(x))$$

is an example of local constraints.

Suppose f_4 is a feature of **MkSpag** that maps an instance of **MkSpag** to its **GetSpag** component, and f_1 is a feature of **MkNdl**, two examples of percolation constraints are:

$$\forall x, v. \;\; \mathbf{MkSpag}(x) \wedge \mathbf{GetSpag}(f_4(x)) \wedge time(f_4(x)) = v \longrightarrow time\_f_4(x) = v$$
$$\forall x, v. \;\; \mathbf{MkNdl}(x) \wedge \mathbf{Boil}(f_1(x)) \wedge time(f_1(x)) = v \longrightarrow time\_f_1(x) = v$$

In summary, the knowledge about plans is represented by three sets of FOL formulas. We write `KB` to denote the conjunction of the set of abstraction axioms, feature restriction axioms and the attribute value constraints.

3 Scenarios

A plan recognizer's task is to find an explanation of the observed actions. We define explanations to be consistent scenarios that entail the observations. A scenario is an FOL formula that describes an plan instance and its components. The syntax of a scenario is not defined by BNF, rather, it is defined in terms of walk trees in the plan hierarchy which is the diagrammatic form of the abstraction and feature restriction axioms in **KB**.

Definition 3.1 (Plan Hierarchy) *A plan hierarchy is a directed graph whose nodes represent elements in P and whose links are as follows:*

"isa" and specialization links: *Corresponding to each abstraction axiom* $\forall x.p_1(x) \rightarrow p_2(x)$ *in I, there is an "isa" link* $p_1 \xrightarrow{isa} p_2$*, and a specialization link* $p_2 \xrightarrow{spec} p_1$.

feature links: *Corresponding to each feature restriction axiom:*

$$\forall x.p_1(x) \wedge (f(x) \neq \perp) \rightarrow p_2(f(x))$$

there is a feature link *from* p_1 *to* p_2 *and labeled* f.

We write $\mathcal{H}$ to denote the plan hierarchy for **KB**. The sets of "isa" links and feature links correspond to the abstraction and decomposition hierarchies in [Kautz, 1987] respectively. Figure 1 shows the plan hierarchy of a cooking world. Each of the bidirectional gray arrows represents a pair of "isa" and specialization links. The upward arrow represents the "isa" link and the downward arrow represents the specialization link.

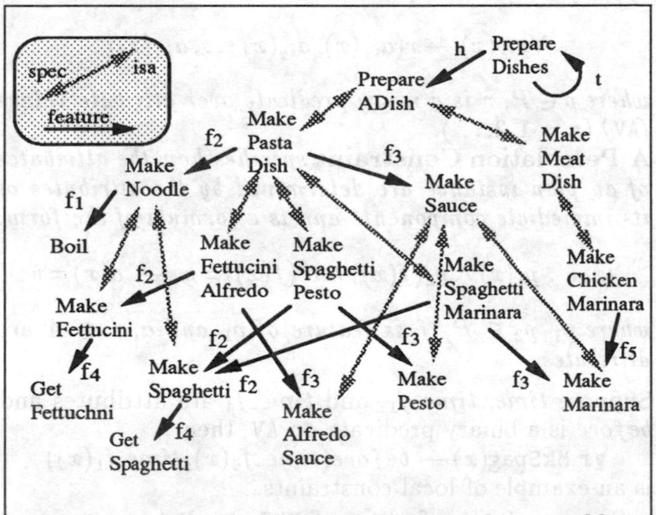

Figure 1: The plan hierarchy of a cooking world

The "isa" links (as well as the specialization links) induce a partial order ("isa" relation) over P. The closure of "isa" relation is denoted by $\xrightarrow{isa}*$ and the non-empty closure is denoted by $\xrightarrow{isa}+$. The meaning of $\xrightarrow{spec}*$ and $\xrightarrow{spec}+$ are similarly defined.

A directed path in the plan hierarchy $\mathcal{H}$ represents a plan–component relationship between the two end nodes of the path. The "isa" links allow plan types to *inherit arguments* from their superclasses. For example, The path from **MkPasta** to **Boil** is an argument that an instance of **MkPasta** has an instance of **Boil** as one of its components. This argument can be inherited by **MkSpagPesto** via the "isa" link from it to **MkPasta**. The specialization links, on the other hand, allow plan types to *inherit explanations* from their superclasses. For example, an explanation of a **MkPasta** instance, together with an assumption that the **MkPasta** instance is a **MkSpagPesto** instance, may also serve as an explanation of the **MkSpagPesto** instance, provided that there does not exist a more direct explanation for the latter. Similar to inheritance reasoning [Touretzky, 1986; Bacchus, 1988], path preemption ensures that only the most specific information is inherited.

Definition 3.2 (Path Preemption)

Generalization Preemption: *A path* $p \xrightarrow{isa}+ p_2 \xrightarrow{f} p'$ *is preempted if there exists a path* $p \xrightarrow{isa}* p_1 \xrightarrow{f} p'_1 \xrightarrow{isa}* p'$ *such that* $p_1 \xrightarrow{isa}+ p_2$ *(Figure 2.a).*

Specialization Preemption: *A path* $p \xrightarrow{f} p_2 \xrightarrow{spec}+ p'$ *is preempted if there exists a path* $p \xrightarrow{spec}* p'_1 \xrightarrow{f} p_1 \xrightarrow{spec}* p'$ *such that* $p_2 \xrightarrow{spec}+ p_1$ *(Figure 2.b).*

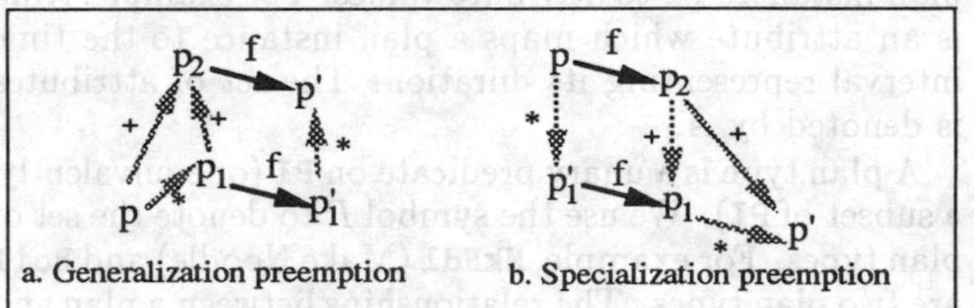

Figure 2: Path Preemption

An observed action can be related to some higher level plan by a path, which identifies the action as a possible component of achieving the plan. The plan recognizer's task, however, is not just to explain the observed actions separately. Rather, it must find a set of coherent relationships which relate all the observations to a higher level plan. To accomplish this, we introduce the notion of walk tree. The definition of a walk tree is built recursively upon the concept of a local tree, which identifies the relationships between a plan and its immediate components.

Definition 3.3 (Local Tree) *A local tree of* $\mathcal{H}$ *is a directed subtree* T *of* $\mathcal{H}$ *such that the paths from the root of* T *to the leaves of* T *are sequences of zero or more "isa" links followed by one feature link and the labels of the feature links are different.*

An example of Local Tree is shown in Figure 3.a

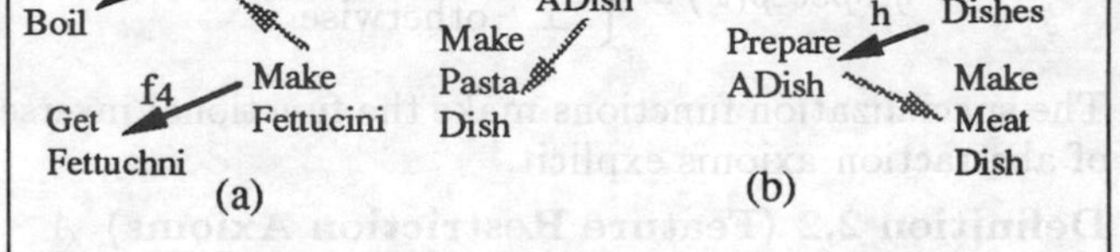

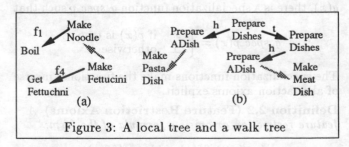

Figure 3: A local tree and a walk tree

Definition 3.4 (Walk Tree) *A walk tree of the plan hierarchy* $\mathcal{H}$ *is defined recursively as follows:*

1. *The local trees of $\mathcal{H}$ are also walk trees of $\mathcal{H}$.*
2. *Suppose α is a walk tree of $\mathcal{H}$. If a leaf node of α is labeled p and β is a local tree or a specialization link in $\mathcal{H}$, with the root labeled p, then the tree formed by joining the node p in α and the root of β is also a walk tree of $\mathcal{H}$.*
3. *All walk trees are either one of the above.*

A walk tree is said to be *valid* if it does not contain any preempted paths. A walk tree is more general than a tree in that there may be multiple occurrences of the same node in $\mathcal{H}$, and therefore can be used to represent iterative or recursive plan components. For example, Figure 3.b shows a valid walk tree, where there are two instances of **PrepareADish**.

An *attribute assignment* of a plan instance x is a set of assignments of attribute values to x and is denoted by $V(x)$. That is $V(x) \equiv \bigwedge_{i=1}^{k} a_i(x) = v_i$, where $a_i \in A$ and v_i's are constants in AV. For example, $time(x) = [0,1] \wedge agent(x) = john$ is an attribute assignment of x.

Definition 3.5 (Scenario) *Let T be a valid walk tree of $\mathcal{H}$. Let $f_1^*, f_2^*, \ldots f_m^*$ be the compositions of the feature and specialization functions along the path from the root of T to the leaf nodes of the local trees in T. Let $p_1, p_2, \ldots p_m$ be the corresponding plan types represented by the nodes. Then T and a set of attribute assignments $V_1, V_2, \ldots, V_m$ define a scenario α, which is an FOL formula:*

$$\alpha \equiv \exists x. \bigwedge_{i=1}^{m} (p_i(f_i^*(x)) \wedge V_i(f_i^*(x))).$$

For example, suppose *time* is an attribute of plans. Let α denote the scenario in Figure 4, where the intervals beside the nodes denote the values of their time attribute. Then α is the following formula:

$$\begin{aligned}\alpha \equiv\ & \exists x \mathtt{MkSpagMari}(x) \wedge time(x) = [0,2] \wedge \\ & \mathtt{MkMari}(x) \wedge time(f_3(x)) = [1,2] \wedge \\ & \mathtt{MkSpag}(f_2(x)) \wedge time(f_2(x)) = [0,2] \wedge \\ & \mathtt{GetSpag}(f_4(f_2(x))) \wedge time(f_4(f_2(x))) = [0,1] \wedge \\ & \mathtt{Boil}(f_1(f_2(x))) \wedge time(f_1(f_2(x))) = [1,2]\end{aligned}$$

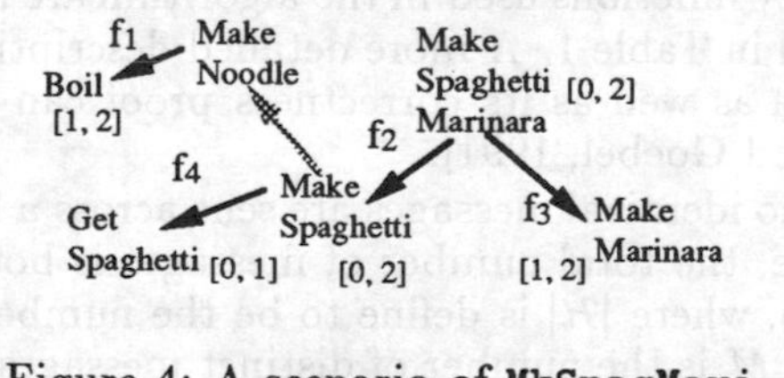

Figure 4: A scenario of **MkSpagMari**

4 The Plan Recognition Problem

An observation is an assertion that there exists a plan instance of certain type and possessing certain attributes.

Definition 4.1 (Observation) *An observation is a formula of the form:*

$$o \equiv \exists x.p(x) \wedge V(x).$$

where p is a plan type and V is an attribute assignment.

Definition 4.2 (Explanation) *Given* KB *and a set of observations $o_1, \ldots, o_k$, an explanation of the observations is a scenario α such that*

1. *α is consistent with* KB, *i.e.,* $\mathtt{KB} \wedge \alpha \not\models false$.
2. $\mathtt{KB} \wedge \alpha \models o_1 \wedge \ldots \wedge o_k$.

Definition 4.3 (Plan Recognition Problem) *Given* KB *and a set of observations $\{o_1, \ldots, o_k\}$, the plan recognition problem is to find the most general explanation α of $\{o_1, \ldots, o_k\}$. That is, there does not exist another explanation β of $\{o_1, \ldots, o_k\}$ such that $root_\alpha \xrightarrow{\text{isa}}{}^{+} root_\beta$, where $root_\alpha$ and $root_\beta$ are the plan type represented by the root nodes of α and β respectively.*

The more general explanation is preferred because a more general statement about a plan instance is more likely to be true. For example, **MkPasta**(x) is more likely to be true than **MkSpagPesto**(x). On the other hand, the validity of the walk tree implies that each explanation contains only the arguments that are the most specific with respect to the observations.

4.1 Examples

Suppose the Abstraction Axioms and Feature Restriction Axioms are represented by Figure 1. The Percolation Constraints are as follows:

$$\forall x, v.\mathtt{MkNdl}(x) \wedge \mathtt{Boil}(f_1(x)) \wedge time(f_1(x)) = v \longrightarrow time\_f_1(x) = v$$

$$\forall x, v.\mathtt{MkSpag}(x) \wedge \mathtt{GetSpag}(f_4(x)) \wedge time(f_4(x)) = v \longrightarrow time\_f_4(x) = v$$

$$\forall x, v.\mathtt{MkPasta}(x) \wedge \mathtt{MkNdl}(f_2(x)) \wedge time(f_2(x)) = v \longrightarrow time\_f_2(x) = v$$

$$\ldots\ldots$$

The Local Constraints are as follows:

$\forall x.\mathtt{MkNdl}(x) \rightarrow before(time\_f_4(x), time\_f_1(x))$

$\forall x.\mathtt{MkNdl}(x) \rightarrow time(x) = union(time\_f_4(x), time\_f_1(x))$

Example 1: Suppose the following observations are made:

$$o_1 \equiv \exists x.\mathtt{GetSpag}(x) \wedge time(x) = [0,1]$$
$$o_2 \equiv \exists x.\mathtt{Boil}(x) \wedge time(x) = [1,2]$$
$$o_3 \equiv \exists x.\mathtt{MkMari}(x) \wedge time(x) = [1,2]$$

Then the scenario that explains $\{o_1, o_2, o_3\}$ is the one shown in Figure 4. Note that the observations do not have to be a sequence of actions. In this example, **Boil** and **MkMari** are concurrent.

Example 2: Suppose the following two observations are made:

$$o_1 \equiv \exists x.\mathtt{MkNdl}(x) \wedge time(x) = [0,1]$$
$$o_2 \equiv \exists x.\mathtt{MkSauce}(x) \wedge time(x) = [1,2]$$

The explanations of $\{o_1, o_2\}$ are shown in Figure 5. Since the explanation in 5.a is more general than those in 5.b, 5.c and 5.d, the solution of the plan recognition problem is the scenario in 5.a.

Example 3: Suppose the observations are:

$$o_1 \equiv \exists x.\mathtt{MkFett}(x) \wedge time(x) = [0,1]$$
$$o_2 \equiv \exists x.\mathtt{MkAlSauce}(x) \wedge time(x) = [1,2]$$

Then the only explanation is the scenario in Figure 5.c. The walk tree shown in Figure 6 is not a valid one because the path:

$$\mathtt{MkPasta} \xrightarrow{f_2} \mathtt{MkNdl} \xrightarrow{spec} \mathtt{MkFett}$$

is preempted by the path

$$\mathtt{MkPasta} \xrightarrow{spec} \mathtt{MkFettAl} \xrightarrow{f_2} \mathtt{MkFett}.$$

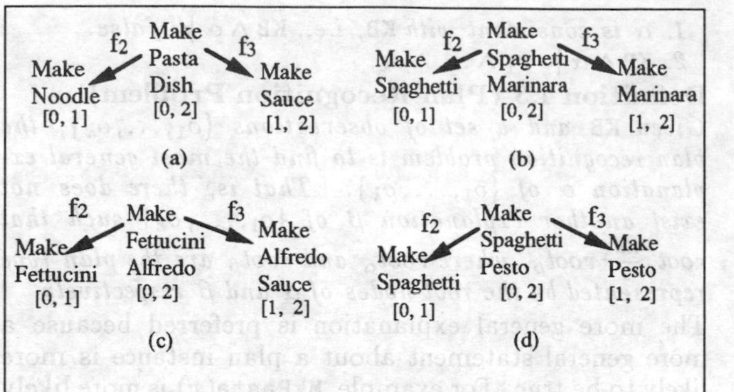

Figure 5: Explanations for {`MkNdl`, `MkSauce`}.

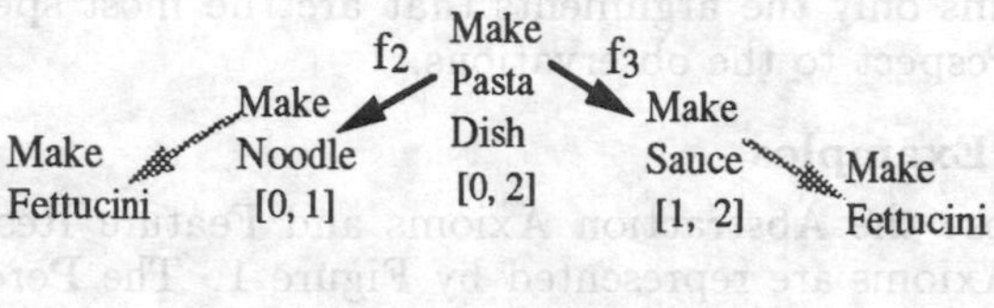

Figure 6: An invalid walk tree

5 A Recognition Algorithm

Since only a restricted subset of FOL is used to represent the observations, scenarios, as well as the domain knowledge, the plan recognition problem may be solved by a specialized inference method. We now present a message passing algorithm for plan recognition. Each node in the plan hierarchy is a computing agent which communicates with other agents by sending messages across the links in the plan hierarchy. A message is a pair: $<V, B>$, where V is an attribute assignment describing a plan instance, and B is a subset of observations. The messages are passed in the reverse direction of the links in the plan hierarchy. If a message $<V, B>$ reaches a node p, then this means that the observations in B can be explained as components of an instance of plan type p that matches the description V. Therefore, the messages represent partial explanations of subsets of the observations. The partial explanations are combined at the nodes to generate explanations for larger subsets of the observations.

Let $\{o_i \equiv \exists x.p_i(x) \wedge V_i(x)\}$ $(i = 1, 2, \ldots, n)$ be a set of observations. The message passing process is initiated by sending the message $<V_i, \{o_i\}>$ to the node p_i, for $i = 1, 2, \ldots, n$. The message passing process stops when no further messages are being sent and the explaining scenarios can then be retrieved from the network by tracing the origins of the messages whose B components are equal to $\{o_1, o_2, \ldots, o_n\}$.

When a node receives a message via a specialization link, the message is forwarded via the incoming specialization and feature links. When a node receives a message $<V, B>$ via an "isa" link or a feature link, the message is first forwarded across the incoming "isa" links, then an item is created and saved into the local memory. An item is a triple $<V, B, F>$, where V and B are the same as in messages, and F is a set of features. The item created when the message $<V, B>$ arrives is $<V', B, \{f\}>$, where V' is determined by V according to the percolation constraints and f is the feature represented by the last feature link traversed by the message. The node then attempts to combine the new item with previously stored items that are compatible with it. Two items $<V_1, B_1, F_1>$ and $<V_2, B_2, F_2>$ are compatible if F_1 and F_2 are disjoint and the unification of V_1 and V_2 satisfies the local constraints. If interleaved plan components are not allowed, B_1 and B_2 must also be consecutive sequences of observations. If shared plan components are not allowed, then the two items are only compatible if $B_1 \cap B_2 = \emptyset$.

The combination of two items $<V_1, B_1, F_1>$ and $<V_2, B_2, F_2>$ is an item $<V_0, B_0, F_0>$, where V_0 is the unification of V_1 and V_2; $B_0 = B_1 \cup B_2$ and $F_0 = F_1 \cup F_2$. If $<V_0, B_0, F_0>$ satisfies all the local constraints, the message $<V_0, B_0>$ is sent further if no identical messages have been previously sent by the current agent.

The message passing algorithm must ensure that the scenarios be consistent with the knowledge base and their walk tree is a valid one, i.e., they must not contain preempted walks. The consistency of the explanations is maintained by checking the percolation and local constraints during the message passing process. The validity of the walk trees of the scenarios is guaranteed by blocking certain messages.

We define a binary relation *preempted* as follows: Let a be a feature link $p \xrightarrow{f} q$ and b be a node in $\mathcal{H}$. *preempted*(a, b) is true iff 1) the path $b \xrightarrow{isa} + p \xrightarrow{f} q$ is preempted; or 2) the path $p \xrightarrow{f} q \xrightarrow{spec} + b$ is preempted.

The relation *preempted* is precomputed and remains unchanged as long as the plan hierarchy is unchanged. A message sent across a "isa" link $c \xrightarrow{isa} b$ is blocked if *preempted*(a, b) is true, where a is the last feature link traversed by the message. A message sent across a feature link a is blocked if *preempted*(a, b) is true, where b is the last node traversed by the message before reaching a via a sequence of specialization link.

The message passing algorithm is shown in Figure 7. The utility functions used in the algorithm are listed and explained in Table 1. A more detailed description of the algorithm as well as its correctness proof can be found in [Lin and Goebel, 1991].

Since no identical messages are sent across a link more than once, the total number of messages is bounded by $O(M|\mathcal{H}|)$, where $|\mathcal{H}|$ is define to be the number of links in $\mathcal{H}$ and M is the number of distinct messages. The total number of items created is bounded by $O(M|\mathcal{H}|2^d)$, where d is the maximum number of immediate components a plan has.

Suppose the same set of restrictions is imposed on the plan hierarchy as in [Vilain, 1990], that is, plan components are linearly ordered and cannot be shared or interleaved. Then the plan recognition algorithm degenerates to a message passing algorithm for context-free grammars [Lin and Goebel, 1990], which has complexity $O(n^3|\mathcal{H}|)$, where n is the number of observations. This is a significant improvement over [Vilain, 1990] which has the complexity $O(n^3|\mathcal{H}|^2)$ because $|\mathcal{H}|$ tends to be a large number in non-trivial domains.

Algorithm 1 Send Message

```
sendViaFeatureLink(Node sender, Message m, Node n)
  foreach feature link l of sender do
      if (not preempted(l, n)) receive(tailOf(l), m, l);
end

sendViaIsaLink(Node sender, Message m, FeatureLink f)
  foreach isa link l of sender do
      if (not preempted(f, tailOf(l))) receive(tailOf(l), m, l);
end

sendViaSpecLink(Node sender, Message m, Node n)
  foreach specialization link l of sender do
      receiveViaSpec(tailOf(l), m, n);
end
```

Algorithm 2 Receive Message

```
receive(Node receiver, Message m, Link b)
  if (isNew(receiver, m)) sendViaIsaLinks(receiver, m, b);
  i ← item(m, b);
  forall items i' such that compatible(receiver, i', i) do
      i'' ← combine(receiver, i, i');
      if (not complete(receiver, i'')) continue;
      m' ← message(i'').
      if (not isNew(receiver, m')) continue;
      sendViaFeatureLinks(receiver, m', nil);
      sendViaSpecLinks(receiver, m', receiver);
  end
end

receiveViaSpec(Node receiver, Message m, Node b)
  if (isNew(receiver, m))
      sendViaSpecLinks(receiver, m, b);
      sendViaFeatureLinks(receiver, m, b);
  end
end
```

Figure 7: A Message Passing Algorithm

Table 1: Utility functions

Function*	Return value
combine(n, i, i');	the combination of i and i'
compatible(n, i, i');	true if i and i' are compatible at node n.
complete(n, i);	true if i satisfies all the local constraints;
isNew(n, m);	true if m has not previously been sent by n;
item(m, l);	the item $<V, B, f_l>$, where $<V, B> = m$ and f_l is the feature represented by l.
message(i);	the message $<V, B>$, where $<V, B, F> = i$.

*n is a Node; i and i' are Items; m is a Message; l is a Link;

If the plan components are partially ordered, but are not shared or interleaved, the complexity of our plan recognition algorithm is the same as the complexity of direct ID (Immediate Dominance) rule parsing in [Lin and Goebel, 1990], i.e., $O(n^2|\mathcal{H}|2^d)$, where d is the maximum number of features of a plan type.

6 Conclusion

We have presented a message passing algorithm for plan recognition, which has an asymptotic upper bound that is an improvement on previous related work. Our representation scheme is more general than Kautz's in its ability to accommodate optional and recursive plan components, but more restrictive in the pattern of constraints that can be specified. The logical representation of plans is made computationally explicit as a graph structure in which plans are manifest as a special kind of graph walk. Explanations of the observations are defined to be valid scenarios that are consistent with the knowledge base and, together with knowledge base, logically entail the observations. A scenario is valid if it consists only of arguments that are the most specific with respect to the observations. In case of multiple possible explanations, the most general one is preferred over the others.

Acknowledgement

Peter van Beek has read two drafts of this paper and provided valuable comments. Thanks are also due to critics and suggestions from anonymous reviewers. This research is done while the first author is at the Department of Computing Science, University of Alberta.

References

[Bacchus, 1988] Fahiem Bacchus. *Representing and Reasoning with Probabilistic Knowledge.* PhD thesis, University of Alberta, Edmonton, Alberta, Canada, 1988.

[Goodman and Litman, 1990] B. Goodman and D. Litman. Plan recognition for intelligent interfaces. In *Proceedings of the IEEE Conference on Artificial Intelligence Applications*, pages 297–303, 1990.

[Kautz, 1987] Henry A. Kautz. A formal theory of plan recognition. Technical Report 215, Department of Computer Science, University of Rochester, May 1987.

[Lin and Goebel, 1990] Dekang Lin and Randy Goebel. Context free grammar parsing by message passing. (Unpublished), 1990.

[Lin and Goebel, 1991] Dekang Lin and Randy Goebel. A message passing algorithm for plan recognition. Technical Report 91–7, Department of Computing Science, University of Alberta, Edmonton, Alberta, Canada, 1991.

[Litman and Allen, 1991] D. Litman and J. Allen. Discourse processing and commonsense plans. In *Intensions in Communication.* MIT Press, 1991.

[Lochbaum *et al.*, 1990] Karen E. Lochbaum, Barbara J. Grosz, and Candace L. Sidner. Models of plans to support communication: an initial report. In *Proceedings of AAAI-90*, pages 485–490, 1990.

[Touretzky, 1986] David Touretzky. *The Mathematics of Inheritance Systems.* Morgan Kaufmann, 1986.

[Vilain, 1990] Marc Vilain. Getting serious about parsing plans: a grammatical analysis of plan recognition. In *Proceedings of AAAI-90*, pages 190–197, Boston, MA, July 1990. The MIT Press.

The Downward Refinement Property

Fahiem Bacchus and Qiang Yang*
Department of Computer Science
University of Waterloo
Waterloo, Ontario, Canada
N2L-3G1

Abstract

Using abstraction in planning does not guarantee an improvement in search efficiency; it is possible for an abstract planner to display worse performance than one that does not use abstraction. Analysis and experiments have shown that good abstraction hierarchies have, or are close to having, the *downward refinement property*, whereby, given that a concrete-level solution exists, *every* abstract solution can be refined to a concrete-level solution without backtracking across abstract levels. Working within a semantics for ABSTRIPS-style abstraction we provide a characterization of the downward refinement property. After discussing its effect on search efficiency, we develop a semantic condition sufficient for guaranteeing its presence in an abstraction hierarchy. Using the semantic condition, we then provide a set of sufficient and polynomial-time checkable syntactic conditions that can be used for checking a hierarchy for the downward refinement property.

1 Introduction

Plan formation is concerned with finding sequences of operators that bring about certain goal states from certain initial states. This task is particularly difficult because of the exponential nature of the search spaces involved. Abstraction [1, 2, 3, 4] is a widely adopted strategy for lessening this computational burden.

It is well-known that if one has a good abstraction hierarchy, then search can be made exponentially more efficient. Korf [5] has shown that by using macro-operators (a form of abstraction), the average time complexity of planning search can drop from exponential to linear. Similar speed-up results have been reported by Knoblock [2] for ABSTRIPS-style abstraction. However, close examination reveals that the *downward refinement property* (DRP) is a major assumption underlying both analyses. This property simply states that if a non-abstract, concrete level solution to the planning problem exists, then *any* abstract solution can be refined to a concrete solution *without backtracking* across abstraction levels. That is, once a solution is found at the abstract level it need never be reconsidered, just refined.

Furthermore, experiments with Abstrips [1] and Abtweak [4] have shown that abstraction only increases search efficiency in hierarchies that are close to having the DRP, i.e., in hierarchies where most abstract solutions can be refined. In hierarchies where this is not the case, using abstraction can in fact decrease the efficiency of the planner. Hence, it is important to characterize those hierarchies that have the DRP. Such a characterization could be to used to *check* whether a given abstraction hierarchy has the DRP. In the presence of the DRP a modified search strategy is applicable that runs exponentially faster without giving up completeness. A characterization could also be used to *generate* an abstraction hierarchy for a given domain guaranteed to have the DRP.

In this paper, we will provide a semantics for ABSTRIPS-style abstraction. We will then use this semantics to give a definition of the DRP. After examining the effect of the DRP on search efficiency, we will give a semantic condition that is sufficient to ensure the DRP. This semantic condition yields both a better understanding of the nature of the DRP and collection of syntactic conditions that are sufficient for guaranteeing its presence. To be useful, we have focused on conditions that can be tested in polynomial time, allowing a specification of a domain hierarchy to be checked quickly for the DRP.

2 The Planning Representation

We will focus on planning problems that can be described with a quantifier-free language, $\mathcal{L}$, consisting of a collection of predicates, of various arities; constants; and variables, used to describe parameterized operators. Such a language can be given a semantics by a traditional first-order model, with a domain of discourse, relations over the domain, and an interpretation function mapping the symbols of the language to semantic entities. The result of such a model will be the assignment of a truth-value to every formula of the language. Abstracting away from the models we can focus on their end product: the truth-value assignments. Treating these assignments as functions from the formulas to TRUE/FALSE, we can view distinct truth-value functions as alternate

*This work is supported by grants from the Natural Science and Engineering Council of Canada. The authors' e-mail addresses are fbacchus@logos.waterloo.ca and qyang@logos.waterloo.ca.

realities or possible worlds as described by $\mathcal{L}$. We will call these distinct truth-value functions possible worlds, and will use $\mathcal{W}$ to denote the set of *all* possible worlds. We say that a possible world w ***satisfies*** a formula $\lambda \in \mathcal{L}$ (set of formulas S) if it assigns the truth-value TRUE to λ (to every member of S), and we will use $w \models \lambda$ to denote this.

Now consider a collection of formulas of $\mathcal{L}$, S. If this collection is consistent (i.e., if there is at least one possible world that satisfies S), then in general there will be many possible worlds which satisfy S. We will use the notation Σ_S to refer to the set of *all* worlds $w \in \mathcal{W}$ that satisfy S.[1] If we add new formulas to S then Σ_S will shrink in size, and if we remove formulas from S, Σ_S will increase.[2] Furthermore, it can be the case that a syntactically distinct set of formulas T will be such that $\Sigma_T = \Sigma_S$ (in the case where T is logically equivalent to S).

State Descriptions. In planning, $\mathcal{L}$ is used to write state descriptions: collections of formulas that are partial descriptions of the state of the world. We restrict our attention to planning problems where the state descriptions are finite, consistent collections of ground literals (a typical situation for STRIPS-style planners). By the above, each such state description, S, corresponds semantically to a set of possible worlds Σ_S. Furthermore, because of our restriction to literals we have that $\Sigma_{S1} = \Sigma_{S2}$ if and only if $S1 = S2$.[3] This follows from the fact that for each set of ground literals there exists a possible world that satisfies those literals and no other literals.

Operators. In addition to state descriptions, planning systems contain operators that, in the case of STRIPS-style planners, are partial functions between state descriptions. A STRIPS-style operator α is defined by three sets of literals, its preconditions, $\mathsf{Pre}(\alpha)$, its add list, $\mathsf{Add}(\alpha)$, and its delete list, $\mathsf{Del}(\alpha)$. Applying an operator α to a state description S results in a new state description $\alpha(S)$, which is obtained by removing from S all the literals in $\mathsf{Del}(\alpha)$, and then adding to S the literals in $\mathsf{Add}(\alpha)$. That is, $\alpha(S) = (S \setminus \mathsf{Del}(\alpha)) \cup \mathsf{Add}(\alpha)$, where '\' is the set difference operator.

Semantically, operators correspond to partial functions between sets of possible worlds. More precisely, consider the power set of $\mathcal{W}$. A subset of this power set is the set of *describable* sets of worlds, $\mathcal{DW}$. This collection is defined by the condition that for each $\Sigma \in \mathcal{DW}$ there exists a legal state description S (finite collection of literals by the above definition) such that $\Sigma = \Sigma_S$.[4]

[1] Hence, Σ_S satisfies "All I know is S" in the sense of Levesque [6].

[2] These notions mirror the possible worlds notion of knowledge, where more knowledge corresponds to a smaller set of accessible worlds [7].

[3] This would not be true if we allow arbitrary formulas in our state descriptions. For example, $\{P(a), P(a) \rightarrow Q(a)\}$ and $\{P(a), Q(a)\}$ are distinct sets of formulas but they have identical sets of satisfying worlds.

[4] Not every set of possible worlds is definable by a finite collection of literals. For example, a set consisting of a single world might require an infinite number of literals in its definition.

Furthermore, as we noted above, the set of literals S is unique. Thus, an operator α corresponds semantically to a partial function $\hat{\alpha}$ from $\mathcal{DW}$ to $\mathcal{DW}$, such that:

1. $\Sigma \in \mathcal{DW}$ is in the domain of $\hat{\alpha}$ if and only if $\Sigma \subseteq \Sigma_{\mathsf{Pre}(\alpha)}$.
2. $\hat{\alpha}(\Sigma) = \Sigma_{\alpha(S)}$, where S is the unique state description corresponding to Σ.[5]

In general, a planning system will contain operator templates instead of operators. These templates contain variables which specify parameterized versions of the actual operators. The operators themselves are generated by instantiating the variables in the template. We will often refer to these operator templates as if they were actual operators. In these cases we are implicitly referring to all of the template's instantiations.

Planning Problems and Plans A plan Π is a sequence of operators $\alpha_1, \ldots, \alpha_n$. A planning problem is a pair of state descriptions $\langle I, G \rangle$, where I is the initial state, and G is the goal state. If we apply the plan Π to the initial state I the operators in Π will define a sequence of state descriptions $S_0, \ldots, S_n$ resulting from the application of the operators: $S_0 \overset{\alpha_1}{\mapsto} S_1 \overset{\alpha_2}{\mapsto} \ldots \overset{\alpha_n}{\mapsto} S_n$, where $S_0 = I$. A plan Π is a *solution* a planning problem $\langle I, G \rangle$, or is *correct* with respect to $\langle I, G \rangle$, if the sequence of state descriptions generated by applying Π to I satisfies two conditions: (1) $\mathsf{Pre}(\alpha_i) \subseteq S_{i-1}$, and (2) $G \subseteq S_n$. That is, the plan is correct if the preconditions of each operator are satisfied in the state to which it is applied, and the final state satisfies the goal G.

Semantically, a planning problem corresponds to a pair of sets from $\mathcal{DW}$, $\langle \Sigma_I, \Sigma_G \rangle$. A correct plan Π for $\langle I, G \rangle$ corresponds to a semantic solution $\hat{\Pi}$ consisting of a sequence of functions $\hat{\alpha}_1, \ldots, \hat{\alpha}_n$ that traverse through $\mathcal{DW}$ such that Σ_I is in the domain of $\hat{\alpha}_1$, each intermediate set of possible worlds, $\Sigma_{S_{i-1}}$, is in the domain of the function next applied, $\hat{\alpha}_i$, and the final set of possible worlds Σ_{S_n} is a subset of Σ_G. It is not difficult to see that every syntactic solution has a corresponding semantic solution and vice versa.

3 Abstraction

The type of abstraction we consider here is of the ABSTRIPS-style, where abstract operators are generated by eliminating preconditions. This type of abstraction has been widely used in planning research [1, 4, 9, 10]. Every literal L in the language $\mathcal{L}$ is assigned one of a finite number of integer criticality values denoted by $crit(L)$. The number of levels of abstraction is equal to the number of distinct criticality values. In particular, let there be $k+1$ different criticality values corresponding to the integers $\{0, 1, \ldots, k\}$, where the highest level of abstraction is k and level 0 corresponds to the concrete level where no abstraction occurs.

[5] These semantics differ in important ways from the semantics for STRIPS provided by Lifschitz [8]. Future work will explore these semantics in more detail, and will treat the more general case where the restriction to literals is removed.

Abstract Operators and Plans Given these abstraction levels we can define an abstraction operator Abs which maps a state description S to its i-th level abstraction $\mathsf{Abs}(i, S)$, where $0 \leq i \leq k$. This abstract state is defined by removing from S all literals with criticality value less than i. We can extend Abs so that it can be applied to an operator α to yield an abstract operator $\mathsf{Abs}(i, \alpha)$. The abstract operator has the same add and delete lists as α but it has a abstracted precondition list. That is, $\mathsf{Add}(\mathsf{Abs}(i, \alpha)) = \mathsf{Add}(\alpha)$ and $\mathsf{Del}(\mathsf{Abs}(i, \alpha)) = \mathsf{Del}(\alpha)$ but $\mathsf{Pre}(\mathsf{Abs}(i, \alpha)) = \mathsf{Abs}(i, \mathsf{Pre}(\alpha))$. Extending Abs further we can apply it to plans. If Π is a plan, then $\mathsf{Abs}(i, \Pi)$ is an i-th level abstract plan where every operator $\alpha \in \Pi$ has been replaced by its i-th level abstraction $\mathsf{Abs}(i, \alpha)$. Note that the ordering of the operators has not been disturbed.

Finally, say that an i-th level abstract plan $\mathsf{Abs}(i, \Pi)$ is a i-th level *abstract solution* to the planning problem $\langle I, G \rangle$ if it is correct with respect to the problem with an abstracted goal. That is, if $\mathsf{Abs}(i, \Pi)$ is a solution to $\langle I, \mathsf{Abs}(i, G) \rangle$. A 0-th level solution is called a *concrete* solution: it involves no abstractions.

It should be noted that as a consequence of our notation $\mathsf{Abs}(0, \alpha) = \alpha$, $\mathsf{Abs}(0, S) = S$, and $\mathsf{Abs}(i, S) \subseteq \mathsf{Abs}(i-1, S)$. Further, if Π is correct with respect $\langle I, G \rangle$ then $\mathsf{Abs}(i, \Pi)$ will be a solution to $\langle I, \mathsf{Abs}(i, G) \rangle$, i.e., an i-level abstract solution. However, if $\mathsf{Abs}(i, \Pi)$ is an abstract solution, Π will probably not be a solution as some of its operators might have unsatisfied lower level preconditions.

Semantically, this style of abstraction has an easy description. The abstraction of a state description will correspond to a larger set of possible worlds, i.e., $\Sigma_S \subseteq S_{\mathsf{Abs}(i,S)}$, $i > 0$. The semantic function corresponding to the abstract operator has the same definition as the concrete level function, it simply has a (potentially) larger domain. In particular it now includes all $\Sigma \in \mathcal{DW}$ such that $\Sigma \subseteq \Sigma_{\mathsf{Abs}(i, \mathsf{Pre}(\alpha))}$. The semantic function denoting $\mathsf{Abs}(i, \alpha)$ is $\mathsf{Abs}(i, \hat{\alpha})$. Similarly, if S is the set of literals that defines $\Sigma \in \mathcal{DW}$, then $\mathsf{Abs}(i, \Sigma)$ is simply $\Sigma_{\mathsf{Abs}(i,S)}$.

Since abstraction preserves the property that the state descriptions are collections of literals, we continue to have a one-to-one correspondence between abstract solutions (plans) and sequences of semantic function applications, where the semantic functions now correspond to abstract operators.

To simplify our subsequent discussion, we further restrict our attention to a special case where criticalities are assigned to predicates only. That is, an atomic formula and its negation always have the same criticality value.

4 The Downward Refinement Property

Let us fix an arbitrary planning problem $\langle I, G \rangle$. All of our subsequent discussion will be about plans, at various levels of abstraction, that are intended as solutions to this fixed problem. For simplicity, we will augment every such plan with special initial and terminal operators. The initial operator α_0, has no preconditions and has I as its add list. The terminal operator α_{n+1} has G as its preconditions and an empty add list. Both have empty delete lists. Semantically, $\hat{\alpha}_0$ is a function whose domain is all of $\mathcal{DW}$ and whose range is Σ_I; $\hat{\alpha}_{n+1}$ is an identity function whose domain is $\{\Sigma | \Sigma \subseteq \Sigma_G\}$. Hence, Π will have the form $\overset{\alpha_0}{\mapsto} S_0 \ldots S_n \overset{\alpha_{n+1}}{\mapsto} S_{n+1}$, where $S_0 = I$ and $S_n = S_{n+1}$. The advantage of this convention is that all of the states in the sequence of states defined by the non-augmented Π are sandwiched by a pair of operators in the augmented Π. Note also that α_0 is unaffected by abstraction, as it has no preconditions, but α_{n+1} is affected, as it has the goal as its preconditions and the goal is altered by abstraction.

We can now give a semantic definition of the DRP. Let $\hat{\Pi}$ be a semantic solution to a planning problem $\langle \Sigma_I, \Sigma_G \rangle$. Using the convention of augmented plans, this solution is a sequence of function applications with a corresponding sequence of semantic states: $\overset{\hat{\alpha}_0}{\mapsto} \Sigma_{S_0} \overset{\hat{\alpha}_1}{\mapsto} \ldots \overset{\hat{\alpha}_n}{\mapsto} \Sigma_{S_n} \overset{\hat{\alpha}_{n+1}}{\mapsto}$, where $\Sigma_{S_0} = \Sigma_I$, $\Sigma_{S_n} \subseteq \Sigma_G$, and each $\Sigma_{S_i} \in \mathrm{Domain}(\hat{\alpha}_{i+1})$.

Forward Justification A plan may contain extraneous operators. Justification is a notion that characterizes some of the redundant operators in $\hat{\Pi}$; i.e., operators that can be removed without affecting its correctness. In particular, in the version of justification we define, an operator is called justified in $\hat{\Pi}$ if it is the last operator in the sequence to guarantee that a particular literal is satisfied before it is required as a precondition for a subsequent operator or in the goal state.

Justification plays an important role in determining what is a "good" refinement of an abstract plan.

Definition 1 (Forward Justified Plans) Let L be a literal. We say that $\hat{\Pi}$ is *correct with respect to* L, if and only if, whenever $\mathrm{Domain}(\hat{\alpha}_i) \subseteq \Sigma_L$, then $\Sigma_{i-1} \subseteq \Sigma_L$. That is, correctness with respect to L ensures that whenever L is required as a precondition, it is supplied.

The first operator in the plan $\hat{\alpha}_1$ is forward justified with respect to L if and only if upon removing it from $\hat{\Pi}$, $\hat{\Pi}$ is no longer correct with respect to L.

Inductively, let Q_i be the set of operators in $\hat{\Pi}$ that precede $\hat{\alpha}_i$ and that are *not* forward justified with respect to L. Then $\hat{\alpha}_i$ is forward justified with respect to L if and only if upon removing $\hat{\alpha}_i$ and all of the operators in Q_i from $\hat{\Pi}$, $\hat{\Pi}$ is no longer correct with respect to L.

Now, we can define $\hat{\Pi}$ to be *forward justified* if and only if for every operator $\hat{\alpha}_i$ in $\hat{\Pi}$ there is some literal L such that $\hat{\alpha}_i$ is forward justified with respect to L. ■

This definition of forward justification is equivalent to a syntactic definition given in [11]. It is not, perhaps, the most natural definition of non-redundant plans from a semantic point of view, and we have examined a number of alternatives. However, for the purposes of this particular paper our definition has the advantage that it corresponds with concepts previously defined in [11].

If a plan $\hat{\Pi}$ is not forward justified, then it can be converted to a forward justified plan by simply removing the non-justified operators. Furthermore, it is not difficult to demonstrate that if $\hat{\Pi}$ is a correct plan (with respect to our fixed planning problem) then its forward justified version will also be correct.

Monotonic Refinement The idea behind monotonic refinement is that it defines a "good" refinement of an abstract plan. It captures the intuition that when an abstract plan at level i is refined to level $i-1$ we want to preserve as much of the work done at the abstract level as is possible. That is, we would not be gaining much advantage from abstraction if we continually replanned achievements of the higher level at the lower level. One way such an undesirable effect could occur is to refine the abstract plan by reversing all of the high-level operators and then plan at the lower level from scratch. Restricting the legal refinements to be monotonic guarantees that such wasteful behavior will not occur.

Definition 2 (Monotonic Refinement) Let $\hat{\Pi}_1$ and $\hat{\Pi}_2$ be forward justified abstract solutions, with $\hat{\Pi}_1$ being an i-th level solution and $\hat{\Pi}_2$ an $i-1$-th level solution, $0 < i \leq k$.

We say that $\hat{\Pi}_2$ is a *monotonic refinement* of $\hat{\Pi}_1$, if when we forward justify $\mathrm{Abs}(i, \hat{\Pi}_2)$ we obtain $\hat{\Pi}_1$. ∎

Note that a monotonic refinement must be a correct plan, i.e., a solution. When we refine an abstract plan we push the operators in that plan to a lower level of abstraction, generating additional preconditions for those operators. Monotonic refinement essentially means that when we add new operators to refine the plan, i.e., to make it correct again, they are added solely to achieve these new preconditions or lower level goal conditions, not to achieve previously satisfied conditions. Hence, when we drop the new conditions again, by abstraction, all of the operators we added during refinement will be come redundant. Thus, rejustifying the plan will yield the original abstract plan.

Our definition of monotonic refinement is the semantic version of a syntactic definition given in [11]. Hence, by results from that work it can be shown that in every ABSTRIPS-type abstraction hierarchy, completeness is preserved even when search is restricted by considering only monotonic refinements of abstract solutions [4].

The Downward Refinement Property

Definition 3 (DRP) An abstraction hierarchy has the *downward refinement property* if and only if for every forward justified i-th level abstract solution $\hat{\Pi}$, there is a monotonic refinement of $\hat{\Pi}$ at level $i-1$, for $0 < i \leq k$. ∎

In other words, a hierarchy has the DRP if every solution at an abstract level can be monotonically refined to a solution at the next lower level of abstraction.

Example 1 Consider the Towers of Hanoi domain with 3 pegs, Peg_1, Peg_2, Peg_3 and 2 disks *Big*, *Small*. Using predicates $OnBig(x)$ and `OnSmall(x)`, where x is a peg, we can represent the location of the two disks. The initial state is $\{OnBig(Peg_1), OnSmall(Peg_1)\}$ and the goal state $\{OnBig(Peg_3), OnSmall(Peg_3)\}$. We can define two operators $MoveBig(x,y)$ which moves the big disk from peg x to y, and $MoveSmall(x,y)$ which similarly moves the small disk. We have that $\mathrm{Pre}(MoveSmall(x,y))$ is $\{IsPeg(x), IsPeg(y), OnSmall(x)\}$; $\mathrm{Add}(MoveSmall(x,y))$ is $\{OnSmall(y)\}$; and $\mathrm{Del}(MoveSmall(x,y))$ is $\{OnSmall(x)\}$. For the other operator we have $\mathrm{Pre}(MoveBig(x,y))$ is $\{IsPeg(x), IsPeg(y), \neg OnSmall(y), \neg OnSmall(x), OnBig(x)\}$; $\mathrm{Add}(MoveBig(x,y))$ is $\{OnBig(y)\}$; and $\mathrm{Del}(MoveBig(x,y))$ is $\{OnBig(x)\}$.

Predicates that are not modifiable by any action, like *Ispeg*, act as constraints at all levels of abstraction. For example, the *Ispeg* preconditions insure that the parameters can only refer to pegs regardless of the level of abstraction. Hence, we always place these "type" predicates at the highest level of abstraction, i.e., level k.[6]

There are two ways to construct an abstraction hierarchy. We can put *OnBig* on the abstract level and *OnSmall* on the concrete level, or we can assign the criticalities the other way around. As we will demonstrate later, the first choice produces a hierarchy that has the DRP, while the second choice produces one that does not.

5 Effects on Search Efficiency

The main reason for being concerned with the DRP is its profound effect on search efficiency.

In planning, it is reasonable to require that completeness is preserved when an one-level planning system is extended to a multiple-level system. Hence, if a non-abstract solution to a problem exists, the abstract planner should also be able to find a concrete solution.

To preserve the completeness of abstract planning, a search method that is complete *across* abstraction levels has to be adopted [4]. Typically, this means that one cannot abandon alternate abstract paths in the search tree when a solution is found at an abstract level. Instead, all paths have to be kept in the open list to be explored later. This can greatly hamper the efficiency of search.

On the other hand, one can do considerably better in hierarchies that satisfy the downward refinement property. At any level of abstraction, search for alternate abstract plans can be terminated once a single correct plan has been found. In other words, search never backtracks to a previously explored abstract level. The DRP guarantees that any abstract solution can be refined to a concrete level one. Thus, if there is a concrete level solution, search in this manner will find it without having to considering alternate abstract plans.

Let b be the average branching factor of the search, and d be the length of an optimal solution. Then breadth-first search without abstraction will take on average $O(b^d)$. On the other hand, say we have k levels of abstraction and assume that the branching factor is constant and equal to b in each abstract level. Further assume that at each level of refinement approximately k/d new operators are inserted.[7] Then, if the DRP is not satisfied and we assume that there is only a 50% chance that an abstract solution can be refined to a solution at the next lowest level, it can be shown that the average case complexity remains $O(b^d)$. With the DRP,

[6] In actuality, since they are not changed by any action, type predicates do not play a role in determining the DSP.

[7] These assumptions are similar to those made in [12].

however, it can be shown that the average case complexity becomes $O(k \times b^{(d/k)})$. That is, the search is exponentially, in k, more efficient.

The downward refinement property has been implemented as an option in the ABTWEAK planner [4]. And experiments done in Towers of Hanoi domain with three disks have shown that there can be as much as a 10 fold improvement in search time and space when using the DRP. This often makes the difference between termination and non-termination.

6 Semantic Conditions for the DRP

Given an abstraction hierarchy, one would like to tell whether it has the DRP. Alternatively, from a domain specification one may want to generate a hierarchy with the DRP guaranteed. We will now provide a set of conditions sufficient to guarantee that the DRP holds. This is done by first providing a semantic condition, and then, in the next section, we will consider various syntactic realizations of this condition.

First we provide a sufficient condition for monotonic refinement.

Lemma 1 Let $\hat{\Pi}_1$ and $\hat{\Pi}_2$ be forward justified abstract solutions, with $\hat{\Pi}_1$ being an i-th level solution and $\hat{\Pi}_2$ an $i-1$-th level solution. $\hat{\Pi}_2$ is a monotonic refinement of $\hat{\Pi}_1$ if the following two conditions hold.

1. $\hat{\Pi}_1$ is a subsequence of $\mathsf{Abs}(i, \hat{\Pi}_2)$.
2. Let $\hat{\alpha}_1$ and $\hat{\alpha}_2$ be any pair of adjacent operators in $\hat{\Pi}_1$, and let Σ be the semantic state between these two operators in $\hat{\Pi}_1$. Now by condition (1) there are two corresponding operators $\hat{\alpha}_1^-$ and $\hat{\alpha}_2^-$ in $\hat{\Pi}_2$ that are the $i-1$ level refined versions of $\hat{\alpha}_1$ and $\hat{\alpha}_2$. Let Σ' be any semantic state in $\hat{\Pi}_2$ lying between $\hat{\alpha}_1^-$ and $\hat{\alpha}_2^-$. The second condition is then stated as the requirement that $\Sigma' \subseteq \mathsf{Abs}(i, \Sigma)$. ■

Now we can give a condition for the downward refinement property.

Theorem 1 Let $\hat{\Pi}_1$ be any forward justified i-th level abstract solution to any planning problem that has a concrete solution. Let $\hat{\alpha}_1$ and $\hat{\alpha}_2$ be any pair of adjacent operators in $\hat{\Pi}_1$, and let Σ be the semantic state between these two operators in $\hat{\Pi}_1$. Let $\hat{\alpha}_1^-$ and $\hat{\alpha}_2^-$ denote the $i-1$ level refined versions of $\hat{\alpha}_1$ and $\hat{\alpha}_2$. Suppose that for every semantic state Σ_1 such that $\Sigma_1 \in \mathrm{Range}(\hat{\alpha}_1^-)$ and $\Sigma_1 \subseteq \mathsf{Abs}(i, \Sigma)$, there exists a state Σ_2, such that

1. $\Sigma_2 \subseteq \mathsf{Abs}(i, \Sigma)$, and $\Sigma_2 \in \mathrm{Domain}(\hat{\alpha}_2^-)$, and
2. a solution $\hat{\Pi}_2$ consisting of $i-1$ level operators exists for the problem $\langle \Sigma_1, \Sigma_2 \rangle$, such that for every state Σ' in $\hat{\Pi}_2$, $\Sigma' \subseteq \mathsf{Abs}(i, \Sigma)$.

Then the DRP is satisfied by the hierarchy. ■

Intuitively, when we refine an abstract solution it may no longer be a solution because of newly introduced and as yet unsatisfied low level preconditions. Hence, looking at the situation between two adjacent operators in the abstract solution we see that the semantic state that is the result of the first operator may no longer be in the domain of the second operator, because of unsatisfied low level preconditions. Our DRP condition states that the hierarchy has the property that a sequence of new operators can be found that will reconnect the two operators. Furthermore, this sequence has the property that it does not affect any higher level conditions; i.e., at the i-th level nothing is changed.

7 Syntactic Checks for The DRP

In this section, we present some sufficient syntactic conditions for the DRP. These conditions are presented in order of increasing sophistication, and range of applicability. Each of these conditions is a syntactic realization of Theorem 1.

Complete Independence We start by considering the most trivial case for the DRP. Suppose that the $k+1$ criticality levels decompose the operators into $k+1$ disjoint subsets, $\mathcal{O}_0, \ldots, \mathcal{O}_k$, so that all of the literals in the precondition, add and delete lists of each operator in $\mathcal{O}_i$ have the same criticality value, i. This condition, which we call *complete independence* insures that no operator used to achieve a condition in an i-th level solution will have any effect on any other levels, and furthermore it will not require any preconditions from other levels either.

It is not hard to see that complete independence ensures the DRP. On the semantic level, the $k+1$ abstraction levels define $k+1$ independent subproblems. Any concatenation of the solution paths at two adjacent levels of abstraction returns a monotonic refinement of the abstract solution. Thus, we have

Theorem 2 Complete independence is sufficient to guarantee the DRP.

Example 2 Consider again the Tower of Hanoi domain. Assume that there are two copies of the 2-disk version of the problem. Given the restriction that no disk for one problem is allowed to be moved to a peg for the other problem, a complete-independence hierarchy can be trivially built by putting one copy of the problem on the abstract level, and the other one on the concrete level.

Complete low-level connectivity The second condition we can place on the preconditions is more useful than complete independence.

Definition 4 (Complete Low-Level Connectivity) Let S_1 and S_2 be any states such that $\mathsf{Abs}(i, S_1) = \mathsf{Abs}(i, S_2)$. That is, S_1 and S_2 only differ with respect to literals at criticality levels less than i. Complete low-level connectivity is satisfied if for any two such states at any level of abstraction i, there is an $i-1$ level solution, Π to the planning problem $\langle S_1, S_2 \rangle$ such that no operators in Π add or delete a literal with criticality higher than level $i-1$.

Intuitively, this condition states that we can always achieve lower level preconditions without violating the higher level effects. According to the condition, every pair of states S_1 and S_2 are connected by a path, provided that $\mathsf{Abs}(i, S_1) = \mathsf{Abs}(i, S_2)$. Furthermore, the condition requires that no operators on this path affect a higher level literal. This is equivalent to saying that the path never travels out of a state defined by higher level literals. Thus, the conditions of Theorem 1 are satisfied. Hence, we have the following theorem:

Theorem 3 Complete low-level connectivity is sufficient to guarantee the DRP.

Example 3 Consider again the 2-disk Tower of Hanoi domain. Construct an abstraction hierarchy by placing the predicate *OnBig* on the abstract level, and *OnSmall* on the concrete level. If we fix the position of the big disk we can freely move the small disk from any peg to another. The hierarchy satisfies the complete low-level connectivity condition. Now consider the opposite hierarchy where the predicate *OnSmall* is placed on the abstract level, while *OnBig* is on the concrete level. This hierarchy does not satisfy the complete low-level connectivity restriction, since whether or not the big disk can be moved to another peg depends on where the small disk is located. In this case it is also possible to show that the hierarchy does not have the DRP. For example, there is no monotonic refinement of the abstract plan $MoveSmall(Peg_1, Peg_3)$.

Unfortunately the complete connectivity condition is difficult to check syntactically. However, special cases can be constructed which can be checked. We give one example.

Definition 5 (Checkable Low-Level Connectivity) Complete low-level connectivity holds if for all levels i we have the following:

For any pair of literals L_1 and L_2, such that $crit(L_1) = crit(L_2) = i-1$, there exists α with $\mathsf{Pre}(\alpha) = \{L_1\}$, $\mathsf{Abs}(i-1, \mathsf{Add}(\alpha)) = \{L_2\}$, and $\mathsf{Abs}(i-1, \mathsf{Del}(\alpha)) = \emptyset$.

Necessary Connectivity The third condition we can place on the preconditions is the most general. The previous connectivity condition requires that all low level states be connected. This, however, is too restrictive. All that is actually required is low level connectivity between pairs of states that could be generated during the refinement of a higher level plan. We call this condition *necessary connectivity.*

In particular we have:

Definition 6 (Necessary Connectivity) Let $\mathcal{O}_{\geq i}$ be the set of operators whose add and delete lists contain at least one literal with criticality value greater than or equal to i. The condition of necessary connectivity is satisfied if for every level of abstraction i we have the following.

Let α_1 and α_2 be operators from $\mathcal{O}_{\geq i}$ such that

1. $\mathsf{Abs}(i, \alpha_1(\mathsf{Pre}(\alpha_1))) \cup \mathsf{Abs}(i, \mathsf{Pre}(\alpha_2))$ does not contain both a literal and its negation, where $\alpha_1(\mathsf{Pre}(\alpha_1))$ is the application of α_1 to its own preconditions, and
2. $\mathsf{Abs}(i-1, \mathsf{Pre}(\alpha_2)) \neq \emptyset$.

By these restrictions α_1 and α_2 are operators that could appear in sequence in an i-th level plan, i.e., the weakest postcondition state of α_1 does not contradict the preconditions of α_2 at level i; and α_2 depends on preconditions at level $i-1$ so that there is the possibility of a problem when refining to this level. For every such pair α_1 and α_2 there must exist an operator β such that:

1. β does not add or delete a literal with criticality higher than $i-1$,
2. $\mathsf{Abs}(i-1, \mathsf{Pre}(\beta)) \subseteq \alpha_1(\mathsf{Pre}(\alpha_1))$, i.e., the preconditions of β at abstraction level $i-1$ are satisfied in weakest the postcondition state of α_1, and
3. $\mathsf{Abs}(i-1, \mathsf{Pre}(\alpha_2)) \subseteq \beta(\mathsf{Pre}(\beta))$; i.e., operator β achieves the $i-1$ preconditions of α_2.

Intuitively, this condition is saying the following: for every pair of operators that might be sequenced in a plan at level i, there exists an operator β whose preconditions at abstraction level $i-1$ are satisfied in any state that results from applying α_1, and that be used to achieve the $i-1$-th level preconditions of α_2. Moreover, the operator β does not change any literal whose criticality value is greater than $i-1$. Therefore, on the semantic level, the conditions of Theorem 1 are satisfied. Thus, we have the following:

Theorem 4 Necessary connectivity are sufficient to guarantee the DRP.

Example 4 Consider the following extended Tower of Hanoi domain with two disks, where there is an additional peg, Peg_4 that is completely disconnected from the other three pegs. That is, although initially a disk can be placed on Peg_4, no disk can be moved to or away from it.

If we place *OnBig* at the abstract level and *OnSmall* at the concrete level, then the extended Tower of Hanoi domain satisfies the necessary connectivity condition. However, since Peg_4 is disconnected from the rest of the pegs, the concrete-level states are not completely connected. Therefore, the hierarchy does not satisfy the complete low-level connectivity condition.

Example 5 Consider the robot planning domain described by Sacerdoti [1]. A robot can travel between several rooms, where each pair of rooms is connected by one or more doors. A door can be either opened or closed by the robot. In addition, a number of boxes also exist, which can be either pushed around by the robot. To be more complex, we can also allow the robot to carry a box from one location to another. To carry a box, the robot has to first pick it up.

The domain is described by a number of predicates (see [1] for a complete description). An abstraction hierarchy can be built by assigning criticality values to the predicates in the following way. The highest level of abstraction consists of all type-preconditions, such as *Connects*, which asserts that a door connects two adjacent rooms. The next level down are predicates *Inroom, At* and *Nextto.* Further down are predicates that describe the status of the door, *Status(dx,Open)* or *Status(dx,Closed).* The lowest level are the predicates *Holding* and *Handempty.*

Suppose that all the goals are described by predicates *Inroom* and/or *Nextto.* Then the above hierarchy satisfies the DRP. In particular, the hierarchy satisfies the complete low-level connectivity condition. For example, the robot can either close or open a door once it is next to the door, without changing any location predicates. Similarly, the robot can pick up or put down a box without changing any door status or location predicates.

Example 6 Consider a problem of inter-city traveling by an agent. Assume that the agent can travel between cities by bus, train, or plane. Also assume that within each city, the agent can travel between a number of key locations by means of public transportation. Finally, the agent can travel to particular addresses in the local vicinity of each key location by walking. An abstraction hierarchy for this problem domain can be built by placing city-level locations at the highest level, the key locations at the next level, and the addresses at the concrete level. This hierarchy satisfies the DRP: once the agent is in a particular city he will never have to leave the city to travel between key locations in the city, and once he is at the nearest key location he never travel to another key location to travel between local addresses.

8 Conclusions and Future Work

In this paper, we have formalized the downward refinement property for ABSTRIPS-type of abstraction hierarchies. The DRP guarantees completeness of planning even when search refrains from backtrack across abstraction levels. Our analysis shows that an exponential amount of savings in search can be achieved. We have presented a general semantic condition for guaranteeing the DRP, and have derived a number of syntactic conditions from it. Although we lack the space it can be demonstrated that these conditions can be checked in polynomial time. Another topic we have not addressed is the use of our syntactic checks in the automatic generation of abstraction hierarchies that are guaranteed to have the DRP. It is possible to specify an algorithm that accomplishes this task.

This work is a step towards understanding abstract problem-solving in general. A number of extensions will be made in future work. One such extension is to design a richer set of conditions that allows for a broader range of application. Another is to explore the use of statistical information in the verification and generation of abstraction hierarchies. As stated above, all of our conditions are sufficient for guaranteeing the DRP. In practice, it may be the case that a large portion of a domain satisfies the property, but not all of it. This might cause the statistical phenomena that most, but not all, abstract solutions can be monotonically refined. We intend to explore the ramifications of this type of behavior. For example, if we have additional statistical information, then we may be able to make inferences as to how close the hierarchy is to having the DRP and the effect this would have on search efficiency.

Acknowledgements Thanks to Craig Knoblock and Josh Tenenberg for helpful comments.

References

[1] Earl Sacerdoti. Planning in a hierarchy of abstraction spaces. *Artificial Intelligence*, 5:115–135, 1974.

[2] Craig A. Knoblock. A theory of abstraction for hierarchical planning. In Paul Benjamin, editor, *Proceedings of the Workshop on Change of Representation and Inductive Bias*, Boston, MA, 1989. Kluwer.

[3] David Wilkins. Domain-independent planning: Representation and plan generation. *Artificial Intelligence*, 22, 1984.

[4] Qiang Yang and Josh D. Tenenberg. Abtweak: Abstracting a nonlinear, least commitment planner. In *Proceedings of Eighth National Conference on Artificial Intelligence*, Boston, MA, 1990.

[5] Richard Korf. Planning as search: A quantitative approach. *Artificial Intelligence*, 33:65–88, 1985.

[6] Hector J. Levesque. All I Know: A study in autoepistemic logic. Technical Report KRR–TR 89–3, University of Toronto, Toronto, Ont., Canada M5S 1A4, 1989.

[7] Joseph Y. Halpern and Yorham Moses. A guide to the modal logics of knowledge and belief. In *Proc. International Joint Conference on Artifical Intelligence (IJCAI)*, pages 480–490, 1985.

[8] Vladimir Lifschitz. On the semantics of strips. In *Proceedings of the Workshop on Reasoning about Actions and Plans*, Timberline, Oregon, 1986.

[9] Jens Christensen. A hierarchical planner that generates its own abstraction hieararchies. In *Proceedings of the 8th AAAI*, pages 1004–1009, Boston, MA., 1990.

[10] Craig A. Knoblock. Learning abstraction hierarchies for problem solving. In *Proceedings of Eighth National Conference on Artificial Intelligence*, Boston, MA, 1990.

[11] Craig Knoblock, Josh Tenenberg, and Qiang Yang. Characterizing abstraction hierarchies for planning. In *Proceedings of Ninth National Conference on Artificial Intelligence*, Anaheim, CA., 1991.

[12] Craig Knoblock. *Automatically Generating Abstractions for Problem Solving.* PhD thesis, School of Computer Science, Carnegie Mellon University, 1991. Technical Report CMU–CS–91–120.

AUTOMATED REASONING

Reason Maintenance

A Logically Complete Reasoning Maintenance System Based on a Logical Constraint Solver

J.C. Madre and **O. Coudert**
Bull Corporate Research Center
Rue Jean Jaurès
78340 Les Clayes-sous-bois FRANCE

Abstract

This paper presents a logically complete assumption based truth maintenance system (ATMS) that is part of a complex blast furnace computer aided piloting system [5]. This system is built on an efficient and logically complete propositional constraint solver that has been successfully used for industrial applications in computer aided design.

1 Introduction

A reasoning maintenance system (RMS) is a critical part of a reasoning system, since it is responsible for assuring that the inferences made by that system are valid. The reasoning system provides the RMS with information about each inference it performs, and in return the RMS provides the reasoning system with information about the whole set of inferences.

Several implementations of reasoning maintenance systems have been proposed in the past, remarkable ones being Doyle's truth maintenance system (TMS) [6], and De Kleer's assumption-based truth maintenance system (ATMS) [7]. Both of them suffer from some limitations. The TMS considers only one state at a time so it is not possible to manipulate environments [6]. The ATMS is intended to maintain multiple environments, but it is limited to propositional Horn clauses [7], so it is not logically complete with respect to full standard Propositional Logic.

This paper describes an original assumption-based truth maintenance system that is logically complete. The power of this system comes from the remarkable properties of the *typed decision graph canonical* representation of propositional formulas [1]. This representation originates from researches made in the field of formal verification of hardware. It has been successfully used in PRIAM [10], a formal verifier of digital circuits that has been integrated in Bull's CAD system in 1988, and is now used by all VLSI circuit designers at Bull.

The paper is divided in 4 parts. Part 2 gives the logical specifications of the reasoning maintenance system. Part 3 presents the typed decision graph representation. Part 4 describes the implementation of the RMS based on this representation. Part 5 discusses the experimental results that have been obtained with this system.

2 Functional Specifications

The reasoning maintenance system receives *propositional formulas* from the reasoning system [12]. These propositional formulas are built out of a countably infinite set of propositional variables using the usual logical connectors $\wedge$, $\vee$, $\Rightarrow$, $\Leftrightarrow$ and $\neg$. We note by KB the *knowledge base* of the system, which is the set of propositional formulas that the RMS maintains. The RMS distinguishes two kinds of variables, *assumptions* and *data*, the assumptions being the variables from which the data will be deduced. An *environment* is a set of *literals*, each literal being either a propositional variable or its negation.

Since any formula is a logical consequence of an inconsistent set of formulas, the first task of the RMS is to keep the knowledge base KB *consistent*. If $KB = \{f_1, \ldots, f_n\}$ then it is consistent if and only if there exists at least one assignment of truth values to the variables of $f_1, \ldots, f_n$ for which these formulas all evaluate to *True*. A consistent environment E is consistent with KB if $(KB \cup E)$ is consistent. If this is not the case, the RMS can be asked to compute the *maximal consistent sub-environments* of E that are all the maximal subsets of the set E consistent with KB.

It is critical for the reasoning system to know, at any moment, which data can be believed and which cannot be. The knowledge base KB and the environment E are said to *support* the datum d if and only if d is a logical consequence of the formulas in $(KB \cup E)$, which is expressed by: $KB,\ E \models d$. If this is the case, the RMS can be asked to compute all the minimal subsets of the environment E, called the *minimal supporters*, that also support this datum. Finally the *labels* of a datum d are all the minimal environments made of assumption variables that support d.

3 Typed Decision Graphs

Several normal forms of Propositional Logic have been used in the past as the basis of automated propositional provers and constraint solvers [11]. Some of these normal forms have the remarkable property of being *canonical*. These canonical forms are very appealing because they support very simple proof procedures. Two formulas written in canonical form are equivalent if and only if they are syntactically equal. More generally, since Propositional Logic is sound and complete, the formula

g can be deduced from the assumptions $\{h_1, \ldots, h_n\}$, which is expressed $(h_1, \ldots, h_n \models g)$ if and only if the formula $((h_1 \wedge \cdots \wedge h_n) \Rightarrow g)$ is valid, which is the case if and only if its canonical form is equal to *True*.

The computational cost of a proof procedure based on canonical rewriting depends on the time needed to rewrite the formula to be proved valid into its canonical form. This time is in the worst case, for all canonical forms, exponential with respect to the size of the formula to be rewritten. The problem is that this worst case was very easily obtained for all the canonical forms that were known until very recently [10]. We present here a new canonical representation that has been shown by experience to support a very efficient and simple rewriting process.

Typed decision graphs (TDG) are a new *canonical graph representation* of Propositional Logic [1]. This canonical form is directly inspired by Shannon's decomposition theorem. This theorem states that any Boolean function $f(x_1, \ldots, x_n)$ from the set $\{0,1\}^n$ to the set $\{0,1\}$ can be expressed in terms of a unique couple of Boolean functions (f_0, f_1) from the set $\{0,1\}^{n-1}$ to the set $\{0,1\}$ in the following way:

$$f = (\neg x_1 \wedge f_0) \vee (x_1 \wedge f_1).$$

The decomposition or expansion process defined above can be iterated until all variables are eliminated. It produces, for any Boolean function f and for any propositional formula f, a unique decomposition tree, called Shannon's tree of f, whose leaves are the constant *False* and *True*. The problem is that the decomposition tree of a formula f with n variables has 2^{n-1} vertices and 2^n leaves so it rapidly becomes too large to be computed when n becomes large. However in many cases, a lot of these vertices are redundant and can thus be eliminated. The elimination rule is very simple: a vertex is useless if and only if its left and right subtrees are identical, and it can then be replaced by either of these subtrees. R. E. Bryant showed in [3] that by sharing identical subtrees that are embedded at different places in Shannon's tree of a formula, the memory space required to store this tree can be dramatically reduced, and that the resulting graph representation, called the *binary decision diagram* (BDD) is canonical.

Shannon's tree of a formula f and its binary decision graph are canonical with respect to the decomposition ordering that has been chosen. The size of this graph, defined as the number of its vertices, heavily depends on this variable ordering [3]. For instance there exist formulas that have a BDD whose size is linear with respect to the size of the formula for the best variable ordering and exponential for the worst variable ordering. Though finding the best variable ordering is a NP-complete problem [9], good heuristics have been proposed to compute a good variable ordering from the structure of the syntactic tree of the formulas [13].

More recently, J. P. Billon defined a new canonical graph representation of Propositional Logic, called the *typed decision graphs* (TDG), that holds all the remarkable properties of the binary decision diagrams in addition with the *instantaneous negation* [1]. Instantaneous negation is obtained by using the same graph to represent a formula and its negation, and by using typed edges in the graphs: a positive edge is a standard one, a negative edge indicates that the pointed graph has to be transformed by a negation operation to obtain the equivalent BDD. Figure 1 shows the BDD and the TDG of the formula $f = (a \wedge (c \oplus d)) \vee (b \wedge (c \Leftrightarrow d))$. Typed decision graphs as well as binary decision diagrams support very efficient proof procedures, as well as efficient resolution procedures of Boolean equations [11].

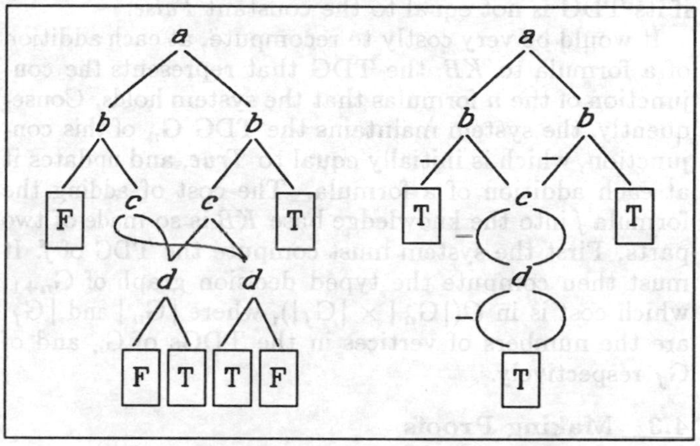

Figure 1: BDD and TDG of the formula $f = (a \wedge (c \oplus d)) \vee (b \wedge (c \Leftrightarrow d))$

Typed decision graphs have been developed in the framework of a research project on formal verification of digital circuits. The automated propositional prover that has been built on the typed decision graphs is the kernel of an industrially used formal verifier of circuits called PRIAM [10]. This tool, which has been integrated in Bull's proprietary computer aided design system in 1988, automatically proves the correctness of circuits with respect to their specification.

4 Implementation of the RMS

This section explains how the typed decision graph representation makes easy and efficient the implementation of the reasoning maintenance system. It gives, for each of the basic tasks that the system must perform, the corresponding procedure and its computational complexity.

4.1 Computing the TDG of a formula

The first task of the system is to compute the typed decision graphs of the formulas that it receives from the reasoning system. The rewriting process takes as input a propositional formula. It performs a depth first traversal of the syntactic tree of this formula, and it computes its TDG in a bottom-up manner by combining the typed decision graphs of its embedded sub-formulas. The leaves of the syntactic tree of the formula are variables whose associated typed decision graphs have only one vertex. These elementary graphs are then combined using the algorithm given in [3], that has been extended to TDG's, until the root of the syntactic tree is reached. The complexity of this rewriting process is in the worst case exponential with respect to the size of the syntactic tree of the formula to be rewritten.

4.2 Keeping the Knowledge Base Consistent

Keeping the knowledge base consistent is trivial. Each time a formula f has to be added to the knowledge base KB, the system first determines whether this formula is consistent, which is the case if and only if its TDG is different from the constant *False*. The system then determines whether this formula can be added to KB without making it becoming inconsistent. If $KB = \{f_1, \ldots, f_n\}$, the resulting base is consistent if and only if the formula $(f_1 \wedge \cdots \wedge f_n \wedge f)$ is satisfiable, which is true if and only if its TDG is not equal to the constant *False*.

It would be very costly to recompute, at each addition of a formula to KB, the TDG that represents the conjunction of the n formulas that the system holds. Consequently, the system maintains the TDG G_n of this conjunction, which is initially equal to *True*, and updates it at each addition of a formula. The cost of adding the formula f into the knowledge base KB is so made of two parts. First the system must compute the TDG of f. It must then compute the typed decision graph of G_{n+1}, which cost is in $O(|G_n| \times |G_f|)$, where $|G_n|$ and $|G_f|$ are the numbers of vertices in the TDGs of G_n and of G_f respectively.

4.3 Making Proofs

Thanks to the canonicity of the graph representation, proofs are also very easy to perform. Consider a literal d, the knowledge base $KB = \{f_1, \ldots, f_n\}$ and the environment $E = \{h_1, \ldots, h_k\}$. The environment E is consistent if and only if the typed decision graph of the formula $(h_1 \wedge \cdots \wedge h_k)$ is different from *False*. In the same way, the environment E is consistent with the knowledge base KB if and only if the formula $C = (f_1 \wedge \cdots \wedge f_n \wedge h_1 \wedge \cdots \wedge h_k)$ does not reduce to *False*. Finally the literal d holds in the environment E of KB if and only if the formula $D = (C \Rightarrow d)$ is valid, which happens if and only if its TDG is equal to *True*.

Computing the TDG of the formula C is in $O(|G_n| \times k)$ where G_n is the TDG of the conjunction of all the formulas in KB. Since the TDG of the literal d has only one vertex, computing the TDG of the formula D is linear with respect to the number of vertices in the TDG of C.

4.4 Minimal Suppporters

Consider the knowledge base $KB = \{f_1, \ldots, f_n\}$ and the environment $E = \{h_1, \ldots, h_k\}$ that support the literal d. The minimal supporters problem is to find all the minimal subsets E' of E that also support d.

Without loss of generality, we will here assume that the literals $h_1, \ldots, h_k$ and d are all positive, i. e. they are propositional variables. If this is not the case we create, for each negative literal l occurring in $\{h_1, \ldots, h_k\} \cup \{d\}$, a new variable pl, then we add the formula $(pl \Leftrightarrow (\neg\, l))$ into the knowledge base, and finally we substitute l with pl in E. The renaming technique defined above allows us to assume, too, that the literal d is not in the set $\{h_1, \ldots, h_k\}$.

A minimal supporter E' of d is a set $\{h'_1, \ldots, h'_m\}$, where $h'_1, \ldots, h'_m$ are elements from the set $\{h_1, \ldots, h_n\}$, such that: $KB,\ E' \models d$. We note by P the conjunction $(f_1 \wedge \cdots \wedge f_n)$, and by H' the conjunction $(h'_1 \wedge \cdots \wedge h'_m)$. The formula given above can be rewritten into $(P, H' \models d)$, which is true if and only if the formula $((P \wedge H') \Rightarrow d)$ is valid.

Shannon's expansion of the formula P with respect to the variable d provides us with a couple of formulas (P_0, P_1) such that $(P \Leftrightarrow ((\neg\, d \wedge P_0) \vee (d \wedge P_1)))$. Since the variable d does not occur in H', Shannon's expansion of the formula $(P \wedge H')$ with respect to the variable d is the couple of formulas $((P_0 \wedge H'), (P_1 \wedge H'))$. Finally, Shannon's expansion of the formula $((P \wedge H') \Rightarrow d)$ with respect to d is $(\neg\, (P_0 \wedge H'), \mathit{True})$ and this formula is a tautology if and only if the formula $(\neg\, (P_0 \wedge H'))$ is valid. This means that the minimal supporters problem comes down to finding all the minimal products H' such that the formula $(\neg\, (P_0 \wedge H'))$ is valid.

These minimal products can be computed in two steps. The first step consists in computing the characteristic function $\chi_{\min}$ of the set of environments built out of the variables $h_1, \ldots, h_k$ that support the literal d. The second step consists in choosing amongst all these sets the minimal ones.

The variables occurring in the formula P_0 are all the variables that have been introduced in the reasoning maintenance system except for the variable d. These variables are the variables $h_1, \ldots, h_k$ and some other variables $x_1, \ldots, x_p$. The first step in the computation of the minimal supporters of d is to get rid of the variables $x_1, \ldots, x_p$ that are not useful for this computation. Any assignment of Boolean values $v_1, \ldots, v_k$ to the variables $h_1, \ldots, h_k$ uniquely defines an environment built out of these variables. This environment supports the datum d if and only if the formula $(\forall x_1 \ldots x_p\ P_0[h_1 \leftarrow v_1] \ldots [h_k \leftarrow v_k])$ is valid. The quantified part of this formula expresses that the formula $(P_0[h_1 \leftarrow v_1] \ldots [h_k \leftarrow v_k])$ evaluates to 1, whatever values are assigned to the variables $x_1, \ldots, x_p$. Using this notation, we can define the characteristic function $\chi_{\min}$ with the equation:

$$\chi_{\min}(h_1, \ldots, h_k) = (\forall x_1 \ldots x_p\ P_0)$$

The TDG G_{min} of $\chi_{\min}$ is directly obtained from the TDG of P_0 by eliminating the variables $x_1, \ldots, x_p$. This elimination is based on the identity:

$$(\forall x_1 \cdots x_p\ f) \quad = \quad (\forall x_1 \ldots x_{p-1}\ (f_0 \wedge f_1))$$

where the couple of formulas (f_0, f_1) is Shannon's expansion of f with respect to the variable x_p.

The second step in the minimal supporters computation consists in computing the minimal products H' such that $(\neg\, (P_0 \wedge H'))$. These minimal products are by definition the prime implicants of the function $\chi_{\min}$ [11], [14]. Finding the prime implicants of a Boolean function f written in normal disjunctive or in normal conjunctive form is a difficult problem [2]. This problem is made much simpler when the function is written in Shannon's canonical form thanks to Shannon's decomposition theorem. We propose in [11] the function `Primes` for computing all the prime implicants of the function f that is based on a depth first traversal of the TDG of the function f and treats each vertex of this graph only once.

This algorithm is a modified version of the algorithm given in [2] for functions in disjunctive normal form.

Note that there exist Boolean functions whose TDG has n vertices and that have 2^n prime implicants. This shows why typed decision graphs are a good representation of propositional formulas, since it means that there are formulas that have an exponential size with respect to the number of their variables when represented in disjunctive or conjunctive (clausal) normal form and that are represented by a TDG of polynomial size.

The computational cost of the minimal supporters computation is the following. Computing Shannon's decomposition of the formula P with respect to the variable d is linear with respect to the size of the TDG of the formula P. Computing the characteristic function $\chi_{\min}$ is in the worst case exponential with respect to the size of the TDG of the formula P_0, but this worst case has never occurred in real world problems. Finally applying the function `Primes` can also be in the worst case exponential with respect to the size of the TDG of the formula $\chi_{\min}$. However in this case this exponential complexity does not depend on the typed decision graph representation but on the size of the set to be computed.

The set of prime implicants that are generated by the function `Primes` for the different vertices of the graph drawn in Figure 2 are the following: $\{(\neg d)\}$ for A, $\{(d)\}$ for B and C, $\{(\neg d)\}$ for D and E, $\{(\neg c), (\neg d)\}$ for F, $\{((\neg c) \wedge d)\}$ for G, $\{((\neg c) \wedge d), (c \wedge (\neg d))\}$ for H, $\{(c \wedge (\neg d))\}$ for I, $\{((\neg c) \wedge d), ((\neg b) \wedge (\neg c)), ((\neg b) \wedge (\neg d))\}$ for J, $\{(c \wedge (\neg d)), ((\neg b) \wedge (\neg c) \wedge d)\}$ for K and $\{((\neg b) \wedge (\neg c) \wedge d), ((\neg a) \wedge (\neg b) \wedge (\neg c)), ((\neg a) \wedge (\neg b) \wedge (\neg d)), ((\neg a) \wedge (\neg c) \wedge d), (a \wedge c \wedge (\neg d))\}$ for L.

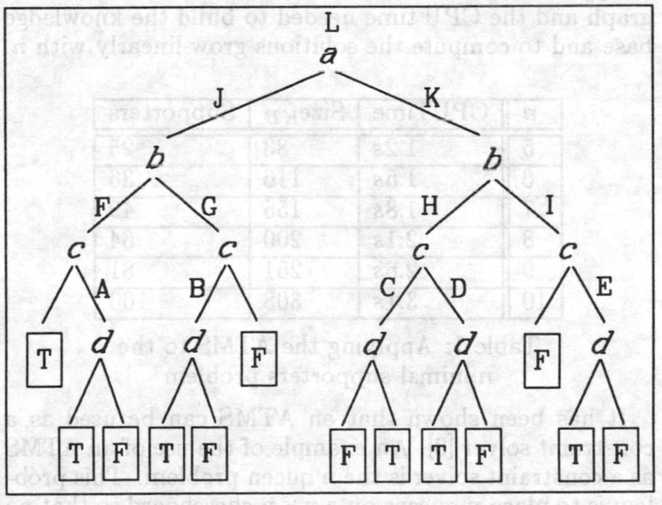

Figure 2: A sample execution of the function `Primes`

4.5 Maximal Consistent Sub-Environments

Consider the knowledge base $KB = \{f_1, \cdots, f_n\}$ and the consistent environment $E = \{h_1, \cdots, h_k\}$ that is inconsistent with KB. The maximal consistent sub-environments problem is to find all the maximal subsets E' of E that are consistent with KB. Without loss of generality, like we did in Section 4.4, we will assume that the literals $h_1, \cdots, h_k$ are positive, i. e. they are propositional variables.

By definition, a maximal consistent sub-environment of E is a subset $E' = \{h'_1, \ldots, h'_m\}$ of E such that E' is consistent with KB et there does not exist a subset E'' of E such that $(E' \subset E'')$ and E'' is consistent with KB. If we note by P the conjunction $(f_1 \wedge \cdots \wedge f_n)$, and by H' the conjunction $(h'_1 \wedge \cdots \wedge h'_m)$, then E' is a maximal consistent sub-environment of E if and only if the formula $(P \wedge H')$ is satisfiable, which is the case if and only if its TDG is not the constant *False*. The problem thus comes down to finding all the maximal sub-products H' of the product $(h_1 \wedge \cdots \wedge h_m)$ such that $(P \wedge H')$ is satisfiable.

These maximal sub-products can be computed using an algorithm that is very similar to the algorithm given in Section 4.4 for the minimal supporters problem. This algorithm works in two steps. The first step consists in computing the characteristic function $\chi_{\max}$ of the set of environments build out of the variables $h_1, \ldots, h_k$ that are consistent with the knowledge base KB. The variables occurring in the formula P are all the variables that have been introduced in the reasoning maintenance system. These variables are the variables $h_1, \ldots, h_k$ and some other variables $x_1, \ldots, x_p$. Using the notation defined in Section 4.4, we can define the function $\chi_{\max}$ with the equation:

$$\chi_{\max}(h_1, \ldots, h_k) = (\exists x_1 \ldots x_p\ P)$$

which expresses that $\chi_{\max}(v_1, \ldots, v_k)$ is equal to *True* if and only if there exists at least one assignment of Boolean values to the variables $x_1, \ldots, x_p$ for which the formula $(P[h_1 \leftarrow v_1] \ldots [h_k \leftarrow v_k])$ evaluates to 1.

The second step in the maximal sub-environments computation consists in computing the maximal products H' such that $(\chi_{\max} \wedge H')$ is satisfiable. If the function $\chi_{\max}$ is the constant *False*, then there are no such products, which means that the set of maximal consistent sub-environments is empty. If the function $\chi_{\max}$ was equal to *True*, then E itself would be the only one maximal consistent sub-environment. Since we assumed that E is inconsistent with KB this situation can not happen. The maximal products searched for can be computed with the function `MaximalProducts` given in [11] using a depth first traversal of the TDG G_{max} of the function $\chi_{\max}$ [11]. During this traversal, the function `MaximalProducts` traverses each vertex of the graph G_{max} only once, and it computes the maximal products associated with this vertex by combining the sets of maximal products that have been obtained for its left and right branches [11]. The cost of the maximal consistent sub-environments computation is the same as the computational cost of the minimal supporters computation.

The set of maximal cubes generated by the function `MaximalProducts` for the different vertices of the graph drawn in Figure 3 are the following: $\{True\}$ for A and B, $\{(d)\}$ for C, $\{True\}$ for D, $\{(c)\}$ for E, $\{(c \wedge d)\}$ for F, $\{(d)\}$ for G, $\{(b \wedge c)\}$ for H, $\{(b \wedge d), (c \wedge d)\}$ for I, $\{(b \wedge c)$ and $(a \wedge b \wedge d), (a \wedge c \wedge d)\ \}$ for J.

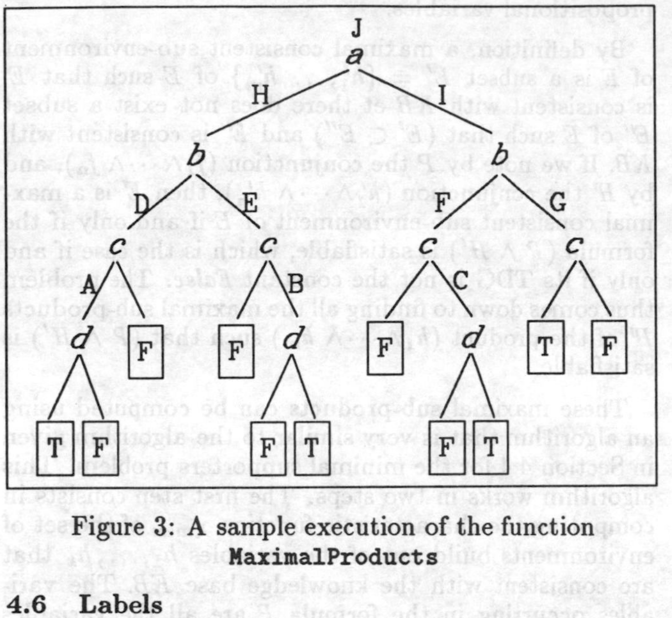

Figure 3: A sample execution of the function `MaximalProducts`

4.6 Labels

The variables that compose the formulas of the knowledge base $KB = \{f_1, \ldots, f_n\}$ are the assumption variables $a_1, \ldots, a_p$ and the datum variables $d_1, \ldots, d_q$. By definition the datum variables have been deduced from the assumption variables. The labels problem is to find all the minimal environments made of assumption variables that support one of the datum variables.

The labels of the datum d are computed in three steps. The first step consists in computing the characteristic function $\chi_{\max}$ of the set of environments built out of the assumption variables that are consistent with the knowledge base KB. This characteristic function, defined by:

$$\chi_{\max}(a_1, \ldots, a_p) = (\exists d_1 \ldots d_q \ P)$$

where we note by P the conjunction $(f_1 \wedge \cdots \wedge f_n)$, can be computed using the procedure defined in Section 4.5. The second step consists in computing the characteristic function $\chi_{\min}$ of all the environments built out of the assumption variables that support the datum d. This characteristic function can be computed using the procedure given in Section 4.4. Finally the third step in the labels computation consists in extracting these labels from $\chi_{\max}$ and $\chi_{\min}$. There are two ways to perform this extraction, depending on whether the characteristic function $\chi_{\max}$ is used *passively* or *actively*:

- The minimal environments that support the datum d can be extracted from the TDG of $\chi_{\min}$ using the function `Primes` presented in Section 4.4. Some of these minimal environments can be inconsistent with the knowledge base KB. These minimal environments that are inconsistent with KB can be eliminated using the characteristic function $\chi_{\max}$ as a *filter*. In this case the characteristic function $\chi_{\max}$ is used passively because all minimal environments that support d are computed, and inconsistent ones are eliminated afterwards.
- Inconsistent environments can be eliminated as soon as possible during the computation of the prime implicants of the characteristic function $\chi_{\min}$. The function `Primes` can be modified to take a second argument that is the TDG of the characteristic function $\chi_{\max}$. During the bottom up generation process, the TDG of $\chi_{\max}$ is used to eliminate the inconsistent environments as soon as they are discovered.

The complexity of this procedure is the same as the complexity of the procedure `Primes` given in Section 4.4.

5 Experimental Results

The reasoning maintenance system presented in this paper has been written in the C language and the results given have been obtained on a Sun Sparc Station. The reasoning maintenance system has an integrated garbage collector that guarantees that the memory use is kept minimal during execution. This garbage collector is incremental which allows the RMS to be used in a real time environment.

The first set of examples given here are minimal supporters computations. We provided the RMS with n environments that support the datum p, and n environments that support the datum q. The environment $\{p, q\}$ supports the datum r. Each of these environments is made of n distinct assumptions variables. This means that the number of assumptions variables used in each of these examples is equal to $2 \times n^2$. The problem is to find the n^2 minimal supporters of r. Table 1 shows the results for these examples. It gives, for each example, the CPU time (**CPU time**) needed to compute the solutions, the number of vertices (**Size**$_{KB}$) of the TDG that denotes the conjunction of all the formulas in the knowledge base and the number of minimal supporters (**Supporters**) to be found. Note that the size of this graph and the CPU time needed to build the knowledge base and to compute the solutions grow linearly with n.

n	CPUTime	Size$_{KB}$	Supporters
5	1.2s	83	25
6	1.5s	116	36
7	1.8s	155	49
8	2.1s	200	64
9	2.6s	251	81
10	3.1s	308	100

Table 1: Applying the ATMS to the minimal supporters problem

It has been shown that an ATMS can be used as a constraint solver [8]. An example of the use of an ATMS as a constraint solver is the n queen problem. This problem is to place n queens on a $n \times n$ chessboard so that no queen dominates any other one. In order to specify the n queen problem, we introduce n^2 propositional variables; each one is associated with one square of the chessboard and indicates whether there is a queen on this square. The formulas or constraints of the n queen problem express that there are no more than one queen on each line, each column and each diagonal of the chessboard.

Table 2 gives the results obtained for $n = 4$ to $n = 9$. For each of these problems, the table gives the CPU time (**Time**$_B$) needed to build the knowledge base, the size

($\mathbf{Size}_{KB}$) of the typed decision graph that represents this base, the CPU time ($\mathbf{Time}_S$) required to compute the solutions and the number of solutions (**Solutions**). These solutions are obtained through a maximal consistent sub-environments request. Note that in this case the size of the TDG that represents the knowledge base grows exponentially with n, while the time needed to compute the solutions grows linearly with the number of solutions to be found.

Queens	$Time_B$	$Size_{KB}$	$Time_S$	Solutions
4	$0.2s$	29	$0.01s$	2
5	$0.6s$	166	$0.1s$	10
6	$1.0s$	129	$0.05s$	4
7	$2.7s$	1098	$0.4s$	40
8	$7.4s$	2450	$1.0s$	92
9	$33.5s$	9556	$7.0s$	352

Table 2: Applying the ATMS to the n-queen problem

6 Conclusion

This paper has presented an original implementation of a logically complete assumption based truth maintenance system. This implementation is based on a new canonical representation of Boolean functions called the typed decision graphs. This canonical form, which is amongst the most compact representations of Boolean functions that are currently known, has remarkable properties that give the system its efficiency. Our approach is quite different from the one followed by De Kleer who proposes an ATMS as a constraint solver [8], since we use here a constraint solver developed for other purposes to build an ATMS. This ATMS has been integrated in the prototype version of a complex blast furnace computer aided piloting system [5]. Within this system the RMS receives formulas from a reasoning system written in Kool [4]. The piloting system is intended to be a real time system so an incremental garbage collection scheme has been developed that guarantees a continuous operation of the RMS.

Acknowledgments

The authors would like to thank Jean Paul Billon for many suggestions and good advice, Jerome Euzénat, Philippe Kirsch, Libéro Maesano and Jean Marc Pugin from Bull Cediag for their help and very helpful criticisms.

References

[1] J. P. Billon. Perfect Normal Forms For Discrete functions. Bull Research Report N°87019, June 1987.

[2] R. K. Brayton, G. D. Hatchel, C. T. McMullen and A. L. Sangiovanni-Vincentelli. *Logic Minimization Algorithms for VLSI Synthesis.* Kluwer Academic Publishers, 1984.

[3] R. E. Bryant. Graph-based Algorithms For Boolean Functions Manipulation. *IEEE transactions on computers*, C35(8):677-691, August 1986.

[4] Bull Cediag. *Kool V2 Reference Manual.* Bull Cediag, June 1989.

[5] Bull, ITMI, CSI. *Consultation pour la réalisation d'un système d'aide à la conduite des hauts fourneaux. Offre technique et Organisationnelle.* Projet Sachem, October 1990.

[6] J. Doyle. A Truth Maintenance System. *Artificial Intelligence*, 12:231-271, 1979.

[7] J. de Kleer. An Assumption-based TMS. *Artificial Intelligence*, 28:127-162, 1986.

[8] J. de Kleer. Comparison of ATMS and CSP Techniques. In *Proceedings of the 89 IJCAI Conference* pages 290-296, Detroit, Michigan, 1989.

[9] S. J. Friedman and K. J. Supowtit. Finding the Optimal Oredring for Binary Decision Diagrams. In *Proceedings of the 24th Design Automation Conference*, June 1987.

[10] J. C. Madre and J. P. Billon. Proving Circuit Correctness using Formal Comparison Between Expected and Extracted Behaviour. In *Proceedings of the 25th Design Automation Conference*, Anaheim, California, June 1988.

[11] J. C. Madre and O. Coudert. A Complete Reasoning Maintenance System Based On Typed Decision Graphs. Bull Research Report N°90006, March 1990.

[12] L. Maesano. *Spécifications fonctionnelles de l'interface programmatique à un Système de Maintien du Raisonnement.* Projet Sachem, June 1989.

[13] S. Minato, N. Ishiura and S. Yajima. Fast Tautology Checking Using Shared Binary Decision Diagrams - Experimental Results. In *Proceedings of the Workshop on Applied Formal Methods for Correct VLSI Design* pages 107-111, Leuven, Belgium, November 1989.

[14] R. Reiter and J. de Kleer. Foundations for Assumption-Based Truth Maintenance Systems. Preliminary Report. In *Proceedings of AAAI-87, American Association for Artificial Intelligence National Conference* pages 183-188, Seattle, July 13-17, 1987,

Contexts for nonmonotonic RMSes

Jérôme Euzenat

SHERPA project,
Laboratoire ARTEMIS/IMAG,
BP 53X,
F-38041 GRENOBLE
internet: Jerome.Euzenat@sherpa.imag.fr, uucp: euzenat@imag.fr

Abstract

A new kind of RMS, based on a close merge of TMS and ATMS, is proposed. It uses the TMS graph and interpretation and the ATMS multiple context labelling procedure. In order to fill in the problems of the ATMS environments in presence of nonmonotonic inferences, a new kind of environment, able to take into account hypotheses that do not hold, is defined. These environments can inherit formulas that hold as in the ATMS context lattice. The dependency graph can be interpreted with regard to these environments; so every node can be labelled. Furthermore, this leads to consider several possible interpretations of a query.

Reason maintenance systems (RMS) are aimed at managing a knowledge base considering different kinds of reasoning. Such a system is connected to a reasoner (or problem solver) which communicates every inference made. The RMS has in charge the maintenance of the reasoner's current belief base. RMSes developed so far focussed on nonmonotonic reasoning or multiple contexts reasoning. They record each inference in a *justification* that relates *nodes* representing propositional formulas plus a special atom ($\perp$) representing contradiction. A justification ($<\{i_1,\ldots i_n\}\{o_1,\ldots o_m\}>: c$) is made of an IN-list ($\{i_1,\ldots i_n\}$) and an OUT-list ($\{o_1,\ldots o_m\}$). Such a justification is said to be valid if and only if all the nodes in the IN-list are known to hold while those in the OUT-list are not; a node, in turn, is known to hold if and only if it is the consequent (c) of a valid justification. The recursion of the definition is stopped by nodes without justification and by the axioms that are nodes with a justification containing empty IN- and OUT-lists.

Jon Doyle's TMS [Doyle, 1979] proceeds by labelling the nodes of the graph with IN and OUT tags which reflect whether they are known to hold or not. A labelling respecting the constraints stated above is an admissble labelling and a labelling which labels the node $\perp$ OUT is a consistent labelling. The TMS algorithm finds a (weakly) founded labelling, i.e. a consistent admissible labelling which relies on no circular argument. The main work of the TMS occurs when it receives a new justification. It then has to integrate the justification in the graph and, if this changes the validity of the formula, it must propagate this validity: all the nodes that could be IN-ed because of the justified node and all those which could be OUT-ed are examined and updated. If an inconsistency occurs following the addition of a justification, the system backtracks on the justifications in order to invalidate a hypothesis — a formula inferred non monotonically — which supports the inconsistency.

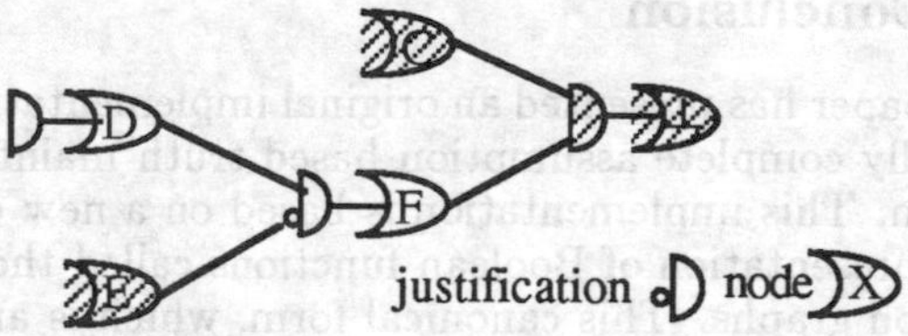

Figure 1. A dependency graph is here represented as a boolean circuit where or-gates are nodes and and-gates are justifications where the nodes in the IN-list come directly while nodes in the OUT-list come through a not-gate. Nodes that have a justification whose IN- and OUT-lists are empty (e.g. D) represent true formulas because they do not need to be inferred. White nodes and justifications are considered valid while hatched ones are invalid. Of course, the value propagation satisfies the rules implied by the circuit components. So, the formulas in the base are ensured to have a valid justification (i.e. corresponding to a valid inference).

Johan De Kleer's assumption-based TMS [De Kleer, 1986; 1988] is rather different. This system considers only monotonic inferences (with only IN-list: $<\{i_1,\ldots i_n\}>: c$), but it deals with several contexts at a time. It considers initial formulas called hypotheses; so, the user can generate and test hypotheses with great efficiency. A set of hypotheses is called an environment and the set of all the environments constitutes a complete lattice structured by the "includes" relation (cf. Figure 2). Instead of labelling absolutely a node (with IN or OUT tags), each node is assigned a label consisting of the set of environments under which it is known to hold. An environment is consistent if $\perp$ is not known to hold in it and the computed labels are minimal in the sense that they do not contain comparable environments. After each inference, the system computes the set of environments that support the inference, inserts it in the label of the inferred node and propagates it through the graph. Then, in order to know if a formula is valid, it compares the current hypothesis set with the label of the node.

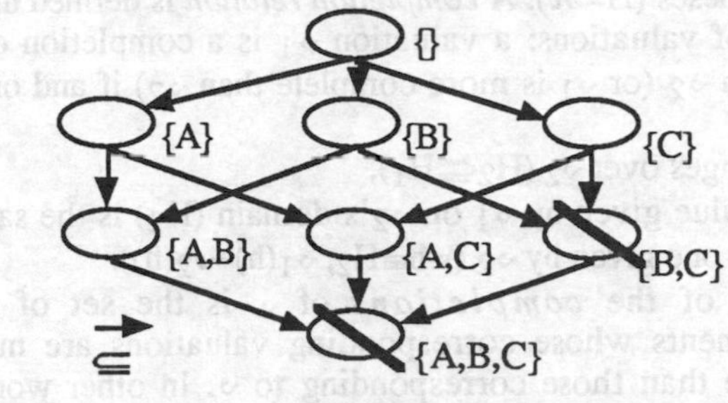

Figure 2. The environment lattice constructed with the hypotheses A, B and C in which the environment {B, C} is known as inconsistent.

As a summary, the TMS handles nonmonotonic inferences and is able to maintain the set of deduced formulas with regard to an axiom set. The ATMS, for its part, cannot accept nonmonotonic inferences, but is able to consider several contexts simultaneously. Merging both systems is needed in order to dispose of a RMS able to deal with nonmonotonicity in multiple contexts. This is the purpose of our context-propagation TMS (CP-TMS).

The first section shows the problem of doing it by extending the ATMS. Section 2 sketches the ideas underlying the CP-TMS. Its construction spreads through sections 3, 4, 5 and 6 by defining the valuations that environments represent, the interpretations that extend valuations to all the formulas, the labels tied to the formulas and their properties of completeness, correctness, minimality and consistency. Section 7 shows that queries can exploit labels in several ways. The last sections are dedicated to the description of a partial implementation (§8), a discussion of some shortcomings of the system (§9) and several solutions to these problems (§10).

1.ATMS and nonmonotonicity

Using an ATMS in order to deal with nonmonotonic reasoning seems attractive. In fact, the introduction of nonmonotonic inferences in the ATMS does not fit well. The main advantage of the ATMS is its use of the context lattice structure in order to infer that if a formula is valid in some environment, it will be under all its supersets. This is the strict definition of monotonicity. So, nonmonotonic inferences lead to important problems in the ATMS (cf. exemple 1).

Example 1.

Deciding under which environment the inference $<\{A\}\{B\}>$:D is valid is not possible. At first sight, {A} is a good candidate because A holds in it while B does not. But, since, in that case, D will be inherited from {A} to {A, B} (cf. Figure 2), in which B holds, {A} is not an adequate environment.

Several authors proposed a special use of the ATMS or similar systems in order to solve these problems [Dressler, 1989; De Kleer, 1988; Giordano and Martelli, 1990]. Here is Oskar Dressler's solution: for each node N, an hypothesis Out(N) can be created whose label represents the set of environments under which N does not hold. Inconsistency between N and Out(N) is dealt with by adding a constraint. and completeness is achieved with the help of a special hyperresolution rule.

With this framework, nonmonotonic justifications can be taken into account. The justification ($<\{i_1,\ldots i_n\}\{o_1,\ldots o_m\}>$: c) is communicated to the ATMS by:

$$\forall k;\ 1\leq k\leq m\ <\{o_k\}>: O$$

and

$$<\{i_1,\ldots\quad i_n,OUT(O)\}>: c.$$

While this approach works well, it suffers from some drawbacks: nonmonotonicity is achieved by multiplying entities. This leads to a "monotonization" of the reasoning and a multiplication of inconsistent contexts (leading, in turn, to intensive hyperresolution). Moreover, additional out-hypotheses are not all significant element for the user.

Since such an approach consists in adding an interface level on the ATMS, it has the advantage to not modify it significantly. But, while it is conceptually simple, it reveals to be a bit cumbersome to work.

2.An alternative

As an alternative solution, a merge between TMS and ATMS is considered which strongly modifies these systems [Euzenat, 1989; 1990]. The main idea consists in using nonmonotonic inferences and the dependency graph of the TMS and labelling the nodes by multi-contexts labels of the ATMS. It means that each node is labelled by the environments such that an absolute (IN/OUT) labelling according to the environment specification will lead the node to hold (be IN).

As pointed out above, representing nonmonotonic inferences in the ATMS context lattice is not possible. Thus, a new kind of environment is defined taking into account the OUTness of a node. *Environments* being built on hypotheses, the new ones will contain the set of holding hypotheses and the set of non holding ones. These new environments are noted by

$$[H_1,\ldots H_n \mid H'_1,\ldots H'_m]$$

or

$$[\{H_1,\ldots H_n\} / \{H'_1,\ldots H'_m\}]$$

where the hypotheses $H_1,\ldots H_n$ hold while the hypotheses $H'_1,\ldots H'_m$ do not. The first set is called *axiom set* while the second is called *restriction*. In order to have a meaningful definition of these environments, the two sets are constrained to be disjoint. At first sight, the idea is not a new one: the two systems ART and MBR [Martins and Shapiro, 1988] have such a kind of environment but they do not share the same semantics.

An environment, for which each possible hypothesis belongs either to the axiom set or the restriction, is called a complete environment. It is assumed to describe the entire world state. Since any environment is generally not complete, it cannot represent *a* state of the world. Its semantics is that it represents the set of complete environments more complete than itself.

So the principle of the system is the same as the ATMS's but the nonmonotonic inferences are taken into account. The absolute labelling of the TMS being manifold, what is meant by a node "holding under an environment", must be set. The possibilities are threefold (cf. Figure 3):

1) For each environment, the TMS chooses the absolute labelling it considers and the node is labelled according to it.
2) The node must hold under every possible labelling according to the environment.
3) The node must hold under at least one possible labelling according to the environment.

We choose the third solution: a node holds under an environment if it holds for at least one labelling according to each completion of the environment.

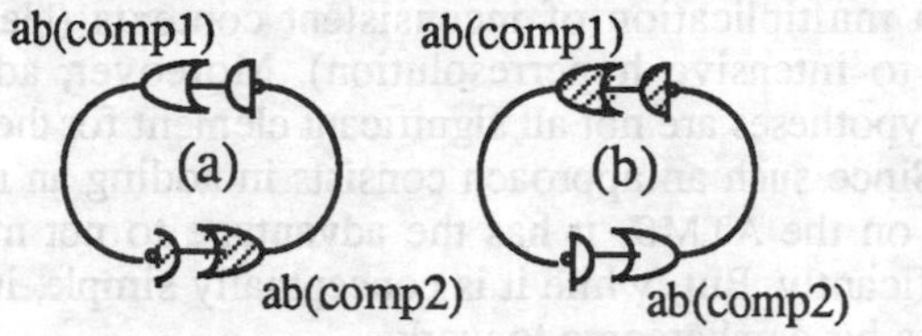

Figure 3. The inferences corresponding to these graphs are: If "Component 1 is abnormal" is not in the base Then hypothesize "Component 2 is abnormal" and If "Component 2 is abnormal" is out of the base Then hypothesize "Component 1 is abnormal". The picture represents the two admissible labelling of the graph.
• If the first option is chosen with (a) as reference labelling, then ab(comp1) holds under the empty environment while ab(comp2) does not.
• If the second option is chosen, then both ab(comp1) and ab(comp2) do not hold (for each one, there exists a labelling for which it does not hold).
• If the last option is chosen, then both ab(comp1) and ab(comp2) hold (for each one, there exists a labelling for which it does hold).

The next sections are dedicated to formally define the new environments and the relations between them. Environment semantics, concerning only hypotheses, are extended toward the whole node base with regard to the dependency graph. Hence, the meaning of labels associated to the nodes can be defined. This work leads to consider several interpretations of the queries against the base.

3. Environments

In the remainder are considered a set $\mathcal{H}$ of hypotheses and a set $\mathcal{N}$ of nodes (with naturally $\mathcal{H} \subset \mathcal{N}$). The set $\mathcal{C}$ of inconsistent nodes will be, without loss of generality, reduced to the set $\{\bot\}$ (thus $\bot \in \mathcal{N} \backslash \mathcal{H}$).

A *valuation* is a boolean function

$$\nu: H \longrightarrow \{0,1\}, \text{ where } H \subseteq \mathcal{H},$$

which states if the hypotheses in the set H hold or not. An environment [A/R] represents the valuation:

$$\begin{array}{rcl} \nu: A \cup R & \longrightarrow & \{0,1\} \\ N & \longmapsto & 1, \text{ if } N \in A \\ & & 0, \text{ if } N \in R \end{array}$$

Of course, A and R must be disjoint in order to avoid valuations that are not functions. Due to the unambiguous mapping between valuations and environments, each one can, subsequently, replace the other.

A valuation is *complete* if it ranges over the whole set of hypotheses ($H=\mathcal{H}$). A *completion relation* is defined upon the set of valuations: a valuation ν_1 is a completion of a valuation ν_2 (or ν_1 is more complete than ν_2) if and only if:

- ν_1 ranges over ν_2 ($H_2 \subseteq H_1$),
- the value given by ν_1 on ν_2's domain (H_2) is the same as the one given by ν_2 ($\forall h \in H_2, \nu_1(h)=\nu_2(h)$).

The set of the *completions* of ν is the set of the environments whose corresponding valuations are more complete than those corresponding to ν. In other words: [A"/R"] is more complete than [A/R] if and only if A is included in (or equal to) A" and R is included in (or equal to) R". The completion set of an environment is defined by:

$$\text{Comp}([A/R]) = \{ [A \cup A'/R \cup R'];\ R' \cup A' \subseteq \mathcal{H} \ \&\ (R \cap A') \cup (R' \cap A) \cup (A' \cap R') = \{\} \}.$$

This completion relation, among the set of environments definable from a set of hypotheses, is a partial order. But the graph representing environments structured by the completion relation is not a complete lattice anymore.

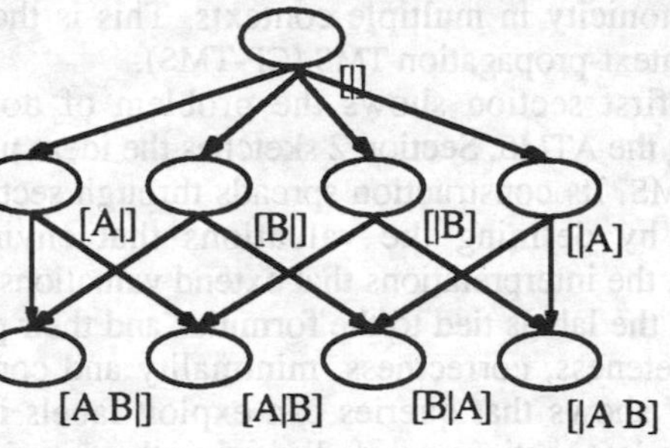

Figure 4. The graph of the completion relation upon the set of hypotheses reduced to {A, B}. There are three completeness levels with regard to the status assigned to the hypotheses. The last level (in which both hypotheses are refered to in the environments) is the set of all the complete environments.

This graph has good properties the ATMS graph lacks. In fact, if F is inferred from B not holding (<{}{B}>:F), then F can have [|B] in its label. Moreover, the node F can be inherited from [|B] to its completions ([A|B] and [|A,B]): they preserve the condition that B does not hold.

A *maximal completion* of a valuation ν is a completion of ν that has the set of all the hypotheses as domain ($H=\mathcal{H}$). So the set of the maximal completions of an environment [A/R] is:

$$\text{Cmax}([A/R]) = \{[A \cup A'/R \cup R'] \in \text{Comp}([A/R]);\ A \cup A' \cup R \cup R' = \mathcal{H} \}.$$

4. Interpretations

Environments, with the help of valuations, allow to valuate hypotheses. In order to design a reason maintenance system, it is necessary to define the valuation of all the nodes. The interpretation notion, as that of logic, extends the valuations to the whole set of nodes. To that extent, the classical interpretation of the TMS dependency graph is used.

An *interpretation* from a valuation ν is a boolean function

$$I: \mathcal{N} \longrightarrow \{0,1\}$$

which respects the three following properties:

environment conformity: $\forall N \in \mathcal{N}, N \in H \Rightarrow I(N) = \smile(N)$

closedness: $\forall N \in \mathcal{N}$,
$\exists J \in$ LISTOFJUST[N];
$\forall N' \in$ IN-list[J] I(N')=1 & $\forall N' \in$ OUT-list[J] I(N')=0
$\Rightarrow$ I(N)=1

(weak) global groundedness: There exists an ordering (<) of nodes whose interpretation is 1 such that:
$\forall N \in \mathcal{N}$, I(N)=1
$\Rightarrow \exists J \in$ LISTOFJUST[N];
$\forall N' \in$ OUT-list[J] I(N')=0
& $\forall N' \in$ IN-list[J] (I(N')=1 & N'<N)

This definition takes into account the (absolute) labelling of the dependency graph in case of nonmonotonic inferences. The conformity requirement to the environment (if $N \in H$ then $I(N) = \smile(N)$) avoids to consider, as an interpretation from that environment, a labelling that justifies a node of the restriction. It means that if the graph contains the justification <{A}{}>:B, there is no interpretation from [A|B] because the only possible labelling constrains B not to hold. This labelling leads, on the other hand, to an interpretation from [A|].

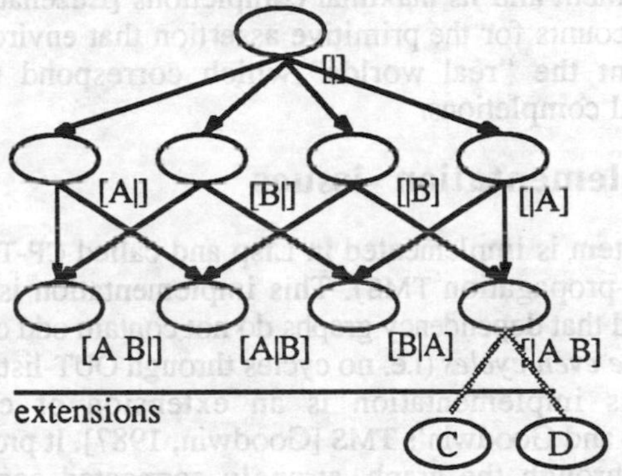

Figure 5. A classical example where the justification set is {<{}{A,B,C}>:D, <{}{A,B,D}>:C}. Under [|A B], there are two possible interpretations: {C} and {D}: the first one where D holds and A, B and C do not and the other where C holds and A, B and D do not.

The recursive definition of interpretations admits several interpretations from a sole valuation. They correspond to the multiple labelling of a TMS graph. The set of interpretations from environment [A/R] is noted IntInd([A/R]) and these interpretations are called *extensions*. They are represented in Figure 5 under the horizontal line.

In order to access extensions through environments, it is possible to bring the line down under the extensions by adding hypotheses C and D. Doing so, extensions will be addressable as maximal completions. But that solution has the drawback of adding hypotheses.

5.Labels

New environments have been defined and interpreted over the whole set of nodes according to the dependency graph. Their main advantage is in representing interpretations in a compact form. At that point, the semantics of labels (which are sets of environments) associated with nodes can be stated.

A *label* for a node N accounts for the set of valuations $\smile$ whose completions admit an interpretation I considering N as holding. So the label definition is the following:
LABEL[N] = {C ; $\forall \smile \in$ Comp(C), $\exists I \in$ IntInd($\smile$); I(N)=1 }.

This is in accordance with the choice made at §2 (i.e. to consider that a node holds under an environment if there exists an interpretation of each completion of it that valuates the node to 1). In other words, the *completeness* property of a label is achieved if

$\forall N \in \mathcal{N}, \forall \smile$,
[$\exists I \in$ IntInd($\smile$); I(N)=1] $\Rightarrow$ [$\exists C \in$ LABEL[N]; $\smile \in$ Comp(C)].

The *correction*, for its part, is expressed by
$\forall N \in \mathcal{N}, \forall C$,
[$C \in$ LABEL[N]] $\Rightarrow$ [$\forall \smile \in$ Comp(C), $\exists I \in$ IntInd($\smile$); I(N)=1].

This choice for label definition is significant. It is noteworthy in Figure 5, that both nodes C and D are labelled with [|A B]. An incorrect understanding of it, could lead to the conclusion that an interpretation from [|A B] exists under which C and D simultaneously hold. Which is not true.

6.Consistency

The RMS task is not only to find a (weakly) founded labelling of the graph but also to avoid inconsistent labelling. Our definition of consistent environments defines those which can appear in labels.

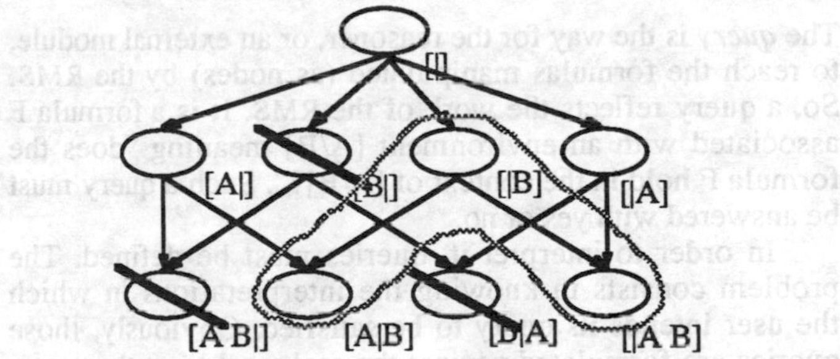

Figure 6. The graph of Figure 5 where the environments in which B holds are inconsistent. So, three of the environments are inconsistent ([B|], [B A|] and [B|A]) and only three of them can be included in labels: [|B], [A|B] and [|B A] (those for which every completion is consistent; they are represented surrounded with a doted line).

An interpretation is called *arguable* (resp. *non arguable*) if and only if $I(\perp)=0$ (resp. $I(\perp)=1$). This definition corresponds really to an inconsistent labelling to be avoided by the RMS. A valuation is said to be *consistent* if none of its interpretations is non arguable (all are arguable). A valuation is called *inconsistent* if it is not consistent. One can adopt another definition, which considers a valuation as consistent if there exists an arguable interpretation from it. Meanwhile, the actual choice for consistency matches the one concerning labels: an inconsistent valuation has a valuation of $\perp$'s label for completion.

For conceptual neatness, it is set that every completion of a valuation in a label must be consistent. Due to its monotonic reasoning, it is obviously true for the ATMS, but in the present framework, the label definition must be changed by adding a constraint on labels:

$\forall N \in \mathcal{N}, \forall C,$
$[C \in LABEL[N]] \Rightarrow [\forall \nu \in Comp(C), \forall I \in IntInd(\nu); I(\perp)=0].$

In order to retrieve the consistent completions of a label, consistent completions of valuations are defined. A *consistent completion* ν' of a valuation ν is a completion of ν such that every interpretation of ν' is arguable. Thus, the set of consistent completions of ν is:

$$Ccons(\nu) = \{\nu' \in Comp(\nu); \forall I \in IntInd(\nu'), I(\perp)=0\}.$$

A *minimal consistent completion* ν' of a valuation ν is a consistent completion of ν which is a consistent completion of no other consistent completion of ν. Thus, the set of minimal consistent completions of ν is

$$Cmin(\nu) = \{\nu' \in Ccons(\nu); \forall \nu'' \in Ccons(\nu), \nu' \in Ccons(\nu'') \Rightarrow \nu''=\nu'\}.$$

In a label, each environment whose valuation has an inconsistent completion is replaced by its minimal consistent completions. This is a maximalist option; some others, weaker, can be adopted without reconsidering the system consistency [Euzenat, 1989]. While the ATMS approach suppresses only environments all the completions of which are inconsistent, the one considered here is closer to MBR's [Martins and Shapiro, 1988] which restricts environments in the same way (with its restriction list).

7.Queries

The *query* is the way for the reasoner, or an external module, to reach the formulas manipulated (as nodes) by the RMS. So, a query reflects the work of the RMS. It is a formula F associated with an environment [A/B] meaning "does the formula F hold in the context of [A/B]?". Such a query must be answered with yes or no.

In order to interpret it, queries must be defined. The problem consists in knowing the interpretations in which the user intends its query to be satisfied. Obviously, those queries are formulated against the real world but the query environment is incomplete with regard to it. Several attitudes can be adopted to face this incompleteness:

1) The formula must hold in every interpretation from every completion of the query environment.
2) The formula must hold in at least one interpretation from each completion of the query environment.
3) The formula must hold in each interpretation from at least one completion of the query environment.
4) The formula must hold in at least one interpretation from at least one completion of the query environment.

Complications can arise if the query environment is not only incomplete but also inconsistent (or it has at least one inconsistent completion). It is then possible to:

1) Report to the user this inconsistency, requiring him/her to complete its environment in a consistent fashion.
2) Compute the minimal consistent completions of the query environment in order to give a safe answer. So, the whole set of query interpretations can, in turn, be applied against the minimal consistent completions.

Some possible interpretations ranging from the stronger to the weaker are presented hereafter. According to the label definition, "to hold in a completion" means that "there exists an interpretation of that completion in which the node corresponding to the formula holds":

a) Does F hold in every completion of the valuation corresponding to [A/R]?
b) Does F hold in every minimal consistent completion of the valuation corresponding to [A/R]?
c) Does F hold in some completion of each minimal consistent completion of the valuation corresponding to [A/R]?
d) Does F hold in each completion of some minimal consistent completion of the valuation corresponding to [A/R]?
e) Does F hold in some completion of some minimal consistent completion of the valuation corresponding to [A/R]?
f) Does F hold in at least one completion of the valuation corresponding to [A/R]?

If there were no restriction on the label meaning, there should be twice as many possible interpretations.

Several sets corresponding to these query interpretations have been characterized. An important result is that these sets can be characterized with regard to both the query environment and its maximal completions [Euzenat, 1990]. This accounts for the primitive assertion that environments represent the "real worlds" which correspond to their maximal completions.

8.Implementation issues

Our system is implemented in Lisp and called CP-TMS (for context-propagation TMS). This implementation is correct provided that dependency graphs do not contain odd cycles or *alternate even cycles* (i.e. no cycles through OUT-lists).

This implementation is an extension of classical Doyle's and Goodwin's TMS [Goodwin, 1987]. It propagates labels through the graph, strongly connected component (SCC) by strongly connected component, and, inside each SCC, node by node. It acts as if labels were logical formulas in disjunctive normal form:

$$(a_{11}\wedge\ldots a_{1p_1}\wedge\neg b_{11}\wedge\ldots\neg b_{1q_1})$$
$$\vee\ldots(a_{n1}\wedge\ldots a_{np_n}\wedge\neg b_{n1}\wedge\ldots\neg b_{nq_n}).$$

Then the propagation strictly conforms to the following rules:

- A node label is the disjunction of its justification labels.
- A justification label is the conjunction of its antecedents (OUT-list plus nodes in the IN-list).
- An OUT-list label is the conjunction of the negation of the labels of all its nodes.

Minimality is tested during disjunction and consistency during conjunction (each negation is followed by a conjunction). In fact, this algorithm is nearly the same as the one proposed by Drew Mac Dermott [Mac Dermott, 1983], except that nodes are ordered before examined and, since hypotheses are allowed to be justified, that the algorithm is not correct in case of alternate even cycles.

Label structure is implemented with bit-vectors and stored in a normalized form (hypotheses are ordered). The system can answer every specified query type.

Consistency recovery was first implemented in a naive way, inspecting each label. But this is not realistic: the size complexity of the resulting system is exponential with the number of hypotheses supporting constraints. The consistency property used in the ATMS is aimed at reducing the label sizes; at the opposite, in the CP-TMS, consistency increases the label size. Several solutions for it are discussed in [Euzenat, 1989], the more radical one drops out the consistency property of labels. It does not matter because consistency is checked at query processing time. This last solution has also been implemented, saving space and time.

9. Discussion

The presented system suffers from several shortcomings we briefly discuss here.

The implementation only partially fulfills the specifications. If the graph contains alternate even cycles, the CP-TMS will miss some extensions (it will choose one). This is due to the propagation algorithm which is local while generating several extensions is a global property of the graph.

The framework presented here sets the interpretation of environments and does not allow another interpretation to coexist. Transforming both the system and established properties for its specifications from "to hold in at least one interpretation" to "to hold in every interpretation" is straightforward. However, both interpretations cannot be considered simultaneously in the same system while this capability can be useful for many applications.

10. Further developments

Filling in the lacks of the algorithm is the most important work; it will lead to reconsider the specifications. To that extent, research on classical TMS and its multiple extensions has been pursued in order to characterize each possible labelling. The aim is to find out the graph configurations (called generators) that lead to multiple extensions. It has begun by further investigating SCC-based propagation algorithms [Quintero, 1989]. While minimal support graph SCC are not sufficient to characterize those extension generators, we used complete support graph SCC.

Once exhibited multiple extension generators, it is possible to design a perfect RMS: the one in which non determinism can be directed during the propagation and backtracking processes. So, any of the admissible extensions can be reached.

This characterization of multiple extension generators is only a first step. This work has to be reintroduced in the work on CP-TMS. As a matter of fact, propagating, through the graph, the configurations that lead to a node holding or not, reveals if the environment must be in the label of the node and so fully implement CP-TMS specifications. A similar work has already been done for network default theories [Lévy, 1989].

This leads to name extensions and so, to manipulate and query them one by one. Hence, the aim of considering both kinds of environment interpretations (a node should hold under at least one or all of its interpretations) will be achieved. To that extent, it will be necessary to adapt the environment structure, taking generators into account.

11. Conclusion

In order to use, in the same RMS, nonmonotonic inferences and multiple context reasoning, the CP-TMS had been designed. It is based on a new definition of the environments and a clear interpretation of them according to the nonmonotonic dependency graph.

A comparison of this work with several others and a theoretical justification of the presented framework can be found in [Euzenat, 1990]. Moreover, an old but detailed description of the implementation, together with several alternative solutions for consistency that should lead to reduce complexity, is discussed in [Euzenat, 1989].

References

[De Kleer, 1986] Johan De Kleer. An assumption-based TMS. *Artificial intelligence*, 28(2):127-162, 1986.

[De Kleer, 1988] Johan De Kleer. A general labeling algorithm for assumption-based truth maintenance. In *Proceedings seventh national conference on artificial intelligence*, pages 188-192, Saint-Paul, MN USA, 1988, American Association for Artificial Intelligence.

[Doyle, 1979] Jon Doyle. A truth maintenance system. *Artificial intelligence*, 12(3):231-272, 1979.

[Dressler, 1989] Oskar Dressler. An extended basic ATMS. *Lecture notes on computer science (Lecture notes on artificial intelligence)*, 346:144-163, 1989.

[Euzenat, 1989] Jérôme Euzenat. Un système de maintenance de la vérité à propagation de contextes (in French). Research report 779-I, IMAG, Grenoble, FR, February 1989.

[Euzenat, 1990] Jérôme Euzenat. Un système de maintenance de la vérité à propagation de contextes (in French). PhD thesis, Université Joseph Fourier, Grenoble, FR, 1990.

[Giordano and Martelli, 1990] Laura Giordano, Alberto Martelli. An abductive characterization of the TMS. Proceedings of the ninth european conference on artificial intelligence, pages 308-313, Stockholm, SE, 1990.

[Goodwin, 1987] James Goodwin. A theory and system for nonmonotonic reasoning. *Linköping studies in science and technology*, 165, 1987.

[Lévy, 1989] François Lévy. Contribution à la réalisation d'un raisonneur à profondeur variable: le système de maintenance (in French). PhD thesis, Université Paris-Nord, Villetaneuse, FR, 1989.

[Mac Dermott, 1983] Drew Mac Dermott. Contexts and data dependencies: a synthesis. *IEEE Transactions on pattern analysis and machine intelligence*, 5(3):237-246, 1983.

[Martins and Shapiro, 1988] João Martins, Stuart Shapiro. A model for belief revision. *Artificial intelligence*, 35(1):25-79, 1988.

[Quintero, 1989] Jose Alejandro Quintero-Garcia. Parallélisation de la maintenance de la vérité tirant parti des composantes fortement connexes (in French). DEA (master) thesis, INPG, Grenoble, FR, 1989.

On Semantics of TMS

Wang Xianchang, Chen Huowang
Department of Computer Science
Changsha Institute of Technology
Changsha, Hunan, P.R. CHINA 410073
Telex:98141 NUDTC CN Fax:86-731-48583

ABSTRACT

In this paper we first give a formal semantics of non-monotonic TMS theory with CP justifications. Then we prove that the model of a theory J is also a model of theory J*(l). Next we conclude that for every TMS theory J, there must be a theory J* such that J* has no CP justifications and all the models of J is also J*'s. Finally we prove that the concept of extension defined by U. Junker and Kurt Konolige is also correct under our definition.

Keywords: TMS, Extension, Semantic, Non-Monotonic, CP, SL, Justification

1. Introduction

TMS (Truth Maintenance System) is first proposed by Doyle in 1979, which is a technique to maintain the consistency of belief and find the source of the contradiction (Dependency-Directed Backtracking). It is more proper to call TMS by BMS (Belief Maintenance System) or RMS (Reason Maintenance System). Traditionally we still call it TMS in this paper. Because TMS plays an important rule in KB, non-monotonic reasoning, pattern recognition, and all the other fields in which the knowledge will be adjusted because of the new knowledge's accumulation or introspection, there has been much researches work on TMS in this decade. In this paper we do not intend to introduce the results in this respect. What we want to point out is that there has been less research on the TMS's basic theory, especially on its formal semantics. This phenomenon can be explained as the following: In this decade, TMS is always studied as a technique, and it seems to be a practical non-monotonic belief maintenance technique by birth. Since TMS is NP-hard, much attention has been attracted to how to make it more practical. The computation complexity of non-monotonic theory has been known since the beginning of 80's, there is still more researches on the beautiful form of non-monotonic reasoning and on the theoretically formal proofs of non-monotonic theory. Although there are some comparison between TMS and non-monotonic reasoning, the results in this field are few and not deep after all.

When we study how to implement a practical non-monotonic reasoning system, we find that it must contain at least two basic parts: one is the non-monotonic inference mechanism, the other is TMS. This opinion complies with the one in reference [B. Smith and G. Kelleher, 1988]. When the default reasoning based on Horn logic is combined with TMS [Wang Xianchang and Chen Huowang, 1990(a),(c)], we find that the first problem we meet is to get the formal semantics of TMS. Only by this way can we ensure the consistency between the non-monotonic inference mechanism and the belief maintenance system. But many of the concepts in TMS are not clear. There are different understandings for these concepts among different people. For example what is the correct meaning of CP justification? What should be a premise node? When we replace a valid CP justification by the so called equally SL justification , is the new TMS theory equal the original theory? We notice that in resent years, there are some researches on the formalization of TMS, but what they study is the TMS with no CP justification. For example, Ulrich Junker and Kurt Konolige make comparison between the relations among TMS which have no CP justification with AEL and DL. They discuss how to translate the AEL, DL to TMS [U. Junker and K. Konolige, 1990]. This kind of work is also very important in our research work [Wang Xianchang and Chen Huowang, 1990(a), (b), (c)].

In this paper, we first define the TMS language and the TMS theory. Then we define the formal semantics of TMS. Next we prove the valid transformation of the CP justification to SL justifications. Finally we discuss the semantic relation between ours and U.Junker semantics of TMS with no CP justification.

2. TMS Theory

The basic language of TMS is a prepositional language. In TMS a statement with variables is not allowed.

Def 1. p,q,p1,q1,...,pi,qi,... are propositions.

Def 2. Suppose r is a proposition, then r and (~r) are nodes.

In general, a TMS theory contains finite nodes. Suppose NS is a set of nodes, here NS is always finite. Node r, (~r) have no semantics relation in TMS. They are formally non-related statements , although we always regard them as excluding each other.

Def 3. SL (Support List) justification

The SL justification on node set NS is a formula as following:

p <-- in(I),out(O)

Here p is in NS, I and O are subset of NS, $I \wedge O = \{\}$. p is called the consequence of above SL justification, (in(I),out(O)) is called one of p's reason. The node in I is called p's premise node, the node in O is called p's default premise node.

Def 4. CP(Conditional Proof) justification

The CP justification on node set NS is a formula as following:

p <-- q, in(I),out(O)

Here p,q are in NS, I and O are subset of NS, $I \wedge O = \{\}$.

The informal meaning of above CP justification is:

If there is a non-monotonic proof of q under premise (in(I),out(O)), then p is believable.

Doyle has not discussed the meaning of CP justification in the case O=/= {}. In this paper we mainly discuss the general case. We ensure that when O==={} the meaning of our definition of CP justification complies with Doyle's original meaning.

Def 5. TMS theory.

A TMS theory J on node set NS is based on finite SL justifications or CP justifications.

Def 6. J(l)

Suppose J is a TMS theory on node set NS, l is a CP justification, l = p <-- q, in(I), out(O), Then we define a TMS theory J(l) as:

J(l)= (J - {l} + { p'<-- l for every p' in I}) - { l1 | l1 is a SL justification of J, and p' is l1's consequence, p' is in O }

Example 1. Consider the following five TMS theories. It is not necessary to list the corresponding node sets of each theory.

J1= { p<-- in(q), q<-- in(p) }

p, q are the premise of each other.

J2= { p<-- out(q), q<-- out(p) }

p, q are the default premise of each other,.

J3= { p<--q, in(q1), q<--in(q1) }

If q1 is a belief of theory J3, then q is also a belief of theory J3; Suppose q1 is believable, if we can get that q is also believable, then p is a belief.

J4 = { p2<--in(p1,p4), p3<--in(p2,p5), p4<--, p5<--, p6<--p3, in(p1) }

This theory can be referred to in [J. Doyle, 1979].

J5 = { p<--q1, q1<-- out(q2),q2<--out(q1) }

If there is a non-monotonic proof of q1 then p is believable.

3. The Semantic Study on TMS Theory.

3.1 Definitions.

Def 1. Assignment f.

Suppose J is a TMS theory on node set NS, then an assignment f of J is a map, f: NS ---> {in out}, such that:

For every node d in NS, f(d)=in iff

Either J has a SL justification, l= d<-- in(I),out(O) such that for every p in I,f(p)=in, and for every node in O, f(p)=out, l is called a valid SL justification.

Or J has a CP justification l = d <-- p, in(I),out(O) such that J(l) has a model f' such that f'(p)=in, l is called a valid CP justification.

Def 2. In assignment f of theory J,we say node p is an in-node if f(p)=in, else we call it out-node.

Suppose p is an in-node, if it has a valid SL justification p<--in(I),out(O), then (I + O) is called p's support set, denoted by Sup(J,f,p). Else,p has an valid CP justification l=p<--q,in(I),out(O) then Rant(J(l), f', I + O, q) is Sup(J, f, p), here f' is the theory J(l)'s model which make q believable. Rant is defined as following.

Def 3. Suppose p is an in-node of theory J in assignment f. We define p's ancestor set, Ant(J,f,p) which is the minimal set satisfying the following conditions:

1. Sup(J,f,p) is a subset of Ant(J,f,p)
2. If in-node q is in Ant(J,f,p), then Sup(J,f,q) is a subset of Ant(J,f,p)

Def 4. Repercussions set.

Suppose J is a TMS theory on node set NS, f is a model of J, for every p in NS we define p's repercussions set , Rep(J,f,p) :

Rep(J,f,p)= {q | q is an in-node and p is in Ant(J,f,q)}

Obviously any node whether it is in-node or out-node,can be one of the reason of an another in-node.

Def 5. Suppose S is a subset of NS, f is an assignment of theory J on node set NS. Then we define Rep(J,f,S) as

1. if S={} then Rep(J,f,S)={}
2. if S= S1 + {p} then Rep(J,f,S)= Rep(J,f,p) + Rep(J,f,S1)

Def 6. Related-ancestors set

Suppose p is an in-node of theory J in assignment f, then the related-ancestors set under premise set S, Rant(J,f,S,p) is the maximal set which satisfies the following conditions:

1. Rant(J,f,S,q) is a subset of Ant(J,f,q)
2. Rant(J,f,S,q) ∧ S = {}
3. Rep(J,f,S) ∧ Rant(J,f,S,p) = {}

The meaning of Rant(J, f, S,q) would be used to define what the premise argument of an valid CP justification.

Suppose CP justification l= p<--q,in(I),out(O) is valid in assignment f of theory J, and f' is a model of theory J(l) such that f'(q)= in. q's related-ancestors set under premise set S= I + O is Rant(J(l), f', S, q). Then we define p's support node set under f is Rant(J(l), f', S, q).

The concept of assignment has involved an undefined concept "model", in the following we will define it recursively.

Def 7. An assignment f of TMS theory J is a model iff

1. For every in-node p of J, p is not in Ant(J, f, p)
2. For every valid CP justification l, J' is defined as def 2 in section 3.4, f is an assignment of J'.

Def 8. We call TMS theory J's assignment f is well-defined iff every in-node p of f, p isn't in set Ant(J, f, p). Obviously the definition of model of TMS theory is very complicated , but it will became very simple and easily understand if the theory has no CP justification. In the following we will discuss the way to translate the CP justification to SL justification, and discuss the correctness of this translation.

3.2 Example 2.

According to the above definitions, we consider the theories of example 1.

J1 = { p<--in(q), q<--in (p)}

J1 has only one model: f1= {p--->out, q--->out}

J2 = { p<--out(q), q<--out(p)}

J2 has only two models:

f2,1 ={ p--->out, q--->in }

f2,2 ={ p--->in, q--->out}

J3 = {p<--q,in(q1), q<--in(q1)}

J3 has only one model: f3 = {p--->in, q--->out, q1--->out }

J4 = {p2<--in(p1,p4), p3<--in(p2,p5),p4<--, p5<--, p6<--p3, in(p1) }

J4 has only one model: f4= {p1--->out,p2--->out, p3--->out, p4---> in, p5--->in, p6--->in}

J5 = {p<--q1,q1<--out(q2), q2<--out(q1) }

J5 has two models:

f5,1 = {p--->in, q1--->in, q2--->out }

f5,2 = {p--->in, q1--->out, q2--->in }

3.3 The Semantics Consideration on CP Justification.

In section 3.1, the meaning of a CP justification is as following: A theory J's CP justification l= p<--q,in(I),out(O) is valid in model f iff there is a model f' of theory J(l) such that f'(q)=in.

Obviously

(a) Whether J's CP justification l is valid in model f has nothing to do with f, its validity only depend upon J.

(b) Suppose |~~~ is a relation :

J |~~~p iff TMS theory J has a model f such that f(p)=in.

Suppose ||~~~ is a relation:

J ||~~~p iff for every model f of TMS theory J f(p)=in.

Then TMS has the following properties:

1. J + {p<--p} ||~~~ p iff J |~~~p
2. Suppose I is a subset of node set NS, then J + {p<-- | p is in I} |~~~q iff J + {q<--q,in(I)} ||~~~q.
3. The validity of CP justification express the "non-monotonic provableness"

For example. a CP justification l = p<--q,in(I),out(O) is valid in theory J iff J(l) |~~~q.

Non-Monotonic properties:

From J |~~~q we can not conclude J + {p<--p} |~~~q

For example. J2 |~~~q, but J2 + {p<--p} |~\~q.

4. if J |~~~q then we have J + { p<--q } ||~~~p.

(c) A TMS theory may have no model.

Example 3.

J6 = {p<--out (p)}

J7 = {p1--out(p2), p2<--out(p3), p3<--out(p1)}

The above two theories have no model. This kind of theory is called paradox theory.

(d) We can modify the semantics definition of CP justification. For example we can modify the "J(l) has a model " of def.1 in section 3.1 by "for all model of J(l)".

Under this interpretation J5 in example 2 will have other two different models:

f'5,1 = {p--->out, q1--->in, q2--->out }

f'5,2 = {p--->out, q1--->out, q2--->in }

(e) It may be very difficulty to give a definition by which the validity of CP justification depends upon both the theory and the present model. The importance to find such definitions is not clear now, but it can be studied further.

3.4 Translation of CP to SL Justification.

In order to simplify the complex of TM processing, Doyle gives a method to translate a valid CP justification to so called "equally" SL justification, maybe it is this unproved "equality" that makes the followed researchers turn to the TMS theory with no CP justification. But our research shows that this "equality " is false.

First we define what is the translated SL justification in theory J under model f through a valid CP justification.

Def 1. Suppose CP justification l= p<--q,in(I),out(O) is valid in model f of theory J, f' is a model of theory J(l) such that f(q)= in. Suppose Sup(J,f,p) is Rant(J(l), f', I + O, q) then we define the translated SL justification of CP justification under J,f,f' is:

p<-- in(I'),out(O') such that

1. I' + O' = Rant(J(l), f', I + O, q)
2. I'∧O'={}
3. For every r in I', f(r)=in;
   For every r in O', f(r)=out.

Example 4. (Continue example 2)

First we consider J3.

J3'=J3(p<--q,in(q1)) = {q<--in(q1), q1<--}, it has only one model f3'= {q1--->in, q-->in}, Rant(J3', f3', {q1}, q) = {}. So the translated SL justification of p<--q,in(q1) under model f3 is:

p<--

Second we consider J4.

J4'=J4(p6<--p3,in(p1)) has only one model f4'={ p1--->in, p2--->in, p3--->in, p4--->in, p5--->in, p6--->out}. Rant(J4', f4', {p1}, p3) = {p4,p5}, so the translated SL justification of p6<--p3,in(p1) is:

p6<--in(p4,p5)

J5'= J5(p<--q1)={q1<--out(q2),q2<--out(q1)}, it has one model f5' = {q1--->in, q2-->out}. Since Rant(J5',f5',{q1},p) = {q2}, the translated SL justification of p<--q1 under (f5,1), f5'is:

p<--out(q2)

The translated SL justification of p<--q1 under (f5,2), f5' is p<-- in(q2)

Def 2. Suppose f is a model of TMS theory J. CP justification l = p<--q,in(I),out(O) is valid in f. Suppose p<--in(I'),out(O') is the translated SL justification of l, then theory J'= J - { l } + { p<--in(I'), out(O') } is called one replaced theory of J under model f.

Obviously we have following theorem.

Theorem 1. Suppose f is a model of theory J, J' is one replaced theory of J under model f. Then f is still a model of J'.

In general some models of J may be not the models of J', and some models of J' may be not J's models.

Example 5. Consider Theory J5 of example 4.

Obviously one replaced theory of J5 under model f5,1 is J'5,1 = { p<--out(q2), q1<--out(q2), q2<--out(q1) }. This theory has two models: one is f5,1 , the other is f'5,2 = {p--->out, q1--->out, q2--->in }. Obviously f'5,2 is not J5's model and the model f5,2 of J5 is also not the model of J'5,1.

Def 3. Suppose J has a valid CP justification l = p<--q, in(I), out(O), we define a translated theory of J as J*(l), which is: J*(l) = J - {l} + { p<--in(I'),out(O') I there is a model f of J such that p<--in(I'),out(O') is a translated SL justification of l under model f}

It is easy to prove

Theorem 2. Suppose l is a valid CP justification in theory J then for every model f of J, f is still a model of J*(l).

Example 6.

Consider TMS theory J4 of example 3. CP justification l4= p6<--p1,in(p3) is valid, it is easy to get that J4*(l4)= { p2<--in(p1, p4), p3<--in(p2, p5), p4<--, p5<--, p3<--in(p4, p5)}. Obviously every model of J4 is also the model of J4*(l4).

Consider TMS theory J5 of example 3. l5= p<--q1 is valid in J5,J5*(l5)={ q1<--out(q2), q2<--out(q1), q<--out(q2), q<--in(q2) }. Obviously all the models of J5 are also J5*(l3)'s models.

Whether the model of J*(l) is the model of J? the answer is not clear now.

From theorem 1 and theorem 2, we can conclude that:

Theorem 3. Suppose J is a TMS theory, then there must be a TMS theory J* such that

1. J* has no CP justifications.
2. Every model of J is also the model of J*.

4. Comparison With U. Junker and Kurt Konolige's Work

U. Junker and Kurt Konolige give a Semantics of TMS theory with no CP justification. Here we do not want to introduce their work, the concepts appeared bellow can be referred in [U. Junker and K. Konolige, 1990]. The following are our main conclusions.

Def 1. Suppose J is a TMS theory on node set NS, f is J's model, then we define T(f) = {c I c is in NS, and f(c)=in } as an extension of J.

Now is U. Junker's extension the same as ours?

In the following all the TMS theories we consider have no CP justifications.

Lemma 1. f is a model of TMS theory J iff

$$apply_{J,T(f)} \quad (T(f)) = T(f)$$

Proof: We can get it from the definition of model f and the function apply.

Lemma 2. For any model f of theory J, we have

$$apply^{*}_{J,T(f)} \quad (\{\}) \subseteq T(f)$$

Proof: Because

$$apply^{*}_{J,T(f)} \quad (\{\}) = \bigcup_{i=0}^{\infty} apply^{i}_{J,T(f)} \quad (\{\})$$

So we can get lemma 2 after we prove the following by inductive method:

for every i=0,1, ..., n,...

$$apply^{i}_{J,T(f)} \quad (\{\}) \subseteq T(f)$$

Lemma 3. If f is a model of TMS theory J, then

$$apply^{*}_{J,T(f)} \quad (\{\}) = T(f)$$

Proof: we can construct a function t:NS--->{0,1,...} such that

1. if p is an out-node of f then t(p) is 0.
2. if SL justification p<--in(I),out(O) is in-node p's valid support justification, then t(p) is defined as
   1 + Max(0, { t(q) I q is in I}

Because every in-node p is not in Ant(J, f, p), the above function t is well defined. It is easy to proof that for every in-node p

$$p \text{ is in } \quad apply^{t(p)}_{J,T(f)} \quad (\{\})$$

so T(f) is a subset of $apply^{*}_{J,T(f)} \quad (\{\})$

From lemma 2 and lemma 3 we can get lemma 4.

Lemma 4. f is a model of TMS theory J iff

$$T(f) = apply^{*}_{J,T(f)} \quad (\{\})$$

Lemma 5. Suppose J is a TMS theory on node set NS. T⊆NS, if

$$T= apply^{*}_{J,T} \quad (\{\})$$

Then the following three properties hold.

a. $T = apply_{J,T} \quad (T)$
b. $T = apply^{*}_{J,T} \quad (\{\})$
c. There is no T0⊂T such that
   $T0 = apply_{J,T0} \quad (T0)$

Proof: The properties a,b can be found in [U. Junker and K. Konolige, 1990]]. Now we prove c. Suppose c is not hold then there must be a T0 such that

T0⊂T and

$T0 = apply_{J,T0}(T0)$

Because $T0 \subset T$, $\{\} \subseteq T0$ so

$apply_{J,T0}(T0) \supseteq apply_{J,T}(T0) \supseteq apply_{J,T}(\{\})$

Suppose for i

$T0 = apply_{J,T0}(T0) \supseteq apply^{i}_{J,T}(\{\})$

then

$$T0 = apply_{J,T0}(T0) \supseteq apply_{J,T}(apply_{J,T0}(T0)) \supseteq apply_{J,T}(apply^{i}_{J,T}(\{\})) = apply^{i+1}_{J,T}(\{\})$$

So we have proven the following by inductive method

for every $i=0,1,...,n,...$

$T0 \supseteq apply^{i}_{J,T}(\{\})$

$$\text{So } T0 \supseteq \bigcup_{i=0}^{\infty} apply^{i}_{J,T}(\{\}) = T$$

So $T0 \supseteq T$, this is contrary to $T0 \subset T$.

c is proved. Q.E.D

From above three lemmas, we can get.

Theorem 6. J is a TMS theory with no CP justification, then E is an extension of what U. Junker and K. Konolige define iff E is also an extension of what we define. In other words, J must have a model f such that $T(f) = E$.

This theorem shows that the extension concept defined by U. Junker and Kurt Konolige is correct in our semantics frame.

5. Conclusion

In this paper we first give a formal semantics of non-monotonic TMS theory with CP justifications. Then we prove that the model of a theory J is also a model of theory J*(I). Next we conclude that for every TMS theory J, there must be a theory J* such that J* has no CP justifications and all the model of J is also J*'s; Finally we prove that the concept of extension defined by U. Junker and Kurt Konolige is the same under our definition. It is necessary to point out that there are more properties of CP justification left for us to study. From our discussion, it seems that the CP justification has a close relation with "non-monotonic provenance".

REFERENCES

[D. Bobrow, 1980] Daniel Bobrow, edit. in chief Artificial Intelligence Vol. 13, 1980 ,North-Holland

[AAAI, 1984] Proceedings 1984 Non-Monotonic Reasoning Workshop AAAI-1984, New Palz, NY.

[P. Besnard,1987] Besnard,P., (1987) An Introduction to DL, Springer-Verlag, Berlin.

[C. Elkan, 1990] Charles Elkan " A Rational Reconstruction of Non-monotonic Truth Maintenance System " AI, vol.42,1990 pp219-234.

[J. Doyle, 1979] J. Doyle "A Truth Maintenance System" AI. vol 12, 1979,p 231-272.

[J. Doyle, 1983] J. Doyle "The ins and outs of Reason Maintenance " in proc. IJCAI-1983, Karlsruke FRG.

[de Kleer, 1984] de Kleer,J. "Choices Without Backtracking" AAAI_84, pp79-85.

[de Kleer, 1986(a)] de Kleer,J. "Assumption Based Truth Maintenance System" AI. vol 28, 1986,pp 127-162.

[de Kleer, 1986(b)] de Kleer, J. "Extending ATMS " AI. vol. 28,1986, pp163-196.

[de Kleer and B. Williams, 1987] de kleer,J. and Williams,B. "Diagnosing Multiple Faults" AI, Vol. 32, 1987, pp97-130

[G.M. Provan, 1988] G. M. Provan "Complexity Analysis of TMS with Applications to High Level vision D.Phil Thesis. University of Oxford (1988)

[M. Reinfrank and U. Dressler, 1989(a)] M. Reinfrank and U. Dressler "On the Relation Between TMS and Non-monotonic Inference" in proc. IJCAI-89, Detroit, MI(1989) pp1206-1212.

[J.F. Horty and R.H. Thomason, 1990] John F. Horty, Richmond H. Thomason, David S. Touretzky " A Skeptical Theory of Inheritance In Non-monotonic Semantic Networks" AI, vol. 42, 1990, num. 2-3, pp311-348.

[K. Konolige, 1986] Kurt Konolige " A Deduction Model of Belief " Ditman, London. Morgan Kaufumann Publishers 1986

[B. Smith and G. Kelleher, 1988] Barbara Smith and Gerald Kelleher (eds.) "Reason Maintenance Systems and Their Applications" Ellis Horwood Likmitted, 1988

[LNAI, 1988] "Proceedings of Second International Workshop on Non-monotonic Reasoning " Lecture Notes In AI, Vol 346 (Springer, NEWYORK, 1988)

[M. Reinfrank and U. Dressler, 1989(b)] M. Reinfrank and U. Dressler 'On The Relation Between TM and AEL " proc. IJCAI-89.

[U. Junker, 1989] Junker, U., "A Correct Non-Monotonic ATMS" IJCAI-89

[U. Junker and K. Konolige, 1990] Junker, U.,and Kurt Konolige "Computing The Extensions of Autoepistemic and Default Logic with a Truth Maintenance System" AAAI-90, pp278-283.

[Wang Xianchang and Chen Huowang, 1990(a)] Wang Xianchang, Chen Huowang "A Non-Monotonic Reasoning System---WMJ " In The Proceedings of The First International Conference on System Integration (ICSI'90), 1990, NEW JERSEY, USA.

[Wang Xianchang and Chen Huowang, 1990(b)] Wang Xianchang, Chen Huowang "On Assumption Reasoning In Multi-Reasoner System" In The Proceedings of Pacific Rim International Conference on AI'90, NAGOYA, JAPAN.

[Wang Xianchang and Chen Huowang, 1990(c)] Wang Xianchang, Chen Huowang " Horn Logic + Default Reasoning + TMS ===> Dynamic Logic Programming?" Technique Report, N0.9006, Changsha Institute of Technology, 1990.

[P.H. Morris, 1987] Paul H. Morris "The Anomalous Extension Problems In Default Reasoning "AAAI-87 or AI., vol.35, 1988, pp383-399.

[K.P. Loui, 1989] K.P. Loui, Defeasible Decisions: What the Proposal Is and Isn't. In proc. Conf. Uncertainty in AI, pages 245-252, 1989.

Prioritized Defaults: Implementation by TMS and Application to Diagnosis

Ulrich Junker
GMD
P O Box 1240
5205 St. Augustin 1
Fed. Rep. of Germany
++49 - 2241/142671
junker@gmdzi.gmd.de

Abstract

We demonstrate the technological value of non-monotonic logics by an example: We use *prioritized defaults* for candidate generation in *diagnosis from first principles.* We implement this non-monotonic logic by *TMS* similar to default logic. Prioritized defaults allow an easy formulation of a diagnosis problem including statements such as *'eletrical parts are more reliable than mechanical ones'* or *'prefer correct models to fault models'* since defaults are put into different levels of reliability. These preferences prune some counterarguments in TMS and thus lead to a reduced network. Moreover, the labelings of this network are exactly the preferred subtheories of its prioritized default theory.

1 Introduction

Although the development of non-monotonic formalisms has been triggered by practical problems most work in this area has been devoted to the study of formal properties of non-monotonic inference. The technological value of non-monotonic formalisms is often ignored or questioned. We argue that non-monotonic logics can serve as *intermediate formalisms* in the development of applications for problems that require the generation and retraction of hypotheses. Good examples are diagnosis and configuration. Thus, we would decompose the design of an application into two steps:

1. **Representation:** First concentrate on the relevant representational decisions (e.g. what statements are encoded by hypotheses, defaults, priorities, counterarguments etc.) without being concerned with technical details. The result of this step should be a comprehensive and implementation-independent solution in terms of a non-monotonic formalism. Like a data-base scheme, it can be kept if the implementation is changed. This step also clarifies whether some properties of non-monotonic logics (e.g. multiple extensions) are really problems or can be useful for applications.

2. **Implementation:** Different techniques can be used for implementing a non-monotonic logic. If they are already available the main task is to select techniques which are efficient for the special case under consideration. Thus, we can benefit from a lot of techniques (e.g. truth maintenance, dependency-directed backtracking) without being in trouble with technical details. Non-monotonic logics serve as a specification for these techniques and show exactly how and in what circumstances they can be applied.

We illustrate this approach by developing a TMS-based system for generating candidates for diagnosis. There are already several (A)TMS-based diagnosis systems (e.g. [de Kleer and Williams, 1987], [Struss and Dressler, 1989], [Dressler and Struss, 1990]). These works contain a lot of innovations how to do diagnosis. Unfortunately, parts of their results are hidden in the code and expressed in system-specific terms like justifications and labels.

Therefore, we consider an intermediate logic to do diagnosis (similar as [Poole, 1989]). We choose prioritized default logic [Brewka, 1989] where defaults are put into different levels of reliability. This allows to express preferences such as *'adders are more reliable than multipliers'* or *'prefer correct models to fault models'.* We discuss this topic in sections 2.2 and 2.3.

In a second step, we provide a general implementation of level-based default theories using TMS. Since they are equivalent to the special case of prioritized circumscription implemented in [Baker and Ginsberg, 1989] we get an alternative method for handling prioritized circumscription. It does not need such notions as rebut and refute. We just map every level of the default theory into a subnetwork of a TMS using the translation in [Junker and Konolige, 1990].

To verify our translation, we need some results on components of TMS-networks. For this purpose, we split networks into independent components which can be labeled in isolation. Extensions of the complete network can be composed of extensions of the subnetworks. The precise results are presented in section 3.2. They are of their own interest because they enable a kind of divide-and-conquer strategy for computing extensions. Thus, we have extended the work of Goodwin [Goodwin, 1987] who uses strongly connected components to guide the search in a particular labeling algorithm.

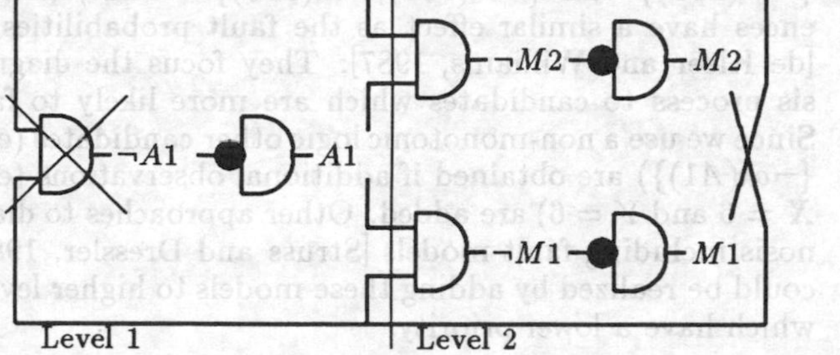

Figure 1: Removing Backpointing Justifications

By linking the subnetworks of every level we obtain a TMS-network that reflects the level-structure of the default theory. Its extensions can be split in the same way as the preferred subtheories of the level-based default theory. This network is also obtained if we first ignore the levels and translate the defaults according to [Junker and Konolige, 1990]. Then we remove all justifications leading from a higher level to a lower level (as illustrated in figure 1). It is difficult to imagine how a direct, ad-hoc approach to diagnosis could yield such a regular TMS-network.

2 From Diagnosis to Defaults

2.1 Prioritized Defaults

In this section, we introduce the non-monotonic formalism which will be used to solve the diagnosis problem. We consider prioritized defaults [Brewka, 1989] which have been introduced by Gerd Brewka to extend the simple formalism of David Poole [Poole, 1988]. Unlike to Poole's Theorist, defaults can there be ordered into different levels L_i of reliability. Defaults in L_i have higher priority than defaults in L_{i+k}.

To formulate this precisely, consider a first-order language $\mathcal{L}$ including a special unsatisfiable constant $\perp$. The first-order consequences of a subset X of $\mathcal{L}$ are defined as $Th(X) := \{q \in \mathcal{L} \mid X \models q\}$.

Defaults are represented by a name q (q is an atomic ground formula from $\mathcal{L}$) and a premise $q \supset \phi$ (where ϕ is an arbitrary formula of $\mathcal{L}$):

Definition 2.1 *A* level-based default theory $\Delta := (W, L)$ *consists of a set* $W \subseteq \mathcal{L}$ *of classical premises and a tupel* $L := (L_1, \ldots, L_k)$ *of disjoint levels* L_i *containing atomic ground formulas from* $\mathcal{L}$.

Preferred subtheories of level-based default theories are defined recursively. A preferred subtheory of level $i+1$ is obtained from a preferred subtheory of level i by adding elements of L_{i+1} as long as consistency with W is ensured:

Definition 2.2 *Let* $\Delta = (W, (L_1, \ldots, L_k))$ *be a level-based default theory.* T *is a preferred subtheory of level* i *iff*

1. $T = \emptyset$ *if* $i = 0$
2. T *is the union of a preferred subtheory* T' *of level* $i-1$ *and a maximal subset of* L_i *s.t.* $T \cup W \not\models \perp$ *if* $i \in \{1, \ldots, k\}$.

The preferred subtheories of Δ *are the preferred subtheories of level* k.

We obtain Poole's Theorist if we consider only a single level. Furthermore, if we already know a preferred subtheory T' of level i we could determine a subtheory of the next level by supplying Theorist with T' as a set of premises and L_{i+1} as a set of hypotheses. This view helps us to get a link to Reiter's default logic and from this to Doyle's TMS using the existing translation. Poole has shown that his simple hypotheses q correspond to prerequisite-free normal defaults $\frac{:q}{q}$ in Reiter's default logic. We define

$$D_L := \{\frac{:q}{q} \mid q \in L\} \tag{1}$$

Then T is a preferred subtheory of level $i+1$ iff T consists of elements of levels and $Th(T \cup W)$ is an extension of a default theory $(D_{L_{i+1}}, W \cup T')$ à la Reiter which is supplied with a preferred subtheory T' of level i

2.2 Diagnosis by Prioritized Defaults

In this section, we sketch how diagnosis problems can be formulated by level-based default theories. This includes statements for ranking different kinds of models (e.g. *'adders are more reliable than multipliers'* or *'prefer correct models to fault models'*).

In the sequel, let O be a set of objects or components. Their normal and faulty behaviour is described by several models[1] that exclude each other. The models of $o \in O$ are named by atomic formulas $m_i(o)$. For the sake of simplicity, we assume that every component has exactly k models. A first-order theory W is used to describe the following facts:

- definition of the models (i.e. the behaviour of the single components)
- connections of pins or relationship between attributes of different components
- values of the pins/attributes (including supplied input values, as well as observed output values)
- exclusion of models ($\forall x. \neg m_i(x) \vee \neg m_j(x)$ for $i \neq j$)
- completeness of models ($\forall x. m_1(x) \vee \ldots \vee m_k(x)$)

We are interested in sets of hypotheses which explain the observed behaviour (i.e. the values of the output pins). A usual approach selects as many model as possible without violating consistency (models are selected by adding their names to the theory above). This method treats every model in the same manner. However, we at least want to prefer normal models to fault models as in [Dressler and Struss, 1990]. A fault model should only be selected if a normal model is inconsistent with the current selection. Furthermore, it is useful to focus the diagnosis process to components that are more likely to fail. For example, cable connections often fail whereas TTL-circuits are reliable. We can easily express these preferences in a level-based default theory consisting of the first-order theory W and different levels $(L_1, \ldots, L_i, L_{i+1}, \ldots, L_{i+k-1})$ containing the names of models:

[1] Models in the sense of model-based diagnosis.

- rank normal models of the components in O according to their reliability and distribute them among the levels $L_1, \ldots, L_i$.
- include the j-th fault model $m_j(o)$ of every component into L_{i+j-1}.

Thus, we have also ranked the different fault models. Other rankings could be used for other approaches to diagnosis. Each preferred subtheory of this level-based default theory corresponds to a diagnosis candidate as defined in [Reiter, 1987] and [de Kleer and Williams, 1987]. To be more precisely, the negation of the correct models of the failing components are derived from the preferred subtheory. It is a maximal consistent subset of the set of models. Due to the preferences we do not obtain every candidate. Thus, diagnosis is focused to less robust components. A similar effect is achieved in [de Kleer, 1990] by preferring diagnoses with less faults.

2.3 Formulating Davis' Familiar Example

We illustrate our approach by the well-known adder-multiplier circuit of Davis. It consists of two adders $A1, A2$ and three multipliers $M1, M2, M3$:

$$\begin{array}{lll} adder(A1) & multiplier(M1) & multiplier(M3) \\ adder(A2) & multiplier(M2) & \end{array} \quad (2)$$

These components are connected as follows:

$$\begin{array}{lll} in1(M1) = A & in2(M1) = C & out(M1) = X \\ in1(M2) = B & in2(M2) = D & out(M2) = Y \\ in1(M3) = C & in2(M3) = E & out(M3) = Z \\ in1(A1) = X & in2(A1) = Y & out(A1) = F \\ in1(A2) = Y & in2(A2) = Z & out(A2) = G \end{array} \quad (3)$$

The correct models are described by a predicate *ok* and:

$$\begin{array}{l} \forall x.adder(x) \wedge ok(x) \supset in1(x) + in2(x) = out(x) \\ \forall x.multiplier(x) \wedge ok(x) \supset in1(x) * in2(x) = out(x) \end{array} \quad (4)$$

The supplied input and observed output values are:

$$\begin{array}{lllll} A = 2 & B = 2 & C = 3 & D = 3 & E = 2 \\ F = 10 & G = 12 & & & \end{array} \quad (5)$$

In this example, we don't consider fault models. Let W be a first-order theory including the formulas above and further axioms for reasoning with equality and arithmetics[2]. Now, we built up a level-based default theory $\Delta_{circ} = (W, L)$ where $L := (L_1, L_2)$ consists of two levels. As a heuristc, we assume that adders are more reliable than multipliers:

$$\begin{array}{l} L_1 := \{ok(A1), ok(A2)\} \\ L_2 := \{ok(M1), ok(M2), ok(M3)\} \end{array} \quad (6)$$

Δ_{circ} has two preferred subtheories, namely:

$$\begin{array}{l} T_1 := \{ok(A1), ok(A2), ok(M2), ok(M3)\} \\ T_1 := \{ok(A1), ok(A2), ok(M1)\} \end{array} \quad (7)$$

Thus, only two of the four diagnosis candidates in [de Kleer and Williams, 1987] are obtained, namely $\{\neg ok(M1)\}$ and $\{\neg ok(M2), \neg ok(M3)\}$. Thus, preferences have a similar effect as the fault probabilities in [de Kleer and Williams, 1987]: They focus the diagnosis process to candidates which are more likely to fail. Since we use a non-monotonic logic other candidates (e.g. $\{\neg ok(A1)\}$) are obtained if additional observations (e.g. $X = 6$ and $Y = 6$) are added. Other approaches to diagnosis including fault models [Struss and Dressler, 1989] could be realized by adding these models to higher levels which have a lower priority.

[2] In practical systems, we realize equality and arithmetics using attached calls of lisp functions and simple propagation rules as in Steele's constraint-system.

3 Results for Doyle's TMS

Before we are able to map level-based default theories to TMS, we need some properties of TMS.

3.1 Relevant Properties of Doyle's TMS

In [Junker and Konolige, 1990], we developed a compact description of Doyle's TMS that is based on closures of operators. For a detailed discussion, we refer the reader to this work. We cite only the prerequisites for the theorems below: An operator *apply* : $2^{\mathcal{L}} \to 2^{\mathcal{L}}$ mapping subsets of $\mathcal{L}$ to subsets of $\mathcal{L}$ is monotonic and compact iff

$$\begin{array}{r} \text{if } X \subseteq Y \text{ then } apply(X) \subseteq apply(Y) \\ \text{if } q \in apply(Y) \text{ then } \exists X \subseteq Y : X \text{ is finite} \\ \text{and } q \in apply(X) \end{array} \quad (8)$$

From this, we obtain a *closure* operation $apply^*$ as follows: $apply^*(X)$ is the minimal superset of X that is closed w.r.t. *apply*. Sometimes, *apply* depends only on a (relevant) part R of its input. In this case, it is sufficient to iterate it on the relevant part to get (the relevant part of) the closure. Hence, we take a restricted operator, which is expressed by the lambda-expression $(\lambda(X).apply(X) \cap R)$:

Lemma 3.1 *Let apply* : $2^{\mathcal{L}} \mapsto 2^{\mathcal{L}}$ *be a monotonic and compact operator and* $R \subseteq \mathcal{L}$ *s.t.* $apply(X) = apply(X \cap R)$ *for all* $X \subseteq \mathcal{L}$. *Then* $apply^*(\emptyset) \cap R = (\lambda(X).apply(X) \cap R)^*(\emptyset)$.

We obtain particular instances of such operators if we consider justification networks (N, J) of Doyle's TMS. N is a set of (arbitrary) nodes q from $\mathcal{L}$ that are justified by non-monotonic justifications in J having the form $\langle in(I), out(O) \to q\rangle$. Their inlists I and outlists O are both finite subsets of N. We obtain a monotonic and compact operator for applying justifications if we use an extra-index to check the outlist:

$$apply_{J,Y}(X) := \{c \mid \langle in(I), out(O) \to c\rangle \in J, \; I \subseteq X \text{ and } O \cap Y = \emptyset\} \quad (9)$$

In contrast to the TMS-translation of unprioritized defaults, we supply justification networks with an input $X \subseteq N$, which is included in every TMS-extension:

Definition 3.1 *Let* $\nu = (N, J)$ *be a justification network and* $X \subseteq N$. T *is an* extension of ν and X *iff* $T = apply^*_{J,T}(X)$. *If* ν *has no extension it is* incoherent.

If $X = \emptyset$ we just say that T is an extension of ν. The extra input X does not make the computation of extensions more difficult. Its elements just get a fixed IN-label.

Now, we consider a set Q of nodes and denote their justifications by

$$J^Q := \{\langle in(I), out(O) \rightarrow c\rangle \in J \mid c \in Q\} \quad (10)$$

If we are only interested in the part of the result of $apply_{J,Y}$ that is in Q we apply only justifications in J^Q:

$$apply_{J,Y}(X) \cap Q = apply_{J^Q,Y}(X) \quad (11)$$

3.2 Clusters in TMS

In the sequel, we explore the structure of TMS-networks. More precisely, we decompose a justification network into components which can be labeled in isolation. These components must not depend on the remaining network. A part of a justification network depends on another part if they are linked by a justification:

Definition 3.2 *Let $\nu = (N, J)$ be a justification network, and C_1, C_2 be two subsets of N. C_2* depends on *C_1 if J^{C_2} contains a justification $\langle in(I), out(O) \rightarrow c\rangle$ s.t. $(I \cup O) \cap C_1 \neq \emptyset$.*

An independent component consists of nodes that have no justification depending on the rest of the network.

Definition 3.3 *Let $\nu = (N, J)$ be a justification network. Then $C \subseteq N$ is an* independent component *of ν iff C does not depend on $N - C$.*

In the sequel, we explore properties of components. Nodes of an independent component C can only be derived from nodes in this component.

$$\begin{aligned} apply_{J^C,Y}(X) &= apply_{J^C,Y}(X \cap C) \\ apply_{J^C,Y}(X) &= apply_{J^C,Y \cap C}(X) \end{aligned} \quad (12)$$

Due to lemma 3.1 and equation 11, these properties can be extended to the closure of $apply_{J,Y}$:

$$\begin{aligned} apply^*_{J,Y}(\emptyset) \cap C &= apply^*_{J^C,Y}(\emptyset) \\ apply^*_{J^C,Y}(\emptyset) &= apply^*_{J^C,Y \cap C}(\emptyset) \end{aligned} \quad (13)$$

This allows to state one important property of independent components: Every extension of the complete network can be split into an extension of the component and an extension of the remaining network and the first extension:

Theorem 3.2 *Let $\nu = (N, J)$ be a justification network, C be an independent component of ν. T is an extension of ν iff*

1. *$T \cap C$ is an extension of (C, J^C)*
2. *T is an extension of (N, J^{N-C}) and $T \cap C$.*

Hence, we get an extension of T if we first find an extension of an independent component and then extend it further. In general, there is no guarantee that we find such an extension of an extension because the remaining network may be incoherent (due to odd loops). For level-based default theories we will however obtain coherent subnetworks.

Networks which can be split into two independent components have an even nicer property: Their extensions can be split completely. Hence, we can ignore the extensions of (C, J^C) if we determine an extension of $(N - C, J^{N-C})$.

Theorem 3.3 *Let $\nu = (N, J)$ be a justification network that can be split into two independent components C and $N - C$. T is an extension of ν iff*

1. *$T \cap C$ is an extension of (C, J^C)*
2. *$T \cap (N - C)$ is an extension of $(N - C, J^{N-C})$*

Due to these results we can take a *divide-and-conquer*-approach for computing extensions. We can compute extensions of independent subnetworks first, record them and then proceed to get extensions of dependent components. Furthermore, we can combine extensions of different independent components without problems.

4 From Prioritized Defaults to TMS

In the next section, we consider the translation of a default theory à la Reiter to a TMS-network and modify it slightly to handle changing premise sets that are obtained as results of lower levels.

4.1 Translating Default Logic to TMS

In [Junker and Konolige, 1990] we extracted two sets of formulas from Reiter's defaults. Let $\Delta = (D, W')$ be a default theory. We consider the set of consequents of defaults and the set of relevant formulas consisting of prerequisites and negated consistency assumptions of defaults:

$$\begin{aligned} C_D = &\ \{c \mid (a : b_1, \cdots, b_k/c) \in D\} \\ \mathcal{L}_D = &\ \{q \mid (a : b_1, \cdots, b_k/c) \in D, \\ &\ q \in \{a, \neg b_1, \ldots, \neg b_k\}\} \end{aligned} \quad (14)$$

Defaults and classical proofs are translated separately into justifications. Every default yields a non-monotonic justification:

$$\begin{aligned} NM_D := &\ \{\langle in(a), out(\neg b_1, \ldots, \neg b_k) \rightarrow c\rangle \mid \\ &\ (a : b_1, \cdots, b_k/c) \in D\} \end{aligned} \quad (15)$$

Furthermore, we need all proofs of relevant formulas from premises W and consequents C_D. For this purpose, we define a set $M_W(U, R)$ of monotonic justifications for a domain $U \subseteq \mathcal{L}$, a range $R \subseteq \mathcal{L}$, and a theory $W \subseteq \mathcal{L}$:

$$\begin{aligned} M_W(U, R) := &\ \{\langle in(Q) \rightarrow q\rangle \mid Q \text{ is a minimal} \\ &\ \text{subset of } U \text{ s.t. } Q \cup W \models q\} \end{aligned} \quad (16)$$

As pointed out in [Junker and Konolige, 1990], these minimal arguments for a goal q can be determined by consequence-finding algorithms based on linear-ordered resolution. The justifications in $M_W(U, R)$ are sufficient to check for every element of R whether it can be derived from *any* subset of U.

In [Junker and Konolige, 1990], we have considered $M_{W'}(C_D, \mathcal{L}_D)$ for a default theory $\Delta = (D, W')$. Here, we take a slightly changed encoding since we want to handle default theories with different premises. For this purpose, we split W' into a fixed part W and a changing part X which is a subset of an upper bound C. Thus, we obtain a set of default theories for D, W, and C:

$$\mathcal{S} := \{(D, W \cup X) \mid X \subseteq C\} \quad (17)$$

These default theories have a common TMS-network. Its non-monotonic justifications are NM_D and its monotonic justifications are $M_W(C_D \cup C, \mathcal{L}_D)$:

$$\nu_{D,W,C} := (C_D \cup \mathcal{L}_D \cup C, NM_D \cup M_W(C_D \cup C, \mathcal{L}_D)) \quad (18)$$

To regain the relevant part of an extension we supply the network with the additional premises $X \subseteq C$ of the selected default theory:

Theorem 4.1 *Let W and C be subsets of $\mathcal{L}$ and D be a set of defaults over $\mathcal{L}$. Let $X \subseteq C$. There exists a bijective mapping of the set of extensions of $(D, W \cup X)$ to the set of TMS-extensions of $\nu_{D,W,C}$ and X.*

Using this network, we can handle default theories which differ in some part of their premise sets.

4.2 Mapping Levels to Clusters

Now, we are ready to map a level-based default theory $(W, (L_1, \ldots, L_k))$ to TMS. We map every level to a TMS-network getting the nodes of lower levels as input. It is important that the different subnetworks are disjoint (i.e. don't share any node). The translation profits from the results in [Junker and Konolige, 1990]: We relate every level to a default theory and map it to a TMS-network using the translation in section 4.1. According to the results of section 3.2 we obtain the extensions of the complete TMS-network by a recursive characterization which is very similar to the definition of a preferred subtheory. Hence, it is not difficult to show that the extensions of this network are exactly the preferred subtheories of the level-based default theory.

Below, we elaborate this in detail. Let $\Delta = (W, (L_1, \ldots, L_k))$ be a level-based default theory. A preferred subtheory of level i is a subset of $L'_i := L_1 \cup \ldots \cup L_i$. As pointed out in section 2.1, we obtain for every level L_i different default theories $\Delta_i := (D_{L_i}, W_i)$ having a varying premise set W_i. Such a set W_i consists of W and a preferred subtheory of the next lower level which is a subset of L'_{i-1}. Then we get the following result:

Theorem 4.2 *Let $\Delta = (W, (L_1, \ldots, L_k))$ be a level-based default theory. Let $\mathcal{S}_i := \{(D_{L_i}, W \cup T') \mid T'$ is a preferred subtheory of level $i-1\}$. Then T is a preferred subtheory of level i iff T is an extension of a default theory in $\mathcal{S}_i$.*

In section 4.1, we extended the TMS-translation of default theories to capture changing premise sets. For level i, the changing part is $C_{D_{L'_{i-1}}}$ containing all consequents of defaults of lower levels. Note that $C_{D_{L_i}} = L_i$ and $C_{D_{L'_i}} = L'_i$ since the defaults in D_{L_i} have the simple form $\frac{:q}{q}$ for $q \in L_i$. Thus, we obtain the network $\nu_i := \nu_{D_{L_i},W,L'_{i-1}}$. If we supply it with a preferred subtheory of level $i-1$ we get a preferred subtheory of level i as an extension of ν_i.

Thus, we could get the preferred subtheories of the level-based default theory if we link the networks of its levels. Let ν_i be equal to (N_i, J_i). First, we consider the networks for the levels 1 to i:

$$\nu_{\Delta,i} := (N_1 \cup \ldots \cup N_i, J_1 \cup \ldots \cup J_i) \qquad (19)$$

The complete network ν_Δ is equal to $\nu_{\Delta,k}$.

Now, we would like to apply the results of section 3.2 in order to relate the extensions of subnetworks to the preferred subtheories of a certain level. First, we have to identify independent components. Since every default is positive and occurs in exactly one level the sets N_i of

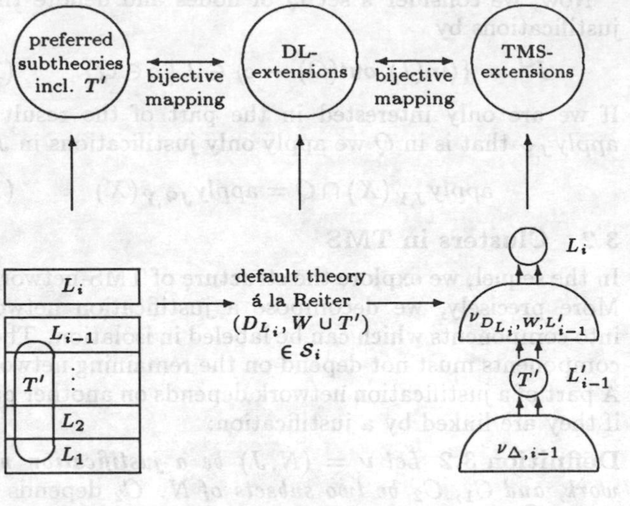

Figure 2: Illustration for theorem 4.4

nodes are mutually disjoint. Hence, there is no justification leading from $N_i - (N_1 \cup \ldots \cup N_{i-1})$ to $N_1 \cup \ldots \cup N_{i-1}$:

Lemma 4.3 *Let $\Delta = (W, (L_1, \ldots, L_k))$ be a level-based default theory. Then the set $N_1 \cup \ldots \cup N_{i-1}$ of the nodes of $\nu_{\Delta,i-1}$ is an independent component of $\nu_{\Delta,i}$.*

After getting all technical prerequisites, we are able to apply theorem 3.2 to the subnetworks of the level-based default theory. Thus, we can prove the following theorem by induction on i using the theorems 4.2, 4.1, and 3.2 (cf. figure 2):

Theorem 4.4 *Let $\Delta = (W, (L_1, \ldots, L_k))$ be a level-based default theory. Then there exists a bijective mapping of the set of extensions of the subnetwork $\nu_{\Delta,i}$ to the set of preferred subtheories of level i.*

The mapping is indeed very simple: Just take the nodes of an extension that are in L'_i to obtain a preferred subtheory. In turn, we get the main result of this paper:

Theorem 4.5 *(Main) Let $\Delta = (W, (L_1, \ldots, L_k))$ be a level-based default theory. Then there exists a bijective mapping of the set of extensions of the network ν_Δ to the set of preferred subtheories of Δ.*

Thus, we have translated a level-based default theory into a TMS-network. It reflects the level-structure of the default theory. It could also be obtained from the network of a level-free default theory by removing justifications leading from a subnetwork of a higher level to a subnetwork of a lower level.

Our approach can also be applied to a restricted kind of *prioritized circumscription* which is obtained by adding unique names assumption and domain closure. Due to [Baker and Ginsberg, 1989], such a circumscription theory can be mapped to a level-based default theory, which is in turn translated to a TMS-network. For circumscription, *goal-directed reasoning* is required. To prove a goal $q \in \mathcal{L}$ we need further justifications for proofs of q. After that, we can get rid of a large part of the network. According to theorem 3.2, we can focus our attention to the minimal independent component containing the goal q because the remaining subnetwork is coherent in this case.

4.3 Network for Davis' Familiar Example

Consider again the circuit example of section 2.3. In this section, we translate the default theory Δ_{circ} into a TMS-network. The relevant first-order proofs can be extracted from the *conflict sets*, i.e. minimal sets of hypotheses that are inconsistent in conjunction with the premises. According to [de Kleer and Williams, 1987], we get two conflict sets:

$$\begin{array}{l} \{ok(M1), ok(M2), ok(A1)\} \cup W \models \bot \\ \{ok(M1), ok(M3), ok(A1), ok(A2)\} \cup W \models \bot \end{array} \tag{20}$$

We get the arguments for the relevant formulas $\neg ok(o)$ by applying the deduction theorem to the conflict sets.

Next, we consider the subnetworks for both levels. The first level contains only adders leading to two non-monotonic justifications. ν_1 consists of

$$\begin{array}{l} \langle out(\neg ok(A1)) \rightarrow ok(A1)\rangle \\ \langle out(\neg ok(A2)) \rightarrow ok(A2)\rangle \end{array} \tag{21}$$

We don't get monotonic justifications in the first level because every conflict set contains some multiplier which belongs to a higher level. For the second level, we obtain a non-monotonic justification for each multiplier:

$$\begin{array}{l} \langle out(\neg ok(M1)) \rightarrow ok(M1)\rangle \\ \langle out(\neg ok(M2)) \rightarrow ok(M2)\rangle \\ \langle out(\neg ok(M3)) \rightarrow ok(M3)\rangle \end{array} \tag{22}$$

Additionally, ν_2 contains justifications for the negations of correct models of multipliers that are obtained from the conflicts of equation 20:

$$\begin{array}{l} \langle in(ok(A1), ok(M2)) \rightarrow \neg ok(M1)\rangle \\ \langle in(ok(A1), ok(A2), ok(M3)) \rightarrow \neg ok(M1)\rangle \\ \langle in(ok(A1), ok(M1)) \rightarrow \neg ok(M2)\rangle \\ \langle in(ok(A1), ok(A2), ok(M1)) \rightarrow \neg ok(M3)\rangle \end{array} \tag{23}$$

This network has two non-monotonic loops sharing $\neg ok(M1)$. To find labelings, we choose a label for this node and proceed with propagation. In general, we first consider networks for lower levels. Since the network lacks monotonic loops no groundedness check is necessary as in [Junker and Konolige, 1990].

5 Conclusion

We pointed out how prioritized default theories [Brewka, 1989] can be used to obtain a TMS-based system for generating *preferred diagnoses*. To achieve this goal, we showed three results, which are of their own interest:

- Prioritized defaults allow to express preferences between models of behaviour in diagnosis from first principles. Thus, the diagnosis process can be focused to candidates that should be investigated first.
- Extensions of TMS-networks having independent components can be split into extensions of subnetworks. Hence, divide-and-conquer methods may be used to compute extensions. An example for this is Goodwin's TMS-algorithm [Goodwin, 1987].
- Levels of defaults are mapped to TMS according to [Junker and Konolige, 1990] and then linked together using the result above. Thus, we get a TMS-based prover for prioritized defaults which is an alternative to Baker's and Ginsberg's prioritized circumscription prover [Baker and Ginsberg, 1989].

Priorities on general defaults have also been considered in [Brewka, 1989]. Our TMS-translation carries over to these defaults provided they don't share components. This condition ensures disjoint subnetworks.

An issue for future work is to see whether prioritized defaults can substitute fault probabilities [de Kleer and Williams, 1987], [de Kleer, 1990] in practical problems.

Acknowledgements

The different ideas presented in this paper arose from discussions with different persons. I would like to thank Prof. M. Richter, Kurt Konolige, Gerd Brewka, and Hans Voss. Peter Struss and Gerhard Friedrich gave helpful comments. This work has been supported by the Federal Ministry for Research and Technology within the joint project TASSO (Grant No. ITW8900A7).

References

[Baker and Ginsberg, 1989] A.B. Baker and M.L. Ginsberg. A theorem prover for prioritized circumscription. In *IJCAI-89*, pages 463–467, 1989.

[Brewka, 1989] G. Brewka. Preferred subtheories: An extended logical framework for default reasoning. In *IJCAI-89*, pages 1043–1048, 1989.

[de Kleer and Williams, 1987] J. de Kleer and B.C. Williams. Diagnosing multiple faults. *Artificial Intelligence*, 32:97–130, 1987.

[de Kleer, 1990] J. de Kleer. Using crude probability estimates to guide diagnosis. *Artificial Intelligence*, 45:381–391, 1990.

[Dressler and Struss, 1990] O. Dressler and P. Struss. Back to defaults: Computing diagnoses as coherent assumption sets. Technical report, Siemens AG, 1990.

[Goodwin, 1987] J.W. Goodwin. *A Theory and System for Non-Monotonic Reasoning*. PhD thesis, University of Linköping, Linköping, Sweden, 1987.

[Junker and Konolige, 1990] U. Junker and K. Konolige. Computing the extensions of autoepistemic and default logics with a truth maintenance system. In *AAAI-90*, pages 278–283, 1990.

[Poole, 1988] D. Poole. A logical framework for default reasoning. *Artificial Intelligence*, 36:27–47, 1988.

[Poole, 1989] D. Poole. Normality and faults in logic-based diagnosis. In *IJCAI-89*, pages 1304–1310, 1989.

[Reiter, 1987] R. Reiter. A theory of diagnosis from first principles. *Artificial Intelligence*, 32:57–952, 1987.

[Struss and Dressler, 1989] P. Struss and O. Dressler. Physical negation - integrating fault models into the general diagnostic engine. In *IJCAI-89*, pages 1318–1323, 1989.

AUTOMATED REASONING

Constraint Satisfaction

On the Feasibility of Distributed Constraint Satisfaction

Zeev Collin
CS, Technion —
Israel Institute of Technology,
Haifa, 32000, Israel

Rina Dechter*
Information and CS, UCI,
Irvine, CA, 92717

Shmuel Katz
CS, Technion —
Israel Institute of Technology,
Haifa, 32000, Israel

Abstract

This paper characterizes connectionist-type architectures that allow a distributed solution for classes of constraint-satisfaction problems. The main issue addressed is whether there exists a **uniform** model of computation (where all nodes are indistinguishable) that guarantees convergence to a solution from every initial state of the system, whenever such a solution exists. We show that even for relatively simple constraint networks, such as rings, there is no general solution using a completely uniform, asynchronous, model. However, some restricted topologies like trees can accommodate the uniform, asynchronous, model and a protocol demonstrating this fact is presented. An **almost-uniform**, asynchronous, network-consistency protocol is also presented. We show that the algorithms are guaranteed to be self-stabilizing, which makes them suitable for dynamic or error-prone environments.

1 Introduction

Consider the distributed version of the graph coloring problem, where each node must select a color (from a given set of colors) that is different from any color selected by its neighbors. This coloring task, whose sequential version is known to be NP-complete, belongs to a class of **Constraint Satisfaction Problems (CSPs)** that present interesting challenges to distributed computation, particularly in the framework of connectionist architectures. We call the distributed versions of such problems **Network Consistency Problems (NCPs)**. We consider what types of distributed models admit a self-stabilizing algorithm (namely, one that converges to a solution from any initial state of the network), and present such algorithms when possible.

Constraints are useful in programming languages, simulation packages and general knowledge representation systems, and the prospects of solving such problems by connectionist networks promise the combined advantages of parallelism, simplicity of design and error correction capabilities.

Indeed, many interesting problems attacked by researchers in neural networks are combinatorial and many involve constraint satisfaction [Ballard *et al.*, 1986, Dahl, 1987]. In fact, any discrete state connectionist network can be viewed as a type of constraint network, with each stable pattern of states representing a consistent solution. However, current connectionist approaches to CSPs lack theoretical guarantees of convergence (to a solution satisfying all constraints), and the terms on which such convergence can be guaranteed (if at all) have not been explored till now.

In this paper we show that widely used connectionist-type architectures in which all nodes run identical procedures cannot admit algorithms that guarantee convergence to a consistent solution, even if such a solution exists (Section 2). We then identify a distributed model that is close in spirit to the connectionist paradigm, for which such guarantees can be established (Section 3). Within this model, we characterize and provide algorithms for a restricted subclass of networks that can be solved uniformly (Section 4).

2 Model and Definitions

2.1 CSP definition

A network of binary constraints involves a set of n variables $X_1, \dots, X_n$, each represented by its domain values, $D_1, \dots, D_n$, and a set of constraints. A **binary constraint** R_{ij} between two variables X_i and X_j is a subset of the Cartesian product $D_i \times D_j$ that specifies which values of the variables are compatible with each other. A solution is an assignment of values to all the variables which satisfies all the constraints, and the constraint satisfaction problems associated with these networks are to find one or all solutions. A binary CSP can be associated with a **constraint-graph** in which nodes represent variables and arcs connect pairs of variables which are constrained explicitly. (General constraint satisfaction problems may involve constraints of any arity, but since network communication is only pairwise we focus on this subclass of problems.) Figure 1a presents a CSP constraint graph.

*This work was partially supported by the National Science Foundation, Grant #IRI-8821444 and by the Air Force Office of Scientific Research, Grant #AFOSR-90-0136.

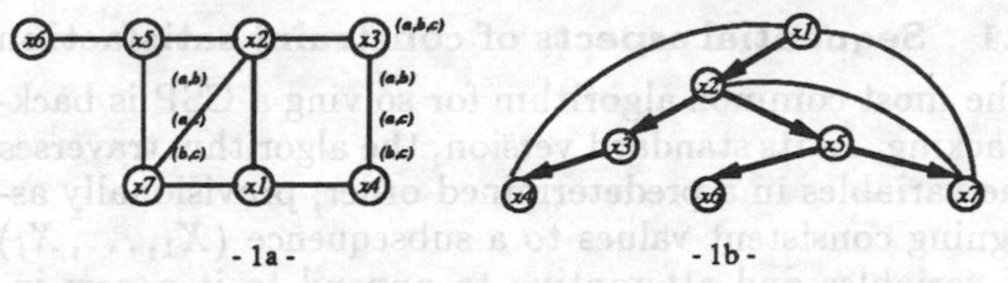

Figure 1: CSP - A constraint graph and its DFS-tree

2.2 The model

Our general communication model is known as the **shared memory multi-reader single-writer** model. A distributed network consists of n nodes, connected by shared communication registers, called **state registers**. The network can be viewed as a **communication graph** where nodes represent processors and arcs correspond to communication registers. The register $state_i$ is written only by node i, but may be read by several nodes (all of i's neighbors). The state register may have several fields, but it is regarded as one unit. A node can be modeled as a finite state-machine where its state is controlled by a **transition function** that is dependent on its current state and the states of its neighbors. In other words, an activated node performs an **atomic step** consisting of reading the states of all its neighbors, deciding whether to change its state and then moving to a new state (by writing in its state register)[1]. The collection of all transition functions is called a **protocol**. The processors are anonymous, i.e. , have no identities (we use the terms node i and processor P_i interchangeably and as a writing convenience only). A configuration c of the system is the state vector of all processors.

The execution of the system can be managed either by **a central demon** (scheduler) defined in [Dijkstra, 1974, Dolev *et al.*, 1990] or by **a distributed demon** defined in [Burns *et al.*, 1987, Dolev *et al.*, 1990]. The distributed demon activates a subset of the system's nodes at each step, while the central demon activates only one processor at a time (and thus can be viewed as a simplified version of the distributed demon). All activated nodes execute a single atomic step simultaneously.

The central demon means that an interleaving is sufficient for the analysis of the protocol. Nevertheless, on the implementation level, truly independent nodes can execute in parallel since they cannot affect each other. Only neighboring nodes in the constraint graph cannot execute at the same atomic step when a central demon is assumed.

We denote $c_1 \rightarrow c_2$ if c_2 is a configuration which is reached from configuration c_1 by some subset of processors simultaneously executing a single atomic step. An **execution** of the system is an infinite sequence of configurations $E = c_1, c_2 \ldots$ such that for every i, $c_i \rightarrow c_{i+1}$. An execution is considered **fair** if every node participates in it infinitely often.

[1] In fact, a finer degree of atomicity, requiring only a **test-and-set** operation, is possible, but is not used here in order to simplify the arguments.

2.3 Self-stabilization

A self-stabilizing protocol [Dijkstra, 1974] is one with a particular convergence property. The system configuration-space is partitioned into two classes — legal, denoted by L, and illegal. The protocol is self-stabilizing if in any infinite fair execution, starting from any initial configuration (and with any input values) and given "enough time", the system eventually reaches a legal configuration, and all subsequently computed configurations are legal. Thus a self-stabilizing protocol converges from any point in its configuration-space to a stable, legal region.

The legality of a configuration depends on the aim of the protocol. In our case, we wish to design a protocol for solving the network consistency problem. Thus, the set of legal configurations are those having a consistent assignment of values to all the nodes in the network, if such an assignment exists, and any set, otherwise. This definition allows the system to oscillate among various solutions, if more than one consistent assignment is possible. However, the protocols that are presented in this paper converge to one of the possible solutions.

2.4 The limits of uniform self-stabilization

A protocol is **uniform** if all the nodes are logically equivalent and identically programmed (i.e. have identical transition functions). Following an observation made by Dijkstra [Dijkstra, 1974] regarding the computational limits of a uniform model for performing the mutual exclusion task, we show that the network consistency problem cannot be solved using a uniform protocol. This is accomplished by presenting a specific constraint network and proving that its convergence cannot be guaranteed using **any** uniform protocol.

Consider the task of numbering a ring of processors in a cyclic ascending order — we call this CSP the **"ring ordering problem"**. The constraint-graph of the problem is a ring of nodes with the domains $\{0, 1, \ldots, n-1\}$. Every arc has the set of constraints $\{(i, (i+1) \bmod n) | 0 \leq i \leq n-1\}$ i.e., the left node is one smaller than the right one. A solution to this problem is a cyclic permutation of the numbers $0, \ldots, n-1$, which means that there are n possible solutions, and in all of them different nodes are assigned different values.

Theorem 1: No uniform, self stabilizing protocol can solve the ring ordering problem, under a central demon policy.

Proof: In order to obtain a contradiction, assume that there exists a uniform self-stabilizing protocol for solving the problem. In particular, it would solve the ring-ordering problem for a ring having a composite number of nodes, $n = r \cdot q$ $(r, q > 1)$. Since convergence to a solution is guaranteed from any initial configuration, it also applies to one where all nodes are in identical states. We construct a fair execution for such a protocol for which the network never converges to a consistent solution, contradicting the self stabilization property of the protocol. Assume the following execution:

$$\begin{array}{lllll} P_0, & P_q, & P_{2q}, & \ldots, & P_{(r-1)q}, \\ P_1, & P_{q+1}, & P_{2q+1}, & \ldots, & P_{(r-1)q+1}, \\ \vdots & & & & \\ P_{q-1}, & P_{2q-1}, & P_{3q-1}, & \ldots, & P_{rq-1}, \\ \vdots & & & & \end{array}$$

Note that nodes $P_0, P_q, P_{2q}, \ldots, P_{(r-1)q}$, after their first activation, move to identical states because their inputs, initial states and transition functions are identical, and when each one of them is activated their neighbors are in identical states too. The same holds for any sequential activation of processors $\{P_{iq+j} \mid 0 \leq i < r,\ 0 \leq j < q\}$. Thus, cycling through the above schedule assures that P_0 and P_q, for instance, move to identical states over and over again an infinite number of times. Since a consistent solution requires their states to be different, the network will never reach a consistent solution, thus yielding a contradiction. □

Theorem 1 implies that it is generally impossible to guarantee convergence to a consistent solution using a uniform protocol. It also implies that such convergence cannot be guaranteed for a class of sequential algorithms using so called "repair" methods, such as in [Minton *et al.*, 1990]. It does not, however, exclude the possibility of existence of uniform protocols for restricted activation policies.

We can also show that, when using a distributed demon, convergence (to a solution) cannot be guaranteed even for **tree-networks.** Consider, for instance, the coloring problem in a tree-network constructed from exactly two connected nodes each having the domain {BLACK, WHITE}. Since the two nodes are topologically identical, If they start from identical initial states and both of them are activated simultaneously, they can never be assigned different values. Consequently, the network does not converge to a legal solution, although one exists. This counterexample can be extended to a large class of trees, where there is no possible way to distinguish between two internal nodes. We will show, however, (section 4) that for a central demon a uniform self stabilizing tree-network consistency protocol does exist.

Having proved that the network consistency problem cannot be solved using a uniform protocol, even with a central demon, we switch to a slightly more relaxed model of an "**almost uniform**" protocol, whereby all nodes but one are identical. We denote the special node as P_0.

3 Consistency-Generation Protocol

Our network consistency protocol is based on a sequential version of a **backtracking** algorithm, called **backjumping.** When implemented on a variable ordering generated by a **depth-first traversal** of the constraint graph, the technique enables a distributed implementation. A preliminary version of this protocol appears in [Collin and Dechter, 1990].

3.1 Sequential aspects of constraint satisfaction

The most common algorithm for solving a CSP is backtracking. In its standard version, the algorithm traverses the variables in a predetermined order, provisionally assigning consistent values to a subsequence $(X_1, \ldots, X_i)$ of variables and attempting to append to it a new instantiation of X_{i+1} such that the whole set is consistent. If no consistent assignment can be found for the next variable X_{i+1}, a deadend situation occurs; the algorithm "backtracks" to the most recent variable, changes its assignment and continues from there.

One useful improvement of backtracking, called **backjumping** [Dechter, 1990] consults the topology of the constraint graph to guide its "backward" phase. Specifically, instead of going back to the most recent variable instantiated it **jumps back** several levels to the first variable **connected** to the deadend variable. It turns out that when using a depth-first search (DFS) on the constraint graph (to generate a DFS tree) and then conducting backjumping in an inorder traversal of the DFS tree, [Even, 1979] the jump-back destination of variable X is the parent of X in the DFS tree.

The nice property of a DFS tree that allows a parallel implementation is that any arc of the graph which is not in the tree connects a node to one of its tree ancestors (i.e. along the path leading to it from the root). Consequently, the DFS tree represents a useful decomposition of the graph: if a variable X and all its ancestors are removed from the graph, the subtrees rooted at X will be disconnected (Figure 1b). This translates to a problem-decomposition strategy: if all ancestors of variable X are instantiated, then the solutions of all its subtrees are completely independent and can be performed in parallel (see also [Freuder and Quinn, 1987]).

3.2 General Network Consistency protocol

The network-consistency (NC) protocol is logically composed of two self-stabilizing subprotocols that can be executed interleaved (we divide the second subprotocol into two parts in order to simplify the explanation):

1. DFS-tree generation
2. (a) graph-traversal protocol
   (b) value-assignment

These subprotocols are unrelated to each other and, thus, can be independently replaced by any other version of implementation.

The basic idea of the protocol is to decompose the network into several independent subnetworks, according to the DFS-tree structure, and to instantiate these subnetworks in parallel. A proper order of value instantiation is guaranteed by the graph traversal protocol.

3.2.1 Neighborhoods and states

A self-stabilizing algorithm for generating a DFS-tree is presented in [Collin and Dolev, 1991] and will not be discussed here. This subprotocol is almost uniform and is the source of non-uniformity for the whole NC protocol. When the algorithm stabilizes each internal node, i, has one adjacent node, *parent*(i), designated as its **parent** in the tree, and a set of **child** nodes denoted *children*(i). Figure 2 indicates the environment of an internal node (2a), the root (2b), and a leaf (2c). The link leading from *parent*(i) to i is called **i's inlink** while the links connecting i to its children are called **i's outlinks**. The set of its neighboring nodes along the path from the **root** to i are called **i's predecessors**. The role of the root is played by the special processor P_0. Each node i (representing variable X_i) has a list of possible values, denoted as $Domain_i$, and a pairwise relation R_{ij} with each neighbor j. The domain and the constraints may be viewed as a part of the system or as inputs that are always valid (though they can be changed during the execution, forcing the network to readjust itself to the changes).

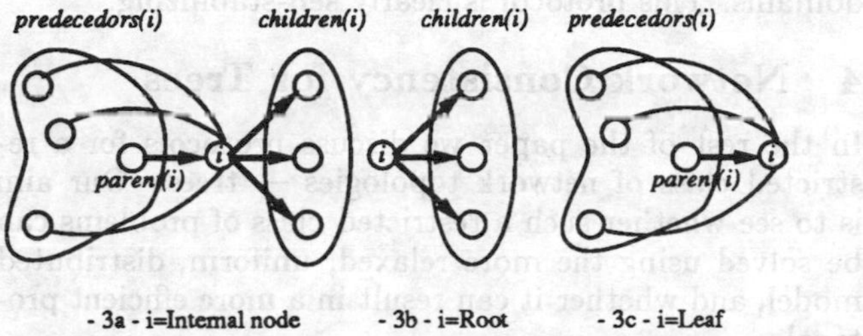

Figure 2: Node's neighborhood set

The state-register of each node contains the following fields:

1. A ***value*** field to which it assigns either one of its domain values or the symbol "$\star$" (to denote a dead-end).
2. A ***mode*** field indicating the node's "belief" regarding the status of the network. A node's mode is ON if its value or its ancestors' values were changed since the last time it was in a forward phase, or otherwise it is OFF. The modes of all nodes also give an indication of whether they have reached a consistent state (all in an OFF mode).
3. Two boolean fields called ***parent_tag*** and ***children_tag***, which are used by the graph-traversal protocol (Section 3.2.2).

3.2.2 Graph-traversal protocol

The graph-traversal protocol is handled by a self-stabilizing **privilege passing mechanism.** According to this protocol a node obtains a privilege to act, granted to it either by its parent or by its children. A node is allowed to change its state only if it is privileged.

Our privilege passing mechanism is an extension of a mutual exclusion protocol for two nodes called **balance-unbalance** [Dijkstra, 1974, Dolev *et al.*, 1990]. Once a DFS-tree is established, this scheme is implemented by having every state register contain two fields: *parent_tag*, referring to its inlink and *children_tag*, referring to all its outlinks. A link is **balanced**, if the *children_tag* and the *parent_tag* on its endpoints have the same value, and the link is **unbalanced** otherwise. A node, i, becomes privileged if its inlink is unbalanced and **all** its outlinks are balanced[2]. The privilege can be passed backwards to the parent by balancing the incoming link or forward to the children by unbalancing the outgoing links (i.e. by changing the *parent_tag* or the *children_tag* value accordingly). A node applies the NC-protocol only when it is privileged, otherwise it leaves its state unchanged.

Denote a **branch** to be a tree-path from the root to a leaf. The privilege-passing mechanism eventually converges to a set of **legally controlled** configurations, in which no more than one node is privileged on every branch. Figure 3 shows such a configuration (the *parent_tag* and the *children_tag* of every node are specified above and below the node respectively). This property assures that eventually a node and its ancestors cannot reassign their values simultaneously. The privileges travel along the branches backwards and forwards. We omit the proof due to space limitations.

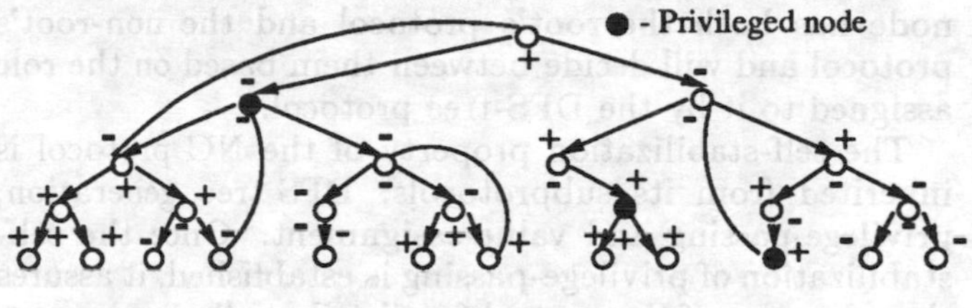

Figure 3: Legally controlled configuration

3.2.3 Value-assignment

The value-assignment has a **forward** and a **backward** phases, corresponding to the two phases of the sequential backtracking algorithm. During the forward phase, nodes in different subtrees assign themselves values consistent with their predecessors or verify the consistency of their assigned values. When a node senses a dead-end it assigns its *value* field a "$\star$" and initiates a backward phase. When the network is consistent (all the processors are in an OFF *mode*) the forward and backward phases continue, where the forward phase is used to verify the consistency of the network and the backward phase just returns the privilege to the root to start a new forward wave. Once consistency verification is violated, the node sensing the violation initiates a new value-assignment. Since the root has no ancestors, it does not check consistency. It only assigns a new value at the end of each backward phase, when needed, and then initiates a new forward phase. A more elaborate description follows.

An internal node can be in one of three situations:

- **Node i is activated by its parent which is in an** ON **mode** (this is the forward phase of value assignments). In that case some change of value in one of its predecessors might have occurred. It, therefore, finds the first value in its domain that is consistent with all its predecessors, puts itself in an ON mode and passes the privilege to its children. If no consistent value exists, it assigns itself the "$\star$"

[2] Note that this is well defined since we prove that eventually all siblings have the same parent-tag.

value (a deadend) and passes the privilege to its parent (initiating a backward phase).

- **Node i is activated by its parent which is in an OFF mode.** In that case it verifies the consistency of its current value with its predecessors. If it is consistent it stays in an OFF mode and passes the privilege to its children. If not, it assigns itself a new value, moves to an ON mode, and passes the privilege to its children[3].
- **Node i is activated by its children** (backward phase). If one of the children has a "$\star$" value, the processor selects the next consistent value from its domain and passes the privilege to the children. If no consistent value is available, it assigns itself a "$\star$" and passes the privilege to its parent[4]. If all children have a consistent value, i passes the privilege to its parent.

The value-assignment protocol is uniform since each node has both the root's protocol and the non-root's protocol and will decide between them based on the role assigned to it by the DFS-tree protocol.

The self-stabilization property of the NC protocol is inherited from its subprotocols; DFS-tree generation, privilege-passing and value-assignment. Once the self-stabilization of privilege-passing is established, it assures the adequacy of the control for distributedly implementing DFS-based backjumping, which guarantees the convergence of the network to a legal solution, if one exists, and if not it keeps checking all the possibilities over and over again.

3.3 Complexity analysis

A crude estimate of the time complexity of the NC protocol can be given by computing the maximal number of state changes from the time the privilege-passing has stabilized until final convergence. The search space that is generated by the sequential DFS-backjumping obeys the following recurrence: $T_m = 1+b\cdot k\cdot T_{m-1}$ with $T_0 = 1$, which yields $T_m = (b\cdot k)^{m+1}$ where T_m stands for the search space generated by sequential DFS-backjumping with depth m or less, b is the maximal branching degree and k bounds the domain sizes. Our bound improves the one presented in [Freuder and Quinn, 1987]. Note that since $b^m < n$ we get that $T_m = O(nk^{m+1})$. Clearly, in the worst parallel execution we get a sequential behavior with the same time complexity — exponential in the depth of the DFS-tree. However, often, due to parallel instantiations of different subtrees, the parallel protocol may have, on the average, a significant speedup over the sequential one. We believe that the speedup (of our protocol over the same sequential algorithm) is of $O(n/m)$. As an extreme example, consider problem instances that have a backtrack-free solution along the DFS ordering. These will be solved in $O(n)$ sequentially, while in $O(m)$ in parallel. To conclude, our protocol convergence can be achieved in polynomial time for networks with a bounded depth of the DFS-tree.

The average performance of the NC protocol can be further improved by adding to it a uniform self-stabilizing **arc-consistency** subprotocol [Mackworth and Freuder, 1985]. A network is said to be **arc-consistent** if for every value in each node's domain there is a consistent value in all its neighbors' domains. Arc-consistency can be achieved by a repeated execution of a "relaxation procedure", where each node reads its neighbors' domains and eliminates any of its own values for which there is no consistent value in one of its neighbors' domains. This protocol is clearly self-stabilizing.

4 Network Consistency for Trees

In the rest of the paper we discuss protocols for a restricted class of network topologies — trees. Our aim is to see whether such a restricted class of problems can be solved using the more relaxed, uniform, distributed model, and whether it can result in a more efficient protocol.

It is well known that the sequential network consistency problem on trees is tractable, and can be achieved in linear time [Mackworth and Freuder, 1985]. A special algorithm for this task is composed of an arc-consistency phase (that can be efficiently implemented on trees), followed by value assignment in an order created by some **rooted tree.** It has been shown that an arc-consistent tree enables backtrack-free value assignment with no deadends [Freuder, 1982]. Applying the general NC protocol together with the arc-consistency protocol to a tree will already result in an improved performance: when arc-consistency is established, one forward phase of the value-assignment protocol will assign values to all the nodes in linear time since no deadends will be encountered (see also [Dechter and Dechter, 1988]). Therefore, the almost-uniform NC protocol if applied to trees is guaranteed to converge in a polynomial number of steps.

Since, the DFS subprotocol of our general algorithm was the source for its non-uniformity, we reexamine the possibility that for trees, a rooted directed tree can be imposed via a uniform protocol. We already showed that when using a distributed demon, a uniform, network-consistency protocol for trees is not feasible. Therefore, the only avenue not yet explored is whether under a central demon such a protocol does exist. We next show that this conjecture is indeed correct.

4.1 A uniform tree-consistency protocol

In principle a uniform tree-consistency (TC) protocol can be extracted from the general NC protocol by only replacing the DFS-tree protocol with a **uniform rooted-tree** protocol, since any rooted-tree is also a DFS-tree. Since the arc-consistency protocol, the value-assignment protocol and the privilege-passing protocol are already uniform, the resulting TC protocol will be uniform, as desired. Nevertheless, we will show that for trees, the value-assignment protocol can be simplified as

[3] A leaf, having no children, is always activated by its parent and always passes the privilege back to its parent (initiating a backward phase).

[4] Due to the privilege passing mechanism, when a parent sees one of its children in a deadend it has to wait until **all** of them have given him the privilege. This is done to guarantee that all subtrees have a consistent view regarding their predecessors' values.

well, while there is no need to have a special privilege-passing mechanism at all.

The TC protocol consists of the following three sub-protocols:

1. arc-consistency
2. tree-directing
3. tree-value-assignment

When the arcs are consistent and the tree has been directed, value assignment is eventually guaranteed by having each node follow the rule (of the **tree-value-assignment** protocol): "CHOOSE A VALUE CONSISTENT WITH YOUR PARENT'S ASSIGNMENT". Such a value must exist, since otherwise the value assigned by the parent would have been removed by the arc-consistency procedure. Since, as we will show, the tree-directing protocol is self-stabilizing, and since the arc-consistency protocol is self-stabilizing as well, the value-assignment protocol eventually converges to a consistent solution.

In order to **direct** the tree, we must break the symmetry reflected by the identical codes and the lack of identifiers, by exploiting the topology of the tree. For this task we use a distributed protocol for finding the **centers** of a tree [Korach *et al.*, 1984]. A center of a tree is a node whose maximal distance from the leaves is minimal. Consider a sequential algorithm that works in phases, so that in every phase the leaves of the previous phase are removed from the tree. In the last phase the tree has either one or two connected nodes left. These nodes are the centers of the tree.

Our protocol distributedly simulates the above algorithm. If only one center exists, it plays the role of a root and all the arcs are directed towards it. When two centers exist, the direction of the link that connects them remains ambiguous and both of them can be viewed as a root since all other links are directed towards them as before. In this case, each one of the two centers considers the other one to be its parent, and the tree-directing protocol, results in a **pseudo-rooted-tree** where the centers (one or two nodes) play the root role.

We claim that this ambiguity will not hurt the tree-value-assignment protocol at all. Note that the "first" center that applies the assignment protocol, assigns itself a value consistent with the other. When the other one is scheduled, it is supposed to assign itself a value that is consistent with the first one. However, its current assignment is already consistent (since the first one has taken care of that already) and thus it remains unchanged. All other nodes assign values that are consistent with their parents as before. The central demon policy assures that only one (neighboring) center will be scheduled each time.

This approach yields a relatively simple uniform tree-directing protocol that simulates the above description. Assume the number of nodes in the network[5] is n. Every node i has the following fields:

$N_i[0..\lfloor n/2 \rfloor]$ – a vector that counts the number of i's neighbors in each phase of the sequential algorithm. $N_i[j]$ records the number of neighbors of i in phase j. If $N_i[j] = 1$ it means that i becomes a leaf in the j-th phase (although it may be initialized incorrectly). $N_i[0]$ is repeatedly initialized to the number of i's neighbors in the network (so that $N_i[0] = 1$ means that i is a leaf in the original tree).

$parent_i$ – a variable assigned the value j if node j becomes the parent of i (the enumeration is local to i). When the network stabilizes, namely when all the N-vectors converge, every node has one neighbor only that is eligible to be its parent, except a single center which has none, and no two nodes are parents of each other except, perhaps, the two centers.

The protocol works by having each node scan its neighbors' N-vectors and compute its own accordingly. Since the j-th entry of vector N_i represents the number of i's neighbors in the j-th phase, its value is recursively computed by decreasing the number of neighbors that became leaves from the entire number of neighbors in the previous phase. Each node chooses as its parent the neighbor that was not removed from the tree earlier than itself. Figure 4 presents a pseudo-code for the protocol. Recall that the code is repeated forever, although from some point on, the tree does not change.

A proper convergence of the N-vectors is guaranteed by the fact that $N_i[j]$ depends only on $N_i[j-1]$ and $\{N_k[j-1] \mid k \in neighbors(i)\}$, which are properly updated earlier. The base of this iterative convergence is applied by assigning to $N_i[0]$ the actual number of neighbors of i in the network.

The complexity of the tree protocol is clearly linear in the network's size since all its subprotocols are, and hence it equals the sequential time complexity. However, the parallel time can be further linearly bounded by the **diameter** of the tree where the diameter is the longest path between any two leaves of the tree.

5 Conclusions

The results presented in this paper establish theoretical bounds on the capabilities of connectionist architectures and other distributed approaches to constraint satisfaction problems.

The paper focuses on the feasibility of solving the network consistency problem using self-stabilizing distributed protocol, namely, guaranteeing a convergence to a consistent solution, if such exists, from any initial configuration. Such property is essential for dynamic environments, where unexpected changes could occur in some of the constraints.

We proved that a uniform protocol, one in which all nodes are identical, cannot solve the network consistency problem even if only one node is activated at a time. Consequently, although such protocols have obvious adventages and are closer in spirit to neural networks architectures, they cannot guarantee convergence to a solution. On the other hand, distinguishing one node from the others is sufficient to guarantee such a convergence

[5]We can overcome the necessity of knowing the size of the network by using dynamic memory allocation. However, for the sake of the simplicity of the code we assume the knowledge of n.

```
procedure tree-directing
Begin
    N_i[0] ← |neighbors(i)|
    j ← 0                    { j is a local counter }
    if N_i[0] ≠ 1 then          { when i is not a leaf }
        while N_i[j] > 1 do       { i is not yet a leaf at the j-th stage }
            j ← j + 1
            { the leaves of the (j − 1)-th stage are removed in the j-th stage }
            N_i[j] ← N_i[j − 1] − |{k | k ∈ neighbors(i) ∧ N_k[j − 1] = 1}|
        od
    if ∃k ∈ neighbors(i) s.t. N_k[j] ≥ 1 then { no more than one such k exists }
        parent_i ← k
    else             { i is the only center }
        parent_i ← NONE
End.
```

Figure 4: Uniform tree-directing procedure for node i

even when sets of nodes are activated simultaneously. A protocol for solving the problem under such conditions is presented.

We then demonstrated that, when the network is restricted to trees, a uniform, self-stabilizing protocol for solving the problem does exist, but only under asynchronous control (one neighboring node is activated at a time).

It is still an open question whether a uniform protocol is feasible under some specific ordering of the asynchronous activation.

Regarding time complexity, we have shown that in the worse-case the distributed and the sequential protocols have the same complexity bound; exponential in the depth of the DFS tree. On the average, however, a linear speed up is feasible for bounded depth networks.

References

[Ballard *et al.*, 1986] D. H. Ballard, P.C. Gardner, and M. A. Srinivas. Graph problems and connectionist architectures. Technical Report 167, University of Rochester, Rochester, NY, March 1986.

[Burns *et al.*, 1987] J. Burns, M. Gouda, and C. L. Wu. A self-stabilizing token system. In *Proceedings of the 20th Annual Intl. Conf. on System Sciences*, pages 218–223, Hawaii, 1987.

[Collin and Dechter, 1990] Z. Collin and R. Dechter. A distributed solution to the network consistency problem. In *Proceedings of the 5-th Intl. Symp. on Methodologies for Intelligent Systems.*, pages 242–251, Tennessee, USA, 1990.

[Collin and Dolev, 1991] Z. Collin and S. Dolev. A self stabilizing protocol for dfs spanning tree generation. in preparation, 1991.

[Dahl, 1987] E. D. Dahl. Neural networks algorithms for an np-complete problem: map and graph coloring. In *Proceedings of the IEEE first Internat. Conf. on Neural Networks*, pages 113–120, San Diego, 1987.

[Dechter and Dechter, 1988] R. Dechter and A. Dechter. Belief maintenance in dynamic constraint networks. In *Proceedings AAAI-88*, St. Paul, Minnesota, August 1988.

[Dechter, 1990] R. Dechter. Enhancement schemes for constraint processing: Backjumping, learning, and cutset decomposition. *Artificial Intelligence Journal*, 41(3):273–312, January 1990.

[Dijkstra, 1974] E. W. Dijkstra. Self stabilizing systems in spite of distributed control. *Communications of the ACM*, 17(11):643–644, 1974.

[Dolev *et al.*, 1990] S. Dolev, A. Israeli, and S. Moran. Self stabilization of dynamic systems assuming only read/write atomicity. In *Proceedings of PODC-90*, pages 103–118, Quebec City, August 1990.

[Even, 1979] S. Even. *Graph Algorithms.* Computer Science Press, Maryland, USA, 1979.

[Freuder and Quinn, 1987] E. C. Freuder and M.J. Quinn. The use of lineal spanning trees to represent constraint satisfaction problems. Technical Report 87-41, University of New Hampshire, Durham, New Hampshire, 1987.

[Freuder, 1982] E.C. Freuder. A sufficient condition for backtrack-free search. *Journal of the ACM*, 29(1):24–32, January 1982.

[Korach *et al.*, 1984] E. Korach, D. Rotem, and N.Santoro. Distributed algorithms for finding centers and medians in networks. *ACM Transactions on Programming Languages and Systems*, 6(3):380–401, July 1984.

[Mackworth and Freuder, 1985] A. K. Mackworth and E.C. Freuder. The complexity of some polinomial network consistency algorithms for constraint satisfaction problem. *Artificial intelligence*, 25:65–74, 1985.

[Minton *et al.*, 1990] S. Minton, M. D. Johnston, A. B. Philips, and P. Laird. Solving large scale constraint satisfaction and scheduling problems using a heuristic repair method. In *Proceedings of AAAI-90*, Boston, 1990.

An Efficient Arc Consistency Algorithm for a Class of CSP Problems

Yves Deville*
University of Namur, 21 rue Grandgagnage
B-5000 Namur (Belgium)
Email: yde@info.fundp.ac.be

Pascal Van Hentenryck
Brown University, Box 1910,
Providence, RI 02912
Email: pvh@cs.brown.edu

Abstract

Consistency Techniques have been studied extensively in the past as a way of tackling Constraint Satisfaction Problems (CSP). In particular various arc consistency algorithms have been proposed, originating from Waltz's filtering algorithm [20] and culminating in the optimal algorithm AC-4 of Mohr and Henderson [13]. AC-4 runs in $O(ed^2)$ in the worst case where e is the number of arcs (or constraints) and d is the size of the largest domain. Being applicable to the whole class of (binary) CSP, these algorithms do not take into account the semantics of constraints.

In this paper, we present a new generic arc consistency algorithm AC-5. The algorithm is parametrized on two specified procedures and can be instantiated to reduce to AC-3 and AC-4. More important, AC-5 can be instantiated to produce an $O(ed)$ algorithm for two important classes of constraints: functional and monotonic constraints.

We also show that AC-5 has an important application in Constraint Logic Programming over Finite Domains [18]. The kernel of the constraint-solver for such a programming language is an arc consistency algorithm for a set of basic constraints. We prove that AC-5, in conjunction with node consistency, provides a decision procedure for these constraints running in time $O(ed)$.

1 Introduction

Many important problems in areas like artificial intelligence, operations research and hardware design can be viewed as Constraint Satisfaction Problems (CSP). A CSP is defined by a finite set of variables taking values from finite domains and a set of constraints between these variables. A solution to a CSP is an assignment of values to variables satisfying all constraints and the problem amounts to finding one or all solutions. Most problems in this class are $\mathcal{NP}$-complete which mean that backtracking search is an important technique for solving them.

Many search algorithms (e.g. [1, 4, 5, 6, 9, 15]), preprocessing techniques and constraint algorithms (e.g. [20, 14, 10, 12, 13]) have been designed and analysed for this class of problems. See the reviews [11, 16] for a comprehensive overview of this area. In this paper, we are mainly concerned with (network) consistency techniques, and arc consistency in particular. Consistency techniques are constraint algorithms that reduce the search space by removing, from the domains and constraints, values that cannot appear in a solution. Arc consistency algorithms work on binary CSP and make sure that the constraints are individually consistent. Arc consistency algorithms have a long story on their own. They originates from Waltz filtering algorithm [20] and were refined several times [10] to culminate in the optimal algorithm AC-4 of Mohr and Henderson [13]. AC-4 runs in $O(ed^2)$ where e is the number of arcs in the network and d is the size of the largest domain.

Consistency techniques have recently[1] been applied in the design of Constraint Logic Programming (CLP) languages, more precisely in the design and implementation of CHIP [18, 3]. CHIP allows for the solving of a variety of constraints over finite domains, including numerical, symbolic, and user-defined constraints. It has been applied to a variety of industrial problems preserving the efficiency of imperative languages, yet shortening the development time significantly. Examples of applications include graph-coloring, warehouse locations, car-sequencing and cutting stock (see for instance [2, 18]). The kernel of CHIP for finite domains is an arc consistency algorithm, based on AC-3, for a set of basic binary constraints. Other (non-basic) constraints are approximated in terms of the basic constraints.

This research originated as an attempt to improve further the efficiency of the kernel algorithm. This paper contains two contributions.

First we present a new generic arc consistency algorithm AC-5. The algorithm is generic in the sense that it is parametrized on two procedures that are specified but whose implementation is left open. It can be reduced to AC-3 and AC-4 by proper implementations of the two procedures. Moreover, we show that AC-5 can be specialized to produce an $O(ed)$ arc consistency algorithm for two important classes of constraints: functional and monotonic constraints.

Second we show that the kernel of CHIP consists precisely of functional and monotonic constraints and that AC-5, in conjunction with node consistency, provides a

*Supported by the Belgian National Fund for Scientific Research as a Research Associate.

[1] Although Mackworth already mentioned as early as 1977 [10] the potential value of consistency techniques for programming languages.

decision procedure for the basic constraints running in time $O(ed)$.

The rest of this paper is organized in the following way. Section 2 fixes the notation used in this paper and contains the basic definitions. Section 3 describes the generic arc consistency algorithm AC-5 and specifies two abstract procedures ArcCons and LocalArcCons. Sections 4 and 5 show how an $O(ed)$ algorithm can be achieved for functional and monotonic constraints by giving particular implementations of the two procedures. Section 6 presents various representations for the domains while Section 7 shows that AC-5, in conjunction with node consistency, provides an $O(ed)$ decision procedure for the basic constraints of CLP over finite domains. Section 8 contains the conclusion of this research.

2 Preliminaries

To describe the CSP, we take the following conventions. Variables are represented by the natural numbers $1, \ldots, n$. Each variable i has an associated finite domain D_i. All constraints are binary and relate two distinct variables. If i and j are variables ($i < j$), there is at most one constraint relating them. This constraint is denoted C_{ij}. As usual, $C_{ij}(v, w)$ denotes the boolean value obtained when variables i and j are replaced by values v and w respectively. We also denote D the union of all domains and d the size of the largest domain.

Arc consistency algorithms generally work on the graph representation of the CSP. We associate a graph G to a CSP in the following way. G has a node i for each variable i. For each constraint C_{ij} relating variables i and j ($i < j$), G has two directed arcs, (i,j) and (j,i). The constraint associated to arc (i,j) is C_{ij} while the constraint associated to (j,i) is C_{ji} which is similar to C_{ij} except that its arguments are interchanged. We denote by e the number of arcs in G. We also use $arc(G)$ and $node(G)$ to denote the set of arcs and the set of nodes of graph G.

We now reproduce the standard definitions of arc consistency for an arc and a graph.

Definition 1 Let $(i,j) \in arc(G)$. Arc (i,j) is *arc consistent wrt* D_i and D_j iff $\forall v \in D_i, \exists w \in D_j : C_{ij}(v,w)$.

Definition 2 Let $\mathcal{P}$ be $D_1 \times \ldots \times D_n$. A graph G is *arc consistent wrt* $\mathcal{P}$ iff $\forall\ (i,j) \in arc(G) : (i,j)$ is arc consistent wrt D_i and D_j.

The next definition is useful to specify the outcome of an arc consistent algorithm.

Definition 3 Let $\mathcal{P}$ be $D_1 \times \ldots \times D_n$. Let $\mathcal{P}' \subseteq \mathcal{P}$. $\mathcal{G}$ is a maximally arc consistent wrt P' in $\mathcal{P}$ iff G is *arc consistent wrt* $\mathcal{P}'$ and there is no other $\mathcal{P}''$ with $\mathcal{P}' \subset \mathcal{P}'' \subseteq \mathcal{P}$ such that G is arc consistent wrt $\mathcal{P}''$.

The purpose of an arc consistency algorithm is to compute, given a graph G and a set P, a set P' such that G is maximally arc consistent wrt P' in P.

3 The new Arc Consistency Algorithm

All algorithms for arc consistency work with a queue containing elements to reconsider. In AC-3, the queue contains arcs (i,j) while AC-4 contains pairs (i,v) where i is a node and v is a value. The novelty in AC-5 is to have a queue containing elements $< (i,j), w >$ where (i,j) is an arc and w is a value which has been removed from D_j and justifies the need to reconsider arc (i,j). As a consequence, AC-5 can be specialized to obtain either AC-3 or AC-4 by giving a particular implementation of Procedures ArcCons and LocalArcCons. Moreover, for certain class of constraints, AC-5 can be specialized to give an $O(ed)$ algorithm.

To present AC-5, we proceed in several steps. We first present the necessary operations on queues. Then we give the specification of the two abstract procedures ArcCons and LocalArcCons. Finally we present the algorithm itself and prove a number of results.

procedure InitQueue(**out** Q)
Post: $Q = \{\}$.
function EmptyQueue(**in** Q): Boolean
Post: EmptyQueue $\Leftrightarrow (Q = \{\})$.
procedure Enqueue(**in** i, Δ, **inout** Q)
Pre: $\Delta \subseteq D_i$ and $i \in node(G)$.
Post: $Q = Q_0 \cup \{< (k,i), v > \mid (k,i) \in arc(G) \text{ and } v \in \Delta\}$.
procedure Dequeue(**inout** Q, **out** i, j, w)
Post: $< (i,j), w > \in Q_0$ and $Q = Q_0 \setminus < (i,j), w >$.

Figure 1: The Queue Module

procedure ArcCons(**in** i, j, **out** Δ)
Pre: $(i,j) \in arc(G)$.
Post: $\Delta = \{v \in D_i \mid \forall w \in D_j : \neg C_{ij}(v,w)\}$.

procedure LocalArcCons(**in** i, j, w, **out** Δ)
Pre: $(i,j) \in arc(G)$ and $w \notin D_j$.
Post: $\Delta_1 \subseteq \Delta \subseteq \Delta_2$,
with $\Delta_1 = \{v \in D_i \mid C_{ij}(v,w) \text{ and } \forall w' \in D_j : \neg C_{ij}(v,w')\}$,
$\Delta_2 = \{v \in D_i \mid \forall w' \in D_j : \neg C_{ij}(v,w')\}$.

Figure 2: Specification of the Procedures

3.1 Operations on Queues

The operations we need are described in Figure 1. Procedure InitQueue simply initializes the queue to an empty set. Function EmptyQueue tests if the queue is empty. Procedure Enqueue(i, Δ, Q) is used when the set of values Δ has been removed from D_i. It introduces elements of the form $< (k,i), v >$ in the queue Q where (k,i) is an arc of the constraint graph and $v \in \Delta$. Procedure Dequeue dequeues one element from the queue. In all specifications, we take the convention that a parameter p subscripted with 0 (i.e., p_0) represents the value of p at call time.

All these operations on queues but Procedure Enqueue can be achieved in constant time. Procedure Enqueue can be implemented to run in $O(s)$ where s is the size of Δ. The only difficulty in fact is Procedure Enqueue. It requires a direct access from a variable to its arcs (which is always assumed in arc consistency algorithms) and a lazy distribution of v on the arcs. To achieve this result, the queue could be organized to contain elements of the form $< v, \{A_1, \ldots, A_m\} >$ where A_k is an arc and v is a value. Procedure Enqueue(i, Δ, v) adds an element $< v, \{A_1, \ldots, A_m\} >$ to the queue, where the A_k are arcs of the form (j,i), for each $v \in \Delta$. Procedure Dequeue picks up an element $< w, \{A_1, \ldots, A_m\} >$ with $m > 0$, remove an $A_k = (i,j)$ from the set, and returns i, j, and w.

3.2 Specification of the Parametric Procedures

Figure 2 gives the specification of the two subproblems. Their implementations for various kinds of con-

Algorithm AC-5
Post: let $\mathcal{P}_0 = D_{1_0} \times \ldots \times D_{n_0}$,
$\mathcal{P} = D_1 \times \ldots \times D_n$
$\mathcal{G}$ is maximally arc consistent wrt $\mathcal{P}$ in $\mathcal{P}_0$.
begin AC-5
1 InitQueue(Q)
2 **for each** $(i, j) \in arc(G)$ **do**
3 **begin**
4 ArcCons(i,j,Δ);
5 Enqueue(i,Δ,Q);
6 Remove(Δ,D_i)
7 **end**;
8 **while not** EmptyQueue(Q) **do**
9 **begin**
10 Dequeue(Q,i,j,w);
11 LocalArcCons(i,j,w,Δ);
12 Enqueue(i,Δ,Q);
13 Remove(Δ,D_i)
14 **end**
end AC-5

Figure 3: The Arc Consistency Algorithm AC-5

procedure InitQueue(**out** Q)
Post: $\forall\ (k, i) \in arc(G) : Status[(k, i), v] =$ **present** if $v \in D_i$
$=$ **rejected** if $v \notin D_i$
function EmptyQueue(**in** Q)
Post: $\forall\ (k, i) \in arc(G)\ \forall v : Status[(k, i), v] \neq$ **suspended**.

procedure Enqueue(**in** i, Δ, **inout** Q)
Pre: $\forall\ (k, i) \in arc(G)\ \forall v \in \Delta : Status[(k, i), v] =$ **present**.
Post: $\forall\ (k, i) \in arc(G)\ \forall v \in \Delta : Status[(k, i), v] =$ **suspended**.
procedure Dequeue(**inout** Q, **out** i, j, w)
Post: $Status[(i, j), w] =$ **rejected**.

Figure 4: The Queue Module on Structure Status

straints will be given in the next sections. They can also be specialized to produce AC-3 and AC-4 from AC-5.

Procedure ArcCons(i, j, Δ) computes the set of values Δ for variable i that are not supported by D_j. Procedure LocalArcCons(i, j, w, Δ) is used to compute the set of values in D_i no longer supported because of the removal of value w from D_j.

Note that the specification of LocalArcCons gives us much freedom for the result Δ to be returned. It is sufficient to compute Δ_1 to guarantee the correctness of AC-5. However the procedure gives the opportunity to achieve more pruning (up to Δ_2) while still preserving the soundness of the algorithm. Interestingly enough, the ability to achieve more pruning turns out to be fundamental, for some classes of constraints (e.g. monotonic constraints), in producing an $O(ed)$ algorithm.

3.3 Algorithm AC-5

We are now in position to present Algorithm AC-5. The algorithm is depicted in Figure 3 and has two main steps. In the first step, all arcs are considered once and arc consistency is enforced on each of them. Procedure Remove(Δ, D) removes the set of values Δ from D. The second step applies LocalArcCons on each of the element of the queue possibly generating new elements in the queue. The correctness of the algorithm is an immediate consequence of the correctness of Algorithm AC-3 [10] that it generalizes. AC-3 is a particular case of AC-5 where the value w is never used in the implementation of Procedure LocalArcCons. AC-4 is a particular case of AC-5 where the implementation of Procedure LocalArcCons does not use node i. Of course, the data-structures used in AC-4 are more sophisticated than those of AC-3.

In order to prove various results on AC-5, we introduce a new data-structure Status which is a two-dimensional array, the first dimension being on arcs and the second on values. We also give the effect of the procedures manipulating the queue on Status in Figure 4. Note that the actual implementation does not need to perform these operations. They are just presented here to ease the presentation and simplify the theorem.

Algorithm AC-5 preserves the following invariant on lines 2 and 8 for Status.

Status$[(k,i),v] =$ **present** iff $v \in D_i$,
$=$ **suspended** iff $v \notin D_i$ & $\langle(k,i),v\rangle \in Q$,
$=$ **rejected** iff $v \notin D_i$ & $\langle(k,i),v\rangle \notin Q$.

We are now in position to prove the following theorem.

Theorem 4 Algorithm AC-5 has the following three properties: (1) The invariant on data-structure Status holds on lines 2 and 8. (2) AC-5 enqueues and dequeues at most $O(ed)$ elements and hence the size of the queue is at most $O(ed)$. (3) If $s_1, \ldots, s_p$ are the size of Δ on each iteration at lines 12, then $s_1 + \ldots + s_p \leq O(ed)$.

Proof

Property 1 holds initially. Assuming that it holds in line 2, it also holds after an iteration of lines 4 to 6. Line 5 makes sure that $< (j, i), v >$ is suspended for all $v \in \Delta$ and put them on the queue while line 6 removes Δ from D_i. So the invariant holds at the first execution of line 8. Execution of lines 10 to 13 preserves the invariant. Lines 10 and 11 maintain it on their own. Lines 12 and 13 respectively make sure that $< (j, i), v >$ is rejected for all $v \in \Delta$ and remove Δ from D_i.

Property 2 holds because each element of Status is only allowed to make two transitions: one from **present** to **suspended** through Procedure Enqueue and one from **suspended** to **rejected** through Procedure Dequeue. Hence there can only be $O(ed)$ dequeues and enqueues.

Property 3 is a direct consequence of Property 2 and the preconditions of Enqueue on the data-structure Status. □

The above theorem can be used to deduce the overall complexity of AC-5 from the complexity of Procedures ArcCons and LocalArcCons. In particular, in AC-3 and AC-4, Procedure ArcCons is necessarily $O(d^2)$ which implies that the overall complexity is at least $O(ed^2)$ since lines 4 to 6 are executed e times. There is no other possibility to reduce the complexity than considering particular classes of constraints, allowing to implement, in particular, Procedure ArcCons in $O(d)$. Note also that an algorithm in $O(ed)$ will be optimal for a subclass of constraints since it is reasonable to assume that we need to check at least once each value in each domain. In the next two sections, we characterize two classes of constraints that guarantee that Procedure ArcCons is $O(d)$ and Procedure LocalArcCons is linearly related to the size of its output set Δ resulting in an AC-5 algorithm for these classes, running in time $O(ed)$. In these sections, we assume a number of primitive operations on domains that are depicted in Figure 5. As the reader will notice, the operations we define on the domains are more sophisticated than those usually required by arc consistency algorithms. In particular, they assume a total ordering on the domain D

```
procedure RemoveElem(in v, inout D)
Post: D = D₀ \ {v}.
function Member(in v, D): Boolean
Post: Member ⇔ (v ∈ D).
function Min(in D): Value
Post: Min = min{v ∈ D}.
function Max(in D): Value
Post: Max = max{v ∈ D}.
function Succ(in v, D): Value
Post: Succ = min{v' ∈ D | v' > v}.
function Pred(in v, D): Value
Post: Pred = max{v' ∈ D | v' < v}
```

Figure 5: The DOMAIN module

```
procedure ArcCons(in i, j, out Δ)
  begin
    Δ := ∅;
    for each v ∈ D_i do
      if f_ij(v) ∉ D_j then
        Δ := Δ ∪ {v}
  end
```

Figure 6: ArcCons for Functional Constraints

for reasons that will become clear later.[2] The additional sophistication is necessary to achieve the bound $O(ed)$ for monotonic constraints. These primitive operations are assumed to take constant time.

4 Functional Constraints

Definition 5 A constraint C is functional wrt a domain D iff for all v (resp. w) $\in D$ there exists at most one w (resp. v) $\in D$ such that $C(v, w)$;

Note that the above definition is parametrized on a domain D. Some constraints might not be functional in general but become functional when restricted to a domain of values.

Convention 6 If C is a functional constraint, we denote by $f_C(v)$ the value w such that $C(v, w)$ and $f_C^{-1}(w)$ the value v such that $C(v, w)$. Since AC-5 works on arcs, we associate a function f_{ij} to each arc (i, j) in such a way that, for constraint C_{ij}, arc (i, j) is assigned $f_{C_{ij}}$ and arc (j, i) is assigned $f_{C_{ij}}^{-1}$.

The results presented in the paper assume that it takes constant time to compute the functions f_C and f_C^{-1} in the same way as arc consistency algorithms assume that $C(v, w)$ can be computed in constant time.

We are now in position to present Procedures ArcCons and LocalArcCons for functional constraints. They are depicted in Figures 6 and 7.

It is clear that the procedures fulfill their specifications. Only one value per arc needs to be checked in Procedure ArcCons since the constraint is functional. Procedure LocalArcCons computes the set Δ_1 in this case and only one value needs to be checked. Procedures ArcCons and LocalArcCons are respectively $O(d)$ and $O(1)$ for functional constraints. Hence we have an optimal algorithm.

[2]Note that if D is made up of several unconnected domains with distinct orderings, it is always possible to transform the underlying partial ordering into a total ordering.

```
procedure LocalArcCons(in i, j, w, out Δ)
  begin
    if f_ji(w) ∈ D_i then
      Δ := {f_ji(w)}
    else
      Δ := ∅
  end
```

Figure 7: LocalArcCons for Functional Constraints

```
procedure ArcCons(in i, j, out Δ)
  begin
    Δ := ∅;
    for each v ∈ D_i do
      if ¬ C_ij(v, first(D_j)) then
        Δ := Δ ∪ {v}
  end
```

Figure 8: ArcCons for Monotonic Constraints

Theorem 7 Algorithm AC-5 is $O(ed)$ for functional constraints wrt D.

Note that functional constraints do not add any requirement for the basic operations on the domains compared to traditional algorithms.

5 Monotonic Constraints

We now consider another class of constraints in this section. This class of constraints requires a total ordering $<$ on D, as mentioned previously. Moreover we assume that, for any constraint C and element $v \in D$, there exists elements w_1, w_2 (not necessarily in D) such that $C(v, w_1)$ and $C(w_2, v)$ hold. This last constraint is used to simplify the algorithms but it is not restrictive in nature.

Definition 8 A constraint C is monotonic wrt D iff there exists a total ordering on D such that, for any value v, w in D, $C(v, w)$ holds implies $C(v', w')$ holds for all values v', w' in D such that $v' \leq v$ and $w' \geq w$.

Convention 9 Since AC-5 is working with arcs, we associate to each arc (i, j) three functions f_{ij}, $first_{ij}$, and $next_{ij}$ and a relation $\succ_{ij}$. Given a monotonic constraint C_{ij}, the functions and relation for arc (i, j) are as follows $f_{ij}(w) = max\{v \mid C(v, w)\}$, $first_{ij} =$ Max, $next_{ij} =$ Pred, $\succ_{ij} = >$ while those for arc (j, i) are $f_{ji}(v) = min\{w \mid C(v, w)\}$, $first_{ji} =$ Min, $next_{ji} =$ Succ, $\succ_{ji} = <$.
Moreover, since Procedures ArcCons and LocalArcCons only use f_{ij}, $first_{ij}$, $next_{ij}$, and $\succ_{ij}$ for arc (i, j),

```
procedure LocalArcCons(in i, j, in w, out Δ)
  begin
    Δ := ∅;
    v := first(D_i);
    while v ≻ f(first(D_j)) do
    begin
      Δ := Δ ∪ {v};
      v := next(v, D_i)
    end
  end
```

Figure 9: LocalArcCons for Monotonic Constraints

Let $S = \{b, \ldots, B\}$
$D_i = \{v_1, \ldots, v_m\} \subseteq S$ with $v_k < v_{k+1}$ and $m > 0$.
Syntax
$D_i.min$: integer $\in S$
$D_i.max$: integer $\in S$
$D_i.element$: array $[b...B]$ of booleans
$D_i.succ$: array $[b...B]$ of integers $\in S$
$D_i.pred$: array $[b...B]$ of integers $\in S$
Semantics
$D_i.min = v_1$
$D_i.max = v_m$
$D_i.element[v]$ iff $v \in D_i$
$D_i.succ[v_k] = v_{k+1}$ $(1 \leq k < m)$
$D_i.pred[v_{k+1}] = v_k$ $(1 \leq k < m)$

Figure 10: DOMAIN of Consecutive Values.

we omit the subscripts in the presentation of the algorithms.

We are now in position to describe the implementation of Procedures ARCCONS and LOCALARCCONS for monotonic constraints. They are depicted in Figures 8 and 9.

Lemma 10 Procedures ARCCONS and LOCALARCCONS fulfill their specifications.

Proof The result for Procedure ARCCONS follows from the monotonicity of the constraint that make sures that the value v can be checked only wrt an extremal value (minimum or maximum depending on the arc).

Procedure LOCALARCCONS computes the set $\Delta = \{v \in D_i \mid v \succ f(first(D_j))\}$. By monotonicity of the constraint, $\Delta \subseteq \Delta_2$, and $\Delta_2 \cap \{v \in D_i \mid v \preceq f(first(D_j))\} = \emptyset$. Hence $\Delta = \Delta_2$ and the postcondition is satisfied. □

Note that, for monotonic constraints, it is more complicated to compute the set Δ_1 as we have no guarantee that the extremal value corresponding to w for variable i is in its domain. If the value is not in the domain, then we have no way to use Procedures PRED and SUCC, and this leads to a non-optimal algorithm.

Procedures ARCCONS is $O(d)$. Procedure LOCALARCCONS has as many iterations in lines 5 and 6 as elements in the resulting set Δ. Hence it follows that we have an optimal algorithm.

Theorem 11 Procedure AC-5 is $O(ed)$ for monotonic constraints wrt D.

It is also clear that AC-5 can be applied at the same time to functional and monotonic constraints keeping the same complexity.

6 Implementation of Domain

In the previous sections, we assume that the primitive operations on domains can be performed in constant time. In this section, we present two data-structures that enable to achieve this result.

The first data-structure assumes a domain of consecutive integer values and is depicted in Figure 10. The fields *min* and *max* are used to pick up the minimum and maximum values, the field *element* to test if a value is in the domain, and the two fields *pred* and *succ* to access in constant time the successor or predecessor of a value in the domain. The operation REMOVEELEMENT must take care updating all fields to preserve the semantics. This can be done in constant time.

When the domain is sparse, the representation is basically the same but it reasons about indices instead of values and uses an hash-table to test membership to the domain. Although the time complexity of membership is theoretically not $O(1)$, under reasonable assumption, the expected time to search for an element is $O(1)$.

7 Application

We describe the application of AC-5 to Constraint Logic Programming over finite domains.

Constraint Logic Programming [7] is a class of languages whose main operation is constraint-solving over a computation domain. A step of computation amounts to check the satisfiability of a conjunction of constraints.

Constraint Logic Programming over finite domains has been investigated in [19, 17, 18]. It is a computation domain where constraints are equations, inequalities and disequations over natural number terms or equations and disequations over constants. Natural number terms are constructed from natural numbers, variables ranging over a finite domain of natural numbers, and the standard arithmetic operators $(+, \times, \ldots)$. Also some symbolic constraints are provided to increase the expressiveness and the user has the ability to define its own constraints. This computation domain is available in CHIP [3] and its constraint-solver is based on consistency techniques, arithmetic reasoning, and branch & bound. It has been applied to numerous applications in combinatorial optimization such as graph-coloring, warehouse location, scheduling and sequencing, cutting-stock, assignment problems, and microcode labeling to name a few (see for instance [2, 18].

Space does not allow us to present the operational semantics of the language. Let us just mention that the kernel of the constraint-solver is an arc consistency algorithm for a set of basic constraints. Other (non-basic) constraints are approximated in terms of the basic constraints and generate new basic constraints. The basic constraints are either *domain* constraints or *arithmetics* constraints, and are as follows (variables are represented by upper case letters and constants by lower case letters):

- domain constraint: $X \in \{a_1, \ldots, a_n\}$;
- arithmetic constraints: $aX \neq b$, $aX = bY + c$, $aX \leq bY + c$, $aX \geq bY + c$ with $a, a_i, b, c \geq 0$ and $a \neq o$.

These constraints have been chosen carefully in order to avoid having to solve an $\mathcal{NP}$-complete constraint satisfaction problem. For instance, allowing two variables in disequations or three variables in inequalities or equations leads to $\mathcal{NP}$-complete problems.

We now show that AC-5 can be the basis of an efficient decision procedure for basic constraints.

Definition 12 A *system of constraints* S is a pair $\langle AC, DC \rangle$ where AC is a set of arithmetic constraints and DC is a set of domain constraints such that any variable occurring in an arithmetic constraint also occurs in some domain constraint of S.

Definition 13 Let $S = \langle AC, DC \rangle$ be a system of constraints. The set D_x is the *domain* of x in S (or in DC) iff the domain constraints of x in DC are $x \in D_1, \ldots, x \in D_k$ and D_x is the intersection of the D_i's.

Let us define a solved form for the constraints.

Definition 14 Let S be a system of constraints. S is in *solved form* iff any unary constraint $C(X)$ in S is node consistent[3] wrt the domain of X in S, and any binary constraint $C(X,Y)$ in S is arc consistent wrt the domains of X, Y in S.

We now study a number of properties of systems of constraints in solved form.

Property 15 Let $C(X,Y)$ be the binary constraint $aX \leq bY + c$ or $aX \geq bY + c$, arc consistent wrt $D_X = \{v_1, \ldots, v_n\}, D_Y = \{w_1, \ldots, w_m\}$. Assume also that $v_1 < \ldots < v_n$ and $w_1 < \ldots < w_m$. Then we have C is monotonic and $C(v_1, w_1)$ and $C(v_n, w_m)$ hold.

Property 16 Let $C(X,Y)$ be the binary constraint $aX = bY + c$ with $a, b \neq 0$, arc consistent wrt $D_X = \{v_1, \ldots, v_n\}, D_Y = \{w_1, \ldots, w_m\}$. Assume also that $v_1 < \ldots < v_n$ and $w_1 < \ldots < w_m$. Then we have C is functional, $n = m$, and $C(v_i, w_i)$ holds.

The satisfiability of a system of constraints in solved form can be tested in a straightforward way.

Theorem 17 Let $S = \langle AC, DC \rangle$ be a system of constraints in solved form. S is satisfiable iff $\langle \emptyset, DC \rangle$ is satisfiable.

Proof It is clear that $\langle \emptyset, DC \rangle$ is not satisfiable iff the domain of some variable is empty in DC. If the domain of some variable is empty in DC, then S is not satisfiable. Otherwise, it is possible to construct a solution to S. By properties 15 and 16, all binary constraints of S hold if we assign to each variable the smallest value in its domain. Moreover, because of node consistency, the unary constraints also hold for such an assignment. □

It remains to show how to transform a system of constraints into an equivalent one in solved form. This is precisely the purpose of the node and arc consistency algorithms.

Algorithm 18 To transform the system of constraints S into a system in solved form S':

1. apply a node consistency algorithm to the unary constraints of $S = \langle AC, DC \rangle$ to obtain $\langle AC, DC' \rangle$;
2. apply an arc consistency algorithm to the binary constraints of $\langle AC, DC' \rangle$ to obtain $S' = \langle AC, DC'' \rangle$.

Theorem 19 Let S be a system of constraints. Algorithm 18 produces a system of constraints in solved form equivalent to S.

We now give a complete constraint-solver for the basic constraints. Given a system of constraints S, Algorithm 20 returns *true* if S is satisfiable and *false* otherwise.

Algorithm 20 To check the satisfiability of a system of constraints S: (1) apply Algorithm 18 to S to obtain $S' = \langle AC, DC \rangle$ and (2) if the domain of some variable is empty in DC', return *false*; otherwise return *true*.

In summary, we have shown that node and arc consistency algorithms provide us with a decision procedure for basic constraints. The complexity of the decision procedure is the complexity of the arc consistency algorithm. Using the specialization of AC-5 for basic constraints, we obtain an $O(ed)$ decision procedure.

[3] As usual, a unary constraint C is *node consistent wrt* D iff $\forall v \in D : C(v)$.

8 Conclusion

A new generic arc consistency algorithm AC-5 has been presented whose specializations include, not only AC-3 and AC-4, but also an $O(ed)$ algorithms for an important subclass of networks containing functional and monotonic constraints. An application of AC-5 to Constraint Logic Programming over finite domains has been described. Together with node consistency, it provides the main algorithms for an $O(ed)$ decision procedure for basic constraints. From a software engineering perspective, AC-5 has the advantage of uniformity. Each constraint may have a particular implementation, based on AC-3, AC-4, or some specific techniques, without influencing the main algorithm. As a consequence, many different implementation techniques can be interleaved together in a natural setting.

Future research on this topic includes the search for other subclasses whose properties allow for an $O(ed)$ algorithm. Path consistency has not been considered seriously in CLP languages and generalizations of the above ideas to path consistency and support for path consistency in CLP languages deserve future attention. Finally, while arc-consistency of functional constraints can also be solved through a reduction to 2-sat [8], it is an open issue to find out if a similar reduction exists for monotonic constraints.

References

[1] R. Dechter and J. Pearl. Network-based heuristics for constraint satisfaction problems. *Artificial Intelligence*, 34:1–38, 1988.

[2] M. Dincbas, H. Simonis, and P. Van Hentenryck. Solving Large Combinatorial Problems in Logic Programming. *Journal of Logic Programming*, 8(1-2):75–93, 1990.

[3] M. Dincbas and al. The Constraint Logic Programming Language CHIP. In *FGCS-88*, Tokyo, 1988.

[4] E.C. Freuder. Synthesizing Constraint Expressions. *CACM*, 21:958–966, 1978.

[5] J. Gaschnig. A Constraint Satisfaction Method for Inference Making. In *Annual Conf. on Circuit System Theory*, 1974.

[6] R.M. Haralick and G.L. Elliot. Increasing Tree Search Efficiency for Constraint Satisfaction Problems. *Artificial Intelligence*, 14:263–313, 1980.

[7] J. Jaffar and S. Michaylov. Methodology and Implementation of a CLP System. In *ICLP-87*, Melbourne 1987.

[8] S. Kasif. On the Parallel Complexity of Discrete Relaxation in Constraint Satisfaction Networks. *AI Journal*, 45:275–286, 1990.

[9] J-L. Lauriere. A Language and a Program for Stating and Solving Combinatorial Problems. *Artificial Intelligence*, 10(1), 1978.

[10] A.K. Mackworth. Consistency in Networks of Relations. *AI Journal*, 8(1):99–118, 1977.

[11] A.K. Mackworth. *Constraint Satisfaction*, volume Encyclopedia of Artificial Intelligence. Wiley, 1987.

[12] A.K. Mackworth and E.C. Freuder. The Complexity of some Polynomial Network Consistency Algorithms for Constraint Satisfaction Problems. *Artificial Intelligence*, 25:65–74, 1985.

[13] R. Mohr and T.C. Henderson. Arc and Path Consistency Revisited. *Artificial Intelligence*, 28:225–233, 1986.

[14] U. Montanari. Networks of Constraints : Fundamental Properties and Applications to Picture Processing. *Information Science*, 7(2):95–132, 1974.

[15] Montanari, U and Rossi, F. Constraint Relaxation May Be Perfect In *To Appear in Artificial Intelligence*.

[16] B. Nadel. Constraint Satisfaction Algorithms. *Computational Intelligence*, 5(4):288–224, 1989.

[17] P. Van Hentenryck. A Framework for Consistency Techniques in Logic Programming. In *IJCAI-87*, Milan, 1987.

[18] P. Van Hentenryck. *Constraint Satisfaction in Logic Programming*. The MIT Press, Cambridge, MA, 1989.

[19] P. Van Hentenryck and M. Dincbas. Domains in Logic Programming. In *AAAI-86*, Philadelphia, PA, August 1986.

[20] D. Waltz. Generating Semantic Descriptions from Drawings of Scenes with Shadows. Technical Report AI271, MIT, MA, 1972.

Where the *Really* Hard Problems Are

Peter Cheeseman
RIACS*

Bob Kanefsky
Sterling Software

William M. Taylor
Sterling Software

Artificial Intelligence Research Branch
NASA Ames Research Center, Mail Stop 244-17
Moffett Field, CA 94035, USA
Email: <last-name>@ptolemy.arc.nasa.gov

Abstract

It is well known that for many NP-complete problems, such as K-Sat, etc., typical cases are easy to solve; so that computationally hard cases must be rare (assuming P $\neq$ NP). This paper shows that NP-complete problems can be summarized by at least one "order parameter", and that the hard problems occur at a critical value of such a parameter. This critical value separates two regions of characteristically different properties. For example, for K-colorability, the critical value separates overconstrained from underconstrained random graphs, and it marks the value at which the probability of a solution changes abruptly from near 0 to near 1. It is the high density of well-separated almost solutions (local minima) at this boundary that cause search algorithms to "thrash". This boundary is a type of phase transition and we show that it is preserved under mappings between problems. We show that for some P problems either there is no phase transition or it occurs for bounded N (and so bounds the cost). These results suggest a way of deciding if a problem is in P or NP and why they are different.

1 Introduction

A common result of AI research is to show that some class of problems is NP-complete (or NP-hard), with the implication that this class of problems is very hard to solve (assuming P $\neq$ NP). On the other hand it is well known that for many of these NP problems, typical instances are easy to solve (e.g. [10]). There is no contradiction here, since NP complexity is usually a worst case analysis for a whole class of problems, and so says nothing about the difficulty of typical instances. However, this situation raises the question "where are the really hard instances of NP problems?". Can a subclass of problems be defined that is typically (exponentially) hard to solve, or do worst cases appear as rare "pathological cases" scattered unpredictably in the problem space?

In this paper we show that for many NP problems one or more "order parameters" can be defined, and hard instances occur around particular critical values of these order parameters. In addition, such critical values form a boundary that separates the space of problems into two regions. One region is underconstrained, so the density of solutions is high, thus making it relatively easy to find a solution. The other region is overconstrained and very unlikely to contain a solution. If there are solutions in this overconstrained region, then they have such deep local minimum (strong basin of attraction) that any reasonable algorithm is likely to find it. If there is no solution, then a backtrack search can usually establish this with ease, since potential solution paths are usually cut off early in the search. Really hard problems occur on the boundary between these two regions, where the probability of a solution is low but non-negligible. At this point there are typically many local minima corresponding to almost solutions separated by high "energy barriers". These almost solutions form deep local minima that may often trap search methods that rely on local information.

Because it is possible to locate a region where hard problems occur, it is possible to predict whether a particular problem is likely to be easy to solve. We expect that in future computer scientists will produce "phase diagrams" for particular problem domains to aid in hard problem identification and for prediction of solution existence probability, such as shown in [6].

We present these ideas by first showing how phase transitions arise in problem solving, and then illustrating particular transitions through several examples with different properties. We then show how some of these examples interrelate when they are mapped onto each other. Finally, we summarize the results and state a strong conjecture based on these results.

2 Phase Transitions

We first review well-studied cases where the behavior of a complex system, including phase transitions, can be described by an order parameter. For example, the probability that a random graph is connected, or contains a Hamilton circuit, or a triangle etc., has a sharp threshold for particular values of the average graph connectivity. In the case of graph connectivity and Hamilton circuits, this threshold depends on the graph size as well. Other

*Research Institute for Advanced Computer Science

properties of random graphs also show interesting behavior around the transition point which is characteristic of phase transitions. In particular, the size of the largest connected sub-graph grows very rapidly as a function of the average connectivity as the critical connectivity is approached from below. Also, the sizes of the subgraphs below the threshold show a fractal distribution—these properties are related to analogous physical systems, e.g. [7].

Our interest in phase transitions arises from the discovery that hard to solve problems occur at such boundaries for many types of problems. The importance of phase transitions for AI is discussed in [4] where it is argued that complex systems composed of many interacting values can often be understood at the macroscopic level in terms of a few order parameters that are characteristic of the system as a whole. Summarizing the properties of complex systems through a small set of parameters is routine in statistical mechanics [2],[7]. This is possible because a large number of local interactions can produce dramatic coordinated macroscopic behavior, such as phase transitions, that do not depend on the detailed interactions within the system. Examples of phase transitions in AI are given in [5],[6].

3 An Example: Hamilton Circuits

A Hamilton Circuit (HC) is a cyclic ordering of a set of nodes such that there is an edge connecting every pair of nodes in the graph in order. The cyclic condition ensures that the circuit is closed, and the requirement that all the nodes be included (with no repeats) ensures that the circuit does not cross over itself, and passes through every node. The problem is to find if a HC exists for a given graph.

The first question we investigate is how the probability of the existence of a HC in a random graph varies with the average connectivity of the graph. The results for several different graph sizes are shown in Fig. 1a. These results were generated by finding the proportion of 20 randomly generated graphs that contained a HC for graphs with different connectivities and numbers of nodes. A fully connected graph always has a HC (all node orderings are a HC), and so an almost fully connected graph has a very high probability of containing a HC. In this region there are a very large number of HCs, and this number drops rapidly as the boundary is approached. At the other extreme, a random graph barely above an average connectivity of 2 is unlikely to even be connected, and so is very unlikely to contain a HC. For some critical value of the average connectivity between these two extremes, the probability of a HC changes steeply from almost 0 to almost 1. Theory predicts that the transition will occur at an average connectivity of $\ln N + \ln \ln N$ [1], and this prediction is supported by our results in Fig. 1a, where the theoretical value is shown by the dashed vertical line. This transition shows the characteristic properties of a phase transition. For example, the size of the largest almost HC grows exponentially below the threshold, and this is the main reason for our next result. The second question we investigate is how the computational cost of

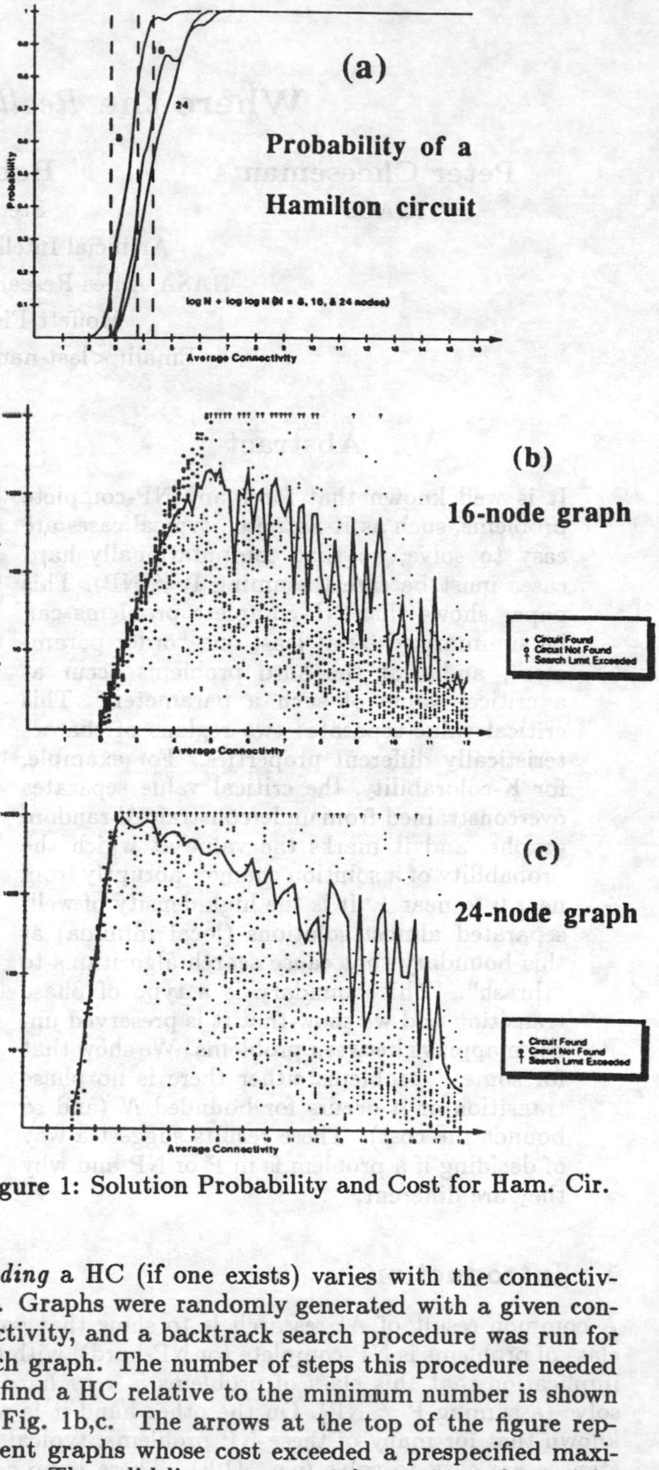

Figure 1: Solution Probability and Cost for Ham. Cir.

finding a HC (if one exists) varies with the connectivity. Graphs were randomly generated with a given connectivity, and a backtrack search procedure was run for each graph. The number of steps this procedure needed to find a HC relative to the minimum number is shown in Fig. 1b,c. The arrows at the top of the figure represent graphs whose cost exceeded a prespecified maximum. The solid line represents the average of 20 trials, but since this average includes the saturated values it severely underestimates the true cost. Despite this underestimation, the existence of a phase transition is clear. The sharpness of the transition increases with increasing graph size (N), as does the location of the critical connectivity. Similar results were obtained for graphs that were guaranteed to contain a HC by construction. An important effect to note in both cases is that the phase transition in cost occurs at the same point at which the probability of a HC drops to zero within the numeric accuracy.

The HC backtrack algorithm uses two heuristics: 1) the initial starting node is the one with the highest connectivity, 2) neighbor nodes of the last node selected are sorted by their connectivity to the remaining unselected nodes—the neighbor with the highest connectivity is selected first. More effective heuristics, such as bidirectional search, may exist, but we do not expect that the behavior observed in Fig. 1b,c would be qualitatively different.

For HCs, the above results show that the average connectivity is an appropriate order parameter, but is this the only one? Another possible order parameter is the *variance* of the average connectivity. Preliminary results show that the phase transition exists for both high and low variance, but the data is insufficient to decide if the variance changes the location of the critical connectivity.

We have shown empirically that for HCs there is a phase transition in computational cost around a critical value of the average connectivity of a graph. The value of this critical connectivity increases with graph size (N), and also gets sharper with N. This critical connectivity occurs at the point at which the probability that there is a HC in a random graph drops to almost zero. In other words, the critical connectivity separates two regions. 1) A low connectivity region where there is almost zero probability of there being a HC—here the backtrack algorithm quickly terminates because all potential HCs are cut off early in the search. If there is a solution in this low probability region, then the algorithm has little trouble finding it, since every other alternative is cut off early. 2) A high connectivity region, on the other hand, has a high density of HCs, and so the backtrack algorithm quickly finds one. It is on the border between these two regions where hard problems occur. On the border there are many almost HCs that are quite different from each other (i.e. it typically takes many changes to transform an almost solution into any other almost solution) and these numerous local minima make it hard to find a HC (if there is one). Any search procedure based on local information will have the same difficulty.

Although the most difficult HC problems occur in the neighborhood of the phase transition, this does not mean that problems not near the transition are easy. For example, strictly 3-connected random graphs with at least one HC (guaranteed by construction) have a solution time that grows exponentially with the size of the graph (using the above backtrack algorithm). This means that even HC problems on random graphs whose connectivity is some distance from the phase transition are very hard—but those on the boundary are even harder. The reason most HC problems are hard, whereas most graph coloring problems are not seems to be a consequence of the global constraint in HCs, but not for K-colorability.

For HC problems there is one global constraint (i.e. a constraint involving all the nodes)—perhaps the phase transition is a result of this property? To investigate this possibility, we next examine graph coloring as an example with only pair-wise local constraints.

4 An Example: Graph Coloring

This is a constraint satisfaction problem, where each variable can take on a number of possible values ("colors"), and there are binary constraints that forbid particular pairs of variables from having the same color. The goal is to see if there is an assignment of colors to the variables that satisfy the constraints and only use K colors, or report that no assignment is possible. This version is the K colorability decision problem; more generally the goal is to find the minimum K that satisfies the constraints (the chromatic number problem). Any solution to a graph coloring problem can be used to generate other solutions by interchanging the colors, implying a color rotation symetry. Many practical constraint satisfaction problems, such as timetable construction, can be mapped into a graph coloring problem.

Graph coloring has been extensively investigated, both theoretically and empirically, e.g., [9],[10]. Even though graph coloring is an NP-complete problem, these authors report that graph coloring is "almost always easy". In particular, a simple backtrack algorithm by Brelaz was found to solve all randomly generated graphs it was tried on with little backtrack [10]. We continue these investigations but restrict our attention to random graphs that have been "reduced". The "reduction operators" decribed below guarantee that if the reduced graph is K-colorable (or not) then the original graph is K-colorable (or not). Any graph that can be reduced to one that is trivially K-colorable (or not) can be solved without search. We only investigate the space of reduced graphs, because the hard problems must be in this space. The particular reduction operators we used for K-colorability are:

1. Remove Underconstrained Nodes—a node with less than K constraints can be removed, because it can always be colored.
2. Remove Subsumed Nodes—a node N can be removed if there is a node M that is connected to everything N is connected to, since any color that works for M will work for N (provided N is not connected to M).
3. Merge nodes that must have the same color—if any nodes are fully connected to a clique of size K-1, then these nodes can be merged into a single node with all the constraints of its constituents, because they must have the same color.

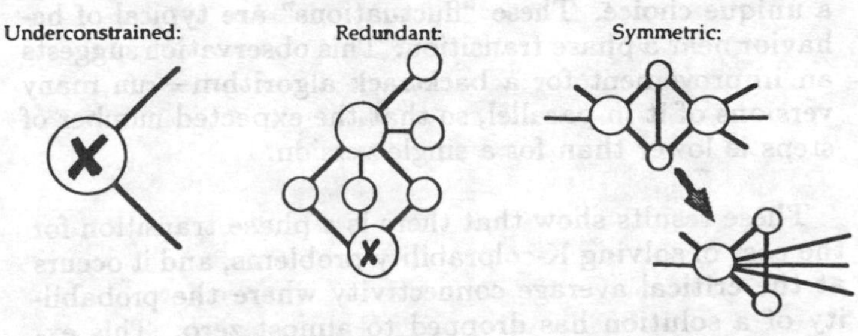

Figure 2: Reduction Operators for 3-Colorability

These reduction operators can be applied in any order, and typically the application of one operator creates a situation where other operators become applicable, producing a reduction cascade. We found that these operators reduced all our carefully hand-constructed "hard" graphs to trivial cases! In particular, all graphs reduced using $K = 2$ reduced to the null graph, showing that 2-colorability is a trivial P problem [3]. Although these are all the reduction operators we could find, they are all that is possible. In particular, we have found reduction operators that eliminate more than one node at a time, but these operators are so rarely applicable we did not use them. The following investigations are all in the space of random reduced graphs because the K-colorability of a reduced graph is equivalent to that of many unreduced graphs. This kind of problem simplification by preprocessing is often overlooked in discussion of algorithms, yet it can make apparently hard problems trivial. The essential difference between problem reduction and problem solving is that problem reduction does not produce disjunctive alternatives (i.e. no search).

We empirically investigated the probability of a solution for K-colorability problems for different values of K and N (number of nodes). The results are shown in Fig. 3a, where each probability point is the average of about 5 trials, but there are no points in the transition region because they are too costly to compute. Two trends are clear from these results. First is the abrupt change in solution probability occurs at higher values of the connectivity for larger K, and the other is the sharpness of the transition increases with N.

We next show how the computational cost varies as a function of the connectivity for different values of K. The results are shown in Figs. 2b,c for random reduced graphs that were generated so that they were guaranteed to have a solution. For both 3-Col and 4-Col the existence of a phase transition is clear, and their location is the same as that for the corresponding solution-probability transition to within the numeric noise level. The transition for 4-Col is much sharper than for 3-Col. Similar results are obtained for random reduced graphs that are not guaranteed to have a K-col solution, and for random graphs restricted to 2-D neighbor connections.

Brelaz's algorithm [10] uses heuristics: Select an uncolored node with the fewest remaining colors; ties are broken by selecting the node connected to the most uncolored nodes; remaining choices are made randomly. This is a very effective algorithm, but its performance at the phase boundary is highly variable, even on the same graph, because the heuristics do not always lead to a unique choice. These "fluctuations" are typical of behavior near a phase transition. This observation suggests an improvement for a backtrack algorithm—run many versions of it in parallel, so that the expected number of steps is lower than for a single version.

These results show that there is a phase transition for the cost of solving K-colorability problems, and it occurs at the critical average connectivity where the probability of a solution has dropped to almost zero. This explains why previous authors [9],[10] found K-colorability an easy problem—they were using *nonreduced* graphs whose effective connectivities did not typically fall near the phase boundary.

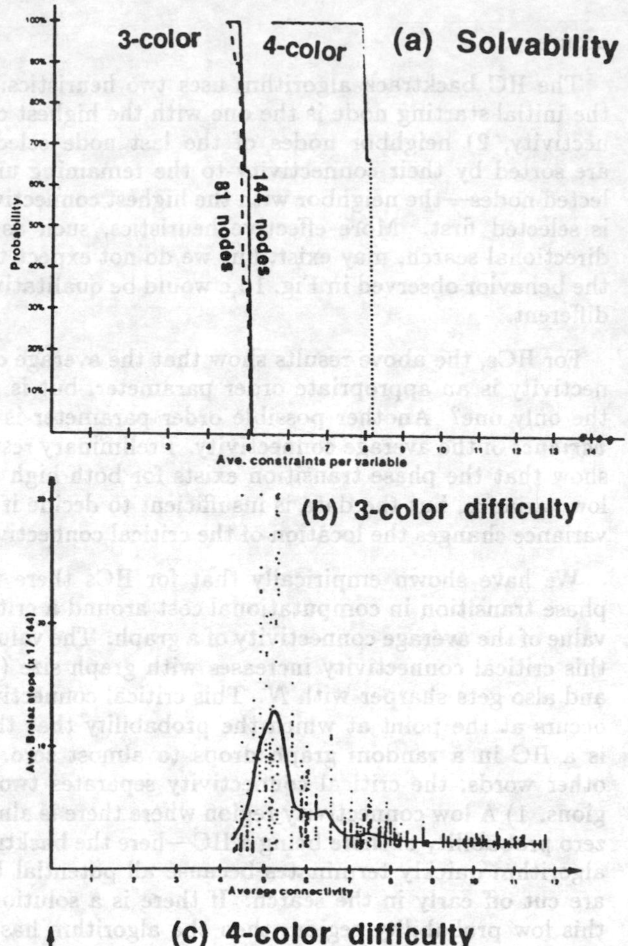

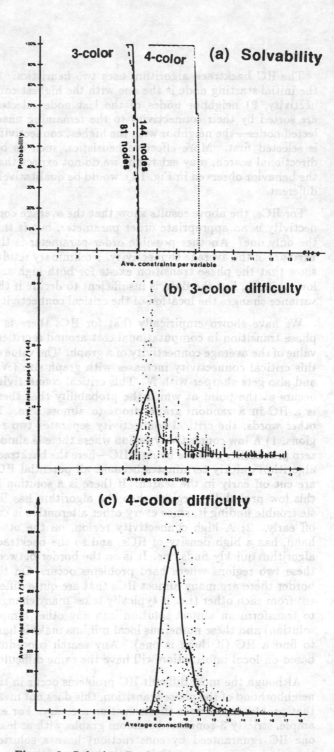

Figure 3: Solution Probability and Cost for K-Col

Examination of Brelaz's algorithm on the hard instances shows that it often backtracks, and sometimes backtracks all the way to the beginning. This "thrashing" occurs because there are many near-solutions available, and they look like solutions to the backtrack algorithm until an assignment is nearly complete. These local minima make it hard to find a solution if one is present—the proverbial needle in a haystack. This observation hints as to why some NP instances are hard; it seems likely that any algorithm based on local information will be fooled by the high number of local minima in problems near the phase boundary. Further experimentation suggests that graphs with a high variance of the average connectivity are generally easier to solve than ones with lower variance, so that the variance of the average connectivity may be an additional order parameter.

An apparent exception to the conjecture that all the NP problems overlap the critical boundary, is to discover if planar graphs with node connectivity ≤ 4) are 3-Col. This is an NP-complete problem [3], yet our 3-Col transition for random reduced graphs occurs at a connectivity ≈ 5.4 (see Fig. 3b)). To compare planar graphs with our results we must first reduce them. Merging destroys the planarity of the graph, reduces the number of nodes and simultaneously increases the connectivity of the merged nodes. The results is increased average connectivity of the previously planar graphs so that they straddle the critical connectivity, thus preserving the conjecture. However, if the proportion of 4-connected nodes in 3,4 planar graphs are sufficiently restricted, the result is a new P class of problems, assuming the conjecture is true.

5 An Example: K-Satisfyability

Since it is possible to map K-colorability problems into K-sat problems and vice versa [3], we next investigate K-sat problems. We used a form of resolution to reduce random K-sat problems before applying a simple backtrack search procedure with a most-constrained-first heuristic. The results are shown in Fig. 4. As for k-colorability, there is a sharp drop in the probability of a solution at some critical value of the graph average connectivity, and this critical value depends on K. Also, the normalized cost of solution shows a phase transition at about the point at which the solution probability drops to near zero. Simjlar results were found for random reduced graphs whose method of construction guaranteed at least one solution. We found that 2-sat does not have a phase boundary, but 3-sat does, as expected, since 2-sat is P and 3-sat is NP.

Large random reduced K-sat problems seem to get easier with large K—the phase transition evident in Fig. 4 becomes weaker with larger K until it disappears altogether (i.e. the backtrack search procedure solves the problem without backtrack). We do not fully understand this behavior, but it is probably due to an incomplete set of reduction operators that leave so may "trivial" problems (for large K) that the relatively few hard problems are missed. This is the same reason that previous authors missed the phase transition for K-colorability; the hard problems are greatly diluted by trivial problems. So far, the only way we have been able to create hard K-sat problems is by mapping equivalent K-colorability problems.

6 An Example: Traveling Salesman

All the previous examples have been constraint satisfaction problems where the order parameter turned out to

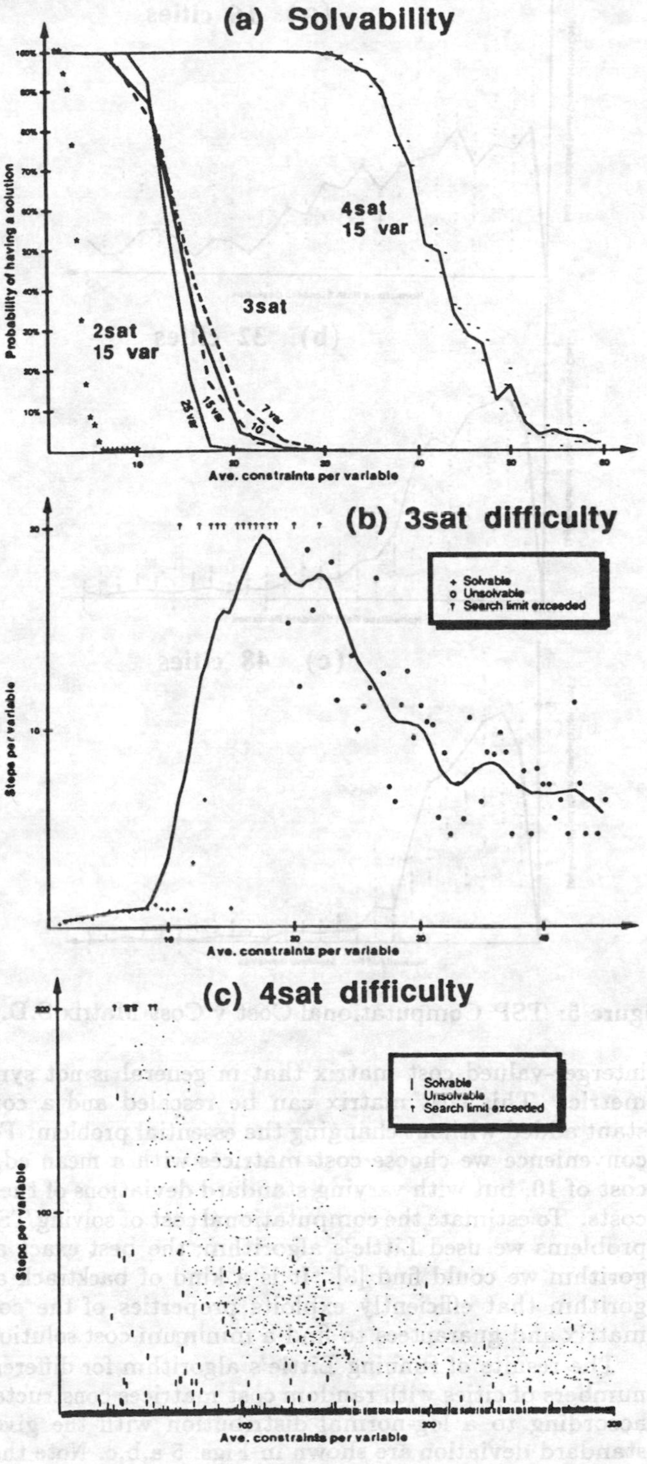

Figure 4: Solution Probability and Cost for K-sat

be the average connectivity of the corresponding graph, and the variance of the average connectivity may be a weak additional order parameter. We now investigate a different order parameter (the standard deviation of the cost matrix) in the context of a minimization problem—the Traveling Salesman Problem (TSP). In a TSP, the goal is to find a Hamilton circuit among a set of nodes ("cities") such that the total cost of the circuit is a minimum. The costs of edges in the graph are given by an

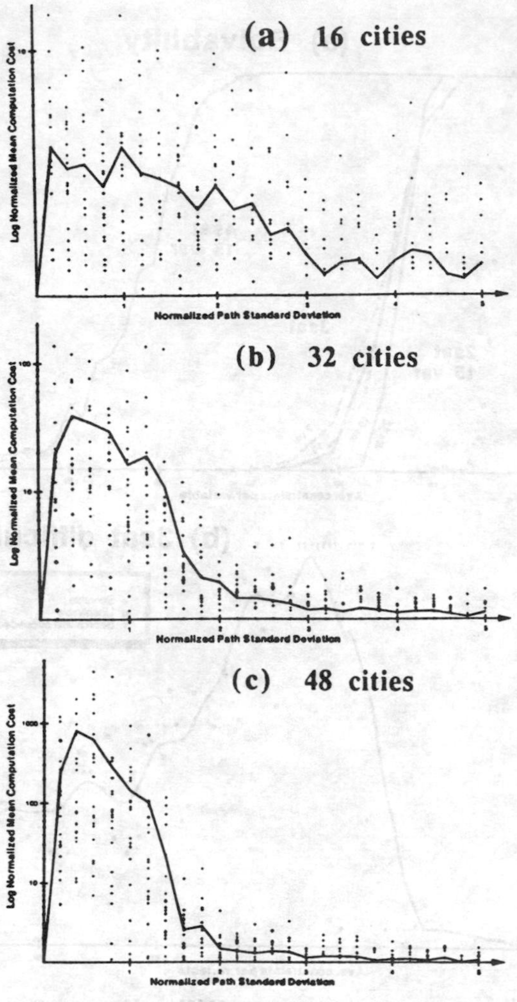

Figure 5: TSP Computational Cost v Cost Matrix S.D.

interger-valued cost matrix that in general is not symmetric. This cost matrix can be rescaled and a constant added without changing the essential problem. For convenience we choose cost matrices with a mean edge cost of 10, but with varying standard deviations of these costs. To estimate the computational cost of solving TSP problems we used Little's algorithm; the best exact algorithm we could find [8]. It is a kind of backtrack algorithm that efficiently exploits properties of the cost matrix and guarantees to find a minimum cost solution.

The results of running Little's algorithm for different numbers of cities with random cost matrices constructed according to a log-normal distribution with the given standard deviation are shown in Figs. 5 a,b,c. Note that the vertical axis is a Log scale, so the phase transition is more dramatic than appears at first sight. The magnitude and sharpness of the phase transition clearly increases with city size.

Because TSP is a minimization problem, there is no probability-of-solution phase transition, such as for Hamilton circuits and graph colorability. However, as for the previous problems, the obvious phase boundary separates two distinct regions. In one region where the standard deviation is high, only the low cost tail of the distribution is considered by Little's algorithm, since any minimum cost circuit will only use these low cost transitions. At the other extreme, where the costs are mostly equal, there are many tours of the same minimum cost, and so finding one of them is not difficult. This is why the curves in Fig. 5 drop precipitously when the standard deviation goes to zero. Once again, a phase boundary has been found between two regions of fundamentally different behavior. Around this boundary the density of local minima of almost equal cost tours forces the search algorithm to investigate many false leads, leading to a dramatic rise in the computational cost.

Note that TSP contains HC as a special case where all the costs are either 1 or 2,(see [3]), where a cost of 1 corresponds to the nodes being connected. Because TSP "contains" HC as a special case, the phase transition in HC would be expected to occur at the same variance value as TSP (when the 1,2 costs are suitably mapped). This behavior has been observed to within the numerical noise limits.

7 Mappings Between Problems

Perhaps the main contribution of the NP-completeness theory is the demonstration that many apparently different problems can be mapped into each other so that solutions are preserved under the mapping. The main conjecture of this paper is that problems whose order parameter is at the critical boundary are typically really hard. If this is true, then an important question is whether the critical boundaries are preserved under these problem mappings, as would be expected if this conjecture is true.

We first investigate what happens when hard-to-K-color reduced graphs are mapped into equivalent K-sat problems. By introducing Boolean variables to represent propositions such as "Node 10 is Red", and translating the constraints into conjunctive normal form, K-col can be mapped into a K-sat problem. This direct mapping can be further reduced by applying resolution to the clauses. This shows that mapping a reduced problem in one space into an equivalent problem in another space does not necessarily produce a reduced problem in the new space. Using this mapping, we found that hard to color K-col graphs translate into hard to solve K-sat problems, as expected.

Another interesting question is what happens to a P problem if it is mapped into an NP problem in the same family? Do P problems avoid the critical region in such a mapping? As an example, consider the mapping of 2-sat (a P problem) into 3-sat (an NP problem). Such a mapping is given in [3], where a 2-sat clause, such as $(a \vee \bar{b})$ goes into two clauses $(a \vee \bar{b} \vee x)$ and $(a \vee \bar{b} \vee \bar{x})$. Since every such transformation introduces an extra variable (e.g. x) which only occurs in two clauses, the average connectivity of all the variables is dragged below the critical threshold. In other words, just transforming 2-sat into 3-sat by trivial variable addition does not produce hard problems since the transformed problems do not overlap the critical region.

In view of these results it is tempting to conjecture that the difference between P and an NP problems is whether a phase boundary exists or not. Unfortunately, this is not true—what matters is whether the phase boundary (if there is one) occurs at a fixed N or not. To explain this distinction, we compare the above results with the N-Queens problem [9], which is a known to be P. For Hamilton circuits, the phase boundary occurs at an average connectivity given approximately by $\ln N + \ln \ln N$, while for K-col the boundary occurs at particular values of the average connectivity that depend on K but not on N. However, for the N-Queens problem the number of variables increases as N^2, while number of constraints only increases as $O(N)$. This means the average connectivity of the variables decreases with increasing N and cannot be freely chosen. For low N the problem is overconstrained and for high N the problem is very underconstrained. There is a phase transition at $N = 4$, but because this phase transition occurs for a fixed (low) N, the amount of computation is strongly bounded, as expected for a P problem.

8 Discussion

Because of the basic equivalence of NP-complete problems, we expect phase boundaries in NP complete problems other than those investigated here. However, constrained minimization problems such as graph partition, integer partition, maximal clique, Ramsey numbers etc., may have a different order parameters. Some of these problems show a "spin glass like" transition [2].

An objection to the above results may be that they are all based on heuristic backtrack search, so that they may be a result of this choice rather than intrinsic to the problem. For graph coloring, a "local repair" algorithm [9] and a probablistic search procedure also had difficulties with reduced graphs in the critical connectivity range, adding confirmation that the phase phenomenon is intrinsic. The difficulties experienced by all these algorithms seems to be due to the large number of local minima.

9 Conclusions and Conjectures

The results reported above suggest the following conjecture:

> All NP-complete problems have at least one order parameter and the hard to solve problems are around a critical value of this order parameter. This critical value (a phase transition) separates one region from another, such as overconstrained and underconstrained regions of the problem space. In such cases, the phase transition occurs at the point where the solution probability changes abruptly from almost zero to almost 1.

The converse conjecture is:

> P problems do not contain a phase transition or if they do it occurs for bounded N (and so has bounded cost).

We have presented empirical evidence for these conjectures for particular problem classes, and have shown in some cases that the hard problems in one space map into hard problems in the other space, thus preserving the phase boundary under the mapping. We have also shown cases where the distinction between P and NP was whether the the P class was excluded from the critical region. If these conjectures are true, then all that is needed to turn an NP problem into a P problem is to add restrictions so problems near the critical value of the order parameter are excluded. Note that these results depend on using only reduced problems, which may explain why these particular results have not been previously noticed.

There are many outstanding questions, such as: "What happens for NP-hard problems"; "Can hard problems occur in the non-critical region?", "Do other types of problems, such as optimization problems, games, etc. have the same properties?"; and so on.

Acknowledgements

We wish to gratefully acknowledge the many stimulating discussions and ideas of W. Buntine, E. Gamble, S. Minton, A. Philips, A. Meyer, O. Hansen and B. Pell.

References

[1] Bollobas, B. "*Random Graphs*", Academic Press, London, 1985.

[2] Fu, Y. "*The Uses and Abuses of Statistical Mechanics in Computational Complexity*", in " Lectures in the Sciences of Complexity", Ed. D. L. Stein, pp 815-826, Addison Wesley, 1989.

[3] Garey M. R. and Johnson D. S., "*Computers and Intractability': A Guide to the Theory of NP-Completeness*", Freeman, 1979.

[4] Huberman, B. A. and Hogg, T., "*Phase Transitions in Artificial Intelligence Systems*", Artificial Intelligence, 33, 155-171, 1987.

[5] Karp, R. M. and Pearl, J., "*Searching for an Optimal Path in a Tree with Random Costs*", Artificial Intelligence,21, (1,2), 99-116, 1983.

[6] Purdom, P. W., "*Search Rearrangement Backtracking and Polynomial Average Time*", Artificial Intelligence,21, (1,2), 117-134, 1983.

[7] Kirkpatrick, S. and Swendsen, R. H., "Statistical Mechanics and Disordered Systems", Comm. ACM, 28, 4, 363-373, April 1985

[8] Little, J. D. C., et al., "*An Algorithm for the Traveling Salesman Problem*", O.R.S.A., 11, 972-989, 1963.

[9] Minton, S. et al, "*Solving Large-Scale Constraint Satisfaction and Scheduling Problems Using a Heuristic Repair Method*", Proc. 8th. Nat. Conf. on A.I. (AAAI-90), 17-24, 1990.

[10] Turner, J. S., "*Almost All k-Colorable Graphs are Easy to Color*", Journal of Algorithms, 9, 63-82, 1988.

COGNITIVE MODELING

How situated is cognition?

Jacobijn Sandberg and **Bob Wielinga**
Social Science Informatics
University of Amsterdam
Roeterstraat 15
1018 WB Amsterdam
The Netherlands
Telephone: (31) 20 5256789
email: sandberg@swi.psy.uva.nl

Abstract

This paper discusses the recent views on knowledge, representations, and memory as presented by different researchers under the flag of 'situated cognition'. The situated view implies a radical shift of paradigm. We argue that there are no strong reasons to leave the traditional paradigm of cognitive science and AI. Four main issues are addressed: the role of computational models in theories of cognition, theories on knowledge and memory, the frame of reference problem and implications for learning and instruction. The main conclusion of the paper is that 'situationism' is throwing out the baby with the bath water. Consolidated achievements of Cognitive Science and AI still stand, even if the architectures that are assumed to underly traditional models of cognition can be challenged.

1 Introduction

The last few years the term "situated" appears more and more in articles on the subject of learning and teaching [Brown *et al.*, 1989]; [Suchman, 1987];[Harel and Papert, 1990];[Pea, in press]., The use of this term reflects a major shift in thinking about "knowledge", "information", "representation", and even "memory". This rethinking of basic terms related to learning and teaching is not limited to the educational field but has recently penetrated the field of AI [Clancey, in press];[Clancey, 1990b]. What does this shift entail and what is the importance of the concept "situated"? In short, the shift states that knowledge can no longer be viewed as a self-contained substance. Knowledge is inherently indexical of the environment, it can not be separated from its context, knowledge is essentially *situated*. Knowledge is not objective but subjective, embedded in a particular frame of reference. Knowledge is always relative, and open to reinterpretation. For the educators this new view on knowledge has major educational implications. They see learning as a process of enculturation. By joining a community of practice, whatever the practice may be, one gets to know the culture of the community, the jargon used, the beliefs held, the problems raised, the solving methods used. The educators claim that involvement in a community of practice is the only way to learn [Brown *et al.*, 1989]. Formal schooling does present students with a culture, but this school culture has nothing to do with the cultures that surround the subjects to be taught. Thus, students are engaged in tasks and endeavours that have no authenticity, no real-life value. Students do not learn the subjects themselves, but they learn *about* subjects [Brown *et al.*, 1989] No wonder, the educators say, that formal education fails. It is no use to try to transfer isolated, decontextualised bits of knowledge. Knowledge can only be gained in authentic activity, it is not a substance, but gets constructed in action. If you want your students to learn mathematics you have to give them the opportunity to act as mathematicians.

This is the situated view on education. How does this view relate to Artificial Intelligence? Work in the field of autonomous agents has clearly adopted a situated view by stressing the interaction of the agent with its environment [Rosenschein, 1985];[Agre, 1988];[Brooks, 1991]. More recently, the situated view has been taken much further by Clancey, by adopting it as a framework for an architecture for cognition and AI at large. He claims that his proposed framework dramatically changes our views on knowledge, representations and memory. He argues, in line with the educators, that knowledge is not a substance, and following from there that representations are not structures in the minds of people, but external, perceivable structures, open to debate, negotiation and reinterpretation. People create representations in their actions. For instance, in speech we do not translate a stored structure into words but construct a new representation each time we speak. Memory can no longer be seen as a storage place for representations - there are no representations left to store - but in Clancey's view should be considered "a capacity for creating and recombining phrases of behavior" [Clancey, in press, page 60].

Thus the representations we equip, for example, our expert systems with do not reflect structures that cause expert behaviour, but are our interpretations of expert behaviour over time. And the expert system does not use or view these representations in the same way people do. To the system these representations are structures to be manipulated syntactically, not semantically. We as observers interpret them semantically, the system however cannot.

In this article we investigate whether the situated view really implies a radical change in our thinking on knowledge, representations and memory and to what extent the suggested implications for learning and teaching are supported by theory and empirical findings. Since the literature on situated cognition is diverse and not all issues raised can be addressed in a short paper, we will focus on four main issues: the role of computational models in the study of cognition, theories of knowledge and memory, the frame of reference problem, and the implications for learning and instruction.

2 The Identity Hypothesis

An important objection that situationists from different camps raise against traditional views on cognition is that intelligent behaviour should not be seen as driven by a knowledge base stored in memory. Knowledge is not to be viewed as stored structures similar to the knowledge representations that we embody in AI programs [Clancey, in press]. In a similar spirit, [Brown *et al.*, 1989] reject the separation between knowledge and doing, which -they claim- treats knowledge as an "integral, self-sufficient substance". They blame traditional education for viewing instruction as the transfer of declarative structures into the head of the pupil.

The situationists' attack on traditional cognitive and instructional sciences, however, starts from an incorrect assumption. This assumption is what we call the *identity hypothesis*, which states that the information and knowledge that we manipulate and represent in our computer programs and teach in our schools are identical or at least very similar to whatever people have in their brains. This assumption does not do justice to much work in cognitive psychology and cognitive science. Cognitive science is building *models* in terms of computer programs or otherwise, which are *abstractions* from the real thing. Such models generate predictions in terms of behaviour, which can be tested, and as such they can be seen as instances of theories of cognition, but only at a certain level of abstraction. An expert system that solves problems through behaviour similar to that of a human expert, can be viewed as a theory of the problem solving behaviour of that expert. However, good fit between model and data does not necessarily mean that all underlying machinery (representations, processes, hardwetware) is identical. The identity hypothesis is a composite one in the sense that it covers different levels of abstraction. The identity hypothesis not only implies an identity relation at the level of observable behaviour, but also at the level of the structures that are being manipulated by certain processes, and at the level of the mechanisms that make it possible to operate on these structures. We think that the identity-hypothesis was never widely held in this strict sense. What might then be the communal view on the relation between human thinking and machine operating as provided by cognitive theory? We view this relation in terms of what we call the *functional-equivalence hypothesis.* To illustrate this point we cite Dennett [1981]: "When an AI model of some cognitive phenomenon is proposed, the model is describable at many different levels, from the most global phenomenological level at which the behaviour is described (with some presumptuousness) in ordinary mentalistic terms down through various levels of implementation, all the way down to the level of program code - and even further down, to the level of fundamental hardware operations, if anyone cares. No one supposes that the model maps onto the process of psychology and biology all the way down". This last sentence is crucial, for it rejects the identity hypothesis. Dennett continues by saying: "The claim is only that for some high level or levels below the phenomenological level (which merely sets the problem) there is a mapping of model features onto what is being modelled: the cognitive processes in living creatures, human or otherwise. It is understood that all implementation details below the level of intended modelling will consist of cognitive wheels - bits of unbiological computer activity mimicking the gross effects of cognitive subcomponents by using methods utterly unlike the methods still to be discovered in the brain". We quote Dennett at length to clarify the issue at hand. Most cognitive theories are high-level theories. They are not committed to statements about lower levels. However, to be implemented, the lower levels have to be there as well. That is where the cognitive wheels introduced by Dennett come in. They are purely technical devices, solely there to make the program work. They are not intended or assumed to bear any relation to what might be found in the human brain. However, at the higher level at which the statements of a cognitive theory lie, functional equivalence is hypothesized. The knowledge structures we describe, the representations we form, are assumed to be functionally equivalent to whatever devices humans use to solve problems, in the sense that they give rise to similar behaviour. The functional-equivalence hypothesis reflects the view generally held by the AI community better than the identity hypothesis as assumed and consequently attacked by Clancey in press. A further reason to refrain from any form of identity hypothesis is clearly stated by Anderson [1978, 1979]. He has pointed out that there are problems with the use of behavioural criteria in deciding upon the psychological validity of a particular computational representation. Different computational representations (imagery representations versus propositional representations, for example) can in principle predict the same behaviour. There are no objective criteria - as yet - to favour one type of representation over another.

In the field of education, the identity hypothesis crops up in critiques of traditional instructional methods. The essence of this criticism is that instruction in the school context is aimed too much at the transfer of knowledge in declarative, decontextualised form, out of context, and disconnected from its use. However, instructional psychology has been well aware of the problems with the teaching of declarative knowledge [Simon, 1980]. Many studies, e.g. in the fields of mathematics and physics problem solving, have shown that just learning the declarative subject matter is insufficient for operational use of the acquired knowledge. The main problem however has always been how to design teaching methods that both teach the declarative subject matter and its *use* [Mettes and Pilot, 1980] in a representative set of contexts. The problem then is how to choose a set that facilitates generalisation of use of the declarative subject matter. In any case, the assumption that traditional instruction is solely based on the identity hypothesis, is an oversimplification.

In summary, the situationists' reaction against traditional views on cognition, is overstated, because it attacks a position not held by many. Many cognitive scientists and educationers have been well aware of the limitations of their theories and methods.

3 Knowledge and Memory

The situated view on cognition leads Clancey to the view that knowledge is not something that we store as structures in memory. Clancey calls this the *externalisation move*. Through this externalisation Clancey places knowledge (as understood at the knowledge level [Newell, 1982] as well as symbolic representations *outside* the thinking agent. Knowledge and its symbolic representations are the results of a sense-making process in which an observer describes patterns of behaviour of an intelligent agent.

Clancey then proceeds with the description of a functional architecture which will support this view and in which perception plays a key role. The central role attributed to perception is crucial to the externalisation move. According to Clancey, we can only know what we can perceive. Constructing a representation means seeing something in a new light. Each act of speaking is a complete act of perceiving in itself. By speaking we create new meanings which are perceivable by ourselves and others and thus open to reinterpretation.

Memory, i.e. what is retained from previous activity, is a capability for replaying previously enacted sequences of behaviour ("phrases"). New phrases can be constructed through substitution of actions and recombination of phrases.

How, one may ask, does the functional architecture that Clancey proposes relate to classical theory and the phenomena it tries to explain? Classical theory offers explanations for, amongst others, phenomena of recall, expertise and recognition. Does Clancey's functional architecture explain these phenomena any better?

3.1 Recall

First, there is the obvious observation that people can recall things. We can recall names, numbers, sentences from a poem, laws of physics and so on. Although empirical evidence clearly shows that recall is much better in contexts similar to the context where the information was acquired, recall of decontextualised information is possible and even desirable in problem solving. Remembering Newton's law in the form F=ma does not remind us of all the physical situations in which we have applied this law, nor of the teachers and professors that have explained the law to us. So, how does Clancey's functional architecture explain recall of decontextualised information? We have to assume that some process is replayed that generates the symbolic representation of Newton's law. If such a memory capability exists, why not call it a piece of knowledge? Why can we not create such a memory phrase through explicit communication (i.e. teaching decontextualised subject matter)? Even if in the neural machinery that implements the functional architecture there is no recognisable *place* where a behavioural phrase is stored, at least functionally it can be viewed as a unit that can be activated as such.

3.2 Expertise

Recent experiments on the nature of expertise, show that it is possible to teach new strategies to experts which normally use other, sub-optimal procedures [Staszewski, 1988]. Such instruction not only changes the expert's behaviour, but also enhances performance. In terms of Clancey's functional architecture, this means that process memory is extended with new phrases through the perception of external representations (symbols explaining a new procedure), not through actual acting. It is not clear to us whether this corresponds to the reflection process postulated by Clancey, but in any case the functionality of the classical memory model can explain this phenomenon just as well as the process memory architecture, if not better.

A second point concerning expertise is that there is ample evidence that experts in various fields have the capability of recognising large amounts of patterns that can occur in problem situations [de Groot, 1966]; [Ericsson and Polson, 1988]; [Chase and Ericsson, 1981]. Such patterns can be identified empirically and can sometimes be verbalised. Admittedly such patterns are primarily indexical and functional. They impose structure on the observed reality and through that structure make a focussed problem solving process possible. However, there appears to be no good reason why such patterns can not be viewed as a psychological reality. The fact that an observer or an experimenter interprets eye-movement data or verbal utterances of an expert in terms of knowledge structures, and that consequently statements about that knowledge are subjective, relative to the observer, does not change the fact that such patterns can be induced by explicit instruction, or can be elicited in knowledge acquisition. Again there does not appear to be a compelling reason why a process memory should give a better account of these phenomena than a classical theory of memory.

3.3 Constructive memory

A third point concerns the observation that memory is constructive and dynamic. Knowledge evolves continually as it is being used [Brown *et al.*, 1989, page 33]. Indeed there is ample evidence that memory is (re-) constructive. Not only Bartlett's [1977] seminal work on remembering provides strong evidence of this, but many, more experiments support this. For example, the experiments by Bransford nd Franks [1971] and other, similar experiments, clearly indicate that what is remembered is not often the exact stimulus, but the gist, the meaning of a linguistic utterance. In reconstructing the original stimulus, inferences are made and other knowledge is used.

Again, the process memory does not seem to give us much more than conventional theories of memory storage, memory retrieval and depth of processing. The depth of processing of a sentence will determine the manner in which it is stored in semantic memory, and will determine to what extent it can be reproduced or recognised. The deeper the processing, the more decontextualised the information that is stored will be.

Thus, even though many of the observations about knowledge - implied by the functional architecture proposed by Clancey - e.g. its indexical nature, better recall in context etc., are relevant and consistent with empirical evidence, there appears to be no compelling need for a radical change in the paradigm of AI with respect to the notions of knowledge and memory. Of course, it is more likely that an architecture based on neural processes resembles what goes on in our heads than a von Neuman architecture. But that is not the point. As Marr [1977] has pointed out, we are studying information processing *problems* and not in the first place mechanisms.

As to the issue whether knowledge can be viewed as a substance, all evidence cited above strongly suggests the conclusion that knowledge can still be viewed at the functional level as "mental substance" more or less of which can be available to a thinker. Moreover, this substance has internal structure which can be made explicit in empirical studies. Whether this "substance" is stored as symbolic structures, as states of neural nets or as process memories, as Clancey suggests, is immaterial for the present discussion, although it is of course an important question from the architectural point of view. What is our concern here, however, is the evidence that knowledge can at least functionally be viewed as a substance that can be communicated in such a way that it can be used.

4 The frame of reference problem

The externalization move [Clancey, in press] as described above is related to what Clancey calls the frame of reference problem. It says that "theories are only true with respect to a frame of reference. AI and cognitive science research has been based on the contrary point of view that theories (representations and language) correspond to a reality that can be objectively known ..." [Clancey, in press, page 20]. There is no objective reality out there. By saying that there are no internal representations stored in any form, and that we can only know the things we can perceive, it follows that all knowledge is relative to the observer. Our perception is biased, and perceiving implies conceptualizing, interpreting. What we perceive is an interpretation in itself.

We agree that any science must operate within a certain frame of reference: the ontology it has chosen, the distinctions it deems relevant, the type of scientific justifications it allows and so on. However, this does not mean that scientific knowledge -and other knowledge for that matter- has no constancy or psychological validity. Both in KBS development and in education we strive to create systems or to coach pupils which *do it right* according to some framework. Although, at the highest level, one may correctly say that all we know is relative to a frame of reference, within a particular frame of reference there exist agreed upon criteria of ***right*** and ***wrong***. For instance, at school it is a particular framework of arithmetic and elementary mathematics that we are trying to convey to our pupils. Of course, the number facts and procedures are important, but the acceptance of the framework, i.e. learning that certain relations hold, certain solution methods are valid, for example accepting that 1+1=2 and not 3, is a major aim. Within that frame it is useful and necessary to talk about the adequacy of solutions being put forward by pupils, not solely in terms of right or wrong, but in terms of elegancy, efficiency, applicability or whatever criteria the frame of reference accepts. These criteria all are related to decontextualisation and naturally go together. The more abstract, formal procedures are the more elegant, more efficient, and more applicable ones. Thus modern physics teaching is aimed at changing fundamental preconceptions, e.g. that a force needs to be continuously applied to a mass in order for it to move with a constant speed, into the more abstract principles of physics. It is exactly this process which requires abstraction from the situation: decontextualisation. It is clear that human cognition is not very well equipped for the decontextualisation process: it is difficult, prone to error, and does not proceed autonomously. That does not mean, however, that one should not try to guide students through a process of decontextualisation.

Here a major flaw in the situationist argument appears to emerge. The fact that all knowledge is relative to a frame of reference, does not mean that humans have to be aware of that frame of reference, in fact most often they are not. Nor does the ever changing nature of frames of reference imply a parallelism in human memory which then no longer leaves room for stable symbolic structures. Working and thinking within a particular frame of reference provides stability and logical consequence to one's thinking. It is probably a good thing to teach students at some point in their career that these - different - frames of reference exist, but it is not at all a necessary condition for acquiring knowledge within a certain framework.

A major problem is the way in which we teach knowledge. How is knowledge applied?

5 Educational implications? How situated should our education be?

Brown et al. and Clancey claim that their revision of how to think of knowledge, representations and memory has strong implications for education. What do these implications boil down to? The central point is that knowledge is fluid, learning goes on all the time, learning entails creating new representations in speaking and acting and are part of every day life. Knowledge can never be simply transferred. People are actively creating representations while engaging in a community of practice. To learn a subject means to take part in a particular community of practice. This entails what is termed "cognitive apprenticeship". Educational researchers advocating this view on learning provide a lot of anecdotical evidence to support their claims [Resnick, 1988]; [Schoenfeld, 1985]; [Pea, in press]. What can we say about the promises of cognitive apprenticeship? What empirical findings do or do not support its claims? One of the consequences of the situated stance is to refrain from decontextualising, from abstracting the particularities of a problem situation. Formal education, as we know it, emphasizes decontextualisation. Its aim is to provide formalized tools that have broad applicability, their use is not restricted to a particular problem in a particular context. Let us take up an example provided by Brown et al 1989.

5.1 A situated example

In this example the inventiveness of a weight-watcher solving a fractions problem by other means than a formal procedure is described. The weight-watcher confronted with the problem of measuring out three quarters of two thirds of cottage cheese does so by making a round shape of cottage cheese, and subsequently dividing this shape into three parts, and then dividing two of these three parts in halves. Brown et al. claim this solution to be adequate, the situation the weight-watcher finds himself in provides him with a solution-path tuned to the problem at hand. There is no need to fall back on a formal solution. One could ask whether the solution described is indeed adequate. What if the weight-watchers material would have been some liquid? Then his procedure would break down. Formal multiplication of the fractions, however, would break down in neither case, and thus has a broader applicability [Elshout, in press]. Isn't that just what you would like to provide your students with: knowledge and procedures that are broadly applicable, decontextualised? Wouldn't cognitive apprenticeship have the risk that decontextualisation will never take place, so the student would become an able practitioner in a limited set of situations, without the possibility to solve problems in slightly different contexts? One could answer that formal education does not show much transfer of this kind either? That may be true. But, whether this lack of transfer is to be blamed on the efforts of decontextualisation is another matter. Could it be that lack of transfer is related to other factors than decontextualisation per se? Elshout [in press] argues convincingly that "at the

root of failure to transfer lies failure to comprehend complex information". The subjects taught at school are inherently difficult. The more abstracted the methods that can be used to solve problems, the more difficult the problems that can be solved. It is evident that many of us do not digest the material offered at school in full. Knowledge remains partial, half remembered and not completely understood. Cognitive apprenticeship in itself is no remedy. It does not reduce the inherent complexity of the subject. And it may be feared that it only conceals this complexity, by offerering the opportunity to "solve" a problem in a situated manner, like the weight-watcher, and thus failing to abstract from the particular context.

5.2 More on cognitive apprenticeship

Clancey is rather optimistic about the questions that students in cognitive apprenticeship would be able to pose [Clancey, 1990a]. Instead of simply taking in what is being put forward as the expert view, they would become aware of the differences of opinion that characterize the field. For a medical student this would mean asking questions like: if I know something, what other people will know it too, nurses or only particular doctors, or what if I were to travel to another part of the world, would I be able to talk to practitioners of medicine in the same terms? Rather high-brow questions for a student to ask? Is Clancey not expecting too much. Would a student in a cognitive apprenticeship not lack the necessary background experience to be able to pose such questions, and would he or she not be overwhelmed by the complexities of the field in action? Are there not just as many sound arguments against cognitive apprenticeship as there are in favour?

Formal education is not available world-wide. To many so called traditional societies, cognitive apprenticeship is the only educational path available. How does this compare to western, formal education? Is there any reason to claim that the cognitive apprenticeship that exists today is in any way superior to the formal education we provide our students with? We do not see one.

6 Conclusion

This paper argues that the situated stance in both AI and in education makes unfounded claims. Clancey arrives at the situationist stance by attacking the identity-hypothesis of which we say that it was never widely held anyway. The educators seek support for the situated view of education in case studies of cognitive apprenticeship. We find that these examples hardly justify a strong preference for situated learning. As we have said, decontextualisation does not come naturally to people. This supports the situated view, as it reflects how people normally act and learn in everyday life. However, it does not necessarily entail that formal education has to proceed in the same manner. On the contrary, formal education exists to free students from particular contexts. Without formal education, the necessary abstraction would not take place.

The conclusion of this paper must be that much of the situated cognition work today appears to throw away the baby with the bath water. It is all very well to postulate new architectures and mechanisms for cognition, but disregarding existing, viable theories on the grounds that they do not hold for the full range of complex phenomena, is too drastic as long as new theories do not have a wider explanatory power. In fact, there is a danger of reductionism, i.e. reducing the mind to a simple organism interacting with its environment and producing complex behaviour through the application of simple behavioural rules. Psychological evidence disfavours this view. It takes a long time to acquire even basic skills, to become an expert requires hard work and a long training period.

It is not our opinion that situationism is entirely wrong. Psychological evidence about everyday thinking certainly supports the view that thinking is largely situated. What we argued against is the complete shift of paradigm that situationists claim. Disregarding evidence and achievements of Cognitive and Instructional Sciences, and AI, is in our view overstating the issues. There is as yet enough room within the traditional theories, to advance towards a full theory of intelligent behaviours.

From an AI point of view it is, of course, perfectly legitimate to investigate roads leading to new architectures, but stating that AI, and indeed educational science, have been built on faulty assumptions is too extreme a view for us to accept.

References

[Agre, 1988] P.E. Agre. *The Dynamic Structure of Everyday Life*. PhD thesis, MIT, 1988.

[Anderson, 1978] J.R. Anderson. Arguments concerning representations for mental imagery. *Psychological Review*, 85:249–277, 1978.

[Anderson, 1979] J.R. Anderson. Further arguments concerning representations for mental imagery: A response to hayes-roth and pylyshyn. *Psychological Review*, 86:395–406, 1979.

[Bartlett, 1977] F.C. Bartlett. *Remembering: A Study in Experimental and Social Psychology*. Cambridge University Press, Cambridge, 1977.

[Bransford and Franks, 1971] J.D. Bransford and J.J. Franks. The abstraction of linguistic ideas. *Cognitive Psychology*, 2:331–350, 1971.

[Brooks, 1991] R.A. Brooks. Intelligence without representation. *Artificial Intelligence*, 47:139–159, 1991.

[Brown *et al.*, 1989] J.S. Brown, A. Collins, and P. Duguid. Situated cognition and the culture of learning. *Educational Researcher*, 18:32–42, 1989.

[Chase and Ericsson, 1981] W.G. Chase and K.A. Ericsson. Skilled memory. In J.R. Anderson, editor, *Cognitive Skills and their Acquisition*. Lawrence Erlbaum Associates, Hillsdale, N.J., 1981.

[Clancey, 1990a] W.J. Clancey. Invited talk at the DELTA, 1990.

[Clancey, 1990b] W.J. Clancey. Why today's computers do not learn the way people do. Paper presented at the annual meeting of AERA, Boston, April, 16-20, 1990.

[Clancey, in press] W.J. Clancey. The frame of reference problem in ai. In K. VanLehn and A. Newell, editors, *Architectures for Intelligence: The Twenty-Second Carnegie Symposium on Cognition*. Lawrence Erlbaum Associates, Hillsdale, NJ, in-press.

[de Groot, 1966] A.D. de Groot. Perception and memory versus thought: some old ideas and recent findings. In B. Kleinmuntz, editor, *Problem solving: Research, method and theory*, pages 19–51. John Wiley and Sons, New York, 1966.

[Dennett, 1981] D.C. Dennett. Cognitive wheels: The frame problem of ai. In C. Hookway, editor, *Minds Machines, and Evolution: Philosophical Studies*, pages 129–151. Cambridge University Press, Cambridge, 1981.

[Elshout, in press] J.J. Elshout. Formal education versus everyday learning. In E. de Corte, M.Linn, H. Mandl, and L. Verschaffel, editors, *Computer-Based Learning Environments and Problem Solving*. Springer-Verlag, Berlin, in-press.

[Ericsson and Polson, 1988] K.A. Ericsson and P.G. Polson. A cognitive analysis of exceptional memory for restaurant orders. In M.T.H. Chi, R. Glaser, and M.J. Farr, editors, *The nature of expertise*. Lawrence Erlbaum Associates, Hillsdale, NJ, 1988.

[Harel and Papert, 1990] I. Harel and S. Papert. Software design as a learning environment. *Interactive Learning Environments*, 1:1–32, 1990.

[Marr, 1977] D. Marr. Artificial intelligence: A personal view. *Artificial Intelligence*, 9:37–48, 1977.

[Mettes and Pilot, 1980] C.T.C.W. Mettes and A. Pilot. *Over het oplossen van natuurwetenschappelijke problemen (On the solving of physics problems)*. PhD thesis, University of Twente, 1980. Enschede: Educational Center.

[Newell, 1982] A. Newell. The knowledge level. *Artificial Intelligence*, pages 87–127, 1982.

[Pea, in press] R.D. Pea. Distributed intelligence and education. In D. Perkins and B.Simmons, editors, *Teaching for Understanding in an Age of Technology*. in-press.

[Resnick, 1988] L. Resnick. Learning in school and out. *Educational Researcher*, 16:13–20, 1988.

[Rosenschein, 1985] S.J. Rosenschein. Formal theories of knowledge in ai and robotics. Technical Report 362, SRI, 1985.

[Schoenfeld, 1985] A.H. Schoenfeld. *Mathematical Problem Solving*. Academic Press, Orlando, FL, 1985.

[Simon, 1980] H.A. Simon. Problem solving and education. In D.T. Tuma and F. Reif, editors, *Problem Solving and Education*, pages 81–92. Lawrence Erlbaum Associates, Hillsdale, NJ, 1980.

[Staszewski, 1988] J.J. Staszewski. Problem solving and education. In R. Glaser M.T.H. Chi and M.J. Farr, editors, *The Nature of Expertise*. Lawrence Erlbaum Associates, Hillsdale, NJ, 1988.

[Suchman, 1987] L.A. Suchman. *Plans and situated actions*. Cambridge University Press, Cambridge, 1987.

Index Transformation Techniques for Facilitating Creative use of Multiple Cases

Katia P. Sycara and **D. Navinchandra**
katia@cs.cmu.edu dchandra@cs.cmu.edu
School of Computer Science
Carnegie Mellon University
Pittsburgh, PA 15213

Abstract

Using cases to find innovative solutions to problems is mainly the result of two processes: (1) cross-contextual remindings, and (2) composition of multiple cases or case parts. Although the ability to use cases taken from across contextual boundaries is desirable, there is a tension between representing and accessing cases across contexts and in using parts of multiple cases to synthesize a solution. One way of alleviating this difficulty is through index transformation. In this paper, we represent two index transformation techniques that facilitate both cross-contextual remindings and the access of multiple appropriate case parts. The mechanisms are general and principled (based on a qualitative calculus). They are also behavior-preserving, a needed requirement for case synthesis in many domains of interest. The transformation techniques have been implemented in CADET, a case-based problem solver that operates in the domain of mechanical design.

1. Introduction

Case based reasoning [Kolodner.Simpson.Sycara 85] is the method of using previous cases to guide solving of new problems. Given a new problem solving situation, appropriate previous cases are retrieved from memory, the best is selected, and differences as well as similarities between the previous and current case are identified. These similarities and differences are used to adapt the retrieved case to fit current circumstances. At the end of problem solving, the solved case is stored as a new case to be used in the future.

Using cases to find innovative solutions to problems is mainly the result of two processes: (1) cross-contextual remindings [Gordon 61], and (2) composition of multiple cases or case parts [Koestler 64]. Each one of these processes imposes requirements on case representation, memory organization, and indexing. The work presented in this paper focuses on the issue of indexing, in terms both of a domain-independent indexing vocabulary and index transformation techniques to facilitate the access and composition of cases and case pieces. We illustrate our claims in the domain of mechanical design. The abstract index representation and transformation techniques presented in this paper have been implemented in CADET, a case-based design problem solver [Sycara & Navinchandra 89, Navinchandra et.al. 91].

A memory that allows retrieval based on similarity is an important component of a case-based system [Schank 82]. The natural way to implement similarity recognition and retrieval based on similarity, is to index memory such that similar cases share common indices and can consequently be retrieved together. But what kind of similarity should this process use? Although surface features have been used successfully to retrieve cases in some CBR systems (e.g., [Simoudis & Miller 90]), it is clearly more useful to index cases in terms of abstract features so that the solution indexed with a particular case is applicable to other cases that share those abstract features, and may share few, if any, surface features. If a case is to have broad applicability, the indexing vocabulary must be at an appropriate level of generality and must reflect some thematic abstraction [Owens 88]. We advocate the use of qualitative influences as an appropriate vocabulary for expressing thematic abstractions.

Qualitative influences express abstract causal interactions among problem variables. An influence is a qualitative differential (partial or total) *relation* between two variables one of which is a dependent variable and the other an independent variable. We use graphs of these influences to represent the behavior of physical artifacts. Behavioral descriptions are good thematic abstractions that result in interesting and useful cross-contextual remindings. For example, an electronic sensing device could be used to sense water level in the design of a flush tank. This is a cross-contextual reminding (electronic device used in a hydraulic domain) that results in an innovative solution.

Retrieving cases from different domains make it difficult

This research is being supported by DARPA and AFOSR under contract number: F49620-90-C-0003.

to access case parts that could be used in the composition. Useful parts may be buried in the case where subpart boundaries may be difficult to identify. One approach for addressing the difficulty of indexing and accessing appropriate case parts is to use index transformation. Our earlier work on the PERSUADER [Sycara 87] and CYCLOPS [Navinchandra 87, Navinchandra 91] used pieces from multiple previous cases to come up with a proposed new solution. Redmond's [Redmond 90] work on diagnosis uses pieces from multiple cases, where conventional subgoaling is used to indicate the appropriate snippets. The snippets are indexed under their corresponding subgoals.

By contrast, in engineering design, a subgoal decomposition that would facilitate snippet indexing and retrieval cannot be identified a priori. This is a consequence of the fact that there is no one to one correspondence between device components and desired device subfunctions. In addition, since design goals change during problem solving, the cases in memory may not always be compatible with the current goal. Therefore, it becomes necessary to transform the goal during problem solving. This is done in CADET through index transformation techniques that are behavior preserving. In the design domain, a stringent constraint on the retrieved case parts is that their *combined behavior must be equivalent to the original behavioral specification of the desired artifact*. In this paper, we present two index transformation techniques that allow such behavior-preserving retrieval of case parts.

2. CBR in Design

Design is the act of devising an artifact that satisfies a useful need, in other words, performs some function. It is an interesting domain for conducting research in Case Based Problem Solving because: *designs are often synthesized by combining several parts of different design cases taken from different contexts, where each part delivers a portion of the overall behavior of the final artifact*. A design, hence, can contain parts taken from design cases that are, on the surface, functionally dissimilar to the current design problem.

For example, consider the design of a device which controls the flow of water into a flush tank. The behavior can be specified as follows: *as the depth of water (D) in the tank increases, the rate of flow of water into the tank (Q) should decrease*. This specification may be used as a set of indices to find relevant cases in memory. If there are no cases that directly match the specifications, then it would be useful to consider using parts of several cases. In this instance, an analogically relevant case is a hot-cold water faucet shown in Figure 2-1. The faucet is specified as a device that allows for the independent control of the temperature and flow rate of water by appropriately mixing the hot and cold water streams. By extracting portions of the faucet, such as the see-saw part, it is possible to design the flush tank device as shown in in Figure 2-2.

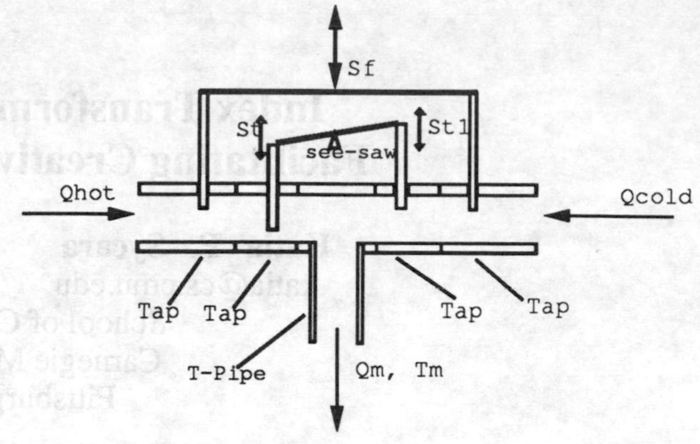

Figure 2-1: A Simple Hot-Cold Water Faucet

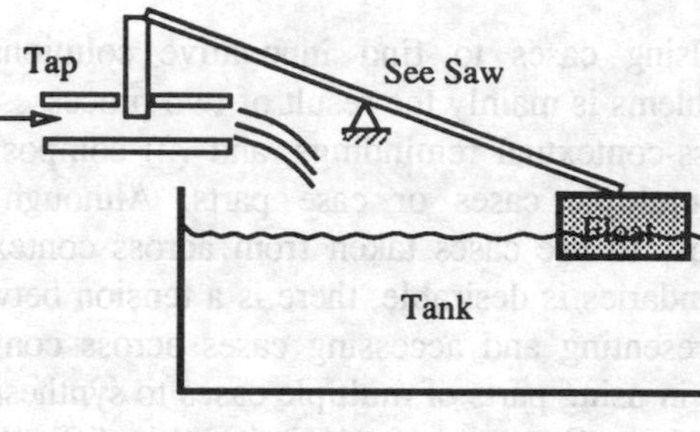

Figure 2-2: A flush tank

The relevance of the faucet case to the design of the flush tank would not have been possible to recognize because: (a) the functional descriptions of the two devices are completely different, and (b) the whole faucet is not relevant to the target problem. The relevance recognition process has two parts: similarity recognition and sub-behavior matching. First, the goal specification is elaborated by applying transformation operators. This process, in essence, generates several alternative behavior descriptions that are equivalent to the original goal. These alternatives are then matched against the cases in memory. The matching process tries to find entire cases or parts of cases that share common "sub-behaviors" with the elaborated goal.

We present an approach to accomplish recognition of shared "sub-behaviors" based on behavior preserving transformations that uses qualitative reasoning methods. The transformation is done in two ways: (a) If it is known what physical laws and principles are going to govern the solution, then the given goal is transformed by relying on the laws to achieve certain sub-behaviors. (b) If, however, the relevant laws are not known *a priori*, sub-behaviors are hypothesized and the case memory is searched to find ways in which the required behavior may be achieved. This is in contrast to other approaches that assume *a priori* knowledge of the domain laws and models that will be part of the solution [Williams 90]. If CADET cannot complete a design because it is not given the relevant physical laws, it hypothesizes new behaviors and looks for cases which embody those behaviors. The approach has the following advantages: (1) the system at each point in the search, is aware of what behavior it is trying to achieve, (2) because cases embody design optimizations, the accessed components correspond to already optimized physical structures, (3) solutions may involve the use of principles outside the current domain, that have been successful in a prior design, (4) the problem solver does not have to re-solve every problem from scratch.

3. Behavior Representation in the Cases

Device behavior is represented as a collection of influences organized in the form of a graph. The notion of influence graphs is a very general one. It applies to any domain in which behavior can be characterized as a set of quantities that relate to one-another. Given such an influence graph, it is possible to predict possible outcomes of given perturbations [Sycara 87].

Consider, for example, a gated water tap that has two inputs: a water source and a signal to regulate the rate of flow of water (Figure 3-1). The flow rate is given by **Q** and the position of the gate is given by **X**. The position of the gate controls the flow rate. This behavior is represented as an influence $Q \xleftarrow{+} X$, which is read as follows: "The flow rate (Q) increases (+) monotonically with an increase in the signal (X)". This influence represents the "tap" principle.

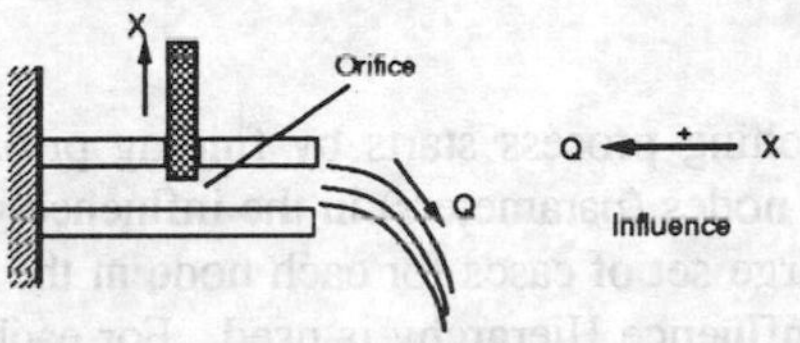

Figure 3-1: A gated-tap

Sets of qualitative influences can be combined to capture the behavior of more complex devices. The see-saw shown in Figure 3-2 has three major behavioral parameters: Ω, the angular position of the see-saw and the positions of the two ends of the see-saw ($X1$ and $X2$). The main influences are $X1 \xleftarrow{+} \Omega$, $X2 \xleftarrow{-} \Omega$ and $X2 \xleftarrow{-} X1$. These influences form a directed graph.

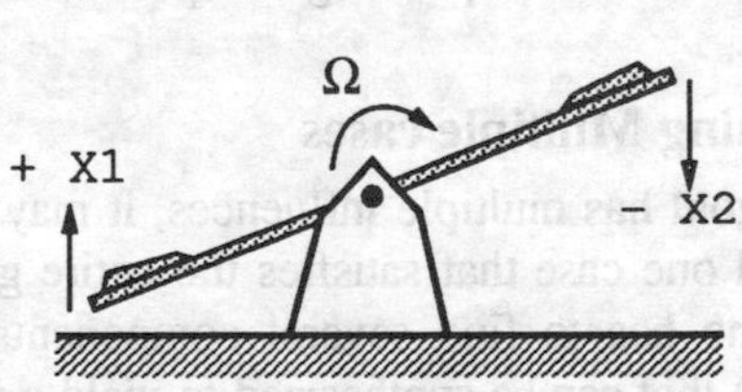

Figure 3-2: A see-saw

3.1. Influence Graphs and Components

The various components of a design work together to deliver its composite behavior. The influence graph that describes the overall behavior has sub-graphs that correspond to individual components. This provides a mapping between behavior and the structure of the case.

Let's re-consider the hot-cold water faucet (Figure 2-1). The behavior of this device can be represented as shown below (Figure 3-3). Two input signals St and Sf control the mix temperature and the mix flow-rate. When St is increased, then the total quantity of hot water Qh increases. At the same time, due to the see-saw principle, the signal $St1$ decreases, causing the total quantity of cold water Qc to proportionately decrease.

Note also, that single and multi-influence subgraphs of the faucet's influence graph corresponds to the various components of the faucet. This information serves as handles for snippet (component) identification and extraction.

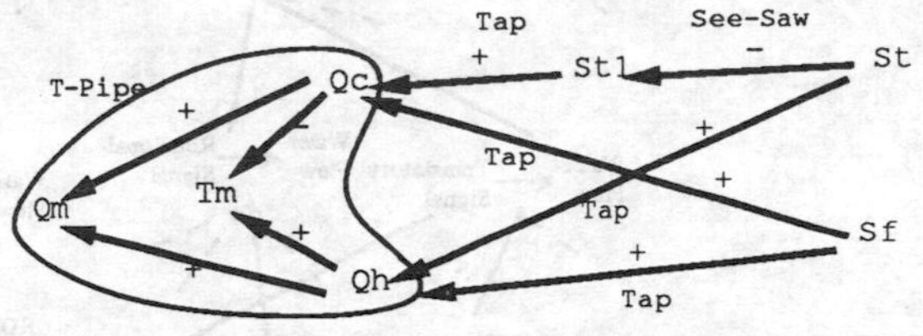

Figure 3-3: Faucet's Influence Graph

When this behavior representation is incorporated in a device case base, it becomes possible to retrieve cases which match given behavior specifications. If retrieval using the design specification fails to retrieve relevant cases, the system should be able to recognize how a combination of component behaviors could produce the required effect. This is done by transforming the indices. In the next section we will cover case indexing and retrieval, followed by a section on index transformation.

4. Case Retrieval

Most CBR systems retrieve cases using indices that match specific attributes about cases. In engineering design, the case matching problem includes matching graphs of influences. Behavior matching for case retrieval is carried out in several ways:

4.1. Abstract Matching

The nodes in the influences are matched using object and concept hierarchies. For example, the simple tap is described by the influence $Q \xleftarrow{+} X$. The node Q which is a flow of water is abstracted to be a liquid-flow, a material flow, and finally a design-parameter. The quantity X is a translatory-signal, a physical-signal, a signal, and finally a design-parameter. Every design parameter is entered in such a hierarchy.

4.2. Matching a sub-part of a larger case

Design cases are often composed of many other cases (or parts thereof). Each part is indexed separately. For example, the faucet is composed of a see-saw, a rigid-body, four gated-taps, and a right angle t-pipe. All these cases are indexed in an abstraction hierarchy. The gated-tap's abstractions are: a tap, a flow-control device, a hydro-mechanical device, and finally a device. In addition to this hierarchy, each influence in the case's behavior graph is indexed in an Influence Hierarchy.

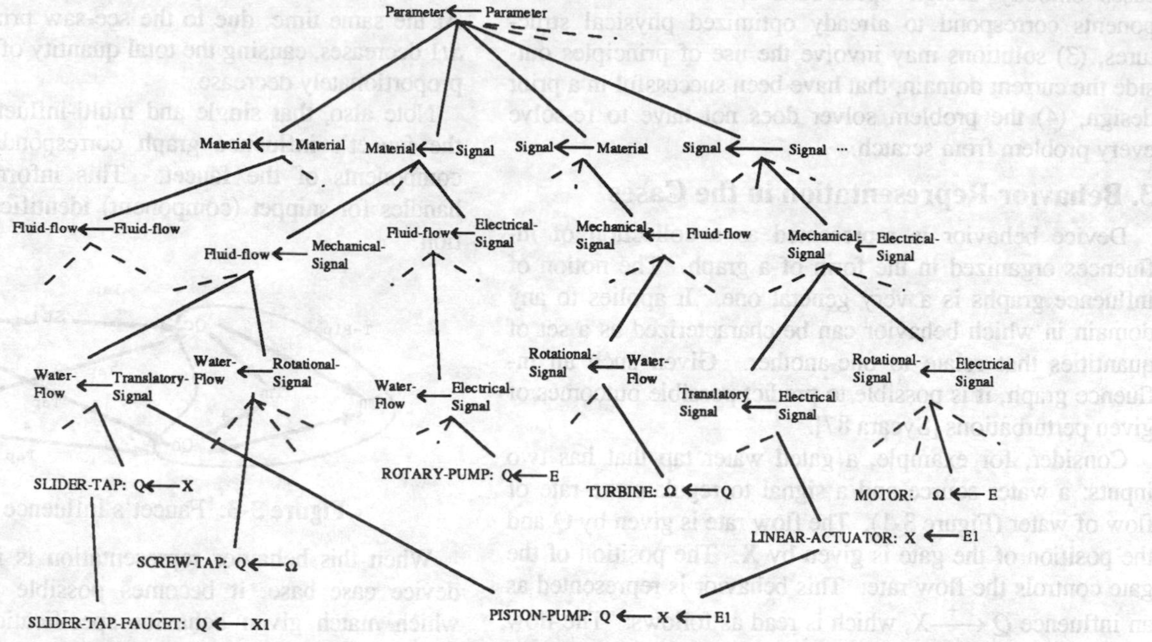

Figure 4-1: Partial Influence Hierarchy

The root of the influence hierarchy is the most generic influence: *Parameter* ⟵ *Parameter*. The parameters can be either materials, energy, or signals. This gives us nine possible influences. This hierarchy is expanded all the way down to the influences in the cases, thus providing a direct access *into* the innards of a case. A part of the influence hierarchy is shown below. The lowest level in the hierarchy points to actual cases or components inside cases. For example, the influence $Qh \xleftarrow{+} X1$ corresponds to the case: SLIDER-TAP-FAUCET which is a slider-tap inside the faucet case. Note that this is different from the general SLIDER-TAP case because the tap in the faucet has been modified to interface with other components in the faucet. The behavior may look the same, but the cases are physically different. We will see, later, why this distinction is important to maintain.

When CADET is given an influence as a goal, it can retrieve all cases that contain the goal. This can include all cases that match an abstraction of the goal. For example, the influence $Q \xleftarrow{+} Y$, can be abstracted to the influence *Water–flow* ⟵ *Translatory–Signal*. In this way, CADET is able to find components of larger cases that match a given goal specification, making it possible to find all "taps" in the case base, even if they are embedded in larger cases.

4.3. Multiple Influences in the Goal

The goal may consist of several influences arranged in the form of a graph. The aim of case matching is to find cases that have behaviors which correspond to the influences in the given goal.

The matching process starts by finding prior cases that contain the nodes (parameters) in the influence graph. This returns a large set of cases for each node in the goal graph. Next, the Influence Hierarchy is used. For each individual influence in the goal statement, the hierarchy is used to identify all the cases that contain that influence. An intersection of the sets of cases that match each influence and each node yields a smaller set of cases that contain the goal influences. This does not, however, guarantee that the topology of the influences in the cases will match that of the goal. The final step involves checking each of the retrieved cases for the goal graph. If the entire graph is matched, then the corresponding components in the case is extracted.

4.4. Matching Multiple cases

When a goal has multiple influences, it may not be possible to find one case that satisfies the entire goal. In this situation, one has to find several components (from different cases) that can be synthesized to yield a final design. The process is as follows: For each influence, we first identify sets of cases that contain that influence. These sets can be viewed as possible colors that can be assigned to the various links in the goal graph. The next step is to select a case for each influence, such that a minimum number of cases are required to cover all the influences in the goal. A heuristic, polynomial-time, algorithm is used to find partitions of the influence graph. The algorithm works as follows: first, the largest contiguous set of influences that share a common case name is identified; next, the set is removed from the graph; and finally, the process is repeated till no unassigned influences are left.

Reconsider the flush tank design problem. The overall goal is to achieve: $Q \xleftarrow{-} D$. Instead of this goal, assume we are given the following elaboration of subgoals: $Q \xleftarrow{+}$ *Mechanical–Signal* $\xleftarrow{-}$ *Mechanical–Signal* $\xleftarrow{+} D$. Each influence in the graph is used to identify relevant cases. In this instance, the influence: $Q \xleftarrow{+}$ *Mechanical–Signal* will match a regular tap, the tap in the faucet, and a pump. The next influence: *Mechanical–Signal* $\xleftarrow{-}$ *Mechanical–Signal* would match a regular see-saw, the see-saw in the faucet, a pulley, and a wedge. The remaining influence will match a simple float. The only case that is common for the first two influences is the faucet. The resulting design (Figure 2-2) is composed of the tap and see-saw combination taken from the faucet, and a float.

4.5. Exploiting Novel Combinations

A question that is often asked about the Case Based Problem Solving approach is: "If design problems can be solved by finding and synthesizing components such as taps, levers, and gears; then why should be keep larger cases in memory? The component hierarchy should be sufficient, why should the system have to find components embedded in the cases?"

In the mechanical design domain, cases provide useful sub-assembly "packages" of components. These sub-assemblies can reflect good design principles. For example, components are often made to share functions and may incorporate decisions that take advantage of, or compensate for incidental components interactions. The components in a prior design are often coupled efficiently to work as a sub-assembly of the larger design. These components are structurally modified to appropriately mesh with one-another. In addition, special connectors and fixtures may be used to interface the components. When a new design calls for the combination of two components behaviors, the modifications and interfaces need not be re-determined from scratch if relevant cases can be identified.

5. Index Transformation

In the example above, we said that the flush tank's goal behavior is given by a set of influences. If, however, we were only given the original influence $Q \xleftarrow{-} D$, then it would not have been possible to recognize that the gated-tap, the see-saw, and the float can be combined to solve the problem.

In our domain, it often happens that the goal description does not correspond to the appropriate cases in memory. A deliberate attempt has to be made to recognize what sub-behaviors can achieve the goal and how these sub-behaviors can be physically realized. We approach this problem in two steps: (1) If the goal description fails to retrieve cases from memory, then the goal is elaborated using certain behavior preserving transformations. (2) The elaborated goal is then used as indices to find relevant cases. Index transformation is a way to change the given salient features of the current problem to match the indices under which previous cases have been stored, thus making accessible to the problem solver previously inaccessible cases. The transformation technique described here is applicable to any domain in which behavior can be modeled as a graph of influences.

We will now examine two rules which are used to transform given goals into more elaborate sets of influences that are behaviorally equivalent to the goal. The hypothesis is that, if one cannot find a case relevant to a given goal, then it might be possible to find several cases or parts of cases that are relevant to elaborations of the given goal.

Design Rule 1. If the goal is to have x influence z, and if it is known *a priori* that u influences z, then the goal could be achieved by making x influence u.

Design Rule 2. If the goal is to have x influence z and if it is known *a priori* that some two quantities p and q influence z then, the goal could be achieved by making x influence p or q, or both.

The two design rules transform a given influence into a more detailed set of influences that are behaviorally equivalent to the original influence. In CADET, the transformation is done in two ways: (1) by using domain laws and, (2) by hypothesizing new variables.

5.1. Elaboration Using Domain Laws

The influences implied by domain laws may be used to elaborate given goals. For example, assume it is our goal to achieve the influence: $z \longleftarrow x$, also assume that there are no known designs that can achieve this effect directly. If, however, there is some domain principle which states that some quantity u influences z, then the goal may be achieved by having x influence u. The goal is hence elaborated to: $z \longleftarrow u \longleftarrow x$. This new influence graph is used as a new index into the case base. If cases or part of cases with influences that match the goal are found, they are retrieved and used.

5.2. Elaboration by Hypothesizing new variables

If the given domain laws are unable to find elaborations that can be realized by the cases in memory, one can try to hypothesize variables. The idea is to hypothesize new influences and then find cases which may be used to achieve those influences. For example, the goal $z \longleftarrow x$ may be elaborated to $z \longleftarrow Var1 \longleftarrow x$ using design rule 1. A new variable $Var1$ is hypothesized as an intermediary. The elaboration is then used to find cases in memory. This time however, the system looks for two influences which match the goal and bind the unknown variable $Var1$.

As new variables are introduced, corresponding new influences are hypothesized. In addition, as influences are all supposed to be based on physical laws or principles, the introduction of new variables implies that laws or principles, unknown to CADET, are being hypothesized. After hypothesizing influences, the case base is used to find prior designs which may embody some physical law or principle that matches the hypothesized influence. With this approach, one often retrieves cases from outside the current design domain that are analogically related to the current design problem. It is for this reason that CADET's solutions are innovative. Through the process of influence hypothesis and matching, the system is able to use physical laws and principles embedded in prior design cases to achieve its current goals.

Let's return to the flush tank example. Another possible elaboration of the original influence for the flush tank is: $Q \xleftarrow{+} Var2 \xleftarrow{+} Var1 \xleftarrow{-} D$. The first influence $Var1 \xleftarrow{} D$, says that as the water level increases, some quantity $Var1$ decreases. An ultrasonic distance measuring device, held over the water surface, could provide this behavior. The output of this device is an electrical signal. Let's call it Sig and bind it to $Var1$. The influence $Q \xleftarrow{+} Var2$ matches a basic tap by binding $Var2$ to X (which is a linear movement). Finally, we are left with the influence $X \xleftarrow{+} Sig$ which says that when an electrical signal increases a body moves linearly in the X direction. A positioning device with a linear ratchet and motor can provide this function. The resulting design is shown in Figure 5-1.

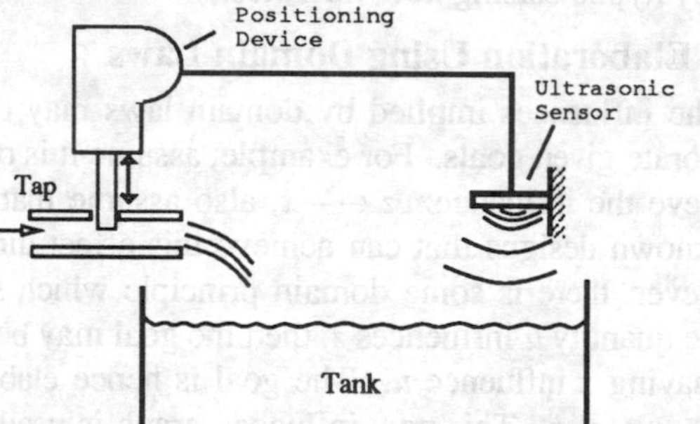

Figure 5-1: A flush tank exploiting extra-domain principle

6. Conclusions

We have presented an approach to the conceptual design of mechanical systems using a case base of previous designs that realize subfunctions of the desired artifact. The process consists of applying behavior-preserving transformations, based on a qualitative calculus, to an abstract description of the desired behavior until a description is found that closely corresponds to some collection of relevant cases. The major benefits of the approach are: (a) it allows for retrieval of relevant cases and case parts based on behavioral thematic abstractions that enable use of cases from contexts other than hydraulics (e.g., electrical, electronic. chemical), (b) it does not impose a predetermined decomposition of the design, (c) it is a generative approach that utilizes knowledge of design principles, such as simplicity, and behavioral constraints to reason from design goals to possible solution structures, (d) it can identify "missing" cases, necessary for completion of the design, and (e) the resulting transformations are guaranteed to be behaviorally equivalent to the original specification.

References

[Goel & Chandrasekaran 89] Goel A., B. Chandrasekaran, ''Integrating Model-based Reasoning and Case-Based Reasoning for Design Problem Solving,'' *Proceedings of the AAAI Design Workshop*, Expected in 1989.

[Gordon 61] Gordon W.J., *Synectics: The development of Creative Capacity*, Harper & Row, Publishers, NY, 1961.

[Koestler 64] Koestler, A., *The act of creation*, McMillan Publication Co., 1964.

[Kolodner.Simpson.Sycara 85] Kolodner, J.L., Simpson, R.L., and Sycara-Cyranski, K., ''A Process Model of Case-Based Reasoning in Problem Solving,'' *Proceedings of the Ninth Joint International Conference on Artificial Intelligence (IJCAI-85)*, Los Angeles, CA, 1985, pp. 284-290.

[Navinchandra 87] Navinchandra, D., *Exploring for Innovative Designs by Relaxing Criteria and reasoning from Precedent-Based Knowledge*, PhD dissertation, M.I.T., 1987.

[Navinchandra 91] Navinchandra, D., *Exploration and Innovation in Design: Towards a Computational Model*, Springer-Verlag series on Symbolic Computation, 1991.

[Navinchandra et.al. 91] Navinchandra D., K.P. Sycara, S. Narasimhan, ''Behavioral Synthesis in CADET, A Case-Based Design Tool,'' *Proceedings of the Seventh Conference on Artificial Intelligence Applications*, IEEE, Miami, Florida, Feb, 1991 .

[Owens 88] Owens, C., ''Domain-Independent Prototype Cases for Planning,'' *Proceedings of the 1988 Case-Based Reasoning Workshop*, Clearwater, Fla., 1988, pp. 302-311.

[Redmond 90] Redmond, M., ''Distributed Cases for Case-Based Reasoning; Facilitating Use of Multiple Cases,'' *Proceedings of the Eigth National Conference on Artificial Intelligence, AAAI-90*, 1990, pp. 304-309.

[Schank 82] Schank, R.C., *Dynamic Memory*, Cambridge University Press, Cambridge, 1982.

[Simoudis & Miller 90] Simoudis, E., J. Miller, ''Validated Retrieval in Case-Based Reasoning,'' *Proceedings of the Eigth National Conference on Artificial Intelligence, AAAI-90*, 1990, pp. 310-315.

[Sycara 87] Sycara, K., *Resolving Adversarial Conflicts: An Approach Integrating Case-Based and Analytic Methods*, PhD dissertation, School of Information and Computer Science Georgia Institute of Technology, 1987.

[Sycara & Navinchandra 89] Sycara, K, D. Navinchandra, ''A Process Model of Case Based Design,'' *Proceedings of the Cognitive Science Society Conference*, Ann Arbor, Michigan, 1989.

[Williams 90] Williams, B., ''Interaction-Based Invention: Designing Novel Devices from First Principles,'' *Proceedings of AAAI-90*, Boston, MA, 1990, pp. 349-356.

Plan Debugging in an Intentional System

Gregg Collins, Lawrence Birnbaum, Bruce Krulwich, and Michael Freed

Northwestern University
The Institute for the Learning Sciences
Evanston, Illinois USA

Abstract

We have developed a model-based approach to learning from plan failures in which an agent uses a model of itself to determine where in its planning or execution the cause of a failure lies. We believe that such an approach constitutes the most promising basis for developing learning models that are capable of deciding for themselves what needs to be learned from a given experience. In addition, such methods appear capable of learning about planning at a very abstract level, and thus of supporting the transfer of knowledge from experience in one domain or task to other domains or tasks.

1 Introduction

Any approach to learning by debugging, or *failure-driven* learning (see, e.g., Sussman, 1975; Schank, 1982; Hayes-Roth, 1983; Kolodner, 1987; Birnbaum and Collins, 1988; Simmons, 1988; Hammond, 1989a), must begin by answering a rather obvious question: What exactly is being debugged? When this paradigm has been applied to the problem of learning to plan, it has generally been taken for granted that the answer is, simply, "plans" (see, e.g., Sussman, 1975; Simmons, 1988).[1] This has historically made a great deal of sense, inasmuch as classical planning work in AI has taken plans to be self-contained, monolithic structures that completely specify the sequence of actions that must be carried out in order to achieve a goal. That is, within the classical tradition, plans have been assumed to be something very much like computer programs. Concomitantly, *planners* have been viewed as devices that take goals and situational constraints as inputs and produce these sorts of complete, program-like structures as outputs; and *plan executors* have been taken to be essentially general-purpose mechanisms for the execution of such program-like structures.

However, this conception of planning has become increasingly untenable as the role of reactivity in goal-directed behavior has become more clearly understood (see, e.g., Hayes-Roth and Hayes-Roth, 1979; Brooks, 1986; Agre and Chapman, 1987; Firby, 1989; Hammond, 1989b). This shift towards reactive models of planning is in part motivated by the recognition that, since the conditions under which an agent's plans will be carried out cannot be completely anticipated, much of the responsibility for determining the particular actions that the agent will perform at a given time must lie in the plan execution component of that agent, rather than resting exclusively with the plans themselves. In order to be capable of carrying out the additional responsibilities required by these models, however, the plan execution component can no longer be taken to be a simple, general-purpose program interpreter. Rather, it must be seen as a highly articulated set of components, each devoted to controlling a particular aspect of behavior.

Consider, for example, a simple plan for keeping a piece safe in chess, formulated as a self-contained, program-like structure:

```
while the piece is on the board do
  if a threat against the piece is detected
  then either   a. move the piece
                b. guard the piece
                c. interpose another piece
                d. remove the threat
                e. ...etc.
```

There are two key points to notice about this plan. First, an agent cannot yield total control of its behavior to a plan of this sort, because the plan will never relinquish control unless a threat is successfully executed and the piece is taken, and the agent cannot

[1] An important exception to this concentration on the individual plans themselves, albeit not within a failure-driven framework, is Carbonell (1986).

afford to execute such a plan to the exclusion of all others. Second, the details of the actions to be carried out in service of this plan cannot be specified in very much detail in advance of detecting a particular threat.

A standard approach to problems of this sort involves *timesharing* or *multitasking*. Applying a similar approach to the current example entails that the above plan must relinquish control of the agent's computational, perceptual, and behavioral resources until such time as a threat against the piece is actually detected. This in turn implies that some executive component of the agent must be charged with the responsibility of returning control to the plan at the appropriate time, i.e., when such a threat is detected. Thus, a task that was formerly the responsibility of individual plans—threat detection—now becomes the responsibility of some specialized component of the agent's architecture.

The increased specialization entailed by this approach also offers opportunities to increase efficiency in much the same way that manufacturing efficiency exploits specialization of workers and equipment on an assembly line: By breaking plans up into constituent pieces, and distributing responsibility for those pieces among components of the agent specialized for those purposes, we can optimize each component for its particular purpose.

In light of the above discussion, we need to reconsider our original question of what is being debugged in a failure-driven approach to learning how to plan. Since a great deal of responsibility for determining what to do has now been shifted to the agent's plan executor, it follows that any adequate approach to learning by debugging must be capable of determining the causes of, and repairs for, performance errors arising from the operation of the plan executor. Approaches that consider only the plans themselves as the objects to be debugged are obviously incapable of making such determinations. In other words, as more responsibility is shifted to the plan executor, the focus of debugging must be shifted there as well.

Changing the focus of debugging in this way yields another benefit: Errors that arise from the operation of the plan executor are the very sorts of errors that are most likely to yield lessons of broad applicability. Because all plans depend upon the plan executor, repairing bugs in this resource has the potential to improve the execution of any plan, regardless of the domain in which it is intended to function. Furthermore, this argument applies not only to the plan executor, but to *any* component of the intentional architecture: Once ubiquitous functions such as threat detection have been assigned to specialized components of the agent's architecture, any improvement in a particular component benefits all plans utilizing that component. Thus, learning that occurs in the context of one task or domain may subsequently yield improved performance in other tasks and domains. In other words, this model serves as the basis for a straightforward approach to achieving *transfer* of learning across tasks and domains, one of the key issues in learning (see, e.g., Krulwich *et al.*, 1990). To enlarge upon our assembly line analogy, when a faulty item is discovered coming out of a factory, one might simply repair that item and continue on; but it is obviously more sensible to determine where in the manufacturing process the fault was introduced, and to see whether anything can be done to avoid such problems in the future. Our thesis is that a similar approach can be applied when learning how to plan. In other words, *when a plan fails, debug the planner, not just the plan.*

The process of debugging an intentional system must, from this perspective, involve determining which component of that system is responsible for the fault. This is a difficult problem inasmuch as the architecture of the agent is, as we have argued above, a rather complex mechanism. Our approach to this problem utilizes *model-based reasoning*, a methodology that has been developed in AI for reasoning about and debugging complex mechanisms such as electronic circuits (see, e.g., Stallman and Sussman, 1977; Davis, 1984; deKleer and Williams, 1987). In this paradigm for debugging, the diagnostic system uses a model of the device being debugged to generate predictions about what the behavior of the device would be if it were functioning properly. These predictions are then compared with measurements performed on the device itself. When a discrepancy is detected, the diagnostic system attempts to determine which of a set of possible device faults is the underlying cause of the discrepancy.

Applied to our problem of learning to plan by debugging, this paradigm becomes the following: A model of the agent's intentional architecture is used to generate predictions about the performance of its plans; deviations from these predictions can then be used to pinpoint where in the mechanism the fault lies. In other words, an intentional agent needs a model of itself in order to adequately diagnose and repair its failures (Birnbaum *et al.*, 1990; Collins and Birnbaum, 1990). Given such a model, the system is able to determine for itself what it needs to learn from a given failure.

The need for a self-model can be justified on psychological grounds as well. Many plans, such as cooking, require waiting for the appropriate moment to perform a particular task. As in the case of detecting and blocking threats described above, an agent cannot afford to idle its resources while waiting for this moment to arrive. A standard technique in such cases is for the agent to set an *alarm* that will return its attention to the activity when the task needs to be performed. To set up such an alarm, the agent must have some notion of the kinds of events that its control allocation component is sensitive to—in other words, a model of the properties of this component. Mnemonic devices, for example the proverbial string tied around one's finger, employ similar techniques to attack a slightly different problem, that of retrieving a piece of information at the appropriate time. To develop and employ such techniques, the agent must not only have a model of its attention focussing mechanisms, but also of how its memory works. To the extent that these techniques work, the naive psychological models upon which they are based must reflect something real about the underlying structure of the agent.

2 Modelling the agent: Threat detection

A central issue in our approach is the development of explicit models for intentional agents that can be used in debugging their performance. We have developed simple models of a number of important planning components, including threat detection, execution scheduling, projection, and case retrieval and adaptation, and applied them to learning within the context of competitive games such as chess and checkers (see, e.g., Collins *et al.*, 1989; Birnbaum *et al.*, 1990; Birnbaum *et al.*, 1991). In this section we will describe our model of threat detection in a simple agent.

We model threat detection as a simple rule-based process (Birnbaum *et al.*, 1990). The planner's threat detection knowledge is encoded as a set of condition-action rules, with each rule being responsible for recognizing a particular type of threat. In chess, for example, the planner could be expected to possess rules specifying, among other things, the various board configurations that indicate that an attack on a piece is imminent.

A set of threat recognition rules does not, in itself, completely determine the behavior of a threat detection mechanism, since the planner must still decide how and when these rules should be evaluated, and what will be done with the results. In particular, the planner can vary the particular rules to be evaluated, the frequency with which they are checked, the domain over which they are evaluated, and the extent to which previously detected threats are cached in memory as opposed to being recomputed each time the rules are evaluated.

Threats are placed on a threat queue when detected:

$\forall x \exists t \;\; t \leq ert(x) \;\&\; detect(x, t) \rightarrow added\text{-}to(x, T, t)$

Threats remain on the threat queue until explicitly removed:

$\forall x, t_1, t_2 \;\; added\text{-}to(x, T, t_1) \;\&\; t_2 \leq ert(x) \;\&$
$\sim\exists t_r \;\; (t1 \leq t_r \leq t2 \;\&\; removed\text{-}from(x, T, t_r))$
$\rightarrow member\text{-}of(x, T, t_2)$

A rule is capable of detecting a threat at a particular time if there exist bindings such that evaluating the rule with those bindings at that time would result in the detection of the threat:

$\forall x, r, t, \theta \;\; could\text{-}detect(r, x, t, \theta) \leftrightarrow$
$evaluate\text{-}rule(r, \theta, t) \rightarrow detect(x, t)$

A rule can detect a threat in time if there is a time while that threat is active, but before it can be realized, when the rule could detect that threat:

$\forall x, r, \theta \;\; could\text{-}detect\text{-}in\text{-}time(r, x, \theta) \leftrightarrow$
$\exists t \; active(x, t) \;\&\; t \leq ert(x) \;\&\; could\text{-}detect(r, x, t, \theta)$

Our rules are capable of detecting all active threats in time:

$\forall x \;\; \exists r, \theta \;\; could\text{-}detect\text{-}in\text{-}time(r, x, \theta)$

Any threat that could be detected without attention focussing can still be detected with such focussing:

$\forall x \;\; (\exists r, \theta \;\; could\text{-}detect\text{-}in\text{-}time(r, x, \theta)) \rightarrow$
$(\exists r, \theta, t \;\; subset\text{-}of(\theta, focus\text{-}results(t)) \;\&$
$active(x, t) \;\&\; t \leq ert(x) \;\&\; could\text{-}detect(r, x, t, \theta))$

The bindings available at a given time are the results of applying all of the focus rules at that time:

$\forall t \;\; focus\text{-}results(t) =$
$union\text{-}over(F, focus\text{-}rule\text{-}evaluation\text{-}result(f, t))$

At each turn, all of the threat rules are applied using bindings provided by the focus rules:

$\forall r, t \;\; evaluate\text{-}rule(r, focus\text{-}results(t), t)$

A threat is removed from the threat queue when it is no longer active:

$\forall x, t \;\; remove\text{-}from(x, T, t) \leftrightarrow$
$member\text{-}of(x, T, t) \;\&\; \sim active(x, t)$

Figure 1: Partial model of threat-detection[2]

---

[2] The predicate "ert" stands for *earliest realization time*, i.e., the earliest time at which the threatened action can be expected to occur.

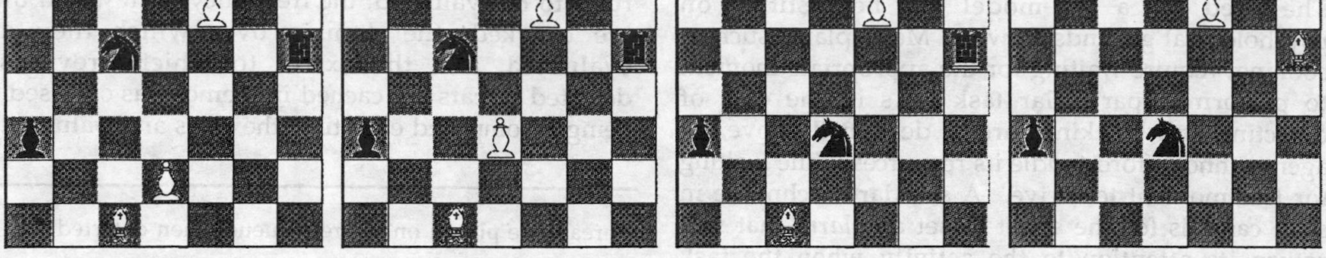
(a) (b) (c) (d)

Figure 2: A discovered attack

Let's consider this last issue in more detail. Broadly speaking, the planner has a choice between two strategies for threat detection: It can recompute the set of outstanding threats each time it checks its rules, or it can incrementally compute this set by noting the changes that have occurred since the previous check. In turn-taking games, such as chess, the latter approach is arguably more efficient, and indeed appears to be the one employed by humans.

In order to benefit from the incremental approach, however, a planner must find a way to ensure that it can detect new threats without having to *re*-detect all of the old threats, since otherwise it is in effect doing all of the work entailed by the recomputation approach. Given the rule-based framework for threat-detection described above, focussing on threats resulting from changes can be implemented as a set of restrictions on the domain of application of the threat detection rules. In our model these restrictions are themselves implemented as a set of *focus rules* that specify the domain over which the threat detection rules will be applied.

The above is a rather brief outline of the threat detection model we have developed. A portion of the model is shown in figure 1.

3 A case study: Discovered attacks

The model of threat detection described above was developed as part of an account of learning in competitive situations—in particular, chess. A central prediction of the model is that if a threat exists, it will be detected. In our application of the model to competitive planning, this prediction is crucial, inasmuch as the decision to block a particular threat depends upon the assumption that all outstanding threats have been taken into consideration, in order to rule out the possibility that a higher priority threat exists. There are, however, a number of reasons why this prediction might fail, and each of these presents an opportunity to learn a different lesson.

Consider, in particular, the example of *discovered attacks* in chess, in which the movement of one piece opens a line of attack for another piece. Novices often fall prey to such attacks, and the key point is that this is *not* because they fail to understand the mechanism of the threat, i.e., the way in which the piece can move to make the capture. Instead, the problem appears to be one of focus: Novices simply fail to consider new threats arising from pieces other than the one just moved. In other words, the problem lies not in their ability to detect the given threat in principle, but rather in their decisions about where to look for threats in practice. In fact, without such a distinction—e.g., if the method for detecting threats were non-incremental in the sense discussed earlier, and entailed scanning the entire board after each move—the problem of discovered attacks, and the need to distinguish them from other sorts of attacks, would not even arise. The model of threat detection described in the last section reflects this distinction by introducing a notion of *focus rules* that limit the application of *threat detection rules*. The former embody knowledge of where to look; the latter, of what to look for. Our system is capable of learning both sorts of rules, depending upon the cause of the failure in a given situation.

The following example depicts a scenario in which the system falls prey to a discovered attack, and thereby learns to improve the attention-focusing portion of its threat detection component. In figure 2(a), the system's opponent is to move. In figure 2(b), we see the result of the opponent's move, which is to advance one of its pawns one square. This opens a discovered attack by the opponent's bishop on the system's rook. However, because of overly restrictive attention-focusing, the system fails to notice this threat, despite the fact that it has a threat detection rule which, if applied to the appropriate portions of the board, would have in fact detected the threat. In figure 2(c), we see that the system has chosen to capture the opponent's pawn with its knight, leaving the threat on the rook unaddressed. Finally, in figure 2(d), the opponent carries out the threat and captures the rook.

Let's examine the system's decision-making in some detail. Any decision to make a particular move must be based upon some assessment of how well that move compares to the available alternatives. Such a comparison, in turn, depends upon the ability to project the implications of each alternative considered. Once an alternative is selected, relevant aspects of the projection made in service of that choice become, in effect, predictions about the future course of events upon which the rationality of the system's chosen action depends. These predictions, in turn, depend upon assumptions stemming from the system's self-model, for example, the assumption that its threat detection component is capable of detecting all outstanding threats. The failure of one of these predictions leads the system to attempt to determine which component of its decision-making process was at fault, as described above. Our approach to this problem entails determining how and why the faulty prediction was originally formulated. A record of the reasoning by which the model gave rise to the predictions is kept in the form of explicit *justification structures* (see, e.g., deKleer, Doyle, Steele, and Sussman, 1977; Doyle, 1979). Diagnosis, then, consists of tracing back through these justification structures in order to determine where the fault lies.

In this particular case, the relevant prediction is that capturing the opponent's pawn would be of greater value than blocking any extant threat. When the opponent takes the system's rook, this prediction is violated. The justification structure underlying the prediction is roughly the following: The system believes that no such threat exists because it has not detected such a threat and it assumes that it can detect all threats. The latter assumption, in turn, is justified by the assumption that there is a threat rule capable of detecting any given threat, and the assumption that the threat rules have been evaluated using appropriate bindings. Finally, the latter is justified by the assumption that the system's focus rules have generated the appropriate bindings. This justification structure, and the assumptions it contains, are derived from the model of threat detection described above.

There are two components of interest that might be at fault in this case: the *threat rules*, and the *focus rules*. Determining which component is at fault means exonerating all of the alternatives. In general, exonerating an alternative can require an arbitrary amount of inference. However, in this case the model's formulation of attention focussing includes the assumption that any threat which can be detected without using the focus rules to delimit the bindings utilized by the threat rules can also be detected using only those bindings (see figure 1 above). Attempting to fault this assumption means attempting to show its negation, which suggests the following experiment: First, evaluate all threat rules over the situation without using any focus rules to delimit their bindings. If this process results in the system detecting the threat, then the fault lies in the set of attention focusing rules; if not, it lies in the set of threat rules. In this instance, the problem lies in the focus rules. Once that has been determined, the system retrieves a specification for focus rules, and uses this specification in conjunction with the current circumstances to acquire a new focus rule via explanation-based learning (see, e.g., DeJong and Mooney, 1986; Mitchell *et al.*, 1986). This example has been implemented in our test-bed system (described in Collins, Birnbaum, and Krulwich, 1989). Once the system has uncovered and repaired the deficiency in its attention focussing, it no longer falls prey to discovered attacks, regardless of the particular pieces involved or their location on the board.

4 Conclusion

We have developed a model-based approach to learning from plan failures in which an agent uses a model of itself to determine where in its planning or execution the cause of a failure lies. We believe that such an approach constitutes the most promising basis for developing learning models that are capable of deciding for themselves what needs to be learned from a given experience. In addition, such methods appear capable of learning about planning at a very abstract level, and thus of supporting the transfer of knowledge from experience in one domain or task to other domains or tasks.

Acknowledgments

We thank Matt Brand and Louise Pryor for many useful discussions. This work was supported in part by the Office of Naval Research under contract N00014-89-J-3217, and by the Defense Advanced Research Projects Agency, monitored by the Air Force Office of Scientific Research under contract F49620-88-C-0058. The Institute for the Learning Sciences was established in 1989 with the support of Andersen

Consulting, part of The Arthur Andersen Worldwide Organization. The Institute receives additional support from Ameritech, an Institute Partner, and from IBM.

References

Agre, P., and Chapman, D. 1987. Pengi: An implementation of a theory of activity. *Proceedings of the 1987 AAAI Conference*, Seattle, WA, pp. 268-272.

Birnbaum, L., and Collins, G. 1988. The transfer of experience across planning domains through the acquisition of abstract strategies. *Proceedings of the 1988 Workshop on Case-Based Reasoning*, Clearwater Beach, FL, pp. 61-79.

Birnbaum, L., Collins, G., Brand, M., Freed, M., Krulwich, B., and Pryor, L. 1991. A model-based approach to the construction of adaptive case-based planning systems. To appear in *Proceedings of the 1991 Workshop on Case-Based Reasoning*, Washington, DC.

Birnbaum, L., Collins, G., Freed, M., and Krulwich, B. 1990. Model-based diagnosis of planning failures. *Proceedings of the 1990 AAAI Conference*, Boston, MA, pp. 318-323.

Brooks, R. 1986. A robust layered control system for a mobile robot. *IEEE Journal of Robotics and Automation*, vol. 2, no. 1.

Carbonell, J. 1986. Derivational analogy: A theory of reconstructive problem solving and expertise acquisition. In R. Michalski, J. Carbonell, and T. Mitchell, eds., *Machine Learning: An Artificial Intelligence Approach, Volume II*, Morgan Kaufmann, Los Altos, CA, pp. 371-392.

Collins, G., and Birnbaum, L. 1990. Problem-solver state descriptions as abstract indices for case retrieval. *Working Notes of the 1990 AAAI Spring Symposium on Case-Based Reasoning*, Stanford, CA, pp. 32-35.

Collins, G., Birnbaum, L., and Krulwich, B. 1989. An adaptive model of decision-making in planning. *Proceedings of the Eleventh IJCAI*, Detroit, MI, pp. 511-516.

Davis, R. 1984. Diagnostic reasoning based on structure and behavior. *Artificial Intelligence*, vol. 24, pp. 347-410.

DeJong, G., and Mooney, R. 1986. Explanation-based learning: An alternative view. *Machine Learning*, vol. 1, pp. 145-176.

deKleer, J., Doyle, J., Steele, G., and Sussman, G. 1977. AMORD: Explicit control of reasoning. *Proceedings of the ACM Symposium on Artificial Intelligence and Programming Languages*, Rochester, NY, pp. 116-125.

deKleer, J., and Williams, B. 1987. Diagnosing multiple faults. *Artificial Intelligence*, vol. 32, pp. 97-130.

Doyle, J. 1979. A truth maintenance system. *Artificial Intelligence*, vol. 12, pp. 231-272.

Firby, R. 1989. Adaptive execution in complex dynamic worlds. Research report no. 672, Yale University, Dept. of Computer Science, New Haven, CT.

Hammond, K. 1989a. *Case-Based Planning: Viewing Planning as a Memory Task.* Academic Press, San Diego.

Hammond, K. 1989b. Opportunistic memory. *Proceedings of the Eleventh IJCAI*, Detroit, MI, pp. 504-510.

Hayes-Roth, F. 1983. Using proofs and refutations to learn from experience. In R. Michalski, J. Carbonell, and T. Mitchell, eds., *Machine Learning: An Artificial Intelligence Approach, Vol. 1*, Tioga, Palo Alto, CA, pp. 221-240.

Kolodner, J. 1987. Capitalizing on failure through case-based inference. *Proceedings of the Ninth Cognitive Science Conference*, Seattle, WA, pp. 715-726.

Krulwich, B., Collins, G., and Birnbaum, L. 1990. Cross-domain transfer of planning strategies: Alternative approaches. *Proceedings of the Twelfth Cognitive Science Conference*, Cambridge, MA, pp. 954-961.

Mitchell, T., Keller, R., and Kedar-Cabelli, S. 1986. Explanation-based generalization: A unifying view. *Machine Learning*, vol. 1, pp. 47-80.

Schank, R. 1982. *Dynamic Memory: A Theory of Reminding and Learning in Computers and People.* Cambridge University Press, Cambridge, England.

Simmons, R. 1988. A theory of debugging plans and interpretations. *Proceedings of the 1988 AAAI Conference*, St. Paul, MN, pp. 94-99.

Stallman, R., and Sussman, G. 1977. Forward reasoning and dependency-directed backtracking in a system for computer-aided circuit analysis. *Artificial Intelligence*, vol. 9, pp. 135-196.

Sussman, G. 1975. *A Computer Model of Skill Acquisition.* American Elsevier, New York.

COGNITIVE MODELING

Cognitive Modeling 2

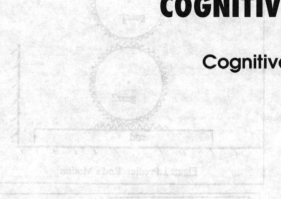

Reasoning Visually about Spatial Interactions

N. Hari Narayanan and B. Chandrasekaran
Laboratory for Artificial Intelligence Research
Department of Computer and Information Science
The Ohio State University
Columbus, Ohio 43210
U. S. A.

Abstract

This paper is concerned with how diagrams can be used for reasoning about spatial interactions of objects. We describe a computational approach that emulates the human capability of predicting interactions of simple objects depicted in two dimensional diagrams. Three core aspects of this approach are a visual representation scheme that has symbolic and imaginal parts, the use of visual processes to manipulate the imaginal part and to extract spatial information, and visual cases that encode experiential knowledge and play a central role in the generation of spatial inferences. These aspects are described and the approach is illustrated with an example. Then we show that reasoning with images is an emerging and promising area of investigation by discussing computational and cognitive research on imagery.

1 Introduction

Humans quite often make use of spatial information implicit in diagrams to make inferences. For example, anyone familiar with the operation of gears will be able to solve the problem posed in Figure 1 by imagining the rotary motion of gear1 being transmitted to the rod through gear2, resulting in the horizontal translation of the rod until it hits the wall. In such situations humans reason about spatial interactions not only by using conceptual knowledge, but also by extracting constraints on such interactions from a perceived image. This integrated use of visual knowledge (about spatial configurations) from the diagram and conceptual knowledge (such as the rigidity or plasticity of objects involved) is a very interesting phenomenon. In this paper we illustrate a computational approach that emulates this capability for solving simple motion prediction problems.

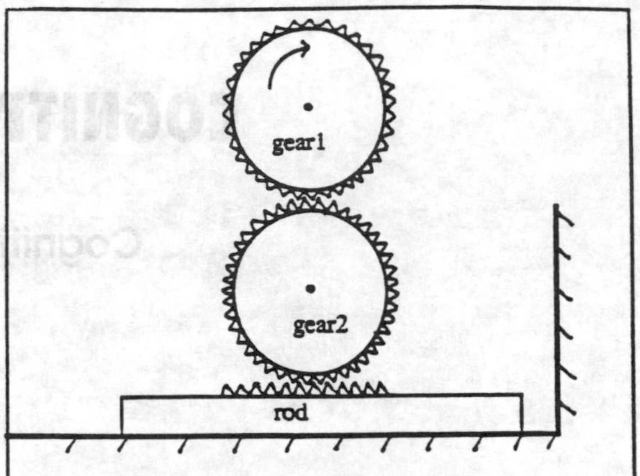

Figure 1. Predict Rod's Motion

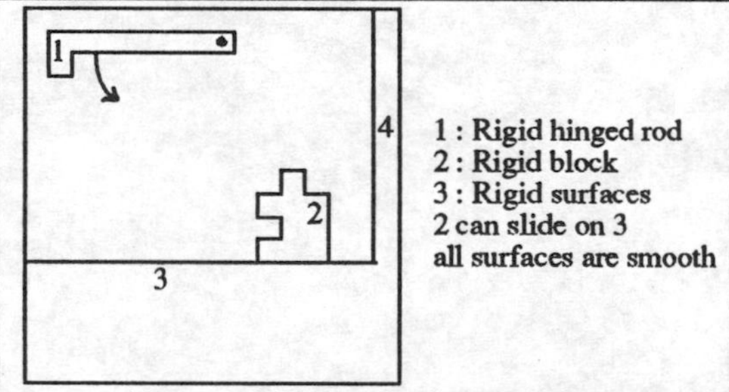

Figure 2. A Motion Prediction Problem

2 The Approach

2.1 Motion Prediction Problems

The class of problems we address is the following: given a two dimensional diagram of the spatial configuration of a set of objects, one or more initial motions of objects and relevant conceptual information about them, predict the subsequent dynamics of the configuration. Figure 2 shows a typical example.

2.2 Cognitive Inspiration

There is considerable evidence in cognitive science for the use of mental images by people when solving problems [Kosslyn, 1981]. Furthermore, introspective reports of people when given a diagram like Figures 1 or 2 and asked to predict motions indicated that by looking at the diagram they were able to visualize the motion of one object causing that of another through physical contact. They appeared to be using (the image of) the diagram in front of them directly to simulate motions in their minds. These reports indicated the following.

(1) Given a diagram depicting the problem, humans quite rapidly focus on localities of potential interactions.

(2) People also seem to simulate or project the motion to determine the nature of interactions that will occur.

(3) For reasoning about the dynamics (e.g., how will motion be transmitted after a collision?) humans bring conceptual knowledge (e.g., gears are rigid objects) and experiential knowledge (e.g., if an object collides with another, it typically transmits motion in the same direction) to bear on the problem.

We have developed an approach that emulates these capabilities.

2.3 Representation

The specification of a motion prediction problem consists of a scene depicting the spatial configuration of the objects involved and conceptual information about their properties (see Figure 2). The spatial configuration is represented using a "visual representation" while conceptual information about object properties is represented declaratively and linked with corresponding object descriptions in the visual representation. In our computer model the visual representation of a problem specification is interactively constructed prior to problem solving, whereas in the case of humans perceptual processes deliver such representations.

Mental representation of visual information and its relation to the phenomenon of mental imagery have been the foci of considerable research in cognitive science [Biederman, 1990; Finke, 1989; Kosslyn, 1981; Pylyshyn, 1981]. A central issue here is the question of how mental imagery that appears to be analogic in nature can arise from underlying representations that are considered to be propositional. One hypothesis regarding this issue [Chandrasekaran and Narayanan, 1990] is that representations for different sensory modalities are operated upon by interpreters that provide privileged operations specific to that modality, including binding the symbols in the representation to perceptual primitives in the corresponding sensory domain. Thus our answer to the above question is that symbolic representations of visual information are interpreted by mechanisms that are specialized to the visual modality and which provide operations tailored to this modality. These operations construct mental images using perceptual primitives in the visual domain. Visual representations in our computer model are therefore structured as multi-level hierarchies that contain *imaginal* descriptions and *symbolic* descriptions of the object configuration. Each level of the hierarchy contains a symbolic description and an imaginal description of the configuration at a certain resolution. The symbolic description is built from parametrized shape primitives like circles, rectangles, etc., whereas the imaginal description is a two dimensional pixel array of fixed width and height in which a configuration is depicted by object boundaries and is implemented as a bitmap. In the rest of the paper we will use the term "diagram" to refer to this boundary-based rendering of the object configuration. Thus the visual representation is dual (symbolic and imaginal) in nature. The two types of mental representations (surface images and deep encodings) that Kosslyn [1981] proposes reflect a similar duality.

The most interesting property of this representation is that it simultaneously provides abstract symbolic descriptions of an object configuration and directly captures, in the imaginal descriptions, specific spatial information about the object configuration (the extent of contact between two surfaces, for example). The justification for our decision to structure the symbolic descriptions in terms of parametrized shape primitives stems from shape representation theories that utilize primitives like geons [Biederman, 1990] and generalized cones [Marr and Nishihara, 1976]. Multiple levels of description are provided in the representation to allow visual processes to operate at different levels of resolution.

2.4 Reasoning

The basic model of reasoning is as follows. The system goes through a sequence of deliberative states. This sequence corresponds to the changes that the initial object configuration undergoes due to motion and interaction of objects. Each deliberative state represents a particular configuration that the objects assume at some point during this evolution of behavior. What distinguishes a deliberative state from other states is that it represents a configuration in which an interaction (such as collision) has occurred that will change the subsequent behavior of objects. The term deliberative refers to the necessity of "deliberation" that arises at these states in order to predict future behavior of objects. A significant characteristic of this deliberation is the combined use of perceptual information from the diagram and conceptual knowledge relevant to the situation.

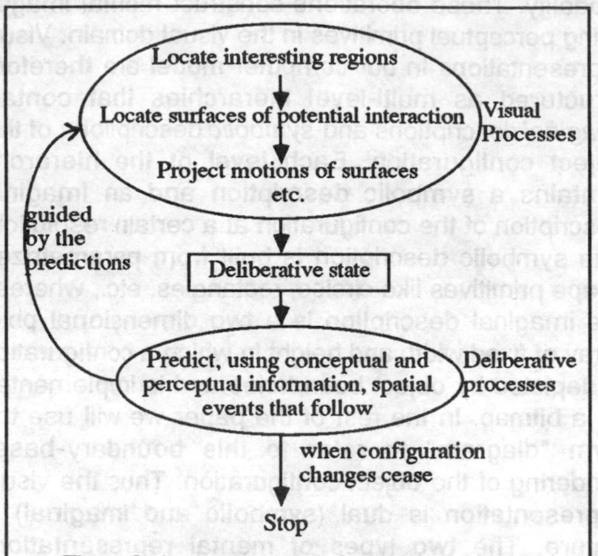

Figure 3. A process model of visual reasoning

The transition between deliberative states is accomplished by two groups of processes. In one, purely visual operations such as attention-focussing, scanning, boundary-tracking, and contact-detection are used to identify significant aspects of the current object configuration from the diagram (e.g., locating interesting regions, identifying surfaces of potential interaction, etc.), to reason about how the configuration will evolve (e.g., project surface motions), and to detect the next deliberative state. A deliberative state is detected by watching out for certain events as the configuration depicted in the diagram changes. The establishment of a new contact between objects, the elimination of a previously existing contact, the establishment of a new support relationship between objects, and the removal of a support relationship are some examples of events which indicate a deliberative state. Motivations behind and justifications for these processes derive from the extensive literature on mental imagery, some of which are discussed in section 3, and the work of Chapman [1990] and Ullman [1985] on visual routines. This group of processes corresponds to the human cognitive process of "imagining".

The second group of processes accomplish the aforementioned task of deliberation. Here knowledge about how interacting physical objects tend to behave under various conditions is used to predict the behavior of objects following the current deliberative state. We take a specific position on the form in which this knowledge is available and the way in which it is utilized. This is described next. A process model of visual reasoning is shown in Figure 3.

We believe that the knowledge humans bring to

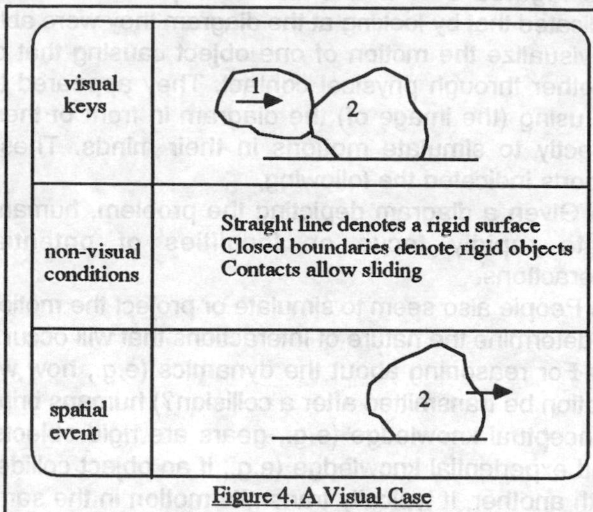

Figure 4. A Visual Case

bear on making spatial inferences in similar situations is mostly acquired through experience, and so in the computer model experiential knowledge has been given a central role in deciding how to proceed from a deliberative state. Experiential memory is considered to be an organized and indexed collection of cases [Schank, 1982] and case-based reasoning is a computational paradigm for modelling the role of experience in problem solving [Kolodner and Simpson, 1989]. Therefore, representational structures called "visual cases" have been developed to encode knowledge applicable at deliberative states and to facilitate inferencing. Each case represents a typical spatial event. Since cases represent experiential knowledge, they may not be logically parsimonious or mutually exclusive. A visual case has three parts. One is information about spatial configurations to which the case is applicable. Cases are called "visual" because this information is visual in nature and is the "key" by which relevant cases get selected during reasoning. It may also be viewed as an "abstract" image that depicts the essential aspects of configurations to which the case is applicable. Because of this abstractness a case can be matched with a variety of specific configurations. This property obviates the need for a large number of cases. The second part is non-visual information that qualifies the visual part further and it is used for deciding the applicability of a case to a particular situation. The third part is a predicted event affecting objects in the spatial configuration represented by the case. This event may specify a state change (e.g., a directional force being applied on an object), a continuous change (e.g., an object moving in a particular direction), etc.

Humans are skilled at blending perceptual and conceptual information in generating spatial inferences. To illustrate this, first consider your

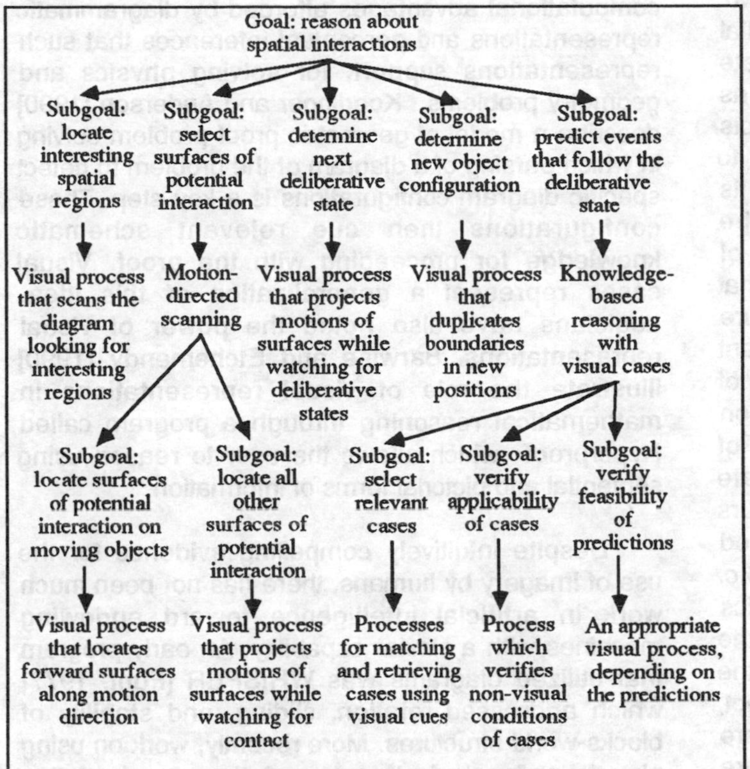

Figure 5. Execution trace for the example

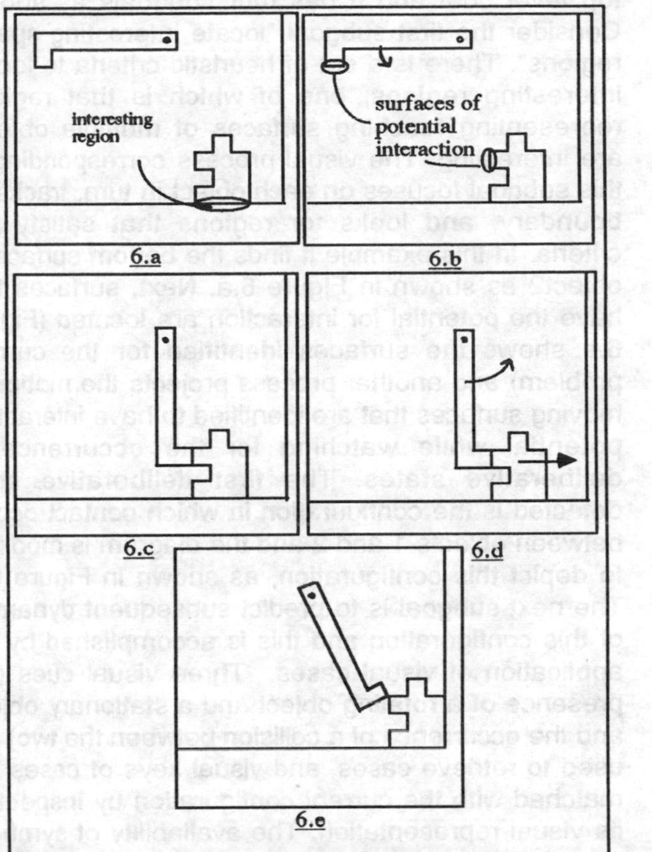

Figure 6. Diagram Snapshots

prediction about the motion of object2 after object1 collides with it, given the problem specification of Figure 2, and then notice how this prediction will change if the specifications were changed to indicate that object1 is non-rigid (say, made of rubber) and that object2 is fixed on surface3. The visual and non-visual parts of a case explicitly capture this aspect. Thus the intent of visual cases is to represent simple chunks of experiential knowledge about spatial events that humans typically have, and to model the blending of conceptual and perceptual information in making spatial inferences. An example of typical knowledge about spatial events is "a rigid object resting on a rigid flat surface, when collided by a moving rigid object, will tend to slide in the same direction". The schematic of a corresponding visual case is shown in Figure 4.

After a deliberative state is detected, visual cases are retrieved and applied to predict events that follow. The retrieval of cases relevant to the spatial configuration in the diagram is based on visual cues. From among the retrieved cases, applicable ones are selected by using information about object properties (which is available as part of problem specification) to verify the non-visual parts of the cases. Events predicted by the applicable cases are further pruned by verifying, through visual processes, their feasibility in the current object configuration. The remaining events serve to guide subsequent steps of reasoning. Since a case brings conceptual knowledge to bear on visual reasoning, this mechanism of inference may be viewed as a computational realization of cognitive penetrability or the influence of tacit knowledge on mental imagery [Pylyshyn, 1981].

2.5 An Example

In this section we present a problem solving episode in some detail. The specification of the problem, which includes a depiction of an initial configuration of objects, an initial motion and relevant non-visual properties of the objects, is shown in Figure 2. The goal is to predict all resulting motions by reasoning about spatial interactions that will occur among the objects. In our computer model control of reasoning is done by a procedure that generates goals and subgoals, and activates relevant processes to achieve them. Thus an execution trace will appear as a tree consisting of goals, subgoals, and processes. The goal generation follows the process model in Figure 3.

Figure 5 shows a partial execution trace for this example. "Reason about spatial interactions" is the top level goal and it has four subgoals as shown. Consider the first subgoal "locate interesting spatial regions". There is a set of heuristic criteria to locate interesting regions, one of which is that regions representing touching surfaces of multiple objects are interesting. The visual process corresponding to this subgoal focuses on each object in turn, tracks its boundary, and looks for regions that satisfy the criteria. In this example it finds the bottom surface of object2 as shown in Figure 6.a. Next, surfaces that have the potential for interaction are located (Figure 6.b shows the surfaces identified for the current problem) and another process projects the motion of moving surfaces that are identified to have interaction potential while watching for the occurrence of deliberative states. The first deliberative state detected is the configuration in which contact occurs between objects 1 and 2 and the diagram is modified to depict this configuration, as shown in Figure 6.c. The next subgoal is to predict subsequent dynamics of this configuration and this is accomplished by the application of visual cases. Three visual cues (the presence of a rotating object and a stationary object, and the occurrence of a collision between the two) are used to retrieve cases, and visual keys of cases are matched with the current configuration by inspecting its visual representation. The availability of symbolic descriptions as well as diagrams in the visual representation allows the matching of visual keys to proceed at an abstract level without recourse to techniques like template matching. A visual case similar to the one shown in Figure 4 (except that the moving object is undergoing rotation) is found to be relevant and applicable, and the event that it predicts is found to be feasible in the current configuration. Non-visual conditions associated with this case are similar to those in Figure 4 and are easily verified from the problem specification. The resulting prediction is shown in Figure 6.d. As the process model shows, after this step the entire cycle is repeated and in the next detected deliberative state object2 has collided with surface4. This time a case that predicts cessation of motion gets applied and Figure 6.e shows the final configuration.

3 Related Work

In this section we present computational and cognitive research which touches upon imagery, in support of our contention that imaginal reasoning is an emerging research area that is highly promising. Cognitive scientists have demonstrated not only the powerful role of imagery in human problem solving but also the advantages of incorporating similar reasoning capabilities in computer programs. For example, Larkin and Simon [1987] persuasively argue for the computational advantages afforded by diagrammatic representations and perceptual inferences that such representations support, for solving physics and geometry problems. Koedinger and Anderson [1990] describe a model of geometric proof problem solving in which parsing of a diagram of the problem to detect specific diagram configurations is a key step. These configurations then cue relevant schematic knowledge for proceeding with the proof. Visual cases represent a generalization of this idea. Logicians have also noted the power of visual representations. Barwise and Etchemendy [1990] illustrate the role of visual representations in mathematical reasoning through a program called Hyperproof which allows the user to reason using sentential and pictorial forms of information.

Despite intuitively compelling evidence for the use of imagery by humans, there has not been much work in artificial intelligence toward endowing machines with a similar capability. An early program that utilized diagrams was WHISPER [Funt, 1977] which addressed rotation, sliding, and stability of blocks-world structures. More recently, work on using pictorial or "analogical" representations for simulating the behavior of strings and liquids in space has been reported [Gardin and Meltzer, 1989]. Shrager [1990] describes a computational model of understanding laser operation in which reinterpretation processes utilize event depictions in an iconic memory as well as in a propositional memory. The research on computational modelling of the cognitive process of spatial reasoning with diagrams [Narayanan, 1991] is yet another step towards realizing the full potential of imaginal reasoning by computers.

4 Concluding Remarks

We have described a novel approach to reasoning about spatial interactions. Since our aim in this paper has been to provide the reader with an overview of all significant aspects of visual reasoning within the limited space available, the descriptions have been necessarily schematic in character. Further details on components of this approach - structure of visual representations, how visual processes are composed from basic visual operations, indexing and adaptation of visual cases, the computer program that implements this model, etc. - can be obtained from [Narayanan, 1991].

The advantages of using diagrams in this approach arise from the property that spatial information such as obstacles to motion or pathways that guide motion are directly evident in images. Our approach is not only intuitive, but flexible as well.

Objects which have irregular shapes that will make their algebraic representations complex can be represented and reasoned about in the same way as regular objects if diagrams are used.

As Forbus and colleagues rightly point out [Forbus *et al.*, 1987], there can be no purely qualitative method for spatial reasoning. What is required is to integrate qualitative and quantitative methods so that qualitative ones provide approximate solutions that serve to focus the application of quantitative methods to only those aspects of the initial solutions that require more precision or further refinement. With this goal in mind, we are currently investigating the integration of visual reasoning with other qualitative and quantitative methods [Narayanan and Chandrasekaran, 1991].

Acknowledgments

A discussion with Stephen Kosslyn provided inspiration during the early stages and Jeff Shrager and Janet Kolodner helped clarify many issues during the course of this research. We also thank the anonymous referees for their suggestions. This research is supported by DARPA & AFOSR contract # F-49620-89-C-0110 and by AFOSR grant # 890250.

References

[Barwise and Etchemendy, 1990] J. Barwise and J. Etchemendy. Visual information and valid reasoning. In W. Zimmerman, (Ed.), *Visualization in Mathematics.* Mathematical Association of America, Washington D. C., 1990.

[Biederman, 1990] I. Biederman. Higher-level vision. In D. N. Osherson, S. M. Kosslyn, and J. M. Hollerbach, (Eds.), *An Invitation to Cognitive Science, Volume 2: Visual Cognition and Action*, MIT Press, Cambridge, MA, 1990.

[Chandrasekaran and Narayanan, 1990] B. Chandrasekaran and N. H. Narayanan. Integrating imagery and visual representations. In *Proc. 12th Annual Conference of the Cognitive Science Society*, pp. 670-678, Boston, MA, 1990.

[Chapman, 1990] D. Chapman. Intermediate vision: architecture, implementation, and use. Technical Report TR-90-06, Teleos Research, Palo Alto, CA, 1990.

[Finke, 1989] R. A. Finke. *Principles of Mental Imagery.* MIT Press, Cambridge, MA, 1989.

[Forbus *et al.*, 1987] K. D. Forbus, P. Nielsen, and B. Faltings. Qualitative kinematics: a framework. In *Proc. 10th International Joint Conference on Artificial Intelligence*, pp. 430-436, Milano, Italy, 1987.

[Funt, 1977] B. V. Funt. WHISPER: a problem solving system utilizing diagrams and a parallel processing retina. In *Proc. 5th International Joint Conference on Artificial Intelligence*, pp. 459-464, Cambridge, MA, 1977.

[Gardin and Meltzer, 1989] F. Gardin and B. Meltzer. Analogical representations of naive physics. *Artificial Intelligence Journal*, 38:139-159, 1989.

[Koedinger and Anderson, 1990] K. R. Koedinger and J. R. Anderson. Abstract planning and perceptual chunks: elements of expertise in geometry. *Cognitive Science*, 14:511-550, 1990.

[Kolodner and Simpson, 1989] J. L. Kolodner and R. L. Simpson. The MEDIATOR: analysis of an early case-based problem solver. *Cognitive Science*, 13:507-549, 1989.

[Kosslyn, 1981] S. M. Kosslyn. The medium and the message in mental imagery: a theory. *Psychological Review*, 88:46-66, 1981.

[Larkin and Simon, 1987] J. H. Larkin and H. A. Simon. Why a diagram is (sometimes) worth ten thousand words. *Cognitive Science*, 11:65-99, 1987.

[Marr and Nishihara, 1976] D. Marr and H. K. Nishihara. Representation and recognition of the spatial organization of three dimensional shapes. AI Memo 377, Artificial Intelligence Laboratory, MIT, Cambridge, MA, 1976.

[Narayanan, 1991] N. H. Narayanan. A study of representations and processes for reasoning visually about spatial interactions. Doctoral Dissertation, Department of Computer & Information Science, The Ohio State University, Columbus, OH, forthcoming.

[Narayanan and Chandrasekaran, 1991] N. H. Narayanan and B. Chandrasekaran. Integration of qualitative and quantitative methods in visual reasoning. In *Proc. 2nd Conference on AI, Simulation and Planning in High Autonomy Systems*, pp. 272-278, Cocoa Beach, FL, 1991.

[Pylyshyn, 1981] Z. W. Pylyshyn. The imagery debate: analogue media versus tacit knowledge. *Psychological Review*, 88:16-45, 1981.

[Schank, 1982] R. Schank. *Dynamic Memory: A Theory of Learning in Computers and People.* Cambridge University Press, New York, 1982.

[Shrager, 1990] J. Shrager. Commonsense perception and the psychology of theory formation. In J. Shrager and P. Langely, (Eds.), *Computational Models of Scientific Discovery and Theory Formation.* Morgan Kaufmann, San Mateo, CA, 1990.

[Ullman, 1985] S. Ullman. Visual routines. In S. Pinker, (Ed.), *Visual Cognition.* MIT Press, Cambridge, MA, 1985.

A Cognitive Model of Figure Segregation

Akira SHIMAYA and **Isamu YOROIZAWA**
NTT Human Interface Laboratories
1-2356 Take Yokosuka-shi Kanagawa 238-03 Japan
E-mail: shimaya%nttcvg.NTT.jp@relay.cs.net yoro%nttcvg.NTT.jp@relay.cs.net

Abstract

When humans look at a complex and ambiguous figure, they divide it into several elemental figures. This human visual characteristic is called figure segregation. There is a problem when constructing a cognitive model for figure segregation. That is, one interpretation is selected by most people for some figures, and several interpretations are selected almost equally for other figures. This paper discusses the deciding selection frequency problem. First, a geometrical function is introduced for describing line figures. Next, several Gestalt features (such as symmetry, continuity, etc) are defined using the function. Then, by applying linear multiple regression analysis, the characteristic value of each interpretation is obtained, and the selection frequency is calculated. The results of a psychological experiment show that the model proposed here can simulate human visual perception in figure segregation fairly well.

1 Introduction

What is figure segregation ? When humans look at a complex and ambiguous figure, they divide it into several elemental figures (Figure 1). In psychology, this characteristic of human visual perception is called figure segregation. How can we construct a cognitive model of figure segregation ? Why is it difficult ? It is difficult because there are two processes to be considered.

(1) How to create a small number of natural interpretations from an infinite number of possible interpretations.

(2) How to decide selection frequencies among those interpretations. (in other words, how to estimate which interpretation will be selected by what percentage.)

Although research on figure segregation modeling is very limited, some research has been reported [Uesaka and Tajima, 1976] [Tuijl, 1980]. However, these models do not include process (1) at all and treat only process (2), and even in the process (2), there are the problems stated below.

(a) they decide segregation characteristic vale with a single measure; therefore, their algorithms are not robust and hard to improve.

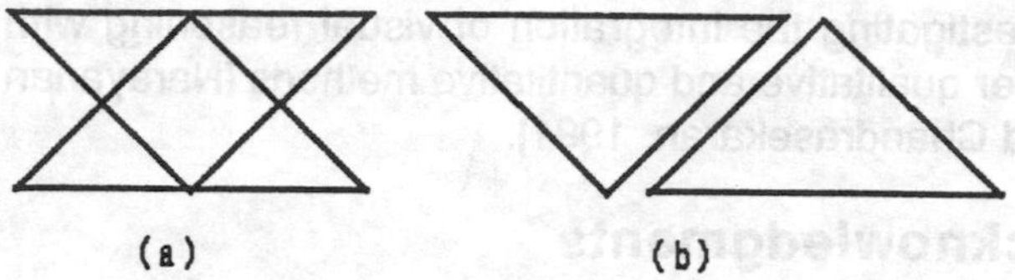

(a) An overlapped figure
(b) An Interpretation of (a)
Figure. 1 An example of figure segregation

(b) their algorithms only estimate which interpretation is likely to be selected more; therefore, they cannot estimate selection frequency.

We have already reported the automatic creation of reasonable interpretations for complex and ambiguous figures to cover process (1) [Shimaya and Yoroizawa, 1990a]. This paper discusses process (2). In order to solve problems (a) and (b), it is necessary to simulate human visual perception. We first introduce a generalized total curvature function for describing line figures in section 2. Five Gestalt factors(such as symmetry, continuity, etc) of each subfigure are defined with the total curvature function in section 3. Two more factors among the subfigures are defined in section 4. The effectiveness of each factor is examined from the results of a psychological experiment in section 5. Then by applying linear multiple regression analysis, the characteristic value of each interpretation is obtained, and the selection frequency is calculated in section 6. Section 7 is the conclusion that the model proposed here can simulate the human visual perception in figure segregation fairly well.

2 Description of a line figure

In order to check the geometrical characteristics of an interpretation, it is necessary to describe each subfigure in the interpretation. Initially, the subfigure is a closed line figure of two dimensions. Curvature can completely describe any two-dimensional smooth line figure. Let s be the length of a line from a starting point and $(x(s), y(s))$ represents a point using X-Y co-ordinates. Then curva-

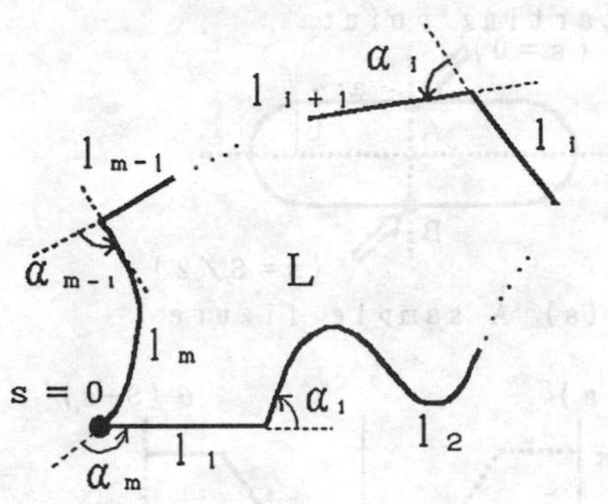

Figure. 2 Description of a line figure

ture k(s) of the point is given as

$$k(s) = \frac{dX(s)}{ds}\frac{d^2Y(s)}{ds^2} - \frac{dY(s)}{ds}\frac{d^2X(s)}{ds^2} \quad (1)$$

However, the curvature itself is not suitable for describing line figures because it is not defined at the corners. Therefore, we introduce the total curvature function $\theta(s)$ in order to describe general line figures. The total curvature function is originally the integral of curvature and defined with only smooth curves, but it can be applied to non-smooth curves by adding the angles at the discontinuous points in curvature[Uesaka and Tajima, 1976]. Now let's consider the line figure L (Figure 2). Let L be composed of m pieces of smooth arcs $l_1, l_2, ..., l_m$. α_i is the discrete part between l_i and l_{i+1}. Let s_i be the length from the starting point to the end point of arc i. Then $\theta(s)$ at a point at distance s ($s_n \le s < s_{n+1}$) from the starting point is defined as

$$\theta(s) = \sum_{i=1}^{n}\{\int_{s_{i-1}}^{s_i} k_i(s)ds + \alpha_i\} + \int_{s_n}^{s} k_{n+1}(s)ds \quad (2)$$

where
$k_i(s)$: curvature of a point on line segment i
α_i : the angle from the tangent at the end point of l_i to the tangent at the starting point of l_{i+1}. Let $-\pi < \alpha_i \le \pi$.

An example of $\theta(s)$ is shown in Figure 3. Note that if the starting point and tracing direction of a line figure is given, then $\theta(s)$ of the figure is uniquely decided and that if $\theta(s)$ is given, the line figure is uniquely decided.

3 Description of Gestalt factors

Figure segregation has been discussed in psychology, especially by Gestalt psychologists. They claimed that several factors(symmetry, continuity, etc) play an important role in figure segregation [Metzger, 1953] [Spoehr and Lehmkule, 1982]. However, they only claimed the general effect of those Gestalt factors in figure segregation. In other words, their analyses were qualitative. In order to construct a cognitive figure segregation model,

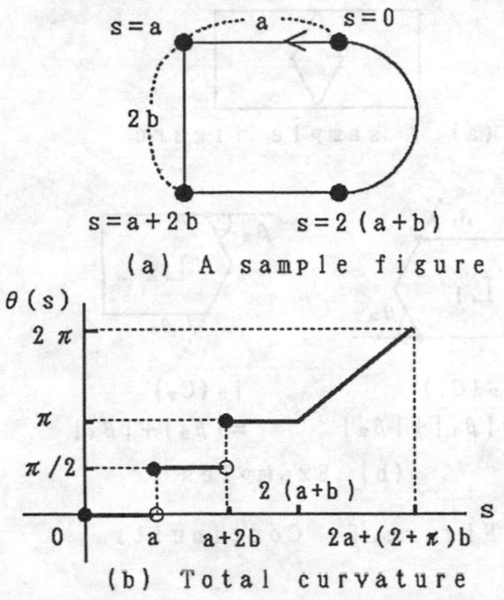

(a) A sample figure

(b) Total curvature

Figure. 3 An example of total curvature function

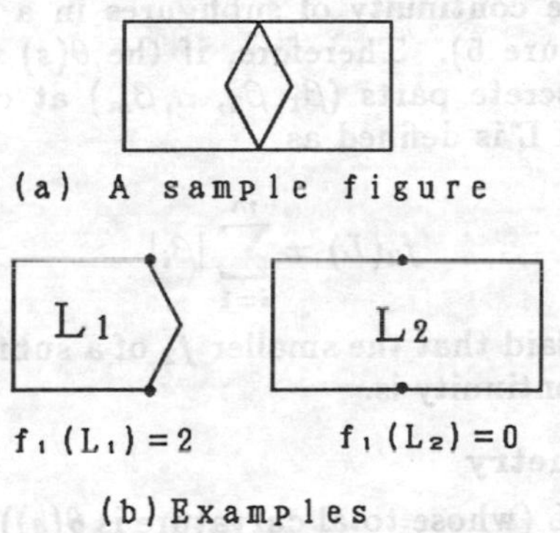

(a) A sample figure

(b) Examples

Figure. 4 Simplicity

it is necessary to give quantitative measure to those factors [Shimaya and Yoroizawa, 1988]. Therefore, we give quantitative definitions of the Gestalt factors in each subfigure with total curvature function. In this section, simplicity, continuity, symmetry, regularity, and convexity of subfigures are defined with $\theta(s)$.

3.1 Simplicity

The number of discrete points in $\theta(s)$ at the cross points of a subfigure represents the simplicity of the figure(Figure 4). Therefore, if $\theta(s)$ of subfigure L has m discreation at cross points, then the simplicity of L is defined as

$$f_1(L) = m \quad (3)$$

It can be said that the smaller f_1 of a subfigure is, the simpler it is.

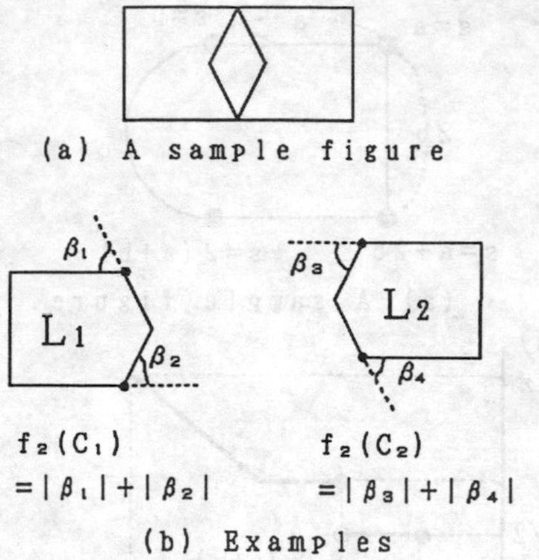

Figure. 5 Continuity

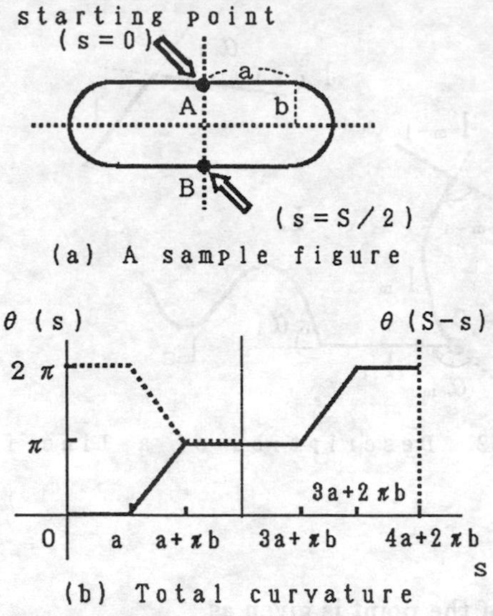

Figure. 6 Symmetry with regard to axes

3.2 Continuity

The discrete parts of $\theta(s)$ at the cross points correspond to the continuity of subfigures in a certain segregation(Figure 5). Therefore, if the $\theta(s)$ of subfigure L has m discrete parts $(\beta_1, \beta_2, ..., \beta_m)$ at cross points, continuity of L is defined as

$$f_2(L) = \sum_{i=1}^{m} |\beta_i| \quad (4)$$

It can be said that the smaller f_2 of a subfigure is, the better it's continuity is.

3.3 Symmetry

If subfigure L (whose total curvature is $\theta(s)$) is symmetric with respect to an axis, there exists a starting point which satisfies the following equation(Figure 6).

$$\theta(s) + \theta(S - s) = \theta(S)$$

$$0 \leq s \leq \frac{S}{2} \quad (5)$$

where S is the total length of L. The line which connects the starting point and the point at a distance of S/2 becomes the symmetrical axis.

Thus, symmetry of L with regard to axes can be defined as

$$A_L = min\frac{1}{S}\int_0^S |\theta_x(s) + \theta_x(S-s) - \theta(S)|ds \quad (6)$$

where $\theta_x(s)$ is the generalized total curvature of L when the starting point is x. This definition means that the symmetry of a subfigure corresponds to the minimum distance of $\theta(s)$ between the subfigure and a symmetrical figure which has the same length.

Similarly, if subfigure L is symmetric with regard to n th order of rotation (in other words, if L returns to it's original shape by rotating at least $360/n$ degree), then there exists a starting point which satisfies the following equation(Figure 7).

$$\theta(s) + \theta(\frac{S}{n}) = \theta(s + \frac{S}{n})$$

$$0 \leq s \leq S - \frac{S}{n} \quad (7)$$

Thus, symmetry of L with regard to rotation can be defined as

$$R_L = min\frac{1}{S}\int_0^S |\theta_x(s) + \theta_x(\frac{S}{n}) - \theta_x(s + \frac{S}{n})|ds \quad (8)$$

Then, symmetry of L is defined as

$$f_3(L) = min(A_L, R_L) \quad (9)$$

if L has n symmetrical axes and also is symmetric with m th order of rotation, then $f_3(L)$ is redefined as follows.

$$f_3(L) = min(\frac{1}{n}, \frac{1}{m-1}) \quad (10)$$

This means that parallelograms and trapezoids that have a symmetrical axis are the same level of symmetry. It can be said that the smaller f_3 of a subfigure is, the more symmetric it is.

3.4 Regularity

It is difficult to say how much regular a figure is. Humans feel circular arcs and straight lines are very regular. Therefore, in order to check the regularity of a subfigure, we first approximate $\theta(s)$ of component lines to that of straight lines or circular arcs. The curvature of circular arcs is constant and the curvature of straight lines is 0, therefore, both of their $\theta(s)$ can be described by a linear

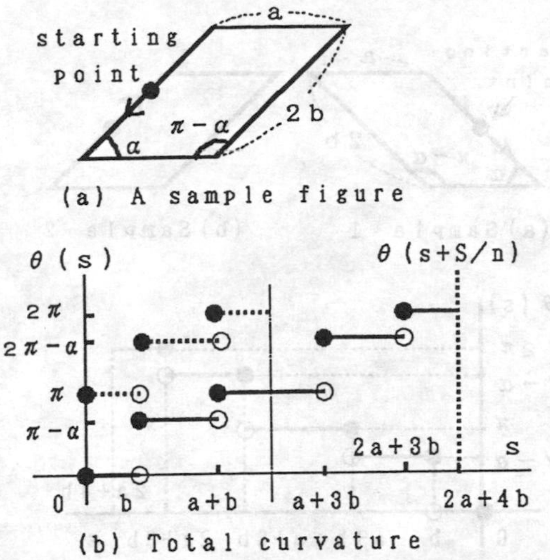

Figure. 7 Symmetry with regard to rotation

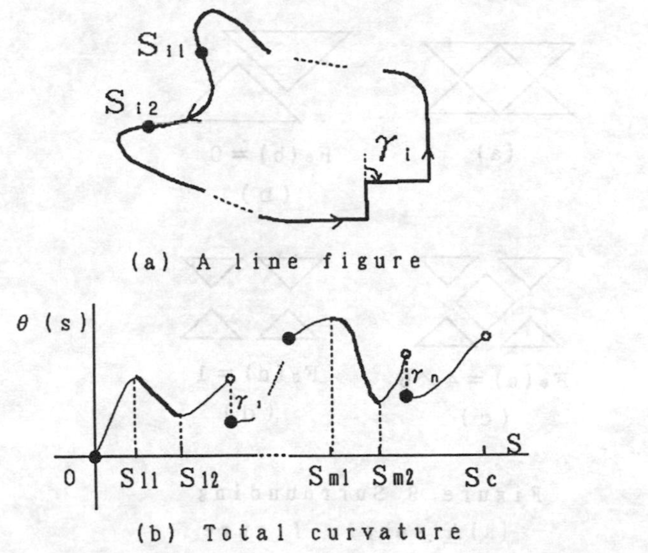

Figure. 8 Convexity

function of s. If a given figure L is composed of m pieces of smooth lines($l_1, l_2, ..., l_m$), it is approximated as

$$D(L) = min \sum_{i=1}^{m} \frac{1}{L_i} \int_{s_{i-1}}^{s_i} |\theta(s) - (a_i s + b_i)| ds \qquad (11)$$

where

L_i : length of line l_i

s_i : length of the line from starting point to the end of line l_i

$\theta(s)$: total curvature of L

a_i, b_i : constants

Further, if a subfigure is composed of only circular arcs and straight lines, the figure is considered to be more regular. Therefore, regularity of subfigure L is defined as

$$f_4(L) = min(D_c(L), D_s(L)) \qquad (12)$$

where $D_c(L)$ is the $D(L)$ when all the arcs of L is approximated by circular arcs, and $D_s(L)$ is the $D(L)$ approximated by straight lines. It can be said that the smaller f_4 of a subfigure is, the more regular it is.

3.5 Convexity

Convexity and concavity may have something to do with the selection of interpretations. Convex lines have a positive curvature, and concave lines have a negative curvature. Note one line may have both concave and convex segments in any order. Remember that the total curvature is originally the integral of curvature. Thus, decreasing $\theta(s)$ values indicate that the subfigure is concave at these points. Note that there are two ways in which $\theta(s)$ values decrease: continuous and discontinuous.

If $\theta(s)$ of subfigure L is composed of m continuously decreasing parts and n discontinuously decreasing parts(Figure 8), then the convexity of L is defined as

$$f_5(L) = \sum_{i=1}^{m} |\theta(s_{i1}) - \theta(s_{i2})| + \sum_{i=1}^{n} |\gamma_i| \qquad (13)$$

It can be said that the smaller f_5 of a subfigure is, the more convex it is.

3.6 Gestalt factors of an interpretation

Five Gestalt factors of a subfigure have been defined. In figure segregation, several subfigures are combined into an interpretation of the complex and ambiguous figure. Each subfigure has five Gestalt factors and by averaging the corresponding factors of the subfigures, an equivalent set of five Gestalt values can be created for each interpretation.

If interpretation I is composed of m subfigures, then the Gestalt values of each interpretation are defined as

$$F_i(I) = \frac{1}{m} \sum_{k=1}^{m} f_i(k)$$

$$i = 1, 2, 3, 4, 5 \qquad (14)$$

where $f_i(k)$ is the Gestalt value of subfigure k.

4 Characteristics among the subfigures

The five Gestalt factors mentioned in section 3 are defined with each subfigure. However, it seems that there exist some characteristics that are defined among several subfigures [Shimaya and Yoroizawa, 1990b]. Therefore, we introduce two more characteristics.

4.1 Overlap

In figure segregation, it is felt that subfigures overlap each other or just connect with each other(Figure

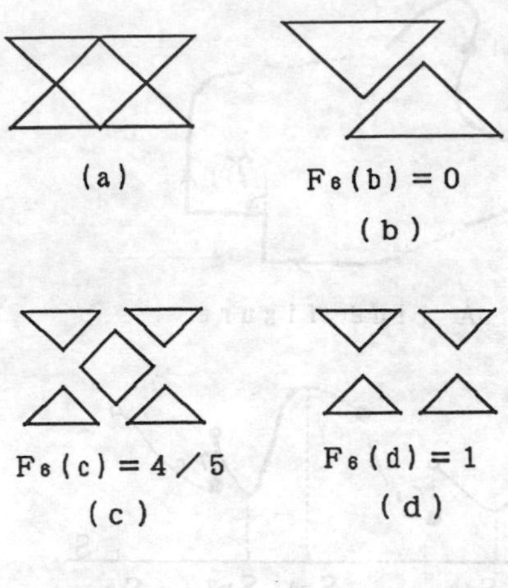

Figure. 9 Surrounding
(a) A sample figure
(b) - (d) Examples

9). This may have something to do with the selection frequency. Let interpretation I has n subfigures $C_1, C_2, ..., C_n$. then, the overlap of I is defined as

$$F_6(I) = \frac{1}{n}\sum_{i=1}^{n} f_6(C_i) \qquad (15)$$

where

$f_6(C_i) = 0$: if C_i satisfies condition 1 or condition 2 but $f_6(C_i) = 1$: otherwise

condition 1: C_i does not share line elements in common with other subfigures and C_i overlaps other subfigures.

condition 2: all the line elements of C_i are inner lines (lines that are not the border lines between the original figure and the background), and all of them are shared with some other subfigures which do not include one another.

The value of F_6 is small when the original figure is interpreted as several subfigures that overlap(Figure 9(b)). If the original figure is interpreted otherwise, then F_6 becomes smaller if there exist subfigures that are surrounded by other subfigures(Figure 9(c),(d)).

4.2 Similarity

It seems that subfigures resembling each other may have something to do with figure segregation. Humans feel two figures look like each other when they are similar or when they are mirror images of each other.

Suppose $\theta_i(s)$ is the total curvature of subfigure C_i, and $\theta_j(s)$ is that of C_j, S_i is total length of C_i, and S_j is that of C_j. Let $S_i \leq S_j$.

If subfigures C_i and C_j are similar, then there exists a start point which satisfies the following equation.

$$\theta_i(s) = \theta_j^*(s)$$
$$0 \leq s \leq S_1 \qquad (16)$$

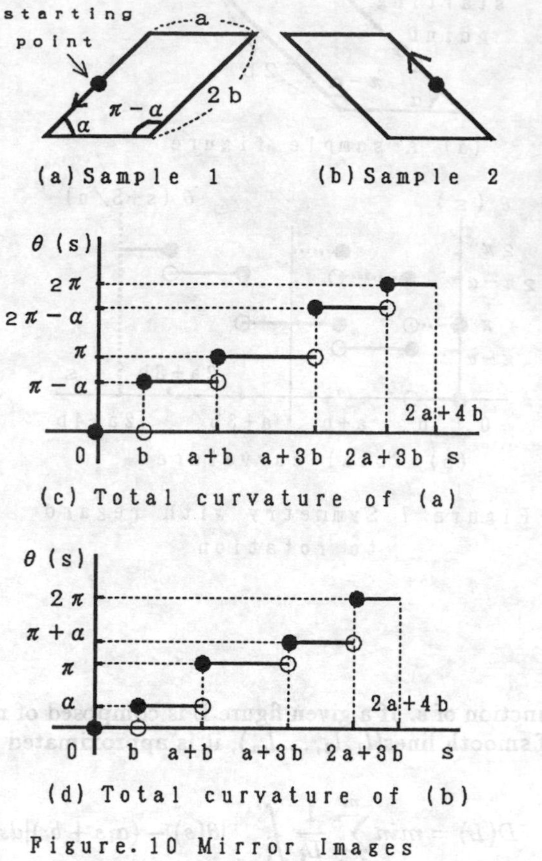

Figure. 10 Mirror Images

where

$$\theta_j^*(s) = \theta_j(s * \frac{S_i}{S_j}) \qquad (17)$$

Thus, similarity of C_i and C_j can be defined as

$$T_s = min\frac{1}{S_i}\int_0^{S_i} |\theta_{ix}(s) - \theta_{jx}^*(s)|ds \qquad (18)$$

where $\theta_{ix}(s), \theta_{jx}^*(s)$ is $\theta_i(s), \theta_j^*(s)$ when the starting point is x.

Mirror images are not similar, but humans think they look like each other. If C_i and C_j are mirror images of each other, then there exists a start point which satisfies the following equation(Figure 10).

$$\theta_i(s) + \theta_j^*(S_i - s) = \theta_i(S_i)$$
$$0 \leq s \leq S_1 \qquad (19)$$

Thus, similarity of C_i and C_j concerning mirror image can be defined as

$$T_m = min\frac{1}{S_i}\int_0^{S_i} |\theta_{ix}(s) + \theta_{jx}^*(S_i - s) - \theta_i(S_i)|ds \qquad (20)$$

Thus, similarity of C_i and C_j can be defined as

$$T_{ij} = min(T_s, T_m) \qquad (21)$$

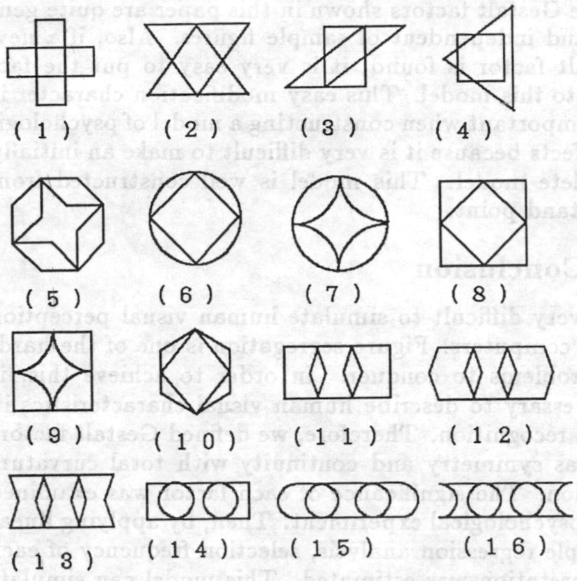

Figure 11 Sample figures

If interpretation I has k subfigures, then similarity of I can be defined as the average of T_{ij}.

$$F_7(I) = \frac{1}{nC2} \sum_{i=1}^{k-1} \sum_{j=i+1}^{k} T_{ij} \quad (22)$$

It can be said that the smaller F_7 of an interpretation is, the more similar the subfigures are in it.

5 Significance of each Gestalt factor

In order to check the significance of the seven Gestalt factors, a psychological experiment was conducted. Sixteen ambiguous figures were shown to twenty subjects. Figure 11 shows the sample figures. Each subject was asked to draw the most natural interpretation for each sample figure. Fifty-six kinds of different interpretations were obtained. Gestalt values of each interpretation can be calculated as shown in sections 3 and 4.

The significance of each Gestalt factor is calculated from the correlation coefficient between the Gestalt values and the selection result as shown as Table 1. In Table 1, column G corresponds with the number of subjects who drew each interpretation.

Statistics give the limit of significance γ_M, by the next equation.

$$\gamma_M = \frac{e^{2T} - 1}{e^{2T} + 1} \quad (23)$$

where

$$T = \frac{t_{n-1}(\epsilon)}{\sqrt{n-3}} \quad (24)$$

n: number of samples
ϵ: risk

	F_1	F_2	F_3	F_4	F_5	F_6	F_7	G
F_1	1.00	0.50	0.28	0.16	0.21	0.71	-0.10	-0.68**
F_2		1.00	0.05	0.03	0.67	0.62	-0.03	-0.41**
F_3			1.00	0.29	-0.04	0.37	-0.42	-0.60**
F_4				1.00	0.02	0.16	-0.19	-0.29*
F_5					1.00	0.27	0.09	-0.14
F_6						1.00	-0.26	-0.66**
F_7							1.00	0.40**
G								1.00

* ···significant with 5% risk
** ···significant with 0.5% risk

Table 1 Correlation coefficient

$t_{n-1}(\epsilon)$: t-distribution with $n-1$ degrees of freedom and with the risk of ϵ

Because the number of samples is 56, the limit of significance γ_M is as follows.

$$\gamma_M = 0.23(with5\%risk)$$
$$\gamma_M = 0.32(with1\%risk) \quad (25)$$
$$\gamma_M = 0.35(with0.5\%risk)$$

The following results can be seen in Table 1.

(1) SimplicityF_1, symmetryF_3, and overlapF_6 are much more significant with 0.5% risk. Therefore, they are very important factors in figure segregation.

(2) ContinuityF_2 and similarityF_7 are significant with 0.5% risk. Therefore, these two are also important factors.

(3) RegularityF_4 is significant with 5% risk.

(4) Is is generally believed that humans prefer convex figures rather than concave figures [Kanizsa, 1979]. However, according to this psychological experiment, convexityF_5 is not significant. It can be said that in figure segregation, even if the convexity seems significant, there exist other more significant factors.

6 Figure segregation estimation

Linear multiple regression analysis was conducted using Gestalt values as predictor variables and the number of the people who selected the interpretation as the criterion variable. By doing this, an equation which estimates the interpretation selection frequency is obtained as follows.

	β_0	β_1	β_2	β_3	β_4	β_5	β_6	β_7
coefficient	11.36	-5.53	-1.98	-4.36	-1.24	0.75	-1.09	2.20
t-value		3.70	1.09	3.62	0.88	0.47	0.64	1.87

Table 2 Partial regression coefficient and t-value

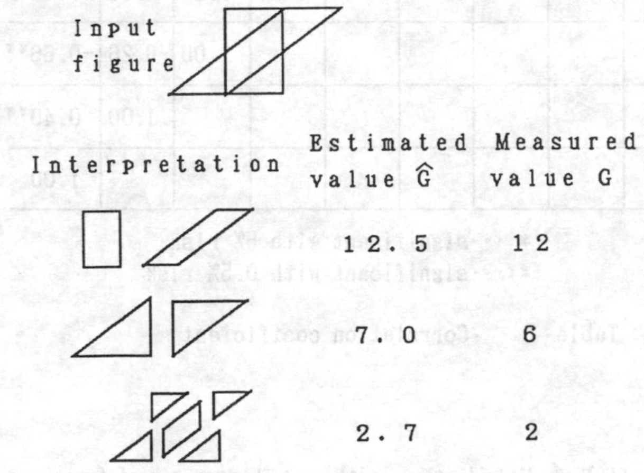

Figure 12 An estimation example

$$\hat{G}(I) = \beta_0 + \sum_{j=1}^{7} \beta_j * F_j(I)$$

$$j = 1, 2, ..., 7 \qquad (26)$$

where $\hat{G}(I)$: the criterion variable of interpretation I.
β_0: a constant.
β_j: the partial regression coefficient.
F_j: Gestalt values of interpretation I.

Table 2 shows the partial regression coefficients and their t-values. Figure 12 shows an example. $\hat{G}$ is the frequency selection value obtained by equation (26) and G is the number of people who actually selected the interpretation.

Multiple correlation R between $\hat{G}$ and G is,

$$R = 0.84 \qquad (27)$$

This indicates that equation (26) agrees fairly well with the experimental results. The characteristics of this model are as follows.

1) Ability of estimation

Figure segregation models have been reported, but they only indicate which interpretation is most likely to be selected. This model can completely estimate which interpretation is selected most and in addition to that, can estimate the selection frequency of each interpretation fairly well.

2) Robustness of the algorithm

The Gestalt factors shown in this paper are quite general and independent of sample figures. Also, if a new Gestalt factor is found, it is very easy to put the factor into this model. This easy modification character is very important when constructing a model of psychological effects because it is very difficult to make an initially complete model. This model is well constructed from this stand point.

7 Conclusion

It is very difficult to simulate human visual perception using computers. Figure segregation is one of the hardest problems to conquer. In order to achieve this, it is necessary to describe human visual characteristics in figure recognition. Therefore, we defined Gestalt factors such as symmetry and continuity with total curvature function. The significance of each factor was examined by a psychological experiment. Then, by applying linear multiple regression analysis, selection frequency of each interpretation was estimated. This model can simulate human visual perception in figure segregation very well. Also, it should be noted that the model proposed here and in [Shimaya and Yoroizawa, 1990a] is quite general and easy to apply to practical applications such as map recognition or technical parts recognition.

References

[Kanizsa, 1979] G. Kanizsa. *Organization in Vision: Essays on Gestalt Perception.* Praeger Publishers, 1979.

[Metzger, 1953] W. Metzger. *GESETZE DES SEHENS.* Verlag von Waldemar Kramer, Frankfurt am Main, 1953.

[Shimaya and Yoroizawa, 1988] A. Shimaya and I. Yoroizawa. A figure segregation criterion based on human visual characteristics. *IEICE Technical Report*, PRU88-72, 1988. (in Japanese).

[Shimaya and Yoroizawa, 1990a] A. Shimaya and I. Yoroizawa. Automatic creation of reasonable interpretations for complex line figures. *Proc. of 10th International Conference on Pattern Recognition*, Vol. I:pages 480–484, 1990.

[Shimaya and Yoroizawa, 1990b] A. Shimaya and I. Yoroizawa. Quantitative analysis on figure segregation. *ITEJ Technical Report*, VAI'90-18:pages 55–60, 1990. (in Japanese).

[Spoehr and Lehmkule, 1982] K. T. Spoehr and S. W. Lehmkule. *Visual Information Processing.* W. h. Freeman and Company, New York, 1982.

[Tuijl, 1980] H.F.J.M.van Tuijl. Perceptual interpretation of complex line patterns. *journal of Experimental Psychology: Human Perception and Performance*, vol.6, No.2, 1980.

[Uesaka and Tajima, 1976] Y. Uesaka and K. Tajima. An interpretative model of figure segregation. *Trans. of IEICE*, Vol.59, D-1, 1976. (in Japanese).

An MFIS for Computing a Raw Cognitive Map

W.K. Yeap, M.E. Jefferies and P.S. Naylor
AI Laboratory,
Computer and Information Science
University of Otago, New Zealand

Ph.+64 03 4798586
COSCWKY@OTAGO.AC.NZ
COSCMEJ@OTAGO.AC.NZ

Abstract

This paper extends Yeap's [1988] computational theory of cognitive maps, focusing on the problem of computing a raw cognitive map by an autonomous agent. In addition to having a 150° view of the environment as input, the agent also maintains a representation of her immediate surroundings. This representation is referred to as an MFIS, a Memory For one's Immediate Surroundings. Arguments for the use of the MFIS are presented. The main questions that we ask in implementing our ideas are: (i) what frame of reference is appropriate for the MFIS? and (ii) how does the MFIS change as the agent moves through the environment? A program has been implemented successfully and the main algorithms used and the results of running the program are presented.

1 Introduction

Psychologists have long suggested that humans and animals compute a representation of the environment (i.e. a cognitive map) which allows them to find their way about in it and return to places of interest [Tolman, 1948]. More recently, a computational theory of cognitive maps was developed which further suggested that the cognitive mapping process (CMP) computes a raw map and a full map [Yeap, 1988]. This paper describes further extensions of this theory dealing specifically with the raw map. In particular, we focus on the problem of computing a raw map of a large environment, based on one's memory of one's immediate surroundings (a structure which is referred to as an MFIS) rather than on one's immediate perception. Results from our simulation studies are presented and briefly discussed.

A raw map is a representation of the physical environment computed from one's sensory perception of the world. This representation forms the basic input to the later cognitive mapping processes. Hence, the input for computing a raw map is information from the senses and the output is a representation containing explicit information about our physical world which is relevant for later tasks. We adhere to a modular structure for the CMP similar to that suggested by Marr [1982] in his study of the visual process since we view the CMP as a natural extension of Marr's theory of vision at the level of the 2D Sketch. Hence, the next module to compute after the 2½D Sketch is the raw map, not the 3D Sketch as suggested by Marr and Nishihara [1978]. We shall digress briefly to discuss this point in a little more depth because, as Marr pointed out, one key problem in formulating a computational study is to identify clearly the likely modularisation.

Marr argued convincingly why we need a 2½D Sketch and abandoned trying to segment an image using specialised knowledge about the nature of the scenes. His argument was that "since most early visual processes extract information about the visible surface, it is these surfaces, their shape and disposition relative to the viewer, that need to be made explicit at this point in the processing". Following his argument, we suggest that the next module should compute the spatial layout of these surfaces as the viewer moves among them rather than forming 3D descriptions of the individual surfaces. The latter task should come much later in the process since not all information necessary for computing a 3D description is available at the initial encounter. This observation is further supported by some recent psychological experiments which demonstrated that a viewer-centered description and not an object-centered description of objects is remembered by subjects in an object recognition task [Tarr and Pinker, 1989; Rock *et al* 1989]. Like Marr's argument for computing the 2½D Sketch which does not preclude the fact that higher-level knowledge is useful, we are also not suggesting that we do not compute 3D objects. It is, however, unlikely that they should be computed *immediately* from the 2½D Sketch. Doing so would be like perceiving the objects without a spatial context and this would be contrary to the way we normally perceive our environment. That objects appear to us with a spatiality that we should not ignore has been raised sporadically in several areas of research [Yeap and Handley, 1990]. Furthermore, computing a 3D Sketch is only one aspect of a more general problem of concept formation and we must therefore begin by asking why objects are formed and how, before suggesting specific algorithms to compute any aspect of it.

In the theory, it is suggested that the raw map is a network of Absolute Space Representations (ASRs), i.e. representations of individual local environments which have been visited (or entered) by the viewer. In this paper, we describe a program which simulates an agent moving with a 150° view through the environment. Information from each view is used to update the MFIS from which ASRs are computed. The questions that need to be asked are:

(i) how to compute an ASR from the MFIS?,
(ii) what frame of reference would be appropriate for the MFIS?, and
(iii) how does the MFIS change as the agent moves through the environment?

Computing ASRs from the MFIS implies that they are no longer computed directly from what could be perceived in a single view (either 360° or smaller) but from one's memory of one's immediate surroundings. This was not considered before in the earlier work and in robotics research concerned with building autonomous mobile robots [Chatila, 1982; Iyengar *et al*, 1985; Rueb and Wong, 1987]. A new algorithm was designed to compute an ASR from the MFIS and is described in detail in [Yeap *et al*, 1990]. Section 2 briefly describes the idea of computing an ASR from the MFIS. The second and third questions are the main concern of this paper. Section 3 discusses these problems and related work. Section 4 describes the algorithm and presents the results of our implementation. Section 5 concludes the paper with some comments on the usefulness of our simulation study.

2 Background on Computing an ASR from Memory

Consider an agent who has just entered a new space and remains stationary at a point. To compute an ASR, one is faced with the problem of identifying the surfaces (unfamiliar or otherwise) in this new environment which, to the agent, appear to enclose her and separate this part of the environment from the rest of it. As well as the surfaces which can be seen from the current viewing position, there are surfaces which are hidden from the agent's view because they are occluded or behind her. If these surfaces were a part of the agent's recent experience of the environment then they, along with the surfaces which can actually be seen, are used to compute an ASR. As Attneave and Farrar [1977] pointed out, "our internal representation of the world around us is based in part on current sensory input, but in much greater part on past sensory inputs, i.e., upon memory".

The key to successfully computing an ASR is to identify which surfaces (in memory) are best combined at each step of the construction process. This is usually straightforward where two surfaces are already connected but in a complex, cluttered environment, there are gaps in walls and obstacles of various sizes which occlude walls and other obstacles so that it is not immediately clear which surface should form the next part of the boundary. Our algorithm tackles this problem by characterising six possible connections which may occur between any two adjacent surfaces. Depending on the type of connection, imaginary surfaces are used to fill in gaps between real surfaces and real surfaces may be clipped forming sub-surfaces. A different weight is applied to each surface so that, for example, real surfaces are normally selected in preference to imaginary ones. At each stage of the construction process a preferred subset of all the possible connections is "grown" until the initial surface is reached. The set of surfaces which form the minimum weighted boundary defines the ASR for the current local space. For details of the algorithm see earlier work [Yeap *et al*, 1990].

3 The MFIS

Early AI models on cognitive maps [Kuipers, 1978; Davis, 1984] used a kind of "You Are Here" pointer to identify a person's current position in the environment. Such a pointer obviously under-represents the amount of information available at one's current position but it nonetheless indicates the usefulness of such information for computing a cognitive map. Furthermore, based upon the observations of our own visual system, such as a limited view and limited range vision, and our visual behaviour, such as the need for active scanning [Norton and Stark, 1971], psychologists have also suggested that we need to integrate the different views to form a more complete picture of what we perceive of our surroundings (e.g. [Gibson, 1979]). Robotics researchers have shown that it is necessary for their robots to compute a global representation of the whole environment in addition to partitioning the environment into smaller spaces [Yeap *et al*, 1990]. Although computing a global representation of the *whole* environment is not necessary, computing a global representation of the immediate surroundings seems to be desirable [Yeap and Handley, 1990]. There are also advantages for doing so. For example, using it, one can detect that one is re-visiting a local space which has just been visited [Yeap, 1988] (and see below) and it provides a richer description of the environment for computing an ASR [Yeap *et al*, 1990].

Information in the immediate surroundings can be represented using either an egocentric (defining spatial positions in relation to the self) or an allocentric (defining spatial positions external to the self) frame of reference. It is clear that from an implementation viewpoint, it is inefficient to use an egocentric reference frame. To use an allocentric reference frame, one has to specify where the reference frame should be centered. The choice of this external point need not be chosen arbitrarily if one uses the current ASR as the frame of reference. An ASR is defined by a boundary (see section 2) and any part of it would be suitable. In the implementation we choose to use the entrance to the current ASR as the center of the reference frame. When the agent moves out of the current ASR, the MFIS is shifted to center on the entrance to the next ASR. Figure 1 shows how the MFIS defined as such, would follow the viewer as she moves through the environment.

The extent of the MFIS can be defined arbitrarily but, more importantly, need not be defined exactly, say, in metrical terms. Varying its size is a tradeoff between how much information is remembered (and hence how useful the MFIS is) and how much effort is required to compute it. Given an MFIS with a fixed size, part of an ASR will often be excluded as it lies outside the area covered by the MFIS (Figure 1). Figure 2 demonstrates that one advantage of having the MFIS is to help one recognise that nearby local spaces were visited before. We therefore do not want to remove a part of an ASR just because it falls outside the area covered by the MFIS. Since its extent is defined arbitrarily, it is better to include the whole ASR if a part of it lies within the area covered by the MFIS. Figure 3 shows how the MFIS defined as such would grow and shrink as the viewer moves through the environment.

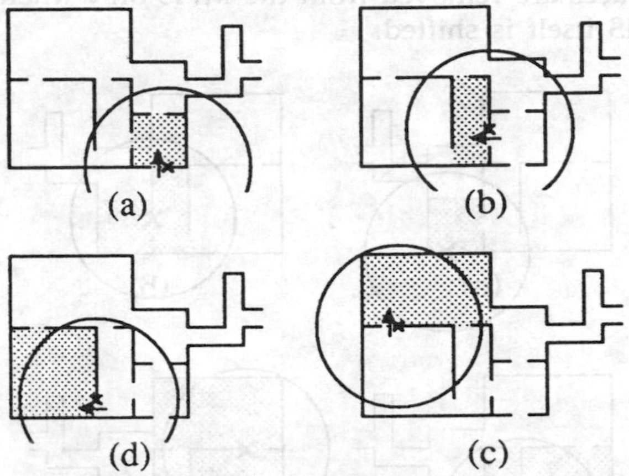

Figure 1 Defining an MFIS using the current ASR at the point marked X as shown from (a) to (d). When the viewer moves out of the ASR, the MFIS is shifted to centre on the new ASR. The arrow indicates the position of the viewer.

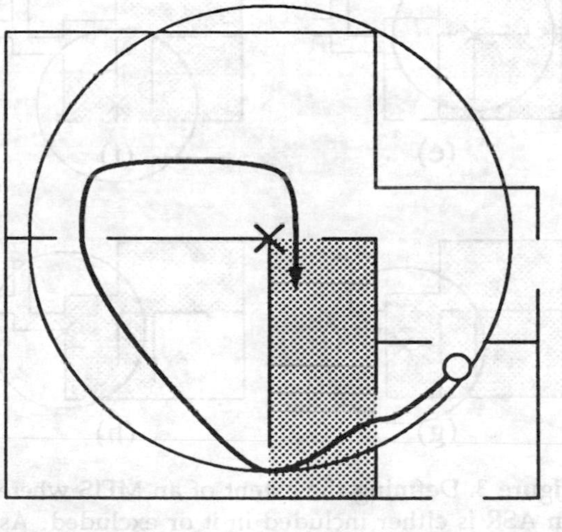

Figure 2. Recognising a local space using the viewer's position in the MFIS. The solid line shows the viewer's path through the environment. The viewer is currently re-visiting the shaded area. One can recognise that one has been to this place by noting the global position of where things are in the MFIS.

In addition to those surfaces defined as part of an ASR, two other types of surfaces are also included in the MFIS. The first are those surfaces which are currently in view and the second are those surfaces which were previously in view but do not belong to an ASR. The former are included in the MFIS every time the MFIS is updated with information from the current view. As such, it does not matter where these surfaces lie. The latter must fall within the boundary of the MFIS and if not, they are removed from the MFIS. Note that in the current implementation, surfaces are removed from the MFIS only when the MFIS itself is shifted.

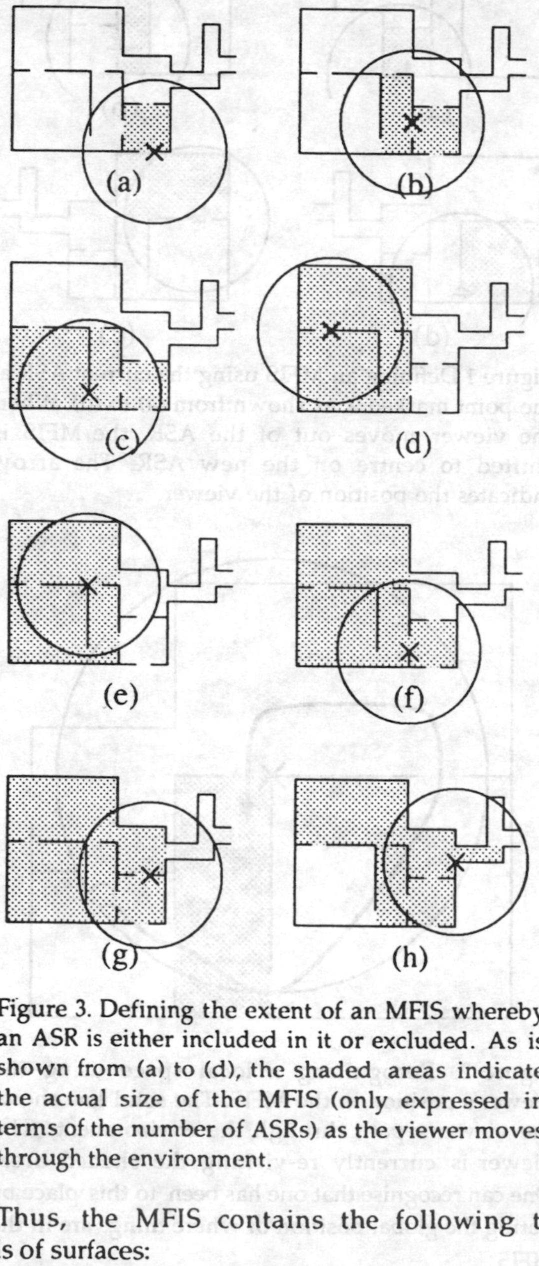

Figure 3. Defining the extent of an MFIS whereby an ASR is either included in it or excluded. As is shown from (a) to (d), the shaded areas indicate the actual size of the MFIS (only expressed in terms of the number of ASRs) as the viewer moves through the environment.

Thus, the MFIS contains the following three kinds of surfaces:

(i) those which are part of an ASR - the whole ASR must be included in the MFIS,

(ii) those which are currently in view - by current, we mean those surfaces which are perceived when in the current ASR. These surfaces are added to the MFIS irrespective of whether they fall within or outside the area covered by the MFIS, and

(iii) those which were perceived when outside the current ASR and are not part of any ASR - these are the least important surfaces and one's ability to remember them is influenced by a wide variety of other factors. They must lie within the area covered by the MFIS.

4 Implementation and Results

Figure 4 shows the steps taken to maintain the MFIS for computing a raw map. As in earlier work [Yeap, 1988], we detect the re-visiting of a local environment using three kinds of information, namely: the exit information, the viewer's position in the MFIS, and the shape of the local environment. However, the difference in this implementation is that the MFIS now "moves" with the viewer as she moves through the environment and ASRs are computed at each appropriate point in the environment rather than being given.

In the implementation, we continue to use a cartesian co-ordinate system, both in describing the surfaces in each view and in the MFIS. In the former, the co-ordinate system is centered on the viewer. Transforming the MFIS is straightforward and the algorithm need not be presented here. The algorithm, RETAIN_SURFACES, which decides which surfaces to remove from the MFIS once it is transformed is given below.

RETAIN_SURFACES

```
;;  MFIS_L is a list of all the surfaces which lie
;;  within the area covered by MFIS before it was
;;  shifted.
;;  MFIS_ASRs is the list of ASRs in the MFIS and
;;  CV is the list of surfaces in the current view.
;;  MFIS_ASRs, MFIS_L and CV are all global data
;;  structures.
```

1. Remove all surfaces from MFIS_L belonging to any ASR which is no longer in the current MFIS.

2. With the remaining surfaces in MFIS_L Do

   2.1 Retain surfaces in it which belong to the current view (CV).

   2.2 Retain surfaces in it which belong to an ASR in MFIS_ASRs.

   2.3 Retain surfaces which do not meet the criteria of 2.1 and 2.2 only if they lie within the boundary of the shifted MFIS.

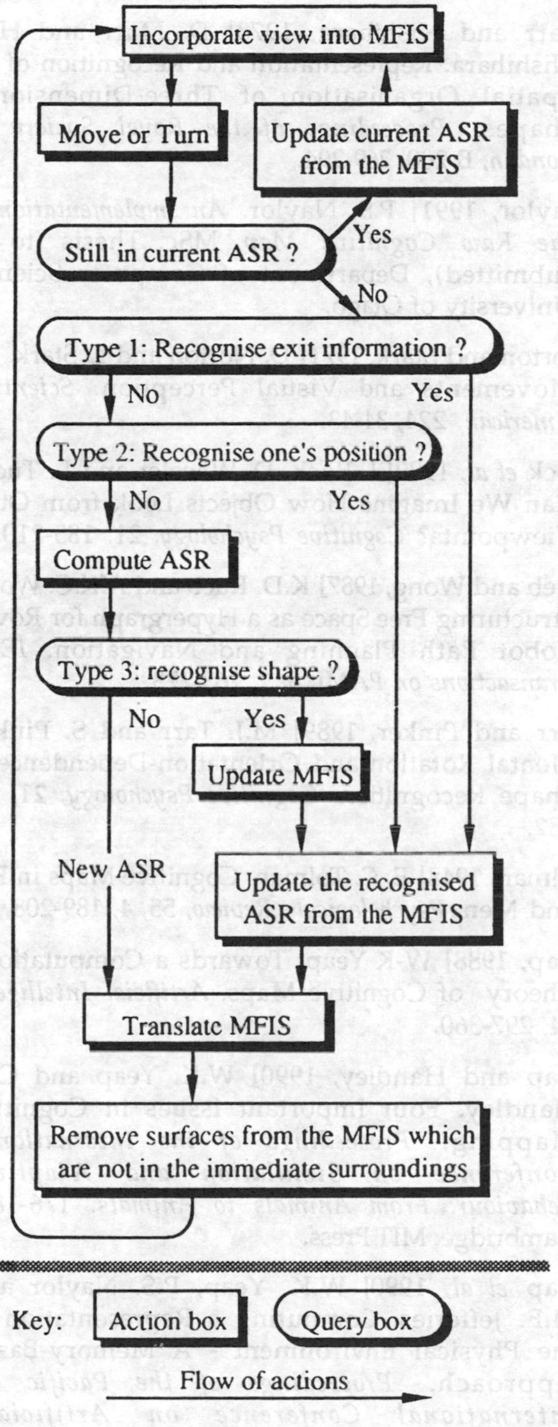

Figure 4. A Flowchart for maintaining the MFIS, from which a Raw Cognitive Map is computed.

Note that in the implementation we use two different boundaries to indicate the size of the MFIS. The reason is as follows. Since we have argued that an ASR must either be retained completely or removed from the MFIS, the designated area for their inclusion need not be large. But, we find that this area would be too small for those surfaces which are not part of any ASR. Hence, one solution is to have two extents for the MFIS.

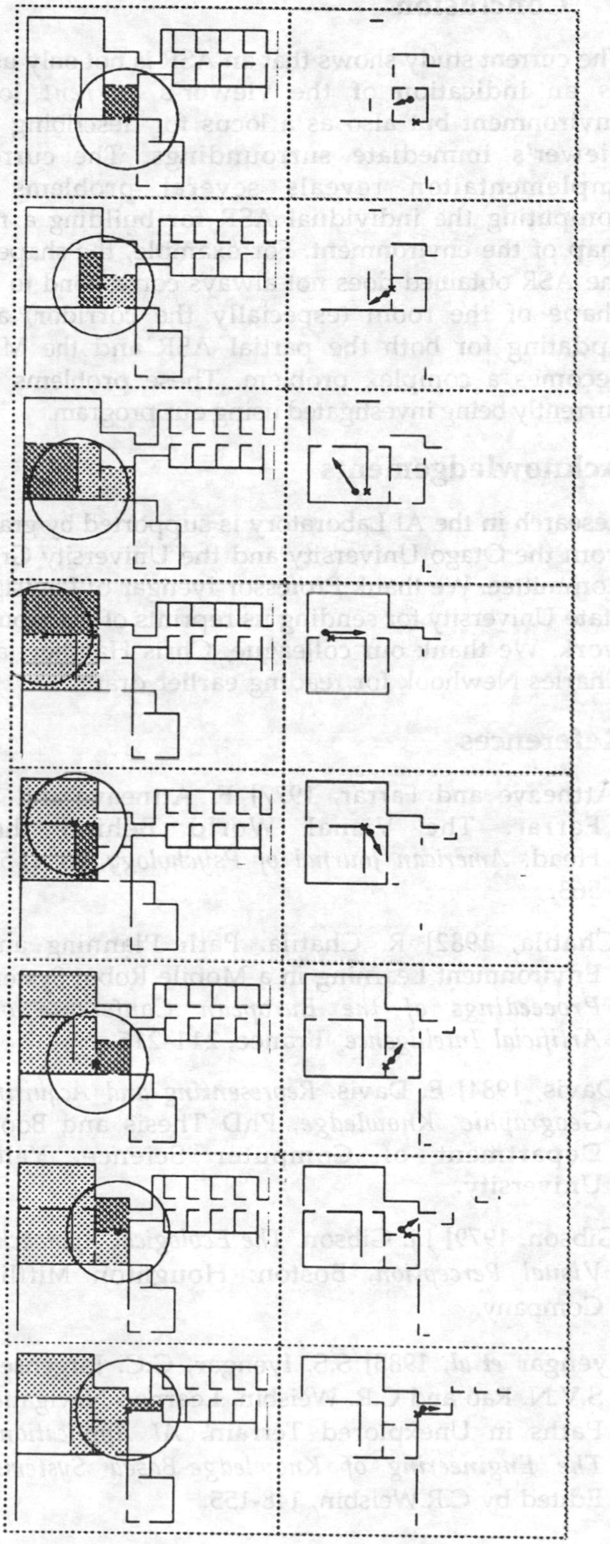

Figure 5. shows how the MFIS (*right*) changes as the viewer moves through the environment (*left*).

Examples of how the MFIS changes as the viewer moves through this environment are shown in Figure 5. For a complete result, see [Naylor, 1991].

5 Conclusion

The current study shows that an ASR is not only used as an indication of the viewer's *current* local environment but also as a locus for describing the viewer's immediate surroundings. The current implementaiton reveals several problems in computing the individual ASR for building a raw map of the environment. For example, the shape of the ASR obtained does not always correspond to the shape of the room (especially the corridor) and updating for both the partial ASR and the MFIS becomes a complex problem. These problems are currently being investigated using our program.

Acknowledgements

Research in the AI Laboratory is supported by grants from the Otago University and the University Grant Committee. We thank Professor Iyengar of Louisiana State University for sending us reprints of his group's work. We thank our colleague, Chris Handley, and Charles Newhook for reading earlier drafts.

References

[Attneave and Farrar, 1977] F. Attneave and P. Farrar. The Visual World Behind the Head. *American Journal of Psychology*, 90, 4, 549-563.

[Chatila, 1982] R. Chatila. Path Planning and Environment Learning in a Mobile Robot System. *Proceedings of the European Conference on Artificial Intelligence*, France, 211-215.

[Davis, 1984] E. Davis. *Representing and Acquiring Geographic Knowledge*. PhD Thesis and Book. Department of Computer Science, Yale University.

[Gibson, 1979] J.J. Gibson. *The Ecological Approach to Visual Perception*. Boston: Houghton Mifflin Company.

[Iyengar *et al*, 1985] S.S. Iyengar, C.C. Jorgensen, S.V.N. Rao and C.R. Weisbin. Learned Navigation Paths in Unexplored Terrain. *AI Applications: The Engineering of Knowledge-Based Systems*, Edited by C.R.Weisbin, 148-155.

[Kuipers, 1978] B. Kuipers. Modelling Spatial Knowledge. *Cognitive Science*, 2, 129-153.

[Marr, 1982] D. Marr. *Vision*. New York: W.H. Freeman and Company.

[Marr and Nishihara, 1978] D. Marr and H.K. Nishihara. Representation and Recognition of the Spatial Organisation of Three-Dimensional shapes. *Proceedings of the Royal Society of London*, B 200, 269-294.

[Naylor, 1991] P.S. Naylor. *An Implementation of the Raw Cognitive Map*. MSc. Thesis (to be submitted), Department of Computer Science, University of Otago.

[Norton and Stark, 1971] D. Norton and L. Stark. Eye Movements and Visual Perception. *Scientific American*, 224, 34-43.

[Rock *et al*, 1989] I. Rock, D. Wheeler and L. Tudor. Can We Imagine How Objects Look from Other Viewpoints? *Cognitive Psychology*. 21, 185-210.

[Rueb and Wong, 1987] K.D. Rueb and A.K.C. Wong. Structuring Free Space as a Hypergraph for Roving Robot Path Planning and Navigation. *IEEE Transactions on PAMI*, 9, 2, 263-273.

[Tarr and Pinker, 1989] M.J. Tarr and S. Pinker. Mental Rotation and Orientation-Dependence in Shape Recognition. *Cognitive Psychology*, 21, 233-282.

[Tolman, 1948] E. C. Tolman. Cognitive Maps in Rats and Men. *Psychological Review*, 55, 4, 189-208.

[Yeap, 1988] W-K Yeap. Towards a Computational Theory of Cognitive Maps. *Artificial Intelligence*, 34, 297-360.

[Yeap and Handley, 1990] W.K. Yeap and C.C. Handley. Four Important Issues in Cognitive Mapping. *Proceedings of the International Conference on Simulation and Adaptive Behaviour: From Animals to Animats*. 176-183. Cambridge: MIT Press.

[Yeap *et al*, 1990] W.K. Yeap, P.S. Naylor and M.E. Jefferies. Computing a Representation of the Physical Environment - A Memory-Based Approach. *Proceedings of the Pacific Rim International Conference on Artificial Intelligence*, Nagoya, 847-852.

KNOWLEDGE REPRESENTATION

Nonmonotonic Reasoning—Modal Logics

Nonmonotonic Databases and Epistemic Queries*

Vladimir Lifschitz
Department of Computer Sciences
and Department of Philosophy
University of Texas at Austin
Austin, TX 78712, U. S. A.

Abstract

The approach to database query evaluation developed by Levesque and Reiter treats *databases* as first order theories, and *queries* as formulas of the language which includes, in addition to the language of the database, an epistemic modal operator. In this epistemic query language, one can express questions not only about the external world described by the database, but also about the database itself—about what the database knows. On the other hand, epistemic formulas are used in knowledge representation for the purpose of expressing *defaults*. Autoepistemic logic is the best known epistemic nonmonotonic formalism; the logic of grounded knowledge, proposed recently by Lin and Shoham, is another such system. This paper brings these two directions of research together. We describe a new version of the Lin/Shoham logic, similar in spirit to the Levesque/Reiter theory of epistemic queries. Using this formalism, we can give meaning to epistemic queries in the context of nonmonotonic databases, including logic programs with negation as failure.

1 Introduction

The approach to database query evaluation developed by Levesque [1984] and Reiter [1990] treats *databases* as first order theories, and *queries* as formulas of the language which includes, in addition to the language of the database, an epistemic modal operator. In this epistemic query language, one can express questions not only about the external world described by the database, but also about the database itself—about what the database knows. For instance, one can ask not only whether John teaches any classes this semester, but also whether there is a known class that John teaches. The first question will be expressed by a formula like $\exists x\, Teaches(John, x)$; the second, by the epistemic formula $\exists x \mathrm{K}\, Teaches(John, x)$. The difference between these queries becomes essential when the database contains incomplete (for instance, disjunctive) information. Reiter [1988] argues that epistemic formulas are appropriate also for expressing integrity constraints.

On the other hand, epistemic formulas are used in knowledge representation for the purpose of expressing *defaults*. Autoepistemic logic ([Moore, 1985], [Levesque, 1990]) is the best known epistemic nonmonotonic formalism. One of the reasons why autoepistemic logic is important is that *general logic programs* can be naturally viewed as autoepistemic theories [Gelfond, 1987]. This is no longer the case, however, for "extended" logic programs, which are capable of handling incomplete information [Gelfond and Lifschitz, 1990]. In order to express extended rules by formulas, one has to use other epistemic nonmonotonic formalisms. The logic of "grounded knowledge," proposed by Lin and Shoham [1990], is one of the possibilities.[1]

This paper brings these two directions of research together. We describe a new version of the Lin/Shoham system, similar in spirit to the Levesque/Reiter theory of epistemic queries. Our formulation is simpler than that of [Lin and Shoham, 1990], and, unlike the latter, it is not restricted to the propositional case. Using this formalism, we can give meaning to epistemic queries in the context of logic programming; we can ask *what a logic program knows.* Because our system contains also (some forms of) default logic [Reiter, 1980] and circumscription [McCarthy, 1986], we can give meaning to epistemic queries in the context of a default theory or a circumscriptive theory as well.

The system of Lin and Shoham, unlike most other epistemic nonmonotonic formalisms, uses *two* epistemic operators. One of them represents "minimal knowledge"[2]; the other is closely related to the concepts of "justification" in default logic and of "negation as failure" in logic programming. The main technical idea of this paper is to identify the former with the epistemic operator K used by Levesque and Reiter.

*This research was supported in part by NSF grant IRI-89-04611 and by DARPA under Contract N00039-84-C-0211.

[1] Other modifications of autoepistemic logic that can be used for this purpose were developed in [Marek and Truszczyński, 1989], [Siegel, 1990] and [Truszczyński, 1991].

[2] The idea of minimal knowledge (or "maximal ignorance") was formalized, in various ways, by several authors, including Konolige [1982], Halpern and Moses [1984], Shoham [1986] and Lin [1988].

We concentrate here entirely on the semantical issues, and leave aside, for the time being, the computational problems of query evaluation in this framework.[3]

2 Propositional MKNF: Formulas and Interpretations

The formulas of the propositional logic of minimal knowledge with negation as failure (MKNF) are built from propositional symbols (atoms) using the standard propositional connectives and two modal operators: K and *not*.[4] A *theory* is a set of formulas (*axioms*).

If a formula or a theory doesn't contain the negation as failure operator *not*, we call it *positive*. If it contains neither K nor *not*, it is *objective*.

An *interpretation* is a set of atoms. The set of all interpretations will be denoted by $\mathcal{I}$. Our first goal is to define when a set $S \subset \mathcal{I}$ is a model of a theory T. As a preliminary step, let us consider the case of positive theories.

3 Positive Theories

For an interpretation I and a set of interpretations S, we define when a positive formula F is *true* in (I, S), as follows. (For simplicity, we assume that all propositional connectives are expressed in terms of the primitives $\neg$ and $\wedge$.)

1. If F is an atom, F is true in (I, S) iff $F \in I$.
2. $\neg F$ is true in (I, S) iff F is not true in (I, S).
3. $F \wedge G$ is true in (I, S) iff F and G are both true in (I, S).
4. KF is true in (I, S) iff, for every $J \in S$, F is true in (J, S).

A *model* of a positive theory T is any maximal set $S \subset \mathcal{I}$ such that, for every $I \in S$, the axioms of T are true in (I, S).

The maximality condition expresses the idea of "minimal knowledge": The larger the set of "possible worlds" is, the fewer facts are known.

In the special case when T is objective, the requirement that all axioms of T be true in (I, S) means simply that I is a model of T in the sense of classical propositional logic. Consequently, the set *Mod*(T) of the "classical models" of T is the only model of T in the sense of MKNF.

As another example, consider the case when T is $\{\mathrm{K}F\}$, where F is an objective formula. The models of T are the maximal sets $S \subset \mathcal{I}$ such that every interpretation from S is a classical model of F. It is clear that *Mod*(F) is the only such set. More generally, if F is an objective formula and T_0 a set of objective formulas, then $T_0 \cup \{\mathrm{K}F\}$ has a unique model; it is the same as the model of $T_0 \cup \{F\}$, that is, *Mod*$(T_0 \cup \{F\})$.

If $T = \{\mathrm{K}F_1 \vee \mathrm{K}F_2\}$, where F_1, F_2 are objective, then the models of T are the maximal sets $S \subset \mathcal{I}$ that satisfy the condition: Every interpretation from S is a classical model of F_1 or every interpretation from S is a classical model of F_2; symbolically:

$$S \subset \mathit{Mod}(F_1) \text{ or } S \subset \mathit{Mod}(F_2).$$

If neither F_1 nor F_2 is a logical consequence of the other, then neither of the sets *Mod*(F_1), *Mod*(F_2) contains the other, and T has two models: *Mod*(F_1) and *Mod*(F_2).

4 Propositional MKNF: Models

How can we extend the definition of a model to the general case, when the axioms contain *not*?

In the presence of both K and *not*, truth will be defined relative to a triple (I, S^k, S^n), where S^k and S^n are sets of interpretations; S^k serves as the set of possible worlds for the purpose of defining the meaning of K, and S^n plays the same role for the operator *not*. Then a model will be defined as any set S^n that satisfies a certain fixpoint condition.

For an interpretation I and two sets of interpretations S^k, S^n, we define when a formula is F *true* in (I, S^k, S^n), as follows.

1. If F is an atom, F is true in (I, S^k, S^n) iff $F \in I$.
2. $\neg F$ is true in (I, S^k, S^n) iff F is not true in (I, S^k, S^n).
3. $F \wedge G$ is true in (I, S^k, S^n) iff F and G are both true in (I, S^k, S^n).
4. KF is true in (I, S^k, S^n) iff, for every $J \in S^k$, F is true in (J, S^k, S^n).
5. *not* F is true in (I, S^k, S^n) iff, for some $J \in S^n$, F is not true in (J, S^k, S^n).

The truth condition for *not* F expresses that F is not known to be true provided that S^n is the set of worlds that are considered "possible."

This definition is a generalization of the definition of truth for positive formulas given in the previous section, in the sense that a positive formula is true in (I, S^k, S^n) iff it is true in (I, S^k).

For any theory T and any set $S \subset \mathcal{I}$, by $\Gamma(T, S)$ we denote the set of all maximal sets $S' \subset \mathcal{I}$ which satisfy the condition:

$$\text{For every } I \in S', \text{ the axioms of } T \text{ are true in } (I, S', S). \tag{1}$$

If $S \in \Gamma(T, S)$, then we say that S is a *model* of T.

It is easy to see that, for positive theories, this is equivalent to the definition given earlier. Indeed, if T is positive, then $\Gamma(T, S)$ does not depend on S, and is simply the set of all models of T in the sense defined in the previous section.

As an example of a theory whose axioms are not positive, consider the theory T whose only axiom is

$$\mathit{not}\, F \supset G, \tag{2}$$

where F and G are objective. The condition (1) says in this case:

$$\text{For every } I \in S', \text{ (2) is true in } (I, S', S).$$

This is equivalent to:

[3] An algorithm for the evaluation of epistemic queries in the monotonic case is proposed in [Reiter, 1990].

[4] The "assumption operator" A from [Lin and Shoham, 1990]) corresponds, in our notation, to the combination $\neg$*not*.

If, for some $J \in S$, F is false in J, then, for every $I \in S'$, G is true in I,

or

If $S \not\subset Mod(F)$ then $S' \subset Mod(G)$.

Consequently $\Gamma(T, S)$ is $\{\mathcal{I}\}$ if $S \subset Mod(F)$, and $\{Mod(G)\}$ otherwise. We conclude that the models of (2) can be characterized as follows:

1. If F is a tautology, then $\mathcal{I}$ is the only model of (2).
2. If F is a not a tautology but is a logical consequence of G, then (2) has no models. For instance, *not* $F \supset F$ has no models.
3. If F is a not a logical consequence of G, then the only model of (2) is $Mod(G)$. For instance, *not* $p \supset q$, where p and q are distinct atoms, has one model, $Mod(q)$.

5 Relation to Logic Programming

In this section we show that logic programs of some kinds can be viewed as theories in the sense of MKNF. We will consider three classes of programs, moving gradually towards greater generality. In the semantics of logic programming, it is customary to view a rule with variables as shorthand for the set of its ground instances; for this reason, we can restrict our attention to propositional programs.

A *positive logic program* is a set of rules of the form

$$A_0 \leftarrow A_1, \ldots, A_m, \tag{3}$$

where $m \geq 0$, and each A_i is an atom. According to van Emden and Kowalski [1976], the semantics of a positive program Π is defined by the smallest set of atoms which is closed under its rules (that is to say, which includes A_0 whenever it includes $A_1, \ldots, A_m$, for every rule (3) from Π). This set of atoms is known as the "minimal model" of Π, and we will denote it by $MM(\Pi)$.

In order to relate the semantics of positive programs to MKNF, let us agree to identify a rule (3) with the formula

$$\mathrm{K}A_1 \wedge \ldots \wedge \mathrm{K}A_m \supset \mathrm{K}A_0.$$

For any interpretation J, let $\omega(J)$ be the set of all interpretations I such that $J \subset I$.

Theorem 1, Part A. *Every positive program* Π *has one model,* $\omega(MM(\Pi))$.

For instance, let the rules of Π be

$$p \leftarrow q;\ r \leftarrow s;\ s \leftarrow . \tag{4}$$

Then $MM(\Pi)$ is $\{r, s\}$. Viewed as a theory in the sense of MKNF, Π is the set of 3 axioms:

$$\mathrm{K}q \supset \mathrm{K}p,\ \mathrm{K}s \supset \mathrm{K}r,\ \mathrm{K}s;$$

its model $\omega(MM(\Pi))$ is

$$\{\{r,s\},\{p,r,s\},\{q,r,s\},\{p,q,r,s\}\}. \tag{5}$$

A *general logic program* is a set of rules of the form

$$A_0 \leftarrow A_1, \ldots, A_m, not\ A_{m+1}, \ldots, not\ A_n, \tag{6}$$

where $n \geq m \geq 0$, and each A_i is an atom. Several approaches to defining a semantics for general logic programs have been proposed. One of them is based on the notion of a "stable model" [Gelfond and Lifschitz, 1988]. A stable model of Π is an interpretation satisfying some fixpoint condition. We will denote the set of such interpretations by $SM(\Pi)$. It is clear from the definition of a stable model that, in the special case when Π is positive, $SM(\Pi) = \{MM(\Pi)\}$.

A rule (6) will be identified with the formula

$$\mathrm{K}A_1 \wedge \ldots \wedge \mathrm{K}A_m \wedge not\ A_{m+1} \wedge \ldots \wedge not\ A_n \supset \mathrm{K}A_0.$$

Theorem 1, Part B. *The set of models of a general program* Π *is*

$$\{\omega(M)\ :\ M \in SM(\Pi)\}.$$

For instance, the program with the rules

$$p \leftarrow not\ q;\ q \leftarrow not\ r$$

has one stable model, $\{q\}$. These rules can be written as

$$not\ q \supset \mathrm{K}p,\ \ not\ r \supset \mathrm{K}q.$$

The only model of these axioms is

$$\{\{q\},\{p,q\},\{q,r\},\{p,q,r\}\}.$$

Finally, we will consider the class of (extended) disjunctive databases in the sense of [Gelfond and Lifschitz, 1991], in which classical negation and a form of disjunction are allowed. A *disjunctive database* is a set of rules of the form

$$L_1 \mid \ldots \mid L_l \leftarrow L_{l+1}, \ldots, L_m, not\ L_{m+1}, \ldots, not\ L_n, \tag{7}$$

where $n \geq m \geq l \geq 0$, and each L_i is a literal (an atom possibly preceded by $\neg$). The semantics of disjunctive databases defines when a set of literals is an "answer set" of a given database. We will denote the set of answer sets of a disjunctive database Π by $AS(\Pi)$. If Π is a general logic program, then $AS(\Pi) = SM(\Pi)$.

A rule (7) will be identified with the formula

$$\mathrm{K}L_{l+1} \wedge \ldots \wedge \mathrm{K}L_m \wedge not\ L_{m+1} \wedge \ldots \wedge not\ L_n \supset \mathrm{K}L_1 \vee \ldots \vee \mathrm{K}L_l. \tag{8}$$

In order to extend Theorem 1 to disjunctive databases, we need to generalize the definition of the operator ω. So far, $\omega(M)$ is defined when M is an interpretation, that is, a set of atoms. Now M is allowed to be a set of literals. For any set of literals M, M^+ is the set of atoms that belong to M, and M^- the set of atoms whose negations belong to M; $\omega(M)$ stands for the set of interpretations I such that $M^+ \subset I$ and $M^- \cap I = \emptyset$.

Theorem 1, Part C. *The set of models of a disjunctive database* Π *is*

$$\{\omega(M)\ :\ M \in AS(\Pi)\}.$$

For instance, the disjunctive database whose only rule is

$$p \mid \neg q \leftarrow not\ r \tag{9}$$

has two answer sets: $\{p\}$ and $\{\neg q\}$. This rule is the same as the formula

$$not\ r \supset \mathrm{K}p \vee \mathrm{K}\neg q;$$

the models of this axiom are

$$\{\{p\},\{p,q\},\{p,r\},\{p,q,r\}\}$$

and

$$\{\emptyset,\{p\},\{r\},\{p,r\}\}.$$

6 Propositional MKNF: The Consequence Relation

We say that a positive formula F is a *theorem* of a theory T, or a *consequence* of its axioms (symbolically, $T \models F$), if, for every model S of T and every interpretation $I \in S$, F is true in (I, S). Thus theoremhood is defined for positive formulas only. (We do not see any reasonable way to define theoremhood for formulas containing *not*.)

To illustrate this definition, consider first the special case when all axioms of T are objective. If F is objective also, then $T \models F$ if and only if F is a consequence of T in the sense of classical propositional logic. If F is allowed to contain K, then the definition of $\models$ turns into (the propositional case of) the definition of $\approx$ from [Reiter, 1990].

If, for instance, the only axiom of T is $p \vee q$, then $\neg Kp$ is a theorem. If $\neg q$ is added as another axiom, this theorem will be lost. Thus the consequence relation $\models$ is nonmonotonic even for objective T.

If Π is a general logic program or a disjunctive database, we can ask whether a positive formula F is a consequence of Π. For instance, $q \supset p$ is not a consequence of the program (4), because it is false in one of the interpretations from (5). Theorem 1 (Part C) shows that a literal is a consequence of Π if and only if it belongs to all answer sets of Π.

We conclude this section with two remarks about general properties of the consequence relation. First, we would like to say that every axiom is a theorem, but this makes sense for positive axioms only. It is easy to check, however, that the result of replacing all occurences of *not* by $\neg K$ in an axiom is a theorem. Second, let F_1 and F_2 be positive formulas; if $KF_1 \supset KF_2$ is provable in $S5$, and $T \models F_1$, then $T \models F_2$. In this sense, the set of theorems is closed under $S5$.

7 Quantification

Our next goal is to extend the definitions given above to languages with quantification. For simplicity, we consider first-order quantifiers only; extension to the higher-order case is straightforward.

Consider the language obtained from a first-order language $\mathcal{L}$ by adding the modal operators K and *not*. A *theory* is now a set of sentences of this language; an *interpretation* is a structure for $\mathcal{L}$. The universe of an interpretation I will be denoted by $|I|$. For any nonempty set U, by $\mathcal{I}_U$ we denote the set of all interpretations with the universe U.

Let I be an interpretation, and let S^k, S^n be subsets of $\mathcal{I}_{|I|}$. We will define when a sentence is *true* in (I, S^k, S^n). To this end, we need to extend the language by object constants representing all elements of $|I|$; these constants will be called *names*. Truth will be defined for all sentences of the extended language. We assume that all propositional connectives and quantifiers are expressed in terms of $\neg$, $\wedge$ and $\forall$.

1. If F is an atomic sentence, F is true in (I, S^k, S^n) iff F is true in I.
2. $\neg F$ is true in (I, S^k, S^n) iff F is not true in (I, S^k, S^n).
3. $F \wedge G$ is true in (I, S^k, S^n) iff F and G are both true in (I, S^k, S^n).
4. $\forall x F(x)$ is true in (I, S^k, S^n) iff, for every name ξ, $F(\xi)$ is true in (I, S^k, S^n).
5. KF is true in (I, S^k, S^n) iff, for every $J \in S^k$, F is true in (J, S^k, S^n).
6. $not\, F$ is true in (I, S^k, S^n) iff, for some $J \in S^n$, F is not true in (J, S^k, S^n).

For any theory T, nonempty set U, and subset S of $\mathcal{I}_U$, by $\Gamma_U(T, S)$ we denote the set of all maximal sets $S' \subset \mathcal{I}_U$ which satisfy the condition:

For every $I \in S'$, the axioms of T are true in (I, S', S).

If $S \in \Gamma_U(T, S)$, then we say that (U, S) is a *model* of T.

If all axioms of T are objective, then the models of T are the pairs $(U, Mod_U(T))$, where $Mod_U(T)$ stands for the set of classical models of T with the universe U.

With quantification available, we can represent logic programs as axiom sets in a more direct way, without first replacing rules by their ground instances. A disjunctive database can be identified with the axiom set consisting of (i) the universal closures of the formulas (8) corresponding to its rules (7), and (ii) appropriate equality axioms (see [Clark, 1978]). This semantics differs from the one presented in Section 5 in that it permits "non-Herbrand models."[5]

A positive sentence F is a *theorem* of a theory T if, for every model (U, S) of T and every interpretation $I \in S$, F is true in (I, S). The two properties of the propositional consequence relation stated at the end of the previous section apply to the first-order case also.

8 Relation to Default Logic and Circumscription

In accordance with the idea of Lin and Shoham [1990], we identify a default

$$\alpha : \beta_1, \ldots, \beta_m / \gamma \tag{10}$$

with (the universal closure of) the formula

$$K\alpha \wedge not\neg\beta_1 \wedge \ldots \wedge not\neg\beta_m \supset K\gamma. \tag{11}$$

The following theorem refers to "default logic with a fixed universe"—a modification of the system of [Reiter, 1980] proposed in [Lifschitz, 1990]. The main difference is that, in the standard default logic, parameters of an open default are treated as metavariables for ground terms, whereas the modified system handles parameters as genuine object variables.

Theorem 2. *An objective sentence F is a fixed-universe consequence of (D, W) iff $D \cup W \models F$.*

This theorem shows that the translation (11) embeds default logic with a fixed universe into MKNF.

In [Lifschitz, 1990] we showed how to embed circumscription (with all nonlogical constants varied) into default logic with a fixed universe. The composition of

[5]See [Przymusinski, 1989] on the role of non-Herbrand models in logic programming.

these two transformations reduces the circumscription of P in a sentence $F(P)$ to the formula

$$F(P) \wedge \forall x(not\ P(x) \supset \neg P(x)).$$

The objective consequences of this formula in the sense of MKNF are exactly the sentences that follow from the circumscription in classical logic.

9 Conclusion

The logic of minimal knowledge with negation as failure provides a unified framework for several nonmonotonic formalisms and for the Levesque/Reiter theory of epistemic queries. Its semantics, like the semantics of circumscription and of default logic with a fixed universe, is a generalization of the standard concept of a model of a first order theory; we consider this an important advantage.

However, this unification is not entirely satisfactory, for two reasons. First, the logic of minimal knowledge (even in the propositional case and without negation as failure) has the following puzzling and unintuitive property.[6] When a theory T is extended by an "explicit definition" of an atom p—by an axiom $p \equiv F$, where p occurs neither in the axioms of T nor in F—this may affect the class of theorems that do not contain p. In other words, in the logic of minimal knowledge, a "definitional" extension is not necessarily "conservative." This observation seems to point to a serious defect of the idea of minimal knowledge. Second, MKNF does not cover the important concept of "strong introspection," introduced recently by Gelfond [1991].

Acknowledgments

I would like to thank Michael Gelfond, Katsumi Inoue, Hector Levesque, Fangzhen Lin, Ray Reiter, Grigorii Schwarz and Miroslaw Truszczyński for useful discussions on the subject of this paper.

References

[Clark, 1978] Keith Clark. Negation as failure. In Herve Gallaire and Jack Minker, editors, *Logic and Data Bases*, pages 293–322. Plenum Press, New York, 1978.

[Emden and Kowalski, 1976] Maarten van Emden and Robert Kowalski. The semantics of predicate logic as a programming language. *Journal of the ACM*, 23(4):733–742, 1976.

[Gelfond and Lifschitz, 1988] Michael Gelfond and Vladimir Lifschitz. The stable model semantics for logic programming. In Robert Kowalski and Kenneth Bowen, editors, *Logic Programming: Proc. of the Fifth Int'l Conf. and Symp.*, pages 1070–1080, 1988.

[Gelfond and Lifschitz, 1990] Michael Gelfond and Vladimir Lifschitz. Logic programs with classical negation. In David Warren and Peter Szeredi, editors, *Logic Programming: Proc. of the Seventh Int'l Conf.*, pages 579–597, 1990.

[6] Grigorii Schwarz, personal communication.

[Gelfond and Lifschitz, 1991] Michael Gelfond and Vladimir Lifschitz. Classical negation in logic programs and disjunctive databases. *New Generation Computing*, 1991. To apppear.

[Gelfond, 1987] Michael Gelfond. On stratified autoepistemic theories. In *Proc. AAAI-87*, pages 207–211, 1987.

[Gelfond, 1991] Michael Gelfond. Strong introspection. In *Proc. AAAI-91*, 1991. To apppear.

[Halpern and Moses, 1984] Joseph Halpern and Yoram Moses. Towards a theory of knowledge and ignorance: preliminary report. Technical Report RJ 4448 (48136), IBM, 1984.

[Konolige, 1982] Kurt Konolige. Circumscriptive ignorance. In *Proc. of AAAI-82*, pages 202–204, 1982.

[Levesque, 1984] Hector Levesque. Foundations of a functional approach to knowledge representation. *Artificial Intelligence*, 23(2):155–212, 1984.

[Levesque, 1990] Hector Levesque. All I know: a study in autoepistemic logic. *Artificial Intelligence*, 42(2,3):263–310, 1990.

[Lifschitz, 1990] Vladimir Lifschitz. On open defaults. In John Lloyd, editor, *Computational Logic: Symposium Proceedings*, pages 80–95. Springer, 1990.

[Lin and Shoham, 1990] Fangzhen Lin and Yoav Shoham. Epistemic semantics for fixed-points nonmonotonic logics. In Rohit Parikh, editor, *Theoretical Aspects of Reasoning about Knowledge: Proc. of the Third Conf.*, pages 111–120, 1990.

[Lin, 1988] Fangzhen Lin. Circumscription in a modal logic. In Moshe Vardi, editor, *Theoretical Aspects of Reasoning about Knowledge: Proc. of the Second Conf.*, pages 113–127, 1988.

[Marek and Truszczyński, 1989] Wiktor Marek and Miroslaw Truszczyński. Relating autoepistemic and default logic. In Ronald Brachman, Hector Levesque, and Raymond Reiter, editors, *Proc. of the First Int'l Conf. on Principles of Knowledge Representation and Reasoning*, pages 276–288, 1989.

[McCarthy, 1986] John McCarthy. Applications of circumscription to formalizing common sense knowledge. *Artificial Intelligence*, 26(3):89–116, 1986.

[Moore, 1985] Robert Moore. Semantical considerations on nonmonotonic logic. *Artificial Intelligence*, 25(1):75–94, 1985.

[Przymusinski, 1989] Teodor Przymusinski. On the declarative and procedural semantics of logic programs. *Journal of Automated Reasoning*, 5:167–205, 1989.

[Reiter, 1980] Raymond Reiter. A logic for default reasoning. *Artificial Intelligence*, 13(1,2):81–132, 1980.

[Reiter, 1988] Raymond Reiter. On integrity constraints. In Moshe Vardi, editor, *Theoretical Aspects of Reasoning about Knowledge: Proc. of the Second Conf.*, pages 97–111, 1988.

[Reiter, 1990] Raymond Reiter. On asking what a database knows. In John Lloyd, editor, *Computational Logic: Symposium Proceedings*, pages 96–113. Springer, 1990.

[Shoham, 1986] Yoav Shoham. Chronological ignorance: Time, nonmonotonicity, necessity and causal theories. In *Proc. of AAAI-86*, pages 389–393, 1986.

[Siegel, 1990] Pierre Siegel. A modal language for nonmonotonic logic. Presented at the DRUMS/CEE Workshop, Marseille, 1990.

[Truszczyński, 1991] Miroslaw Truszczyński. Modal interpretations of default logic. In *Proc. of IJCAI-91*, 1991.

Commonsense Entailment: A Modal Theory of Nonmonotonic Reasoning

Nicholas Asher
Center for Cognitive Science, GRG 220
University of Texas at Austin
Austin TX 78712, USA
asher@sygmund.cgs.utexas.edu

Michael Morreau
IMS, University of Stuttgart
Keplerstrasse 17
7000 Stuttgart 1, Deutschland
mimo@adler.philosophie.uni-stuttgart.de

Abstract

In this paper, we construct a truth conditional semantics for generic sentences, which treats arbitrarily deep nestings of generic sentences. The resulting notion of logical entailment captures intuitively valid argument forms involving generics. A dynamic semantics is built on top of the truth conditional one, and the resulting inference notion captures nonmonotonic argument patterns familiar from the artificial intelligence literature by exploiting constraints on modal frames alone, without the use of ordering principles on rules, abnormality or "relevance" predicates.

1. Introduction

Potatoes contain vitamin C, amino acid, protein and thiamin expresses a true generalization about potatoes. *John smokes a cigar after dinner*, understood in its generic sense as expressing a regularity in John's behaviour after dinner, can be true, and it can be false. This realist conviction inspires the theory of generic propositions which is the subject of this paper. The difficulty with generic propositions is that their truth is loosly but clearly connected with particular facts. For instance, potatoes contain vitamin C, even though large numbers of them are boiled for so long that it is lost. Potatoes would contain vitamin C even if *all* of them were to be boiled for so long that it is lost. Nevertheless, the generic fact that potatoes contain vitamin C furnishes all the evidence we need to be justified in concluding that this potato, in the absence of any other conflicting information, contains vitamin C. The curious relation between generic and particular facts has for a decade or more frustrated efforts in artificial intelligence, linguistics, and philosophy to provide generic sentences with a rigorous semantics. We offer such a semantics here for one kind of genericity.

Researchers in AI have produced many theories of non-monotonic reasoning that be seen also as attempting to give a semantics for genericity. As motivation for our theory, we argue for three desiderata of a semantics for genericity and defaults which other theories of genericity do not simultaneously satisfy. A first requirement is that any theory of genericity should explain the ways in which we reason with generic sentences. Logical entailment is one form of reasoning. We think that the truth conditions of generic sentences can be captured by using ordinary quantification and a non-monotonic conditional operator; so in what follows we shall write *φ's normally ψ* as $\forall x(\varphi > \psi)$.[1] There are a few forms involving generic sentences that seem clearly to be cases of logical entailment (⊧). One is WEAKENING OF THE CONSEQUENT. Suppose ζ is a logical consequence of ψ; then:

$$\forall x(\varphi > \psi) \models \forall x(\varphi > \zeta).$$

Among the intuitively valid generic sentences, those which are entailed by everything, we count *Lions are lions*, and the nested generic sentence *People who don't like to eat out don't like to eat out.* We take this last sentence to be nested because it says that people possessing a characteristic property -- namely the property of typically not liking to eat out-- typically have this property.

While the logic of generic sentences seems to support few valid argument forms, it does seem to support many "reasonable inference patterns." Among the things not entailed by the generic statement that potatoes contain vitamin C is the particular conclusion that *this* potato contains vitamin C. Nevertheless, the generic fact makes it somehow reasonable to expect this potato to contain vitamin C, without at the same time making it reasonable to expect any number of other things which are not entailed, like say that the moon is made of green cheese. Researchers in the field of nonmonotonic reasoning have discovered a wealth of such patterns of invalid but reasonable generic inference, of which some examples are given below. We will symbolize reasonable inference by $\approx\!\!\!|$ (⊨≈).

The main patterns come in three distinguishable groups. In this paper we will present in some detail an interpretation of generic sentences in which the following generally acknowledge patterns of nonmonotonic reasoning hold.

DEFEASIBLE MODUS PONENS $\forall x(\varphi > \psi), \varphi(\delta) \mathrel{|\!\approx} \psi(\delta)$,
but not $\forall x(\varphi > \psi), \varphi(\delta), \neg \psi(\delta) \mathrel{|\!\approx} \psi(\delta)$

NIXON DIAMOND not$\{ \forall x(\varphi > \psi), \forall x(\zeta > \neg\psi), \varphi(d), \zeta(d) \mathrel{|\!\approx} \psi(d)$ (or $\neg \psi(d))\}$

POINTWISE DEFEASIBLE TRANSITIVITY $\forall x(\varphi > \psi), \forall x(\psi > \zeta), \varphi(\delta) \mathrel{|\!\approx} \zeta(\delta)$
but not $\{ \forall x(\varphi > \psi), \forall x(\psi > \zeta), \forall x(\varphi > \neg\zeta), \varphi(\delta) \mathrel{|\!\approx} \varphi(\delta)\}$

[1] Assuming a generic quantifier makes more linguistic sense than what we have done above; however, such a quantifier is definable in terms of ∀ and >, given our semantics.

POINTWISE DEFEASIBLE STRENGTHENING OF THE ANTECEDENT: $\forall x(\varphi > \psi), \varphi(\delta) \& \zeta(\delta) \mid\!\approx \psi(\delta)$, but not $\{\forall x(\varphi > \psi), \varphi(\delta) \& \zeta(\delta), \forall x((\varphi \& \zeta) > \neg\psi) \mid\!\approx \psi(\delta)\}$.

PENGUIN PRINCIPLE: $\forall x(\varphi > \psi), \forall x(\psi > \zeta), \forall x(\varphi > \neg\zeta), \varphi(\delta) \mid\!\approx \neg\psi(\delta)$.

EMBEDDED DEFEASIBLE MODUS PONENS: $\forall x(\zeta > \forall y(\varphi > \psi)), \gamma(\delta), \forall u(\gamma > \exists y\varphi) \mid\!\approx \exists y\psi(\delta)$.

In all of these forms of reasoning, we observe that $\mid\!\approx$ is very sensitive to "relevant premises" that may affect conclusions that may be reasonably drawn from a subset of those premises. Capturing such inferences has been a major challenge for AI. But further these forms of reasoning may interact, but they should not interact in "bizarre" ways. Here is one bizarre interaction that we want to avoid. For while we have

$$\forall x(\varphi > \psi) \models \forall x(\varphi > (\psi \vee \zeta))$$

and we have defeasible modus ponens, we do not get the undesirable inference,

DEFEASIBLE IRRELEVANCE: $\forall x(\varphi > \psi), \varphi(\delta), \neg\, \psi(\delta) \mid\!\approx \zeta(\delta)$

for then we would defeasibly conclude that from *birds fly* and *Tweety is a bird that does not fly*, that Tweety is a locomotive!

A second class of inferences that we believe to be plausible are the following "rule versions" of the pointwise, defeasible transitivity and strengthening of the antecedent rules.

DEFEASIBLE TRANSITIVITY $\forall x(\varphi > \psi), \forall x(\psi > \zeta) \mid\!\approx \forall x(\varphi > \zeta)$, but not $\{\forall x(\varphi > \psi), \forall x(\psi > \zeta), \forall x(\varphi > \neg\zeta) \mid\!\approx \forall x(\varphi > \zeta)\}$.

DEFEASIBLE STRENGTHENING OF THE ANTECEDENT: $\forall x(\varphi > \psi) \mid\!\approx \forall x((\varphi \& \zeta) > \psi)$ but not $\{\forall x(\varphi > \psi), \forall x((\varphi \& \zeta) > \neg\psi) \mid\!\approx \forall x((\varphi \& \zeta) > \psi)$.

Finally there is a third group of reasonable inferences that depend on a view of normality on which normality comes in degrees.

GRADED NORMALITY AND DEFASIBLE MODUS PONENS: $\forall x(\varphi > \psi_1), \ldots, \forall x(\varphi > \psi_n), \varphi(\delta), \neg\psi_1(\delta) \mid\!\approx \psi_2(\delta) \& \ldots \& \psi_n(\delta)$ but not $\{\forall x(\varphi > \psi_1), \ldots, \forall x(\varphi > \psi_n), \varphi(\delta), \neg \psi_1(\delta) \mid\!\approx \psi_1(\delta) \& \ldots \& \psi_n(\delta)\}$.

GRADED NORMALITY AND DEFASIBLE TRANSITIVITY: $\forall x(\varphi > \psi), \forall x(\psi > \zeta), \forall x(\psi > \psi_1), \forall x(\varphi > \neg\psi_1) \mid\!\approx \forall x(\varphi > \zeta)$, but not $\{\forall x(\varphi > \psi), \forall x(\psi > \zeta), \forall x(\psi > \psi_1), \forall x(\varphi > \neg\psi_1) \mid\!\approx \forall x(\varphi > \psi_1)\}$.

Although we have worked out a semantics on which these last two groups of inferences hold, we cannot give a detailed account here. We give a brief description in the penultimate section of the paper; we will concentrate on presenting a minimal system of commonsense entailment.

In any case, an acceptable theory of genericity will respect the distinction between logical entailment and reasonable inference, and it must realistically model the reasoning belonging to each area. In particular, the semantics must capture the feature that these defeasible patterns of inference introduce a dependence on epistemic contexts which is not at all present in the case of the valid patterns. Their conclusions are defeated *as one obtains information* which brings them into doubt, not as the world changes in whatever way. Realistically modelling such defeasible reasoning will lead us to model these epistemic contexts explicitly in the semantics of generic sentences.

A second requirement for theories of genericity is that they be sufficiently general. The correct theory must provide interpretations not only for simple generic sentences like most of those we have seen up until now, but also for composite sentences in which genericity mixes with counterfactuality, belief, knowledge, and even with more genericity, as in the case of nested generic sentences like *healthy cats jump at small moving objects*, or *people who work late at nights do not wake up early.* Here is an example of generics interacting with counterfactuality and propositional attitudes: *John knows that Mary loves kissing him, and he would be unhappy if she were were to like it less.* A theory of what generics mean ought at least to extend to a theory of what they mean in such contexts.

The third desideratum for theories of genericity is a methodological one. In one respect most of the formalisms (including the one to be presented below) for representing and reasoning with generic information are alike: they are empirically inadequate. In another respect, however, they differ greatly. Some theories cover up the deficiencies of the underlying mechanisms that purport to explain nonmonotonic reasoning by introducing devices foreign to those mechanisms. One case in point is the way in which theories treat the penguin principle, the pattern of reasoning where specific information takes precedence. This is the familiar problem of multiple extensions. Formalizing the premises of the penguin principle in the way done in circumscription by means of a multitude of "abnormality predicates," for example, we find that minimization of abnormality results in two kinds of minimal models: there are models where Tweety is an abnormal bird but a normal penguin, and so does not fly. But in addition there are others where he is a normal bird but an abnormal penguin, and does fly. Because of these latter, undesirable models it then does not follow that Tweety does not fly, and we see that circumscription does not handle the penguin principle adequately. Similar problems confront default logic and autoepistemic logic. The solution which proponents of these theories have suggested is as familiar as the problem: the order in which default rules fire needs to be constrained; the predicates to be minimized in the case of circumscription need to be prioritized. They thus commit themselves to the

HYPOTHESIS OF THE GHOST IN THE MACHINE

> That specific information takes precedence over general information is not to be accounted for by the semantics of generic statements itself. Rather, it is due to the intervention of a power which is extraneous to the semantic machinery, but which guides this machinery to have this effect (by ordering the defaults, deciding the priorities of predicates to be minimized, or whatever).

Whatever kind of reasoning generic reasoning is, more specific information takes precedence is intrinsic to it. The penguin principle should emerge naturally from the semantics of generic sentences without the intervention of a user who decides how the reasoning is to be applied. We want to exorcise the ghost from the machine.

Emulating the possible worlds analysis of conditional sentences, we construct first a semantics assigning truth values to (nested) generic sentences relative to possible worlds. The truth conditional part of our semantics, with its standard notion of entailment, accounts for the valid argument forms we mentioned. Because it is a conventional possible worlds theory, we can insert the semantics of generics within general, possible worlds frameworks that yield semantics for counterfactuals, propositional attitudes and so on. It is thus in principle very clear how to interpret complex sentences such as those discussed above.

On top of the truth conditional semantics, we build a second, dynamic, partial theory, which accounts for defeasible patterns of reasonable inference. Our intuitive picture of what goes on when one reasons by defeasible modus ponens is this: first one assumes the premises *birds fly* and *Tweety is a bird*, and no more than this. Second, one assumes that Tweety is as normal a bird as is consistent with these premises. Finally, one then looks to see whether one believes that Tweety flies or not, and finds that he does. In our view *all* of the patterns of defeasible reasoning outlined in the introduction arise in this way, from assuming just their premises, then assuming everyone and everything as normal as is epistemically possible, and finally seeing whether one believes their conclusions. The dynamic semantic models such epistemic reasoning by means of information states, which are sets of possible worlds taken from the truth conditional model theory. We define two functions on these information states: updating and normalization. The first of these is eliminative, simply removing from information states all those possible worlds where the sentences with which one is updating are not true. Assuming just the premises of an argument can then be modelled as updating a distinguished informationally minimal state ☺ with those premises. The second of these functions, normalization, encodes in the semantics the notion of assuming everyone and everything as normal as possible. Normalizing the result of updating ☺ with a set of premises Γ yields a set of information states which are fixpoints of the normalization process. The conclusions of reasonable inferences from premises Γ are all those sentences that are true at all the worlds in all of these fixpoints. The figure below graphically depicts our dynamic theory of reasonable inference;+ represents update, the arrows the normalization process.

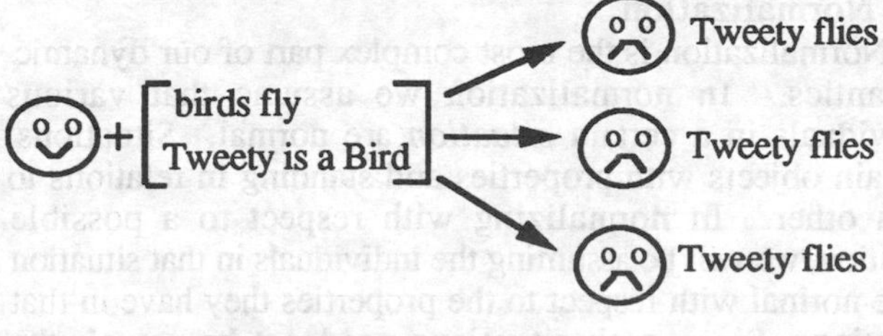

2. The Truth Conditional Semantics of Generics

2.1 The Language

In the following we are working with a first-order language L augmented with a binary conditional operator >. The formulas of the language $L_>$ are defined by the usual clauses, together with the following one:

If φ and ψ are formulas, then φ > ψ is a formula.

This definition allows for arbitrarily deep nesting of the conditional > in formulas.

2.2 The Truth Conditional Semantics

The underlying semantic idea in interpreting the language $L_>$ is that a generic sentence $\forall x(\varphi > \psi)$ is true at a possible world just in case, at that world, being a normal φ involves being a ψ. The modal frames encode what being a normal φ invariably involves by means of a worlds accessibility function *, which assigns to each possible world w and proposition p a set of worlds. This gives a basic semantics for $L_>$ and a simple system of commonsense entailment.

DEFINITION: A $L_>$ frame is a triple $F = \langle W, D, *\rangle$ where

i) W is a non-empty set of worlds,
ii) D is a non-empty set of individuals, and
iii) $*: W \times \wp(W) \rightarrow \wp(W)$

*(w, p) contains only worlds in which, intuitively speaking, the proposition p holds together with everything else which, in world w, is normally the case when p holds. For example, let p be the proposition that Big Bird of *Sesame Street* fame is a bird. Let w be the actual world, where it is true that birds fly, that birds have feathers, and that birds lay eggs. Then *(w, p) contains only worlds where Big Bird flies, has feathers and lays eggs. World w may in fact not be in *(w, p), given that the television character is, as birds go, not at all typical.

Note that what is normally the case when a proposition p holds is allowed to vary from possible world to possible world. We want there to be, for example, possible worlds where Tweety is a perfectly normal bird and doesn't fly, these quite simply being those possible worlds where it is not true that birds fly. Note also that it is important that we do not suppose any absolute normality order on possible worlds. In particular, we explicitly reject the idea that *(w, p) is to be identified with those most normal of all possible worlds where p holds.

Up until now * has been left virtually unconstrained, and indeed in view of the weak logic of generics only a few constraints are needed.[2] The first of these is

FACTICITY: $*(w, p) \subseteq p$

Worlds where p holds together with other propositions which are normally associated with p are, no matter how few of these other propositions hold, in any case worlds where p holds. One of the most important patterns of defeasible reasoning which we want to capture is the penguin principle. We capture the penguin principle by introducing a constraint on *. When we build the dynamic semantics, this constraint

[2]One constraint on * which is familiar from the literature on conditional logic but which we certainly do not want to impose here is

CENTERING If $w \in p$, then $w \in *(w, p)$

That w is a world where p holds is no guarantee that w is a world where everything holds which is normally associated with p.

will interact with the normalization function in such a way as to give us the penguin principle.

SPECIFICITY: If $*(w, p) \subseteq q$, $*(w, p) \cap *(w, q) = \emptyset$, and $*(w, p) \neq \emptyset$, then $*(w, q) \cap p = \emptyset$.

Suppose that p is the proposition that Tweety is a penguin, q the proposition that he is a bird; suppose further that if Tweety is a normal bird he flies but that if he is a normal penguin he doesn't fly. Then specificity says that for any world in which Tweety is a normal bird, he's not a penguin. We don't think specificity is all that intuitive by itself, but it yields plausible results when combined with our operation of normalization. In all of the following we will restrict $L_>$ to those which satisfy facticity and specificity.

We now define $L_>$ interpretations in $L_>$ frames in the standard way.

DEFINITION: A *base model* M is a pair $M = \langle F, [\![\,]\!] \rangle$, where
- i) F is an $L_>$ frame, and
- ii) $[\![\,]\!]$ is a function from nonlogical constants of L to appropriate intensions (functions from worlds to appropriate extensions)

The satisfaction definition for $L_>$ sentences islargely familiar and uses assignments α_i: Var $\rightarrow D_M$. Truth is deiined as satisfaction with respect to all assignments.

DEFINITION: For any possible world $w \in W_M$ and model M:

$M, w, \alpha_i \models \varphi$, as usual, for φ an atomic formula of FOL.

$M, w, \alpha_i \models \varphi > \psi$ iff $*(w, \|\varphi\|_{M, \alpha_i}) \subseteq \|\psi\|_{M, \alpha_i}$

The usual clauses for complex formulas involving $\forall, \exists, \vee, \&, \rightarrow, \neg$.

$\|\varphi\|_{M, \alpha_i} = \{w \in W_M: M, w, \alpha_i \models \varphi\}$.

This truth definition implies that a generic sentence is true in a model M at a world w iff for all $\delta \in D_M$, $*(w, \|\varphi\underline{\delta}\|_M) \subseteq \|\psi\underline{\delta}\|_M$. One important novelty in this definition is that unlike the usual definitions in modal or conditional logic, the semantics for generics exploits the instances of the formulas on the left and the right. As a result, the truth of *birds fly* does not imply the existence of worlds where *all* birds are normal fliers. This is an unnatural assumption in many cases.

$L_>$ logical consequence, $\models$, is defined in a completely standard way: $\Gamma \models \varphi$ iff in all $L_>$ models M extending $L_>$ frames satisfying facticity and specificity, if $\forall\gamma \in \Gamma$ $M \models \gamma$, then $M \models \varphi$. A corresponding derivability notion $\vdash$ is given by the following rules and axioms; the resulting derivability notion is denoted $\vdash$.

<u>The Logic T_1</u>

(A1) Truth functional $L_>$ tautologies

(A2) $\forall x\varphi \rightarrow \varphi[t/x]$ for any term t

(A3) $\forall x\, \varphi \leftrightarrow \neg\exists x\neg\varphi x$

(A4) $\forall x(\varphi \rightarrow \psi) \rightarrow (\exists x\varphi \rightarrow \psi)$

(A5) $\varphi > \varphi$.

(A6) $(\varphi > \psi \;\&\; \psi > \zeta \;\&\; \varphi > \neg\zeta) \rightarrow \psi > \neg\varphi$.

(A7) $\forall x(\varphi > \psi) \rightarrow (\varphi > \forall x\psi)$, for x not free in φ.

(R1) $\vdash \varphi$ and $\vdash \varphi \rightarrow \psi \Rightarrow \vdash \psi$

(R2) $\vdash (\psi_1 \;\&\; .. \;\&\; \psi_n) \rightarrow \psi \Rightarrow \vdash (\varphi > \psi_1 \;\&\; .. \;\&\; \varphi > \psi_n) \rightarrow \varphi > \psi$

(R3) $\vdash \varphi \rightarrow \psi[t/x]$, where t is a constant not in φ or $\psi \Rightarrow \vdash \varphi \rightarrow \forall x\psi$

(R4) $\vdash \varphi \Rightarrow \vdash \varphi[t/x]$ where t is a term not in φ.

(R5) $\vdash \varphi \leftrightarrow \psi$ and φ a subformula of $\zeta \Rightarrow \vdash \zeta \leftrightarrow \zeta[\psi/\varphi]$

Using a slight extension of the present language so as to express the Penguin principle and Henkin's technique to construct a canonical model yields the following completeness theorem for T_1.

THEOREM 1: $\Gamma \vdash \varphi$ iff $\Gamma \models \varphi$

3. The Dynamic Semantics of Generic Reasoning

We now show how to model the patterns of invalid but reasonable inference by building on top of the truth conditional semantics a dynamic semantics. We will use four concepts: information states, updating, the state of ignorance, and normalization, which we now spell out.

3.1. Information States, Updates and Ignorance

We take *information states* to be sets of possible worlds taken from the base models already defined. Accordingly, our approach to updating information states with new information is very simple and follows Stalnaker's definition. On updating with *Sam is a dodo*, the set of one's informational possibilities is reduced to those possible worlds where Sam is a dodo. We will define update functions + of this kind. We also will define a support relation $\models$ between belief states and sentences of $L_>$.

In order to capture the notion of believing no more than one has been told, we must define a very particular information state. This is the *informationally minimal* state of the introduction, ☺. This informationally minimal state must support only logical truths. This state must have some particular properties: it must contain enough worlds to verify every possible consistent combination of L sentences, for instance. Furthermore, it must contain worlds w to which are assigned sets of p normal worlds for every proposition p so that the T_1 axioms hold at every w. The Henkin construction procedure for the canonical T_1 model yields the appropriate model M_0 in which to define ignorance. W_0, the set of worlds in M_0, is just ☺. "Knowing no more than Γ" comes to being in the information state ☺ + Γ.

3.2 Normalization

Normalization is the most complex part of our dynamic semantics. In normalization we assume that various individuals in a certain *situation* are normal. Situations contain objects with properties and standing in relations to each other. In normalizing with respect to a possible situation, we will be assuming the individuals in that situation to be normal with respect to the properties they have in that situation. Since such situations need not be actual, the individuals may not actually possess those properties. We limit ourselves here to *simple situations.* A simple situation is one in which a single individual has a simple atomic property; in virtue of the canonical model in which we are working, we may identify a simple situation with an atomic formula or a negation of an atomic formula paired with an individual. To model the notion of assuming everything to be as normal as epistemically possible, we iterate normalization with respect to a set of simple situations.

To get an intuitive feel for normalization with respect to a single, simple situation consider for example a state which contains only the information that birds fly and that Tweety is a bird. Strengthening such a state with the assumption that Tweety is as normal a bird as is consistent with that state will return the information that Tweety flies. An initial state which contains the additional information that Tweety does not fly will, when thus strengthened, not return the information that Tweety flies, since in this case the new assumption is not consistent.

The normalization function makes use of the information about normality contained within whole information states. So we define the notion of a set of normal worlds for information states as follows:

DEFINITION: $*(s, p) := \bigcup_{w \in s} *(w, p)$.

Consider a simple situation ψ $\psi = <\varphi(x), \delta>$ and $\delta \in D_{M_0}$. We will write $\|\psi\|$ to denote the set of worlds in which δ has the property of being a φ. $\underline{N}(s, \psi)$, defined below, stands for the result of strengthening s by assuming δ to be a normal ψ, if this is consistent with s. The definition of normalization uses information about normality to characterize worlds that the state does *not* take to be normal. For ψ as defined above, $\|\psi\| \setminus *(w, \|\psi\|)$ stands for the set of possible worlds in which, according to an isolated w, an individual δ is, though a φ, not a normal φ. So $\|\psi\| \setminus *(s, \|\psi\|)$ is the set of worlds where, according to *all* of the worlds in s, δ is not a normal φ. They all agree that in each world in $\|\psi\| \setminus *(s, \|\psi\|)$, δ lacks at least one of the properties had by a normal φ.

DEFINITION: $\underline{N}(s, \psi) := \{w \in s : w \notin (\|\psi\| \setminus *(s, \|\psi\|))\}$, if $s \cap *(s, \|\psi\|) \neq \emptyset$;
$:= s$, otherwise.

$\underline{N}$ isolates those worlds in s where δ is a normal φ, if this is consistent with s: a world v is excluded from $\underline{N}(s, \psi)$ just in case δ is, *at v itself*, not a normal φ, if this is consistent with s. To see what this means concretely, let us for the moment suppose that it is, intuitively speaking, consistent with s that δ is what (in s) is taken to be a completely normal φ. For example, where φ is *bird*(x) and s contains the information *bird*(δ) and *bird*(x) $>_x$ *fly*(x), we are supposing the sentence *fly*($\underline{\delta}$) to be consistent with s. This state of affairs amounts formally to the case where $s \cap *(s, \|\psi\|) \neq \emptyset$, so then, given the above explanation of what $\|\psi\| \setminus *(s, \|\psi\|)$ stands for, $\underline{N}(s, \psi)$ clearly contains only those worlds in s where δ is, if at all a φ, then as normal a φ as is consistent with s (namely a completely normal one). It is not always consistent with s that δ is a normal φ. This is the case in which $s \cap *(s, \|\psi\|) = \emptyset$. Assuming δ to be a normal φ is in this case hopeless, so the normalization function "gives up" and simply returns the original state s.

Let us now turn to iterated normalization. In normalizing with respect to many individuals and many properties, we iterate the normalization function on information states. One factor affecting such iterated normalization is the order in which the normalizations of the sort discussed in the previous section are performed. Consider for instance a Nixon diamond situation, where the outcome depends on the order in which the different respects in which individuals are assumed normal show up in the iteration. If one first assumes that Dick is a normal republican and only then assumes that he is as normal a quaker as possible, then one will end up with the information that he is a non-pacifist. If one first assumes him to be a normal quaker and then assumes that he is as normal a republican as possible, then one will end up with the information that he is a pacifist. So it is desirable that the order sensitivity of the iterated normalization be cancelled out by taking all different orderings of the iterations into account.

A second point about iterated normalization concerns the situations relevant to normalization. The relevant situations are defined with repsect to the premises Γ in a nonmonotonic inference that one wishes to verify. The relevant situations relative to a set of premises Γ are those situations $<\varphi(x), \delta>$ where $\delta \in D_{M_0}$ and $\varphi(x)$ is either the antecedent of a "positive" occurrence of a universally quantified $>$ conditional in Γ^* or identical with $\delta(x/t)$, where δ is the antecedent of a non quantified $>$ conditional in Γ^*, where Γ^* contains the conjunctive normal form of each sentence in Γ. We call the set of such antecedents Subst(*Ant*(Γ)).

DEFINITION: For $\Gamma \subseteq L_>$, thc *Γ-normalization chain* with respect to an enumeration ν of Subst(Ant(Γ)) is defined to be the following sequence:

$N^0{}_\nu = s$

$N^{\alpha+1}{}_\nu = \underline{N}(N^\alpha{}_\nu, \varphi_i)$, where $\alpha = \lambda + n + 1$, and $\nu(\varphi_i) = n + 1$.

$N^\lambda{}_\nu = \bigcap_{\mu \in \lambda} N^\mu{}_\nu$

There is one such Γ-normalization chain for each state and each enumeration of Subst(Ant(Γ)). Every Γ-normalization chain beginning in a state s reaches a fixed point. That is: for all s and ν, $\exists\alpha\forall\beta \geq \alpha\ N^\beta{}_\nu = N^\alpha{}_\nu$.

3.3 Reasonable Inference

Armed with the notions of information states, ignorance, updating and maximal normality, we can now put together our model theory of non-monotonic reasoning. We define the relevant dynamic information model, as well as the support relation for information states, and then finally our notion of commonsense entailment.

DEFINITION: The *dynamic information model* $\mathcal{A}_0$ is a triple $<\wp(W_{M_0}), +, \underline{N}>$, and:

(i) $+: \wp(W_{M_0}) \times \wp(L_>) \rightarrow \wp(W_{M_0})$ is defined such that $\forall s \in \wp(W_{M_0}), \forall\Gamma \subseteq L_>\ s + \Gamma = s \cap (\bigcap_{\gamma \in \Gamma} \|\gamma\|_{M_0})$.

(ii) $\underline{N}$ is the normalization function on information states.

Note that ☺ $\in \wp(W_{M_0})$.

DEFINITION: For $s \in \wp(W_{M_0})$, $s \models \varphi$ iff for all $w \in s$, $M_0, w \models \varphi$.

DEFINITION: $\Gamma \mid\approx \varphi$ iff for any Γ-normalization chain C beginning from ☺ $+ \Gamma$, $C^* \models \varphi$, where C^* is the fixpoint of C.

Since $\Gamma \models \varphi \rightarrow \Gamma \mid\approx \varphi$, our non-monotonic consequence relation is supraclassical. Further all the T_1 theorems are also $\mid\approx$ valid. Theorem 2 shows that $\mid\approx$. captures the first group of reasonable inference patterns from the introduction.

DEFINITION: φ, ψ and $\zeta$are *independent formulas* just in case for all $\underline{\delta}$, each boolean combination containing at most one instance of each of $\underline{\varphi\delta}$, $\underline{\psi\delta}$, $\underline{\zeta\delta}$ is satisfiable.

THEOREM 2: When φ, ψ, and ζ are restricted to independent formulas, Defeasible Modus Ponens, Pointwise Defeasible Transitivity, Pointwise Defeasible Strengthening of the Antecedent, Nixon Diamond, Penguin Principle, the Embedded Normality patterns as they are stated in the introduction all hold given our interpretation of $\mid\approx$.

Another welcome fact about our interpretation of $\mid\approx$ is that Defeasible Irrelevance does not hold. While this fact follows straightforwardly from the definition of $\mid\approx$, the proof of theorem 3 exploits a construction of particular worlds for each inference pattern that (a) verify the premises of the inference pattern and exist in the state of ignorance, (b) survive the process of normalization, and (c) have the requisite properties to force the normalized state to verify the desired conclusion.

4. Subtheories and Extensions

There are several extensions and subtheories of the basic system. of commonsense entailment we have just described that we will describe at length in a longer paper. For instance, there is a quantifier free version of our system in which the set of nonmonotonic consequences of a finite set of premises Γ is decidable.

We can also extend the system of commonsense entailment in $L_>$ with stronger monotonic inferences. We think, for example, that this inference pattern is valid.

$$\forall x(\varphi > \psi)\ \&\ \forall x(\zeta > \psi) \models \forall x((\varphi \vee \zeta) > \psi)$$

The constraint on * required to validate the Dudley Doorite argument scheme in an $L_>$ complicates, however, the construction of a canonical model.

We may also extend the system by complicaing the definition of normalization.

DEFINITION: $\underline{N}^*(s, \psi) = \underline{N}(s, \psi) \cap X$, where

$X :=$ { $w \in s$: for all situations ζ $*(w, \|\zeta\|) = *(w, \|\zeta\|) \setminus *(s, \|\psi\|)$}, if $*(w, \|\zeta\|) \setminus *(s, \|\psi\|) \neq \emptyset$;

$:= s$ otherwise.

Where $\psi = <\varphi(x), \delta>$ and $\delta \in D_{M_0}$, a world v is excluded from $\underline{N}(s, \psi)$ just in case δ is, *at v itself*, not a normal φ and this is consistent with s. A world v is excluded from set X just in case *the set of normal ζ worlds* of v contains worlds where δ is not a normal φ if this is consistent with other normality information in s. Each set of ζ normal worlds for worlds of s should encode as much normality information of s as is consistent with it. A nonmonotonic consequence relation $\mid\approx^*$ based on $\underline{N}^*$ extends $\mid\approx$ and verifies the rule forms of defeasible transitivity and strengthening of the antecedent.

Yet another extension refines the basic semantics by replacing the sets of normal worlds $*(w, p)$ in $L_>$ models with concentric spheres of worlds $\$(w, p)$. to capture a limited version of the graded normality inferences.[3]

5. Comparisons with Other Work

The theory presented above derives heavily from two traditions in logic which many have thought closely related: modal logic and the theories of nonmonotonic and default reasoning developed during the last decade. Our theory differs considerably from Reiter's default logic. Reiter's default logic augments classical logic with default rules of the form: if φ and it is not inconsistent to assume ψ, then ζ. These rules offer a representation of generic facts, but significantly the theory has no representations for generic sentences in the object language. Thus, there seems to be no way to write down sensible representations for nested defaults and nested generic statements or to reason about them within Reiter's formalism. McCarthy's original proposal concerning circumscription-- or the model theoretic minimization of certain predicates-- has in principle the resources to represent nested generic sentences, on the other hand; but the formalism does not capture most of the desired inferences. Further, the original system as well as subsequent refinements are very unstable. Defeasible modus ponens fails, for example, as soon as we add the new premise that there is a bird that doesn't fly. Further, the refinements get the desired inferences only to the extent that ghosts are imported into the logic. We get the inferences without ghosts.

With Delgrande, we exploit an analogy with conditional logic. Again, however, Delgrande does not give a theory that permits us to reason about or even assign meanings to nested generic statements. Delgrande's theory does not, insofar as we understand it, handle adequately inferences like defeasible strengthening of the antecedent. The reason we get defeasible strengthening in the same breath (though it's a deep one) as default transitivity is because of the very special use of the informationally minimal state and updating. Whereas Delgrande has to appeal to complicated mechanisms to test for "irrelevance," the update of the informationally minimal state with *birds fly* will yield upon normalization that *white birds fly*.

References

[Delgrande, 1987] Jim Delgrande. A Semantics for Defaults Using Conditional Logic. *Artificial Intelligence*, 1987.

[McCarthy, 1980] John McCarthy. Circumscription-- A Form of Non-Monotonic Reasoning. *Artificial Intelligence* 13, pp.27-39, 1980.

[Reiter, 1980] Ray Reiter. A Logic for Default Reasoning. *Artificial Intelligence* 13 , pp.81-132, 1980.

[Stalnaker, 1968] Robert Stalnaker. A Theory of Conditionals. Nicholas Rescher, editor. *Studies in Logical Theory*, Oxford: Basil Blackwell.

[3]We have shown that these inferences may hold if the consequents of conditionals in the premises are restricted to atomic formulas or negations of atomic formulas. These limits are significant; we know that we cannot give a fully general version of the graded normality inferences without trivializing the theory.

Modal Interpretations of Default Logic

Mirosław Truszczyński*
Department of Computer Science
University of Kentucky
Lexington, KY 40506–0027, USA

mirek@ms.uky.edu

Abstract

In the paper we study a new and natural modal interpretation of defaults. We show that under this interpretation there are whole families of modal nonmonotonic logics that accurately represent default reasoning. One of these logics is used in a definition of possible-worlds semantics for default logic. This semantics yields a characterization of default extensions similar to the characterization of stable expansions by means of autoepistemic interpretation.

We also show that the disjunctive information can easily be handled if disjunction is represented by means of *modal disjunctive defaults* — modal formulas that we use in our interpretation.

Our results indicate that there is no single modal logic for describing default reasoning. On the contrary, there exist whole ranges of modal logics, each of which can be used in the embedding as a "host" logic.

1 Introduction

The default logic of Reiter [1980] is a nonmonotonic formalism based on the paradigm of "negation as failure to prove" and is defined by means of a certain fixed-point construction. It is a formalism in the language of propositional calculus (or, in a more general variant, in the language of first-order logic). In 1982, McDermott [1982], building on the joint work with Doyle [1980], introduced a large class of modal nonmonotonic logics. He proposed a general scheme which, also using "negation as failure to prove" and a fixed-point construction, assigns to each monotone modal logic its nonmonotonic variant. The autoepistemic logic of Moore [1985], an important modal formalism, belongs to the McDermott-Doyle's family of logics (see [Shvarts, 1990]). In recent years there have been numerous attempts to explain and exploit the nature of the relationship between the default logic and modal nonmonotonic logics. There are two main reasons behind the interest in this particular research area. Firstly, modal nonmonotonic logics often have clear, intuitive semantics (for example, list semantics [Moore, 1985], possible-world semantics [Moore, 1984; Konolige, 1988], or preference semantics [Shoham, 1987]), and the default logic lacks one. By embedding the default logic into a modal nonmonotonic logic with an elegant semantics, insights into semantic aspects of default logic can be gained. Secondly, the automated inference methods for the "host" modal nonmonotonic logic could be used as a uniform tool for handling default theories.

The default logic was first embedded into a variant of autoepistemic logic by Konolige [1988]. Marek and Truszczynski [1989; 1990] proposed to embed default logic into the nonmonotonic variant of the logic of *necessitation* **N** — the modal logic that does not contain any modal axiom schemata and uses modus ponens and necessitation as inference rules. Recently, Lin and Shoham [1990] defined yet another, this time bimodal, nonmonotonic logic, which they called the logic of *grounded knowledge* (denoted **GK**), and provided an interpretation of the default logic within logic **GK**.

Each of these approaches has some disadvantages. We discuss them briefly in the next section. In this paper we consider another interpretation of defaults in the modal language. It is somewhat related to the approach of Siegel [1990] to modal nonmonotonic logic[1]. We argue that our translation avoids the problems of the translations used in the earlier approaches. We show that under this new interpretation, default logic can be faithfully embedded into any of the whole range of modal nonmonotonic logics. As a consequence, possible-worlds semantics for these modal logics yield possible-worlds semantics for default logic, and their automated proof methods (whenever exist) can be applied to default theories. For example, in Section 4, we choose logic **S4F**, that has a particularly well-structured possible-world semantics, to obtain possible-world semantics for default logic.

An important feature of the new translation is that it easily lends itself to an extension suitable for default

*This work was partially supported by Army Research Office under grant DAAL03-89-K-0124, and by National Science Foundation and the Commonwealth of Kentucky EPSCoR program under grant RII 8610671.

[1] I would like to thank Vladimir Lifschitz who informed me about the work of Siegel after seeing the preliminary version of my paper.

reasonings with indefinite information in the form of disjunction, and generalizes the formalism for such reasonings introduced recently by Gelfond [1990]. In Section 5, we introduce this extension, relate it to an earlier work of [Gelfond, 1990] and [Gelfond *et al.*, 1991], and apply our formalism to discuss the "broken hand" example of Poole [1989].

Our results bring up the following general question: how essential in explaining default reasonings are those aspects of modal logics that are specifically concerned with properties of the modality? Earlier investigations [Konolige, 1988], [Marek and Truszczyński, 1990], [Siegel, 1990], implicitly suggested that there may be some relationship between the properties of the modality and default logic by centering around the question of what is the right modal logic for the embedding to work (logics **K45** [Konolige, 1988], **N** [Marek and Truszczyński, 1990] and **T** [Siegel, 1990] were considered). But there seem to be no reason for any connection between default reasonings and modal axioms to exist. Default reasonings first use a certain mechanism ("negation as failure to prove") to establish defaults applicable in a given situation and then proceed like in a classical first-order case. In the whole process there is no place where properties of the modality (like standard modal axiom schemata) might intervene.

Our results support this view by showing that there is a significant degree of freedom in the choice of the "host" modal nonmonotonic logic — any out of the whole family of (drastically different) modal nonmonotonic logics will do. An analysis of the translation proposed by Konolige reveals the same "insensitivity" to the choice of modal logic (see [Truszczyński, 1991a]), and Lin and Shoham [1990] make a similar observation in the case of their approach.

2 Previous approaches to the problem of representing default logic as a modal system

Theories in default logic are pairs (D, W), where W is a collection of formulas in some propositional language $\mathcal{L}$, and D is a collection of nonstandard inference rules, called ***defaults***, that are of the form

$$\frac{\alpha, M\beta_1, \ldots, M\beta_n}{\gamma}. \tag{1}$$

To apply default (1) and conclude γ, as in the case of standard inference rules, one first has to establish all its premises. The premises of defaults are of two types. Premise α is treated in a standard way — α has to be proved before the default can be applied. Premises $M\beta_i$ are treated differently. This is the place when we depart from standard monotone systems. We interpret $M\beta_i$ as "β_i is possible" (which is emphasized by the use of the modal operator M) and define this as consistency of β_i with some theory S (the potential collection of consequences of a default theory). Thus, $M\beta_i$ is established if $S \not\vdash \neg\beta_i$.

Such treatment of the premises of defaults leads to a nonstandard consequence operator, $\Gamma_{D,W}(S)$ [Reiter, 1980]. For a theory $W \subseteq \mathcal{L}$, $\Gamma_{D,W}(S)$ consists of all facts that can be proven from W by means of propositional calculus and defaults in D, applied as explained above (with S used in consistency checking). If theory S coincides with the set $\Gamma_{D,W}(S)$ of such consequences of W, that is, if

$$S = \Gamma_{D,W}(S), \tag{2}$$

then S is called an *extension* of a default theory (D, W) and is regarded as a candidate (many theories S may satisfy (2)) for the set of nonmonotonic consequences of (D, W).

A similar approach to nonmonotonicity but within the language of modal logic $\mathcal{L}_L$ — an extension of $\mathcal{L}$ by a modal operator L interpreted as "is known" — was proposed by McDermott and Doyle [1980] and McDermott [1982]. The operator M, mentioned earlier, is simply an abbreviation for $\neg L \neg$. The idea was that modal formulas would play the role of defaults, and the standard consequence operator $Cn_{\mathcal{S}}$ for a selected modal logic $\mathcal{S}$ would replace the nonstandard consequence operator $\Gamma_{D,\cdot}(S)$. To achieve nonmonotonicity, the theory I encoding the knowledge of a reasoning agent was extended by the formulas expressing "negation as failure to prove" that is, by the formulas $\neg L\varphi$ for $\varphi \notin T$. Theory T (playing the same role as S for default logic) is potentially the collection of nonmonotonic consequences of I. If T agrees exactly with consequences in logic $\mathcal{S}$ of $I \cup \{\neg L\varphi : \varphi \notin T\}$ that is, if

$$T = Cn_{\mathcal{S}}(I \cup \{\neg L\varphi : \varphi \notin T\}), \tag{3}$$

then T is called an $\mathcal{S}$-expansion of I, and is regarded as a candidate (equation (3) may have multiple solutions) for the set of nonmonotonic $\mathcal{S}$-consequences of I.

A variant of nonmonotonic modal logic was recently introduced by Kaminski [1991] and further studied in [Truszczyński, 1991b] (see also [Konolige, 1988]). Instead of extending I by all formulas given by "negation as failure to prove", I is extended only by the results of application of this rule to modal-free formulas of T. Formally, theory T is a ground $\mathcal{S}$-expansion of I if

$$T = Cn_{\mathcal{S}}(I \cup \{\neg L\varphi : \varphi \in \mathcal{L} \setminus T\}). \tag{4}$$

This approach, by restricting the applicability of the "negation as failure to prove" rule to modal-free formulas, results in nonmonotonic formalisms more robust to updates in the initial theory I. In addition, since modal nonmonotonic logics based on (4) apply "negation as failure" only to modal-free formulas — all that is required in default logic — they seem especially suitable for studying default reasonings.

Before we continue, let us recall one more important notion. A theory $T \subseteq \mathcal{L}_L$ is ***stable*** if it is closed under propositional consequence and necessitation, and if for every $\varphi \notin T$, $\neg L\varphi \in T$. It is well-known that $\mathcal{S}$-expansions and ground $\mathcal{S}$-expansions are stable (for the latter to hold, we require that $\mathcal{S}$ be normal). Stable sets are uniquely determined by their objective part [Moore, 1985; Konolige, 1988]. That is, for each $S \subseteq \mathcal{L}$ there is exactly one stable set T such that $T \cap \mathcal{L} = Cn(S)$, where Cn stands for the consequence operator of propositional calculus. We will denote this unique stable set by $St(S)$.

There have been several attempts to embed default logic into a modal nonmonotonic logic.

(1) Konolige [Konolige, 1988] proposed to interpret a default d given by (1) by the formula

$$emb_K(d) = L\alpha \wedge \neg L \neg \beta_1 \wedge \ldots \wedge \neg L \neg \beta_n \Rightarrow \gamma \quad (5)$$

This translation can be extended to a default theory (D, W) by setting

$$emb_K(D, W) = W \cup \{emb_K(d) \colon d \in D\}.$$

Under this interpretation no modal nonmonotone logic is known to faithfully capture default reasoning. An additional modification of $emb_K(D, W)$ is needed. This modification, involving a stable theory T, yields a subtheory of $emb_K(D, W)$ referred to as the *reduct of* $emb_K(D, W)$ *with respect to* T. Konolige proved that a consistent and closed under provability theory S is an extension of a default theory (D, W) if and only if $St(S)$ is a ground **K45**-expansion of the reduct of $emb_K(D, W)$ with respect to $St(S)$. For the same interpretation, Marek and Truszczynski [1989] showed a similar result: a consistent and closed under provability theory S is an extension of a default theory (D, W) if and only if $St(S)$ is an **N**-expansion of the reduct of $emb_K(D, W)$ with respect to $St(S)$.

The problem with the approach of Konolige is that the concept of reduct is representation dependent — logically equivalent theories may have reducts that are not logically equivalent. Consequently, in modal systems using the concept of reduct, syntactically different but logically equivalent theories may have different consequences. Moreover, as we will argue later, this translation cannot be used to handle reasonings with disjunction.

(2) In another paper Marek and Truszczynski [1990] introduced a different translation of the default (1):

$$L\alpha \wedge \neg LL \neg \beta_1 \wedge \ldots \wedge \neg LL \neg \beta_n \Rightarrow \gamma. \quad (6)$$

Under this interpretation consistent extensions of (D, W) correspond exactly to **N**-expansions of the translation of (D, W). This was the first result which embedded default logic into a modal nonmonotonic logic in McDermott-Doyle's family. The main disadvantage of this approach is that the interpretation used does not have a natural, intuitive justification.

(3) Lin and Shoham [Lin and Shoham, 1990] do not use the scheme of McDermott and Doyle. They introduce a modal nonmonotonic logic with two modalities. They define semantics of this logic by modifying the concept of preference semantics and faithfully embed default logic into their logic. The solution is elegant but requires two modalities, which introduces an extra degree of complexity.

3 New modal representation of default logic

The translation we propose is based on the most natural interpretation of a default $d = \frac{\alpha, M\beta_1, \ldots, M\beta_n}{\gamma}$: if α, $M\beta_1, \ldots, M\beta_n$ are known to an agent then the agent knows γ. Such interpretation treats defaults in the same way as standard inference rules are treated — all premises must be known — the only difference is that premises are of two types. This new interpretation can be encoded faithfully in the language of modal logic by the formula

$$emb(d) = L\alpha \wedge LM\beta_1 \wedge \ldots \wedge LM\beta_n \Rightarrow L\gamma. \quad (7)$$

We extend now this definition to the case of default theories. Let (D, W) be a default theory. A modal theory representing (D, W) is defined by

$$emb(D, W) = \{L\varphi \colon \varphi \in W\} \cup \{emb(d) \colon d \in D\}. \quad (8)$$

In the rest of the paper, we assume familiarity with basic concepts of (monotone) modal logic. For all undefined concepts the reader is referred to Hughes and Cresswell [1984]. All modal logics considered in this paper contain propositional calculus and use *necessitation* $(\varphi / L\varphi)$ as an additional inference rule. Besides standard modal logic systems like **K, T, S4, S5** and **K45**, we will consider the following two logics:

1. $\mathbf{T}^-$ — the logic containing only axiom schema T,
2. **S4F** — the logic determined by the class of Kripke frames with the accessibility relation of the form $(M_1 \times M_1) \cup (M_1 \times M_2) \cup (M_2 \times M_2)$, where M_1 and M_2 are disjoint (M_1 may be empty) and contain all the worlds of the model. Logic **S4F** contains logic **S4** and is included in logic **S5**. It can be axiomatized by the axiom schemata of **S4** and thc followng additional axiom F: $\varphi \wedge ML\psi \Rightarrow L(M\varphi \vee \psi)$ (see [Segerberg, 1971]).

Our first theorem contains the main result of the paper.

Theorem 3.1 *Let* (D, W) *be a default theory and let* $S \subseteq \mathcal{L}$ *be consistent and closed under propositional consequence. The following conditions are equivalent:*

1. S *is an extension of* (D, W);
2. $St(S) = Cn_{\mathbf{T}^-}(emb(D, W) \cup \{\neg L\varphi \colon \varphi \notin St(S)\})$;
3. $St(S) = Cn_{\mathcal{S}}(emb(D, W) \cup \{\neg L\varphi \colon \varphi \notin St(S)\})$, *for any modal logic* $\mathcal{S}$ *such that* $\mathbf{T}^- \subseteq \mathcal{S} \subseteq \mathbf{S4F}$;
4. $St(S) = Cn_{\mathbf{S4F}}(emb(D, W) \cup \{\neg L\varphi \colon \varphi \notin St(S)\})$.

Thus, under the translation (7) — (8) for any of a big range of modal logics ($\mathbf{T}^-$ — **S4F**) its nonmonotonic variant (exactly as introduced in [McDermott and Doyle, 1980; McDermott, 1982]) can be used to express default reasonings, without the need for representation-dependent concepts like reduct.

Let us now consider representing default reasoning in ground modal nonmonotonic logics. We will again use our new translation of defaults. A similar result to the previous one holds: there is a whole range of logics that can be used for an embedding.

Theorem 3.2 *Let* $\mathcal{S}$ *be any logic such that* $\mathbf{T} \subseteq \mathcal{S} \subseteq$ **S4F**. *A consistent and closed under propositional provability theory* S *is an extension of a default theory* (D, W) *if and only if* $St(S)$ *is a ground* $\mathcal{S}$*-expansion of* $emb(D, W)$.

This theorem will be used in the next section in a definition of a possible-words semantics for default logic, where logic **S4F**, which has a relatively simple Kripke-model characterization is selected as a modal counterpart of default logic.

Even larger range of equivalent logics, in the sense of faithful representation of default reasoning, can be found if the concept of ground expansion is combined with the concept of the reduct of *emb*(D, W) In such case any of the logics from the range **T** — **S5** can be used. Similarly, for the original approach of Konolige [1988] (translation emb_K combined with the concept of reduct), we can prove that any of the modal logics in the range **K** — **S5**, and not only logic **K45** used in [Konolige, 1988], allows us to faithfully encode default logic (see [Truszczyński, 1991a] for details).

4 Possible-worlds semantics for default logic

In the previous section we have presented two results embedding default logic into nonmonotonic modal logics of McDermott and their ground variants. In each case we have a significant degree of freedom in choosing the underlying monotone logic. In this section, we make use of this freedom. Our approach is based on Theorem 3.2, and for logic $\mathcal{S}$ we choose **S4F**.

A (*default*) *model* is a triple $\mathcal{M} = \langle M_1, M_2, V\rangle$, where M_1 and M_2 are sets such that $M_1 \cap M_2 = \emptyset$ and $M_2 \neq \emptyset$, and V is a function assigning to each $m \in M$ a propositional valuation $V(m)$.

We say that a formula φ is true (holds) in a world m of $M_1 \cup M_2$ if φ is true in the valuation $V(m)$ (in symbols: $(\mathcal{M}, m) \models \varphi$). We say that a pair $(\mathcal{M}, m)$, where $m \in M_1$, satisfies default (1) (in symbols, $(\mathcal{M}, m) \models d$) if whenever α is true in all worlds in $M_1 \cup M_2$ and each β_i holds in at least one world of M_2, then γ holds in all worlds in $M_1 \cup M_2$. We say that a pair $(\mathcal{M}, m)$, where $m \in M_2$, satisfies default (1) ($(\mathcal{M}, m) \models d$) if whenever α is true in all worlds in M_2 and each β_i holds in at least one of the worlds in M_2, then γ holds in all worlds in M_2. In a standard way, we define now satisfiability of a default by a model. Namely, $\mathcal{M} \models d$, if $(\mathcal{M}, m) \models d$ for each $m \in M_1 \cup M_2$. In a similar fashion, we define satisfiability of a formula by a model: for $\varphi \in \mathcal{L}$, $\mathcal{M} \models \varphi$ if φ is true in all worlds from $M_1 \cup M_2$.

Note that for each model $\mathcal{M}$ there is an equivalent model $\mathcal{M}' = (M_1', M_2', V')$ (that is, for each default d, $\mathcal{M} \models d$ if and only if $\mathcal{M}' \models d$) such that valuations assigned to worlds in M_i', $i = 1, 2$, are distinct. Consequently, if $\mathcal{L}$ has only finitely many propositional variables, then each model has an equivalent finite model.

In commonsense reasoning we often restrict the class of models by imposing additional conditions. For example, Moore's autoepistemic interpretations of the language $\mathcal{L}_L$ [Moore, 1985] are defined with respect to a theory $T \subseteq \mathcal{L}_L$, called the *modal index* of an interpretation. A valuation v of $\mathcal{L}_L$ is *autoepistemic with respect to* T if $v(L\varphi) = 1$ if and only if $\varphi \in T$. The class of autoepistemic interpretation has been used by Moore to define the concept of *stable expansion* and the nonmonotonic formalism called *autoepistemic logic*.

In this paper, we proceed similarly. Let $S \subseteq \mathcal{L}$. A model $\mathcal{M}$ is called *strongly consistent with* S

$$\{\varphi \in \mathcal{L} : v(\varphi) = 1, \text{ for every } v \in V_2\} \subseteq S.$$

Let (D, W) be a default theory. We say that (D, W) S-*entails* a, where a stands for a default or for a formula from $\mathcal{L}$, if a is satisfied in all models strongly consistent with S in which (D, W) is satisfied. We denote the relation of S-entailment by $\models_S$. We have the following theorem providing a characterization of extensions analogous to Moore's definition of stable expansions by means of autoepistemic interpretations.

Theorem 4.1 *Let (D, W) be a default theory. Let $S \subseteq \mathcal{L}$. Theory S is an extension of (D, W) if and only if*

$$S = \{\varphi \in \mathcal{L} : (D, W) \models_S \varphi\},$$

that is, if S is exactly the set of all formulas true in all S-models of (D, W).

5 Effective disjunction

One of the problems of nonmonotonic formalisms often is that the semantics of the disjunction operator does not accurately capture the intuitive understanding of disjunction [Poole, 1989; Gelfond, 1990]. We will show that our embedding of defaults can be used to handle disjunction. In commonsense reasoning we often use a "constructive" or "effective" disjunction — knowing $a \vee b$, each belief set an agent will construct will contain a or b instead of the classical, nonconstructive interpretation in which we may know $a \vee b$ without knowing which of the two disjuncts is true. The distinction between the two can easily be achieved in the modal language. The "constructive" disjunction can be expressed as $La \vee Lb$ and the "noneffective" one by $L(a \vee b)$.

Let us consider the following example due to Poole [Poole, 1989]. Suppose that normally people's left (resp. right) arms are usable and people with broken left (resp. right) arms are exceptions. Suppose also that we remember seeing a friend with a broken arm, but we cannot remember which. Intuitively, we should not conclude that both his arms are usable. A straightforward default encoding of this situation by a default theory (D, W) is as follows:

$$D = \{\frac{M\neg ab_l}{u_l}, \frac{M\neg ab_r}{u_r}\},$$

and

$$W = \{b_l \Rightarrow ab_l, b_r \Rightarrow ab_r, b_l \vee b_r\}.$$

Clearly, this default theory has exactly one extension and it contains the formula $u_l \wedge u_r$, contrary to the intuition.

The reason for the inadequacy of the default logic to handle such situations is that default logic does not have a mechanism to deal with effective disjunction. Recently an extension of default logic was proposed in [Gelfond *et al.*, 1991] which commonsense disjunction is expressed by means of a new connective. In this extension of default logic the abovementioned paradox disappears.

Let us now consider the encoding of the above situation using *modal disjunctive defaults* of the form:

$$L\alpha \wedge LM\beta_1 \wedge \ldots \wedge LM\beta_n \Rightarrow L\gamma_1 \vee \ldots \vee L\gamma_k. \quad (9)$$

Using such formulas, the Poole's example can be encoded as follows (recall that $M = \neg L \neg$):

$$I = \{L\neg Lab_l \Rightarrow Lu_l, L\neg Lab_r \Rightarrow Lu_r,$$
$$L(b_l \Rightarrow ab_l), L(b_r \Rightarrow ab_r), Lb_l \vee Lb_r\}.$$

Consider now logic **S4**. In [Shvarts, 1990; Marek *et al.*, 1990] **S4**-expansions are characterized and algorithms to compute them described. Using these results, one can find that the above theory has two **S4**-expansions: one generated by $\{ab_l, b_l, u_r\}$ and the other generated by $\{ab_r, b_r, u_l\}$, which coincides with the intuition. The same result can be obtained for any logic from the range $\mathbf{T}^- - \mathbf{S4F}$.

In fact, more can be shown. Namely, each nonmonotonic logic $\mathcal{S}$, for logics $\mathcal{S}$ such that $\mathbf{T}^- \subseteq \mathcal{S} \subseteq \mathbf{S4}$, and each ground nonmonotonic logic $\mathcal{S}$, for logics $\mathcal{S}$ such that $\mathbf{T} \subseteq \mathcal{S} \subseteq \mathbf{S4F}$, can be used as a nonmonotonic system capable of distinguishing between "effective" and "noneffective" disjunction. These issues will be discussed in detail in the full version of the paper.

Let us briefly mention here that formulas used to represent default proposed by Konolige [1988] and Marek and Truszczynski [1990] cannot be extended to handle disjunction, because they use modal-free formulas to represent consequents of defaults and, thus, cannot distinguish between the "effective" and "noneffective" interpretations of disjunction.

6 Conclusions

In the paper we presented a new and natural interpretation of defaults as modal formulas. We have shown that under this interpretation there are whole families of modal nonmonotonic logics that accurately represent default reasoning. We proposed a semantics for default logic based on the embedding we found.

We also have shown that the disjunctive information can easily be handled within our modal system. disjunctive defaults.

A very important conclusion of this research is that there is no single, distinguished modal logic for describing default reasoning. On the contrary, there exist whole ranges of modal logics, each of which can be used in the embedding as a "host" logic. This shows that, in agreement with the intuition, in order to capture default reasoning the most important step is to translate into a nonmonotonic modal system the principle of "negation as failure to prove". Once this is made, then the choice of particular modal axiom schemata is of secondary importance, in fact, there is a large degree of freedom in which of them to choose.

7 Proof of Theorem 3.1

Let us define in a precise way the operator $\Gamma_{D,W}(S)$. To this end, let us introduce a formal system $\mathbf{PC} + (D, S)$ as the formal system containing propositional calculus and an additional set D_S of inference rules, where $D_S = \{\frac{\alpha}{\gamma}: \frac{\alpha, M\beta_1, \ldots, M\beta_n}{\gamma} \in D$ and $S \not\vdash \neg\beta_i$, $1 \leq i \leq n\}$. By $\Gamma_{D,W}(S)$ we denote the set of all formulas that have a proof from W in the system $\mathbf{PC} + (D, S)$. It is well-known that $\Gamma_{D,W}(S)$ can alternatively be defined as the minimal set closed under provability in $\mathbf{PC}{+}(D, S)$ that is, the minimal set closed under propositional provability and the rules in D_S (this is the original definition of $\Gamma_{D,W}(S)$ given in [Reiter, 1980]).

Throughout the proof we use the following abbreviations: $T = St(S)$ and $I = emb(D, W)$. The *reduct of* $emb(D, W)$ *with respect to* $St(S)$ (in symbols: I_R) is the theory containing $\{L\varphi: \varphi \in W\}$ and formulas $L\alpha \Rightarrow L\gamma$, such that for some $\beta_1, \ldots \beta_n$, $\frac{\alpha, M\beta_1, \ldots, M\beta_n}{\gamma} \in D$ and for all $i, \neg\beta_i \notin S$. $I_R = R(emb(D, W), St(S))$. We will also use the following facts listed below:

P1: For a normal modal logic $\mathcal{S}$, and for $S \subseteq \mathcal{L}$, if $S \subseteq Cn_{\mathcal{S}}(I \cup \{\neg L\varphi: \varphi \in \mathcal{L} \setminus St(S)\})$, then $St(S) \subseteq Cn_{\mathcal{S}}(I \cup \{\neg L\varphi: \varphi \in \mathcal{L} \setminus St(S)\})$ ([Truszczyński, 1991b]). For any modal logic $\mathcal{S}$ containing necessitation, and for $S \subseteq \mathcal{L}$, if $S \subseteq Cn_{\mathcal{S}}(I \cup \{\neg L\varphi: \varphi \notin St(S)\})$, then $St(S) \subseteq Cn_{\mathcal{S}}(I \cup \{\neg L\varphi: \varphi \notin St(S)\})$ ([Marek and Truszczyński, 1990]);

P2: If $\mathcal{S} \subseteq \mathcal{T} \subseteq \mathbf{S5}$ are two modal logics with necessitation, then each $\mathcal{S}$-expansion of I is a $\mathcal{T}$-expansion of I ([McDermott, 1982]);

P3: Logic **S5** is complete with respect to the class of universal Kripke models that is, models with a universal accessibility relation ([Hughes and Cresswell, 1984]);

P4: Each consistent stable set is of the form $\{\varphi: \mathcal{M} \models \varphi\}$, for some universal Kripke model $\mathcal{M}$ [Moore, 1984];

P5: Stable sets are closed under provability in **S5** ([McDermott, 1982]);

P6: A theory $S \subseteq \mathcal{L}$ closed under propositional consequence, is closed under rules in D_S if and only if $emb(D, W) \subseteq St(S)$ if and only if $I_R \subseteq St(S)$ (straightforward to prove).

$1 \Rightarrow 2$. Assume that $S = \Gamma_{D,W}(S)$. Then, if $\varphi \in S$, φ has a proof $\varphi_1, \ldots, \varphi_n (= \varphi)$ from W in the system $\mathbf{PC} + D_S$. We will show, by induction on the length of the proof, that $\varphi \in Cn_{\mathbf{T}^-}(emb(D, W) \cup \{\neg L\varphi: \varphi \notin T\})$. Assume that the claim holds for all formulas in S with proofs of length $< n$. If $\varphi_n (= \varphi)$ is a tautology or is a member of W, then $\varphi \in Cn_{\mathbf{T}^-}(emb(D, W) \cup \{\neg L\varphi: \varphi \notin T\})$. If φ_n is obtained from φ_i, φ_j, where $i, j < n$, by means of modus ponenes, then the induction hypothesis applies and $\varphi_i, \varphi_j \in Cn_{\mathbf{T}^-}(emb(D, W) \cup \{\neg L\varphi: \varphi \notin T\})$. Consequently, $\varphi \in Cn_{\mathbf{T}^-}(emb(D, W) \cup \{\neg L\varphi: \varphi \notin T\})$.

The last possibility is that φ_n is obtained from φ_i, $i < n$, by means of a rule $\frac{\varphi_i}{\varphi_n} \in D_S$. Then, there is a default $d = \frac{\varphi_i, M\beta_1, \ldots, M\beta_m}{\varphi_n} \in D$ such that all $\neg\beta_i \notin S$. Consequently, all $L\neg L\neg\beta_i \in Cn_{\mathbf{T}^-}(emb(D, W) \cup \{\neg L\varphi: \varphi \notin T\})$. By the induction hypothesis, $\varphi_i \in Cn_{\mathbf{T}^-}(emb(D, W) \cup \{\neg L\varphi: \varphi \notin T\})$. Thus, $L\varphi_i \in Cn_{\mathbf{T}^-}(emb(D, W) \cup \{\neg L\varphi: \varphi \notin T\})$. Moreover, $emb(d) = L\varphi_i \wedge L\neg L\neg\beta_1 \wedge \ldots \wedge L\neg L\neg\beta_m \Rightarrow L\varphi_n$ is a member of $Cn_{\mathbf{T}^-}(emb(D, W) \cup \{\neg L\varphi: \varphi \notin T\})$ (recall that $M = \neg L \neg$). Thus, $L\varphi_n \in Cn_{\mathbf{T}^-}(emb(D, W) \cup \{\neg L\varphi: \varphi \notin T\})$. Applying axiom T, we get that $\varphi_n (= \varphi) \in Cn_{\mathbf{T}^-}(emb(D, W) \cup \{\neg L\varphi: \varphi \notin T\})$.

By P1, it follows that $St(S) \subseteq Cn_{\mathbf{T}^-}(emb(D, W) \cup \{\neg L\varphi: \varphi \notin T\})$. To prove the converse inclusion, observe that $St(S)$ is closed under provability in $\mathbf{T}^-$ (by P5), $St(S) \supseteq emb(D, W)$ (since S is an extension of (D, W), S is closed under rules from D_S and P6 applies). Finally, since $T = St(S)$ and $St(S)$ is stable, $\{\neg L\varphi : \varphi \notin T\} \subseteq St(S)$.

$2 \Rightarrow 3$ and $3 \Rightarrow 4$. These implications follow by P2.

$4 \Rightarrow 1$. The definition of the reduct yields

$Cn_{\mathbf{S4F}}(I \cup \{\neg L\varphi : \varphi \notin T\}) = Cn_{\mathbf{S4F}}(I_R \cup \{\neg L\varphi : \varphi \notin T\})$. Thus, $St(S) = Cn_{\mathbf{S4F}}(I_R \cup \{\neg L\varphi : \varphi \notin St(T)\})$.

Next, we will show that

$$St(S) = Cn_{\mathbf{S5}}(I_R \cup \{\neg L\varphi : \varphi \in \mathcal{L} \setminus T\}).$$

Since T is stable, T is closed under provability in **S5** (by P5). In addition, $\{\neg L\varphi : \varphi \in \mathcal{L} \setminus T\} \subseteq T$. Thus, $Cn_{\mathbf{S5}}(I_R \cup \{\neg L\varphi : \varphi \in \mathcal{L} \setminus T\}) \subseteq T$. To prove the converse inclusion it suffices, by P1, to show that

$$S \subseteq Cn_{\mathbf{S5}}(I_R \cup \{\neg L\varphi : \varphi \in \mathcal{L} \setminus T\}).$$

Consider $\varphi \in S$ and any universal Kripke model $\mathcal{M} = \langle M, R, V \rangle$ such that $\mathcal{M} \models I_R \cup \{\neg L\varphi : \varphi \in \mathcal{L} \setminus T\}$. Let $\mathcal{M}' = \langle M', R', V' \rangle$, $M \cap M' = \emptyset$, be a universal Kripke model such that $T = \{\psi : \mathcal{M}' \models \psi\}$ (apply P4). Define $\mathcal{N} = \langle M'', R'', V'' \rangle$, by letting $M'' = M \cup M'$, $R'' = R \cup (M \times M') \cup R'$ and $V'' = V \cup V'$. It follows from the definition of $\mathcal{N}$ that $\mathcal{N}, m' \models \{\neg L\varphi : \varphi \notin T\}$, for every $m' \in M'$. Thus, also for every $m \in M$, $\mathcal{N}, m \models \{\neg L\varphi : \varphi \notin T\}$. Next, it is easy to see that if $\psi \in \mathcal{L}$ then $\mathcal{N}, m \models \psi$ if and only if $\mathcal{M}, m \models \psi$, and $\mathcal{N}, m \models L\psi$ if and only if $\mathcal{M}, m \models L\psi$. Thus, for every $m \in M$, $\mathcal{N}, m \models I_R$. Since $I_R \subseteq T$, $\mathcal{M}', m \models I_R$, for every $m \in M'$. Consequently, $\mathcal{N}, m \models I_R$, for every $m \in M'$. Summarizing, $\mathcal{N} \models I_R \cup \{\neg L\varphi : \varphi \notin T\}$. By the definitions of the model $\mathcal{N}$ and of the logic **S4F**, it follows that $\mathcal{N} \models \varphi$. Thus, $\mathcal{M} \models \varphi$ and, by P3, $\varphi \in Cn_{\mathbf{S5}}(I_R \cup \{\neg L\varphi : \varphi \in \mathcal{L} \setminus T\})$.

Now, $St(S)$ is a ground **S5**-expansion of I_R and, by a result of Kaminski [Kaminski, 1991], $St(S)$ is a minimal stable theory containing I_R. Consequently, S is a minimal set closed under rules from D_S. Hence, S is an extension of (D, W). □

References

[Gelfond *et al.*, 1991] M. Gelfond, V. Lifschitz, H. Przymusinska, and M. Truszczynski. Disjunctive defaults. In *Second International Conference on Principles of Knowledge Representation and Reasoning, KR '91*, Cambridge, MA, 1991.

[Gelfond, 1990] M. Gelfond. Reasoning in knowledge systems. A manuscript, 1990.

[Hughes and Cresswell, 1984] G.E. Hughes and M.J. Cresswell. *A companion to modal logic*. Methuen and Co. Ltd., London, 1984.

[Kaminski, 1991] M. Kaminski. Embedding a default system into nonmonotonic logic. *Fundamenta Informaticae*, 14:345 – 354, 1991.

[Konolige, 1988] K. Konolige. On the relation between default and autoepistemic logic. *Artificial Intelligence*, 35:343–382, 1988.

[Lin and Shoham, 1990] F. Lin and Y. Shoham. Epistemic semantics for fixed-points non-monotonic logics. In *Proceedings of TARK-90*, pages 111–120, San Mateo, CA., 1990. Morgan Kaufmann.

[Marek and Truszczyński, 1989] W. Marek and M. Truszczyński. Relating autoepistemic and default logics. In *Principles of Knowledge Representation and Reasoning*, pages 276–288, San Mateo, CA., 1989. Morgan Kaufmann.

[Marek and Truszczyński, 1990] W. Marek and M Truszczyński. Modal logic for default reasoning. *Annals of Mathematics and Artificial Intelligence*, 1:275 – 302, 1990.

[Marek *et al.*, 1990] W. Marek, G.F. Shvarts, and M. Truszczynski. Classification of expansions in modal nonmonotonic logics. Technical Report 168-90, Department of Computer Science, University of Kentucky, 1990.

[McDermott and Doyle, 1980] D. McDermott and J. Doyle. Nonmonotonic logic i. *Artificial Intelligence*, 13:41–72, 1980.

[McDermott, 1982] D. McDermott. Nonmonotonic logic ii: Nonmonotonic modal theories. *Journal of the ACM*, 29:33–57, 1982.

[Moore, 1984] R.C. Moore. Possible-world semantics autoepistemic logic. In R. Reiter, editor, *Proceedings of the workshop on non-monotonic reasoning*, pages 344–354, 1984.

[Moore, 1985] R.C. Moore. Semantical considerations on non-monotonic logic. *Artificial Intelligence*, 25:75–94, 1985.

[Poole, 1989] D. Poole. What the lottery paradox tells us about default reasoning. In *Principles of Knowledge Representation and Reasoning*, pages 333–340, San Mateo, CA., 1989. Morgan Kaufmann.

[Reiter, 1980] R. Reiter. A logic for default reasoning. *Artificial Intelligence*, 13:81–132, 1980.

[Segerberg, 1971] K. Segerberg. *An essay in classical modal logic*. Uppsala University, Filosofiska Studier, 13, 1971.

[Shoham, 1987] Y. Shoham. Nonmonotonic logics: meaning and utility. In *Proceedings of IJCAI-87*, San Mateo, CA., 1987. Morgan Kaufmann.

[Shvarts, 1990] G.F. Shvarts. Autoepistemic modal logics. In R. Parikh, editor, *Proceedings of TARK 1990*, pages 97–109, San Mateo, CA., 1990. Morgan Kaufmann.

[Siegel, 1990] P. Siegel. A modal language for nonmonotonic logic. Workshop DRUMS/CEE, Marseille, France, 1990.

[Truszczyński, 1991a] M. Truszczyński. Embedding default logic into modal nonmonotoninc logics. *to appear* in Proceedings of the Workshop on Logic Programming and Non-Monotoninc Reasoning, Washington, July, 1991, 1991.

[Truszczyński, 1991b] M. Truszczyński. Modal nonmonotonic logic with restricted application of the negation as failure to prove rule. *Fundamenta Informaticae*, 14:355 – 366, 1991.

Constructive Tightly Grounded Autoepistemic Reasoning*

Ilkka N.F. Niemelä
Department of Computer Science
Helsinki University of Technology
Otakaari 1, 02150 ESPOO, FINLAND

Abstract

The key concept of autoepistemic logic introduced by Moore is a stable expansion of a set of premises, i.e., a set of beliefs adopted by an agent with perfect introspection capabilities on the basis of the premises. Moore's formalization of a stable expansion, however, is nonconstructive and produces sets of beliefs which are quite weakly grounded in the premises. A new more constructive definition of the sets of beliefs of the agent is proposed. It is based on classical logic and enumerations of formulae. Considering only a certain subclass of enumerations, *L-hierarchic* enumerations, an attractive class of expansions is captured to characterize the sets of beliefs of a fully introspective agent. These L-hierarchic expansions are stable set minimal, very tightly grounded in the premises and independent of the syntactic representation of premises. Furthermore, Reiter's default logic is shown to be a special case of autoepistemic logic based on L-hierarchic expansions.

1 Introduction

Nonmonotonic reasoning is one of the most important and active areas of research in knowledge representation and reasoning. Autoepistemic logic introduced by Moore [1985] appears to be one of the best available tools for studying nonmonotonic reasoning as recent results [Elkan, 1990; Konolige, 1989; Marek and Truszczyński, 1989] on the relationship between autoepistemic logic and other forms of nonmonotonic reasoning suggest that it offers a unifying approach to a large part of nonmonotonic reasoning.

Autoepistemic logic is a modal logic with an operator L which is read 'is believed'. It was originally introduced as a reconstruction of McDermott and Doyle's [1980] nonmonotonic logic to avoid some peculiarities of this logic. Autoepistemic logic models the beliefs of an ideally rational agent who is capable of perfect introspection. The interesting question is to determine the set of beliefs of the agent given a set of formulae as the initial assumptions of the agent. The agent's rationality is interpreted as requiring that the beliefs of the agent have to be logical consequences of the initial assumptions and the beliefs of the agent. The agent is capable of using both positive introspection (if χ is a belief, so is $L\chi$) and negative introspection (if χ is not a belief, then $\neg L\chi$ is). The agent is also ideal: if a formula is a logical consequence of the beliefs of the agent, then it belongs to the set of beliefs of the agent.

The informal description of the set of beliefs of the agent given above is circular: the set of beliefs is defined using the set of beliefs. Moore [1985] offers a formal definition where the sets of beliefs, the *stable expansions* of the initial assumptions, are defined as the fixed points of an operator given with the aid of the logical consequence relation used by the agent. Moore's formalization is elegant but in connection with some sets of premises it produces sets of beliefs which are quite weakly grounded in the premises. Another problem is that Moore's formalization is non-constructive. It yields no direct method of enumerating or constructing a set of beliefs of the agent given a set of premises. It merely states a condition to be satisfied by any proper set of beliefs based on the premises.

We propose a new more constructive definition of the set of beliefs of the agent. It is based on classical logic and enumerations of formulae. It produces sets of beliefs which are a proper subclass of the stable expansions defined by Moore. In fact, the class coincides with iterative expansions defined by Marek and Truszczynski [1989]. Iterative expansions have many desirable properties. In particular, autoepistemic logic based on iterative expansions can be regarded as a generalization of the other leading nonmonotonic logic, default logic [Reiter, 1980]. The basic problem of iterative expansions is that they are not necessarily stable set minimal which suggests that autoepistemic logic based on iterative expansions is not a proper generalization of default logic. This problem is analysed and shown be the result of the possibility of introspecting a formula before introspecting its subformulae when constructing an iterative expansion. When using the new definition where the enumeration specifies the order of introspection tighter groundedness can be ensured by restricting the order of the formulae in the

*The research has been supported in part by the Jenny and Antti Wihuri Foundation and the Foundation of Technology.

enumeration, i.e., the order of introspection.

In this paper we propose a new class of expansions based on a special subclass of enumerations, *L-hierarchic* enumerations, as the sets of beliefs adopted by an ideal agent with perfect introspection capabilities. L-hierarchic expansions turn out to be more tightly grounded than iterative expansions because they are always stable set minimal. However, autoepistemic logic based on L-hierarchic expansions still remains a generalization of default logic.

The outline of the paper is as follows. First we introduce autoepistemic logic. Then we present a short survey of the groundedness notions proposed previously. After that we introduce the enumeration based expansions and show that Reiter's default logic is a special case of autoepistemic logic based on L-hierarchic expansions.

2 Autoepistemic logic

We can view autoepistemic logic being induced by some underlying logic CL whose language is $\mathcal{L}$. In our case CL is the propositional logic. We build an autoepistemic logic CL_{ae} on top of CL. We extend $\mathcal{L}$ by adding a monadic operator L and obtain an autoepistemic language $\mathcal{L}_{ae}$ which is the language of CL_{ae}. $\mathcal{L}_{ae}$ is defined recursively as $\mathcal{L}$ but containing an extra formation rule: if $\phi \in \mathcal{L}_{ae}$, then $L\phi \in \mathcal{L}_{ae}$.

Autoepistemic logic models an ideal agent's reasoning about his own beliefs. The agent reasons according to a consequence relation based on the underlying logic and can reflect on his own beliefs. The consequence relation of the underlying logic CL is extended to the richer language $\mathcal{L}_{ae}$ simply by treating $L\phi$ formulae as atomic. Thus the consequence relation $\models$ used by the agent is defined as follows. A formula ϕ is a consequence of a set of formulae Σ ($\Sigma \models \phi$) if ϕ is true in every interpretation in which every formula in Σ is true. The interpretations treat $L\phi$ formulae as atomic formulae.

The key objects in autoepistemic logic are the sets of total beliefs of the agent given a set of premises as the agent's initial assumptions. These sets are called *stable expansions* of the premises and they are the fixed points of an operator defined with the aid of the underlying consequence relation in the following way.

Definition 2.1 *[Moore, 1985] Δ is a stable expansion of Σ iff Δ satisfies the following fixed point equation.*

$$\Delta = \{\phi \in \mathcal{L}_{ae} \mid \Sigma \cup L(\Delta) \cup \neg L(\overline{\Delta}) \models \phi\} \tag{1}$$

where $L(\Delta) = \{L\phi \mid \phi \in \Delta\}$, $\neg\Delta = \{\neg\phi \mid \phi \in \Delta\}$, and $\overline{\Delta} = \mathcal{L}_{ae} - \Delta$. Thus $\neg L(\overline{\Delta}) = \{\neg L\phi \mid \phi \in \mathcal{L}_{ae} - \Delta\}$.

3 Groundedness

It can be argued that stable expansions are too weakly grounded in the premises. We start by an example clarifying the problem.

Example 1 Consider the following premise where p is an atomic formula.

$$Lp \rightarrow p \tag{2}$$

The premise has two stable expansions: one containing p and the other not containing p. The stable expansion containing p can be considered too weakly grounded because the agent's belief p is based on the fact that the agent believes p, thus obtains Lp by positive introspection and from this and the premise deduces p. This kind of a belief based on a circular argument is rather weakly grounded in the premises and a stronger form of groundedness is often required. ■

In this chapter we survey the various groundedness notions proposed in the literature and show in what respects they are not satisfactory.

Konolige [1988] presents two stronger notions of groundedness leading to *moderately grounded and strongly grounded expansions.* His basic motivation is to find a class of stable expansions which would capture extensions in default logic [Reiter, 1980] under a suitable translation of default logic to autoepistemic logic. To eliminate circularly based beliefs Konolige introduces the concept of a moderately grounded expansion. He shows that a set of formulae Δ moderately grounded in Σ is in fact a stable expansion of Σ which is minimal in the following sense: there is no stable set[1] S which contains Σ such that $S \cap \mathcal{L} \subset \Delta \cap \mathcal{L}$, i.e. formulae of S without the L operator are a proper subset of formulae of Δ without the L operator. Such expansions are said to be *stable set minimal* for Σ.

Moderately grounded expansions (or stable set minimal expansions) do not quite capture extensions in default logic and, moreover, are still rather weakly grounded as can be seen from the following example also discussed by Konolige [1988].

Example 2 Consider the following set of premises Σ where p, q are atomic.

$$\{Lp \rightarrow p, \neg Lp \rightarrow q\} \tag{3}$$

Σ has two stable expansions: one containing p but not q and one containing q but not p. Both are stable set minimal but the first one contains the belief p which is based on the belief p, i.e., the same circular argument as in the previous example. ■

To capture extensions in default logic Konolige proposes the notion of an expansion strongly grounded in the premises. The notion is defined only for autoepistemic formulae in a normal form:

$$\neg L\alpha \vee L\beta_1 \vee \ldots \vee L\beta_n \vee \gamma \tag{4}$$

where α, β_i, and γ are all in $\mathcal{L}$. Strongly grounded expansions are also moderately grounded. However, Marek and Truszczynski [1989] have discovered that strongly grounded expansions do not capture extensions in default logic. Marek and Truszczynski [1989] report that Konolige has introduced a corrected version of the definition of strongly grounded expansions. Neither definition of strong groundedness is satisfactory because different expansions could be grounded in different subsets of the premises and strongly grounded expansions depend on the syntactic representation of premises. This

[1] A set S is stable if it is closed under propositional consequence and satisfies the conditions (1) if $\phi \in S$ then $L\phi \in S$ and (2) if $\phi \in \overline{S}$ then $\neg L\phi \in S$.

means that classically equivalent premises do not have the same strongly grounded expansions. For example, $(Lp \rightarrow p) \wedge (\neg Lp \rightarrow p)$ is equivalent to p in propositional logic but the former has none and the latter has one strongly grounded expansion (according to the corrected definition of strong groundedness).

Marek and Truszczynski [1989] present an interesting notion of groundedness in their study of the relationship of default logic and autoepistemic logic. It is based on a monotone operator A defined as follows.

$$A(\Sigma) = Cn(\Sigma \cup L(\Sigma)) \tag{5}$$

where $Cn(\Sigma) = \{\phi \mid \Sigma \models \phi\}$. The operator A is equipped with a context parameter $\Delta \subseteq \mathcal{L}_{ae}$ and given a set of premise $\Sigma \subseteq \mathcal{L}_{ae}$ the operator A^{Δ} is iterated in the following way.

$$A_0^{\Delta}(\Sigma) = Cn(\Sigma \cup \neg L(\overline{\Delta})) \tag{6}$$

$$A_{n+1}^{\Delta}(\Sigma) = A(A_n^{\Delta}(\Sigma)) \tag{7}$$

$$A^{\Delta}(\Sigma) = \bigcup_{n=0}^{\infty} A_n^{\Delta}(\Sigma) \tag{8}$$

Marek and Truszczynski [1989] note that $A^{\Delta}(\Sigma)$ is the set of formulae provable from $\Sigma \cup \neg L(\overline{\Delta})$ using propositional logic and the necessitation rule. They define a new class of expansions based on the operator A.

Definition 3.1 *(Marek and Truszczynski [1989])* Δ *is an* iterative expansion *of* Σ *iff* $\Delta = A^{\Delta}(\Sigma)$.

They prove that iterative expansions are in fact stable expansions. The class of iterative expansions is an attractive candidate for the sets of beliefs adopted by a fully introspective agent. In particular, because in a later paper Marek and Truszczynski [1990] show that iterative expansions generalize nicely reasoning in Reiter's default logic. They show that under the translation tr_T of the defaults D in a default theory (D, W)

$$tr_T(\frac{\alpha : \beta_1, \ldots, \beta_n}{\gamma}) = (L\alpha \wedge \neg LL\neg\beta_1 \wedge \ldots \wedge \neg LL\neg\beta_n) \rightarrow \gamma \tag{9}$$

default logic can be seen as a fragment of autoepistemic logic based on iterative expansions, i.e., E is an extension of a default theory (D, W) iff $E = \Delta \cap \mathcal{L}$ for an iterative expansion Δ of $tr_T(D, W)$.

Marek and Truszczynski [1990] already observed a basic groundedness problem of iterative expansions and gave the following example which shows that iterative expansions are not necessarily stable set minimal. Thus iterative expansions may be regarded too weakly grounded.

Example 3 Consider a set

$$\Sigma = \{\neg L\neg Lp \rightarrow p\} \tag{10}$$

where p is atomic. The set Σ has two stable expansions: one containing p and the other not. Both are iterative but only the second one is minimal. Technically the problem seems to be that the definition of $A^{\Delta}(\Sigma)$ allows the adoption of a belief (in the context Δ) which is justified (indirectly) on the basis of the same belief. This is what happens in the first iterative expansion. If p is put to the context Δ but $\neg Lp$ is not, then by negative introspection we have that $\neg L\neg Lp \in A_0^{\Delta}(\Sigma)$ and $p \in A_0^{\Delta}(\Sigma)$. Thus $Lp \in A_1^{\Delta}(\Sigma)$. Hence $p \in A^{\Delta}(\Sigma)$ and $Lp \in A^{\Delta}(\Sigma)$. It cannot be the case that $\neg Lp \in A^{\Delta}(\Sigma)$ (unless $A^{\Delta}(\Sigma)$ is inconsistent, which it is not). Thus the justification of p is indirectly based on the belief p. ■

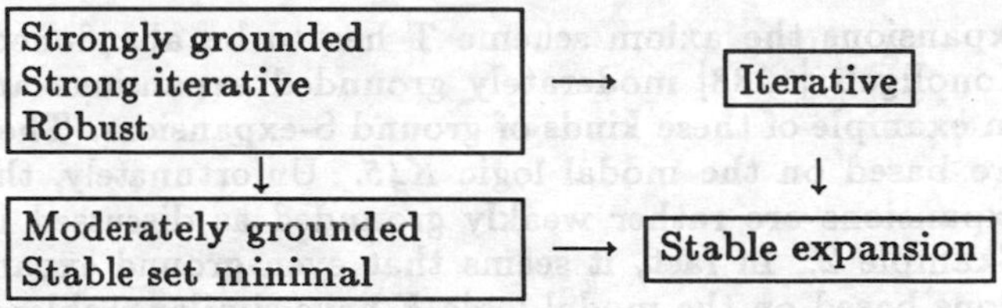

Figure 1: Relationships of groundedness concepts.

Marek and Truszczynski [1989] show how to capture extensions in default logic using two new classes of expansions: ***strongly iterative expansions*** (a strengthened form of iterative expansions) and ***robust expansions.*** These classes of expansions are equivalent with Konolige's strongly grounded expansions and are also defined only for premises in the normal form (4). They suffer from the same unnatural properties as discussed in connection with Konolige's strongly grounded expansions, especially, the dependence on the syntactic representation of premises.

Figure 1 displays a summary of the various groundedness conditions discussed above and their relationships. The arrow is interpreted as implies. E.g., strong groundedness implies stable set minimality.

It seems clear that to get tighter grounded expansions the construction of an expansion should start from the formulae without the L operator. Marek and Truszczynski [1989] present such a construction which builds a stable set out of its L-free part. This method does not seem to be applicable to building expansions from premises, however, because expansions cannot be constructed using such a layered method where, roughly speaking, all formulae having the same depth of L operators are decided at the same time. E.g., consider the set of premises $\{\neg Lq \rightarrow q, \neg LLp \rightarrow q\}$.

Another related idea is to restrict the set of formulae subject to direct introspection and accomplish further introspection by applying some modal logic. Tiomkin and Kaminski [1990] propose ***nonmonotonic ground logics*** based on modal logics *T, S4*, and *S5* where only negative introspection restricted to L-free formulae is applied directly. The set of beliefs is defined using the following fixed point equation

$$\Delta = \{\phi \mid \Sigma \cup \{\neg L\psi \mid \psi \in \mathcal{L} - \Delta\} \vdash_S \phi\} \tag{11}$$

where $\vdash_S$ is the derivability relation of the underlying modal logic (*T, S4, S5*). It seems, however, that these ***ground S-expansions*** are not necessarily stable expansions. E.g., the premise $\neg Lp \rightarrow p$ has no stable expansions. But all the underlying logics *T, S4*, and *S5* contain the axiom scheme T ($L\phi \rightarrow \phi$) which produces an S-expansion containing p. So to stay within stable expansions the axiom scheme T has to be abandoned. Konolige's [1988] moderately grounded expansions are an example of these kinds of ground S-expansions. They are based on the modal logic *K45*. Unfortunately, the expansions are rather weakly grounded as discussed in Example 2. In fact, it seems that even ground expansions based on the modal logic *K* have similar problems of weak groundedness as discussed in Example 2. Consider the set of premises $\{\neg Lp \rightarrow q, \neg L\neg Lp \rightarrow p\}$. It seems that it has two ground *K*-expansions: one containing p and the other containing q. However, the first one is quite weakly grounded in the premises.

4 Enumeration Based Expansions

Our aim is to find a proper characterization of the sets of beliefs of an agent with full introspection capabilities. These sets should be stable expansions of the premises but more tightly grounded in the premises. At least they should be stable set minimal and, in addition, multiple stable set minimal expansions should be excluded in the situations like in Example 2. Iterative expansions suggested by Marek and Truszczynski [1989] are a step in the right direction but are still too weakly grounded as they are not necessarily stable set minimal. Strong iterative expansions (which are the same as strongly grounded and robust expansions) are stable set minimal but are not satisfactory, especially, because of their dependence on the syntactic representation of premises. Another goal is to find a more constructive basis for defining expansions.

We propose a new more constructive definition of the sets of beliefs of an introspective agent which produces tightly grounded sets of beliefs. The definition is based on enumerations of the formulae of $\mathcal{L}_{ae}$. Davis [1980] used this idea in connection with McDermott and Doyle's [1980] nonmonotonic logic to characterize the intersection of fixed points in McDermott and Doyle's logic. The author [Niemelä, 1988] has extended the work of Davis and shown that also individual fixed points in McDermott and Doyle's logic can be characterized using enumerations of the formulae.

The idea is to build a set of beliefs from premises Σ by applying introspection to formulae in the order given by an enumeration ε. A set $\mathbf{B}^\varepsilon(\Sigma)$ is constructed which contains all the results of introspection in the order ε starting from the premises Σ. The set $\mathbf{B}^\varepsilon(\Sigma)$ together with Σ induces the set of beliefs $\mathbf{SE}^\varepsilon(\Sigma)$ of a fully introspective agent having initial assumptions Σ after introspecting formulae in the order ε.

Definition 4.1 *Let $\Sigma \subseteq \mathcal{L}_{ae}$. Let $\varepsilon = \psi_1, \psi_2, \ldots$ be an enumeration of all the formulae of $\mathcal{L}_{ae}$. Let $\mathbf{B}^\varepsilon_0(\Sigma) = \emptyset$.*

Define $\mathbf{B}^\varepsilon_{i+1}(\Sigma)$ for $i = 0, 1, \ldots$ as follows:

$$\mathbf{B}^\varepsilon_{i+1}(\Sigma) = \begin{cases} \mathbf{B}^\varepsilon_i(\Sigma) \cup \{L\psi_{i+1}\} & \text{if } \Sigma \cup \mathbf{B}^\varepsilon_i(\Sigma) \models \psi_{i+1} \\ \mathbf{B}^\varepsilon_i(\Sigma) \cup \{\neg L\psi_{i+1}\} & \text{otherwise} \end{cases}$$

Finally let

$$\mathbf{B}^\varepsilon(\Sigma) = \bigcup_{i=0}^{\infty} \mathbf{B}^\varepsilon_i(\Sigma)$$

$$\mathbf{SE}^\varepsilon(\Sigma) = \{\phi \in \mathcal{L}_{ae} \mid \Sigma \cup \mathbf{B}^\varepsilon(\Sigma) \models \phi\}.$$

We would like $\mathbf{SE}^\varepsilon(\Sigma)$ to be a stable expansion of Σ induced by the enumeration ε. Unfortunately, this not the case for all enumerations.

Example 4 Consider a set of premises

$$\Sigma = \{\neg Lp \rightarrow q\} \tag{12}$$

and take an enumeration $\varepsilon = q, p, \ldots$ Then $\mathbf{B}^\varepsilon_1(\Sigma) = \{\neg Lq\}$ as $\Sigma \not\models q$ and $\mathbf{B}^\varepsilon_2(\Sigma) = \{\neg Lq, \neg Lp\}$ as $\Sigma \cup \mathbf{B}^\varepsilon_1(\Sigma) \not\models p$. But now $q \in \mathbf{SE}^\varepsilon(\Sigma)$ and $\neg Lq \in \mathbf{SE}^\varepsilon(\Sigma)$ but $Lq \notin \mathbf{SE}^\varepsilon(\Sigma)$. Thus $\mathbf{SE}^\varepsilon(\Sigma)$ does not satisfy the fixed point equation (1) of a stable expansion. ■

To stay within stable expansions we must require enumerations to be acceptable in the following sense.

Definition 4.2 *An enumeration ε is Σ-acceptable if there is no i and no formula ϕ such that $\neg L\phi \in \mathbf{B}^\varepsilon_i(\Sigma)$ but $\Sigma \cup \mathbf{B}^\varepsilon_i(\Sigma) \models \phi$.*

Theorem 4.3 *For all Σ-acceptable enumerations ε, $\mathbf{SE}^\varepsilon(\Sigma)$ is a stable expansion of Σ.*

Proof. We prove that $\mathbf{SE}^\varepsilon(\Sigma) = \{\phi \mid \Sigma \cup \mathbf{B}^\varepsilon(\Sigma) \models \phi\}$ is a stable expansion of Σ by showing that $\mathbf{B}^\varepsilon(\Sigma) = L(\mathbf{SE}^\varepsilon(\Sigma)) \cup \neg L(\overline{\mathbf{SE}^\varepsilon(\Sigma)})$.

If $L\psi_i \in \mathbf{B}^\varepsilon(\Sigma)$, then $\Sigma \cup \mathbf{B}^\varepsilon_{i-1}(\Sigma) \models \psi_i$ and as $\mathbf{B}^\varepsilon_{i-1}(\Sigma) \subseteq \mathbf{B}^\varepsilon(\Sigma)$, $\psi_i \in \mathbf{SE}^\varepsilon(\Sigma)$ and thus $L\psi_i \in L(\mathbf{SE}^\varepsilon(\Sigma))$. If $\neg L\psi_i \in \mathbf{B}^\varepsilon(\Sigma)$, then $\Sigma \cup \mathbf{B}^\varepsilon_{i-1}(\Sigma) \not\models \psi_i$. Assume that $\Sigma \cup \mathbf{B}^\varepsilon(\Sigma) \models \psi_i$. Then there exists a $k \geq i$ such that $\Sigma \cup \mathbf{B}^\varepsilon_k(\Sigma) \models \psi_i$ but $\neg L\psi_i \in \mathbf{B}^\varepsilon_k(\Sigma)$, which is a contradiction as ε is Σ-acceptable. Thus $\psi_i \notin \mathbf{SE}^\varepsilon(\Sigma)$ and $\neg L\psi_i \in \neg L(\overline{\mathbf{SE}^\varepsilon(\Sigma)})$. This shows that $\mathbf{B}^\varepsilon(\Sigma) \subseteq L(\mathbf{SE}^\varepsilon(\Sigma)) \cup \neg L(\overline{\mathbf{SE}^\varepsilon(\Sigma)})$.

If $\neg L\psi_i \in \neg L(\overline{\mathbf{SE}^\varepsilon(\Sigma)})$, then $\Sigma \cup \mathbf{B}^\varepsilon(\Sigma) \not\models \psi_i$. This implies that $\Sigma \cup \mathbf{B}^\varepsilon_{i-1}(\Sigma) \not\models \psi_i$ as $\mathbf{B}^\varepsilon_{i-1}(\Sigma) \subseteq \mathbf{B}^\varepsilon(\Sigma)$. Thus $\neg L\psi_i \in \mathbf{B}^\varepsilon(\Sigma)$. If $L\psi_i \in L(\mathbf{SE}^\varepsilon(\Sigma))$, then $\Sigma \cup \mathbf{B}^\varepsilon(\Sigma) \models \psi_i$. Assume that $\Sigma \cup \mathbf{B}^\varepsilon_{i-1}(\Sigma) \not\models \psi_i$. Then there exists a $k \geq i$ such that $\Sigma \cup \mathbf{B}^\varepsilon_k(\Sigma) \models \psi_i$ but $\neg L\psi_i \in \mathbf{B}^\varepsilon_k(\Sigma)$, which is a contradiction as ε is Σ-acceptable. Thus $\Sigma \cup \mathbf{B}^\varepsilon_{i-1}(\Sigma) \models \psi_i$ and $L\psi_i \in \mathbf{B}^\varepsilon(\Sigma)$. Hence $\mathbf{B}^\varepsilon(\Sigma) = L(\mathbf{SE}^\varepsilon(\Sigma)) \cup \neg L(\overline{\mathbf{SE}^\varepsilon(\Sigma)})$. □

Σ-acceptable enumerations offer a constructive way to define stable expansions. The expansion is directly built from the premises and the enumeration. It should be noted that even the acceptability condition is in a sense local to each $\mathbf{B}^\varepsilon_i(\Sigma)$ as only those formula ψ_j have to be checked for which $j \leq i$ because they are the only formulae for which $\neg L\psi_j \in \mathbf{B}^\varepsilon_i(\Sigma)$ could hold.

However, enumerations are not capable of capturing every stable expansion. Consider the premise $Lp \rightarrow p$ discussed in Example 1. It has two stable expansions: one containing p and the other not containing p. Only the second one is characterizable using enumerations because in enumeration based expansions Lp cannot be used in deriving p directly. This leads one to assume that enumerations might produce minimal expansions. However, this is not the case as shown by the following example.

Example 5 Consider the set

$$\Sigma = \{\neg L\neg Lp \rightarrow p\} \tag{13}$$

where p is atomic. Σ has two stable expansions which are both characterizable using enumerations. The first one not containing p using an enumeration $p, \neg Lp, \ldots$ and the second containing p using an enumeration $\neg Lp, p, \ldots$ Let us look what happens in the second enumeration ε. $\mathbf{B}_1^\varepsilon(\Sigma) = \{\neg L\neg Lp\}$ as $\Sigma \not\models \neg Lp$. But then $\mathbf{B}_2^\varepsilon(\Sigma) = \{\neg L\neg Lp, Lp\}$ as $\Sigma \cup \mathbf{B}_1^\varepsilon(\Sigma) \models p$ ■

Thus the enumeration method fails to capture stable set minimal expansions exactly in the same situation where iterative method fails. This is no coincidence because enumeration based expansions and iterative expansions are closely related. Enumerations produce always iterative expansions and at least for finite sets of premises for every iterative expansion there is a corresponding enumeration producing it.

Theorem 4.4 *For all Σ-acceptable enumerations ε, $\mathbf{SE}^\varepsilon(\Sigma)$ is an iterative expansion of Σ.*

Proof. We have to show that for $\Delta = \mathbf{SE}^\varepsilon(\Sigma)$, $A^\Delta(\Sigma) = \Delta$ holds. First we show that for all $i = 0, 1, 2, \ldots$

$$\mathbf{B}_i^\varepsilon(\Sigma) \subseteq L(A_i^\Delta(\Sigma)) \cup \neg L(\overline{\Delta}). \quad (14)$$

For $i = 0$ this holds trivially. If $L\psi_i \in \mathbf{B}_i^\varepsilon(\Sigma)$, then $\Sigma \cup \mathbf{B}_{i-1}^\varepsilon(\Sigma) \models \psi_i$. By the induction hypothesis $\Sigma \cup L(A_{i-1}^\Delta(\Sigma)) \cup \neg L(\overline{\Delta}) \models \psi_i$ which implies that $\psi_i \in A_i^\Delta(\Sigma) = Cn(A_{i-1}^\Delta(\Sigma) \cup L(A_{i-1}^\Delta(\Sigma)))$ because $\Sigma \cup \neg L(\overline{\Delta}) \subseteq A_n^\Delta(\Sigma)$ for all $n = 0, 1, \ldots$ Thus $L\psi_i \in L(A_i^\Delta(\Sigma))$. If $\neg L\psi_i \in \mathbf{B}_i^\varepsilon(\Sigma)$, then $\psi_i \notin \Delta$ as ε is Σ-acceptable. Thus $\neg L\psi \in \neg L(\overline{\Delta})$. Hence $\mathbf{B}_i^\varepsilon(\Sigma) \subseteq L(A_i^\Delta(\Sigma)) \cup \neg L(\overline{\Delta})$.

This result implies $\Delta \subseteq A^\Delta(\Sigma)$ in the following way. Let $\phi \in \Delta$. Then there exists i such that $\Sigma \cup \mathbf{B}_{i-1}^\varepsilon(\Sigma) \models \phi$. By (14) $\Sigma \cup L(A_{i-1}^\Delta(\Sigma)) \cup \neg L(\overline{\Delta}) \models \phi$ which implies that $\phi \in A_i^\Delta(\Sigma) \subseteq A^\Delta(\Sigma)$.

We show that for all $i = 0, 1, 2, \ldots$ $A_i^\Delta(\Sigma) \subseteq \Delta$ which implies $A^\Delta(\Sigma) \subseteq \Delta$ and thus $A^\Delta(\Sigma) = \Delta$. Let $\phi \in A_0^\Delta(\Sigma)$. Then $\Sigma \cup \neg L(\overline{\Delta}) \models \phi$. So $\phi \in \Delta = \{\phi \mid \Sigma \cup L(\Delta) \cup \neg L(\overline{\Delta}) \models \phi\}$. Let $\phi \in A_i^\Delta(\Sigma)$. Then $A_{i-1}^\Delta(\Sigma) \cup L(A_{i-1}^\Delta(\Sigma)) \models \phi$. By the induction hypothesis $A_{i-1}^\Delta(\Sigma) \subseteq \Delta$ and thus $L(A_{i-1}^\Delta(\Sigma)) \subseteq L(\Delta) \subseteq \Delta$. Thus $\phi \in \Delta$. □

Theorem 4.5 *For each iterative expansion Δ of a finite set of premises Σ there is a Σ-acceptable enumeration ε such that $\Delta = \mathbf{SE}^\varepsilon(\Sigma)$.*

Proof. It can be shown that a Σ-acceptable enumeration ε which induces Δ can be constructed from Δ in the following way if Σ is finite.

1. Let the first formulae in ε be the formulae $\psi_i \notin \Delta$ for which $L\psi_i \in Sf^L(\Sigma)$[2].
2. The next formulae in ε are those $\psi_i \in \Delta$ for which $L\psi_i \in Sf^L(\Sigma)$ in the order they are produced by the iteration of A^Δ.
3. All the rest of the formulae in $\mathcal{L}_{ae}$ are ordered such that if $L\psi_i \in Sf^L(\{\psi_j\})$, then $i < j$.

[2] $Sf^L(\Sigma)$ is the set of the $L\chi$ subformulae of the formulae in Σ.

The set Σ has to be finite for the conditions 1 and 2 to be satisfied by an enumeration of formulae. The question whether there exists a Σ-acceptable enumeration ε which induces Δ for any iterative expansion Δ of an infinite set of premises Σ remains open. □

Thus enumeration based expansions provide an alternative way of defining iterative expansions. Example 5 reveals also why iterative expansions are not necessarily stable set minimal. It is possible to introspect a formula ϕ without first introspecting the subformulae of ϕ which can effect the result of the introspection of ϕ. In the case of Example 5 it is possible to introspect $\neg Lp$ and obtain $\neg L\neg Lp$ without first checking the status of p.

So it seems as a very natural requirement to demand that in order to get tightly grounded beliefs all subformulae of a given formula ϕ that can effect the result of the introspection of ϕ must be examined before ϕ. This new groundedness requirement can be incorporated easily to the definition of enumeration based stable expansions. We require the enumerations to be *L-hierarchic*. This means that a formula ϕ can appear in the enumeration only after all ψ such that $L\psi$ is a subformula of ϕ have appeared in the enumeration. It is unclear how to incorporate this kind of a requirement into the definition of iterative expansions.

Definition 4.6 *Let ε be an enumeration $\psi_1, \psi_2, \ldots$ of all the formulae in $\mathcal{L}_{ae}$. ε is* L-hierarchic *if for all ψ_i, ψ_j holds that if $L\psi_i \in Sf^L(\{\psi_j\})$, then $i < j$.*

Definition 4.7 $\mathbf{SE}^\varepsilon(\Sigma)$ *is an* L-hierarchic expansion *of Σ if ε is a Σ-acceptable L-hierarchic enumeration.*

It turns out that the simple requirement on the order of the formulae in the enumerations guarantees that L-hierarchic expansions are stable set minimal.

Theorem 4.8 *Every L-hierarchic expansion $\mathbf{SE}^\varepsilon(\Sigma)$ of Σ is a stable set minimal stable expansion of Σ (a moderately grounded expansion of Σ).*

Proof. We denote $\mathbf{SE}^\varepsilon(\Sigma)$ by Δ. Assume that there exists a stable set S containing Σ such that $S \cap \mathcal{L} \subseteq \Delta \cap \mathcal{L}$. We prove that $\Delta = S$ by showing that for all $i = 1, 2, \ldots$, $\psi_i \in \Delta$ iff $\psi_i \in S$. This proves that Δ is stable set minimal for Σ.

If $\psi_1 \in S$, then as ε is L-hierarchic $\psi_1 \in \mathcal{L}$ and $\psi_1 \in \Delta$. If $\psi_1 \in \Delta$, then $\Sigma \models \psi_1$ as ε is Σ-acceptable. Thus $\psi_1 \in S$ as $\Sigma \subseteq S$ and S is stable.

If $\psi_i \in \Delta$, then $\Sigma \cup \mathbf{B}_{i-1}^\varepsilon(\Sigma) \models \psi_i$ as ε is Σ-acceptable. By the induction hypothesis $\mathbf{B}_{i-1}^\varepsilon(\Sigma) \subseteq S$. Thus $\psi_i \in S$ as $\Sigma \subseteq S$ and S is stable. Let $\psi_i \notin \Delta$. The formula ψ_i can be transformed into a normal form $\psi_i' = d_1 \wedge \ldots \wedge d_n$ where each d_i is of the form

$$\gamma \vee L\alpha_1 \vee \ldots \vee L\alpha_m \vee \neg L\beta_1 \vee \ldots \vee \neg L\beta_l$$

where $\gamma \in \mathcal{L}$ and $\alpha_i, \beta_i \in \mathcal{L}_{ae}$. It holds that $\psi_i \in \Delta$ iff $\psi_i' \in \Delta$. So $\psi_i' \notin \Delta$. Thus there exists a disjunction $d_j \notin \Delta$. As Δ is a stable set, $d_j \notin \Delta$ iff $\gamma \notin \Delta, \alpha_1 \notin \Delta, \ldots, \alpha_m \notin \Delta, \beta_1 \in \Delta, \ldots, \beta_l \in \Delta$. The normal form transformation does not go into the $L\chi$ formulae. Thus $Sf^L(\{\psi_i\}) = Sf^L(\{\psi_i'\})$ and so each α_i and β_i is some ψ_j such that $j < i$ because the enumeration is L-hierarchic. Thus by the induction hypothesis

$\alpha_1 \notin S, \ldots, \alpha_m \notin S, \beta_1 \in S, \ldots, \beta_l \in S$. As $\gamma \in \mathcal{L}$ and $\gamma \notin \Delta$, $\gamma \notin S$. Thus $d_j \notin S$ which implies that $\psi_i' \notin S$. As ψ_i is equivalent to ψ_i', $\psi_i \notin S$. Hence $\Delta = S$ □

Thus an L-hierarchic expansion of Σ is a stable set minimal iterative expansion which is not dependent on the syntactic representation of premises. E.g., $\{Lp \rightarrow p, \neg Lp \rightarrow p\}$ and $\{p\}$ have both the same unique L-hierarchic expansion. So L-hierarchic expansions are not necessarily strongly grounded (or strongly iterative/robust).

It turns out that in the case of T-clauses which are of the form

$$(L\alpha_1 \wedge \ldots \wedge L\alpha_m \wedge \neg LL\beta_1 \wedge \ldots \wedge \neg LL\beta_n) \rightarrow \gamma \quad (15)$$

where $\alpha_i, \beta_i, \gamma \in \mathcal{L}$ all iterative expansions of every finite set of premises are also L-hierarchic expansions. It can be shown that the conditions in the proof of Theorem 4.5 for an enumeration inducing an iterative expansion are also satisfied by an L-hierarchic enumeration for each iterative expansion of every finite set of T-clauses. So for T-clauses iterative and L-hierarchic expansions coincide. This shows that L-hierarchic expansions are adequate to capture extensions in Reiter's default logic using the translation proposed by Marek and Truszczynski (9) because this translation produces T-clauses.

Theorem 4.9 *$E \subseteq \mathcal{L}$ is an extension of a finite default theory (D, W)*[3] *iff $E = \mathbf{SE}^{\epsilon}(tr_T(D, W)) \cap \mathcal{L}$ for a $tr_T(D, W)$-acceptable L-hierarchic enumeration ϵ.*

Thus autoepistemic logic based on L-hierarchic expansions is a generalization of default logic which provides an alternative definition of an extension (Reiter [1980] gave originally a fixed point characterization). On the other hand, default logic is a special case of this kind of autoepistemic logic where only formulae of the form $(L\alpha \wedge \neg LL\neg\beta_1 \wedge \ldots \wedge \neg LL\neg\beta_n) \rightarrow \gamma$ are allowed.

The question of a general semantics approach to L-hierarchic expansions remains open. In the case of T-programs which are T-clauses where $\alpha_i, \beta_i, \gamma \in \mathcal{L}$ are literals Marek and Truszczynski [1990] have given a semantic characterization of consistent iterative expansions and as in this case iterative and L-hierarchic expansions coincide this semantics applies also to consistent L-hierarchic expansions of T-programs.

5 Conclusions

We have introduced a new class of expansions in autoepistemic logic called *L-hierarchic expansions*. L-hierarchic expansions are very promising candidates for the sets of conclusions derived by an ideally rational agent with full introspection capabilities on the basis of given premises. This new class of expansions has a number of attractive properties. Instead of a fixed point characterization an L-hierarchic expansion is constructed directly from the premises and an enumeration of the formulae of the language. The construction is given in terms of classical logic, e.g., no modal logic is needed. L-hierarchic expansions are independent of the syntactic representation of premises. They are very tightly grounded in the premises. They are iterative expansions [Marek and Truszczyński, 1989] and, in addition, always stable set minimal. Furthermore, autoepistemic logic based on L-hierarchic expansions captures default reasoning: it is shown that Reiter's default logic is a special case of this new logic. One of the most important open problems is the question of existence of a semantic characterization of L-hierarchic expansions in the general case.

[3]For a finite default theory (D, W) $D \cup W$ is a finite set.

References

[Davis, 1980] M. Davis. The mathematics of nonmonotonic reasoning. *Artificial Intelligence*, 13:73–80, 1980.

[Elkan, 1990] C. Elkan. A rational reconstruction of nonmonotonic truth maintenance systems. *Artificial Intelligence*, 43:219–234, 1990.

[Konolige, 1988] K. Konolige. On the relation between default and autoepistemic logic. *Artificial Intelligence*, 35:343–382, 1988.

[Konolige, 1989] K. Konolige. On the relation between autoepistemic logic and circumscription. In *Proceeding of the 11th International Joint Conference on Artificial Intelligence*, pages 1213–1218, Detroit, Michigan, August 1989. International Joint Conferences on Artificial Intelligence.

[Marek and Truszczyński, 1989] W. Marek and M. Truszczyński. Relating autoepistemic and default logics. In *Proceedings of the 1st International Conference on Principles of Knowledge Representation and Reasoning*, pages 276–288, Toronto, Canada, May 1989.

[Marek and Truszczyński, 1990] W. Marek and M. Truszczyński. Modal logic for default reasoning. In *Preprints of the 3rd International Workshop on Nonmonotonic Reasoning*, pages 247–258, South Lake Tahoe, California, May 1990.

[McDermott and Doyle, 1980] D. McDermott and J. Doyle. Non-monotonic logic I. *Artificial Intelligence*, 13:41–72, 1980.

[Moore, 1985] R.C. Moore. Semantical considerations on nonmonotonic logic. *Artificial Intelligence*, 25:75–94, 1985.

[Niemelä, 1988] I. Niemelä. On the complexity of the decision problem in propositional nonmonotonic logic. In *Proceedings of the 2nd Workshop on Computer Science Logic*, pages 226–239, Duisburg, FRG, October 1988. Springer-Verlag.

[Reiter, 1980] R. Reiter. A logic for default reasoning. *Artificial Intelligence*, 13:81–132, 1980.

[Tiomkin and Kaminski, 1990] M. Tiomkin and M. Kaminski. Nonmonotonic default modal logics. In *Proceedings of the Third Conference on Theoretical Aspects of Reasoning about Knowledge*, pages 73–83, Pacific Grove California, March 1990.

KNOWLEDGE REPRESENTATION

Nonmonotonic Reasoning—Conditional Logics

A Unified View of Consequence Relation, Belief Revision and Conditional Logic

Hirofumi Katsuno
NTT Basic Research Laboratories
Musashino-shi, Tokyo 180
Japan
katsuno@ntt-20.ntt.jp

Ken Satoh
ICOT Research Center
1-4-28 Mita, Minato-ku, Tokyo 108
Japan
ksatoh@icot.or.jp

Abstract

The notion of *minimality* is widely used in three different areas of Artificial Intelligence: nonmonotonic reasoning, belief revision, and conditional reasoning. However, it is difficult for the readers of the literature in these areas to perceive the similarities clearly, because each formalization in those areas uses its own language sometimes without referring to other formalizations. We define *ordered structures* and *families of ordered structures* as the common ingredient of the semantics of all the works above. We also define the logics for ordered structures and families. We present a uniform view of how minimality is used in these three areas, and shed light on deep reciprocal relations among different approaches of the areas by using the ordered structures and the families of ordered structures.

1 Introduction

The notion of *minimality* is proving to be a key unifying idea in three different areas of Artificial Intelligence: nonmonotonic reasoning, belief revision, and conditional reasoning. However, it is difficult for the readers of the literature in these areas to perceive the similarities clearly. The models used differ, sometimes superficially, sometimes in depth, and the notation is different, making it hard to apply results on, say, conditional logic to, say, belief revision. Even within the same area there is confusion, as, for example, different authors use different formalisms for conditional logic, sometimes without relating their proposals to the literature. We present a uniform view of how minimality is used in these three areas, shedding light on deep connections among the areas. We clarify differences and similarities between different approaches by classifying them according to the notion of minimality that they are based on.

The first field in which minimality plays a crucial role is nonmonotonic reasoning. Shoham [1987] proposes a uniform approach to subsuming various formalisms of nonmonotonic reasoning in terms of *preferential relations* among interpretations. Kraus, Lehmann and Magidor [1990] propose several *consequence relations* that capture general patterns of nonmonotonic reasoning. A consequence relation, denoted by $\mu \mid\sim \phi$, means that μ is a good enough reason to believe ϕ, or that ϕ is a plausible consequence of μ. We can regard their work as an extension of Shoham's work since some consequence relations can be characterized in terms of preferential relations among possible worlds.

The second field in which minimality is discussed is knowledge base *revision* and *update*. Alchourrón, Gärdenfors and Makinson [1985] propose, on philosophical grounds, a set of rationality postulates that belief revision operators must satisfy. Katsuno and Mendelzon [1989; 1991a] show that the AGM postulates precisely characterize revision operators that accomplish a modification with minimal change among models of knowledge bases expressed in a finitary propositional logic.

Katsuno and Mendelzon [1991b] clarify a fundamental distinction between knowledge base revision and update. They propose update postulates in the spirit of the AGM revision postulates, and show that the update postulates precisely characterize minimal change update operators just as the revision postulates characterize minimal change revision.

The third field is conditional logic, which is concerned with the logical and semantical properties of *counterfactuals*, statements such as "if I were a bird then I could fly." Many applications of counterfactuals in Artificial Intelligence are pointed out by Ginsberg [1986]. Delgrande [1988] uses a conditional logic to formalize default reasoning.

There are several different conditional logics, and some of them can be formulated in terms of minimal change [Nute, 1984]. According to this minimality view, a counterfactual, $\mu > \phi$, is true if we add its antecedent μ to our set of beliefs, modify the set as little as possible to preserve consistency, and then its consequent ϕ is true under the modified set of beliefs. Gärdenfors [1988] shows the difficulties associated with using revision to model this view of counterfactuals; Katsuno and Mendelzon [1991b] suggest using update instead of revision. This suggestion is carried out by Grahne [1991] in a logic of updates and counterfactuals.

Lewis [1973] proposes conditional logics called VC and VW. In the semantics of VC and VW, total pre-orders (in Lewis' terminology, "systems of spheres") play a key role. Pollock [Pollock, 1981; Nute, 1984] proposes another conditional logic, called SS, the semantics of which is determined by changing total pre-orders in VC to partial orders.

In this paper, we discuss fundamental similarities and differences among the above works, and give a unified view of all the above in terms of notions of minimality.

A good deal of previous work has been done, especially recently, on comparisons among consequence relations, knowledge base revision and conditional logics. Kraus, Lehmann and Magidor [1990] point out a relationship between one of their consequence relations and conditional logics. We extend their result and show more accurate semantic and syntactic correspondences.

Makinson and Gärdenfors [Makinson and Gärdenfors, 1991; Gärdenfors, 1990] show the relationship between the AGM postulates for revision and postulates for nonmonotonic consequence relations. Gärdenfors [1988] also investigates the relationship between knowledge base revision and conditional logic based on Ramsey test in terms of syntax. He shows that although there are close resemblances between his postulates for revision and axioms of conditional logic, it is impossible to formulate conditional logic by knowledge base revision and Ramsey test. We show the distinctions between conditional logic and knowledge base revision in light of their semantics, and show that there is a close relationship between knowledge base update and conditional logic. Grahne [1991] proposes a new logic in which counterfactual and update are treated in a unified way.

Bell [1989] proposes using a conditional logic, called C, to extend Shoham's work. The C logic is no more than SS, although the semantics of C seems to be slightly different from the semantics of SS.

Boutilier [1990a; 1990b] establishes a mapping between two conditional logics, called CT4 and CT4D, and consequence relations. We show the differences between his conditional logics and other conditional logics in light of notions of minimality. We also extend these results to other conditional logics.

The outline of the paper is as follows. We define, in Section 3, *ordered structures* and *families of ordered structures* as the common ingredient of the semantics of all the works above, based on the observation that an order among possible worlds is a key concept in all of them. We define logics for ordered structures and families, and give sound and complete axiomatizations for them. In Section 4, we consider in detail each of the three areas – nonmonotonic logic, belief revision, and conditional logic – and show how the works in each area fit into our framework. Finally, in Section 5 we use our framework to derive new cross-connections among the areas.

2 Preliminaries

Let L be a language of propositional logic that may have an infinite number of propositional letters. Let L_n be a finitary propositional language that has exactly n propositional letters. We denote the set consisting of all the interpretations of L_n by $\mathcal{I}_n$. Throughout this paper, we use ψ, μ and ϕ to denote a well-formed formula of L.

A pre-order $\leq$ over a set W is a reflexive and transitive relation. We denote the strict order of $\leq$ by $<$. An element w is a *minimum* with respect to $\leq$ if $w < w'$ for any $w' \in W - \{w\}$. Let W' be a subset of W. An element w is *minimal* in W' with respect to $\leq$ if w is a member of W' and for any $w' \in W'$, $w' \leq w$ implies $w \leq w'$. We denote by $Min(W', \leq)$ the set of minimal elements in W' with respect to $\leq$. We can define a total pre-order and a partial order in a usual way.

3 Common Language

We define a common language $L_{\leadsto}$ to discuss consequence relations, knowledge base revision, update and conditional logics in a unified way. The language $L_{\leadsto}$ is a language augmented L with a binary connective $\leadsto$. The connective $\leadsto$ is directly related to the connective $\mid\!\sim$ in the context of consequence relations and the conditional connective $>$ of conditional logics.

We define $Wff_{\leadsto}$ as the set consisting of all the well formed formulas of $L_{\leadsto}$. We also define $S\text{-}Wff_{\leadsto}$ as the set of formulas that have no nesting of $\leadsto$. For example, $\phi \leadsto (\psi \leadsto \mu)$ is not a formula of $S\text{-}Wff_{\leadsto}$. We define $Wff_{n,\leadsto}$ as the set consisting of all the formulas in $Wff_{\leadsto}$ such that every propositional letter occurred in the formula is a propositional letter of L_n.

3.1 Ordered Structure

An ordered structure is one of the central notions in the semantics of the works that involve minimality. We can give semantics of the formulas in $S\text{-}Wff_{\leadsto}$ by using ordered structures. An ordered structure is a special case of Kripke structure used in modal logics.

We define an *ordered structure* $\mathcal{O}$ as a triple $\langle W, \leq, V\rangle$, where W is a nonempty set of worlds, $\leq$ is a pre-order over W satisfying the smoothness property defined later, and V is a function that maps a pair of each propositional letter of L and an element of W to T or F.

For an ordered structure $\mathcal{O} = \langle W, \leq, V\rangle$, we define truth of each formula in $S\text{-}Wff_{\leadsto}$ as follows. First, we recursively define the truth of formulas at a world w by using $\mathcal{O}, w \models$.

$$
\begin{array}{lll}
\mathcal{O}, w \models p & \text{iff} & V(p, w) = \mathrm{T} \\
\mathcal{O}, w \models \neg\alpha & \text{iff} & \mathcal{O}, w \not\models \alpha, \\
\mathcal{O}, w \models \alpha \wedge \beta & \text{iff} & \mathcal{O}, w \models \alpha \text{ and } \mathcal{O}, w \models \beta, \\
\mathcal{O}, w \models \phi \leadsto \varphi & \text{iff} & Min(\|\phi\|, \leq) \subseteq \|\varphi\|,
\end{array}
$$

where $\|\phi\| = \{w \mid V(\phi, w) = \mathrm{T}\}$.

We say that a formula α in $S\text{-}Wff_{\leadsto}$ is true under an ordered structure $\mathcal{O}$, denoted by $\mathcal{O} \models \alpha$, if $\mathcal{O}, w \models \alpha$ for any w in $Min(W, \leq)$, that is, α is true at every minimal world of W.

Note the following facts.

1. If $w_1 \leq w_2$ means w_1 is a more natural world than w_2, then the semantics defined above shows that $\phi \leadsto \varphi$ is true under $\mathcal{O}$ if and only if all most natural worlds that satisfy ϕ also satisfy φ.
2. If W is an infinite set, there might exist infinite descending chains of elements of W. Then, although some $\|\phi\|$ is not empty, $Min(\|\phi\|, \leq)$ might be empty.

The smoothness condition, mentioned in the definition of ordered structure, precludes the possibility of the above emptiness problem. A pre-order $\leq$ satisfies the *smoothness condition* if, for any formula ϕ of L and any $w \in \|\phi\|$, there is some world w' such that $w' \leq w$ and w' is minimal in $\|\phi\|$ with respect to $\leq$.

We consider various restrictions on an ordered structure $\mathcal{O} = \langle W, \leq, V\rangle$. If the pre-order $\leq$ is a total pre-order (or a partial order), then we say that $\mathcal{O}$ is a *totally ordered structure* (or *partially ordered structure*). If W is finite, we say that $\mathcal{O}$ is a *finite ordered structure*. If, for any two different worlds, w_1 and w_2, there is some formula ϕ of L such that $V(\phi, w_1) \neq V(\phi, w_2)$, then we say that $\mathcal{O}$ is a *distinguishable ordered structure*. If $\mathcal{O}$ is a distinguishable ordered structure then no two worlds represent the same interpretation of L. If the pre-order $\leq$ has a minimum in W, we say that $\mathcal{O}$ is an *ordered structure with a minimum*. The ordered structures with a minimum are used to give semantics to formulas of $Wff_{\rightsquigarrow}$.

The readers who are familiar with ranked models and preferential models of consequence relations may easily notice that totally (resp. partially) ordered structures are very similar to ranked (resp. preferential) models.

Another restriction is the case where a finitary propositional logic L_n is used instead of L. An *ordered L_n-structure* is an ordered structure $\langle W, \leq, V\rangle$ such that if a propositional letter p is not in L_n then $V(p, w)$ is undefined. We can also define various restrictions (total, partial, finite, distinguishable, with a minimum) on ordered L_n-structures.

Next, we consider a collection of ordered structures in order to give semantics to any formula of $Wff_{\rightsquigarrow}$. A *family of ordered structures* $\widehat{\mathcal{O}} = (\mathcal{O}_w)_{w\in W}$ is a collection of ordered structures such that W is a nonempty set of worlds, each $\mathcal{O}_w = \langle W_w, \leq_w, V\rangle$ is an ordered structure, W_w is a nonempty subset of W, w is minimal in W_w with respect to $\leq_w$, and a stronger smoothness condition defined later is satisfied. For a family of ordered structures $\widehat{\mathcal{O}} = (\langle W_w, \leq_w, V\rangle)_{w\in W}$, if each w is the minimum of W_w with respect to $\leq_w$ then we say that $\widehat{\mathcal{O}}$ is a *family of ordered structures with minimum*. We can also define various restrictions on a family of ordered structures (with minimum) in a similar way to the case of ordered structures.

For a family of ordered structures $\widehat{\mathcal{O}} = (\mathcal{O}_w)_{w\in W}$, we recursively define the truth of formulas at each world w in W as follows.

$$\begin{array}{lll}
\widehat{\mathcal{O}}, w \models p & \text{iff} & V(p, w) = \mathrm{T}, \\
\widehat{\mathcal{O}}, w \models \neg A & \text{iff} & \widehat{\mathcal{O}}, w \not\models A, \\
\widehat{\mathcal{O}}, w \models A \wedge B & \text{iff} & \widehat{\mathcal{O}}, w \models A \text{ and } \widehat{\mathcal{O}}, w \models B, \\
\widehat{\mathcal{O}}, w \models A \rightsquigarrow B & \text{iff} & Min(\|A\|^{\widehat{\mathcal{O}}} \cap W_w, \leq_w) \subseteq \|B\|^{\widehat{\mathcal{O}}},
\end{array}$$

where $\|A\|^{\widehat{\mathcal{O}}} = \{w \mid \widehat{\mathcal{O}}, w \models A\}$. Intuitively, the set $\|A\|^{\widehat{\mathcal{O}}}$ denotes all the worlds under which A is true. We say that A is true under a family of ordered structures $\widehat{\mathcal{O}}$ if $\|A\|^{\widehat{\mathcal{O}}} = W$.

The stronger smoothness condition for a family of ordered structures $\widehat{\mathcal{O}}$ is: for any formula A in $Wff_{\rightsquigarrow}$ and any $w \in W$, if $w' \in \|A\|^{\widehat{\mathcal{O}}} \cap W_w$ then there is some world $w'' \in W_w$ such that $w'' \leq w'$ and w'' is minimal in $\|A\|^{\widehat{\mathcal{O}}} \cap W_w$ with respect to $\leq_w$.

3.2 Validity

We investigate the relationship between ordered structures and families of ordered structures (with minimum) in light of the validity of formulas. We also show how various restrictions on those structures are related to the interpretation of formulas.

First, we can show that there is no difference between ordered structures and families of ordered structure in light of the validity of formulas of $S\text{-}Wff_{\rightsquigarrow}$.

Theorem 3.1 *For any formula α in $S\text{-}Wff_{\rightsquigarrow}$, α is valid under totally (resp. partially) ordered structures if and only if α is valid under families of totally (resp. partially) ordered structures.*

The validity under families of ordered structures and the validity under families of ordered structures with minimum are *different*. We show, at the end of this subsection, that the two validities are equivalent for some restricted formulas.

Next, we can show that all the restrictions on totally ordered structures introduce no distinction as long as we consider formulas of $S\text{-}Wff_{\rightsquigarrow}$ in the context of L_n. This result implies that none of the restrictions influence the validity of each formula α.

Theorem 3.2 *For any totally ordered structure $\mathcal{O}$, there exists a finite, distinguishable, totally ordered L_n-structure $\mathcal{O}'$ such that for any formula α in $S\text{-}Wff_{n,\rightsquigarrow}$, α is true under $\mathcal{O}$ if and only if α is true under $\mathcal{O}'$.*

The case of partially ordered structures is different from the case of totally ordered structures. The validity under finite, distinguishable, partially ordered L_n-structures is exceptional.

Theorem 3.3 *For any partially ordered structure $\mathcal{O}$, there exists a finite, partially ordered L_n-structure $\mathcal{O}'$ such that for any formula α in $S\text{-}Wff_{n,\rightsquigarrow}$, α is true under $\mathcal{O}$ if and only if α is true under $\mathcal{O}'$.*

We can show similar theorems about families of ordered structures (with minimum) in the context of $Wff_{\rightsquigarrow}$.

Third, we can define a conditional Horn formula by regarding $\mu \rightsquigarrow \phi$ as an atom. For example, a formula $(\mu_1 \rightsquigarrow \phi_1) \wedge \ldots \wedge (\mu_k \rightsquigarrow \phi_k) \supset (\mu \rightsquigarrow \phi)$ is a conditional Horn formula. Then, we can prove that the validity of a conditional Horn formula is independent of whether total pre-order or partial order is used in ordered structures. This fact is interesting in light of axiomatizations, because in the axiomatic systems proposed in various works, non-Horn axioms are used to discriminate total pre-order cases from partial order cases.

Furthermore, we can show that the validity of a conditional Horn formula under families of ordered structures is the same as the validity under families of ordered structures with minimum.

3.3 Axiomatization

We show axiomatic systems for ordered structures and families of ordered structures (with minimum). As we see later, the axiomatic system for ordered structures is the same as the axiomatic system for families of ordered structures except for the fact that a variable of the former system ranges over a formula in either $S\text{-}Wff_{\rightsquigarrow}$ or L, but a variable of the latter system ranges over a formula in $Wff_{\rightsquigarrow}$.

First, let ζ, η and ξ be formula variables that range over formulas of L. Let γ and δ be formula variables that range over formulas of $S\text{-}Wff_{\rightsquigarrow}$. Let X, Y and Z be formula variables that range over formulas of $Wff_{\rightsquigarrow}$. An axiomatic system TO is a set of the following axiomatic schemas and inference rules.[1]

Axiom Schemas

(PC)	Truth-functional tautologies.
(ID)	$\zeta \rightsquigarrow \zeta$.
(MP)	$(\zeta \rightsquigarrow \eta) \supset (\zeta \supset \eta)$.
(AND)	$(\zeta \rightsquigarrow \eta) \wedge (\zeta \rightsquigarrow \xi) \supset (\zeta \rightsquigarrow (\eta \wedge \xi))$.
(OR)	$(\zeta \rightsquigarrow \xi) \wedge (\eta \rightsquigarrow \xi) \supset ((\zeta \vee \eta) \rightsquigarrow \xi)$.
(CE)	$(\zeta \rightsquigarrow \eta) \wedge (\eta \rightsquigarrow \zeta) \wedge (\zeta \rightsquigarrow \xi) \supset (\eta \rightsquigarrow \xi)$.
(RM)	$(\zeta \rightsquigarrow \xi) \wedge \neg(\zeta \rightsquigarrow \neg\eta) \supset ((\zeta \wedge \eta) \rightsquigarrow \xi)$.

Inference Rules

(Mp)	From δ and $\delta \supset \gamma$ infer γ.
(RCM)	From $\eta \supset \xi$ infer $(\zeta \rightsquigarrow \eta) \supset (\zeta \rightsquigarrow \xi)$.

Another axiomatic system PO is the axiomatic system obtained from TO by removing the axiomatic schema (RM).

We can show a kind of the completeness theorem.

Theorem 3.4 *A formula α in $S\text{-}Wff_{\rightsquigarrow}$ is a theorem of TO (resp. PO) if and only if α is valid under totally (resp. partially) ordered structures.*

Next, let us give an axiomatization for families of ordered structures. An axiomatic system FTO (resp. FPO) is the axiomatic system obtained from TO (resp. PO) by replacing the formula variables ζ, η, ξ, δ and γ with X, Y, Z, X and Y, respectively.

Theorem 3.5 *A formula A in $Wff_{\rightsquigarrow}$ is a theorem of FTO (resp. FPO) if and only if A is valid under families of totally (resp. partially) ordered structures.*

Third, we consider an axiomatization of families of ordered structures with minimum. An axiomatic system FTOM (resp. FPOM) is the axiomatic system obtained from FTO (resp. FPO) by adding an axiomatic schema:

(CS) $(X \wedge Y) \supset (X \rightsquigarrow Y)$.

Theorem 3.6 *A formula A in $Wff_{\rightsquigarrow}$ is a theorem of FTOM (resp. FPOM) if and only if A is valid under families of totally (resp. partially) ordered structures with minimum.*

For each axiomatic system above, we can construct a kind of canonical model such that a set consists of all the true formulas at a world of the model if and only if the set is a maximally consistent set under the axiomatic system. A later version of this paper will provide the details.

Finally, we note that we can prove nonexistence of axiomatic systems, such as PO, for finite, distinguishable, partially ordered L_n-structures. Despite this, Katsuno and Mendelzon [1991a] give a kind of axiomatization of finite, distinguishable, partially ordered L_n-structures in the context of knowledge base revisions. They achieve this by introducing a revision operator that corresponds to a kind of function mapping a formula to another formula.

4 Comparison

4.1 Consequence Relation

A consequence relation represents a well-behaved set of conditional assertions, where a conditional assertion $\mu \mid\!\sim \phi$ intuitively shows that μ is a good enough reason to believe ϕ. Kraus, Lehmann and Magidor [Kraus *et al.*, 1990; Lehmann, 1989] define preferential (resp. rational) consequence relations as a set of conditional assertions that is closed under a set of inference rules, **P** (resp. **R**). They also define preferential models and ranked models to discuss the semantics of the consequence relations. They show that preferential (resp. rational) consequence relations can be characterized by preferential (resp. ranked) models. It is easy to define a bijection between preferential (resp. ranked) models and partially (resp. totally) ordered structures.

By associating the connective $\rightsquigarrow$ to the connective $\mid\!\sim$, we can transform the results on TO or PO to the results on consequence relations, and vice versa. A superficial difference between consequence relations and TO or PO is the way of representations of rules and axioms. Gentzen-style rules are used in consequence relations, while a Hilbert-style axiomatization is used for ordered structures. Since a transformation between the two styles is straightforward, we can easily find a counterpart of each rule of **R** or **P** in the axioms, the inference rules, or the theorems of TO or PO. However, note that: when we consider the converse transformation, there is no counterpart to (MP) in the rules of consequence relations.

Another difference is that some logical combinations of conditional assertions are not allowed in rules of consequence relations, while all combinations are allowed in $S\text{-}Wff_{\rightsquigarrow}$. For example, $((\mu_1 \mid\!\sim \phi_1) \vee (\mu_2 \mid\!\sim \phi_2)) \supset \mu$ is not allowed, but $((\mu_1 \rightsquigarrow \phi_1) \vee (\mu_2 \rightsquigarrow \phi_2)) \supset \mu$ is allowed. Boutilier [1990a; 1990b] also extends the syntax of consequence relation so that we may use logical combinations of conditional assertion. However, his semantics of an extended formula is different from ours.

Although the above differences exist, Theorem 4.1 shows that there is no essential distinction between **R** (resp. **P**) and TO (resp. PO). For any subset Γ of $S\text{-}Wff_{\rightsquigarrow}$, we define $Con(\Gamma)$ as a set of conditional assertions such that $Con(\Gamma) = \{\mu \mid\!\sim \phi \mid \mu \rightsquigarrow \phi \in \Gamma\}$.

Theorem 4.1 *A set of conditional assertions C is a ranked (resp. preferential) consequence relation if and only if there is some deductively closed set Γ of $S\text{-}Wff_{\rightsquigarrow}$ under TO (resp. PO) such that $C = Con(\Gamma)$.*

4.2 Knowledge Base Revision

A major problem for knowledge base management is how to revise a knowledge base (KB) when new information

[1] TO and the other axiomatic systems given are based on the axiomatization of Bell's C logic [Bell, 1989].

that is inconsistent with the current KB is obtained. Alchourrón, Gärdenfors and Makinson [1985] propose rationality postulates for the revision operation. Katsuno and Mendelzon [1989; 1991a] characterize the AGM postulates in terms of minimal change with respect to an ordering among interpretations. We discuss the relationship between those works and the results on ordered structures.

Gärdenfors and his colleagues [Alchourrón *et al.*, 1985; Gärdenfors, 1988; Gärdenfors and Makinson, 1988] represent a KB as a *knowledge set*. A knowledge set is, in our context, a deductively closed set of formulas in L. Given knowledge set K and sentence μ, $K^*\mu$ is the revision of K by μ. $K^+\mu$ is the smallest deductively closed set containing K and μ. $K_\perp$ is the set consisting of all the propositional formulas. The AGM postulates consist of the following eight rules. See [Gärdenfors, 1988] for a discussion of the intuitive meaning and formal properties of these postulates.

(K*1) $K^*\mu$ is a knowledge set.

(K*2) $\mu \in K^*\mu$

(K*3) $K^*\mu \subseteq K^+\mu$

(K*4) If $\neg\mu \notin K$, then $K^+\mu \subseteq K^*\mu$

(K*5) $K^*\mu = K_\perp$ only if μ is unsatisfiable.

(K*6) If $\mu \equiv \phi$ then $K^*\mu = K^*\phi$.

(K*7) $K^*(\mu \wedge \phi) \subseteq (K^*\mu)^+\phi$

(K*8) If $\neg\phi \notin K^*\mu$ then $(K^*\mu)^+\phi \subseteq K^*(\mu \wedge \phi)$

We note that (K*3) and (K*4) imply the condition: if new knowledge μ is consistent with a knowledge set K then the revised knowledge set $K^*\mu$ is $K^+\mu$. We call this condition an *expansion condition*.

Makinson and Gärdenfors [1991] discuss similarities between these postulates and rules of consequence relations by fixing a knowledge set K and by using the transformation rule: $\phi \in K^*\mu$ iff $\mu \mid\!\sim \phi$. Since the rules of consequence relations can be translated into formulas in $S\text{-}Wff_{\leadsto}$, we can apply their discussion to the relationship between the postulates and formulas in $S\text{-}Wff_{\leadsto}$.

We give a semantic characterization of the postulates (K*1)~(K*8) by using the ordered structures. We can capture a revision operator $*$ by a collection of totally ordered structures, where a totally ordered structure is assigned to each knowledge set. The total ordered structure $\mathcal{O}_K = \langle W_K, \leq_K, V_K \rangle$ assigned to a knowledge set K must satisfy a *covering condition*[2]: for any satisfiable formula μ there is some world $w \in W_K$ such that $V_K(\mu, w) = \text{T}$. The expansion condition of the postulates implies a remarkable property (the third condition of Theorem 4.2): each consistent knowledge set K consists of all the propositional formulas that are true under every minimal world of $\mathcal{O}_K$. The second condition of Theorem 4.2 corresponds to the transformation rule proposed by Makinson and Gärdenfors.

Theorem 4.2 *A revision operator $*$ satisfies (K*1)~(K*8) if and only if for each knowledge set K, there is a total ordered structure $\mathcal{O}_K$ such that*

1. *$\mathcal{O}_K$ satisfies the covering condition,*
2. *$K^*\mu = \{\phi \mid \mathcal{O}_K \models \mu \leadsto \phi\}$,*
3. *$K = \{\phi \mid \mathcal{O}_K \models \phi\}$ if $K \neq K_\perp$.*

Katsuno and Mendelzon [1989; 1991a] consider knowledge base revision in the framework of a finitary propositional logic L_n. They represent a KB as a formula of L_n, since a computer-based KB must be finitely representable. We note that every knowledge set K (i.e., deductively closed set) can be represented in the context of L_n by a formula ψ of L_n such that $K = \{\phi \mid \psi \vdash \phi\}$. We denote by $\psi \circ \mu$ the revision of a KB ψ by μ, where $\circ$ is a revision operator.

Katsuno and Mendelzon show the six postulates (R1)~(R6) for a revision operator $\circ$ that are equivalent to (K*1)~(K*8). By introducing total pre-orders among interpretations of L_n, they characterize all the revision operators satisfying (R1)~(R6) in light of minimal change with respect to the introduced total pre-orders. It is possible to rephrase the characterization in terms of finite, distinguishable, totally ordered L_n-structures, and show a theorem similar to Theorem 4.2.

Katsuno and Mendelzon [1991a] show postulates for a revision operator that is defined by minimal change with respect to *partial* orders among interpretations. The postulates consist of (R1)~(R5) and other two postulates (R7) and (R8). Due to space limitation let us only state the (R8) postulate.

(R8) $(\psi \circ \mu_1) \wedge (\psi \circ \mu_2)$ implies $\psi \circ (\mu_1 \vee \mu_2)$.

The postulate (R8) is noteworthy in light of the axiomatization of finite, distinguishable, partially ordered L_n-structures, because it is difficult to find a counterpart to (R8) in formulas of $S\text{-}Wff_{\leadsto}$.

We can show the relationship between revision operators satisfying (R1)~(R5), (R7), (R8) and finite, distinguishable, partially ordered L_n-structures. To do so, we need a restriction on partially ordered L_n-structures. We say that a partially ordered L_n-structure $\mathcal{O} = \langle W, \leq, V \rangle$ has a *minimum set* if it satisfies the condition: for any $w \in Min(W, \leq)$ and any $w' \in W$, if $w' \notin Min(W, \leq)$ then $w < w'$ holds. The reason why we must impose this condition is related to the expansion condition which requires that every model of ψ be less than any non-model with respect to the order that characterizes minimal change.

Theorem 4.3 *A revision operator $\circ$ satisfies (R1)~(R5), (R7) and (R8) if and only if for each formula ψ of L_n, there is a finite, distinguishable, partially ordered L_n-structure, $\mathcal{O}_\psi$, such that*

1. *$\psi \circ \mu \equiv \bigwedge\{\phi \mid \mathcal{O}_\psi \models \mu \leadsto \phi\}$,*
2. *$\mathcal{O}_\psi$ satisfies the covering condition and has a minimum set,*
3. *$\psi \equiv \bigwedge\{\phi \mid \mathcal{O}_\psi \models \phi\}$ if ψ is consistent,*
4. *if ψ and ψ_1 are logically equivalent then $\mathcal{O}_\psi$ is equal to $\mathcal{O}_{\psi_1}$.*

The fourth condition of Theorem 4.3 says that revision is independent of the syntactic representation of a KB ψ.

[2] This property is related to (K*5).

Table 1: Conditional Logic and Axiomatization

Conditional Logic	Axiomatization
VW ([Lewis, 1973; Nute, 1984])	FTO
VC ([Lewis, 1973; Nute, 1984])	FTOM
SS or C ([Nute, 1984; Bell, 1989])	FPOM

4.3 Knowledge Base Update

We discuss the relationship between knowledge base update and families of ordered structures with minimum. The revision discussed in Section 4.2 is used to modify a KB when we obtain new information about a static world, while we need another operation, *update*, to bring the KB up to date when the world described by it changes. The distinctions between update and revision are discussed in [Katsuno and Mendelzon, 1991b].

Katsuno and Mendelzon propose postulates (U1)∼(U8) for an update operator under L_n, and characterize all the update operators that satisfy the postulates in terms of partial orders among interpretations. The postulates (U1)∼(U8) are defined along the same lines as (R1)∼(R8). However, two important differences exist; one is that (U1)∼(U8) do not require the expansion condition, that is, even if a KB ψ and new information μ are consistent, the new KB $\psi \diamond \mu$ is not necessarily equivalent to $\psi \wedge \mu$. The other difference is that an update operator should satisfy a "disjunction rule" (U8) guaranteeing that each possible world of the KB is given independent consideration.

(U8) $(\psi_1 \vee \psi_2) \diamond \mu \equiv (\psi_1 \diamond \mu) \vee (\psi_2 \diamond \mu)$.

We can show that an update operator satisfying (U1)∼(U8) can be identified with a family of finite, distinguishable, partially ordered L_n-structures with minimum, where an ordered structure is assigned to each interpretation of L_n.

Theorem 4.4 *An update operator $\diamond$ satisfies (U1)∼(U8) if and only if there is a family of finite, distinguishable, partially ordered L_n-structures with minimum $\widehat{\mathcal{O}} = (\mathcal{O}_I)_{I \in \mathcal{I}_n}$ such that*

1. *$\mathcal{O}_I$ satisfies the covering condition,*
2. *the minimum of $\mathcal{O}_I$ is I,*
3. *$\psi \diamond \mu \equiv \bigwedge\{\phi \mid \widehat{\mathcal{O}} \models \psi \supset (\mu \rightsquigarrow \phi)\}$.*

4.4 Conditional Logic

The conditional logics consist of the propositional logic augmented with a conditional connective denoted by $>$. If we replace $\rightsquigarrow$ with $>$, we can regard $L_{\rightsquigarrow}$ as a language of conditional logics.

The various conditional logics are surveyed in [Nute, 1984]. Table 1 shows a correspondence between the proposed conditional logics and the axiomatization in Section 3.3.[3] For instance, the table states that FTO is an axiomatization of VW.

[3] We have not found any conditional logic proposed in the literature that corresponds to FPO.

Conditional logics that are not appeared in [Nute, 1984] are CT4 and CT4D proposed by Boutilier [1990a; 1990b]. The logics are formalized to represent and reason with "normality". The semantics of $\mu > \phi$ under CT4 (or CT4D) is that ϕ is true under the most *normal* situation where μ is true. Roughly speaking, he considers an order such that the more distant a world is from w, the more normal the world is. A later version of this paper will provide a formal analysis on the relationship between Boutilier's semantics and the notion of ordering.

5 Reciprocal Relation

5.1 Consequence Relation versus Revision

If we fix a knowledge set K, we can identify a revision operator $*$ satisfying (K*1)∼(K*8) with a rational consequence relation determined by a ranked model satisfying the covering condition. The identification is established by Condition 2 of Theorem 4.2. In general, a revision operator $*$ satisfying (K*1)∼(K*8) corresponds to some collection of rational consequence relations.

The discussion in Section 4, in light of **P** or PO, suggests a way of determining the rationality postulates for revision to knowledge sets that correspond to preferential consequence relations.

5.2 Consequence Relation versus Conditional Logic

Consequence relations are, in some sense, equivalent to "nesting-free" conditional logics. We can show the following theorem[4] by extending the discussion of Section 4.1 and by using Theorems 3.1 and 3.5.

Theorem 5.1 *For any rule α that holds in all rational (resp. preferential) consequence relations, the corresponding formula α' of conditional logic is a theorem of VW (resp. FPO). Conversely, for any theorem α' of VW (resp. FPO) that is a restricted formula of S-Wff* [5]*, the corresponding rule α holds in all rational (resp. preferential) consequence relations.*

5.3 Revision versus Conditional Logic

Gärdenfors [1988] investigates the relationship between the postulates for revision and the conditional logic VC in light of the Ramsey test: $\beta \in K^*\alpha$ iff $\alpha > \beta \in K$. He shows that the Ramsey test is incompatible with the postulate (K*4) (intuitively, the expansion condition) in his framework. Since he considers a knowledge set constructed from formulas of $L_>$ whereas we use a knowledge set as a set of propositional formulas, we can not translate his results into our context.

A revision operator satisfying (K*1)∼(K*8) is equivalent to some collection of totally ordered structures. However, the semantics of VC is determined by a family of totally ordered structures with minimum. The two differences, i.e., having minimum or not and different types

[4] Boutilier [1990a; 1990b] shows a similar theorem in terms of CT4 and CT4D.

[5] Note that the syntax of rules of consequence relations is restricted as discussed in Section 4.1; for example, neither $p \mid\!\sim (q \mid\!\sim r)$ nor $r \wedge (p \mid\!\sim q)$ is allowed.

of collection, suggest an incompatibility result similar to the incompatibility obtained by Gärdenfors.

5.4 Update versus Conditional Logic

The update operators satisfying (U1)~(U8) are characterized by families of finite, distinguishable, partially ordered L_n-structures with minimum. The semantics of the conditional logic SS (or equivalently C) is determined by families of partially ordered structures with minimum. We can expect more similarities of update to conditional logic than those of revision from the above two facts. To develop the correspondence, we must define an update operator in the context of knowledge sets, and find postulates for the update that correspond to (U1)~(U8).

Grahne [1991] proposes a conditional logic VCU^2 having an update operator, and shows the Gärdenfors' incompatibility result does not hold in VCU^2.

6 Concluding Remarks

We define ordered structures and families of ordered structures (with minimum) as tools to develop a unified view of existing work on consequence relations, knowledge base revision, update and conditional logics. By using ordered structures and families of ordered structures, we can show reciprocal relations among the different approaches.

Acknowledgements

The authors are grateful to Alberto O. Mendelzon for discussions on this work and many insightful comments on drafts of this paper. The authors are also grateful to Yves Lespérance and anonymous referees for their helpful comments.

References

[Alchourrón *et al.*, 1985] Carlos E. Alchourrón, Peter Gärdenfors and David Makinson. On the logic of theory change: partial meet contraction and revision functions. *Journal of Symbolic Logic*, 50:510–530, 1985.

[Bell, 1989] John Bell. The logic of nonmonotonicity. *Artificial Intelligence*, 41:365–374, 1989/90.

[Boutilier, 1990a] Craig Boutilier. Conditional logics of normality as modal systems. In *Proceedings of the Eighth National Conference on Artificial Intelligence*, pages 594–599, 1990.

[Boutilier, 1990b] Craig Boutilier. Viewing conditional logics of normality as extensions of the modal system S4. Technical Report KRR-TR-90-4, Department of Computer Science, University of Toronto, June 1990.

[Delgrande, 1988] James P. Delgrande. An approach to default reasoning based on a first-order conditional logic: revised report. *Artificial Intelligence*, 36:63–90, 1988.

[Gärdenfors and Makinson, 1988] Peter Gärdenfors and David Makinson. Revisions of knowledge systems using epistemic entrenchment. In *Proceedings of the Second Conference on Theoretical Aspects of Reasoning about Knowledge*, pages 83–95, 1988.

[Gärdenfors, 1988] Peter Gärdenfors. *Knowledge in Flux: Modeling the Dynamics of Epistemic States.* Bradford Books, MIT Press, Cambridge, MA, 1988.

[Gärdenfors, 1990] Peter Gärdenfors. Belief revision and nonmonotonic logic: two sides of the same coin? In *Proceedings of the Ninth European Conference on Artificial Intelligence*, pages 768–773, 1990

[Ginsberg, 1986] Matthew L. Ginsberg. Counterfactuals. *Artificial Intelligence*, 30:35–79, 1986.

[Grahne, 1991] Gösta Grahne. Updates and counterfactuals. to appear in *Proceedings of the Second International Conference on Principles of Knowledge Representation and Reasoning*, 1991

[Katsuno and Mendelzon, 1989] Hirofumi Katsuno and Alberto O. Mendelzon. A unified view of propositional knowledge base updates. In *Proceedings of the Eleventh International Joint Conference on Artificial Intelligence*, pages 1413–1419, 1989.

[Katsuno and Mendelzon, 1991a] Hirofumi Katsuno and Alberto O. Mendelzon. Propositional knowledge base revision and minimal change. to appear in *Artificial Intelligence*, 1991

[Katsuno and Mendelzon, 1991b] Hirofumi Katsuno and Alberto O. Mendelzon. On the difference between updating a knowledge base and revising it. to appear in *Proceedings of the Second International Conference on Principles of Knowledge Representation and Reasoning*, 1991

[Kraus *et al.*, 1990] Sarit Kraus, Daniel Lehmann, and Menachem Magidor. Nonmonotonic reasoning, preferential models and cumulative logics. *Artificial Intelligence*, 44:167–207, 1990.

[Lehmann, 1989] Daniel Lehmann. What does a conditional knowledge base entail? In *Proceedings of the First International Conference on Principles of Knowledge Representation and Reasoning*, pages 212–222, 1989.

[Lewis, 1973] D. K. Lewis. *Counterfactuals.* Blackwell, Oxford, 1973.

[Makinson and Gärdenfors, 1991] David Makinson and Peter Gärdenfors. Relations between the logic of theory change and nonmonotonic logic. In A. Fuhrmann and M. Morreau, editors, *The Logic of Theory Change*, Lecture Notes in Artificial Intelligence 465, Springer-Verlag, 1991.

[Nute, 1984] Donald Nute. Conditional logic. In Dov M. Gabbay and Franz Guenthner, editors, *Handbook of Philosophical Logic*, D. Reidel, Dordrecht, 1984.

[Pollock, 1981] John L. Pollock. A refined theory of counterfactuals. *Journal of Philosophical Logic*, 10:239–266, 1981.

[Shoham, 1987] Yoav Shoham. A semantical approach to nonmonotonic logics. In *Proceedings of the Tenth International Joint Conference on Artificial Intelligence*, pages 1413–1419, 1987.

Inaccessible Worlds and Irrelevance: Preliminary Report

Craig Boutilier
Department of Computer Science
University of Toronto
Toronto, Canada M5S 1A4
Email: cebly@ai.toronto.edu

Abstract

Recently, the relationship between several forms of default reasoning based on conditional defaults has been investigated. In particular, the systems based on ε-semantics, preferential models, and (fragments of) modally-defined conditional logics have been shown to be equivalent. These systems form a plausible core for default inference, but are too weak in general, failing to deal adequately with irrelevance. We propose an extension of the (modal) conditional logics in which one can express the truth of sentences at inaccessible possible worlds and show how this logic can be used to axiomatize a simple preference relation on the modal structures of this logic. This preferential semantics is shown to be equivalent to 1-entailment and rational closure. We suggest that many meta-logical systems of default inference can be axiomatized within this logic, using the notion of inaccessible worlds.

1 Introduction

Recently, the focus of much research on default reasoning has centered on the representation of default rules as conditional sentences in various conditional logics. While the motivation and underlying semantics for these logics often diverge, most allow "In the most normal situations in which A is true, B is true" as a profitable interpretation of the conditional $A \rightarrow B$. Each of these logics can be viewed as enforcing some type of normality ordering on states of affairs, or possible worlds. For instance, the logic of ε-semantics (Adams 1975; Pearl 1988) is based on a probability distributions over sets of worlds, and a conditional $A \rightarrow B$ is true iff B is true at the most probable (as ε approaches 0) A-worlds; hence, more probable worlds can be viewed as more normal under such an ordering. The preferential logics of (Kraus, Lehmann and Magidor 1990) embody an explicit normality ordering on situations, and the conditional logics of (Boutilier 1990) are similar, incorporating normality as a modal accessibility relation.

Given that these logics can be regarded in such a similar fashion, it is not surprising that they have been shown to be essentially equivalent (Boutilier 1990; Kraus, Lehmann and Magidor 1990), giving credence to their underlying motivation. Unfortunately, while each can be considered a "core" for default reasoning (Pearl 1989), they are too weak to sanction all of the patterns of default inference we would like. In particular, the conclusions authorized by such systems are often rendered invalid in the face of irrelevant information. For example, given that birds fly ($B \rightarrow F$) we cannot conclude that green birds fly ($G \wedge B \rightarrow F$).

To circumvent such difficulties, many schemes have been proposed which augment the logics under consideration with extra-logical machinery for deriving the appropriate conclusions (Delgrande 1988; Lehmann 1989; Pearl 1990; Goldszmidt, Morris and Pearl 1990). Goldszmidt and Pearl (1990) have shown that Pearl's 1-entailment corresponds to Lehmann's rational closure, demonstrating that these reasonable extensions (as well as the logical cores) of ε-semantics and preferential logics determine the same default conclusions.

We can view these logics as being able to express what is true at "more normal" possible worlds; hence, sentences can force worlds (which don't satisfy these constraints) to be less normal. The meta-logical extensions of these systems, conversely, attempt to force worlds to be more normal than is required. In this paper, we will show that the conditional logics of (Boutilier 1990) can also be extended in a manner which corresponds exactly to these systems. This extension is based on a simple preference relation over modal structures, one that prefers structures in which possible worlds are as normal as possible. Furthermore, we extend the logic itself such that we can make reference to inaccessible worlds in addition to accessible worlds; thus we can express truth at less normal worlds and force worlds to be more normal. With this capability, we can axiomatize a default theory making the derivable conclusions exactly those sanctioned by the preferential semantics. Just as the second-order circumscription axiom conforms to truth in (predicate) minimal models (McCarthy 1986), so too does this closure correspond to preferred models. We suggest that, to the extent any meta-logical default system forces worlds to be more normal, it can be axiomatized within this extended conditional logic.

A more detailed presentation and proofs may be found in (Boutilier 1991c).

2 Inaccessible Worlds and the Logic CO

As in (Boutilier 1990), we will present a Kripke-style possible worlds semantics for a conditional logic capable of representing and reasoning with statements of normality or prototypicality. A sentence $A \Rightarrow B$ is intended to mean "A normally implies B". Following a suggestion of Delgrande (1988), we will interpret the truth conditions for such a statement roughly as "In the most normal situations in which A holds, B is true as well". The ordering of normality presupposed by such a reading will be represented as an accessibility relation on possible worlds; world v is accessible to w (wRv) iff v is *at least as normal as* w. In (Boutilier 1990), it is argued that such a relation should be, at a minimum, reflexive and transitive, and that a further restriction of total-connectedness[1] gives rise to a reasonable extension, namely the logic CT4D. It is also shown that CT4D is equivalent to the standard modal logic S4.3, in the sense that the conditional connective $\Rightarrow$ can be defined in terms of the modal operator $\Box$, and vice versa. In the sequel, we will take the modal connective to be basic and define the conditional within the modal language.

In (Boutilier 1990) it is shown that CT4D captures many of the properties we expect of normal implication, such as allowing exceptions to prototypical statements, and capturing rules such as cautious and rational monotony. It is also shown that (a fragment of) CT4D is equivalent to the logic of ranked preferential models of (Lehmann 1989).

The following approach to default reasoning using CT4D immediately presents itself. Let KB be (the conjunction of) a finite knowledge base of sentences of CT4D. It is reasonable to ask what is true at the most normal worlds in which all the facts in KB hold; that is a default reasoner could conclude α whenever $\vdash_{CT4D} KB \Rightarrow \alpha$ (see also Delgrande's (1988) *Assumption of Normality*). However, a serious problem arises when we consider certain classes of default inferences, specifically those involving irrelevant properties. If KB consists of two facts, *Bird* and *Bird* $\Rightarrow$ *Fly*, then $KB \Rightarrow$ *Fly* is derivable. However, if we add *Green* to KB, then $KB \Rightarrow$ *Fly* is no longer a theorem, for the most normal *Green* $\wedge$ *Bird*-worlds need not satisfy *Fly*, as long as these are not among the most normal *Bird*-worlds. In other words, greenness may be an exceptional property of birds (with respect to flying), as "penguinness" is.

The problem of irrelevance has been addressed using a number of extra-logical techniques, such as rational closure, assumptions of irrelevance (Delgrande 1988), and 1-entailment. We will approach the problem from a perspective which may in the future lead to a purely logical account of default inference, and, at present, provides some new insights into irrelevance.

Consider some normality ordering on all possible states of affairs, W, and refer to the most normal A-worlds in this ordering as $n(A)$. Then $A \Rightarrow C$ is true iff $n(A) \subseteq \|C\|$.[2] Of course, A must hold at all such worlds, so we can write this as $n(A) \subseteq \|A \wedge C\|$. Now, to say that B is irrelevant to the truth of this conditional is to say (roughly) that $A \wedge B \Rightarrow C$ is true. For this to be the case it is sufficient to insist that some B-world exist among those in $n(A)$, making this a most normal $A \wedge B$-world. In general, we want this to be true for arbitrary properties α (consistent with $A \wedge C$), so that $A \wedge \alpha \Rightarrow C$ holds. Hence, we need only insist that $\|A \wedge C\| \subseteq n(A)$. Together with the converse, this implies that $A \wedge \alpha \Rightarrow C$ for any such α. In other words, we would like to assume, if we know $A \Rightarrow C$, that the most normal A-worlds are *exactly* all $A \wedge C$-worlds.

These constraints are analogous to those used by Levesque (1990) to define the semantics of OL, the logic of "only knowing". In an entirely similar fashion, $A \Rightarrow C$ can be read as "at the most normal A-worlds, *at least* $A \wedge C$ is known".[3] Supposing a new connective $>$, we say $A > C$ is true iff $\|A \wedge C\| \subseteq n(A)$. We can read this, then, as "at the most normal A-worlds, *at most* $A \wedge C$ is known". Together, $A \Rightarrow C$ and $A > C$ tell us that exactly $A \wedge C$ is known at the most normal A-worlds, and allow us to conclude that all (consistent) properties are irrelevant. This captures the intuition that if some fact (other than A) were relevant to concluding C we would know this to be the case. Since we "haven't been told", we assume nothing else should affect our deliberations.

In order to formalize this discussion, we will provide a semantics and axiomatization for the connectives $\Rightarrow$ and $>$. As mentioned, we can define $\Rightarrow$ in terms of the standard modal operator $\Box$. However, in a similar manner we can define $>$ in terms of a new modal connective $\overleftarrow{\Box}$. This connective corresponds to Levesque's N, and $\overleftarrow{\Box}\,\alpha$ will hold exactly when α is true at all inaccessible worlds.

Our language **L** will be formed from a denumerable set **P** of propositional variables, together with the connectives $\neg$, $\supset$, $\Box$ and $\overleftarrow{\Box}$. The connectives $\wedge$, $\vee$ and $\equiv$ are defined in terms of these in the usual way.

Definition A *CO-model* is a triple $M = \langle W, R, \varphi \rangle$, where W is a set (of possible worlds), R is a transitive totally-connected binary relation on W (the accessibility relation), and φ maps **P** into 2^W ($\varphi(A)$ is the set of worlds where A is true).

The truth of a formula α at w in M is defined in the usual inductive manner, with the interesting cases being:

$M \models_w \Box\alpha$ iff for each v such that wRv, $M \models_v \alpha$.

$M \models_w \overleftarrow{\Box}\,\alpha$ iff for each v such that not wRv, $M \models_v \alpha$.

[1] R is total-connected iff vRw or wRv for all v, w. In (Boutilier 1990) we use *forward-connectedness*, but this stronger condition results in an equivalent logic (Hughes and Cresswell 1984), and the distinction is important later.

[2] Formally, $n(A)$ need not exist, but the technical details which follow will not depend on this. We use this notation only informally, to illustrate the ideas which follow. $\|\alpha\|$ stands for the set of all possible worlds which satisfy α, and again, in our informal discussion, we take this to mean all logically possible worlds rather than those from the set W of some formal structure.

[3] We use "known" here in a much less technical sense than Levesque. More accurately, we could say if $n(A)$ were the only worlds an agent considered possible, then it would know at least $A \wedge C$.

We can define several new connectives as follows: $\Diamond\alpha \equiv_{df} \neg\Box\neg\alpha$; $\overleftarrow{\Diamond}\,\alpha \equiv_{df} \neg\,\overleftarrow{\Box}\,\neg\alpha$; $\overleftrightarrow{\Box}\,\alpha \equiv_{df} \Box\alpha \wedge \overleftarrow{\Box}\,\alpha$; and $\overleftrightarrow{\Diamond}\,\alpha \equiv_{df} \Diamond\alpha \vee \overleftarrow{\Diamond}\,\alpha$. It is easy to verify that these connectives have the following truth conditions: $\Diamond\alpha$ ($\overleftarrow{\Diamond}\,\alpha$) is true at some world if α holds at all accessible (inaccessible) worlds; $\overleftrightarrow{\Box}\,\alpha$ ($\overleftrightarrow{\Diamond}\,\alpha$) holds iff α holds at all (some) worlds, whether accessible or inaccessible. Validity is defined in a straightforward manner, a sentence α being *CO-valid* ($\models_{CO} \alpha$) just when every CO-model M satisfies α. Finally, we define the connectives:

$$A \Rightarrow B \equiv_{df} \overleftrightarrow{\Box}\,\neg A \vee \overleftrightarrow{\Diamond}\,(A \wedge \Box(A \supset B)).$$ [4]

$$A > B \equiv_{df} \overleftarrow{\Box}\,(A \supset (\overleftarrow{\Box}\,(A \supset \neg B) \wedge \Diamond(A \wedge B))) \wedge \overleftrightarrow{\Diamond}\,A.$$

$A \Rightarrow B$ will be true vacuously if there is no world in the model at which A holds. Otherwise, it is true iff there is some world where A holds, and B holds at all more normal A-worlds The dual of this is $A > B$ which states that at most $A \wedge B$ is known at the most normal A-worlds. This is only true if A holds at some world (condition $\overleftrightarrow{\Diamond}\,A$), otherwise there would exist no such worlds and everything would be trivially satisfied ("known") by this (empty) set. Furthermore, $A > B$ can only hold if, at each A-world, $A \supset \neg B$ is true at every inaccessible world (otherwise this world would be strictly more normal than some $A \wedge B$-world); and if at each A-world, $A \wedge B$ is true at some more normal world (since such worlds are the most normal A-worlds, each A-world should "see" one). It is easy to verify that $A > B$ holds iff all $A \wedge B$-worlds are mutually accessible (equally normal) and no A-world is strictly more normal than these. In other words, by asserting that $\neg B$ holds at each inaccessible A-world, we force all $A \wedge B$-worlds to be accessible to, or at least as normal as, every other A-world.

We call the logic associated with this semantics CT4D-O, or CO for short, the extension of CT4D allowing conditionalized "only knowing". Completeness is proven using a technique of Humberstone (1983).

Definition The conditional logic CO is the smallest $S \subseteq \mathbf{L}$ such that S contains classical propositional logic and the following axiom schemata, and is closed under the following rules of inference:

K $\Box(A \supset B) \supset (\Box A \supset \Box B)$

K′ $\overleftarrow{\Box}\,(A \supset B) \supset (\overleftarrow{\Box}\,A \supset \overleftarrow{\Box}\,B)$

T $\Box A \supset A$

4 $\Box A \supset \Box\Box A$

4′ $\overleftarrow{\Box}\,A \supset \overleftarrow{\Box}\,\overleftarrow{\Box}\,A$

S $A \supset \overleftarrow{\Box}\,\Diamond A$

H $\overleftrightarrow{\Diamond}\,(\Box A \wedge \overleftarrow{\Box}\,B) \supset \overleftrightarrow{\Box}\,(A \vee B)$

Nes From A infer $\overleftrightarrow{\Box}\,A$.

MP From $A \supset B$ and A infer B.

Theorem 1 *The system* CO *is characterized by the class of CO-models.*

That the connective $\Rightarrow$, as defined, captures a reasonable notion of normal implication has been discussed in (Boutilier 1990). It should also be clear that the connective $>$ captures the dual notion of (conditional) "knowing at most", and that together, $A \Rightarrow B$ and $A > B$ allow us to extend the conditional to include all irrelevant properties. Consider the following theorem of CO (for propositional A, B, and α):

$$(A \Rightarrow B \wedge A > B) \supset (\overleftrightarrow{\Diamond}\,(A \wedge B \wedge \alpha) \supset (A \wedge \alpha \Rightarrow B)).$$

This theorem states that if both $A \Rightarrow B$ and $A > B$ are true, then we can conclude that all properties α are irrelevant to the truth of the original conditional.

Notice that the extension of $A \Rightarrow B$ is conditional on the possibility of $A \wedge B \wedge \alpha$. If we insist that all logically possible worlds be contained in W, then we can derive $A \wedge \alpha \Rightarrow B$ directly (provided $A \wedge B \wedge \alpha$ is logically consistent). Levesque (1990) enforces a similar constraint. This gives rise to the following extension of CO:

Definition CO* is the smallest extension of CO closed under all rules of CO and containing the following:

LP $\overleftrightarrow{\Diamond}\,\alpha$ for all satisfiable propositional α.[5]

Definition A *CO*-model* is any CO-model $M = \langle W, R, \varphi\rangle$, such that $\{w^* : w \in W\} \supseteq \{f : f \text{ maps } \mathbf{P} \text{ into } \{0,1\}\}$.[6]

Theorem 2 *The system* CO* *is characterized by the class of CO*-models.*

The logic CO* addresses the difficulty of having to conditionalize extensions of normative conditionals on the possibility of the antecedent (since all consistent such antecedents are possible). Hence a theorem of CO* (for satisfiable $A \wedge B \wedge \alpha$) is $(A \Rightarrow B \wedge A > B) \supset (A \wedge \alpha \Rightarrow B)$.

The notion of irrelevance sketched here is rather undermotivated. While it's clear in examples such as the case of green birds that *Green* should be irrelevant to *Fly*, the question remains: what do we mean by *irrelevance*? Space limitations preclude anything resembling a reasonable discussion of this point, but a few words are in order. Gärdenfors (1978) has presented and discussed a number of postulates which should be satisfied by any notion of relevance, motivated by the consideration that p is relevant to r (given evidence e), written $p\mathcal{R}_e r$, iff the

[4] This definition of $A \Rightarrow B$ is different from that of (Boutilier 1990). It is more similar in spirit to the connective $\mid\!\sim$ of (Kraus, Lehmann and Magidor 1990), whereby if $A \Rightarrow B$ holds at any world in a model then it holds at all worlds. Previously, $A \Rightarrow B$ could hold "vacuously" if there were no *accessible* worlds at which A is true. While this is in accord with an epistemic reading of the relation R, it does not conform to our normative interpretation. It is entirely unreasonable to expect only more normal worlds to determine which normative statements we take to be true. Worlds which are exceptional should also play a role in such deliberations. One advantage of our approach is that the connective $\overleftarrow{\Box}$ allows us to define the truth conditions of $\Rightarrow$ at individual worlds, whereas the truth conditions of $\mid\!\sim$ can only be defined with respect to entire structures.

[5] Alternatively, we could use Levesque's schema: $\overleftarrow{\Box}\,\alpha \supset \neg\Box\alpha$ for all falsifiable α.

[6] For all $w \in W$, w^* is defined as the map from $\mathbf{P}$ into $\{0,1\}$ such that $w^*(A) = 1$ iff $w \in \varphi(A)$; in other words, w^* is the valuation associated with w.

conditional probability of r given $p \wedge e$ is different than that of r given e alone (i.e. $P(r|p \wedge e) \neq P(r|e)$). Postulates (R0) to (R4) are presented as reasonable restrictions on the relevance relation.[7] In (Boutilier 1991b) we define a notion of *statistical relevance* (*s-relevance*) which roughly states that $p\mathcal{R}_e r$ if learning the truth (or falsity) of p affects our judgement as to the truth of r. Assuming $e \Rightarrow r$ means we are willing to accept r based on evidence e, p is relevant to r if $p \wedge e \not\Rightarrow r$ or $\neg p \wedge e \not\Rightarrow r$ (similar definitional clauses apply when $e \Rightarrow \neg r$, or $e \not\Rightarrow r$ and $e \not\Rightarrow \neg r$). We show this definition to satisfy the postulates, and that asserting $e > r$ ensures that any sentence contingent on $e \wedge r$ is irrelevant to r in this sense.

We also define a weaker notion of *commonsense relevance* (*c-relevance*), violating the postulate (R2) which asserts that $p\mathcal{R}_e r$ iff $\neg p\mathcal{R}_e r$. Defined in terms of conditional independence, s-relevance must satisfy (R2). If learning p increases the probability of r, then learning $\neg p$ must decrease it. If the magnitudes of the changes are vastly different, this may seem a counterintuitive notion of relevance. For instance, if I'm about to cross a bridge a someone tells me to go ahead because there will be no earthquakes ($\neg Q$) in the next minute, I'm liable to dismiss my informant as a lunatic and discount $\neg Q$ as being irrelevant. However, if I am told there *will* be an earthquake (Q), I will surely consider this information to be relevant. Intuitively, $\neg Q$ is irrelevant because (statistically) it changes the probability of a safe crossing negligibly (assuming the prior probability of Q is very low), while Q changes the probability radically. We capture this potential failure of (R2) by saying that p is c-relevant to r if, e.g., $p \wedge e \not\Rightarrow r$ when $e \Rightarrow r$, and discounting the possible effect of learning $\neg p$. It often seems that p is only regarded as relevant if its *truth* can change the status of r as an accepted belief, not its falsehood.

Other reasons for disassociating conditional independence and irrelevance are mentioned in (Gärdenfors 1978) and we discuss our definition of irrelevance and how inaccessible worlds capture this concept in detail in (Boutilier 1991b).

While the logic CO* seems able to express the concept of irrelevance, it is not clear how a default reasoner should proceed given such a logic and a set of facts KB. A modest proposal is to simply assert $A > B$ for each $A \Rightarrow B$ in KB, so long as the result is consistent. This works on a wide variety of examples; for instance, if $KB = \{Bird \Rightarrow Fly\}$, then asserting $Bird > Fly$, we can derive conditionals such as $Bird \wedge Green \Rightarrow Fly$. If $Penguin \Rightarrow \neg Fly$ and $\Box(Penguin \supset Bird)$ are added to KB, $B > F$ is no longer consistent. However, $B \wedge \neg P \Rightarrow F$ and $B \wedge P \Rightarrow \neg F$ are both derivable and it is consistent to assert $B \wedge P > \neg F$ and $B \wedge \neg P > F$. Adding these to KB, we obtain the following theorems:

1. $(KB \wedge Bird) \Rightarrow Fly$
2. $(KB \wedge Bird \wedge Green) \Rightarrow Fly$
3. $(KB \wedge Penguin) \Rightarrow \neg Fly$
4. $(KB \wedge Penguin \wedge Green) \Rightarrow \neg Fly$

Such an approach, however, has limitations. Consider a KB of two independent conditionals $A \Rightarrow B$ and $C \Rightarrow D$. In this case, it is inconsistent to assert both $A > B$ and $C > D$, and it is not clear what "extendible" conditionals of interest are derivable from such a KB. Thus, the use of the connective $>$ for dealing with irrelevance requires further investigation. Another simple proposal, which adequately handles this KB, can be described as follows: since the material counterparts of these sentences, $A \supset B$ and $C \supset D$, must be normally true (that is $\top \Rightarrow (A \supset B \wedge C \supset D)$), it should be the case that $\top > (A \supset B \wedge C \supset D)$ holds as well. Extending this idea, we will show that the connective $>$ is capable of representing a certain form of default reasoning, namely 1-entailment or rational closure.

3 A Simple Preference Relation

A common approach to default reasoning is to use the notion of *preferred models* (Shoham 1986). Given a set of CO-models, we will suggest the preferred models are those in which possible worlds are as normal as possible. Consider again a KB containing only $Bird \Rightarrow Fly$. A model of KB will contain some $Bird \wedge Fly$-world which is more normal than any $Bird \wedge \neg Fly$-world. In general, we want to derive sentences like $Bird \wedge Green \Rightarrow Fly$, but the most normal worlds with green birds need not satisfy Fly. However, assuming that some $Green \wedge Bird \wedge Fly$-world is as normal as the most normal $Bird$-worlds violates no constraints imposed by KB. This assumption forces such a world to be more normal than we originally supposed, so if preferred models force worlds to be as normal as possible, $Bird \wedge Green \Rightarrow Fly$ will be derivable.

We must formulate the conditions under which one model will be more normal than another. Let $M_1 = \langle W, R_1, \varphi \rangle$ and $M_2 = \langle W, R_2, \varphi \rangle$ be CO-models.[8] To ensure that M_1 is at least as "normal" as M_2, each world in W should be as normal in M_1 as in M_2; so we will insist (in general) that each world "see" at least as many worlds in R_1 as in R_2. There are two cases to consider when a world w has fewer accessible worlds in R_1. First, some world v might be less normal in R_1 than in R_2, in which case it is inaccessible to (some) w in R_1 to which it was accessible in R_2. In such a case M_1 should not be preferred to M_2. However, in the second case, w may have become more normal in R_1, in which case it *should* see fewer worlds (since fewer will be more normal than it). In this circumstance, M_1 may well be preferable to M_2, and we relax the restriction that w see as many worlds in R_1. More formally, assume M_1 and M_2 are defined as above.

Definition $w \in W$ is *more normal in* R_1 than in R_2 (written $N(w, R_1, R_2)$) iff there is some $v \in W$ such that vR_1w, wR_1v, and not vR_2w.

[7] Gärdenfors also presents postulate (R5) — which leads to a triviality result — and two possible replacements, one of which (R7) is deemed acceptable. The notion of relevance defined below is a simple one, but can be extended easily to incorporate (R7) (see (Boutilier 1991b) for details).

[8] We will only compare models which agree on possible worlds; however, it should be clear that the idea can be extended by taking preference relative to the subset of worlds two models have in common. See (Boutilier 1991c).

Definition M_1 is *as preferable as* M_2 (written $M_1 \leq M_2$) iff for all $w \in W$, $N(w, R_1, R_2)$ is false only if $\{v : wR_2v\} \subseteq \{v : wR_1v\}$. M_1 is *preferred to* M_2 ($M_1 < M_2$) iff $M_1 \leq M_2$ and $M_2 \not\leq M_1$.

Definition Let $T \subseteq \mathbf{L}$ be a set of facts. M is a *minimal model of* T iff $M \models T$ and for all M' such that $M' \models T$, $M' \not\leq M$. α is a *default conclusion* based on T (written $T \models_{\leq} \alpha$) iff $M \models \alpha$ for each minimal model M of T.[9]

We examine the consequences of these definitions in the following section.

4 Equivalence to 1-entailment

Pearl (1990) describes a natural ordering on default rules named the *Z-ordering*, and uses this to define a nonmonotonic entailment relation, 1-entailment. While put forth as an extension of ε-semantics, this entailment relation is essentially based on using preferred models of a sort similar to those described in the previous section. In fact, we will show these notions correspond exactly, and that, while 1-entailment is defined in terms of a particular theory T and orders only models of T, it can be described in terms of our theory-independent preference criterion, whereby all logical interpretations are ordered.

In this section, we will assume a language with a finite set of propositional variables, and CO*-models only will be treated. The default rules r of (Pearl 1990) have the form $\alpha \rightarrow \beta$, where α and β are propositional formulae. These will correspond to our conditional sentences $\alpha \Rightarrow \beta$. We say a valuation (possible world) w *verifies* the rule $\alpha \rightarrow \beta$ iff $w \models \alpha \wedge \beta$, *falsifies* the rule iff $w \models \alpha \wedge \neg\beta$, and *satisfies* the rule iff $w \models \alpha \supset \beta$. Let T be a finite set of such rules. From (Pearl 1990):

Definition T *tolerates* $\alpha \rightarrow \beta$ iff there is some world which verifies $\alpha \rightarrow \beta$, and falsifies no rule in T; that is, $\{\alpha \wedge \beta\} \cup \{\gamma \supset \delta : \gamma \rightarrow \delta \in T\}$ is satisfiable.

This notion of toleration can be used to characterize probabilistic ε-consistency (Adams 1975; Pearl 1988) in a manner that also captures the CO-consistency of a set of rules.[10] Furthermore, toleration can be used to define a natural ordering on default rules (or conditionals) by partitioning T as follows (Pearl 1990):

Definition $T_i = \{r : r \text{ is tolerated by } T - T_0 - T_1 - \cdots T_{i-1}\}$, for $i \geq 0$.

Assuming T is ε-consistent, this results in an ordered partition $T = T_0 \cup T_1 \cup \cdots T_n$. Now to each rule $r \in T$ we assign a rank (the *Z-ranking*), $Z(r) = i$ whenever $r \in T_i$. The idea is that lower ranked rules are more general, or have lower priority. Given this ranking, we can rank possible worlds according to the highest ranked rule they falsify:

$$Z(w) = \min\{n : w \text{ satisifes } r, \text{ for all } r \in T \text{ where } Z(r) \geq n\}.$$

Lower ranked worlds are to be considered more normal. Now, a propositional formula α can be ranked according to the lowest ranked world which satisfies it: $Z(\alpha) = \min\{Z(w) : w \models \alpha\}$. Given that lower ranked worlds are considered more normal, we can say that a normative conditional $\alpha \Rightarrow \beta$ should hold iff the rank of $\alpha \wedge \beta$ is lower than that of $\alpha \wedge \neg\beta$. This leads to the following definition (Pearl 1990):

Definition Formula β is *1-entailed* by α with respect to T (written $\alpha \vdash_1 \beta$) iff $Z(\alpha \wedge \beta) < Z(\alpha \wedge \neg\beta)$.

For details regarding the types of conclusions 1-entailment draws, see (Pearl 1990). It should be fairly clear that 1-entailment can be viewed as asserting a preference on models of theory T, namely that worlds should have their lowest possible rank (without violating the rules of T). In other words, worlds should be as normal as possible. Not surprisingly then 1-entailment corresponds to the preferential entailment relation of the preceding section. For a fixed theory T, we define the CO*-model Z_T as:

Definition $Z_T = \langle W, R, \varphi\rangle$ where wRv iff $Z(w^*) \geq Z(v^*)$.

Theorem 3 *$T \models_{\leq} \alpha \Rightarrow \beta$ iff $\alpha \vdash_1 \beta$ with respect to T.*

This means that the minimal Z-ranking of worlds corresponds to a theory-dependent instance of the more general preferential ranking of CO*-models. Furthermore, the explicit nature of this Z-ranking allows us to capture the exact nature of the (unique) preferred model Z_T. In particular, if T is ε-consistent and is partitioned as $T_0, \cdots, T_n$, then Z_T consists of $n + 2$ "clusters" of mutually accessible (or equally normal) worlds; cluster 0 consists of all worlds of rank 0, cluster 1 consisting of all worlds of rank 1, and so on, with the most exceptional worlds being those of rank $n + 1$.

Since the preferred model of T is unique, we can capture the exact structure of Z_T using sentences in the logic CO containing the connective $>$, since worlds in each cluster can be characterized by the rules they violate (see (Boutilier 1991c) for details).

Let T be a finite set of conditionals, partitioned as $T_0, T_1, \cdots, T_n$.

Definition Let $R^{\wedge}_{-1} \equiv_{\text{df}} \bot$. For $0 \leq i \leq n+1$, let $R^{\wedge}_i \equiv_{\text{df}} \bigwedge\{\alpha \supset \beta : \alpha \Rightarrow \beta \in T - T_0 - \cdots T_{i-1}\}$. We assume $\bigwedge \emptyset \equiv_{\text{df}} \top$ (hence $R^{\wedge}_{n+1} \equiv \top$).

Definition For theory T as above, the *closure* of T is $Cl(T) = T \cup \{\neg R^{\wedge}_i > R^{\wedge}_{i+1} : -1 \leq i \leq n\}$.

Theorem 4 *$Cl(T) \models_{CO*} \alpha \Rightarrow \beta$ iff $T \models_{\leq} \alpha \Rightarrow \beta$.*

Corollary 1 *$Cl(T) \models_{CO*} \alpha \Rightarrow \beta$ iff $\alpha \vdash_1 \beta$ with respect to T.*

Just as the (second-order) circumscriptive axiom applied to a theory T closes that theory to correspond to (predicate) minimal models, so too does this closure correspond to our notion of minimality. Theorem 4 shows that $Cl(T)$ can be regarded as an axiomatization of the notion of preference described in the previous section,

---

[9] Strictly speaking, T should consist only of conditional sentences and α should be conditional as well. See (Boutilier 1991c) for details on how to extend this relation.

[10] T is ε-consistent iff every non-empty subset of T contains some rule tolerated by all others. If T is the corresponding set of conditionals, this condition holds iff T is "non-vacuously" satisfiable; that is, if $T \cup \{\overleftrightarrow{\Diamond}\alpha : \alpha \Rightarrow \beta \in T\}$ is CO-consistent.

and of the implicit preference ordering determined by System-Z. Hence, the types of conclusions sanctioned by 1-entailment (see (Pearl 1990)) are also determined by this form of closure. This implies, given the results of (Goldszmidt and Pearl 1990), that $Cl(T)$ determines the same consequence relation as that of rational closure (Lehmann 1989).

5 Concluding Remarks

We have presented a modal logic CO in which truth at inaccessible worlds is expressible. In this logic we can define not only the normative conditional $\Rightarrow$ of conditional "knowing at least", as in (Boutilier 1990), but also the dual connective $>$ of conditional "knowing at most". This provides us with a conditional version of Levesque's (1990) "only knowing". We discussed briefly the relationship of conditional only knowing to the problem of irrelevance in default reasoning, and have shown how a simple preference relation (corresponding to 1-entailment and rational closure) which deals with irrelevance can be axiomatized within this logic.

Much work remains to be done on the application of conditional only knowing to problems in default reasoning. Levesque's characterization is semantically very clear and elegant, but has the drawback of relying on an autoepistemic interpretation of default rules (see e.g. (Reiter 1987) for problems with this interpretation). Ultimately, we would like to push the "closure" of our default theories into the logic via some connective analogous to Levesque's O operator, thereby consolidating the semantic clarity of only knowing with the compelling conditional interpretation of default rules. We expect the expressive power gained by the use of inaccessible worlds makes this goal achievable.

In this connection, we have begun exploring the use of the logic CO to capture a number of other types of reasoning. In (Boutilier 1991a) we provide a logical calculus for belief revision within CO, and show how revision, subjunctive reasoning and default reasoning (including such varied approaches as autoepistemic logic, ε-semantics and normative conditionals) can be unified using a framework which exploits the power of inaccessible worlds.

Other avenues to pursue include the weakening of these logics, along the same lines suggested in (Boutilier 1990), providing other versions of "only knowing" (e.g. based on S4). A further task is to investigate how the logic CO can be used to capture other default reasoning systems, such as the maximum entropy formalism of (Goldszmidt, Morris and Pearl 1990), which makes finer-grained distinctions on the ordering of possible worlds. We suggest that most approaches to default reasoning which can be viewed as restricting the degree of abnormality of worlds may be axiomatized using some logic of inaccessible worlds, or conditional only knowing.

Acknowledgements

Thanks to Ray Reiter, Hector Levesque and especially Moisés Goldszmidt for helpful discussion and criticism. Financial support of NSERC and the University of Toronto is gratefully acknowledged.

References

Adams, E. W. 1975. *The Logic of Conditionals.* D.Reidel, Dordrecht.

Boutilier, C. 1990. Conditional logics of normality as modal systems. In *Proc. of AAAI*, pages 594–599, Boston.

Boutilier, C. 1991a. Belief revision as a modally defined conditional. Technical report, University of Toronto. forthcoming.

Boutilier, C. 1991b. *Conditional Logics for Default Reasoning and Belief Revision.* PhD thesis, University of Toronto. Forthcoming.

Boutilier, C. 1991c. Preliminary report on inaccessible worlds and irrelevance. Technical Report KRR-TR-91-1, University of Toronto.

Delgrande, J. P. 1988. An approach to default reasoning based on a first-order conditional logic: Revised report. *Artificial Intelligence*, 36:63–90.

Gärdenfors, P. 1978. On the logic of relevance. *Synthese*, 37(3):351–367.

Goldszmidt, M., Morris, P., and Pearl, J. 1990. A maximum entropy approach to nonmonotonic reasoning. In *Proc. of AAAI*, pages 646–652, Boston.

Goldszmidt, M. and Pearl, J. 1990. On the relation between rational closure and system Z. In *Nonmon. Reasoning Workshop*, pages 130–140, South Lake Tahoe.

Hughes, G. E. and Cresswell, M. J. 1984. *A Companion to Modal Logic.* Methuen, London.

Humberstone, I. L. 1983. Inaccessible worlds. *Notre Dame Journal of Formal Logic*, 24(3):346–352.

Kraus, S., Lehmann, D., and Magidor, M. 1990. Nonmonotonic reasoning, preferential models and cumulative logics. *Artificial Intelligence*, 44:167–207.

Lehmann, D. 1989. What does a conditional knowledge base entail? In *Proc. of KR'89*, pages 212–222, Toronto.

Levesque, H. J. 1990. All I know: A study in autoepistemic logic. *Artificial Intelligence*, 42:263–309.

McCarthy, J. 1986. Applications of circumscription to formalizing commonsense reasoning. *Artificial Intelligence*, 28:89–116.

Pearl, J. 1988. *Probabilistic Reasoning in Intelligent Systems: Networks of Plausible Inference.* Morgan Kaufmann, San Mateo.

Pearl, J. 1989. Probabilistic semantics for nonmonotonic reasoning: A survey. In *Proc. of KR'89*, pages 505–516, Toronto.

Pearl, J. 1990. System Z: A natural ordering of defaults with tractable applications to default reasoning. In Vardi, M., editor, *Proc. of TARC*, pages 121–135. Morgan Kaufmann, San Mateo.

Reiter, R. 1987. Nonmonotonic reasoning. *Annual Reviews of Computer Science*, 2:147–186.

Shoham, Y. 1986. Reasoning about change: Time and causation from the standpoint of artificial intelligence. Technical Report YALEU/CSD/RR#507, Yale University, New Haven.

Possibilistic logic, preferential models, non-monotonicity and related issues

Didier DUBOIS – Henri PRADE
Institut de Recherche en Informatique de Toulouse (I.R.I.T.)
Université Paul Sabatier, 118 route de Narbonne
31062 TOULOUSE Cedex – FRANCE

Abstract

The links between Shoham's preference logic and possibilistic logic, a numerical logic of uncertainty based on Zadeh's possibility measures, are investigated. Starting from a fuzzy set of preferential interpretations of a propositional theory, we prove that the notion of preferential entailment is closely related to a previously introduced notion of conditional possibility. Conditional possibility is then shown to possess all properties (originally stated by Gabbay) of a well-behaved non-monotonic consequence relation. We obtain the possibilistic counterpart of Adams' ε–semantics of conditional probabilities which is the basis of the probabilistic model of non-monotonic logic proposed by Geffner and Pearl. Lastly we prove that our notion of possibilistic entailment is the one at work in possibilistic logic, a logic that handles uncertain propositional formulas, where uncertainty is modelled by degrees of necessity, and where partial inconsistency is allowed. Considering the formerly established close links between Gärdenfors'epistemic entrenchment and necessity measures, what this paper proposes is a new way of relating belief revision and non-monotonic inference, namely via possibility theory.

1 Introduction

For more than ten years, Artificial Intelligence researchers have devoted a lot of efforts for developing various approaches to the handling of incomplete, uncertain or partially inconsistent knowledge in reasoning processes. At a superficial level a dichotomy is usually made between purely symbolic approaches and approaches which rely on the use of numerical scales for grading uncertainty. This obvious and sometimes convenient distinction turns out to have a limited significance when we observe that the numerical and the non-numerical methods can deal with the same kind of examples and that there may exist more fundamental differences between two symbolic, or between two numerical approaches than between a symbolic and a numerical one in some cases ; see the comparative study by Léa Sombé [1990] on these points.

Moreover different kinds of unifying results have been provided at the theoretical level in the recent past years. On the symbolic side, Kraus, Lehmann and Magidor [1990], following pioneering works by Gabbay [1985] and Makinson [1989], have studied non-monotonic logic systems from an axiomatic point of view. They have related these systems to the preference relation-based logic advocated by Shoham [1988] for unifying non-monotonic inference systems at the semantic level. Also on the symbolic side, more recently, Makinson and Gärdenfors have established connections between non-monotonic logic and belief revision mechanisms (see [Gärdenfors, 1990] for a summary sketch). They are based on so-called epistemic entrenchment relations [Gärdenfors, 1988].

On the numerical side, probabilistic semantics of defaults have been proposed by Geffner [1988] and Pearl [1988] on the basis of Adams [1975]'s logic of conditionals. This logic displays all properties of a well-behaved non-monotonic logic. Neufeld et al. [1990] also try to equip defaults with probabilistic semantics related to the confirmation property "*p* favours *q*", i.e. the fact that the probability of assertion *q* is strictly increased when the truth of assertion *p* is established. Besides, qualitative necessity relations [Dubois, 1986], whose unique numerical counterparts are necessity measures, are characterized by a system of axioms which was recently proved to be equivalent to the one characterizing epistemic entrenchment relations [Dubois and Prade, 1990b], where necessity measures are just the dual of possibility measures introduced by Zadeh [1978]. With this result in mind, the ability of possibilistic logic —a logic of classical formulas weighted in terms of necessity measures— to deal with partially inconsistent knowledge bases and to exhibit in that case non-monotonic reasoning behaviors, is not very surprizing [Dubois, Lang and Prade, 1989]. Besides, several researchers, including Goodman and Nguyen [1988], Dubois and Prade [1989, 1990a] have developed a new model of measure-free conditioning, trying to give a mathematical and a logical meaning to conditional objects q | p independently of the notion of probability, but still in agreement with this notion in the sense that Prob(q | p) can indeed be considered as the probability of the entity q | p. As already suggested in Dubois and Prade [1989], there is more than an analogy between the logical calculus developed on conditional objects and non-monotonic consequence relation systems ; more precisely, it has been recently shown that there is a one-to-one correspondence between the inference rules governing the non-monotonic consequence relation |~ and ordering relationships between conditional objects equipped with a conjunction operation [Dubois and Prade, 1991]. Moreover conditional objects correspond to a qualitative view of conditioning which is compatible not only with probability but also with other uncertainty models including possibility measures and Shafer belief functions.

The aim of this paper is to pursue this exploration of the links between formalisms aiming at mechanizing reasoning under incomplete and uncertain information, by showing the close relationship between Shoham's preference relation-based semantics and possibilistic logic ; this is not unexpected if we remember that possibilistic logic has a semantics [Dubois, Lang and Prade, 1989] in terms of a weight distribution on the set of worlds or interpretations, which clearly induces a total ordering among the possible worlds. More generally, possibilistic logic will be advocated as a simple numerical formalism for non-monotonic inference and belief revision which is in complete agreement with purely symbolic approaches.

In Section 2, after introducing the necessary background, we establish the link between Shoham's preference relation-based semantics and conditional possibility measures. Section 3 shows that conditional possibilities enjoy properties similar to the ones of non-monotonic consequence relations. Section 4 relates conditional possibility measures to possibilistic logic and its semantics (which is itself in close relationship with epistemic entrenchment relations and belief revision processes as already said).

2 Preference logic and conditional possibility

Let $(\mathcal{B}, \wedge, \vee, \neg)$ be a Boolean algebra induced by a set of classical propositions of interest. Let Ω be the set of atoms of $\mathcal{B}$, i.e. the set of possible interpretations relative to $\mathcal{B}$. Ω is assumed finite here for simplicity. If the proposition p is true in the interpretation $\omega \in \Omega$, we shall write $\omega \models p$, which reads "ω satisfies p". Starting with a preference relation denoted by $\sqsubset$ ($\omega \sqsubset \omega'$ reads ω' is preferred over ω) which equips Ω with a strict partial order, Shoham [1988] says that ω preferentially satisfies p, written $\omega \models_{\sqsubset} p$, when $\omega \models p$ and $\nexists \omega'$, $\omega \sqsubset \omega'$ and $\omega' \models p$. Then preferential entailment is defined by Shoham [1988] as follows :

$$p \models_{\sqsubset} q \Leftrightarrow (\forall \omega, \omega \models_{\sqsubset} p \Rightarrow \omega \models q) \quad (1)$$

where $p \models_{\sqsubset} q$ reads "p preferentially entails q". In other words, p preferentially entails q iff the set of interpretations that make q true (i.e. the set of models of q) includes the preferred models of p, which has a fairly intuitive meaning. Note that if p is a contradiction (i.e. $\nexists \omega$, $\omega \models p$), $p \models_{\sqsubset} q$ trivially holds because the set of preferred models of p is empty. The intuitive appeal of preferential entailment is then lost in that particular situation.

Let π be a function from Ω to [0,1] called a possibility distribution on Ω that describes the fuzzy set of preferred interpretations. For each $\omega \in \Omega$, π assigns a numerical value which can be viewed as the assessment of a level of possibility or acceptability of interpretation ω. $\pi(\omega) = 0$ means that the interpretation ω is totally impossible, totally excluded, while $\pi(\omega) = 1$ only means that ω is among the most plausible interpretations (there may be distinct ω and ω' such that $\pi(\omega) = \pi(\omega')$). Obviously, as soon as, $\pi(\omega) < \pi(\omega')$, we can say that ω' is preferred to ω, which will be written $\omega \sqsubset_{\pi} \omega'$, i.e. π induces a strict partial order on Ω (as well as a total order $\omega \sqsubseteq_{\pi} \omega' \Leftrightarrow \pi(\omega) \leq \pi(\omega')$). Then a possibility measure Π is defined on $\mathcal{B}$, following Zadeh [1978], by

$$\forall p \in \mathcal{B}, \Pi(p) = \max\{\pi(\omega) \mid \omega \in \Omega \text{ and } \omega \models p\} \quad (2)$$

and $\Pi(\bot) = 0$, $\Pi(T) = 1$, where $\bot$ and T denote the bottom (contradiction) and the top (tautology) elements of $\mathcal{B}$, respectively. The conditional possibility measure $\Pi(\cdot \mid p)$ is defined as the maximal solution of the equation (first proposed by Hisdal [1978]) :

$$\forall q \neq \bot, \Pi(p \wedge q) = \min(\Pi(q \mid p), \Pi(p)) \quad (3)$$

and $\Pi(\bot \mid p) = 0$. This solution has been first suggested in [Dubois and Prade, 1986] and reads :

$$\Pi(q \mid p) = 1 \text{ if } \Pi(p) = \Pi(p \wedge q) ;$$
$$\Pi(q \mid p) = \Pi(p \wedge q) \text{ if } \Pi(p) > \Pi(p \wedge q) \quad (4)$$

since we always have $\Pi(p) \geq \Pi(p \wedge q)$ (indeed if $\omega \models p \wedge q$ then $\omega \models p$ and Π is monotonic with respect to entailment). Justifications for (3) can be found in Dubois and Prade [1990a] ; in any case, the meaning of (3) is intuitively clear since it looks like Bayes rule with product changed into min. In the framework of possibility theory, the choice of the maximal solution is based on the so-called minimum specificity principle (e.g. [Dubois and Prade, 1988]) which calls for the assignment of the greatest possibility degrees compatible with the constraint(s) under consideration. Indeed as already said the smallest the possibility degree, the stronger the information that it conveys (recall that $\pi(\omega) = 0$ means that ω is totally impossible while $\pi(\omega) = 1$ only means that ω is among the most plausible interpretations, but does not mean at all that we are (somewhat) certain that ω is *the* right interpretation).

Let us observe that as soon as p entails q (i.e. $\forall \omega$, $\omega \models p \Rightarrow \omega \models q$) then $p \equiv p \wedge q$ (where $\equiv$ denotes the equivalence) and thus $\Pi(p) = \Pi(p \wedge q)$ and $\Pi(q \mid p) = 1$, which is satisfying. Let us also note that if $1 \geq \Pi(p) > \Pi(p \wedge q)$ then $\Pi(q \mid p) = \Pi(p \wedge q) < 1$. Moreover $\Pi(q \mid p)$ is defined even if $\Pi(p) = 0$ and in that case $\Pi(q \mid p) = \Pi(\neg q \mid p) = 1$ when $q \neq \bot$, thus expressing total ignorance about q when p is impossible. By duality a so-called necessity measure N (e.g. [Dubois and Prade, 1988]) is associated with Π, i.e.

$$\forall p, N(p) = 1 - \Pi(\neg p) \quad (5)$$

which expresses that we become somewhat certain of something when the contrary turns out to be more or less impossible. (5) requires the normalization of π, $\exists \omega \in \Omega$, $\pi(\omega) = 1$ which guarantees $\Pi(T) = 1$. This also applies to conditional possibility measures, and yields

$$\forall p, N(q \mid p) = 1 - \Pi(\neg q \mid p) = \begin{cases} 0 \text{ if } N(p \to q) = N(\neg p) \\ N(p \to q) \text{ if } N(p \to q) > N(\neg p) \end{cases} \quad (6)$$

where $p \to q$ denotes material implication ($\neg p \vee q$).

Let us show now that conditional possibility is in agreement with Shoham's preferential entailment.

<u>Definition 1</u> : ω is said to be a π-preferential model of $p \in \mathcal{B}$ (denoted $\omega \models_{\pi} p$) if and only if $\omega \models p$, $\Pi(p) > 0$,

and $\nexists\omega'$ such that $\omega' \models p$ and $\pi(\omega) < \pi(\omega')$.

Lemma 1 : $\omega \models_\pi p \Leftrightarrow \Pi(p) = \pi(\omega) > 0$

Proof : obvious since $\forall\omega', \omega' \models p \Rightarrow \pi(\omega') \leq \pi(\omega)$. Q.E.D.

The π-preferential entailment $p \models_\pi q$ is then defined by

$$p \models_\pi q \Leftrightarrow \exists\omega, \omega \models_\pi p \text{ and } \forall\, \omega \models_\pi p, \omega \models q \quad (7)$$

This definition is equivalent to (1) where $\sqsubset$ has been changed into $\sqsubset_\pi$ and the condition $\Pi(p) > 0$ is forced. This extra condition enables preferential entailment to exclude the case when p is a contradiction.

Proposition 1 : $p \models_\pi q \Leftrightarrow \Pi(q \mid p) > \Pi(\neg q \mid p)$

Proof :

(7) $\Leftrightarrow \forall\omega, (\omega \models p \text{ and } \Pi(p) = \pi(\omega) > 0) \Rightarrow \omega \models q$
$\Leftrightarrow \{\omega, \omega \models p, \Pi(p) = \pi(\omega) > 0\} \subseteq \{\omega, \omega \models q\}$
$\Leftrightarrow \Pi(p) = \Pi(p \wedge q) > \Pi(p \wedge \neg q)$ (since no preferential interpretation of p is an interpretation of $\neg q$)
$\Leftrightarrow \Pi(q \mid p) = 1 \geq \Pi(p \wedge q) > \Pi(p \wedge \neg q) = \Pi(\neg q \mid p)$
Q.E.D.

Thus given a possibility distribution π over the set of interpretations, the set NMC($\mathcal{K}$) of non-monotonic consequences of a (consistent) knowledge base $\mathcal{K}$, viewed as a conjunction of (classical) formulas, will be defined by $\text{NMC}(\mathcal{K}) = \{q \mid \Pi(q \mid \mathcal{K}) > \Pi(\neg q \mid \mathcal{K})\}$. Our conventions suggest that $\text{NMC}(\mathcal{K}) = \emptyset$ when $\mathcal{K}$ is inconsistent. It can be easily seen that $\Pi(q \mid p) > \Pi(\neg q \mid p)$ does not imply $\Pi(q \mid p \wedge r) > \Pi(\neg q \mid p \wedge r)$, since the supremum of π over the interpretations of $p \wedge q$ corresponds to interpretation(s) which do(es) not necessarily belong to the set of interpretations of $p \wedge q \wedge r$ (recall that $\Pi(q|p) > \Pi(\neg q \mid p)$ means that all the interpretations of p which maximize π are among the interpretations of q). This explains the non-monotonic behavior of $\Pi(q \mid p)$ when greater than $\Pi(\neg q \mid p)$. Note that $\Pi(q \mid p) > \Pi(\neg q \mid p)$ implies $\Pi(q \mid p) = 1$ (the converse being false). However if $\Pi(q \mid p) < 1$ then $\Pi(q \mid p) = \Pi(p \wedge q)$ and monotonicity is recovered.

An immediate corollary of Proposition 1 is obtained for necessity measures

$$p \models_\pi q \Leftrightarrow N(q \mid p) > 0 \qquad (8)$$

i.e. p preferentially entails q (in the sense of the ordering induced by π) if we are at least somewhat certain about the truth of q in the context p. (8) is easily obtained noticing that $\Pi(q \mid p) > \Pi(\neg q \mid p)$ is equivalent to $\Pi(\neg q \mid p) < 1$, since $\Pi(q \mid p) = 1$ in that case. Note also that $N(q \mid p) > 0 \Rightarrow N(\neg q \mid p) = 0$ due to (5). We now investigate the behavior of conditional possibility from a proof-theoretic point of view and mention its relation to the framework of conditional objects.

3 Conditional possibility and the non-monotonic consequence relation

Starting from a logical point of view, Gabbay [1985] proposed several properties that a non-monotonic deduction operation $\mid\!\sim$ should satisfy, and especially the cut and the restricted or cautious monotonicity, i.e. :

$$\frac{p \mid\!\sim q \,;\, p \wedge q \mid\!\sim r}{p \mid\!\sim r} \text{ (cut)} \quad \text{and} \quad \frac{p \mid\!\sim q \,;\, p \mid\!\sim r}{p \wedge q \mid\!\sim r} \text{ (restricted monotonicity)}$$

Note that in the above patterns of inference, the terms $p \mid\!\sim r$ and $p \wedge q \mid\!\sim r$ are exchanged, as pointed out by Makinson [1989]. It is then possible to put these two patterns together and claim that given $p \mid\!\sim q$, the non-monotonic deductions $p \wedge q \mid\!\sim r$ and $p \mid\!\sim r$ are equivalent. This is what Makinson [1989] calls the cumulativity condition.

Moreover the following property [Adams, 1975] is also worth considering

$$\frac{p \mid\!\sim q \qquad r \mid\!\sim q}{p \vee r \mid\!\sim q} \text{ (OR rule)}$$

It can be checked that these properties, stated in terms of conditional possibility, do hold, interpreting $p \mid\!\sim q$ as $p \models_\pi q$, and using the equivalence between $p \models_\pi q$ and $\Pi(\neg q \mid p) < 1$:

Proposition 2 : Cut

$$\Pi(\neg q \mid p) < 1 \text{ and } \Pi(\neg r \mid p \wedge q) < 1 \Rightarrow \Pi(\neg r \mid p) < 1 \qquad (9)$$

Proof : the two premisses of (9) are equivalent to $\Pi(p) > \Pi(p \wedge \neg q)$ and $\Pi(p \wedge q) > \Pi(p \wedge q \wedge \neg r)$; then $\Pi(p \wedge \neg r) = \max(\Pi(p \wedge q \wedge \neg r), \Pi(p \wedge \neg q \wedge \neg r)) \leq \max(\Pi(p \wedge q \wedge \neg r), \Pi(p \wedge \neg q)) < \max(\Pi(p \wedge q), \Pi(p)) = \Pi(p)$ Q.E.D.

Proposition 3 : Restricted monotonicity

$$\Pi(\neg q \mid p) < 1 \text{ and } \Pi(\neg r \mid p) < 1 \Rightarrow \Pi(\neg r \mid p \wedge q) < 1 \qquad (10)$$

Stated positively, (10) simply means that if all maxima of π over the models of p are at the same time among the models of q and among the models of r then these maxima are also those of π over the models of $p \wedge q$ and they are among the models of r. A formal proof as the one of (9) is as easy.

Proposition 4 : OR property

$$\Pi(\neg q \mid p) < 1 \text{ and } \Pi(\neg q \mid r) < 1 \Rightarrow \Pi(\neg q \mid p \vee r) < 1 \qquad (11)$$

Proof : from (4), $\Pi(\neg q \wedge p) < \Pi(p)$, $\Pi(\neg q \wedge r) < \Pi(r)$. Using the axiom of possibility measures, it follows $\Pi(\neg q \wedge (p \vee r)) < \Pi(p \vee r)$. Q.E.D.

Other requirements for non-monotonic consequence relations proposed by Kraus et al. [1990] hold as well. The reflexivity axiom $p \mid\!\sim p$ obviously holds since $\Pi(p \mid p) = 1$ and $\Pi(\neg p \mid p) = 0$ except if p is a contradiction. Right weakening, i.e. $\dfrac{\models p \rightarrow q \,;\, r \mid\!\sim p}{r \mid\!\sim q}$ corresponds to $\Pi(\neg p \mid r) < 1 \Rightarrow \Pi(\neg q \mid r) < 1$, if p entails q, which holds (since we have $\Pi(\neg q \mid r) \leq \Pi(\neg p \mid r)$ in this case). Left logical equivalence $\dfrac{\models p \leftrightarrow q \,;\, r \mid\!\sim p}{q \mid\!\sim r}$ holds with conditional possibility since if $\models p \leftrightarrow q$ then $\Pi(r \mid p) = \Pi(r \mid q)$ due to $\Pi(p) = \Pi(q)$.

Kraus et al. [1990] have shown that other rules can be derived from the so-called system C (consisting of reflexivity, cut, cautious monotonicity, right weakening and left equivalence), e.g. the equivalence rule $\dfrac{p \mid\!\sim q \,;\, q \mid\!\sim p \,;\, p \mid\!\sim r}{q \mid\!\sim r}$. In terms of conditional possibility, it reads :

$\Pi(\neg q \mid p) < 1$, $\Pi(\neg p \mid q) < 1$ and $\Pi(\neg r \mid p) < 1$ entail $\Pi(\neg r \mid q) < 1$.

Inference based on conditional possibility is actually a model for the non-monotonic inference system P of Kraus et al. [1990] (i.e. C and the OR rule), as well as a model for the non-monotonic system of Geffner [1988] after Adams

[1975]. We have seen that the counterpart of the non-monotonic consequence relation $p \mid\!\sim q$ is $\Pi(\neg q \mid p) < 1$ or equivalently $N(q \mid p) > 0$ in the conditional possibility model. As pointed out in Pearl [1988], a probabilistic counterpart is $\text{Prob}(q \mid p) \geq 1 - \varepsilon$ where ε is infinitely small, using results by Adams [1975] who showed that the rules, named cut, cautious monotonicity and the OR rule later on, are in full agreement with this semantics. However this semantics is not very realistic in practice for default rules since then the exceptions should have an infinitely small probability to be encountered. By contrast, it may seem more natural to view a "default rule" $p \mid\!\sim q$ as a rule which means that q is more possible than $\neg q$ in the context p (as seen above this is exactly what $N(q \mid p) > 0$ means).

In [Dubois and Prade, 1989] it has been shown that the cut, the cautious monotonicity and the OR rule have exact counterparts in the framework of symbolic conditional objects. Counterparts of the other rules of Kraus et al.' system P are also discussed in this framework in [Dubois and Prade, 1991]. Conditional objects offer a natural qualitative basis for defining conditional measures of uncertainty. It can be shown [Dubois and Prade, 1989, 1991] that various conditional measures of uncertainty can be built on top of conditional objects. It holds in particular for probability, possibility measures and belief functions. Hence the fact that conditional possibility leads to a system of non-monotonic inference should not be too surprizing (since conditional objects behave in a non-monotonic way).

To the reader, it must be clear that results presented above do not require the use of the unit interval [0,1]. Any totally ordered set V can be used to express degrees of possibility, 0 and 1 standing for the least and the greatest element of V. (2), (3), Definition 1, (7), and all Propositions remain true, as long as we stick to possibility measures, and we obviate necessity measures (although the latter could be properly defined on V). Beyond the obvious convenience of a real-valued scale for possibility degrees, the main reason to use [0,1] explicitly is that it enables the link between degrees of possibility and degrees of probability to be preserved. It is well known indeed that degrees of possibility can also be viewed as upper probabilities or degrees of plausibility in the sense of Shafer's evidence theory [Dubois and Prade, 1988].

4 Preferential entailment in possibilistic logic

A necessity-valued knowledge base $\mathcal{K}$ in possibilistic logic is a collection of pairs (p_i,α_i), $i = 1,n$, where p_i is a classical logic formula, here a proposition for the sake of simplicity, and α_i is a number belonging to (0,1] interpreted as a lower bound of the value of a necessity measure N for p_i, i.e. $N(p_i) \geq \alpha_i$, $i = 1,n$. This necessity measure N is associated with a possibility distribution π on the set of interpretations Ω, which represents the semantics of $\mathcal{K}$ and which can be built in the following way [Dubois, Lang and Prade, 1989]. To (p_i,α_i) is associated the fuzzy set of interpretations

$$\mu_i(\omega) = 1 \text{ if } \omega \models p_i \;;\; \mu_i(\omega) = 1 - \alpha_i \text{ if } \omega \models \neg p_i$$

Then π is obtained by intersection of these fuzzy sets (since $\mathcal{K}$ is viewed as the conjunction of the pairs (p_i,α_i)), i.e. $\pi(\omega) = \min_{i=1,n} \mu_i(\omega)$. It can be checked that the necessity measure N defined from π, namely

$$N(p) = \min\{1 - \pi(\omega), \omega \models \neg p\}$$

is such that $\forall\ i = 1,n$, $N(p_i) = \alpha_i$. In other words, in agreement with the principle of minimum specificity, the least restrictive, i.e. the largest, possibility distribution π on Ω, which saturates the constraints $N(p_i) \geq \alpha_i$, is in accordance with the semantics associated with $\mathcal{K}$. Note that here the possibility distribution π on the set of interpretations is built from the weights given in $\mathcal{K}$ and is not given a priori, as in Section 2, for defining $\sqsubset_\pi$. The degree of inconsistency of $\mathcal{K}$, $\text{Inc}(\mathcal{K})$ is defined from π, by $\text{Inc}(\mathcal{K}) = 1 - \max\{\pi(\omega), \omega \in \Omega\}$. In other words, $\mathcal{K}$ is all the more inconsistent as π is subnormalized. When $\text{Inc}(\mathcal{K}) = 0$, $\mathcal{K}$ is said to be consistent. It can be shown [Dubois, Lang and Prade, 1989] that the three following statements are equivalent : i) $\text{Inc}(\mathcal{K}) = 0$; ii) K is consistent in the usual sense where K is the set of propositions obtained from $\mathcal{K}$ by ignoring the weights α_i ; iii) the assignment of the α_i's is such that $\forall p$, $\min(N(p),N(\neg p)) = 0$. When $1 > \text{Inc}(\mathcal{K}) = \alpha > 0$, $\mathcal{K}$ is said to be α-inconsistent and we have $\forall p$, $\min(N(p),N(\neg p)) = \text{Inc}(\mathcal{K})$ (indeed $\max(\Pi(p),\Pi(\neg p)) = \max\{\pi(\omega), \omega \in \Omega\} = 1 - \text{Inc}(\mathcal{K})$).

Semantic entailment from such a possibilistic knowledge base $\mathcal{K}$ is defined by

$$\exists\, \beta > \text{Inc}(\mathcal{K}),\ \mathcal{K} \models (p,\beta) \Leftrightarrow N(p) > N(\neg p) \quad (12)$$

where N is defined from the possibility distribution π associated with $\mathcal{K}$. Then $N(\neg p) = \text{Inc}(\mathcal{K}) = 1 - \Pi(p)$ since $\min(N(p),N(\neg p)) = \text{Inc}(\mathcal{K})$, and $\exists\beta$, $N(p) \geq \beta > \text{Inc}(\mathcal{K})$. Let $\ker(\mathcal{K}) = \{\omega \in \Omega, \pi(\omega) = 1 - \text{Inc}(\mathcal{K})\}$ be the set of preferred interpretations with respect to the $\text{Inc}(\mathcal{K})$-inconsistent possibilistic knowledge base $\mathcal{K}$. Then we have the equivalence

$$N(p) > N(\neg p) \Leftrightarrow \ker(\mathcal{K}) \subseteq \{\omega \in \Omega, \omega \models p\} \quad (13)$$

Indeed $N(p) > N(\neg p) \Leftrightarrow 1 - \text{Inc}(\mathcal{K}) = \Pi(p) > \Pi(\neg p)$ (using the duality between Π and N), which makes the result obvious since $\Pi(p) = \max\{\pi(\omega), \omega \models p\}$.

Now let us prove the following equivalence which relates, in the possibilistic framework, non-monotonicity and belief revision

<u>Proposition 5</u> : $N(q \mid p) > 0 \Leftrightarrow \exists\beta > \text{Inc}(\mathcal{K} \cup \{(p,1)\})$, $(\mathcal{K} \cup \{(p,1)\}) \models (q,\beta)$ where N is the necessity measure defined from the possibility distribution associated with $\mathcal{K}$.

<u>Proof</u> : $N(q \mid p) > 0 \Leftrightarrow p \models_\pi q \Leftrightarrow \{\omega \in \Omega \mid \pi(\omega) = \Pi(p) > 0\} \subseteq \{\omega \in \Omega, \omega \models q\}$ $\Leftrightarrow$ $\{\omega \in \Omega \mid \pi(\omega) = 1 - \text{Inc}(\mathcal{K} \cup \{(p,1)\}) > 0\} \subseteq \{\omega \in \Omega, \omega \models q\}$
(since $\text{Inc}(\mathcal{K} \cup \{(p,1)\}) = 1 - \max\{\min(\pi(\omega),\mu_{M(p)}(\omega)), \omega \in \Omega\} = 1 - \max\{\pi(\omega), \omega \models p\} = 1 - \Pi(p)$ where M(p) is the non-empty set of models of p)
$\Leftrightarrow \ker(\mathcal{K} \cup \{(p,1)\}) \subseteq \{\omega \in \Omega, \omega \models q\}$
$\Leftrightarrow \exists\, \beta > \text{Inc}(\mathcal{K} \cup \{(p,1)\})$, $(\mathcal{K} \cup \{(p,1)\}) \models (q,\beta)$ using (12-13) Q.E.D.

The above equivalence illustrates, in the possibilistic framework, the translation in the sense of [Gärdenfors, 1990] of a non-monotonic formalism, namely $N(q \mid p) > 0$ playing the role of $p \mid\!\sim_K q$ (where K is a belief set representing our background beliefs), into a belief revision statement $q \in K^*_p$, using Gärdenfors [1988, 1990]'s notations, where K^*_p denotes the result of the revision of K when adding p, here expressed in our framework by $(\mathcal{K} \cup \{(p,1)\}) \models (q,\alpha)$. Moreover note that it is also equivalent to preferential entailment in the sense of Shoham (upto the trivial entailment from contradictory propositions), here denoted $p \models_\pi q$. Here, instead of a belief set K, closed under deduction, we use any weighted set $\mathcal{K}$ of propositions, and we derive a preference relation on interpretations.

A machinery described elsewhere [Dubois, Lang and Prade, 1987, 1989], based on extended resolution and refutation implements this non-monotonic/belief revision mechanism. Let us briefly restate the main points before giving an illustrative example. The necessity-valued possibilistic knowledge base $\mathcal{K}$ with which we start is supposed to be put in clausal form. This is not constraining since if a formula p is the conjunction of n formulas $p_1, \ldots, p_n$, then $N(p) \geq \alpha \Leftrightarrow N(p_1 \wedge \ldots \wedge p_n) = \min(N(p_1), \ldots, N(p_n)) \geq \alpha \Leftrightarrow \forall\, i = 1,n,\ N(p_i) \geq \alpha$. Extended resolution corresponds to the following pattern $\dfrac{(c,\alpha) \quad (c',\beta)}{(\mathrm{Res}(c,c'),\ \min(\alpha,\beta))}$ where Res(c,c') is the classical resolvent of clauses c and c'. The refutation consists in adding to $\mathcal{K}$ the set of clauses generated by the negation $(\neg p,1)$ of the proposition p of interest, with the weight 1 (total certainty). Then it can be shown that any weight obtained with the empty clause by the repeated application of the resolution pattern on $\mathcal{K} \cup \{(\neg p,1)\}$ is indeed a lower bound of the value of the necessity measure (associated with $\mathcal{K}$) for the event "p is true". So we are interested in obtaining the empty clause with the greatest possible lower bound. A procedure yielding such a refutation with the best possible weight first has been implemented using an ordered search method. Let us denote by $\mathcal{K} \vdash (p,\alpha)$ the fact that $(\bot,\alpha)$ can be obtained by a refutation from $\mathcal{K} \cup \{(\neg p,1)\}$ (here α does not necessarily correspond to the best lower bound). Then the following soundness and completeness results holds, whether $\mathcal{K}$ is totally consistent [Dubois, Lang and Prade, 1989] or partially inconsistent [Lang et al., 1990] :

$$\mathcal{K} \vdash (p,\alpha) \Leftrightarrow \mathcal{K} \models (p,\alpha), \text{ for } \alpha > \mathrm{Inc}(\mathcal{K})$$

which guarantees the perfect agreement of the extended refutation machinery with the semantics presented above.

Let us now give an illustrative example

Let $\mathcal{K}$ be the following knowledge base :

C1. If Bob attends a meeting, then Mary does not.
C2. Bob comes to the meeting to-morrow.
C3. If Betty attends a meeting, then it is likely that the meeting will not be quiet.
C4. If is only somewhat certain that Betty comes to the meeting to-morrow.
C5. If Albert comes to-morrow and Mary does not, then it is almost certain that the meeting will not be quiet.
C6. It is likely that Mary or John will come to-morrow.
C7. If John comes to-morrow, it is rather likely that Albert will come.
C8. If John does not come to-morrow, it is almost certain that the meeting will be quiet.

This can be represented by the following weighted clauses :
C1 $(\neg\mathrm{Bob}(x) \vee \neg\mathrm{Mary}(x)\ 1)$; C2 $(\mathrm{Bob}(m)\ 1)$
C3 $(\neg\mathrm{Betty}(x) \vee \neg\mathrm{quiet}(x)\ 0.7)$; C4 $(\mathrm{Betty}(m)\ 0.3)$
C5 $(\mathrm{Mary}(m) \vee \neg\mathrm{Albert}(m) \vee \neg\mathrm{quiet}(m)\ 0.8)$
C6 $(\mathrm{John}(m) \vee \mathrm{Mary}(m)\ 0.7)$; C7 $(\mathrm{John}(m) \vee \mathrm{quiet}(m)\ 0.8)$
C8 $(\neg\mathrm{John}(m) \vee \mathrm{Albert}(m)\ 0.6)$

If we want to try to prove that the meeting to-morrow will not be quiet, we add the clause C0 : $(\mathrm{quiet}(m)\ \ 1)$. Then it can be checked that there exist two possible refutations : one from C0, C3, C4 which gives $(\bot,0.3)$ and another from C0, C5, C1, C2, C6, C8 which gives $(\bot,0.6)$. The last refutation is the optimal one. We proved that $N(\neg\mathrm{quiet}(m)) \geq 0.6$, i.e. it is rather likely that the meeting to-morrow will not be quiet.

Moreover, adding to a consistent knowledge base $\mathcal{K}$, a clause (c,α) that makes it partially inconsistent, produces a non-monotonic behavior. Namely, if from $\mathcal{K}$ a conclusion (p,β) can be obtained by refutation, it may happen that, from $\mathcal{K}' = \mathcal{K} \cup \{(c,\alpha)\}$, an opposite conclusion $(\neg p,\gamma)$ with $\gamma > \mathrm{Inc}(\mathcal{K}') \geq \beta$ can be derived.

Suppose we add to $\mathcal{K}$ in the above example the clause $(\neg\mathrm{John}(m),1)$, i.e. $\alpha = 1$, expressing that we are now certain that John will not come to-morrow. Let $\mathcal{K}'$ be the new knowledge base. The inconsistency degree of $\mathcal{K}'$ is 0.7, i.e. $\mathrm{Inc}(\mathcal{K}') = 0.7$ (as given by refutation from C1, C2, C6 and $(\neg\mathrm{John}(m),\ 1)$). Now the proof of $(\neg\mathrm{quiet}(m),0.6)$ (it corresponds to $\beta = 0.6$) is no longer valid ; but we can prove $(\mathrm{quiet}(m),0.8)$, i.e. $\gamma = 0.8$; which is obtained by a refutation from $(\neg\mathrm{quiet}(m),1)$, C7 and $(\neg\mathrm{John}(m),1)$, using only a consistent subpart of $\mathcal{K} \cup \{(\neg\mathrm{John}(m),1)\}$. Thus a non-monotonic behaviour can be captured in this framework.

The above example shows not only the ability of possibilistic logic to cope with partial inconsistency but also that a revision mechanism is implicitly working in it. The deep reason for that has been recently discovered [Dubois and Prade, 1990b]. It is basically due to the equivalence between the system of axioms defining the so-called epistemic entrenchment relations (on which well-behaved revision processes should be based [Gärdenfors, 1988]) and the systems of axioms characterizing qualitative necessity relations. Qualitative necessity relations [Dubois, 1986] are binary relations denoted $\leq$ where $p \leq q$ means q is at least as certain as p, are the perfect qualitative counterpart of necessity measures in the sense that for any necessity measure N there exists a qualitative necessity relation $<$ such that the following equivalence holds $\forall\, p, q,\ p < q \Leftrightarrow N(p) \leq N(q)$. Conversely only necessity measures are numerical representations of such kinds of ordering.This emphasizes the qualitative nature of possibility and necessity measures and points out that the numbers which are used in practice, as in the above example, have mainly an ordinal meaning.

5 - Conclusion

This paper has tried to take one more step towards the unification of symbolic and numerical knowledge representation approaches for reasoning under uncertainty. Namely possibilistic logic belongs to the family of non-monotonic systems based on preferential models. Moreover the identity of axioms between necessity measures and epistemic entrenchment puts possibilistic logic in the current stream of ideas on belief revision. Stated compactly, any possibilistic knowledge base $\mathcal{K}$ induces a preference relation among interpretations. This preference relation is consistent with an epistemic entrenchment relation over formulas that can be deduced from $\mathcal{K}$; adding a new formula to $\mathcal{K}$ produces a revision effect, in accordance with this epistemic entrenchment relation, that is achieved by applying the resolution principle extended to necessity valued clauses. Moreover, deduction from a partially inconsistent possibilistic knowledge base has all properties of a well-behaved non-monotonic deduction. Note that our investigation parallels the one of Pearl and others on probabilistic semantics of default, but here in a purely non-probabilistic framework .

A further topic of interest would be to try to bridge the gap between possibilistic logic and conditional logic, following the path opened by Bell [1990] who reinterprets Shoham's preference logic in the framework of conditional logics. This would enable Delgrande [1986]'s logic of typicality to be better understood in its links with other non-monotonic logics. Note that our notion of conditional possibility and certainty have symbolic counterparts in Bell's logic.

Moreover the definition of these conditional measures of uncertainty is based on the minimum operation here ($\Pi(p \wedge q) = \min(\Pi(p \mid q),\Pi(q))$), but clearly most of the results obtained here carry over to the case where min is changed into product, i.e. conditional possibility is then in accordance with Dempster rule of conditioning. This fact suggests that the close relationships displayed here between non-monotonic reasoning, belief revision and possibility theory might extend to belief functions .

Lastly, there is an obvious proximity of ideas between possibilistic logic and constraint-directed programming where constraints have various levels of priority [Satoh, 1990]. This topic will also be investigated in the future, interpreting a necessity-valued clause as a soft constraint.

Acknowledgements : The authors are grateful to a referee for pointing out the problem of preferential entailment from inconsistent premises, and for various other remarks that significantly improved the presentation of the paper. This work has been partially supported by the European ESPRIT Basic Research Action n° 3085 entitled "Defeasible Reasoning and Uncertainty Management Systems (DRUMS)".

References

[Adams, 1975] E.W. Adams. *The Logic of Conditionals*. Reidel, Dordrecht, The Netherlands, 1975.

[Bell, 1990] J. Bell. The logic of nonmonotonicity. *Artificial Intelligence*, 4(3):365–374, 1990.

[Delgrande, 1986] J.P. Delgrande. A first-order conditional logic for prototypical properties. *Artificial Intelligence*, 33:105–130, 1986.

[Dubois, 1986] D. Dubois. Belief structures, possibility theory and decomposable confidence measures on finite sets. *Computers and Artificial Intelligence*, 5(5):403–416, 1986.

[Dubois, Lang, Prade, 1987] D. Dubois, J. Lang, and H. Prade. Theorem proving under uncertainty – A possibility theory-based approach. *Proc. IJCAI-87*, pages 984-986, Milan, Italy, 1987.

[Dubois, Lang, Prade, 1989] D. Dubois, J. Lang, and H. Prade. Automated reasoning using possibilistic logic : semantics, belief revision and variable certainty weights. *Proc. 5th Workshop on Uncertainty in Artificial Intelligence*, pages 81-87, Windsor, Ontario, 1989.

[Dubois, Prade, 1986] D. Dubois, and H. Prade. Possibilistic inference under matrix form. In *Fuzzy Logic in Knowledge Engineering* (H. Prade, C.V. Negoita, eds.), Verlag TÜV Rheinland, pages 112–126.

[Dubois, Prade, 1988] D. Dubois, and H. Prade (with the collaboration of H. Farreny, R. Martin-Clouaire, C. Testemale). *Possibility Theory – An Approach to Computerized Processing of Uncertainty*. Plenum Press, New York, 1988.

[Dubois, Prade, 1989] D. Dubois, and H. Prade. Measure-free conditioning, probability and non-monotonic reasoning. *Proc. IJCAI-89*, pages 1110-1114, Detroit, Michigan, 1989.

[Dubois, Prade, 1990a] D. Dubois, and H. Prade. The logical view of conditioning and its application to possibility and evidence theory. *Int. J. of Approximate Reasoning*, 4(1): 23–46, 1990.

[Dubois, Prade, 1990b] D. Dubois, and H. Prade. Epistemic entrenchment and possibilistic logic. In Tech. Report IRIT/90-2/R, IRIT, Univ. P. Sabatier, Toulouse, France. *Artificial Intelligence*, to appear.

[Dubois, Prade, 1991] D. Dubois, and H. Prade. Conditional objects and non-monotonic reasoning. *2nd Inter. Conf. on Principles of Knowledge Representation and Reasoning (KR'91)*, Cambridge, Mass.

[Gabbay, 1985] D.M. Gabbay. Theoretical foundations for non-monotonic reasoning in expert systems. *Proc. NATO Advanced Study Institute on Logics and Models of Concurrent Systems*, pages 439-457, La Colle-sur-Loup, France (K.R. Apt, ed.), Springer Verlag, Berlin, 1985.

[Gärdenfors, 1988] P. Gärdenfors. *Knowledge in Flux – Modeling the Dynamics of Epistemic States*. The MIT Press, Cambridge, Mass, 1988.

[Gärdenfors, 1990] P. Gärdenfors. Belief revision and nonmonotonic logic : two sides of the same coin ?. *Proc. 9th Europ. Conf. on Artificial Intelligence*, pages 768-773, Stockholm, Sweden, 1990.

[Geffner, 1988] H. Geffner. On the logic of defaults. *Proc. 7th. AAAI National Conference on Artificial Intelligence*, pages 449-454, St Paul, Mn., 1988.

[Goodman, Nguyen, 1988] I.R. Goodman, and H.T. Nguyen. Conditional objects and the modeling of uncertainties. In *Fuzzy Computing – Theory, Hardware and Applications* (M.M. Gupta, T. Yamakawa, eds.), North-Holland, Amsterdam, pages 119–138.

[Hisdal, 1978] E. Hisdal. Conditional possibilities – Independence and non-interactivity. *Fuzzy Sets and Systems*, 1:283–297, 1978.

[Kraus, Lehmann, Magidor, 1990] S. Kraus, D. Lehmann, and M. Magidor. Nonmonotonic reasoning, preferential models and cumulative logics. *Artificial Intelligence*, 44(1-2): 137–207, 1990.

[Lang, Dubois, Prade, 1990] J. Lang, D. Dubois, and H. Prade. A logic of graded possibility and certainty coping with partial inconsistency, Tech. Report IRIT/90-54/R, Univ. P. Sabatier, Toulouse, France.

[Léa Sombé, 1990] Léa Sombé (P. Besnard, M.O. Cordier, D. Dubois, L. Fariñas del Cerro, C. Froidevaux, Y. Moinard, H. Prade, C. Schwind, and P. Siegel). Reasoning Under Incomplete Information in Artificial Intelligence : A Comparison of Formalisms Using a Single Example. *Int. J. of Intelligent Systems*, 5(4):323–471, 1990, available as a monograph, Wiley, New York.

[Makinson, 1989] D. Makinson. General theory of cumulative inference. In *Non-Monotonic Reasoning* (2nd Inter. Workshop, Grassau, FRG, June 1988) (M. Reinfrank, J. De Kleer, M.L. Ginsberg, E. Sandewall, eds.), Lecture Notes in Computer Science, Vol. 346, Springer Verlag, Berlin, 1989, pages 1-18.

[Neufeld, Poole, Aleliunas, 1990] E. Neufeld, D. Poole, and R. Aleliunas. Probabilistic semantics and defaults. In *Uncertainty in Artificial Intelligence 4* (R.D. Shachter, T.S. Levitt, L.N. Kanal, J.F. Lemmer, eds.), North-Holland, Amsterdam, pages 121-131, 1990.

[Pearl, 1988] J. Pearl. *Probabilistic Reasoning in Intelligent Systems : Networks of Plausible Inference*. Morgan Kaufmann, Los Altos, Ca., 1988.

[Satoh, 1990] K. Satoh. Formalizing soft constraints by interpretation ordering. *Proc. Europ. Conf. on Artificial Intelligence (ECAI-90)*, pages 585-590, Stockholm, 1990.

[Shoham, 1988] Y. Shoham. *Reasoning About Change – Time and Causation from the Standpoint of Artificial Intelligence*. The MIT Press, Cambridge, Mass., 1988.

[Zadeh, 1978] L.A. Zadeh. Fuzzy sets as a basis for a theory of possibility. *Fuzzy Sets and Systems*, 1:3–28, 1978.

KNOWLEDGE REPRESENTATION

Nonmonotonic Reasoning—Circumscription

Query Answering in Circumscription

Nicolas Helft *
Artificial Intelligence Center
SRI International
333 Ravenswood Ave.
Menlo Park, CA 94025

Katsumi Inoue
ICOT Research Center
Mita Kokusai Bldg. 21F.
1-4-28 Mita, Minato-ku
Tokyo 108, Japan

David Poole
Department of Computer Science
University of British Columbia
Vancouver, B.C.
Canada V6T 1W5

Abstract

We address the problem of answering queries in circumscription and related nonmonotonic formalisms. The answering process we describe uses resolution-based theorem provers recently developed for circumscription. In a way analogous to query answering techniques in classical predicate logic, the process extracts information from a proof of the query. Circumscriptive theorem provers consist of two processes, generating explanations for the theorem to be proved and showing that these explanations cannot be refuted. In general, many explanations compete in supporting the theorem. We show that queries can be answered by finding certain combinations of explanations, and present results to search the space of explanations, while carrying out significant pruning on this space. The results are relevant to other nonmonotonic formalisms having explanation-based proof procedures.

1 Introduction

For the first-order predicate logic, techniques developed by Green [1969a] are the basis for query-answering systems extensively used in deductive databases, logic programming and synthesis problems such as planning. These techniques rely on resolution-based theorem provers that attempt to prove the query while keeping track of the information generated during the proof. Theorem provers can decide whether a query follows from a given theory, and thus answer questions such as "Is there a coffee cup?"; the corresponding query-answering procedure computes the instance for which the query holds and can provide answers to questions such as "Where is the coffee cup?".

This paper addresses the query answering problem for logic databases augmented with a circumscription axiom [McCarthy, 1986] and related nonmonotonic formalisms. As in the first-order case, the answering procedure we present extracts information from a proof of the query. We build on existing proof procedures for circumscription that have recently been developed [Przymusinski, 1989; Ginsberg, 1989; Inoue and Helft, 1990].

While existing theorem provers for circumscription can correctly answer whether or not a formula follows from a circumscription, Green's techniques, although necessary, are not sufficient to provide answer extraction. The reason is the following. Circumscriptive theorem provers are based on finding explanations, or arguments, for the theorem to be proved, and showing that these explanations cannot be refuted. In general, many explanations compete in supporting the theorem, and a certain combination of these has to be found. We show that to an informative answer corresponds a particular combination of explanations, and present a procedure to find these combinations, together with results to search this space and carry out significant pruning.

Although we focus on circumscription, the results we present obviously apply to its restrictions, as for example logic databases using different types of closed-world assumptions, and similar default reasoning systems having explanation-based proof theories [Geffner, 1990; Poole, 1989].

The next section is a summary of results concerning circumscription and its theorem provers. Section 3 illustrates the problem through an example, and Section 4 provides the main results on extracting answers from a proof.

2 Background

This section gives a very brief survey on circumscription and its proof procedures. Additional background can be found in [McCarthy, 1986; Lifschitz, 1985].

2.1 Circumscription

The circumscription of a first-order theory T is its augmentation with a second-order axiom $CIRC(T; P; Z)$, where P and Z denote sets of predicate symbols of T, whose model-theoretic characterization is based on the following definition and result.

Definition 2.1 Let M_1 and M_2 be models of T. Then $M_1 \leq_{P,Z} M_2$ if M_1 and M_2 differ only in the way they interpret predicates from P and Z, and the extension of every predicate from P in M_1 is a subset of its extension

*Supported by the NTT Corporation, and by the Office of Naval Research under Contract No. N00014-89-C-0095.

in M_2. A model M of T is (P,Z)-*minimal* if for no other model M' of T it is the case that $M' \leq_{P,Z} M$.[1]

The predicates in P are said to be *minimized* and those in Z to be *variables*; Q denotes the rest of the predicates, called *parameters*.

Theorem 2.2 *CIRC*$(T;P;Z) \models F$ if and only if $M \models F$, for every (P,Z)-minimal model M of T.[2]

2.2 Theorem Proving Results

General circumscription is highly uncomputable [Schlipf, 1986], and existing theorem proving results apply to restrictions of circumscriptive theories. From now on, T is a first-order theory without equality, consisting of finitely many *clauses*, each of which is a disjunction of possibly negated atoms called *literals*, augmented with the Unique Names Assumptions, that is, different ground terms denote different elements of the domain. We also assume that the Domain Closure Assumption is satisfied since this is necessary to guarantee the soundness of the query answering procedure described in this paper. Queries to be answered are restricted to existentially quantified formulas (note that this includes ground formulas).

Theorem proving techniques for circumscription are based on the following results [Gelfond *et al.*, 1989; Przymusinski, 1989; Ginsberg, 1989].

Definition 2.3 Let T be a theory, *CIRC*$(T;P;Z)$ its circumscription, F a formula, and let P^+ (P^-) denote the set of positive (negative) literals whose predicate symbol belongs to P.

1. $P^- + Q$[3] is called the ***explanation vocabulary.***
2. A finite conjunction E of literals from the explanation vocabulary is an ***elementary explanation for*** F relative to T if
   (a) $T + E \models F$, and
   (b) $T + E$ is consistent.

   A disjunction of elementary explanations is called an ***explanation.***
3. Let E be an explanation. An elementary explanation for $\neg E$ is called a ***counter*** to E.
4. If an explanation has no counters it is ***valid.***
5. A valid explanation E is ***minimal*** if there is no other valid explanation E' such that $E' \models E$.

Theorem 2.4 *CIRC*$(T;P;Z) \models F$ if and only if there exist a valid explanation for F relative to the theory T.

Example 2.5 Consider the theory

$$T = \{ \ \forall x \ bird(x) \wedge \neg ab(x) \supset flies(x), \quad bird(tweety) \ \},$$

where $P = \{ab\}$, $Q = \{bird\}$ and $Z = \{flies\}$, so that the explanation vocabulary is $\{ab\}^- + \{bird\}^+ + \{bird\}^-$. Let us consider the query

$$F = flies(tweety).$$

Now, $\neg ab(tweety)$ is an explanation for F, as it implies F together with T and belongs to the explanation vocabulary. It has no counters, as no formula from the explanation vocabulary can be consistently added to T to deduce $ab(tweety)$. F is thus a theorem of *CIRC* $(T;\{ab\};\{flies\})$.

Next, let

$$T' = T \cup \{ \ ab(tweety) \vee ab(sam) \ \}.$$

Then $\neg ab(sam)$ is a counter to $\neg ab(tweety)$ relative to T'. As no other valid explanation for F exists, F is not a theorem of the circumscription of T'.

2.3 Query Answering Procedure

In line with the above results, the task of a query answering procedure for circumscription is to search for explanations of the query and test their validity.

To do so, the answering procedure can rely on an *explanation-finding algorithm*. Such an algorithm is provided with a set of clauses T, a clause F, and a vocabulary, and returns an explanation E, that is, a conjunction of literals from the vocabulary, consistent with T, such that $T + E \models F$. The computation of explanations is based on the observation that such T, F and E verify

(a) $T + \neg F \models \neg E$, and
(b) $T \not\models \neg E$.

Explanations can thus be obtained by computing the set

$$New(T, \neg F) = Th(T + \neg F) - Th(T)$$

that belong to the vocabulary $P^+ + Q$. We call these the *new theorems* of $\neg F$ relative to T.[4] The negation of each of such clauses (a conjunction of literals from the explanation vocabulary) is an elementary explanation and any disjunction of these is an explanation.

Testing the validity of an explanation represents the same computational problem: if an explanation E has no counter, then there is no new theorem of E relative to T, belonging to the vocabulary $P^+ + Q$. In symbols, given an algorithm to compute the set $New(T, F)$, we are interested in

$$Explanations(T, F) = \neg New(T, \neg F)$$

and

$$Valid(E, T) \Leftrightarrow New(T, E) = \emptyset.$$

Algorithms based on ordered-linear resolution [Chang and Lee, 1973] are known to perform this computation [Przymusinski, 1989; Oxusoff and Rauzy, 1989; Siegel, 1987; Inoue, 1991], and are used in many abductive procedures [de Kleer, 1986; Poole, 1989]. The explanation-finding algorithm is not a concern of this paper. The results we present concern how to *combine* explanations in order to extract answers from a proof. We thus assume such an algorithm exist and return the correct explanations, and concentrate on the query answering procedure. The following one has been shown to correctly return yes/no answers, and is used in [Ginsberg, 1989; Przymusinski, 1989].

[1] We will often just say minimal models, P and Z being clear from the context.

[2] $\models$ is classical first-order.

[3] We identify Q with the set of all literals whose predicate symbols are parameters.

[4] Note that $New(T, \neg F)$ does not include clauses implied by T alone because their negations are inconsistent with T and they cannot be counters. The predicates of P have their sign changed because we look for the negation of E.

Algorithm 2.6 (Yes/No Answering Procedure)

Step 1. (Generate Elementary Explanations)
Compute elementary explanations of F relative to T.

Step 2. (Combine Elementary Explanations)
Set the explanation E to the disjunction of all elementary explanations, and represent it in conjunctive normal form (i.e., as a set of clauses).

Step 3. (Test Validity)
Test if E has no counter, in which case answer "Yes"; otherwise answer "No".

This query answering procedure is not an exact implementation of Theorem 2.4 in one respect. The Theorem stipulates the need for an arbitrary valid explanation, while the answering procedure, in Step 2, only tests one for validity, namely the disjunction of all the elementary ones generated in Step 1. This is enough to return yes/no answers. The reason is that if a certain disjunction of valid explanations exist, then the maximal disjunction is valid. This maximal disjunction is then tested for validity. The example we present next illustrates the inability of this procedure to provide answer-extraction.

3 Example

I have to do some Prolog and Lisp programming this morning, and I need the manuals. Asking people around, I collect information about who has recently been using them. I know the office number of my colleagues, and I also know that normally people leave books in their offices. However, there are exceptions to this rule: for example, some of my colleagues work at home and don't bring back the books to the office. The information I have can be expressed with the following theory T, where predicate symbols and constants have obvious intended interpretations:

$$\forall x \forall y \forall z\ had(x, y) \wedge office(x, z) \wedge \neg ab(x) \supset at(y, z),$$
$$had(fred, prolog\text{-}manual) \vee had(mary, prolog\text{-}manual),$$
$$had(harold, prolog\text{-}manual),$$
$$had(kurt, lisp\text{-}manual),$$
$$office(fred, EJ225),$$
$$office(mary, EJ230),$$
$$office(harold, EJ235),$$
$$office(kurt, EJ240),$$
$$\forall x \forall y \forall z\ different(y, z) \supset \neg at(x, y) \vee \neg at(x, z),$$
$$different(EJ225, EJ230) \wedge \ldots$$
$$\cdots \wedge different(EJ235, EJ240).$$

Where should I look for the manuals? Suppose I submit to the theorem prover the query

$$F = \exists x \exists y\ at(x, y)\,.$$

I am not really interested in knowing whether F is true or not. I would like to know how to get the manuals back, and do so without inspecting all the offices around.

If we set $P = \{ab\}$ and let the rest of the predicates vary, the minimal models of T can be divided in three groups, in each of which exactly one of $\neg ab(harold)$, $\neg ab(mary)$ or $\neg ab(fred)$ is true. In the first group of these

$$at(prolog\text{-}manual, EJ235)$$

holds. In the second and the third groups,

$$at(prolog\text{-}manual, EJ225) \vee at(prolog\text{-}manual, EJ230)$$

holds. Thus

$$at(prolog\text{-}manual, EJ225) \vee at(prolog\text{-}manual, EJ230) \vee at(prolog\text{-}manual, EJ235)$$

holds in all minimal models, and no subdisjunction does. Moreover, in all minimal models $\neg ab(kurt)$ is true, which means that

$$at(lisp\text{-}manual, EJ240)$$

is another theorem of the circumscription. These two smallest disjunction of answers provide me with information about where the manuals are.

However, Algorithm 2.6 produces the following.

Step 1. Three elementary explanations are computed:

$$E1 = \neg ab(fred) \wedge \neg ab(mary)$$
$$E2 = \neg ab(harold)$$
$$E3 = \neg ab(kurt)$$

Step 2. The disjunction $E1 \vee E2 \vee E3$ is transformed to conjunctive normal form. This is the conjunction of the following clauses:

$$\neg ab(fred) \vee \neg ab(harold) \vee \neg ab(kurt)$$
$$\neg ab(mary) \vee \neg ab(harold) \vee \neg ab(kurt)$$

Step 3. These clauses, when added to T, produce no new theorem in the vocabulary of positive ab predicates, showing that the disjunction of explanations is valid, as it has no counters. The procedure correctly answers "Yes".

There is no way instances of the query can be returned with this procedure. The reason is that the actual substitution for the variable in the query is lost in step 2, when the explanation is converted from disjunctive to conjunctive normal form. The rest of the paper describes a methodology and results on how to combine elementary explanation in a more careful way in order to produce the informative answers.

4 Answer Extraction

We consider informative answers to a query F relative to a circumscription $CIRC(T; P; Z)$ to be the most specific instances of F entailed by the circumscription; in the sequel we simply call them *answers* to the query.

Definition 4.1 Let $CIRC(T; P; Z)$ be a circumscriptive theory, F an existentially quantified query. An *answer* to F is a formula A such that

1. $CIRC(T; P; Z) \models A$,
2. $A \models F$, and
3. No A' different from A satisfies (1), (2) and $A' \models A$.

We now show how to produce such answers.

4.1 Obtaining Instances of the Query

As we said before, we assume that an explanation-finding algorithm returns explanations for the query. The problem we address is that of finding answers, that is, most specific disjunction of instances of the query entailed by the circumscription. To compute such instances of the query, we use Green's techniques for first-order logic [Green, 1969a; Green, 1969b], that consist of associating with F the clause

$$F' = \neg F \vee Ans(\mathbf{x})$$

where $\mathbf{x} = x_1, \ldots, x_n$ stands for the variables appearing in F. During the proof of F, Ans keeps track of the substitutions for which F holds at no extra cost. The explanation-finding algorithm is thus the same resolution-based algorithm used by existing theorem provers for circumscription [Ginsberg, 1989; Przymusinski, 1989], but instead of supplying the negation of the query F to compute $\neg New(T, \neg F)$, we supply F' and compute $New(T, F')$.[5] Accordingly, instead of obtaining explanations

$$E_1, \ldots, E_n$$

for F, we obtain

$$E_1 \supset Ans_1, \; \ldots, \; E_n \supset Ans_n,$$

where each Ans_i keeps the substitutions for a disjunction F_i of instances of F explained by E_i, that is,

$$T + E_i \models F_i \; (i = 1, \ldots, n).$$

4.2 Computing Answers

Given a query, the explanation-finding algorithm can compute the candidate answers $F_1, F_2, \ldots$, the explanations for each of these $E_{11}, E_{12}, \ldots$, and their counters $C_{111}, C_{112}, \ldots$. An answer is a shortest disjunction of F_i that has a valid explanation, that is, for which at least one explanation exists with no counter.

Suppose two instances of the query F_1 and F_2 have elementary explanations E_1 and E_2, neither of which is valid. E_1 and E_2 thus have counters C_1 and C_2. Now $C = C_1 \wedge C_2$ is a candidate counter for $E = E_1 \vee E_2$ in the sense that as $T + C_i \models \neg E_i$, obviously $T + C_1 \wedge C_2 \models \neg E$. But still C might not be a counter to E because, although each C_i is consistent with T, C might not be. If C is not consistent with T, and no other counter exist, E will be a valid explanation for $F_1 \vee F_2$.

Thus while certain explanations may have counters, their disjunction might not, as the corresponding conjunction of potential counters is inconsistent. Thus, compared with theorem provers that return yes/no answers, *the only additional computation needed is the consistency check on combinations of counters.*

So the search problem consists of finding the disjunctions of instances of the query such that the potential counters of their explanations are inconsistent. A counter C is inconsistent with T if and only if $T \models \neg C$; and such counters belong to a particular vocabulary. It is thus rewarding to compute the following set of clauses.

[5] The answer predicate Ans is added to the vocabulary $P^+ + Q$.

Definition 4.2 Let $CIRC(T; P; Z)$ be a circumscriptive theory. A *characteristic clause* of $CIRC(T; P; Z)$ is a clause C that satisfies the following.

1. Every literal of C belongs to $P^+ + Q$.
2. $T \models C$.
3. No other clause C' satisfies (1), (2) and $C' \models C$.

These are the restriction of the *prime implicates* [Reiter and de Kleer, 1987] of T to a particular vocabulary. They can be computed with the same linear resolution algorithm used by the explanation-finding procedure, as shown by [Inoue, 1991].

We can take advantage of this set in at least the following ways.

1. Let E be an elementary explanation, and C a counter to E. Then $T + C \models \neg E$, and thus $T \models \neg C \vee \neg E$. As the explanation-finding algorithm returns the shortest of such clauses, $\neg C \vee \neg E$ *is a characteristic clause of the circumscription.* In other words, to compute counters to an explanation, we consider the negation of its elementary components. The counters are the negation of the complement within a characteristic clause.
2. If $T + C$ is inconsistent, and thus $T \models \neg C$, then $\neg C$ *is implied by a characteristic clause of the circumscription.* This means that the consistency test on a combination of counters can be performed by entailment tests on the characteristic clauses.

The above ideas can be implemented using different search strategies, which are not our concern. The following is a possible implementation of an algorithm[6] to return informative answers to a query in a circumscriptive theory.

Algorithm 4.3 (Query Answering Procedure)

Step 1. (Compilation)
Compute the characteristic clauses of the circumscription.

Step 2. (Generate Elementary Explanations)
Compute elementary explanations of F relative to T.

Step 3. (Compute Counters)
A counter to an explanation is the complement of its elementary components within the characteristic clauses. If an explanation has no counters, output the instance of the query explained by it.

Step 4. (Combinations of Counters)
Compute the conjunctions of counters whose negation is entailed by a characteristic clause. Such a conjunction of counters is inconsistent with T, and the corresponding disjunction of elementary explanations is valid. If such an explanation has no other counters, the corresponding disjunction of instances of the query is an answer.

[6] Strictly speaking, this is not an "algorithm". The reason is, in Step 1 or 2, it may produce an infinite number of characteristic clauses or elementary explanations.

4.3 Example

We consider again the example of section 3.

Step 1. Since *ab* is the only minimized predicate, the only characteristic clause of the circumscription is:

$$ab(harold) \lor ab(fred) \lor ab(mary).$$

Step 2. We provide the explanation-finding algorithm with the clause

$$\neg at(x,y) \lor Ans(x,y),$$

and the answer predicate *Ans*.

Then we obtain the new clause

$$ab(fred) \lor ab(mary) \lor Ans(prolog\text{-}manual, EJ225) \lor Ans(prolog\text{-}manual, EJ230),$$

indicating that

$$E_1 = \neg ab(fred) \land \neg ab(mary)$$

explains

$$A_1 = at(prolog\text{-}manual, EJ225) \lor at(prolog\text{-}manual, EJ230).$$

In a similar way,

$$E_2 = \neg ab(harold)$$

explains

$$A_2 = at(prolog\text{-}manual, EJ235),$$

and

$$E_3 = \neg ab(kurt)$$

explains

$$A_3 = at(lisp\text{-}manual, EJ240).$$

Step 3. $C_1 = \neg ab(harold)$, is a counter to E_1. $C_2 = \neg ab(fred) \land \neg ab(mary)$, is a counter to E_2. E_3 has no counters, thus A_3 is output.

Step 4. The only characteristic clause subsumes (in fact, is equivalent to) the disjunction of the negation of the two counters C_1 and C_2. This indicates that $T + C_1 \land C_2$ is inconsistent, and as $E_1 \lor E_2$ has no other counter, it is a valid explanation for $A_1 \lor A_2$.

5 Conclusion

Nonmonotonic theorem provers often consist in a two-step classical deduction — making a default proof in which explanations are collected and checking validity of the explanations. We showed that the substitutions needed for query answering are lost in this process, and a combination of theses need to be found to produce the required answers.

We presented a procedure for combining explanations in order to obtain informative answers, and results that enable an answering procedure to return the interesting answers with minimal search.

The importance of the results presented lies in their applicability to a wide class of systems that are either a restriction of circumscription, for example, databases using different types of closed-world assumptions (see [Przymusinski, 1989; Gelfond *et al.*, 1989]), or similar default reasoning systems having explanation-based proof theories [Poole, 1989; Geffner, 1990].

Acknowledgment

We are grateful to Martin Abadi and Vladimir Lifschitz for their comments on earlier drafts.

References

[Chang and Lee, 1973] Chin-Liang Chang and Richard Char-Tung Lee. *Symbolic Logic and Mechanical Theorem Proving.* Academic Press, New York, 1973.

[de Kleer, 1986] Johan de Kleer. An assumption-based TMS. *Artificial Intelligence*, 28: 127–162, 1986.

[Etherington, 1988] David W. Etherington. *Reasoning with Incomplete Information.* Pitman, London, 1988.

[Geffner, 1990] Hector Geffner. Causal theories for nonmonotonic reasoning. In *Proceedings of the 8th AAAI*, pages 524–530, Boston, MA, 1990.

[Gelfond *et al.*, 1989] Michael Gelfond, Halina Przymusinska, and Teodor Przymusinski. On the relationship between circumscription and negation as failure, *Artificial Intelligence*, 38: 75–94, 1989.

[Ginsberg, 1989] Matthew L. Ginsberg. A circumscriptive theorem prover. *Artificial Intelligence*, 39: 209–230, 1989.

[Green, 1969a] Cordell Green. Theorem-proving by resolution as a basis for question-answering systems. In: B. Meltzer and D. Michie, editors, *Machine Intelligence 4*, pages 183–205, Edinburgh University Press, Edinburgh, 1969.

[Green, 1969b] Cordell Green. Application of theorem proving to problem solving. In *Proceedings of the IJCAI*, pages 219–239, Washington D.C., 1969.

[Inoue and Helft, 1990] Katsumi Inoue and Nicolas Helft. On theorem provers for circumscription. In *Proceedings of the 8th Biennial Conference of the Canadian Society for Computational Studies of Intelligence*, pages 212–219, Ottawa, Ontario, 1990.

[Inoue, 1991] Katsumi Inoue. Consequence-finding based on ordered linear resolution. In *Proceedings of the 12th IJCAI*, Sydney, Australia, 1991.

[Lifschitz, 1985] Vladimir Lifschitz. Computing circumscription. In *Proceedings of the 9th IJCAI*, pages 121–127, Los Angeles, CA, 1985.

[McCarthy, 1986] John McCarthy. Applications of circumscription to formalizing common-sense knowledge. *Artificial Intelligence*, 28: 89–116, 1986.

[Minicozzi and Reiter, 1972] Eliana Minicozzi and Raymond Reiter. A note on linear resolution strategies in consequence-finding. *Artificial Intelligence*, 3: 175–180, 1972.

[Oxusoff and Rauzy, 1989] Laurent Oxusoff and Antoine Rauzy. L'evaluation sémantique en calcul propositionnel. Thèse de Doctorat, Université d'Aix-Marseille II, Luminy, France, 1989.

[Poole, 1989] David Poole. Explanation and prediction: an architecture for default and abductive reasoning. *Computational Intelligence*, 5: 97–110, 1989.

[Przymusinski, 1989] Teodor C. Przymusinski. An algorithm to compute circumscription. *Artificial Intelligence*, 38: 49–73, 1989.

[Reiter and de Kleer, 1987] Raymond Reiter and Johan de Kleer. Foundations of assumption-based truth maintenance systems: preliminary report. In *Proceedings of the 6th AAAI*, pages 183–187, Seattle, WA, 1987.

[Schlipf, 1986] John S. Schlipf. How uncomputable is general circumscription? In *Proceeings of the 1st IEEE Symposium on Logic in Computer Science*, pages 92–95, Cambridge, MA, 1986.

[Siegel, 1987] Pierre Siegel. Représentation et utilisation de la connaissance en calcul propositionnel. Thèse d'État. Université d'Aix-Marseille II, Luminy, France, 1987.

Circumscription and Definability

Yves Moinard
IRISA, Campus de Beaulieu
35042 RENNES-Cedex, FRANCE
tel.: (33) 99-36-20-00
E-mail: moinard@irisa.fr

Raymond Rolland
IRMAR, Campus de Beaulieu
35042 RENNES-Cedex, FRANCE.
tel.: (33) 99-28-60-19

Abstract

Thanks to two stronger versions of predicate circumscription (one of the best known non-monotonic reasoning methods), we give a definitive answer to two old open problems. The first one is the problem of expressing domain circumscription in terms of predicate circumscription. The second one is the problem of definability of the circumscribed predicates, asked by Doyle in 1985, and never answered since. These two results, and the way used to obtain them, could help an "automatic circumscriptor".

1 Introduction

Firstly, McCarthy defined domain circumscription which reduces the set of individuals (§2). Later, he defined predicate circumscription, which reduces the extensions of some relations (§3). McCarthy has stated [1980] that domain circumscription is a particular case of predicate circumscription. [Etherington and Mercer, 1987] reaffirmed the importance of domain circumscription and contested McCarthy's statement. We show (§8) why this contestation is not fully justified and we provide two improvements of McCarthy's translation. To obtain our results, we define (§4) a variant of the strong pointwise circumscription of [Lifschitz, 1988a]. Cases of equivalence with standard circumscrition (§5) allow us to answer the central question in [Doyle, 1985]: when does circumscription define the predicates (§6)? A stronger circumscription, "definabilization" (§7), simplifies the expression, and hopefully the computation, of domain circumscription. We make precise the expression of domain circumscription in terms of predicate circumscription. Throughout the text we provide the semantics for each kind of "circumscription" defined, thus all of them, including the first order versions, may be considered as preferential entailment notions.

2 Domain circumscription

In many situations only the objects named are supposed to exist. Domain circumscription ([McCarthy, 1980], amended by [Morreau, 1985, Etherington and Mercer, 1987]) formalizes this idea. A theory $\mathcal{T}$ is a set of formulas in a first order language $\mathcal{L}$. Φ or $\Phi[x_0]$, is a formula in $\mathcal{L}$, $\Phi[x]$ denotes the formula obtained by substituting the free variable x for every free occurrence of x_0 in Φ (x not bound in $\Phi[x_0]$).

Definitions 2.1 **a)** $Axiom_{\mathcal{L}}(\Phi)$ denotes $\{\exists x_0 \ \Phi[x_0]\}$, together with the set of formulas
$\{\forall \mathbf{x} \ (\widehat{\Phi[\mathbf{x}]} \Rightarrow \Phi[f(\mathbf{x})])/f$ is a function symbol in $\mathcal{L}\}$. $\mathbf{x}$ is a tuple $(x_1, ..., x_k)$ of free variables, k is the arity of f, and $\widehat{\Phi[\mathbf{x}]}$ is $\Phi[x_1] \wedge ... \wedge \Phi[x_k]$ ($TRUE$ if $k=0$).

b) $\mathcal{T}^{\Phi}$, the *relativization of* $\mathcal{T}$ *to* Φ, is $\mathcal{T}$ in prenex form, where for each variable symbol y, we replace $\forall y \ (\cdots)$ by $\forall y \ (\Phi[y] \Rightarrow (\cdots))$ and
$\exists y \ (\cdots)$ by $\exists y \ (\Phi[y] \wedge (\cdots))$ (thus $P(a)$ by $\Phi[a] \wedge P(a)$).

c) **Circd**$(\mathcal{T})$, the *domain circumscription of* $\mathcal{T}$, adds the following axiom schema to $\mathcal{T}$:

(SDC) $(Axiom_{\mathcal{L}}(\Phi) \wedge \mathcal{T}^{\Phi}) \Rightarrow \forall x_0 \ \Phi[x_0]$,
for each formula Φ in $\mathcal{L}$.

Notations Our models are normal (equality interpreted as identity). If μ is an interpretation over $\mathcal{L}$, D_μ is its domain. For each predicate P (resp. function f) of arity k in $\mathcal{L}$, the subset $|P|_\mu$ of D_μ^k (resp. the application f_μ of D_μ^k in D_μ) denotes its extension in μ.

$\mathcal{L}_\mu$, the *language of* μ, adds to $\mathcal{L}$ a name for each element in D_μ.

Definition 2.2 (see e.g. [Enderton, 1972] p.90–91) μ and ν are interpretations over $\mathcal{L}$. We denote $\nu < \mu$, if and only if: 1) $D_\nu \subset D_\mu$ (strict inclusion),
2) for each function f in $\mathcal{L}$, if $e \in D_\nu^k$, then $f_\mu(e) = f_\nu(e)$,
3) for each predicate P in $\mathcal{L}$, $|P|_\mu \cap D_\nu^k = |P|_\nu$.

Definition 2.3 $\mathcal{R}$ is a binary relation between interpretations over $\mathcal{L}$. A model μ of $\mathcal{T}$ is *minimal for* $\mathcal{R}$ when no model ν of $\mathcal{T}$ is such that $\nu \mathcal{R} \mu$.

Theorem 2.1 (Davis [1980]) Any model of $\mathcal{T}$ minimal for $<$ is a model of **Circd**$(\mathcal{T})$.

The converse needs a more sophisticated relation:

Definition 2.4 (see e.g.[Enderton, 1972] p.88–89 and ex. 24 p.97): A subset S of D_μ^k is *definable with parameters in* μ when there exists a formula Φ in $\mathcal{L}_\mu$, of arity k, such that $S = |\Phi|_\mu$.

Definition 2.5 If $\nu < \mu$ and if D_ν is definable with parameters in μ, we note $\nu <^\delta \mu$.

Theorem 2.2 ([Morreau, 1985], or §8) The models of **Circd**$(\mathcal{T})$ are the models of $\mathcal{T}$ minimal for $<^\delta$.

Here is an example showing how domain circumscription reduces the domain to the minimum allowed by the axioms of the given theory (note that here, it does not matter whether we use $<$ or $<^{\delta}$).

Example 2.1 $\mathcal{T}$ is $P(a) \wedge \exists x \neg P(x)$.
$Axiom_{\mathcal{L}}(\Phi)$ is $\Phi[a]$, $\mathcal{T}^{\Phi}$ is $\Phi[a] \wedge P(a) \wedge \exists x(\Phi[x] \wedge \neg P(x))$ (SDC) is: $\mathcal{T}^{\Phi} \Rightarrow \forall x\, \Phi[x]$ (for every Φ in $\mathcal{L}$). Choosing $(x = a \vee x = y)$ as $\Phi[x]$ in (SDC) gives: $\mathbf{Circd}(\mathcal{T}) \equiv P(a) \wedge \exists y(\neg P(y) \wedge \forall x\,(x = a \vee x = y))$. The models of $\mathbf{Circd}(\mathcal{T})$ are the models of $\mathcal{T}$ with only two elements.

3 Predicate circumscription

Definition 3.1 ([McCarthy, 1986]) **a)** Let $\mathcal{T}$ be a finite set of first order formulas in which the lists of predicates $\mathbf{P} = (P_1, \cdots, P_n)$ and $\mathbf{Q} = (Q_1, \cdots, Q_m)$ occur. The *first order circumscription* of $\mathbf{P}$ in $\mathcal{T}$ with $\mathbf{Q}$ varying, noted $\mathbf{Circ_1}(\mathcal{T}\text{: } \mathbf{P};\ \mathbf{Q})$ ($\mathbf{Circ_1}(\mathcal{T}\text{: } \mathbf{P})$ if $\mathbf{Q}$ is empty), adds the following axiom schema to $\mathcal{T}$, (SAC):
$\{\mathcal{T}[\mathbf{p}, \mathbf{q}] \wedge \forall \mathbf{x}\, (\mathbf{p[x]} \Rightarrow \mathbf{P(x)})\} \Rightarrow \forall \mathbf{x}\, (\mathbf{P(x)} \Rightarrow \mathbf{p[x]})$,
for every $\mathbf{p} = (p_1, \cdots, p_n)$, $\mathbf{q} = (q_1, \cdots, q_m)$ lists of first order formulas in $\mathcal{L}$.

$\mathcal{T}[\mathbf{p,q}]$ is $\mathcal{T}$ where each occurrence of P_i (resp. Q_j) is replaced by p_i (resp. q_j). $\mathbf{p[x]} \Rightarrow \mathbf{P(x)}$ is $(p_1[\mathbf{x_1}] \Rightarrow P_1(\mathbf{x_1})) \wedge \cdots \wedge (p_n[\mathbf{x_n}] \Rightarrow P_n(\mathbf{x_n}))$.

The square brackets mean that $p_i[x_i]$ may have free variables not included in $\mathbf{x_i} = \{x_{i,1}, \cdots, x_{i,k_i}\}$ (k_i arity of P_i) (see [Besnard *et al.*, 1989] and ex. 8.1 below).

b) The *second order circumscription* $\mathbf{Circ_2}(\mathcal{T}\text{: } \mathbf{P};\ \mathbf{Q})$ adds the following axiom to $\mathcal{T}$, (AC):
$\forall \mathbf{pq}\ \{[\mathcal{T}[\mathbf{p,q}] \wedge (\forall \mathbf{x}\ (\mathbf{p(x)} \Rightarrow \mathbf{P(x)})] \Rightarrow \forall \mathbf{x}\ (\mathbf{P(x)} \Rightarrow \mathbf{p(x)})\}$,
$\mathbf{p}$ and $\mathbf{q}$ are lists of predicate variables, each p_i (resp. q_j) having the arity of P_i (resp. Q_j).

Circ denotes either $\mathbf{Circ_1}$ or $\mathbf{Circ_2}$.

Definition 3.2 Let μ and ν be two interpretations over $\mathcal{L}$. We write $\mu =_{\mathbf{P};\mathbf{Q}} \nu$ when μ and ν are identical except that there is no condition on the extensions of the P_j's $(1 \leq j \leq n)$ and Q_j's $(1 \leq j \leq m)$. Furthermore, if each $|P_i|_\mu$ and $|Q_j|_\mu$ is definable with parameters in ν, we write $\mu =^{\delta}_{\mathbf{P};\mathbf{Q}} \nu$. If Q is empty, we write $=_{\mathbf{P}}$ or $=^{\delta}_{\mathbf{P}}$.

$=_{\mathbf{P};\mathbf{Q}}$ is an equivalence relation, $=^{\delta}_{\mathbf{P}}$ is reflexive and transitive but it is not symmetrical (ex. 5.3).

Definition 3.3 $\mu <_{\mathbf{P};\mathbf{Q}} \nu$ (respectively $\mu <^{\delta}_{\mathbf{P};\mathbf{Q}} \nu$) means $\mu =_{\mathbf{P};\mathbf{Q}} \nu$ (respectively $\mu =^{\delta}_{\mathbf{P};\mathbf{Q}} \nu$), and $|P_i|_\mu \subseteq |P_i|_\nu$ $(1 \leq i \leq n)$ with some $|P_i|_\mu \subset |P_i|_\nu$.

If $\mathbf{Q} = \emptyset$, we note $<_{\mathbf{P}}$ or $<^{\delta}_{\mathbf{P}}$.

Definition 3.4 (Lifschitz [1986]) $\mathcal{T}$ is *(**P**; **Q**)-well founded* when for every model μ of $\mathcal{T}$, not minimal for $<_{\mathbf{P};\mathbf{Q}}$, there exists a model ν of $\mathcal{T}$ minimal for $<_{\mathbf{P};\mathbf{Q}}$ with $\nu <_{\mathbf{P};\mathbf{Q}} \mu$.

Universal theories are (**P**; **Q**)-well founded [Bossu and Siegel, 1985, Etherington *et al.*, 1985, Lifschitz, 1986].

Theorem 3.1 a) *Soundness* (see [McCarthy, 1980, Lifschitz, 1986]): Every model of $\mathcal{T}$ which is minimal for $<_{\mathbf{P};\mathbf{Q}}$ is a model of $\mathbf{Circ}(\mathcal{T}\text{: } \mathbf{P};\ \mathbf{Q})$.
b) [Lifschitz, 1986] The models of $\mathbf{Circ_2}(\mathcal{T}\text{: } \mathbf{P};\ \mathbf{Q})$ are the models of $\mathcal{T}$ minimal for $<_{\mathbf{P};\mathbf{Q}}$.
c) [Besnard, 1989] The models of $\mathbf{Circ_1}(\mathcal{T}\text{: } \mathbf{P};\ \mathbf{Q})$ are the models of $\mathcal{T}$ minimal for $<^{\delta}_{\mathbf{P};\mathbf{Q}}$.
A model minimal for $<_{\mathbf{P};\mathbf{Q}}$ is minimal for $<^{\delta}_{\mathbf{P};\mathbf{Q}}$.

As it is one of the purposes of this text, we give now an example where a seemingly stronger axiom is in fact equivalent to the circumscription axiom (first order or second order version).

Example 3.1 $\mathcal{T}$ is $P(0) \wedge \forall x\ (P(x) \Rightarrow P(s(x)))$.

$\mathbf{Circ_1}(\mathcal{T} : P)$, adds the following axiom schema to $\mathcal{T}$: for each formula p in $\mathcal{L}$: (SAC) $\{p[0] \wedge \forall x\ (p[x] \Rightarrow p[s(x)]) \wedge \forall x\ (p[x] \Rightarrow P(x))\} \Rightarrow \forall x\ (P(x) \Rightarrow p[x])$. Let (SAR) be the axiom schema of (Peano's) recurrence: for each p in $\mathcal{L}$: $\{p[0] \wedge \forall x\ (p[x] \Rightarrow p[s(x)])\} \Rightarrow \forall x\ (P(x) \Rightarrow p[x])$. Clearly (SAR) entails (SAC), so $\mathcal{T} \cup$ (SAR) entails $\mathbf{Circ_1}(\mathcal{T} : P)$. Here the converse is true (§5).

4 A strong predicate circumscription

We reinforce and simplify (SAC) the circumscription schema, or the axiom (AC).

Definition 4.1 The first order strong circumscription of $\mathbf{P}$ in $\mathcal{T}$, with $\mathbf{Q}$ varying, $\mathbf{Circf_1}(\mathcal{T}\text{: } \mathbf{P};\ \mathbf{Q})$, adds to $\mathcal{T}$ the schema (SACf): $\mathcal{T}[\mathbf{p,q}] \Rightarrow \forall \mathbf{x}\ (\mathbf{P(x)} \Rightarrow \mathbf{p[x]})$. The 2nd order version $\mathbf{Circf_2}(\mathcal{T}\text{: } \mathbf{P};\ \mathbf{Q})$, adds (ACf) $\equiv \forall \mathbf{pq}\ \{\mathcal{T}[\mathbf{p,q}] \Rightarrow \forall \mathbf{x}\ (\mathbf{P(x)} \Rightarrow \mathbf{p(x)})\}$ to $\mathcal{T}$.

Circf denotes either $\mathbf{Circf_1}$ or $\mathbf{Circf_2}$.

$\mathbf{Circf}(\mathcal{T}\text{: } \mathbf{P};\ \mathbf{Q}) \vdash \mathbf{Circ}(\mathcal{T} : \mathbf{P};\ \mathbf{Q})$.

Here is the semantics for this strong circumscription.

Definitions 4.2 We write $\nu \prec_{\mathbf{P};\mathbf{Q}} \mu$ (respectively $\nu \prec^{\delta}_{\mathbf{P};\mathbf{Q}} \mu$) when $\nu =_{\mathbf{P};\mathbf{Q}} \mu$ (respectively $\nu =^{\delta}_{\mathbf{P};\mathbf{Q}} \mu$) and $|P_i|_\mu - |P_i|_\nu \neq \emptyset$ for at least one i $(1 \leq i \leq n)$. "$-$" denotes the set difference.

If $\mathbf{Q}$ is empty, then we write $\prec_{\mathbf{P}}$ or $\prec^{\delta}_{\mathbf{P}}$.

Theorem 4.1 The models of $\mathbf{Circf_2}(\mathcal{T}\text{: } \mathbf{P};\ \mathbf{Q})$ (respectively $\mathbf{Circf_1}(\mathcal{T}\text{: } \mathbf{P};\ \mathbf{Q})$) are the models of $\mathcal{T}$ minimal for $\prec_{\mathbf{P};\mathbf{Q}}$ (respectively $\prec^{\delta}_{\mathbf{P};\mathbf{Q}}$).

Remarks 4.1 a) The proofs are as the proofs of theorem 3.1.
b) If $\nu <_{\mathbf{P};\mathbf{Q}} \mu$, then $\nu \prec_{\mathbf{P};\mathbf{Q}} \mu$.
c) $\prec_{\mathbf{P};\mathbf{Q}}$ is neither transitive nor antisymmetrical.
d) $(\nu \prec_{P_1,P_2\,;\,\mathbf{Q}} \mu)$ if and only if
$(\nu \prec_{P_1\,;\,P_2,\mathbf{Q}} \mu)$ or $(\nu \prec_{P_2\,;\,P_1,\mathbf{Q}} \mu)$.
b), c) and d) also hold with $^{\delta}$-relations.

Example 4.1 $\mathcal{T}$ is $(P(a) \vee P(b)) \wedge a \neq b$.
— $\mathbf{Circ}(\mathcal{T} : P)$ is consistent, being equivalent to
$a \neq b \wedge (\forall x\ (P(x) \Leftrightarrow x = a) \vee \forall x\ (P(x) \Leftrightarrow x = b))$.
— From $\mathbf{Circf}(\mathcal{T} : P)$, $\neg P(a)$ can be proved (choose $x = b$ as $p[x]$ in (SACf)), as can $\neg P(b)$ (choose $p[x] \equiv x = a$). Thus $\mathbf{Circf}(\mathcal{T} : P)$ is inconsistent.
— Here are 3 models of $\mathcal{T}$, with the same domain

$\{a,b,e\}$: $|P|_\mu = \{a,b,e\}$, $|P|_\nu = \{a\}$, $|P|_{\nu'} = \{b\}$. ν and ν', minimal for $<_P$, are models of **Circ**($\mathcal{T}$: P): $\nu <_P \mu$, $\nu' <_P \mu$. $\nu \prec_P \mu$, $\nu' \prec_P \mu$, $\nu \not\prec_P \nu'$ and $\nu' \not\prec_P \nu$: there is no model minimal for $\prec_P$. Here, the domain is finite and so the $^\delta$-relations coincide with these relations.

Here is a result about strong circumscription (proof: remark 4.1-d, which is obvious):

Theorem 4.2 **Circf**($\mathcal{T}$: $(P_1, ..., P_n)$; Q) is equivalent to $\bigcup_{j=1}^{n}$ **Circf**($\mathcal{T}$: P_j; $P_1, ..., P_{j-1}, P_{j+1}, ..., P_n$, Q).

Now, this strong circumscription is not as new as it may seem, although the presentation and the semantics are new:

Definition 4.3 ([Lifschitz, 1988b]) The *strong pointwise circumscription* adds to $\mathcal{T}$ the schema (SAPf): $\forall \mathbf{x}\ \neg(P(x) \wedge \neg p[x] \wedge \mathcal{T}[p,\mathbf{q}])$, for every tuple of formulas $(p, \mathbf{q})$ in $\mathcal{L}$.

We have: (SAPf) $\equiv \forall \mathbf{x}\ (\mathcal{T}[p,\mathbf{q}] \Rightarrow (P(\mathbf{x}) \Rightarrow p[\mathbf{x}])) \equiv$ $(\mathcal{T}[p,\mathbf{q}] \Rightarrow \forall \mathbf{x}\ (P(\mathbf{x}) \Rightarrow p[\mathbf{x}])) \equiv$ (SACf).

Lifschitz defines only *individual* strong pointwise circumscription (for one P at a time), and uses unions. We allow tuples **P** in *parallel* strong circumscription. Theorem 4.2 shows that these two ways are equivalent. As this circumscription is not pointwise at all, we prefer our name "strong circumscription".

Lifschitz gives an elegant second order formula

$$\mathbf{Circf}_2(\mathcal{T} : \mathbf{P}; \mathbf{Q}) \equiv \mathcal{T} \wedge \forall \mathbf{x}\ \{\mathbf{P}(\mathbf{x}) \Leftrightarrow (\mathrm{L})\}, \text{ with}$$
$$(\mathrm{L}) \equiv \forall \mathbf{pq}\ (\mathcal{T}[\mathbf{p},\mathbf{q}] \Rightarrow \mathbf{p}(\mathbf{x})).$$

Also, the *"modal strong circumscription"* of [Perlis, 1988], differs from (SACf) only in the fact that $\mathbf{P}(\mathbf{x})$ is replaced by $K\mathbf{P}(\mathbf{x})$, where K is a modal operator, attenuating this otherwise too strong circumscription.

5 When strong and standard circumscriptions coincide

Definitions 5.1 **a)** A theory $\mathcal{T} \equiv \mathcal{T}[\mathbf{P};\mathbf{Q}]$ is *stable for extended conjunction in* (**P**; **Q**) (first order version) if, for every tuple of formulas **p**, **q**, **p'**, **q'** in $\mathcal{L}$:

$\mathcal{T}[\mathbf{p},\mathbf{q}] \cup \mathcal{T}[\mathbf{p}',\mathbf{q}'] \vdash \mathcal{T}[\mathbf{p} \wedge \mathbf{p}' \wedge \mathbf{p}'', \mathbf{q}'']$ for some tuples $\mathbf{p}''$, $\mathbf{q}''$ of formulas in $\mathcal{L}$.

p, **p'**, **p''** have the same length as the tuple of predicates **P**, and **q**, **q'**, **q''** have the length of **Q**. $\mathbf{p} \wedge \mathbf{p}' \wedge \mathbf{p}''$ denotes the tuple of the $p_i \wedge p'_i \wedge p''_i$'s involved.

b) $\mathcal{T}$ is *stable for extended conjunction in* (**P**; **Q**) (second order version) if $\forall \mathbf{p}\,\mathbf{q}\,\mathbf{p}'\,\mathbf{q}'\ \exists \mathbf{p}''\,\mathbf{q}''\ \{(\mathcal{T}[\mathbf{p},\mathbf{q}] \wedge \mathcal{T}[\mathbf{p}',\mathbf{q}']) \Rightarrow \mathcal{T}[\mathbf{p} \wedge \mathbf{p}' \wedge \mathbf{p}'', \mathbf{q}'']\}$ is true in $\mathcal{T}$. **p**, **q**, **p'**, **q'**, **p''**, **q''** are tuples of predicate variables of suitable lengths and arities.

If there is no **p''**, $\mathcal{T}$ is *stable for conjunction in* **P**.

Theorem 5.1 If $\mathcal{T}$ is stable for extended conjunction in (**P**; **Q**), then **Circf**($\mathcal{T}$: **P**; **Q**) $\equiv$ **Circ**($\mathcal{T}$: **P**; **Q**).

Proof: This theorem is true for the 1st and for the 2nd order versions of definitions 3.1, 4.1 and 5.1. We give the 1st order version.

Circf$_1$($\mathcal{T}$: **P**; **Q**) entails **Circ**$_1$($\mathcal{T}$: **P**; **Q**), we need the converse. **Circ**$_1$($\mathcal{T}$: **P**; **Q**) is: $\mathcal{T}$ and (SAC). Suppose we also have $\mathcal{T}[\mathbf{p},\mathbf{q}]$. $\mathcal{T} \equiv \mathcal{T}[\mathbf{P},\mathbf{Q}]$, so we get (definition 5.1) $\mathcal{T}[\mathbf{p} \wedge \mathbf{P} \wedge \mathbf{p}'', \mathbf{q}'']$, for some **p''**, **q''**. The instance of (SAC) associated with $(\mathbf{p} \wedge \mathbf{P} \wedge \mathbf{p}'', \mathbf{q}'')$ gives $\forall \mathbf{x}\ (\mathbf{P}(\mathbf{x}) \Rightarrow (\mathbf{p}[\mathbf{x}] \wedge \mathbf{P}(\mathbf{x}) \wedge \mathbf{p}''[\mathbf{x}]))$. Thus $\mathcal{T}[\mathbf{p},\mathbf{q}] \Rightarrow \forall \mathbf{x}\ (\mathbf{P}(\mathbf{x}) \Rightarrow \mathbf{p}[\mathbf{x}])$, i.e. (SACf)

Horn theories are stable for conjunction in (**P**; **Q**) (generalize a well-known result of [van Emden and Kowalski, 1976]). Thus, for Horn theories (or for stratified logic programs, see [Moinard, 1990]) we may simplify the circumscription axiom. So in example 3.1, **Circf**$_1$($\mathcal{T}$: P), which is $\mathcal{T} \cup$ (SAR) in this case, is equivalent to **Circ**$_1$($\mathcal{T}$: P).

Definition 5.2 A theory $\mathcal{T}$ has the property of *extended intersection in* (**P**; **Q**) if and only if, for every models μ and ν of $\mathcal{T}$ such that $\nu =_{\mathbf{P};\mathbf{Q}} \mu$, there exists a model μ' of $\mathcal{T}$ such that $\mu' =_{\mathbf{P};\mathbf{Q}} \mu$, with $|\mathbf{P}|_{\mu'} \subseteq |\mathbf{P}|_\mu \cap |\mathbf{P}|_\nu$.

Theorem 5.2 **a)** A theory $\mathcal{T}$ is stable for extended conjunction in (**P**; **Q**) (second order version), if and only if $\mathcal{T}$ has the property of extended intersection in (**P**; **Q**).

b) If $\mathcal{T}$ is (**P**; **Q**)-well founded, then **Circ**$_2$($\mathcal{T}$: **P**; **Q**) is equivalent to **Circf**$_2$($\mathcal{T}$: **P**; **Q**) if and only if $\mathcal{T}$ has the property of extended intersection in (**P**; **Q**).

Proof: **a)** Details lengthy, but obvious (see [Moinard and Rolland, 1991].

b) Theorem 5.1 gives one way. **Circ**$_2$($\mathcal{T}$: **P**; **Q**) $\equiv$ **Circf**$_2$($\mathcal{T}$: **P**; **Q**) if and only if: for every model μ' of $\mathcal{T}$ minimal for $<_{\mathbf{P};\mathbf{Q}}$, if μ is a model of $\mathcal{T}$ and $\mu =_{\mathbf{P};\mathbf{Q}} \mu'$, we have: $|\mathbf{P}|'_\mu \subseteq |\mathbf{P}|_\mu$ (see remark 4.1 b). Let μ and ν be two models of $\mathcal{T}$ with $\nu =_{\mathbf{P};\mathbf{Q}} \mu$. As $\mathcal{T}$ is (**P**; **Q**)-well founded, there exists μ' model of $\mathcal{T}$, minimal for $<_{\mathbf{P};\mathbf{Q}}$ with ($\mu' <_{\mathbf{P};\mathbf{Q}} \mu$ or $\mu' = \mu$). $\mu' =_{\mathbf{P};\mathbf{Q}} \mu$, so $|\mathbf{P}|_{\mu'} \subseteq |\mathbf{P}|_\mu$. Also, $\mu' =_{\mathbf{P};\mathbf{Q}} \nu$ thus $|\mathbf{P}|_{\mu'} \subseteq |\mathbf{P}|_\nu$ and $|\mathbf{P}|_{\mu'} \subseteq |\mathbf{P}|_\mu \cap |\mathbf{P}|_\nu$.

If $\mathcal{T}$ is (**P**; **Q**)-well founded, we may refine this result:

Definition 5.3 $\mathcal{T} \equiv \mathcal{T}[\mathbf{P};\mathbf{Q}]$ has the property of *unique minimal model in* (**P**; **Q**) if and only if, for every models μ and ν of $\mathcal{T}$ minimal for $<_{\mathbf{P};\mathbf{Q}}$ and such that $\mu =_{\mathbf{P};\mathbf{Q}} \nu$, we have $|\mathbf{P}|_\mu = |\mathbf{P}|_\nu$ (i.e. $\mu =_{\mathbf{Q}} \nu$).

Theorem 5.3 **a)** If $\mathcal{T}$ has the property of extended intersection in (**P**; **Q**), then $\mathcal{T}$ has the property of unique minimal model in (**P**; **Q**).

b) If $\mathcal{T}$ is (**P**; **Q**)-well founded, then $\mathcal{T}$ has the property of extended intersection in (**P**; **Q**) if and only if $\mathcal{T}$ has the property of unique minimal model in (**P**; **Q**).

Proof: **a)** Obvious.

b) Let μ and ν be models of $\mathcal{T}$ with $\mu =_{\mathbf{P};\mathbf{Q}} \nu$. There exist models μ' and ν' of $\mathcal{T}$ minimal for $<_{\mathbf{P};\mathbf{Q}}$ with ($\mu' =_{\mathbf{P};\mathbf{Q}} \mu$, $|\mathbf{P}|_{\mu'} \subseteq |\mathbf{P}|_\mu$) and ($\nu' =_{\mathbf{P};\mathbf{Q}} \nu$, $|\mathbf{P}|_{\nu'} \subseteq |\mathbf{P}|_\nu$). Thus $\mu' =_{\mathbf{P};\mathbf{Q}} \nu'$, and $|\mathbf{P}|_{\mu'} = |\mathbf{P}|_{\nu'}$.

Example 5.1 $\mathcal{T}$: $P(a)$, $P(b) \Rightarrow (P(c) \vee P(d))$, $\{a \neq b, b \neq c, b \neq d, c \neq d, a \neq c, a \neq d\}$ {(S1)}.

— **Circf**($\mathcal{T}$: P) $\equiv$ **Circ**($\mathcal{T}$: P) $\equiv$ (S1) $\wedge (\forall x\ (P(x) \Leftrightarrow x = a)$ (choose $p(x) \equiv x = a$ in AC).

— $\mathcal{T}$ is not stable for conjunction in P, but $\mathcal{T}$ is stable for extended conjunction in P ($p''(x) \equiv x = a$). $\mathcal{T}$ is

P-well founded, and has the property of unique minimal model in P. This example shows that we must use the *extended* conjunction in theorem 5.2.

Example 5.2 $\mathcal{T}$ is:

$P(0) \vee \exists x \{P(x) \wedge \forall y (P(y) \Rightarrow (P(s(y)) \wedge x \neq s(y)))\}$,
$\forall x \forall y (s(x) = s(y) \Rightarrow x = y), \forall x (s(x) \neq 0)$ (S2)

— $\mathcal{T}$ is not P-well founded (right-hand side of disjunction).

— $\mathbf{Circ_2}(\mathcal{T} : P) \equiv$ (S2) $\wedge \forall x (P(x) \Leftrightarrow x = 0)$ (consistent).

$\mathbf{Circf_2}(\mathcal{T} : P)$ entails $P(0)$ (choose $x = 0$ as $p(x)$ in (SACF)), and also $\neg P(0)$ ($p(x) \equiv x \neq 0$), thus it is inconsistent.

— $\mathcal{T}$ has the property of unique minimal model in P: for every model μ of $\mathcal{T}$ minimal for $<_P$, $|P|_\mu = \{0_\mu\}$. $\mathcal{T}$ does not have the property of extended intersection in P: take $D_\mu = \mathbb{N} = \{0, 1, 2, 3, \ldots\}$, s_μ successor function in $\mathbb{N}$, $|P|_\mu = \{0\}$, $0_\mu = 0$; $\nu =_P \mu$, $|P|_\nu = \{1, 2, 3, \ldots\}$. μ and ν are two models of $\mathcal{T}$, $|P|_\mu \cap |P|_\nu = \emptyset$, and as $\mathcal{T}$[FALSE] is not true, no model μ' of $\mathcal{T}$ verifies $\mu' =_P \mu$ and $|P|_{\mu'} \subseteq |P|_\mu \cap |P|_\nu$. μ is minimal for $<_P$, ν is not (choose $|P|_{\nu'} = \{2, 3, 4, \ldots\}$). $\nu \prec_P \mu$, μ is not minimal for $\prec_P$ (no model is minimal for $\prec_P$). This example shows that we need the well-foundedness condition in theorem 5.3-b.

Other examples [Moinard and Rolland, 1991] show the importance of the well foundedness condition also for theorem 5.2 b or show that, since theorem 5.2, the main results are false with the first order versions (even with an adapted notion of well-foundedness). Thus, in the end of this section and in the following section, we deal only with the second order versions. Here we give only a simple example of one problem encountered with first order versions:

Example 5.3 $\mathcal{T}$: $P(0) \wedge \forall x (P(x) \Rightarrow P(s(x)))$.

(cf example 3.1). It is easy to find two models of $\mathbf{Circf_1}(\mathcal{T} : P)$ with $\mu =_P \nu$ and $|P|_\mu \neq |P|_\nu$. Choose $\mathbb{N} \cup \mathbf{Z}$ for domain, $|P|_\mu = \mathbb{N}$, $|P|_\nu = \mathbb{N} \cup \mathbf{Z}$. The problem is that $\mu =_P^\delta \nu$ is false ($|P|_\mu$ is not definable with parameters in ν) thus $\mu <_P^\delta \nu$ is false.
(Note that $\nu =_P^\delta \mu$ is true: $|P|_\nu = D_\mu$ is definable in μ).

6 Definability of the circumscribed predicate

Here are two definitions reminded by [Doyle, 1985]. This definability *in a theory* must not be confused with the definability *in a model* of definition 2.4.

Definition 6.1 A first order theory $\mathcal{T}$ *implicitly defines* P if and only if whenever μ and ν are two models of $\mathcal{T}$ such that $\nu =_P \mu$, then they are identical.

Definition 6.2 A first order theory $\mathcal{T}$ *explicitly defines* P if and only if there exists a first order formula Φ in $\mathcal{L}$, not involving P, such that: $\mathcal{T} \vdash \forall x (P(x) \Leftrightarrow \Phi)$.

The *Beth's definability theorem* (see [Chang and Keisler, 1973, Doyle, 1985]), states that implicit definability is equivalent to explicit definability. Now, we give a definition adapted to circumscription with variable predicates:

Definition 6.3 A 2nd *order circumscription* of $\mathbf{P}$ in $\mathcal{T}$ with $\mathbf{Q}$ varying *implicitly defines* $\mathbf{P}$ if and only if $\mathcal{T}$ has the property of unique minimal model in $(\mathbf{P}; \mathbf{Q})$.

This is a natural extension of definition 6.1, when "varying predicates" are involved. As already mentioned, we must use the second order circumscription, but $\mathcal{T}$ is a first order theory, and we may consider only first order models. If $\mathbf{Q}$ is empty, definition 6.3 coincides with definition 6.1: $\mathbf{Circ_2}(\mathcal{T} : P)$ implicitly defines P (definition 6.3) if and only if whenever μ and ν are models of $\mathbf{Circ_2}(\mathcal{T} : P)$ such that $\nu =_P \mu$, then $\mu = \nu$ (cf definition 6.1). So, the theorems 5.2 and 5.3 give:

Theorem 6.1 a) If $\mathcal{T}$ is such that $\mathbf{Circ_2}(\mathcal{T}: \mathbf{P}; \mathbf{Q})$ is equivalent to $\mathbf{Circf_2}(\mathcal{T}: \mathbf{P}; \mathbf{Q})$, then $\mathbf{Circ_2}(\mathcal{T}: \mathbf{P}; \mathbf{Q})$ implicitly defines $\mathbf{P}$.

b) If $\mathcal{T}$ has the property of extended conjunction in $(\mathbf{P}; \mathbf{Q})$ (second order version),then $\mathbf{Circ_2}(\mathcal{T}: \mathbf{P}; \mathbf{Q})$ implicitly defines $\mathbf{P}$.

c) If $\mathcal{T}$ is $(\mathbf{P}; \mathbf{Q})$-well founded, then $\mathbf{Circ_2}(\mathcal{T}: \mathbf{P}; \mathbf{Q})$ implicitly defines $\mathbf{P}$ if and only if $\mathbf{Circ_2}(\mathcal{T}: \mathbf{P}; \mathbf{Q})$ is equivalent to $\mathbf{Circf_2}(\mathcal{T}: \mathbf{P}; \mathbf{Q})$, that is if and only if $\mathcal{T}$ is stable for extended conjunction in $(\mathbf{P}; \mathbf{Q})$ (second order version).

This gives the answer to the central problem in [Doyle, 1985], asking when P is definable in the circumscribed theory. Also it strengthens the importance of formula (L), given at the end of §4, with standard circumscription. (L) does not involve $\mathbf{P}$ nor $\mathbf{Q}$, so for well-founded theories, (L) gives the explicit second order definition of $\mathbf{P}$ in $\mathbf{Circ_2}(\mathcal{T}: \mathbf{P}; \mathbf{Q})$ in all the cases where such a definition does exist. Note however that (L) being a second order formula is **not** the Φ of definition 6.2; such a Φ does not necessarily exist because $\mathbf{Circ_2}(\mathcal{T}: \mathbf{P}; \mathbf{Q})$ is a second order theory (cf example below).

Examples In examples 5.1, 5.2 and 5.3, $\mathbf{Circ_2}(\mathcal{T} : P)$ implicitly defines P. We may even give an explicit first order definition (for first or second order circumscription) in examples 5.1 ($P(x) \equiv x = a$) and 5.2 ($P(x) \equiv x = 0$). In example 5.3, $\mathbf{Circ_1}(\mathcal{T} : P)$ does not implicitly defines P. Also it is a case where no first order explicit definition exists for P in $\mathbf{Circ_2}(\mathcal{T} : P)$.

7 Definabilization (a stronger circumscription)

Definition 7.1 $\mathbf{Def_1}(\mathcal{T}: \mathbf{P}; \mathbf{Q})$, the *first order definabilization of* $\mathbf{P}$ in $\mathcal{T}$ with $\mathbf{Q}$ varying, adds to $\mathcal{T}$ the axiom schema (SADf): $\mathcal{T}[\mathbf{p}, \mathbf{q}] \Rightarrow \forall \mathbf{x} (\mathbf{P}(\mathbf{x}) \Leftrightarrow \mathbf{p}[\mathbf{x}])$. The 2nd order version $\mathbf{Def_2}(\mathcal{T}: \mathbf{P}; \mathbf{Q})$ adds to $\mathcal{T}$ (ADf) $\equiv \forall \mathbf{p}, \mathbf{q} \{\mathcal{T}[\mathbf{p}, \mathbf{q}] \Rightarrow \forall \mathbf{x} (\mathbf{P}(\mathbf{x}) \Leftrightarrow \mathbf{p}(\mathbf{x}))\}$.

Def denotes $\mathbf{Def_1}$ or $\mathbf{Def_2}$.

$\mathbf{Def}(\mathcal{T}: \mathbf{P}; \mathbf{Q}) \vdash \mathbf{Circf}(\mathcal{T}: \mathbf{P}; \mathbf{Q})$.

Doyle [1985] uses a similar notion without variable predicate, and calls it "implicit definability" (cf definition 6.1). A specific name makes a clear difference between a theory having this property and the addition of an axiom schema to any theory.

Example 7.1 $\mathcal{T}$: $P(a)$ (Horn theory).

— **Circf**($\mathcal{T}: P$) $\equiv$ **Circ**($\mathcal{T}: P$) $\equiv \forall x\ (P(x) \Leftrightarrow x=a)$.
— **Def**($\mathcal{T}: P$) $\equiv P(a) \wedge \forall x\ (x=a)$
(Choose $p[x] \equiv x=a$, then $p[x] \equiv x=x$, in (SADf)).

Example 7.2 $\mathcal{T}$: $P(a)$, $\exists x \neg P(x)$ (cf example 2.1).
— **Circf**($\mathcal{T}: P$) $\equiv$ **Circ**($\mathcal{T}: P$) $\equiv \forall x\ (P(x) \Leftrightarrow x = a) \wedge \exists x \neg P(x)$. ($\mathcal{T}$ is stable for conjunction in P, and $|P|_\mu = \{a_\mu\}$ in every model μ minimal for $<_P$).
— **Def**($\mathcal{T}: P$) $\equiv$
$\forall x\ (P(x) \equiv x=a) \wedge \exists y\ (y \neq a \wedge \forall x\ (x=a \vee x=y))$.
(Choose $p[x] \equiv x=a$, getting $\forall x\ (P(x) \equiv x=a)$, then $p[x] \equiv x \neq y$ which gives $y \neq a \Rightarrow \forall x\ (P(x) \Leftrightarrow x \neq y)$).

So definabilization minimizes the extensions of the predicates and the domain, as precised now:

Theorem 7.1 a) If $\mathcal{T} \equiv \mathcal{T}[\mathbf{P}, \mathbf{Q}]$ entails $\mathcal{T}[\mathbf{TRUE}, \mathbf{q}]$ for some tuple of formulas **q**, then **Def**($\mathcal{T}$: **P**; **Q**) entails $\forall \mathbf{x}\ \mathbf{P}(\mathbf{x})$. (**TRUE** is the tuple $(\mathbf{x}_1 = \mathbf{x}_1, \ldots, \mathbf{x}_n = \mathbf{x}_n)$).
b) **Def**($\mathcal{T}$: **P**; **Q**) $\vdash$ **Circ**($\mathcal{T}$: **P**; **Q**).
$\{\forall \mathbf{x}\ \mathbf{P}(\mathbf{x})\} \cup$ **Circ**($\mathcal{T}$: **P**; **Q**) $\vdash$ **Def**($\mathcal{T}$: **P**; **Q**).
c) If $\mathcal{T} \vdash \mathcal{T}[\mathbf{TRUE}, \mathbf{q}]$, then
Def($\mathcal{T}$: **P**; **Q**) $\equiv \{\forall \mathbf{x}\ \mathbf{P}(\mathbf{x})\} \cup$ **Circ**($\mathcal{T}$: **P**; **Q**).

Proof: **a)** Choose (**TRUE**, **q**) as (**p**,**q**) in (SADf) or (ADf) (depending of the version).
b) — Obvious.
— $\{\forall \mathbf{x}\ \mathbf{P}(\mathbf{x})\} \cup$ **Circ**($\mathcal{T}$: **P**; **Q**) is: $\mathcal{T} \cup \{\forall \mathbf{x}\ \mathbf{P}(\mathbf{x})\} \cup$ (SAC). $\forall \mathbf{x}\ \mathbf{P}(\mathbf{x})$ gives $\forall x\ (\mathbf{p}[\mathbf{x}] \Rightarrow \mathbf{P}(\mathbf{x}))$, thus (SAC) gives (SADf). Adaptation easy for the 2nd order version.

Definitions 7.2 We write $\nu \#_{\mathbf{P};\mathbf{Q}} \mu$ (resp. $\nu \#^{\delta}_{\mathbf{P};\mathbf{Q}} \mu$) when $\nu =_{\mathbf{P};\mathbf{Q}} \mu$ (resp. $\nu =^{\delta}_{\mathbf{P};\mathbf{Q}} \mu$) and $|P_i|_\mu \neq |P_i|_\nu$ for at least one i $(1 \leq i \leq n)$.

Theorem 7.2 The models of **Def**$_2$($\mathcal{T}$: **P**; **Q**) (respectively **Def**$_1$($\mathcal{T}$: **P**; **Q**)) are the models of $\mathcal{T}$ minimal for $\#_{\mathbf{P};\mathbf{Q}}$ (respectively $\#^{\delta}_{\mathbf{P};\mathbf{Q}}$).

Proofs obvious. As Doyle [1985] has noted, definabilization is generally too strong, here is an example:

Example 7.3 $\mathcal{T}$: $P(a) \Rightarrow P(b)$, $a \neq b$ (Horn theory).
— **Circf**($\mathcal{T}: P$) $\equiv$ **Circ**($\mathcal{T}: P$) $\equiv a \neq b \wedge \forall x \neg P(x)$
— **Def**($\mathcal{T}: P$) is inconsistent:
choosing $p[x] \equiv x=b$ proves $\neg P(a)$, then
choosing $p[x] \equiv (x=a \vee x=b)$ proves $P(a)$.
— Here are 3 models of $\mathcal{T}$, with the same domain $\{a, b\}$: $|P|_\mu = \{b\}, |P|_\nu = \{a, b\}, |P|_{\mu'} = \emptyset$.
$\mu' <_P \mu <_P \nu$. μ', minimal for $<_P$ and $\prec_P$, is a model of **Circ**($\mathcal{T}: P$) and **Circf**($\mathcal{T}: P$). $\mu' \#_P \mu$, $\mu \#_P \mu'$, etc... There is no model minimal for $\#_P$.

8 From domain to predicate circumscription

We will use only the first order versions (cf §2). Here is the way McCarthy [1980] uses to transform a domain circumscription into a predicate circumscription:

Definition 8.1 U being a new unary predicate symbol, we note: $\mathcal{T}_U \equiv Axiom_{\mathcal{L}}(U) \wedge \mathcal{T}^U$ and
$\mathcal{T}\langle U \rangle \equiv$ **Circ**$_1$($\mathcal{T}_U : U$) $\cup \{\forall x\ U(x)\}$.
$\mathcal{L}(U)$ denotes $\mathcal{L}$ augmented by U. $Axiom_{\mathcal{L}}(U)$ is also $Axiom_{\mathcal{L}(U)}(U)$, as $\mathcal{L}$ and $\mathcal{L}(U)$ have the same function symbols, and we will often note $Axiom(U)$.

Theorem 8.1 (McCarthy [1980]) $\mathcal{T}\langle U \rangle$ simulates the domain circumscription of $\mathcal{T}$: $\mathcal{T}\langle U \rangle$ entails **Circd**($\mathcal{T}$). The converse is true: every formula Φ in $\mathcal{L}$ entailed by $\mathcal{T}\langle U \rangle$, is entailed by **Circd**($\mathcal{T}$). That is, $\mathcal{T}\langle U \rangle$ is a *conservative extension* of **Circd**($\mathcal{T}$).

In a contestation of this method, Etherington and Mercer [1987] argue that consistency is not guaranteed when adding $\forall x\ U(x)$. However, no example is given. We prove that in fact, if an inconsistency has to appear, then it is detected in the circumscription of U:

Theorem 8.2 If **Circ**$_1$($\mathcal{T}_U : U$) is consistent,
then $\mathcal{T}\langle U \rangle$ is consistent.

Proof: Let μ be a model of **Circ**$_1$($\mathcal{T}_U : U$), that is a model of $\mathcal{T}_U$, minimal for $<^{\delta}_P$. We define μ_U (μ *restricted to* U): $\mu_U < \mu$; $D_{\mu_U} = |U|_{\mu_U} = |U|_\mu$. μ_U is a model of $\forall x\ U(x)$. μ is a model of $\mathcal{T}_U$, and so is μ_U. Let us suppose that there exists ν, model of $\mathcal{T}_U$, with $\nu <^{\delta}_U \mu_U$. Let ϕ be a formula in $\mathcal{L}_{\mu_U}$ with: $|\phi|_{\mu_U} = |U|_\nu$ (see definitions 3.3, 2.4). We define μ': $\mu' <_U \mu$, $|U|_{\mu'} = |\phi|_{\mu_U}$. Let Φ be a prenex formula in $\mathcal{L}_{\mu_U}$, we may prove by induction on the length of Φ that: $|\Phi|_{\mu_U} = |\Phi^U|_\mu$ [Moinard and Rolland, 1991]. First, this proves that μ' is a model of $\mathcal{T}^U$. Also, ν is a model of $Axiom_{\mathcal{L}}(U)$, and so is μ', thus μ' is a model of $\mathcal{T}_U$. From: $|U|_{\mu'} = |\phi|_{\mu_U} = |\phi^U|_\mu$, we get $\mu' <^{\delta}_U \mu$ contradicting the fact that μ is a model of $\mathcal{T}_U$ minimal for $<^{\delta}_U$. So there exists no ν and μ_U is a model of $\mathcal{T}_U$ minimal for $<^{\delta}_U$, i.e. a model of **Circ**$_1$($\mathcal{T}_U : U$). If there exists a model (μ) of **Circ**$_1$($\mathcal{T}_U : U$), there exists a model (μ_U) of $\mathcal{T}\langle U \rangle$. (Proof simpler for the 2nd order version).

Thus, McCarthy's way of expressing domain circumscription into predicate circumscription is justified. One of the main problems in any circumscription is the possibility of unexpected inconsistency. Here, if inconsistency arises it is detected in the circumscribing process, not in the addition of the last axiom $\forall x\ U(x)$ which is harmless.

However, there is a little problem remaining. Any known method of circumscription adds axioms to the initial theory. Here, we leave the initial theory for a while (neither $\mathcal{T}_U$ nor **Circ**$_1$($\mathcal{T}_U : U$) entails $\mathcal{T}$), and at the end, we recover $\mathcal{T}$. This does not simplify the matter if we are to automatize the process: for this purpose, we do not want to prove any axiom of $\mathcal{T}$, we need to know that these formulas are true. One theoretical solution meeting this requirement is to introduce $\mathcal{T}$ in the circumscription involved. That is why we propose to circumscribe U in $\mathcal{T} \wedge \mathcal{T}_U$, instead of $\mathcal{T}_U$ alone. As U does not occur in $\mathcal{T}$, we get: **Circ**$_1$($\mathcal{T}_U : U$) $\wedge\ \mathcal{T} \equiv$ **Circ**$_1$($\mathcal{T}_U \wedge \mathcal{T} : U$). As $\mathcal{T}\langle U \rangle$ entails $\mathcal{T}$, we have:

Theorem 8.3 $\mathcal{T}\langle U \rangle \equiv$ **Circ**$_1$($\mathcal{T}_U \wedge \mathcal{T} : U$) $\cup \{\forall x\ U(x)\}$.
Again, inconsistency cannot be provoqued by the addition of $\forall x\ U(x)$.
If $\mathcal{T}$ is universal, we get a simplification:
$\mathcal{T}\langle U \rangle \equiv$ **Circ**$_1$($Axiom(U) \wedge \mathcal{T} : U$) $\cup \{\forall x\ U(x)\}$.
(Indeed, $\mathcal{T}$ entails $\mathcal{T}^U$).

With this simulation of domain circumscription, we are closer to the other known kinds of circumscription: we add an axiom schema to $\mathcal{T}$. "More work is done by the circumscription of U" (the final addition of $\forall x\, U(x)$ eliminates fewer models). As with McCarthy's method, if we had an automatic demonstrator including a predicate circumscriptor (we may tend towards this goal), then we would also have a domain circumscriptor. We cannot avoid adding $\forall x \;\; U(x)$ if we want to use a predicate circumscription (see [Etherington *et al.*, 1985, Etherington and Mercer, 1987]). But now we show how, using definabilization, we may greatly simplify the process and avoid the need for $\forall x\, U(x)$.

Theorem 8.4 $\mathcal{T}\!<\!U\!>\equiv \mathbf{Circ}_1(\mathcal{T}_U \wedge \mathcal{T} : U) \cup \{\forall x\, U(x)\}$
$\equiv \mathbf{Def}_1(\mathcal{T}_U \wedge \mathcal{T} : U)$.

Proof: $\mathcal{T}_U$[TRUE] is $\mathcal{T}^U$[TRUE] $\wedge$ Axiom(TRUE), i.e. $\mathcal{T}\wedge$ Axiom(TRUE), i.e. $\mathcal{T}$, and $\mathcal{T}$[TRUE] is $\mathcal{T}$ because U does not occur in $\mathcal{T}$. Thus: $\mathcal{T}_U[U] \wedge \mathcal{T}[U]$ entails $\mathcal{T}_U$[TRUE] $\wedge$ $\mathcal{T}$[TRUE]. Use theorems 7.1 and 8.1.

Example 8.1 $\mathcal{T}$: $P(a) \wedge \exists x\, \neg P(x)$ (cf ex. 2.1, 7.2).

$Axiom(U) \equiv U(a)$; $\mathcal{T}^U \equiv \mathcal{T}_U \equiv U(a) \wedge \exists x\; (U(x) \wedge \neg P(x))$. $\mathbf{Circ}_1(\mathcal{T}_U : U) \equiv \mathcal{T}_U \cup \{\, [u[a] \wedge \exists x\; (u[x] \wedge \neg P(x)) \wedge \forall x\; (u[x] \Rightarrow U(x))] \Rightarrow \forall x\; (U(x) \Rightarrow u[x])$, for any formula u in $\mathcal{L}(U)\,\}$. We choose $u[x] \equiv (x=a \vee x=y)$, which gives: $(U(y) \wedge \neg P(y)) \Rightarrow \forall x\; (U(x) \Rightarrow (x=a \vee x=y))$. Adding $\forall x\; U(x)$, we get $\neg P(y) \Rightarrow \forall x\; (x=a \vee x=y)$, which together with $P(a) \wedge \exists x\; \neg P(x)$ gives: $P(a) \wedge \exists y\; (\neg P(y) \wedge \forall x\; (x=a \vee x=y)$, that is $\mathbf{Circd}(\mathcal{T})$ (cf example 2.1).

$\mathbf{Def}_1(\mathcal{T}_U : U) \equiv \mathcal{T}_U \cup \{[u[a] \wedge \exists x\; (u[x] \wedge \neg P(x))] \Rightarrow \forall x\; (U(x) \Leftrightarrow u[x])$, for every formula u in $\mathcal{L}(U)\,\}$. We choose $u[x] \equiv (x=a \vee x=y)$, which gives: $\neg P(y) \Rightarrow \forall x\; (U(x) \Leftrightarrow (x=a \vee x=y))$, then we choose $u[x] \equiv x=x$, which gives: $\forall x\; (x=a \vee x=y))$.

Theorem 8.5 If $\mathcal{T}$ is universal, then we get a simplification: $\mathcal{T}\!<\!U\!>\equiv \mathbf{Def}_1(\mathcal{T} \wedge Axiom(U) : U) \equiv \mathcal{T} \wedge \mathbf{Def}_1(\text{Axiom}(U) : U)$ (U does not appear in $\mathcal{T}$).

The axiom schema of definabilization is simpler than the axiom schema of domain circumscription, so this is an application of definabilization.

9 Conclusion

We have precised the definitions, semantics, and possible uses, of two kinds of "super circumscriptions". We have given new cases where the circumscription schema may be simplified, a result which is of theoretical and practical importance, as it could be of some help in the process of automatization of circumscription. These results have solved an old question: when does circumscription uniquely define the circumscribed predicates? Our answer is complete for well founded theories. At last, we have precised and justified the passage from domain circumscription to predicate circumscription. We have shown that this passage is safe: it cannot bring inconsistancy. Also we have given two new methods. The first one enhances the role of predicate circumscription, which is useful if we want to use an automatic predicate circumscriptor for domain circumscription. The second one greatly simplifies the schemas involved.

Acknowledgement We are glad to thank Philippe Besnard who initiated this work.

References

[Besnard *et al.*, 1989] P. Besnard, R. Mercer, and Y. Moinard. The importance of open and recursive circumscription. *Artificial Intel.*, 39:251–262, 1989.

[Besnard, 1989] Philippe Besnard. *An Introduction to Default Logic*. Springer Verlag, 1989.

[Bossu and Siegel, 1985] G. Bossu and P. Siegel. Saturation, nonmonotonic reasoning and the closed-world assumption. *Artificial Intelligence*, 25:13–63, 1985.

[Chang and Keisler, 1973] C.C. Chang and H.J. Keisler. *Model Theory*. North-Holland, 1973.

[Davis, 1980] M. Davis. The mathematics of non-monotonic reasoning. *Artificial Intel.*, 13:73–80, 1980.

[Doyle, 1985] Jon Doyle. Circumscription and implicit definability. *Automated Reasoning*, 1:391–405, 1985.

[Enderton, 1972] Herbert B. Enderton. *A Mathematical introduction to logic*. Academic Press, 1972.

[Etherington and Mercer, 1987] D.W. Etherington and R. Mercer. Domain circumscription: a reevaluation. *Computational Intelligence*, 3:94–99, 1987.

[Etherington *et al.*, 1985] D.W. Etherington, R. Mercer, and R. Reiter. On the adequacy of predicate circumscription for closed-world reasoning. *Computational Intelligence*, 1:11 15, 1985.

[Lifschitz, 1986] V. Lifschitz. On the satisfiability of circumscription. *Artificial Intelligence*, 28:17–27, 1986.

[Lifschitz, 1988a] V. Lifschitz. On the declarative semantics of logic programs with negation. In J. Minker, ed., *Foundations of Deductive Databases and Logic Programs*, pp. 177–192. Morgan-Kaufmann, 1988.

[Lifschitz, 1988b] V. Lifschitz. Pointwise circumscription. *Readings in Nonmonotonic Reasoning*, Ginsberg ed., pp. 179–193. Morgan-Kaufmann, 1988.

[McCarthy, 1980] John McCarthy. Circumscription–a form of non-monotonic reasoning. *Artificial Intelligence*, 13:27–39, 1980.

[McCarthy, 1986] John McCarthy. Application of circumscription to formalizing common sense knowledge. *Artificial Intelligence*, 28:89–116, 1986.

[Moinard and Rolland, 1991] Circumscription and definability (2). T.R., IRISA, Rennes, 1991.

[Moinard, 1990] Y. Moinard. Circumscription and Horn theories. In *ECAI*, pages 449–454, 1990.

[Morreau, 1985] M.P. Morreau. Circumscription: A sound and complete form of non-monotonic reasoning. Technical Report 15, University, Amsterdam, 1985.

[Perlis, 1988] Donald Perlis. Autocircumscription. *Artificial Intelligence*, 36:223–236, 1988.

[van Emden and Kowalski, 1976] M.H. van Emden and R.A. Kowalski. The semantics of predicate logic as a programming language. *JACM*, 23(4):841–862, 1976.

CIRCUMSCRIBING DEFAULTS

Zhaogang Qian and **Keki B. Irani**
Artificial Intelligence Laboratory
Department of Electrical Engineering and Computer Science
The University of Michigan
Ann Arbor, Michigan 48109-2122, USA

Abstract

One of the questions in understanding the relation between circumscription and consistency-based nonmonotonic logic is – can default logic be expressed in circumscription? While it seems impossible to express default logic in existing forms of circumscription, is it nevertheless possible to express default logic in a certain extension of circumscription? This paper presents a construction of "default logic" in the spirit of circumscription. It has been shown that the new formalism, *circumscriptive extension*, is indeed an extension of circumscription. The equivalence of the new formalism and default logic is shown to hold under certain conditions, which demonstrates that default logic can be expressed by merely classical logic with a fixed point operator.

1 Introduction

Various logics have been developed to formalize nonmonotonic reasoning [Rei87]. They mainly fall into two camps: consistency-based logics, such as default logic [Rei80] and autoepistemic logic [Moo85], and minimal model-based logics, such as various forms of circumscriptions[McC80, Lif85]. Understanding the relation between the two is important. It will not only enable us to compare the relative expressive powers of these logics, but it may also suggest a logic with the advantages of both approaches.

To compare the expressive powers of these logics, two questions are asked: can circumscription be expressed in default logic or autoepistemic logic, and vice versa.

The former question has been answered by Etherington [Eth87] and Konolige [Kon89]. Etherington showed that circumscription can be translated to default logic under the domain closure assumption. Konolige extended the autoepistemic logic so that it can handle 'quantifying-in', and then showed that circumscription can be translated to the extended autoepistemic logic.

The latter, expressing default logic in circumscription*[Gro84], seems to be more interesting. One of the reasons is that circumscription is within the framework of classical logic, which has been well-studied and has many known properties. In addition, circumscription avoids consistency checks; it seems more attractive computationally.

While it is desirable to express default logic in the existing forms of circumscription, it is, unfortunately, impossible to do so. Imielinski[Imi87] proved that default logic could not be modularly translated to circumscription in general. Informally, circumscription seems to correspond to default logic with a special form of default – that is, normal default without prerequisites. It has difficulty in expressing non-normal default, which is very useful in dealing with certain problems in common sense reasoning[Mor88, Gel88].

A natural question then, is whether it is possible to extend circumscription so that it has the expressive power of default logic. That is, is it possible to construct a "default logic" in the spirit of circumscription? Since circumscription is nothing but an axiomatization of a certain nonmonotonic reasoning in classical logic, the above question then becomes – is it possible to axiomatize the type of nonmonotonic reasoning permitted by consistency-based logics in terms of classical logic, without referring to modal operators, non-language expressions (such as defaults, which need consistency tests), and fixed points?

Some of the extensions of circumscription, such as autocircumscription[Per88] and introspective circumscription[Lif89], do extend the expressive power of circumscription. In particular, they can express certain non-normal defaults. However, a closer examination shows that they are still not as expressive as default logic or autoepistemic logic, in the sense that inconsistency may arise in some cases where default logic and/or autoepistemic logic are consistent†.

The results in this paper demonstrate that certain limitations of the expressive power of circumscription are not due to the language (first-order in most cases, plus a certain second-order formula) itself. Almost all the expressive power of default logic can be achieved by mere

*Since the equivalence between default logic and autoepistemic logic has been established[Kon87], the solution to the problem of expressing default logic in circumscription will automatically lead to the solution to a similar problem for autoepistemic logic.

†Application of autocircumscription or introspective circumscription to the Yale Shooting Problem in [Gel88]'s formulation is one of the examples.

classical logic with a fixed point operator. This further clarifies the relation between circumscription and default logic.

This paper is organized as follows. We begin with an informal discussion which leads to the formal definition and semantics of a *circumscriptive extension* for a default theory. We then show that the new formalism is indeed an extension of circumscription. We proceed to show that the circumscriptive extension and the original extension of default logic, as defined by Reiter[Rei80], are equivalent under the domain closure assumption and the unique names assumption. Finally, we show the applications of the new formalism to some well-known problems in default reasoning, problems that involve non-normal defaults.

2 Consistency, Minimization and Fixed Point

In this section, we discuss what is necessary and what is not necessary for default reasoning. We also suggest how circumscription can be extended so that it will have the expressive power of default logic.

Classical logic allows us to represent our knowledge about the world by sentences of a logical language and to derive more facts about the world through its deductive system. However, our knowledge about the world is in most cases incomplete. To fill in the gaps, assumptions are often made in default reasoning. These assumptions are often based on what is known, as well as what is not known. In order to formalize this, nonmonotonic logic augments the classical logic with certain mechanisms which can permit assumptions to be made under certain conditions.

In default logic, rules called "default" are used for this purpose. A default correctly captures the patterns in default reasoning: assume γ whenever α is known and $\neg\beta$ is not known. Although a default looks simple, it turns out to be quite expressive. For instance, Konolige [Kon87] shows that every set of sentences in autoepistemic logic, which involve complicated constructions as embedded L-operators, can be effectively rewritten as a default theory. However, default logic departs from classical logic in that it expresses the defaults neither in the language of classical logic, nor as inference rules. Also, default logic requires an explicit consistency test, which is not even semidecidable.

On the other hand, circumscription is a second-order formula, which means that it requires nothing more than classical logic. In particular, ignorance of knowledge is detected by formula or predicate minimization instead of by an explicit consistency test. Circumscription seems, however, incapable of expressing non-normal defaults. The main reason is that it always forces the predicate circumscribed to be minimal in itself. In fact, finding a minimal extension of a formula (or a maximal extension of the negation of the formula) is very closely related to the consistency test of a formula. Consider a sentence T and a predicate Q, for an individual a in the universe. $T \not\vdash \neg Q(\dot{a})$ ($Q(\dot{a})$ is consistent with T) is equivalent to the following: there exists a model M of T, such that $M \models Q(\dot{a})$. Assuming that models of T have the same universe and denotation functions, a set of all a such that $T \not\vdash \neg Q(\dot{a})$ is clearly the union of extensions of Q in all those models [‡]. The union of all such extensions, similar to a minimal extension of a predicate, can be expressed by a second-order formula, which can be used as the basis for sanctioning other formulas. This will allow us to have a formalism with full expressive power of default logic but still within the classical logic. In addition, we will gain the ability to reason about open domain freely, as we shall show later.

In both default logic and autoepistemic logic, the consistency of a formula is tested globally (with respect to the final set of beliefs, instead of the premises). This is especially necessary when non-normal defaults are involved, because otherwise, inconsistency may arise when new assumptions are added. To test the consistency of a formula globally, the concept of a fixed point seems to be inevitable. The use of fixed point does not change the language itself, but it complicates the logic. It seems that this is the price we have to pay to gain the full expressive power of the default logic.

In what follows, we show how defaults can be represented by second-order formulas, and how an extension of a default theory can be defined as a fixed point.

3 Circumscriptive Extension

A *default* is an expression of the form $\alpha(\mathbf{x}) : \beta(\mathbf{x})/\gamma(\mathbf{x})$, where α ($\mathbf{x}$), β ($\mathbf{x}$) and γ ($\mathbf{x}$) are first-order formulas whose free variables are among those of $\mathbf{x} = x_1, ..., x_n$. In the rest of the paper, we will use x for $\mathbf{x}$, if confusion does not arise from the context. A default is *closed* iff α, β and γ contain no free variables; otherwise, it is *open*. A *default theory* is a pair (A, D) where A is a set of first-order sentences and D is a set of defaults. A default theory is open if at least one default in D is open.

Given a default theory (A, D), for each default $\alpha_i(x) : \beta_i(x)/\gamma_i(x) \in D$, we introduce new predicate constants P_i and Q_i and add an axiom $\forall x(\alpha_i(x) \leftrightarrow P_i(x)) \wedge \forall x(\beta_i(x) \leftrightarrow Q_i(x))$ to A. The default $\alpha_i(x) : \beta_i(x)/\gamma_i(x)$ can then be rewritten as $P_i(x) : Q_i(x)/\gamma_i(x)$. We assume that all default theories (A, D) in this paper have been rewritten in this way.

Let S,T be sentences. Let P_i, Q_i be some predicate constants in S,T and let Z be a tuple of all other predicate constants in S,T. We write $S(p_i, q_i, z)$ and $T(p_i, q_i, z)$ for the sentences resulting from substituting all occurrences of P_i, Q_i and Z by corresponding predicate variables p_i, q_i and corresponding tuple of predicate variables z, respectively.

Definition 3.1 *Given a default theory (A, D) where both A and D are finite, we define an operator Δ on two sentences S, T as follows:*
$\Delta(S,T) \equiv$

$$S \wedge \bigwedge_{P_i(x):Q_i(x)/\gamma_i(x)\in D} \forall x[\forall p_i q_i z(S(p_i, q_i, z) \rightarrow p_i(x)) \wedge \exists p_i q_i z(T(p_i, q_i, z) \wedge q_i(x)) \rightarrow \gamma_i(x)]$$

[‡]This discussion is informal. The intuition is formalized in lemmas 5.1 and 5.2 in section 5.

Definition 3.2 *Given a default theory (A, D) where both A and D are finite, let*

$$B_0 \equiv A$$
$$B_{j+1} \equiv \Delta(B_j, B).$$

A first-order sentence B is defined to be a circumscriptive extension *of (A, D) iff $Mod(B) = Mod(\bigcup_{j=0}^{\infty} B_j)$ where $Mod(T) = \{M | M \models T\}$.*

Informally, the sentence $\forall x[\forall p_i q_i z(S(p_i, q_i, z) \rightarrow p_i(x)) \wedge \exists p_i q_i z(T(p_i, q_i, z) \wedge q_i(x)) \rightarrow \gamma_i(x)]$ says that if $\alpha_i(x)$ follows from S and $\neg\beta_i(x)$ does not follow from T, then $\gamma_i(x)$ is true. By iterating with the operator Δ and defining circumscriptive extension as a fixed point of the iteration, we make sure that $\gamma_i(x)$ is in the circumscriptive extension whenever 1) $\alpha_i(x)$ can be derived only from the premises A and the assumptions which have been made up to each point of an iterative step, and 2) $\beta_i(x)$ is consistent with the circumscriptive extension.

We have the following proposition, which follows from definition 3.2 directly.

Proposition 3.1 [§] *If B is a circumscriptive extension of a default theory (A, D), then $Cn(B) = Cn(\bigcup_{i=0}^{\infty} B_i)$ where $Cn(T) = \{\varphi | \varphi$ is a first-order sentence and $T \models \varphi\}$.*

In what follows, we give some examples to illustrate the usage of circumscriptive extensions.

Example 1 Let $A \equiv P(a) \wedge P(b) \wedge (\neg P = Q)$ [¶]. and $D = \{: \neg P(x) / \neg P(x)\}$.

There is only one circumscriptive extension of (A, D), namely, $B \equiv A \wedge \forall x(x \neq a \wedge x \neq b \rightarrow \neg P(x))$. Note that this is exactly equivalent to circumscription of P in A.

Example 2 Let $A \equiv (P(a) \vee P(b)) \wedge (\neg P = Q)$ and $D = \{: \neg P(x) / \neg P(x)\}$.

There are two circumscriptive extension of (A, D), namely, $B_1 \equiv A \wedge \forall x(x \neq a \rightarrow \neg P(x))$ and $B_2 \equiv A \wedge \forall x(x \neq b \rightarrow \neg P(x))$. Note that $B_1 \vee B_2$ is equivalent to circumscription of P in A.

Example 3 Let $A \equiv T(a) \wedge T(b) \wedge B(a) \wedge a \neq b \wedge (\neg ab1 = Q_1) \wedge (\neg ab2 = Q_2)$. Let $D = \{T(x) : \neg ab1(x) / \neg F(x), B(x) : \neg ab2(x) / F(x), B(x) : \neg ab2(x) / ab1(x)\}$. This is a simplified version of the Bird Problem under Morris' formulation[Mor88]. Note that T stands for 'thing', B stands for 'bird', and F stands for 'fly'. There is a unique circumscriptive extension for this default theory (A,D), which is $B \equiv A \wedge \forall x(x = a \rightarrow F(x)) \wedge \forall x(x = b \rightarrow \neg F(x)) \wedge \forall x(x = a \rightarrow ab1(x))$. It follows that, $B \vdash \neg F(b)$ and $B \vdash F(a)$. Note that this problem involves non-normal defaults, which cannot be handled by ordinary circumscription.

Semantically, circumscriptive extension can be characterized as follows. Let A be a sentence, and P be a predicate constant. Let $Mod(A)$ be the class of all the models of A. Let M be a structure. Using the notations similar to that in [Lif89], let X be a set of tuples of elements in the universe of M such that the length of each tuple in X equals the arity of P. We write $M[X/P]$ for the structure which differs from M in that it interprets some or all predicate constants differently, in particular it interprets P as X. In addition, we use $M[\![P]\!]$ to denote the interpretation of P in M (sometimes P could be a wff); $|M|$ denotes the universe (domain) of M. Let $\mathcal{M}$ be a class of structures. We define a sequence of classes of structures in the following way: let

$$\mathcal{N}_0 = Mod(A)$$
$$\mathcal{N}_{j+1} = \Omega(\mathcal{N}_j, \mathcal{M})$$

where

$$\Omega(\mathcal{N}, \mathcal{M}) = \{M | M \in \mathcal{N} and \text{ for all } P_i(x) : Q_i(x)/\gamma_i(x) \in D \bigcap_{M[X_i/P_i] \in \mathcal{N}} X_i \cap \bigcup_{M[Y_i/Q_i] \in \mathcal{M}} Y_i \subseteq M[\![\gamma_i]\!]\}$$

Theorem 3.1 *A class of structures $\mathcal{M}$ is the class of all the models of a circumscriptive extension B of a default theory (A, D) iff $\mathcal{M} = \bigcap_{j=0}^{\infty} \mathcal{N}_j$.*

Proof Note that for any structure M,

$$M \models \forall x[\forall pqz(S(p, q, z) \rightarrow p(x)) \wedge \exists pqz(T(p, q, z) \wedge q(x)) \rightarrow \gamma(x)]$$

$$\Longleftrightarrow \bigcap_{M[X/P] \models S} X \cap \bigcup_{M[Y/Q] \models T} Y \subseteq M[\![\gamma]\!].$$

□

Note that, unlike the conventional semantics of classical logic, the satisfaction relation between *a* structure and a circumscriptive extension cannot be defined without referring to other structures. This is similar to modal logic where the satisfaction relation between a structure and a modal sentence is defined in terms of a set of possible worlds. However, in our case, the "possible worlds" are the very structures which satisfy the circumscriptive extension. Therefore, we define the class of all the models of a circumscriptive extension as a fixed point of a sequence of applications of the operator Ω. The operator $\Omega(\mathcal{N}, \mathcal{M})$ picks up the structures in $\mathcal{N}$ which satisfy the relation

$$\bigcap_{M[X_i/P_i] \in \mathcal{N}} X_i \cap \bigcup_{M[Y_i/Q_i] \in \mathcal{M}} Y_i \subseteq M[\![\gamma_i]\!]$$

for each default in D. Consider the structures with the same universe and interpretations for object and function constants as M. Let $\Omega_{\alpha_i}(M)$ be the intersection of extensions of P_i in all such structures in $\mathcal{N}$ and $\Omega_{\beta_i}(M)$ be the union of extensions of Q_i in all such structures in $\mathcal{M}$. $\Omega(\mathcal{N}, \mathcal{M})$ then picks up those structures in $\mathcal{N}$ such that the intersection of $\Omega_{\alpha_i}(M)$ and $\Omega_{\beta_i}(M)$ is a subset of the interpretation of γ_i in M for all defaults in D.

---

§Proofs of proposition, lemmas, and theorems are either omitted or sketched in this paper due to space restriction. Interested readers are referred to [Qia91]

¶$\neg P = Q$ stands for $\forall x(\neg P(x) \leftrightarrow Q(x))$. This conjunct is necessary for A, so that the wff $\neg P(x)$ in the default can be replaced by a new predicate constant Q.

4 Circumscriptive Extension and Circumscription

In this section, we will show that circumscriptive extension is indeed an extension of circumscription.

Circumscription exists in many different versions. Here, we compare circumscriptive extension with a model-theoretic definition of circumscription. Let A be a first-order sentence and P be a tuple of predicate constants to be circumscribed. Semantically, circumscription is defined as sentences that are true in all P-minimal models of A. Given two models M and N of A with the same domain and the same interpretations of object and function constants, $M \leq_P N$ if the extension of P_i in M is a subset of the extension of P_i in N for all P_i in P. A P-minimal model of A is then a model M of A minimal with respect to the relation $\leq_P$.

As we mentioned earlier, circumscription itself seems to correspond to a special case of default reasoning, namely, the default reasoning with defaults ": $\neg P(x)/\neg P(x)$." Let B_n be a circumscriptive extension of (A, D) where $D = \{: \neg P_i(x)/\neg P_i(x) | P_i \in P\}$. Obviously, B_n satisfies the following equation:

$Cn(B_n) \equiv$

$$Cn(A \wedge \bigwedge_{P_i \in P} \forall x [\exists p_i z (B_n(p_i, z) \wedge \neg p_i(x)) \rightarrow \neg P_i(x)])$$

Lemma 4.1 *Models of B_n are P-minimal models of A.*

Lemma 4.2 *If M is a P-minimal model of A, then M satisfies some B_n.*

Theorem 4.1 *A first-order formula φ is true in all P-minimal models of A iff it follows from all B_n.*

Proof The theorem follows directly from lemmas 4.1 and 4.2. □

Since the first-order sentences that follow from circumscription are true in all P-minimal models of A, circumscription corresponds to the sentences that follow from all circumscriptive extensions of $(A, \{: \neg P(x)/\neg P(x)\})$. This reflects the different attitude between default logic and circumscription towards nonmonotonic reasoning, as pointed out by [Eth87]. Default logic is a "brave" reasoner while circumscription is "cautious". In defining circumscriptive extension, we follow the "brave" approach of default logic. To be "cautious", one can always just believe the sentences that follow from all circumscriptive extensions.

In addition, in a more general definition of circumscription, some of the predicates are considered as variables and the others are fixed. While in translating default theory to circumscriptive extension, however, all the predicates are considered as variables. As has been proven in [DeK89], fixed predicates are not essential in circumscription. In other words, fixed predicates can be eliminated by circumscribing a slightly different set of axioms A, while allowing all predicates to vary. Because of this, the above results can be extended to circumscription with fixed variables.

5 Circumscriptive Extension and Default Logic Extension

In this section, we establish a relation between circumscriptive extension with default logic extension. First, we review the definition of an extension of a default theory.

Given a closed default theory (A, D), Reiter[Rei80] defines an extension of (A, D) as a fixed point of an operator Γ. For any set of wffs S, $\Gamma(S)$ is the smallest set such that: 1) it contains A, 2) it is closed under logical consequence, and 3) it contains γ whenever $\alpha : \beta/\gamma \in D$ and $\alpha \in \Gamma(S)$ and $\neg\beta \notin S$. An extension of an open default theory is defined as an extension of a closed default theory $(A, CLOSED(D))$, where $CLOSED(D)$ is a set of closed defaults resulting from instantiating each open default in D by ground terms constructible from all the object constants, function constants and the Skolem functions of the Skolemized form of the default theory.

It is obvious that, in default logic, the *domain closure assumption* (DCA) is implicitly made. The domain closure assumption essentially assumes that the domain contains only those individuals which are explicitly referred to in the theory. In circumscriptive extension, however, we do not make this assumption, and therefore, we can make conjectures about individuals in "open domain." For instance, the extension of the default theory for the example 1 is $Cn(A)$. No conjecture is made about individuals without names; whereas in circumscriptive extension, we have $\forall x(x \neq a \wedge x \neq b \rightarrow \neg P(x))$. However, comparison between circumscriptive extension and default theory extension can be made under DCA.

The other difference concerns equality. In default logic, one can make conjectures about equalities. For example, an extension of a default theory $(\phi, \{: a \neq b/a \neq b\})$ contains $a \neq b$. Etherington [Eth88] pointed out that circumscription has difficulty in deriving such a conjecture. The same is true for circumscriptive extension. In the above example, one needs to maximize inequality. However, $\Omega_\beta(M)$ gives us the union of extensions of β in different structures with the same universe and denotation functions. This will not enable us to pick up the structures which interpret a and b differently. Therefore, we add the *unique-names assumption* (UNA) explicitly, in order to compare default logic extension and circumscriptive extension. UNA says that each individual in the universe has a unique name.

One can express DCA and UNA in first-order logic if the language of default theory has a finite number of object constants and is function-free. In fact, DCA can be expressed by the first-order sentence $\forall x(x = c_1 \vee ... \vee x = c_n)$, where c_i's are the set of all object constants in the language, and UNA can be expressed by the conjunction of $c_i \neq c_j$ for each pair of distinct object constants in the language.

As discussed in the previous section, in circumscriptive extension, a second-order formula is used to replace the consistency test in the definition of extension in default logic. The first published result directly relating consistency test to first-order schema is in [Per88]. The following lemmas make this relation more general. They also establish the major link between circumscriptive extension and default logic extension.

Lemma 5.1 *Let T be a sentence. Let Q be a predicate constant in T, and let Z be a tuple of all other predicate constants in T. If $\exists qz(T(q, z) \wedge q(a))$ is satisfiable, then*

$T \not\models \neg Q(a)$.

Lemma 5.2 *Let T be a sentence such that $T \models DCA \wedge UNA$. Let Q, Z be the same as in lemma 5.1. If $T \not\models \neg Q(a)$ then $DCA \wedge UNA \models \exists qz(T(q,z) \wedge q(a))$.*

Proof Suppose $T \not\models \neg Q(a)$, then there exists a model M of T such that $M \models Q(a)$. For if this is not true, then for all model M of T, $M \models \neg Q(a)$. This means that $T \models \neg Q(a)$ which contradicts the hypothesis.

To show that $DCA \wedge UNA \models \exists q, z(T(q,z) \wedge q(a))$, it suffices to show that for all the models M of $DCA \wedge UNA$, $M \models \exists q, z(T(q,z) \wedge q(a))$. Let M be an arbitrary model of $DCA \wedge UNA$. From above, there exists a structure M' such that $M' \models T \wedge Q(a)$. In the following, we show that M' is isomorphic to M^* which is a structure the same as M except for the interpretation of all predicate constants in T.

Let f and g be functions which map all the ground terms in T to $|M|$ and $|M'|$ respectively. Since $T \models DCA \wedge UNA$ and since both M and M' satisfy $DCA \wedge UNA$, both f and g are bijections. Obviously f^{-1} exists and is a bijection too. Let $h = g \circ f^{-1}$. Since both g and f^{-1} are bijections, h is a bijection from M to M'. Let M^* be a structure, the same as M, except that it interprets the predicate symbols in the following way. For n-place predicate symbol Q, and for each n-tuple $< a_1, ..., a_n >$ of elements of $|M^*|$,

$$< a_1, ..., a_n > \in M^*[\![Q]\!] \text{ iff } < h(a_1), ..., h(a_n) > \in M'[\![Q]\!]$$

Similarly, for each n-place predicate symbol P in Z,

$$< a_1, ..., a_n > \in M^*[\![P]\!] \text{ iff } < h(a_1), ..., h(a_n) > \in M'[\![P]\!]$$

Since M^* has the same domain and interpretation of all the constant symbols as M, for all i, $h(M^*[\![c_i]\!]) = M'[\![c_i]\!]$. Clearly, h is an isomorphism from M^* onto M'. Hence, M' and M^* are isomorphic. Therefore, they are elementarily equivalent and since $M' \models T \wedge Q(a)$, $M^* \models T \wedge Q(a)$. Let $X = M^*[\![Q]\!]$ and $Y = M^*[\![Z]\!]$, then $M[X/Q, Y/Z] = M^* \cong M'$. Since $M[X/Q, Y/Z] \models T(Q,Z) \wedge Q(a)$, $M \models \exists qz(T(q,z) \wedge q(a))$. Since M is an arbitrary model of $DCA \wedge UNA$, $DCA \wedge UNA \models \exists qz(T(q,z) \wedge q(a))$. □

To establish the relation between circumscriptive extension and extension as defined in default logic, we also need the following lemmas.

Lemma 5.3 *Let T be a sentence. Let P be a predicate constant in T, and let Z be a tuple of all other predicate constants in T. If $T \models P(a)$ then $\forall pz(T(p,z) \rightarrow p(a))$.*

Lemma 5.4 *Let T be a sentence such that $T \models DCA \wedge UNA$. Let P, Z be the same as in lemma 5.3. if there is a structure M such that $M \models DCA \wedge UNA$, and $M \models \forall pz(T(p,z) \rightarrow p(a))$, then $T \models P(a)$.*

Proof Similar to the proof of lemma 5.2. □

Now, we are able to present the theorem which shows that circumscriptive extension and default theory extension are equivalent under DCA and UNA.

Theorem 5.1 *Given a default theory (A, D) where $A \models DCA \wedge UNA$. A finitely axiomatizable theory E is an extension of $(A, CLOSED(D))$ iff $E = Cn(B)$ and B is a circumscriptive extension of (A, D).*

The theorem demonstrates that circumscriptive extension essentially has the same expressive power as extension except for UNA. Specifically, circumscriptive extension can handle non-normal defaults. Moreover, it can also make conjectures about individuals in open domain.

6 Applications

Example 4 (Yale Shooting Problem)

This is a well known problem suggested by Hanks and McDermott [HaM87] to demonstrate that nonmonotonic logics have difficulty in reasoning about a class of problems including the frame problem. It essentially shows that for this problem, two extensions could be derived using either default logic or circumscription. While one extension corresponds to intuition, the other is counterintuitive. Morris [Mor88]presented a simple solution to the problem. He used standard default logic. The only difference between his and Hanks and McDermott's formulations is that Morris used non-normal default to represent frame axiom. Gelfond [Gel88] also showed that the Yale shooting problem could be solved by autoepistemic logic using a formulation similar to that of Morris. Below, we show a solution to this problem by finding the circumscriptive extension for a default theory under Morris' formulation. Axioms A is a conjunction of UNA and the followings:

$$t(ALIVE, S_0) \quad (1)$$
$$\forall s(t(LOADED, result(LOAD, s))) \quad (2)$$
$$\forall s(t(LOADED, s) \rightarrow ab(ALIVE, SHOOT, s)) \quad (3)$$
$$\forall s(t(LOADED, s) \rightarrow t(DEAD, result(SHOOT, s))) \quad (4)$$

Also, there is a set of actions:

$$S_1 = result(LOAD, S_0) \quad (5)$$
$$S_2 = result(WAIT, S_1) \quad (6)$$
$$S_3 = result(SHOOT, S_2) \quad (7)$$

We have one default for the frame axiom:

$$t(f,s) : \neg ab(f,e,s)/t(f, result(e,s)) \quad (8)$$

For this default theory (A, D), there is a unique circumscriptive extension.

$$\begin{aligned} A \wedge \forall f,e,s(\quad & (f = ALIVE \wedge (s = S_0 \vee s = S_1 \vee s = S_2)) \vee \\ & (f = LOADED \wedge s \neq S_0) \vee \\ & (f = DEAD \wedge (s \neq S_0 \wedge s \neq S_1 \wedge s \neq S_2)) \wedge \\ & \neg(f = ALIVE \wedge e = SHOOT \wedge s \neq S_0)) \\ & \rightarrow t(f, result(s))) \end{aligned}$$

Obviously, $t(DEAD, S_3)$ is in the circumscriptive extension. Notice that inconsistency will arise for both this and the next examples, when introspective circumscription and autocircumscription are applied.

Example 5 (Nixon Diamond)

This is another well known example originally suggested by Reiter to demonstrate the situation of multiple extensions. Using non-normal defaults, it can be formulated as follows:

$$Quaker(nixon) \wedge Republican(nixon) \quad (9)$$
$$quaker \neq republican \quad (10)$$
$$Quaker(x) : \neg ab(x, quaker, pacifist)/ \; Pacifist(x) \quad (11)$$
$$Republican(x) : \neg ab(x, republican, pacifist)/ \; \neg Pacifist(x) \quad (12)$$
$$Quaker(x) : \neg ab(x, quaker, pacifist)/ \; ab(x, republican, pacifist) \quad (13)$$
$$Republican(x) : \neg ab(x, republican, pacifist)/ \; ab(x, quaker, pacifist) \quad (14)$$

where A is a conjunction of (9) and (10), and D contains (11) to (14).

There are two circumscriptive extensions for this default theory.

$$B_1 \equiv A \wedge \forall x(x = nixon \rightarrow (Pacifist(x) \wedge ab(x, republican, pacifist)))$$
$$B_2 \equiv A \wedge \forall x(x = nixon \rightarrow (\neg Pacifist(x) \wedge ab(x, quaker, pacifist)))$$

7 Conclusion

In this paper, we constructed a "default logic" in the spirit of circumscription. We showed that it is indeed an extension of circumscription and it has the expressive power of default logic. These lead us to conclude that: 1. Default logic can be expressed by classical logic with a fixed point operator. Certain syntactic structures in consistency-based logics such as modal operator, non-language expressions like defaults, and consistency test are not essential. Fixed point construction, however, is necessary. 2. The method of circumscription provides some flexibility in reasoning about "open domain". 3. Our extension of circumscription still cannot conjecture the unique-names assumption‖.

References

[DeK89] de Kleer, J., Konolige, K.,"Eliminating the Fixed Predicates from a Circumscription", *Artificial Intelligence* **39** (1989)

[Eth87] Etherington, D. W., "Relating Default Logic and Circumscription", *Proceedings IJCAI 87*, Milan, Italy, (1987)

[Eth88] Etherington, D. W., *Reasoning with Incomplete Information*, Morgan Kaufmann (1988)

[Gel88] Gelfond, M., " Autoepistemic Logic and Formalization of Commonsense Reasoning:Preliminary Report", *Proceedings Non-Monotonic Reasoning: 2nd. International Workshop*, Grassau, FRG (1988)

[Gro84] Grosof, B., "Default Reasoning as Circumscription", *Proceedings Non-Monotonic Reasoning Workshop*, Mohonk Mountain House, New Paltz, NY (1984)

[HaM87] Hanks,S., McDermott, D. "Nonmonotonic Logic and Temporal Projection", *Artificial Intelligence* **33** (1987)

[Imi87] Imielinski, T., "Results on Translating Defaults to Circumscription", *Artificial Intelligence***32** (1987)

[Kon87] Konolige, K., "On the Relation between Default Theories and Autoepistemic Logic" *Proceedings IJCAI 87*, Milan, Italy, (1987)

[Kon89] Konolige, K., "On the Relation between Autoepistemic Logic and Circumscription:Preliminary Report", *Proceedings IJCAI 89*, Detroit, Michigan, (1989)

[Lif85] Lifschitz, V. "Computing Circumscription", *Proceedings IJCAI 85*, Los Angeles, CA (1985)

‖An extension of circumscription which does that can be found in [RaW89].

[Lif89] Lifschitz, V., "Between Circumscription and Autoepistemic Logic", *Proceedings KR'89*, Toronto, Ontario, (1989)

[McC80] McCarthy, J., "Circumscription - A Form of Non-Monotonic Reasoning", *Artificial Intelligence* **13** (1980)

[McC86] McCarthy, J., "Applications of Circumscription to Formalizing Common-Sense Knowledge", *Artificial Intelligence* **28** (1986)

[Moo85] Moore, R., "Semantical Considerations on Nonmonotonic Logic", *Artificial Intelligence* **25** (1985)

[Mor88] Morris, P. H., "The Anomalous Extension Problem in Default Reasoning", *Artificial Intelligence* **35** (1988)

[Per88] Perlis, D. "Autocircumscription", *Artificial Intelligence* **36** (1988)

[Qia91] Qian, Z. "Nonmonotonic Reasoning: Semantics and Applications to Induction" Ph. D. thesis, The University of Michigan, Ann Arbor, forthcoming

[RaW89] Rathmann, P. K., Winslett, M., "Circumscribing Equality" , *Proceedings IJCAI 89*, Detroit, Michigan, (1989)

[Rei80] Reiter, R., "A Logic for Default Reasoning", *Artificial Intelligence* **13** (1980)

[Rei87] Reiter, R., "Nonmonotonic Reasoning", in *Annual Reviews of Computer Science* **2** (1987)

KNOWLEDGE REPRESENTATION

Concept Languages

Augmenting Concept Languages by Transitive Closure of Roles: An Alternative to Terminological Cycles

Franz Baader*
German Research Center for Artificial Intelligence
Projektgruppe WINO, Postfach 2080
W-6750 Kaiserslautern, Germany
baader@dfki.uni-kl.de

Abstract

In Baader (1990,1990a), we have considered different types of semantics for terminologicial cycles in the concept language $\mathcal{FL}_0$ which allows only conjunction of concepts and value-restrictions. It turned out that greatest fixed-point semantics (gfp-semantics) seems to be most appropriate for cycles in this language. In the present paper we shall show that the concept defining facilities of $\mathcal{FL}_0$ with cyclic definitions and gfp-semantics can also be obtained in a different way. One may replace cycles by role definitions involving union, composition, and transitive closure of roles.

This proposes a way of retaining, in an extended language, the pleasant features of gfp-semantics for $\mathcal{FL}_0$ with cyclic definitions without running into the troubles caused by cycles in larger languages. Starting with the language $\mathcal{ALC}$ of Schmidt-Schauß&Smolka (1988)—which allows negation, conjunction and disjunction of concepts as well as value-restrictions and exists-in-restrictions—we shall disallow cyclic concept definitions, but instead shall add the possibility of role definitions involving union, composition, and transitive closure of roles. In contrast to other terminological KR-systems which incorporate the transitive closure operator for roles, we shall be able to give a sound and complete algorithm for concept subsumption.

1 Introduction

In knowledge representation (KR) languages based on KL-ONE (Brachman&Schmolze (1985)), one starts with atomic concepts and roles, and can use the language formalism to define new concepts and roles. Concepts can be considered as unary predicates which are interpreted as sets of individuals whereas roles are binary predicates which are interpreted as binary relations between individuals. The languages (e.g., $\mathcal{FL}$ and $\mathcal{FL}^-$ of Levesque&Brachman (1987), $\mathcal{TF}$ and $\mathcal{NTF}$ of Nebel (1990)) differ in what kind of constructs are allowed for the definition of concepts and roles. Their common feature—besides the use of concepts and roles—is that the meaning of the constructs is defined with the help of a model-theoretic semantics. Most of these languages do not go beyond the scope of first-order predicate logic, and they usually have very restricted formalisms for defining roles.

However, for many applications it would be very useful to have means for expressing things like transitive closure of roles. For example, if we have a role child (resp. is-direct-part-of) we might want to use its transitive closure offspring (resp. is-part-of) in order to define concepts like "man who has only male offsprings" (resp. "car which has only functioning parts"). Obviously, we cannot just introduce a new role offspring without enforcing the appropriate relationship between offspring and child. Since the transitive closure of binary relations cannot be expressed in first-order predicate logic (see Aho&Ullman (1979)), the concept languages mentioned above cannot be used for that purpose.

There are two possibilities to overcome this problem. On the one hand, one may introduce a new role-forming operator trans, and define its semantics such that, for any role R, trans(R) is interpreted as the transitive closure of R. This operator is e.g. contained in the terminological representation language LOOM (MacGregor&Bates (1987)). However, LOOM does not have a complete algorithm to determine subsumption relationships between concepts.

On the other hand, cyclic concept definitions together with an appropriate fixed-point semantics can be used to express value-restrictions with respect to the transitive closure of roles (see Baader (1990,1990a)). However, cyclic definitions are prohibited in most terminological knowledge representation languages because, from a theoretical point of view, their semantics is not clear and, from a practical point of view, existing inference algorithms cannot handle cycles.

The first thorough investigation of cycles in terminological knowledge representation languages can be found in Nebel (1990,1990a). Nebel has introduced three different kinds of semantics—namely, least fixed-point semantics (lfp-semantics), greatest fixed-point semantics (gfp-semantics), and what he called descriptive semantics—for cyclic definitions in his language $\mathcal{NTF}$. Baader (1990,1990a) considers terminological cycles in a small KL-ONE-based language which allows only concept conjunctions and value-restrictions. For this language, which will be called $\mathcal{FL}_0$ in the following, the effect of the three above mentioned types of semantics can be completely described with the help of finite automata. As a consequence, subsumption determination for each type of semantics can be reduced to a well-known decision problem for finite automata. For the language $\mathcal{FL}_0$, the gfp-semantics comes off best. The characterization of this

* This work was supported by the German "Bundesministerium für Forschung und Technologie" under Grant ITW 8903 0.

semantics is easy and has an obvious intuitive interpretation. It also shows that gfp-semantics is the appropriate semantics for expressing value-restrictions with respect to the transitive closure of roles.

However, the results described in Baader (1990a) have two major drawbacks which we intend to overcome in the present paper. First, the language $\mathcal{FL}_0$ is too small to be sufficient for practical purposes. As shown in Baader (1990), the results can be extended to the language $\mathcal{FL}^-$ of Levesque&Brachman (1987), and it seems to be relatively easy to include number-restrictions. However, as soon as we also consider disjunction of concepts and exists-in-restrictions (see Def. 2.1), the unpleasant features which lfp-semantics had for $\mathcal{FL}_0$ (see Baader (1990,1990a)) also occur for gfp-semantics in this larger language. If we should like to have general negation of concepts, least or greatest fixed-points may not even exist, thus rendering fixed-point semantics impossible.

Second, the characterization of gfp-semantics for $\mathcal{FL}_0$—though relatively easy and intuitive—still involves notions from formal language theory such as regular languages and finite automata. In the present paper we shall show that the concept defining facilities of $\mathcal{FL}_0$ with cyclic definitions and gfp-semantics can also be obtained in a different way. One may prohibit cycles and instead allow role definitions using union, composition, and transitive closure of roles. The regular languages which occur in the characterization of gfp-semantics for $\mathcal{FL}_0$ can directly be translated into role definitions in this new language.

This proposes a way of retaining, in an extended language, the pleasant features of gfp-semantics for $\mathcal{FL}_0$ with cyclic definitions without running into the troubles caused by cycles in larger languages. Starting with the language $\mathcal{ALC}$ of Schmidt-Schauß&Smolka (1988)—which allows negation, conjunction and disjunction of concepts as well as value-restrictions and exists-in-restrictions—we shall disallow cyclic concept definitions, but instead shall add the possibility of role definitions involving union, composition, and transitive closure of roles. In contrast to other terminological KR-systems which incorporate the transitive closure operator for roles, we shall be able to give a sound and complete algorithm for concept subsumption.

Because of the space limitations it is not possible to include a complete formal description of this algorithm into the present paper. Instead we shall first recall by an example how the subsumption algorithm for $\mathcal{ALC}$ works. It will then be explained how the ideas underlying this algorithm can be generalized to the extended language. Two more examples will be used to demonstrate what kind of new problems may occur. A complete description of the algorithm, together with the proof of its correctness can be found in Baader (1990b).

2 The Languages $\mathcal{ALC}$ and $\mathcal{FL}_0$

The language which we shall use as a starting point for the extension described in Section 4 is called "attributive concept description language with unions and complements", for short $\mathcal{ALC}$ (Schmidt-Schauß&Smolka (1988)). The reason for choosing $\mathcal{ALC}$ was that it is large enough to exhibit most of the problems connected with such an extension. Taking a larger language (e.g., including number restrictions) would only mean more work without bringing new insights.

Definition 2.1. (concept terms and terminologies)
Let **C** be a set of concept names and **R** be a set of role names. The set of *concept terms* of $\mathcal{ALC}$ is inductively defined. As a starting point of the induction, any element of C is a concept term (*atomic terms*). Now let C and D be concept terms already defined, and let R be a role name. Then C ⊓ D (*conjunction*), C ⊔ D (*disjunction*), ¬C (*negation*), ∀R:C (*value-restriction*), and ∃R:C (*exists-in-restriction*) are concept terms.
Let A be a concept name and let D be a concept term. Then A = D is a terminological axiom. A *terminology* (T-box) is a finite set of terminological axioms with the additional restriction that no concept name may appear more than once as a left hand side of a definition. ❑

The sublanguage $\mathcal{FL}_0$ of $\mathcal{ALC}$ is defined as follows: the concept defining operators are restricted to concept conjunction and value-restriction.

A T-box T contains two different kinds of concept names. *Defined concepts* occur on the left hand side of a terminological axiom of T. The other concepts are called *primitive concepts*. Cycles in terminologies are defined as follows. Let A, B be concept names and let T be a T-box. We say that A *directly uses* B in T iff B appears on the right hand side of the definition of A. Let *uses* denote the transitive closure of the relation *directly uses*. Then T contains a *terminological cycle* iff there exists a concept name A in T such that A uses A

For example, assume that we want to describe all "aliens having only melmacian ancestors on the mother's side", using the primitive roles father, mother, and the primitive concepts Alien, Melmacian. In $\mathcal{FL}_0$, this concept (for short Mam) is defined by the cyclic terminology Mam = Alien ⊓ ∀mother:Ma, Ma = Melmacian ⊓ ∀mother:Ma ⊓ ∀father:Ma, which introduces the auxiliary concept Ma for "aliens having only melmacian ancestors".

The next definition gives a model-theoretic semantics for the language introduced in Definition 2.1.

Definition 2.2. (interpretations and models)
An *interpretation* I consists of a set dom(I), the domain of the interpretation, and an interpretation function which associates with each concept name A a subset A^I of dom(I), and with each role name R a binary relation R^I on dom(I), i.e., a subset of dom(I) × dom(I).
The interpretation function—which gives an interpretation for atomic terms—can be extended to arbitrary terms as follows: Let C, D be concept terms and R be a role name. Assume that C^I and D^I are already defined. Then $(C \sqcap D)^I := C^I \cap D^I$, $(C \sqcup D)^I := C^I \cup D^I$, $(\neg C)^I := \mathrm{dom}(I) \setminus C^I$, $(\forall R{:}C)^I := \{x \in \mathrm{dom}(I);$ for all y such that $(x,y) \in R^I$ we have $y \in C^I\}$, and $(\exists R{:}C)^I := \{x \in \mathrm{dom}(I);$ there exists y such that $(x,y) \in R^I$ and $y \in C^I\}$.
An interpretation I is a *model* of the T-box T iff it satisfies $A^I = D^I$ for all terminological axioms A = D in T. ❑

An important service terminological representation systems provide is computing the *subsumption hierarchy*.

Let T be a terminology and let A, B be concept names. Then we say that B *subsumes* A with respect to T (symbolically $A \sqsubseteq_T B$) iff $A^I \subseteq B^I$ for all models I of T.

3 Extensions of $\mathcal{FL}_0$

The semantics we have given in Definition 2.2 is not restricted to non-cyclic terminologies. But for cyclic terminologies this kind of semantics, which will be called *descriptive semantics* in the following, turns out to be unsatisfactory (see Baader (1990a), Example 2.3). For this reason, alternative types of semantics for terminological cycles have been considered, namely *greatest fixed-point semantics* (gfp-semantics) and *least fixed-point semantics* (lfp-semantics). Roughly speaking, gfp-semantics (lfp-semantics) means that, with respect to a given interpretation of the primitive concepts and roles, the defined concepts are interpreted as large (small) as possible in gfp-models (lfp-models) of the terminology (see Nebel (1990,1990a) or Baader (1990,1990a) for details).

In Baader (1990,1990a) it was shown that a finite automaton $\mathcal{A}_T$ can be associated to each terminology T of $\mathcal{FL}_0$. The alphabet of $\mathcal{A}_T$ is the set $\mathbf{R}_T$ of all role names occurring in T, the states of $\mathcal{A}_T$ are the concept names occurring in T, and the transitions of $\mathcal{A}_T$ are defined by the terminological axioms of T (see Baader (1990,1990a) for details). This automaton was used to describe the effect of the three above mentioned types of semantics with the help of well-known notions from automata theory. The characterization of gfp-semantics is easy, and it involves only regular languages over the alphabet of role names. More precisely, the automaton $\mathcal{A}_T$ defines a regular languages L(A,B) for each pair of concepts A, B occurring in T. For an interpretation I and a word $W = R_1R_2...R_n$ over $\mathbf{R}_T$, W^I denotes the composition $R_1{}^I \circ R_2{}^I \circ ... \circ R_n{}^I$ of the binary relations $R_1{}^I, R_2{}^I, ..., R_n{}^I$. For the empty word ε, ε^I denotes the identity relation, i.e., $\varepsilon^I = \{(d,d);\ d \in dom(I)\}$.

Theorem 3.1. Let T be a terminology of $\mathcal{FL}_0$, and let $\mathcal{A}_T$ be the corresponding automaton. Let I be a gfp-model of T, and let A be a concept name occurring in T.
For any $d \in dom(I)$ we have $d \in A^I$ iff for all primitive concepts P, all words $W \in L(A,P)$, and all individuals $e \in dom(I)$, $(d,e) \in W^I$ implies $e \in P^I$. ❑

In our example which is about aliens from Melmac, we have L(Mam,Melmacian) = (mother(father∪mother)*)

The characterization in Theorem 3.1 means that, if we start with an individual d = ALF and consider first his mother, and then arbitrarily mothers or fathers of the individuals already obtained, then ALF is an alien having only melmacian ancestors on the mother's side if and only if all the individuals reached that way come from Melmac.

Theorem 3.1 motivates the definition of regular value-restrictions in the following "regular extension" of $\mathcal{FL}_0$.

Definition 3.2. (1) Let L be a regular language over the set of role names, and let C be a concept term already defined. Then $\forall L{:}C$ is a *regular value-restriction*. Its semantics is defined as $(\forall L{:}C)^I := \{d \in dom(I);$ for all words $W \in L$ and all individuals $e \in dom(I)$, $(d,e) \in W^I$ implies $e \in C^I\}$.

(2) In the *regular extension* $\mathcal{FL}_{reg}$ of $\mathcal{FL}_0$ we allow to use regular value-restrictions and concept conjunction as concept forming operators. ❑

Theorem 3.1 implies that, with respect to gfp-semantics, cyclic terminologies of $\mathcal{FL}_0$ can be expressed by acyclic terminologies of $\mathcal{FL}_{reg}$. On the other hand, it can be shown that any acyclic terminology of $\mathcal{FL}_{reg}$ can be expressed by a possibly cyclic terminology of $\mathcal{FL}_0$. Moreover, any cyclic terminology of $\mathcal{FL}_{reg}$ (considered with gfp-semantics) can be transformed into an equivalent acyclic terminology of $\mathcal{FL}_{reg}$ (Baader (1990b)). In our example, we can describe Mam by the following concept term of $\mathcal{FL}_{reg}$:

Alien ⊓ ∀(mother(father∪mother)*):Melmacian

Proposition 3.3. Possibly cyclic terminologies of $\mathcal{FL}_0$ considered with gfp-semantics, acyclic terminologies of $\mathcal{FL}_{reg}$, and possibly cyclic terminologies of $\mathcal{FL}_{reg}$ considered with gfp-semantics have the same expressive power. ❑

In place of cyclic definitions or regular languages in value-restrictions, we shall now allow role terms involving union, composition and transitive closure of roles in the following "transitive extension" of $\mathcal{FL}_0$. All these role forming operators have already been considered in KL-ONE based systems, though not necessarily together. It will turn out that we get a language having exactly the same expressiveness as $\mathcal{FL}_{reg}$.

Definition 3.4. (1) Let **R** be a set of role names. The set of *role terms* is inductively defined as follows. As a starting point of the induction, any role name is a role term (*atomic role*), and the symbol Ø is a role term (*empty role*). Now assume that R and S are role terms already defined. Then R ⊔ S (*union*), R∘S (*composition*), and trans(R) (*transitive closure*) are role terms. The semantics of the role forming operators is defined in the obvious way: $Ø^I := Ø$, $(R \sqcup S)^I := R^I \cup S^I$, $(R \circ S)^I := R^I \circ S^I$, and $(trans(R))^I := \bigcup_{n\geq 1}(R^I)^n$, i.e., $(trans(R))^I$ is the transitive closure of R^I.
(2) In the *transitive extension* $\mathcal{FL}_{trans}$ of $\mathcal{FL}_0$ we allow to use role terms instead of simply roles in value-restrictions. ❑

It is now easy to see that there is a direct correspondence between the regular languages in value-restrictions of $\mathcal{FL}_{reg}$ and the role terms in value-restrictions of $\mathcal{FL}_{trans}$. Consequently, acyclic (resp. cyclic) terminologies of $\mathcal{FL}_{trans}$ have the same expressive power as acyclic (resp. cyclic) terminologies of $\mathcal{FL}_{reg}$, and thus as possibly cyclic terminologies of $\mathcal{FL}_0$ considered with gfp-semantics.

In $\mathcal{FL}_{trans}$ we can use the following term to define the concept Mam of our example:

Alien ⊓ ∀mother:Melmacian ⊓
∀(mother∘trans(father⊔mother)):Melmacian.

4 The Extension of $\mathcal{ALC}$

In the previous section we have seen that the expressiveness of possibly cyclic terminologies of $\mathcal{FL}_0$ considered with gfp-semantics can also be obtained without involving cyclic definitions; we just have to include the appropriate role forming operators into the language. These role forming operators can now be integrated into the larger language $\mathcal{ALC}$ without causing any of the troubles we should have with cyclic definitions in $\mathcal{ALC}$.

Definition 4.1. (1) In the *transitive extension* $\mathcal{ALC}_{trans}$ of $\mathcal{ALC}$ we allow to use role terms (as defined in part (1) of Definition 3.4) instead of simply roles in value-restrictions and exists-in-restrictions. The semantics of $\mathcal{ALC}_{trans}$ is defined as in Definition 2.2 and 3.4.
(2) In the *regular extension* $\mathcal{ALC}_{reg}$ of $\mathcal{ALC}$ we allow to use regular value-restrictions and regular exists-in-restrictions in place of the usual restrictions of $\mathcal{ALC}$. The semantics of the regular value-restrictions is defined as in part (1) of Definition 3.2. The semantics of the regular exists-in-restrictions will be defined in a way such that $\neg(\exists L{:}C)$ is equivalent to $\forall L{:}(\neg C)$. That means that we define $(\exists L{:}C)^I := \{d \in dom(I)$; there exists a word $W \in L$ and an individual $e \in dom(I)$ such that $(d,e) \in W^I$ and $e \in C^I\}$. ❑

Please note that the regular exists-in-restriction is very similar to what is called "Functional Uncertainty" in computational linguistic (see Kaplan&Maxwell (1988)).

As for $\mathcal{FL}_{reg}$ and $\mathcal{FL}_{trans}$, acyclic terminologies of $\mathcal{ALC}_{trans}$ and acyclic terminologies of $\mathcal{ALC}_{reg}$ have the same expressive power. This shows that we may restrict our attention to one of these two languages. The definition of $\mathcal{ALC}_{trans}$ is more intuitive, and thus $\mathcal{ALC}_{trans}$ may be more appropriate if we want to apply the language to actual representation problems. But $\mathcal{ALC}_{reg}$ turns out to be more convenient for describing the subsumption algorithm. We can now state the main result of the paper.

Theorem 4.2. There exists a sound and complete algorithm for testing subsumption relationships w.r.t. acyclic terminologies of $\mathcal{ALC}_{reg}$ (or equivalently $\mathcal{ALC}_{trans}$). ❑

All the existing system which incorporate transitive closure of roles have only sound but incomplete algorithms, i.e., these algorithms may sometimes fail to detect subsumption relationships.

Since we only allow acyclic terminologies of $\mathcal{ALC}_{reg}$, subsumption with respect to terminologies can be reduced to subsumption of concept terms by expanding concept definitions (see e.g., Nebel (1990)). For two concept terms C, D we say that C is subsumed by D (symbolically $C \sqsubseteq D$) iff $C^I \subseteq D^I$ for all interpretations I. As for $\mathcal{ALC}$, the subsumption problem for concept terms can further be reduced to the satisfiability problem, where a concept term C is called satisfiable iff there exists an interpretation I such that $C^I \neq \emptyset$. In fact, for concept terms C, D and an interpretation I, we have $C^I \subseteq D^I$ iff $C^I \setminus D^I = \emptyset$, i.e., iff $(C \sqcap \neg D)^I = \emptyset$. This shows that C is subsumed by D iff $C \sqcap \neg D$ is unsatisfiable. Thus it is sufficient to have an algorithm which decides satisfiability of concept terms.

This algorithm will use the idea of constraint propagation, as proposed by Schmidt-Schauß&Smolka (1988) for $\mathcal{ALC}$, and successfully used by Hollunder et al. (1990) and Hollunder&Nutt (1990) for various other languages. However, an algorithm for $\mathcal{ALC}_{reg}$ has to treat regular restrictions of the form $\exists L{:}C$, $\forall L{:}C$ instead of simple restrictions $\exists R{:}C$, $\forall R{:}C$.

In order to clarify this difference, let us first recall by an example how satisfiability can be checked for concept terms of $\mathcal{ALC}$ (see Schmidt-Schauß&Smolka (1988), and Hollunder&Nutt (1990) for details).

4.1 The Satisfiability Test for $\mathcal{ALC}$

Assume that C is a concept term of $\mathcal{ALC}$ which has to be checked for satisfiability. In a first step we can push all negations as far as possible into the term using the fact that the terms $\neg\neg D$ and D, $\neg(D \sqcap E)$ and $\neg D \sqcup \neg E$, $\neg(D \sqcup E)$ and $\neg D \sqcap \neg E$, $\neg(\exists R{:}D)$ and $\forall R{:}(\neg D)$, as well as $\neg(\forall R{:}D)$ and $\exists R{:}(\neg D)$ are equivalent. We end up with a term C' in negation normal form where negation is only applied to concept names.

Example 4.3. Assume that we want to know whether the term $\exists R{:}A \sqcap \exists R{:}B$ is subsumed by $\exists R{:}(A \sqcap B)$. That means that we have to check whether the term $C := \exists R{:}A \sqcap \exists R{:}B \sqcap \neg(\exists R{:}(A \sqcap B))$ is unsatisfiable. The negation normal form of C is the term $C' := \exists R{:}A \sqcap \exists R{:}B \sqcap \forall R{:}(\neg A \sqcup \neg B)$.

In a second step, we try to construct a finite interpretation I such that $C'^I \neq \emptyset$. That means that there has to exist an individual in dom(I) which is an element of C'^I. Thus the algorithm generates such an individual b and imposes the constraint $b \in C'^I$ on it. In the example, this means that b has to satisfy the following constraints: $b \in (\exists R{:}A)^I$, $b \in (\exists R{:}B)^I$, and $b \in (\forall R{:}(\neg A \sqcup \neg B))^I$.

From $b \in (\exists R{:}A)^I$ we can deduce that there has to exist an individual c such that $(b,c) \in R^I$ and $c \in A^I$. Analogously, $b \in (\exists R{:}B)^I$ implies the existence of an individual d with $(b,d) \in R^I$ and $d \in B^I$. We should not assume that c = d since this would possibly impose too many constraints on the individuals newly introduced to satisfy the exists-in-restrictions on b. Thus the algorithm introduces for any exists-in-restriction a new individual as role-successor, and this individual has to satisfy the constraints expressed by the restriction.

Since b also has to satisfy the value-restriction $\forall R{:}(\neg A \sqcup \neg B)$, and c, d were introduced as R^I-successors of b, we also get the constraints $c \in (\neg A \sqcup \neg B)^I$, and $d \in (\neg A \sqcup \neg B)^I$. Now c has to satisfy the constraints $c \in A^I$ and $c \in (\neg A \sqcup \neg B)^I$ whereas d has to satisfy the constraints $d \in B^I$ and $d \in (\neg A \sqcup \neg B)^I$. Thus the algorithm uses value-restrictions in interaction with already defined role-relationships to impose new constraints on individuals.

Now $c \in (\neg A \sqcup \neg B)^I$ means that $c \in (\neg A)^I$ or $c \in (\neg B)^I$, and we have to choose one of these possibilities. If we assume $c \in (\neg A)^I$, this clashes with the other constraint $c \in A^I$. Thus we have to choose $c \in (\neg B)^I$. Analogously, we have to choose $d \in (\neg A)^I$ in order to satisfy the constraint $d \in (\neg A \sqcup \neg B)^I$ without creating a contradiction to $d \in B^I$. Thus, for disjunctive constraints, the algorithm tries both possibilities in successive attempts. It has to backtrack, if it reaches a contradiction, i.e., if the same individual has to satisfy complementary constraints.

In the example, we have now satisfied all the constraints without getting a contradiction. This shows that C' is satisfiable, and thus $\exists R{:}A \sqcap \exists R{:}B$ is not subsumed by

$\exists$R:(A $\sqcap$ B). We have generated an interpretation I as witness for this fact: dom(I) = {b, c, d}; R^I = {(b,c), (b,d)}; A^I = {c} and B^I = {d}. For this interpretation, b $\in$ C'^I. That means that b $\in$ ($\exists$R:A $\sqcap$ $\exists$R:B)^I, but b $\notin$ ($\exists$R:(A $\sqcap$ B))^I.

Termination of the algorithm is ensured by the fact that the newly introduced constraints are always smaller than the constraints which enforced their introduction.

4.2 The Generalization to $\mathcal{ALC}_{reg}$

A satisfiability algorithm for $\mathcal{ALC}_{reg}$ has to treat regular restrictions of the form $\exists$L:C and $\forall$L:C instead of simple restrictions $\exists$R:C and $\forall$R:C. In order to satisfy a constraint of the form b $\in$ ($\exists$R:C)^I, the algorithm described above introduces a new individual c which has to satisfy bR^Ic and c $\in$ C^I. This is not so easy if we have to satisfy a regular constraint of the form b $\in$ ($\exists$L:C)^I. All we know is that there has to exist some word W $\in$ L and an individual c such that bW^Ic and c $\in$ C^I. But we do not know which W does the job, and if L is infinite, there are infinitely many canditates. Thus trying them one after another will not do.

Obviously, the concept terms $\exists$L:C and C $\sqcup$ $\exists$(L \ {ε}):C are equivalent. For that reason we may without loss of generality assume that L does not contain the empty word. Thus the correct word W $\in$ L has some role symbol R as its first symbol. That means that there exists a word U such that W = RU. The alphabet of role symbols over which L is built is finite, and thus there are only finitely many possibilities for choosing a symbol R. Once we have chosen R, we still do not know which word U does the job. All we know about U is that it is an element of the set $R^{-1}L$:= {V; RV $\in$ L}.

Definition 4.4. Let L be a language and let W be a word. The left quotient $W^{-1}L$ of L with respect to W is defined as $W^{-1}L$:= { V; WV $\in$ L }. ❑

For a regular language L, the language $W^{-1}L$ is also regular (see Eilenberg (1974), p. 37), and obviously, this is also true for $W^{-1}L$ \ {ε}. For words V, W we have $(VW)^{-1}L$ = $W^{-1}(V^{-1}L)$. For example, let L be the regular language $(RS)^+$. Then $R^{-1}L$ = $S(RS)^*$, $S^{-1}L$ = Ø, and $(RS)^{-1}L$ = $S^{-1}(R^{-1}L)$ = $(RS)^*$.

In the satisfiability test, we can now choose between two possibilities: U $\in$ $R^{-1}L$ can be the empty word (provided that R $\in$ L) or U can be nonempty (provided that $R^{-1}L$ \ {ε} ≠ Ø). If we assume U = ε, then the new individual c has to satisfy bR^Ic and c $\in$ C^I, and the exists-in-restriction is worked off. If we assume U ≠ ε, then b$(RU)^I$c ensures the existence of an individual d such that bR^Id, dU^Ic, and c $\in$ C^I. We still do not know the appropriate U, but the existence of such a word U and an individual c with dU^Ic, and c $\in$ C^I can be expressed by the constraint d $\in$ ($\exists$($R^{-1}L$ \ {ε}):C)^I.

Thus we have seen how the treatment of exists-in-restrictions in the satisfiability algorithm for $\mathcal{ALC}$ can be generalized to $\mathcal{ALC}_{reg}$. We shall now turn to value-restrictions.

Assume that we have a constraint b $\in$ ($\forall$L:C)^I, and—to satisfy an exists-in-constraint on b—we have introduced an individual c such that bR^Ic. Obviously, if R $\in$ L, we have to add the constraint c $\in$ C^I; but this is not sufficient for the following reason. Assume that U is an element of $R^{-1}L$ \ {ε}, i.e., U is a nonempty word such that RU $\in$ L. If, in some step of the algorithm, an individual d is introduced such that cU^Id holds, then d has to satisfy the constraint d $\in$ C^I. This is so because b$(RU)^I$d, RU $\in$ L, and b has to satisfy b $\in$ ($\forall$L:C)^I. We can keep track of this possibility by imposing the constraint c $\in$ ($\forall$($R^{-1}L$ \ {ε}):C)^I on c.

Unlike the situation for $\mathcal{ALC}$ one can no longer be sure of the termination of the algorithm, unless one imposes an appropriate control structure, and tests for cycles. The problem of nontermination will be demonstrated by the following example.

Example 4.5. We consider the following concept term of $\mathcal{ALC}_{reg}$: C := A $\sqcap$ $\exists$R:A $\sqcap$ $\forall R^+$:($\exists$R:A).
(1) We introduce an individual a_0 which has to satisfy the constraints a_0 $\in$ A^I, a_0 $\in$ ($\exists$R:A)^I, a_0 $\in$ ($\forall R^+$:($\exists$R:A))^I.
(2) Because of the exists-in-restriction for a_0 we introduce a new individual a_1 such that $a_0R^Ia_1$, and this individual has to satisfy the constraint a_1 $\in$ A^I.
(3) Now the interaction between $a_0R^Ia_1$ and the value-restriction a_0 $\in$ ($\forall R^+$:($\exists$R:A))^I has to be taken into account. Because of R $\in$ R^+ we obtain the constraint a_1 $\in$ ($\exists$R:A)^I. In addition, we have $R^{-1}R^+$ \ {ε} = R^+ ≠ Ø, which yields the constraint a_1 $\in$ ($\forall R^+$:($\exists$R:A))^I. To sum up, a_1 has to satisfy the constraints a_1 $\in$ A^I, a_1 $\in$ ($\exists$R:A)^I, and a_1 $\in$ ($\forall R^+$:($\exists$R:A))^I, i.e., the same constraints as previously a_0. If we continue with the constraints on a_1 we get an individual a_2 which, in the end, has to satisfy the same constraints as a_1. This yields an individual a_3, and so on. In other words, the algorithm has run into a cycle.
On the other hand, we could just identify a_0 with a_1. This would yield the following interpretation J: dom(J) := {a_0}; R^J := { (a_0,a_0) }; A^J := {a_0}. It is easy to see that this interpretation satisfies a_0 $\in$ C^J. ❑

The phenomenon that such cycles may occur is not particular for this example. After sufficiently long computation, the algorithm will always reproduce sets of constraints which have already been considered. Basically, this is a consequence of the following fact, which in turn is an easy consequence of the quotient criterion for regular languages (see Eilenberg (1974), Theorem 8.1).

Proposition 4.6. Let **K** be a finite set of regular languages. Then the set {$W^{-1}L$ \ {ε}; where L $\in$ **K** and W is a word} is also finite. ❑

However, it turns out that there are two different types of cycles: "good cycles" and "bad cycles". The cycle of Example 4.5 is a "good cycle"; its occurrence indicated that the concept term under consideration is in fact satisfiable. The following example will demonstrate how "bad cycles" may arise.

Example 4.7. We consider the following concept term of $\mathcal{ALC}_{reg}$: D := ¬A $\sqcap$ $\exists R^+$:A $\sqcap$ $\forall R^+$:(¬A).
(1) We introduce an individual a_0 which has to satisfy a_0 $\in$ (¬A)^I, a_0 $\in$ ($\exists R^+$:A)^I, and a_0 $\in$ ($\forall R^+$:(¬A))^I.
(2) Because of the exists-in-restriction for a_0 we introduce a new individual a_1 such that $a_0R^Ia_1$. But now we have R $\in$ R^+ as well as $R^{-1}R^+$ \ {ε} = R^+ ≠ Ø. Thus we have to choose between two possibilities for the constraint on a_1.

(3) First, we may consider the constraint $a_1 \in A^I$ (corresponding to the case $U = \varepsilon$ from above). But $a_0R^Ia_1$ together with the value-restriction $a_0 \in (\forall R^+:(\neg A))^I$ yields $a_1 \in (\neg A)^I$, and we have a clash with $a_1 \in A^I$.
(4) Thus we have to backtrack and choose the constraint $a_1 \in (\exists R^+:A)^I$ (corresponding to the case $U \neq \varepsilon$ from above). As before, $a_0R^Ia_1$ together with the value-restriction on a_0 yields $a_1 \in (\neg A)^I$ and $a_1 \in (\forall R^+:(\neg A))^I$. Thus a_1 has to satisfy the same constraints as previously a_0. This shows that we have again run into a cycle; but this time the situation is different. In fact, it is easy to see that the concept term D is unsatisfiable whereas the term C of Example 4.5 was satisfiable. ❑

We may now ask what makes the difference between the cycle of Example 4.5 and that of Example 4.7. In the second example we have postponed satisfying the exists-in-restriction for a_0 by introducing the new exists-in-restriction for a_1. It is easy to see that we should have to postpone satisfying the restriction forever because trying to actually satisfy it will always result in a clash. In the first example however, we had already satisfied the exists-in-restriction before the cycle occurred.

Building up on these ideas, an algorithm for deciding satisfiability of concept terms of $\mathcal{ALC}_{reg}$ is presented, and proved to be sound, complete, and terminating in Baader (1990b). The algorithm uses so-called concept trees (which are similar to AND/OR search trees) to impose an appropriate control on the search for a finite model. This makes it possible to detect cycles at the right moment, and to distinguish between good ones and bad ones. The termination proof mainly depends on Proposition 4.6, that is, on a result from formal language theory.

5 Conclusion

Augmenting $\mathcal{ALC}$ by a transitive closure operator for roles means not just adding yet another construct to this languages, and thus getting a language and an algorithm which are only slightly different from those previously considered. The transitive closure is of a rather different quality.

This claim is substantiated by the following observations. Firstly, by adding transitive closure, we are leaving the realm of first order logic. Secondly, the algorithm depends on new methods, namely on the use of results from formal language theory, and on a more sophisticated data structure to cope with the nontermination problem. Thirdly, adding features (i.e., functional roles) and feature agreements would make the subsumption problem undecidable (Baader et al. (1991)), whereas this was never a problem for the languages considered by Hollunder&Nutt (1990).

Finally, the expressiveness of $\mathcal{ALC}_{reg}$ is also demonstrated by the fact that concept terms of this language can be used to simulate general concept equations, i.e., equations of the form C = D where both C and D may be complex concept terms of $\mathcal{ALC}$ or $\mathcal{ALC}_{reg}$ (see Baader (1990b), Section 6, Baader et al. (1991)). For this reason, the algorithm for $\mathcal{ALC}_{reg}$ can be used to decide satisfiability and subsumption of concepts with respect to finite sets of concept equations. As a special case, one thus gets algorithms for satisfiability and subsumption of concepts with respect to cyclic T-boxes of $\mathcal{ALC}$, provided that these T-boxes are interpreted with descriptive semantics.

References

Aho, A.V., and Ullman, J.D. 1979. Universality of Data Retrieval Languages. In Proceedings of the 6th ACM Symposium on Principles of Programming Languages, 110–120.

Baader, F. 1990. Terminological Cycles in KL-ONE-based KR-languages. Research Report, RR-90-01, DFKI, Kaiserslautern.

Baader, F. 1990a. Terminological Cycles in KL-ONE-based Knowledge Representation Languages. Proceedings of the *8th National Conference on Artificial Intelligence*, AAAI-90.

Baader, F. 1990b. Augmenting Concept Languages by Transitive Closure of Roles: An Alternative to Terminological Cycles. DFKI Research Report RR-90-13, DFKI, Kaiserslautern.

Baader, F., Bürckert, H.-J., Nebel, B., Nutt, W., Smolka, G. 1991. On the Expressivity of Feature Logics with Negation, Functional Uncertainty, and Sort Equations. Research Report, RR-91-01, DFKI, Kaiserslautern.

Brachman, R.J., and Schmolze, J.G. 1985. An Overview of the KL-ONE Knowledge Representation System. *Cognitive Science* 16: 171–216.

Eilenberg, S. 1974. *Automata, Languages and Machines, Vol. A.* New York/London: Academic Press.

Hollunder, B., Nutt, W., Schmidt-Schauß, M. (1990). Subsumption Algorithms for Concept Languages. Proceedings of the *9th European Conference on Artificial Intelligence*, ECAI-90.

Hollunder, B., Nutt, W. 1990. Subsumption Algorithms for Concept Languages. Research Report RR-90-04, DFKI, Kaiserslautern.

Kaplan, R.M., Maxwell III, J. T. 1988. An Algorithm for Functional Uncertainty. Proceedings of the COLIN 88.

Levesque, H.J., and Brachman, R.J. 1987. Expressiveness and Tractability in Knowledge Representation and Reasoning. *Computational Intelligence* 3: 78–93.

MacGregor, R., and Bates, R. 1987. The Loom Knowledge Representation Language. Technical Report ISI/RS-87-188, Information Science Institute, Univ. of Southern California.

Nebel, B. 1990. *Reasoning and Revision in Hybrid Representation Systems.* Lecture Notes in Artificial Intelligence, Subseries of Lecture Notes in Computer Science 422.

Nebel, B. 1990a. Terminological Cycles: Semantics and Computational Properties. To appear in Sowa, J. ed. 1990. *Formal Aspects of Semantic Networks.*

Schmidt-Schauß, M., Smolka, G. 1988. Attributive Concept Descriptions with Unions and Complements. SEKI Report SR-88-21. To appear in Artificial Intelligence.

A Scheme for Integrating Concrete Domains into Concept Languages

Franz Baader* and **Philipp Hanschke**†
German Research Center for AI (DFKI)
Postfach 2080
W-6750 Kaiserslautern, Germany

Abstract

A drawback which concept languages based on KL-ONE have is that all the terminological knowledge has to be defined on an abstract logical level. In many applications, one would like to be able to refer to concrete domains and predicates on these domains when defining concepts. Examples for such concrete domains are the integers, the real numbers, or also non-arithmetic domains, and predicates could be equality, inequality, or more complex predicates. In the present paper we shall propose a scheme for integrating such concrete domains into concept languages rather than describing a particular extension by some specific concrete domain. We shall define a terminological and an assertional language, and consider the important inference problems such as subsumption, instantiation, and consistency. The formal semantics as well as the reasoning algorithms can be given on the scheme level. In contrast to existing KL-ONE based systems, these algorithms are not only sound but also complete. They generate subtasks which have to be solved by a special purpose reasoner of the concrete domain.

1 Introduction

Concept languages based on KL-ONE [Brachman and Schmolze, 1985] are used to represent the taxonomical and conceptual knowledge of a particular problem domain on an abstract logical level. To describe this kind of knowledge, one starts with atomic concepts and roles, and defines new concepts using the operations provided by the language. Examples for atomic concepts may be Human and Female, and for roles child. If the logical connective conjunction is present as language construct, one may describe the concept Woman as "humans who are female", and represent it by the expression Human $\sqcap$ Female. Many languages provide quantification over role fillers which allows for example to describe the concept Mother by the expression Woman $\sqcap$ $\exists$child.Human.

KL-ONE was first developed for the purpose of natural language processing [Brachman *et al.*, 1979], and some of the existing systems are still mostly used in this context (see e.g., SB-ONE [Kobsa, 1989]). However, its success in this area has also led to applications in other fields (see e.g., MESON [Edelmann and Owsnicki, 1986] which is used for computer configuration tasks, CLASSIC [Borgida *et al.*, 1989] which is e.g. used in the area of CAD/CAM, or K-Rep [Mays *et al.*, 1988] which is used in a financial marketing domain).

A drawback which pure KL-ONE languages have is that all the terminological knowledge has to be defined on the abstract logical level. In many applications, one would like to be able to refer to concrete domains and predicates on these domains when defining concepts. An example for such a concrete domain could be the set of nonnegative integers. In the above example, one might think that being human and female is not enough to make a woman. As an additional property one could require that she should be old enough, e.g., at least 21. Thus one would like to introduce a new role age, and define Woman by an expression of the form Human $\sqcap$ Female $\sqcap \geq_{21}$(age). Here $\geq_{21}$ stands for the unary predicate $\{n; n \geq 21\}$ of all nonnegative integers greater or equal 21. Stating such properties directly with reference to a given concrete domain seems to be easier and more natural than encoding them somehow into abstract concept expressions.[1] Though this drawback already appears in natural language processing, it becomes even more important if one has other applications in mind. For example, in a technical application the adequate representation of geometrical concepts requires to relate points in a coordinate system. For that purpose one would e.g. like to have access to real arithmetic. Similar motivations have already led to extensions of KL-ONE in the above mentioned systems MESON, CLASSIC, and K-Rep. The MESON system provides "a separate hierarchy for de-

*Supported by the BMFT research project AKA-WINO
†Supported by the BMFT research project ARC-TEC

[1] See e.g. [Brachman and Schmolze, 1985], Section 9.2, where so-called Structural Descriptions are used to encode the concrete predicate "less than one hour". From a computational point of view, Structural Descriptions are as bad as Role Value Maps which cause undecidability of subsumption [Schmidt-Schauß, 1989].

scribing non-concepts (e.g., integer ranges and strings)" ([Patel-Schneider *et al.*, 1990], p. 8) which are given as user-defined or machine-defined predicates. Similar features are provided by the "test" construct in CLASSIC. In K-Rep "the roles of concepts may in turn be other (complex) concepts, as well as numbers, strings and ... arbitrary Lisp objects" ([Mays *et al.*, 1988], p. 62).

For similar reasons, Logic Programming has been extended to Constraint Logic Programming (CLP). The constraints in CLP languages "state properties directly in the domain of discourse as opposed to having these properties encoded into Prolog terms" ([Lassez, 1987], p. 2).

Before describing our approach for extending a concept language by concrete domains we shall state some of the properties which such an extension should satisfy:

- The extension should still have a formal declarative semantics which is as close as possible to the usual semantics employed for concept languages.
- It should be possible to combine existing inference algorithms for concept languages with well-known reasoning algorithms in the concrete domain in order to get the appropriate algorithms for the extension.
- One should provide a scheme for extending concept languages by various concrete domains rather than constructing a single ad hoc extension for a specific concrete domain. The formal semantics as well as the combination of the algorithms should already be treated on this scheme level.

In order to satisfy these properties it is important to choose an appropriate interface between the concept language and the concrete domain. The interface which we shall use in the present paper was inspired by a construct which is e.g. present in the CLASSIC system, namely coreference constraints (also called agreements) between chains of single-valued roles (also called features).[2] With such a coreference constraint one can for example express the concept of all women whose father and husband are of the same age by the expression Woman $\sqcap$ (father age) $\downarrow$ (husband age). But one cannot express that the husband is even older than the father. This becomes possible if we take the set of nonnegative integers as concrete domain. Then we can simply write Woman $\sqcap \geq$(husband age, father age) where $\geq$ stands for the binary predicate $\{(n,m); n \geq m\}$ on nonnegative integers. More general, our extension will allow to state that feature chains satisfy a (nonnecessarily binary) predicate which is provided by the concrete domain in question.

The next section will contain a formal definition of what we mean by the notion "concrete domain". Section 3 describes our scheme for extending a concept language by an arbitrary concrete domain. As a starting point for this extension we use the language $\mathcal{ALC}$ of [Schmidt-Schauß and Smolka, 1991]. The reason for choosing this language was that it is large enough to exhibit most of the problems connected with such an extension. Taking a larger language (e.g., including number restrictions) would only mean more work without bringing new insights. Section 4 describes how an assertional component for such an extended concept language can be defined. For both the terminological and the assertional part of our formalism we shall introduce the important inference problems. Because of the space limitations it is not possible to present the algorithm which can be used to decide all of these problems. A complete presentation of the algorithm, and a proof of its correctness can be found in [Baader and Hanschke, 1991]. It is important to note that this algorithm is not only sound but also complete.[3]

2 Concrete Domains

The following definition formalizes the notion "concrete domain" which has until now only been used in an intuitive sense.

Definition 2.1 *A concrete domain $\mathcal{D}$ consists of a set dom($\mathcal{D}$), the domain of $\mathcal{D}$, and a set pred($\mathcal{D}$), the predicate names of $\mathcal{D}$. Each predicate name P is associated with an arity n, and an n-ary predicate $P^{\mathcal{D}} \subseteq dom(\mathcal{D})^n$.*

We shall now give some examples of concrete domains.

- In the examples of the introduction we have considered the concrete domain $\mathcal{N}$ which has the set of nonnegative integers as its domain. We have also used the binary predicate name $\geq$, and one of the unary predicate names $\geq_n$.
- The concrete domain $\mathcal{R}$ is defined as follows. The domain of $\mathcal{R}$ is the set of all real numbers, and the predicates of $\mathcal{R}$ are given by formulae which are built by first order means (i.e., by using logical connectives and quantifiers) from equalities and inequalities between integer polynomials in several indeterminates.[4] For example, $x + z^2 = y$ is an equality between the polynomials $p(x,z) = x + z^2$ and $q(y) = y$; and $x > y$ is an inequality between very simple polynomials. From these equalities and inequalities one can e.g. build the formulae $\exists z(x + z^2 = y)$ and $\exists z(x + z^2 = y) \vee (x > y)$. The first formula yields a predicate name of arity 2 (since it has two free variables), and it is easy to see that the associated predicate is $\{(r,s);\ r$ and s are real numbers and $r \leq s\}$. Consequently, the predicate associated to the second formula is $\{(r,s);\ r$ and s are real numbers$\} = dom(\mathcal{R}) \times dom(\mathcal{R})$.
- The concrete domain $\mathcal{Z}$ is defined as $\mathcal{R}$ with the only difference that $dom(\mathcal{Z})$ is the set of all integers instead of all real numbers.
- Our next example leaves the realm of numbers and arithmetic. Assume that $\mathcal{DB}$ is an arbitrary relational database equipped with an appropriate query

[2] Agreements on feature chains are just the restriction of Role Value Maps to single-valued (i.e., functional) roles; but unlike Role Value Maps they usually do not cause undecidability of subsumption [Hollunder and Nutt, 1990].

[3] All the above mentioned systems employ sound but incomplete algorithms.

[4] For the sake of simplicity we assume here that the formula itself is the predicate name.

language. Then $\mathcal{DB}$ can be seen as a concrete domain where $dom(\mathcal{DB})$ is the set of atomic values in the database. The predicates of $\mathcal{DB}$ are the relations which can be defined over $\mathcal{DB}$ with the help of the query language.

As mentioned in the introduction, we want to combine inference algorithms for the given concept language with reasoning algorithms for the concrete domain in order to get inference algorithms for the extended concept language. This is only possible if the concrete domain satisfies some additional properties.

For technical reasons we shall have to push negation into concept terms. To make this possible we have to require that the set of predicate names of the concrete domain is *closed under negation*, i.e., if P is an n-ary predicate name in $pred(\mathcal{D})$ then there has to exist a predicate name Q in $pred(\mathcal{D})$ such that $Q^{\mathcal{D}} = dom(\mathcal{D})^n \setminus P^{\mathcal{D}}$. In addition, we need a unary predicate name which denotes the predicate $dom(\mathcal{D})$. The domain $\mathcal{N}$ from above does not satisfy these properties. We should have to add the predicate names $<, <_n$. The domains $\mathcal{R}$ and $\mathcal{Z}$ satisfy the properties. Whether a domain of the form $\mathcal{DB}$ satisfies these properties depends on the query language.

The property which will be formulated now clarifies what kind of reasoning mechanisms are required in the concrete domain. Let $P_1, \ldots, P_k$ be k (not necessarily different) predicate names in $pred(\mathcal{D})$ of arities $n_1, \ldots, n_k$. We consider the conjunction

$$\bigwedge_{i=1}^{k} P_i(\underline{x}^{(i)}).$$

Here $\underline{x}^{(i)}$ stands for an n_i-tuple $(x_1^{(i)}, \ldots, x_{n_i}^{(i)})$ of variables. It is important to note that neither all variables in one tuple nor those in different tuples are assumed to be distinct. Such a conjunction is said to be *satisfiable* iff there exists an assignment of elements of $dom(\mathcal{D})$ to the variables such that the conjunction becomes true in $\mathcal{D}$.

For example, let $P_1(x, y)$ be the predicate $\exists z(x + z^2 = y)$ in $pred(\mathcal{R})$, and let $P_2(x, y)$ be the predicate $x > y$ in $pred(\mathcal{R})$. Obviously, neither the conjunction $P_1(x, y) \wedge P_2(x, y)$ nor $P_2(x, x)$ is satisfiable.

Definition 2.2 *A concrete domain $\mathcal{D}$ is called* admissible *iff* (i) *the set of its predicate names is closed under negation and contains a name for $dom(\mathcal{D})$, and* (ii) *the satisfiability problem for finite conjunctions of the above mentioned form is decidable.*

The concrete domain $\mathcal{R}$ is admissible. This is a consequence of Tarski's decidability result for real arithmetic [Tarski, 1951]. The concrete domain $\mathcal{Z}$ is not admissible since Hilbert's Tenth Problem—one of the most prominent undecidable problems [Matijacevič, 1970]—is a special case of its satisfiability problem.

3 The Concept Language

We shall now present our scheme for integrating an arbitrary concrete domain $\mathcal{D}$ into the concept language $\mathcal{ALC}$. The result of this integration will be called $\mathcal{ALC}(\mathcal{D})$.

3.1 Syntax and Semantics

In addition to the usual language constructs of $\mathcal{ALC}$, the language $\mathcal{ALC}(\mathcal{D})$ allows features (i.e., functional roles) in value restrictions, and predicate names of $\mathcal{D}$ applied to feature chains. For a set F of feature names, a feature chain is just a nonempty word over F.

Definition 3.1 *Let* C, R, *and* F *be disjoint sets of concept, role, and feature names. The set of* concept terms *of $\mathcal{ALC}(\mathcal{D})$ is inductively defined. As a starting point of the induction, any element of* C *is a concept term* (atomic terms). *Now let C and D be concept terms, let R be a role name or feature name, $P \in pred(\mathcal{D})$ be an n-ary predicate name, and $u_1, \ldots, u_n$ be feature chains. Then the following expressions are also concept terms:*

1. $C \sqcup D$ (disjunction), $C \sqcap D$ (conjunction), *and* $\neg C$ (negation),

2. $\exists R.C$ (exists-in restriction) *and* $\forall R.C$ (value restriction),

3. $P(u_1, \ldots, u_n)$ (predicate restriction).

Let A be a concept name and let D be a concept term. Then $A = D$ is a terminological axiom. *A* terminology (T-box) *is a finite set $\mathcal{T}$ of terminological axioms with the additional restrictions that* (i) *no concept name appears more than once as a left hand side of a definition, and* (ii) *$\mathcal{T}$ contains no cyclic definitions.*[5]

Please note that the exists-in and the value restrictions are not only defined for roles but also for features.

The following is an example of a T-box in $\mathcal{ALC}(\mathcal{N})$. Let Human, Female, Mother, Woman be concept names, let child be a role name, and let age be a feature name. The T-box—which proposes yet another definition of the concept woman—consists of the following axioms:

$$\begin{aligned}\mathsf{Mother} &= \mathsf{Human} \sqcap \mathsf{Female} \sqcap \exists\mathsf{child}.\mathsf{Human} \\ \mathsf{Woman} &= \mathsf{Human} \sqcap \mathsf{Female} \sqcap (\mathsf{Mother} \sqcup \geq_{21}(\mathsf{age}))\end{aligned}$$

The reason for choosing child as role and age as feature is that an individual can have more than one child, but (s)he has only one age. The next definition gives a model-theoretic semantics for the languages introduced in Definition 3.1.

Definition 3.2 *An* interpretation *$\mathcal{I}$ for $\mathcal{ALC}(\mathcal{D})$ consists of a set* dom($\mathcal{I}$), *the abstract domain of the interpretation, and an interpretation function. The abstract domain and the given concrete domain have to be disjoint, i.e.,* dom($\mathcal{D}$) $\cap$ dom($\mathcal{I}$) $= \emptyset$. *The interpretation function associates with each concept name A a subset $A^{\mathcal{I}}$ of* dom($\mathcal{I}$), *with each role name R a binary relation $R^{\mathcal{I}}$ on* dom($\mathcal{I}$), *i.e., a subset of* dom($\mathcal{I}$) $\times$ dom($\mathcal{I}$), *and with each feature name f a partial function $f^{\mathcal{I}}$ from* dom($\mathcal{I}$) *into* dom($\mathcal{I}$) $\cup$ dom($\mathcal{D}$).
For such a partial function $f^{\mathcal{I}}$ the expression $f^{\mathcal{I}}(x) = y$ is sometimes written as $(x, y) \in f^{\mathcal{I}}$. If $u = f_1 \ldots f_n$ is a feature chain, then $u^{\mathcal{I}}$ denotes the composition $f_1^{\mathcal{I}} \circ \ldots \circ f_n^{\mathcal{I}}$ of the partial functions $f_1^{\mathcal{I}}, \ldots, f_n^{\mathcal{I}}$.[6]

[5] See [Nebel, 1989; Baader, 1990] for a treatment of cyclic definitions in concept languages.

[6] The composition should be read from left to right, i.e., $f_1^{\mathcal{I}} \circ \ldots \circ f_n^{\mathcal{I}}$ means apply first $f_1^{\mathcal{I}}$, then $f_2^{\mathcal{I}}$, and so on.

The interpretation function—which gives an interpretation for atomic terms—can be extended to arbitrary concept terms as follows: Let C and D be concept terms, let R be a role name or feature name, $P \in pred(\mathcal{D})$ be an n-ary predicate name, and $u_1, \ldots, u_n$ be feature chains. Assume that $C^{\mathcal{I}}$ and $D^{\mathcal{I}}$ are already defined. Then

1. $(C \sqcup D)^{\mathcal{I}} = C^{\mathcal{I}} \cup D^{\mathcal{I}}$, $(C \sqcap D)^{\mathcal{I}} = C^{\mathcal{I}} \cap D^{\mathcal{I}}$, *and* $(\neg C)^{\mathcal{I}} = dom(\mathcal{I}) \setminus C^{\mathcal{I}}$,
2. $(\forall R.C)^{\mathcal{I}} = \{x \in dom(\mathcal{I});\ \forall y\colon (x,y) \in R^{\mathcal{I}} \rightarrow y \in C^{\mathcal{I}}\}$, $(\exists R.C)^{\mathcal{I}} = \{x \in dom(\mathcal{I});\ \exists y\colon (x,y) \in R^{\mathcal{I}} \wedge y \in C^{\mathcal{I}}\}$,
3. $P(u_1, \ldots, u_n)^{\mathcal{I}} = \{x \in dom(\mathcal{I}); \exists r_1, \ldots, r_n \in dom(\mathcal{D})\colon u_1^{\mathcal{I}}(x) = r_1, \ldots, u_n^{\mathcal{I}}(x) = r_n \ \wedge\ (r_1, \ldots, r_n) \in P^{\mathcal{D}}\}$.

An interpretation $\mathcal{I}$ is a model *of the T-box $\mathcal{T}$ iff it satisfies $A^{\mathcal{I}} = D^{\mathcal{I}}$ for all terminological axioms $A = D$ in $\mathcal{T}$.*

The philosophy underlying this definition is that we assume that the concrete domain $\mathcal{D}$ is sufficiently structured by the predicates in $pred(\mathcal{D})$. That means that we do not want to define new classes of elements of $dom(\mathcal{D})$ or new relations between elements of $dom(\mathcal{D})$ with the help of our concept language. Consequently, concept terms are always interpreted as subsets of the abstract domain, i.e., an individual of the concrete domain cannot be element of a concept.

3.2 Terminological Reasoning

An important service terminological representation systems provide is computing the subsumption hierarchy, i.e., computing the subconcept-superconcept relationships between the concepts of a T-box. Let $\mathcal{T}$ be a T-box and let A, B be concept names. Then B *subsumes* A with respect to $\mathcal{T}$ (symbolically $A \sqsubseteq_{\mathcal{T}} B$) iff $A^{\mathcal{I}} \subseteq B^{\mathcal{I}}$ holds for all models $\mathcal{I}$ of $\mathcal{T}$.

In our example, it is very easy to see that Woman subsumes Mother. However, in general it is not at all trivial to determine such relationships. Until recently, sound and complete subsumption algorithms were only known for rather trivial concept languages (see [Levesque and Brachman, 1987]). Consequently, all the existing KL-ONE systems use only sound, but incomplete algorithms. If such an algorithm gives a positive answer, a subsumption relationship really exists; but if its answer is negative, then we do not know anything. A subsumption relationship may or may not exist. In [Schmidt-Schauß and Smolka, 1991] a sound and complete subsumption algorithm for $\mathcal{ALC}$ is described. The underlying method of constraint propagation was used in [Hollunder *et al.*, 1990] to derive algorithms for various other concept languages. This method can—with appropriate modifications—also be applied to the languages of the form $\mathcal{ALC}(\mathcal{D})$. As a subtask, such an algorithm for $\mathcal{ALC}(\mathcal{D})$ will have to decide satisfiability of conjunctions of the form $\bigwedge_{i=1}^{k} P_i(\underline{x}^{(i)})$ in the concrete domain. Thus we shall have to require that $\mathcal{D}$ is admissible.

In [Baader and Hanschke, 1991] we do not directly give a subsumption algorithm for $\mathcal{ALC}(\mathcal{D})$. Instead we reduce the subsumption problem to a problem which will be introduced in the next section: the consistency problem for A-boxes.

4 The Assertional Language

The terminological formalism introduced in the previous section allows to describe knowledge about classes of objects (the concepts) and relationships between these classes (e.g., subsumption relationships which are consequences of the descriptions). Many applications, however, require that one can also say something about objects in the world. For this reason, most KL-ONE systems provide additional assertional capabilities. This assertional part of the system uses the concept terms for making statements about parts of a given world. The expressiveness of this component varies between the rather weak formalism employed in the original KL-ONE system [Brachman and Schmolze, 1985] to full first order predicate logic as used in KRYPTON [Brachman *et al.*, 1985]. We shall now show how to integrate a concrete domain into an assertional language which is similar to the ones used in KANDOR [Patel-Schneider, 1984], MESON [Edelmann and Owsnicki, 1986], CLASSIC [Borgida *et al.*, 1989], or BACK [Nebel and von Luck, 1988].

4.1 Syntax and Semantics

Let $\mathcal{D}$ be an arbitrary concrete domain. We have seen in Section 3 that we have to deal with two different kinds of objects: the individuals of the concrete domain and the individuals in the abstract domain (see Definition 3.2). The names for objects of the concrete domain will come from a set OC of object names, and the names for objects of the abstract domain from a set OA.

Definition 4.1 *Let* OC *and* OA *be two disjoint sets of object names. The set of all* assertional axioms *is defined as follows. Let C be a concept term of $\mathcal{ALC}(\mathcal{D})$, R be a role name, f be a feature name, P be an n-ary predicate name of $\mathcal{D}$, and let a, b be elements of* OA *and $y, y_1, \ldots, y_n$ be elements of* OC*. Then the following are assertional axioms:*

$$a : C,\quad (a,b) : R,\quad (a,b) : f,\quad (a,y) : f,\quad (y_1, \ldots, y_n) : P.$$

An A-box *is a finite set of such assertional axioms.*

The assertional language can for example be used to express the facts that the woman Lolita, the daughter of Humbert, is married to Vladimir, a man older than Humbert, by the assertional axioms

LOLITA : Woman, (LOLITA, HUMBERT) : father, (LOLITA, VLADIMIR) : husband, (HUMBERT, A1) : age, (VLADIMIR, A2) : age, (A2, A1) : >.

Here LOLITA, HUMBERT, and VLADIMIR are elements of OA, and A1 and A2 are elements of OC.

It may seem to be a drawback of the above defined assertional language that it disallows the use of specific elements of $dom(\mathcal{D})$ in the assertions. For example, we are not allowed to write the axiom (LOLITA, 12) : age. However, if we have a predicate name for the singleton set $\{12\}$, say $=_{12}$, then we can express the same fact by the two axioms (LOLITA, A3) : age and $=_{12}$(A3). In A-boxes of $\mathcal{ALC}(\mathcal{R})$ one can use algebraic numbers such as $\sqrt{2}$ because the corresponding singleton set $\{\sqrt{2}\}$ corresponds to a predicate name in $\mathcal{R}$, namely $(x^2 = 2) \wedge x \geq 0$.

Definition 4.2 *An* interpretation *for the assertional language is simply an interpretation for $\mathcal{ALC}(\mathcal{D})$ which, in addition, assigns an object $a^{\mathcal{I}} \in dom(\mathcal{I})$ to each object name $a \in$ OA, and an object $x^{\mathcal{I}} \in dom(\mathcal{D})$ to each object name $x \in$ OC. Such an interpretation satisfies an assertional axiom*

$$a : C \text{ iff } a^{\mathcal{I}} \in C^{\mathcal{I}}, \qquad (a,b) : R \text{ iff } (a^{\mathcal{I}}, b^{\mathcal{I}}) \in R^{\mathcal{I}},$$
$$(a,b) : f \text{ iff } f^{\mathcal{I}}(a^{\mathcal{I}}) = b^{\mathcal{I}}, \qquad (a,y) : f \text{ iff } f^{\mathcal{I}}(a^{\mathcal{I}}) = y^{\mathcal{I}},$$
$$(y_1, ..., y_n) : P \text{ iff } (y_1^{\mathcal{I}}, ..., y_n^{\mathcal{I}}) \in P^{\mathcal{D}}.$$

An interpretation is a model of an A-box $\mathcal{A}$ *iff it satisfies all the assertional axioms of* $\mathcal{A}$, *and it is a* model of an A-box $\mathcal{A}$ together with a T-box $\mathcal{T}$ *iff it is a model of* $\mathcal{T}$ *and a model of* $\mathcal{A}$.

The definition shows that we do not require unique names for the objects occurring in an A-box.[7] For example, assume that we have the abstract names VLADIMIR and LOLITA'S_FATHER in our A-box. As our knowledge about the world increases, we may learn that Vladimir is in fact Lolita's father. Similarly, if we introduce concrete names A1, A2 for the ages of two persons PERSON1, PERSON2 into the A-box, we do not want to assume automatically that these two numbers are different.

4.2 Assertional Reasoning

In the following, $\mathcal{A}$ will always denote an A-box, $\mathcal{T}$ a T-box, C, D concept terms, $a, b \in$ OA names of abstract objects, and $x, y \in$ OC names of concrete objects.

An obvious requirement on the represented knowledge is that it should not be contradictory. Otherwise, it would be useless to deduce other facts from this knowledge since logically, everything follows from an inconsistent set of assumptions. However, a given A-box together with a given T-box need not have a model. For example, an A-box containing the axioms $a : C$ and $a : \neg C$, or the axioms $(a, b) : f$, $(a, y) : f$ for a feature name f is contradictory, and thus cannot have a model.

We say that an A-box together with a T-box is *consistent* iff it has a model. Otherwise, it is called *inconsistent*.

For the above mentioned reason it is important to have an algorithm which decides consistency of a given A-box together with a T-box. In addition, it will turn out that such an algorithm can also be used to solve the other important inference problems, namely subsumption between concepts and the so-called instantiation problem.

This last problem is defined as follows. The abstract object a is an *instance* of C with respect to $\mathcal{A}$ together with $\mathcal{T}$ iff $a^{\mathcal{I}} \in C^{\mathcal{I}}$ for all models of $\mathcal{A}$ together with $\mathcal{T}$.

As an example, we consider the T-box defining the concepts Mother and Woman of Section 3, and an A-box containing the axioms (LOLITA, A3) : age, $=_{12}$(A3) and LOLITA : Woman. Then LOLITA is an instance of Mother with respect to the A-box together with the T-box.

The instantiation problem can be reduced to the consistency problem as follows: a is an instance of C with respect to $\mathcal{A}$ together with $\mathcal{T}$ iff the A-box $\mathcal{A} \cup \{a : \neg C\}$ together with $\mathcal{T}$ is inconsistent.

[7] Many KL-ONE based systems have a unique name assumption for their A-box individuals; but for example KL-TWO [Vilain, 1985] does not assume unique names.

Finally, the subsumption problem can also be reduced to the instantiation problem, and thus to the consistency problem for A-boxes. In fact, C is subsumed by D with respect to $\mathcal{T}$ iff the abstract object a is an instance of D with respect to the A-box $\{a : C\}$ together with $\mathcal{T}$.

In [Baader and Hanschke, 1991] a sound and complete algorithm is described which decides the consistency problem for $\mathcal{ALC}(\mathcal{D})$, provided that the concrete domain $\mathcal{D}$ is admissible. Such an algorithm for $\mathcal{ALC}$ without concrete domain and features can be found in [Hollunder, 1990]. Since the other inference problems introduced above can be reduced to the consistency problem, we thus have

Theorem 4.3 *Let $\mathcal{D}$ be an admissible concrete domain. Then there exists a sound and complete algorithm which is able to decide the following problems for $\mathcal{ALC}(\mathcal{D})$: the subsumption problem w.r.t. a T-box, the instantiation problem w.r.t. an A-box together with a T-box, and the consistency problem for an A-box together with a T-box.*

5 Conclusion

We have proposed a KL-ONE based knowledge representation and reasoning system which is hybrid in two respects. On the one hand, it makes the usual distinction between two epistemological different kinds of knowledge, the terminological knowledge and the assertional knowledge. On the other hand, the terminological and assertional language, which usually describes the knowledge on an abstract logical level, is extended by allowing to refer to concrete domains and predicates on these domains.

The different parts of the system are integrated with the help of a unified model-theoretic semantics. Reasoning in the terminological and the assertional part can be done with the help of a single basic reasoning algorithm. This algorithm creates subtasks which have to be solved by the special purpose reasoner of the concrete domain. But there is no other interaction necessary between our basic reasoning algorithm and the reasoner on the concrete domain.

Our approach differs from other extensions of KL-ONE which were done for similar reasons in several respects. Firstly, we have proposed a scheme for such an extension, and not a particular extension by some specific concrete domains. The formal semantics and the algorithm are given on this scheme level. Secondly, the basic reasoning algorithm is not only sound but also complete with respect to this semantics. In addition, we can utilize special purpose reasoners which may already exist for the concrete domain in question. This shows another difference to e.g. the MESON system where the important relationships between the user-defined or machine-defined predicates have to be explicitely supplied by the user.

An advantage other systems have compared to our approach is that their incomplete algorithms are usually polynomial, whereas our complete algorithm is of complexity at least PSPACE (depending on the concrete domain). However, one should keep in mind that these complexity results are worst case results. The algorithm may behave much better for "typical" knowledge bases.

Our main motivation for developing the presented KL-ONE extension was to represent knowledge in a mechanical engineering domain. In particular, we wanted to describe both geometric and other attributes of lathe work pieces in a unified framework. For that purpose we intend to use the language $\mathcal{ALC}(\mathcal{R})$ where geometric properties can be described with the help of predicates over real numbers. Currently, we are experimenting with a prototypical implementation which uses a relatively small fragment of real arithmetics as its concrete domain.

References

[Baader and Hanschke, 1991] F. Baader and P. Hanschke. A scheme for integrating concrete domains into concept languages. Research Report RR-91-10, DFKI, Kaiserslautern, 1991.

[Baader, 1990] F. Baader. Terminological cycles in KL-ONE-based knowledge representation languages. In *Proceedings of the Eighth National Conference on Artificial Intelligence*, volume 2, pages 621–626. AAAI, 1990.

[Borgida *et al.*, 1989] A. Borgida, R. J. Brachman, D. L. McGuinness, and L. A. Resnick. CLASSIC: A structural data model for objects. In *International Conference on Management of Data*. ACM SIGMOD, 1989.

[Brachman and Schmolze, 1985] R. J. Brachman and J. G. Schmolze. An overview of the KL-ONE knowledge representation system. *Cognitive Science*, 9(2):171–216, 1985.

[Brachman *et al.*, 1979] R. J. Brachman, R. J. Bobrow, P. R. Cohen, J. W. Klovstad, B. L. Webber, and W. A. Woods. Research in natural language understanding, annual report. Tech. Rep. No. 4274, Cambrige, MA, 1979. Bolt Beranek and Newman.

[Brachman *et al.*, 1985] R. J. Brachman, V. Pigman Gilbert, and H. J. Levesque. An essential hybrid reasoning system: knowledge and symbol level accounts in KRYPTON. In *Proceedings of the 9th International Joint Conference on Artificial Intelligence*, pages 532–539, 1985.

[Edelmann and Owsnicki, 1986] J. Edelmann and B. Owsnicki. Data models in knowledge representation systems: a case study. In GWAI-86 *und 2. Östereichische Artificial-Intelligence-Tagung*, volume 124 of *Informatik-Fachberichte*, pages 69–74. Springer, 1986.

[Hollunder and Nutt, 1990] B. Hollunder and W. Nutt. Subsumption algorithms for concept languages. Research Report RR-90-04, DFKI, Kaiserslautern, 1990.

[Hollunder *et al.*, 1990] B. Hollunder, W. Nutt, and M. Schmidt-Schauß. Subsumption algorithms for concept description languages. In *9th European Conference on Artificial Intelligence (ECAI'90)*, pages 348–353, 1990.

[Hollunder, 1990] B. Hollunder. Hybrid inferences in KL-ONE-based knowledge representation systems. In GWAI-90*; 14th German Workshop on Artificial Intelligence*, volume 251 of *Informatik-Fachberichte*, pages 38–47. Springer, 1990.

[Kobsa, 1989] A. Kobsa. The SB-ONE knowledge representation workbench. In *Preprints of the Workshop on Formal Aspects of Semantic Networks*, 1989. Two Harbors, Cal.

[Lassez, 1987] C. Lassez. Constraint logic programming. In *Constraint Logic Programming: A Reader*, 1987. Fourth IEEE Symposium on Logic Programming, San Francisco.

[Levesque and Brachman, 1987] H. J. Levesque and R. J. Brachman. Expressiveness and tractability in knowledge representation and reasoning. *Computational Intelligence*, 3:78–93, 1987.

[Matijacevič, 1970] Y. Matijacevič. Enumerable sets are diophantine. *Soviet Math. Doklady*, 11:354–357, 1970. English translation.

[Mays *et al.*, 1988] E. Mays, C. Apté, J. Griesmer, and J. Kastner. Experience with K-Rep: an object centered knowledge representation language. In *Proceedings of* IEEE CAIA-88, pages 62–67, 1988.

[Nebel and von Luck, 1988] B. Nebel and K. von Luck. Hybrid reasoning in BACK. In Z. W. Ras and L. Saitta, editors, *Methodologies for Intelligent Systems*, volume 3, pages 260–269. North-Holland, 1988.

[Nebel, 1989] B. Nebel. Terminological cycles: Semantics and computational properties. In *Proceedings of the Workshop on Formal Aspects of Semantic Networks*, 1989. Two Harbors, Cal.

[Patel-Schneider *et al.*, 1990] P. F. Patel-Schneider, B. Owsnicki-Klewe, A. Kobsa, N. Guarino, R. McGregor, W. S. Mark, D. McGuiness, B. Nebel, A. Schmiedel, and J. Yen. Report on the workshop on term subsumption languages in knowledge representation. AI *Magazine*, 11(2):16–23, 1990.

[Patel-Schneider, 1984] P. F. Patel-Schneider. Small can be beautiful in knowledge representation. In *Proceedings of the* IEEE *Workshop on Principles of Knowledge-Based Systems*, pages 11–16. Denver, Colo., 1984.

[Schmidt-Schauß and Smolka, 1991] M. Schmidt-Schauß and G. Smolka. Attributive concept descriptions with complements. To appear in Journal of Artificial Intelligence, 47, 1991.

[Schmidt-Schauß, 1989] M. Schmidt-Schauß. Subsumption in KL-ONE is undecidable. In R. J. Brachman, editor, *First International Conference on Principles of Knowledge Representation and Reasoning*, pages 421–431, 1989.

[Tarski, 1951] A. Tarski. *A Decision Method for Elementary Algebra and Geometry.* U. of California Press. Berkley, 1951.

[Vilain, 1985] M. Vilain. The restricted language architecture of a hybrid representation system. In *Proceedings of the 9th International Joint Conference on Artificial Intelligence*, pages 547–551, 1985.

Tractable Concept Languages

Francesco M. Donini
Maurizio Lenzerini
Daniele Nardi
Dipartimento di Informatica e Sistemistica,
Università di Roma "La Sapienza"
Via Salaria 113, I-00198, Roma, Italy

Werner Nutt
Deutsches Forschungszentrum für
Künstliche Intelligenz
Postfach 2080, D-6750 Kaiserslautern
Germany

Abstract

We present two concept languages, called $\mathcal{PL}_1$ and $\mathcal{PL}_2$, which are extensions of $\mathcal{FL}^-$. We prove that the subsumption problem in these languages can be solved in polynomial time. Both languages include a construct for expressing inverse roles, which has not been considered up to now in tractable languages. In addition, $\mathcal{PL}_1$ includes number restrictions and negation of primitive concepts, while $\mathcal{PL}_2$ includes role conjunction and role chaining.

By exploiting recent complexity results, we show that none of the constructs usually considered in concept languages can be added to $\mathcal{PL}_1$ and $\mathcal{PL}_2$ without losing tractability. Therefore, on the assumption that languages are characterized by the set of constructs they provide, the two languages presented in this paper provide a solution to the problem of singling out an optimal trade-off between expressive power and computational complexity.

1 Introduction

Concept languages provide a means for expressing knowledge about hierarchies of concepts, i.e. classes of objects with common properties. They have been investigated following the ideas initially embedded in many frame-based and semantic-network-based languages, especially the KL-ONE language [Brachman and Schmolze, 1985]. In contrast to earlier formalisms, concept languages are given a Tarski style declarative semantics that allows them to be conceived as sublanguages of predicate logic [Brachman and Levesque, 1984].

The basic reasoning tasks on concepts are unsatisfiability and subsumption checking. A concept is unsatisfiable if it always denotes an empty set. A concept C is subsumed by a concept D if C always denotes a subset of D.

Since the performance of any application developed using concept languages will heavily rely on the above reasoning tasks, it is important both to characterize their computational complexity and to devise algorithms as much efficient as possible.

Recent results allow us to draw a fairly complete picture of the complexity of a wide class of concept languages [Schmidt-Schauß and Smolka, 1988,Donini et al., 1990]. Such results have been obtained by exploiting a general technique for satisfiability checking in concept languages. The technique relies on a form of tableaux calculus, and has been proved extremely useful for studying both the correctness and the complexity of the algorithms.

The outcomes of this body of research go far beyond a mere complexity analysis. In particular, we think that they shed light on three basic aspects related to the use of concept languages in knowledge representation.

First of all, since the complexity of both satisfiability and subsumption depends upon the constructs allowed in the language, we have now an appropriate framework for the study of the trade-off between the expressive power of the languages and their inherent complexity, which was the initial motivation of the seminal work by Brachman and Levesque (see [Levesque and Brachman, 1987]).

Secondly, the design of concept languages and the associated reasoning procedures can now be realized through the application of the above mentioned technique, which provides an algorithmic framework that is parametric with respect to the language constructs.

Thirdly, the study of the computational behaviour of concept languages has led to a clear understanding of the properties of the language constructs and their interaction. The knowledge about the structure of concept languages can thus be used in the design of intelligent reasoning procedures, that—by looking at the form of concepts—can reason about the deductive service, for example estimating the difficulty of performing the required deduction, attempting to provide quick answers to subproblems, or trying possible simplification of the problem.

The work reported in this paper is concerned with the first of the above three points. Our goal was the design of languages including the most powerful set of constructs, while retaining the tractability of subsumption, in particular extending the basic polynomial language $\mathcal{FL}^-$ [Brachman and Levesque, 1984]. $\mathcal{FL}^-$ includes conjunction of concepts (written $C \sqcap D$), universal role quantification ($\forall R.C$), and unqualified existential role quantification ($\exists R$). Various extensions of $\mathcal{FL}^-$ with a polynomial subsumption problem have already been considered:

This work was partly funded by the ESPRIT BRA 3012 (Compulog), the Italian CNR under Progetto Finalizzato Sistemi Informatici e Calcolo Parallelo, contract 90.00681.PF69, and the German BMFT under grant ITW 8903 0.

- $\mathcal{FL}^-$ + role concatenation (also called role chaining) [Brachman and Levesque, 1984];
- $\mathcal{FL}^-$ + number restrictions [Nebel, 1988];
- $\mathcal{FL}^-$ + role conjunction [Nebel, 1988];
- $\mathcal{FL}^-$ + negation of primitive concepts [Schmidt-Schauß and Smolka, 1988].

The result of our work is the definition of two new extensions of $\mathcal{FL}^-$, called $\mathcal{PL}_1$ and $\mathcal{PL}_2$. We show that subsumption in both languages can be solved in polynomial time. Moreover, they are maximally expressive, in the sense that no construct can be added to them without losing tractability.

In particular, $\mathcal{PL}_1$ extends $\mathcal{FL}^-$ with number restrictions, negation of primitive concepts, and inverse roles, and is therefore maximally expressive relative to the costructs available for concepts. On the other hand, $\mathcal{PL}_2$ extends $\mathcal{FL}^-$ with role conjunction, role concatenation, and inverse roles, and is therefore maximally expressive relative to the costructs available for roles. Notice that the construct for inverse roles has not been considered up to now in tractable languages.

The paper is organized as follows. In Section 2 we summarize the main notions used in the formalization of concept languages. In Section 3 we describe the technique used for subsumption checking. In Sections 4 and 5 we present the languages $\mathcal{PL}_1$ and $\mathcal{PL}_2$, together with the corresponding subsumption algorithms. Finally, conclusions are drawn in Section 6. For the sake of brevity, the proofs of the theorems are omitted; they are fully reported in [Donini et al., 1991b].

2 Basic Notions on Concept Languages

In this section we provide the essential notions about the concept languages considered in the paper. For a general presentation, see [Nebel and Smolka, 1990].

We start by considering the language $\mathcal{FL}^-$, where *concepts* (denoted by the letters C and D) are built out of *primitive concepts* (denoted by the letter A) and *primitive roles* (denoted here by the letter R) according to the syntax rule

$$C, D \longrightarrow A \mid C \sqcap D \mid \forall R.C \mid \exists R$$

An *interpretation* $\mathcal{I} = (\Delta^\mathcal{I}, \cdot^\mathcal{I})$ consists of a set $\Delta^\mathcal{I}$ (the *domain* of $\mathcal{I}$) and a function $\cdot^\mathcal{I}$ (the *interpretation function* of $\mathcal{I}$) that maps every concept to a subset of $\Delta^\mathcal{I}$ and every role to a subset of $\Delta^\mathcal{I} \times \Delta^\mathcal{I}$ such that the following equations are satisfied:

$$\begin{aligned}(C \sqcap D)^\mathcal{I} &= C^\mathcal{I} \cap D^\mathcal{I}\\ (\forall R.C)^\mathcal{I} &= \{a \in \Delta^\mathcal{I} \mid \forall b.\, (a,b) \in R^\mathcal{I} \rightarrow b \in C^\mathcal{I}\}\\ (\exists R)^\mathcal{I} &= \{a \in \Delta^\mathcal{I} \mid \exists b.\, (a,b) \in R^\mathcal{I}\}.\end{aligned}$$

An interpretation $\mathcal{I}$ is a *model* for a concept C if $C^\mathcal{I}$ is nonempty; C is *subsumed* by D if $C^\mathcal{I} \subseteq D^\mathcal{I}$ for every interpretation $\mathcal{I}$. A concept is *satisfiable* if it has a model and *unsatisfiable* otherwise. Notice that since $\mathcal{FL}^-$ does not include any form of negation, every $\mathcal{FL}^-$-concept is satisfiable.

Other constructs have been considered in the literature to define more general languages. They are:

- the empty concept and the universal concept, defined by $\bot^\mathcal{I} = \emptyset$ and $\top^\mathcal{I} = \Delta^\mathcal{I}$, respectively;
- disjunction of concepts: $(C \sqcup D)^\mathcal{I} = C^\mathcal{I} \cup D^\mathcal{I}$;
- negation of concepts (also called complement): $(\neg C)^\mathcal{I} = \Delta^\mathcal{I} \setminus C^\mathcal{I}$; sometimes negation can only be applied to primitive concepts (in this case we use the notation $\neg A$);
- qualified existential role quantification: $(\exists R.C)^\mathcal{I} = \{a \in \Delta^\mathcal{I} \mid \exists (a,b) \in R^\mathcal{I}.\, b \in C^\mathcal{I}\}$;
- number restrictions: $(\geq n\, R)^\mathcal{I} = \{a \in \Delta^\mathcal{I} \mid |\{b \in \Delta^\mathcal{I} \mid (a,b) \in R^\mathcal{I}\}| \geq n\}$, and $(\leq n\, R)^\mathcal{I} = \{a \in \Delta^\mathcal{I} \mid |\{b \in \Delta^\mathcal{I} \mid (a,b) \in R^\mathcal{I}\}| \leq n\}$.
- role conjunction: $(Q \sqcap R)^\mathcal{I} = Q^\mathcal{I} \cap R^\mathcal{I}$;
- inverse of roles: $(R^{-1})^\mathcal{I} = \{(a,b) \in \Delta^\mathcal{I} \times \Delta^\mathcal{I} \mid (b,a) \in R^\mathcal{I}\}$;
- role chaining: $(R_1 \circ R_2)^\mathcal{I} = \{(a,b) \in \Delta^\mathcal{I} \times \Delta^\mathcal{I} \mid \exists c.\, (a,c) \in R_1^\mathcal{I}, (c,b) \in R_2^\mathcal{I}\}$.

In the following, we consider concept languages obtained as combinations of the above constructs. Several such combinations have been taken into account in the design of concept languages. In general, the constructs for role formation have been introduced only in the most sophisticated and powerful languages. In particular, the construct for the description of inverse roles has been considered very rarely, and never in tractable languages. This is somewhat surprising, especially if one consider its importance in the description of complex concepts.

For example, let child be a primitive role, and let young be a primitive concept. It is easy to see that the concept "someone that has at least one child and all of whose parents are young" cannot be defined in a language without inverse roles. Indeed, the introduction of a new primitive role parent would not solve the problem, because child and parent would be completely unrelated. On the other hand, the notion of parent is obviously captured by the inverse of the role child. Therefore, in a language with inverse roles, the above concept can be defined as: $\exists \text{child} \sqcap \forall \text{child}^{-1}.\text{young}$.

One of the goals of this paper is to study the impact of inverse roles in the tractability of concept languages. In fact, we show in Sections 4 and 5 that the construct for inverse roles can be added to $\mathcal{FL}^-$ without increasing the complexity of subsumption.

3 Checking Subsumption Using Constraint Systems

In this section we present the basic features of a technique for checking concept satisfiability. The technique is a refinement of the one used in [Schmidt-Schauß and Smolka, 1988], and is fully described in [Donini et al., 1990].

We assume that there exists an alphabet of variable symbols, which will be denoted by the letters x, y, and z. The calculus operates on constraints consisting of variables, concepts, and roles. A *constraint* is a syntactic object of one of the forms $x\colon C$, xRy where C is a concept and R is a role.

Let $\mathcal{I}$ be an interpretation. An *$\mathcal{I}$-assignment* is a function α that maps every variable to an element of $\Delta^{\mathcal{I}}$. We say that α *satisfies* the constraint $x{:}C$ if $\alpha(x) \in C^{\mathcal{I}}$, and α *satisfies* xRy if $(\alpha(x), \alpha(y)) \in R^{\mathcal{I}}$. A constraint c is *satisfiable* if there is an interpretation $\mathcal{I}$ and an $\mathcal{I}$-assignment α such that α satisfies c. A *constraint system* S is a finite, nonempty set of constraints. An $\mathcal{I}$-assignment α *satisfies* S if α satisfies every constraint in S. S is *satisfiable* if there is an interpretation $\mathcal{I}$ and an $\mathcal{I}$-assignment α such that α satisfies S. Using the results reported in [Schmidt-Schauß and Smolka, 1988], it is easy to see that a concept C is satisfiable if and only if the constraint system $\{x{:}C\}$ is satisfiable.

In order to check whether a concept C is satisfiable we start with the constraint system $S = \{x{:}C\}$, and in subsequent steps, we add constraints according to a set of propagation rules, until the resulting system is *complete*, i.e. none of the propagation rules is applicable. At that point, either the complete system S' contains a contradiction (called *clash*), or an interpretation satisfying C can be obtained from S'. Each propagation rule deals with one of the constructs allowed in the language, and the computational complexity of the method crucially depends on their form. It is interesting to observe that, from the logical viewpoint, the method is essentially a tableaux calculus modified with suitable control mechanisms.

In order to use the above technique for subsumption, we can rephrase subsumption in terms of unsatisfiability, exploiting the fact that C is subsumed by D if and only if $C \sqcap \neg D$ is unsatisfiable. The problem with this approach is that, in general, $C \sqcap \neg D$ may include constructs which are not present in the language in which C and D are expressed. We show in the following how to deal with this problem for the language $\mathcal{FL}^-$.

We first define a useful property of a class of concept languages, which includes $\mathcal{FL}^-$. A concept is said to be *conjunction-free* if it contains no conjunction of concepts (i.e. it does not contain the symbol $\sqcap$ applied to concepts). It is easy to see that in a language including neither disjunction nor qualified existential quantification, a concept D can be rewritten into an equivalent concept of the form $D_1 \sqcap \ldots \sqcap D_n$, where each D_i is conjunction-free, and is called a *conjunction-free component* of D. This can be done by means of the following rewriting rule:

$$\forall R.(C \sqcap D) \longrightarrow \forall R.C \sqcap \forall R.D$$

Theorem 3.1 *For every pair of concepts C,D of a language including neither union nor qualified existential quantification, C is subsumed by D iff for every conjunction-free component D_i of D, $C \sqcap \neg D_i$ is unsatisfiable.*

Notice that, although the concept $\neg D_i$ may contain the negation of a non-primitive concept, it can be rewritten in linear time into an equivalent *simple* concept (i.e. a concept where negation occurs only in front of primitive concepts) by using suitable rewriting rules.

When $\mathcal{FL}^-$ is the language used to express C and D, the simple concept resulting from the rewriting of $C \sqcap \neg D_i$ does not belong to the original language, not only because primitive concepts are negated, but for new constructs introduced through the rewriting rules. In particular, it is easy to see that $C \sqcap \neg D_i$ is a concept of $\mathcal{ALE}$, an extension of $\mathcal{FL}^-$ with qualified existential quantification and negation of primitive concepts. It follows from the results reported in [Schmidt-Schauß and Smolka, 1988] that the propagation rules for satisfiability checking in $\mathcal{ALE}$ are:

1. $S \rightarrow_{\sqcap} \{x{:}C_1,\ x{:}C_2\} \cup S$
   if $x{:}C_1 \sqcap C_2$ is in S, and either $x{:}C_1$ or $x{:}C_2$ is not in S
2. $S \rightarrow_{\exists} \{xRy,\ y{:}C\} \cup S$
   if $x{:}\exists R.C$ is in S, there is no z such that both xRz and $z{:}C$ are in S, and y is a new variable
3. $S \rightarrow_{\forall} \{y{:}C\} \cup S$
   if $x{:}\forall R.C$ is in S, xRy is in S, and $y{:}C$ is not in S.

Notice that the complete constraint system S' obtained from $S = \{x{:}C\}$ by applying the above rules, may have a number of constraints that is exponential in the size of C, in particular because of the number of variables generated by the $\rightarrow_{\exists}$-rule. It has recently been shown that this is due to the interaction of existential and universal quantification, which makes the unsatisfiability problem (and therefore subsumption) in $\mathcal{ALE}$ NP-complete [Donini et al., 1990].

This problem does not arise when computing subsumption in $\mathcal{FL}^-$. Indeed, if we look at the form of the concept obtained by negating the candidate subsumer and rewriting it into a simple concept, we realize that the body of a qualified existential quantification may contain only a universal quantification of the form $\forall R.\bot$. This implies that the inherent complexity given by the interaction of existential and universal quantification in $\mathcal{ALE}$ is not present in the extension of $\mathcal{FL}^-$ used to compute subsumption.

This allows us to modify the $\rightarrow_{\exists}$-rule in such a way that only one variable y is generated for all the constraints of the forms $x{:}\exists R.C$, $x{:}\exists R$. The correctness of this method stems from the fact that, even if different variables are generated for each of the above constraints, they all share the same properties of y. Therefore, in order to check whether a contradiction arises in the system, it is sufficient to consider only the variable y.

The above modification directly leads to a polynomial time algorithm for subumption in $\mathcal{FL}^-$. In the following sections, similar techniques are used to show the tractability of two extensions of $\mathcal{FL}^-$.

4 The Language $\mathcal{PL}_1$

The language considered in this section, called $\mathcal{PL}_1$, is an extension of $\mathcal{FL}^-$ with negation of primitive concepts, number restrictions and inverse roles. Its syntax is specified by the following rules:

$$C, D \longrightarrow A \mid \neg A \mid \top \mid \bot \mid C \sqcap D \mid \forall R.C \mid (\geq n\, R) \mid (\leq n\, R)$$

$$R \longrightarrow P \mid P^{-1}$$

where R denotes a role, and P a primitive role[1].

In order to deal with subsumption in $\mathcal{PL}_1$, we reduce this problem to the unsatisfiability problem in a suitable extension of $\mathcal{PL}_1$.

Notice that, since $\mathcal{PL}_1$ includes neither disjunction nor qualified existential quantification C is subsumed by D iff for every conjunction-free component D_i of D, $C \sqcap \neg D_i$ is unsatisfiable. Moreover, as pointed out in Section 3, $\neg D_i$ can be rewritten into an equivalent simple concept. The resulting concept may not belong to the language $\mathcal{PL}_1$, because $\neg\forall R.C$ is rewritten as $\exists R.\neg C$. We call $\mathcal{PL}_1{}^+$ the language constituted by concepts of one of the form: C, D, $C \sqcap D$, where C is a concept of $\mathcal{PL}_1$, and D is a simple concept resulting from rewriting a conjunction-free $\mathcal{PL}_1$-concept. In the rest of the section, we always refer to concepts of $\mathcal{PL}_1{}^+$, unless otherwise stated. As a notation, we say that xRy *holds* in a $\mathcal{PL}_1{}^+$-constraint system S if:

- R is a primitive role P and $xPy \in S$;
- R is P^{-1} and $yPx \in S$.

The propagation rules for $\mathcal{PL}_1{}^+$-constraint system are as follows:

1. $S \rightarrow_{\sqcap} \{x: C_1,\ x: C_2\} \cup S$
   if $x: C_1 \sqcap C_2$ is in S, and either $x: C_1$ or $x: C_2$ is not in S
2. $S \rightarrow_{\forall} \{y: C\} \cup S$
   if $x: \forall R.C$ is in S, xRy holds in S, and $y: C$ is not in S
3. $S \rightarrow_{-1} \{yPx\} \cup S$
   if $xP^{-1}y$ is in S and yPx is not in S
4. $S \rightarrow_{\leq} [y/z]S$
   if $x: (\leq 1\, R)$ is in S, xRy and xRz hold in S with $y \neq z$, and $[y/z]S$ is obtained from S by replacing y with z
5. $S \rightarrow_{\geq} \{xRy\} \cup S$
   if $x: (\geq n\, R)$ is in S, with $n > 0$, y is a new variable, and there is no z such that xRz holds in S
6. $S \rightarrow_{\exists} \{xRy,\ y: C\} \cup S$
   if $x: \exists R.C$ is in S, y is a new variable and there is no z such that both xRz holds in S and $z: C$ is in S

Notice that the construct $(\geq n\, R)$ is treated like the unqualified existential $\exists R$, and, as discussed in Section 3 for $\mathcal{FL}^-$, only one variable is generated for all the constraints of the forms $x: (\geq n\, R)$, $x: \exists R.C$. We show in the sequel that this simplification, which is crucial for the tractability of the method, does not affect its correctness. Notice also that the construct $(\leq n\, R)$ is taken into account only if $n = 1$. This is because using the above rules, no more than 2 variables may be linked to the same variable through a given role.

In a $\mathcal{PL}_1{}^+$-constraint system a clash is a set of constraints of one of the following forms:

1. $\{x: \bot\}$;
2. $\{x: A, x: \neg A\}$;
3. $\{x: (\geq n\, R), x: (\leq m\, R)\}$, with $n > m$;
4. $\{x: (\leq 0\, P), xPy\}$;
5. $\{x: (\leq 0\, P^{-1}), yPx\}$.

The next theorem states that the above propagation rules preserve satisfiability.

Theorem 4.1 *Let S be a constraint system. If S' is obtained from S by the application of the above propagation rules, then S is satisfiable if and only if S' is satisfiable.*

We say that S' is a *completion* of $\{x: C\}$, if S' is complete, and is obtained from $\{x: C\}$ by giving priority to the application of the $\rightarrow_{\exists}$-rule. It is easy to see that, up to variable renaming, only one completion can be derived from $\{x: C\}$.

It is important to notice that, differently from the case of $\mathcal{ALE}$-constraint systems, there is not a direct correspondence between a clash-free completion of $\{x: C\}$ and an assignment satisfying it. This is due to the $\rightarrow_{\geq}$-rule dealing with concepts of the form $(\geq n\, R)$, which are treated as $\exists R$, independently of the value of n. However, the crucial point is that it is always possible to obtain from a clash-free completion S' an interpretation $\mathcal{I}$ and an $\mathcal{I}$-assignment α that satisfies S'. In particular, $\mathcal{I}$ and α are built in such a way that to each variable in S' there corresponds a suitable number of objects in the domain of $\mathcal{I}$, all with the same properties, in order for α to satisfy all constraints of the form $x: (\geq n\, R)$.

Theorem 4.2 *Let C be a $\mathcal{PL}_1{}^+$-concept, and let S' be the completion of the constraint system $\{x: C\}$. Then S' is satisfiable if and only if it contains no clash.*

The entire method for testing subsumption in $\mathcal{PL}_1$—and satisfiability as a special case—can be summed up as follows. In order to check if C is subsumed by D, we compute the conjunction-free components $D_1, \ldots, D_n$ of D, and for each i we rewrite $\neg D_i$ into the simple concept $D_i{}'$. Finally, we check if for each i, the completion of $C \sqcap D_i{}'$ contains a clash.

The tractability of subsumption in $\mathcal{PL}_1$ can be proved by showing that computing the completion of a constraint system $\{x: C \sqcap \neg D_i\}$ requires polynomial time. The proof is based on the following observations. First of all, giving priority to the $\rightarrow_{\exists}$-rule leads to a constraint system of the form $S = \{x: C, xR_1y_1, y_1R_2y_2, \ldots, y_{h-1}R_hy_h, y_h: F\}$, where F is not of the form $\exists R.E$. Second, the number of variables generated in the completion of a constraint system of the form S is bounded by $(g+1)\cdot(h+1)$, where g is the number of subconcepts (i.e. substrings that are concepts) of C of the form $(\geq n\, R)$. Finally, the cost of the entire method is polynomially bounded by the number of variables in the computed completion.

Theorem 4.3 *The subsumption problem in $\mathcal{PL}_1$ can be solved in polynomial time.*

[1]Note that $\mathcal{PL}_1$ allows for the representation of unqualified existential role quantification: indeed, $\exists R$ can be expressed as $(\geq 1\, R)$.

It is interesting to observe that none of the constructs presented in Section 2 can be added to $\mathcal{PL}_1$ without sacrificing tractability. In particular, it follows from the results reported in [Nebel, 1988] that the addition of role conjunction leads to co-NP-hardness of subsumption. Also, adding negation of non-primitive concepts leads to PSPACE-hardness, whereas adding union makes subsumption co-NP-hard [Schmidt-Schauß and Smolka, 1988]. Moreover, the addition of qualified existential quantification results in the language $\mathcal{ALE}$, and therefore leads to NP-hardness of subsumption [Donini et al., 1990].

We now show that the same problems arise when $\mathcal{PL}_1$ is extended with role chaining. In particular, any concept D of $\mathcal{ALE}$ can be translated into a concept D' of $\mathcal{PL}_1$ + role chaining such that D is satisfiable if and only if D' is satisfiable. D' is obtained from D by substituting each subconcept of D having the form $\exists P.C$ with $(\geq 1\ (P \circ Q)) \sqcap \forall(P \circ Q \circ Q^{-1}).C$, where Q is a new primitive role used only in the substitution of that subconcept. Since the above translation is clearly polynomial, we can conclude that unsatisfiability—and therefore subsumption—in $\mathcal{PL}_1$ with role chaining is NP-hard.

5 The language $\mathcal{PL}_2$

The language considered in this section, called $\mathcal{PL}_2$, is an extension of $\mathcal{FL}^-$ with role conjunction, role chaining, and inverse roles. Its syntax is specified by the following rules:

$$C, D \longrightarrow A \mid C \sqcap D \mid \forall R.C \mid \exists R$$
$$R \longrightarrow P \mid R^{-1} \mid R_1 \sqcap R_2 \mid R_1 \circ R_2$$

where P is a primitive role, and R, R_1 and R_2 are arbitrary roles. Notice that, as for $\mathcal{FL}^-$, every $\mathcal{PL}_2$-concept is satisfiable.

It is possible to verify that every role of $\mathcal{PL}_2$ can be written in a so-called normal form, where the constructor for the inverse role is applied only to primitive roles. The following rewriting rules can be used to transform any role into an equivalent role having such a form. In the sequel, we only refer to roles in normal form.

$$(R_1 \sqcap R_2)^{-1} \longrightarrow R_1^{-1} \sqcap R_2^{-1}$$
$$(R_1 \circ R_2)^{-1} \longrightarrow R_2^{-1} \circ R_1^{-1}$$
$$(R^{-1})^{-1} \longrightarrow R$$

As done for $\mathcal{PL}_1$, we reduce the subsumption problem in $\mathcal{PL}_2$ to the unsatisfiability problem in a suitable extension of the language. Moreover, since $\mathcal{PL}_2$ includes neither disjunction nor qualified existential quantification, it is sufficient to consider the unsatisfiability problem for concepts of the form $C \sqcap \neg D$, where D is conjunction-free.

We call $\mathcal{PL}_2{}^+$ the language constituted by concepts of one of the forms: C, $\neg D$, $C \sqcap \neg D$, where C is a concept of $\mathcal{PL}_2$, and D is a conjunction-free concept of $\mathcal{PL}_2$. In the rest of this section we always refer to concepts of $\mathcal{PL}_2{}^+$, unless otherwise stated.

In order to present the propagation rules for $\mathcal{PL}_2{}^+$-constraint systems, we need the following definition. We say that xRy *holds in* a $\mathcal{PL}_2{}^+$-constraint system S if:

- R is a primitive role P and $xPy \in S$;
- R is P^{-1} and $yPx \in S$;
- R is $R_1 \sqcap R_2$, and both xR_1y and xR_2y hold in S;
- R is $R_1 \circ R_2$ and there is a z such that both xR_1z and zR_2y hold in S.

The propagation rules for $\mathcal{PL}_2{}^+$-constraint systems are the $\rightarrow_\sqcap$-rule, $\rightarrow_\forall$-rule, and the $\rightarrow_{-1}$-rule already defined for $\mathcal{PL}_1$, plus the following ones:

4. $S \rightarrow_{\neg\forall} \{xRy, y{:}\neg C\} \cup S$
   if $x{:}\neg\forall R.C$ is in S, y is a new variable and there is no z such that $z{:}\neg C$ is in S
5. $S \rightarrow_{\sqcap_\rho} \{xR_1y, xR_2y\} \cup S$
   if $x(R_1 \sqcap R_2)y$ is in S, and either xR_1y or xR_2y is not in S
6. $S \rightarrow_\circ \{xR_1z, zR_2y\} \cup S$
   if $x(R_1 \circ R_2)y$ is in S, z is a new variable and there is no w such that both xR_1w and wR_2y are in S

Notice that variables are only generated by the $\rightarrow_{\neg\forall}$-rule. In particular only one variable is generated for each constraint of the form $x{:}\neg\forall R.C$. On the other hand, no rule is needed for constraints of the form $x{:}\exists R$, since we can avoid to produce new variables for them. This is crucial for keeping the size of the system polynomial. Indeed, even if one generates only one variable for each constraint of the form $x{:}\exists R$ (as done in $\mathcal{FL}^-$), the presence of role conjunction may lead to an exponential number of variables in the completion of the system.

It is easy to see that, up to variable renaming, only one completion can be derived from a $\mathcal{PL}_2{}^+$-constraint system. The following theorem states that the above rules preserve satisfiability.

Theorem 5.1 *Let S be a constraint system. Then, if S' is obtained from S by application of the above rules, then S is satisfiable if and only if S' is satisfiable.*

In $\mathcal{PL}_2{}^+$-constraint systems, a *clash* is defined as a set of constraints of one of the following forms:

1. $\{x{:}A, x{:}\neg A\}$;
2. $\{x{:}\exists R_1, x{:}\neg\exists R_2\}$,
   where the completion of the new constraint system $\{xR_1y, x{:}\forall R_2.B\}$ (B is a new symbol denoting a primitive concept) contains a constraint $z{:}B$, for some variable z.

Notice that checking whether a completion of a constraint system S has a clash may require to compute the completion of other systems, each one constituted by two constraints of the form $\{xR_1y, x{:}\forall R_2.B\}$. It is easy to see that if such a completion contains a constraint $z{:}B$, then the existence of an object y related to x through the role R_1 implies that x is also related to an object z through the role R_2, and the pair of constraints $\{x{:}\exists R_1, x{:}\neg\exists R_2\}$ is unsatisfiable.

Theorem 5.2 *Let S be the completion of the constraint system $\{x{:}C \sqcap \neg D\}$. Then S is satisfiable if and only if it contains no clash.*

The tractability of subsumption in $\mathcal{PL}_2$ can be proved by showing that computing the completion S' of a constraint system $\{x{:}C \sqcap \neg D_i\}$ requires polynomial time, and moreover checking whether S' has a clash is also a polynomial task. With regard to the first point, the basic observation is that for every subconcept C' of $C \sqcap \neg D$ at most one constraint of the form $z{:}C'$ can be contained in S'. Therefore, the number of constraints in S' is bounded by the size of $C \sqcap \neg D$. With regard to the second point, notice that the worst case requires considering every pair of constraints of S', and checking if they constitute a clash of the form $\{x{:}\exists R_1, x{:}\neg\exists R_2\}$. Since the cost of such a check is polynomially bounded by the size of R_1 and R_2, we can state the following theorem.

Theorem 5.3 *The subsumption problem in $\mathcal{PL}_2$ can be solved in polynomial time.*

As for $\mathcal{PL}_1$, it is possible to show that none of the constructs presented in Section 2 can be added to $\mathcal{PL}_2$ without sacrificing tractability. In particular, the addition of number restrictions leads to co-NP-hardness of subsumption [Nebel, 1988]. The addition of the negation of primitive concepts results in a language that is a superset of a language called $\mathcal{ALR}$, shown intractable in [Donini et al., 1991a], whereas the addition of qualified existential quantification results in a superset of $\mathcal{ALE}$. Finally, it is possible to show that adding union to $\mathcal{PL}_2$ makes subsumption intractable. In fact, one can prove that even the simpler problem of checking whether C is subsumed by $D_1 \sqcup \cdots \sqcup D_n$, where $C, D_1, \ldots, D_n$ are $\mathcal{FL}^-$-concepts is already intractable (see [Lenzerini and Schaerf, 1991]).

6 Conclusion

We have presented two concept laguages, called $\mathcal{PL}_1$ and $\mathcal{PL}_2$, that include as many as possible of the constructs usually considered in terminological reasoning, while avoiding combinations that are proved harmful for tractability.

It is interesting to observe that we can extend both $\mathcal{PL}_1$ and $\mathcal{PL}_2$ with functional roles, functional role value map and disjunction of primitive concepts without endangering the tractability of subsumption.

The algorithms for checking subsumption in $\mathcal{PL}_1$ and $\mathcal{PL}_2$ have been designed by exploiting a general technique for satisfiability checking in concept languages. Such a technique is the basis of recent complexity results about a wide class of concept languages [Schmidt-Schauß and Smolka, 1988,Donini et al., 1991a]. These results allow us to derive lower bounds for the complexity of almost all the possible combinations of the constructs presented in Section 2. There is in fact one single exception, because it is still unknown if subsumption is tractable in the language obtained from $\mathcal{FL}^-$ by adding number restrictions and role chaining. It turns out that we can state an interesting property of $\mathcal{PL}_1$ and $\mathcal{PL}_2$: *Let $\mathcal{L}$ be a language extending $\mathcal{FL}^-$ with any combination of the constructs presented in Section 2, except for the combination of number restrictions and role chaining; if the subsumption problem in $\mathcal{L}$ is tractable, then $\mathcal{L}$ is a sublanguage of either $\mathcal{PL}_1$ or $\mathcal{PL}_2$.*

Therefore, on the assumption that languages are characterized by the set of constructs they provide, the two languages presented in this paper provide a solution to the problem of singling out an optimal trade-off between expressive power and computational complexity.

References

[Brachman and Levesque, 1984] R. J. Brachman, H. J. Levesque. "The tractability of subsumption in frame-based description languages." In *Proceedings of the Fourth National Conference on Artificial Intelligence*, pp. 34–37, Austin, Texas, 1984.

[Brachman and Schmolze, 1985] R. J. Brachman, J. Schmolze, "An overview of the KL-ONE knowledge representation system." *Cognitive Science*, 9(2):171–216, 1985.

[Donini et al., 1990] F.M. Donini, B. Hollunder, M. Lenzerini, A. Marchetti Spaccamela, D. Nardi, W. Nutt. "The complexity of existential quantification in concept languages." DFKI-Report, DFKI, Postfach 2080, D-6750 Kaiserslautern, Germany, 1990.

[Donini et al., 1991a] F.M. Donini, M. Lenzerini, D. Nardi, W. Nutt. "The complexity of concept languages." To appear in *Proceedings of the Second International Conference on Principles of Knowledge Representation and Reasoning*, Boston, 1991.

[Donini et al., 1991b] F.M. Donini, M. Lenzerini, D. Nardi, W. Nutt. "Tractable concept languages." Technical Report D.1.2.b,c, ESPRIT Basic Research Action 3012 Compulog, 1991.

[Lenzerini and Schaerf, 1991] M. Lenzerini, A. Schaerf. "Concept languages as query languages." To appear in *Proceedings of the Ninth National Conference on Artificial Intelligence*, Anaheim, 1991.

[Levesque and Brachman, 1987] H. J. Levesque, R. J. Brachman. "Expressiveness and tractability in knowledge representation and reasoning." *Computational Intelligence*, 3:78–93, 1987.

[Nebel, 1988] B. Nebel. "Computational complexity of terminological reasoning in BACK." *Artificial Intelligence*, 34(3):371–383, 1988.

[Nebel and Smolka, 1990] B. Nebel, G. Smolka. "Representation and reasoning with attributive descriptions." in K.H. Bläsius, U. Hedtstück, C.-R. Rollinger (Eds.) *Sorts and Types in Artificial Intelligence*, Lecture Notes in Artificial Intelligence 418, Springer Verlag, pp. 112–139, 1990.

[Schmidt-Schauß and Smolka, 1988] M. Schmidt-Schauß, G. Smolka. "Attributive concept descriptions with unions and complements." SEKI Report SR-88-21, FB Informatik, Universität Kaiserslautern, D-6750, Kaiserslautern, Germany, 1988. To appear in *Artificial Intelligence*.

KNOWLEDGE REPRESENTATION

Concept Languages, Inheritance Reasoning

A Correspondence Theory for Terminological Logics: Preliminary Report*

Klaus Schild
Technische Universität Berlin
Projekt KIT-BACK, Sekr. FR 5-12
Franklinstraße 28/29
D-1000 Berlin 10, FRG

Abstract

We show that the terminological logic $\mathcal{ALC}$ comprising Boolean operations on concepts and value restrictions is a notational variant of the propositional modal logic $\mathbf{K}_{(\mathbf{m})}$. To demonstrate the utility of the correspondence, we give two of its immediate by-products. Namely, we axiomatize $\mathcal{ALC}$ and give a simple proof that subsumption in $\mathcal{ALC}$ is PSPACE-complete, replacing the original six-page one.

Furthermore, we consider an extension of $\mathcal{ALC}$ additionally containing both the identity role and the composition, union, transitive-reflexive closure, range restriction, and inverse of roles. It turns out that this language, called $\mathcal{TSL}$, is a notational variant of the propositional dynamic logic *converse*-PDL. Using this correspondence, we prove that it suffices to consider finite $\mathcal{TSL}$-models, show that $\mathcal{TSL}$-subsumption is decidable, and obtain an axiomatization of $\mathcal{TSL}$.

By discovering that features correspond to deterministic programs in dynamic logic, we show that adding them to $\mathcal{TSL}$ preserves decidability, although violates its finite model property. Additionally, we describe an algorithm for deciding the coherence of inverse-free $\mathcal{TSL}$-concepts with features. Finally, we prove that universal implications can be expressed within $\mathcal{TSL}$.

1 Motivation

We shall establish correspondences between terminological logics and propositional modal and dynamic logics. These correspondences turn out to be highly productive because formerly unrelated fields are brought together. In the area of terminological logics, running systems such as BACK, CLASSIC, KL-ONE, KRYPTON, and LOOM have been developed since the late seventies. Only recently theoretical investigations have been undertaken mainly concerning the computational complexity of terminological logics.[1] In the very contrast to that, elaborated theories for modal and dynamic logics have been developed much earlier.[2] Particularly for modal logic there is—apart from first order logic—the most elaborated theory, and dynamic logic has benefited from these results. By detecting these correspondences, we gain new insights into terminological logics solely by expounding the theorems of modal and dynamic logic as theorems of the corresponding terminological logic. There can also be redundant research if correspondences are overlooked. For instance, Ladner [1977] showed that the propositional modal logic $\mathbf{K}_{(\mathbf{m})}$ is PSPACE-complete, and twelve years later this was reproved by Schmidt-Schauß and Smolka [1991] for its notational variant $\mathcal{ALC}$.

*This work was partially supported by the Commission of the European Communities and is part of the ESPRIT Project 5210.

2 Preliminaries

To understand the complexity results to be presented, you should know the complexity classes P, NP, PSPACE, and EXPTIME: P is the class of problems decidable in deterministic polynomial time, NP are those problems decidable in nondeterministic polynomial time, PSPACE are the problems decidable in deterministic polynomial space, and EXPTIME are those problems decidable in deterministic exponential time. Furthermore, you should know that a problem L is *PSPACE-complete* iff both $L \in$ PSPACE and each problem in PSPACE is log space reducible to L; a problem M is *log space reducible* to L iff there is a function $f : M \rightarrow L$ computable in space log (and therefore also computable in polynomial time) such that for all x, $x \in M$ iff $f(x) \in L$. Be aware of the complexity hierarchy P $\subseteq$ NP $\subseteq$ PSPACE $\subseteq$ EXPTIME for which it is only *known* that P $\neq$ EXPTIME.

3 Terminological Logics and Modal Logics

We first consider a terminological logic investigated by Schmidt-Schauß and Smolka [1991], named $\mathcal{ALC}$. Like any other terminological logic, $\mathcal{ALC}$ comprises *concepts*,

[1] Confer [Nebel, 1990] for a good overview of the systems and the complexity results.

[2] For the history of modal logic confer [Hughes and Cresswell, 1984], and for that of dynamic logic confer [Harel, 1984].

denoting sets, as well as *roles*, which denote binary relations. Contrary to roles, concepts can be compound, viz. by intersection $\sqcap$, union $\sqcup$, complementation $\neg$, and the *value restrictions* $\forall.$ and $\exists.$ taking a role and a concept as their arguments. $\forall R.C$ is to be read as "all objects for which all R's are in C," whereas $\exists R.C$ is to be read as "all objects for which there exists an R in C." So we can express concepts such as 'mothers having only sons' by the $\mathcal{ALC}$-expression

$$women \sqcap \neg men \sqcap (\exists child.men) \sqcap \forall child.(men \sqcap \neg women).$$

Formally, $\mathcal{ALC}$ is given by the following formation rules, where c denotes a concept symbol and r a role symbol:

$$\begin{array}{rcl} C, D & \rightarrow & c \mid \top \; C \sqcap D \mid \neg C \mid \forall R.C \\ R & \rightarrow & r \end{array}$$

As usually, we specify the formal semantics of $\mathcal{ALC}$ by an *extension function*. Let $\mathcal{D}$ be any set, called the *domain*. An *extension function* $\mathcal{E}$ *over* $\mathcal{D}$ is a function mapping concepts to subsets of $\mathcal{D}$ and roles to subsets of $\mathcal{D} \times \mathcal{D}$ such that

$$\begin{array}{rcl} \mathcal{E}[\top] & = & \mathcal{D} \\ \mathcal{E}[C \sqcap D] & = & \mathcal{E}[C] \cap \mathcal{E}[D] \\ \mathcal{E}[\neg C] & = & \mathcal{D} \setminus \mathcal{E}[C] \\ \mathcal{E}[\forall R.C] & = & \{d \in \mathcal{D} : \forall \langle d, e\rangle \in \mathcal{E}[R].e \in \mathcal{E}[C]\} \end{array}$$

Using extension functions, we can define the semantic notions *subsumption*, *equivalence*, and *coherence*: D *subsumes* C, written $\models C \sqsubseteq D$, iff for each extension function $\mathcal{E}$, $\mathcal{E}[C] \subseteq \mathcal{E}[D]$, whereas C and D are *equivalent*, written $\models C = D$, iff for each extension function $\mathcal{E}$, $\mathcal{E}[C] = \mathcal{E}[D]$. Finally, C is *coherent* iff there is an extension function $\mathcal{E}$ with $\mathcal{E}[C] \neq \emptyset$, called a *model for* C; otherwise C is *incoherent*. The following lemma justifies merely investigating subsumption in $\mathcal{ALC}$:

Lemma 1 *Subsumption, equivalence, and incoherence are log space reducible to each other in any terminological logic comprising Boolean operations on concepts.*

Proof: Since $\models C \sqsubseteq D$ iff $\models C \sqcap D = C$, subsumption is log space reducible to equivalence in presence of $\sqcap$. Equivalence in turn is log space reducible to incoherence in presence of $\sqcap$ as well as $\neg$ because $\models C = D$ iff $(C \sqcap \neg D) \sqcup (D \sqcap \neg C)$ is incoherent. And finally, incoherence clearly is log space reducible to subsumption in presence of $\neg\top$ since C is incoherent iff $\models C \sqsubseteq \neg\top$. □

We take the union of concepts $\sqcup$ and the operation $\exists.$ dual to $\forall.$ with $\mathcal{E}[\exists R.C] = \{d \in \mathcal{D} : \exists \langle d, e\rangle \in \mathcal{E}[R].e \in \mathcal{E}[C]\}$ as abbreviations for linearly length-bounded $\mathcal{ALC}$-expressions:

$$\begin{array}{rcl} C \sqcup D & \stackrel{\text{def}}{=} & \neg(\neg C \sqcap \neg D) \\ \exists R.C & \stackrel{\text{def}}{=} & \neg \forall R.\neg C \end{array}$$

It is well known that $\mathcal{ALC}$ is a sublanguage of first order logic since atomic concepts correspond to one-place predicates and atomic roles to two-place predicates. The $\mathcal{ALC}$-concept $\neg c_1 \sqcup \forall r.(c_2 \sqcap c_3)$, for instance, can be expressed by the first order formula $\neg c_1(x) \vee \forall y.r(x,y) \Rightarrow c_2(y) \wedge c_3(y)$.

Viewing $\mathcal{ALC}$ from the modal logic perspective, atomic concepts simply can be expounded as atomic *propositional* formulae, and can be interpreted as the set of worlds in which the atomic propositional formula holds. In this case $\forall.$ becomes a modal operator since it is applied to formulae. Thus $\neg c_1 \sqcup \forall r.(c_2 \sqcap c_3)$ can be expressed by the propositional modal formula $\neg c_1 \vee \mathbf{K_r}(c_2 \wedge c_3)$. $\mathbf{K_r}(c_2 \wedge c_3)$ is to be read as "agent r *knows* proposition $c_2 \wedge c_3$," and means that in every world accessible for r, both c_2 and c_3 hold. Actually

- the domain of an extension function can be read as a set of *worlds*.
- atomic concepts can be interpreted as the set of worlds in which they hold, if expounded as atomic formulae.
- atomic roles can be interpreted as *accessibility relations*.

Hence $\forall R.C$ can be expounded as "all worlds in which agent R knows proposition C" instead of "all objects for which all R's are in C."

It is not essential for the following to know propositional modal logic except for establishing the correspondence. To begin with, we inductively fix the syntax of $\mathbf{K_{(m)}}$. The atomic propositions $p_1, p_2, \ldots$ as well as *true* are $\mathbf{K_{(m)}}$-formulae, and, if α and β are $\mathbf{K_{(m)}}$-formulae, so are $\alpha \wedge \beta$, $\neg\alpha$, $\mathbf{K_1}\alpha, \ldots$, and $\mathbf{K_m}\alpha$. The meaning of a $\mathbf{K_{(m)}}$-formula is given by a *Kripke structure* $M = \langle \mathcal{D}, \pi, \mathcal{P}_1, \ldots, \mathcal{P}_m \rangle$, where $\mathcal{D}$ is any set of worlds, $\mathcal{P}_1, \ldots, \mathcal{P}_m \subseteq \mathcal{D} \times \mathcal{D}$ are accessibility relations, and π is a truth assignment mapping atomic propositions to subsets of $\mathcal{D}$. $d \in \pi(p)$ says that p holds in the world d, and $d\mathcal{P}_i e$ denotes that in world d agent i considers world e to be possible. We call $\mathbf{K_{(m)}}$ *normal* because there are no restrictions on the accessibility relations. The denotation of arbitrary formulae is given by a *valuation* v_M mapping $\mathbf{K_{(m)}}$-formulae to subsets of $\mathcal{D}$. v_M is uniquely defined w.r.t. a Kripke structure $M = \langle \mathcal{D}, \pi, \mathcal{P}_1, \ldots, \mathcal{P}_m \rangle$ by $v_M(true) = \mathcal{D}$, $v_M(p_i) = \pi(p_i)$, $v_M(\alpha \wedge \beta) = v_M(\alpha) \cap v_M(\beta)$, $v_M(\neg\alpha) = \mathcal{D} \setminus v_M(\alpha)$, and $v_M(\mathbf{K_i}\alpha) = \{w \in \mathcal{D} : \forall \langle w, w'\rangle \in \mathcal{P}_i.w' \in v_M(\alpha)\}$. Now a $\mathbf{K_{(m)}}$-formula α is *satisfiable* iff there is a valuation v_M with $v_M(\alpha) \neq \emptyset$, and α is *valid* iff $\neg\alpha$ is not satisfiable. For a slightly more comprehensive introduction to $\mathbf{K_{(m)}}$ confer [Halpern and Moses, 1985].

To establish the correspondence, consider the function f mapping $\mathcal{ALC}$-concepts to $\mathbf{K_{(m)}}$-formulae with $f(c) = c$, $f(\top) = true$, $f(C \sqcap D) = f(C) \wedge f(D)$, $f(\neg C) = \neg f(C)$, and $f(\forall R.C) = \mathbf{K_R} f(C)$. It could easily be shown by induction on the complexity of $\mathcal{ALC}$-concepts that f is a linearly length-bounded isomorphism such that an $\mathcal{ALC}$-concept C is coherent iff the $\mathbf{K_{(m)}}$-formula $f(C)$ is satisfiable. Hence we can conclude:

Theorem 1 *$\mathcal{ALC}$ is a notational variant of the propositional modal logic $\mathbf{K_{(m)}}$, and satisfiability in $\mathbf{K_{(m)}}$ has the same computational complexity as coherence in $\mathcal{ALC}$.*

By this correspondence, several theoretical results for $\mathbf{K_{(m)}}$ can easily be carried over to $\mathcal{ALC}$. We immediately know, for example, that without loss of generality, it suffices to consider either finite $\mathcal{ALC}$-models of exponential size or a single infinite *canonical* $\mathcal{ALC}$-model (cf. e.g. [Hughes and Cresswell, 1984]). We shall expose two other outcomes of the correspondence, namely an axiomatization of $\mathcal{ALC}$ and the complexity of $\mathcal{ALC}$ somewhat closer.

Proposition 1 (An Axiomatization of $\mathcal{ALC}$) *The axioms forcing $\langle \top, \sqcap, \neg \rangle$ to be a Boolean algebra together with*

$$\forall R.\top = \top$$
$$\forall R.(C \sqcap D) = (\forall R.C) \sqcap (\forall R.D)$$

are a sound and complete axiomatization of $\mathcal{ALC}$-equivalence [Lemmon, 1966].

Now we shall prove that deciding subsumption in $\mathcal{ALC}$ is PSPACE-complete. Of course, this is not a new result, but its proof is much simpler than the original six-page one in [Schmidt-Schauß and Smolka, 1991]. The reason is that Ladner [1977] proved the PSPACE-completeness of validity in $\mathbf{K_{(m)}}$ for $m = 1$, and, as Halpern and Moses [1985] noted, this result also holds for each $m \geq 1$. Using Theorem 1 and Lemma 1, we can immediately conclude:

Proposition 2 (Complexity of $\mathcal{ALC}$) *Deciding subsumption in $\mathcal{ALC}$ is PSPACE-complete, even if involving only a single atomic role [Ladner, 1977].*

An algorithm for deterministically computing coherence in $\mathcal{ALC}$ in quadratic space is also given in [Ladner, 1977].

4 Terminological Logics and Dynamic Logics

Although concepts can be composed in $\mathcal{ALC}$, we are not able to form compound roles. To overcome this deficiency, we shall introduce an extension of $\mathcal{ALC}$, named $\mathcal{TSL}$. Based on the role *parent*, for instance, we can express in $\mathcal{TSL}$ its transitive-reflexive closure by $parent^*$, its inverse role 'has child' by $parent^{-1}$, and the union of the roles *parent* and $parent^{-1}$, for example, by $parent \sqcup parent^{-1}$. Thus in $\mathcal{TSL}$ we could formalize the concept 'human beings' as follows:

$$\forall parent^*.(\exists parent.women \sqcap \exists parent.men)$$
$$\sqcap\ \forall(parent \sqcup parent^{-1})^*.((women \sqcap \neg men) \sqcup (men \sqcap \neg women))$$

Beside these operations, $\mathcal{TSL}$ comprises the composition of roles $\circ$ and the operation id with $\mathsf{id}(C)$ denoting the identity relation over C. Using both we can express, for instance, the role 'mother' by $parent \circ \mathsf{id}(women)$.

To be exact, $\mathcal{TSL}$ is given by the same concept-formation rule as $\mathcal{ALC}$ together with the role-formation rule

$$R, S \rightarrow r \mid R \circ S \mid R \sqcup S \mid R^* \mid R^{-1} \mid \mathsf{id}(C).$$

To specify the formal semantics of $\mathcal{TSL}$, we additionally require an extension function $\mathcal{E}$ to be a mapping with

$$\mathcal{E}[R \circ S] = \mathcal{E}[R] \circ \mathcal{E}[S]$$
$$\mathcal{E}[R \sqcup S] = \mathcal{E}[R] \cup \mathcal{E}[S]$$
$$\mathcal{E}[R^*] = \mathcal{E}[R]^*$$
$$\mathcal{E}[R^{-1}] = \{\langle d, e \rangle : \langle e, d \rangle \in \mathcal{E}[R]\}$$
$$\mathcal{E}[\mathsf{id}(C)] = \{\langle d, d \rangle : d \in \mathcal{E}[C]\}$$

The identity role self, the *range restriction* $\angle$ defined by $\mathcal{E}[R \angle C] = \{\langle d, e \rangle \in \mathcal{E}[R] : e \in \mathcal{E}[C]\}$, and the transitive closure of roles $^+$ all can be defined within $\mathcal{TSL}$:

$$\mathsf{self} \stackrel{\text{def}}{=} \mathsf{id}(\top)$$
$$R \angle C \stackrel{\text{def}}{=} R \circ \mathsf{id}(C)$$
$$R^+ \stackrel{\text{def}}{=} R \circ R^*$$

However, only the first and the second definition are linearly bounded in their length whereas the third generally is not. Remarkably, we could have introduced the range restriction $\angle$ and the role self into the logic and then define $\mathsf{id}(C)$ as $\mathsf{self} \angle C$.

Now it is important to realize that roles not only can be interpreted as accessibility relations but also as nondeterministic programs. In this case $\langle d, e \rangle \in \mathcal{E}[R]$ denotes that there is an execution of the program R starting in state d and ending in state e. To achieve this interpretation

- the domain of an extension function is to be read as a set of program *states.*
- atomic concepts are to be interpreted as the set of states in which they hold, if expounded as atomic formulae.
- atomic roles are to be interpreted as *atomic nondeterministic programs.*

Using this interpretation, compound $\mathcal{TSL}$-expressions can be expounded as follows:

- $\forall R.C$ as "whenever program R terminates, proposition C holds on termination"
- $R_1 \circ R_2$ as "run R_1 and R_2 consecutively"
- $R_1 \sqcup R_2$ as "nondeterministically do R_1 or R_2"
- R^* as "repeat program R a nondeterministically chosen number of times ≥ 0"
- R^{-1} as "run R in reverse"
- $\mathsf{id}(C)$ as "proceed without changing the program state iff proposition C holds"

This illustrates that $\mathcal{TSL}$ corresponds to propositional dynamic logic. Indeed, $\mathcal{TSL}$ could easily be shown to be a notational variant of *converse*-PDL as given in [Fischer and Ladner, 1979]. There, $\top$ is written as *true*, $C \sqcap D$ as $C \wedge D$, $\neg C$ as $\sim C$, $\forall R.C$ as $[R]C$, $\exists R.C$ as $\langle R \rangle C$, $R \circ S$ as $R;S$, $R \sqcup S$ as $R \cup S$, R^{-1} as R^-, and $\mathsf{id}(C)$ as $C?$.

Theorem 2 *$\mathcal{TSL}$ is a notational variant of converse-PDL, the propositional dynamic logic PDL with the converse-operator. Moreover, satisfiability in converse-PDL has the same computational complexity as coherence in $\mathcal{TSL}$.*

For an excellent introduction to dynamic logic you may confer [Harel, 1984]. There, one can find a survey of interesting theorems of dynamic logic which can now be expounded as theorems of $\mathcal{TSL}$. Hence, for instance, we can narrow down the computational complexity of $\mathcal{TSL}$. Fischer and Ladner [1979] showed that PDL-validity is EXPTIME-hard, even if involving only a single atomic program and its transitive-reflexive closure as programs. Using Theorem 2, we can infer:

Proposition 3 (Lower Compl. Bound of $\mathcal{TSL}$)
Deciding subsumption in $\mathcal{ALC}$ extended with the transitive-reflexive closure of roles is EXPTIME-hard, even if involving only a single atomic role [Fischer and Ladner, 1979].

Concerning the upper comlexity bound, Pratt [1979] gave an algorithm for deciding PDL-satisfiability requiring at most exponential time. As Harel [1984, Section 2.5.6] pointed out, the algorithm can easily be extended to deal with $^{-1}$. The reason is that without loss of generality, we can assume $^{-1}$ applied only to atomic roles. To see this, realize that for each $\mathcal{E}$, $\mathcal{E}[(R \circ S)^{-1}] = \mathcal{E}[S^{-1} \circ R^{-1}]$, $\mathcal{E}[(R \sqcup S)^{-1}] = \mathcal{E}[R^{-1} \sqcup S^{-1}]$, and $\mathcal{E}[(R^*)^{-1}] = \mathcal{E}[(R^{-1})^*]$. Using Theorem 2, we know that $\mathcal{TSL}$-coherence is contained in EXPTIME, and therefore $\mathcal{TSL}$-subsumption is in co-EXPTIME. However, co-EXPTIME is the same as EXPTIME. So we have:

Proposition 4 (Upper Compl. Bound of $\mathcal{TSL}$)
Subsumption in $\mathcal{TSL}$ can be decided in exponential time [Pratt, 1979, Harel, 1984, Section 2.2/2.5.6].

As another by-product of the correspondence we gain an axiomatization of $\mathcal{TSL}$ which assumes $^{-1}$ to be applied only to atomic roles.

Proposition 5 (An Axiomatization of $\mathcal{TSL}$)
Let $C \sqsubseteq D$ be defined as $C \sqcap D = C$. The axioms for $\mathcal{ALC}$ together with

$$\begin{aligned}
\forall R \sqcup S.C &= (\forall R.C) \sqcap (\forall S.C) \\
\forall R \circ S.C &= \forall R.\forall S.C \\
\forall \mathsf{id}(C).D &= \neg C \sqcup D \\
\forall R^*.C &= C \sqcap \forall R^+.C \\
C \sqcap \forall R^*.(\neg C \sqcup \forall R.C) &\sqsubseteq \forall R^*.C \\
C &\sqsubseteq \forall r.\exists r^{-1}.C \\
C &\sqsubseteq \forall r^{-1}.\exists r.C
\end{aligned}$$

are a sound and complete axiomatization of $\mathcal{TSL}$-equivalence [Pratt, 1979, Harel, 1984, Section 2.5.6].

By the way, the first three axioms indicate that $\mathcal{TSL}$ without * and $^{-1}$ is reduced to $\mathcal{ALC}$ since $\sqcup$, $\circ$, id can be eliminated linearly.

The correspondence theorem additionally provides us with an elaborated model theory. The main model theorem for *converse*-PDL says that it suffices to consider only finite connected models of exponential size. To carry over this result, we call an extension function $\mathcal{E}$ over $\mathcal{D}$ mapping the atomic roles $r_1, ..., r_m$ *connected* iff for every $d, e \in \mathcal{D}$, $\langle d, e \rangle \in \mathcal{E}[(r_1 \sqcup r_1^{-1} ... \sqcup r_m \sqcup r_m^{-1})^*]$. Furthermore, $l(C)$ denotes the length of the concept C regarded as a string over $\top, \sqcap, \sqcup, \neg, \forall., \circ, ^*, ^{-1}$, and atoms.

Proposition 6 (Finite $\mathcal{TSL}$-Models)
Every coherent $\mathcal{TSL}$-concept C has a connected model over $\mathcal{D}$ with $|\mathcal{D}| \leq 2^{l(C)}$ [Fischer and Ladner, 1979].

In contrast to that, the finite model property does not hold for $\mathcal{TSL}$ augmented with the intersection of roles, called $\mathcal{TSLR}$. The reason is that every model $\mathcal{E}$ for

$$\forall r^*.((\exists r.\top) \sqcap \forall (r^+ \sqcap \mathsf{self}).\neg\top)$$

has an infinite acyclic $\mathcal{E}[r]$-chain.

Proposition 7 (Infinite $\mathcal{TSLR}$-Models)
There is a coherent $\mathcal{TSLR}$-concept which has no finite model [Harel, 1984, Theorem 2.35].

Note that this does not mean that $\mathcal{TSLR}$ is undecidable. Actually, the decidability of $\mathcal{TSLR}$ seems to be unknown. It is known, however, that $\mathcal{TSL}$ extended with the complementation of roles is undecidable [Harel, 1984, Theorem 2.34], and that $\mathcal{TSLR}$ with features is highly undecidable as we shall see in the next section.

4.1 $\mathcal{TSL}$ with Features

In $\mathcal{TSL}$ we are able to force, for instance, that something has at least two parents, namely a female and a male one:

$$(\exists parent \angle women.\neg men) \sqcap (\exists parent \angle men.\neg women)$$

Unfortunately, this expression does not stipulate that something has exactly two parents. The reason is that we have expressed 'has mother' as the role $parent \angle women$. However, 'has mother' rather is a partial function than a relation. If something has a mother, it has exactly one. This suggests to extend $\mathcal{TSL}$ with *features*, denoting atomic partial functions. If *mother* and *father* were features, the above expression indeed would force that each human being has exactly one mother and father.

We define $\mathcal{FSL}$ by the same formation rules as $\mathcal{TSL}$ execpt that an $\mathcal{FSL}$-role additionally can be a *feature* symbol. Moreover, we require an extension function $\mathcal{E}$ over $\mathcal{D}$ to be a mapping such that for each feature symbol f, $\mathcal{E}[f]$ is a partial function mapping $\mathcal{D}$ to $\mathcal{D}$.

Note that $f_1 \circ f_2$ and $\mathsf{id}(C)$ denote partial functions, whereas $f_1 \sqcup f_2$, f^*, and f^{-1} generally denote binary relations.

Clearly, features correspond to *atomic deterministic programs* considered in dynamic logic. Thus [Parikh, 1979, §7] can be read to show that any atomic role r is expressible by $f_r \circ (f_{new})^*$, where f_r is the feature uniquely corresponding to r and f_{new} is a new feature. In this manner each non-feature atomic role in a $\mathcal{TSL}$-expression can be eliminated without increasing its length more than linearly.[3] Thus we can assume that the only atomic roles which $\mathcal{FSL}$ comprises are features. So, it is obvious that $\mathcal{FSL}$ is a notational variant of the deterministic version of *converse*-PDL.

Theorem 3 *$\mathcal{FSL}$ is a notational variant of converse-DPDL, the deterministic propositional dynamic logic DPDL with the converse-operator. Moreover, satisfiability in converse-DPDL has—up to linear time—the same computational complexity as coherence in $\mathcal{FSL}$.*

Ben-Ari *et al.* [1982] showed that DPDL-satisfiability is contained in EXPTIME, and Vardi [1985] pointed out that satisfiability in *converse*-DPDL can be decided in double exponential time. Utilizing Theorem 3 and Lemma 1, we can conclude:

Proposition 8 (Complexity of $\mathcal{FSL}$)
Subsumption in $\mathcal{FSL}$ without $^{-1}$ can be decided in exponential time [Ben-Ari et al.*, 1982], and deciding subsumption in $\mathcal{FSL}$ can be done in double exponential time*

[3] By the way this means that in the presence of * deciding subsumption in feature logics is at least as hard as deciding subsumption in the corresponding terminological logic.

[Vardi, 1985]. Furthermore, both problems are EXPTIME-hard [Parikh, 1979, § 7].

We now present a sound and complete algorithm for deciding coherence of $^{-1}$-free $\mathcal{FSL}$-concepts in deterministic exponential time as described in [Ben-Ari *et al.*, 1982]. To test the coherence of a concept C, the algorithm builds a tree with nodes labelled by sets of $\mathcal{FSL}$-concepts with root $\{C\}$, where double negations occurring in concepts are assumed to be eliminated. The algorithm uses three functions to build the tree, namley $\wedge$-*succ*, $\vee$-*succ*, and f-*succ*. $\wedge$-*succ* and $\vee$-*succ* are nondeterministic functions to generate necessary and possible consequences of a set of $\mathcal{FSL}$-concepts represented by an and-or-tree.

$$\wedge\text{-}succ(\Gamma) \stackrel{\text{def}}{=} \Gamma \cup \begin{cases} \{C, D\} & \text{if } C \sqcap D \in \Gamma \\ \{C, D\} & \text{if } \exists \mathrm{id}(C).D \in \Gamma \\ \{\exists R.\exists S.C\} & \text{if } \exists R \circ S.C \in \Gamma \\ \{\forall R.\forall S.C\} & \text{if } \forall R \circ S.C \in \Gamma \\ \{\forall R.C, \forall S.C\} & \text{if } \forall R \sqcup S.C \in \Gamma \\ \{C, \forall R.\forall R^*.C\} & \text{if } \forall R^*.C \in \Gamma \end{cases}$$

$$\vee\text{-}succ(\Gamma) \stackrel{\text{def}}{=}$$

$$\begin{cases} \langle \Gamma \cup \{C\}, \Gamma \cup \{D\} \rangle & \text{if } C \sqcup D \in \Gamma \\ \langle \Gamma \cup \{\neg C\}, \Gamma \cup \{D\} \rangle & \text{if } \forall \mathrm{id}(C).D \in \Gamma \\ \langle \Gamma \cup \{\exists R.C\}, \Gamma \cup \{\exists S.C\} \rangle & \text{if } \exists R \sqcup S.C \in \Gamma \\ \langle \Gamma \cup \{C\}, \Gamma \cup \{\exists R.\exists R^*.C\} \rangle & \text{if } \exists R^*.C \in \Gamma \end{cases}$$

f-*succ* is a function to generate the f-successors of a node, defined for each feature f by

$$f\text{-}succ(\Gamma) \stackrel{\text{def}}{=} \{C : \exists f.C \in \Gamma\} \cup \{C : \forall f.C \in \Gamma\}.$$

To compute the coherence of an $^{-1}$-free $\mathcal{FSL}$-concept, the algorithm performs the following steps:

1. Replace each occurrence of a non-feature atomic role r in C by $f_r \circ (f_{new})^*$, where f_r is the feature uniquely corresponding to r and f_{new} is a new feature.
2. Take the tree consisting solely of the root $\{C\}$ as the current tree.
3. Apply $\wedge$-*succ* and $\vee$-*succ* to the not yet eliminated leaves until every node thus obtainable already is on the tree.
4. Repeatedly eliminate each leaf Γ violating either (a) $S \subseteq \Gamma$ for every $S = \wedge\text{-}succ(\Gamma)$, (b) $S_1 \subseteq \Gamma$ or $S_2 \subseteq \Gamma$ for every $\langle S_1, S_2 \rangle = \vee\text{-}succ(\Gamma)$, or (c) $C \in \Gamma$ iff $\neg C \notin \Gamma$ for each C. Call the set of nodes of the current tree N.
5. For each feature f, apply f-*succ* to all not yet eliminated leaves where two nodes $f\text{-}succ(\Gamma)$ and $f'\text{-}succ(\Gamma)$ are to be identified if they are equal. Now define for each feature f, $\mathcal{E}[f] \subseteq N \times N$ such that $\langle \Gamma_s, \Gamma_t \rangle \in \mathcal{E}[f]$ iff Γ_t is a node of the tree with root $f\text{-}succ(\Gamma_s)$ generated by $\wedge$-*succ* and $\vee$-*succ*. For each node $\Gamma_s \in N$ check (in polynomial time) whether for every $\exists R.D \in \Gamma_s$ there is a Γ_t such that $\langle \Gamma_s, \Gamma_t \rangle \in \mathcal{E}[R]$ and $D \in \Gamma_t$. Eliminate each node not satisfying this condition and all edges leading from and to that node. Continue with 3. until all leaves do satisfy the condition.
6. Return 'yes' if C is an element of a not eliminated node; otherwise return 'no.'

To test $\exists f^*.c$, for instance, the algorithm first generates the root $\Gamma_0 = \{\exists f^*.c\}$ and its $\vee$-successors $\Gamma_1 = \{\exists f^*.c, c\}$ and $\Gamma_2 = \{\exists f^*.c, \exists f.\exists f^*.c\}$. Then the f-successor of Γ_2, $\Gamma_3 = \{\exists f^*.c\}$, is generated. $\mathcal{E}[f]$ is defined as $\{\langle \Gamma_2, \Gamma_0 \rangle, \langle \Gamma_2, \Gamma_1 \rangle, \langle \Gamma_2, \Gamma_2 \rangle\}$ because Γ_1 as well as Γ_2 are $\vee$-successors of $f\text{-}succ(\Gamma_2)$. Now for each $\exists R.C \in \Gamma_2$ there is a node Γ such that $\langle \Gamma_2, \Gamma \rangle \in \mathcal{E}[R]$ and $C \in \Gamma$. Therefore no leaf has to be eliminated. The algorithm halts returning 'yes' because each $\vee$-successor of Γ_3 is already on the tree and $\exists f^*.c \in \Gamma_0$.

Surprisingly, allowing the intersection of roles does not preserve the decidability of $\mathcal{FSL}$.

Proposition 9 (Undecidability of $\mathcal{FSLR}$)
Subsumption in $\mathcal{FSL}$ augmented with role intersection is highly undecidable, even if involving only features as atomic roles [Harel, 1984, Theorem 2.36].

With Theorem 3 we gain new model theoretic insights into $\mathcal{FSL}$. For the ability to force an $\mathcal{FSL}$-model to be infinite, both features and $^{-1}$ are essential. To see this, first realize that each model $\mathcal{E}$ for

$$c \sqcap \forall (f^{-1})^*.\exists f^{-1}.\neg c$$

has an infinite acyclic $\mathcal{E}[f]$-chain if f is a feature. Requiring f to be a feature is necessary to preclude cyclic models such as $\mathcal{E}$ over $\mathcal{D} = \{d, e\}$ with $\mathcal{E}[c] = \{e\}$ and $\mathcal{E}[f] = \{\langle d, e \rangle, \langle d, d \rangle\}$, where $\mathcal{E}[f]$ is not functional.

Proposition 10 (Infinite $\mathcal{FSL}$-Models)
There is a coherent $\mathcal{FSL}$-concept which has no finite model [Vardi, 1985].

In contrast to this result, the finite model property holds for $^{-1}$-free $\mathcal{FSL}$.

Proposition 11 (Finite Models for $^{-1}$-free $\mathcal{FSL}$)
Every coherent $^{-1}$-free $\mathcal{FSL}$-concept C has a connected model over $\mathcal{D}$ with $|\mathcal{D}| \leq 4^n n^2$, where $n = l(C)$ [Ben-Ari et al.*, 1982].*

4.2 Concept Equations and Inequations

The terminological logics investigated seem to be very expressive. Nevertheless, they do not support concept definitions and constraints. We could want to define, for instance, human beings by

(1) $\qquad human \; = \; \forall parent.human$

Of course, we want to know the consequences of such definitions and constraints. Like in dynamic logic we say, for example, that $human \sqsubseteq \forall parent^*.human$ is a *global consequence* of the set $\Gamma = \{(1)\}$ and write:

$$\Gamma \models human \sqsubseteq \forall parent^*.human$$

Formally, we pin this down as follows: Let $\Gamma \cup \{E\}$ be a set of concept equations and inequations. E is a *global consequence* of Γ, written $\Gamma \models E$, iff each extension function $\mathcal{E}$ satisfying all elements of Γ, also satisfies E; where $\mathcal{E}$ *satisfies* $C = D$ iff $\mathcal{E}[C] = \mathcal{E}[D]$, and $\mathcal{E}$ *satisfies* $C \neq D$ iff $\mathcal{E}[C] \neq \mathcal{E}[D]$.

We treat $C \sqsubseteq D$ as an abbreviation for $C \sqcap D = C$, and each element of Γ of this form is called *universal implication.*

Now there is the question whether the ability to define and constrain sets actually increases the expressive power of $\mathcal{TSL}$. It will turn out that for finite Γ, global consequence in $\mathcal{TSL}$ is reducible to subsumption in $\mathcal{TSL}$. To show this, we need two lemmata. The first signifies that only connected models are relevant for global consequence in $\mathcal{TSL}$. This can easily be proved by utilizing the so-called *collapsed model property* of $\mathcal{TSL}$ stating that every $\mathcal{TSL}$-model can be collapsed into a finite connected one [Harel, 1984, Theorem 2.13].

Lemma 2 *Let $\Gamma \cup \{E\}$ be a set of $\mathcal{TSL}$-concept equations and inequations. Then $\Gamma \models E$ iff each connected extension function $\mathcal{E}$ satisfying all elements of Γ, also satisfies E.*

The following lemma states that universally quantified expressions are expressible in connected models—viz. by $c(C)$ defined as $\forall(r_1 \sqcup r_1^{-1} ... \sqcup r_m \sqcup r_m^{-1})^*.C$, where $r_1, ..., r_m$ are the atomic roles and features of the language in question. Note that c owes its name to the common knowledge operator (cf. [Halpern and Moses, 1985]).

Lemma 3 *Let C be any $\mathcal{TSL}$-concept and $\mathcal{E}$ any connected extension function over $\mathcal{D}$. $\mathcal{E}[C] = \mathcal{D}$ iff $\mathcal{E}[c(C)] = \mathcal{D}$, and moreover $\mathcal{E}[c(C)] \neq \mathcal{D}$ iff $\mathcal{E}[c(C)] = \emptyset$.*

Theorem 4 *For finite sets of concept equations and inequations, global consequence in $\mathcal{TSL}$ is log space reducible to subsumption in $\mathcal{TSL}$.*

Proof: Let $eq(C, D)$ be $c(\neg C \sqcup D) \sqcap c(\neg D \sqcup C)$. According to the last two lemmata, it is obvious that $\{C_1 = D_1\} \cup \Gamma \models C \sqsubseteq D$ iff $\Gamma \models eq(C_1, D_1) \sqcap C \sqsubseteq D$ and that $\{C_1 \neq D_1\} \cup \Gamma \models C \sqsubseteq D$ iff $\Gamma \models \neg eq(C_1, D_1) \sqcap C \sqsubseteq D$. Taking this as induction step, it can be easily shown by induction on $|\Gamma|$ that all elements of Γ can be eliminated linearly. □

However, the proof does not work for infinite Γ since $\mathcal{TSL}$ lacks compactness. This becomes obvious when considering the infinite set $\Gamma = \{c \sqsubseteq \forall r.d, c \sqsubseteq \forall r \circ r.d, ...\}$. Clearly, $c \sqsubseteq \forall r^+.d$ is a global consequence of Γ but not a global consequence of any finite subset of Γ. In fact, global consequence in $\mathcal{TSL}$ is known to be highly undecidable [Harel, 1984, Section 2.4]. However, Theorem 4 also holds for $\mathcal{FSL}$ since Vardi [1985] proved the collapsed model property for $\mathcal{FSL}$.

5 Conclusions

So far we have seen that correspondences between terminological logics and propositional modal and dynamic logics can be used to gain new insights into the nature of terminological logics. However, this work can be extended in two ways. First, we can further exploit the correspondences already established by carefully studying the corresponding theories of modal and dynamic logic. For example, we proved that a syntactically restricted form of global consequence in $\mathcal{TSL}$, known in dynamic logic as *partial completeness assertions*, is NP-complete. Secondly, we can establish further correspondences. *Constants* in terminological logics, for instance, correspond to *names* (atomic formulae denoting single element sets) in dynamic logic. Similarly, temporal expressions can be integrated into terminological logics.

References

[Ben-Ari *et al.*, 1982] Mordechai Ben-Ari, Joseph Y. Halpern, and Amir Pnueli. Deterministic propositional dynamic logic: Finite models, complexity, and completeness. *Journal of Computer and System Science*, 25:402–417, 1982.

[Fischer and Ladner, 1979] Michael J. Fischer and Richard E. Ladner. Propositional dynamic logic of regular programs. *Journal of Computer and System Science*, 18:194–211, 1979.

[Halpern and Moses, 1985] Joseph Y. Halpern and Yoram Moses. A guide to the modal logics of knowledge and belief. In *Proceedings of the 9th International Joint Conference on Artificial Intelligence*, pages 480–490, Los Angeles, Cal., 1985.

[Harel, 1984] David Harel. Dynamic logic. In D. Gabbay and F. Guenther, editors, *Handbook of Philosophical Logic*, volume 2, pages 497–604. Reidel, Dordrecht, Holland, 1984.

[Hughes and Cresswell, 1984] George E. Hughes and M. J. Cresswell. *A Companion to Modal Logic.* Methuen, London, 1984.

[Ladner, 1977] Richard E. Ladner. The computational complexity of provability in systems of modal propositional logic. *SIAM Journal of Computing*, 6(3):467–480, 1977.

[Lemmon, 1966] E. J. Lemmon. Algebraic semantics for modal logic I. *Journal of Symbolic Logic*, 31(1):46–65, 1966.

[Nebel, 1990] Bernhard Nebel. *Reasoning and Revision in Hybrid Representation Systems.* Lecture Notes in Artificial Intelligence. Springer-Verlag, Berlin, West Germany, 1990.

[Parikh, 1979] Rohit Parikh. Propositional dynamic logics of programms: A survey. In E. Engeler, editor, *Proceedings of the Workshop on Logic of Programs*, volume 125 of *Lecture Notes in Computer Science*, pages 102–144, Berlin, West Germany, 1979. Springer-Verlag.

[Pratt, 1979] Vaughan R. Pratt. Models of program logics. In *Proceedings of the 20th Annual Symposium on Foundations of Computer Science*, pages 115–122, San Juan, Puerto Rico, 1979.

[Schmidt-Schauß and Smolka, 1991] Manfred Schmidt-Schauß and Gert Smolka. Attributive concept descriptions with complements. *Artificial Intelligence*, 48(1):1–26, 1991. A prelimenary version of this paper is available as IBM Germany Scientific Center, IWBS, Stuttgart, Germany, 1989.

[Vardi, 1985] Moshe Y. Vardi. The taming of converse: Reasoning about two-way computations. In R. Parikh, editor, *Proceedings of the Workshop on Logic of Programs*, volume 193 of *Lecture Notes in Computer Science*, pages 413–424, Berlin, West Germany, 1985. Springer-Verlag.

Generalizing Term Subsumption Languages to Fuzzy Logic

John Yen*
Department of Computer Science
Texas A&M University
College Station, TX 77843
Yen@CSSUN.TAMU.EDU

Abstract

During the past decade, knowledge representation research in AI has generated a class of languages called term subsumption languages (TSL), which is a knowledge representation formalism with a well-defined logic-based semantics. Due to its formal semantics, a term subsumption system can automatically infer the subsumption relationships between concepts defined in the system. However, these systems are very limited in handling vague concepts in the knowledge base. In contrast, fuzzy logic directly deals with the notion of vagueness and imprecision using fuzzy predicates, fuzzy quantifiers, linguistic variables, and other constructs. Hence, fuzzy logic offers an appealing foundation for generalizing the semantics of term subsumption languages. Based on a test score semantics in fuzzy logic, this paper first generalizes the semantics of term subsumption languages. Then, we discuss impacts of such a generalization to the reasoning capabilities of term subsumption systems. The generalized knowledge representation framework not only alleviates the difficulty of conventional AI knowledge representation schemes in handling imprecise and vague information, but also extends the application of fuzzy logic to complex intelligent systems that need to perform high-level analyses using conceptual abstractions.

1 Introduction

During the past decade, knowledge representation works in AI have generated a class of languages called term subsumption languages (TSL), which is a knowledge representation formalism with a well-defined logic-based semantics. Using a TSL, a knowledge engineer can explicitly describe defining characteristics of concepts (unary terms) and roles (binary terms) [Patel-Schneider *et al.* 1990][1]. The major strength of term subsumption systems is their reasoning capabilities offered by a *classifier*. The classifier is a special purpose reasoner that automatically infers and maintains a consistent and accurate taxonomic lattice of logical subsumption relations between terms [Schmolze and Lipkis 1983]. These formalisms generally descend from the ideas presented in KL-ONE [Brachman and Schmolze 1985]. Term subsumption languages are a generalization of both semantic networks and frames because the languages have well-defined semantics, which is often missing from frames and semantic networks [Woods 1975, Brachman 1983].

Term subsumption languages are limited to expressing crisp concept definitions. However, many useful concepts that are needed by an intelligent system do not have well-defined boundaries, i.e., they are vague concepts. For instance, we may say that a baseball player is a good hitter if the person's hitting ratio is *fairly high*. In an intelligent monitoring and control system, we may wish to define a critical valve as a valve that has a *low tolerance* of pressure. In all these examples, a concept is defined by referring to other vague terms such as "fairly high hitting ratio" and "low pressure tolerance". It is the difficulty to express these vague concepts in term subsumption languages that motivates us to generalize the languages.

Fuzzy logic, which is a generalization of conventional logic, directly deals with the notion of vagueness and imprecision using fuzzy predicates, fuzzy quantifiers, linguistic variables, and other constructs. Thus, it offers an appealing foundation for generalizing TSL to capture imprecise and vague linguistic terms. In particular, the test score semantics in fuzzy logic allows us to easily generalize the term forming expression in TSL into elastic constraints, which can be satisfied to a degree.

In the following sections, we first introduce the basics of term subsumption languages and test score semantics as a background. Section 3 generalizes the semantics of term subsumption languages and describes a complete and sound subsumption test algorithm for a simple fuzzy term subsumption language. A discussion of related works then follows. Finally, we summarize the potential benefits of our approach.

---

*This research was supported by Engineering Excellence Fund at Texas A&M University.

[1] A role in a TSL corresponds to a slot in other frame-based systems.

2 Background

2.1 Term Subsumption Languages

A term subsumption languages (TSL) distinguishes two kinds of concepts: primitive concepts and defined concepts. A primitive concept is a concept whose definition can not be stated in the language; a defined concept is a concept whose definition is described using other concepts and a set of concept forming expressions provided by the language. *Value restriction* and *number restriction* are two concept forming constructs that are offered by almost all TSL's. A value restriction restricts the type of a role value (i.e., slot value), while a number restriction constrains the cardinality of a role value. In this paper, a value restriction will be expressed in the form of `(:all R C)` which means that all values of the role R are of type C. A number restriction can be either in the form of `(:at-least n R)`, which means that the role R has at least n values, or in the form of `(:at-most n R)`, which states that the role R has at most n values.

To describe the formal semantics of these concept forming constructs in TSL's, we need to introduce the following terminology. A terminological knowledge base, denoted by $\mathcal{T}$, consists of concepts and roles (which are also called relations in some TSL's) defined using a term subsumption language. An interpretation $\mathcal{I}_{\mathcal{T}}$ of $\mathcal{T}$ is a pair ($\mathcal{D}$, $\mathcal{E}$) where $\mathcal{D}$ is a set of individuals described by terms in $\mathcal{T}$ and $\mathcal{E}$ is an *extension function* that maps concepts in $\mathcal{T}$ to subsets of $\mathcal{D}$, and roles in $\mathcal{T}$ to subsets of the Cartesian product, $\mathcal{D} \times \mathcal{D}$. Based on these notations, we describe the semantics of some term forming expressions in TSL's below [Nebel 1988]:

$$\mathcal{E}[(\textbf{:and } C_1 ... C_n)] = \mathcal{E}[C_1] \cap \cdots \cap \mathcal{E}[C_n],$$

$$\mathcal{E}[(\textbf{:all} \text{ R C})] = \{x \in D | \forall y :< x,\ y > \in \mathcal{E}[R] \Rightarrow y \in \mathcal{E}[C]\},$$

$$\mathcal{E}[(\textbf{:at-least} \text{ n R})] = \{x \in \mathcal{D} |\ \|\ \{y \in \mathcal{D} | < x,\ y > \in \mathcal{E}[R]\}\ \| \geq n\},$$

$$\mathcal{E}[(\textbf{:at-most} \text{ n R})] = \{x \in \mathcal{D} |\ \|\ \{y \in \mathcal{D} | < x,\ y > \in \mathcal{E}[R]\}\ \| \leq n\},$$

$$\mathcal{E}[(\textbf{:range} \text{ R C})] = \{< x,\ y > \in \mathcal{D} \times \mathcal{D} | < x,\ y > \in \mathcal{E}[R] \wedge y \in \mathcal{E}[C]\}.$$

2.2 Test Score Semantics

In 1981, while the first KL-ONE workshop was being held, Lotfi A. Zadeh was advocating a meaning-representation language called PRUF based on possibility theory in fuzzy logic [Zadeh 1978b]. The semantics underlying PRUF is what Zadeh referred to as *test score semantics*, which interprets the meaning of a predicate as having an *elastic constraint* on objects in the database [Zadeh 1981, Zadeh 1982]. In PRUF, a query is processed by first applying a sequence of tests to database objects, yielding a collection of test scores. By aggregating these test scores, the system obtains an overall test score that measures the compatibility between the query and the database.

Test-score semantics is more general than the semantics of term subsumption languages, in which test scores are limited to true and fals. Unlike KL-ONE, however, PRUF was not concerned about developing efficient special purpose reasoners. By combining works in these two areas, we can develop a knowledge representation system that takes advantage of both the generality of test score semantics and the efficient reasoning capabilities of term subsumption systems.

3 Generalizing the Semantics of Term Subsumption Languages

In this section, we generalize the semantics of term subsumption language. First, we generalize the extension of a term and the subsumption relationship between terms. Then we describe how various concept forming expressions can be generalized into elastic constraints using test score semantics in fuzzy logic.

3.1 Generalizing the Extension Function and the Subsumption Relationship

We first generalize the extension function $\mathcal{E}$ such that the extension of a concept is a fuzzy subset of $\mathcal{D}$, and the extension of a role is a fuzzy subset of $\mathcal{D} \times \mathcal{D}$. A fuzzy subset C of $\mathcal{D}$is characterized by a membership function μ_{C} that maps elements of $\mathcal{D}$to the interval [0, 1]. The degree to which an element x of $\mathcal{D}$ belongs to a concept C is denoted as $\mu_{\mathrm{C}}(x)$. Similarly, the degree to which an ordered pair $< x, y >$ belongs to a role R is denoted as $\mu_{\mathrm{R}}(x, y)$. Moreover, we can generalize the extension of a term forming expression to a fuzzy set and denote the degree to which an object x satisfies a term forming expression e by $\mu_e(x)$.

A concept C_1 subsumes a concept C_2 if and only if the extension of the former is a fuzzy superset of the extension of the latter. More formally, we say that C_1 subsumes C_2 if and only if for any set $\mathcal{D}$ and any extension function $\mathcal{E}$ over $\mathcal{D}$ the following holds:

$$\forall d \in \mathcal{D} : \mu_{C_1}(d) \geq \mu_{C_2}(d) \quad (1)$$

3.2 Soft Value Restriction

A value restriction in a terminological language constrains all the role values of an object to be instances of a given class. For instance, a type of valve can be defined by restricting its pressure tolerance to an interval. We can generalize this kind of constraint to an "elastic constraint" or "soft constraint" (e.g., `(:all Pressure-Tolerance Low-pressure)`) in two ways. The logic implication in the original semantics

$$\forall y \; \texttt{Pressure-Tolerance}(x, y) \Rightarrow \texttt{Low-pressure}(y) \quad (2)$$

can be generalized to a fuzzy implication operator. Thus, the degree to which a value restriction is satisfied by an instance x is determined by the degree to which the implication is true for x. This can be formulated as follows:

$$\mu_{(\text{:all R C})}(x) = \inf_{y_i} [\mu_{\mathrm{R(x,y)} \Rightarrow \mathrm{C(y)}}(x, y_i)] \quad (3)$$

where $\mu_{\mathrm{R(x,y)} \Rightarrow \mathrm{C(y)}}(x, y_i)$ can be defined using various fuzzy implication operators [Magrez and Smets 1989].

An alternative approach to generalizing the semantics of a value restriction is to use the notion of conditional necessity in possibility theory [Zadeh 1978a, Dubois and Prade 1988]:

$$\mu_{(\text{:all R C})}(x) = Nec(\text{C}(y)|\text{R}(x,y)) \quad (4)$$

$$= 1 - Poss(\neg\text{C}(y)|\text{R}(x,y)) \quad (5)$$

$$= 1 - \frac{\max_y \{\min[1-\mu_{\text{C}}(y), \mu_{\text{R}}(x,y)]\}}{\max_y \mu_{\text{R}}(x,y)} \quad (6)$$

In essence, this formula computes a measure that a Pressure-Tolerance of x is *necessarily* a college graduate. It is easy to verify that both generalizations of the value restriction above are consistent with the original semantics. For the rest of our discussion, we will be using Equation 6 as the generalized semantics of value restrictions.

3.3 Soft Number Restriction

The cardinality of a fuzzy set is defined using sigma-counts in test-score semantics[Zadeh 1981]:

$$\Sigma COUNT(A) = \sum_{i=1}^{n} \mu_A(x_i) \quad (7)$$

where A is a fuzzy set characterized by a membership function μ_A. We can thus generalize the number restriction in terminological languages to a "soft" number restriction using sigma-counts and fuzzy numbers:

$$\mu_{(\text{:at-least n R2})}(x) = \mu_{at-least-n}\left(\sum_y \mu_{R2}(x,y)\right) \quad (8)$$

$$\mu_{(\text{:at-most n R2})}(x) = \mu_{at-most-n}\left(\sum_y \mu_{R2}(x,y)\right) \quad (9)$$

where at-least-n and at-most-n are fuzzy subsets of real numbers characterized by the following membership functions:

$$\mu_{at-least-n}(z) = \begin{cases} 0 & z \leq n-1 \\ z-n+1 & n-1 \leq z \leq n \\ 1 & z \geq n \end{cases}$$

$$\mu_{at-most-n}(z) = \begin{cases} 1 & z \leq n \\ n+1-z & n \leq z \leq n+1 \\ 0 & z \geq n+1 \end{cases}$$

where z is a real number.

3.4 Fuzzy Conjunction

Finally, the degree an instance satisfies a conjunction of sub-expressions can be computed using the "min" operator in fuzzy set theory. For instance, suppose **Critical-Valve** is defined as a valve whose pressure tolerance is low. This can be expressed as

```
(defconcept Critical-Valve (:and Valve
   (:all Pressure-Tolerance Low-pressure)))
```

The degree to which an instance is a **Critical-Valve** can thus be defined as follows:

$$\mu_{\text{Critical-Valve}}(x) = \min\{\mu_{\text{Valve}}(x), \mu_{(\text{:all PT L})}(x)\} \quad (10)$$

where PT and L stand for "Pressure-Tolerance" and "Low-pressure" respectively.

It should be noted, however, that other Triangular Norms operators could be used to represent the conjunction of the sub-expressions. Moreover, by considering the bounds imposed by all Triangular Norms, we could represent the lower and upper bounds of such intersection as:

$$\mu_{\text{Critical-Valve}}(x) = [\max\{0, \mu_{\text{Valve}}(x) + \mu_{(\text{:all PT L})}(x) - 1\}, \min\{\mu_{\text{Valve}}(x), \mu_{(\text{:all PT L})}(x)\}] \quad (11)$$

3.5 Defining Fuzzy Concepts Using Membership Functions

A fuzzy concept can also be defined by describing its membership function explicitly, or by modifying the membership function of an existing fuzzy concept. To do the former, we also need to specify the domain of the membership function, which is called *the universe of discourse* in fuzzy set theory. For instance, we may define the fuzzy concept **Low-pressure** by specifying its membership function and its universe of discourse as follows:

```
(defconcept Low-pressure
   :universe-of-discourse Air-pressure
   :membership-fx (lambda (p) (low p)))
```

where low is a function that returns the membership degree for a given pressure. Once such a fuzzy set is completely specified, we can define many other fuzzy sets using modifiers (also called hedges in fuzzy logic) such as NOT, VERY, SLIGHTLY, etc. This can be expressed in a generalized term subsumption language as follows:

```
(defconcept Very-Low-pressure
     (:VERY Low-pressure) ).
```

4 Subsumption Test

The major component of a term subsumption system's reasoner is a subsumption test, which determines whether a term description subsumes (i.e., is more general than) another term description. In our generalized term subsumption systems, a term a subsumes another term b if and only if the extension of a is a fuzzy superset of the extension of b (i.e., $\forall x \in \mathcal{D}\ \mu_a(x) \geq \mu_b(x)$).

In a landmark paper that discussed the tradeoff between the expressiveness and the tractability of subsumption test, Ronald J. Brachman and Hector J. Levesque described a simple term subsumption language $\mathcal{FL}^-$ that has a sound and complete algorithm for the subsumption test [Brachman and Levesque 1984][2]. In this section, we show that a similar fuzzy term subsumption language, called $\mathcal{FTSL}^-$, also has a sound and complete algorithm for the subsumption test. The grammar of a $\mathcal{FTSL}^-$ is shown below.

[2]Even though Brachman and Levesque's algorithm for computing the subsumption of concept descriptions in $\mathcal{FL}^-$ has polynomial time complexity, Bernhard Nebel has recently shown that the problem of determining the subsumption of terms, in general, is intractable[Nebel 1989].

<term-definition> ::=
  <primitive-concept-definition>
  | <defined-concept-definition>
  | <primitive-role-definition>
<primitive-concept-definition> ::=
  (defconcept <c-name>
    (:and <c-name>* :primitive))
<defined-concept-definition> ::=
  (defconcept <c-name>
    (:and <concept-forming-expr>+))
  | (defconcept <c-name>
    :universe-of-discourse <c-name>
    :membership-fx <lambda expression>)
  | (defconcept <c-name>
    (<modifier> <c-name>))
<modifier> ::= :NOT | :VERY | :SLIGHTLY
<concept-forming-expr> ::= <c-name>
  | (:all <r-name> <c-name>)
  | (:some <r-name>)
<primitive-role-definition> ::=
  (defrole <r-name> :primitive)

The subsumption algorithm for $\mathcal{FTSL}^-$ is a slightly modified version of that of $\mathcal{FL}^-$ presented in [Brachman and Levesque 1984]:

Subsumption Algorithm for $\mathcal{FTSL}^-$: SUBS?[a,b]

1. If a and b are both defined by membership functions, then return true if they have the same universe of discourse and their membership functions satisfy the condition[3]:
$$\forall x \in U \mu_a(x) \geq \mu_b(x)$$
where U is the universe of discourse of these concepts. Otherwise, return false.
2. If only one of the two concepts are defined using membership functions, return false.
3. If both a and b are defined using concept forming expressions, normalize their descriptions by recursively replacing all non-primitive concepts in the descriptions by their definitions.
4. Flatten the normalized concept description by removing all nested `:and` operators.
5. Collect all arguments to an `:all` for a given role.
6. Assuming the description of a is now (`:and` a_1 ... a_n) and the description of b is now (`:and` b_1 ... b_m), then return true iff for each a_i
   (a) if a_i is an atom (i.e., the name of a primitive concept) or a `:some`, then one of the b_j is a_i.
   (b) if a_i is (`:all` r c_1), then one of the b_j is (`:all` r c_2) where SUBS?[c_1,c_2].

By slightly modifying Brachman and Levesque's proof about the soundness and completeness of $\mathcal{FL}^-$'s subsumption algorithm in [Brachman and Levesque 1984], we can show that the algorithm above is both complete and sound. To prove the soundness of the algorithm, we must show that if SUBS?[a,b] is true, then a indeed subsumes b. Suppose SUBS?[a,b] is true, a and b must be in one of cases below:

1. Both a and b have the same universe of discourse and their membership functions satisfy the test that a is a fuzzy superset of b.
2. Both a and b are defined using concept forming expressions. For any conjunct in a, say a_i, either a_i is among the b_j or it is of the form (`:all` r c_1). In the latter case, there is an (`:all` r c_2) among the b_j where SUBS?[c_1,c_2]. To prove by induction, we need to show that if $\mathcal{E}[c_1] \supseteq \mathcal{E}[c_2]$, then
$$\mathcal{E}[(\texttt{:all}\ r\ c_1)] \supseteq \mathcal{E}[(\texttt{:all}\ r\ c_2)]. \quad (12)$$
Since $\mathcal{E}[c_1] \supseteq \mathcal{E}[c_2]$, we have
$$\forall y\ \mu_{c_1}(y) \geq \mu_{c_2}(y).$$
Using the generalized semantics for :all (i.e., Equation 6), we get
$$\mu_{(\texttt{:all}\ r\ c_1)}(x) \geq \mu_{(\texttt{:all}\ r\ c_2)}(x).$$
Equation 12 thus follows. So no matter what a_i is, the extension of b (which is the conjunction of all the b_j's) must be a subset of a_i. Since this is true for every a_i, the extension of b must also be a subset of the extension of a.

So, whenever SUBS?[a,b] is true, a subsumes b.

To prove the completeness of the algorithm, we need to show that anytime SUBS?[a,b] is false, there is an extension function $\mathcal{E}$ such that $\mathcal{E}[a] \not\supseteq \mathcal{E}[b]$. There are five cases that may cause SUBS?[a,b] to return false.

1. Assume that a, b are both defined by membership functions, but they have different universe of discourse or there exists an x_i such that $\mu_a(x_i) < \mu_b(x_i)$. In either case, the extension of a is not a superset of the extension of b.
2. Assume that a is defined by concept expressions, and b is defined by a membership function. Let * be an object not in b's universe of discourse, we can construct an extension function $\mathcal{E}$ that assigns * to all concepts defined by concept expressions, and assigns <*,*> to all roles. Hence, * is in the extension of a, but not that of b.
3. Assume that some atom a_i does not appear among the b_j. Let $\mathcal{E}$ assign the ordered pairs <0,1>,<1,1> to every role and 0,1 to every primitive concept except a_i, to which it assigns 1. Hence, 0 is in the extension of b, but not that of a.
4. Assume that a_i is (`:some` r), which does not appear among the b_j. Let $\mathcal{E}$ assign 0,1 to every primitive concepts and <0,1>,<1,1> to every role except r, to which it assigns only <1,1>. Hence, 0 is in the extension of b, but not that of a.
5. Assume that a_i is (`:all r` c_1), where if (`:all` r c_2) appears among the b_j, then, by induction, c_1 does not subsume c_2. Let $\mathcal{E}^*$ be an extension function not using 0 or 1 but such that some object

[3] We assume that before testing the subsumption of a concept that is defined using modifiers, the system has computed its membership function using the standard interpretation of those modifiers in fuzzy logic.

* has a higher membership degree in c_2 than in c_1 (i.e., $\mu_{c_1}(*) < \mu_{c_2}(*)$). Then, let $\mathcal{E}$ contain $\mathcal{E}^*$ and assign 0,1 to every primitive concepts and <0,1>,<1,1> to every role except r, to which it assigns <1,1>,<0,*>. Based on the generalized semantics of `:all` construct, we have

$$\mu_a[0] = \mu_{a_i}[0] = 1 - (1 - \mu_{c_1}(*)) = \mu_{c_1}(*) \quad (13)$$

$$\mu_b[0] = \mu_{(:\texttt{all}\ r\ c_2)}[0] = \mu_{c_2}(*) \quad (14)$$

$$(15)$$

It then follows that the membership degree of 0 in a is less than that in b.

In all cases, we have shown that $\mathcal{E}$[a] is not a fuzzy superset of $\mathcal{E}$[b]. So, a does not subsume b when SUBS?[a,b] is false. Therefore, we have proved that the subsumption algorithm is sound and complete.

5 Related Work

Most existing works in extending frame-based knowledge representation languages for uncertainty management lie in the category of probabilistic extensions. Lokendra Shastri has developed a framework, based on the principle of maximum entropy, for dealing with uncertainty in semantic networks [Shastri and Feldman 1985, Shastri 1989]. His approach is based on the assumption that the system has certain statistical data (e.g., the number of red apples, the number of sweet apples, ...). Based on these statistical data, Shastri's evidential theory answers questions of the following kind: *Given that an instance, x, is red and sweet, is x more likely to be an apple or a grape ?* The major shortcoming of Shastri's theory is the difficulty in obtaining marginal probability judgements that are required by his model.

Heinsohn and Owsnicki-Klewe recently proposed a model of probabilistic reasoning in hybrid term subsumption systems[Heinsohn and Owsnicki-Klewe 1988]. Probabilistic knowledge is represented as *probabilistic implications* in the form of $C_1 \Rightarrow_s C_2$ where s denotes the conditional probability $P(C_2(x)|C_1(x))$, C_1 and C_2 are concepts defined in the terminological knowledge base. The reasoning mechanism of their model is *probabilistic inheritance* (i.e., the inheritance of probabilistic implications in concept taxonomy). The issue of nonmonotonicity of probabilistic inheritance has also been discussed in [Grosof 1986].

Even though these probabilistic extensions to frame-based reasoning could potentially enlarge the applicability of term subsumption systems, they do not directly address the issue of representing and reasoning about the subsumption relationships between vague concepts.

6 Summary

We have described an approach for generalizing term subsumption languages to fuzzy logic. Using test score semantics, we have generalized the concept forming constructs in term subsumption languages into elastic constraints. By slightly modifying previous works in term subsumption languages, we are able to show a complete and sound subsumption algorithm for a simple fuzzy term subsumption language. The generalized knowledge representation framework not only alleviates the difficulty of conventional AI knowledge representation schemes in handling imprecise and vague information in an intelligent system, but also enables an intelligent system to construct an abstraction hierarchy automatically based on the semantics of elastic concept descriptions, some of which may be vague and imprecise. Hence, our approach facilitates the development of complex intelligent systems where the system's capability in performing high-level analysis using conceptual abstraction and analyzing vague and imprecise information are both essential.

Acknowledgements

I am grateful to many discussions with Lotfi A. Zadeh, Robert MacGregor, Piero Bonissone, and Jonathan Lee. I would also like to thank the referees for their comments on an earlier draft of the paper.

References

[Brachman and Levesque, 1984] Ronald J. Brachman and Hector J. Levesque. The tractability of subsumption in frame-based description languages. In *Proceedings of AAAI-84*, pages 34–37, Austin, Texas, August 1984.

[Brachman and Schmolze, 1985] R.J. Brachman and J.G. Schmolze. An overview of the KL-ONE knowledge representation system. *Cognitive Science*, 9(2):171–216, August 1985.

[Brachman, 1983] R. J. Brachman. What is-a is and isn't: An analysis of taxonomic links in semantic networks. *Computer*, 16(10):30–36, October 1983.

[Dubois and Prade, 1988] D. Dubois and H. Prade. *Possibility Theory.* Plenum Press, New York, N.Y., 1988.

[Grosof, 1986] B. N. Grosof. Non-monotonicity in probabilistic reasoning. In *Proceedings of the AAAI Workshop on Uncertainty and Probability in Artificial Intelligence*, pages 91–98, Philadelphia, PA, August 1986. AAAI and RCA.

[Heinsohn and Owsnicki-Klewe, 1988] Jochen Heinsohn and Bernd Owsnicki-Klewe. Probabilistic inheritance and reasoning in hybrid knowledge representation systems. In *Proceedings of the 12th German Workshop on Artificial Intelligence (GWAI-88)*, pages 51–60, Springer, Berlin, 1988.

[Magrez and Smets, 1989] P. Magrez and P. Smets. Fuzzy modus ponens: A new model suitable for applications in knowledge-based systems. *International Journal of Intelligent Systems*, 4:181–200, 1989.

[Nebel, 1988] Bernhard Nebel. Computational complexity of terminological reasoning in back. *Artificial Intelligence*, 34(3), April 1988.

[Nebel, 1989] Bernhard Nebel. Terminological reasoning is inherently intractable. Technical Report IWBS Report 82, IWBS, IBM Deutschland, W. Germany, October 1989.

[Patel-Schneider *et al.*, 1990] Peter F. Patel-Schneider, Bernd Owsnicki-Klewe, Alfred Kobsa, Nicola Guarino, Robert MacGregor, William S. Mark, Deborah McGuinness, Bernhard Nebel, Albrecht Schmiedel, and John Yen. Term subsumption languages in knowledge representation. *AI Magazine*, 11(2):16–23, 1990.

[Schmolze and Lipkis, 1983] James Schmolze and Thomas Lipkis. Classification in the kl-one knowledge representation system. In *Proceedings of the Eighth International Joint Conference on Artificial Intelligence*. IJCAI, 1983.

[Shastri and Feldman, 1985] Lokendra Shastri and Jerome A. Feldman. Evidential reasoning in semantic networks. In *Proceedings of IJCAI-85*, pages 18–23, Los Angeles, California, August 1985.

[Shastri, 1989] Lokendra Shastri. Default reasoning in semantic networks: A formalization of recognition and inheritance. *Artificial Intelligence*, 39(3):283–355, July 1989.

[Woods, 1975] William A. Woods. Whats's in a link: Foundations for semantic networks. In Daniel Bobrow and Allan Collins, editors, *Representation and Understanding: Studies in Cognitive Science*. Academic Press, 1975.

[Zadeh, 1978a] L. A. Zadeh. Fuzzy sets as a basis for a theory of possibility. *Fuzzy Sets and Systems*, 1:3–28, 1978.

[Zadeh, 1978b] L. A. Zadeh. PRUF - a meaning representation language for natural languages. *Int. J. Man-Machine Studies*, 10:395–460, 1978.

[Zadeh, 1981] L. A. Zadeh. Test-score semantics for natural languages and meaning representation via pruf. In Burghard B. Rieger, editor, *Empirical Semantics*, pages 281–347. Studienverlag Dr. N. Brockmeyer, Bochum, 1981.

[Zadeh, 1982] L. A. Zadeh. Test-score semantics for natural languages. In *Proceedings of the Ninth International Conference on Computational Linguistics*, pages 425–430, Prague, 1982.

A Skeptic's Menagerie: Conflictors, Preemptors, Reinstaters, and Zombies in Nonmonotonic Inheritance

David S. Touretzky
School of Computer Science
Carnegie Mellon
Pittsburgh, PA 15213

Richmond H. Thomason
Intelligent Systems Program
University of Pittsburgh
Pittsburgh, PA 15260

John F. Horty
Institute for Advanced Computer Studies
University of Maryland
College Park, MD 20742

Abstract

Subtle differences in the method of constructing arguments in inheritance systems can result in profound differences in both the conclusions reached and the efficiency of inference. This paper focuses on issues surrounding the defeat of arguments in nonmonotonic inheritance. Looking primarily at skeptical reasoners, we analyze several types of defeat that may be encountered, especially the defeat of defeaters. Finally, we raise some questions specific to networks that mix strict and defeasible links.

1 Introduction

In earlier work we presented a *skeptical* approach to nonmonotonic inheritance reasoning [4] that differed in several respects from Touretzky's original *credulous* approach [15]. The main difference is that conflicting paths such as the well-known Nixon diamond generate multiple extensions in a credulous reasoner, while a skeptical reasoner produces a single extension in which all conflicted paths are excluded. As discussed in our "Clash of Intuitions" paper [16], inheritance systems of either type may differ in several other technical respects, such as the direction in which arguments are extended in computing inheritance (upward vs. downward reasoning), the precise definition of the preemption relation, the treatment of negative information, and the admission of strict (as opposed to defeasible) links.

In this paper we analyze another major point of difference among nonmonotonic reasoners: the treatment of defeated paths, primarily in skeptical systems. We define several types of possible interactions among paths according to the types of defeat involved. This "skeptics's menagerie" provides new insights into inheritance reasoning, and helps us to evaluate the computational consequences of alternative axiomatizations.

2 Defeat in Inheritance Systems

Let Γ be an inheritance network containing defeasible positive or negative links of form $x \rightarrow y$ or $x \not\rightarrow y$. A path σ through a network is a sequence of links, e.g., the path $x \rightarrow y \not\rightarrow z$ is composed of the links $x \rightarrow y$ and $y \not\rightarrow z$. Let Φ be the extension of Γ containing all paths through Γ permitted by some upward skeptical inheritance rule, such as the one in [4]. By definition, $\Gamma \subseteq \Phi$. We say that Γ "permits" σ (written $\Gamma \mathrel{|\!\!\!>} \sigma$) iff $\sigma \in \Phi$.

Definition 1 A path ρ is a *situator* of $x \rightarrow \tau \rightarrow w \not\rightarrow y$ with respect to $x \rightarrow \sigma \rightarrow z \rightarrow y$ iff ρ has the form $x \rightarrow \tau_1 \rightarrow w \rightarrow \tau_2 \rightarrow z$. (Similarly for paths of opposite polarity.)

A situator establishes the "betweenness" required by the inferential distance metric for preemption to hold. The above definition produces "off-path preemption" [16], originally proposed by Sandewall [11]. For "on-path preemption" we require a closer relationship between the subject path and the situator: $x \rightarrow \sigma \rightarrow z$ must be a subpath of ρ.

Definition 2 A path $x \rightarrow \sigma \rightarrow z \rightarrow y$ is *preempted* in Γ iff $\Gamma \mathrel{|\!\!\!>} x \rightarrow \sigma \rightarrow z$ and there is a preemptor path $x \rightarrow \tau \rightarrow w \not\rightarrow y$ with a permitted situator. (Similarly for paths of opposite polarity.)

In the famous "Clyde the elephant" example, the path Clyde $\rightarrow$ Elephant $\rightarrow$ Gray is defeated by the preemptor Clyde $\rightarrow$ Royal-Elephant $\not\rightarrow$ Gray, since Γ permits the situator Clyde $\rightarrow$ Royal-Elephant $\rightarrow$ Elephant. In our definition the situator must be a permitted path, but some inheritance schemes only require the two subpaths $x \rightarrow \tau_1 \rightarrow w$ and $w \rightarrow \tau_2 \rightarrow z$ to be permitted [2; 6]. Inheritance systems also disagree about whether the preemptor must be permitted; some require only the initial segment $x \rightarrow \tau \rightarrow w$ to be permitted.

Definition 3 A *conflictor* of a path $x \rightarrow \sigma \rightarrow y$ is a path $x \rightarrow \tau \not\rightarrow y$ having no permitted situator with respect to the former path. (Similarly for paths of opposite polarity.)

Definition 4 A path $x \rightarrow \sigma \rightarrow y$ is *conflicted* in Γ iff $\Gamma \mathrel{|\!\!\!>} x \rightarrow \sigma$ and there is a conflictor $x \rightarrow \tau \not\rightarrow y$ such that $\Gamma \mathrel{|\!\!\!>} x \rightarrow \tau$. (Similarly for paths of opposite polarity.)

In the classic Nixon diamond example, the conflicted paths are Nixon $\rightarrow$ Quaker $\rightarrow$ Pacifist and Nixon $\rightarrow$ Republican $\not\rightarrow$ Pacifist. Each is a conflictor of the other because neither is situated with respect to the other.

Conflictors, being unsituated, always generate multiple extensions in a credulous theory, or no conclusion in a skeptical theory, unless they are preempted by a direct link. We view direct links as preemptors and not conflictors because a direct link $x \not\rightarrow y$ is always situated with respect to any path from x to y; therefore it can never generate multiple extensions or no conclusion the way a true conflictor can. Returning to the elephant example, the direct link Royal-Elephant $\not\rightarrow$ Gray preempts the path Royal-Elephant $\rightarrow$ Elephant $\rightarrow$ Gray, but does not conflict with it.

Definition 5 An inheritance *defeater* is either a conflictor or a situated preemptor.

The concept of a defeater as a general category of paths that interfere with a particular argument is due originally to Pollock [9; 10]. Since his overall theoretical framework is so different from ours, however, it is hard to find any exact correspondence between his notion of a defeater and the one presented here.

The definition of inheritability varies depending on whether one is using upward or downward reasoning. For upward reasoning we have:

Definition 6 A path $x \rightarrow \sigma \rightarrow y \rightarrow z$ is *inheritable* iff $x \rightarrow \sigma \rightarrow y$ is permitted and $y \rightarrow z \in \Gamma$. (Similarly for negative paths.)

All links in Γ are permitted. Permission of longer paths is defined in terms of inheritability and defeat:

Definition 7 A path is *permitted* if it is inheritable and has no defeaters.

Finally, we need to define the conclusions an inheritance theory allows one to draw from a network:

Definition 8 Γ *supports* the conclusion $x \rightarrow y$ iff its extension contains some path $x \rightarrow \sigma \rightarrow y$. (Similarly for negative paths.)

3 Defeater Defeaters

Some inheritance systems prohibit defeated paths from themselves acting as defeaters. In such a system, the ability of a path to act as a defeater may itself be defeated by some other path. Thus, these systems are said to admit "defeater-defeaters," another term due to Pollock, and later used by Loui [7]. Since in these systems defeating a path prevents it from defeating other paths, adding a defeater-defeater to a nonmonotonic network can reinstate a previously defeated path. Given the two types of inheritance defeat defined in the preceding section, there are five types[1] of defeater-defeater in an inheritance system:

- preemptor-preemptor
- preemptor-conflictor
- conflictor-preemptor
- conflictor-conflictor
- situator-preemptor

These different types of defeater-defeater can have different effects in inheritance networks, and in some cases there is disagreement about the best way to handle them. We shall consider several of these issues in the following sections.

4 Reinstatement

Consider the network in Figure 1. The path X → Chicken ↛ Flies is a preemptor of X → Chicken → Bird → Flies; it is situated by X → Chicken → Bird. It is not necessary that X → Chicken ↛ Flies actually be a permitted path for it to be a preemptor. (In fact, X → Chicken ↛ Flies is defeated by the direct link X → Flies.) But suppose we decided that preemptors must be permitted. This would cause the longer path to go through, since it has no *permitted* preemptor. In this case the path X → Flies would be acting as a "reinstater" of X → Chicken → Bird → Flies.

[1]This missing type, situator-conflictor, will be discussed in section 5.

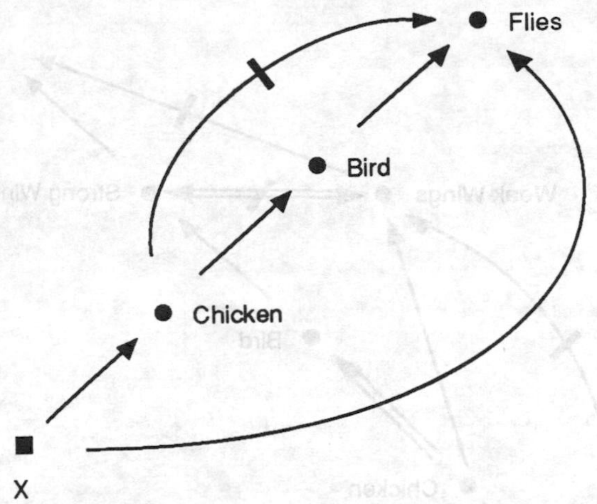

Figure 1: The intuitiveness of reinstatement seems to depend on the identity of the node X.

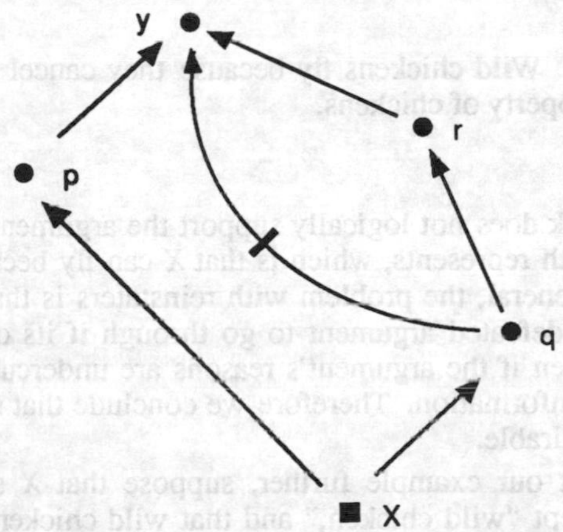

Figure 2: Conflictors can be reinstaters only in credulous theories.

Definition 9 A *reinstater* is a path whose permission defeats preemptors of other paths to the same conclusion, thereby allowing them to also go through.

Reinstaters are a type of defeater-defeater; specifically, they are preemption defeaters. In skeptical systems, reinstaters must be preemptor-preemptors, not preemptor-conflictors, since a reinstating path by definition must be permitted; in a skeptical system conflictors are never permitted. But in credulous reasoners conflictors will be permitted in some extensions, and can therefore act as reinstaters there. In Figure 2, for example, note that $x \rightarrow p \rightarrow y$ is a conflictor of $x \rightarrow q \not\rightarrow y$, which is in turn a preemptor of $x \rightarrow q \rightarrow r \rightarrow y$. The path $x \rightarrow p \rightarrow y$ will be permitted in one of the two credulous extensions, and in that extension it can reinstate $x \rightarrow q \rightarrow r \rightarrow y$ if the inheritance axioms permit reinstatement.

Reinstatement may not be desirable in inheritance reasoning. Suppose node *X* in Figure 1 stands for the concept "chicken with a jet pack." We have directly asserted that chickens with jet packs can fly, but the reason for their flying has nothing to do with their being birds. Therefore the

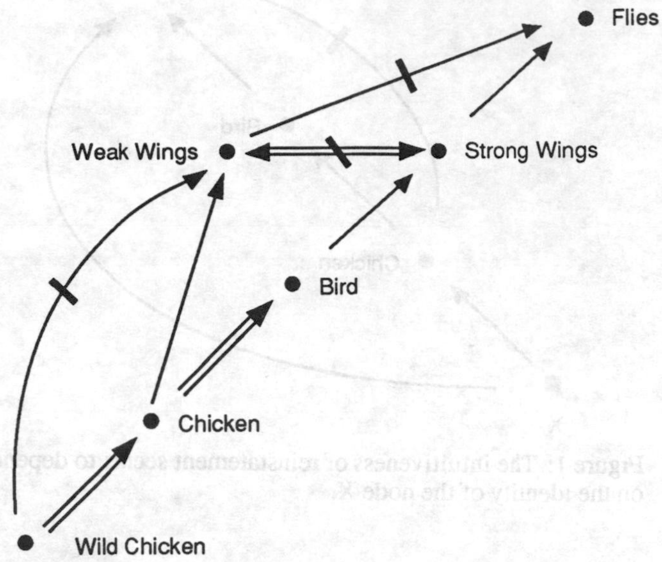

Figure 3: Wild chickens fly because they cancel an exceptional property of chickens.

direct link does not logically support the argument the reinstated path represents, which is that X can fly because birds fly. In general, the problem with reinstaters is that they allow *any* defeated argument to go through if its conclusion holds, even if the argument's reasons are undercut by more specific information. Therefore we conclude that reinstaters are undesirable.

To test our example further, suppose that X stands for the concept "wild chicken," and that wild chickens, having stronger wings than their domestic cousins, can fly. In this case the wild chicken's flying ability really is a consequence of its being a bird. This may seem to be evidence in favor of reinstatement, but what it really shows, we believe, is that the network of Figure 1 doesn't capture all of our knowledge about the relationship of wild chickens to ordinary chickens. In particular, it doesn't express the fact that the reason why wild chickens fly is that they cancel precisely those exceptional properties of chickens that prevent them from flying. Figure 3 shows one way to express this knowledge. The network mixes strict and defeasible links, and under the definition of inheritance given in [3], the path Wild-Chicken $\Rightarrow$ Chicken $\Rightarrow$ Bird $\rightarrow$ Strong-Wings $\rightarrow$ Flies is permitted. It is not, however, "reinstated" (as we have defined the term), as there is no preemptor that could have defeated it. This follows from the fact that no positive path from Wild-Chicken can reach Weak-Wings.

Reinstatement can affect not just the arguments a network permits, but also the conclusions it reaches. In Figure 4, if we do not allow reinstatement, the link $x \rightarrow o$ does not cause Γ to permit the situator path $x \rightarrow m \rightarrow n \rightarrow o$. Therefore the two paths $x \rightarrow m \not\rightarrow y$ and $x \rightarrow o \rightarrow y$ conflict, and so a skeptical reasoner will draw no conclusion about whether x is a y. But if reinstatement is allowed, the permitted situator $x \rightarrow m \rightarrow n \rightarrow o$ causes $x \rightarrow m \not\rightarrow y$ to preempt $x \rightarrow o \rightarrow y$, causing us to conclude $x \not\rightarrow y$.

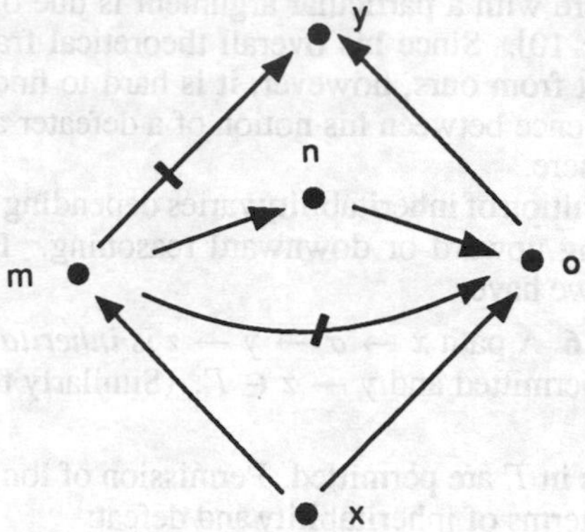

Figure 4: A network where reinstatement affects the conclusions that can be drawn.

Although reinstatement may be semantically undesirable, the parallel marker propagation algorithms described in [4] for defeasible nets and [17] for mixed nets depend on this property in order to compute preemption efficiently. One of the lemmas in the correctness proof of the algorithm in [4] states (roughly) that if $x \rightarrow z_1 \in \Gamma$, $z_i \rightarrow z_{i+1} \in \Gamma$ for i from 1 to $n-1$, and Γ supports $x \rightarrow z_i$ for i from 1 to n, then $\Gamma \models x \rightarrow z_1 \rightarrow \ldots \rightarrow z_n$.

Consider what happens when the inheritance query algorithm is asked to determine whether x is a y in Figure 4. Processing nodes in degree order, the algorithm puts the "true" mark M_T on x, m, n, and o, indicating that Γ supports $x \rightarrow m$, $x \rightarrow n$, and $x \rightarrow o$. Then it is ready to determine whether Γ supports the conclusion $x \rightarrow y$ or $x \not\rightarrow y$. It marks all nodes with M_T having a direct positive or negative link to y with marker M_{dir}; both m and o are so marked. Next, any nodes on preempted paths must be eliminated. A preemption mark, M_{pre}, is used to kill off nodes whose link to y is preempted by some lower node. This is done in a very simple way: Every node with M_{dir} sends M_{pre} up "$\rightarrow$" links, and M_{pre} is propagated upward across "$\rightarrow$" links into nodes with M_T as far as it will go. So node m first sends M_{pre} to node n, and node o sends it nowhere because no node above o has M_T. Propagation then causes M_{pre} to spread upward from n to o, killing off o. Finally, only those nodes that have M_{dir} and not M_{pre} are allowed to send M_T up "$\rightarrow$" links or M_F up "$\not\rightarrow$" links to y. Since m is the only node meeting these conditions, y is marked with M_F, meaning Γ supports $x \not\rightarrow y$.

The important thing to note here is that the preemption marker M_{pre} that originates at m flows from n to o precisely because m, n, and o are all marked with M_T, meaning Γ supports $x \rightarrow m$, $x \rightarrow n$, and $x \rightarrow o$. But the preemption is only valid because, as the lemma tells us, this guarantees that $\Gamma \models x \rightarrow m \rightarrow n \rightarrow o$. The lemma holds for the system in [4] because its definition of inheritance requires that preemptors not have preemptors of their own; this is what produces reinstatement.

In more recent work, Horty has developed an alternative axiomatization of skeptical preemption that does not admit reinstaters [5]. In this scheme preempters need not be permitted; they can defeat other paths even if they themselves are preempted by more specific paths.

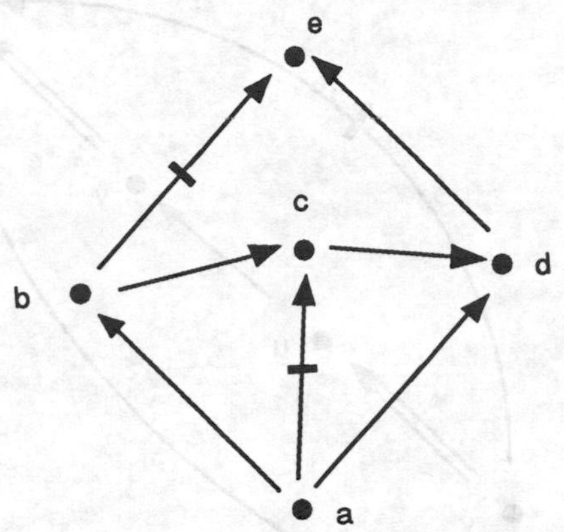

Figure 5: An example of a situator-preemptor.

It is an open question whether preemption without reinstatement can be computed efficiently without enumerating all possible situator paths. It cannot be done using just parallel marker propagation with a bounded number of markers. The reason is that, referring to Figure 4 again, there can be an arbitrary number of paths between m and o. Only one of these need go through in order to situate the preemptor $x \rightarrow m \not\rightarrow y$ with respect to $x \rightarrow o \rightarrow y$, and each situator must be examined independently.

Thus we see the possiblity for an interesting tradeoff between inheritance definitions: some give the most "correct" results, while others have efficient algorithms that are correct in most cases, but will produce different results in certain situations.[2]

5 Defeat of Situators

The previous section looked at defeat of preemption by defeating the preemptor. It's also possible to defeat preemption by defeating the situator. This form of defeat can result in a conflict (skepticism or multiple extensions) rather than the replacement of a conclusion with its opposite.

Figure 5 shows an example of a situator-preemptor. The path $a \rightarrow d \rightarrow e$ has preemptor $a \rightarrow b \not\rightarrow e$, with situator $a \rightarrow b \rightarrow c \rightarrow d$. But the preemptor isn't situated because the situator isn't permitted; the link $a \not\rightarrow c$ preempts its initial segment $a \rightarrow b \rightarrow c$. Unsituated preemptors are conflictors, so we must be skeptical about whether a is an e.

Situator-conflictors are excluded from our list of defeater-defeaters because they have no independent effect. Let ρ be a path of form $x \rightarrow \tau_1 \rightarrow w \rightarrow \tau_2 \rightarrow z$. Suppose ρ is a situator of $x \rightarrow \tau \rightarrow w \not\rightarrow y$, a potential preemptor of the subject path, $x \rightarrow \sigma \rightarrow z \rightarrow y$. Then a conflictor ξ of ρ must

[2]The tradeoff is further complicated by the fact that *theoretical* well-behavedness may not be the same as intuitive correctness. In [5], it is shown that skeptical extensions allowing reinstatement can be defined directly through a fixedpoint equation, while the only known definitions of skeptical extensions without reinstatement rely on an iterative process using degree. To the extent that fixedpoint approaches in nonmonotonic reasoning seem more declarative than iterative definitions, this may provide a theoretical reason for preferring reinstatement.

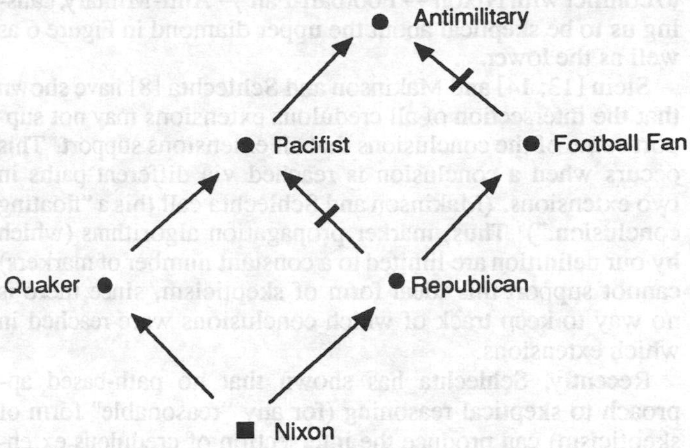

Figure 6: A conflicted conflictor.

be of form $x \rightarrow \mu \not\rightarrow z$, which also makes it a conflictor of $x \rightarrow \sigma \rightarrow z$, an initial segment of the subject path. In all skeptical definitions, if an initial segment of a subject path is conflicted, the subject path is not even potentially inheritable; it will not be permitted. It therefore does not matter whether the subject path's preemptors have permitted situators.

In credulous theories there are two cases to consider. Let ξ be a conflictor of the situator ρ. In extensions that support $x \not\rightarrow z$ (because ξ is permitted), the subject path has a conflicted initial segment and will not be inheritable. In extensions that support $x \rightarrow z$, ρ will be a permitted path, and hence the situator will not be conflicted. So in credulous as well as skeptical theories, situator-conflictors do not function as defeater-defeaters.

6 Conflicted Paths

An important difference between defeat by preemptors vs. defeat by conflictors is that preempted paths cannot be extended further; they are dead. Conflicted paths will hold in some credulous extension, and thus can be extended there, perhaps giving rise to other instances of defeat.

Since skeptical reasoning as defined in [4] does not allow conflicted paths to be extended, one way of making a path go through is to conflict some initial segment of its defeater. In the double-diamond example reproduced in Figure 6, because Nixon is conflicted about Pacifist, the negative path to Anti-Military goes through unopposed. Thus, the path Nixon $\rightarrow$ Republican $\not\rightarrow$ Pacifist is acting as a conflictor-conflictor, another type of defeater-defeater.

An alternative notion of skepticism to the one presented here is one where the extension is the intersection of all credulous extensions. In [16] we called this "ambiguity propagation," and Stein and others view it as a more rational or pure form of skepticism [14; 8]. Conflicted paths in such a system cannot be salvaged by conflictor-conflictors. This observation has led Makinson and Schlechta to propose the notion of "zombies:" conflicted paths that are dead but can still kill other paths [8]. In their proposal, conflictor-conflictors would not be defeater-defeaters. Thus, even though we are conflicted about Nixon's pacifism, we would still go on to form the zombie path Nixon $\rightarrow$ Quaker $\rightarrow$ Pacifist $\rightarrow$ Anti-Military to conflict with Nixon → Football-Fan $\not\to$ Anti-Military, causing us to be skeptical about the upper diamond in Figure 6 as well as the lower.

Stein [13; 14] and Makinson and Schlechta [8] have shown that the intersection of all credulous extensions may not support some of the conclusions that all extensions support. This occurs when a conclusion is reached via different paths in two extensions. (Makinson and Schlechta call this a "floating conclusion.") Thus, marker propagation algorithms (which by our definition are limited to a constant number of markers) cannot support this ideal form of skepticism, since there is no way to keep track of which conclusions were reached in which extensions.

Recently, Schlechta has shown that no path-based approach to skeptical reasoning (for any "reasonable" form of skepticism) can produce the intersection of credulous extensions [12]. Hence, we cannot even axiomatize ideal skepticism in our purely path-based formalism. However, the analysis of various defeater-defeater situations reported here applies to other formulations of inheritance as well.

7 Defeat in Mixed Nets

Networks that mix strict and defeasible links, as in [3] and [5], use similar definitions of defeat to the ones presented here, except that strict extensions of paths must be taken into account. (The strict extension of a path is the set of nodes reachable by purely strict links from the path's conclusion.) For example, a reinstater need not have the same conclusion as the reinstated path; the reinstated path's conclusion simply needs to be in the reinstater's strict extension.

One very interesting idea for mixed nets is to require that situators be strict paths. This is in accordance with Brachman's observation [1] that inclusion in natural hierarchies is strict; only properties are defeasible. Note that our proposal does not reduce the network to a simple class/property system as defined in [15], since it is still possible to chain off of defeasible links, defeasible inferences can have strict extensions, and they can generate conflicts. However, the preemption relation is simplified by requiring situators to be strict, since only defeasible paths have the potential to be reinstated, and these can never be situators.

Unfortunately, we still cannot allow reinstatement without affecting the conclusions the system will reach. Figure 7 shows an example of why this is true. The path $x \Rightarrow v \not\to m \Leftarrow y$ preempts $x \Rightarrow v \Rightarrow u \to y$, with a strict situator $x \Rightarrow v \Rightarrow u$. The preemptor is itself preempted by the direct link $x \to m$. But with no reinstatement, this does not restore any path from x to y. Therefore we should reach no conclusion about y. An axiomatization in which preemptors must be unpreempted (leading to reinstatement) would conclude that x is a y.

8 Conclusions

Inheritance theory has a richer structure than we previously imagined. Complex patterns of defeat and reinstatement were known to exist, but had not been systematically analyzed. Even within a narrow family of reasoners, such as skeptical, upward, purely defeasible systems, we find that differences in axiomatization can affect both the results produced and the efficiency of inference.

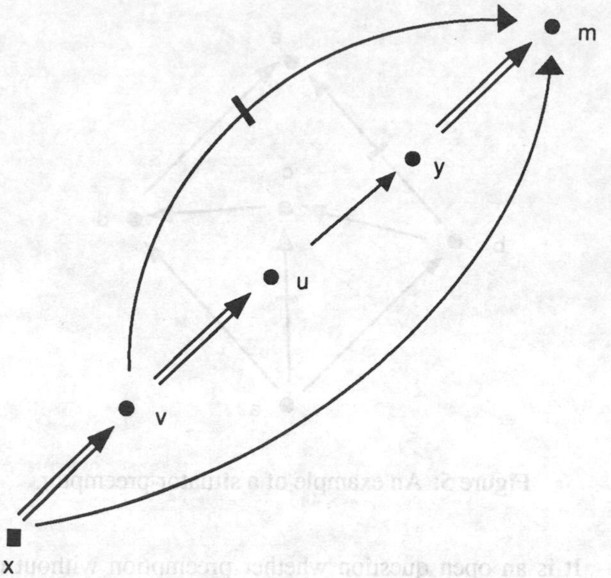

Figure 7: A mixed network whose conclusions are affected by reinstatement.

There are two immediate observations to be drawn from our investigations. First, axiomatizations of inheritance should avoid reinstatement, because it is semantically undesirable. But, second, marker propagation systems[3] have implicitly relied on reinstatement, by assuming that preemptors will be permitted paths, in order to compute permission efficiently. Since they also cannot implement ideal skepticism, we conclude that simple marker propagation architectures may not be as well-suited to inheritance reasoning as previously thought. They may still be useful as fast query/retrieval devices, provided that the correctness of the query algorithm is enforced by other means, such as the conditioning algorithms of [15], or is shown experimentally to provide correct results for most naturally occurring networks.

Acknowledgements

This work was funded by National Science Foundation grant IRI-9003165. We thank Bart Selman and one of the anonymous referees for helpful discussions.

References

[1] Brachman, R. J. (1985) "I lied about the trees" or, Defaults and definitions in knowledge representation. *AI Magazine*, vol. 6 (Fall 1985), pp. 80-93.

[2] Geffner, H., and Verma, V. (1989) Inheritance = chaining + defeat. In Z. Ras and M. Zemankova (eds.), Methodologies for Intelligent Systems, 4. Amsterdam: North-Holland.

[3] Horty, J. F., and Thomason, R. H. (1988) Mixing Strict and Defeasible Inference. Proceedings of AAAI-88. Minneapolis, MN, July, 1988.

[3] As we have defined them, using a small, fixed number of markers with no internal structure.

[4] Horty, J. F., Thomason, R. H., and Touretzky, D. S. (1990) A skeptical theory of inheritance in nonmonotonic semantic nets. *Artificial Intelligence* 42(2-3):311-348, April 1990. An abbreviated version appeared in Proceedings of AAAI-87, pp. 358-363.

[5] Horty, J. F. (forthcoming) Some direct theories of nonmonotonic inheritance. Forthcoming in *Handbook of Logic in Artificial Intelligence and Logic Programming*, D. Gabbay and C. Hogger (eds.), Oxford University Press.

[6] Krishnaprasad, T., Kifer, M., and Warren, D. S. (1989) On the declarative semantics of inheritance networks. Proceedings of IJCAI-89, pp. 1099-1103. Detroit, MI, August, 1989.

[7] Loui, R. P. (1988) Defeat among arguments II: Renewal, rebuttal, and referral. Unpublished manuscript.

[8] D. Makinson and K. Schlechta. (1991) Floating conclusions and zombie paths: two deep difficulties in the "directly skeptical" approach to defeasible inheritance nets. *Artificial Intelligence*, vol. 48, pp. 199-209.

[9] Pollock, J. (1974) *Knowledge and Justification*. Princeton, NJ: Princeton University Press.

[10] Pollock, J. (1987) Defeasible reasoning. *Cognitive Science*, vol. 11, pp. 481-518.

[11] Sandewall, E. (1986) Non-monotonic inference rules for multiple inheritance with exceptions. *Proceedings of the IEEE* 74, pp. 1345-1353.

[12] Schlechta, K. (1990) Directly sceptical inheritance cannot capture the intersection of extensions. Proceedings of the Sankt Augustin Workshop on Nonmonotonic Reasoning.

[13] Stein, L. J. (1989) Skeptical inheritance: computing the intersection of credulous extensions. Proceedings of IJCAI-89, pp. 1153-1158,. Detroit, August, 1989.

[14] Stein, L. J. (1990) Resolving Ambiguity in Nonmonotonic Reasoning. Ph.D. Dissertation, technical Report No. CS-90-18, Brown University, Providence, 1990.

[15] Touretzky, D. S. (1986) The Mathematics of Inheritance Systems. San Mateo, CA: Morgan Kaufmann Publishers.

[16] Touretzky, D. S., Horty, J. F., and Thomason, R. H. (1987) A clash of intuitions: the current state of nonmonotonic multiple inheritance systems. Proceedings of IJCAI-87, pp. 476-482. Milan, Italy, August, 1987.

[17] Touretzky, D. S., and Thomason, R. H. (1990) An inference algorithm for networks that mix strict and defeasible inheritance. In Z. W. Ras, M. Zemankova, and M. L. Emrich (eds.), *Methodologies for Intelligent Systems, 5*, pp. 212-225. Amsterdam: North-Holland. Proceedings of the Fifth International Symposium on Methodologies for Intelligent Systems, October 25-27, Knoxville, TN.

KNOWLEDGE REPRESENTATION

Belief

A NEW LOGIC OF BELIEFS: MONOTONIC AND NON-MONOTONIC BELIEFS - Part I

Sukhamay Kundu
Computer Science Department
Louisiana State University
Baton Rouge, LA 70803, USA

Abstract

We present here a new formalization of beliefs, which has a simpler semantics than the previous formalizations, and develop an inference method for it by generalizing the resolution method. The usual propositional formulas are embedded in our logic as a special type of belief formulas. One can obtain a non-monotonic logic of beliefs by applying, say, circumscription to the basic belief-logic developed here which is monotonic in nature. One can also apply the technique repeatedly to construct a hierarchy of belief-logics $\mathbf{BL}_k$, $k \geq 1$, where $\mathbf{BL}_k \supset \mathbf{BL}_{k-1}$ and $\mathbf{BL}_k$ can handle formulas involving up to level k nested applications of the belief operator B.

1. Introduction

The fundamental assumption in this paper is that the distinction between the notion of truth of the belief of a proposition P and that of P lies in the underlying contexts of worlds. In the case of beliefs, the context is a set of worlds whereas in the case of propositions the context is a single world. We say that P is *believed* by an agent in the context W, which is a set of worlds, if P is true in every world $w_j \in$ W. Put another way, the agent believes in any thing unless there is evidence to the contrary. Why does the context being a set of worlds make a significant difference? First, the meaning of negation as in B¬P is now different from the meaning of negation as in ~BP.[1] By B¬P = "believe in negation of P", we mean that P is false in each $w_j \in$ W, which is quite different from ~BP, meaning that P is false for at least one $w_j \in$ W. Thus, B¬P ≠ ~BP. Second, it is possible that an agent believes neither P nor ¬P. It is also possible that he believes both P and ¬P simultaneously, i.e., assert BP ∧ B¬P, which can happen only in the extreme case W = ∅. Note that every thing is believed when W = ∅, including the propositional false-formula, denoted by □.

[1]We use "~" for negations applied to beliefs, to distinguish it from the negation "¬" applied to propositional formulas.

In defining a logic for beliefs, one of the first questions that arises is what is its relationship to the standard logic. For example, if ϕ_1 and ϕ_2 are two equivalent propositional formulas, then is $B\phi_1$ considered to be equivalent to $B\phi_2$? More generally, if ϕ_1 is believed and ϕ_1 logically implies ϕ_2, then should ϕ_2 be also believed? Note that if the answer to the second question is 'yes', then the same is true for the first question. For the belief-logic defined here, both the answers are 'yes'. A different belief-logic is defined in [Levesque, 1984] specifically to allow $B\phi_1$ not to be equivalent to $B\phi_2$ even though ϕ_1 and ϕ_2 may be equivalent as propositional formulas. This is achieved by considering a general notion of a world w_j in which the truth value of a proposition P may be true (T), false (F), undefined, or simultaneously true and false (i.e., P does not have a unique truth value). These general worlds are used for modeling the "explicit" beliefs whereas the "implicit" beliefs are modeled (for the most part) by the standard worlds, with each proposition having a unique truth value.

For the logic of belief described here, only the standard worlds are considered. We do not distinguish thus the explicit beliefs from the implicit beliefs. More importantly, we consider each propositional formula ϕ as a special kind of belief-formula ϕ' whose truth value is evaluated in the same way as that of the general belief-formulas. This is not the case in [Levesque, 1984]. Another interesting property of the belief-logic given here is that one can apply the construction repeatedly to obtain a hierarchy of belief-logics $\mathbf{BL}_k$, $k \geq 1$, where $\mathbf{BL}_k$ can handle formulas involving up to level k nested applications of the belief-operator B. Thus, the formula $B(\phi' \vee B\psi)$ – note the use ϕ' instead of ϕ – can be handled in $\mathbf{BL}_2$. The belief-logic in [Levesque, 1984] can consider such nested formulas directly. However, we feel that our formulation of belief-logic is actually more natural in that it explicitly recognizes the inherent higher complexity of the formulas with higher nested levels of B and handles them in a higher level (larger value of k) logic $\mathbf{BL}_k$.

We give here a simple inference technique for the new belief-logic (= $\mathbf{BL}_1$) by generalizing the resolution method in propositional logic. A similar generalization of the resolution rules for $\mathbf{BL}_{k-1}$ immediately gives the resolution rules for $\mathbf{BL}_k$, $k \geq 2$. In Part-I, we present only the basic monotonic form of the belief-logic $\mathbf{BL}_1$. The construction of a non-monotonic form of $\mathbf{BL}_1$ (and other $\mathbf{BL}_k$, $k > 1$) by using the circumscription is presented elsewhere [Kundu, 1991b]. Note that the separation of the non-monotonic aspects from the monotonic aspects of beliefs makes it easier to model a world and control the inferencing in it.

2. Basic Notions

We formally define a formula of the form $B\phi$, where ϕ is a propositional formula, to be an *atomic* belief-formula. A general *belief-formula* is defined to be an atomic belief-formula or a formula which is obtained by logical combination of other belief-formulas via $\wedge$, $\vee$, and ~. We use "$\rightarrow$" as an abbreviation for the usual logical combination of $\vee$ and $\neg$ (or ~). Thus, $\sim B\neg P \vee B(P \rightarrow Q)$ is a belief-formula, but $BB\neg P$ is not. Note that the operator B is considered to have higher precedence than $\wedge$, $\vee$, and $\rightarrow$.

Let $\{P_1, P_2, ..., P_n\}$ be the basic propositions in our universe of discourse. We denote by Ω_n the set of 2^n individual worlds defined by the combination of T/F values of the P_j's. For $W \subseteq \Omega$, we say $B\phi$ has the truth value T at W if ϕ is true at each $w_j \in W$. In that case, the set W is said to be a *model* of $B\phi$. The truth value of a complex belief-formula is defined in the usual way by combining the truth values of its subformulas via the connectives $\{\wedge, \vee, \neg$, and $\rightarrow\}$. In particular, $\sim B\phi$ is true at W if and only if ϕ is false at at least one world $w_j \in W$. Clearly, the only model of $B\Box$ is the empty subset $\varnothing \subseteq \Omega$ and the models of $\sim B\Box$ are all non-empty subsets of Ω. On the other hand, the models of $B\phi \wedge \sim B\Box$ are the set of all non-empty models of $B\phi$, i.e, the non-empty subsets of the set of models of ϕ; the only model of $B\phi \wedge B\neg\phi$ is $W = \varnothing$. We write $\Omega(\beta)$ for the set of models of a belief-formula β and write $\Omega(\phi)$ also for the set of models of a propositional formula ϕ. By abuse of notation, we let $\Box$ denote also the false belief-formula, which should not cause any confusion; similarly, we write $\mathbf{T} = \sim\Box$. The belief-formula β is said to be a *tautology* or valid if $\Omega(\beta) = 2^{\Omega}$. It is easy to see that $B\phi$ is valid if and only if ϕ is a valid propositional formula. The notion of satisfiability of a set of belief-formulas and its models are defined in the usual way.

We say a belief-formula β_1 is *equivalent* to another belief-formula β_2 if they have the same models, in which case we write $\beta_1 = \beta_2$. Table 1 shows some simple equivalences of belief-formulas. Note that $B\Box \neq \Box$ and, in general, $B\phi_1 \vee B\phi_2 \neq B(\phi_1 \vee \phi_2)$.

We say β_1 *implies* β_2 or β_2 can be *inferred* from β_1, if $\beta_1 \rightarrow \beta_2$ is valid. In symbols, we write $\beta_1 \Rightarrow \beta_2$. It is clear that $B\phi_1 \vee B\phi_2$ implies $B(\phi_1 \vee \phi_2)$, but as we noted above the converse may not be true. One can derive $[B\phi_1 \vee B\phi_2] \Rightarrow B[\phi_1 \vee \phi_2]$ by repeated application of Theorem 1 below. First, since $\phi_1 \Rightarrow \phi_1 \vee \phi_2$, we get $B\phi_1 \Rightarrow B[\phi_1 \vee \phi_2]$ and, similarly, $B\phi_2 \Rightarrow B[\phi_1 \vee \phi_2]$. In propositional logic, we

TABLE 1. Some simple equivalences of belief-formulas.

$B\phi_1 \wedge B\phi_2$	$= B(\phi_1 \wedge \phi_2)$
$B\phi_1 \wedge (B\phi_2 \vee B\phi_3)$	$= [B\phi_1 \wedge B\phi_2] \vee [B\phi_1 \wedge B\phi_3]$
$B\phi_1 \vee (B\phi_2 \wedge B\phi_3)$	$= [B\phi_1 \vee B\phi_2] \wedge [B\phi_1 \vee B\phi_3]$
$\sim\sim B\phi_1$	$= B\phi_1$
$\sim[B\phi_1 \wedge B\phi_2]$	$= \sim B\phi_1 \vee \sim B\phi_2$
$\sim[B\phi_1 \vee B\phi_2]$	$= \sim B\phi_1 \wedge \sim B\phi_2$
$B\phi_1 \wedge B\phi_2$	$= B\phi_2 \wedge B\phi_1$
$B\phi_1 \vee B\phi_2$	$= B\phi_2 \vee B\phi_1$
$B\Box \vee B\phi$	$= B\phi$
$\sim B\neg\Box$	$= \Box$ (i.e., $\mathbf{BT} = \mathbf{T}$)

also have $\phi_1 \Rightarrow \psi$ and $\phi_2 \Rightarrow \psi$ implies $[\phi_1 \vee \phi_2] \Rightarrow \psi$. The same is true if ϕ_1, ϕ_2, and ψ are replaced by arbitrary belief-formulas. By putting $B\phi_1$ in place of ϕ_1, $B\phi_2$ in place of ϕ_2, and $B[\phi_1 \vee \phi_2]$ in place of ψ, we get that $B\phi_1 \vee B\phi_2 \Rightarrow B[\phi_1 \vee \phi_2]$. The following Modus-ponens for belief-formulas is also immediate from the definitions.

If β_1 and $\beta_1 \rightarrow \beta_2$ are valid belief-formulas,
then β_2 is a valid belief-formula.

Theorem 1. For any two propositional formulas ϕ_1 and ϕ_2, we have

(1) $\phi_1 \Rightarrow \phi_2$ if and only if $B\phi_1 \Rightarrow B\phi_2$ if and only if $\sim B\phi_2 \Rightarrow \sim B\phi_1$.
(2) $\sim B(\phi_1 \vee \phi_2) \Rightarrow \sim B(\phi_1) \wedge \sim B(\phi_2)$.
(3) $B(\neg\phi_1) \wedge \sim B\Box \Rightarrow \sim B\phi_1$.

Proof. Immediate from the definitions. ■

The following theorem shows that belief formulas are sufficiently powerful to describe any family K of subsets of Ω, i.e., $K \subseteq 2^{\Omega}$. In particular, if $N = |\Omega| = 2^n$, then the number of distinct (non-equivalent) belief-formulas over the propositions $\{P_1, P_2, ..., P_n\}$ is 2^{2^N} whereas the number of distinct propositional formulas is only 2^N.

Theorem 2. If K is an arbitrary family of subsets of Ω, then there is a belief-formula β_K whose set of models equals K, i.e., $\Omega(\beta_K) = K$. Moreover, β is unique up to equivalence.

Proof. If $K = \varnothing$, then we take $\beta_K = \Box$. Now let $K = \{W_1, W_2, ..., W_m\}$. We first show that there is a belief-formula β_W which has a unique model W for any $W \subseteq \Omega$. If $W = \varnothing$, then $\beta_W = B\Box$. Now assume that $W \neq \varnothing$. For each world $w_j \in W = \{w_1, w_2, ..., w_q\}$, let C_j be the conjunction of the form $Z_1 \wedge Z_2 \wedge ... \wedge Z_n$, where each $Z_i = P_i$ or $\neg P_i$, such that the propositional formula C_j has exactly one model w_j. The belief-formula $\beta_W = B(C_1 \vee C_2 \vee ... \vee C_q) \wedge \sim B\neg C_1 \wedge \sim B\neg C_2 \wedge ... \wedge \sim B\neg C_q$ then has the unique model W. If we write β_j for the formula whose unique model is $W_j \in K$, then $\beta_K = \beta_1 \vee \beta_2 \vee ... \vee \beta_m$ satisfies the theorem. The uniqueness of β_K is immediate. ■

The belief-formula β_K obtained in the proof of Theorem 2 may be called the *disjunctive normal form* of a belief-formula whose models are $K = \{W_1, W_2, ..., W_m\}$. Example 1 shows some families of subsets of Ω_2 and the associated disjunctive normal form belief-formulas. The proof of Theorem 2 suggests the notation $N\phi = \sim B\neg C_1 \wedge \sim B\neg C_2 \wedge ... \wedge \sim B\neg C_q$, where $\phi = C_1 \vee C_2 \vee ... \vee C_q$ is a disjunctive normal form propositional formula. The formula $N\phi$, which may be read as "necessarily contains (or implied by) ϕ", has the models $\{W: \Omega(\phi) \subseteq W\}$. In particular, the models of $N\Box$ is 2^Ω and thus $N\Box = \mathbf{T}$.

Example 1. Consider the universe of discourse consisting of two proposition $\{P_1, P_2\}$. Thus $\Omega = \{w_0, w_1, w_2, w_3\}$, where w_0 corresponds to $P_1 = F = P_2$, w_1 corresponds to $P_1 = F$ and $P_2 = T$, etc. Table 2 shows some of the families $K \subseteq 2^\Omega$ and their associated disjunctive normal form belief-formulas β_K. Here, we write $P_1 \wedge P_2$ in short as P_1P_2, $\neg P_1 \wedge P_2$ as $\neg P_1P_2$, etc. ■

TABLE 2. Examples of disjunctive normal form belief-formulas in the propositions P_1 and P_2.

$K \subseteq 2^\Omega$	The disjunctive normal form β_K
$\varnothing$	$\Box$
$\{\varnothing\}$	$B\Box$
$\{\{w_0\}\}$	$B(\neg P_1\neg P_2) \wedge \sim B(P_1 \vee P_2)$
$\{\{w_0\}, \{w_1\}\}$	$[B(\neg P_1\neg P_2) \wedge \sim B(P_1 \vee P_2)] \vee$ $[B(\neg P_1 P_2) \wedge \sim B(P_1 \vee \neg P_2)]$
$\{\{w_0, w_1\}\}$	$B(\neg P_1\neg P_2 \vee \neg P_1 P_2) \wedge$ $\sim B(P_1 \vee P_2) \wedge \sim B(P_1 \vee \neg P_2)$
$\{\{w_0\}, \{w_0, w_1\}\}$	$[B(\neg P_1\neg P_2) \wedge \sim B(P_1 \vee P_2)] \vee$ $[B(\neg P_1\neg P_2 \vee \neg P_1 P_2) \wedge \sim B(P_1 \vee P_2)$ $\wedge \sim B(P_1 \vee \neg P_2)]$

In view of Theorem 2, we can associate a belief-formula ϕ' with each propositional formula ϕ in an one-to-one fashion such that the set of models of ϕ' is given by $\Omega(\phi') = \{\{w_j\}: w_j \in \Omega(\phi)\}$. In particular, $\Box' = \Box$ though $\mathbf{T}' \neq \mathbf{T}$. The mapping from ϕ to ϕ' is consistent with the logical operations $\wedge$ and $\vee$ in the sense that

$$(\phi_1 \wedge \phi_2)' = \phi_1' \wedge \phi_2' \text{ and } (\phi_1 \vee \phi_2)' = \phi_1' \vee \phi_2'.$$

In general, $(\neg\phi)' \neq \sim(\phi')$, which should not be surprising since $B(\neg\phi) \neq \sim B\phi$. Nevertheless, if ϕ_1 and ϕ_2 are two propositional formulas and $\phi_1 \Rightarrow \phi_2$, i.e., $\neg\phi_1 \vee \phi_2$ is a tautology in propositional logic, then we have $\phi_1' \Rightarrow \phi_2'$ for the associated belief formulas, i.e., $\sim(\phi_1') \vee \phi_2'$ is a tautology in belief-logic. The following theorem, where ϕ may also be $\Box$ or a tautology, is immediate and is illustrated in Table 3.

Theorem 3. For any propositional formulas ϕ_1 and ϕ_2, we have $\phi_1' \Rightarrow B\phi_1$ and $B\neg\phi_1 \Rightarrow \sim(\phi_1')$. Also, $\phi_1 \Rightarrow \phi_2$ if and only if $\phi_1' \Rightarrow \phi_2'$. ■

TABLE 3. Illustration of Theorem 3 for the universe of propositions $\{P_1, P_2\}$; $\Omega = \{w_0, w_1, w_2, w_3\}$.

Formula	Models
P_1	$\{w_2, w_3\}$
$\neg P_1$	$\{w_0, w_1\}$
P_1'	$\{\{w_2\}, \{w_3\}\}$
$\sim(P_1')$	$2^\Omega - \{\{w_2\}, \{w_3\}\}$
BP_1	$\{\varnothing, \{w_2\}, \{w_3\}, \{w_2, w_3\}\}$
$B\neg P_1$	$\{\varnothing, \{w_0\}, \{w_1\}, \{w_0, w_1\}\}$

3. Resolution Method for Beliefs

The inference problem in a belief-logic consists of determining whether a given goal belief-formula β_0 is implied by a finite set of belief-formulas $S = \{\beta_1, \beta_2, ...\beta_k\}$, called facts. We present a resolution method for inferencing in the belief-logic, which is a generalization of the resolution method for the propositional logic. The derivation of $\Box$ in the belief-logic often involves as a substep the derivation of $B\Box$, meaning that the facts which are believed are contradictory to each other (as in $B\phi$ and $B\neg\phi$). The final derivation of $\Box$ shows that the beliefs themselves are in contradiction with each other (as in $B\phi$ and $\sim B\phi$).

We begin by defining the notion of literals, clauses, and the resolvent. If C is a propositional-clause, including the case $C = \Box$, then BC and ~BC are said to be *belief-literals*; BC is said to be a *positive* literal and ~BC a *negative* literal. A *belief-clause* is a disjunction of zero or more belief-literals. We sometimes use the term "literal" as a short form of "belief-literal" and also of "propositional-literal", when no confusion is likely; similarly, the term "clause" is used for both "belief-clause" and "propositional-clause". It is clear from Table 1 that each belief-formula is equivalent to a conjunction of belief-clauses.

We define the notion of subsumption between two belief-clauses β_1 and β_2 in such a way that the following holds: If β_1 subsumes β_2, then each model of β_1 is a model of β_2, i.e., $\beta_1 \rightarrow \beta_2$ is valid. This means, in particular, that we can remove a clause β_j from a set S if it is subsumed by some other clause in S without affecting the satisfiability or unsatisfiability of S. Formally, we define the subsumption as follows:

(1) If C_1 and C_2 are two propositional clauses such that C_1 subsumes C_2, then we say BC_1 *subsumes* BC_2 and $\sim BC_2$ *subsumes* $\sim BC_1$. (It is not possible for a positive belief-literal BC_1 to subsume a negative belief-literal $\sim BC_2$ because $\Box \in \Omega(BC_1) - \Omega(\sim BC_2)$. The only case where a negative belief-literal subsumes a positive belief-literal is $\sim BT = \Box$ subsuming BC_2, C_2 being arbitrary, and $\sim BC_1$ subsuming $BT = T$.)

(2) More generally, a belief-clause β_1 is said to *subsume* another belief-clause β_2 if each literal in β_1 equals or subsumes some literal in β_2. The empty belief-clause $\Box$, which has no literals in it, subsumes all other belief-clauses.

Thus, $\sim BP_1 \vee BP_2$ is subsumed by $\sim BP_1$; also, $\sim BP_1$ is subsumed by $\sim B(P_1 \vee P_2)$ or, more generally, by a clause of the form

$$\sim B(P_1 \vee C_1) \vee \sim B(P_1 \vee C_2) \vee \ldots \vee \sim B(P_1 \vee C_k),\ k \geq 1.$$

We first define two types of resolvents for belief-literals, called Type-I and Type-II. These are then generalized to the case of arbitrary belief-clauses. Finally, we define a third type of resolvents, called Type-III. One can actually generalize the other two resolvents to include the Type-III resolvent, but we choose to formulate it separately for the sake of clarity. In each case, we make sure that the resolvent is logically implied by the parent clauses from which it is derived.

(1°) *Type-I* resolvent.
If BC_1 and BC_2 are two belief-literals such that C_1 and C_2 are propositionally resolvable, then we say that BC_1 and BC_2 are *resolvable* and we define their *resolvent* to be the literal given by (R.1).

(R.1) $\text{res}(BC_1, BC_2) = B(\text{res}(C_1, C_2))$.

Thus, we have $\text{res}(B(P \vee \neg Q), B(Q \vee R)) = B(P \vee R)$. It is clear that $BC_1 \wedge BC_2 \Rightarrow B(\text{res}(C_1, C_2))$. Note that this type of resolvent can be at best $B\Box$, but not $\Box$.

(2°) *Type-II* resolvent.
Let $C_1 = L_1 \vee L_2 \vee \ldots \vee L_m$ and $C_2 = L_{k+1} \vee L_{k+2} \vee \ldots \vee L_m \vee C'_2$ be two propositional clauses, where $0 \leq k < m$ and each L_j is a propositional literal; C'_2 may be the empty clause. Then, we say that BC_1 and $\sim BC_2$ are *resolvable* and we define their *resolvent* to be the clause given by (R.2).

$$\text{(R.2)}\quad \text{res}(BC_1, \sim BC_2) = \sim B(\neg L_1 \wedge \neg L_2 \wedge \ldots \wedge \neg L_k) = \sim B(\neg L_1) \vee \ldots \vee \sim B(\neg L_k) = \Box, \text{ if } k = 0.$$

Two special cases of (R.2) that are worth noting are: $\text{res}(B\Box, \sim BC_2) = \Box = \text{res}(BC_2, \sim BC_2)$, and $\text{res}(BC_1, \sim B\Box) = \sim B(\neg L_1) \vee \sim B(\neg L_2) \vee \ldots \vee \sim B(\neg L_m)$. Once again, we have $BC_1 \wedge \sim BC_2 \Rightarrow \text{res}(BC_1, \sim BC_2)$.

(3°) Generalization of (R.1) and (R.2).
Two belief-clauses $\beta_1 = X_1 \vee X_2 \vee \ldots \vee X_m$ and $\beta_2 = Y_1 \vee Y_2 \vee \ldots \vee Y_n$ are said to be *resolvable* if there is a literal in β_1 (say, X_m) which can be resolved with a literal in β_2 (say, Y_1) using (R.1) or (R.2). We define the resolvent $\text{res}(\beta_1, \beta_2)$ to be the clause given by (R.3) below. We say (R.3) is of Type-I or Type-II according as $\text{res}(X_m, Y_1)$ is of Type-I or Type-II. Note that β_1 and β_2 may contain several pairs of literals with respect to which we can form $\text{res}(\beta_1, \beta_2)$ and we may obtain different resolvents in this way. (This is unlike the case of propositional logic, where one obtains a unique resolvent no matter how it is resolved.)

$$\text{(R.3)}\quad \text{res}(\beta_1, \beta_2) = X_1 \vee X_2 \vee \ldots \vee X_{m-1} \vee \text{res}(X_m, Y_1) \vee Y_2 \vee \ldots \vee Y_n.$$

If the right hand side of (R.3) contains duplicate literals, i.e., $X_i = Y_j$ for some $i \leq m-1$ and $j \geq 2$, or $\text{res}(X_m, Y_1)$ equals some of the other literals, then we simplify it by removing the duplicate literals. That $\beta_1 \wedge \beta_2 \Rightarrow \text{res}(\beta_1, \beta_2)$ follows from the corresponding properties of (R.1) and (R.2).

(4°) *Type-III* resolvent.
Let $\beta = X_1 \vee X_2 \vee \ldots \vee X_m$, $m \geq 2$, where each $X_j = \sim B(C \vee C_j)$ is a negative literal and C is the largest common subclause of the propositional clauses $\{C \vee C_j : 1 \leq j \leq m\}$, i.e., there is no literal common to all C_j. Then β is subsumed by $\sim BC$ and we define the resolvent $\text{res}(\beta)$ to be the literal given by (R.4).

(R.4) $\text{res}(\beta) = \sim BC$.

A *derivation* of a belief-clause β from a set S of belief-clauses is defined to be a sequence $D = (D_1, D_2, \ldots, D_m)$, where each $D_k \in S$ or is a resolvent of some previous clause(s) in the sequence D and $D_m = \beta$. A *refutation proof* of a goal β_0 from a set of facts $\{\beta_1, \beta_2, \ldots, \beta_k\}$ is a derivation of □ from the union of the sets of clauses obtained from β_j, $1 \leq j \leq k$, and the clauses obtained from $\neg\beta_0$. There is no restriction on how the clauses of β_j and of $\sim\beta_0$ are formed.

Example 2. Shown below are the minimal unsatisfiable sets of clauses S in a single proposition P, which do not contain □.[2]

(1) B□ and one of {~BP, ~B¬P, ~B□}
(2) {~BP, BP}
(3) {~B¬P, B¬P}
(4) {BP, ~B□, B¬P}
(5) {~BP ∨ B□, BP ∨ B¬P, ~B¬P ∨ B□, ~B□}

It is easy to see that □ can be derived in each case. There are three ways of deriving □ in case (4). One of the many possible ways of deriving □ in case (5) is shown in Fig. 1. If we replace one or more of the input clauses by their alternate representations (e.g., replace ~BP ∨ B□ by ~BP ∨ B¬P), then one can still derive □. ■

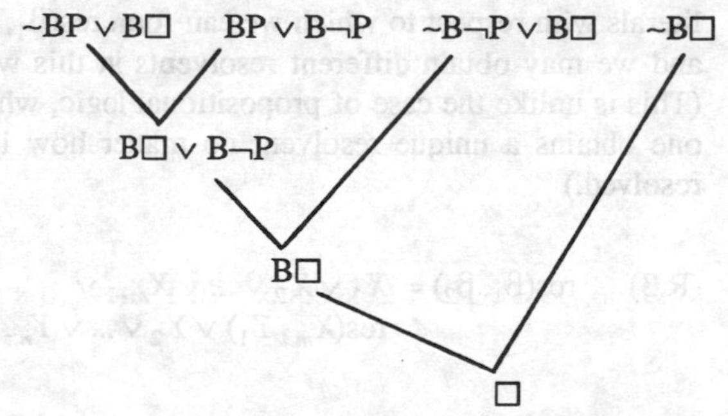

Figure 1. A derivation of □ from the belief-clauses {~BP ∨ B□, BP ∨ B¬P, ~B¬P ∨ B□, ~B□}.

Example 3. Suppose our universe of discourse consists of the basic propositions P = "Tweety has wings" and Q = "Tweety flies". Let B be the belief operator "Kundu believes ...". We consider the following facts (1)-(2) and the goal (3):

(1) "Kundu believes that if Tweety has wings, then Tweety flies". This is represented by B(P → Q) = B(¬P ∨ Q).
(2) "Kundu does not believe that Tweety does not have wings". This is represented by ~B¬P.

[2] The minimality of S means that S does not contain a proper subset which is also unsatisfiable. In particular, no clause in S is subsumed by another clause in S.

(3) "Kundu does not believe that Tweety cannot fly". This is represented by ~B¬Q.

One expects that perhaps (3) can be proved from (1)-(2). Fig. 2 shows a refutation proof of (3). If we replace (2) by the stronger fact BP ∧ ~B□, then we can indeed still prove the goal (3). We first resolve BP with B(¬P ∨ Q), giving the resolvent BQ. Now, obtain B□ = res(BQ, B¬Q), which can be then resolved with ~B□ to obtain the desired empty-clause □. Note the use of ~B□ here, without which we cannot obtain □ in this case. This is not surprising because the empty set of worlds ∅ is a model for {BP, B(P → Q), B¬Q}. We can actually derive a stronger goal BQ ∧ ~B□ in this case.

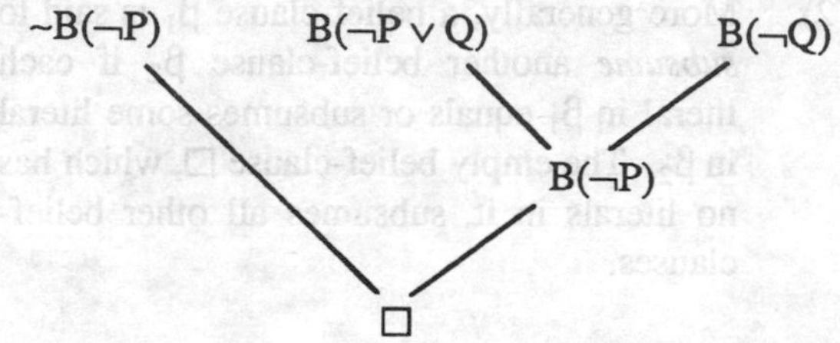

Figure 2. An illustration of resolution proof for beliefs.

If we consider the goal (3′) = BQ = "Kundu believes that Tweety flies", which is stronger than (3), then it may not be so obvious if (3′) can be proved from (1)-(2). Fig. 3 shows all possible resolvents that can be obtained from {(1), (2), ~(3′)} and, in particular, that □ cannot be derived. The set of worlds W = {TT, FF}, where TT means P = T = Q and similarly for FF, forms a model of {(1), (2), ~(3′)}. ■

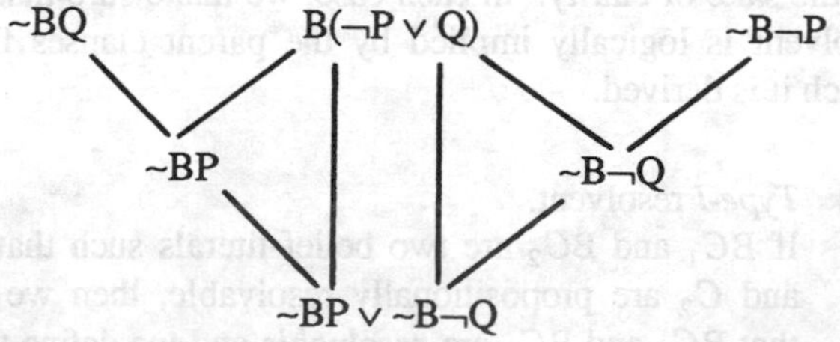

Figure 3. An example where □ cannot be derived.

The main result of this paper is the following theorem. We omit the proof for want of space, but it can be found in [Kundu, 1991a]. We point out that the resolution rules given here can be seen to be closely related to that for predicate logic (without function symbols). One could almost say that the completeness of the belief-logic inference method follows from that of predicate logic without function symbols, except for the slight difference of the empty set of worlds being a possible model for a given belief-formulas.

Theorem 4 (Completeness and soundness of the resolution method). Let S be an arbitrary finite set of belief-clauses. The set S is unsatisfiable if and only if there is a derivation of □ from S. ■

4. Conclusion

We have presented here a new belief-logic for propositional facts (i.e., without variables and quantifiers), including a resolution proof method for this logic, which can be thought of as a generalization of the resolution method for propositional logic. Our formulation of the belief-logic differs from the other belief-logics in two fundamental ways: (1) The ordinary propositional logic is imbedded within our belief-logic. Each propositional formula ϕ is mapped to a belief-formula ϕ' in an one-to-one to fashion in such a way that if ϕ implies ψ as propositional formulas, then ϕ' implies ψ' as belief-formulas, and conversely. Also, the truth value of ϕ' is evaluated in the same way as for general belief-formulas. (2) The belief-logic developed here is monotonic in nature and its construction can be applied repeatedly to obtain a hierarchy of belief-logics $\mathbf{BL}_k$, $k \geq 1$, such that $\mathbf{BL}_k \supset \mathbf{BL}_{k-1}$ and $\mathbf{BL}_k$ can handle all belief-formulas involving up to level k nested applications of the belief-operator B. We obtain a non-monotonic belief-logic from $\mathbf{BL}_k$ by applying circumscription to it, for instance. This is the approach taken in [Kundu, 1991b].

Acknowledgements: The author wishes to express sincere thanks to an anonymous referee for indicating the close connection between the resolution rules given here and those of predicate logic.

Appendix: Consider the universe $\Omega = \{w_0, w_1\}$ of a single proposition P. Shown below are all the belief-literals and their models. There are only three belief-clauses which are not equivalent to a belief-literal or **T**, namely, $\sim BP \vee B\Box = \sim BP \vee B\neg P$, $\sim B\neg P \vee B\Box = \sim B\neg P \vee BP$, and $BP \vee B\neg P$. The set of models for these clauses are given by $\{\varnothing, \{w_0\}, \{w_0, w_1\}\}$, $\{\varnothing, \{w_1\}, \{w_0, w_1\}\}$, and $\{\varnothing, \{w_0\}, \{w_1\}\}$, respectively.

The belief-literals in proposition P.

B□	~B□	BP	~BP	B¬P	~B¬P
$\varnothing$	$\{w_0\}$	$\varnothing$	$\{w_0\}$	$\varnothing$	$\{w_1\}$
		$\{w_1\}$	$\{w_1\}$	$\{w_0, w_1\}$	$\{w_0\}$
		$\{w_0, w_1\}$			

The following diagram shows the subsumption relationships among the belief-clauses other than **T**, where a clause β_1 is shown below another clause β_2 if β_1 subsumes β_2.

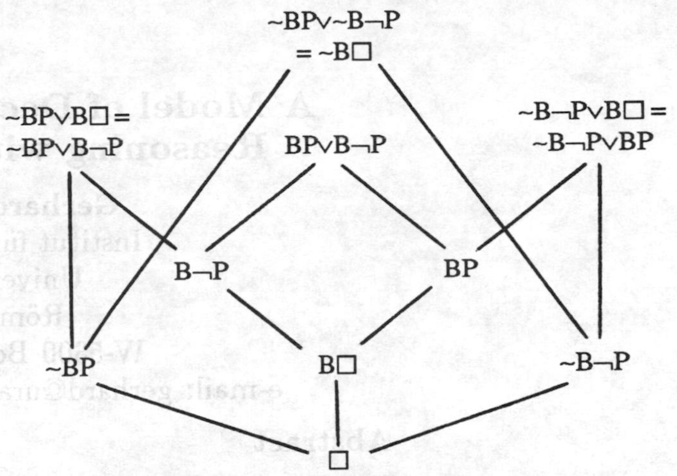

The subsumption relationships among the belief-clauses in a single proposition P.

References:

[Anderson and Belnap, 1975] A. R. Anderson and N. D. Belnap. *Entailment, the logic of relevance and necessity*, Princeton University Press, 1975.

[Hintikka, 1962] J. Hintikka. *Knowledge and belief: An introduction to the logic of the two notion*, Cornell University Press, 1962.

[Levesque, 1990] H. J. Levesque. All I know: a study in autoepistemic logic, *Artificial Intelligence*, 42(1990), pp. 263-309.

[Levesque, 1984] H. J. Levesque. A logic of implicit and explicit belief, *Proceedings of National Conference on Artificial Intelligence, AAAI-84*, Aug. 6-10, 1984, pp. 198-202.

[Kundu, 1991a] S. Kundu. A new logic of beliefs: monotonic and non-monotonic beliefs - Part I, *Tech Rept.*, 91-003, Louisiana State University, Computer Sc. Dept., 1991.

[Kundu, 1991b] S. Kundu. A new logic of beliefs: monotonic and non-monotonic beliefs - Part II, in preparation.

A Model of Decidable Introspective Reasoning with Quantifying-In

Gerhard Lakemeyer*
Institut für Informatik III
Universität Bonn
Römerstr. 164
W-5300 Bonn 1, Germany
e-mail: gerhard@uran.informatik.uni-bonn.de

Abstract

Since knowledge is usually incomplete, agents need to introspect on what they know and do not know. The best known models of introspective reasoning suffer from intractability or even undecidability if the underlying language is first-order. To better suit the fact that agents have limited resources, we recently proposed a model of decidable introspective reasoning in first-order knowledge bases (KBs). However, this model is deficient in that it does not allow for quantifying-in, which is needed to distinguish between *knowing that* and *knowing who*. In this paper, we extend our earlier work by adding quantifying-in and equality to a model of limited belief that integrates ideas from possible-world semantics and relevance logic.

1 Introduction

Since agents rarely have complete information about the world, it is important for them to introspect on what they know and, more importantly, do not know. For example,

> if somebody tells you that Sue's father is a teacher and you have no other information about Sue's father, then introspection (in addition to deduction) allows you to conclude that there is a teacher and that you do *not know who* that teacher is, that is, as far as you know, Sue's father could be any of a number of individuals.

There have been various attempts to formalize introspective reasoning, most notably in the guise of the so-called *autoepistemic logics* (e.g. [18, 17]). While providing a very elegant framework for introspection, these logics have a major drawback in that they assume an ideal reasoner with infinite resources. In particular, in the first-order case, reasoning is undecidable. It is therefore of particular interest to devise models of introspective reasoning which are better suited for agents with limited resources.

For that purpose, a model of a tractable introspective reasoner was proposed for a propositional language in [12]. Since its obvious first-order extension leads to an undecidable reasoner, we proposed a modification which retains decidability in [13]. However, this proposal is still too limited since it lacks the expressiveness to deal with incomplete knowledge as exhibited in our initial example. In particular, it does not allow us to make distinctions between *knowing that* and *knowing who* because the underlying language does not provide for *quantifying-in* [6], that is, the ability to use variables *within* a belief[1] that are bound *outside* the belief. With quantifying-in, the above example can easily be expressed as (we use the modal operator **B** for belief)

$$\exists x \mathtt{Teacher}(x) \wedge \neg \mathbf{B}\mathtt{Teacher}(x),$$

a sentence that should follow from an introspective KB that contains only the sentence $\mathtt{Teacher}(\mathit{father}(\mathit{sue}))$.

In this paper, we extend the results of [13] by considering a language with quantifying-in and equality. It is not at all obvious whether adding quantifying-in allows us to retain a decidable reasoner. As Konolige observed [8], while introspective reasoning in classical monadic predicate calculus is decidable, it becomes undecidable if we add quantifying-in. As a result, Konolige makes the following comment:

> Thus the presence of quantifying-in seems to pose an inherently difficult computational problem for introspective systems.

In this paper we show that, given an arbitrary first-order KB, it is decidable for a large class of sentences with quantifying-in whether or not these sentences follow from the KB.

One way to formalize reasoning is to view the problem as one of modeling belief. In a nutshell, a model of belief tells us what the possible sets of beliefs or *epistemic states* of an agent are. One then needs to specify for any given KB which epistemic state it represents. Under this view, reasoning reduces to testing for membership in the appropriate epistemic state.

As in [12, 17], we use an approach that allows us to model the beliefs of a KB directly within the logic. Intuitively, a KB's epistemic state can be characterized as the set of all sentences that are believed given that the sentences in the KB are *all* that is believed or, as we

*This work was conducted at the University of Toronto.

[1] We use the terms *knowledge* and *belief* interchangeably in this paper, even though belief is the more appropriate term, since we allow an agent to have false beliefs.

will say for short, *only-believed*. We formalize this idea using a modal logic with two modal operators **B** and **O** for belief and only-believing, respectively. This allows us to say that a KB believes a sentence α just in case $\mathbf{O}\text{KB} \supset \mathbf{B}\alpha$ is a valid sentence[2] of the logic, thus characterizing the epistemic state of the KB. The complexity of reasoning then reduces to the complexity of solving this validity problem.

In related work, Konolige [8] also addresses the issue of modeling introspection under resource limitations. However rather than proposing an actual instance of a computationally attractive reasoner, he presents a general framework in which one can be formalized. Since we consider a limited introspective reasoner who is able to perform full introspection and is only limited in his deductive component, work on limited deduction alone is also relevant [7, 2, 19, 4]. In particular, as discussed in [13], [19] is a special case of ours. Finally, in preliminary work [11], we proposed a model of limited belief with quantifying-in yet without nested beliefs. As a result, the corresponding reasoner was purely deductive and not able to make use of quantifying-in himself.

In the next section, we introduce the logic *OBLIQUE*,[3] which defines the model of belief and only-believing. In Section 3, we take a closer look at the epistemic states of KB's as defined by *OBLIQUE*. Section 4 shows the computational pay-off of using this particular limited form of belief. In Section 5, we use the logic to define a KR service that allows a user to query a KB and to add new information to it. Finally, we end the paper with a brief summary and an outlook on future work.

2 The Logic *OBLIQUE*

We begin with a discussion of belief and only-believing.

Belief

As in in [13], belief is modeled by integrating ideas from possible-world semantics [5, 9] and relevance logic [1, 3]. Roughly, an agent believes a sentence just in case that sentence holds in all states of affairs or *situations* the agent imagines. In order to obtain agents with perfect introspection we require that, similar to a semantics of the modal logic *weak S5*, that every model has one globally accessible set of situations. Situations are a four-valued extension of classical worlds. Instead of facts being either true or false, situations assign them independent *true* and *false-support*, which corresponds to the use of four truth values {}, {`true`}, {`false`}, and {`true`, `false`}, an idea originally proposed to provide a semantics for a fragment of relevance logic called *tautological entailment* [1, 3].[4]

In order to be able to distinguish between ***knowing that*** and ***knowing who***, we follow [17] and use a language with both *rigid* and *non-rigid* designators (see [10]). The non-rigid designators are the usual terms of a first-order language such as $father(sue)$, which may vary in their interpretation. The rigid designators are special unique identifiers called *standard names*. For simplicity, the standard names are taken to be the universe of discourse in our semantics.

Employing four-valued situations instead of worlds has the effect that beliefs are no longer closed under *modus ponens*, e.g. $\mathbf{B}(p \vee q)$ and $\mathbf{B}(\neg q \vee r)$ may be true and $\mathbf{B}(p \vee r)$ may be false at the same time. As discussed in [13], a further restriction is needed in order to use this model of belief as a basis for a decidable reasoner. In particular, the link between disjunction and existential quantification is weakened in the sense that an agent may believe $\mathtt{P}(a) \vee \mathtt{P}(b)$, yet fail to believe $\exists x \mathtt{P}(x)$. In the case of beliefs without quantifying-in, this can be achieved semantically by requiring that an agent who believes the existence of an individual with a certain property must be able to name or give a description of that individual. More concretely, in order to believe $\exists x \mathtt{P}(x)$ there must be a closed term t (e.g. $father(sue)$) such that $\mathtt{P}(t)$ is true in all accessible situations (see [13]).

In the case of beliefs with quantifying-in, this idea of simply substituting terms for existentially quantified variables does not suffice. E.g., given the belief $\exists x \mathtt{Teacher}(x) \wedge \neg\mathbf{B}\mathtt{Teacher}(x)$, if we replace x by any term, say $father(sue)$, then the resulting belief is inconsistent because for an introspective agent to believe that $\mathtt{Teacher}(father(sue)) \wedge \neg\mathbf{B}\mathtt{Teacher}(father(sue))$ means that he both believes and does not believe that $\mathtt{Teacher}(father(sue))$. What is wrong is that we should not have substituted $father(sue)$ for the second occurrence of x (within the context of **B**). Instead, what we really want at its place is the *denotation* of $father(sue)$ so that, while $\mathtt{Teacher}(father(sue))$ holds at every situation the agent imagines, the agent does not know *of* the denotation of $father(sue)$ at any given situation that he is a teacher, that is, the agent does not know *who* the father of Sue is. To make this distinction between a term and its denotation we introduce a so-called *level marker* **.0** which is attached to a term whenever the term is substituted *within* the context of a modal operator. In our example, the substitution results in $\mathtt{Teacher}(father(sue)) \wedge \neg\mathbf{B}\mathtt{Teacher}(father(sue).0)$. Later we will return to this example and demonstrate formally how the use of level markers has the desired effect.[5]

Only-Believing

An agent who only-believes a sentence α believes α and, intuitively, believes as little else as possible. In other words, the agent is maximally ignorant while still believing α.

As demonstrated in [12, 17], if belief is modeled by a set of situations, independent of whether they are four-valued or two-valued as in classical possible-world se-

[2]Whenever KB occurs within a logical sentence, we mean the conjunction of all the sentences in the KB.

[3]Thanks to Hector Levesque, who suggested that name to me. It may be read as "Only Belief Logic with Quantifiers and Equality."

[4]Levesque [16] was the first to introduce the notion of four-valued situations to model a limited form of belief in a propositional framework.

[5]In the logic, we allow an infinite number of distinct level markers. While not apparent in this paper, this choice was made for technical convenience. The reader may simply ignore all level markers other than .0.

mantics, only-believing has a particularly simple characterization: an agent only-believes a sentence α if he or she believes α and the set of situations M is as large as possible, i.e., if we were to add any other situation to M, the agent would no longer believe α.[6]

With the special treatment of existential quantification as outlined above, we need to pay special attention to the case of only-believing sentences that contain existential quantifiers (see also [13]). Consider the example of only-believing $\alpha = \exists x \mathtt{P}(x)$. Since α is believed, we need a term t such that $\mathtt{P}(t)$ is believed as well. However, t should not carry any information about the world (where should the information come from?). Thus t has to be a generic term much like a Skolem function.

For that reason, we introduce a special set of function symbols called *sk-functions*, which must be used when substituting existentials in the context of only-believing. To obtain the desired effect, we allow KB's to contain sk-functions while excluding them from epistemic states. This way, given an sk-function t_{sk} and a KB $= \mathtt{P}(t_{sk})$, the beliefs that follow from KB are the same as if KB $= \exists x \mathtt{P}(x)$.

2.1 The Languages $\mathcal{L}$ and $\mathcal{BL}$

We introduce a language $\mathcal{L}$, which allows us to talk *about* the beliefs of a KB and a language $\mathcal{BL}$, which is a sublanguage of $\mathcal{L}$ and which contains all the sentences that qualify as possible beliefs of a KB. For example, the operator **O** may be used to talk about the beliefs of a KB but it may not appear within a belief itself.[7]

The language $\mathcal{L}$ is a modal first-order dialect with equality and function symbols, which form a countably infinite set $\mathcal{F}$, which itself is partitioned into two countably infinite sets $\mathcal{F}_{\mathrm{REG}}$ and $\mathcal{F}_{\mathrm{SK}}$ of every arity. The latter contains the sk-functions mentioned earlier. The language also contains a countably infinite set $N = \{\#1, \#2, \ldots\}$ of standard names, which are syntactically treated like constants. Finally the **level markers** form a countably infinite and totally ordered set with a least element. They are written as **.i**, where i is a natural number. The ordering is $.0 < .1 < .2 < .3 < \ldots$

Given the usual definitions of **terms**, a **primitive term** is a term with only standard names as arguments. Given a term t, an **extended term** $\hat{t}$ is obtained from t by appending zero or more subterms of t with level markers such that, if u.i occurs in $\hat{t}$, then u is not a variable and does not contain level markers.[8] Atomic formulas (or atoms) are predicate symbols whose arguments are extended terms. **Primitive formulas** are atoms with standard names as arguments.

The **formulas** of $\mathcal{L}$ are constructed in the usual way from the atomic formulas, the connectives $\neg$ and $\vee$, the quantifier $\exists$,[9] and the modal operators **B** and **O**. To simplify the technical presentation below, we also require that no variable is bound more than once within the scope of a modal operator of a formula. Formulas without any occurrences of **B** or **O** are called **objective**, formulas without occurrences of **O** are called **basic**, and formulas whose predicate symbols all occur within the scope of a modal operator are called **subjective. Sentences** are, as usual, formulas without free variables.

The language $\mathcal{BL}$, over which the epistemic states of KB's will be defined, is a sublanguage of $\mathcal{L}$ and consists of all those basic formulas of $\mathcal{L}$ that contain neither level markers nor sk-functions. We often use the terms **$\mathcal{BL}$-formulas** and **$\mathcal{BL}$-sentences** to refer to the formulas and sentences of $\mathcal{BL}$.

Notation: Sequences of terms or variables are sometimes written in vector notation. E.g., a sequence of variables $\langle x_1, \ldots, x_k \rangle$ is abbreviated as $\vec{x}$. Also, $\exists \vec{x}$ stands for $\exists x_1 \ldots \exists x_k$. If a formula α contains the free variables $x_1, \ldots, x_k$, $\alpha[x_1/t_1, \ldots, x_k/t_k]$ (abbreviated as $\alpha[\vec{x}/\vec{t}]$) denotes α with every occurrence of x_i replaced by t_i. If the context is clear, we omit the variables and write $\alpha[t_1, \ldots, t_k]$ or $\alpha[\vec{t}]$ instead. The truth values `true` and `false` are used as shorthand for $(\#1 = \#1)$ and $(\#1 \neq \#1)$, respectively.

The following definitions are needed for the semantics of **B** and **O**. In particular, Definitions 2 and 3 describe what terms can be substituted for the existentially quantified variables when interpreting **B** and **O**, respectively.

Definition 1 *A variable occurs (is bound) at the* **objective level** *of α if it occurs (is bound) outside the scope of any modal operator in α.*

Let α be a formula in $\mathcal{L}$. Let x be a variable that is bound at the objective level of some formula β such that either $\beta = \alpha$ or $\mathbf{B}\beta$ is a subformula of α. x is said to be **existentially (universally) quantified** *in α iff x is bound within in the scope of an* **even (odd)** *number of $\neg$-operators in β.*

For example, in $\exists x \neg \mathbf{B} \exists y \mathtt{P}(x, y)$, both x and y are considered existentially quantified.

Definition 2 *Admissible Terms*

Let α be a formula and x existentially quantified in α. A term t is said to be an **admissible** *substitution for x with respect to α iff every variable y in t is universally quantified in α and x occurs within the scope of y.*

If the context is clear, we often say t is admissible for *x or t* is admissible.

Definition 3 *Sk-terms*

Let α be a sentence and x an existentially quantified variable bound at the objective level of α. Let $U(x)$ be a sequence of the universally quantified variables in whose scope x is bound. Let $f \in \mathcal{F}_{\mathrm{SK}}$ be a function symbol of arity $|U(x)|$ occurring nowhere else in α. Then $f(U(x))$ is called an **sk-term** *(for x).*

Definition 4 *Let α be a sentence and let $\vec{x} = \langle x_1, \ldots, x_k \rangle$ be a sequence of the existentially quantified variables bound at the objective level of α. $\alpha^{\not\exists}$ denotes α with all $\exists x_i$ removed.*

---

[6] M need not be unique for the same reasons as there are multiple extensions in autoepistemic logic (see [12, 17]).

[7] This restriction of $\mathcal{BL}$ was chosen to simplify the technical treatment. Besides, there seems to be little practical use for beliefs about whether something is *all* that is believed.

[8] E.g., given a term $f(a)$ (a constant), $f(a.0)$ and $f(a).14$ are extended terms, but $f(a).1.3$ and $f(a.1).14$ are not.

[9] Other logical connectives like $\wedge$, $\supset$, and $\equiv$ and the quantifier $\forall$ are used freely and are defined in the usual way in terms of $\neg$, $\vee$, and $\exists$.

Example 2.1 Let $\alpha = \exists w \forall x \exists y \mathrm{P}(w,x,y) \wedge \mathbf{B}\exists z \mathrm{Q}(z)$. Then $\alpha^{\sharp} = \forall x \mathrm{P}(w,x,y) \wedge \mathbf{B}\exists z \mathrm{Q}(z)$. Note that existential quantifiers within modalities are left untouched.

Definition 5 *Let α be a formula with free variables $\vec{x} = \langle x_1, \ldots, x_k \rangle$. ($\alpha$ may contain other free variables as well.) Let $\vec{t} = \langle t_1, \ldots, t_k \rangle$ be a sequence of terms.* *$\alpha[\![\vec{x}/\vec{t}]\!]$ is α with every occurrence of x_i at the objective level replaced by t_i and every occurrence of x_i inside the scope of a modal operator replaced by $t_i.0$.*

Example 2.2
Let $\alpha = \mathrm{P}(x_1) \wedge \mathbf{B}(\neg \mathrm{Q}(x_1) \vee \mathrm{R}(x_2))$. Then $\alpha[\![x_1/a, x_2/b]\!] = \mathrm{P}(a) \wedge \mathbf{B}(\neg \mathrm{Q}(a.0) \vee \mathrm{R}(b.0))$. **Note** the difference to $\alpha[x_1/a, x_2/b] = \mathrm{P}(a) \wedge \mathbf{B}(\neg \mathrm{Q}(a) \vee \mathrm{R}(b))$, that is, [...] indicates regular substitutions, while [\[...]\] indicates that substitutions within modalities are appended with level marker .0.

2.2 A Formal Semantics

We first define situations, which are a four-valued extension of classical (two-valued) Kripke worlds [9]. Situations are defined over a fixed universe of discourse, which is the set of standard names of the language. This allows us to describe the true- and false-support of predicates in terms of the primitive formulas. Closed terms are interpreted by mapping them into the standard names.

Definition 6 *Denotation Function*
A **denotation function** *d is a mapping from closed terms into the standard names such that $d(n) = n$ for all $n \in N$ and $d(f(t_1, \ldots, t_k)) = d(f(d(t_1), \ldots, d(t_k)))$ for all closed non-rigid terms $f(t_1, \ldots, t_k)$. We extend d to apply to terms with level markers. If t is a closed term and .i a level marker, then $d(t.i) = d(t)$.*

Definition 7 *First-Order Situations*
A situation s is a triple $s = \langle T, F, d \rangle$, where T and F are subsets of the set of primitive formulas and d is a denotation function.

T and F can be arbitrary sets of primitive formulas except for equality, which has a fixed interpretation, that is, $(n = m) \in T$ [$(n = m) \in F$] iff n and m are identical [distinct] standard names.

Notice that equality has a standard two-valued interpretation. The main reason why we have chosen such a strong form of equality is to obtain Theorem 2.

Definition 8 *Worlds*
A situation w is called a **world**, *iff $\mathrm{P}(\vec{n}) \in T_w \Leftrightarrow \mathrm{P}(\vec{n}) \notin F_w$ for all primitive formulas $\mathrm{P}(\vec{n})$.*

Definition 9 *Let α be a sentence and $s = \langle T_s, F_s, d_s \rangle$ a situation.*

- *$\alpha^{\blacktriangledown}$ is α with every level marker .i replaced by .i-1 for all .i > .0.*
- *α^{s} is obtained from α by replacing every occurrence of $t.0$ by the standard name $d_s(t)$, if t is closed, and by t otherwise.*

Example 2.3 If $\alpha = \mathrm{P}(a.0) \wedge \forall x \mathbf{B}(\mathrm{Q}(f(x).0) \vee \mathrm{R}(g(x).1))$ and $s = \langle T_s, F_s, d_s \rangle$ with $d_s(a) = \#1$, then $\alpha^{s\blacktriangledown} = \mathrm{P}(\#1) \wedge \forall x \mathbf{B}(\mathrm{Q}(f(x)) \vee \mathrm{R}(g(x).0))$.

Note that $\alpha^{s\blacktriangledown}$ is always well defined, since α^{s} does not contain any occurrences of the level marker .0.

The true- and false-support for the sentences of $\mathcal{L}$ can now be defined. Let $s = \langle T_s, F_s, d_s \rangle$ be a situation and M a set of situations. Let $\mathrm{P}(\vec{t})$ be an atomic sentence and let α and β be sentences except in rule 4 where α may contain the free variable x.

1. $M, s \models_{\mathrm{T}} \mathrm{P}(\vec{t}) \iff \mathrm{P}(d_s(\vec{t})) \in T_s$
   $M, s \models_{\mathrm{F}} \mathrm{P}(\vec{t}) \iff \mathrm{P}(d_s(\vec{t})) \in F_s$
2. $M, s \models_{\mathrm{T}} \neg\alpha \iff M, s \models_{\mathrm{F}} \alpha$
   $M, s \models_{\mathrm{F}} \neg\alpha \iff M, s \models_{\mathrm{T}} \alpha$
3. $M, s \models_{\mathrm{T}} \alpha \vee \beta \iff M, s \models_{\mathrm{T}} \alpha$ or $M, s \models_{\mathrm{T}} \beta$
   $M, s \models_{\mathrm{F}} \alpha \vee \beta \iff M, s \models_{\mathrm{F}} \alpha$ and $M, s \models_{\mathrm{F}} \beta$
4. $M, s \models_{\mathrm{T}} \exists x \alpha \iff$ for some $n \in N$, $M, s \models_{\mathrm{T}} \alpha[x/n]$
   $M, s \models_{\mathrm{F}} \exists x \alpha \iff$ for all $n \in N$, $M, s \models_{\mathrm{F}} \alpha[x/n]$

   Let $\vec{x} = \langle x_1, \ldots, x_k \rangle$ be a sequence of the existentially quantified variables bound at the objective level of α.
5. $M, s \models_{\mathrm{T}} \mathbf{B}\alpha \iff$ there are admissible $\vec{t}$ such that for all s', if $s' \in M$ then $M, s' \models_{\mathrm{T}} \alpha^{s\blacktriangledown\sharp}[\![\vec{x}/\vec{t}]\!]$
   $M, s \models_{\mathrm{F}} \mathbf{B}\alpha \iff M, s \not\models_{\mathrm{T}} \mathbf{B}\alpha$
6. $M, s \models_{\mathrm{T}} \mathbf{O}\alpha \iff$ there is a sequence of sk-terms $\vec{t}_{\mathrm{SK}}$ for $\vec{x}$ such that for all s', $s' \in M$ iff $M, s' \models_{\mathrm{T}} \alpha^{s\blacktriangledown\sharp}[\![\vec{x}/\vec{t}_{\mathrm{SK}}]\!]$
   $M, s \models_{\mathrm{F}} \mathbf{O}\alpha \iff M, s \not\models_{\mathrm{T}} \mathbf{O}\alpha$

Example 2.4 Let $M = \{s \mid s \models_{\mathrm{T}} \mathrm{P}(a)\}$ for some constant a. Then $M \models_{\mathrm{T}} \mathbf{B}(\exists x \mathrm{P}(x) \wedge \neg \mathbf{B}\mathrm{P}(x))$.
Proof: Let $\alpha = \exists x \mathrm{P}(x) \wedge \neg \mathbf{B}\mathrm{P}(x)$. By definition, $M \models_{\mathrm{T}} \mathbf{B}\alpha$ iff $\forall s \in M$, $M, s \models_{\mathrm{T}} \alpha^{s\blacktriangledown\sharp}[\![x/t]\!]$ for some admissible t. Note that, in this case, $\alpha^{s\blacktriangledown} = \alpha$ because α does not contain any level markers.
Then $\alpha^{s\blacktriangledown\sharp}[\![x/a]\!] = \mathrm{P}(a) \wedge \neg \mathbf{B}\mathrm{P}(a.0)$. It suffices to show that for all $s \in M$, $M, s \models_{\mathrm{T}} \mathrm{P}(a) \wedge \neg \mathbf{B}\mathrm{P}(a.0)$. Let $s = \langle T_s, F_s, d_s \rangle$ be any situation in M. $M, s \models_{\mathrm{T}} \mathrm{P}(a)$ follows immediately from the definition of M.
To show that $M, s \models_{\mathrm{T}} \neg \mathbf{B}\mathrm{P}(a.0)$, assume that $d_s(a) = n$ for some standard name n. By the definition of M, there must be a situation $s' \in M$ with a different denotation function such that $s' \not\models_{\mathrm{T}} \mathrm{P}(n)$. Therefore, $M, s \models_{\mathrm{T}} \neg \mathbf{B}\mathrm{P}(n)$ which implies $M, s \models_{\mathrm{T}} \neg \mathbf{B}\mathrm{P}(a.0)$.

Truth, logical consequence, validity, and *satisfiability* are defined with respect to worlds and sets of situations. A sentence α is *true* at a set of situations M and a world w if $M, w \models_{\mathrm{T}} \alpha$. α is *false* if $M, w \not\models_{\mathrm{T}} \alpha$. A sentence α is *valid* ($\models\alpha$) iff α is true at every world w and every set of situations M. α is *satisfiable* iff $\neg\alpha$ is not valid.[10]

2.3 Quantifying-in

For sentences without quantifying-in and without level-markers, *OBLIQUE* reduces essentially to the logic *OBL* in [13].[11] For example, we obtain the same limitations of belief such as no *modus ponens* ($\not\models \mathbf{B}p \wedge$

[10] In this semantics, the basic beliefs of an epistemic state (represented by a set of situations) do not completely determine what is only-believed at that state. As shown in [14], this problem can be overcome. Since this issue is independent from the main concern of this paper, we have chosen to ignore it here.

[11] A minor distinction is that we allow the empty set of situations in the definition of truth and validity, while we excluded it in [13].

$\mathbf{B}(p \supset q) \supset \mathbf{B}q)$ and no existential generalization from disjunctions ($\not\models \mathbf{B}(\mathtt{P}(a) \vee \mathtt{P}(b)) \supset \mathbf{B}\exists x \mathtt{P}(x)$).

Here we focus on the additional feature of *quantifying-in*, which allows us to properly distinguish between *knowing that* and *knowing who*. For example, $\models \mathbf{B}\mathtt{Teacher}((father(sue))) \supset \mathbf{B}\exists x \mathtt{Teacher}(x)$ while $\not\models \mathbf{B}\mathtt{Teacher}((father(sue))) \supset \exists x \mathbf{B}\mathtt{Teacher}(x)$. In other words, knowing the non-rigid designator of a teacher ($father(sue)$) allows an agent to conclude only the existence of a teacher, but the agent does not necessarily know who it is. On the other hand, if he knows the teacher's standard name, say #27, then he knows who the teacher is:
$\models \mathbf{B}(\mathtt{Teacher}(f(sue)) \wedge f(sue) = \#27) \supset \exists x \mathbf{B}\mathtt{Teacher}(x)$.
In general, we obtain $\models \exists x \mathbf{B}\alpha \supset \mathbf{B}\exists x \alpha$ for all α.

The *Barcan formula* ($\forall x \mathbf{B}\alpha \supset \mathbf{B}\forall x \alpha$) is not valid in general. In a sense, the agent is not able to perform arbitrary universal generalization. However, if we restrict α to formulas where no existentially quantified variable is bound at the objective level of α, the Barcan formula is indeed valid. Finally, the converse of the Barcan formula, $\models \mathbf{B}\forall x \alpha \supset \forall x \mathbf{B}\alpha$, is valid for all α.

3 Epistemic States of First-Order KB's

Besides offering us a model of limited belief with quantifying-in, *OBLIQUE* specifies for every objective KB a unique corresponding epistemic state, if we take $\mathcal{BL}$ to be the agent's language of belief.[12]

Theorem 1 *Let* KB *be an objective sentence. For any basic* α *in* $\mathcal{BL}$*, exactly one of* $\models \mathbf{O}\mathrm{KB} \supset \mathbf{B}\alpha$ *and* $\models \mathbf{O}\mathrm{KB} \supset \neg\mathbf{B}\alpha$ *holds.*[13]

One important property of such epistemic states is that the question whether or not an arbitrary belief follows from an objective KB reduces to the question whether an *objective* belief, that is a belief that itself does not mention any **B**'s, follows from the KB. For example, let KB = $\mathtt{Teacher}(\#27) \wedge (\mathtt{Teacher}(father(sue)) \wedge (father(sue) \neq \#27)$, where #27 is a standard name. Then determining the validity of $\mathbf{O}\mathrm{KB} \supset \mathbf{B}(\exists x \mathtt{Teacher}(x) \wedge \neg \mathbf{B}\mathtt{Teacher}(x))$ reduces to determining the validity of $\mathbf{O}\mathrm{KB} \supset \mathbf{B}(\exists x \mathtt{Teacher}(x) \wedge \neg(x = \#27))$, that is, the formula $\mathbf{B}\mathtt{Teacher}(x)$ is replaced by an equality expression which describes the set of all standard names who are known to be teachers. In general, it turns out that, even if the set of instances that are known to have a certain property is infinite, there is always a finite equality expression that describes it (Definitions 10 and 11).[14]

Definition 10 *Let* KB *be an objective sentence and let* α *be a* $\mathcal{BL}$*-formula, possibly containing free variables. Let* $n_1, \ldots, n_m$ *be all the standard names occurring in* KB *or* α*, and let* n^* *be a standard name not occurring in* KB *or* α.

1. If α is closed then
$$\mathbf{RES_B}(\mathrm{KB}, \alpha) = \begin{cases} \mathtt{true} & \models \mathbf{O}\mathrm{KB} \supset \mathbf{B}\alpha \\ \mathtt{false} & \models \mathbf{O}\mathrm{KB} \supset \neg\mathbf{B}\alpha \end{cases}$$
2. Otherwise let α contain the free variable x. Then
$$\mathbf{RES_B}(\mathrm{KB}, \alpha) = \begin{cases} \bigvee((x = n_i) \wedge \mathbf{RES_B}(\mathrm{KB}, \alpha^x_{n_i})) \vee \\ (\bigwedge(x \neq n_i) \wedge \mathbf{RES_B}(\mathrm{KB}, \alpha^x_{n^*})^{n^*}_x) \end{cases}$$

The next definition shows how to apply $\mathbf{RES_B}$ recursively to all occurrences of **B** within a belief and thus obtain an objective belief.

Definition 11 *Let* KB *be an objective sentence and let* α *be a* $\mathcal{BL}$*-formula.*

$$\begin{array}{lcl} \|\alpha\|_{\mathrm{KB}} & = & \alpha, \text{ for objective } \alpha \\ \|\neg\alpha\|_{\mathrm{KB}} & = & \neg\|\alpha\|_{\mathrm{KB}} \\ \|\alpha \vee \beta\|_{\mathrm{KB}} & = & \|\alpha\|_{\mathrm{KB}} \vee \|\beta\|_{\mathrm{KB}} \\ \|\exists x \alpha\|_{\mathrm{KB}} & = & \exists x \|\alpha\|_{\mathrm{KB}} \\ \|\mathbf{B}\alpha\|_{\mathrm{KB}} & = & \mathbf{RES_B}(\mathrm{KB}, \|\alpha\|_{\mathrm{KB}}) \end{array}$$

Lemma 3.1 $\|\alpha\|_{\mathrm{KB}}$ *is objective.*

Theorem 2 *Let* KB *be an objective sentence and* α *a* $\mathcal{BL}$*-sentence. Then* $\models \mathbf{O}\mathrm{KB} \supset \mathbf{B}\alpha$ iff $\models \mathbf{O}\mathrm{KB} \supset \mathbf{B}\|\alpha\|_{\mathrm{KB}}$.

This result is crucial in obtaining decidability results for the reasoner specified by *OBLIQUE*.

4 A Computational Pay-Off

While *OBLIQUE* specifies an admittedly weak reasoner, we gain a clear computational pay-off in return. In particular, we obtain a decidable reasoner for a large class of sentences including ones with quantifying-in. Let us call an equality expression $t = t'$ *ground* if both t and t' are closed terms.

Theorem 3 *Let* $\mathrm{KB} = \mathrm{KB}' \wedge E$ *be an objective sentence, where* KB′ *contains no equality and* E *is a conjunction of ground equalities and inequalities. Let* α *be a* $\mathcal{BL}$*-sentence such that every free variable* x *in a subformula* $\mathbf{B}\gamma$ *in* α *is universally quantified. (In other words, only universally quantified variables may participate in quantifying-in.) In addition we require that every term in an equality expression in* α *is either a universally quantified variable or a closed term. Then the validity of* $\mathbf{O}\mathrm{KB} \supset \mathbf{B}\alpha$ *is decidable.*

Proof : (Sketch) While the proof is rather involved, it is instructive to sketch the main ideas.

First, it can be shown that we can assume, without loss of generality, that the existentially quantified variables in KB′ are skolemized and KB′ is in prenex conjunctive normal form.

Next, given Theorem 2, a simple induction on the nesting of **B**'s shows that $\models \mathbf{O}\mathrm{KB} \supset \mathbf{B}\alpha$ is decidable iff the same holds for *objective* α. (Note that the $\|.\|_{\mathrm{KB}}$-transformation introduces only equalities that satisfy the restrictions of the theorem.) Thus let us assume from now on that α is objective. Also, let $\vec{x}$ and $\vec{y}$ be the existentially and universally quantified variables of α, respectively, and let α' be the matrix of α (all the quantifiers removed) in conjunctive normal form.

For an objective α it is easy to see that $\models \mathbf{O}\mathrm{KB} \supset \mathbf{B}\alpha$ iff $\models \mathbf{B}\mathrm{KB} \supset \mathbf{B}\alpha$. Next, $\models \mathbf{B}\mathrm{KB} \supset \mathbf{B}\alpha$ iff there are admissible terms for $\vec{x}$ in α such that for all the substitutions of standard names $\vec{n} \in I^l$ $\models \mathbf{B}\mathrm{KB} \supset \forall \vec{y} \mathbf{B}(\alpha'[\vec{x}/\vec{t}])[\vec{y}/\vec{n}]$, where $I = \{n \mid n \text{ occurs in KB or } \alpha\} \cup \{n^*_1, \ldots, n^*_l\}$. ■

[12] If the KB is not objective, the logic may not give us a unique epistemic state for the same reasons as there are multiple extensions in autoepistemic logic [18].

[13] Proofs are generally omitted for lack of space (see [14]).

[14] The same process works for Levesque [17] in the case of an ideal reasoner with unlimited resources.

Allowing arbitrary equalities within a KB is problematic because equality has a 2-valued semantics, which would result in hard reasoning such as *modus ponens*.

On the other hand, while we have not yet proven that reasoning remains decidable if we allow arbitrary forms of quantifying-in, results in [14] strongly suggest that this is indeed the case. In any event, Theorem 3 can be used to prove the decidability of special cases such as $\models \mathbf{O}\mathrm{KB} \supset \mathbf{B}(\exists x\alpha \wedge \neg\mathbf{B}\beta)$, where α and β are objective formulas containing the free variable x.

5 ASK and TELL

In this section, we apply the results of this paper to the specification of a KR service in the sense of [15], which allows a user to query a KB and to add new information to it using $\mathcal{BL}$ as the interaction language.

Definition 12 `ASK` ***and*** `TELL`

Let KB *be an objective sentence and* α *a* $\mathcal{BL}$*-sentence.*

$$\mathtt{ASK}(\mathrm{KB},\alpha) = \begin{cases} \text{YES} & \text{if } \models \mathbf{O}\mathrm{KB} \supset \mathbf{B}\alpha \wedge \neg\mathbf{B}\neg\alpha \\ \text{NO} & \text{if } \models \mathbf{O}\mathrm{KB} \supset \mathbf{B}\neg\alpha \wedge \neg\mathbf{B}\alpha \\ \text{UNK} & \text{if } \models \mathbf{O}\mathrm{KB} \supset \neg\mathbf{B}\alpha \wedge \neg\mathbf{B}\neg\alpha \\ \text{INC} & \text{if } \models \mathbf{O}\mathrm{KB} \supset \mathbf{B}\alpha \wedge \mathbf{B}\neg\alpha \end{cases}$$

$$\mathtt{TELL}(\mathrm{KB},\alpha) = \mathrm{KB} \wedge \|\alpha\|_{\mathrm{KB}}\,.$$

Note that the way TELLing a sentence α to a KB is handled. Any occurrence of a $\mathbf{B}\gamma$ within α is first evaluated with respect to the *old* KB and replaced by an (objective) equality expression. Thus, if we start out with an initially empty KB_0, successive TELL-operations are guaranteed to always produce an objective KB. However, TELL is not prevented from returning a KB that lies outside the class of KB's for which reasoning is decidable. A simple check would be to require that the KB is in the form $\mathrm{KB}' \wedge E$ as in Theorem 3 or can be easily transformed into that form by rearranging conjuncts.

$$\mathrm{KB} = \left\{ \begin{array}{l} \mathtt{Teacher}(jack), \mathtt{Teacher}(jill) \\ \mathtt{Emp}(jack), \mathtt{Emp}(jill), \mathtt{Emp}(sue) \\ \mathtt{Teach}(jack, csc378), \mathtt{Teach}(jill, csc484) \end{array} \right\}$$

$\mathtt{ASK}(\mathrm{KB}, \forall x(\mathtt{Teacher}(x) \supset \mathtt{Emp}(x))) = \mathrm{UNK}$.

The answer is UNK because there may be teachers who are not known to the KB and who are not employees.[15]

$\mathtt{ASK}(\mathrm{KB}, \forall x(\mathbf{B}\mathtt{Teacher}(x) \supset \mathtt{Emp}(x)) = \mathrm{YES}$.

Note the difference to the previous query. Here the KB is only asked about the ***known*** teachers.

$\mathtt{ASK}(\mathrm{KB}, \forall x(\mathbf{B}\mathtt{Emp}(x) \supset \mathbf{B}\mathtt{Teacher}(x))) = \mathrm{NO}$.

The answer is NO because Sue, who is a known employee, is not known to be a teacher.

$\mathtt{ASK}(\mathrm{KB}, \forall x(\mathbf{B}\mathtt{Teacher}(x) \supset \exists y \mathtt{Teach}(x,y))) = \mathrm{UNK}$.

The answer is UNK because there is no admissible term for y which would work for all known teachers. To obtain the answer YES, we need to rephrase the question as $\forall x[\mathbf{B}\mathtt{Teacher}(x) \supset \exists y_1 \exists y_2(\mathtt{Teach}(x,y_1) \vee \mathtt{Teach}(x,y_2))]$. Now it is possible to substitute different admissible terms for y_1 and y_2.

6 Summary and Future Work

In this paper, we extended earlier work on limited belief by adding quantifying-in and equality. We established that reasoning is decidable if the KB is first-order and where queries can range over a large class of modal sentences with quantifying-in. In the future we hope to prove the conjecture that decidability holds if we allow arbitrary forms of quantifying-in. It is also important to identify classes of sentences where reasoning is not just decidable but provably tractable as well. Finally, one should investigate to what extent modalities can be allowed in the KB itself without sacrificing decidability.

Acknowledgements

I am grateful to Hector Levesque for many inspiring discussions on limited belief.

References

[1] Belnap, N. D., A Useful Four-Valued Logic, in G. Epstein and J. M. Dunn (eds.), *Modern Uses of Multiple-Valued Logic*, Reidel, 1977.

[2] Davis, M., Obvious Logical Inferences, in *Proc.IJCAI-81*, Vancouver, B.C., 1981, pp. 530–531.

[3] Dunn, J. M., Intuitive Semantics for First-Degree Entailments and Coupled Trees, *Philosophical Studies* **29**, 1976, pp. 149–168.

[4] Frisch, A. M., *Knowledge Retrieval as Specialized Inference*, Ph.D. Thesis, University of Rochester, 1986.

[5] Hintikka, J., *Knowledge and Belief: An Introduction to the Logic of the Two Notions*, Cornell University Press, 1962.

[6] Kaplan, D., Quantifying In, in L. Linsky (ed.), *Reference and Modality*, Oxford University Press, Oxford, 1971.

[7] Ketonen, J. and Weyhrauch, R., A Decidable Fragment of Predicate Calculus, *Theoretical Computer Science* **32**, 1984, pp. 297–307.

[8] Konolige, K., A Computational Theory of Belief Introspection. In *Proc. IJCAI-85*, Los Angeles, 1985, pp. 502-508.

[9] Kripke, S. A., Semantical Considerations on Modal Logic, *Acta Philosophica Fennica* **16**, 1963, pp. 83–94.

[10] Kripke, S. A., *Naming and Necessity*, Harvard University Press, Cambridge, MA, 1980.

[11] Lakemeyer, G., Steps Towards a First-Order Logic of Explicit and Implicit Belief, in *Proc. of the Conference on Theoretical Aspects of Reasoning about Knowledge*, Asilomar, California, 1986, pp. 325–340.

[12] Lakemeyer, G. and Levesque, H. J., A Tractable Knowledge Representation Service with Full Introspection, in *Proc. of the Second Conference on Theoretical Aspects of Reasoning about Knowledge*, Asilomar, California, 1988, pp. 145–159.

[13] Lakemeyer, G., Decidable Reasoning in First-Order Knowledge Bases with Perfect Introspection, in *Proc.AAAI-90*, Boston, MA, August 1990, pp. 531–537.

[14] Lakemeyer, G., *Models of Belief for Decidable Reasoning in Incomplete Knowledge Bases*, Ph.D. thesis, University of Toronto, 1990.

[15] Levesque, H. J., Foundations of a Functional Approach to Knowledge Representation, *Artificial Intelligence*, **23**, 1984, pp. 155-212.

[16] Levesque, H. J., A Logic of Implicit and Explicit Belief, in *Proc. AAAI-84*, Austin, TX, 1984, pp. 198–202.

[17] Levesque, H. J., All I Know: A Study in Autoepistemic Logic, *Artificial Intelligence*, North Holland, **42**, 1990, pp. 263–309.

[18] Moore, R. C., Semantical Considerations on Nonmonotonic Logic, in *Proc. IJCAI-83*, Karlsruhe, FRG, 1983, pp. 272–279.

[19] Patel-Schneider, P. F., *Decidable, Logic-Based Knowledge Representation*, Ph.D thesis, University of Toronto, 1987.

[15] All names in KB are assumed to be standard names.

Asymmetry Thesis and Side-Effect Problems in Linear-Time and Branching-Time Intention Logics*

Anand S. Rao and **Michael P. Georgeff**
Australian Artificial Intelligence Institute
Carlton, Victoria 3053
Australia
Email: anand@aaii.oz.au and georgeff@aaii.oz.au

Abstract

In this paper, we examine the relationships between beliefs, goals, and intentions. In particular, we consider the formalization of the *Asymmetry Thesis* as proposed by Bratman [1987]. We argue that the semantic characterization of this principle determines if the resulting logic is capable of handling other important problems, such as the side-effect problem of belief-goal-intention interaction. While Cohen and Levesque's [1990] formalization faithfully models some aspects of the asymmetry thesis, it does not solve all the side-effect problems; on the other hand the formalization provided by Rao and Georgeff [1991] solves all the side-effect problems, but only models a weak form of the asymmetry thesis. In this paper, we combine the intuition behind both these approaches and provide a semantic account of the asymmetry thesis, in both linear-time and branching-time logics, for solving many of these problems.

1 Introduction

Formalizations of intentions and their relationships with other propositional attitudes such as beliefs and goals have received increased attention in recent years [Cohen and Levesque, 1990, Konolige and Pollack, 1990, Werner, 1990, Rao and Georgeff, 1991, Konolige, 1991]. Some of these formalizations have been influenced by the philosophical work of Bratman [1987]. He argues, convincingly, that intentions involve a characteristic form of commitment, play a distinct role in practical reasoning, and are not reducible to beliefs and desires (or goals).

According to Bratman, it is irrational for an agent to intend to do an act a and at the same time believe that he will not do a. However, it is rational for him to intend to do a and not believe that he will do a. In other words, it is irrational for an agent to have beliefs that are inconsistent with his intentions, but perfectly rational to have incomplete beliefs about his intentions. Bratman refers to these two principles of *intention-belief consistency* and *intention-belief incompleteness* as the *asymmetry thesis.* One can also extend the asymmetry thesis to the relationship between intentions and goals, and goals and beliefs. Thus, it is reasonable to require a rational agent to have *intention-goal consistency* and *goal-belief consistency*, but allow *intention-goal incompleteness* and *goal-belief incompleteness.*

The way in which the relationships between beliefs, goals, and intentions are captured can have a significant impact on the design of a rational agent. In particular, if not represented properly, it can lead to the *side-effect problem* and the *transference* problem. The side-effect problem has received a great deal of attention in the literature [Allen, 1990, Bratman, 1987, Cohen and Levesque, 1990, Konolige and Pollack, 1990, Rao and Georgeff, 1991, Konolige, 1991]. It can be stated as follows: an agent who intends to do a should not be forced to intend to do b, no matter how strongly he believes that doing a will force him to do b. Bratman [1987] provides the example of a strategic bomber[1] who intends to bomb a munitions factory and also believes that doing so would kill all the children in a nearby school. In this case, one can argue that the strategic bomber does not intend to kill the children in the school but brings it about as a side-effect of bombing the munitions factory. The same principle extends to the relationship between goals and beliefs.

A related problem is the problem of transference. An agent who believes that the formula ϕ will be inevitably true some time in the future should not be forced to have a goal to achieve ϕ nor be forced to intend it. For example, an agent believing that "it is inevitable that the sun will rise in the east tomorrow morning" should not be required to have this condition as a goal nor to intend it.

Cohen and Levesque [1990] were the first to formalize some of these ideas. They present a possible-worlds model for beliefs and goals. Each possible world is a *time-line* representing a sequence of events, temporally

*This research was in part supported by a *Generic Industry Research and Development Grant* from the Department of Industry, Technology and Commerce, Australia and in part by the Australian Civil Aviation Authority.

[1] A more sensitive reader can consider the example of a person intending to water rose plants, without intending to water the weeds at the base of the rose plants, even though he strongly believes that watering the rose plants will result in watering the weeds.

extended infinitely into the past and the future. Formulas are evaluated with respect to a given world and an index into the course of events defining the world. Accessibility relations $\mathcal{B}$ and $\mathcal{G}$ are relations between the world at an index to a set of worlds or courses of events. These worlds are called belief-accessible and goal-accessible worlds, respectively. Intuitively, an agent believes a proposition in a world at a particular index if and only if the proposition is satisfied in all the belief-accessible worlds. A similar relationship holds between goals and goal-accessible worlds.

In the Cohen–Levesque formalism, one would intuitively expect the goal-accessible worlds to be some subset of the agent's belief-accessible worlds. This constraint, called *realism* by Cohen and Levesque [1990], ensures that the worlds chosen by an agent are not ruled out by his beliefs. This constraint also realises some aspects of Bratman's asymmetry thesis. However, as we shall see later, it also leads to certain problems concerning the side effects of actions (as observed by Cohen and Levesque [1990] and Allen [1990]). Additionally, it is unsatisfactory in that any beliefs about the future thereby become adopted as goals.

Elsewhere [Rao and Georgeff, 1991], we have provided an alternative possible-worlds formalism where each world is a branching-time structure with a single past and multiple futures. Accessibility relations $\mathcal{B}$, $\mathcal{G}$, and $\mathcal{I}$ are used to represent the beliefs, goals, and intentions of the agent, respectively.

As with Cohen and Levesque's formalism, each possible world represents, according to the agent, the way the world could turn out to be. However, it differs in that the branches within each of these possible worlds represent the *choice* available to the agent in determining what actions to perform. Thus the formalism distinguishes between the choice available to the agent (represented by the branching structure within each possible world) and the chance (or lack of knowledge of the agent) concerning in which world he is possibly situated.

In our approach, the notion of realism is captured by requiring that for every belief-accessible world there exists a goal-accessible world that is a sub-world of that belief-accessible world. However, there can be goal-accessible worlds that do not have corresponding belief-accessible worlds. A similar relationship holds between goal-accessible worlds and intention-accessible worlds. Thus, moving from belief to goal to intention worlds amounts to successively pruning the paths of the time tree; intuitively, to making increasingly selective choices about one's future actions.

Thus stated, this property turns out to be a somewhat stronger notion of realism than that used by Cohen and Levesque. It essentially states that an agent can only have a goal towards some proposition if he believes that, *no matter how the world turns out*, he has the *option* of eventually achieving that goal. While the agent may contemplate possible failure along the way, he believes that he can eventually recover from such failures and ultimately achieve his goals. A similar constraint applies to the relationship between goals and intentions. This restriction on goals and intentions is desirable when one wants to ensure that a system (agent) will only adopt goals or intentions towards ends over which it has control. However, it is too strong for modeling rational agents. We thus call this constraint *strong realism* [Rao and Georgeff, 1991].

The realism constraint for linear-time intention logic proposed by Cohen and Levesque can be weakened to a constraint that requires only that the intersection of belief and goal-accessible worlds be non-empty, i.e. there is *at least* one world common to the belief and goal-accessible worlds. We shall call this the *weak-realism* constraint for linear-time intention logic.

Similarly, we can weaken the strong-realism constraint for branching-time intention logic to a weak-realism constraint. In particular, instead of requiring that for every belief-accessible world there exists a corresponding goal-accessible world, we simply require that there exists *at least one* belief-accessible world with a corresponding goal-accessible world (as before, this goal-accessible world must be a sub-world of the belief-accessible world).

In this paper, we shall show that, although the weak-realism constraint appears extremely weak and inadequate, it is all that is needed to satisfy all aspects of the asymmetry thesis and to avoid the side-effect and transference problems. We also show that, by adding this semantic constraint to the formalism proposed by Cohen and Levesque, some of the stronger side-effect problems in their logic can be avoided. However, even with this semantic constraint, the strong case of side-effects between intentions and goals cannot be avoided. If intentions are defined as basic entities, irreducible to the other basic attitudes of belief and desire, this side-effect can also be avoided.

2 Belief-Goal-Intention Interaction

In this section, we formally define some of the properties discussed above. We characterise these principles for linear-time intention logics. Although we provide a language for expressing these principles and also talk about satisfiability or validity of these principles with respect to a model, we do not provide a specific model in this section. In other words, any model (be it possible-worlds [Cohen and Levesque, 1990, Rao and Georgeff, 1991], situation-semantics [Werner, 1990] or representationalist [Konolige and Pollack, 1990]) has to satisfy at least these principles. In later sections we shall examine specific models.

The language we use to capture these properties for any linear-time model is as follows.[2] BEL(ϕ), GOAL(ϕ), and INTEND(ϕ) denote the belief, goal, and intention in ϕ, where ϕ is a first-order formula.[3] In addition to the above, temporal formulas $\Box\phi$ (always) and $\Diamond\phi$ (sometimes) are also defined.

[2]The language we use here is essentially that of Cohen and Levesque [1990] with some additions from [Rao and Georgeff, 1991]. However, we do not require beliefs, goals, and intentions to be treated as modal operators in this section.

[3]For the sake of simplicity we have dropped the agent argument from all these propositional attitudes.

Asymmetry Thesis

Bratman argues that it is irrational for an agent to intend do an action and also believe that he will not do it. Thus he does not allow *intention-belief inconsistency* (BI-ICN). On the other hand, he does allow a rational agent to intend to do an action but not believe that he will do it. Thus *intention-belief incompleteness* (BI-ICM) is allowed. These two principles put together is called the *Asymmetry thesis.* More formally,

(BI-ICN) $\not\models \mathsf{INTEND}(\phi) \wedge \mathsf{BEL}(\neg\phi)$
(BI-ICM) there exists a model M such that
$M \models \mathsf{INTEND}(\phi) \wedge \neg\mathsf{BEL}(\phi)$.

The asymmetry thesis can be extended to hold between intentions and goals, and goals and beliefs as well. That is we must not allow intention-goal (GI-ICN) and goal-belief inconsistency (BG-ICN), whereas we should allow intention-goal (GI-ICM) and goal-belief incompleteness (BG-ICM).

Side-Effect-Free Principle

The belief-intention side-effect-free principle states that, if an agent intends ϕ, he should not be forced to intend a side-effect ψ, no matter how strong the belief about $\phi \supset \psi$. As described by Cohen and Levesque, the strength of the belief could be either one of the following:[4] $\mathsf{BEL}(\phi \supset \psi)$, $\mathsf{BEL}(\Box(\phi \supset \psi))$, or $\Box\mathsf{BEL}(\Box(\phi \supset \psi))$. The strongest side-effect-free principle is stated as:

(BI-SE3) there exists a model M such that
$M \models \mathsf{INTEND}(\phi) \wedge \Box\mathsf{BEL}(\Box(\phi \supset \psi)) \wedge \neg\mathsf{INTEND}(\psi)$.

Substituting the second conjunct of BI-SE3 by the weaker forms of beliefs, yields BI-SE1 and BI-SE2. The side-effect problem exists, not only between intentions and beliefs, but also between intentions and goals, and goals and beliefs. Thus analogous to (BI-SE1) – (BI-SE3), we have (GI-SE1) – (GI-SE3) and (BG-SE1) – (BG-SE3).

Non-Transference Principle

One aspect of the non-transference principle states that no matter how strongly an agent believes in a proposition, he should not be forced to adopt it as a goal. This non-transference principle can be stated as follows:

(BG-NT) there exists a model M such that
$M \models \mathsf{BEL}(\phi) \wedge \neg\mathsf{GOAL}(\phi)$.

This transference problem exists, not only between beliefs and goals, but also between goals and intentions and beliefs and intentions. Thus analogous to (BG-NT), we have (GI-NT) and (BI-NT).

A rational agent is one who satisfies all the above principles. More formally,

Proposition 1 *: The necessary conditions for an agent to be called rational are as follows:*

(a) the asymmetry thesis principles BI-ICN, BG-ICN, and GI-ICN regarding consistency and BI-ICM, BG-ICM, and GI-ICM regarding incompleteness are satisfied;

(b) all the side-effect-free principles BI-SE1 – BI-SE3, BG-SE1 – BG-SE3, and GI-SE1 – GI-SE3 are satisfied; and

(c) all the non-transference principles BI-NT, BG-NT, and GI-NT are satisfied.

[4]In reality, there are nine different cases, namely $\mathsf{BEL}(\gamma)$, $\mathsf{BEL}(\Diamond\gamma)$, $\mathsf{BEL}(\Box\gamma)$ $\Diamond\mathsf{BEL}(\gamma)$, $\Diamond\mathsf{BEL}(\Diamond\gamma)$, $\Diamond\mathsf{BEL}(\Box\gamma)$, $\Box\mathsf{BEL}(\gamma)$, $\Box\mathsf{BEL}(\Diamond\gamma)$, $\Box\mathsf{BEL}(\Box\gamma)$, where γ is $\phi \supset \psi$.

3 Linear-Time Intention Logic

In this section we present a linear-time intention logic which has all the desirable properties of Proposition 1. We take Cohen and Levesque's [1990] logic as the starting point for our logic and make two major modifications: (a) in addition to the accessibility relations $\mathcal{B}$ and $\mathcal{G}$ for beliefs and goals, we introduce the relation $\mathcal{I}$ for intentions; and (b) instead of the realism constraint between belief-accessible and goal-accessible worlds, we introduce the weak-realism constraint between belief- and goal-, goal- and intention-, and belief- and intention- accessible worlds.

Similar to Cohen and Levesque's logic, we consider a possible-worlds model where each possible world is a sequence of events, temporally extended infinitely in past and future. Formulas are evaluated with respect to an interpretation M, a variable assignment v, a given world w, and an index t into the course of events defining the world. The interpretation M is a fairly standard possible worlds structure with accessibility relations $\mathcal{B}$, $\mathcal{G}$ and $\mathcal{I}$ that map a world at an index to a set of worlds. We use B_t^w to denote the set of belief-accessible worlds from world w and index t, i.e., $B_t^w = \{ w' \mid <w, t>\mathcal{B}w'\}$. The sets G_t^w and I_t^w are defined likewise. Except for intentions, our semantics is identical to that of Cohen and Levesque. While Cohen and Levesque define intentions in terms of persistent goals, we define intentions in the same way as beliefs and goals, using the intention-accessibility relation $\mathcal{I}$.

The weak-realism constraint (WC) requires that there be at least one world common to belief- and goal-accessible worlds, and similarly for belief- and intention-accessible worlds and goal- and intention-accessible worlds. More formally,

(WC-BG) $G_t^w \cap B_t^w \neq \emptyset$ (i.e., $\mathcal{G} \cap \mathcal{B} \neq \emptyset$)
(WC-GI) $I_t^w \cap G_t^w \neq \emptyset$ (i.e., $\mathcal{I} \cap \mathcal{G} \neq \emptyset$)
(WC-BI) $I_t^w \cap B_t^w \neq \emptyset$ (i.e., $\mathcal{I} \cap \mathcal{B} \neq \emptyset$).

The above semantic constraints correspond to the following weak-realism axioms (WA):

(WA-BG) $\models \mathsf{GOAL}(\phi) \supset \neg\mathsf{BEL}(\neg\phi)$
(WA-GI) $\models \mathsf{INTEND}(\phi) \supset \neg\mathsf{GOAL}(\neg\phi)$
(WA-BI) $\models \mathsf{INTEND}(\phi) \supset \neg\mathsf{BEL}(\neg\phi)$.

The weak-realism axiom WA-BG states that if an agent has the goal ϕ then he will not believe in the negation of ϕ. If the formula ϕ is $\Diamond p$ then the above axiom states that if the agent has chosen the goal to achieve p in the future then he will not believe that it is impossible to achieve p.

One can impose a somewhat stronger constraint; namely, that there be at least one world that is common to belief-, goal-, and intention-accessible worlds. Formally, this translates to $\mathcal{B} \cap \mathcal{G} \cap \mathcal{I} \neq \emptyset$. This stronger constraint implies the above weak-realism constraints but not vice versa.

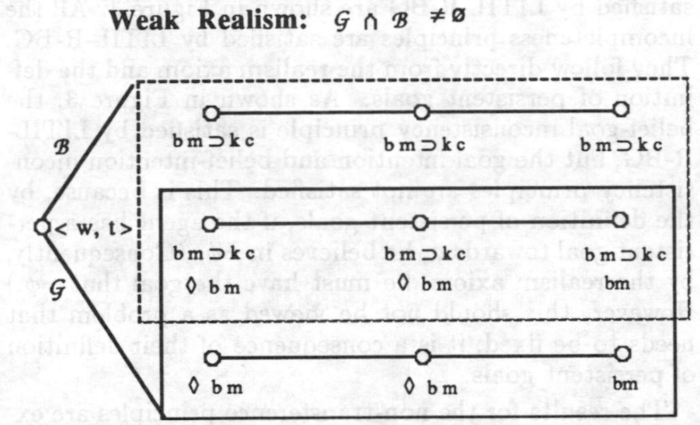

Figure 1: Weak realism between belief-accessible and goal-accessible worlds

The semantic constraint of weak-realism is shown in Figure 1 for the strategic bomber example. Note that we have two belief-accessible worlds and two goal-accessible worlds, but only one world is both belief- and goal-accessible. The agent in world w at index t believes always that bombing the munitions factory (bm) will result in killing the children (kc), i.e. $\mathsf{BEL}(\Box(bm \supset kc))$ is satisfiable in w at t. Also, the agent has the goal to eventually bomb the munitions factory, i.e., $\mathsf{GOAL}(\Diamond bm)$ is satisfiable in w at t. However, the formula $\mathsf{GOAL}(\Box(bm \supset kc))$ is not satisfiable because there is a goal-accessible world that is not a belief-accessible world. Intuitively, the goal-accessible worlds which are not belief-accessible worlds are those possible worlds that may turn out to be the real world but are not strong enough to be considered as belief-accessible worlds. For example, the strategic bomber may consider the possibility of the children being moved from the school in which case the implication will not hold [Bratman, 1987]. However, this possibility is not strong enough for him to consider it to be a belief-accessible world. On the other hand, if such a scenario did arise (namely, the children being moved from the school), he would still like to bomb the munitions factory and hence makes it one of his goal-accessible worlds.

To summarise, we shall adopt the following set of axioms and inference rules for our logic: (a) weak-S5 (or KD45) axioms and belief-necessitation inference rule for beliefs; (b) K and D axioms and goal-necessitation inference rule for goals; (c) K and D axioms and intention-necessitation inference rule for intentions; (d) S5 (or KT45) axioms and $\Box$-necessitation inference rule for $\Box$; and (e) the three weak-realism axioms (WA-BG, WA-BI, WA-GI) connecting beliefs, goals, and intentions. The class of models which correspond to the above axiom system can be easily constructed. Apart from the standard constraints on belief, goal, and intention relations (e.g., serial, transitive, and euclidean for $\mathcal{B}$, and serial for $\mathcal{G}$ and $\mathcal{I}$) we also have the three weak-realism constraints mentioned above. We shall refer to the Linear-Time Intention Logic with the above axiom system and class of models as LITIL-W-BGI.[5]

Now we want to show that LITIL-W-BGI satisfies Proposition 1. The various inconsistency properties of beliefs, goals, and intentions are reformulations of the weak-realism axioms. The incompleteness principles and different versions of the non-transference principles hold because each relation is not a subset of any other relation. For example, the intention-belief incompleteness principle holds because (a) there exists a model where all intention-accessible worlds satisfy ϕ and (b) there is a belief-accessible world which is not an intention-accessible world in which ϕ is not satisfied. The non-transference principle is essentially the reverse of this; by substituting intentions with beliefs and vice versa in the above argument we can show that belief-intention transference does not arise.

The different versions of the side-effect-free principles are satisfied for the same reason as the non-transference principles. Consider the case of the intention-belief side-effect-free principle BI-SE2. No matter how strong the beliefs of an agent are, one can postulate an intention-accessible world where ϕ is true but $\phi \supset \psi$ is false, and hence the agent does not intend ψ. A similar argument holds for the side-effect-free principles involving the other propositional attitudes.

In the case of the strategic bomber, the agent is not required to have the goal that it is always the case that bombing the munitions factory will result in the children being killed, even though he might have such a belief. Therefore, the agent is not forced to have the goal that eventually the children will be killed nor is he forced to intend to kill the children.

Note that the above line of reasoning does not appeal to possible changes of belief and hence can be applied to the stronger version, namely the BI-SE3 principle. This is illustrated in the following example by Allen [1990]. Consider an agent who, for the sake of winning a bet, intends to drink a full bottle of wine within the next five minutes and always believes that it is always true that drinking for five minutes will cause him to get drunk. By a similar line of reasoning to that above, the agent can intend to drink the entire bottle of wine without intending to get drunk. Thus having intended the primary action the agent is not forced to intend one of its side-effects no matter how strong his beliefs about these side-effects. These results are summarised in Figure 3. The symbols Y and N denote the satisfaction and non-satisfaction of the principles, respectively.

4 Other Linear-Time Intention Logics

In this section we consider two other linear-time intention logics – Cohen and Levesque's logic, and a modified version of Cohen and Levesque's logic with the weak-realism constraint between beliefs and goals.

Using beliefs, goals, and actions, as basic entities, Cohen and Levesque [1990] define the notion of persistent goals and intentions. An agent has a ***persistent goal*** or $\mathsf{PGOAL}(\phi)$ if and only if the agent currently believes $\neg\phi$,

[5]W indicates weak-realism and BGI indicates that there are independent relations for Beliefs, Goals, and Intentions.

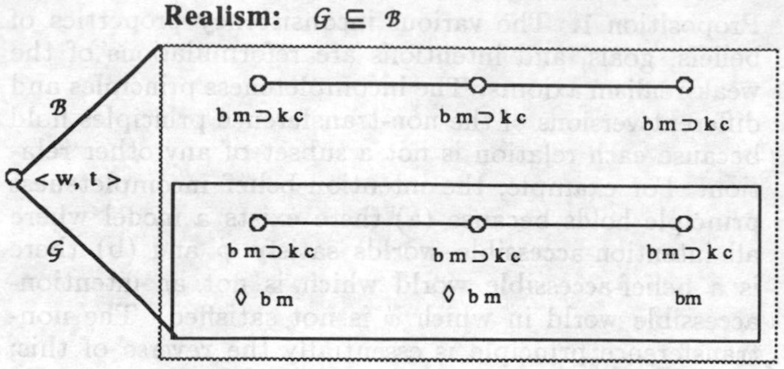

Figure 2: Realism between belief-accessible and goal-accessible worlds

has the goal to eventually make ϕ true, and maintains this goal until he either comes to believe in ϕ or comes to believe that ϕ is impossible. They capture the notion of intention as a special type of persistent goal. More specifically, an agent intends an action a if and only if he has a persistent goal to have done the action a and, until he has done it, maintains his belief that he is doing it. Although the above notion of intention is based on a fanatical commitment by the agent, Cohen and Levesque also define other notions of intention based on less severe forms of commitment, namely, relativized commitment. For the purposes of this paper, however, we shall not be concerned with these differences. Our primary concern here is to examine the constraints imposed on beliefs and goals, and see how these affect the properties discussed earlier.

As they define persistent goals and intentions in terms of the beliefs, goals, and actions of the agent, Cohen and Levesque have only two relations: the belief-accessibility relation $\mathcal{B}$ and the goal-accessibility relation $\mathcal{G}$. The realism constraint (RC) and its corresponding axiom (RA) (Proposition 3.26 of [Cohen and Levesque, 1990]) between beliefs and goals are as follows:

(RC-BG) $G_t^w \subseteq B_t^w$ (i.e., $\mathcal{G} \subseteq \mathcal{B}$)
(RA-BG) $\models$ BEL(ϕ) $\supset$ GOAL(ϕ).

The axiom states that if an agent believes in ϕ he also has it as a goal. In other words, if ϕ is taken to be $\Diamond p$, the axiom states that, if the agent believes that eventually p will be true, he will adopt it as a goal. Note that the realism axiom implies the weak-realism axiom but not vice versa.[6]

The object of an intention as defined by Cohen and Levesque can only be an action formula. However, as intentions are just a special type of persistent goal and the object of a persistent goal can be a well-formed formula, we shall treat PGOAL(ϕ) as being synonymous with INTEND(ϕ) as discussed in Section 2. Hence, we shall consider all the properties of Section 2 with INTEND substituted by PGOAL.

[6]From the realism axiom BEL($\neg\phi$) $\supset$ GOAL($\neg\phi$) and the D-axiom GOAL($\neg\phi$) $\supset$ $\neg$GOAL(ϕ), we have BEL($\neg\phi$) $\supset$ $\neg$GOAL(ϕ). Taking the contrapositive of this, we obtain the weak-realism axiom GOAL(ϕ) $\supset$ $\neg$BEL($\neg\phi$).

We shall refer to Cohen and Levesque's logic as LITIL-R-BG. A summary of some of the important properties satisfied by LITIL-R-BG are shown in Figure 3. All the incompleteness principles are satisfied by LITIL-R-BG. They follow directly from the realism axiom and the definition of persistent goals. As shown in Figure 3, the belief-goal inconsistency principle is satisfied by LITIL-R-BG, but the goal-intention and belief-intention inconsistency principles are not satisfied. This is because, by the definition of persistent goals, if the agent has a persistent goal towards ϕ, he believes in $\neg\phi$. (Consequently, by the realism axiom, he must have the goal that $\neg\phi$.) However, this should not be viewed as a problem that needs to be fixed; it is a consequence of their definition of persistent goals.

The results for the non-transference principles are exactly the opposite and are given in Figure 3. The realism axiom forces belief-goal transference. However, as Cohen and Levesque note, the agent may adopt the goal while reluctantly believing that, if he comes to change his beliefs about the inevitability of ϕ in the future, he might drop the goal. The lack of a similar axiom between goals and persistent goals avoids goal-intention and belief-intention transference.

We illustrate the side-effect-free principle for LITIL-R-BG using the strategic bomber example as shown in Figure 2. As before, the formulas BEL($\Box(bm \supset kc)$) and GOAL($\Diamond bm$) are satisfiable in w at t. The realism constraint requires that all goal-accessible worlds be belief-accessible, which forces GOAL($\Box(bm \supset kc)$) also to be satisfiable. However, the bomber need not have the goal to kill the children because at the next time point (or some time in the future before he bombs the munitions factory) he can change his beliefs such that the implication does not hold. Consequently, he also need not intend to kill the children. Thus both BG-SE2 and BI-SE2 principles are satisfied. However, as noted by Cohen and Levesque [1990] and Allen [1990], the same reasoning does not apply to the stronger SE3 principles for non-trivial cases.

A similar result holds for the side-effects involving intentions and goals, i.e., GI-SE1 and GI-SE2 are satisfied, but GI-SE3 is not satisfied. As beliefs imply goals, all three side-effect problems involving goals and beliefs exist, i.e., BG-SE1, BG-SE2, and BG-SE3 are not satisfied. A summary of the strongest form of the side-effect-free principles, namely SE3, is shown in Figure 3. The table considers only the non-trivial cases of the SE3 principle; the trivial cases of SE3 are satisfied by all the logics.

Next we consider Cohen and Levesque's logic with the realism constraint replaced by the weak-realism constraint. We shall refer to this logic as LITIL-W-BG. The properties satisfied by LITIL-W-BG are summarised in Figure 3. The important points to note are that LITIL-W-BG does not suffer from belief-goal transference nor does it have belief-goal or belief-intention side-effect problems. The same line of reasoning as in Section 3 can be applied to prove these results. Note that the intention-goal side-effect problem remains in LITIL-W-BG. This is because intentions are defined in terms of beliefs and goals. This manifests itself when we consider the side-effect-free principles regarding intentions and goals. We cannot use the same reasoning as above to solve the strong case of intention-goal side-effect problem GI-SE3 and we still have to appeal to the change in goals from one time point to another to solve the weaker intention-goal side-effect problem GI-SE2.

While the desirability of the GI-SE3 principle may be debatable, we have provided the constraint WC-GI that satisfies this principle. One can either adopt this constraint or not independent of whether one wants to introduce intentions as basic entities or define them in terms of beliefs and goals.

However, we believe that the intention relation plays an important role in means-end reasoning. In essence, the goals of an agent represent his pro-attitudes and his intentions represent the refinement of these goals into realizable means (or conduct-controlling pro-attitudes [Bratman, 1987]). In particular, this distinction allows an agent to maintain his goals, even if his intentions towards the means for achieving these goals fail. If intentions are defined in terms of goals, such means-end reasoning is not transparent and can only be captured by resorting to various book-keeping mechanisms.

Logic	*ICN Principle*			*ICM Principle*		
	BG	GI	BI	BG	GI	BI
LITIL-W-BGI	Y	Y	Y	Y	Y	Y
LITIL-R-BG	Y	N	N	Y	Y	Y
LITIL-W-BG	Y	N	N	Y	Y	Y

Logic	*SE3 Principle*			*NT Principle*		
	BG	GI	BI	BG	GI	BI
LITIL-W-BGI	Y	Y	Y	Y	Y	Y
LITIL-R-BG	N	N	N	N	Y	Y
LITIL-W-BG	Y	N	Y	Y	Y	Y

Figure 3: Principles satisfied by Linear-Time Logics

5 Branching-Time Intention Logic

The language we use for branching-time intention logic is a CTL^* [Emerson and Srinivasan, 1989] branching-time logic within a possible-worlds framework (see [Rao and Georgeff, 1991] for more details). In addition to the operators of linear-time intention logic, the branching-time logic has two additional operators: $\mathsf{inevitable}(\phi)$, meaning that in all future paths ϕ is true; and $\mathsf{optional}(\phi)$, meaning that in at least one future path ϕ is true. Well-formed formulas that contain no positive occurrences of inevitable (or negative occurrences of optional) outside the scope of belief, goal, or modal operators will be called O-formulas and will be denoted by α.

An ideal theory of rational agency, in the case of branching-time intention logic, should also satisfy Proposition 1, namely, the asymmetry thesis, side-effect-free and non-transference principles.

Now we briefly describe the strong-realism constraint introduced elsewhere [Rao and Georgeff, 1991]. First, we define the notion of a sub-world. Intuitively, a sub-world is a sub-tree of a given world with the same truth assignment and accessibility relations. More formally, we say that w' is a sub-world of w, denoted by $w' \sqsubseteq w$, iff (a) the index points of w' are a subset of the index points of w; (b) the same events occur between two index points in w' and w; (c) the assignment of truth values for predicate symbols for w' and w are identical; and (d) the accessibility relations for w' and w are also identical. Sometimes, we shall also say that w is a super-world of w'. The strong-realism constraint (SC) (between belief and goal-accessible worlds) requires that for every belief-accessible world there exists a goal-accessible world that is a sub-world of the belief-accessible world. A similar constraint holds for goal- and intention-accessible worlds.

(SC-BG) $\forall w' \in \mathcal{B}_t^w\ \exists w'' \in \mathcal{G}_t^w$ such that $w'' \sqsubseteq w'$
(denoted by $\mathcal{B}_t^w \subseteq_{super} \mathcal{G}_t^w$)

(SC-GI) $\mathcal{G}_t^w \subseteq_{super} \mathcal{I}_t^w$.

The strong-realism constraint is equivalent to the following two axioms (as before, α is taken to be an O-formula):

(SA-BG) $\models \mathsf{INTEND}(\alpha) \supset \mathsf{GOAL}(\alpha)$
(SA-GI) $\models \mathsf{GOAL}(\alpha) \supset \mathsf{BEL}(\alpha)$.

In other words, even if the agent intends optionally to do an action, he should have a goal that optionally he is going to do the action, and also believe that he will optionally do it. Thus the intention-goal, goal-belief, and intention-belief incompleteness principles are not satisfied. However, as we have shown previously [Rao and Georgeff, 1991], none of the side-effect problems arise with this semantic constraint. This is because there are goal-accessible worlds that are not belief-accessible and there are intention-accessible worlds that are not goal-accessible. Also, none of the transference problems arise for the same reasons. We refer to this Branching-Time Intention Logic with the above strong realism axioms and other axioms given elsewhere [Rao and Georgeff, 1991] as the BRITIL-S-BGI system. Some of the properties of BRITIL-S-BGI are summarised in Figure 4.

The weak-realism constraint (WC) (between belief and goal-accessible worlds) states that there is at least one belief-accessible world such that there exists a goal-accessible world that is a sub-world of this belief-accessible world. A similar constraint holds between goal and intention-accessible worlds, and belief and intention-accessible worlds.

(WC-BG) $\exists w' \in \mathcal{B}_t^w$ such that $\exists w'' \in \mathcal{G}_t^w$ and $w'' \sqsubseteq w'$
(denoted by $\mathcal{B}_t^w \cap_{super} \mathcal{G}_t^w \neq \emptyset$)

(WC-GI) $\mathcal{G}_t^w \cap_{super} \mathcal{I}_t^w \neq \emptyset$
(WC-BI) $\mathcal{B}_t^w \cap_{super} \mathcal{I}_t^w \neq \emptyset$.

The weak-realism axioms for branching-time intention logic are the same as the weak-realism axioms for linear-time intention logic.

We can show that the strong-realism axioms imply the weak-realism axioms but not vice versa. With the semantic constraint of weak-realism we can satisfy the asymmetry thesis and also avoid the side-effect and transference problems. We shall refer to this branching-time intention logic with the above weak-realism constraints and axioms as the BRITIL-W-BGI system. The properties of this system are summarised in Figure 4.

Logic	ICN Principle			ICM Principle		
	BG	GI	BI	BG	GI	BI
BRITIL-S-BGI	Y	Y	Y	N	N	N
BRITIL-W-BGI	Y	Y	Y	Y	Y	Y

Logic	SE3 Principle			NT Principle		
	BG	GI	BI	BG	GI	BI
BRITIL-S-BGI	Y	Y	Y	Y	Y	Y
BRITIL-W-BGI	Y	Y	Y	Y	Y	Y

Figure 4: Principles satisfied by Branching-Time Logics

6 Conclusion

Bratman [1987] and others [Bratman *et al.*, 1988, Cohen and Levesque, 1990] have stated certain properties that are desirable for the design of rational agents. This paper formalizes some of these properties and examines different logics that satisfy some or all of these properties.

The primary contribution of this paper is in defining the semantic constraint of weak-realism that has all the desirable properties for both linear-time and branching-time intention logics. Replacing the realism constraint in Cohen and Levesque's logic with the weak-realism constraint allows us to avoid all cases of intention-belief side-effect problems without appealing to changing beliefs or goals, which was one of the main criticisms of the formalism by Allen [1990]. However, if intentions are modeled as independent entities, the intention-goal side-effect problem is also avoided. This problem remains in a formalism that treats intentions as being definable in terms of beliefs and persistent goals.

We have also shown how the strong-realism constraints used in our branching-time intention logic [Rao and Georgeff, 1991] can be weakened to satisfy additional properties; namely, the incompleteness principles.

Acknowledgements

The authors would like to thank the reviewers for their valuable comments.

References

[Allen, 1990] J. Allen. Two views of intention: Comments on Bratman and on Cohen and Levesque. In P. R. Cohen, J. Morgan, and M. E. Pollack, editors, *Intentions in Communication*. MIT Press, Cambridge, Ma., 1990.

[Bratman *et al.*, 1988] M. E. Bratman, D. Israel, and M. E. Pollack. Plans and resource-bounded practical reasoning. *Computational Intelligence*, 4:349–355, 1988.

[Bratman, 1987] M. E. Bratman. *Intentions, Plans, and Practical Reason*. Harvard University Press, Massachusetts, 1987.

[Cohen and Levesque, 1990] P. R. Cohen and H. J. Levesque. Intention is choice with commitment. *Artificial Intelligence*, 42(3), 1990.

[Emerson and Srinivasan, 1989] E. A. Emerson and J. Srinivasan. Branching time temporal logic. In J. W. de Bakker, W.-P. de Roever, and G. Rozenberg, editors, *Linear Time, Branching Time and Partial Order in Logics and Models for Concurrency*, pages 123–172. Springer-Verlag, Berlin, 1989.

[Konolige and Pollack, 1990] K. Konolige and M. Pollack. A representationalist theory of intention. Technical Report (to be published), SRI International, Menlo Park, California, 1990.

[Konolige, 1991] K. Konolige. Intention, commitment and preference. Technical Report (to be published), SRI International, Menlo Park, California, 1991.

[Rao and Georgeff, 1991] A. S. Rao and M. P. Georgeff. Modeling rational agents within a BDI-architecture. In J. Allen, R. Fikes, and E. Sandewall, editors, *Proceedings of the Second International Conference on Principles of Knowledge Representation and Reasoning*. Morgan Kaufmann, San Mateo, 1991.

[Werner, 1990] E. Werner. Cooperating agents: A unified theory of communication and social structure. In L. Gasser and M. N. Huhns, editors, *Distributed Artificial Intelligence: Volume II*. Morgan Kaufmann Publishers, Inc., 1990.

KNOWLEDGE REPRESENTATION

Topics in Knowledge Representation

A Model of Events and Processes*

Periklis Belegrinos
Department of Computer Science
The University of Melbourne
Parkville, Victoria

Michael Georgeff
Australian Artificial Intelligence Institute
1 Grattan Street
Carlton, Victoria

Abstract

The aim of this paper is to provide a basis for a theory of events and processes that can be used for reasoning about arbitrarily complex dynamic domains involving multiple agents. The approach is based on a model of events that explicitly represents the domain of influence of each event. By scoping an event's domain of influence, most of the problems that have plagued the more conventional stated-transition models of events can be avoided. The effect of performing events, either in isolation or concurrently with other events, is described. To represent constraints among events, a model of processes is developed. This allows the modelling of arbitrarily complex behaviours. Finally, a representation of causal influence is provided that allows the ramifications of any given event occurrence to be modelled.

1 Introduction

Representing and reasoning about events (or actions) has been a continuing problem for researchers in Artificial Intelligence (AI). What apparently makes it so hard is the difficulty in describing, in a tractable and natural way, the effects that events have — or, more particularly, do not have — on the world.

The standard approach within AI is to assume that, at any given instant, the world is in a particular *world state*. Various properties or propositions may hold of these states. A given world state has no duration; the only way the passage of time can be observed is through some change of state. The world changes its state by the occurrence of *events*.

A representation of events has to allow us to determine the outcome of performing an event in some given world state — that is, what propositions hold in the resulting world state given that certain ones hold in the initial state. The normal way to do this is to introduce a formalism, such as the situation calculus [McCarthy and Hayes, 1969], to describe world states and the propositions that hold in those states. Then one writes down certain axioms about how the performance of a given event affects the propositions holding in the world.

There are two problems here. The first is that, in any sizable domain, there are a large number of properties that do not change from one state to the next, and writing down the axioms to express these facts is simply untenable. This is what is conventionally known as the *frame problem*. The second problem is that, in most real-world domains, the effects of an event can be quite complex, depending on the situation in which the event is performed and the causal properties of the domain. This is known as the *ramification problem*. These problems become even more severe when we allow events to be performed in parallel (concurrently), as one then has to be able to specify the results of performing any event in conjunction with every other set of possible events.

Most of the recent approaches to these problems utilize nonmonotonic reasoning mechanisms. There are numerous ways this can be done, including nonmonotonic logic, circumscription, closest possible worlds (or models), and circumscriptive ignorance. These are complex devices, and every now and then someone finds a significant flaw in one or other approach [Hanks and McDermott, 1987].

We believe that much of the problem rests with viewing events as *transitions* between world states. Clearly, the performance of an event results in the world undergoing a transition from one state to another. But, in reality, an event affects only a small part of the world, and the model of events we choose should reflect this localization property. This paper proposes a model of events and processes based on this idea.

2 Informal Description

We consider the world to consist of a set of properties or relations among individuals. A world state is defined to be an assignment of truth or falsity (or, more generally, some value) to each of these properties. We view an event or action as a black box that has certain input ports and certain output ports. The input and output ports are associated with properties of particular individuals, and the values obtaining at these ports represent the values of the associated properties. The aim is to specify the transition table for the input and output ports of the event, rather than the transition table for

*This work was supported in part by a *Generic Industry Research and D...elopment Grant* from the Australian Department of Industry, Technology and Commerce and by Carlton and United Breweries Ltd.

the world as a whole.

To determine what state transitions are possible given an occurrence of an event, we simply require that the properties associated with the input and output ports of the event have the specified values in the initial and final states, respectively. What happens to other properties depends on what other events are, or are not, occurring at the same time.

Of course, all that we are doing here is specifying explicitly which properties are affected by an event and which are not. But this is very important. Most representations or formalisms for describing events do not explicitly specify the domain of influence of an event; instead, they determine the scope of influence by resorting to nonmonotonic mechanisms.

Such explicit specification, however, would seem to prevent solution of the ramification problem — the manner in which the occurrence of a given event affects the world can be very complex and extensive. To handle this problem, we introduce notions of causality and process. Intuitively, although the domain of influence of a particular event may be quite limited, the event can cause the occurrence of other events or processes and in this way have a far more extensive effect upon the world.

3 Modelling Events

We base our model of events on situation semantics [Barwise and Perry, 1983]. We consider a set of *individuals* or *objects* I and a set of n-ary *properties*, F, over these individuals. A *situation type* (or, simply, *situation*) is an assignment of *values* V to a set of properties from F. Each assignment in a given situation s is called a *constituent* of s. For example,

$$s = \{open(door1)\colon \mathbf{t}\ ,\ distance(room1, room2)\colon 8\}$$

is a situation in which *door*1 is open[1] and the distance between *room*1 and *room*2 is 8; nothing is said about other individuals or the values of other properties.

A *state* is a complete situation where all property values for all individuals are specified. We let $s_\emptyset$ represent the null situation (i.e., the situation with no constituent). We will denote the set of all possible states in a given domain by W. An example of a state in the living-room world introduced by Ginsberg and Smith [1988] is given as A1 in the Appendix.

A situation s is *coherent* if s does not assign two different values to any property. Situations s and t are *compatible* if their union is coherent. A sequence of situations is called a *history*.

An *atomic event type* (or simply *event*) is a mapping from an *event name* to a pair of situation types.[2] For an event e, the first element of this pair is called the *precondition* of e, denoted $pre(e)$, and the second element the *postcondition* of e, $post(e)$. The properties comprising the precondition and postcondition of e are called, respectively, the domain of e, denoted $dom(e)$, and the range of e, $ran(e)$.

[1]The symbols t and f represent true and false, respectively.

[2]This definition can be generalized to allow sets of transitions between situation types without affecting the results given in this paper.

For example,

$$o(door1) = (\{open(door1)\colon \mathbf{f}\}\ ,\ \{open(door1)\colon \mathbf{t}\})$$

denotes an atomic event type representing the opening of *door*1. An example of an event from the living-room world is given as A2 in the Appendix.

We let $e_\| = (s_\emptyset, s_\emptyset)$. If either the precondition or postcondition of an event is not coherent, we denote the event by e_+. Intuitively, $e_\|$ corresponds to a no-op and e_+ is an event that can never be performed.

An event e can *occur* in a history between adjacent situations s and t if and only if $pre(e)$ is contained in s and $post(e)$ is contained in t. Intuitively, the precondition of the event must be satisfied in the initial situation and the postcondition must be satisfied in the resulting (final) situation.

It is important to note that the precondition of an event acts like a guard; that is, the event simply cannot occur unless the precondition is satisfied. This is different to many event formalisms in AI, in which the event can occur without the precondition being satisfied, but possibly with unpredictable results.

4 Concurrent Events

Consider two events occurring concurrently (i.e., occurring between the same two situations) in any given history. It follows directly from the condition on event occurrence given above that the preconditions of both events must be compatible and that their postconditions must be compatible. Intuitively, two events can be performed concurrently provided they do not interfere with one another.

We can also define new events consisting of the composition of two or more concurrent atomic events. More formally, we represent the concurrent combination of two atomic events e_1 and e_2, denoted by $e_1 \| e_2$, as

$$e_1 \| e_2 = (pre(e_1) \cup pre(e_2), post(e_1) \cup post(e_2)).$$

The resulting event can only occur if both its precondition and postcondition are coherent; otherwise, it reduces to the event e_+. An example of a concurrent event is given as A3 in the Appendix.

As the union of two situations is itself a situation, it follows that the concurrent event $e_1 \| e_2$ is also an atomic event. It can therefore be combined concurrently with other atomic events. The operator $\|$ can be shown [Belegrinos, 1991] to be reflexive, commutative and associative, with $e_\|$ and e_+ playing the role of the unit and zero elements, respectively. With the above definition, we can therefore replace any set of concurrently occurring events $e_1, e_2, \ldots e_n$ by the single atomic event $e_1 \| e_2 \| \ldots \| e_n$. We denote the closure of a set of atomic events E under the operator $\|$ by $\overline{E}$.

Elsewhere [Belegrinos, 1991] we develop a method for representing more general classes of events using a greater range of event operators. For the present discussion, however, atomic events are sufficient.

5 Performing Events

We have already stated conditions that have to be satisfied for an event to occur in a particular history. We now introduce further constraints upon events and the situations over which they occur.

Intuitively, we wish to only allow changes in properties from one situation to the next if an event occurs that brings about that change [Georgeff, 1987]. In our event representation, it is an immediate consequence that the value of any property outside the range of the events occurring between the two situations will remain unchanged.

Consider a pair of adjacent situations s and t in a given history. Let the set of all (concurrent) atomic events occurring between these situations be represented by the single atomic event e, as defined above. Then the following conditions must be observed between the situations s and t:

$$pre(e) \subset s$$
$$post(e) \subset t, \text{ and}$$
$$t|_{R-ran(e)} = s|_{R-ran(e)} \qquad (1)$$

where $u|_Q$ represents the restriction of u to the properties in Q and R is the set of properties in the situation t.

Note that the resulting situation t is fully determined by the event e and the initial situation s, provided s includes all the properties in t not included in the range of e. In the particular case when s and t are states (i.e., complete situations), e fully specifies the transition between the states. We will denote this state by $result(e, s)$. Formally, we have

$$result(e,s)|_{ran(e)} = post(e), \text{ and}$$
$$result(e,s)|_{F-ran(e)} = s|_{F-ran(e)}$$

Note that *result* is a partial function and is undefined for some states. In particular, we write $result(e, s) = \bot$ if $pre(e)$ is not compatible with s.

Because the domain of influence of an event is fully prescribed, describing events and their effects upon the world is not subject to the frame problem. That is, the effects of an event can be fully delineated without having to use either frame axioms or nonmonotonic mechanisms [Georgeff, 1987].

Now consider the occurrence of an event e, possibly concurrently with other events from a set of events E. The set of all possible transitions between states, called the ***transition relation*** of e with respect to W and E, is given by

$$T_e = \bigcup_{s \in W} T_{e,s} \text{ where } T_{e,s} = \bigcup_{d \in \overline{E}} result(e\|d, s)$$

The set T_e corresponds to the conventional view of events in the AI literature, i.e., as transition relations over world states [McDermott, 1982]. It is straightforward to prove that $T_{e_1\|e_2} = T_{e_1} \cap T_{e_2}$, as expected.

While this indicates that, for every event e in a specified domain of world states W and events E, there is a corresponding transition relation, the converse is not true. This is quite important. It means that our notion of an event is more restrictive than notions in which arbitrary transitions are allowed. But we can represent any transition relation as a *set* of atomic events, and thus can represent any possible world history.

Moreover, the fact that our notion of events is more restrictive allows for simpler logical representations and possibly more effective reasoning techniques. For example, the model of events as proposed can be used to provide a formal semantics for the standard STRIPS representation [Fikes and Nilsson, 1971] of events and is suggestive of its straightforward extension for reasoning about concurrent events. Provided that one has some means for specifying any domain-specific constraints on the occurrence of events, and extends the STRIPS representation to allow event sets and concurrency, the approach is fully general. The model proposed here can also be used for providing the formal semantics for other more powerful logics of events and actions.

6 Constraints Among Events

The above model of events is quite general and can be used to represent arbitrary histories of events and situations. However, to reason about events and their possible ramifications, we need to add to this representation some means for specifying domain-specific constraints among events.

6.1 Processes

The world can be viewed as consisting of various mechanisms or causal relationships which place constraints upon the events that can be performed. These constraints determine both which events can or must occur concurrently and which events can or must occur sequentially. Most AI formalisms have limited expressive capability for describing these kinds of causal and temporal relations among events (a notable exception being the work of Lansky [1987]). To model these constraints on behaviour in a fully general way, we therefore introduce the notion of *process*.

While there are a number of different process models that would be suitable to this end, we choose herein to use the model of Communicating Sequential Processes (CSP) as introduced by Hoare [1985]. Following this approach, we represent a process as a pair of sets. The first set, called the ***alphabet*** of the process, is the set of atomic events in which the process can engage. The alphabet of a process P is denoted by $\alpha(P)$. The second set, called the ***traces*** of the process, is a set of sequences of atomic events.

Each trace describes the behaviour of the process up to a particular point in time, and each event that appears in a trace is a possibly concurrent combination of the atomic events contained in the alphabet of the process. The traces of a process P are denoted by $traces(P)$ and the trace that consists of the sequence of events m_1 followed by m_2 and so on up to m_n is denoted by $<m_1, m_2, \ldots, m_n>$. The first event of a trace $m \neq <>$ is denoted by m_1 and the trace which results from removing the first event of m is denoted by m'.

This notion of process is important in a number of ways that parallel our representation of events. First, it depends on an explicit representation of the events that can possibly engage in the process, as defined by the process alphabet. Second, it is local. That is, it does not attempt to define the constraints between events as they occur globally, but restricts attention to their local influence over one another. The fact that an event e_2 directly follows another event e_1 in a process P does not prevent other events, not in the alphabet of P, from occurring between the occurrences of e_1 and e_2. These ideas are important for the definition of process concurrency, which we introduce below, and are essential to providing compositionality of the representation. Moreover, the ability to represent localized constraints on events is critical for achieving computational tractability [Lansky, 1988].

Rather than specifying the traces of a process directly, Hoare introduces an equivalent method for representing processes. This method consists of the following recursive rules.

1. The process $STOP_B$ (where B is a set of atomic events and $\alpha(STOP_B) = B$) denotes a process that never performs any of the events in B.

2. The process $e \rightarrow P$ (where $e \in \overline{\alpha(P)}$) denotes a process that performs the event e and then behaves like P.

3. The process $e_1 \rightarrow \underline{P_1} \mid e_2 \rightarrow \underline{P_2}$ (where $\alpha(P_1) = \alpha(P_2)$ and $e_1 \in \alpha(P_1)$, $e_2 \in \alpha(P_2)$ and $e_1 \neq e_2$) denotes a process that first performs either e_1 or e_2 and then behaves like P_1 if e_1 was performed first and like P_2 if e_2 was performed first.

The above rules can be conveniently expressed using the notation $P = e : B \rightarrow P(e)$, where B is a set of atomic events and $P(e)$ is an expression denoting a process for each of the different events e in B. The process $e : B \rightarrow P(e)$ denotes a process that first performs an event $e \in B$ and then behaves like $P(e)$. The traces of this process are expressed as follows:

$$traces(e : B \rightarrow P(e)) = \{m : m = \langle\rangle \text{ or } (m_1 \in B \text{ and } m' \in traces(P(m_1)))\}$$

6.2 Concurrent Processes

Different agents (or machines) and the environment in which they are situated can be modelled by different processes. It remains to specify how these processes evolve when they are brought together. For this we need the notion of concurrent processes.

The definition we adopt is similar to that of Hoare. That is, events that are unique to one process can be performed whenever that process is ready to perform them and events that are in the alphabets of more than one process must be performed simultaneously (synchronously). However, we extend Hoare's approach to allow the simultaneous occurrence of events of different types.

Formally, we represent the concurrent combination of two processes P_1 and P_2, denoted $P_1 \| P_2$, as follows:

$$\alpha(P_1 \| P_2) = \alpha(P_1) \cup \alpha(P_2)$$

$$traces(P_1 \| P_2) = \{m : m!\alpha(P_1) \in traces(P_1) \text{ and } m!\alpha(P_2) \in traces(P_2) \text{ and } m_i \in \overline{\alpha(P_1 \| P_2)} \text{ for all } m_i \text{ in } m\}$$

The expression $m!\alpha$ is the restriction of the events in m to the events in α. If no events in m are contained in α, $m!\alpha = \langle\rangle$.

6.3 Relationship to Situation Histories

The notion of process as defined above allows us to represent arbitrary constraints among events[3] and to compose these in various ways. We now have to determine how these sequences of events relate to situation and state histories.

We do this by extending the notion of event occurrence between two situations within a given history. In particular, we say that an event trace can occur over a given interval within a given history just in case each element of the trace can occur between successive situations in the interval. More formally, we have $e = \langle e_1, e_2, \ldots, e_n \rangle$ can *occur* over an interval $s = s_0, s_1, \ldots, s_n$ of a history if and only if e_i can occur between situations s_{i-1} and s_i for $i = 1, \ldots, n$.[4]

If we have a set of concurrent processes P representing the constraints among all the events of a given domain, the traces of P will fully determine which events can occur from one moment to the next. Thus, for any such trace to occur in a particular history, the conditions given as Equation 1 in Section 5 must also be satisfied. In the case that the history is over complete states, it follows that each trace of P determines a unique history, given the state of the history in which P is initiated.

Given a set of concurrent processes P, we will say a trace $e = \langle e_1, \ldots, e_n \rangle$ of P is *realizable* with respect to a state $s \in W$ if and only if

$$result(e_n, (result(e_{n-1}, \cdots (result(e_1, s)) \cdots))) \neq \perp$$

where we let $result(e, \perp) = \perp$. We take the empty trace to be realizable with respect to any state.

7 Causality

One of the most important relationships between events is that of *causation*. This is particularly so in our case, because it is by this mechanism that we can represent the ramifications of any given event. In this section, we show how to model causation using processes.

Following earlier work [Georgeff, 1987], we consider two types of causation: *sequential* and *simultaneous*. Let us first consider simultaneous causation. An atomic event e_1 is said to simultaneously cause an atomic event e_2 under conditions ϕ if, whenever e_1 occurs and the condition ϕ holds, event e_2 also occurs. This form of causation can be modelled by the following process:

$$P_C = (e_1 \| e_2) \rightarrow P_C \mid (e_1 \| e_{\neg\phi}) \rightarrow P_C \mid e_2 \rightarrow P_C$$

where $e_{\neg\phi}$ is an atomic event that tests if ϕ is false (i.e., has $\neg\phi$ as its precondition).

This process is such that, whenever e_1 is performed under condition ϕ, the event e_2 is forced to occur concurrently. However, if ϕ is not true, e_1 can occur by

[3] This is not quite true. The process model given here cannot represent nondeterministic machines. However, the extension to this case, which requires the notion of *failure sets*, is relatively straightforward.

[4] A set of event traces can be considered a complex (i.e., non-atomic) event (see also the work of Lansky [1987]). The above definition thus defines under what circumstances such an event can occur in a history.

itself. The third alternative branch in the above process (i.e., as represented by the choice e_2) is necessary so that the occurrence of e_2 can occur unconstrained by the occurrence or otherwise of e_1.

Sequential causation models the case in which the occurrence of an event e_1 causes the subsequent occurrence of an event e_2, though possibly other events may occur between the occurrences of these events. The causation may also be dependent upon some condition ϕ holding when e_1 is performed. This form of causation can be represented by a process similar to that given above.

Other examples of causal processes are given as A4 in the Appendix.

8 Mapping Properties to Processes

We have introduced above a model for representing events and situations and for representing arbitrarily complex relations among those events. We have defined under what conditions an event or set of events can occur (or be performed), and how such occurrences affect the situations over which the event(s) take place.

This model can be used as a basis for the semantics of various logics and calculi for reasoning about events, situations, and plans. However, in some circumstances, it is desirable to be able to reason entirely within a process framework. Therefore, in this section, we describe how to transform the current representation into an equivalent process representation.

Hoare's representation of processes is purely event based and contains no explicit representation of state properties. Determining the behaviour of a set of processes is thus simply a matter of determining how the event traces of the participating process can be combined, given the restrictions on event execution defined above. However, once we allow state properties to be introduced, events can indirectly influence one another through the effect one event has on the properties that affect performance of another. In essence, the state properties provide yet other constraints on the performance of events.

One way to represent the influence of state properties is to introduce further processes that force these constraints to be observed. We call such processes *property processes*, and introduce one for each property p in F. The property process for a property p can be viewed as an n state machine, where n is the number of values that can be assigned to p. Each state represents a different value of p; the current state represents the current value of p. A change in state of the machine results by performing an event e such that $pre(e)$ is compatible with the current assignment to p. The resulting state of the machine is the state which represents the value specified by $post(e)$.

To keep the description of the property processes relatively simple, we introduce the events $d^p_v = (\{p\colon v\}\ ,\ s_\emptyset)$ and $r^p_v = (s_\emptyset\ ,\ \{p\colon v\})$ for each different value v that can be assigned to p. Intuitively, d^p_v is an event that tests whether p has value v and r^p_v assigns the value v to p. We let the set of all such events for the property p be denoted by E_p.

Any event can be described as a concurrent combination of d^p_v and r^p_v events with different p and v. This relationship can be captured by constructing a causal process for each event e, such that e causes the simultaneous occurrence of the events d^p_v (or r^p_v), for each valuation of p in the domain (range) of e.

The property process P^p for property p is then constructed as follows:

$P^p = init^p_{v_1} \rightarrow P^p_{v_1} \mid \cdots \mid init^p_{v_n} \rightarrow P^p_{v_n}$, where
$v_1, \ldots, v_n$ are the different assignments to p,
$init^p_{v_1}, \ldots, init^p_{v_n}$ are distinguished atomic events,
$\alpha(P^p) = \alpha(P^p_{v_i}) = \{init^p_{v_1}, \ldots init^p_{v_n}\} \cup E_p$,
and where

$$P^p_{v_i} = e : C^p_{v_i} \rightarrow P^p_{v_i}(e),$$
$$C^p_{v_i} = C^p_{v_{i1}} \cup \cdots \cup C^p_{v_{in}}$$
$$C^p_{v_{ii}} = \{d^p_{v_i}, r^p_{v_i}, d^p_{v_i} \| r^p_{v_i}\}$$
$$C^p_{v_{ij}} = \{r^p_{v_j}, d^p_{v_i} \| r^p_{v_j}\}\ (j \neq i)$$

and

$$P^p_{v_i}(e) = P^p_{v_j} \text{ if } e \in C^p_{v_{ij}}$$

The purpose of the events $init^p_{v_i}$ is simply to set the initial state of the property process; their form is straightforward and is given elsewhere [Belegrinos, 1991]. Intuitively, $P^p_{v_i}$ represents the state in which p has the value v_i and the events in $C^p_{v_{ij}}$ represent those events $e \in \overline{E_p}$ that change the value of the property p from v_i to v_j. Note that these processes correspond directly to the constraints used by Lansky [1987] to represent event properties, with the events r^p_v playing the role of Lansky's "adders" (v = **t**) and "deleters" (v = **f**) for property p and d^p_v representing the constraints on event preconditions.

Given an arbitrary process P and a set of property processes as described above, it can be shown [Belegrinos, 1991] that the traces of P executed concurrently with the property processes are exactly those traces that would result from executing P, taking into account the influence of state properties. That is, the traces are exactly the realizable traces of P.

9 Conclusions

The aim of this paper has been to determine the basic foundations for a theory of events, situations, and processes that can be used for reasoning about arbitrarily complex dynamic domains. The essential elements of the approach are: (1) A model of events that explicitly represents the domain of influence of the event; (2) A model of processes that can represent arbitrarily complex behaviours; (3) An extension of that process model to represent the influence of events upon state properties and the influence, in turn, of those properties upon other events; and (4) A representation of causality that allows the ramifications of a given event occurrence to be modelled.

We have also shown how to map the representation of a problem domain described in terms of high-level events, state properties, and causality into a more-or-less standard process model. Having done this, we can then draw on all the work in process theory and its application to help solve complex, real-world problems.

Although we have not directly addressed the frame problem, it should be clear that, by scoping the domain of influence of events, the problem as conventionally viewed will not arise. In essence, we have transferred the problem of reasoning about the effects of events and actions to one of reasoning about which events are occurring at any given moment of time. While we believe that process models provide the basis for doing this reasoning in a tractable way, this claim has yet to be demonstrated. We also need to develop a logic of events and situations that is well suited to this model and to examine the semantic foundations, in terms of this model, of previous formalisms.

Appendix

We illustrate here how our approach can be used to reason about the living-room world introduced by Ginsberg and Smith [1988]. For simplicity, we consider only a subset of this world. In particular, we assume that the room contains a television, a plant, a shelf, and two ventilation ducts located under the floor. If an object is on a duct, that duct is blocked; if both ducts are blocked, the room will become stuffy. We can represent this world by taking

$$F = \{pos(\text{tv}), pos(\text{plant}), blocked(\text{duct1}), blocked(\text{duct2}), stuffy(\text{room})\},$$

where

pos can take the values $\{floor, shelf, duct1, duct2\}$ and *blocked* and *stuffy* the values $\{\mathbf{t}, \mathbf{f}\}$.

The initial state of the world is represented by the state s as follows:

$$s = \{pos(\text{tv}): \text{shelf}\ ,\ pos(\text{plant}): \text{duct2}\ ,\ blocked(\text{duct1}): \mathbf{f}\ ,\ blocked(\text{duct2}): \mathbf{t}\ ,\ stuffy(\text{room}): \mathbf{f}\} \quad \text{(A1)}$$

Suppose we can perform two events in this world: move the television from the shelf to duct1 (denoted by e_1) and move the plant from duct2 to the floor (denoted by e_2). We can represent these events and their concurrent combination as follows:

$$e_1 = (\{pos(\text{tv}): \text{shelf}\ ,\ blocked(\text{duct1}): \mathbf{f}\}\ \{pos(\text{tv}): \text{duct1}\ ,\ blocked(\text{duct1}): \mathbf{t}\})$$
$$e_2 = (\{pos(\text{plant}): \text{duct2}\ ,\ blocked(\text{duct2}): \mathbf{t}\}\ \{pos(\text{plant}): \text{floor}\ ,\ blocked(\text{duct2}): \mathbf{f}\}) \quad \text{(A2)}$$

$$e_1 \| e_2 = (\{pos(\text{tv}): \text{shelf}\ ,\ blocked(\text{duct1}): \mathbf{f}\ ,\ pos(\text{plant}): \text{duct2}\ ,\ blocked(\text{duct2}): \mathbf{t}\}\ ,\ \{pos(\text{tv}): \text{duct1}\ ,\ blocked(\text{duct1}): \mathbf{t}\ ,\ pos(\text{plant}): \text{floor}\ ,\ blocked(\text{duct2}): \mathbf{f}\}) \quad \text{(A3)}$$

Let P_A be an agent process that performs the event e_1 followed by e_2. That is, $\alpha(P_A) = \{e_1, e_2\}$ and $P_A = e_1 \rightarrow e_2 \rightarrow STOP_{\alpha(P_A)}$.

The indirect effects (ramifications) of these events on the property *stuffy*(room) are handled by introducing the events e_{stuffy} and e_{clear}, defined as follows:

$$e_{clear} = (s_\emptyset\ ,\ \{stuffy(\text{room}): \mathbf{f}\})$$
$$e_{stuffy} = (s_\emptyset\ ,\ \{stuffy(\text{room}): \mathbf{t}\})$$

Depending upon which causal rules one adopts, we can force the room to become stuffy immediately the two ducts are blocked or some time after both are blocked. For this example, we will assume the former. This leads to the following causal processes:

$$P_{C_1} = (e_2 \| e_{clear}) \rightarrow P_{C_1}$$
$$P_{C_2} = (e_1 \| e_\phi \| e_{stuffy}) \rightarrow P_{C_2}\ \mid\ (e_1 \| e_{\neg\phi}) \rightarrow P_{C_2}$$

where

$$e_\phi = (\{blocked(\text{duct2}): \mathbf{t}\}\ ,\ s_\emptyset)$$
$$e_{\neg\phi} = (\{blocked(\text{duct2}): \mathbf{f}\}\ ,\ s_\emptyset) \quad \text{(A4)}$$

Putting these processes together, it is not too hard to show that $< init_s, (e_1 \| e_\phi \| e_{stuffy}), (e_2 \| e_{clear}) >$ is the only realizable trace of P, where $init_s$ is the event that sets the initial state properties to s.

Acknowledgments

The authors wish to thank David Morley, Anand Rao, and Liz Sonenberg for their contributions to this work.

References

[Barwise and Perry, 1983] J. Barwise and J. Perry. *Situations and Attitudes.* MIT Press, Cambridge, Massachusetts, 1983.

[Belegrinos, 1991] P. Belegrinos. A Model of Actions and Processes. Technical Report 91/6, The University of Melbourne, Parkville, Victoria, 1991.

[Fikes and Nilsson, 1971] R. E. Fikes and N. J. Nilsson. STRIPS: A New Approach to the Application of Theorem Proving to Problem Solving. *Artificial Intelligence*, 2:189–208, 1971.

[Georgeff, 1987] M. P. Georgeff. Actions, Processes, and Causality. In *Reasoning about Actions and Plans: Proceedings of the 1986 Workshop*, pages 99–122. Morgan Kaufmann, Mountain View, California, 1987.

[Ginsberg and Smith, 1988] M. L. Ginsberg and D. E. Smith. Reasoning about Action I: A Possible Worlds Approach. *Artificial Intelligence*, 35:165–195, 1988.

[Hanks and McDermott, 1987] S. Hanks and D. McDermott. Nonmonotonic Logic and Temporal Projection. *Artificial Intelligence*, 33:379–412, 1987.

[Hoare, 1985] C. A. R. Hoare. *Communicating Sequential Processes.* Prentice-Hall International, UK, 1985.

[Lansky, 1987] A. L. Lansky. A Representation of Parallel Activity Based on Events, Structure, and Causality. In *Reasoning about Actions and Plans: Proceedings of the 1986 Workshop*, pages 123–159. Morgan Kaufmann, Mountain View, California, 1987.

[Lansky, 1988] A. L. Lansky. Localized Event-Based Reasoning for Multiagent Domains. *Computational Intelligence*, 4:319–340, 1988.

[McCarthy and Hayes, 1969] J. McCarthy and P. J. Hayes. Some Philosophical Problems from the Standpoint of Artificial Intelligence. *Machine Intelligence*, 4:463–502, 1969.

[McDermott, 1982] D. McDermott. A Temporal Logic for Reasoning about Processes and Plans. *Cognitive Science*, 6:101–155, 1982.

Parameter Structures for Parametrized Modal Operators

Hans Jürgen Ohlbach
Max Planck Institut für Informatik
Im Stadtwald
D-6600 Saarbrücken 11, Germany
email: ohlbach@mpi.uni-sb.de

Andreas Herzig
IRIT, Université Paul Sabatier
118 route de Narbonne
F-31062 Toulouse Cedex, France
email: herzig@irit.fr
Tel. ...33 6155 6764

Abstract*

The parameters of the parameterized modal operators [p] and <p> usually represent agents (in the epistemic interpretation) or actions (in the dynamic logic interpretation) or the like. In this paper the application of the idea of parametrized modal operators is extended in in two ways: First of all a modified neighbourhood semantics is defined which permits among others the interpretation of the parameters as probability values. A formula [.5] F may for example express the fact that in at least 50% of all cases (worlds) F holds. These probability values can be numbers, qualitative descriptions and even arbitrary terms. Secondly a general theory of the parameters and in particular of the characteristic operations on the parameters is developed which unifies for example the multiplication of numbers in the probabilistic interpretation of the parameters and the sequencing of actions in the dynamic logic interpretation.

Key words: Modal Logic, Probability Logic, Epistemic Logic, Temporal Logic.

Introduction

Modal logics are used with various interpretations, as epistemic logic to express the knowledge of an agent, as doxastic logic to express belief, as temporal logic to express temporal relationships, as action logic to express the effect of actions in the world etc. Many of these interpretations require the modal operators to be parametrized with agents, actions, etc.

One interpretation of the parameters however has not yet been tried, namely the interpretation as probability values, such that for example [p]F with $p \in [0,1]$ expresses that F holds in at least (exactly, at most) p*100% of all cases (worlds). The reason might be that in this application numerical (or symbolic) computations with these parameters have to be an essential part of the calculus. For example [.5][.6]F which expresses that in 50% of all cases it is true that in 60% of their subcases F holds, should imply [.3]F. That means we have to integrate the operations on the parameters very deeply into the logic.

When we adopt the interpretation that [p]F means *at least* p*100% (the other versions are similar) then there are more rules we would like to have:

$(p \geq q \wedge [p]F) \Rightarrow [q]F$, i.e. $[.6]F \Rightarrow [.5]F$,

$([p]F \wedge [q]G) \Rightarrow \max(0, p+q-1)(F \wedge G)$,

i.e. $([.6]F \wedge [.7]F) \Rightarrow [.3]F$ (conservative estimation for probability of simultaneous events based on minimal overlaps),

$([p]F \wedge [q]F) \Leftrightarrow [\max(p,q)]F$,

$([p]F \vee [q]F) \Leftrightarrow [\min(p,q)]F$,

$\neg[p]F \Leftrightarrow [1\text{-}p]^{+}\neg F$, i.e. $\neg[.4]F \Leftrightarrow [.6]^{+}\neg F$,

where $[.6]^{+}F$ is true if F holds in more than 60% of all cases.

Unfortunately it turned out that the standard relational Kripke semantics for modal logic is not sufficient to support these rules. In classical modal logics there is one (or several) binary relations on worlds which is used to determine for the "actual world" the set of all accessible worlds [Kripke 59,63]. □F is true in the actual world iff F is true in all accessible worlds. At first glance it should be possible to use the standard accessibility relation and interpret [p]F: There is a p*100% subset $\mathcal{U}$ of the worlds accessible from the actual world and F holds in all these worlds $\mathcal{U}$. This version, however, fails to support the rule $[p][q]F \Rightarrow [p{*}q]F$. The following picture of a typical possible worlds structure shows what goes wrong.

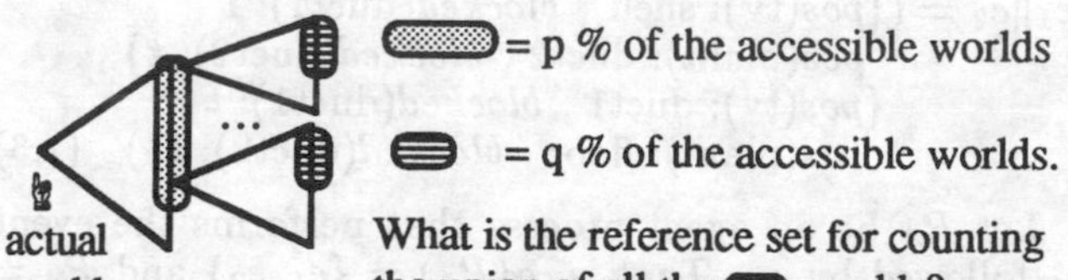

What is the reference set for counting the union of all the worlds?

In order to overcome this problem we have to keep not only an actual world, but also an **actual world set** which serves as reference set against which to count the worlds. To this end we switch from the relational possible worlds structure to a kind of neighbourhood semantics [Rautenberg 79] or minimal model semantics [Chellas 80] and replace the accessibility relation by an **access function** $\varphi(p, \mathcal{U})$ which

* This work has been supported by the ESPRIT project MEDLAR and the SFB 314 of the German Science Foundation (DFG).

Thanks to Luis Fariñas del Cerro for useful discussions.

computes for a parameter p and an actual *world set* $\mathcal{U}$ a set of sets of accessible worlds (neighbourhood structure). For example $\varphi(.5,\mathcal{U})$ may compute the set of all at least (exactly, at most) 50% subsets of $\mathcal{U}$. If $\mathcal{U}$ is the actual world set then [p]F is interpreted: there is a set $\mathcal{V} \in \varphi(p,\mathcal{U})$ (a p*100% subset of $\mathcal{U}$) and F holds in all worlds of $\mathcal{V}$. The nesting of operators is no problem any longer. If $\mathcal{V} \in \varphi(.5,\mathcal{U})$ and $\mathcal{V}' \in \varphi(.6,\mathcal{V})$ then $\mathcal{V}' \in \varphi(.3,\mathcal{U})$. Thus, [.5][.6] $\Rightarrow$ [.3]F.

To our surprise it turned out that with this simple idea we have discovered a very general principle which permits a uniform treatment of many kinds of operations on parameters in may applications of modal logic, new and old ones.

In order to demonstrate that the theory is of general nature we use the following five very different applications of the logic:

1. Epistemic logic with a single agent.
   [p]F means, agent p knows F.
2. Epistemic logic with a set of agents.
   [p]F means, every agent in the set p knows F.
3. Temporal Logic with duration parameters.
   [p]F means there is an interval I of length p and F holds at each instant in I.
4. Action Logic. [p]F means, after performing p, F holds.
5. Probabilistic Logic. [p]F means, F holds in at least p* 100 % of all cases. (Note that although we only use the interval [0...1] for probability values, there can be arbitrary qualifications such as "may be", "very likely", etc.)

Common aspects which have shown up are for example that the multiplication of probability values corresponds (the same laws hold) to the sequencing of actions in the action logic interpretation. The operation max(0, p+q-1) corresponds to parallel execution of independent actions.

In order to cover as many applications as possible we introduce generic operations on the parameters which have to be instantiated with concrete operations in each particular application. For each generic operation a correspondence between a characteristic axiom schema (like [p][q]F $\Rightarrow$ [p$\otimes$q]F) and a characteristic property of the access function φ is shown. This correspondence plays the same rôle as for example the correspondence between the rule $\Box$F $\Rightarrow$ F in classical modal logic and the reflexivity of the accessibility relation. Correspondences of this kind are essential for incorporating desired axiom schemas efficiently into semantics based deduction calculi [Fitting 83, Ohlbach 88, Herzig 89, Auffray & Enjalbert 89]. In this paper however we present only the basic logic itself and prove the correspondence theorems. The applications – the probabilistic application as well – are used to illustrate the ideas. They are not investigated themselves.

The logic we present is first order and permits arbitrary nesting of modal operators and quantifiers. For example ∀x:human [.5]male(x) and [.5]∀x:human male(x) are both allowed formulae, but with totally different meaning. This is one of the differences to standard theories for dealing with uncertainty where this is usually not possible, as for example in probability theory [Frost 86], certainty theory [Shortcliff & Buchanan 75], Dempster Schafer theory of evidence [Schafer 76], possibility theory [Zadeh 78] or incidence calculus [Bundy 84]. In [Halpern 89] there has been given a possible worlds model for a probability logic where this problem is solved by introducing two different notions: probabilities on the world and probabilities on the domain.

The reader is assumed to be familiar with modal logic ([Hughes & Cresswell 86], [Chellas 80], [Fitting 83]).

In the sequel we use the following notational conventions for writing formulae: Syntactic objects are written in standard letters, whereas semantic objects are written in italics. For example if x is a variable symbol, then χ denotes its interpretation with respect to a given variable assignment. F, G, H are used as meta symbols for formulae.

Syntax and Semantics

The logic is defined as an extension of many sorted first order logic. For the purpose of this paper it is not necessary to fix the particular kind of the sort structure. Any kind of logic which allows different sorts will do, for example logics of [Walther 87, Schmidt-Schauß 89, Cohn 87]. We only distinguish one sort as a "parameter sort". In the sequel we use "P" as the name of this sort and we call terms of sort P "P-terms". For this sort we further presuppose the existence of the following function and predicate symbols: function symbols ⊓, ⊔, ⩎, ⩏ and $\otimes$, all of them of sort P×P→P, a function symbol ~ of sort P→P and a predicate symbol ⊑ of sort P×P. The sort P together with these symbols make up the **parameter signature** Σ_P = (P, ⊓, ⊔, ⩎, ⩏, $\otimes$, ~, ⊑).

The formulae are built in the usual way using the logical connectives and quantifiers ¬, ∧, ∨, ⇒, ⇔, ∀, ∃. Furthermore there are the parametrized modal operators [p] and <p>. The syntax rule for these operators is: If p is a P-term and F a formula then [p]F and <p>F are formulae. The <p> operator is used as an abbreviation for ¬[p]¬.

Algebras and homomorphisms [Grätzer 79] are the basic building blocks for the definition of the semantics of well sorted terms and well formed formulae. A **Σ-algebra** $\mathcal{A}$ for a signature Σ containing the available syntactic objects consists of a carrier set $D_{\mathcal{A}}$ and a set of functions which correspond to Σ in the right way. The carrier set is divided into subsets according to Σ's sort structure. A special Σ-algebra is the algebra of free terms where the carrier set consists of the well sorted terms themselves and the functions are constructor functions for terms. This fact can be exploited to define the semantics of terms just by an homomorphism from the free term algebra into a corresponding Σ-algebra. A Σ-algebra does not contain objects that correspond to predicate symbols. Therefore **Σ-structures** are Σ-algebras together with relations as denotations for the predicate symbols. We write $Q_{\mathcal{A}}$ for the interpretation of the symbol Q in the Σ-structure or Σ-algebra $\mathcal{A}$.

Definition 1 Semantics

A **frame** Φ = ($\mathcal{W}$, $\mathcal{P}$, φ) over a parameter signature Σ_P, i.e. a signature containing the syntactic components of the parameter sort P, consists of

- a set $\mathcal{W}$ of **worlds**,
- a Σ_P-structure $\mathcal{P}$ of **parameter values**,

- φ is a function $\varphi: \mathcal{P} \times 2^{\mathcal{W}} \to 2^{2^{\mathcal{W}}}$, i.e. φ computes for a parameter and a set of worlds the neighbourhood as a set of sets of worlds. We call φ the **access function.**

For a signature Σ containing Σ_P, a **Σ-interpretation** $\Im = (\Phi, \mathcal{U}, u, \Xi, \Theta)$ consists of

- a frame $\Phi = (\mathcal{W}, \mathcal{P}, \varphi)$,
- the actual world set $\mathcal{U} \subseteq \mathcal{W}$,
- the actual world $u \in \mathcal{U}$,
- an assignment Ξ of worlds to Σ-structures. The substructure corresponding to Σ_P is the same in all worlds, and
- a variable assignment Θ, i.e. a mapping from variables to domain elements.

We say the interpretation $\Im$ is Φ-based.

In the sequel $\Im[x/\chi]$ is like $\Im$ and $\Theta[x/\chi]$ is like Θ except that Θ maps the variable x to the value χ. There is an induced homomorphism $\Im_h$ which interprets terms in the actual world u. We usually write $\Im(t)$ instead of $\Im_h(t)$ to denote t's value in the particular interpretation $\Im$.

- The satisfiability relation $\models$ is defined as follows: Let $\Im = (\Phi, \mathcal{U}, u, \Xi, \Theta)$ be an interpretation.
- $\Im \models P(t_1,\ldots,t_n)$ iff $(\Im(t_1),\ldots,\Im(t_n)) \in P_{\Xi(u)}$.
- $\Im \models \forall x{:}S\ F$ iff for all $\chi \in S_{\Xi(u)}$ $\Im[x/\chi] \models F$.
- $\Im \models [p]\ F$ iff there is a set $\mathcal{V} \in \varphi(\Im(p), \mathcal{U})$ such that $v \in \mathcal{V}$ iff $(\Phi, \mathcal{V}, v, \Xi, \Theta) \models F$. (We say that F holds exactly in V.)
- The interpretation of the logical connectives $\neg, \wedge, \vee, \Rightarrow, \Leftrightarrow, \exists$ and <p> is as usual.

For a frame Φ:

- $\Phi \models F$ iff $\Im \models F$ for all Φ-based interpretations $\Im$.

A frame satisfying a formula, i.e $\Phi \models F$ is called a **model** for F. If every frame satisfies F we say that F is **valid.** ♦

Like in standard modal logics, the differenciation between frames and interpretations allows us to fix certain properties of the semantic structure for all interpretations based on a frame. Traditionally these are properties of the accessibility relation like reflexivity etc. Classes of frames with the same property then make up a logic (e.g. K, T, S4 etc.). We included in the definition of a frame not only the access function φ as a substitute for the accessibility relation, but also the parameter structure. This permits the distinction of logics according to certain properties of the access function and the parameter structure.

Our semantics differs in a key point from standard neighbourhood semantics. We need the neighbourhood not of the actual world, but of the actual world set. Therefore the function φ accepts a set of worlds as input and returns the neighbourhood of this set. In the case of unparametrized modal operators this makes no difference to standard neighbourhood semantics. For the parameterized case, however it is essential for interpreting the parameters as probability values which count worlds.

In the concrete definition of the access function φ, the intuition about the actual application can be manifested. For example in the epistemic interpretation with a single agent, φ returns the basic set of worlds the agent considers in his mind together with its supersets. If different frames of mind are to be modeled in which the agent may believe controversial things then several different basic sets are returned [Fagin & Halpern 88]. In the epistemic interpretation with a set of agents, φ returns a single basic set with the union of all worlds the agents consider (again together with their supersets). In the temporal interpretation with duration parameter, $\varphi(p, ..)$ returns the set of intervals with length p. In the action logic interpretation, φ returns the sets of worlds which are caused by each action. Finally in the probabilistic interpretation, $\varphi(p, \mathcal{U})$ returns the set of subsets of $\mathcal{U}$ with at least p*100% of its elements.

Some theorems which carry over from modal logic with standard neighbourhood semantics are collected in the following lemma [Chellas 80, Rautenberg 79].

Lemma 2

a) If $F \Leftrightarrow G$ is valid then $[p]F \Leftrightarrow [p]G$ is valid.

b) For all frames Φ the following statements are equivalent:
   1. If $F \Rightarrow G$ is valid then $[p]F \Rightarrow [p]G$ is valid in Φ.
   2. The access function φ is **upwardly closed**, i.e. if $\mathcal{V} \in \varphi(p,\mathcal{U})$ then all supersets of $\mathcal{V}$ are in $\varphi(p,\mathcal{U})$.

c) In frames with upwardly closed access functions the following axiom schemas are valid:
   $[p](F \wedge G) \Rightarrow [p]F \wedge [p]G$ and
   $[p]F \vee [p]G \Rightarrow [p](F \vee G)$.

The converse implications do not hold. ♦

From now on we choose "F holds in at least p*100% of all cases" as the probabilistic reading of [p]F, and require thus φ to be upwardly closed in this case.

Characterizing the Parameter Structure

In a sequence of theorems we investigate the correlations between the operations $\sqsubseteq, \sqcap, \sqcup, ⋒, ⋓, \otimes, \sim$ on the parameter structure and characteristic formula schemas. We start with the $\sqsubseteq$-relation.

Theorem 3 For evey frame $\Phi = (\mathcal{W}, \mathcal{P}, \varphi)$ the following statements are equivalent:

1) $\Phi \models (p \sqsubseteq q \wedge [q]F) \Rightarrow [p]F$.

2) For $p, q \in \mathcal{P}$, $p \sqsubseteq q$ implies for all $\mathcal{U}$: $\varphi(q, \mathcal{U}) \subseteq \varphi(p, \mathcal{U})$.

<u>Proof</u>: "1→2": Let $p \sqsubseteq q$ and $\mathcal{V} \in \varphi(q, \mathcal{U})$ for some $\mathcal{U}$. Take a predicate F and a Φ-based interpretation $\Im$ with actual world set $\mathcal{V}$ where F holds *exactly* in $\mathcal{V}$'s worlds. $\Im$ satisfies [q]F and $p \sqsubseteq q$ and, by 1) also [p]F. Therefore there is a $\mathcal{V}' \in \varphi(p, \mathcal{U})$ and F holds exactly in $\mathcal{V}'$. Since F holds exactly in $\mathcal{V}$, $\mathcal{V}' = \mathcal{V} \in \varphi(p, \mathcal{U})$.

"2→1": If F holds in a set $\mathcal{V}$ of worlds computed by $\varphi(q, \mathcal{U})$, and $\varphi(q, \mathcal{U}) \subseteq \varphi(p, \mathcal{U})$ where $p \sqsubseteq q$, $\mathcal{V} \in \varphi(p, \mathcal{U})$. Thus, $\mathcal{F}$ holds also in a set of worlds computed by $\varphi(p, \mathcal{U})$ and therefore the implication 1) must be true. ♦

Possible meanings of the $\sqsubseteq$-predicate in the different applications of the logic are as follows. In the epistemic interpretation with a single agent, $p \sqsubseteq q$ means that p knows everything q knows. In the epistemic interpretation with a set of agents, p ⊑ q is just the subset relation. In the temporal interpretation with duration parameters, p ⊑ q enforces that q denotes a shorter period than p. In the action logic interpretation, p ⊑ q is a specialization relation. For example move ⊑ walk expresses that everything that can be achieved with the action 'move' can also be achieved with the action 'walk'. In the probability interpretation ⊑ is just the less equal relation on numbers.

If the ⊑-relation has top and bottom element – assume they are denoted by 1 and 0 – according to theorem 3 the axioms [1]F ⇒ [p]F and [p] ⇒ [0]F hold. This allows for some interesting interpretations of these top and bottom elements. In the epistemic interpretation with a single agent, a top element is a gossip. What he knows everybody knows. A bottom element is "big brother". He knows everything the other agents know. In the epistemic interpretation with a set of agents, 0 denotes the empty set and 1 denotes the set of all agents. In the temporal interpretation with duration parameters, 0 denotes the empty period and 1 a longest period (day, month or whatsoever). In the action logic interpretation, there is no meaningful bottom element. A top element might be "do-something". In the probability interpretation the top and bottom elements are simply the numbers 1 and 0 expressing "certainly" and "no information".

Next we consider the ⩀ operation which corresponds to the intersection of sets of accessible worlds.

Theorem 4 For all frames $\Phi = (\mathcal{W}, \mathcal{P}, \varphi)$ the following statements are equivalent:

1) For all operator free formulae F and G:
$\Phi \models ([p]F \wedge [q]G) \Rightarrow [p⩀q](F \wedge G)$.
2) For all $p, q \in \mathcal{P}$, for all $\mathcal{U}$:
$\varphi(p, \mathcal{U}) ⩀ \varphi(q, \mathcal{U}) \subseteq \varphi(p ⩀ q, \mathcal{U})$ where
$A ⩀ B =_{def} \{a \cap b \mid a \in A, b \in B\}$

Proof: "1→2": Let $\mathcal{V} \in \varphi(p, \mathcal{U}) ⩀ \varphi(q, \mathcal{U})$.
There are $\mathcal{V}_p \in \varphi(p, \mathcal{U})$ and $\mathcal{V}_q \in \varphi(q, \mathcal{U})$ with $\mathcal{V} = \mathcal{V}_p \cap \mathcal{V}_q$. Take predicates F and G and a Φ-based interpretation $\mathfrak{I}$ where F holds *exactly* in $\mathcal{V}_p$'s worlds and G holds *exactly* in $\mathcal{V}_q$'s worlds. Thus, [p]F ∧ [q]G is satisfied and therefore, by 1) also [p⩀q](F ∧ G). That means, F ∧ G holds exactly in a set $\mathcal{V}' \in \varphi(p ⩀ q, \mathcal{U})$. Since F holds exactly in $\mathcal{V}_p$ and G holds exactly in $\mathcal{V}_q$, $\mathcal{V}' = \mathcal{V}_p \cap \mathcal{V}_q = \mathcal{V} \in \varphi(p ⩀ q, \mathcal{U})$.
"2→1": If [p]F ∧ [q]G is satisfied then F holds exactly in a set $\mathcal{V}_p \in \varphi(p, \mathcal{U})$ and G holds exactly in a set $\mathcal{V}_q \in \varphi(q, \mathcal{U})$. Since F and G are operator free, F ∧ G holds exactly in $\mathcal{V}_p \cap \mathcal{V}_q$ and because of 2), $\mathcal{V}_p \cap \mathcal{V}_q \in \varphi(p ⩀ q, \mathcal{U})$ and therefore [p⩀q](F ∧ G) is satisfied as well. ♦

There are meanings of ⩀ in all applications we considered. In the epistemic interpretation with a single agent, ⩀ computes a common close confidant (maybe a father confessor) who knows everything the two agents know. In the epistemic interpretation with sets of agents, ⩀ computes the intersection of two sets of agents. In the action logic interpretation, p ⩀ q means parallel execution of independent actions. In the temporal interpretation, ⩀ computes minimal overlaps with respect to a maximal interval length. For example from [12h]shining(sun) and [13h]¬shining(sun) with respect to a maximal interval length of 24 hours we get [1h = 12h⩀13h] (shining(sun) ∧ ¬shining(sun)), i.e. a contradiction. In the probabilistic interpretation ⩀ also computes minimal overlaps. In this case p ⩀ q = max(0, p+q-1). This is the lower bound for the intersection of events. Therefore for example [.6]F ∧ [.7]G yields [.3](F ∧ G).

The result for ⊓ is slightly stronger than that for ⩀:

Theorem 5 For all frames $\Phi = (\mathcal{W}, \mathcal{P}, \varphi)$ the following statements are equivalent:
1) For operator free formulae: $\Phi \models ([p]F \wedge [q]F) \Leftrightarrow [p⊓q]F$.
2) For all $p, q, \mathcal{U}$: $\varphi(p, \mathcal{U}) \cap \varphi(q, \mathcal{U}) = \varphi(p ⊓ q, \mathcal{U})$.

Proof: "1→2": The proof of the "⊆"-direction is similar to that for the ⩀ operation. To establish the inclusion in the other direction, let $\mathcal{V} \in \varphi(p ⊓ q, \mathcal{U})$. Take a predicate F and a Φ-based interpretation $\mathfrak{I}$ with actual world set $\mathcal{U}$ where F holds exactly in $\mathcal{V}$'s worlds. Thus, $\mathfrak{I}$ satisfies [p⊓q]F and with 1) [p]F ∧ [q]F as well. Therefore there are sets $\mathcal{V}_p \in \varphi(p,\mathcal{U})$ and $\mathcal{V}_q \in \varphi(q,\mathcal{U})$ such that F holds exactly in $\mathcal{V}_p$ and in $\mathcal{V}_q$. Since F holds exactly in $\mathcal{V}$, $\mathcal{V}_p = \mathcal{V}_q = \mathcal{V} \in \varphi(p,\mathcal{U}) \cap \varphi(q,\mathcal{U})$.
"2→1": For the ⇒ direction, let[p]F ∧ [q]F hold exactly in $\mathcal{U}$, i.e. F holds exactly in a set $\mathcal{V}_p \in \varphi(p,\mathcal{U})$ and in a set $\mathcal{V}_q \in \varphi(q,\mathcal{U})$. As F is operator free, $\mathcal{V}_p = \mathcal{V}_q$. Using 2) we get that $\mathcal{V}_p \in \varphi(p ⊓ q, \mathcal{U})$. Thus, [p⊓q]F holds as well.
The proof of the "⇐" direction is similar. ♦

Note that in the case of upwardly closed φ, validity of the formula ([p]F ∧ [q]F) ⇔ [p⊓q]F entails validity of the formula ([p]F ∧ [q]G) ⇒ [p⊓q](F ∨ G) by Lemma 2.b). In the probabilistic interpretation ⊓ computes lower bounds for the union of events: In this case p⊓q = max(p,q). The validity of ([p]F ∧ [q]G) ⇒ [p⊓q](F ∨ G) can be interpreted as follows: "If the probability of F is at least p and that of G at least q, then that of F ∨ G is at least max(p,q)". E.g. [.6]F ∧ [.7]G yields [.7](F ∨ G). Dual to ⊓ is ⊔.

Theorem 6 For every frame $\Phi = (\mathcal{W}, \mathcal{P}, \varphi)$ the following statements are equivalent:
1) For all formulae F: $\Phi \models ([p]F \vee [q]F) \Leftrightarrow [p⊔q]F$.
2) For all $p, q, \mathcal{U}$: $\varphi(p, \mathcal{U}) \cup \varphi(q, \mathcal{U}) = \varphi(p ⊔ q, \mathcal{U})$.

Proof: The proof is similar to the previous one. ♦

Dually, in the case of upwardly closed φ, validity of the formula ([p]F ∨ [q]F) ⇔ [p⊔q]F entails validity of the formula [p⊔q](F ∧ G) ⇒ [p]F ∨ [q]G by Lemma 2.b). In the probabilistic interpretation ⊔ computes upper bounds for the intersection of events: In this case p⊔q = min(p,q). Now the validity of (¬[p]F ∧ ¬[q]G) ⇒ ¬[p⊔q](F ∧ G) can be interpreted as follows: "If the probability of F is less than p and that of G less than q, then that of F ∧ G is less than min(p,q)". E.g. ¬[.6]F ∧ ¬[.7]G yields ¬[.6](F ∧ G).

Next we consider the multiplication operation ⊗ which allows to collapse sequences of operators into a single operator. On the semantic side, $p \otimes q$ must be a parameter such that $\varphi(p \otimes q, \mathcal{U})$ collects the sets of worlds, that correspond to applying first $\varphi(p\ldots)$ and then $\varphi(q\ldots)$ to its results.

Theorem 7 For every frame $\Phi = (\mathcal{W}, \mathcal{P}, \varphi)$ the following statements are equivalent:

1) $\Phi \models [p][q]F \Leftrightarrow [p\otimes q]F$.
2) For all $p, q, \mathcal{U}$: $\bigcup_{\mathcal{V}\in\varphi(p,\mathcal{U})} \varphi(q, \mathcal{V}) = \varphi(p\otimes q, \mathcal{U})$.

Proof: "1→2, ⊆ part": Let $\mathcal{V}' \in \bigcup_{\mathcal{V}\in\varphi(p,\mathcal{U})} \varphi(q, \mathcal{V})$. Take a predicate F and a Φ-based interpretation $\Im$ where F holds exactly in $\mathcal{V}'$'s worlds. As there is a $\mathcal{V}\in\varphi(p, \mathcal{U})$ such that $\mathcal{V}' \in \varphi(q, \mathcal{V})$, [p][q]F is satisfied and with 1) [p⊗q]F as well. Therefore there is a set $\mathcal{V}'' \in \varphi(p\otimes q, \mathcal{U})$ and F holds in $\mathcal{V}''$. Since F holds exactly in $\mathcal{V}'$, $\mathcal{V}'' = \mathcal{V}' \in \varphi(p\otimes q, \mathcal{U})$.
"1→2, ⊇ part": The proof is similar.
"2→1": [p][q]F is satisfied iff there is a set $\mathcal{V}\in\varphi(p, \mathcal{U})$ such that F holds exactly in a set $\mathcal{V}' \in \varphi(q, \mathcal{V})$. By 2) this is equivalent to F holds exactly in a set $\mathcal{V}' \in \varphi(p\otimes q, \mathcal{U})$, which means that [p⊗q]F is satisfied. ♦

In the epistemic interpretations there is no obvious interpretation of the multiplication function. In the temporal interpretation p⊗q = q. For example [12h][6h]shinig(sun)⇒ [6h]shinig(sun). In the action logic, ⊗ obviously denotes sequencing of actions. Finally in the probability interpretation ⊗ can be used to compute the overall probability of nested probabilities. For example [.6][.5]F ⇒ [.3]F.

The inverse operation ~ we are going to introduce now is useful for turning negative information into positive information using the equivalence ¬[p]F ⇔ $[\sim p]^+\neg F$. The motivation comes again from the probabilistic interpretation where we want to express something like: if it is not the case that F holds in at least p% of all worlds then ¬F must hold in *more* than 100-p % of all worlds. This schema, however holds only under a number of restrictions to the access function (which are fulfilled in the probabilistic application). Therefore we first introduce a couple of additional notions.

Definition 8 For a set A of sets let
basis(A) $=_{def}$ {B ∈ A | there is no subset of B in A}.
u-cl(A,$\mathcal{U}$) $=_{def}$ $\{B \cup C \mid B \in A, C \in 2^{\mathcal{U}}\}$,
i.e. u-cl(A,$\mathcal{U}$) contains all supersets in $\mathcal{U}$ of all its sets.
Hence an access function φ in a frame $\Phi = (\mathcal{W}, \mathcal{P}, \varphi)$ is upwardly closed iff u-cl($\varphi(p,\mathcal{U}),\mathcal{W}$) = $\varphi(p,\mathcal{U})$. Let
$\overline{\varphi}(p,\mathcal{U})) =_{def}$ u-cl($\{\mathcal{U}\setminus\mathcal{V} \mid \mathcal{V}\in$ basis($\varphi(p,\mathcal{U})$)$\}$, $\mathcal{W}$).
An access function φ is called

- **restricting** iff basis($\varphi(p,\mathcal{U})$) $\subseteq 2^{\mathcal{U}}$, i.e. φ yields subsets of $\mathcal{U}$.
- **covering** iff it is restricting and for all $\mathcal{V}\in$ basis($\varphi(p, \mathcal{U})$) all other subsets of $\mathcal{U}$ with the same cardinality as $\mathcal{V}$ are also in $\varphi(p, \mathcal{U})$.

The formal semantics of the $[p]^+$ operator is:
$\Im \models [p]^+F$ iff F holds in a proper superset of some set $\mathcal{V}\in\varphi(p, \mathcal{U})$. ♦

Theorem 9 For all frames $\Phi = (\mathcal{W}, \mathcal{P}, \varphi)$ *with upwardly closed and covering access function* φ the following statements are equivalent:

1) For all formulae F: $\Phi \models \neg[p]F \Leftrightarrow [\sim p]^+\neg F$
2) For all $p\in\mathcal{P}$, for all $\mathcal{U}$: $\overline{\varphi}(p,\mathcal{U}) = \varphi(\sim p, \mathcal{U})$.

Proof: "1→2, ⊆ part": Let $\mathcal{V}\in\overline{\varphi}(p,\mathcal{U})$.
Case 1: $\mathcal{V}\in$ basis($\overline{\varphi}(p,\mathcal{U})$), i.e. there is a $\mathcal{V}^c \in \varphi(p, \mathcal{U})$ with $\mathcal{V} = \mathcal{V}^c\setminus\mathcal{U}$. If $\mathcal{V}^c = \emptyset$ then $\mathcal{V} = \mathcal{U}\in\varphi(\sim p, \mathcal{U})$ because φ is restricting and $\varphi(\sim p, \mathcal{U})$ is upwardly closed. Therefore assume $\mathcal{V}^c \neq \emptyset$. Take a predicate F and a Φ-based interpretation $\Im$ where ¬F holds exactly in a set $\mathcal{V}\cup\{w\} \neq \mathcal{V}$. That means F holds only in a proper subset of $\mathcal{V}^c$. Since $\mathcal{V}^c\in$ basis($\varphi(p, \mathcal{U})$), no proper subsets of $\mathcal{V}^c$ are in $\varphi(p, \mathcal{U})$. Therefore $\Im$ does not satisfy [p]F, but, by 1) $\Im$ satisfies $[\sim p]^+\neg F$, i.e. ¬F holds in a proper superset $\mathcal{V}''$ of some set $\mathcal{V}' \in \varphi(\sim p, \mathcal{U})$. Since ¬F holds exactly in $\mathcal{V}\cup\{w\}$, $\mathcal{V}' \subseteq \mathcal{V}\cup\{w\}$, and therefore $|\mathcal{V}'| \leq |\mathcal{V}|$. Since φ is covering, $\varphi(\sim p, \mathcal{U})$ contains a subset of $\mathcal{V}$ and with φ being upwardly closed, we obtain $\mathcal{V} \in \varphi(\sim p, \mathcal{U})$.
Case 2: If $\mathcal{V}\notin$ basis($\overline{\varphi}(p,\mathcal{U})$)) there is a subset of $\mathcal{V}$ in basis($\overline{\varphi}(p,\mathcal{U})$)) which by case 1 is also in $\varphi(\sim p(p), \mathcal{U})$ and because φ is upwardly closed, $\mathcal{V}\in\varphi(\sim p(p), \mathcal{U})$.
"1→2, ⊇ part": Let $\mathcal{V}\in\varphi(\sim p(p),\mathcal{U})$ and $\mathcal{V}^c = \mathcal{U}\setminus\mathcal{V}$. If $\mathcal{V}^c = \emptyset$ then again $\mathcal{V} = \mathcal{U}\in\overline{\varphi}(p,\mathcal{U})$). Therefore assume $\mathcal{V}\neq\emptyset$. Take a Φ-based interpretation $\Im$ where ¬F holds exactly in a set $\mathcal{V}\cup\{w\}\neq\mathcal{V}$. Thus, $\Im$ satisfies $[\sim p]^+\neg F$ and with 1) ¬[p]F as well. If there was a $\mathcal{V}' \in$ basis($\varphi(p),\mathcal{U}$) with $|\mathcal{V}'| \leq |\mathcal{U}\setminus(\mathcal{V}\cup\{w\})|$ then coveringness and upward closedness would enforce $\mathcal{U}\setminus(\mathcal{V}\cup\{w\}) \in \varphi(p,\mathcal{U})$. In this case, however, F is satisfied in $\mathcal{U}\setminus(\mathcal{V}\cup\{w\})$ which contradicts ¬[p]F. Therefore for all $\mathcal{V}'\in$ basis($\varphi(p,\mathcal{U})$) $|\mathcal{V}'| \geq |\mathcal{V}^c|$ and $|\mathcal{U}\setminus\mathcal{V}'| \leq |\mathcal{V}|$. Coveringness and upward closedness of φ now yields $\mathcal{V}\in\overline{\varphi}(p,\mathcal{U})$.
"2→1, ⇒ part": Let $\Im$ be a Φ-based interpretation with actual world set $\mathcal{U}$, and let $\Im$ satisfy ¬[p]F. Let $\mathcal{N}$ be the set of $\mathcal{U}$'s subsets satisfying ¬F. $\mathcal{N}$ can be ordered by ⊂. Since all elements of $\mathcal{N}$ are subsets of $\mathcal{U}$, every ordered chain in $\mathcal{N}$ has a maximal element. Applying the lemma of Zorn we obtain a maximal element $\mathcal{U}'\in\mathcal{N}$ and ¬F holds in $\mathcal{U}'$. That means every $\mathcal{V}\in\varphi(p,\mathcal{U})$ must intersect $\mathcal{U}'$, otherwise [p]F would hold. Since φ is covering, there is a $\mathcal{V}\in$ basis($\varphi(p,\mathcal{U})$) with $\mathcal{V}^c = \mathcal{U}\setminus\mathcal{V} \subset \mathcal{U}'$. Furthermore $\mathcal{V}^c \in \overline{\varphi}(p,\mathcal{U}) = \varphi(\sim p,\mathcal{U})$ (by 2) and therefore ¬F holds in a proper superset of $\mathcal{V}^c \in \varphi(\sim p, \mathcal{U})$. Thus, $[\sim p]^+\neg F$ is satisfied as well.
"2→1, ⇐ part": Assume $[\sim p]^+\neg F$ holds, i.e. ¬F holds in a proper superset of some $\mathcal{V}\in$ basis($\varphi(\sim p, \mathcal{U})$). Using 2) we obtain $\mathcal{V}^c = \mathcal{U}\setminus\mathcal{V}\in$ basis($\overline{\varphi}(p,\mathcal{U})$). Every set satisfying F must be a proper subset of $\mathcal{V}^c$ and cannot be in ~($\varphi(p,\mathcal{U}),\mathcal{U}$). Therefore, ¬[p]F must hold as well. ♦

The most obvious meaning the inverse function can have is in the probability interpretation. In this case ~p is defined as 1-p. This means e.g. ¬[.6]F ⇒ $[.4]^+\neg F$, i.e. if it is not the case that in at least 60% of all cases F holds then its negation must hold in at least 40% of all cases. There is an analogous meaning in the temporal case where the interval lengths are determined relative to the actual interval.

Conclusion

We have presented an extended possible worlds semantics for modal logics. It is based on the idea of neighbourhood semantics and it supports the incorporation of correlations between different parameters into the logic in applications requiring parameterized modal operators. This permits new applications of the idea of possible worlds semantics. For each application, the theory we have presented gives a concrete guidance for the development of the parameter structure and the corresponding operations on these parameters.

In particular there is an interpretation as a probabilistic logic where the modal operator [p]F expresses that F holds in at least p*100% of all cases. Since the logic is full first order, probability values and quantifiers can be arbitrarily mixed. Non-numerical parameters are also allowed.

The way to develop applications of our general framework is as follows: As usual in modal logic, truth is defined relative to a class of frames. For each application there is a class of frames which best approximates the intuition behind the application. The buttons we can turn in order to specify the class of frames are the properties of the access functions and the properties of the parameter structure. The weak homomorphism conditions in the statements 2 of the theorems 3-9, however, set the limits on these manipulations. The stronger we restrict the class of parameter structures we allow in an application, the stronger we restrict the class of access functions. Therefore it has always to be proved that there is still at least one access function that satisfies these weak homomorphism conditions. Typically, however, we proceed the other way round. We define a class of access functions first. Then we have to look how far we can restrict the class of parameter structures without further restricting the class of access functions.

There are of course still a lot of things to do. An additional implication $\mapsto$ can be introduced which is more natural e.g. in the probabilistic application. It permits the interpretation of $P \mapsto [.2]Q$ as "Q holds in 20 % of the cases where P holds".

A logic without a calculus is as useless as a programming language without an interpreter or compiler. Therefore the most important step is to develop a calculus for this logic. Experience with classical (first order) modal logics has shown that it is no good idea to develop a calculus operating on the original logic directly. Therefore we aim at a translation method which permits the translation of modal formulae into predicate logic such that standard predicate logic deduction methods can be applied [Ohlbach 88, Herzig 89, Fariñas & Herzig 90]. Applied to our case the method translates for example a formula [p]Q into $\exists X\ \forall x\ x \in X(p) \Rightarrow Q'(x)$. The interpretation of this translated formula is: X is a function which, applied to p yields a particular set of functions x mapping the actual world to some world where the predicate Q' holds.

Since our logic has no built in assumptions at all it contains none of the paradoxes, other theories of certainty suffer from. Moreover, it should be possible to axiomatize the other theories within our framework. For example the statistic probability of independent events multiplies whereas we have the logically sound, but sometimes too weak minimal solution max(0, p+q-1). We can however easily add an axiom $\forall p,q\ [p]P \land [q]Q \Rightarrow [p*q](P \land Q)$ such that for particular P and Q where $[p*q](P \land Q)$ can be derived, this subsumes the built in inference $[\max(0, p+q-1)]\ (P \land Q)$. We have to investigate how far we can go in this direction.

References

[Auffray & Enjalbert 89] Y. Auffray, P. Enjalbert. *Modal Theorem Proving: An Equational Viewpoint*. IJCAI, 1989.

[Bundy 84] A. Bundy. *Incidence Calculus: A Mechanism for Probabilistic Reasoning*. Research Paper No. 216, Dept. of Artificial Intelligence, Edinburgh University, 1984.

[Chellas 80] B.F. Chellas. *Modal logic - An Introduction*. Cambridge University Press, 1980.

[Cohn 87] A.G. Cohn. *A More Expressive Formulation of Many-Sorted Logic*. Journal of Automated Reasoning 3,2, pp. 113-200, 1987.

[Fagin & Halpern 88] R. Fagin, J.Y. Halpern. *Belief, Awareness and Limited Reasoning*. Artificial Intelligence 34, pp. 39-76, 1988.

[Fariñas & Herzig 89] L. Fariñas, A. Herzig. *Deterministic Modal Logics for Automated Deduction*. ECAI, 1989.

[Fitting 83] M.C. Fitting. *Proof Methods for Modal and Intuitionistic Logics*. Vol. 169 of Synthese Library, D. Reidel Publishing Company, 1983.

[Frost 86] R.A. Frost. *Introduction to Knowledge Base Systems*, Collins, 1976.

[Grätzer 79] G. Grätzer. *Universal Algebra*. Springer, 1979.

[Halpern 89] J. Halpern. *An Analysis of First-Order Logics of Probability*. IJCAI, 1989.

[Herzig 89] A. Herzig. *Raisonnement automatique en logique modale et algorithmes d'unification*. Thèse de doctorat de l'Université Paul-Sabatier de Toulouse, 1989.

[Hughes & Cresswell 86] G. Hughes, M. Cresswell. *A Companion to Modal Logic*. Methuen & Co., 1986.

[Kripke 59] S. Kripke. *A Completeness Theorem in Modal Logic*. J. of Symbolic Logic, Vol 24, 1959, pp 1-14.

[Kripke 63] S. Kripke. *Semantical analysis of modal logic I, normal propositional calculi*. Zeitschr. für math. Logik und Grundlagen der Mathematik, Vol. 9, 1963, pp 67-96.

[Ohlbach 88] H.J. Ohlbach. *A Resolution Calculus for Modal Logics*. Proc. of 9th CADE, Argonne, Springer LNCS 310, pp. 500-516, 1988.
Full version: SEKI Report SR-88-08, FB Informatik, Univ. of Kaiserslautern, Germany, 1988.

[Rautenberg 79] W. Rautenberg. *Klassische und nichtklassische Áussagenlogik*, Vieweg Verlag, Braunschweig 1979.

[Schafer 76] G. Schafer. *A Mathematical Theory of Evidence*. Princeton University Press.

[Schmidt-Schauß 89] M. Schmidt-Schauß. *Computational Aspects of an Order-Sorted Logic with Term Declarations*. Springer Lecture Notes in AI 395, 1989.

[Shortcliff & Buchanan 75] E.H. Shortcliff and B.G. Buchanan. *A Model of Inexact Reasoning in Medicine*. Mathematical Bioscience 23, pp. 351-379.

[Walther 87] C. Walther. *A Many-sorted Calculus Based on Resolution and Paramodulation*. Research Notes in Artifical Intelligence, Pitman Ltd., London, M. Kaufmann Inc., Los Altos, 1987.

[Zadeh 78] L. A. Zadeh, *Fuzzy Sets as a Basis for a Theory of Possibility*. in Fuzzy Sets and Systems, North Holland.

Measuring and Improving the Effectiveness of Representations

Russell Greiner*
Department of Computer Science
University of Toronto
Toronto, Ontario M5S 1A4
greiner@cs.toronto.edu

Charles Elkan†
Department of Computer Science
University of California, San Diego
La Jolla, California 92093-0114
elkan@cs.ucsd.edu

Abstract

This report discusses what it means to claim that a representation is an effective encoding of knowledge. We first present dimensions of merit for evaluating representations, based on the view that usefulness is a behavioral property, and is necessarily relative to a specified task. We then provide methods (based on results from mathematical statistics) for reliably measuring effectiveness empirically, and hence for comparing different representations. We also discuss weak but guaranteed methods of improving inadequate representations. Our results are an application of the ideas of formal learning theory to concrete knowledge representation formalisms.

1 Introduction

A principal aim of research in knowledge representation and reasoning is to design good formalisms for representing knowledge about the world. This paper gives operational criteria for evaluating the goodness of a "representation".[1] Many areas of AI research can use these results. For example, many papers on nonmonotonic logic [Reiter, 1987] implicitly or explicitly make the claim that one formalism leads to *better* representations than the others. Similarly, the aim of an explanation-based learning (EBL) system [Mitchell *et al.*, 1986; DeJong and Mooney, 1986; DeJong, 1988] is to transform one problem-solving representation into a *better* one. However these articles do not specify precisely what it means to say that one representation is better than another. This paper addresses this shortcoming.

Our research has a pragmatic objective: to develop methods for deciding, for example, what type of representation should be installed in Robbie the Robot to enable it to retrieve keys located several miles away. The criteria for Robbie's success are fundamentally behavioral — what is critical is the correctness of Robbie's interactions with the world. This paper therefore adopts an "external" perspective, in which the goodness of a representation depends on its observable outputs.

One alternative perspective is worth mentioning. The "internal" perspective asks questions about a representation, such as whether it is elegant, concise, or simple. These properties may be desirable for certain tasks, such as communicating information to another agent.[2] However, while it is possible to provide operational criteria for evaluating internal properties of a representation, these properties necessarily reflect some subjective choices, and their correlation with the usefulness of a representation is usually difficult to gauge. External criteria, on the other hand, can directly guide the design of useful AI systems.

So, what behavioral features do good representations exhibit? Accuracy and coverage are two: everything else held equal, a representation should state only true facts,

*Supported by an Operating Grant from Canada's Natural Science and Engineering Research Council. Both authors would like to thank William Cohen, Dave Mitchell and the anonymous referees for their useful comments.

†Supported by a grant from the Powell foundation. This research was performed while at the University of Toronto.

[1] "Representation" is an abbreviation for "representational system", which refers to a process that answers questions; see Section 2. *N.b.*, it is not just a data structure, but will include a reasoning process as well.

[2] Much of the work on nonmonotonic formalisms is motivated by internal criteria of goodness. The notorious frame problem, in its simplest guise, is to find a formalism that admits concise representations of actions and their effects; and conciseness is an internal criterion.

and it should state as many true facts as possible. Timeliness is another important property: an accurate answer to a question can be worthless if the answer arrives too late. (The correct information that "stock X will go up tomorrow" is useless unless it arrives before the end of today's trading.) In general we have to settle for representations that are not both universally accurate and fast; *c.f.*, [Nagel and Newman, 1958; Simon, 1981; Levesque and Brachman, 1985]. Any single-valued metric for evaluating representations must embody decisions as to the relative importance of accuracy, coverage, and timeliness. The tradeoffs chosen will depend on the context: for example, fast responses are more important when predicting future events than in most design tasks. This measure must also be relative to the anticipated set of problems. (*E.g.*, it may be acceptable for a representation to return incorrect answers to certain questions, but only if those questions occur very rarely; hence, we need to know how often those questions will appear.)

This report shows how to define measures of the effectiveness of a representation, how to score representations according to these measures, and how to transform representations in ways that increase their scores. Section 2 discusses the dimensions of merit just mentioned and proposes combined utility measures. Sections 3 and 4 show how to use a set of observations to determine with confidence whether a representation is acceptable, and to improve a "deficient" representation, or even to find an approximately optimal representation, with high probability.

2 Framework

Our aim here is not to debate what representations really are; as a working definition, we take it that a representation is some sort of system capable of answering questions about the world. Mathematically, a representation is a function that maps queries to answers. In practice, representations are typically combinations of a data structure encoding aspects of the outside world and an inference procedure; see Section 4 for examples.

Our concern is with the effectiveness of a representation as perceived by an external observer, who wants to use the representation to perform some task. Here, performing a task involves asking the representation questions and receiving its answers. Formally, we assume that there is a set $\mathcal{Q}$ of all relevant questions that the representation may be asked.

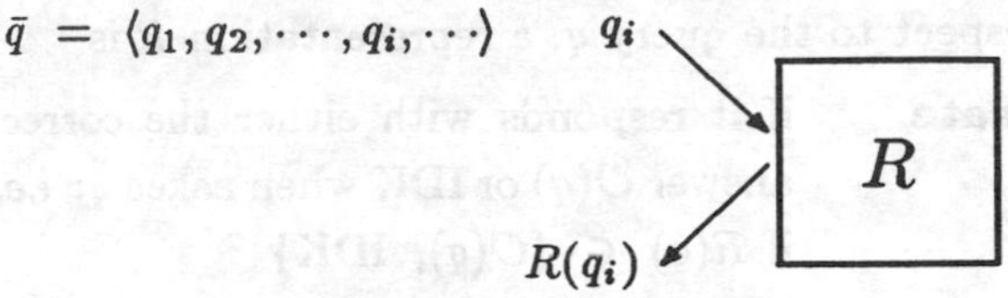

Figure 1: General view of a representation.

In Figure 1, R is the name of a representation that takes as input a sequence of queries $\bar{q} = \langle q_1, q_2, \ldots, q_i, \ldots \rangle$ and after each query q_i, produces a candidate answer $R(q_i)$. Each q_i is drawn randomly from $\mathcal{Q}$ according to an arbitrary, stationary probability distribution.

For simplicity we shall assume that the response to any query is one of {Yes, No, IDK}, where IDK is read as "I don't know." In order to talk about the accuracy and coverage of representations, we need a specification of when responses are correct. Formally, we posit the existence of an oracle, $\mathcal{O}(\cdot)$, that maps each query onto its unique correct answer Yes or No.[3] Finally, to discuss the speed of a representation, we need a time function $\tau(R, q_i)$ that returns the time required by R to respond to the query q_i.[4]

One example of a representation is a set of axioms in any standard logic, together with an appropriate inference procedure. If the collection of axioms is insufficient, or if the inference procedure is incomplete, then the representation's response to some queries may be IDK. If some of the axioms in the set are false, or if the inference procedure is unsound, then some Yes or No answers may be incorrect.[5]

Dimensions of merit: Criteria for the effectiveness of a representation depend on the expected use of the representation. Some tasks require complete accuracy, while others can allow some inaccuracy in exchange for increased efficiency, and so on. Nevertheless, it is possible to identify some orthogonal dimensions of merit.

[3]The existence of $\mathcal{O}(\cdot)$ presupposes that queries have unique answers. This condition could be relaxed. In addition, the answers to questions could also provide extra information, such as a witness for an existential query, or information about the derivation path used to solve a problem. See [Greiner and Elkan, 1991].

[4]We could use the τ function to deal with resource requirements in general, including space usage, power consumption, etc., as well as time.

[5]If the logic used by the representation has a model-theoretic semantics, the notional oracle that defines the correct answers of queries can be identified with an intended model.

With respect to the query q, a representation R is

accurate if it responds with either the correct answer $\mathcal{O}(q)$ or IDK when asked q: *i.e.*, if $R(q) \in \{\mathcal{O}(q), \text{IDK}\}$

categorical if it responds either Yes or No but not IDK: *i.e.*, if $R(q) \in \{\text{Yes}, \text{No}\}$

t-efficient if, when asked q, it responds in at most t time units: *i.e.*, if $\tau(R, q) \leq t$.

These three properties are orthogonal, in the sense that a representation can possess any combination of them. As a simple example, the "ignorant" representation that immediately answers every question with IDK, is universally accurate and ϵ-efficient for some small ϵ, but it is sadly uncategorical.

The three dimensions of merit listed above are not exhaustive: *i.e.*, they do not span the space of external criteria of merit for representations. In particular, [Segre, 1988] identifies a number of further dimensions of merit that are important if the world being modeled by the representation is uncertain. Our dimensions are still quite general; we show below that linear combinations cover many standard situations.

Utility measures: A utility measure evaluates a representation with respect to the set $\mathcal{Q}$ of all questions it will be asked. Taking into account the probability distribution over $\mathcal{Q}$, the measure $\mathcal{M}(R)$ of a representation R is defined as the expected value of $g_{\mathcal{M}}$ over $\mathcal{Q}$, where $g_{\mathcal{M}}$ is a function that returns the score of R on a single query; the arguments of $g_{\mathcal{M}}$ are the query, its correct answer, the representation's answer to the query, and the time required. If $\bar{q}$ is an infinite sequence of queries, such that each element of $\bar{q}$ is drawn independently from $\mathcal{Q}$ according to the fixed probability distribution, then $\mathcal{M}(R)$ can also be defined by the following equation:

$$\mathcal{M}(R) = \lim_{k\to\infty} \frac{1}{k} \sum_{i=1}^{k} g_{\mathcal{M}}(q_i, R(q_i), \mathcal{O}(q_i), \tau(R, q_i)).$$

We shall only consider utility measures whose scoring functions are bounded above and below; *i.e.*, in the class U_λ for some $\lambda \in \mathcal{R}^+$, where

$$U_\lambda = \left\{ g_{\mathcal{M}} \mid \begin{array}{l} \exists a \in \mathcal{R}^+ \, \forall R \, \forall q \in \mathcal{Q}. \\ a \leq g_{\mathcal{M}}(q_i, R(q_i), \mathcal{O}(q_i), \tau(R, q_i)) \leq a + \lambda \end{array} \right\}$$

This property is technically convenient for proving the results of the following sections, but similar results hold for the class U of all utility measures.

Since a perfectly accurate, categorical, and efficient representation is usually unobtainable, and the relative importance of the three dimensions depends on the task for which the representation is to be used, we now define a class of utility measures that incorporate task-specific tradeoffs. This class consists of weighted linear combinations of an accuracy value, a categoricity value, and a timeliness value; as shown below:

$$g(q, R(q), \mathcal{O}(q), \tau(R, q)) =$$

$$\left\{ \begin{array}{ll} \alpha_+ & \text{if } R(q_i) = \mathcal{O}(q_i) \\ -\alpha_0 & \text{if } R(q_i) = \text{IDK} \\ -\alpha_- & \text{otherwise} \end{array} \right\} - \alpha_t \cdot \tau(R, q_i).$$

This equation characterizes the entire class of bounded, linearly separable utility measures, where the time penalty is linear.[6] There are several important special cases: Setting $\alpha_t = 0$ indicates that efficiency is unimportant; setting $\alpha_0 = \alpha_-$ discriminates only between correct and incorrect answers, etc.

3 Appraising and Comparing Representations

Appraising utility: Suppose someone hands you a black-box representation and claims that the $\mathcal{M}$ value of this representation is above some threshold. How confident should you be with that assessment? There are clearly several approaches. First, you might trust the supplier of the representation — some people really do think they are purchasing the Brooklyn Bridge. Second, you could analyze the internals of the representation. For example, imagine that the representation's answers are the result of running a sound proof procedure on a collection of true facts. You can then be completely confident that all its answers will be accurate. If you know, furthermore, that all facts have a certain syntactic form (*e.g.*, all are DATALOG definite clauses), you can know that all answers are obtainable in polynomial time. The remainder of this section presents a third approach, in which a sequence of examples of the representation's behavior is used to approximate its real utility.

Our objective is to determine the worth of a representation *for some specific application*; that is, we want to know how it will perform over the particular distribu-

[6] We assume that $\tau(R, q)$ "tops off" at some upper limit. Notice this assumption holds for all of the utility measures discussed in Section 4.

tion of queries it will eventually see. The only empirical method that is guaranteed to provide this information involves observing the representation perform throughout its entire lifetime; a most impractical approach. Fortunately, however, we can obtain good estimates, based on a small set of samples, using "Chernoff bounds" [Chernoff, 1952]:

> Let $\{X_i\}$ be a set of independent, identically distributed random variables with mean μ, whose values are all in the range $[a, a+\lambda]$; and let $S_n = \frac{1}{n}\sum_{j=1}^{n} X_j$ be the sample mean of n variables. We expect this average to tend to the population mean, μ, as $n \to \infty$. Chernoff bounds tell us the probable rate of convergence: the probability that "S_n is more than $\mu+\beta$" goes to 0 exponentially fast as n increases; and, for a fixed n, exponentially as β increases. Formally, [Bollobás, 1985, p. 12]
>
> $$Pr[\, S_n > \mu + \beta \,] \;\leq\; e^{-2n\left(\frac{\beta}{\lambda}\right)^2} \qquad (1)$$

Recall now that a representation's utility is defined as the mean of its scores over its distribution of possible queries. Now suppose that the value of the scoring function is always in the range $[-3, -3+5]$, say, and that the average observed score of the representation R is $S_{1000} = 1.7$ after $n = 1000$ queries. Equation 1 says that the probability that the representation's real utility is greater than, say, $\beta = 0.25$ over the real utility is less than $e^{-2n(\beta/\lambda)^2} = e^{-2\times1000\times(\frac{0.25}{5})^2} \approx 0.0067$.

We can therefore use the performance of a representation on a sampling of queries to approximate the representation's true utility. The following lemma supplies the sample complexity required to estimate a representation's utility to high accuracy (within ϵ) with high probability (at least $1-\delta$).[7]

Lemma 1 *Let ϵ, $\delta > 0$ be given constants, R be a representation, $\mathcal{M}(\cdot) \in U_\lambda$ be a utility measure, and $\hat{\mathcal{M}}^{N_1}(R)$ be the approximation to $\mathcal{M}(\cdot)$ obtained as the average score on $N_1 \stackrel{def}{=} \lceil \frac{1}{2}\left(\frac{\lambda}{\epsilon}\right)^2 \ln\frac{2}{\delta} \rceil$ sample queries. Then*

$$Pr\left[\, |\mathcal{M}(R) - \hat{\mathcal{M}}^{N_1}(R)| \,\leq\, \epsilon \,\right] \;\geq\; 1-\delta.$$

This means we can approximate the representation's true utility, with provably high probability to arbitrarily high accuracy, by watching its behavior over enough samples. Notice the estimate $\hat{\mathcal{M}}^{N_1}(R)$, like the real $\mathcal{M}(R)$, depends on the distribution of queries that R will encounter; it therefore is more likely to provide a good indication of R's true utility than we would get by testing R on worst case queries, a set of concocted queries, a sample drawn randomly from a uniform distribution [Goldberg, 1979], or any particular collection of "benchmark challenge problems" [Keller, 1987].

[7] [Greiner and Elkan, 1991] provides the proofs for all of the lemmas and theorems presented in this short paper.

Comparing representations: If we had an analytic technique for evaluating the utility of representations with respect to a distribution of queries, and knew this distribution of queries, we could directly determine which of two representations was better. In general we have neither analytic technique nor distribution, but we can fall back on an empirical technique — of "running" both contenders; *i.e.*, finding the "paired-t confidence" [Law and Kelton, 1982].

Lemma 2 *Let $\delta > 0$ be a given constant, and $\mathcal{M}(\cdot) \in U_\lambda$ be a utility measure. Given any two representations, R_1 and R_2, let $\hat{\mathcal{M}}^N(R_1)$ (respectively $\hat{\mathcal{M}}^N(R_2)$) be the approximation to $\mathcal{M}(R_1)$ (respectively $\mathcal{M}(R_2)$) obtained as the average score on $N \in \mathcal{Z}^+$ samples. If*

$$\hat{\mathcal{M}}^N(R_2) - \hat{\mathcal{M}}^N(R_1) \quad > \quad \lambda\sqrt{\frac{2}{N}\ln\frac{1}{\delta}}$$

then $\mathcal{M}(R_2) > \mathcal{M}(R_1)$ holds with confidence $\geq 1-\delta$. (Hence, we may believe that R_2 is $\mathcal{M}$-better than R_1).

4 Improving a Representation

This section discusses various ways to improve a deficient representation. The lemmas of the previous section directly suggest a "generate and test" procedure for improving representations. Other approaches search the space of alternative representations more intelligently. They use a set of "training examples" (perhaps $\langle q_i, \mathcal{O}(q_i)\rangle$ query/answer pairs) to construct a new representation that is $\mathcal{M}$-better than the original, with provably high probability.

Due to space limitations, this short paper can only summarize a few individual algorithms associated with various type of utility measures. The extended paper, [Greiner and Elkan, 1991], presents these algorithms (and others) in detail, and proves their correctness.

Improving efficiency (preserving accuracy): Suppose that a representation is producing the correct answers, but too slowly. As an example, consider the knowledge base shown in Figure 2, that states that we will buy a car if it is fast or cheap. Furthermore, our

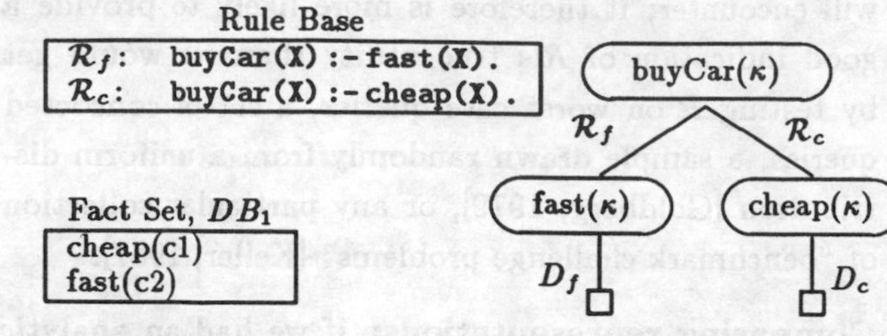
Rule Base
$\mathcal{R}_f$: buyCar(X) :- fast(X).
$\mathcal{R}_c$: buyCar(X) :- cheap(X).
Fact Set, DB_1
cheap(c1)
fast(c2)
buyCar(κ)
$\mathcal{R}_f$
$\mathcal{R}_c$
fast(κ)
cheap(κ)
D_f
D_c

Figure 2: Rule base and associated inference graph.

representation R_1 searches this "inference graph" in a left-to-right order — *i.e.*, given a query **buyCar(c$_i$)** (for some constant **c$_i$**), it would first use the $\mathcal{R}_f$ rule to reduce **buyCar(c$_i$)** to the subgoal **fast(c$_i$)**, and then determine whether this proposition is in the fact set, DB_1. If so (for example in the case where the top query was **buyCar(c2)**), R_1 would return **Yes** and terminate. If not, it would then follow the $\mathcal{R}_c$ rule to the **cheap(c$_i$)** subgoal, and ask if it is in the database. R_1 would then return **Yes** or **IDK**, depending on the success of that retrieval. Here, we say that R_1's *strategy* is $\langle \mathcal{R}_f, D_f, \mathcal{R}_c, D_c \rangle$.

Now imagine we find that R_1 is relatively slow — perhaps because the queries all dealt with **c1**, meaning R_1 "wasted" its time on the $\langle \mathcal{R}_f, D_f \rangle$ path, before finding the appropriate $\langle \mathcal{R}_c, D_c \rangle$ path. One obvious proposal would be to change R_1 to a new representation, R_2, that uses the different strategy, $\langle \mathcal{R}_c, D_c, \mathcal{R}_f, D_f \rangle$. Notice this R_2 would be strictly better than R_1, if all of the queries were **buyCar(c1)**. In general, we can compute which the relative utilities of R_1 and R_2 if we know the costs of the various paths (*e.g.*, the cost of following the $\langle \mathcal{R}_c, D_c \rangle$ path), and the frequencies of the various possible queries (*e.g.*, that 80% of the queries would be **buyCar(c1)**, 5% would be **buyCar(c2)**, and 15% would be **buyCar(c)** for some **c** such that **buyCar(c)** is not provable; see [Greiner, 1991]).

In general, we do not know this distribution information. We can, however, use a set of samples to estimate it, and use this information to determine whether R_2 would be better than R_1, with high confidence. In fact, we can obtain reasonable estimates of this distribution by running R_1 *alone*; see [Greiner and Cohen, 1991a]. That paper also shows how to extend this learning system to handle more elaborate classes of inference graphs (with many different paths from query to retrieval, involving conjunctions, etc.), and other types of modifications (besides simply rearranging the strategy). It also

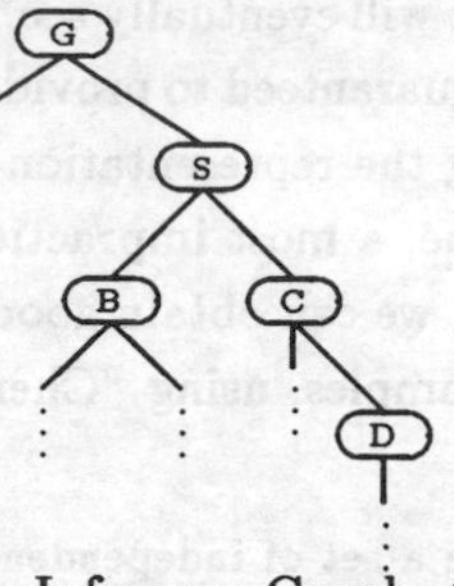

Figure 3: Inference Graph, G_M

presents an efficient algorithm, PALO, that can "hill-climb" in the space of representations, reaching a representation that is, with high probability, close to a local optimum. The PAO system [Greiner and Orponen, 1991] is another variant of this idea: it uses a set of training examples to identify a strategy that is, with high probability, arbitrarily close to the globally optimal strategy.

Increasing efficiency by decreasing accuracy: The previous subsection deals with speedup learning (performing only "symbol-level" modifications [Dietterich, 1986]), whose objective is new performance systems that are as accurate and as categorical as the original system, but (we hope) faster. This subsection removes this constraint, and considers techniques that are allowed to produce systems that are less accurate or less categorical. The utility-based approach introduced in this paper allows us to quantify the tradeoffs among the various performance attributes of a representation. In particular, the relative values of α_+ and α_- versus α_t specify how much accuracy or categoricity we are willing to lose, in exchange for how much improvement in speed.

As a simple example of an application of this idea, consider the G_M inference graph shown in Figure 3. As above, each node represents a (sub)goal, and each arc, a rule that reduces one goal to a subgoal. Some arcs are "probabilistic", meaning that whether a representation can traverse such an arc can depend on the contents of the fact set, or the particular query posed, etc. A representation returns **Yes** if it reachs any leaf node. (More details appear in [Greiner and Cohen, 1991a].)

The R_1 representation answers G(·) queries by exploring the entire G_M graph. Imagine the subgraph under the B node is extensive, meaning it is expensive to search, and furthermore, that R_1 seldom find answers in that subgraph, over the distribution of G(·) queries.

Now consider the R_2 representation, which traverses

some of the arcs in G_M, in the same order as R_1; but R_2 completely skips B and its children. Of course, this R_2 will not reach any node under B, and so can produce an incorrect answer. It will, however, require less time to produce that answer. Is it better than R_1? This depends on the relative values of α_t versus $\alpha_+ + \alpha_0$, and on the actual cost of searching under B, versus the frequency with which solutions will appear there.

We can consider this "delete subgraph" process as an operation. As above, we can provide conditions under which it (is likely to) produce a superior new representation, and build a PALO-like learning system that hill-climbs in this space to a representation that is, with arbitrarily high probability, close to local optimum.

Two final notes: [1] We can use this same approach to deal with SAT problems: here, the inference graph is a complete binary tree, where each node corresponds to a literal, and one descending arc indicates that this literal should be positive, and other, that is should be negative. [2] Several previous systems have implicitly dealt with this theme, of gaining efficiency at the expense of accuracy or categoricity; see [Cohen, 1990], [Subramanian and Genesereth, 1987], [Levesque, 1986; Selman and Kautz, 1988; Etherington *et al.*, 1989; Borgida and Etherington, 1989], [Selman and Kautz, 1991]. None, however, have explicitly quantified the tradeoffs.

Improving accuracy (ignoring efficiency): One standard issue with default logic is the "multiple extension problem" [Reiter, 1987]: For example, knowing the facts $\mathcal{F}_1 = \{B(T), P(T)\}$ and the defaults $\mathcal{D}_1 = \left\{ d_1\!: \frac{B(x):\,F(x)}{F(x)},\ d_2\!: \frac{P(x):\,\neg F(x)}{\neg F(x)} \right\}$, one could conclude either F(T), based on the first fact and first default, d_1; or $\neg$F(T), based on the second fact and second default, d_2.[8]

One way around this problem involves prioritizing the defaults [Przymusiński, 1987; Brewka, 1989]. Here, for example, we could specify $d_2 \prec d_1$, meaning we should use the d_2 default if it applies, and only if it does not should we consider d_1. Hence, R_1, the default-based representation that uses this ordering, would conclude $\neg$F(T) as desired, and not F(T).

Unfortunately, there is not always an appropriate order of the defaults; consider, for example, the famous "Nixon diamond", based on the facts $\mathcal{F}_2 = \{Q(N), R(N)\}$ and the defaults $\mathcal{D}_2 = \left\{ d_3\!: \frac{Q(x):\,P(x)}{P(x)},\ d_4\!: \frac{R(x):\,\neg P(x)}{\neg P(x)} \right\}$. Here, one could either use d_3 to conclude P(N), or use d_4 to conclude $\neg$P(N).[9]

Which ordering is appropriate: $d_3 \prec d_4$ or $d_4 \prec d_3$? Our paper takes a pragmatic approach to answering this question: the proper order is the one that produces the correct answer most often. This, of course, depends on the distribution of queries. For example, imagine we knew that the only individual that mattered (*i.e.*, the only n such that Q(n) and R(n) held, and that appeared in any "P(n)?" query) was $\mathfrak{n}_1$, and that this $\mathfrak{n}_1$ was a pacifist — *i.e.*, the oracle (that emulates the "real world") claims P($\mathfrak{n}_1$). The "pragmatically correct" ordering, here, is $d_3 \prec d_4$, as this leads to the correct answer. Similarly, if we knew that there were many relevant individuals, but very few were pacifists, then we would know that $d_4 \prec d_3$ is appropriate.

In general, however, we do not know the distribution. [Greiner and Cohen, 1991b] presents a PAO-like algorithm that uses a set of samples to approximate the distribution, to obtain an estimate that is sufficiently close to guarantee that the total ordering based on it will be close to the global optimal, with high probability. It also shows this task to be NP-hard, even in the simple case when only a single default is used in any derivation. That paper then discusses a PALO-like hill-climbing system that finds a representation that is usually arbitrarily close to a local optimum.

We close with a few final comments. [1] Notice we are only concerned with the *accuracy* of the resulting representation, but not with its efficiency. Hence, this learning process corresponds to a utility measure with $\alpha_t = 0$. [2] The "accuracy" of the resulting representation is improved with respect to the $\mathcal{O}$ oracle. While we think of this oracle as an encoding of the real world, this is not necessary; this overall learning system can be viewed as a way of obtaining a increasingly more correct "simulation" of an arbitrary function. [3] There are other approaches to this challenge. One obvious one is to remove the defaults (here usually called "hypotheses", etc.) that are inconsistent with the data. Essentially all inductive inference systems fit into the framework; see

[8] B = "Bird"; P = "Penguin"; T = "Tweety"; F = "Fly".

[9] N = "Nixon"; Q = "Quaker"; R = "Republican"; P = "Pacifist".

[Russell and Grosof, 1987], [Haussler, 1988].

5 Conclusion

The principal claim of many papers on knowledge representation is that one proposed representation is appropriate, or that one is better than another: *e.g.*, that this axiomatization of liquids is good, or that this EBL process does produce improved problem-solvers, and so on. The work reported here provides a way for future papers to add teeth to such claims, by defining a general approach to evaluating and comparing representations. The approach is based on the position that whether a representation is appropriate, or better than another, is a *behavioral* property, that must be defined relative to a specified task. In this paper, tasks are modelled as distributions of anticipated queries, and the desired behavior of a representation is specified using a scoring function. In the spirit of traditional scientific methodology, the notion of representation usefulness is given an operational definition that has no dependence on any subjective observer.

After settling on a precise definition of usefulness, this paper provides a method for reliably (but approximately) measuring usefulness, and presents several transformations capable of improving an inadequate representation. The space of techniques for improving representations is open-ended. We hope other researchers will formulate their mechanisms in this framework, and so contribute to the growing class of useful transformations.

References

[Bollobás, 1985] B. Bollobás. *Random Graphs.* Acad. Press, 1985.

[Borgida and Etherington, 1989] A. Borgida and D. Etherington. Hierarchical knowledge bases and efficient disjunctive reasoning. In *KR-89*, 1989.

[Brewka, 1989] G. Brewka. Preferred subtheories: An extended logical framework for default reasoning. In *IJCAI-89*, 1989.

[Chernoff, 1952] H. Chernoff. A measure of asymptotic efficiency for tests of a hypothesis based on the sums of observations. *Annals of Mathematical Statistics*, 23, 1952.

[Cohen, 1990] W. Cohen. Using distribution-free learning theory to analyze chunking. In *CSCSI-90*, 1990.

[DeJong and Mooney, 1986] G. DeJong and R. Mooney. Explanation-based learning: An alternative view. *Machine Learning*, 1(2), 1986.

[DeJong, 1988] G. DeJong. AAAI workshop on Explanation-Based Learning. Sponsored by AAAI, 1988.

[Dietterich, 1986] T. Dietterich. Learning at the knowledge level. *Machine Learning*, 1(3), 1986.

[Etherington *et al.*, 1989] D. Etherington, A. Borgida, R. Brachman, and H. Kautz. Vivid knowledge and tractable reasoning: Preliminary report. In *IJCAI-89*, 1989.

[Goldberg, 1979] A. Goldberg. An average case complexity analysis of the satisfiability problem. In *Proceedings of the 4th Workshop on Automated Deduction*, 1979.

[Greiner and Cohen, 1991a] R. Greiner and W. Cohen. EBL systems that (almost) always improve performance. Technical report, Univ. of Toronto, 1991.

[Greiner and Cohen, 1991b] R. Greiner and W. Cohen. Producing more accurate theories. Technical report, Univ. of Toronto, 1991.

[Greiner and Elkan, 1991] R. Greiner and C. Elkan. Effective representations. Technical report, Univ. of Toronto, 1991.

[Greiner and Orponen, 1991] R. Greiner and P. Orponen. Probably approximately optimal derivation strategies. In *KR-91*. Morgan Kaufmann, 1991.

[Greiner, 1991] R. Greiner. Finding the optimal derivation strategy in a redundant knowledge base. *Artificial Intelligence*, 1991.

[Haussler, 1988] D. Haussler. Quantifying inductive bias: AI learning algorithms and Valiant's learning framework. *Artificial Intelligence*, 1988.

[Keller, 1987] R. Keller. Defining operationality for explanation-based learning. In *AAAI-87*, 1987.

[Law and Kelton, 1982] A. Law and W. Kelton. *Simulation Modeling and Analysis.* McGraw-Hill Book Co., 1982.

[Levesque and Brachman, 1985] H. Levesque and R. Brachman. A fundamental tradeoff in knowledge representation and reasoning. In *Readings in Knowledge Representation.* Morgan Kaufmann Publishers, Inc., 1985.

[Levesque, 1986] H. Levesque. Making believers out of computers. *Artificial Intelligence*, 30(1), 1986.

[Mitchell *et al.*, 1986] T. Mitchell, R. Keller, and S. Kedar-Cabelli. Example-based generalization: A unifying view. *Machine Learning*, 1(1), 1986.

[Nagel and Newman, 1958] E. Nagel and J. Newman. *Gödel's Proof.* New York University Press, 1958.

[Przymusiński, 1987] T. Przymusiński. On the declarative semantics of stratified deductive databases and logic programs. In *Foundations of Deductive Databases and Logic Programming.* Morgan Kaufmann Pub., Inc., 1987.

[Reiter, 1987] R. Reiter. Nonmonotonic reasoning. In *Annual Review of Computing Sciences*, volume 2. Annual Reviews Incorporated, 1987.

[Russell and Grosof, 1987] S. Russell and B. Grosof. A declarative approach to bias in concept learning. In *AAAI-87*, 1987.

[Segre, 1988] A. Segre. Operationality and real-world plans. In *AAAI Workshop on Explanation-Based Learning*, 1988.

[Selman and Kautz, 1988] B. Selman and H. Kautz. The complexity of model-preference default theories. In *CSCSI-88*, 1988.

[Selman and Kautz, 1991] B. Selman and H. Kautz. Knowledge compilation using horn approximations. In *AAAI-91*, 1991.

[Simon, 1981] H. Simon. *The Sciences of the Artificial.* M.I.T. Press, 1981.

[Subramanian and Genesereth, 1987] D. Subramanian and M. Genesereth. The relevance of irrelevance. In *IJCAI-87*, 1987.

Propositional Non-Monotonic Reasoning and Inconsistency in Symmetric Neural Networks *

Gadi Pinkas
Department of Computer Science,
Washington University,
St. Louis, MO 63130, U.S.A.

Abstract

We define a model-theoretic reasoning formalism that is naturally implemented on symmetric neural networks (like Hopfield networks or Boltzman machines). We show that every symmetric neural network, can be seen as performing a search for a satisfying model of some knowledge that is wired into the network's weights. Several equivalent languages are then shown to describe the knowledge embedded in these networks. Among them is propositional calculus extended by augmenting propositional assumptions with penalties. The extended calculus is useful in expressing default knowledge, preference between arguments, and reliability of assumptions in an inconsistent knowledge base. Every symmetric network can be described by this language and any sentence in the language is translatable into such a network. A sound and complete proof procedure supplements the model-theoretic definition and gives an intuitive understanding of the non-monotonic behavior of the reasoning mechanism. Finally, we sketch a connectionist inference engine that implements this reasoning paradigm.

1 Introduction

Recent non-monotonic (NM) systems are quite successful in capturing our intuitions about default reasoning. Most of them, however, are still plagued with intractable computational complexity, sensitivity to noise, inability to combine other sources of knowledge (like probabilities, utilities...) and inflexibility to develop personal intuitions and adjust themselves to new situations. Connectionist systems may be the missing link. They can supply us with a fast, massively parallel platform; noise tolerance can emerge from their collective computation; and their ability to learn may be used to incorporate new evidence and dynamically change the knowledge base. We shall concentrate on a restricted class of connectionist models, called symmetric networks ([Hopfield 82], [Hinton, Sejnowski 86]).

We shall demonstrate that symmetric neural networks (SNNs) are natural platforms for propositional defeasible reasoning and for noisy knowledge bases. In fact we shall show that every such network can be seen as encapsulating a body of knowledge and as performing a search for a satisfying model of that knowledge.

Our objectives in this paper are first to investigate the kind of knowledge that can be represented by those SNNs, and second, to build a connectionist inference engine capable of reasoning from incomplete and inconsistent knowledge. Proofs and detailed constructions are omitted and will appear in the extended version of the article.

2 Reasoning with World Rank Functions

We begin by giving a model-theoretic definition for an abstract reasoning formalism independently of any symbolic language. Later we shall use it to give semantics for the knowledge embedded in SNNs, and for the reasoning mechanism that will be defined.

DEFINITION **2.1** A *World Rank Function* (WRF) with respect to a set of possible worlds (models) M is a function $k : M \to \mathcal{R}$ that ranks each of the possible worlds with a number that is in $(-\infty \ldots \infty]$.[1] A WRF is *propositional* iff it is defined over the set of truth assignments (i.e., $dom(k) = \{0,1\}^n$).

DEFINITION **2.2** A model $\Omega \in M$ *satisfies* a WRF k iff it minimizes the function to a value that is less than ∞. Let Γ_k be the set of all satisfying models of WRF k. We say that k *entails* k' ($k \models k'$) iff all the models that satisfy k satisfy also k'; i.e., $\Gamma_k \subseteq \Gamma_{k'}$.

3 Connectionist energy functions

3.1 Symmetric connectionist models

Connectionist networks with symmetric weights (SNNs) use gradient descent to find a minimum for quadratic energy functions. A k-order energy function is a function

*This research was supported in part by NSF grant 22-1321 57136.

[1]The symbol ∞ denotes a real positive number that is larger than any other number mentioned explicitly in a formula (practically infinity.

$E : \{0,1\}^n \rightarrow \mathcal{R}$ that can be expressed in a sum-of-products form with product terms of up to k variables. We denote this sum-of-products form by:

$\sum_{1 \le i_1 < i_2 < \cdots < i_k \le n} w_{i_1,\ldots,i_k} x_{i_1} \cdots x_{i_k} + \sum_{1 \le i_1 < \cdots < i_{k-1} \le n} w_{i_1,\ldots,i_{k-1}} x_{i_1} \cdots x_{i_{k-1}} + \cdots + \sum_{1 \le i \le n}^{1} w_i x_i$.

Quadratic energy functions are special cases of energy functions in the form :

$$E(x_1, \ldots, x_n) = \sum_{1 \le i < j \le n} w_{ij} x_i x_j + \sum_{i \le n} w_i x_i.$$

We can arbitrarily divide the variables of an energy function into two sets: visible variables and hidden variables. An energy function with $x_1 \ldots x_n$ visible variables and $t_1 \ldots t_k$ hidden variables is denoted by $E(\vec{x}, \vec{t})$. There is a direct mapping between quadratic energy functions and SNNs that minimize them. Variables map into neuron units (nodes), and weighted terms map into weighted connections (arcs). Hyper-graphs with Sigma-Pi units can be used for minimizing high-order energy functions.

3.2 WRFs and energy functions

A SNN can be viewed as an implementation of a propositional WRF. A model is a zero/one truth-assignment to the visible variables of the function. For each such assignment we can compute a *rank* by clamping the visible variables to the zero/one values of the assignment and letting the free variables $\vec{t}$ (the hidden units) settle to values that minimize the function.

DEFINITION 3.1 The *rank* associated with an energy function $E(\vec{x}, \vec{t})$ is the function $rank_E(\vec{x}) = MIN_{\vec{t}}\{E(\vec{x}, \vec{t})\}$.

A search performed by the SNN for a global minimum may therefore be interpreted as a search for a satisfying model of the WRF $rank_E$. We will interchangeably use energy functions, rank functions and graph descriptions to represent the functional behavior of SNNs.

4 Symbolic languages to describe WRFs

Our next step is to describe symbolically the knowledge that is encapsulated in a network. We shall allow transformation from one form of knowledge representation to another, and for that purpose, we define several types of equivalence relations that preserve basic properties of the knowledge.

DEFINITION 4.1 A calculus is a triple $< \mathcal{L}, m(), M >$ where $\mathcal{L}$ is a language, M is a set of possible worlds, and $m : \mathcal{L} \rightarrow \{k \mid k \text{ is a WRF }\}$ is a function that returns for each sentence of the language $\mathcal{L}$ a WRF. $m(s)$ is called the *interpretation* of the sentence s.

Let $s, s', e, k \in \mathcal{L}$; a model Ω *satisfies* s $(\Omega \models s)$ iff it satisfies $m(s)$. Similarly, a sentence s *entails* sentence s' $(s \models s')$ iff the WRF $m(s)$ entails the WRF $m(s')$. A conjunction of a background sentence (k) with an evidence sentence (e) [2] is interpreted as the addition of their corresponding WRFs; i.e., $k, e \models s$ iff $(m(e) + m(k)) \models m(s)$.

[2] NM systems "jump" to conclusions based on evidence given, and later may retract those conclusions based on new evidence. It is convenient therefore to divide the knowledge from which we reason, to background knowledge and evidence (see [Geffner 89].

Both predicate logic and propositional logic can be viewed as calculi whose languages describe WRFs.

EXAMPLE 4.1 Propositional calculus is a triple $< \mathcal{L}, m(), \{0,1\}^n >$, where $\mathcal{L}$ is the language of propositional well formed formulae (WFFs) and $m()$ outputs the function $(\infty \times (1 - H_s))$, when given a WFF s. $H_s(\vec{x})$ is the characteristic function of the WFFs and is recursively defined as:

$H_{X_i}(\vec{x}) = X_i$
$H_{\neg s}(\vec{x}) = 1 - H_s(\vec{x})$
$H_{s_1 \vee s_2}(\vec{x}) = H_{s_1}(\vec{x}) + H_{s_2}(\vec{x}) - H_{s_1}(\vec{x}) \times H_{s_2}(\vec{x})$

The reader can easily observe that any propositional WFF describes a WRF that returns 0 for truth assignments that satisfy the WFF and ∞ for assignments that do not satisfy it.

DEFINITION 4.2 Let $s \in \mathcal{L}_1$ and $s' \in \mathcal{L}_2$ be sentences of two (possibly different) calculi $< \mathcal{L}_1, m, M >$ and $< \mathcal{L}_2, m', M >$; we define equivalence between them:

1. s is *strongly equivalent* to s' $(s \overset{s}{\approx} s')$ iff their corresponding WRFs are equal, up to a constant difference; i.e., $m(s) = m'(s') + c$. We call this equivalence "magnitude preserving" or *s*-equivalence.
2. s is weakly equivalent to s' $(s \overset{w}{\approx} s')$ iff their corresponding WRFs have the same sets of satisfying models; i.e., $\Gamma_{m(s)} = \Gamma_{m'(s')}$. We call this equivalence "minima preserving" or w-equivalence. [3]

OBSERVATION 4.1 *1. If two background sentences are strongly equivalent, then for any given evidence function e, the two corresponding WRFs entail the same set of conclusions; i.e., if $k \overset{s}{\approx} k'$ and e is* any *evidence, then for every WRF f, $(m(k) + e) \models f$ iff $(m'(k') + e) \models f$.*[4]

2. If two sentences k, k' are weakly equivalent, then for every WRF f, $m(k) \models f$ iff $m'(k') \models f$. We can't guarantee this property to hold once we try to add evidence to both k and k'.

If all we want is to preserve the set of conclusions achievable from a piece of knowledge, we may use transformations which only preserve the minima (weak equivalence). If however we would like to be able to combine evidence to our transformed knowledge, we need to perform "magnitude preserving" transformations (strong equivalence). The transformations we use in the reminder of this paper are all "magnitude preserving".

We define now an equivalence between two calculi.

DEFINITION 4.3 A calculus $\mathcal{C}_1 =< \mathcal{L}, m, M >$ is (s-/w-) equivalent to a calculus $\mathcal{C}' =< \mathcal{L}', m', M >$ iff for every $s \in \mathcal{L}$ there exists a (s-/w-) equivalent $s' \in \mathcal{L}'$ and for every $s' \in \mathcal{L}'$ there exists a (s-/w-) equivalent $s \in \mathcal{L}$.

[3] A third equivalence, one that preserves the order of the worlds, is also possible, but is beyond the scope of this article.

[4] In addition, two strongly equivalent WRFs have the same probabilistic interpretation since $P(\Omega_1)/P(\Omega_2) = e^{(k(\Omega_1) - k(\Omega_2))} = e^{((k'(\Omega_1)+c) - (k'(\Omega_2)+c))}$.

We thus can use the language $\mathcal{L}$ to represent every WRF that is representable using the language $\mathcal{L}'$, and vice versa. In the sections to come we shall present several equivalent calculi and show that all of them describe the knowledge embedded in SNNs.

5 Calculi for describing symmetric neural networks

The algebraic notation that was used to describe energy functions as sum-of-products can be viewed as a propositional WRF. The *calculus of energy functions* is therefore $< \{E\}, m(), \{0,1\}^n >$, where $\{E\}$ is the set of all strings representing energy functions written as sum-of-products, and $m(E) = Erank_E$. Two special cases are of particular interest: the calculus of quadratic functions and the calculus of high-order energy functions with no hidden variables.

Using the algorithms given in [Pinkas 90] we can conclude that the calculus of high-order energy functions with no hidden units is strongly equivalent to the calculus of quadratic functions. Thus, we can use the language of high-order energy functions with no hidden units to describe any symmetric neural network (SNN) with arbitrary number of hidden units.

In [Pinkas 90] we also gave algorithms to convert any satisfiable WFF to a weakly equivalent quadratic energy function (of the same order of length), and every energy function to a weakly equivalent satisfiable WFF. As a result, propositional calculus is weakly equivalent to the calculus of quadratic energy functions and can be used as a high-level language to describe SNNs. However, two limitations exist: 1) The algorithm that converts an energy function to a satisfiable WFF may generate an exponentially long WFF; and 2) Although the WFF and the energy function have the same set of satisfying models, evidence can not be added and the a probabilistic interpretation is not preserved.

In the next section we define a new logic calculus that is strongly equivalent to the calculus of energy functions and does not suffer from these two limitations.

6 Penalty calculus

We now extend propositional calculus by augmenting assumptions with penalties (as in [Derthick 88]). The extended calculus is able to deal with an inconsistent knowledge base (noise, errors in observations...) and will be used as a framework for defeasible reasoning.

DEFINITION 6.1 A *Penalty Logic WFF* (PLOFF) ψ is a finite set of pairs. Each pair is composed of a real positive number (including ∞), called *penalty*, and a standard propositional WFF, called an *assumption* ; i.e., $\psi = \{< \rho_i, \varphi_i >| \rho_i \in \mathcal{R}^+, \varphi_i$ is a WFF, $i = 1...n\}$.
The *violation-rank* of a PLOFF ψ ($Vrank_\psi(\vec{x})$) assigns a real-valued rank to each of the truth assignments. It is computed by summing the penalties for the assumptions of ψ that are violated by the assignment; i.e., $Vrank_\psi(\vec{x}) = \sum_i \rho_i H_{\neg\varphi_i}(\vec{x})$. *Penalty calculus* is the triple $< \mathcal{L}, m(), \{0,1\}^n >$, where $\mathcal{L}$ is the set of all PLOFFs and $m(\psi) = Vrank_\psi$.

We may conclude that a truth assignment $\vec{x}$, satisfies a PLOFF ψ iff it minimizes the violation-rank of ψ to a finite value (we call such models, "preferred models"). A sentence ψ therefore semantically entails φ iff any preferred model of ψ is also a preferred model of φ.

7 Proof-theory for penalty calculus

Although our inference engine will be based on the model-theoretic definition, a proof procedure still gives us valuable intuition about the reasoning process and about the role of the penalties.

DEFINITION 7.1 T is a *sub-theory* of a PLOFF ψ if T is a consistent subset of the assumptions in ψ; i.e., $T \subseteq \{\varphi_i \mid < \rho_i, \varphi_i > \in \psi\} = \mathcal{U}_\psi$, (note that $\mathcal{U}_\psi$ may be inconsistent).
The *penalty* of a sub-theory T of ψ is the sum of the penalties of the assumptions in ψ that are not included in T; The *penalty function* of ψ is: $penalty_\psi(T) = \sum_{\varphi_i \in (\mathcal{U}_\psi - T)} \rho_i$.
A *Minimum Penalty* sub-theory (MP-theory) of ψ is a sub-theory T that minimizes the penalty of ψ; i.e., $penalty_\psi(T) = MIN_S\{penalty_\psi(S) \mid S$ is a sub-theory of $\psi\}$.

DEFINITION 7.2 Let $T_\psi = \{T_i\}$ the set of all MP-theories of ψ, and let $T_\varphi = \{T'_j\}$ the set of all MP-theories of φ. We say that ψ entails φ ($\psi \vdash \varphi$) iff all the MP-theories of ψ entails (in the classic sense) the disjunction of all the MP-theories of φ; i.e, $\psi \vdash \varphi$ iff $\bigvee T_i \vdash \bigvee T'_j$ (when φ is consistent then $\psi \vdash \varphi$ iff all MP-theories of ψ entail φ).

Intuitively, conflicting sub-theories compete among themselves and those who win are the preferred sub-theories (with the minimum sum of penalties). φ must follow from all the preferred (winning) sub-theories.

THEOREM 7.1 *The proof procedure is sound and complete; i.e.,* $\psi \models \varphi$ *iff* $\psi \vdash \varphi$.
The theorem follows from the observation that the penalty of a maximal consistent subset $T \subseteq \mathcal{U}_\psi$ is equal to the violation rank ($Vrank$) of the models that satisfy T.

This entailment mechanism is useful both for dealing with inconsistency in the knowledge base and for defeasible reasoning. For example, in a noisy knowledge base, when we detect inconsistency we usually want to adopt a sub-theory with maximum cardinality (we assume that only a minority of the observations are erroneous). When all the penalties are one, minimum penalty means maximum cardinality. Penalty logic is therefore a generalization of the maximal cardinality principle.

For defeasible reasoning, the notion of conflicting sub-theories can be used to decide between conflicting arguments. Intuitively, an argument A_1 defeats a conflicting argument A_2 if A_1 is supported by a "better" sub-theory than all those that support A_2.

EXAMPLE 7.1 Two levels of blocking ([Brewka 89]):

1	meeting	I tend to go to the meeting.
10	sick $\rightarrow$($\neg$ meeting)	If sick, I don't go.
100	cold-only $\rightarrow$ meeting	If only a cold, I still go.
1000	cold-only $\rightarrow$ sick	If I've cold it means I'm sick.

Without any additional evidence, all the assumptions are consistent, and we can infer that "meeting" is true (from the first assumption). However, given the evidence that "sick" is true, we prefer models that falsify "meeting" and "cold-only", since the second assumption has greater penalty than the competing first assumption (the only MP-theory, does not include the first assumption). If we include the evidence that "cold-only" is true, we prefer again the models where "meeting" is true, since we prefer to defeat the second assumption rather than the third or the fourth assumptions.

EXAMPLE 7.2 Nixon diamond (skeptical reasoning):

10	$N \rightarrow Q$	Nixon is a quaker.
10	$N \rightarrow R$	Nixon is a republican.
1	$Q \rightarrow P$	Quakers tend to be pacifists.
1	$R \rightarrow \neg P$	Republicans tend to be not pacifists.

When Nixon is given, we reason that he is both republican and quaker. We cannot decide however, whether he is pacifist or not, since in both preferred models (those with minimal $Vrank$) either the third or fourth assumption is violated; i.e., there are two MP-theories: one that entails $\neg P$, whereas the other entails P.

8 Penalty logic and energy functions

In this section we show that penalty calculus is strongly equivalent to the calculus of quadratic energy functions. We give algorithms to convert a PLOFF into a strongly equivalent quadratic energy function and vice-versa. We first show that every PLOFF can be reduced into a quadratic energy function.

THEOREM 8.1 *For every PLOFF* $\psi = \{< \rho_i, \varphi_i >| i = 1 \ldots n\}$ *there exists a strongly equivalent quadratic energy function* $E(\vec{x}, \vec{t})$ *such that* $Vrank_\psi = Erank_E$.

We construct E from ψ using the following procedure:

1. "Name" all φ_i's using new hidden atomic propositions T_i and construct $\psi' = \{< \infty, T_i \leftrightarrow \varphi_i >\} \cup \{< \rho_i, T_i >\}$. The high penalty guarantees that the "naming" will always be satisfied, while the T_i's (with the original penalty) compete with each other.
2. Construct the energy function $\sum_i \infty E_{T_i \leftrightarrow \varphi_i} - \sum_j \rho_j T_j$, where E_φ is the energy function that describes φ (using the algorithm from [Pinkas 90]).

EXAMPLE 8.1 Converting the "meeting" example:

<1000, $T_1 \leftrightarrow$ meeting>,
<1000, $T_2 \leftrightarrow$ (sick $\rightarrow$($\neg$ meeting))>,
<1000, $T_3 \leftrightarrow$ (cold-only $\rightarrow$ meeting)>,
<1000, $T_4 \leftrightarrow$ (cold-only $\rightarrow$ sick)>,
<1, T_1 >, <10, T_2 >, <100, T_3 >, <1000, T_4 >

The energy function we get by summing the energy terms of the assumptions is: $1000(T_1 - 2T_1M + M) + 1000(T_2SM - 2T_2 - S - M + T_2S + T_2M) + 1000(-T_3 - C + 2T_3C + M - T_3M - T_3CM) + 1000(-T_4 - C + 2T_4C + S - T_4S - T_4CS) - 1T_1 - 10T_2 - 100T_3 - 1000T_4$. The corresponding network appears in fig 1.

THEOREM 8.2 *Every energy function* E *is strongly equivalent to some PLOFF* ψ, *such that* $rank_E = Vrank_\psi + c$.

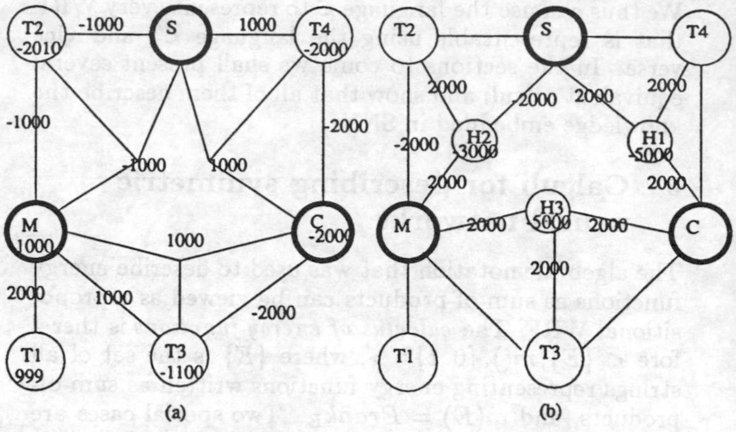

Figure 1: Equivalent SNNs (the meeting example). The numbers in the circles are thresholds. a) Cubic network; b) Quadratic network after adding hidden units.

The following algorithm generates a strongly equivalent PLOFF ψ from an energy function E:

1. Eliminate hidden variables from the energy function using the algorithm of [Pinkas 90].
2. The energy function (with no hidden variables) is now brought into a sum-of-products form and is converted into a PLOFF in the following way: Let $E(\vec{x}) = \sum_{i=1}^{m} w_i \prod_{n=1}^{k_i} x_{i_n}$ be the energy function. We construct a PLOFF $\psi = \{< -w_i, \bigwedge_{n=1}^{k_i} x_{i_n} >| w_i < 0\} \cup \{< w_l, \neg \bigwedge_{n=1}^{k_l} x_{l_n} >| w_l > 0\}$.

The size of the generated PLOFF is of the same order as the size of the original function.

Penalty logic is therefore strongly equivalent to the calculus of quadratic energy functions and can be used as a language to describe SNNs. It is expressive enough to represent in a compact way every such network, and for every sentence in this language we can generate a SNN that represents the same WRF. The transformations are efficient and generate a linear size output.

9 A sketch of a connectionist inference engine

Suppose a background PLOFF ψ, an evidence PLOFF e, and a WFF φ. We would like to construct a network to answer one of the possible three answers: 1) $\psi \cup e \models \varphi$; 2) $\psi \cup e \models (\neg\varphi)$; or 3) both $\psi \not\models \varphi$ and $\psi \not\models (\neg\varphi)$ ("unknown"). For simplicity let us first assume that the evidence e is a monomial (a conjunction of literals) and that φ is a single literal. Later we'll describe a general solution.

Intuitively, our connectionist engine is built out of two sub-networks, each that is trying to find a satisfying model for $\psi \cup e$. The first sub-network is biased to search for a model which satisfies *also* φ, while the second is biased to search for a model which satisfies *also* $\neg\varphi$. If two such preferred models exist then we conclude that φ is "unknown" ($\psi \cup e$ entails neither φ nor $\neg\varphi$). If no preferred model of $\psi \cup e$ satisfies φ, we conclude that

$\psi \cup e \models \neg\varphi$, and if no preferred model satisfies $\neg\varphi$, we conclude that $\psi \cup e \models \varphi$.

To implement this intuition we first need to duplicate our background knowledge ψ and create a copy ψ' by naming all the atomic propositions A using A'. For each proposition Q that might participate in a query, we then add two more propositions: "$QUERY_Q$" and "$UNKNOWN_Q$". $QUERY_Q$ is used to initiate a query Q: it will be externally clamped by the user, when inquiring about Q. $UNKNOWN_A$ represents the answer of the system. It will be set to TRUE if we can conclude neither that ψ entails φ nor that ψ entails φ.

Our inference engine can therefore be described (using the high-level language of penalty logic) by:

ψ /* searches for a model that satisfies also Q*/
$\cup\psi'$ /* searches for a model that satisfies also $\neg Q$ */
$\cup\{<\epsilon, (QUERY_Q \rightarrow Q)>\}$ /*bias Q */
$\cup\{<\epsilon, (QUERY_Q \rightarrow (\neg Q'))>\}$ /* bias $(\neg Q')$ */
$\cup\{<\epsilon, (Q \wedge \neg Q') \rightarrow UNKNOWN_Q>\}$
$\cup\{<\epsilon, (Q \leftrightarrow Q') \rightarrow (\neg UNKNOWN_Q)>\}$

Using the algorithm of Theorem 8.1, we generate the corresponding energy function and network.

To initiate a query about propositional Q the user externally clamps the unit $QUERY_Q$. This causes a small positive bias ϵ to be sent to unit Q and a negative bias $-\epsilon$ to be sent to Q'. Each of the two sub-networks ψ and ψ', searches for a global minimum (a satisfying model) of the original PLOFF. The bias (ϵ) is small enough so it does not introduce new global minima. It may however, constrain the set of global minima: if a satisfying model that also satisfies the bias exists then it is in the new set of global minima. The network tries to find preferred models that satisfy also the bias rules. If it succeeds ($Q \wedge \neg Q'$), we conclude "UNKNOWN", otherwise we conclude that all the satisfying models agree on the same truth value for the query. The "UNKNOWN" unit is then set to "false" and the answer whether $\psi \models \varphi$ or whether $\psi \models \neg\varphi$ can be found in the proposition Q.

When the evidence is a monomial, we can add it to the background network simply by clamping the appropriate atomic propositions. In the general case we need to combine an arbitrary evidence e, and an arbitrary WFF φ as a query. We do this by adding to ψ, the energy terms that correspond to $e \cup \{<\infty, Q \leftrightarrow \varphi>\}$ and querying Q.

The network that is generated converges to the correct answer if it manages to find a global minimum. An annealing schedule as in [Hinton, Sejnowski 86] may be used for such search. A slow enough annealing will find a global minimum and therefore the correct answer, but it might take exponential time. Since the problem is NP-hard, we shall probably not find an algorithm that will always give us the correct answer in polynomial time. Traditionally in AI, knowledge representation systems traded the expressiveness of the language they use with the time complexity they allow.[5] The accuracy of the answer is usually not sacrificed. In our system, we trade the time with the accuracy of the answer. We are given limited time resources and we stop the search when this limit is reached. Although the answer may be incorrect, the system is able to improve its guess as more time resources are given.

[5]Connectionist systems like [Shastri,Ajjanagadde 90] trade expressiveness with time complexity, while systems like [Hölldobler 90] trade time with size.

10 Related work

Derthick [Derthick 88] was the first to observe that weighted logical constraints (which he called "certainties") can be used for non-monotonic connectionist reasoning. There are however, two basic differences: 1) Derthick's "Mundane" reasoning is based on finding a most likely single model; his system is never skeptical. Our system is more cautious and closer in its behavior to recent symbolic NM systems. 2) Our system can be implemented using standard low-order units, and we can use models like Hopfield nets or Boltzman machines that are relatively well studied (e.g., a learning algorithm exists).

Another connectionist non-monotonic system is [Shastri 85]. It uses evidential reasoning based on maximum likelihood to reason in inheritance networks. Our approach is different; we use low-level units and we are not restricted to inheritance networks.[6] Shastri's system is guaranteed to work, whereas we trade the correctness with the time.

Our WRFs have a lot in common with Lehmann's ranked models [Lehmann 89]. His result about the relationship between rational consequence relations and ranked models can be applied to our paradigm; yielding a rather strong conclusion: for every conditional knowledge base we can build a ranked model (for the rational closure of the knowledge base) and implement it as a WRF using a symmetric neural net. Also, any symmetric neural net is implementing some rational consequence relation.

Our penalty logic has some similarities with systems that are based on the user specifying priorities to defaults. The closest system is [Brewka 89] that is based on levels of reliability. Brewka's system for propositional logic can be mapped to penalty logic by selecting large enough penalties. Systems like [Poole 88] (with strict specificity) can be implemented using our architecture, and the penalties can therefore be generated automatically from conditional languages that do not force the user to associate explicitly numbers or priorities to the assumptions. Brewka however is concerned with maximal consistent sets in the sense of set inclusion, while we are interested in sub-theories with maximum cardinality (generalized definition). As a result we prefer theories with "more" evidence. For example consider the Nixon diamond of example 7.2 when we add $<10, N \rightarrow FF>$ and $<1, FF \rightarrow \neg P>$ (Nixon is also a football fan and football fans tend to be not pacifists). Most other NM systems (like [Touretzky 86], [Geffner 89],[Simari,Loui 90]) will still be skeptical about P. Our system decides $\neg P$ since it is better to defeat the one assumption sup-

[6]We can easily extend our approach to handle inheritance nets, by looking at the atomic propositions as predicates with free variables. Those variables are bound by the user during query time.

porting P, than the two assumptions supporting $\neg P$. We can correct this behavior however, by multiplying the penalty for $Q \rightarrow P$ by two. Further, a network with learning capabilities can adjust the penalties autonomously and thus develop its own intuition and non-monotonic behavior.

Because we do not allow for arbitrary partial orders ([Shoham 88] [Geffner 89]) of the models, there are other fundamental problematic examples where our system (and all systems with ranked models semantics) concludes the truth (or falsity) of a proposition while other systems are skeptical. Such examples are beyond the scope of this article. On the positive side, every skeptical reasoning mechanism with ranked models semantics can be mapped to our paradigm.

11 Conclusions

We have developed a model theoretic notion of reasoning using world-rank-functions independently of the use of symbolic languages. We showed that any SNN can be viewed as if it is searching for a satisfying model of such a function, and every such function can be approximated using these networks.

Several equivalent high-level languages can be used to describe SNNs: 1) quadratic energy functions; 2) high-order energy functions with no hidden units; 3) propositional logic, and finally 4) penalty logic. All these languages are expressive enough to describe any SNN and every sentence of such languages can be translated into a SNN. We gave algorithms that perform these transformations, which are magnitude preserving (except for propositional calculus which is only weakly equivalent).

We have developed a calculus based on assumptions augmented by penalties that fits very naturally the symmetric models' paradigm. This calculus can be used as a platform for defeasible reasoning and inconsistency handling. Several recent NM systems can be mapped into this paradigm and therefore suggest settings of the penalties. When the right penalties are given, penalty calculus features a non-monotonic behavior that matches our intuition. Penalties do not necessarily have to come from a syntactic analysis of a symbolic language; since those networks can learn, they can potentially adjust their WRFs and develop their own intuition.

Revision of the knowledge base and adding evidence are efficient if we use penalty logic to describe the knowledge: adding (or deleting) a PLOFF is simply computing the energy terms of the new PLOFF and then adding (deleting) it to the background energy function. A local change to the PLOFF is translated into a local change in the network.

We sketched a connectionist inference engine for penalty calculus. When a query is clamped, the global minima of such network correspond exactly to the correct answer. Although the worst case for the *correct* answer is still exponential, the mechanism however, trades the soundness of the answer with the time given to solve the problem.

Acknowledgment Thanks to John Doyle, Hector Geffner, Sally Goldman, Dan Kimura, Stan Kwasny, Fritz Lehmann and Ron Loui for helpful discussions and comments.

References

[Brewka 89] G. Brewka, "Preferred sub-theories: An extended logical framework for default reasoning.", *IJCAI* 1989, pp. 1043-1048.

[Derthick 88] M. Derthick, "Mundane reasoning by parallel constraint satisfaction", PhD Thesis, TR. CMU-CS-88-182, Carnegie Mellon 1988.

[Geffner 89] H. Geffner, "Defeasible reasoning: causal and conditional theories", PhD Thesis, UCLA, 1989.

[Hinton, Sejnowski 86] G.E Hinton and T.J. Sejnowski "Learning and Re-learning in Boltzman Machines" in McClelland, Rumelhart, *"Parallel Distributed Processing"* , Vol I MIT Press 1986

[Hölldobler 90] S. Hölldobler, "CHCL, a connectionist inference system for horn logic based on connection method and using limited resources", *International Computer Science Institute* TR-90-042, 1990.

[Hopfield 82] J.J. Hopfield "Neural networks and physical system with emergent collective computational abilities," *Proc. of the Nat. Acad. of Sciences* , 79,1982.

[Lehmann 89] D. Lehmann, "What does a conditional knowledge base entail?", KR-89, *Proc. of the int. conf. on knowledge representation,* 89.

[Pinkas 90] G. Pinkas, "Energy minimization and the satisfiability of propositional calculus", *Neural Computation* Vol 3-2, 1991.

[Poole 88] D. Poole , "A logical framework for default reasoning", *Artificial Intelligence* 36,1988.

[Shastri 85] L. Shastri, "Evidential reasoning in semantic networks:A formal theory and its parallel implementation", *PhD thesis, TR 166, University of Rochester*, Sept. 1985.

[Shastri,Ajjanagadde 90] L. Shastri, V. Ajjanagadde, "From simple associations to systematic reasoning: a connectionist representation of rules, variables and dynamic bindings " TR. MS-CIS-90-05 *University of Pennsylvania, Philadelphia*, 1990.

[Shoham 88] Y. Shoham, "Reasoning about change" *The MIT press*, Cambridge, Massachusetts, London, England 1988.

[Simari,Loui 90] G. Simari, R.P. Loui , "Mathematics of defeasible reasoning and its implementation", *Artificial Intelligence*, to appear.

[Touretzky 86] D.S. Touretzky,"The mathematics of inheritance systems", Pitman, London, 1986.

KNOWLEDGE REPRESENTATION

Reasoning with Inconsistency

CONTEXTUAL NEGATIONS AND REASONING WITH CONTRADICTIONS

Walter Alexandre CARNIELLI*
University of Campinas-IMECC
C. P. 6065
13081 Campinas, SP – Brasil
walterc@ccvax.unicamp.ansp.br

Luis FARIÑAS del CERRO†
Université Paul Sabatier-IRIT
118, Route de Narbonne
31062 Toulouse – France
farinas@irit.fr

Mamede LIMA MARQUES ‡
Université Paul Sabatier-IRIT
118, Route de Narbonne
31062 Toulouse – France
mamede@irit.fr

Abstract

This paper introduces the logical basis for modelling the phenomenon of reasoning in the presence of contradiction, by identifying this problem with the notion of change of context. We give here the basic definitions of a new semantics, which works by interpreting one logic into a family of logics via translations, which we call *semantics of translations*. As a particular application we show that a simple logic supporting contradictions can be constructed translating classical logic into three-valued logics. This translation semantics offers a new interpretation to certain paraconsistent logics which allows the application of them to automated reasoning and knowledge representation.

1 Introduction

In some previous work we have defended the idea that any system which tries to formalise reasoning should be able to treat the question of contradiction (cf. [Carnielli and Lima Marques, 1990] and [Carnielli, 1990]).

A similar point has been raised (more or less independently) by several authors, and some solutions involving simple many–valued logics and non–monotonic logics, for example, have already been proposed.

Such solutions, however, fail to consider the difference between *local* (or *contextual*) inconsistencies, and *global* inconsistencies.

This is an important point, first because this distinction is apparently very familiar to real reasoners, and second because by failing to consider these points the existing solutions try to reestablish consistency as soon as contradictions appear, and are thus obliged to maintain a costly and cumbersome process of revision.

It is then very natural to consider the possibility of approaching this problem by means of some logic which can support local inconsistencies.

In modal logics, for instance, simultaneous utterances of A *is possible* and $\neg A$ *is possible* are perfectly acceptable, if we understand *possibility* as a contextual notion: in this case we are just not referring to the same world.

We want to propose that *trueness* in certain cases can be interpreted in a similar way: so if our theory has to analyse A *is true* and $\neg A$ *is true* and the theory is sufficiently prepared, it *may* regard that discrepancy as an intrinsic difference of context between the two assertions, thus avoiding collapsing and at the same time gaining more information while recognising that difference of context.

The objectives of this paper are:

1. To propose a new definition of *semantics of translations*, in order to give a formal approach to the problem of characterizing the notion of distinct contexts or situations that affect the truth of a sentence, and
2. In particular, to illustrate how semantics of this sort can be obtained for a certain logic which supports contradictions in the process of reasoning.

In the particular application, we will be using as underlying logics certain three-valued logics (see, e.g. [Ginsberg, 1988], and [Delahaye and Thibau, 1988] for related uses of many-valued logics).

The method introduced here is general, and can be used for instance in connection to other logics (many-valued or not). The restriction to three-valued logics, however, is interesting because of the connection with *paraconsistent logic*.

Paraconsistent logic, in particular the propositional systems $\mathcal{C}_n$ $(1 \leq n < \omega)$ and $\mathcal{C}_\omega$ and their first–order counterparts make it possible to separate inconsistency from triviality in formal systems. The importance of this point in terms of reasoning strategy is discussed in [Carnielli and Lima Marques, 1990].

Although all such paraconsistent systems are known to be sound and complete with respect to semantics of two–valued functions (see e.g. [da Costa, 1974] and [Alves, 1984]) some non–intuitive aspects of those semantics have prevented their applications in automated reasoning.

We show how to obtain a new semantic interpretation for paraconsistent logics in such a way that negation in those logics could be seen as a kind of *contextual negation*.

In this way, as we argue, it is possible to obtain a logical framework which gives a quite natural account of the idea of reasoning under contradiction.

*Supported by the Alexander von Humboldt Foundation (FRG) and CNPq (Brasil).
†Supported by BRA: (MEDLAR).
‡Supported by CAPES (Brasil) and BRA: (MEDLAR).

2 Translation Semantics

The idea of translation semantics and its applications was introduced in elsewhere (cf. [Carnielli, 1990]). In this section we give a more general treatment to this notion, refining the appropriate concepts.

Let L be a logic whose language $\mathcal{L}(L)$ has connectives $(\vee, \wedge, \rightarrow, \neg)$ and quantifiers $(\forall, \exists)$. Let also M be another logic whose language $\mathcal{L}(M)$ contains *sets* of corresponding connectives and quantifiers, that is, $\mathcal{L}(M)$ contains sets

$$S_\vee = \{\vee_1, ..., \vee_{n_1}\} \quad S_\wedge = \{\wedge_1, ..., \wedge_{n_2}\}$$
$$S_\rightarrow = \{\rightarrow_1, ..., \rightarrow_{n_3}\} \quad S_\neg = \{\neg_1, ..., \neg_{n_4}\}$$
$$S_\forall = \{\forall_1, ..., \forall_{n_5}\} \quad S_\exists = \{\exists_1, ..., \exists_{n_6}\}$$

We suppose that $\mathcal{L}(M)$ and $\mathcal{L}(L)$ contain all the familiar logical symbols and that all the usual syntactic definitions hold for them. A situation such as that occurs naturally when M is a many–valued logic, for example, where several connectives can be defined. It is usual to classify them as conjunctions, disjunctions, etc., and we use this classification here, assuming only that the sets $S_\sharp$ (where $\sharp$ is in $\{\vee, \wedge, \neg, \rightarrow, \exists, \forall\}$) are non–empty if the corresponding $\{\vee, \wedge, \neg, \rightarrow, \exists, \forall\}$ are present in L. Of course each connective and quantifier can be seen as a distinct logical symbol.

We define a *translation* from L to M as a function $\mathcal{T} : \mathcal{L}(L) \mapsto \mathcal{L}(M)$ such that:

1. $\mathcal{T}(p)$ is a wff of $\mathcal{L}(M)$, for p an atomic wff of $\mathcal{L}(L)$
2. $\mathcal{T}(\neg A) = \neg_{i_1} \mathcal{T}(A)$ for some i_1
3. $\mathcal{T}(A \vee B) = \mathcal{T}(A) \vee_{i_2} \mathcal{T}(B)$ for some i_2
4. $\mathcal{T}(A \wedge B) = \mathcal{T}(A) \wedge_{i_3} \mathcal{T}(B)$ for some i_3
5. $\mathcal{T}(A \rightarrow B) = \mathcal{T}(A) \rightarrow_{i_4} \mathcal{T}(B)$ for some i_4
6. $\mathcal{T}(\forall x A) = \forall_{i_5} \mathcal{T}(A)$ for some i_5
7. $\mathcal{T}(\exists x A) = \exists_{i_6} \mathcal{T}(A)$ for some i_6

satisfying the following properties:

$$\Lambda \models_L A \text{ iff } \mathcal{T}(\Lambda) \models_M \mathcal{T}(A)$$

where $\mathcal{T}(\Lambda) = \{\mathcal{T}(X) : X \in \Lambda\}$ and $\models_L$, $\models_M$ denote the respective satisfiability relations in L and M.

The indices i_1 to i_6 above are fixed in advances or can vary according to prescribed conditions.

For example, the well-known Gentzen translation from classical propositional calculus (PC) to intuitionistic logic (INT) is given by:

$$\mathcal{T} : \mathcal{L}(PC) \mapsto \mathcal{L}(INT)$$

where

$$\mathcal{T}(p) = \neg\neg p$$
$$\mathcal{T}(\neg A) = \neg(\mathcal{T}(A))$$
$$\mathcal{T}(A \rightarrow B) = \mathcal{T}(A) \rightarrow \mathcal{T}(B)$$
$$\mathcal{T}(A \wedge B) = \mathcal{T}(A) \wedge \mathcal{T}(B)$$
$$\mathcal{T}(A \vee B) = \neg(\neg\mathcal{T}(A) \wedge \neg\mathcal{T}(B))$$

In this case there are no quantifiers, and the sets $S_\sharp$ in INT are all singletons (consequently, the indices i_1 to i_6 are all fixed).

It is clear that our definition includes many distinct translations depending upon the cardinalities of $S_\sharp$.

Other properties and examples of translations are given in [Epstein, 1990].

The cases when M is a many–valued logic are of especial interest because those logics have semantics described by simple algebraic conditions (through logic matrices).

We shall concentrate on the particular case of three–valued logics, showing that there exists a semantics of translations between the paraconsistent calculus $\mathcal{C}_1$ and the three–valued logic LCD containing two negations (all other connectives and quantifiers appearing just one time). In order to render the analysis more intuitive, we can consider two different logics, LD and CD, instead of one single logic LCD containing two negations.

3 Three–valued Logics, Continous and Local Default

Let us consider a fixed language L containing the following symbols (as the usual language for first–order theories):

(a) primitive connectives: $\neg$ (negation), $\vee$ (disjunction), $\wedge$ (conjunction), $\rightarrow$ (implication),

(b) quantifiers: $\forall$ (universal), $\exists$ (existential)

(c) a denumerable stock of variables, constants, functions symbols and predicate symbols.

We denote the collection of all well–formed formulas by Wff and a well–formed formula by wff.

All the usual syntactic definitions such as substitution, etc. (with their usual proviso on variables) hold also here.

We define now the calculus of *continuous truth–default* CD and the calculus of *local truth default* LD as three–valued systems in the language L, whose interpretation is given by the following logical matrices:

1. Logic values: T, F, I, of which T and I are *designated;*
2. The connectives $\wedge$, $\vee$, and $\rightarrow$ are interpreted by the following tables:

$\wedge$	T	I	F
T	T	I	F
I	I	I	F
F	F	F	F

$\vee$	T	I	F
T	T	I	T
I	I	I	I
F	T	I	F

$\rightarrow$	T	I	F
T	T	I	F
I	I	I	F
F	T	I	T

and the two negations, respectively, in CD and LD are interpreted by the *negation of continuous default* $\neg_{\mathsf{C}}$, and by the *negation of local default* $\neg_{\mathsf{L}}$:

	T	I	F
$\neg_C$	F	I	T

	T	I	F
$\neg_L$	F	F	T

We call a *3-valuation for* CD (respectively, for LD) any function extended from the atomic sentences to all sentences by these tables. We assume that the reader is familiar with the usual definitions of many–valued structures $\mathcal{A}$; it is sufficient to know that the routine syntactic and semantic notions can be defined for those logics. In particular, $\mathcal{L}(\mathcal{A})$ stands for the *extended language* obtained from $\mathcal{A}$ by adding new constants as names for all elements of the universe $|\mathcal{A}|$ of $\mathcal{A}$. For both systems, the valuations for the quantified case are extended as follows:

if v is 3-valuation then

$$v(\forall x A) = max\{v(A_x[i]) : i \in \mathcal{L}(\mathcal{A})\}$$

and

$$v(\exists x A) = \begin{cases} \bullet\ I \text{ if there exists } i \text{ in } \mathcal{L}(\mathcal{A}) \\ \quad \text{such that } v(A_x[i]) = I \\ \bullet\ min\{v(A_x[i]) : i \in \mathcal{L}(\mathcal{A})\} \text{ otherwise} \end{cases}$$

where $T < I < F$.

These conditions are sufficient to characterize completely a many valued logic in terms of syntactic rules for which these tables are sound and complete (see [Carnielli, 1987]).

In order to make clear that we are referring to CD or LD we underline the connectives and quantifiers, and write $\neg_C$ or $\neg_L$ for the negations.

We want to argue that the logic values and the matrices for CD and LD can be viewed as a basis for a model of reasoning by default, inspired by suggestions of Epstein in [Epstein, 1990]. For this purpose consider the following interpretation of the logic values:

1. F means *definitely false*, and thus a sentence A receives values F only when there is positive evidence of falsehood;
2. Duble negations are reducible, that is, A and $\neg\neg A$ receive the same logic value.
3. There cannot be positive evidence of falsehood for both A and $\neg A$.
4. We assume that T is assigned to A (resp., to $\neg A$) when there is positive evidence of falsehood for $\neg A$ (resp., to A) and in this case $\neg A$ (resp., to A) receives value F.
5. We further assume that positive evidence of trueness is not possible; so this implies that a sentence of the form A or $\neg A$ receives value T by ***default*** when there is positive evidence of the falsehood of the other one; that is, T is the *default* value, which is assumed to hold if there is no other indication.
6. If it happens that neither A nor $\neg A$ have positive evidence of falsehood, we accept that in principle A is not yet determined, thus assigning to it the value I.
7. As a final assumption, we agree that positive information for falsehood of *negated* sentences may be obtained in the future, but not for positive sentences, i.e. ones not beginning with T (this can be justified, for example, imagining a process of limited resources, where after a first attempt to find evidence for the positive sentences, we concentrate our efforts on the negative ones).

If we are careful reasoners we should keep track of our deductions made on the basis of I values; we thus assume that any valuation which relates to I is assigned I *unless* it is granted by some value F: this is clearly guaranteed by the tables for $\vee$, $\wedge$ and $\rightarrow$ above, and by the interpretation of the quantifiers.

This explains why we *do not* define, in the tables for "$\vee$" and "$\rightarrow$" $T \vee I = T$, $I \vee T = T$, $I \rightarrow T = T$, $F \rightarrow I = T$. The intuitive idea is that I is the indeterminated value, which can be turned into T or F in the presence of further information, but also that we want to be able to keep track of all wff's which somehow involve I values.

The reader will notice that, defining $T \vee I = I \vee T = T$, for example (which incidentally would give the relevant system RM3 of relevant logic [Anderson and Belnap, 1975]) would make we too loose this property of keeping track of I values.

As a consequence of our assumptions, it follows that neither T nor F can be changed, but the value I *can* be changed in the light of future information. There are two possibilities for the course of events of a given sentence A having value I:

case (a) This situation continues forever, and thus $\neg A$ is also evaluated as I; this explains the table for $\neg_C$ and justifies calling CD a logic for continuous default.

case (b) As a consequence of assumption (7) above, in a given moment A stops being regarded as I, but gains the status of T, because new positive information on the falsehood of $\neg A$ has been obtained. Thus $\neg A$ has to be evaluated as F, and this explains the table for $\neg_L$ and justifies calling LD a logic for local default.

We want to remark that while LD is a three-valued version of classical logic, CD is a genuinely new system: it does not coincide with any of the well-known three-valued systems.

We can regard the union (in the obvious sense as simply a logic in $\mathcal{L}(\neg_L, \neg_C, \vee, \wedge, \rightarrow)$) LCD of CD and LD as a three–valued logic also, and all the definitions (like 3–valuations, etc.) extend to LCD.

4 Paraconsistent Backgrounds

Paraconsistent logics are formal systems designed to serve as the basis for inconsistent but non-trivial theories, with the additional characteristic of being as conservative as possible with respect to the postulates of classical logic. We refer to [da Costa, 1974] and [Alves, 1984] for the axiomatics of C_1 and its first–order extension C_1^*.

We are using here the version of [Alves, 1984] where $(\neg\neg A \leftrightarrow A)$ is an axiom.

The semantic interpretation of $C_1^\star$ is described as follows: if L is a language of $C_1^\star$ (i.e., the basic alphabet plus a class of function symbols, predicate symbols, variables and constants), we define a *structure* in the usual way as a nonempty domain $|\mathcal{A}|$ plus the interpretations for the elements of L. $\mathcal{L}(\mathcal{A})$ as explained above, denotes the extended language. Here i and j denote names.

A *paraconsistent valuation based on the structure* $\mathcal{A}$ is a function v from a wff to $\{t, f\}$ such that:

1. if $p^\star = pa_1 \cdots a_n$ then $v(p^\star) = t$ iff $p_\mathcal{A}(\mathcal{A}(a_1), \cdots, \mathcal{A}(a_n))$ for p a predicate, $p_\mathcal{A}$ its interpretation, a_i variable-free terms and $\mathcal{A}(a_i)$ their interpretations;
2. $v(A \rightarrow B) = t$ iff $v(A) = f$ or $v(B) = t$
3. $v(A \vee B) = t$ iff $v(A) = t$ or $v(B) = t$
4. $v(A \wedge B) = t$ iff $v(A) = t$ and $v(B) = t$
5. $v(\neg\neg A) = t$ iff $v(A) = t$
6. if $v(A) = f$ then $v(\neg A) = t$
7. if $v(B^\circ) = v(A \rightarrow B) = v(A \rightarrow \neg B) = t$ then $v(A) = t$

   where X° is defined as $\neg(X \wedge \neg X)$ for any wff X.
8. if $v(A^\circ) = v(B^\circ) = t$ then $v((A \sharp B)^\circ) = t$ for $\sharp$ in $\{\vee, \wedge, \rightarrow\}$
9. $v(\forall x A) = t$ iff $v(A_x[i]) = t$ for all i in $\mathcal{L}(\mathcal{A})$
10. $v(\exists x A) = t$ iff $v(A_x[i]) = t$ for some i in $\mathcal{L}(\mathcal{A})$
11. if $v(\forall x A^\circ) = t$ then $v((\forall x A)^\circ) = v((\exists x A)^\circ) = t$
12. $v(A) = v(A')$ if A and A' are variants obtained by renaming variables.

Note that from (6) and (7) it follows that $v(A) \neq v(\neg A)$ iff $v(A^\circ) = t$. Thus, in the cases where $v(A^\circ) = f$ we *do* have $v(A) = v(\neg A) = t$, since clause (6) forbids $v(A) = v(\neg A) = f$.

The proof of completeness given in [Alves, 1984] for $C_1^=$ (i.e. $C_1^\star$ plus the predicate $=$ for equality) can be modified in minor details to show that $C_1^\star$ is correct and complete with respect to the paraconsistent valuations.

Theorem 4.1 *The systems C_1 and $C_1^\star$ are not finite many-valued logics.*

Proof : It is sufficient to show that the propositional system C_1 is not finite many-valued.

The proof is an adaptation of the proof by Gödel [Gödel, 1932] about the non-characterizability of the intuitionistic propositional calculus by many-valued logics, using the following logic matrix $\mathcal{M}$, whose logic values are the ordinals in $\omega + 1$ and ω the set of distinguished logic values and whose operations $\bigvee$, $\bigwedge$, $\neg$, $\longrightarrow$ are defined by:

1. $x \bigvee y = min\{x, y\}$
2. $x \bigwedge y = max\{x, y\}$
3. $\neg x = \begin{cases} \omega \text{ if } x = 0 \\ 0 \text{ if } x = \omega \\ x + 1 \text{ otherwise} \end{cases}$
4. $x \longrightarrow y = \begin{cases} max\{x, y\} & \text{if } x, y \in \omega \\ \omega & \text{if } x < \omega \text{ and } y = \omega \\ y & \text{if } x = \omega \text{ and } y < \omega \\ 0 & \text{if } x = y = \omega \end{cases}$

□

The previous theorem shows that paraconsistent logic (at least the systems C_1 and $C_1^\star$ and their cognates) cannot be interpreted as a finite many–valued logic. The relationship between paraconsistent and many–valued logics is, however, much more subtle: we prove that paraconsistent semantics can be characterized by classes of translations involving simultaneously *more* than one many–valued systems, as explained in section (5).

5 Contradictions and Contextual Negation

A *translation* between $C_1^\star$ and LCD $=$ CD $\cup$ LD is a function $\mathcal{T}$ from the language of $C_1^\star$ into the union of the languages of CD and LD such that the following conditions hold (underlined symbols belong to the common language of CD and LD):

1. For $p^\star$ an atomic formula:
   (a) $\mathcal{T}(p^\star) = \underline{p}^\star$, where $\underline{p}^\star$ is an atomic sentence in $\mathcal{L}(\text{LCD})$
   (b) $\mathcal{T}(\neg p^\star) = \begin{cases} \neg_\mathsf{C}(\mathcal{T}(p^\star)) \text{ or} \\ \neg_\mathsf{L}(\mathcal{T}(p^\star)) \end{cases}$
2. For non–atomic formulas
   (a) $\mathcal{T}(A \sharp B) = \mathcal{T}(A) \,\underline{\sharp}\, \mathcal{T}(B)$ where $\sharp \in \{\vee, \wedge, \rightarrow\}$;
   (b) $\mathcal{T}(QxA) = \underline{Qx}\mathcal{T}(A)$ for $Q \in \{\forall, \exists\}$;
   (c) $\mathcal{T}(\neg QxA) = \begin{cases} \neg_\mathsf{L}\, \mathcal{T}(QxA) \text{ if } \mathcal{T}(\neg A) = \neg_\mathsf{L}\, \mathcal{T}(A) \\ \qquad\qquad \text{and } x \text{ is free in } A \\ \neg_\mathsf{L}\, \mathcal{T}(QxA) \text{ or } \neg_\mathsf{C}\, \mathcal{T}(QxA) \\ \qquad\qquad \text{otherwise} \end{cases}$
   (d) If $\mathcal{T}(\neg A) = \neg_\mathsf{L}\, \mathcal{T}(A)$ and $\mathcal{T}(\neg B) = \neg_\mathsf{L}\, \mathcal{T}(B)$ then $\mathcal{T}\neg(A \sharp B) = \neg_\mathsf{L}\, \mathcal{T}(A \sharp B)$

A translation $\mathcal{T}$ is called a *$C_1^\star$–translation* if it is subjected to the following conditions:

1. $\mathcal{T}(\neg\neg A) = \neg_\mathsf{C} \neg_\mathsf{C} \mathcal{T}(A)$ or $\mathcal{T}(\neg\neg A) = \neg_\mathsf{L} \neg_\mathsf{L} \mathcal{T}(A)$;
2. If $\mathcal{T}(\neg A) = \neg_\mathsf{C}\mathcal{T}(A)$ then $\mathcal{T}(\neg(A \wedge \neg A)) = \neg_\mathsf{L}(\mathcal{T}(A \wedge \neg A))$ and $\mathcal{T}(\neg(\neg A \wedge A)) = \neg_\mathsf{L}(\mathcal{T}(\neg A \wedge A))$

In intuitive terms, the above definitions mean:

(a) translations of double neighbour negations cannot mix, and

(b) for the sentences of the form A°, if the internal negation is regarded as continuous default then the external one has to be local default.

Note that a translation will not be determined by the atomic level: thus, for example, all the following formulas can be obtained by distinct translations of $\neg(\neg A \vee B)$: $\neg_\mathsf{C}(\neg_\mathsf{C} A \vee B)$, $\neg_\mathsf{C}(\neg_\mathsf{L} A \vee B)$, $\neg_\mathsf{L}(\neg_\mathsf{C} A \vee B)$ and $\neg_\mathsf{L}(\neg\neg_\mathsf{L}\, A \vee B)$ for A, B atomic.

All the above clauses which treat negation make clear that the negation in $C_1^\star$ is being translated into two distinct *contexts* (namely, the distinct negations in LD and CD).

Given a $C_1^\star$–translation $\mathcal{T}$ and a 3-valuation ν in LCD, we say that $(\mathcal{T},\nu)$ *satisfies* a $C_1^\star$–sentence X iff $\nu(\mathcal{T}(X)) \in \{T, I\}$; this is denoted in symbols as

$$(\mathcal{T},\nu) \models X$$

The sentence X is said to be ***valid in the translation*** $\mathcal{T}$ (respectively, ***valid in the valuation*** ν) if there exists a valuation ν (respectively, a translation $\mathcal{T}$) such that $(\mathcal{T},\nu) \models X$; and X is a ***tautology*** if it is valid for all translations $\mathcal{T}$ and valuations ν.

The following theorem can be proved:

Theorem 5.1 *Let $\mathcal{T}$ be a $C_1^\star$–translation. Then each model $(\mathcal{T},\nu)$ determines a paraconsistent valuation v such that $(\mathcal{T},\nu) \models A$ iff $v(A) = t$, for all wff's A.* □

Now it remains to prove that we can define a 3–valuation and an appropriate translation based on paraconsistent valuations.

Theorem 5.2 *Each paraconsistent valuation v (based on the structure $\mathcal{A}$) determines a $C_1^\star$–translation model $(\mathcal{T},\nu)$ such that $v(A) = t$ iff $(\mathcal{T},\nu) \models A$, for all sentences A.*

Proof : Let $\mathsf{L}(\mathcal{A})$ and v be the given structure and paraconsistent valuation; the proof is carried out by constructing simultaneously a 3–valuation ν and a $C_1^\star$–translation $\mathcal{T}$ having the desired property, by induction on the length of formulas:

1. For atomic sentences $p^\star$, define

$$\nu(p^\star) = \begin{cases} F \text{ if } v(p^\star) = f \\ I \text{ if } v(p^\star) = t \text{ and } v(\neg p^\star) = t \\ T \text{ if } v(p^\star) = t \text{ and } v(\neg p^\star) = f \end{cases}$$

   and set $\mathcal{T}(p^\star) = \underline{p}^\star$. Then clearly the result holds.

2. For non-atomic cases the proof involves a detailed analyses by cases, defining inductively (on the length of formulas) the required valuation ν and $C_1^\star$–translation $\mathcal{T}$.

□

Theorems (5.1) and (5.2) establish then the proposed translation semantics for $C_1^\star$. This offers a meaning for the negation in $C_1^\star$ as a contextual negation: each instance of negation in this logic is interpreted differently according to which logic scenario the reasoner is accepting for this particular instance (namely, CD or LD).

6 Applications

The deep significance of this idea is that we *can* use the two usual logic values t and f, and almost all the usual logic laws (as guaranteed by the axioms of $C_1^\star$).

When contradiction of the form $v(A) = t$ and $v(\neg A) = t$ occurs, this is interpreted by the system (by virtue of the translation semantics) as a situation where A and $\neg A$ would take the value I, interpreted as a situation caused by each of information. The system is prepared, then, not only to ***support*** such a situation, but also to *correct* it in the light of further information.

We believe that our analysis gives a precise and intuitively acceptable account of a theory of reasoning which supports local inconsistency, with both theoretical and practical interest. As for applications, in [Carnielli and Lima Marques, 1990] we give examples of automated reasoners who can, for example, discover a liar in a group interview, or who can handle paradoxes like the Barber's Paradox.

An application of our analysis consists in obtaining a clear account of the method of analysis of contradictions which we have developed in [Carnielli and Lima Marques, 1990]. We give here a example (the same given in the mentioned paper) of how such ideas can be applied to a controversial investigation:

Suppose that in the course of an investigation there is some information concerning three persons α, β, γ; the system has to answer who, among α, β, γ, are the men and who the women, based on the following knowledge, which is possibly incomplete and contradictory:

1. All men are using hats.
2. All persons using earrings are women.
3. Each person is either a man or a woman.
4. γ is sure not to be using a hat.
5. γ is using an earring.
6. Either β is using an earring or γ is a man.
7. If γ is using an earring, then β is not.
8. It is sure that no two of α, β, γ are women

Note that, according to the analysis of section (3), clauses (4) and (8) are the only to be prefixed with F; the remaining clauses are assumed to be true by default.

Using the tableau version of $C_1^\star$ developed in [Carnielli and Lima Marques, 1990], where the prefixes T and F are interpreted as ***it is true that*** and ***it is false that*** respectively, these conditions are formalized as follows:

1. $T(\forall x(M(x) \rightarrow H(x))$
2. $T(\forall x(E(x) \rightarrow W(x))$
3. $T(\forall x(M(x) \vee W(x))$
4. $F(H(\gamma))$
5. $T(E(\gamma))$
6. $T(E(\beta) \vee M(\gamma))$
7. $T(E(\gamma) \rightarrow \neg E(\beta))$
8. $F(W(\alpha) \wedge W(\beta)) \vee (W(\alpha) \wedge W(\gamma)) \vee (W(\beta) \wedge W(\gamma))$

Analysing this set of formulas using the tableau method referred to above, we obtain as a solution the following information:

$$T(M(\alpha)), T(M(\beta)), T(W(\gamma)), T(E(\beta)), F(E(\beta)^\circ)$$

meaning that:

1. α and β are men
2. γ is a woman

and the extra information $T(E(\beta))$ and $F(E(\beta)^\circ)$ convey that β is using an earring, but this has to be revised.

These examples show that the system can identify the critical points where contradictions appear, and give a solution taking the critical points into consideration, in accordance with the clauses of the problem.

Problems of this sort and their solutions show the real applicability of the systems supporting contradiction when they are based on an intuitively clear and well founded semantics. Since such semantics, in the way we have studied, are based on the idea of translations, it also suggests the interest about investigating other logics from this point of view.

References

[Alves, 1984] Elias H. Alves. Paraconsistent logic and model theory. *Studia Logica*, XLIII/1(2):17–32, 1984.

[Anderson and Belnap, 1975] A.R. Anderson and N.D. Jr. Belnap. *Entailment: the logic of relevance and necessity*, volume 1. Princeton University Press, 1975.

[Carnielli and Lima Marques, 1990] W. A. Carnielli and M. Lima Marques. Reasoning under inconsistent knowledge. Technical Report IRIT/90-15R, Institut de Recherche en Informatique de Toulouse–IRIT, France, 1990. revised edition of 1988.

[Carnielli, 1987] Walter A. Carnielli. Systematization of the finite many-valued logics through the method of tableaux. *The J. of Symbolic Logic*, 52:473–493, 1987.

[Carnielli, 1990] Walter A. Carnielli. Many-valued logics and plausible reasoning. In *Proceedings of Intl. Symp. on Multiple-valued Logic*, Charlotte, 1990. IEEE.

[da Costa, 1974] Newton C.A. da Costa. On the theory of inconsistent formal system. *Notre Dame Journal of Formal Logic*, 11:497–510, 1974.

[Delahaye and Thibau, 1988] J. P. Delahaye and V. Thibau. Programmation en logique trivaluée. In *Journé Européennes sur les Méthodes Logiques en Intelligence Artificielle*, pages 27–30, Roscoff, 1988. JELIA 88.

[Epstein, 1990] R. L. Epstein. *The Semantic Foundation of Logic: Propositional Logics*, volume 1. Kluwer Academic Publishers, 1990.

[Ginsberg, 1988] M. L. Ginsberg. Multivalued logic. In M. L. Ginsberg, editor, *Non-Monotonic Reasoning*, pages 251–257. Morgan Kaufman, 1988.

[Gödel, 1932] K. Gödel. Zum intuitionistichen Aussagenkalkül. *Anzeiger d. Ak. Wiss Wlen, Math. nat Klasse*, 69:65–66, 1932.

Ex contradictione nihil sequitur*

Gerd Wagner
Gruppe Logik, Wissenstheorie und Information
Institut für Philosophie, Freie Universität Berlin
Habelschwerdter Allee 30, 1000 Berlin 33
Germany

Abstract

In the logical semantics of knowledge bases (KB) the handling of contradicitions poses a problem not solvable by standard logic. An adequate logic for KBs must be capable of tolerating inconsistency in a KB without losing its deductive content. This is also the bottom line of so-called paraconsistent logics. But paraconsistent logic does not address the question whether contradictory information should be accepted or not in the derivation of further information depending on it. We propose two computational logics based on the notions of support and acceptance handling contradictions in a conservative, resp. skeptical, manner: they neither lead to the break-down of the system nor are they accepted as valid pieces of information.

1 Introduction

Dating back to Aristotle, the classical principle *ex contradictione sequitur quodlibet* has been considered fundamental by most logicians and philosophers. Clearly, it makes sense for mathematics[1] where it amounts to the postulate that contradictions in a theory must not be tolerated and have to be removed, otherwise the theory as a whole should be rejected as meaningless. This postulate, however, is neither acceptable for the logical modeling of cognitive processes nor for a semantics of databases, respectively knowledge bases, where the logic is required to be an adequate tool for information processing rather than a metaphysically correct theory.

In AI, notably in the field of knowledge representation and automated reasoning, inconsistency handling plays a crucial role:

- it is a real problem for expert system shells which don't seem to deal with it in a principled way
- it is the main issue of many nonmonotonic formalisms such as default logic, inheritance networks, defeasible reasoning and belief revision
- it will be a major issue in logic programming where – this is a forecast – negative conclusions will be allowed in future systems[2]

There have been several suggestions to apply paraconsistent logics in AI.[3] But the principle of paraconsistency, $\{p, \sim p\} \not\vdash q$, does not imply an answer to the question whether a derivation may rely on possibly contradictory information or not. Also in the aforementioned work this question was not addressed.[4] Usually, in paraconsistent logics contradictory sentences are accepted as a basis for further derivations. This corresponds to the 'dialethic' standpoint of e.g. Priest [1989] according to which a contradictory sentence counts as both true and false, simultaneously: $\{p, \sim p\} \vdash p$ as well as $\{p, \sim p\} \vdash \sim p$.

From an information processing point of view, however, it seems to be more natural to discard contradictory information as neither true nor false, so it cannot be used in the derivation of further information: $\{p, \sim p\} \not\vdash p$ as well as $\{p, \sim p\} \not\vdash \sim p$. This view seems to be shared by Perlis [1989]: "when a contradiction is found in our reasoning we tend to notice that fact and take corrective action, such as temporarily suspending beliefs in one or both conflicting beliefs."

While in many other formalisms (in belief revision[5], for instance) the logic is extended by adding a certain higher-level apparatus, our aim is to establish a basic-level logical system capable of handling contradictory information in a satisfactory way.

*The present paper extends ideas presented in [Wagner 1990a].

[1] But even for mathematics some people, e.g. Wittgenstein [1956], have questioned it.

[2] The theoretical basis for this is discussed in [Pearce & Wagner 1989], [Gelfond & Lifschitz 1990], [Kowalski & Sadri 1990], [Wagner 1990b].

[3] e.g. [Blair & Subrahmanian 1989], [Kifer & Lozinskii 1989], [da Costa et al. 1990], [Subrahmanian 1990]

[4] Subrahmanian [1990] remarks as a criticism of the 4-valued approach of [Blair & Subrahmanian 1989] that we should not be allowed to use inconsistent information to draw further conclusions. However, no solution to this problem is offered.

[5] cf. [Gärdenfors 1988]

2 Informal Presentation

We assume that a KB consists of rules, *conclusion* $\leftarrow$ *premise*, representing positive, resp. negative, conditional information. A fact can be represented as a rule with an empty premise, or, in an alternative notation, with premise 1, the *verum*, which is trivially accepted. Instead of *conclusion* $\leftarrow$ 1 we shall also simply write *conclusion* as an abbreviation. The following is an example of a KB in this sense:

Example 1 $KB_1 = \{p, \sim q, s, \sim p, q \leftarrow p, r \leftarrow q\}$

2.1 Liberal Reasoning

The notions of liberal support and acceptance are defined by the following clauses:

(1) 1 is supported.

(support) A conclusion is supported if the KB contains a rule for it the premise of which is supported.

(accept) A conclusion is accepted if it is supported.

We denote the consequence operation collecting all liberally accepted conclusions by LC,

$$LC(KB_1) = \{p, q, \sim p, \sim q, r, s\}$$

Notice that certain conclusions are accepted together with their resp. contraries, i.e. they are simultaneously accepted and rejected. In order to avoid this strange situation acceptance should be defined in another way.

2.2 Semi-liberal Reasoning

The simplest contradiction banning modification of liberal reasoning would be to delete all contradictory conclusions from LC(KB). The definitions of (1) and (support) from liberal reasoning are retained. Additionally, we have

(doubt) A conclusion is doubted if its contrary is supported.

(accept) A conclusion is accepted if it is supported and not doubted.

(reject) A conclusion is rejected if it is doubted and not supported.

The resulting consequence operation, collecting all semi-liberally accepted conclusions, is denoted by LC′. In our example KB_1, p and q are no longer accepted consequences, since they are not only supported but also doubted. Only r and s are accepted, $LC'(KB_1) = \{r, s\}$. At first glance this looks like we had cleaned up the mess of $LC(KB_1)$. But if we really don't want to accept contradictory conclusions we should also ban them from entering into derivations. Consequently, r should not be derivable since it depends on q which is contradictory.

One possible solution consists in a seemingly small change in the definition of support.

2.3 Conservative Reasoning

Conservative reasoning requires the premise of a rule to be accepted (and not only supported) in order that the conclusion be supported. (1), (doubt), (accept) and (reject) are as above. Additionally, we have now

(support) A conclusion is supported if the KB contains a rule for it the premise of which is accepted.

Concerning KB_1, this means that p is not accepted, since it is both supported and doubted, consequently q is not supported by $q \leftarrow p$, but only doubted, by $\sim q$, hence $\sim q$ is accepted. Also, s is accepted, and r is not. Thus, we obtain the following set of conservative consequences, $CC(KB_1) = \{\sim q, s\}$. The interesting point here is that, by our redefinition of support, we have also redefined the concept of contradiction. So, in comparison with liberal and semi-liberal reasoning, we not just lose conclusions based on contradictions, but we also lose contradictions, and consequently, gain new conclusions.

2.4 Skeptical Reasoning

We might not want to rely on conclusions which are, although not conservatively, but liberally doubted. As real skeptics we are not willing to accept any possibly inconsistent information. That is, we would not accept $\sim q$ as a conclusion from KB_1, since there is some evidence for the premise of a contrary rule, p (though there is evidence for $\sim p$, as well). This is achieved by (1), (support), (accept) and (reject) as in conservative reasoning, and a stronger notion of doubt,

(doubt) A conclusion is doubted if its contrary is liberally supported.

According to skeptical reasoning we obtain the following set of skeptical consequences, $SC(KB_1) = \{s\}$.

2.5 Discussion

LC′, CC and SC are nonmonotonic: the addition of new information to the KB may cause new contradictions invalidating previously accepted conclusions. The question now is: which of LC, LC′, CC and SC is the most appropriate consequence operation for knowledge bases. From the above example it becomes clear that LC′ is not a good choice. It represents a bad compromise between liberal and skeptical reasoning. Obviously, LC is computationally cheaper than CC and SC which require twofold recursion.[6] So, it could make sense first to check the liberal derivability of a query, and if it succeeds, check

[6] SC seems to be computationally cheaper than CC.

in a second step whether it is grounded in noncontradictory information, i.e. conservatively, or even skeptically, derivable.

But there might also be domains of application where the liberal rationale is perfectly reasonable and the conservative and skeptical reasoning procedures are too restrictive.

Example 2 *Consider*

$$\mathrm{KB} = \left\{ \begin{array}{rcl} \text{treatment\_A} & \leftarrow & \text{symptom\_1} \wedge \text{fever} \\ \text{treatment\_B} & \leftarrow & \text{symptom\_1} \wedge \sim\text{fever} \\ \text{fever} & \leftarrow & \text{measure}(x) \wedge x > 37 \\ \sim\text{fever} & \leftarrow & \text{measure}(x) \wedge x \leq 37 \end{array} \right.$$

It is conceivable that in certain cases both treatments are applicable since, due to the vagueness of the measurement method, the first measurement might yield 37.3 and the second one 36.8, so we would obtain fever *and also* ~fever *by liberal reasoning. Both by conservative and skeptical reasoning the patient would not get any treatment, since neither* fever *nor* ~fever *would hold.*

The difference between conservative and skeptical reasoning consists in the resp. concept of contradiction. A conclusion is considered contradictory if it is both supported and doubted. Skeptical doubt is much stronger than its conservative counterpart which allows for conclusions not acceptable to a skeptic.

We propose to use LC, CC and SC as complementary options in knowledge-based reasoning.

3 The Formal System

The language of KBs consists of the logical operator symbols $\wedge, \vee, \sim$ and 1 standing for conjunction, disjunction, negation and the verum, respectively, predicate symbols, constant symbols, and variables. Notice that there are no function symbols and no explicit quantifiers.

A *literal* is either an atom or a negated atom (if it is neither 1 nor ~ 1 it is called *proper*). We use $a, b, \ldots, l, k, \ldots$ and $F, G, H, \ldots$ as metavariables for atoms, literals and formulas, respectively. A variable-free expression is called *ground*. A KB consists of clauses of the form $l \leftarrow F$. We consider such clauses as specific inference rules expressing conditional facts, and not as implicational formulas. A rule with premise 1 is also called a *fact*, and we abbreviate $l \leftarrow 1$ by l. Examples of clauses are $\sim$flies$(x) \leftarrow$ emu$(x) \vee$penguin(x) or switch_on_light $\leftarrow$ dark $\wedge \sim$illuminated.

We consider a KB containing non-ground clauses as a dynamic representation of the corresponding set of ground clauses formed by means of the current domain of individuals U and denoted by $[\mathrm{KB}]_U$. Formally,

$$[\mathrm{KB}]_U \;=\; \{l\sigma \leftarrow F\sigma : l \leftarrow F \in \mathrm{KB}, \text{ and } \sigma : \mathrm{Var}(l, F) \rightarrow U\}$$

where σ ranges over all mappings from the set of variables of l and F into the Herbrand universe U. We call σ a ***ground substitution*** for $l \leftarrow F$ and $[\mathrm{KB}]_U$ the ***Herbrand expansion*** of KB with respect to a certain Herbrand universe U. We shall write [KB] for the Herbrand expansion of KB with respect to the Herbrand universe U_{KB} of KB.

We shall formulate our system proof-theoretically[7] by defining a derivability relation between a KB and a well-formed formula in the style of a natural deduction system by means of the introduction rules (l),$(\wedge)$,$(\sim\wedge)$, $(\sim\sim)$ and (x).[8] We first present the deduction rules for complex formulas. We write "$\mathrm{KB} \vdash F, G$" as an abbreviation of "$\mathrm{KB} \vdash F$ and $\mathrm{KB} \vdash G$".

$$(\wedge)\ \frac{\mathrm{KB} \vdash F, G}{\mathrm{KB} \vdash F \wedge G} \qquad (\sim\sim)\ \frac{\mathrm{KB} \vdash F}{\mathrm{KB} \vdash \sim\sim F}$$

$$(\sim\wedge)\ \frac{\mathrm{KB} \vdash \sim F}{\mathrm{KB} \vdash \sim(F \wedge G)} \qquad \frac{\mathrm{KB} \vdash \sim G}{\mathrm{KB} \vdash \sim(F \wedge G)}$$

where F and G are ground formuas, and a non-ground formula is provable if some ground instance of it is,

$$(x)\ \frac{\mathrm{KB} \vdash F(c) \quad \text{for some constant } c}{\mathrm{KB} \vdash F(x)}$$

We also stipulate that for any KB, $\mathrm{KB} \vdash 1$. The rules for disjunction, $(\vee)$ and $(\sim\vee)$, are derivable according to the DeMorgan identities.

In order to complete this definition of derivability relative to a KB we have to specify what it means for a ground literal to be derivable, i.e. the rule (l). While liberal, conservative and skeptical derivabiltity have the same rules for complex formulas, $(\wedge)$, $(\sim\wedge)$, $(\sim\sim)$, (x), they differ in the base case, (l), which is defined in the next sections.

Notice that we do not have a 'trivialization rule', so as to conclude anything from a contradiction. The principle *ex contradictione sequitur quodlibet*, $\{F, \sim F\} \vdash G$, which is fundamental in classical and intuitionistic logic, has been dropped. Furthermore, in the conservative and in the skeptical system, we replace it by the principle *ex contradictione nihil sequitur.*

4 Well-founded KBs

Concerning the recursive structure of a KB, the most straightforward way to define *liberal derivability* for ground literals is the following

$$(l)_l \quad \mathrm{KB} \vdash_l l \quad \text{iff} \quad \exists (l \leftarrow F) \in [\mathrm{KB}] : \mathrm{KB} \vdash_l F$$

[7] Notice that this seems to be the most natural way to define cognitively interesting nonstandard logics such as relevance logics, default logic, or the defeasible reasoning procedure of Nute, which all have in common that they have no simple and intuitively convincing model theory.

[8] There is no need for elimination rules because $\vdash$ does not allow for arbitrary formulas in the premise.

However, this definition only works for 'well-behaved' KBs which we call *well-founded* according to the definition below. In other cases it enters a loop.[9]

In order to say what it means for a KB to be well-founded we need a few definitions. We define DNS(F), the ***disjunctive normal set*** of a formula F as follows:

$$\begin{aligned}\mathrm{DNS}(l) &= \{\{l\}\}\\ \mathrm{DNS}(F\wedge G) &= \{K\cup L : K\in \mathrm{DNS}(F),\\ &\qquad L\in \mathrm{DNS}(G)\}\\ \mathrm{DNS}(\sim(F\wedge G)) &= \mathrm{DNS}(\sim F)\cup \mathrm{DNS}(\sim G)\\ \mathrm{DNS}(\sim\sim F) &= \mathrm{DNS}(F)\end{aligned}$$

With this the ***disjunctive normal form*** of a formula G can be obtained as

$$\mathrm{DNF}(G) = \bigvee_{K\in \mathrm{DNS}(G)} \bigwedge K$$

For a ground literal l we define $\mathrm{Pre}^1(l)$, the set of its single-step literal predecessors, $\mathrm{Pre}^i(l)$, the set of its ith-step literal predecessors, and $\mathrm{Pre}(l)$, the set of all proper ground literals preceeding it in KB:

$$\begin{aligned}\mathrm{Pre}^1(l) &= \bigcup\{K-\{1\} : K\in \mathrm{DNS}(F)\\ &\qquad \&\ l\leftarrow F\in[\mathrm{KB}]\}\\ \mathrm{Pre}^{i+1}(l) &= \bigcup\{\mathrm{Pre}^1(k) : k\in \mathrm{Pre}^i(l)\}\\ \mathrm{Pre}(l) &= \mathrm{Pre}^1(l)\cup\bigcup\{\mathrm{Pre}(k) : k\in \mathrm{Pre}^1(l)\}\end{aligned}$$

Intuitively speaking, Pre(l) collects all ground literals on which the derivability of l possibly depends.

A KB is called *well-founded*, if for every $l\leftarrow F\in[\mathrm{KB}]$ we have $l\notin \mathrm{Pre}(l)$. It is called *strongly well-founded* if for every $l\leftarrow F\in[\mathrm{KB}]$ we have $l\notin \mathrm{Pre}(l)$ and also $\tilde{l}\notin \mathrm{Pre}(l)$, where $\widetilde{\tilde{a}}=a$ and $\tilde{a}=\sim a$.

For example, $\mathrm{KB}=\{q, p\leftarrow q, q\leftarrow \sim p\}$ is well-founded but not strongly well-founded since $\sim p\in \mathrm{Pre}(p)$.

For strongly well-founded KBs we can define *conservative* and *skeptical derivability*, $\vdash_c$ and $\vdash_s$, as follows:

$(l)_c$ $\mathrm{KB}\vdash_c l$ iff $\exists(l\leftarrow F)\in[\mathrm{KB}] : \mathrm{KB}\vdash_c F$, and $\forall(\tilde{l}\leftarrow G)\in[\mathrm{KB}] : \mathrm{KB}\not\vdash_c G$

$(l)_s$ $\mathrm{KB}\vdash_s l$ iff $\exists(l\leftarrow F)\in[\mathrm{KB}] : \mathrm{KB}\vdash_s F$, and $\forall(\tilde{l}\leftarrow G)\in[\mathrm{KB}] : \mathrm{KB}\not\vdash_l G$

Notice that these definitions are twofold recursive. Conservative derivability excludes only those contradictory information the derivation of which does not itself rest on other contradictions, whereas skeptical derivability also discards information as contradictory if its inconsistency is caused by other contradictory information.

We denote the resp. consequence operations associating the set of liberal, conservative and skeptical consequences with a KB, $\{F : \mathrm{KB}\vdash_* F\}$ where $*=l,c,s$, by LC(KB), CC(KB) and SC(KB).

[9] This problem does not arise in standard logic where the notion of derivability is not operational but simply requires the existence of a proof.

Observation 1 *$SC(KB)\subseteq CC(KB)\subseteq LC(KB)$*

Example 3 *$\mathrm{KB}_2=\{\sim p, r, q\leftarrow\sim p, s\leftarrow r, \sim q\leftarrow r, \sim r\leftarrow p, \sim s\leftarrow q\wedge r\}$ is strongly well-founded. Thus, applying the resp. recursive derivability procedures we obtain*

$$\begin{aligned}\mathrm{LC}(\mathrm{KB}_2) &= \{\sim p, r, q, \sim q, s, \sim s\}\\ \mathrm{CC}(\mathrm{KB}_2) &= \{\sim p, r, s\}\\ \mathrm{SC}(\mathrm{KB}_2) &= \{\sim p, r\}\end{aligned}$$

5 Non-Well-Founded KBs

The simplest case of a non-well-founded knowledge base is $\mathrm{KB}=\{p\leftarrow p\}$. Clearly, we are interested in a decidable derivation procedure yielding $\mathrm{KB}\not\vdash p$. In order to intercept such looping situations in the course of derivation we introduce an 'index' to the derivability relation. Let L be an arbitrary set of ground literals. First, we stipulate that $\langle \mathrm{KB}, L\rangle\vdash_* 1$ for $*=l,c,s$. Then we define

$\langle \mathrm{KB}, L\rangle\vdash_l l$ iff $\exists(l\leftarrow F)\in[\mathrm{KB}]\,\exists K\in \mathrm{DNS}(F)$:
(i) $K\cap(L\cup\{l\})=\emptyset$, and
(ii) $\forall k\in K : \langle \mathrm{KB}, L\cup\{l\}\rangle\vdash_l k$

Natural cases of not strongly well-founded rules arise, for example, when incompatibility between predicates is expressed like in $\mathrm{KB}_3=\{r(n), \sim q(x)\leftarrow r(x), \sim r(x)\leftarrow q(x)\}$ where r and q ('being a republican' and 'being a quaker') are incompatible. Although such incompatibility rules are not strongly well-founded we want to employ them in derivations if possible. So, we want to be able to conclude from KB_3 that Nixon, since being a republican, is not a quaker. For an arbitrary set A of ground atoms and an arbitrary KB we define:

$\langle \mathrm{KB}, A\rangle\vdash_c l$ iff $\exists(l\leftarrow F)\in[\mathrm{KB}]\,\exists K\in \mathrm{DNS}(F)$:
(i) $\hat{K}\cap(A\cup\{\hat{l}\})=\emptyset$, and
(ii) $\forall k\in K : \langle \mathrm{KB}, A\cup\{\hat{l}\}\rangle\vdash_c k$, and
(iii) $\forall(\tilde{l}\leftarrow G)\in[\mathrm{KB}]\,\forall K\in \mathrm{DNS}(G)$ $\exists k\in K : \langle \mathrm{KB}, A\cup\{\hat{l}\}\rangle\not\vdash_c k$

$\langle \mathrm{KB}, A\rangle\vdash_s l$ iff $\exists(l\leftarrow F)\in[\mathrm{KB}]\,\exists K\in \mathrm{DNS}(F)$:
(i) $\hat{K}\cap(A\cup\{\hat{l}\})=\emptyset$, and
(ii) $\forall k\in K : \langle \mathrm{KB}, A\cup\{\hat{l}\}\rangle\vdash_s k$, and
(iii) $\forall(\tilde{l}\leftarrow G)\in[\mathrm{KB}]\,\forall K\in \mathrm{DNS}(G)$ $\exists k\in K : \langle \mathrm{KB}, A\cup\{\hat{l}\}\rangle\not\vdash_l k$

where $\hat{a}=\widehat{\sim a}=a$ and $\hat{K}=\{\hat{k} : k\in K\}$.

Notice that condition (i) in the above definitions provides a kind of loop-checking.

Observation 2 *(i) For every well-founded KB,* $\mathrm{KB}\vdash_l l$ *iff* $\langle \mathrm{KB},\emptyset\rangle\vdash_l l$.
(ii) For every strongly well-founded KB, $\mathrm{KB}\vdash_* l$ *iff* $\langle \mathrm{KB},\emptyset\rangle\vdash_* l$ *for* $*=c,s$.

This is because well-foundedness guarantees that condition (i) of the definition will be satisfied (proof by induction on the degree of l). Thus, we can define derivability for general, not necessarily (strongly) well-founded, KBs by

$$(l)_* \quad \text{KB} \vdash_* l \quad \text{iff} \quad \langle \text{KB}, \emptyset \rangle \vdash_* l \quad \text{for } * = l, c, s$$

Example 4 *The following KB (about the barber shaving anyone not shaving himself) is not strongly well-founded,*

$$\text{KB}_4 \quad = \quad \begin{cases} s(b,x) & \leftarrow \;\sim s(x,x) \\ \sim s(b,b) \\ \sim s(c,c) \end{cases}$$

We have $SC(\text{KB}_4) = \{\sim s(b,b), \sim s(c,c), s(b,c)\}$ since the only contrary rule for $\sim s(b,b)$ fails through the loop check: $\langle \text{KB}_4, \{\widehat{\sim s(b,b)}\} \rangle \not\vdash_s s(b,b)$.

6 Relation to Other Formalisms

The logics of liberal, conservative and skeptical reasoning are non-classical. For instance, the law of the excluded middle is not a tautological consequence: in general, $p \vee \sim p$ is neither valid in liberal, nor in conservative, nor in skeptical reasoning. Rather, liberal derivability corresponds to a certain fragment of the **paraconsistent constructive logic** N^- of Nelson [1949; Almukdad & Nelson 1984].

While liberal derivability is adequate with respect to general partial models[10], or, equivalently, 4-valued models[11], the model theory for conservative and skeptical reasoning is still under investigation. It seems that a preferred model approach within **general partial semantics** is needed.

Conservative and skeptical reasoning can be viewed as generalizations of ambiguity-blocking and ambiguity-propagating **skeptical inheritance**. In fact, Ex. 1 is the logical representation of a net which illustrates the difference between these two strategies.

Conservative reasoning corresponds to **Nute's defeasible reasoning** procedure in the following way: if all clauses of a KB are considered to be defeasible rules in the sense of [Nute 1988], then our concept of conservative consequence essentially agrees with the concept of consequence in Nute's formalism (without specificity defeat).

There is also a close connection to the partial **logic of normal defaults**[12] which is defined as follows. Let D be a set of normal 'conclusion unary' defaults, $F : l \,/\, l$, and Γ_D an operator taking a set of literals to a set of literals, $\Gamma_D : 2^{\text{Lit}} \rightarrow 2^{\text{Lit}}$ with $\Gamma_D(X)$ defined as the smallest set such that $l \in \Gamma_D(X)$ whenever $\Gamma_D(X) \vdash F$ & $\tilde{l} \notin X$ for all ground defaults $F : l \,/\, l \in [D]$. E is called a *partial default extension* for D if $\Gamma_D(E) = E$. Now, if all the clauses of a KB are considered to be normal defaults, i.e. $l \leftarrow F$ is identified with $F : l \,/\, l$, we can state

Observation 3 *For every KB, and every partial default extension E of KB, we have $SC(KB) \subseteq E \subseteq LC(KB)$.*

[10] cf. [Langholm 1988]

[11] cf. [Belnap 1977]

[12] Default logic was introduced by Reiter [1980].

7 Future Work

The logics of liberal, conservative and skeptical reasoning can be extended by adding another negation allowing for the processing of implicit negative information in the spirit of negation-as-failure. This has been done for liberal reasoning in [Wagner 1991] where the resulting system is called *vivid logic*. This system and its conservative and skeptical variants seem to be a kind of common background logic for such areas like default logic, defeasible inheritance, generalized deductive databases[13] and generalized logic programs[14].

For the model theory of the above systems we think that general partial semantics is a promising framework. As soon as we want to add a genuine implication to our systems we expect to end up with some kind of possible worlds semantics.

The addition of inconsistent hypothesis to a KB does not require any belief revision in our system. It should be interesting to compare the approach to inconsistency handling described in this paper with the 'consistency maintenance' approach of belief revision formalisms where contradictions have to be detected and eliminated. We expect computational advantages of our approach.

8 Concluding Remarks

We have presented a simple and natural nonmonotonic formalism for dealing with contradictory information. Since it is given by a recursive proof theory, it is computationally feasible.[15] By comparison with default logic and defeasible inheritance we obtained some evidence that it might be the logical kernel of inconsistency-tolerant reasoning.

References

[Almukdad & Nelson 1984] A. Almukdad and D. Nelson: Constructible Falsity and Inexact Predicates, *JSL 49/1* (1984), 231–233

[13] see [Wagner 1991]

[14] see [Gelfond & Lifschitz 1990]

[15] It is a straightforward matter to implement an inference engine for liberal, conservative and skeptical reasoning in Prolog, for instance.

[Belnap 1977] N.D. Belnap: A Useful Four-valued Logic, in G. Epstein and J.M. Dunn (eds.), *Modern Uses of Many-valued Logic*, Reidel, 1977, 8–37

[Blair & Subrahmanian 1989] H. Blair and V.S. Subrahmanian: Paraconsistent Logic Programming, *Theoretical Computer Science* 68 (1989), 135–154

[da Costa et al. 1990] N.C.A. da Costa, L.J. Henschen, J.J. Lu and V.S. Subrahmanian: Automatic Theorem Proving in Paraconsistent Logics, *Proc. of 10th Int. Conf. on Automated Deduction 1990*, Springer LNAI 449

[Gärdenfors 1988] P. Gärdenfors: *Knowledge in Flux*, MIT Press, Cambridge 1988

[Gelfond & Lifschitz 1990] M. Gelfond and V. Lifschitz: Logic Programs with Classical Negation, *Proc. ICLP-90*, MIT Press

[Kifer & Lozinskii 1989] M. Kifer and E.L. Lozinskii, RI: A Logic for Reasoning with Inconsistency, *Proc. of 4th IEEE Symp. on Logic in Computer Science 1989*, 253–262

[Langholm 1988] T. Langholm: *Partiality, Truth and Persistence*, CSLI Lecture Notes No. 15, University of Chicago Press, 1988

[Nelson 1949] D. Nelson: Constructible falsity, *JSL 14* (1949), 16–26

[Nute 1988] D. Nute, Defeasible Reasoning: A Philosophical Analysis in Prolog, in J.H. Fetzer (ed.), *Aspects of AI*, 1988, 251–288

[Pearce & Wagner 1989] D. Pearce and G. Wagner: Reasoning with Negative Information I – Strong Negation in Logic Programs, LWI Technical Report 4/1989, Freie Universität Berlin; also in L. Haarparanta (ed.), *Proc. of Symposium on the Philosophy of Jaako Hintikka 1989*, Helsinki, 1991

[Perlis 1989] D. Perlis: Truth and Meaning, *AI* 39 (1989), 245–250

[Priest 1989] G. Priest: Reasoning about Truth, *AI* 39 (1989), 231–244

[Reiter 1980] R. Reiter: A Logic for Default Reasoning, *AI* 13 (1980), 81–132

[Subrahmanian 1990] V.S. Subrahmanian, Y-Logic: A Framework for Reasoning about Chameolonic Programs with Inconsistent Completions, *Fundamenta Informatice* XIII (1990), 465–483

[Wagner 1990a] G. Wagner: The Two Sources of Nonmonotonicity in Vivid Logic – Inconsistency Handling and Weak Falsity, *Proc. of GMD Workshop on Nonmonotonic Reasoning 1989*, Gesellschaft für Mathematik und Datenverarbeitung, Bonn - St. Augustin, 1990

[Wagner 1990b] G. Wagner: Logic Programming with Strong Negation and Inexact Predicates, LWI Technical Report 11/1990, Freie Universität Berlin, to appear in *Journal of Logic and Computation*

[Wagner 1991] G. Wagner: A Database Needs Two Kinds of Negation, *Proc. of Int. Conf. on Mathematical Fundamentals of Database and Knowlege Base Systems MFDBS-91*, Springer LNCS, 1991

[Wittgenstein 1956] L. Wittgenstein: *Remarks on the Foundations of Mathematics*, MacMillan, New York 1956

PANELS

Panel: The Role of Chess in Artificial Intelligence Research

Robert Levinson (Chairperson)
Computer and Information Sciences
Applied Sciences Building
University of California at Santa Cruz
Santa Cruz, CA 95064
(408)459-2087
ARPANET:levinson@cis.ucsc.edu
FAX:429-0146

Feng-hsiung Hsu
IBM T.J. Watson Research Center
PO Box 704
Yorktown Heights
NY 10598

Jonathan Schaeffer
Computing Science
University of Alberta
Edmonton
Canada T6G 2H1

T. Anthony Marsland
Computing Science
University of Alberta
Edmonton
Canada T6G 2H1

David E. Wilkins
SRI International EJ227
333 Ravenswood Ave
Menlo Park
CA 94025

Abstract

Our eminent researchers including John McCarthy, Allen Newell, Claude Shannon, Herb Simon, Ken Thompson and Alan Turing put significant effort into computer chess research. Now that computers have reached the grandmaster level, and are beginning to vie for the World Championship, the AI community should pause to evaluate the significance of chess in the evolving objectives of AI, evaluate the contributions made to date, and assess what can be expected in the future. Despite the general interest in chess amongst computer scientists and the significant progress in the last twenty years, there seems to be a lack of appreciation for the field in the AI community. On one hand this is the fruit of success (brute force works, why study anything else?), but also the result of a focus on performance above all else in the chess community. Also, chess has proved to be too challenging for many of the AI techniques that have been thrown at it. We wish to promote chess as the fundamental test bed recognized by our founding researchers and increase awareness of its contribution to date.

Panel Summary

The factors that make chess an excellent domain for AI research include:

- Richness of the problem-solving domain.
- Ability to monitor and record progress accurately through competition and rating, because of its well-defined structure.
- Chess has been around for centuries – the basics are well-understood internationally, expertise is readily available and is (generally!) beyond proprietary or nationalistic interests. Has been considered a "game of intelligence." Many players of the game feel mentally "stretched."
- Detailed psychological studies of chess playing exist. These studies suggest that human players use different reasoning modes from those in current chess programs. Further, the reasoning modes are also used in many other problem-solving domains.
- Excellent test bed for uncertainty management schemes – the basis of most expert problem-solving. The well-definedness and discreteness of the game have led many to ignore this.

The above factors make chess a useful tool regardless of the strength of the current programs. Because of the success of the current methods there remains a vast arena of other methods that have not been explored. The most obvious lack is in the application and development of machine learning techniques to chess, but other areas, including knowledge representation and compilation, planning and control, also seem to be applicable. AI researchers should be encouraged to use chess as a test bed for their techniques, with the understanding that chess is not the end in itself. Chess may provide the avenue by which bridges may be built between cognitive science, AI and connectionist modeling.

With the current and future battle for the World Human-Computer Championship the AI community should be made more sensitive to the issues involved and their bearing on intelligence research: Is search sufficient? How much detailed chess knowledge is required? How is this knowledge implemented and incorporated with search? We are fortunate to have a World Champion who promotes creativity over the chess board and is willing to face the challenge from computers head-on.

The members of the panel and the presentations have been designed to address these topics in a way that supports our objectives to make chess an important and respected AI tool in this new decade. *Jonathan Schaeffer* will emphasize those areas of computer chess research that have been ignored, because the approach has been a competitive/engineering one instead of scientific. *Feng-hsiung Hsu* of the Deep Thought team will discuss the role of knowledge in current chess programming and argue that more responsibility for the knowledge should be put on the machines themselves. *Tony Marsland* will present specific open research issues in computer chess that will require AI solutions. *Robert Levinson* will describe an alternative model of chess computation, a self-learning pattern-oriented chess program ("Morph") whose knowledge is learned incrementally from experience, without many examples being stored (and with little guidance about relevant features). *David Wilkins* will provide balance to the discussion by pointing out the limitations of chess and claiming that Go is a better domain. He will also describe a new type of games tournament that prevents the human tailoring of evaluation functions and encourages the use of learning and more robust approaches.

The timing for this panel is particularly good with the current World Championship having completed, a more powerful Deep Thought on the scene, a recent article in Scientific American [Hsu *et al.*, 1990] and new books by Levy and Newborn [1991], and by Marsland and Schaeffer [1990].

Presentations

Computer Chess: Science or Engineering?

Jonathan Schaeffer
University of Alberta

Research into artificial intelligence using chess as the application domain has produced several important contributions to AI:

- The effectiveness of brute-force search. Chess has clearly demonstrated that simple, brute-force approaches should not be quickly discarded.
- Iterative search. Some of the ideas developed for alpha-beta search, iterative deepening in particular, are applicable to other search domains.
- The inadequacy of conventional AI techniques for realtime computation. No competitive computer chess program uses AI languages or knowledge representation methods. Why? They are too slow for a real-time, high performance application.

Although these (and other, lesser contributions) have enhanced our knowledge, it is not clear whether the effort expended justifies the results obtained.

It is easy to question the usefulness of computer chess research. It is important to distinguish between computer chess research and research using chess as a test bed. Unfortunately, the latter has evolved into the former. An entirely new field of "computer chess" has evolved, with the emphasis on chess performance and chess research – not generally of much interest to the AI community. There is a much deserved credibility problem here. The unfortunate correlation between program speed and performance encourages short-term projects (speeding up a move generator 10%) at the sacrifice of long-term research projects (such as chess programs that learn).

After over 30 years of work on chess programs, where are the scientific advances in:

- knowledge-based search algorithms? There has been some good work in this area, but none has progressed enough to be used in competitive chess programs. Alpha-beta simplifies the programming task, but the exponential search limits what can be achieved.
- knowledge representation and acquisition? These areas are of considerable importance to chess programs, yet the computer chess community has done embarrassing little research in this area.
- error analysis? While extensive error analysis has been done on search algorithms, little has been done to quantify errors in evaluation functions and how they interact with the search.
- tool development? With the right tool, work that might take days could be done in minutes. No tools are being developed to help build chess programs. For example, why isn't someone working on tools for defining chess knowledge?

If the community were committed to research, many of these problems would have been addressed by now. Sadly, much of the work currently being done on computer chess programs is engineering, not science. For example, the engineering of special-purpose VLSI chips to increase the speed of a chess program only underlines the importance chess programmers attach to speed.

In my opinion, conventional computer-chess methods will yield little of further interest to the AI community. I believe they will be inadequate to defeat the human World Champion in a match for a long time to come. It is still very easy to set up a position for which the computer has no idea what is going on – even if you speed up the machine 1000-fold. The current computer chess work will only underscore the need for better ways of adding and manipulating knowledge reliably.

The defeat of the human World Chess Champion sooner rather than later will help artificial intelligence. This will help to re-establish chess as an ideal problem domain for experimenting with the fundamental problems of artificial intelligence, as elaborated more fully by Donskoy and Schaeffer [1989].

"Expert Inputs" are Sometimes Harmful

Feng-hsiung Hsu
IBM T.J. Watson Research Center

Experience from the chess machine Deep Thought suggests that inputs from chess experts, while generally useful, cannot be trusted completely. A good example of this is Deep Thought's evaluation function. Several changes by capable human chess experts failed to produce significant improvements and occasionally even affected the machine's performance negatively. Here, human experts, along with their expertise, introduced their own prejudices into the program. One way of solving this problem is to limit the type and the amount of expert inputs allowed into the program; in other words, having an almost "knowledge-free" machine. The availability of on-line high quality chess game databases makes this an attractive approach. Instead of having the value of, say, an isolated pawn set by human experts either explicitly or in functional form, one can simply tell the program that isolated pawns are important features and statistical procedures, with some additional expert inputs, can then be used to decide the functional form and the proper weighting of the features in question.

That more responsibility for knowledge should be placed on machines is consistent with recent efforts to handle the knowledge acquisition problem in expert systems and also in memory-based reasoning schemes where knowledge is generated statistically rather than relying on symbolic learning, abstraction or domain modeling.

Open Problems and Lessons for AI

T. Anthony Marsland
University of Alberta

Based on predicted advances in computer technology, particularly the faster speeds and increasing memory of low cost systems, it is reasonable to assume that within the next decade the World Chess Champion will lose an informal game to a computer, and within twenty-five years lose a 12-game match. The early losses will reflect more breaks in concentration at first and later a recognition of the inevitable, as arose when trains started to out-pace runners. Although the defeat of humans by machines will be significant, it will mean neither the destruction of chess as a pastime and learning medium, nor the end of interest in computer chess *per se*. Instead it will focus attention even more sharply on precisely how and why humans can become so expert at selecting sound (often optimal) variations in seemingly complex situations, without resorting to the exhaustive techniques used by computer programs.

Some fundamental AI questions that will remain are:

- Given a patient and seemingly perfect teacher (that is a superior chess-playing machine), how should one use it to "teach" an AI-based learning program about strategies for playing chess (given that the rules of chess themselves are already perfectly known)?
- A related but perhaps simpler problem comes from the realm of endgame play. Given a perfect N-piece database holding an optimal move for each position (or perhaps only the length of the optimal sequence from that position, or even less, whether the position was won), develop a program that can deduce a sound set of rules or strategies for playing the endgame perfectly (or at least better than any other expert).
- Given endgame positions which cannot be solved by search or databases alone, deduce a plan or playing strategy that will transform the position into a known (win/draw) state. In one class of positions the remaining pieces are held to few squares. Progress can only be made by a freeing move that converts a short-term loss of material (or perhaps position) to the achievement of a later, more significant goal. Consider the Duchess-Chaos game [Frey, 1983, pp. 269–274], which is still thought to be beyond brute force search. Related examples abound, for instance giving up a passed pawn on one side of the board to win a pawn race on the other.
- Given a well-defined threat (for example mate) deep in the tree, identify un-examined moves at an earlier level along the current path that have the potential to deny the threat explicitly. This a form of dynamic re-ordering of moves, but is also (if no potential denials exist) a good forward pruning criteria – providing evidence to abandon this line of play.

The first two projects rely on perfect domain knowledge and the availability of an un-tiring teacher to whom questions can be posed. The need for convergence to a solution within some arbitrary or unreasonably short time-frame will thus be eliminated. The learning mechanisms used will have the benefit of drawing on results obtained by exhaustive means. Even simple rote learning, for example, has its place in Artificial Intelligence. Scherzer *et al.* [1990] have shown how to use the moves made during a series of chess games to ensure that a poor move sequence will eventually not be replayed. By holding the computer's memory of played games in a hash table the information can be used to extend the depth of search during later play. In related work, the expert knowledge from an encyclopedia of games has been optically read into a computer which also corrected the typographical computer to play through all known games, identify "losing moves" and by back-tracking develop "innovations" that correct the flaws. It is not trivial work because it requires making a plausible re-construction from imperfect data, but Ken Thompson has shown the way here [Marsland, 1987] Finally, once errors are found, a backtracking mechanism will be needed to find the best place earlier in the game-tree path to correct (avoid) the flaw that follows. The approach of recording, correcting and innovating appears to be fundamental to Artificial Intelligence.

The remaining problems are linked closely to formal or probabilistic pruning methods. Computer chess is computationally expensive enough that one can afford to expend considerable time eliminating parts of the search space by deduction. Over the years humans have developed techniques that allow them to reduce the search space through judicious use of forward pruning (that is, by temporarily abandoning certain variations) and either deducing by analogy that further consideration would be irrelevant, or (upon questioning the validity of the pruning) force reconsideration of the omitted lines. Pruning by analogy is a powerful general-purpose tool and if developed satisfactorily for a perfect information game like chess would almost certainly be applicable to related decision-tree searches. The intent is to be more selective about variations that are to be expanded fully. Methods like the null-move heuristic [Beal, 1989], conspiracy number search and singular extensions [Anantharaman *et al.*, 1988] all do this by expanding non-quiescent lines of play. On the other hand, the more formal probabilistic methods [Palay, 1985] attempt to limit the width of search at any node by estimating the probability that a better move exists in the moves that remain to be searched (Kozdrowicki and Cooper's [1973] so called "Fischer Set"). In effect this problem requires looking again at the method of analogies [Adelson-Velsky *et al.*, 1975]. It is remarkable that no significant improvement has been made to that method, despite the passage of 15 years. Not even attempts to implement simple forms of the idea in serious chess programs. The fundamental work here is to determine how best to make the method of analogies pay for itself. In this era of faster processors and parallel computation this must be a topic that is ripe for xploitation.

One important lesson for the AI community is the importance of competitive testing and performance comparison of algorithms. In a sense 20 years of computer chess championships have provided a long-running series of experiments proving conclusively that progress has been made, identifying clearly those methods that have been effective and making a direct comparison from year to year possible. In principle theorem proving programs could be tested the same way, as indeed could language translation systems. These forms of comparison are standard for pattern recognition systems, why not for natural language understanding? In conclusion AI would benefit if more of its work were done on a direct competitive basis to identify more sharply those methods that are truly generally applicable.

Morph: An Adaptive, Pattern-Oriented Chess System

Robert Levinson
University of California

Although chess computers now are competitive at master and grandmaster levels, that is where their resemblance to human players ends. Psychological evidence indicates that human chess players search very few positions, and base their positional assessments on structural/perceptual patterns learned through experience. Morph is a computer chess program that has been developed to be more consistent with the cognitive models.

The main objectives of the project are to demonstrate capacity of the system to learn, to deepen our understanding of the interaction of knowledge and search, and to build bridges in this area between AI and cognitive science.

The current model of chess programming came into its own in the 70's and early 80's and has been refined ever since [Slate and Atkin, 1977]. The main characteristic of the model is the use of brute-force alpha-beta minimax search with selective extensions for special situations such as forcing variations. This has been further enhanced by special purpose hardware. This model has been so successful that little else has been tried.

The alternative AI approaches have not fared well, perhaps because of the expense in applying the "knowledge" that had been supplied to the system. When chess has been used as a test bed [Flann and Dietterich, 1989; Minton, 1984; Pitrat, 1976; Quinlan, 1983; Wilkins, 1982] only a small sub-domain of the game was used, so that fundamental efficiency issues that AI must grapple with have been largely unaddressed. However, we feel that there is a third approach that relies neither on search nor on the symbolic computation approach of knowledge-oriented AI. In what we shall call the "pattern-oriented approach," configurations of interaction between squares and pieces are stored along with their significance. A uniform (and hence efficient method) is used to combine the significance in a given position to reach a final evaluation for that position. That such an approach is possible is evidenced by psychological models of human chess play [de Groot, 1965; Pfleger and Treppner, 1987].

Morph[1] is a system developed over the past 3 years that implements the pattern oriented approach [Levinson, 1989; Levinson and Snyder, 1991]. It is not conceivable that the detailed knowledge required to evaluate positions in this way could be supplied directly to the system, thus learning is required.

To strengthen the connections with the cognitive literature the system's knowledge is to come from its own playing experience, no sets of pre-classified examples are given and beyond its chess pattern representation scheme little chess knowledge such as the fact that having pieces is valuable (leave alone their values) has been provided to the system. Further, the system is limited to using only 1-ply of search.[2]

System Design Morph makes a move by generating all legal successors of the current position, evaluating each position using the current pattern database and choosing the position that is considered least favorable to the opponent. After each game patterns are created, deleted and generalized and weights are changed to make its evaluations more accurate, based on the outcome of the game. A more detailed summary of the design has recently appeared [Levinson and Syn-

[1]The name "Morph" comes from the Greek *morph* meaning form and the chess great, Paul Morphy.

[2]Though nothing in the method except perhaps efficiency, prevents deeper search.

der, 1991].

Morph stores two types of pattern: Graph patterns which represent attacks and defends relationships between pieces and squares and Material patterns that are vectors giving the relative material difference between the players, e.g. "up 2 pawns and down 1 rook," "even material," and so on. Along with each pattern is stored a weight that reflects the significance of the pattern. The weight is a real number in [0,1] that is an estimate of the expected true minmax evaluation of states that satisfy the pattern.

Results with Morph There have been many encouraging signs in the three months since Morph was fully implemented, and some preliminary results have been published [Levinson and Snyder, 1991].

Relationship of Morph to other approaches The chess system combines threads of a variety of machine-learning techniques that have been successful in other settings. It is this combination, and exactly what is done to achieve it, that is the basis for Morph's contributions. The learning-method areas and their involvement in Morph include genetic algorithms [Goldberg, 1989], neural nets (weight updating), temporal-difference learning, explanation-based generalization (EBG), and similarity-based learning. To combine these methods some design constraints usually associated with these methods are relaxed. With genetic algorithms, structured patterns rather than bit strings are used. In contrast to neural networks the nodes in Morph's hierarchy are assigned particular semantic/structural values. Temporal-difference learning is usually applied to methods with fixed evaluation function forms (in which the features are known but not their weights) but here the features change and the hierarchical database organization produce atypical discontinuities in the function.

Once a chess graph is constructed from a game board, the semantics of the nodes and edges in the graphs are unknown to the system. The only information a pattern contains as far as the system is concerned is the significance (weight) that has been attached to the pattern , in no place after pattern creation do we special case pieces or edges. Such a syntactic approach to the learning of search knowledge is substantially different from many of the traditional symbolic AI approaches to chess and to the learning of control knowledge.

In summary, in addition to a unique combination of methods, what distinguishes Morph is:

- A uniform representation of search knowledge.
- A syntactic approach to playing and learning.
- An attempt to play a complete game of chess rather than a small subdomain.
- Rejection of a learning-by-examples framework for an experiential framework that is more cognitively-inspired.
- Responsibility for feature discovery given to the system.
- Non-reliance on search (though at some point small guided search may be incorporated, bringing us even closer to the cognitive model).

Chess Was Good for AI Research.

David E. Wilkins
SRI International

Over the years, chess has proven to be a fertile ground for ideas and techniques that have spread to other areas of AI. These include database enumeration techniques [Bratko, 1978], chunking [Campbell, 1988], search techniques (minimax, alpha-beta, iterative deepening), and the utility of information [Good, 1977]. Considering the lack of funding for chess, it is significant that it has produced so many results.

Chess has been fertile because it provides a complex reasoning problem from a simple domain with a built-in performance criteria. The simple domain permits research to progress with little initial overhead. Having a hostile opponent adds complexity to the reasoning. In many domains (natural language understanding comes to mind), progress can be hindered by lack of performance criteria – it can be hard to tell whether the latest thesis is an improvement on the current state of the art. Chess provides precise answers to performance questions.

However, hardware advances have made chess a less fertile ground for addressing the basic issues of AI. The game is small enough that brute-force search techniques have dominated competitive computer chess, and I see little AI interest in squeezing out the last few hundred points on the chess ratings, except for the psychological impact of having a computer beat the human world champion.

Obviously, many basic issues in AI are not naturally addressed in a game-playing environment and should be explored in other domains. These include communication, forming models of one's environment, sensor analysis and integration, and (perhaps) reasoning about uncertainty. In addition, real-world domains force AI researchers to address issues such as economy of scale, noise, realtime response, failed actions, novel phenomena, and multiple agents – issues that can be ignored in chess.

Of the AI areas well-suited to a game-playing domain, there are better domains than chess. In particular, Go has all the advantages of chess but provides more complex reasoning and an even simpler domain. A successful symbolic Go program would have to plan, would have to use goal-directed search, would encourage machine learning, and would promote visual reasoning – all basic AI research issues that are now ignored in competitive computer chess.

Even better than Go, Barney Pell [1991] has proposed an event where programs compete against each other, but are only given a description of the game to be played at the beginning of the match. Chess is particularly well suited to this adaptation. One could, for example, have a competition using a chess board and pieces, where the match begins by giving the programs a declarative statement of how the pieces move, how they capture, the initial position, and what the objective of the game is. The programs would have to play this newly defined game under time constraints. A longish series of games could be required. This would require machine learning and a robust symbolic problem-solving capability that is not tailored to a specific game. For each new game, the programs would have to learn evaluation functions (if needed), learn what goals are advantageous to attempt, and learn heuristics or features for selecting moves. Brute force techniques would be disadvantaged by the lack of opportunity to fine tune both an evaluation function and a quiescence search for the game at hand.

References

[Adelson-Velsky *et al.*, 1975] G. Adelson-Velsky, V. Arlazarov, and M. Donsky. Some methods of controlling the tree search in chess programs. *Artificial Intelligence*, 6(4):361–371, 1975.

[Anantharaman *et al.*, 1988] T. Anantharaman, M. S. Campbell, and F. H. Hsu. Singular extensions: Adding selectivitly to brute force search. *Intern. Computer Chess Assoc. Journal*, 11(4):135–143, 1988.

[Beal, 1989] D. Beal. Experiments with the null move. In *Advances in Computer Chess 5*, pages 65–79. Elsevier, 1989.

[Bratko *et al.*, 1978] I. Bratko, D. Kopek, and D. Michie. Pattern-based representation of chess end-game knowledge. *Computer Journal*, 21(2):149–153, May 1978.

[Campbell, 1988] M. S. Campbell. *Chunking as an Abstraction Mechanism.* PhD thesis, Carnegie Mellon University, 1988.

[de Groot, 1965] A. D. de Groot. *Thought and Choice in Chess.* The Hague, 1965.

[Donskoy and Schaeffer, 1989] M. Donskoy and J. Schaeffer. Perspectives on falling from grace. *Intern. Computer Chess Assoc. Journal*, 12(3):155–163, 1989. Reprinted by Marsland and Schaeffer [1990, pages 259–268].

[Flann and Dietterich, 1989] N. S. Flann and T. G. Dietterich. A study of explanation-based methods for inductive learning. *Machine Learning*, 4:187–226, 1989.

[Frey, 1983] P. W. Frey, editor. *Chess Skill in Man and Machine.* Springer-Verlag, 1983.

[Goldberg, 1989] D. E. Goldberg. *Genetic Algorithms in Search, Optimization and Machine Learning.* Addison-Welsley, Reading, MA, 1989.

[Good, 1977] I. J. Good. Dynamic probability, computer chess, and the measurement of knowledge. In E. W. Elcock and D. Michie, editors, *Machine Intelligence 8*, pages 139–150. Ellis Horwood, Chichester, 1977.

[Hsu *et al.*, 1990] F. Hsu, T. Anantharaman, M. S. Campbell, and A. Nowatzyk. A grandmaster chess machine. *Scientific American*, 263(4):44–50, 1990.

[Kozdrowicki and Cooper, 1973] E. Kozdrowicki and D. Cooper. COKO III: The cooper-koz chess program. *Comm. ACM*, 16(7):411–427, 1973.

[Levinson and Snyder, 1991] R. Levinson and R. Snyder. Adaptive pattern oriented chess. In *Proceedings of AAAI-91.* Morgan-Kaufman, 1991.

[Levinson, 1989] R. Levinson. A self-learning, pattern-oriented chess program. *Intern. Computer Chess Assoc. Journal*, 12(4):207–215, December 1989.

[Levy and Newborn, 1991] D. Levy and M. Newborn. *How Computers Play Chess.* Computer Science Press, New York, NY, 1991.

[Marsland and Schaeffer, 1990] T. A. Marsland and J. Schaeffer, editors. *Computers, Chess and Cognition.* Springer-Verlag, 1990.

[Marsland, 1987] T.A. Marsland. Workshop report: Theory and practice in computer chess. *Intern. Computer Chess Assoc. Journal*, 10(4):205–210, 1987.

[Michalski and Negri, 1977] R. S. Michalski and P. Negri. An experiment on inductive learning in chess end games. In E. W. Elcock and D. Michie, editors, *Machine Intelligence 8*, pages 175–192. Ellis Horwood, Chichester, 1977.

[Minton, 1984] S. Minton. Constraint based generalization-learning game playing plans from single examples. In *Proceedings of AAAI-84*, pages 251–254. AAAI, 1984.

[Niblett and Shapiro, 1981] T. Niblett and A. Shapiro. Automatic induction of classification rules for chess endgames. Technical Report MIP-R-129, Machine Intelligence Research Unit, University of Edinburgh, 1981.

[Palay, 1985] A.J. Palay. *Searching with Probabilities.* Pitman, 1985.

[Pell, 1991] B. Pell. A computer game-learning tournament. (In Preparation), 1991.

[Pfleger and Treppner, 1987] H. Pfleger and G. Treppner. *Chess: The Mechanics of the Mind.* The Crowood Press, North Pomfret, VT, 1987.

[Pitrat, 1976] J. Pitrat. A program for learning to play chess. In *Pattern Recognition and Artificial Intelligence.* Academic Press, 1976.

[Quinlan, 1983] J. R. Quinlan. Learning efficient classification procedures and their application to chess end games. In R. S. Michalski, J. G. Carbonell, and T. M. Mitchell, editors, *Machine Learning*, pages 463–482. Morgan Kaufmann, San Mateo, CA, 1983.

[Scherzer *et al.*, 1990] T. Scherzer, L. Scherzer, and D. Tjaden. Learning in Bebe. In T. A. Marsland and J. Schaeffer, editors, *Computers, Chess and Cognition*, chapter 12, pages 197–216. Springer-Verlag, 1990.

[Slate and Atkin, 1977] D. J. Slate and L. R. Atkin. Chess 4.5–the northwestern university chess program. In P. W. Frey, editor, *Chess Skill in Man and Machine*, pages 82–118. Springer-Verlag, 1977.

[Tadepalli, 1989] P. Tadepalli. Lazy explanation-based learning: A solution to the intractable theory problem. In *Proceedings of the Eleventh International Joint Conference on Artificial Intelligence*, Detroit, MI, 1989. Morgan Kaufmann.

[Wilkins, 1982] D. Wilkins. Using knowldge to control tree searching. *Artificial Intelligence*, 18(1):1–51, 1982.

Multiple Approaches to Multiple Agent Problem Solving

James Hendler (Chair)
Computer Science Department
University of Maryland
College Park, Md. 20742, USA

Danny Bobrow
Xerox Palo Alto Research Center, USA
bobrow.pa@xerox.com

Les Gasser
Ecole des Mines, France
gasser@usc.edu

Carl Hewitt
MIT, USA
hewitt@ai.mit.edu

Marvin Minsky
MIT, USA
minsky@ai.mit.edu

Pick up any modern operating systems textbook, and you will find sections on distributed processing – the sharing of computation among multiple physical processors. Familiarity with this literature brings the reader into contact with a jargon filled with the sorts of terms that computer science thrives on: *load balancing, network topology, routing strategies, circuit switching, collision detection, job migration,* and the like. The discussion centers on how the bits of data that make up a computation can be physically moved among machines.

If, however, one picks up a book on distributed AI processing[1], the papers are very different. Instead of solely seeing the technical jargon of computer science, the pages are full of terms borrowed from sociology: *negotiation, interaction, contracts, agreement, organization, cohesion, social order, and collaboration,* to name but a few. This is not to say that serious AI scientists aren't concerned with the issues in the underlying computation, but rather that concentrating on the issues involved in determining how a set of separate agents can give rise to global "intelligent" behavior forces the researcher to go beyond consideration of the computation itself.

It is clear that an understanding of how multiple agents can jointly achieve the solution of complex problems demands insights into the bases of communication and social organization. For example, consider a group of humans working together to build a house. Such an endeavour requires a number of instances of cooperation and organization, in particular, the communication of information between participants and the organization of the activity so that specialists in one area (electricians, carpenters, architects) can cooperate with those working in another, all organized so as to achieve a shared goal. These same features emerge, however, as a swarm of bees work together to establish a hive. The similarities and differences between these situations brings us to the topic of this panel: what are some of the differences in perspective arising from differing views of multiple agent problem solving? The goal of this panel is to bring together researchers attacking multiagency in different ways and to explore the similarities and differences between their approaches.

[1]for example, *Readings in Distributed Artificial Intelligence,* A. Bond and L. Gasser (eds.), Morgan-Kaufman, 1988.

The panelists represent a set of very different approaches to understanding multiagent problem solving. These include:

- *Collaborative Work:* Danny Bobrow has been studying issues involved in enabling a set of humans to work together in the solving of complex problems. His work involves both the observation of humans attacking complex problems across a wide spectrum of activities and an examination of computer systems aimed at supporting such collaborative work. A large part of this work focuses on the establishment of a "common ground" for the agents involved in the problem solving — no agent can fully describe its languages or its assumptions to another, and yet they must work together with shared assumptions if they are to solve problems without conflict. Theories must be developed to explain how actors can come to establish mutually compatible languages, sets of assumptions (e.g., common defaults), and other common bases for interaction given the absence of global semantics.

- *Social Conceptions of Knowledge and Action:* Les Gasser's work focuses on "identifying the principles that underly a fundamentally multi-agent (social) conception of action and knowledge for Distributed AI research" (Gasser, 1991). This work investigates foundational issues in understanding and representing the existence and interaction of multiple agents. Important issues include how to integrate the multiple perspectives arising among different participants, how to integrate the situated information arising from an individual's particular problem-solving context into the group's more general knowledge, and how to understand the relationships between the autonomy of an individual agent and an externally imposed social order.

- *Open Information Systems Semantics:* Carl Hewitt's work focuses on the building of large scale open information systems (OIS), those "which are always subject to unanticipated outcomes in their operation and which can receive new information from outside themselves at any time." One major aspect of this work is the development of a semantics for such systems. The work involves the development of a framework in which concepts such as commitment, cooperation, negotiation, conflict, and distributed problem solving can be made rigorous. In addition, his work raises the question of how the important AI concept of *deduction* is changed when it is viewed in a multiagent framework.
- *Abstraction and Reaction:* James Hendler has been investigating planning systems which can react to dynamic change in the world. His system is based on the use of a number of asynchronously processing "monitors" which observe conditions in the world and report their observations to effectors and to other monitors. The monitors, arranged in an abstraction hierarchy, thus form a distributed network of cooperating entities, in essence a social order is imposed on a network of agents with very limited autonomy. One of the key questions under consideration is how this sort of multiagency can achieve complex problem solving tasks.
- *The Society of Mind:* Marvin Minsky's work looks at multiagent problem solving from a very different perspective. In his model "mind" (or thought) arises from the interaction of a myriad of simple agents, none of which by themselves can be characterized as having thoughts. He raises questions as to how these agents function, how they are embodied, how they communicate, what happens when they "disagree," how they are differentiated, and, most importantly of all, how such a group of agents can have a competence far beyond that of any of the single agents.

The panelists will address basic questions as to how their different perspectives on the nature of the agents, the means of communication, and the social organization of agents affect their views of multiagent problem solving. Issues to be addressed include:

1. What implications result from the differing views of the "granularity" of agents (from individual humans through mindless agents)?
2. What are the tradeoffs between autonomy and order in the different models?
3. What does each approach have to say about the basic nature of multi-agent communication?
4. In each model, what information does an agent need to know about itself? About others?
5. How does each account for the arising of globally desirable behavior from interactions of between independent individual agents?

References

Bobrow, D, Fogelsong, D. and Miller M, "Definition Groups: making sources into first-class objects," in Wegner, P. and Shriver, B (editors) *Research directions in object-oriented programming,* MIT Press 1987

Bond, A. and Gasser,L. eds. *Readings in Distributed Artificial Intelligence.* Morgan Kaufman Publishers, San Mateo, CA., 1988.

Gasser, L. "Social Conceptions of Knowledge and Action: Distributed Artificial Intelligence and Open Systems Semantics," *Artificial Intelligence,* January/February 1991.

Gasser, L. "The Integration of Computing and Routine Work," *ACM Transactions on Office Information Systems,* Vol 4:3, July 1986, pp. 225-250.

Hendler, J. *Integrating Marker-Passing and Problem Solving,* Lawrence Erlbaum Associates, Hillsdale, NJ. 1987.

Hendler, J., Tate, A., and Drummond, M. "AI Planning:Systems and Techniques" i. *AI Magazine* 11(2), May, 1990. ii. Reprinted (Japanese Translation) in *Nikkei Artificial Intelligence,* Nikkei Business Publications, Japan, Oct., 1990.

Hewitt, C. "Open Information Systems Semantics for Distributed Artificial Intelligence" *Journal of Artificial Intelligence* , Vol. 14, No. 1, January 1991.

Hewitt, C. "Towards Open Information Systems Semantics," *Towards Open Information Systems Science,* Hewitt, C. E. , Manning, C. R. , Inman, J. .T. , and Agha, G. (eds.), MIT Press, Spring 1991.

Hewitt, C. "Scientific Communities and Open Information Systems," *Towards Open Information Systems Science,* Hewitt, C. E. , Manning, C. R. , Inman, J. .T. , and Agha, G. (eds.), MIT Press, Spring 1991.

Hewitt, C. and Inman, J. "DAI Betwixt and Between: From Intelligent Agents to Open Systems Science" *IEEE Transactions on Systems, Man, and Cybernetics* Special Issue on Distributed Artificial Intelligence, 1991.

Minksy, M. *The Society of Mind.* Simon and Schuster, New York, 1987.

Minsky, M. Preface. in Connectionist Models and Their Implications: Readings from Cognitive Science, eds. D. L. waltz and J. Feldman vii-xvi. Norwood, N.J.: Ablex, 1988

Minsky, M. "Logical vs. analogical or symbolic vs. connectionist or neat vs. scruffy." In Patrick H. Winston with Sara A. Shellard, editor, *AI at MIT: Expanding Frontiers,* MIT Press, 1990.

Sanborn, J. and Hendler, J. "Monitoring and Reacting: Planning in dynamic domains" *International Journal of AI and Engineering,* 3(2), April, 1988.

Tatar, D., Foster, G., and Bobrow, D. "Reflections on a face-to-face Multiuser System," IJMMS, Special Issue, 1991

AI in Telecommunications

Andrew Jennings (Chairperson)
Telecom Australia Research Laboratories
Melbourne, Australia

Akira Kurematsu
President,
ATR Interpreting Telephone Laboratories
Kyoto , Japan

Adam Irgon
Bell Communications Research
New Jersey, USA

Greg Vessonder and **Jon R. Wright**
AT&T Bell Laboratories
New Jersey, USA

Abstract

The telecommunications industry has been a fertile field of application for AI. Some of the earliest field applications of expert sytems were in telecommunications. So when we are looking to the future we wish to examine the current status of AI in telecommunications. Is telecommunications to continue to be at the center of application of AI? If so what are the applications that will be explored?

Introduction

AI has found a wide application in improving the efficiency of the telecommunications infrastructure. Some of the world's first practical expert systems were employed to improve operations and maintenance of telecommunications networks and services. With the growth in complexity of networks, there will be ample opportunity for the application of AI to this future infrastructure. Several of the panel members will present their contributions in this direction.

Future telecommunication services are very complex, and if they are to be promulgated to a wide audience they will require a much easier user interface. AI holds the promise of overcoming these difficulties and playing a major role in the widespread promulgation of new services. How do we construct new environments that are suitable for this task ? What are the key research issues in creating these service environments? What role will speaker understanding have in this progression ?

Others hold the hope of AI techniques overcoming the difficulties that different languages present. The future promise of translation of language as part of a communication network has profound implications for all of us. Whilst this is a long term goal, the implications are very far seeking. It is timely to review progress in this direction, and to assemble the issues that need addressing. With progress towards high rate international communication networks, there are great opportunities for adding high level services such as translation.

Future information services offer the promise of delivering a wide range of information sources to a very large audience. Yet we are only now beginning to grapple with the issues of how to present these services to new customers. Many hold the promise of AI techniques playing a large part in the new information society. New techniques for natural language processing and knowledge acquisition are very important in this area.In many ways AI may be one of the key enabling technologies for the creation of these new services. This panel will highlight the research issues that are important for this new phase we are entering.

Given that we have some experience in the application of AI, it is timely to review the important issues in this application. What are the prerequisites to successful application and what issues are important for the future? How will this experience contribute to better methods of building AI Systems? Clearly we would like to take the lessons of the past to give a direction to the future of AI in telecommunications.

This panel will present a view of the state of AI in telecommunications from the viewpoint of a number of international contributors. It presents a view of the current status of AI in telecommunications, and examines the key issues for the near future.

The perspective of Automatic Telephone Interpretation

Akira Kurematsu
President
ATR Interpreting Telephone Laboratories
Kyoto , Japan

An automatic telephone interpretation system will transform a spoken dialogue from the speaker's language to the listener's automatically and simultaneously. Creation of such a system will require developing various constituent technologies: speech recognition, machine translation and speech synthesis. Technology to integrate individual subsystems to form an automatic telephone interpretation system is also important. A significant requirement for an automatic telephone interpretation system is two-way spoken language interpretation between persons speaking different languages. The recent progress in the technologies on speech recognition, machine translation of dialogues, and speech synthesis allows a promising forecast of the feasibility of an automatic telephone interpretation system in an goal-oriented dialogue in a specific domain. The perspective of an automatic telephone interpretation system will be discussed in this panel.

Bellcore's R&D Program in AI

Adam Irgon
Bell Communications Research
New Jersey, USA

A wide range of issues drive Bellcore's R&D program in AI, from communicating with customers to providing new types of service to day-to-day management of the network. Communicating effectively and efficiently with customers is one problem motivating a program in natural language processing, which includes work on the lexicon, parsing, and generation, and on the acquisition, analysis, management, and delivery of massive document collections. As new telecommunications services become increasingly complex, predicting their behavior becomes correspondingly crucial. This is one problem motivating work in logic programming, including deductive databases and extending the expressive power of logic programming languages. A program in neural networks and connectionist learning, including the development of neural network chips, addresses issues that cannot be handled easily by traditional methods. Moreover, the ubiquity of software in today's telecommunications business is leading us to address a range of software engineering problems through AI. Finally, we observe that the American telecommunications industry now has fewer people who are expected to learn how to do more and more complex tasks, which motivates work in Intelligent Tutoring Systems with emphasis on ITS authoring. We explore Bellcore's current R&D effort in these and other areas and identify some opportunities and issues yet to be addressed.

A Decade of Applying AI at AT&T

Greg Vessonder & Jon R. Wright
AT&T Bell Laboratories
New Jersey, USA

AT&T has been involved in applying artificial intelligence for over a decade. Our first commercial application of artificial intelligence was the expert system ACE, a diagnostic system that assists analysts in the local telephone loop network. Since that time we have developed systems that are in regular use for both telecommunications and non-telecommunications applications. During this period, we passed through several generations of techniques and tools used for building AI systems.

We will describe several systems that we have developed during the past decade and discuss some of the lessons we have learned during that period.

Massively Parallel Artificial Intelligence

Hiroaki Kitano (Chairperson)
Carnegie Mellon University NEC Corporation
Pittsburgh, PA, 15213 Tokyo 108, Japan
hiroaki@cs.cmu.edu

James Hendler
University of Maryland, USA
hendler@cs.umd.edu

Tetsuya Higuchi
Electrotechnical Laboratory, Japan
higuchi@etl.go.jp

Dan Moldovan
University of Southern California, USA
moldovan@gringo.usc.edu

David Waltz
Thinking Machines Corporation, USA and
Brandeis University, USA
waltz@think.com

Abstract

Massively Parallel Artificial Intelligence is a new and growing area of AI research, enabled by the emergence of massively parallel machines. It is a new paradigm in AI research. A high degree of parallelism not only affects computing performance, but also triggers drastic change in the approach toward building intelligent systems; memory-based reasoning and parallel marker-passing are examples of new and redefined approaches. These new approaches, fostered by massively parallel machines, offer a golden opportunity for AI in challenging the vastness and irregularities of real-world data that are encountered when a system accesses and processes Very Large Data Bases and Knowledge Bases. This article describes the current status of massively parallel artificial intelligence research and positions of each panelist.

1 Introduction

The goal of the panel is to highlight current accomplishments and future issues in the use of massively parallel machines for artificial intelligence research, a field generally called *massively parallel artificial intelligence*. The importance of massively parallel artificial intelligence has been recognized in recent years due to three major reasons:

1. increasing availability of massively parallel machines,
2. increasing interest in memory-based reasoning and other highly-parallel AI approaches,
3. development efforts on Very Large Knowledge Bases (VLKB).

Despite wide recognition of massively parallel computing as an important aspect of high performance computing and general interest in the AI community on highly parallel processing, only a small amount of attention has been paid to exploring the full potential of the massive parallelism offered on currently available machines. One of the causes of this is that little communication has occurred between hardware architects and AI researchers. Hardware architects design without actually recognizing the processing, memory, and performance requirements of AI algorithms. AI researchers have developed their theories and models assuming idealizations of massive parallelism. Further, with few exceptions, the AI community has often taken parallelism as a mere "implementation detail" and has not yet come up with algorithms and applications which take full advantage of the massively parallelism available.

The panel intends to rectify this situation by inviting panelists knowledgeable and experienced in both hardware and application aspects of massively parallel computing in artificial intelligence. There are two interrelated issues which will be addressed by the panel: (1) the design of massively parallel hardware for artificial intelligence, and (2) the potential applications, algorithms and paradigms aimed at fully exploring the power of massively parallel computers for symbolic AI.

2 Current Research in Massively Parallel AI

2.1 Massively Parallel Machines

Currently, there are a few research projects involving the development of the massively parallel machines and a few commercially available machines being used for symbolic AI. Three projects of particular importance are:

- The CM-2 Connection Machine (Thinking Machines Corporation),
- The Semantic Network Array Processor (University of Southern California)
- The IXM2 Associative Memory Processor (Electrotechnical Laboratory, Japan).

These machines provide an extremely high-level of parallelism (8K - 256K) and promise even more in the future. Table 1 shows the specification of these machines.

Machine	CM-2	SNAP-1	IXM2
Architecture	Array Processor SIMD	Array Processor MIMD/SIMD	Associative Processor MIMD/SIMD
Connection	Hyper-Cube	Modified Hyper-Cube	Full Connection
PE Type	1 bit PE	TMS320C30 DSP	T800 Transputer
PE Number	64K	160	64
Maximum Parallelism	64K	160	256K
Maximum Nodes	64K (VPR = 1)	16K	256K
Word Length	1 bit	32 bit	32 bit
Peak Throughput	28 GFlops (single precision)	3.4 GFlops	7.2 GOPS
Communication Channels	24576	96 8-bit channels	224 Serial links
Channel Bandwidth	5 Mbit/sec	32 MBits/sec	19.2 MBits/sec
Broadcast/Collection Bus	1 bit	32 bit	32 bit and 2.4Mbyte/sec serial
Application Controller	Vax/SUN	Custom Dual Processor	SUN
Message Processing	Foreground	Background	Foreground
Message Control	Central Controller	Local via Propagation Rules	Local

Table 1: Comparison of the major massively parallel machines

There are two major approaches to designing a massively parallel machine: the Array Processor and the Associative Processor. CM-2 and SNAP are examples of the array processor architecture, and IXM2 is an example of the associative processor architecture. While the array processor architecture attains parallelism by the number of physical processors available, the associative processor attains parallelism by the associative memory assigned to each processor. Thus, the parallelism attained by the associative processor architecture is beyond the number of processors in the machine, whereas the array processor attains parallelism equal to the number of actual processors. This is why the IXM2 attains 256K parallelism with 64 processors. However, operations carried out by associative memories are limited to bit-marker passing and relatively simple arithmetic operations. When more complex operations are necessary, the parallelism will be equal to the number of processors.

Regarding the parallelism, the next version of the IXM2 (may be called IXM3) will aim at over one million parallelism using up-to-data processors and high density associative memory chips. The SNAP project is planning to develop a custom VLSI to attain a one million processor-scale machine. DARPA (Defense Advanced Research Projects Agency) is funding a project to attain TeraOps by 1995 [Waltz, 1990].

2.2 Massively Parallel AI Paradigm

In addition to designing new hardware architectures, the strategies and perhaps even the paradigms for designing and building AI systems may need to be changed in order to take advantage of the full potential of massively parallel machines. Emergence of massively parallel machines offers a new opportunity for AI in that large-scale DB/KB processing can be made possible in real-time. Waltz's talk at AAAI-90 [Waltz, 1990] envisioned the challenge of massively parallel AI. Two of the major ideas that play central roles in massively parallel AI are: memory-based reasoning and marker-passing.

Memory-based reasoning and case-based reasoning assume that memory is a foundation of intelligence. Systems based on this approach store a large number of memory instances of past cases, and modify them to provide solutions to new problems. Computationally, the memory-based reasoning is an attractive approach to AI on massively parallel machines due to the memory-intensive and data-parallel nature of its operation. Traditional AI work has been largely constrained by the performance characteristics of serial machines. Thus, for example, the memory efficiency and optimization of serial rule application has been regarded as a central issue in expert systems design. However, massively parallel machines may take away such constraints by the use of highly parallel operations based on the idea of data-parallelism. The memory-based reasoning fits perfectly with this idea.

Another approach is marker-passing. In the Marker-Passing approach, knowledge is stored in semantic networks, and objects called *markers* are propagated, in parallel, to perform the inference. Marker-passing is a powerful method of performing inferencing on large semantic network knowledge-bases on massively parallel machines, due to the high degree of parallelism that can be attained. One obvious application of this approach is the processing of Very Large Knowledge Bases (VLKB) such as MCC's CYC [Lenat and Guha, 1989], EDR's electric dictionaries [EDR, 1988] (both of which are expected to require millions of network links), and ATR's dialogue database [Ehara et. al., 1990]. It is clear that as KBs grow substantially large (over a million concepts) the complex (and often complete) searches used in many traditional inferencing systems will have to give way to heuristic solutions unless a high degree of parallelism can be exploited. Thus, the use of massively parallel computers for VLKB processing is clearly warranted.

Table 2 shows massively parallel AI systems developed so far. The list is by no means exhaustive, only lists the major systems. Also, there are many other models which match well with massively parallel machines. But, we only list the systems that are actually implemented on massively parallel machines.

System	Task	Machine	Reference
CIS	Concurrent Inference System	CM-1	[Blelloch, 1986]
CFS	Classifier System	CM-1	[Robertson, 1987]
MBRtalk	Word pronunciation by MBR	CM-1	[Stanfill, 1988]
Parallel ATMS	Massively Parallel ATMS	CM-1	[Dixon and de Kleer, 1988]
PHI-PSI	Protein Structure Prediction by MBR	CM-2	[Zhang, et. al., 1988]
PARADYME	Parallel Case Retrieval for CBR	CM-2	[Kolodner, 1988]
DowQuest	Information Retrieval	CM-2	[Stanfill et. al., 1989]
PARKA	Frame-based AI language	CM-2	[Evett et. al., 1990a]
Census	Census data classification by MBR	CM-2	[Creecy et. al., 1990]
PRA*	Massively Parallel Heuristic Search	CM-2	[Evett et. al., 1990b]
ASTRAL	Machine Translation (a version of ΦDMDIALOG)	IXM2	[Kitano and Higuchi, 1991a]
DmSNAP	Machine Translation (a version of ΦDMDIALOG)	SNAP	[Kitano, et. al., 1991b]
GA-1	Rule Learning by Genetic Algorithms	IXM2	[Kitano, et. al., 1991a]

Table 2: Massively Parallel AI Systems

3 Associative Memory Architecture

Tetsuya Higuchi
Electrotechnical Laboratory, Japan

In this talk, we consider the architectural requirements for massively parallel AI applications, based on our experiences of developing a parallel associative processor IXM2 and applications for IXM2. In addition, we introduce the current status of the Electric Dictionary Research project in Japan which is a real example of a very large knowledge base containing 400,000 concepts.

We have developed a parallel associative processor IXM2 which enables 256K parallel operations using a large associative memory. IXM2 consists of 64 associative processors with 256K word large associative memory and 9 communications processors. These are interconnected based on a complete connection scheme to improve marker propagations. Due to its bit-parallel nature, the associative memory is more powerful in fundamental operations of AI such as association and set intersection, compared with 1-bit PEs of SIMD machines like Connection Machine [Thinking Machine Corp., 1989], MPP [Batcher, 1980] and DAP [Bowler, 1984].

The current applications for IXM2 include:
(1) very large knowledge base processing,
(2) memory-based parsing for real-time speech-to-speech translation, and
(3) rule-based learning system using genetic algorithms.

As we develop applications for IXM2, we also compare the results on IXM2 with those on other high performance machines such as Connection Machine (CM-2), Cray-XMP and SUN-4 in order to investigate the architectural requirements for massively parallel AI applications.

Now we enumerate some findings through our experiments.

1. Supercomputers are not necessarily fast for applications of knowledge base processing and memory-based parsing.

   Example 1. Set Intersection: Set intersection can be performed in O(1) on SIMD machines like IXM2 and CM-2, because the data-level parallelism can be utilized by direct mapping of datum to each processing element. On the other hand, supercomputers perform it in O(N). Therefore, there is a difference of two orders of magnitude in execu- tion time between Cray-XMP and CM-2 for 64K data, and a difference of three orders between Cray-XMP and IXM2.

   Example 2. Marker Propagation: Marker propagation is intensively used in processing is-a hierarchy know- ledge base. It actually traverses links of the network structured data. A marker propagation program written in C, which uses recursive procedure call for traversing links, was run both on SUN-4 and Cray-XMP. In spite of the exactly same program, Cray was slightly slower than SUN-4. The main reasons for this are that the overhead of recursive procedure calls is heavy, and that network structured data can not be represented well with array data structures which best fit Cray.

2. Performances on SIMD are heavily influenced by the number of simultaneous activations of communications. SIMD machines prefer applications where:
   (1) Computation can be done in parallel on each PE, and
   (2) Communications between PEs are local and the communication can be done in parallel.

   This is because SIMD machines employ 1-bit PEs and serial(slow) communication links between PEs. Applications with above characteristics are often found in scientific computations. However, AI applications are not necessarily the case. AI applications where all PEs are not always active and the number of simultaneous communications are a few often cause the severe degradation in performance. According to our experiments on knowledge base processing and memory-based parsing, CM-2 is the best for applications with "average" simultaneous communication over 1,000. And for applications under 1,000, IXM2 outperforms CM-2. However, it seems that AI applications with simultaneous activations over 1,000 are not commonly seen.

3. Interaction overheads between the host and SIMD machines.

   The rule-based learning system using genetic algorithms (classifier systems) is one of the typical examples which require frequent interactions between the host processor and SIMD machine. In such applications, the performances of SIMD machines are degraded heavily by the interaction overheads; the communication bandwidth and efficiency between the host and parallel processing modules have to be designed carefully to alleviate the problem. In addition, the introduction of the processing capability located in an intermediate level between the host and parallel processing modules may be very effective for this problem as demonstrated in dedicated architectures for image processing. Medium-grain multicomputers operating in MIMD mode, such as IXM2, MIT J-machine [Dally et. al., 1989], and iWarp [Borkar et. al., 1990] are also promising in this respect.

Inference algorithms to VLKB have to be investigated and evaluated using large-scale knowledge bases such as CYC and EDR. Practical knowledge bases include many exceptions (cancellation of inheritance) and tangled is-a hierarchy. Without such examples, it is very hard to develop efficient and robust inference algorithms.

The EDR electric dictionaries are the promising environment where investigations for VLKB processing techniques should be conducted. The dictionaries consist of a word dictionary, concept dictionary, co-occurrence dictionary and bilingual dictionary. The concept dictionary is especially interesting to VLKB researchers. It contains knowledge on the 400,000 concepts defined by the word dictionary. The knowledge is described in a form similar to semantic network.

4 How to Design a Marker-Passing Architecture for Knowledge Processing

Dan Moldovan
Computer Engineering
University of Southern California
Los Angeles, CA 90089-0781

In this talk we will share our experience in designing a parallel marker-passing computer system dedicated for processing semantic network applications. Over the last few years we have investigated and eventually implemented such a system. It is called SNAP (Semantic Network Array Processor).

We have approached this problem by first understanding the processing requirements of some AI domains and then seeking computer structures to satisfy these requirements. The outcome of our design effort was a parallel computer architecture capable of performing marker and value passing. Some of the architectural innovations of the SNAP machine are its unique high-level instruction set, marker propagation rules, and processor architecture.

A SNAP prototype has been implemented in our laboratory using off the shelf components. The prototype has 160 microprocessors grouped into some 32 clusters. It is capable of storing 16 k node semantic network with approximately 160 k inter-node relations.

The primary application for the SNAP machine is Natural Language Processing. We have found out that SNAP is suitable for NLP. In particular there is a good match between SNAP's distributed memory with its marker-passing features and the new dynamic memory parsing approach. For some limited domains we have observed parsing speeds in the order of millisecond per sentence [Kitano, et. al., 1991b].

5 Massively Parallel AI Applications[1]

David L. Waltz[2]
Thinking Machines Corporation and
Brandeis University

Memory-based and Case-based reasoning methods fit perfectly on massively parallel computers of all varieties; these methods use analogies with previous examples to decide on appropriate courses of action for new examples. In order for memory-based methods to work, one needs, in general, a database of previous examples, along with a "shell" that contains the machinery for matching new with previous examples. The database is of exactly the same sort that is typically used to train artificial neural nets or AI learning systems such as ID3.

Such systems have now been applied to a number of real-world applications; an MBR system that automatic classifies US Census Bureau returns will be described. This system significantly outperforms an expert system devised for the same task, but is most noteworthy because the effort to build it was only about 1/50th that required to build the expert system. Other MBR systems show promise for handling problems that have generally been considered to require rule-based solutions; for instance, Sumita and Iida have recently demonstrated the value of MBR-like methods for machine translation [Sumita and Iida, 1991].

I will argue that for nearly every domain of AI interest, MBR is likely to be more appropriate than rule-based methods. This is because most domains contain both regularities (that seem to encourage rule-based approaches) as well as large number of exceptions or idiosyncrasies (that demand item-by-item treatment). Unfortunately for those who favor rules, the ubiquity and sheer number of exceptions may cause the number of rules needed to handle all phenomena to become extremely large, so large that the number of rules is on the same order as the number of phenomena. MBR systems handle both regularities and exceptions in a uniform and simple-to-program fashion. Trade-offs between different learning and knowledge engineering methods will be discussed, along with implications of new and more powerful hardware and other factors.

6 Massively Parallel Symbolic AI[3]

James A. Hendler
University of Maryland

It has been argued that memory-based reasoning can best be performed on a parallel platform by the application of an associative-memory-type process running over a database of training examples. It is my contention that while such approaches may be useful in applications, they fall far short of

[1]This research was funded in part by the Defense Advanced Research Projects Agency, administered by the U.S. Air Force Office of Scientific Research under contract number F49620-0058, and in part by the United States Bureau of the Census.

[2]Thinking Machines Corporation, 245 First St., Cambridge, MA, 02142, USA.

[3]This research was funded in part by the ONR grant N-00014-88-K-0560 and NSF grant IRI-8907890. Development of the PARKA project has been performed in conjunction with two of my students, Matthew Evett and Lee Spector.

the inferencing needs of complex AI systems. If we are truly to succeed at NLP, planning, and other tasks requiring a richness of knowledge, we will have to automate the sorts of complex inferencing procedures that have been the mainspring of work in the traditional AI symbolic reasoning paradigm. Although the majority of the AI research done to date on actual parallel platforms has focused on vision research or on connectionist modeling, I will demonstrate that symbolic inferencing, in the form of traditional AI frame systems, can also show significant performance gains when using massive parallelism.

My discussion will center on a frame-based knowledge representation system, called PARKA, which runs on the massively parallel Connection Machine. Our research to date has centered on demonstrating that PARKA's performance of common types of inferencing can be far superior to that of serial systems. We have concentrated on two types of inferencing, bottom-up and top-down inheritance, both related to ISA-hierarchy property inheritance. Property inheritance is at the heart of most representation systems. Designing PARKA to have superior performance on property inheritance calculations furnishes a solid platform on which to base PARKA's other representation mechanisms.

For "top-down" inheritance queries, those which must start at the root of the tree and proceed towards the leaves (for example, "what are all the animals") we see that PARKA has worst-case runtime of $O(d)$; linear with respect to the depth d of the network, while serial inheritance programs have a worst-case performance of $O(B^d)$ (where B is the average branching factor in the network). For relatively large networks (over 32K nodes and upwards of 100K links) PARKA can process top-down inheritance queries in under two seconds.

We are currently working on extending the representational power of the PARKA language. One important ability which we are now focusing on is the ability to perform recognition queries, which we will argue are necessary to performing case-based inferencing with any real generality. We will describe a method by which the PARKA system can handle complex recognition queries in time approximating $O(D + M)$, where M is the number of conjuncts in the query. This contrasts dramatically with the $O(M \times B^d)$ time taken by current systems. I will argue that such algorithms are necessary to the success of large "common sense" knowledge-bases, such as the US CYC project or the Japanese electronic dictionary.

7 Designing Massively Parallel AI Systems[4]

Hiroaki Kitano
Carnegie Mellon University and
NEC Corporation, Japan

This talk addresses some of the issues that the designer of the massively parallel AI systems should notice. Some of the issues affect design decisions of the overall design ideas and some issues affects choice of the hardware.

1. Gaining massive parallelism
2. Deciding where to gain parallelism
3. Mapping from logical world to physical world
4. Avoiding PE overload
5. Minimizing Communication

First, a high level of parallelism needs to be attained in order to take advantage of the massively parallel machines. However, if we simply map current AI systems which extensively rely on piecewise rule applications, the level of parallelism attained can only be medium at best. The memory-based approach fits perfectly with massively parallel machines because matching of an input against all cases will be considered in parallel by SIMD operation. For example, the traditional view of natural language processing has been relying upon grammar rules to analyze sentences. However, in reality, natural language is a bulk collection of exceptions, and many serious NLP systems have a large set of rules which cope with each exceptions. Memory-based parsing and memory-based translation theory is a superior and practical model for building practical NLP systems to be delivered to the real-world.

Second, the designer should notice that not all processes can be parallelized. The processes which can be parallelized differ from one architecture to another. For example, the array processor architecture (such as CM-2 and SNAP) can parallelize activation of more than one nodes, but thise architecture does not send markers in parallel – each marker will be send out sequentially from one node. The associative processor (such as IXM2) can send markers in parallel, but activation of nodes will be in serial in each driving PE, thus parallelism will be only 64 for this operation. In some cases, creating/deletion of nodes and links requires controller interrupts which makes this part of process serial. Designers should be well aware of the characteristics of each architecture and should avoid turning a massively parallel machine into a serial machine.

Third, logical structure of the semantic networks is not necessary mapped directly on physical allocation. Suppose we have a node with 10 fanout. All 10 neighbour nodes are within one hop on the logical map. However, if the PE has only 4 physically connected neighbour PEs, at least 6 of the logical neighbours will be allocated on PEs which are more than one hop.

Fourth, there are hardware constraints. For example, if marker-passing algorithm requires propagation of addresses or other information, each node needs to have memory to store the information, or the information will be simply lost. Physical constraints on the memory capacity limits numbers of markers which can be legally acceptable to each node. In addition, fine-grained massively parallel machines do not have powerful PEs assigned to each node, so that heavy operations such as unification would kill entire performance of the system.

Fifth, minimization of communication is critical in designing high performance massively parallel AI systems. Although the massively parallel machine circumvented a Von-Neumann bottleneck, it encounters a communication bottleneck. In some case, over 95% of entire computing time was consumed in communication of data between processors. Physically, a communication between processor is an expensive operation.

These are some of the design issues for massively parallel AI applications. This list may give the impression that designing a massively parallel AI system is a hard task, but it is not true. It simply requires a paradigm change of the view toward intelligent processes. We had been relying on

[4]This research was funded by the National Science Foundation under grant MIP-9009111, and by the Pittsburgh Supercomputing Center under grant IRI-910002P.

somewhat rule-based and serial thinking, which may be due to hardware constraints of the serial machines we have so far. The alternative view which is more oriented toward memory-based and parallel thinking, enables us to build more practical AI applications, and once one get used to massively parallel thinking, and it would be a viable alternative to many of the current AI approaches.

References

[Batcher, 1980] Batcher, K., "Design of a Massively Parallel Processor," *IEEE Transactions on Computers* 29, no.9, September 1980.

[Blelloch, 1986] Blelloch, G. E., *AFS-1: A programming language for massively concurrent computers*, Tech Report 918, MIT AI Lab., 1986.

[Blelloch, 1986] Blelloch, G. E., "CIS: A Massively Concurrent Rule-Based System," *Proceedings of the National Conference on Artificial Intelligence (AAAI-86)*, 1986.

[Borkar et. al., 1990] Borkar, S., Cohn, R., Cox, G., Gross, T., Kung, H. T., Lam, M., Levine, M., Moore, B., Moore, W., Peterson, C., Susman, J., Sutton, J., Urbanski, J., and Webb, J., "Supporting Systolic and Memory Communication in iWarp", *The 17th Annual International Symposium on Computer Architecture*, May 1990.

[Bowler, 1984] K.C.Bowler and G.S.Pawley, "Molecular Dynamics and Monte Carlo Simulation in Solid-State and Elementary Particle Physics," *Proceedings of the IEEE*, 74, January 1984.

[Creecy et. al., 1990] Creecy, R., Masand, B., Smith, S., and Waltz, D., "Trading MIPS and Memory for Knowledge Engineering: Automatic Classification of Census Returns on a Massively Parallel Supercomputer," Thinking Machine Corp., 1990.

[Dally et. al., 1989] Dally, W. J., et. al. "The J-Machine: a fine-grain concurrent computer," Information Processing 89, Elsevier North Holland, 1989.

[Dixon and de Kleer, 1988] Dixon, M. and de Kleer, J., "Massively Parallel Assumption-based Truth Maintenance," *Proceedings of the the National Conference on Artificial Intelligence (AAAI-88)*, 1988.

[Drumheller, 1986] Drumheller, M., "Connection Machine stereomatching," *Proceedings of the National Conference on Artificial Intelligence (AAAI-86)*, 1986.

[EDR, 1988] Japan Electric Dictionary Research Institute, "EDR Electric Dictionaries," Technical Report, Japan Electric Dictionary Research Institute, 1988.

[Ehara et. al., 1990] Ehara, T., Inoue, N., Kohyama, H., Hasegawa, T., Shohyama, F., and Morimoto, T., *Content of the ATR Dialogue Database*, TR-I-0186, ATR Interpreting Telephony Research Laboratories, 1990.

[Evett et. al., 1990a] Evett, M., Hendler, J., and Spector, L., *PARKA: Parallel knowledge representation on the Connection Machine*, Tech Report CS-TR-2409, University of Maryland, 1990.

[Evett et. al., 1990b] Evett, M., Hendler, J., Mahanti, A., and Nau, D., "PRA* A memory-limited heuristic search procedure for the connection machine," *Proceedings – Frontiers of Massively Parallel Computing*, 1990.

[Higuchi et. al., 1991] Higuchi, T., Kitano, H., Furuya, T., Kusumoto, H., Handa, K., and Kokubu, A., "IXM2: A Parallel Associate Processor for Knowledge Processing," *Proceedings of the National Conference on Artificial Intelligence*, 1991.

[Hillis, 1985] Hillis, D., *The Connection Machine*, The M.I.T. Press, 1985.

[Inmos, 1987] Inmos, *IMS T800 Transputer*, 1987.

[Kitano, et. al., 1991a] Kitano, H., Smith, S. F., and Higuchi, T., "GA-1: A Parallel Associative Memory Processor for Rule Learning with Genetic Algorithms," *Proceedings of the International Conference on Genetic Algorithms (ICGA-91)*, 1991.

[Kitano, et. al., 1991b] Kitano, H., Moldovan, D., Um, I., Cha, S., "High Performance Natural Language Processing on Semantic Network Array Processor," *Proceeding of the International Joint Conference on Artificial Intelligence (IJCAI-91)*, 1991.

[Kitano and Higuchi, 1991a] Kitano, H. and Higuchi, T., "High Performance Memory-Based Translation on IXM2 Massively Parallel Associative Memory Processor," *Proceeding of the National Conference on Artificial Intelligence (AAAI-91)*, 1991.

[Kitano and Higuchi, 1991b] Kitano, H. and Higuchi, T., "Massively Parallel Memory-Based Parsing," *Proceeding of the International Joint Conference on Artificial Intelligence (IJCAI-91)*, 1991.

[Kitano, 1990] Kitano, H., "ΦDMDIALOG: A Speech-to-Speech Dialogue Translation," *Machine Translation*, 5, 301-338, 1990.

[Kitano, 1988] Kitano, H., "Multilingual Information Retrieval Mechanism using VLSI," *Proceedings of RIAO-88*, Boston, 1988.

[Kolodner, 1988] Kolodner, J., "Retrieving Events from a Case Memory: A Parallel Implementation," *Proceedings of Case-Based Reasoning Workshop*, 1988.

[Lenat and Guha, 1989] Lenat, D. B. and Guha, R. V., *Building Large Knowledge-Based Systems*, Addison-Wesley, 1989.

[Moldovan et. al., 1990] Moldovan, D., Lee, W., and Lin, C., *SNAP: A Marker-Passing Architecture for Knowledge Processing*, Technical Report PKPL 90-4, Department of Electrical Engineering Systems, University of Southern California, 1990.

[Riesbeck and Martin, 1986] Riesbeck, C. and Martin, C., "Direct Memory Access Parsing," *Experience, Memory, and Reasoning*, Lawrence Erlbaum Associates, 1986.

[Robertson, 1987] Robertson, G., "Parallel Implementation of Genetic Algorithms in a Classifier System," Davis, L., (Ed.) *Genetic Algorithms and Simulated Annealing*, Morgan Kaufmann Publishers, 1987.

[Stanfill et. al., 1989] Stanfill, C., Thau, R., and Waltz, D., "A Parallel Indexed Algorithm for Information Retrieval," *Proceedings of the SIG-IR-89*, 1989.

[Stanfill and Waltz, 1988] Stanfill, C. and Waltz, D., "The Memory-Based Reasoning Paradigm," *Proceedings of the Case-Based Reasoning Workshop*, DARPA, 1988.

[Stanfill and Waltz, 1986] Stanfill, C. and Waltz, D., "Toward Memory-Based Reasoning," *Communications of the ACM*, 1986.

[Stanfill, 1988] Stanfill, C., "Memory-Based Reasoning Reasoning Applied to English Pronunciation," *Proceedings of the National Conference on Artificial Intelligence (AAAI-88)*, 1988.

[Sumita and Iida, 1991] Sumita, E., and Iida, H., "Experiments and Prospects of Example-Based Machine Translation," *Proceedings of the Annual Meeting of the ACL (ACL-91)*, 1991.

[Thinking Machine Corp., 1989] Thinking Machine Corporation, *Model CM-2 Technical Summary*, Technical Report TR-89-1, 1989.

[Waltz, 1987] Waltz, D., "Application of the Connection Machine," *Computer*, Jan., 1987.

[Waltz, 1990] Waltz, D., "Massively Parallel AI," *Proceedings of the National Conference on Artificial Intelligence (AAAI-90)*, 1990.

[Waltz and Stanfill, 1988] Waltz, D. and Stanfill, C., "Artificial Intelligence Related Research on the Connection Machine," *Proceedings of the International Conference on Fifth Generation Computer*, 1988.

[Zhang, et. al., 1988] Zhang, X., Waltz, D., and Mesirov, J., *Protein Structure Prediction by Memory-based Reasoning*, Thinking Machine Corporation, 1988.

Some articles relevant to the topic, but not referred in the text, are also included for the reader's convenience in further investigation of the subject.

PANEL ON AI AND DESIGN

Saul Amarel (Organizer, Chair), Rutgers University
Alvin Despain, University of Southern California
Penny Nii, Stanford University
Louis Steinberg, Rutgers University
Marty Tenenbaum, Enterprise Integration Technologies Corp., and Stanford University
Peter Will, Hewlett Packard Laboratories

1 General Significance

Issues of industrial productivity are of major economic significance at present - not only in the US, but in all parts of the industrialized world. By advancing the science of design, and by creating a broad computer-based methodology for automating the design of artifacts and of industrial processes, we can attain dramatic improvements in productivity.

Recent developments in computer science, especially in AI and in related areas of advance computing, provide us with a unique opportunity to push beyond the present level of computer aided automation technology and to attain substantial advances in the understanding and mechanization of design processes. To attain these goals, we need to build on top of the present state of AI, and to accelerate research and development in areas that are especially relevant to design problems of realistic complexity.

Work in design provides a unifying theme for collaborative research among subfields of AI, and also between AI and other parts of computer science - especially database systems and high performance computing applied to large scale modeling and simulation. Also, it provides an effective vehicle for establishing links between AI and computational science/engineering.

2 Relevance to AI Research

Design is the problem solving activity that results in the generation of a description of an artifact or process (in a given language of design structures) in some domain that satisfies given design specifications, i.e., goals and constraints. Typically, a designer reasons in two spaces - the space of design specifications and the space of design structures. Furthermore, in most engineering problems of realistic complexity the design process is multi-level (hierarchical) in nature - where high levels of the hierarchy correspond to conceptual design, with considerable amount of exploration taking place both in the space of structures and the space of specifications; and lower levels correspond to detailed technical design where specifications are fairly fixed, and complex searches take place in the space of structures.

Looking at basic work in AI from the perspective of design automation, we identify a number of research issues that need special attention. These can be organized in three major groupings: decision making; representations; and knowledge handling, including modeling and simulation.

In the area of decision making, the issues include how to handle poorly defined and incomplete design specification; how to handle multiple interacting goals and constraints, especially in tasks of concurrent design and in those involving tradeoff decisions; how to choose decompositions in various problem solving contexts; how to handle formation problems; how to organize hierarchical reasoning processes in design; and how to handle incremental design and redesign tasks. The complexity of realistic design problems is expected to stress current methods of problem solving (goal-directed, constraint-based, model-based, and case-based), and it is likely to induce the development of new methods.

In the area of representations, the issues include how to represent candidate design structures in ways that facilitate their evaluation and modification in light of given design specifications; how to represent design records so as to facilitate explanation and design reuse; how to represent designs from multiple viewpoints; and how to organize large reusable design knowledge bases. Much current work in Knowledge Representation and Reasoning, in Problem Formulation and Reformulation, and in the Organization of Large Knowledge Bases, is relevant to problems in this area.

In the area of knowledge handling, the issues include how to use domain knowledge for a priori guiding the generation of candidate solutions rather than (in addition to) the a posteriori evaluation of candidate solutions; how to find and exploit useful approximations to domain theories/models to enable reasoning from function to structure and to provide computationally tractable evaluations of solution candidates at various levels of solution construction; how to integrate qualitative and quantitative knowledge of a domain in the context of design problem solving; how to automatically acquire (or refine) domain knowledge; and how to learn from design experience, i.e., how to transform design experience into increased design expertise. Current research in approximate reasoning, qualitative physics, theory formation, and machine learning, is relevant to the concerns of this area.

Progress in handling these research problems will have major impact both on our understanding of design processes and their automation, and also on several fundamental questions that are of intrinsic concern to AI.

3 AI Activities in Design

AI work on specific design tasks has been increasing in scope and volume since the early eighties. Domains/tasks that received considerable attention include digital circuit design (especially, VLSI design), design of small electro-mechanical parts and assemblies, and design of materials.

Recently, AI methods are starting to be explored in the context of design tasks of increased complexity, e.g., design of computer architectures, design of ships, design of aircraft engines, conceptual design of aircraft, design of large static structures. Also, renewed attention is being given to the exploration of AI approaches in large-scale software design - a problem that has been of intense interest to AI since the early days of the field.

Together with the increased levels of research activity in AI and Design, there has been a substantial growth in professional activity in the field, in the form of papers, tutorials in national conferences, workshops, etc.

4 Immediate Background for the Panel

It is as a result of a recent seminal workshop in the field that the idea of the present panel has emerged. The workshop was held in Ithaca, N.Y. on August 14 to 16, 1990 - to assess research issues involved in the creation of a new generation of powerful computer aided systems for engineering design, to identify major research opportunities and difficulties in introducing AI methods and technology into significant design tasks, and to formulate recommendations for a major research program in this area [1].

The workshop, which was sponsored by DARPA, was co-organized by Saul Amarel (Rutgers) and John Hopcroft (Cornell). It had about 60 invited participants from academia and industry, mostly from AI, but also from other areas of computing and from several engineering disciplines with strong interest in advanced approaches to computational design.

Research issues, opportunities and difficulties were viewed at the Ithaca workshop both from the perspective of core science/technology and of significant design domains. The bulk of the workshop activity was conducted in six working groups, each focusing on a specific set of issues. The discussion of AI (and, more generally, computer science) issues in design concentrated in the three areas of design decision making, design representations and information management, and modeling and simulation in design. The three design domains that received primary attention are: design of small electromechanical systems, design of large structures (ships, airplanes, engines), and design of software.

The general sense of the workshop was that the time is ripe to launch a major research program in computational design, with AI as a central component; and specific technical recommendations were formulated for such a program. Also, a set of fundamental issues for AI research surfaced at the workshop.

(i) The choice of representations and domain models strongly depend on the specific design task on hand and on the stage of design. This has strong implications on the development of comprehensive large knowledge bases for design that rely on fixed ontologies and representational conventions. A related issue is that certain problem solving methods are possible only if domain knowledge is available in certain forms and is represented/organized appropriately.

(ii) There is evidence that design (in particular, innovative and high level design) may be so completely dominated and determined by specific domain knowledge that it could not be effectively handled by generic methods and techniques. For example, experts agree that the reasoning involved in introducing an innovative hull configuration in ship design, or an innovative wing-tail configuration in aircraft design, are strongly tied to the physics of each specific situation. This point has important implications on AI methodology.

(iii) The concept of design record seems to be central to work in computational design. Advances in this area seem to be slow, despite progress in related areas of explanation and proof construction in AI. It is important to understand better the difficulties involved.

(iv) To identify critical problems and to test ideas, it is essential to build systems (and conduct experiments) in specific tasks/domains of realistic engineering significance. This implies the need for a substantial infrastructure to support the research, and an organization involving interdisciplinary teams from universities, research labs, and industry. Thus, serious progress in this area requires the commitment of resources that are above some "critical mass".

5 Panel Goals

The panel will review and discuss the scientific/technical assessments, the recommendations for research, and the fundamental AI issues that emerged from the August '90 Ithaca Design workshop.

A major goal is to increase the awareness of opportunities and problems in this area within the international AI community.

Another important goal is to elicit views, and to stimulate discussion, on the open issues (of substance and of research methodology) that AI faces in the context of a major push in computational design. It is essential for this discussion to have participation by AI researchers as well as by researchers who are exploring AI approaches in a variety of engineering domains, and also by those who are concerned about design in the broader context of product development and manufacturing.

6 Outlines of Panel Presentations

Saul Amarel (Chair)

Introduction to the panel: general significance of AI in Design; relevance to AI research; summary of assessments, recommendations, and AI issues from the Ithaca Design Workshop. The case for a major program in AI and Design; features of such a program. Issues of collaborative research between AI and engineering disciplines.

Alvin Despain

Summary of AI approaches to VLSI design and to the design of computer architectures; needs and research ideas in these domains. Issues in hierarchical systems for design problem solving - languages, management of the design process, knowledge acquisition. Experience in applications of AI methods to VLSI design. Problems of complexity, and prospects of handling them via High Performance Computing and via AI methods.

Penny Nii

Summary of discussions/recommendations in the domain of software design from the Ithaca Design Workshop. The Workshop focused on problems associated with programming-in-the-large. There were three major recommendations with AI implications: (i) Build an infrastructure to cumulate and to use design information about both the process and the artifact of design; this has implications on the representation and use of design records. (ii)Build and disseminate domain-specific software architectures; this has implications on the acquisition and structuring of appropriate domain knowledge. (iii) Develop a technology for managing consistency, and for coordinating the efforts of multiple designers of large multi-version systems; this has implications on methods for handling domain and task-specific consistency in addition to syntactic consistency.

Louis Steinberg

Summary of AI research issues in decision-making, representations, and knowledge handling from the Ithaca Design Workshop. Emphasis on overall design frameworks, and their relationship to design tasks of various types. There are a number of dimensions along which a design task can be categorized; the position of the task along these dimensions determines the method which is appropriate for handling it. E.g., the degree of interaction between parts of a task specification affects whether and how a top-down decomposition method can be used. By considering where past and current research falls along some of these dimensions, we can get a good idea of what we know how to do, and where further work is needed.

Marty Tenenbaum

Summary of discussions/recommendations in the domain of small electromechanical parts design from the Ithaca Design Workshop. Needs and research ideas in areas of design knowledge capture and in the building of environments for support of human-machine collaboration in design. Issues in the handling of manufacturing constraints early in the process of designing an artifact. Current state and research directions in AI approaches for design of manufacturing processes.

Peter Will

Summary of research and development issues in the Product Development Process and in Enterprise Automation to support the total life cycle of a product. The issues include support for Design and Manufacturing as well as other functional areas, including: (i) capturing design intent, (ii) knowledge bases of components and sub-assemblies, (iii) simulation and modeling, and (iv) agent oriented manufacturing and distribution.

Reference

[1]Amarel, S. (1991). *Report on DARPA-sponsored Workshop on Design - held on 14-16 August, 1990, in Ithaca, N.Y.*, Technical Report LCSR-TR-160, LCSR, Rutgers University, New Brunswick, N.J. 08903

AWARD AND INVITED PAPERS

Intelligence Without Reason

Rodney A. Brooks
MIT Artificial Intelligence Lab
545 Technology Square
Cambridge, MA 02139, USA

Abstract

Computers and *Thought* are the two categories that together define Artificial Intelligence as a discipline. It is generally accepted that work in Artificial Intelligence over the last thirty years has had a strong influence on aspects of computer architectures. In this paper we also make the converse claim; that the state of computer architecture has been a strong influence on our models of thought. The Von Neumann model of computation has lead Artificial Intelligence in particular directions. Intelligence in biological systems is completely different. Recent work in behavior-based Artificial Intelligence has produced new models of intelligence that are much closer in spirit to biological systems. The non-Von Neumann computational models they use share many characteristics with biological computation.

1 Introduction

Artificial Intelligence as a formal discipline has been around for a little over thirty years. The goals of individual practitioners vary and change over time. A reasonable characterization of the general field is that it is intended to make computers do things, that when done by people, are described as having indicated intelligence. Winston [**Winston 84**] characterizes the goals of Artificial Intelligence as both the construction of useful intelligent systems and the understanding of human intelligence.

There is a temptation (often succumbed to) to then go ahead and define *intelligence*, but that does not immediately give a clearly grounded meaning to the field. In fact there is danger of deep philosophical regress with no recovery. Therefore I prefer to stay with a more informal notion of intelligence being the sort of stuff that humans do, pretty much all the time.

1.1 Approaches

Traditional Artificial Intelligence has tried to tackle the problem of building artificially intelligent systems from the top down. It tackled intelligence through the notions of *thought* and *reason*. These are things we only know about through introspection. The field has adopted a certain *modus operandi* over the years, which includes a particular set of conventions on how the inputs and outputs to thought and reasoning are to be handled (e.g., the subfield of knowledge representation), and the sorts of things that thought and reasoning do (e.g., planning, problem solving, etc.). I will argue that these conventions cannot account for large aspects of what goes into intelligence. Furthermore, without those aspects the validity of the traditional Artificial Intelligence approaches comes into question. I will also argue that much of the landmark work on thought has been influenced by the technological constraints of the available computers, and thereafter these consequences have often mistakenly become enshrined as principles, long after the original impetus has disappeared.

From an evolutionary stance, human level intelligence did not suddenly leap onto the scene. There were precursors and foundations throughout the lineage to humans. Much of this substrate is present in other animals today. The study of that substrate may well provide constraints on how higher level *thought* in humans could be organized.

Recently there has been a movement to study intelligence from the bottom up, concentrating on physical systems (e.g., mobile robots), situated in the world, autonomously carrying out tasks of various sorts. Some of this work is based on engineering from first principles, other parts of the work are firmly based on biological inspirations. The flavor of this work is quite different from that of traditional Artificial Intelligence. In fact it suggests that despite our best introspections, traditional Artificial Intelligence offers solutions to intelligence which bear almost no resemblance at all to how biological systems work.

There are of course dangers in studying biological systems too closely. Their design was not highly optimized from a global systems point of view. Rather they were patched together and adapted from previously working systems, in ways which most expeditiously met the latest environmental pressures. Perhaps the solutions found for much of intelligence are terribly suboptimal. Certainly there are many vestigial structures surviving within humans' and other animals' digestive, skeletal, and muscular systems. One should suppose then that there are many vestigial neurological structures, interactions, and side effects. Their emulation may be a distraction.

1.2 Outline

The body of this paper is formed by ivemain sections: 2 *Robots*, 3 *Computers*, 4 *Biology*, 5 *Ideas* and 6 *Thought*. The theme of the paper is how computers and thought have be intimately intertwined in the development of Artificial Intelligence, how those connections may have led the field astray, how biological examples of intelligence are quite different from the models used by Artificial Intelligence, and how recent new approaches point to another path for both computers and thought.

The new approaches that have been developed recently for Artificial Intelligence arose out of work with mobile robots. Section 2 (Robots) briefly outlines the context within which this work arose, and discusses some key realizations made by the researchers involved.

Section 3 (Computers) traces the development of the foundational ideas for Artificial Intelligence, and how they were intimately linked to the technology available for computation. Neither situatedness nor embodiment were easy to include on the original agenda, although their importance was recognized by many early researchers. The early framework with its emphasis on search has remained dominant, and has led to solutions that seem important within the closed world of Artificial Intelligence, but which perhaps are not very relevant to practical applications. The field of Cybernetics with a heritage of very different tools from the early digital computer, provides an interesting counterpoint, confirming the hypothesis that models of thought are intimately tied to the available models of computation.

Section 4 (Biology) is a brief overview of recent developments in the understanding of biological intelligence. It covers material from ethology, psychology, and neuroscience. Of necessity it is not comprehensive, but it is sufficient to demonstrate that the intelligence of biological systems is organized in ways quite different from traditional views of Artificial Intelligence.

Section 5 (Ideas) introduces the two cornerstones to the new approach to Artificial Intelligence, ***situatedness*** and *embodiment*, and discusses both intelligence and emergence in these contexts.

The last major section, 6 (Thought), outlines some details of the approach of my group at MIT to building complete situated, embodied, artificially intelligent robots. This approach shares much more heritage with biological systems than with what is usually called Artificial Intelligence.

2 Robots

There has been a scattering of work with mobile robots within the Artificial Intelligence community over the years. Shakey from the late sixties at SRI (see **[Nilsson 84]** for a collection of original reports) is perhaps the best known, but other significant efforts include the CART (**[Moravec 82]**) at Stanford and Hilare (**[Giralt, Chatila and Vaisset 84]**) in Toulouse.

All these systems used offboard computers (and thus they could be the largest most powerful computers available at the time and place), and all operated in mostly[1] static environments. All of these robots operated in environments that had been specially engineered for them to some degree at least. They all sensed the world and tried to build two or three dimensional world models of it. Then, in each case, a planner could ignore the actual world, and operate in the model to produce a plan of action for the robot to achieve whatever goal it had been given. In all three of these robots, the generated plans included at least a nominal path through the world model along which it was intended that the robot should move.

Despite the simplifications (static, engineered environments, and the most powerful available computers) all these robots operated excruciatingly slowly. Much of the processing time was consumed in the perceptual end of the systems and in building the world models. Relatively little computation was used in planning and acting.

An important effect of this work was to provide a framework within which other researchers could operate without testing their ideas on real robots, and even without having any access to real robot data. We will call this framework, the ***sense-model-plan-act*** framework, or *SMPA* for short. See section 3.6 for more details of how the SMPA framework influenced the manner in which robots were built over the following years, and how those robots in turn imposed restrictions on the ways in which intelligent control programs could be built for them.

There was at least an implicit assumption in this early work with mobile robots, that once the simpler case of operating in a static environment had been solved, then the more difficult case of an actively dynamic environment could be tackled. None of these early SMPA systems were ever extended in this way.

Around 1984, a number of people started to worry about the more general problem of organizing intelligence. There was a requirement that intelligence be reactive to dynamic aspects of the environment, that a mobile robot operate on time scales similar to those of animals and humans, and that intelligence be able to generate robust behavior in the face of uncertain sensors, an unpredicted environment, and a changing world. Some of the key realizations about the organization of intelligence were as follows:

- Most of what people do in their day to day lives is not problem-solving or planning, but rather it is routine activity in a relatively benign, but certainly dynamic, world. Furthermore the representations an agent uses of objects in the world need not rely on a semantic correspondence with symbols that the agent possesses, but rather can be defined through interactions of the agent with the world. Agents

[1] In the case of Shakey, experiments included the existence of a gremlin who would secretly come and alter the environment by moving a block to a different location. However, this would usually happen only once, say, in a many hour run, and the robot would not perceive the dynamic act, but rather might later notice a changed world if the change was directly relevant to the particular subtask it was executing. In the case of the CART, the only dynamic aspect of the world was the change in sun angle over long time periods, and this in fact caused the robot to fail as its position estimation scheme was confused by the moving shadows.

based on these ideas have achieved interesting performance levels and were built from combinatorial circuits plus a little timing circuitry ([**Agre and Chapman 87**], [**Agre and Chapman 90**]).

- An observer can legitimately talk about an agent's beliefs and goals, even though the agent need not manipulate symbolic data structures at run time. A formal grounding in semantics used for the agent's design can be compiled away. Agents based on these ideas have achieved interesting performance levels and were built from combinatorial circuits plus a little timing circuitry ([**Rosenschein and Kaelbling 86**], [**Kaelbling and Rosenschein 90**]).

- In order to really test ideas of intelligence it is important to build complete agents which operate in dynamic environments using real sensors. Internal world models which are complete representations of the external environment, besides being impossible to obtain, are not at all necessary for agents to act in a competent manner. Many of the actions of an agent are quite separable—coherent intelligence can emerge from subcomponents interacting in the world. Agents based on these ideas have achieved interesting performance levels and were built from combinatorial circuits plus a little timing circuitry ([**Brooks 86**], [**Brooks 90b**], [**Brooks 91a**]).

A large number of others have also contributed to the approach. [**Maes 90a**] is the most representative collection.

There is no generally accepted term to describe this style of work. It has sometimes been characterized by the oxymoron *reactive planning*. I have variously used *Robot Beings* [**Brooks and Flynn 89**] and *Artificial Creatures* [**Brooks 90b**]. Related work on non-mobile, but nevertheless active systems has been called *active vision*, or *animate vision* [**Ballard 89**]. Some workers refer to their beings, or creatures, as *agents*; unfortunately that term is also used by others to refer to somewhat independent components of intelligence within a single physical creature (e.g., the agencies of [**Minsky 86**]). Sometimes the approach is called *behavior-based* as the computational components tend to be direct behavior producing modules[2]. For the remainder of this paper, we will simply call the entities of discussion 'robots' or 'behavior-based robots'.

There are a number of key aspects characterizing this style of work.

- [**Situatedness**] The robots are situated in the world—they do not deal with abstract descriptions, but with the here and now of the world directly influencing the behavior of the system.

- [**Embodiment**] The robots have bodies and experience the world directly—their actions are part of a dynamic with the world and have immediate feedback on their own sensations.

- [**Intelligence**] They are observed to be intelligent—but the source of intelligence is not limited to just the computational engine. It also comes from the situation in the world, the signal transformations within the sensors, and the physical coupling of the robot with the world.

- [**Emergence**] The intelligence of the system emerges from the system's interactions with the world and from sometimes indirect interactions between its components—it is sometimes hard to point to one event or place within the system and say that is why some external action was manifested.

Recently there has been a trend to try to integrate traditional symbolic reasoning, on top of a purely reactive system, both with real robots (e.g., [**Arkin 90**], [**Mitchell 90**],) and in simulation (e.g, [**Firby 89**]). The idea is that the reactive system handles the real-time issues of being embedded in the world, while the deliberative system does the 'hard' stuff traditionally imagined to be handled by an Artificial Intelligence system. I think that these approaches are suffering from the well known 'horizon effect'—they have bought a little better performance in their overall system with the reactive component, but they have simply pushed the limitations of the reasoning system a bit further into the future. I will not be concerned with such systems for the remainder of this paper.

Before examining this work in greater detail, we will turn to the reasons why traditional Artificial Intelligence adopted such a different approach.

3 Computers

In evolution there is a theory [**Gould and Eldredge 77**] of punctuated equilibria, where most of the time there is little change within a species, but at intervals a subpopulation branches off with a short burst of greatly accelerated changes. Likewise, I believe that in Artificial Intelligence research over the last forty or so years, there have been long periods of incremental work within established guidelines, and occasionally a shift in orientation and assumptions causing a new subfield to branch off. The older work usually continues, sometimes remaining strong, and sometimes dying off gradually. This description of the field also fits more general models of science, such as [**Kuhn 70**].

The point of this section is that all those steady-state bodies of work rely, sometimes implicitly, on certain philosophical and *technological* assumptions. The founders of the bodies of work are quite aware of these assumptions, but over time as new people come into the fields, these assumptions get lost, forgotten, or buried, and the work takes on a life of its own for its own sake.

In this section I am particularly concerned with how the architecture of our computers influences our choice of problems on which to work, our models of thought, and our algorithms, and how the problems on which we work, our models of thought, and our algorithm choice puts pressure on the development of architectures of our computers.

[2] Unfortunately this clashes a little with the meaning of *behavior* as used by ethologists as an observed interaction with the world, rather than as something explicitly generated.

Biological systems run on massively parallel, low speed computation, within an essentially fixed topology network with bounded depth. Almost all Artificial Intelligence research, and indeed almost all modern computation, runs on essentially Von Neumann architectures, with a large, inactive memory which can respond at very high speed over an extremely narrow channel, to a very high speed central processing unit which contains very little state. When connections to sensors and actuators are also considered, the gap between biological systems and our artificial systems widens.

Besides putting architectural constraints on our programs, even our mathematical tools are strongly influenced by our computational architectures. Most algorithmic analysis is based on the RAM model of computation (essentially a Von Neumann model, shown to be polynomially equivalent to a Turing machine, e.g., **[Hartmanis 71]**). Only in recent years have more general models gained prominence, but they have been in the direction of oracles, and other improbable devices for our robot beings.

Are we doomed to work forever within the current architectural constraints?

Over the past few centuries computation technology has progressed from making marks on various surfaces (chiselling, writing, etc.), through a long evolutionary chain of purely mechanical systems, then electromechanical relay based systems, through vacuum tube based devices, followed by an evolutionary chain of silicon-based devices to the current state of the art.

It would be the height of arrogance and foolishness to assume that we are now using the ultimate technology for computation, namely silicon based integrated circuits, just as it would have been foolish (at least in retrospect) to assume in the 16th century that Napier's Bones were the ultimate computing technology **[Williams 83]**. Indeed the end of the exponential increase in computation speed for uni-processors is in sight, forcing somewhat the large amount of research into parallel approaches to more computation for the dollar, and per second. But there are other more radical possibilities for changes in computation infrastructure[3]. These include computation based on optical switching (**[Gibbs 85]**, **[Brady 90]**), protein folding, gene expression, non-organic atomic switching.

3.1 Prehistory

During the early 1940's even while the second world war was being waged, and the first electronic computers were being built for cryptanalysis and trajectory calculations, the idea of using computers to carry out intelligent activities was already on people's minds.

Alan Turing, already famous for his work on computability **[Turing 37]** had discussions with Donald Michie, as early as 1943, and others less known to the modern Artificial Intelligence world as early as 1941, about using a computer to play chess. He and others developed the idea of minimaxing a tree of moves, and of static evaluation, and carried out elaborate hand simulations against human opponents. Later (during the period from 1945 to 1950 at least) he and Claude Shannon communicated about these ideas[4]. Although there was already an established field of mathematics concerning a theory of games, pioneered by Von Neumann **[Von Neumann and Morgenstern 44]**, chess had such a large space of legal positions, that even though everything about it is deterministic, the theories were not particularly applicable. Only heuristic and operational programs seemed plausible means of attack.

In a paper titled *Intelligent Machinery*, written in 1948[5], but not published until long after his death **[Turing 70]**, Turing outlined a more general view of making computers intelligent. In this rather short insightful paper he foresaw many modern developments and techniques. He argued (somewhat whimsically, to the annoyance of his employers **[Hodges 83]**) for at least some fields of intelligence, and his particular example is the learning of languages, that the machine would have to be embodied, and claimed success "seems however to depend rather too much on sense organs and locomotion to be feasible".

Turing argued that it must be possible to build a thinking machine since it was possible to build imitations of "any small part of a man". He made the distinction between producing accurate electrical models of nerves, and replacing them computationally with the available technology of vacuum tube circuits (this follows directly from his earlier paper **[Turing 37]**), and the assumption that the nervous system can be modeled as a computational system. For other parts of the body he suggests that "television cameras, microphones, loudspeakers", etc., could be used to model the rest of the system. "This would be a tremendous undertaking of course." Even so, Turing notes that the so constructed machine "would still have no contact with food, sex, sport and many other things of interest to the human being". Turing concludes that the best domains in which to explore the mechanization of thought are various games, and cryptanalysis, "in that they require little contact with the outside world"[6].

Turing thus carefully considered the question of embodiment, and for technical reasons chose to pursue aspects of intelligence which could be viewed, at least in his opinion, as purely symbolic. Minimax search, augmented with the idea of pursuing chains of capture to quiescence, and clever static evaluation functions (the

---

[3]Equally radical changes have occurred in the past, but admittedly they happened well before the current high levels of installed base of silicon-based computers.

[4]Norbert Wiener also outlines the idea of minimax in the final note of the original edition of **[Wiener 48]**. However he restricts the idea to a depth of two or three plays—one assumes for practical reasons, as he does express the general notion for *n* plays. See Section 3.3 for more details on the ways in which cybernetic models of thought were restricted by the computational models at hand.

[5]Different sources cite 1947 and 1948 as the time of writing.

[6]Interestingly, Turing did not completely abstract even a chess playing machine away from embodiment, commenting that "its only organs need be 'eyes' capable of distinguishing the various positions on a specially made board, and means for announcing its own moves".

Turochamp system of David Champernowne and Alan Turing[7], **[Shannon 50]**) soon became the dominant approach to the problem. **[Newell, Shaw and Simon 58]** compared all four known implemented chess playing programs of 1958 (with a total combined experience of six games played), including Turochamp, and they all followed this approach.

The basic approach of minimax with a good static evaluation function has not changed to this day. Programs of this ilk compete well with International Grand Masters. The best of them, *Deep Thought* **[Hsu, Anantharaman, Campbell and Nowatzyk 90]**, uses special purpose chips for massive search capabilities, along with a skillful evaluation scheme and selective deepening to direct that search better than in previous programs.

Although Turing had conceived of using chess as a vehicle for studying human thought processes, this notion has largely gotten lost along the way (there are of course exceptions, e.g., **[Wilkins 79]** describes a system which substitutes chess knowledge for search in the middle game—usually there are very few static evaluations, and tree search is mainly to confirm or deny the existence of a mate). Instead the driving force has always been performance, and the most successful program of the day has usually relied on technological advances. Brute force tree search has been the dominant method, itself dominated by the amount of bruteness available. This in turn has been a product of clever harnessing of the latest technology available. Over the years, the current 'champion' program has capitalized on the available hardware. *MacHack-6* **[Greenblatt, Eastlake and Crocker 67]** made use of the largest available fast memory (256K 36 bits words—about a megabyte or so, or $45 by today's standards) and a new comprehensive architecture (the PDP-6) largely influenced by Minsky and McCarthy's requirements for Lisp and symbolic programming. *Chess 4.0* and its descendants **[Slate and Atkin 84]** relied on the running on the world's faster available computer. *Belle* **[Condon and Thompson 84]** used a smaller central computer, but had a custom move generator, built from LSI circuits. Deep Thought, mentioned above as the most recent champion, relies on custom VLSI circuits to handle its move generation and tree search. It is clear that the success and progress in chess playing programs has been driven by technology enabling large tree searches. Few would argue that today's chess programs/hardware systems are very good models for general human thought processes.

There were some misgivings along the way, however. In an early paper **[Selfridge 56]** argues that better static evaluation is the key to playing chess, so that look-ahead can be limited to a single move except in situations close to mate (and one assumes he would include situations where there is capture, and perhaps exchanges, involved). But, he claims that humans come to chess with a significant advantage over computers (the thrust of the paper is on learning, and in this instance on learning to play chess) as they have concepts such as 'value', 'double threat', the 'centre' etc., already formed. Chess to Selfridge is not a disembodied exercise, but one where successful play is built upon a richness of experience in other, perhaps simpler, situations.

There is an interesting counterpoint to the history of computer chess; the game of Go. The search tree for Go is much much larger than for chess, and a good static evaluation function is much harder to define. Go has never worked out well as a vehicle for research in computer game playing—any reasonable crack at it is much more likely to require techniques much closer to those of human thought—mere computer technology advances are not going to bring the minimax approach close to success in this domain (see **[Campbell 83]** for a brief overview).

Before leaving Turing entirely there is one other rather significant contribution he made to the field which in a sense he predated. In **[Turing 50]** poses the question "Can machines think?". To tease out an acceptable meaning for this question he presented what has come to be known as the *Turing test*, where a person communicates in English over a teletype with either another person or a computer. The goal is to guess whether it is a person or a computer at the other end. Over time this test has come to be an informal goal of Artificial Intelligence[8]. Notice that it is a totally disembodied view of intelligence, although it is somewhat situated in that the machine has to respond in a timely fashion to its interrogator. Turing suggests that the machine should try to simulate a person by taking extra time and making mistakes with arithmetic problems. This is the version of the Turing test that is bandied around by current day Artificial Intelligence researchers[9].

Turing advances a number of strawman arguments against the case that a digital computer might one day be able to pass this test, but he does not consider the need that machine be fully embodied. In principle, of course, he is right. But how a machine might be then programmed is a question. Turing provides an argument that programming the machine by hand would be impractical, so he suggests having it learn. At this point he brings up the need to embody the machine in some way. He rejects giving it limbs, but suspects that eyes would be good, although not entirely necessary. At the end of the paper he proposes two possible paths towards his goal of a "thinking" machine. The unembodied path is to concentrate on programming intellectual activities like chess, while the embodied approach is to equip a digital computer "with the best sense organs that money can buy, and then teach it to understand and speak English". Artificial Intelligence followed the former path, and has all but ignored the latter approach[10].

[7] See *Personal Computing* January 1980, pages 80–81, for a description of this hand simulation of a chess machine.

[8] Turing expresses his own belief that it will be possible for a machine with 10^9 bits of store to pass a five minute version of the test with 70% probability by about the year 2000.

[9] In fact there is a yearly competition with a $100,000 prize for a machine that can pass this version of the Turing test.

[10] An excerpt from Turing's paper is reprinted in **[Hofstadter and Dennett 81]**. They leave out the whole section on learning and embodiment.

3.2 Establishment

The establishment of Artificial Intelligence as a discipline that is clearly the foundation of today's discipline by that name occurred during the period from the famous 'Dartmouth Conference' of 1956 through the publication of the book "Computers and Thought" in 1963 (**[Feigenbaum and Feldman 63]**).

Named and mostly organized by John McCarthy as "The Dartmouth Summer Research Project on Artificial Intelligence" the six-week long workshop brought together those who would establish and lead the major Artificial Intelligence research centers in North America for the next twenty years. McCarthy jointly established the MIT Artificial Intelligence Laboratory with Marvin Minsky, and then went on to found the Stanford Artificial Intelligence Laboratory. Allen Newell and Herbert Simon shaped and lead the group that turned into the Computer Science department at Carnegie-Mellon University. Even today a large portion of the researchers in Artificial Intelligence in North America had one of these four people on their doctoral committee, or were advised by someone who did. The ideas expressed at the Dartmouth meeting have thus had a signal impact upon the field first named there.

As can be seen from interviews of the participants published in **[McCorduck 79]** there is still some disagreement over the intellectual property that was brought to the conference and its relative significance. The key outcome was the acceptance and rise of search as the preeminent tool of Artificial Intelligence. There was a general acceptance of the use of search to solve problems, and with this there was an essential abandonment of any notion of situatedness.

Minsky's earlier work had been involved with neural modeling. His Ph.D. thesis at Princeton was concerned with a model for the brain **[Minsky 54]**. Later, while at Harvard he was strongly influenced by McCulloch and Pitts (see **[McCulloch and Pitts 43]**), but by the time of the Dartmouth meeting he had become more involved with symbolic search-based systems. In his collection **[Minsky 68]** of versions of his students' Ph.D. theses, all were concerned to some degree with defining and controlling an appropriate search space.

Simon and Newell presented their recent work on the *Logic Theorist* **[Newell, Shaw and Simon 57]**, a program that proved logic theorems by searching a tree of subgoals. The program made extensive use of heuristics to prune its search space. With this success, the idea of heuristic search soon became dominant within the still tiny Artificial Intelligence community.

McCarthy was not so affected by the conference that he had organized, and continues to this day to concentrate on epistemological issues rather than performance programs. However he was soon to invent the Lisp programming language **[McCarthy 1960]** which became the standard model of computation for Artificial Intelligence. It had great influence on the models of thought that were popular however, as it made certain things such as search, and representations based on individuals, much easier to program.

At the time, most programs were written in assembly language. It was a tedious job to write search procedures, especially recursive procedures in the machine languages of the day, although some people such as **[Samuel 59]** (another Dartmouth participant) were spectacularly successful. Newell and Simon owed much of their success in developing the Logic Theorist and their later General Problem Solver **[Newell, Shaw and Simon 59]**, to their use of an interpreted language (IPL-V—see **[Newell, Shaw and Simon 61]**) which supported complex list structures and recursion. Many of their student's projects reported in **[Feigenbaum and Feldman 63]** also used this language.

McCarthy's Lisp was much cleaner and simpler. It made processing lists of information and recursive tree searches trivial to program–often a dozen lines of code could replace many hundreds of lines of assembler code. Search procedures now became even easier and more convenient to include in Artificial Intelligence programs. Lisp also had an influence on the classes of representational systems used, as is described in section 3.5.

In **[Minsky 61]**, Artificial Intelligence was broken into five key topics: search, pattern recognition, learning, planning and induction. The second through fourth of these were characterized as ways of controlling search (respectively by better selection of tree expansion operators, by directing search through previous experience, and by replacing a given search with a smaller and more appropriate exploration). Again, most of the serious work in Artificial Intelligence according to this breakdown was concerned with search.

Eventually, after much experimentation **[Michie and Ross 70]**, search methods became well understood, formalized, and analyzed **[Knuth and Moore 75]**, and became celebrated as the primary method of Artificial Intelligence **[Nilsson 71]**.

At the end of the era of establishment, in 1963, Minsky generated an exhaustive annotated bibliography (**[Minsky 63]**) of literature "directly concerned with construction of artificial problem-solving systems"[11]. It contains 925 citations, 890 of which are to scientific papers and books, and 35 of which are to collections of such papers. There are two main points of interest here. First, although the title of the bibliography, "A Selected Descriptor-Indexed Bibliography to the Literature on Artificial Intelligence", refers to Artificial Intelligence, in his introduction he refers to the area of concern as "artificial problem-solving systems". Second, and somewhat paradoxically, the scope of the bibliography is much broader than one would expect from an Artificial Intelligence bibliography today. It includes many items on cybernetics, neuroscience, bionics, information and communication theory, and first generation connectionism.

These two contrasting aspects of the bibliography highlight a trend in Artificial Intelligence that continued for the next 25 years. Out of a soup of ideas on how to build intelligent machines the disembodied and non-situated approach of problem-solving search systems emerged as dominant, at least within the community that referred to its own work as Artificial Intelligence.

[11] It also acted as the combined bibliography for the papers in **[Feigenbaum and Feldman 63]**.

With hindsight we can step back and look at what happened. Originally search was introduced as a mechanism for solving problems that arguably humans used some search in solving. Chess and logic theorem proving are two examples we have already discussed. In these domains one does not expect instantaneous responses from humans doing the same tasks. They are not tasks that are situated in the world.

One can debate whether even in these tasks it is wise to rely so heavily on search, as bigger problems will have exponentially bad effects on search time—in fact **[Newell, Shaw and Simon 58]** argue just this, but produced a markedly slower chess program because of the complexity of static evaluation and search control. Some, such as **[Samuel 59]** with his checker's playing program, did worry about keeping things on a human timescale. **[Slagle 63]** in his symbolic integration program, was worried about being economically competitive with humans, but as he points out in the last two paragraphs of his paper, the explosive increase in price/performance ratio for computing was able to keep his programs ahead. In general, performance increases in computers were able to feed researchers with a steadily larger search space, enabling them to feel that they were making progress as the years went by. For any given technology level, a long-term freeze would soon show that programs relying on search had very serious problems, especially if there was any desire to situate them in a dynamic world.

In the last paragraph of **[Minsky 61]** he does bring up the possibility of a situated agent, acting as a "thinking aid" to a person. But again he relies on a performance increase in standard computing methods (this time through the introduction of time sharing) to supply the necessary time relevant computations.

In the early days of the formal discipline of Artificial Intelligence, search was adopted as a basic technology. It was easy to program on digital computers. It lead to reasoning systems which are not easy to shoe-horn into situated agents.

3.3 Cybernetics

There was, especially in the forties and fifties, another discipline which could be viewed as having the same goals as we have identified for Artificial Intelligence—the construction of useful intelligent systems and the understanding of human intelligence. This work, known as *Cybernetics*, had a fundamentally different flavor from the today's traditional Artificial Intelligence.

Cybernetics co-evolved with control theory and statistical information theory—e.g., see **[Wiener 48, 61]**. It is the study of the mathematics of machines, not in terms of the functional components of a machine and how they are connected, and not in terms of what an individual machine can do here and now, and but rather in terms of *all* the possible behaviors that an individual machine can produce. There was a strong emphasis on characterizing a machine in terms of its inputs and outputs, and treating it as a *black box* as far as its internal workings were unobservable. The tools of analysis were often differential or integral equations, and these tools inherently limited cybernetics to situations where the boundary conditions were not changing rapidly. In contrast, they often do so in a system situated in a dynamically changing world—that complexity needs to go somewhere; either into discontinuous models or changed boundary conditions.

Cybernetics arose in the context of regulation of machinery and electronic circuits—it is often characterized by the subtitle of Wiener's book as the study of "control and communication in the animal and the machine". The model of computation at the time of its original development was analog. The inputs to and outputs from the machine to be analyzed were usually thought of as almost everywhere continuous functions with reasonable derivatives, and the mechanisms for automated analysis and modeling were usually things that today would be characterized as analog components. As such there was no notion of symbolic search—any search was couched in terms of minimization of a function. There was also much less of a notion of representation as an abstract manipulable entity than was found in the Artificial Intelligence approaches.

Much of the work in Cybernetics really was aimed at understanding animals and intelligence. Animals were modeled as machines, and from those models, it was hoped to glean how the animals changed their behavior through learning, and how that lead to better adaptation to the environment for the whole organism. It was recognized rather early (e.g., **[Ashby 52]** for an explicit statement) that an organism and its environment must be modeled together in order to understand the behavior produced by the organism—this is clearly an expression of situatedness. The tools of feedback analysis were used (**[Ashby 56]**) to concentrate on such issues as stability of the system as the environment was perturbed, and in particular a system's *homeostasis* or ability to keep certain parameters within prescribed ranges, no matter what the uncontrolled variations within the environment.

With regards to embodiment there were some experiments along these lines. Many cybernetic models of organisms were rather abstract demonstrations of homeostasis, but some were concerned with physical robots. **[Walter 50, 51, 53]**[12] describes robots built on cybernetic principles which demonstrated goal-seeking behavior, homeostasis, and learning abilities.

The complexity and abilities of Walter's physically embodied machines rank with the purely imaginary ones in the first half dozen chapters of **[Braitenberg 84]** three decades later.

The limiting factors in these experiments were twofold; (1) the technology of building small self contained robots when the computational elements were miniature (a relative term) vacuum tubes, and (2) the lack of mechanisms for abstractly describing behavior at a level below the complete behavior, so that an implementation could reflect those simpler components. Thus in the first in-

[12] Much of the book **[Walter 53]** is concerned with early work on electroencephalography and hopes for its role in revealing the workings of the brain—forty years later these hopes do not seem to have been born out.

stance the models of thought were limited by technological barriers to implementing those models, and in the second instance, the lack of certain critical components of a model (organization into submodules) restricted the ability to build better technological implementations.

Let us return to Wiener and analyze the ways in which the mechanisms of cybernetics, and the mechanisms of computation were intimately interrelated in deep and self limiting ways.

Wiener was certainly aware of digital machines[13] even in his earlier edition of **[Wiener 48]**. He compared them to analog machines such as the Bush differential analyzer, and declares that the digital (or *numerical*, as he called them) machines are superior for accurate numerical calculations. But in some deep sense Wiener did not see the flexibility of these machines. In an added chapter in **[Wiener 61]** he discussed the problem of building a self reproducing machine, and in the Cybernetic tradition, reduced the problem to modeling the input/output characteristics of a black box, in particular a non-linear transducer. He related methods for approximating observations of this function with a linear combination of basis non-linear transducers, and then showed that the whole problem could be done by summing and multiplying potentials and averaging over time. Rather than turn to a digital computer to do this he stated that there were some interesting possibilities for multiplication devices using piezo-electric effects. We see then the intimate tying together between models of computation, i.e., analog computation, and models of the essentials of self-reproduction. It is impossible to tease apart cause and effect from this vantage point. The critical point is the way in which the mathematical proposal is tied to a technological implementation as a certification of the validity of the approach[14].

By the mid sixties it was clear that the study of intelligence, even a study arising from the principles of cybernetics, if it was to succeed needed to be more broad-based in its levels of abstraction and tools of analysis. A good example is **[Arbib 64]**[15]. Even so, he still harbors hope that cybernetic methods may turn out to give an understanding of the "overall coordinating and integrating principles" which interrelate the component subsystems of the human nervous system.

3.4 Abstraction

The years immediately following the Dartmouth conference shaped the field of Artificial Intelligence in a way which has not significantly changed. The next few years, in the main, amplified the abstraction away from situatedness, or connectedness to the world[16]. There were a number of demonstrations along the way which seemed to legitimize this abstraction. In this section I review some of those events, and argue that there were fundamental flaws in the conclusions generally drawn.

At MIT **[Roberts 63]** demonstrated a vision program that could match pre-stored models to visual images of blocks and wedges. This program was the forerunner of all modern vision programs, and it was many years before its performance could be matched by others. It took a grey level image of the world, and extracted a cartoon-like line drawing. It was this line drawing that was then fitted, via an inverse perspective transform to the pre-stored models. To those who saw its results this looked like a straightforward and natural way to process images and to build models (based on the prestored library) of the objective reality in front of the camera.

The unfortunate truth however, is that it is extraordinarily difficult to extract reliable line drawings in any sort of realistic cases of images. In Roberts' case the lighting was carefully controlled, the blocks were well painted, and the background was chosen with care. The images of his blocks produced rather complete line drawings with very little clutter where there should, by human observer standards, be no line elements. Today, after almost thirty years of research on bottom-up, top-down, and middle-out line finders, there is still no line finder that gets such clean results on a single natural image. Real world images are not at all the clean things that our personal introspection tells us they are. It is hard to appreciate this without working on an image yourself[17].

The fallout of Roberts' program working on a very controlled set of images was that people thought that the line detection problem was doable and solved. E.g., **[Evans 68]** cites Roberts in his discussion of how input could obtained for his analogy program which compared sets of line drawings of 2-D geometric figures.

During the late sixties and early seventies the Shakey project **[Nilsson 84]** at SRI reaffirmed the premises of abstract Artificial Intelligence. Shakey, mentioned in section 2, was a mobile robot that inhabited a set of

[13]In the introduction to **[Wiener 48]** he talks about embodying such machines with photoelectric cells, thermometers, strain gauges and motors in the service of mechanical labor. But, in the text of the book he does not make such a connection with models of organisms. Rather he notes that they are intended for many successive runs, with the memory being cleared out between runs and states that "the brain, under normal circumstances, is not the complete analogue of the computing machine but rather the analogue of a single run on such a machine". His models of digital computation and models of thought are too dis-similar to make the connection that we would today.

[14]With hindsight, an even wilder speculation is presented at the end of the later edition. Wiener suggests that the capital substances of genes and viruses may self reproduce through such a spectral analysis of infra-red emissions from the model molecules that then induce self organization into the undifferentiated magma of amino and nucleic acids available to form the new biological material.

[15]Arbib includes an elegant warning against being too committed to models, even mathematical models, which may turn out to be wrong. His statement that the "mere use of formulas gives no magical powers to a theory" is just as timely today as it was then.

[16]One exception was a computer controlled hand built at MIT, **[Ernst 61]**, and connected to the TX-0 computer. The hand was very much situated and embodied, and relied heavily on the external world as a model, rather than using internal representations. This piece of work seems to have gotten lost, for reasons that are not clear to me.

[17]Try it! You'll be amazed at how bad it is.

specially prepared rooms. It navigated from room to room, trying to satisfy a goal given to it on a teletype. It would, depending on the goal and circumstances, navigate around obstacles consisting of large painted blocks and wedges, push them out of the way, or push them to some desired location.

Shakey had an onboard black and white television camera as its primary sensor. An offboard computer analyzed the images, and merged descriptions of what was seen into an existing first order predicate calculus model of the world. A planning program, STRIPS, operated on those symbolic descriptions of the world to generate a sequence of actions for Shakey. These plans were translated through a series of refinements into calls to atomic actions in fairly tight feedback loops with atomic sensing operations using Shakey's other sensors such as a bump bar and odometry.

Shakey was considered a great success at the time, demonstrating an integrated system involving mobility, perception, representation, planning, execution, and error recovery.

Shakey's success thus reaffirmed the idea of relying completely on internal models of an external objective reality. That is precisely the methodology it followed, and it appeared successful. However, it only worked because of very careful engineering of the environment. Twenty years later, no mobile robot has been demonstrated matching all aspects of Shakey's performance in a more general environment, such as an office environment.

The rooms in which Shakey operated were bare except for the large colored blocks and wedges. This made the class of objects that had to be represented very simple. The walls were of a uniform color, and carefully lighted, with dark rubber baseboards, making clear boundaries with the lighter colored floor. This meant that very simple and robust vision of trihedral corners between two walls and the floor, could be used for relocalizing the robot in order to correct for drift in the robot's odometric measurements. The blocks and wedges were painted different colors on different planar surfaces. This ensured that it was relatively easy, especially in the good lighting provided, to find edges in the images separating the surfaces, and thus making it easy to identify the shape of the polyhedron. Blocks and wedges were relatively rare in the environment, eliminating problems due to partial obscurations. The objective reality of the environment was thus quite simple, and the mapping to an internal model of that reality was also quite plausible.

Around the same time at MIT a major demonstration was mounted of a robot which could view a scene consisting of stacked blocks, then build a copy of the scene using a robot arm (see **[Winston 72]**—the program was known as the *copy-demo*). The programs to do this were very specific to the blocks world, and would not have worked in the presence of simple curved objects, rough texture on the blocks, or without carefully controlled lighting. Nevertheless it reinforced the idea that a complete three dimensional description of the world could be extracted from a visual image. It legitimized the work of others, such as **[Winograd 72]**, whose programs worked in a make-believe world of blocks—if one program could be built which understood such a world completely and could also manipulate that world, then it was assumed that programs which assumed that abstraction could in fact be connected to the real world without great difficulty. The problem remained of slowness of the programs due to the large search spaces, but as before, faster computers were always just around the corner.

The key problem that I see with all this work (apart from the use of search) is that it relied on the assumption that a complete world model could be built internally and then manipulated. The examples from Roberts, through Shakey and the copy-demo all relied on very simple worlds, and controlled situations. The programs were able to largely ignore unpleasant issues like sensor uncertainty, and were never really stressed because of the carefully controlled perceptual conditions. No computer vision systems can produce world models of this fidelity for anything nearing the complexity of realistic world scenes—even object recognition is an active and difficult research area. There are two responses to this: (1) eventually computer vision will catch up and provide such world models—I don't believe this based on the biological evidence presented below, or (2) complete objective models of reality are unrealistic—and hence the methods of Artificial Intelligence that rely on such models are unrealistic.

With the rise in abstraction it is interesting to note that it was still quite technologically difficult to connect to the real world for most Artificial Intelligence researchers[18]. For instance, **[Barrow and Salter 70]** describe efforts at Edinburgh, a major Artificial Intelligence center, to connect sensing to action, and the results are extraordinarily primitive by today's standards—both MIT and SRI had major engineering efforts in support of their successful activities. **[Moravec 81]** relates a sad tale of frustration from the early seventies of efforts at the Stanford Artificial Intelligence Laboratory to build a simple mobile robot with visual input.

Around the late sixties and early seventies there was a dramatic increase in the availability of computer processing power available to researchers at reasonably well equipped laboratories. Not only was there a large increase in processing speed and physical memory, but time sharing systems became well established. An individual researcher was now able to work continuously and conveniently on a disembodied program designed to exhibit intelligence. However, connections to the real world were not only difficult and overly expensive, but the physical constraints of using them made development of the 'intelligent' parts of the system slower by at least an order of magnitude, and probably two orders, as compared to the new found power of timesharing. The computers clearly had a potential to influence the models of thought used—and certainly that hypothesis is not

[18]It is still fairly difficult even today. There are very few turnkey systems available for purchase which connect sensors to reasonable computers, and reasonable computers to actuators. The situation does seem to be rapidly improving however—we may well be just about to step over a significant threshold.

contradicted by the sort of micro-world work that actually went on.

3.5 Knowledge

By this point in the history of Artificial Intelligence, the trends, assumptions, and approaches had become well established. The last fifteen years have seen the discipline thundering along on inertia more than anything else. Apart from a renewed flirtation with neural models (see section 3.8 below) there has been very little change in the underlying assumptions about the models of thought. This coincides with an era of very little technical innovation in our underlying models of computation.

For the remainder of section 3, I rather briefly review the progress made over the last fifteen years, and show how it relates to the fundamental issues of situatedness and embodiment brought up earlier.

One problem with micro-worlds is that they are somewhat uninteresting. The blocks world was the most popular micro-world and there is very little that can be done in it other than make stacks of blocks. After a flurry of early work where particularly difficult 'problems' or 'puzzles' were discovered and then solved (e.g., **[Sussman 75]**) it became more and more difficult to do something new within that domain.

There were three classes of responses to this impoverished problem space:

- Move to other domains with equally simple semantics, but with more interesting print names than *block-a* etc. It was usually not the intent of the researchers to do this, but many in fact did fall into this trap. **[Winograd and Flores 86]** expose and criticize a number of such dressings up in the chapter on "Understanding Language".
- Build a more complex semantics into the blocks world and work on the new problems which arise. A rather heroic example of this is **[Fahlman 74]** who included balance, multi-shaped blocks, friction, and the like. The problem with this approach is that the solutions to the 'puzzles' become so domain specific that it is hard to see how they might generalize to other domains.
- Move to the wider world. In particular, represent knowledge about the everyday world, and then build problem solvers, learning systems, etc., that operate in this semantically richer world.

The last of these approaches has spawned possibly the largest recognizable subfield of Artificial Intelligence, known as Knowledge Representation. It has its own conferences. It has theoretical and practical camps. Yet, it is totally ungrounded. It concentrates much of its energies on anomalies within formal systems which are never used for any practical tasks.

[Brachman and Levesque 85] is a collection of papers in the area. The knowledge representation systems described receive their input either in symbolic form or as the output of natural language systems. The goal of the papers seems to be to represent 'knowledge' about the world. However it is totally ungrounded. There is very little attempt to use the knowledge (save in the naive physics **[Hayes 85]**, or qualitative physics **[de Kleer and Brown 84]** areas—but note that these areas too are ungrounded). There is an implicit assumption that someday the inputs and outputs will be connected to something which will make use of them (see **[Brooks 91a]** for an earlier criticism of this approach).

In the meantime the work proceeds with very little to steer it, and much of it concerns problems produced by rather simple-minded attempts at representing complex concepts. To take but one example, there have been many pages written on the problem of penguins being birds, even though they cannot fly. The reason that this is a problem is that the knowledge representation systems are built on top of a computational technology that makes convenient the use of very simple individuals (Lisp atoms) and placing links between them. As pointed out in **[Brooks 90b]**, and much earlier in **[Brooks 91a]**, such a simple approach does not work when the system is to be physically grounded through embodiment. It seems pointless to try to patch up a system which in the long run cannot possibly work. **[Dreyfus 81]**[19] provides a useful criticism of this style of work.

Perhaps the pinnacle of the knowledge-is-everything approach can be found in **[Lenat and Feigenbaum 91]** where they discuss the foundations of a 10-year project to encode knowledge having the scope of a simple encyclopedia. It is a totally unsituated, and totally disembodied approach. Everything the system is to know is through hand-entered units of 'knowledge', although there is some hope expressed that later it will be able to learn itself by reading. **[Smith 91]** provides a commentary on this approach, and points out how the early years of the project have been devoted to finding a more primitive level of knowledge than was previously envisioned for grounding the higher levels of knowledge. It is my opinion, and also Smith's, that there is a fundamental problem still and one can expect continued regress until the system has some form of embodiment.

3.6 Robotics

Section 2 outlined the early history of mobile robots. There have been some interesting developments over the last ten years as attempts have been made to embody some theories from Artificial Intelligence in mobile robots. In this section I briefly review some of the results.

In the early eighties the Defense Advanced Research Projects Agency (DARPA) in the US, sponsored a major thrust in building an Autonomous Land Vehicle. The initial task for the vehicle was to run along a paved road in daylight using vision as the primary perceptual sense. The first attempts at this problem (e.g., **[Waxman, Le Moigne and Srinivasan)]** followed the SMPA methodology. The idea was to build a three-dimensional world model of the road ahead, then plan a path along it, including steering and velocity control annotations. These approaches failed as it was not possible to recover accurate three-dimensional road models from the visual

[19] Endorsement of some of Dreyfus' views should not be taken as whole hearted embrace of all his arguments.

images. Even under fairly strong assumptions about the class of roads being followed the programs would produce ludicrously wrong results.

With the pressure of getting actual demonstrations of the vehicle running on roads, and of having all the processing onboard, radical changes had to made in the approaches taken. Two separate teams came up with similar approaches, **[Turk, Morgenthaler, Gremban, and Marra 88]** at Martin Marietta, the integrating contractor, and **[Thorpe, Hebert, Kanade, and Shafer 88]** at CMU, the main academic participant in the project, both producing vision-based navigation systems. Both systems operated in picture coordinates rather than world coordinates, and both successfully drove vehicles along the roads. Neither system generated three dimensional world models. Rather, both identified road regions in the images and servo-ed the vehicle to stay on the road. The systems can be characterized as reactive, situated and embodied. **[Horswill and Brooks 88]** describe a system of similar vintage which operates an indoor mobile robot under visual navigation. The shift in approach taken on the outdoor vehicle was necessitated by the realities of the technology available, and the need to get things operational.

Despite these lessons there is still a strong bias to following the traditional Artificial Intelligence SMPA approach as can be seen in the work at CMU on the Ambler project. The same team that adopted a reactive approach to the road following problem have reverted to a cumbersome, complex, and slow complete world modeling approach **[Simmons and Krotkov 91]**.

3.7 Vision

Inspired by the work of **[Roberts 63]** and that on Shakey **[Nilsson 84]**, the vision community has been content to work on scene description problems for many years. The implicit intent has been that when the reasoning systems of Artificial Intelligence were ready, the vision systems would be ready to deliver world models as required, and the two could be hooked together to get a situated, or embodied system.

There are numerous problems with this approach, and too little room to treat them adequately within the space constraints of this paper. The fundamental issue is that Artificial Intelligence and Computer Vision have made an assumption that the purpose of vision is to reconstruct the static external world (for dynamic worlds it is just supposed to do it often and quickly) as a three dimensional world model. I do not believe that this is possible with the generality that is usually assumed. Furthermore I do not think it is necessary, nor do I think that it is what human vision does. Section 4 discusses some of these issues a little more.

3.8 Parallelism

Parallel computers are potentially quite different from Von Neumann machines. One might expect then that parallel models of computation would lead to fundamentally different models of thought. The story about parallelism, and the influence of parallel machines on models of thought, and the influence of models of thought on parallel machines has two and a half pieces. The first piece arose around the time of the early cybernetics work, the second piece exploded in the mid-eighties and we have still to see all the casualties. The last half piece has been pressured by the current models of thought to change the model of parallelism.

There was a large flurry of work in the late fifties and sixties involving linear threshold devices, commonly known as perceptrons. The extremes in this work are represented by **[Rosenblatt 62]** and **[Minsky and Papert 69]**. These devices were used in rough analogy to neurons and were to be wired into networks that learned to do some task, rather than having to be programmed. Adjusting the weights on the inputs of these devices was roughly equivalent in the model to adjusting the synaptic weights where axons connect to dendrites in real neurons—this is currently considered as the likely site of most learning within the brain.

The idea was that the network had specially distinguished inputs and outputs. Members of classes of patterns would be presented to the inputs and the outputs would be given a correct classification. The difference between the correct response and the actual response of the network would then be used to update weights on the inputs of individual devices. The key driving force behind the blossoming of this field was the perceptron convergence theorem that showed that a simple parameter adjustment technique would always let a single perceptron learn a discrimination if there existed a set of weights capable of making that discrimination.

To make things more manageable the networks were often structured as layers of devices with connections only between adjacent layers. The directions of the connections were strictly controlled, so that there were no feedback loops in the network and that there was a natural progression from one single layer that would then be the input layer, and one layer would be the output layer. The problem with multi-layer networks was that there was no obvious way to assign the credit or blame over the layers for a correct or incorrect pattern classification.

In the formal analyses that were carried out (e.g., **[Nilsson 65]** and **[Minsky and Papert 69]**) only a single layer of devices which could learn, or be adjusted, were ever considered. **[Nilsson 65]** in the later chapters did consider multi-layer machines, but in each case, all but one layer consisted of static unmodifiable devices. There was very little work on analyzing machines with feedback.

None of these machines was particularly situated, or embodied. They were usually tested on problems set up by the researcher. There were many abuses of the scientific method in these tests—the results were not always as the researchers interpreted them.

After the publication of **[Minsky and Papert 69]**, which contained many negative results on the capabilities of single layer machines, the field seemed to die out for about fifteen years.

Recently there has been a resurgence in the field starting with the publication of **[Rumelhart and McClelland 86]**.

The new approaches were inspired by a new learning algorithm known as *back propagation* (**[Rumelhart, Hinton and Williams 86]**). This algorithm gives a method for assigning credit and blame in fully connected multi-layer machines without feedback loops. The individual devices within the layers have linearly weighted inputs and a differentiable output function, a sigmoid, which closely matches a step function, or threshold function. Thus they are only slight generalizations of the earlier perceptrons, but their continuous and differentiable outputs enable hill climbing to be performed which lets the networks converge eventually to be able to classify inputs appropriately as trained.

Back propagation has a number of problems; it is slow to learn in general, and there is a learning rate which needs to be tuned by hand in most cases. The effect of a low learning rate is that the network might often get stuck in local minima. The effect of a higher learning rate is that the network may never really converge as it will be able to jump out of the correct minimum as well as it can jump out of an incorrect minimum. These problems combine to make back propagation, which is the cornerstone of modern neural network research, inconvenient for use in embodied or situated systems.

In fact, most of the examples in the new wave of neural networks have not been situated or embodied. There are a few counterexamples (e.g., **[Sejnowksi and Rosenberg 87]**, **[Atkeson 89]** and **[Viola 90]**) but in the main they are not based on back propagation. The most successful recent learning techniques for situated, embodied, mobile robots, have not been based on parallel algorithms at all—rather they use a reinforcement learning algorithm such as Q-learning (**[Watkins 89]**) as for example, **[Kaelbling 90]** and **[Mahadevan and Connell 90]**.

One problem for neural networks becoming situated or embodied is that they do not have a simple translation into time varying perception or action pattern systems. They need extensive front and back ends to equip them to interact with the world—all the cited examples above had such features added to them.

Both waves of neural network research have been heralded by predictions of the demise of all other forms of computation. It has not happened in either case. Both times there has been a bandwagon effect where many people have tried to use the mechanisms that have become available to solve many classes of problems, often without regard to whether the problems could even be solved in principle by the methods used. In both cases the enthusiasm for the approach has been largely stimulated by a single piece of technology, first the perceptron training rule, and then the back propagation algorithm.

And now for the last half-piece of the parallel computation story. The primary hope for parallel computation helping Artificial Intelligence has been the Connection Machine developed by **[Hillis 85]**. This is a SIMD machine, and as such might be thought to have limited applicability for general intelligent activities. Hillis, however, made a convincing case that it could be used for many algorithms to do with knowledge representation, and that it would speed them up, often to be constant time algorithms. The book describing the approach is exciting, and in fact on pages 4 and 5 of **[Hillis 85]** the author promises to break the Von Neumann bottleneck by making all the silicon in a machine actively compute all the time. The argument is presented that most of the silicon in a Von Neumann machine is devoted to memory, and most of that is inactive most of the time. This was a brave new approach, but it has not survived the market place. New models of the connection machine have large local memories (in the order of 64K bits) associated with each one bit processor (there can be up to 64K processors in a single Connection Machine). Once again, most of the silicon is inactive most of the time. Connection machines are used within Artificial Intelligence laboratories mostly for computer vision where there is an obvious mapping from processors and their NEWS network to pixels of standard digital images. Traditional Artificial Intelligence approaches are so tied to their traditional machine architectures that they have been hard to map to this new sort of architecture.

4 Biology

We have our own introspection to tell us how our minds work, and our own observations to tell us how the behavior of other people and of animals works. We have our own partial theories and methods of explanation[20]. Sometimes, when an observation, internal or external, does not fit our pre-conceptions, we are rather ready to dismiss it as something we do not understand, and do not need to understand.

In this section I will skim over a scattering of recent work from ethology, psychology, and neuroscience, in an effort to indicate how deficient our everyday understanding of behavior really is. This is important to realize because traditional Artificial Intelligence has relied at the very least implicitly, and sometimes quite explicitly, on these folk understandings of human and animal behavior. The most common example is the story about getting from Boston to California (or vice-versa), which sets up an analogy between what a person does mentally in order to *Plan* the trip, and the means-ends method of planning. See **[Agre 91]** for a more detailed analysis of the phenomenon.

4.1 Ethology

Ethology, the study of animal behavior, tries to explain the causation, development, survival value, and evolution of behavior patterns within animals. See **[McFarland 85]** for an easy introduction to modern ethology.

Perhaps the most famous ethologist was Niko Tinbergen (closely followed by his co-Nobel winners Konrad Lorenz and Karl von Frisch). His heirarchical view of intelligence, described in **[Tinbergen 51]**, is often quoted by Artificial Intelligence researchers in support of their own hierarchical theories. However, this approach was meant to be a neurobiologically plausible theory, but it was described in the absence any evidence. Tinbergen's model has largely been replaced in modern ethology by theories of motivational competition, disinhibition, and dominant and sub-dominant behaviors.

[20] See **[Churchland 86]** for a discussion of folk psychology.

There is no completely worked out theory of exactly how the decision is made as to which behavioral pattern (e.g., drinking or eating) should be active in an animal. A large number of experiments give evidence of complex internal and external feedback loops in determining an appropriate behavior. **[McFarland 88]** presents a number of such experiments and demonstrates the challenges for the theories. The experimental data has ruled out the earlier hierarchical models of behavior selection, and current theories share many common properties with the behavior-based approach advocated in this paper.

4.2 Psychology

The way in which our brains work is quite hidden from us. We have some introspection, we believe, to some aspects of our thought processes, but there are certainly perceptual and motor areas that we are quite confident we have no access to[21]. To tease out the mechanisms at work we can do at least two sorts of experiments: we can test the brain at limits of its operational envelop to see how it breaks down, and we can study damaged brains and get a glimpse at the operation of previously integrated components. In fact, some of these observations call into question the reliability of any of our own introspections.

There have been many psychophysical experiments to test the limits of human visual perception. We are all aware of so-called *optical illusions* where our visual apparatus seems to break down. The journal *Perception* regularly carries papers which show that what we perceive is not what we see (e.g., **[Ramachandran and Anstis 85]**). For instance in visual images of a jumping leopard whose spots are made to artificially move about, we perceive them all as individually following the leopard. The straightforward model of human perception proposed by **[Marr 82]**, and almost universally accepted by Artificial Intelligence vision researchers, does not account for such results. Likewise it is now clear that the color pathway is separate from the intensity pathway in the human visual system, and our color vision is something of an illusion[22]. We are unaware of these deficiencies—most people are not aware that they have a blind spot in each eye the size of the image of the moon—they are totally inaccessible to our consciousness. Even more surprising, our very notion of consciousness is full of inconsistencies—psychophysical experiments show that our experience of the flow of time as we observe things in the world is an illusion, as we can often consciously perceive things in a temporal order inconsistent with the world as constructed by an experimenter (see **[Dennett and Kinsbourne 90]** for an overview).

We turn now to damaged brains to get a glimpse at how things might be organized. This work can better be termed *neuropsychology*. There is a large body of literature on this subject from which we merely pick out just a few instances here. The purpose is to highlight the fact that the approaches taken in traditional Artificial Intelligence are vastly different from the way the human brain is organized.

The common view in Artificial Intelligence, and particularly in the knowledge representation community, is that there is a central storage system which links together the information about concepts, individuals, categories, goals, intentions, desires, and whatever else might be needed by the system. In particular there is a tendency to believe that the knowledge is stored in a way that is independent from the way or circumstances in which it was acquired.

[McCarthy and Warrington 88] (and a series of earlier papers by them and their colleagues) give cause to doubt this seemingly logical organization. They report on a particular individual (identified as TOB), who at an advanced age developed a semantic deficit in knowledge of living things, but retained a reasonable knowledge of inanimate things. By itself, this sounds perfectly plausible—the semantic knowledge might just be stored in a category specific way, and the animate part of the storage has been damaged. But, it happens that TOB is able to access the knowledge when, for example he was shown a picture of a dolphin—he was able to form sentences using the word 'dolphin' and talk about its habitat, its ability to be trained, and its role in the US military. When verbally asked what a dolphin is, however, he thought it was either a fish or a bird. He has no such conflict in knowledge when the subject is a wheelbarrow, say. The authors argue that since the deficit is not complete but shows degradation, the hypothesis that there is a deficit in a particular type of sensory modality access to a particular category subclass in a single database is not valid. Through a series of further observations they argue that they have shown evidence of modality-specific organization of meaning, besides a category specific organization. Thus knowledge may be duplicated in many places, and may by no means be uniformly accessible. There are examples of where the knowledge is shown to be inconsistent. Our normal introspection does not reveal this organization, and would seem to be at odds with these explanations. Below, we call into question our normal introspection.

[Newcombe and Ratcliff 89] present a long discussion of visuospatial disorders in brain damaged patients. Many of these severely tax the model a person as an integrated rational agent. One simple example they report is finger agnosia, where a patient may be quite impaired in the way he can carry out conscious simple tasks using their fingers, but could still do things such as thread a needle, or play the piano well. This suggests the existence of multiple parallel channels of control, rather than some centralized finger control box, for instance.

[Teitelbaum, Pellis and Pellis 90] summarize work which shows that rat locomotion involves a number of reflexes. Drugs can be used to shut off many reflexes so that a rat will appear to be unable to move. Almost all stimuli have no effect—the rat simply remains with its limbs in whatever configuration the experimenter has ar-

[21] This contrasts with a popular fad in Artificial Intelligence where all reasoning of a system is supposed to be available to a meta-reasoning system, or even introspectively to the system itself.

[22] See the techniques used in the current trend of 'colorization' of black and white movie classics for a commercial capitalization on our visual deficiencies.

ranged them. However certain very specific stimuli can trigger a whole chain of complex motor interactions—e.g., tilting the surface on which the rats feet are resting to the point where the rat starts to slide will cause the rat to leap. There has also been a recent popularization of the work of **[Sacks 74]** which shows similar symptoms, in somewhat less understood detail, for humans. Again, it is hard to explain these results in terms of a centralized will—rather an interpretation of multiple almost independent agencies such as hypothesized by **[Minsky 86]** seems a better explanation.

Perhaps the most remarkable sets of results are from split brain patients. It has become common knowledge that we all possess a left brain and a right brain, but in patients whose *corpus callosum* has been severed they really do become separate operational brains in their own rights **[Gazzaniga and LeDoux 77]**.

Through careful experimentation it is possible to independently communicate with the two brains, visually with both, and verbally with the left. By setting up experiments where one side does not have access to the information possessed by the other side, it is possible to push hard on the introspection mechanisms. It turns out that the ignorant half prefers to fabricate explanations for what is going on, rather than admit ignorance. These are normal people (except their brains are cut in half), and it seems that they sincerely believe the lies they are telling, as a result of confabulations generated during introspection. One must question then the ordinary introspection that goes on when our brains are intact.

What is the point of all this? The traditional Artificial Intelligence model of representation and organization along centralized lines is not how people are built. Traditional Artificial Intelligence methods are certainly not necessary for intelligence then, and so far they have not really been demonstrated to be sufficient in situated, embodied systems. The organization of humans is by definition sufficient—it is not known at all whether it will turn out to be necessary. The point is that we cannot make assumptions of necessity under either approach. The best we can expect to do for a while at least, is to show that some approach is sufficient to produce interesting intelligence.

4.3 Neuroscience

The working understanding of the brain among Artificial Intelligence researchers seems to be that it is an electrical machine with electrical inputs and outputs to the sensors and actuators of the body. One can see this assumption made explicit, for example, in the fiction and speculative writing of professional Artificial Intelligence researchers such as **[Dennett 81]** and **[Moravec 88]**. This view, and further reduction, leads to the very simple models of brain used in connectionism (**[Rumelhart and McClelland 86]**).

In fact, however, the brain is embodied with a much more serious coupling. The brain is situated in a soup of hormones, that influences it in the strongest possible ways. It receives messages encoded hormonally, and sends messages so encoded throughout the body. Our electrocentrism, based on our electronic models of computation, has lead us to ignore these aspects in our informal models of neuroscience, but hormones play a strong, almost dominating, role in determination of behavior in both simple (**[Kravitz 88]**) and higher animals (**[Bloom 76]**)[23].

Real biological systems are not rational agents that take inputs, compute logically, and produce outputs. They are a mess of many mechanisms working in various ways, out of which emerges the behavior that we observe and rationalize. We can see this in more detail by looking both at the individual computational level, and at the organizational level of the brain.

We do not really know how computation is done at the lowest levels in the brain. There is debate over whether the neuron is the functional unit of the nervous system, or whether a single neuron can act as a many independent smaller units (**[Cohen and Wu 90]**). However, we do know that signals are propagated along axons and dendrites at very low speeds compared to electronic computers, and that there are significant delays crossing synapses. The usual estimates for the computational speed of neuronal systems are no more than about 1 Kilo-Hertz. This implies that the computations that go on in humans to effect actions in the subsecond range must go through only a very limited number of processing steps—the network cannot be very deep in order to get meaningful results out on the timescales that routinely occur for much of human thought. On the other hand, the networks seem incredibly richly connected, compared to the connection width of either our electronic systems, or our connectionist models. For simple creatures some motor neurons are connected to tens of percent of the other neurons in the animal. For mammals motor neurons are typically connected to 5,000 and some neurons in humans are connected to as many as 90,000 other neurons (**[Churchland 86]**).

For one very simple animal *Caenorhabditis elegans*, a nematode, we have a complete wiring diagram of its nervous system, including its development stages (**[Wood 88]**). In the hermaphrodite there are 302 neurons and 56 support cells out of the animal's total of 959 cells. In the male there are 381 neurons and 92 support cells out of a total of 1031 cells. Even though the anatomy and behavior of this creature are well studied, and the neuronal activity is well probed, the way in which the circuits control the animal's behavior is not understood very well at all.

Given that even a simple animal is not yet understood one cannot expect to gain complete insight into building Artificial Intelligence by looking at the nervous systems of complex animals. We can, however, get insight into aspects of intelligent behavior, and some clues about sensory systems and motor systems.

[Wehner 87] for instance, gives great insight into

[23] See **[Bergland 85]** for a history of theories of the brain, and how they were influenced by the current technologies available to provide explanatory power. Unfortunately this book is marred by the author's own lack of understanding of computation which leads him to dismiss electrical activity of the brain as largely irrelevant to the process of thought.

the way in which evolution has selected for sensor-neurological couplings with the environment which can be very specialized. By choosing the right sensors, animals can often get by with very little neurological processing, in order to extract just the right information about the here and now around them, for the task at hand. Complex world model building is not possible given the sensors' limitations, and not needed when the creature is appropriately situated.

[Cruse 90] and **[Götz and Wenking 73]** give insight into how simple animals work, based on an understanding at a primitive level of their neurological circuits. These sorts of clues can help us as we try to build walking robots–for examples of such computational neuroethology see **[Brooks 89]** and **[Beer 90]**.

These clues can help us build better artificial systems, but by themselves they do not provide us with a full theory.

5 Ideas

Earlier we identified situatedness, embodiment, intelligence, and emergence, with a set of key ideas that have lead to a new style of Artificial Intelligence research which we are calling behavior-based robots. In this section I expound on these four topics in more detail.

5.1 Situatedness

Traditional Artificial Intelligence has adopted a style of research where the agents that are built to test theories in intelligence are essentially problem solvers that work in an symbolic abstracted domain. The symbols may have referents in the minds of the builders of the systems, but there is nothing to ground those referents in any real world. Furthermore, the agents are not situated in a world at all. Rather they are given a problem, and they solve it. Then, they are given another problem and they solve it. They are not participating in a world as would agents in the usual sense.

In these systems there is no external world per se, with continuity, surprises, or ongoing history. The programs deal only with a model world, with its own built-in physics. There is a blurring between the knowledge of the agent and the world it is supposed to be operating in—indeed in many Artificial Intelligence systems there is no distinction between the two—the agent has access to direct and perfect perception, and direct and perfect action. When consideration is given to porting such agents or systems to operate in the world, the question arises of what sort of representation they need of the real world. Over the years within traditional Artificial Intelligence, it has become accepted that they will need an objective model of the world with individuated entities, tracked and identified over time—the models of knowledge representation that have been developed expect and require such a one-to-one correspondence between the world and the agent's representation of it.

The early robots such as Shakey and the Cart certainly followed this approach. They built models of the world, planned paths around obstacles, and updated their estimate of where objects were relative to themselves as they moved. We developed a different approach **[Brooks 86]** where a mobile robot used the world as its own model—continuously referring to its sensors rather than to an internal world model. The problems of object class and identity disappeared. The perceptual processing became much simpler. And the performance of the robot was better in comparable tasks than that of the Cart[24], and with much less computation, even allowing for the different sensing modalities.

[Agre 88] and **[Chapman 90]** formalized these ideas in their arguments for *deictic* (or *indexical-functional* in an earlier incarnation) representations. Instead of having representations of individual entities in the world, the system has representations in terms of the relationship of the entities to the robot. These relationships are both spatial and functional. For instance in Pengi **[Agre and Chapman 87]**, rather than refer to *Bee-27* the system refers to *the-bee-that-is-chasing-me-now*. The latter may or may not be the same bee that was chasing the robot two minutes previously—it doesn't matter for the particular tasks in which the robot is engaged.

When this style of representation is used it is possible to build computational systems which trade off computational depth for computational width. The idea is that the computation can be represented by a network of gates, timers, and state elements. The network does not need long paths from inputs (sensors) to outputs (actuators). Any computation that is capable of being done is done in a very short time span. There have been other approaches which address a similar time-bounded computation issue, namely the *bounded rationality* approach **[Russell 89]**. Those approaches try to squeeze a traditional Artificial Intelligence system into a bounded amount of computation. With the new approach we tend to come from the other direction, we start with very little computation and build up the amount, while staying away from the boundary of computation that takes too long. As more computation needs to be added there is a tendency to add it in breadth (thinking of the computation as being represented by a circuit whose depth is the longest path length in gates from input to output) rather than depth.

A situated agent must respond in a timely fashion to its inputs. Modeling the world completely under these conditions can be computationally challenging. But a world in which it is situated also provides some continuity to the agent. That continuity can be relied upon, so that the agent can use its perception of the world instead of an objective world model. The representational primitives that are useful then change quite dramatically from those in traditional Artificial Intelligence.

The key idea from situatedness is:

The world is its own best model.

5.2 Embodiment

There are two reasons that embodiment of intelligent systems is critical. First, only an embodied intelligent agent is fully validated as one that can deal with the

[24] The tasks carried out by this first robot, *Allen*, were of a different class than those attempted by Shakey. Shakey could certainly not have carried out the tasks that Allen did.

real world. Second, only through a physical grounding can any internal symbolic or other system find a place to bottom out, and give 'meaning' to the processing going on within the system.

The physical grounding of a robot in the world forces its designer to deal with all the issues. If the intelligent agent has a body, has sensors, and has actuators, then all the details and issues of being in the world must be faced. It is no longer possible to argue in conference papers, that the simulated perceptual system is realistic, or that problems of uncertainty in action will not be significant. Instead, physical experiments can be done simply and repeatedly. There is no room for cheating[25]. When this is done it is usual to find that many of the problems that seemed significant are not so in the physical system (typically 'puzzle' like situations where symbolic reasoning seemed necessary tend not to arise in embodied systems), and many that seemed non-problems become major hurdles (typically these concern aspects of perception and action)[26].

A deeper problem is "can there be disembodied mind?". Many believe that what is human about us is very directly related to our physical experiences. For instance **[Johnson 87]** argues that a large amount of our language is actually metaphorically related to our physical connections to the world. Our mental 'concepts' are based on physically experienced exemplars. **[Smith 91]** suggests that without physical grounding there can be no halt to the regress within a knowledge based system as it tries to reason about real world knowledge such as that contained in an encyclopedia (e.g., **[Lenat and Feigenbaum 91]**).

Without an ongoing participation and perception of the world there is no meaning for an agent. Everything is random symbols. Arguments might be made that at some level of abstraction even the human mind operates in this solipsist position. However, biological evidence (see section 4) suggests that the human mind's connection to the world is so strong, and many faceted, that these philosophical abstractions may not be correct.

The key idea from embodiment is:

The world grounds regress.

5.3 Intelligence

[Brooks 91a] argues that the sorts of activities we usually think of as demonstrating intelligence in humans have been taking place for only a very small fraction of our evolutionary lineage. Further, I argue that the 'simple' things to do with perception and mobility in a dynamic environment took evolution much longer to perfect, and that all those capabilities are a necessary basis for 'higher-level' intellect.

Therefore, I proposed looking at simpler animals as a bottom-up model for building intelligence. It is soon apparent, when 'reasoning' is stripped away as the prime component of a robot's intellect, that the dynamics of the interaction of the robot and its environment are primary determinants of the structure of its intelligence.

Earlier, **[Simon 69]** had discussed a similar point in terms of an ant walking along the beach. He pointed out that the complexity of the behavior of the ant is more a reflection of the complexity of its environment than its own internal complexity. He speculated that the same may be true of humans, but within two pages of text had reduced studying human behavior to the domain of crypto-arithmetic problems.

It is hard to draw the line at what is intelligence, and what is environmental interaction. In a sense it does not really matter which is which, as all intelligent systems must be situated in some world or other if they are to be useful entities.

The key idea from intelligence is:

Intelligence is determined by the dynamics of interaction with the world.

5.4 Emergence

In discussing where intelligence resides in an Artificial Intelligence program **[Minsky 61]** points out that "there is never any 'heart' in a program" and "we find senseless loops and sequences of trivial operations". It is hard to point at a single component as the seat of intelligence. There is no homunculus. Rather, intelligence emerges from the interaction of the components of the system. The way in which it emerges, however, is quite different for traditional and behavior-based Artificial Intelligence systems.

In traditional Artificial Intelligence the modules that are defined are information processing, or functional. Typically these modules might be a perception module, a planner, a world modeler, a learner, etc. The components directly participate in functions such as perceiving, planning, modeling, learning, etc. Intelligent behavior of the system, such as avoiding obstacles, standing up, controlling gaze, etc., emerges from the interaction of the components.

In behavior-based Artificial Intelligence the modules that are defined are behavior producing. Typically these modules might be an obstacle avoidance behavior, a standing up behavior, a gaze control behavior, etc. The components directly participate in producing behaviors such as avoiding obstacles, standing up, controlling gaze, etc. Intelligent functionality of the system, such as perception, planning, modeling, learning, etc., emerges from the interaction of the components.

Although this dualism between traditional and behavior-based systems looks pretty it is not completely accurate. Traditional systems have hardly ever been really connected to the world, and so the emergence of intelligent behavior is something more of an expectation in most cases, rather than an established phenomenon. Conversely, because of the many behaviors present in a behavior-based system, and their individual dynamics of interaction with the world, it is often hard to say that

[25] I mean this in the sense of causing self-delusion, not in the sense of wrong doing with intent.

[26] In fact, there is some room for cheating as the physical environment can be specially simplified for the robot—and in fact it may be very hard in some cases to identify such self delusions. In some research projects it may be necessary to test a particular class of robot activities, and therefore it may be necessary to build a test environment for the robot. There is a fine and difficult to define line to be drawn here.

a particular series of actions was produced by a particular behavior. Sometimes many behaviors are operating simultaneously, or are switching rapidly **[Horswill and Brooks 88]**.

Over the years there has been a lot of work on emergence based on the theme of self-organization (e.g., **[Nicolis and Prigogine 77]**). Within behavior-based robots there is beginning to be work at better characterizing emergent functionality, but it is still in its early stages, e.g., **[Steels 90a]**. He defines it as meaning that a function is achieved "indirectly by the interaction of more primitive components among themselves and with the world"

It is hard to identify the seat of intelligence within any system, as intelligence is produced by the interactions of many components. Intelligence can only be determined by the total behavior of the system and how that behavior appears in relation to the environment.

The key idea from emergence is:

Intelligence is in the eye of the observer.

6 Thought

Since late 1984 I have been building autonomous mobile robots in the 'Mobot Lab' at the MIT Artificial Intelligence Laboratory; **[Brooks 86]** gives the original ideas, and **[Brooks 90b]** contains a recent summary of the capabilities of the robots developed in my laboratory over the years.

My work fits within the framework described above in terms of situatedness, embodiment, intelligence and emergence. In particular I have advocated situatedness, embodiment, and highly reactive architectures with no reasoning systems, no manipulable representations, no symbols, and totally decentralized computation. This different model of computation has lead to radically different models of thought.

I have been accused of overstating the case that the new approach is all that is necessary to build truly intelligent systems. It has even been suggested that as an evangelist I have deliberately overstated my case to pull people towards the correct level of belief, and that really all along, I have known that a hybrid approach is necessary.

That is not what I believe. I think that the new approach can be extended to cover the whole story, both with regards to building intelligent systems and to understanding human intelligence—the two principal goals identified for Artificial Intelligence at the beginning of the paper.

Whether I am right or not is an empirical question. Multiple approaches to Artificial Intelligence will continue to be pursued. At some point we will be able to evaluate which approach has been more successful.

In this section I want to outline the philosophical underpinnings of my work, and discuss why I believe the approach is the one that in the end will prove dominant.

6.1 Principles

All research goes on within the constraints of certain principles. Sometimes these are explicit, and sometimes they are implicit. In the following paragraphs I outline as explicitly as I can the principles followed.

The first set of principles defines the domain for the work.

- The goal is to study complete integrated intelligent autonomous agents.
- The agents should be embodied as mobile robots, situated in unmodified worlds found around our laboratory[27]. This confronts the embodiment issue. The environments chosen are for convenience, although we strongly resist the temptation to change the environments in any way for the robots.
- The robots should operate equally well when visitors, or cleaners, walk through their workspace, when furniture is rearranged, when lighting or other environmental conditions change, and when their sensors and actuators drift in calibration. This confronts the situatedness issue.
- The robots should operate on timescales commensurate with the time scales used by humans. This too confronts the situatedness issue.

The specific model of computation used was not originally based on biological models. It was one arrived at by continuously refining attempts to program a robot to reactively avoid collisions in a people-populated environment, **[Brooks 86]**. Now, however, in stating the principles used in the model of computation, it is clear that it shares certain properties with models of how neurological systems are arranged. It is important to emphasize that it only shares certain properties. Our model of computation is not intended as a realistic model of how neurological systems work. We call our computation model the *subsumption architecture* and its purpose is to program intelligent, situated, embodied agents.

Our principles of computation are:

- Computation is organized as an asynchronous network of active computational elements (they are *augmented finite state machines*—see **[Brooks 89]** for details[28]), with a fixed topology network of unidirectional connections.
- Messages sent over connections have no implicit semantics—they are small numbers (typically 8 or 16 bits, but on some robots just 1 bit) and their meanings are dependent on the dynamics designed into both the sender and receiver.
- Sensors and actuators are connected to this network, usually through asynchronous two-sided buffers.

[27] This constraint has slipped a little recently as we are working on building prototype small legged planetary rovers (**[Angle and Brooks 90]**). We have built a special purpose environment for the robots—a physically simulated lunar surface.

[28] For programming convenience we use a higher level abstraction known as the *Behavior Language*, documented in **[Brooks 90c]**. It compiles down to a network of machines as described above.

These principles lead to certain consequences. In particular:

- The system can certainly have state—it is not at all constrained to be purely reactive.
- Pointers and manipulable data structures are very hard to implement (since the model is Turing equivalent it is of course possible, but hardly within the spirit).
- Any search space must be quite bounded in size, as search nodes cannot be dynamically created and destroyed during the search process.
- There is no implicit separation of data and computation, they are both distributed over the same network of elements.

In considering the biological observations outlined in section 4, certain properties seemed worth incorporating into the way in which robots are programmed within the given model of computation. In all the robots built in the mobot lab, the following principles of organization of intelligence have been observed:

- There is no central model maintained of the world. All data is distributed over many computational elements.
- There is no central locus of control.
- There is no separation into perceptual system, central system, and actuation system. Pieces of the network may perform more than one of these functions. More importantly, there is intimate intertwining of aspects of all three of them.
- The behavioral competence of the system is improved by adding more behavior-specific network to the existing network. We call this process *layering*. This is a simplistic and crude analogy to evolutionary development. As with evolution, at every stage of the development the systems are tested—unlike evolution there is a gentle debugging process available. Each of the layers is a behavior-producing piece of network in its own right, although it may implicitly rely on presence of earlier pieces of network.
- There is no hierarchical arrangement—i.e., there is no notion of one process calling on another as a subroutine. Rather the networks are designed so that needed computations will simply be available on the appropriate input line when needed. There is no explicit synchronization between a producer and a consumer of messages. Message reception buffers can be overwritten by new messages before the consumer has looked at the old one. It is not atypical for a message producer to send 10 messages for every one that is examined by the receiver.
- The layers, or behaviors, all run in parallel. There may need to be a conflict resolution mechanism when different behaviors try to give different actuator commands.
- The world is often a good communication medium for processes, or behaviors, within a single robot.

It should be clear that these principles are quite different to the ones we have become accustomed to using as we program Von Neumann machines. It necessarily forces the programmer to use a different style of organization for their programs for intelligence.

There are also always influences on approaches to building thinking machines that lie outside the realm of purely logical or scientific thought. The following, perhaps arbitrary, principles have also had an influence on the organization of intelligence that has been used in Mobot Lab robots:

- A decision was made early on that all computation should be done onboard the robots. This was so that the robots could run tether-free and without any communication link. The idea is to download programs over cables (although in the case of some of our earlier robots the technique was to plug in a newly written erasable ROM) into non-volatile storage on the robots, then switch them on to interact with and be situated in the environment.
- In order to maintain a long term goal of being able to eventually produce very tiny robots (**[Flynn 87]**) the computational model has been restricted so that any specification within that model could be rather easily compiled into a silicon circuit. This has put an additional constraint on designers of agent software, in that they cannot use non-linear numbers of connections between collections of computational elements, as that would lead to severe silicon compilation problems. Note that the general model of computation outlined above is such that a goal of silicon compilation is in general quite realistic.

The point of section 3 was to show how the technology of available computation had a major impact on the shape of the developing field of Artificial Intelligence. Likewise there have been a number of influences on my own work that are technological in nature. These include:

- Given the smallness in overall size of the robots there is a very real limitation on the amount of onboard computation that can be carried, and by an earlier principle all computation must be done onboard. The limiting factor on the amount of portable computation is not weight of the computers directly, but the electrical power that is available to run them. Empirically we have observed that the amount of electrical power available is proportional to the weight of the robot[29].
- Since there are many single chip microprocessors available including EEPROM and RAM, it is becoming more possible to include large numbers of sensors which require interrupt servicing, local calibration, and data massaging. The microprocessors

[29] Jon Connell, a former member of the Mobot Lab, plotted data from a large number of mobile robots and noted the empirical fact that there is roughly one watt of electrical power available for onboard computation for every pound of overall weight of the robot. We call this *Connell's Law*.

can significantly reduce the overall wiring complexity by servicing a local group of sensors (e.g., all those on a single leg of a robot) *in situ*, and packaging up the data to run over a communication network to the behavior-producing network.

These principles have been used in the programming of a number of behavior-based robots. Below we point out the importance of some of these robot demonstrations in indicating how the subsumption architecture (or one like it in spirit) can be expected to scale up to very intelligent applications. In what follows individual references are given to the most relevant piece of the literature. For a condensed description of what each of the robots is and how they are programmed, the reader should see **[Brooks 90b]**; it also includes a number of robots not mentioned here.

6.2 Reactivity

The earliest demonstration of the subsumption architecture was on the robot *Allen* (**[Brooks 86]**). It was almost entirely reactive, using sonar readings to keep away from people and other moving obstacles, while not colliding with static obstacles. It also had a non-reactive higher level layer that would select a goal to head towards, and then proceed to that location while the lower level reactive layer took care of avoiding obstacles.

The very first subsumption robot thus combined non-reactive capabilities with reactive ones. But the important point is that it used exactly the same sorts of computational mechanism to do both. In looking at the network of the combined layers there was no obvious partition into lower and higher level components based on the type of information flowing on the connections, or the state machines that were the computational elements. To be sure, there was a difference in function between the two layers, but there was no need to introduce any centralization or explicit representations to achieve a higher level, or later, process having useful and effective influence over a lower level.

The second robot, *Herbert* (**[Connell 89]**), pushed on the reactive approach. It used a laser scanner to find soda can-like objects visually, infrared proximity sensors to navigate by following walls and going through doorways, a magnetic compass to maintain a global sense of orientation, and a host of sensors on an arm which were sufficient to reliably pick up soda cans. The task for Herbert was to wander around looking for soda cans, pick one up, and bring it back to where Herbert had started from. It was demonstrated reliably finding soda cans in rooms using its laser range finder (some tens of trials), picking up soda cans many times (over 100 instances), reliably navigating (many hours of runs), and in one finale doing all the tasks together to navigate, locate, pickup and return with a soda can[30].

In programming Herbert it was decided that it should maintain no state longer than three seconds, and that there would be no internal communication between behavior generating modules. Each one was connected to sensors on the input side, and a fixed priority arbitration network on the output side. The arbitration network drove the actuators.

In order to carry out its tasks, Herbert, in many instances, had to use the world as its own best model and as a communication medium. E.g., the laser-based soda can object finder drove the robot so that its arm was lined up in front of the soda can. But it did not tell the arm controller that there was now a soda can ready to be picked up. Rather, the arm behaviors monitored the shaft encoders on the wheels, and when they noticed that there was no body motion, initiated motions of the arm, which in turn triggered other behaviors, so that eventually the robot would pick up the soda can.

The advantage of this approach is was that there was no need to set up internal expectations for what was going to happen next; that meant that the control system could both (1) be naturally opportunistic if fortuitous circumstances presented themselves, and (2) it could easily respond to changed circumstances, such as some other object approaching it on a collision course.

As one example of how the arm behaviors cascaded upon one another, consider actually grasping a soda can. The hand had a grasp reflex that operated whenever something broke an infrared beam between the fingers. When the arm located a soda can with its local sensors, it simply drove the hand so that the two fingers lined up on either side of the can. The hand then independently grasped the can. Given this arrangement, it was possible for a human to hand a soda can to the robot. As soon as it was grasped, the arm retracted—it did not matter whether it was a soda can that was intentionally grasped, or one that magically appeared. The same opportunism among behaviors let the arm adapt automatically to a wide variety of cluttered desktops, and still successfully find the soda can.

In order to return to where it came from after picking up a soda can, Herbert used a trick. The navigation routines could carry implement rules such as: ***when passing through a door southbound, turn left.*** These rules were conditionalized on the separation of the fingers on the hand. When the robot was outbound with no can in its hand, it effectively executed one set of rules. After picking up a can, it would execute a different set. By carefully designing the rules, Herbert was guaranteed, with reasonable reliability, to retrace its path.

The point of Herbert is two-fold.

- It demonstrates complex, apparently goal directed and intentional, behavior in a system which has no long term internal state and no internal communication.
- It is very easy for an observer of a system to attribute more complex internal structure than really exists. Herbert appeared to be doing things like path planning and map building, even though it was not.

6.3 Representation

My earlier paper **[Brooks 91a]** is often criticized for advocating absolutely no representation of the world within a behavior-based robot. This criticism is invalid. I make

[30]The limiting factor on Herbert was the mechanical seating of its chips—its mean time between chip seating failure was no more than 15 minutes.

it clear in the paper that I reject traditional Artificial Intelligence representation schemes (see section 5). I also made it clear that I reject explicit representations of goals within the machine.

There can, however, be representations which are partial models of the world—in fact I mentioned that "individual layers extract only those *aspects* of the world which they find relevant—projections of a representation into a simple subspace" **[Brooks 91a]**. The form these representations take, within the context of the computational model we are using, will depend on the particular task those representations are to be used for. For more general navigation than that demonstrated by Connell it may sometimes[31] need to build and maintain a map.

[Mataric 90, 91] introduced *active-constructive representations* to subsumption in a sonar-based robot, *Toto*, which wandered around office environments building a map based on landmarks, and then used that map to get from one location to another. Her representations were totally decentralized and non-manipulable, and there is certainly no central control which build, maintains, or uses the maps. Rather, the map itself is an active structure which does the computations necessary for any path planning the robot needs to do.

Primitive layers of control let Toto wander around following boundaries (such as walls and furniture clutter) in an indoor environment. A layer which detects landmarks, such as flat clear walls, corridors, etc., runs in parallel. It informs the map layer as its detection certainty exceeds a fixed threshold. The map is represented as a graph internally. The nodes of the graph are computational elements (they are identical little subnetworks of distinct augmented finite state machines). Free nodes arbitrate and allocate themselves, in a purely local fashion, to represent a new landmark, and set up topological links to physically neighboring nodes (using a limited capacity switching network to keep the total virtual 'wire length' between finite state machines to be linear in the map capacity). These nodes keep track of where the robot is physically, by observing changes in the output of the landmark detector, and comparing that to predictions they have made by local message passing, and by referring to other more primitive (magnetic compass based) coarse position estimation schemes.

When a higher layer wants the robot to go to some known landmark, it merely 'excites', in some particular way the particular place in the map that it wants to go. The excitation (this is an abstraction programmed into the particular finite state machines used here—it is not a primitive—as such there could be many different types of excitation co-existing in the map, if other types of planning are required) is spread through the map following topological links, estimating total path link, and arriving at the *landmark-that-I'm-at-now* node (a deictic representation) with a recommendation of the direction to travel right now to follow the shortest path. As the robot moves so to does its representation of where it is, and at that new node the arriving excitation tells it where to go next. The map thus bears a similarity to the *internalized plans* of **[Payton 90]**, but it represented by the same computational elements that use it—there is no distinction between data and process. Furthermore Mataric's scheme can have multiple simultaneously active goals—the robot will simply head towards the nearest one.

This work demonstrates the following aspects of behavior-based or subsumption systems:

- Such systems can make predictions about what will happen in the world, and have expectations.
- Such systems can make plans—but they are not the same as traditional Artificial Intelligence plans—see **[Agre and Chapman 90]** for an analysis of this issue.
- Such systems can have goals—see **[Maes 90b]** for another way to implement goals within the approach.
- All these things can be done without resorting to central representations.
- All these things can be done without resorting to manipulable representations.
- All these things can be done without resorting to symbolic representations.

6.4 Complexity

Can subsumption-like approaches scale to arbitrarily complex systems? This is a question that cannot be answered affirmatively right now—just as it is totally unfounded to answer the same question affirmatively in the case of traditional symbolic Artificial Intelligence methods. The best one can do is point to precedents and trends.

There are a number of dimensions along which the scaling question can be asked. E.g.,

- Can the approach work well as the environment becomes more complex?
- Can the approach handle larger numbers of sensors and actuators?
- Can the approach work smoothly as more and more layers or behaviors are added?

We answer each of these in turn in the following paragraphs.

The approach taken at the Mobot Lab has been that from day one always test the robot in the most complex environment for which it is ultimately destined. This forces even the simplest levels to handle the most complex environment expected. So for a given robot and intended environment the scaling question is handled by the methodology chosen for implementation. But there is also the question of how complex are the environments that are targeted for with the current generation of robots. Almost all of our robots have been tested and operated in indoor environments with people unrelated to the research wandering through their work area at will. Thus we have a certain degree of confidence that

[31] Note that we are saying only *sometimes*, not *must*—there are many navigation tasks doable by mobile robots which appear intelligent, but which do not require map information at all.

the same basic approach will work in outdoor environments (the sensory processing will have to change for some sensors) with other forms of dynamic action taking place.

The number of sensors and actuators possessed by today's robots are pitiful when compared to the numbers in even simple organisms such as insects. Our first robots had only a handful of identical sonar sensors and two motors. Later a six legged walking robot was built **[Angle 89]**. It had 12 actuators and 20 sensors, and was successfully programmed in subsumption (**[Brooks 89]**) to walk adaptively over rough terrain. The key was to find the right factoring into sensor and actuator subsystems so that interactions between the subsystems could be minimized. A new six legged robot, recently completed (**[Brooks and Angle 90]**, is much more challenging, but still nowhere near the complexity of insects. It has 23 actuators and over 150 sensors. With this level of sensing it is possible to start to develop some of the 'senses' that animals and humans have, such as a kinesthetic sense—this comes from the contributions of many sensor readings. Rather, than feed into a geometric model the sensors into a estimate of bodily motion. There is also the question of the types of sensors used. **[Horswill and Brooks 88]** generalized the subsumption architecture so that some of the connections between processing elements could be a *retina bus*, a cable that transmitted partially processed images from one site to another within the system. The robot so programmed was able to follow corridors and follow moving objects in real time.

As we add more layers we find that the interactions can become more complex. **[Maes 89]** introduced the notion of switching whole pieces of the network on and off, using an *activation* scheme for behaviors. That idea is now incorporated into the subsumption methodology **[Brooks 90c]**, and provides a way of implementing both competition and cooperation between behaviors. At a lower level a hormone-like system has been introduced (**[Brooks 91b]**) which models the hormone system of the lobster **[Kravitz 88]** (**[Arkin 88]** had implemented a system with similar inspiration). With these additional control mechanisms we have certainly bought ourselves breathing room to increase the performance of our systems markedly. The key point about these control systems is that they fit exactly into the existing structures, and are totally distributed and local in their operations.

6.5 Learning

Evolution has decided that there is a tradeoff between what we know through our genes and what we must find out for ourselves as we develop. We can expect to see a similar tradeoff for our behavior-based robots.

There are at least four classes of things that can be learned:

1. representations of the world that help in some task
2. aspects of instances of sensors and actuators (this is sometimes called calibration)
3. the ways in which individual behaviors should interact
4. new behavioral modules

The robots in the Mobot Lab have been programmed to demonstrate the first three of these types of learning. The last one has not yet been successfully tackled[32]

Learning representations of the world was already discussed above concerning the work of **[Mataric 90, 91]**. The next step will be to generalize active-constructive representations to more classes of use.

[Viola 90] demonstrated calibration of a complex head-eye system modeling the primate vestibulo-ocular system. In this system there is one fast channel between a gyroscope and a high performance pan-tilt head holding the camera, and a slower channel using vision which produces correction signals for the gyroscope channel. The same system was used to learn how to accurately saccade to moving stimuli.

Lastly, **[Maes and Brooks 90]** programmed an early six legged robot to learn to walk using the subsumption architecture along with the behavior activation schemes of **[Maes 89]**. Independent behaviors on each leg monitored the activity of other behaviors and correlated that, their own activity state, and the results from a belly switch which provided negative feedback, as input to a local learning rule which learned under which conditions it was to operate the behavior. After about 20 trials per leg, spread over a total of a minute or two, the robot reliably learns the alternating tripod gait—it slowly seems to emerge out of initially chaotic flailing of the legs.

Learning within subsumption is in its early stages but it has been demonstrated in a number of different critical modes of development.

6.6 Vistas

The behavior-based approach has been demonstrated on situated embodied systems doing things that traditional Artificial Intelligence would have tackled in quite different ways. What are the key research areas that need to be addressed in order to push behavior-based robots towards more and more sophisticated capabilities?

In this section we outline research challenges in three categories or levels[33]:

- Understanding the dynamics of how an individual behavior couples with the environment via the robot's sensors and actuators. The primary concerns here are what forms of perception are necessary, and what relationships exist between perception, internal state, and action (i.e., how behavior is specified or described).

- Understanding how many behaviors can be integrated into a single robot. The primary concerns here are how independent various perceptions and behaviors can be, how much they must rely on, and interfere with each other, how a competent complete robot can be built in such a way as to accommodate all the required individual behaviors, and

[32] We did have a failed attempt at this through simulated evolution—this is the approach taken by many in the Artificial Life movement.

[33] The reader is referred to [Brooks 90a] for a more complete discussion of these issues.

to what extent apparently complex behaviors can emerge from simple reflexes.

- Understanding how multiple robots (either a homogeneous, or a heterogeneous group) can interact as they go about their business. The primary concerns here are the relationships between individuals' behaviors, the amount and type of communication between robots, the way the environment reacts to multiple individuals, and the resulting patterns of behavior and their impacts upon the environment (which night not occur in the case of isolated individuals).

Just as research in Artificial Intelligence is broken into subfields, these categories provide subfields of behavior-based robots within which it is possible to concentrate a particular research project. Some of these topics are theoretical in nature, contributing to a science of behavior-based systems. Others are engineering in nature, providing tools and mechanisms for successfully building and programming behavior-based robots. Some of these topics have already been touched upon by researchers in behavior-based approaches, but none of them are yet solved or completely understood.

At the individual behavior level some of the important issues are as follows:

Convergence: Demonstrate or prove that a specified behavior is such that the robot will indeed carry out the desired task successfully. For instance, we may want to give some set of initial conditions for a robot, and some limitations on possible worlds in which it is placed, and show that under those conditions, the robot is guaranteed to follow a particular wall, rather than diverge and get lost.

Synthesis: Given a particular task, automatically derive a behavior specification for the creature so that it carries out that task in a way which has clearly demonstrable convergence. I do not expect progress in this topic in the near future.

Complexity: Deal with the complexity of real world environments, and sift out the relevant aspects of received sensations rather than being overwhelmed with a multitude of data.

Learning: Develop methods for the automatic acquisition of new behaviors, and the modification and tuning of existing behaviors.

As multiple behaviors are built into a single robot the following issues need to be addressed:

Coherence: Even though many behaviors may be active at once, or are being actively switched on or off, the robot should still appear to an observer to have coherence of action and goals. It should not be rapidly switching between inconsistent behaviors, nor should two behaviors be active simultaneously, if they interfere with each other to the point that neither operates successfully.

Relevance: The behaviors that are active should be relevant to the situation the robot finds itself in—e.g., it should recharge itself when the batteries are low, not when they are full.

Adequacy: The behavior selection mechanism must operate in such a way that the long term goals that the robot designer has for the robot are met—e.g., a floor cleaning robot should successfully clean the floor in normal circumstances, besides doing all the ancillary tasks that are necessary for it to be successful at that.

Representation: Multiple behaviors might want to share partial representations of the world—in fact the representations of world aspects might generate multiple behaviors when activated appropriately.

Learning: The performance of a robot might be improved by adapting the ways in which behaviors interact, or are activated, as a result of experience.

When many behavior-based robots start to interact there are a whole new host of issues which arise. Many of these same issues would arise if the robots were built using traditional Artificial Intelligence methods, but there has been very little published in these areas.

Emergence: Given a set of behaviors programmed into a set of robots, we would like to be able to predict what the global behavior of the system will be, and as a consequence determine the differential effects of small changes to the individual robots on the global behavior.

Synthesis: As at single behavior level, given a particular task, automatically derive a program for the set of robots so that they carry out the task.

Communication: Performance may be increased by increasing the amount of explicit communication between robots, but the relationship between the amount of communication increase and performance increase needs to be understood.

Cooperation: In some circumstances robots should be able to achieve more by cooperating—the form and specification of such possible cooperations need to be understood.

Interference: Robots may interfere with one another. Protocols for avoiding this when it is undesirable must be included in the design of the creatures' instructions.

Density dependence: The global behavior of the system may be dependent on the density of the creatures and the resources they consume within the world. A characterization of this dependence is desirable. At the two ends of the spectrum it may be the case that (a) a single robot given n units of time performs identically to n robots each given 1 unit of time, and (2) the global task might not be achieved at all if there are fewer than, say, m robots.

Individuality: Robustness can be achieved if all robots are interchangeable. A fixed number of classes of robots, where all robots within a class are identical, is also robust, but somewhat less so. The issue then is to, given a task, decide how many classes of creatures are necessary

Learning: The performance of the robots may increase in two ways through learning. At one level, when one robot learns some skill if might be able to transfer it to another. At another level, the robots might learn cooperative strategies.

These are a first cut at topics of interest within behavior-based approaches. As we explore more we will find more topics, and some that seem interesting now will turn out to be irrelevant.

6.7 Thinking

Can this approach lead to thought? How could it? It seems the antithesis of thought. But we must ask first, what is thought? Like intelligence this is a very slippery concept.

We only know that thought exists in biological systems through our own introspection. At one level we identify thought with the product of our consciousness, but that too is a contentious subject, and one which has had little attention from Artificial Intelligence.

My feeling is that thought and consciousness are epiphenomena of the process of being in the world. As the complexity of the world increases, and the complexity of processing to deal with that world rises, we will see the same evidence of thought and consciousness in our systems as we see in people other than ourselves now. Thought and consciousness will not need to be programmed in. They will emerge.

7 Conclusion

The title of this paper is intentionally ambiguous. The following interpretations all encapsulate important points.

- An earlier paper **[Brooks 91a]**[34] was titled *Intelligence without Representation.* The thesis of that paper was that intelligent behavior could be generated without having explicit manipulable internal representations. *Intelligence without Reason* is thus complementary, stating that intelligent behavior can be generated without having explicit reasoning systems present.
- *Intelligence without Reason* can be read as a statement that intelligence is an emergent property of certain complex systems—it sometimes arises without an easily identifiable reason for arising.
- *Intelligence without Reason* can be viewed as a commentary on the bandwagon effect in research in general, and in particular in the case of Artificial Intelligence research. Many lines of research have become goals of pursuit in their own right, with little recall of the reasons for pursuing those lines. A little grounding occasionally can go a long way towards helping keep things on track.
- *Intelligence without Reason* is also a commentary on the way evolution built intelligence—rather than reason about how to build intelligent systems, it used a generate and test strategy. This is in stark contrast to the way all human endeavors to build intelligent systems must inevitably proceed. Furthermore we must be careful in emulating the results of evolution—there may be many structures and observable properties which are suboptimal or vestigial.

We are a long way from creating Artificial Intelligences that measure up the to the standards of early ambitions for the field. It is a complex endeavor and we sometimes need to step back and question why we are proceeding in the direction we are going, and look around for other promising directions.

[34] Despite the publication date it was written in 1986 and 1987, and was complete in its published form in 1987.

Acknowledgements

Maja Mataric reviewed numerous drafts of this paper and gave helpful criticism at every stage of the process. Lynne Parker, Anita Flynn, Ian Horswill and Pattie Maes gave me much constructive feedback on later drafts.

Support for this research was provided in part by the University Research Initiative under Office of Naval Research contract N00014–86–K–0685, in part by the Advanced Research Projects Agency under Office of Naval Research contract N00014–85–K–0124, in part by the Hughes Artificial Intelligence Center, in part by Siemens Corporation, and in part by Mazda Corporation.

References

[Agre 88] "The Dynamic Structure of Everyday Life", Philip E. Agre, *MIT AI TR-1085*, Oct., 1988.

[Agre 91] "The Dynamic Structure of Everyday Life", Philip E. Agre, *Cambridge University Press*, Cambridge, UK, 1991.

[Agre and Chapman 87] "Pengi: An Implementation of a Theory of Activity", Philip E. Agre and David Chapman, *AAAI-87*, Seattle, WA, 1987, 268–272.

[Agre and Chapman 90] "What Are Plans for?", Philip E. Agre and David Chapman, *in* **[Maes 90a]**, 1990, 17–34.

[Angle 89] "Genghis, a Six Legged Autonomous Walking Robot", Colin M. Angle, *MIT SB Thesis*, March, 1989.

[Angle and Brooks 90] "Small Planetary Rovers", Colin M. Angle and Rodney A. Brooks, *IEEE/RSJ International Workshop on Intelligent Robots and Systems*, Ikabara, Japan, 1990, 383–388.

[Arbib 64] "Brains, Machines and Mathematics", Michael A. Arbib, *McGraw-Hill*, New York, NY, 1964.

[Arkin 89] "Homeostatic Control for a Mobile Robot: Dynamic Replanning in Hazardous Environments", Ronald C. Arkin, *SPIE Proceedings 1007, Mobile Robots III, William J. Wolfe* (ed), 1989, 407–413.

[Arkin 90] "Integrating Behavioral, Perceptual and World Knowledge in Reactive Navigation", Ronald C. Arkin, *in* **[Maes 90a]**, 1990, 105–122.

[Ashby 52] "Design for a Brain", W. Ross Ashby, *Chapman and Hall*, London, 1952.

[Ashby 56] "An Introduction to Cybernetics", W. Ross Ashby, *Chapman and Hall*, London, 1956.

[Atkeson 89] "Using Local Models to Control Movement", Christopher G. Atkeson, *in Neural Information Processing 2, David S. Touretzky* (ed), *Morgan Kaufmann*, Los Altos, CA, 1989, 316–324.

[Ballard 89] "Reference Frames for Active Vision", Dana H. Ballard, *Proceedings IJCAI–89*, Detroit, MI, 1989, 1635–1641.

[Barrow and Salter 70] "Design of Low-Cost Equipment for Cognitive Robot Research", H. G. Barrow and S. H. Salter, *Machine Intelligence 5, Bernard Meltzer and Donald Michie* (eds), *American Elsevier Publishing*, New York, NY, 1970, 555–566.

[Beer 90] "Intelligence as Adaptive Behavior", Randall D. Beer, *Academic Press*, San Diego, CA, 1990.

[Bergland 85] "The Fabric of Mind", Richard Bergland, *Viking*, New York, NY, 1985.

[Bloom 76] "Endorphins: Profound Behavioral Effects", F. E. Bloom, *Science 194*, 1976, 630–634.

[Braitenberg 84] "Vehicles: Experiments in Synthetic Psychology", Valentino Braitenberg, *MIT Press*, Cambridge, MA, 1984.

[Brachman and Levesque 85] "Readings in Knowledge Representation", Ronald J. Brachman and Hector J. Levesque, *Morgan Kaufmann*, Los Altos, CA, 1985.

[Brady 90] "Switching Arrays Make Light Work in a Simple Processor", David Brady, *Nature 344*, 1990, 486–487.

[Brooks 86] "A Robust Layered Control System for a Mobile Robot", Rodney A. Brooks, *IEEE Journal of Robotics and Automation, RA-2*, April, 1986, 14–23.

[Brooks 89] "A Robot that Walks: Emergent Behavior from a Carefully Evolved Network", Rodney A. Brooks, *Neural Computation 1:2*, 1989, 253–262.

[Brooks 90a] "Challenges for Complete Creature Architectures", Rodney A. Brooks, *Proc. First Int. Conf. on Simulation of Adaptive Behavior, MIT Press*, Cambridge, MA, 1990, 434–443.

[Brooks 90b] "Elephants Don't Play Chess", Rodney A. Brooks, *in* [Maes 90a], 1990, 3–15.

[Brooks 90c] "The Behavior Language; User's Guide", Rodney A. Brooks, *MIT A.I. Lab Memo* 1227, 1990.

[Brooks 91a] "Intelligence Without Representation", Rodney A. Brooks, *Artificial Intelligence, 47*, 1991, 139–160.

[Brooks 91b] "Integrated Systems Based on Behaviors", Rodney A. Brooks, *special issue of SIGART on Integrated Intelligent Systems*, July, 1991.

[Brooks and Flynn 89] "Robot Beings", Rodney A. Brooks and Anita M. Flynn, *IEEE/RSJ International Workshop on Intelligent Robots and Systems*, Tsukuba, Japan, 1989, 2–10.

[Campbell 83] "Go", J. A. Campbell, *in Computer Game-Playing: Theory and Practice, M. A. Bramer* (ed), *Ellis Horwood*, Chichester, UK, 1983.

[Chapman 90] "Vision, Instruction and Action", David Chapman, *MIT AI TR-1085*, June, 1990.

[Churchland 86] "Neurophilosophy", Patricia Smith Churchland, *MIT Press*, Cambridge, MA, 1986.

[Cohen and Wu 90] "One Neuron, Many Units?", Larry Cohen and Jain-young Wu, *Nature 346*, 1990, 108–109.

[Condon and Thompson 84] "Belle", J. H. Condon and Ken Thompson, *in Chess Skill in Man and Machine, P. W. Frey* (ed), *Springer-Verlag*, 1984.

[Connell 89] "A Colony Architecture for an Artificial Creature", Jonathan H. Connell, *MIT AI TR-1151*, June, 1989.

[Cruse 90] "What Mechanisms Coordinate Leg Movement in Walking Arthropods?", Holk Cruse, *Trends in Neurosciences 13:1*, 1990, 15–21.

[de Kleer and Brown 84] "A Qualitative Physics Based on Confluences", Johann de Kleer and John Seely Brown, *Artificial Intelligence 24*, 1984, 7–83.

[Dennett 78] "Where Am I?", Daniel C. Dennett, *in* [Hofstadter and Dennett 81], 1981.

[Dennett and Kinsbourne 90] "Time and the Observer: the Where and When of Consciousness in the Brain", Daniel Dennett and Marcel Kinsbourne, *Technical Report, Center for Cognitive Studies, Tufts University*, 1990.

[Dreyfus 81] "From Micro-Worlds to Knowledge Representation: AI at an Impasse", Hubert L. Dreyfus, *in Mind Design, John Haugeland* (ed), *MIT Press*, Cambridge, MA, 1981, 161–204.

[Ernst 61] "MH-1. A Computer-Operated Mechanical Hand", Heinrich A. Ernst, *MIT Ph.D. Thesis*, Dec, 1961.

[Evans 68] "A Program for the Solution of Geometric-Analogy Intelligence Test Questions", Thomas G. Evans, *in* [Minsky 68], 1968, 271–353.

[Fahlman 74] "A Planning System for Robot Construction Tasks", Scott E. Fahlman, *Artificial Intelligence 5*, 1974, 1–50.

[Feigenbaum and Feldman 63] "Computers and Thought", Edward A. Feigenbaum and Julian Feldman, *McGraw-Hill*, New York, NY, 1963.

[Firby 89] "Adaptive Execution in Dynamic Domains", R. James Firby, *Ph.D. Thesis*, Yale, 1989.

[Flynn 87] "Gnat Robots (And How They Will Change Robotics)", Anita M. Flynn, *IEEE Micro Robots and Teleoperators Workshop*, Hyannis, MA, Nov., 1989.

[Gazzaniga and LeDoux 77] "The Integrated Mind", Michael S. Gazzaniga and Joseph E. LeDoux, *Plenum*, New York, NY, 1977.

[Gibbs 85] "Optical Bistability: Controlling Light with Light", H. M. Gibbs, *Academic Press*, New York, NY, 1985.

[Giralt, Chatila and Vaisset 84] "An Integrated Navigation and Motion Control System for Multisensory

Robots", Georges Giralt, Raja Chatila, and Marc Vaisset, *Robotics Research 1, Brady and Paul* (eds), *MIT Press*, Cambridge, MA, 191–214.

[Götz and Wenking 73] "Visual Control of Locomotion in the Walking Fruitfly *Drosophilia*", Karl Georg Götz and Hans Wenking, *Journal of Computational Physiology 85*, 1973, 235–266.

[Gould and Eldredge 77] "Punctuated Equilibria: The Tempo and Mode of Evolution Reconsidered", S. J. Gould and N. Eldredge, *Paleobiology 3*, 1977, 115–151.

[Greenblatt, Eastlake and Crocker 67] "The Greenblatt Chess Program", R. D. Greenblatt, D. E. Eastlake and S. D. Crocker, *Am. Fed. Inf. Proc. Soc. Conference Proceedings, 31*, 1967, 801–810.

[Hartmanis 71] "Computational Complexity of Random Access Stored Program Machines", Juris Hartmanis, *Mathematical Systems Theory 5:3*, 1971, 232–245.

[Hayes 85] "The Second Naive Physics Manifesto", Patrick J. Hayes, *in Formal Theories of the Commonsense World, Jerry R. Hobbs and Robert C. Moore* (eds), *Ablex*, Norwood, NJ, 1985, 1–36.

[Hillis 85] "The Connection Machine", W. Daniel Hillis, *MIT Press*, Cambridge, MA, 1985.

[Hodges 83] "Alan Turing: The Enigma", Andrew Hodges, *Simon and Schuster*, New York, NY, 1983.

[Hofstadter and Dennett 81] "The Mind's I", Douglas R. Hofstadter and Daniel C. Dennett, *Bantam Books*, New York, NY, 1981.

[Horswill and Brooks 88] "Situated Vision in a Dynamic World: Chasing Objects", Ian D. Horswill and Rodney A. Brooks, *AAAI-88*, St Paul, MN, 1988, 796–800.

[Hsu, Anantharaman, Campbell and Nowatzyk 90] "A Grandmaster Chess Machine", Feng-hsiung Hsu, Thomas Anantharaman, Murray Campbell and Andreas Nowatzyk, *Scientific American, 263(4)*, Oct. 1990, 44–50.

[Johnson 87] "The Body in the Mind", Mark Johnson, *University of Chicago Press*, Chicago, IL, 1987.

[Kaelbling 90] "Learning in Embedded Systems", Leslie Pack Kaelbling, *Ph.D. Thesis*, Stanford, 1990.

[Kaelbling and Rosenschein 90] "Action and Planning in Embedded Agents", Leslie Pack Kaelbling and Stanley J. Rosenschein, *in* **[Maes 90a]**, 1990, 35–48.

[Knuth and Moore 75] "An Analysis of Alpha-Beta Pruning", Donald E. Knuth and Ronald E. Moore, *Artificial Intelligence 6*, 1975, 293–326.

[Kravitz 88] "Hormonal Control of Behavior: Amines and the Biasing of Behavioral Output in Lobsters", Edward A. Kravitz, *Science 241*, Sep. 30, 1988, 1775–1781.

[Kuhn 70] "The Structure of Scientific Revolutions", Thomas S. Kuhn, *Second Edition, Enlarged, University of Chicago Press*, Chicago, IL, 1970.

[Lenat and Feigenbaum 91] "On the Thresholds of Knowledge", Douglas B. Lenat and Edward A. Feigenbaum, *Artificial Intelligence, 47*, 1991, 185–250.

[Maes 89] "The Dynamics of Action Selection", Pattie Maes, *IJCAI-89*, Detroit, MI, 1989, 991–997.

[Maes 90a] "Designing Autonomous Agents: Theory and Practice from Biology to Engineering and Back", Pattie Maes *(ed)*, *MIT Press*, Cambridge, MA, 1990.

[Maes 90b] "Situated Agents Can Have Goals", Pattie Maes, *in* **[Maes 90a]**, 1990, 49–70.

[Maes and Brooks 90] "Learning to Coordinate Behaviors", Pattie Maes and Rodney A. Brooks, *AAAI-90*, Boston, MA, 1990, 796–802.

[Mahadevan and Connell 90] "Automatic Programming of Behavior-based Robots using Reinforcement Learning", Sridhar Mahadevan and Jonathan Connell, *IBM T.J. Watson Research Report*, Dec., 1990.

[Marr 82] "Vision", David Marr, *Freeman*, San Francisco, CA, 1982.

[Mataric 90] "Navigation with a Rat Brain: A Neurobiologically-Inspired Model for Robot Spatial Representation", Maja J Mataric, *Proc. First Int. Conf. on Simulation of Adaptive Behavior, MIT Press*, Cambridge, MA, 1990, 169–175.

[Mataric 91] "Behavioral Synergy Without Explicit Integration", Maja J Mataric, *special issue of SIGART on Integrated Intelligent Systems*, July, 1991.

[McCarthy 60] "Recursive Functions of Symbolic Expressions", John McCarthy, *CACM 3*, 1960, 184–195.

[McCarthy and Warrington 88] "Evidence for Modality-Specific Systems in the Brain", Rosaleen A. McCarthy and Elizabeth. K. Warrington, *Nature 334*, 1988, 428–430.

[McCorduck 79] "Machines Who Think", Pamela McCorduck, *Freeman*, New York, NY, 1979.

[McCulloch and Pitts 43] "A Logical Calculus of the Ideas Immanent in Nervous Activity", W. S. McCulloch and W. Pitts, *Bull. of Math. Biophysics 5*, 1943, 115–137.

[McFarland 85] "Animal Behavior", David McFarland, *Benjamin/Cummings*, Menlo Park, CA, 1985.

[McFarland 88] "Problems of Animal Behavior", David McFarland, *Lognman*, Harlow, UK, 1988.

[Michie and Ross 70] "Experiments with the Adaptive Graph Traverser", Donald Michie and Robert Ross, *Machine Intelligence 5, Bernard Meltzer and Donald Michie* (eds), *American Elsevier Publishing*, New York, NY, 1970, 301–318.

[Minsky 54] "Neural Nets and the Brain Model Problem", Marvin Minsky, *unpublished Ph.D. dissertation, Princeton University*, 1954, available from University Microfilms, Ann Arbor, MI.

[Minsky 61] "Steps Toward Artificial Intelligence", Marvin Minsky, *Proc. IRE 49*, Jan. 1961, 8–30, also in **[Feigenbaum and Feldman 63]**.

[Minsky 63] "A Selected Descriptor-Indexed Bibliography to the Literature on Artificial Intelligence", Marvin Minsky, *in* **[Feigenbaum and Feldman 63]**, 1963, 453–523.

[**Minsky 68**] "Semantic Information Processing", Marvin Minsky *(ed)*, *MIT Press*, Cambridge, MA, 1968.

[**Minsky 86**] "The Society of Mind", Marvin Minsky, *Simon and Schuster*, New York, NY, 1986.

[**Minsky and Papert 69**] "Perceptrons", Marvin Minsky and Seymour Papert, *MIT Press*, Cambridge, MA, 1969.

[**Mitchell 90**] "Becoming Increasingly Reactive", Tom M. Mitchell, *AAAI-90*, Boston, MA, 1990, 1051–1058.

[**Moravec 81**] "Robot Rover Visual Navigation", Hans P. Moravec, *UMI Research Press*, Ann Arbor, MI, 1981.

[**Moravec 82**] "The Stanford Cart and the CMU Rover", Hans P. Moravec, *Proceedings of the IEEE, 71(7)*, 1982, 872–884.

[**Moravec 88**] "Mind Children", Hans P. Moravec, *Harvard University Press*, Cambridge, MA, 1988.

[**Newcombe and Ratcliff 89**] "Freda Newcombe and Graham Ratcliff", Disorders of Visupspatial Analysis, *in Handbook of Neuropsychology, Vol 2, Elsevier*, New York, NY, 1989.

[**Newell, Shaw and Simon 57**] "Empirical Explorations with the Logic Theory Machine", Allen Newell, J. C. Shaw, Herbert Simon, *Proc. Western Joint Computer Conference 15*, 1957, 218–329, also in [**Feigenbaum and Feldman 63**].

[**Newell, Shaw and Simon 58**] "Chess Playing Programs and the Problem of Complexity", Allen Newell, J. C. Shaw, Herbert Simon, *IBM Journal of Research and Development 2*, Oct. 1958, 320–335, also in [**Feigenbaum and Feldman 63**].

[**Newell, Shaw and Simon 59**] "A General Problem-Solving Program for a Computer", Allen Newell, J. C. Shaw, Herbert Simon, *Computers and Automation 8(7)*, 1959, 10–16.

[**Newell, Shaw and Simon 61**] "Information Processing Language V Manual", Allen Newell, J. C. Shaw, Herbert Simon, *Prentice-Hall*, Edgewood Cliffs, NJ, 1961.

[**Nicolis and Prigogine 77**] "Self-Organization in Nonequilibrium Systems", G. Nicolis and I. Prigogine, *Wiley*, New York, NY, 1977.

[**Nilsson 65**] "Learning Machines", Nils J. Nilsson, *McGraw-Hill*, New York, NY, 1965.

[**Nilsson 71**] "Problem-Solving Methods in Artificial Intelligence", Nils J. Nilsson, *McGraw-Hill*, New York, NY, 1971.

[**Nilsson 84**] "Shakey the Robot", Nils J. Nilsson *(ed)*, *SRI A.I. Center Technical Note 323*, April, 1984.

[**Payton 90**] "Internalized Plans: A Representation for Action Resources", David W. Payton, *in* [**Maes 90a**], 1990, 89–103.

[**Ramachandran and Anstis 85**] "Perceptual Organization in Multistable Apparent Motion", Vilayanur S. Ramachandran and Stuart M. Anstis, *Perception 14*, 1985, 135–143.

[**Roberts 63**] "Machine Perception of Three-Dimensional Solids", Larry G. Roberts, *MIT Lincoln Laboratory, Technical Report No. 315*, May, 1963.

[**Rosenblatt 62**] "Principles of Neurodynamics", Frank Rosenblatt, *Spartan*, New York, NY, 1962.

[**Rosenschein and Kaelbling 86**] "The Synthesis of Machines with Provable Epistemic Properties", Stanley J. Rosenschein and Leslie Pack Kaelbling, *Proc. Conf. on Theoretical Aspects of Reasoning about Knowledge, Joseph Halpern* (ed), *Morgan Kaufmann*, Los Altos, CA, 1986, 83–98.

[**Rumelhart, Hinton and Williams 86**] "Learning Internal Representations by Error Propagation", D. E. Rumelhart, G. E. Hinton, and R. J. Williams, *in* [**Rumelhart and McClelland 86**], 1986, 318–364.

[**Rumelhart and McClelland 86**] "Parallel Distributed Processing", David E. Rumelhart and James L. McClelland, *MIT Press*, Cambridge, MA, 1986.

[**Russell 89**] "Execution Architectures and Compilation", Stuart J. Russell, *Proceedings IJCAI-89*, Detroit, MI, 1989, 15–20.

[**Sacks 74**] "Awakenings", Oliver W. Sacks, *Doubleday*, New York, NY, 1974.

[**Samuel 59**] "Some Studies in Machine Learning Using the Game of Checkers", Arthur L. Samuel, *IBM Journal of Research and Development 3*, July 1959, 211–229, also in [**Feigenbaum and Feldman 63**].

[**Sejnowski and Rosenberg 87**] "Parallel Networks that Learn to Pronounce English Text", T. J. Sejnowski and C. R. Rosenberg, *Complex Systems 1*, 145–168.

[**Selfridge 56**] "Pattern Recognition and Learning", Oliver G. Selfridge, *Proc. Third London Symp. on Information Theory, Colin Cherry* (ed), *Academic Press*, New York, NY, 1956, 345–353.

[**Shannon 50**] "A Chess-Playing Machine", Claude E. Shannon, *Scientific American 182(2)*, February, 1950.

[**Simon 69**] "The Sciences of the Artificial", Herbert A. Simon, *MIT Press*, Cambridge, MA, 1969.

[**Simmons and Krotkov 91**] "An Integrated Walking System for the Ambler Planetary Rover", Reid Simmons and Eric Krotkov, *Proc. IEEE Robotics and Automation*, Sacramento, CA, 1991, ??–??.

[**Slagle 63**] "A Heuristic Program that Solves Symbolic Integration Problems in Freshman Calculus", James R. Slagle, *in* [**Feigenbaum and Feldman 63**], 1963, 191–206 (from a 1961 MIT mathematics Ph.D. thesis).

[**Slate and Atkin 84**] "Chess 4.5–The Northwestern University Chess Program", David J. Slate and Lawrence R. Atkin, *in Chess Skill in Man and Machine, P. W. Frey* (ed), *Springer-Verlag*, 1984.

[**Smith 91**] "The Owl and the Electric Encyclopedia", Brian Cantwell Smith, *Artificial Intelligence, 47*, 1991, 251–288.

[**Steels 90a**] "Towards a Theory of Emergent Functionality", Luc Steels, *Proc. First Int. Conf. on Simulation of Adaptive Behavior, MIT Press*, Cambridge, MA,

1990, 451–461.

[Steels 90b] "Exploiting Analogical Representations", Luc Steels, *in* **[Maes 90a]**, 1990, 71–88.

[Sussman 75] "A Computer Model of Skill Acquisition", Gerald J. Sussman, *Elsevier*, New York, NY, 1975.

[Teitelbaum, Pellis and Pellis 90] "Can Allied Reflexes Promote the Integration of a Robot's Behavior", Philip Teitelbaum, Vivien C. Pellis and Sergio M. Pellis, *Proc. First Int. Conf. on Simulation of Adaptive Behavior, MIT Press*, Cambridge, MA, 1990, 97–104.

[Thorpe, Hebert, Kanade, and Shafer 88] "Vision and Navigation for the Carnegie-Mellon Navlab", Charles Thorpe, Martial Hebert, Takeo Kanade, and Steven A. Shafer, *IEEE Trans. PAMI, 10(3)*, May 1988, 362–373.

[Tinbergen 51] "The Study of Instinct", Niko Tinbergen, *Oxford University Press*, Oxford, UK, 1951.

[Turing 37] "On Computable Numbers with an Application to the Entscheidungsproblem", Alan M. Turing, *Proc. London Math. Soc. 42*, 1937, 230–65.

[Turing 50] "Computing Machinery and Intelligence", Alan M. Turing, *Mind 59*, Oct. 1950, 433–460, also in **[Feigenbaum and Feldman 63]**.

[Turing 70] "Intelligent Machinery", Alan M. Turing, *Machine Intelligence 5, Bernard Meltzer and Donald Michie* (eds), *American Elsevier Publishing*, New York, NY, 1970, 3–23.

[Turk, Morgenthaler, Gremban, and Marra 88] "VITS-A Vision System for Autonomous Land Vehicle Navigation", Matthew A. Turk, David G. Morgenthaler, Keith D. Gremban, and Martin Marra, *IEEE Trans. PAMI, 10(3)*, May 1988, 342–361.

[Viola 90] "Adaptive Gaze Control", Paul A. Viola, *MIT SM Thesis*, 1990.

[Von Neumann and Morgenstern 44] "Theory of Games and Economic Behavior", J. von Neumann and O. Morgenstern, *John Wiley and Sons*, New York, NY, 1944.

[Walter 50] "An Imitation of Life", W. Grey Walter, *Scientific American, 182(5)*, May 1950, 42–45.

[Walter 51] "A Machine That Learns", W. Grey Walter, *Scientific American, 185(2)*, August 1951, 60–63.

[Walter 53] "The Living Brain", W. Grey Walter, *Duckworth*, London, 1953, republished by *Penguin*, Harmondsworth, UK, 1961.

[Watkins 89] "Learning from Delayed Rewards", Christopher Watkins, *Ph.D. Thesis*, King's College, Cambridge, 1989.

[Waxman, Le Moigne and Srinivasan 85] "Visual Navigation of Roadways", Allen M. Waxman, Jacqueline Le Moigne and Babu Srinivasan, *Proc. IEEE Robotics and Automation*, St Louis, MO, 1985, 862–867.

[Wehner 87] "'Matched Filters' – Neural Models of the External World", Rüdiger Wehner, *J. comp. Physiol. A 161*, 1987, 511–531.

[Wiener 48] "Cybernetics", Norbert Wiener, *John Wiley and Sons*, New York, NY, 1948.

[Wiener 61] "Cybernetics", Norbert Wiener, *Second Edition, MIT Press*, Cambridge, MA, 1961.

[Wilkins 79] "Using Patterns and Plans to Solve Problems and Control Search", David E. Wilkins, *Stanford AI Memo 329*, July, 1979.

[Williams 83] "From Napier to Lucas", Michael R. Williams, *Annals of the History of Computing*, (5)3, 1983, 279–96.

[Winograd 72] "Understanding Natural Language", Terry Winograd, *Academic Press*, New York, NY, 1972.

[Winograd and Flores 86] "Understanding Computers and Cognition", Terry Winograd and Fernando Flores, *Addison-Wesley*, Reading, MA, 1986.

[Winston 72] "The MIT Robot", Patrick H. Winston, *Machine Intelligence 7, Bernard Meltzer and Donald Michie* (eds), *John Wiley and Sons*, New York, NY, 1972, 431–463.

[Winston 84] "Artificial Intelligence", Patrick Henry Winston, *Second Edition, Addison-Wesley*, Reading, MA, 1984.

[Wood 88] "The Nematode *Caenorhabditis Elegans*", William B. Wood, *Cold Spring Harbor Laboratory*, Cold Spring Harbor, NY, 1988.

LOGIC PROGRAMMING IN ARTIFICIAL INTELLIGENCE

Robert A. Kowalski
Department of Computing
Imperial College of Science, Technology and Medicine
London SW7 2BZ, UK

1. INTRODUCTION

Logic programming originated in the field of artificial intelligence. It was artificial intelligence that provided both the theorem-proving research for its backward-reasoning execution strategy [42,47,68] and its first intended applications in natural language question-answering [14]. It also provided the controversy (see e.g. [32,81]). between the relative merits of procedural versus declarative representations of knowledge, which helped to motivate the procedural interpretation of Horn clauses, which is the basis of logic programming, even today.

In this short paper I will sketch some of the subsequent developments in logic programming, concentrating especially on extensions which have been developed to make logic programming more suitable for knowledge representation in artificial intelligence. I will focus particularly on developments in non-monotonic reasoning, abduction, and metareasoning. I will also argue that the unrestricted use of full first-order logic might not be necessary or useful for most applications.

2. THE SCOPE OF LOGIC PROGRAMMING FORM

Logic programming was originally restricted to sentences (also called *rules*) in *Horn clause* form:

A if B_1 and ... and B_n

with a single atomic conclusion A and zero or more atomic conditions B_i. All variables, X_1, ... , X_m, occurring in a rule are universally quantified in front of the rule:

for all X_1, ... , X_m [A if B_1 and ... and B_n]

Today the notion of logic programming also includes rules whose conditions are arbitrary formulae of first-order logic. Lloyd and Topor [51,52] showed how to reduce such more general rules to *normal logic programming form,* where each condition is either an atomic formula or the negation of an atomic formula. Similarly the conditions B_i in *queries*

? B_1 and ... and B_n

to a logic program can be arbitrary formulae of first-order logic. Such queries can be reduced to a normal logic program together with a *normal query,* in which all conditions are atomic formulae or negations of atomic formulae.

The basis of logic programming is the interpretation of rules as procedures:

reduce problems of the form A
to subproblems of the form B_1, ... , B_n.

The significance of this *procedural interpretation* is two-fold: Not only can declarative sentences be executed as procedures, but procedures in problem-reduction form can be interpreted declaratively as statements of logic. In this way logic programming reconciles declarative and procedural representations of knowledge.

Today many artificial intelligence applications are explicitly represented in logic programming form, and many of these are implemented in a logic programming language such as Prolog. However, many other applications are represented *de facto* as logic programs, without explicit acknowledgement of the fact. The situation calculus and its application to the Yale shooting problem [31] are among the most interesting examples. The case of the Yale shooting problem is especially interesting, because as pointed out in [2,24,25] the use of negation by failure in logic programming solves the problem of non-monotonic reasoning which arises in the example. The procedural interpretation and operational semantics of negation by failure are discussed in section 4 below.

In addition to these artificial intelligence applications explicitly or implicitly formulated as logic programs, there are many others implemented in "if-then" languages [82], which approximate logic programming form. Most of these languages, many of which are in the EMYCIN family [79], have only the expressive power of variable-free (i.e. propositional) logic programs augmented with some form of "isa-hierarchy" for taxonomic reasoning, compensating for the propositional nature of the rules.

Other applications of logic, not restricted to those exclusively associated with artificial intelligence, such as those to do with the formal specification of programs, the implementation of database systems, and the formalisation of legislation, show a similar bias towards the use of logic programming form. Applications to legislation [44,45,49,70] have special significance for knowledge representation in artificial intelligence, because the law deals with every aspect of human affairs. They also have special significance for logic programming, because they provide a rich source of material for guiding the development of its extensions. It is interesting that the extensions needed for legislation do not seem to include disjunctions in the conclusions of rules or complex forms of quantification.

3. THE IF-AND-ONLY-IF FORM OF LOGIC PROGRAMS

It seems that many applications of logic in artificial intelligence which can not be reduced to normal logic programming form can be understood instead as expressing the only-if halves of if-and-only-if definitions.

Normal logic programs, on the other hand, can be understood as expressing the if-halves of definitions. The program

```
parent(X, Y) if mother(X, Y)
parent(X, Y) if father(X, Y)
mother(mary, jack)
mother(mary, jill)
father(john, jack)
father(john, jill)
```

for example, is the if-half of the if-and-only-if definitions

```
parent(X,Y) iff [mother(X,Y) or father(X,Y)]
mother(X,Y) iff [(X=mary and Y=jack) or
                 (X=mary and Y=jill)]
father(X,Y) iff [(X=john and Y=jack) or
                 (X=john and Y=jill)]
```

augmented with appropriate axioms of equality and inequality, such as

X=X

$s \neq t$, for every pair of distinct terms s,t.

It can be argued [43] that the if-and-only-if form expresses the semantics intended by the if-form.

It seems to be the case that reasoning with the if-halves of definitions can simulate reasoning with the only-if halves and vice-versa. Consider, for example, the assertion

parent(x, jack)

where x is a constant. Reasoning forward using the only-if half of the definitions we can derive first

mother(x, jack) or father(x, jack)

then

(x = mary and jack = jack) or
(x = mary and jack = jill) or
(x = john and jack = jack) or
(x = john and jack = jill).

Simplifying this disjunction, we obtain the final conclusion:

x = mary or x = john.

This conclusion is dual (see e.g. [16]) to the one we obtain by reasoning backward, logic programming style, and deriving all answers to the query

? parent(X, jack)

where X is a variable:

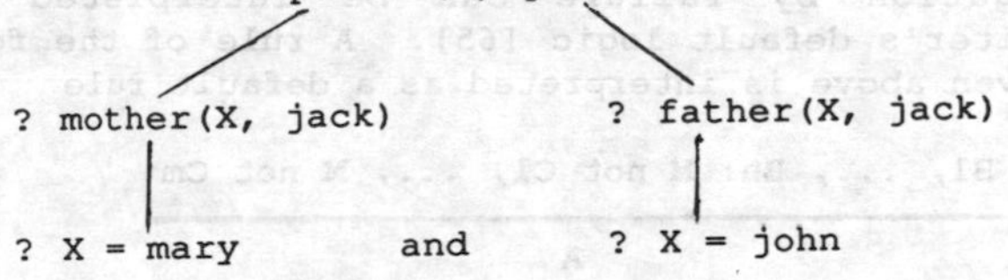

Thus backward reasoning using the if-halves of the definitions simulates forward reasoning with the only-if halves. Moreover implicit reasoning with equality by means of unification simulates explicit reasoning with equality and inequality axioms.

The simulation of only-if halves of definitions by if-halves is also the basis for Clark's result [9] that negation by failure is a correct implementation of classical negation.

4. NON-MONOTONIC REASONING IN LOGIC PROGRAMMING

The execution of negative conditions in logic programs is performed by *negation by failure*:

not P holds if and only if
P fails to hold.

Clark [9] showed that finite failure to demonstrate P using the if-halves of definitions simulates proof of not P using the only-if halves. Reiter [66] showed that the if-and-only-if form (also called the *completion* or *Clark-completion*) of a logic program is "sometimes" equivalent to McCarthy's circumscription [54].

Despite the attractions of the completion as a semantics for negation by failure, it has a number of limitations, which have been addressed by subsequent investigators. Kunen [50] and Fitting [27] for example have proposed three-valued logic for the semantics of the completion. Apt, Blair and Walker [2], Przymuszynski [63,64] and van Gelder [76,77] have proposed extensions of the least fix point and minimal model semantics originally developed for Horn clauses by van Emden and Kowalski [75].

More recently Gelfond [28] showed that negation by failure in logic programming can be interpreted in Moore's autoepistemic logic [58]. A rule of the form

A if B_1 and ... B_n not C_1 and ... not C_m

where B_i and C_i are atomic formulae, can be interpreted as a sentence

A if B_1 and ... B_n and not LC_1 and ... not LC_m

where LC_i means C_i is believed, and therefore not LC_i means C_i is not believed. Gelfond and Lifschitz subsequently showed how to adapt the semantics of autoepistemic logic to obtain a direct *stable model semantics* [29] for normal logic programs.

Marek and Truszczynski [55] showed how negation by failure can be interpreted in Reiter's default logic [65]. A rule of the form given above is interpreted as a default rule

$$\frac{B1, \ldots, Bn: \mathbf{M}\ \text{not}\ C1, \ldots, \mathbf{M}\ \text{not}\ Cm}{A}$$

Eshghi and Kowalski [24] have shown that negation by failure can be interpreted as a case of abduction:

not C_1, ... , not C_m

are hypotheses which are assumed to hold, provided there is no evidence to the contrary. The abductive interpretation of negation by failure has been developed further by Kakas and Mancarella [37] and Dung [22].

5. ABDUCTION

Abduction has many applications in artificial intelligence, including fault diagnosis [8,62], image recognition [19], plan formation [23], plan recognition [8], temporal reasoning [71], and natural language understanding [8,74]. It can also be used for knowledge assimilation [38,39] and default reasoning [24,61].

Various strategies have been developed for generating abductive hypotheses. Most of these are based on resolution [19,26]. The ATMS approach developed by Reiter and deKleer [67] for propositional Horn clauses also uses a form of resolution, together with subsumption, called *consensus*. The use of subsumption guarantees that the hypotheses which are generated are minimal.

Similar strategies have also been developed for generating conditional answers within a logic programming "query-the-user" framework [69]. Instead of failing in a proof when a condition selected for execution fails to unify with the conclusion of any rule or can not be answered by the user, the condition is set aside as a hypothesis for the answer. Thus, for example, given the program

```
wobbly-wheel if broken-spokes
wobbly-wheel if flat-tyre
flat-tyre if punctured-tube
flat-tyre if leaky-valve
```

and the observed conclusion

wobbly-wheel

backward reasoning eventually reduces the conclusion to the hypotheses

broken-spokes
punctured-tube
leaky-valve

each of which is an alternative explanation of the observation.

In the general case such hypotheses have to be tested for compatibility with integrity constraints. In most applications the use of backward reasoning makes it unnecessary to test hypotheses for minimality.

Console, Theseidre Dupré and Torasso [15] have noted that abductive reasoning using the if-halves of if-and-only-if definitions can be replaced by deduction using the only-if halves. For example, using the only-if halves of the completion

```
wobbly-wheel iff [broken-spokes or flat-tyre]
flat-tyre iff [punctured-tube or leaky-valve].
```

forward reasoning from the observation

wobbly-wheel

generates the disjunction

broken-spokes or punctured-tube or leaky-valve.

Thus we see another example of a correspondence between if-halves and only-if halves of the if-and-only-if form of logic programs. Such examples give added support to the thesis that logic programming appropriately extended might provide a general basis for knowledge representation and reasoning in artificial intelligence.

6. "REAL" NEGATION

Recently, extensions of logic programming have been developed in which the conclusions of rules can be negations of atomic formulae. Gelfond and Lifschitz [29] in particular have shown how to extend the stable model semantics to allow logic programs to contain both "real" negation, "¬", as well as negation by failure, "not". Kowalski and Sadri [48] have adapted their semantics so that rules with negative conclusions are interpreted as exceptions to rules with positive conclusions.

Applied to the well-known example

```
 fly(X) if bird(X)
¬fly(X) if ostrich(X)
 bird(X) if ostrich(X)
 ostrich(tom)
```

the semantics gives the result

¬fly(tom)

but not the result

fly(tom).

Equivalent results can also be obtained by combining both forms of negation:

```
fly(X) if bird(X) and not ¬ fly(X)
¬fly(X) if ostrich(X)
bird(X) if ostrich(X)
ostrich(tom).
```

Under this adaptation of the stable model semantics, both formulations are essentially equivalent to a conventional formulation in normal logic programming form

```
fly(X) if bird(X) and not ab(X)
ab(X) if ostrich(X)
bird(X) if ostrich(X)
ostrich(tom)
```

where the negative predicate ¬ fly(X) is renamed as a positive predicate ab(X).

Thus under this semantics, programs combining real negation and negation by failure can be transformed back into normal logic programs with only negation by failure. Nonetheless, empirical studies of the language of legislation [44] suggest that the extension of logic programming to include negation in the conclusion of rules is essential for naturalness of expression in practice.

7. METALOGIC PROGRAMMING

Metaprogramming, in which programs, databases, and "theories" in general are manipulated as data, is an important technique in logic programming methodology [5,43,73]. It is used for such applications as program transformation and verification, knowledge base management, and the implementation of expert system shells. It is commonly used to overcome the limitations of Prolog's simple execution strategy and to implement more sophisticated execution methods.

Metalogic programming is usually carried out with the aid of a one-argument predicate

solve(X), which holds when the goal X can be solved,

or with a two-argument predicate

demo(X, Y), which holds when the goal Y can be solved (or demonstrated) using the program, database, or theory X.

It is common to augment the metapredicate with extra arguments representing such entities as proof, uncertainty, or time.

The metapredicate can be implemented by reflection rules as in Weyhrauch's FOL [80] or Costantini and Lanzaroni's [18] Reflective Prolog. It can, and more usually is, implemented by means of a metainterpreter, as in the following case where the extra argument represents a time point:

```
demo(X, Y, T)   if  demo(X, Y ← Z, T)
                    and demo(X, Z, T)
demo(X, Y ∧ Z, T) if  demo(X, Y, T)
                    and demo(X, Z, T)
demo(example, mortal(X) ← human (X), T)
demo(example, human(socrates), T)
                    if 380 b.c. ≤ T
demo(example, human(turing), T)
                    if 1912 a.d. ≤ T
```

Here "←" and "∧" are infix function symbols naming "if" and "and". The constant symbol "example" names an object level theory.

The computational overheads of running the metainterpreter can be alleviated by "top-down" partial evaluation [74a] or "bottom-up" data-driven, transformation [17]. In the example above, the five rules can be replaced by three:

```
demo(example, mortal(X), T)
                    if demo(example, human(X), T)
demo(example, human(socrates), T)
        if 380 b.c. ≤ T
demo(example, human(turing), T)
        if 1912 a.d. ≤ T
```

These rules can be simplified further. If we rename predicates, replacing

```
demo(example, mortal(X),T)  by  mortal*(X,T)
demo(example, human(X),T)   by  human*(X,T)
```

we obtain the essentially equivalent object level rules:

```
mortal*(X, T) if human*(X, T)
human*(socrates, T) if 380 b.c. ≤ T
human*(turing, T) if 1912 a.d. ≤ T
```

Metalogic programming can also be used to implement more powerful object level reasoning, for example by means of such metarules as

```
demo(X, Y) if  demo(X, Y ∨ Z)
               and demo(X, ¬ Z)
```

where "∨" and "¬" are function symbols naming disjunction and negation respectively. Such use of a restricted metalanguage to implement and reason about a more powerful object language is reminiscent of Hilbert's program to use a finitary metatheory to justify non-constructive mathematics (see e.g. [40]).

The proof predicate

demo(X, Y)

can also be used to represent belief:

X believes Y.

Such an interpretation of belief as provability in artificial intelligence has been advocated in different ways by Konolige [41] and Perlis [60]. The use of the demo predicate within a logic programming framework to represent multi-agent knowledge and belief has been studied by Kowalski and Kim [46].

The use of metalogic is essential also when logic programming is used to represent legislation. It is needed, for example, to represent situations where one statute refers to another, or where one provision refers to another provision of the same statute. It is needed also [45] to represent explicitly the executive agency's reasoning process.

Metalogic gives much of the power of higher order logic. Conversely, higher-order logic, as incorporated in Miller's λ-Prolog [56] for example, can also be used for metaprogramming.

8. TERMINOLOGICAL REASONING

Beginning with the language KLONE [6], there has been much interest in recent years in languages and logics specifically designed for "terminological reasoning". In these logics, terms denote sets, and logical operators such as conjunction, disjunction, negation and quantification, which can be applied to terms, denote operations on sets. The important logical properties of such *structured terms* are whether a term is *satisfiable* (denotes a non-empty set) and whether one term *subsumes* another (denotes a set which includes the set denoted by the other).

Ait Kasi and Nasr [1] have shown how to extend logic programming to include structured terms. Such extensions combine the advantages of logic programming with those of terminological reasoning. More recently, Bürkert [7] and Höhfeld and Smolka [33] have shown that such a combination of logic programming and terminological reasoning can be obtained by incorporating equations over structured terms as constraints within a constraint logic programming framework.

9. CONSTRAINT LOGIC PROGRAMMING

In constraint logic programming, the conditions of rules are partitioned into two kinds. One kind is executed normally by backward reasoning. The other kind is treated in a domain-specific manner as a constraint. Constraints are simplified and tested for satisfiability using algorithms specific to the given problem domain.

The first language incorporating an early notion of constraint logic programming was Colmerauer's Prolog II [13], since extended to Prolog III [12]. The underlying theory was developed by Jaffar, Lassez, and Maher [36]. Some of the most successful applications have been implemented using CHIP [21], the language developed at ECRC.

Constraint logic programming has proved to be a fruitful paradigm for integrating logic programming with special-purpose problem-solving mechanisms for mathematical programming, functional programming, and finite domains. It may be that many of the special-purpose problem solving methods developed in artificial intelligence can usefully be integrated with logic programming in this way.

10. FORMAL METHODS

Logic has traditionally been used to formalise program specifications for program verification and synthesis. For such purposes, logic programming has the advantage over other programming approaches that programs and specifications are written in the same logical formalism. Moreover program execution, verification, and synthesis can all be performed using similar logical reasoning techniques. These characteristics of logic programming have motivated many investigations (e.g. [10,11,34,35]) into the problem of deriving efficient logic programs from more obviously correct, but inefficient, logical specifications. These studies are important for artificial intelligence, because they show how rigorous, formal methods can be applied to artificial intelligence applications.

11. LEARNING

It is not always possible or convenient to rigorously formulate a program specification, either before or after writing a program. In many such cases, however, it is natural to specify the intended program informally by means of examples. The simple form of logic programs makes them especially amenable to such learning methods.

Ehud Shapiro's early work [72] was specifically oriented toward learning logic programs. Many other learning methods generate logic programs implicitly without explicitly acknowledging that fact. It has been shown, for example, that explanation-based learning can be viewed as partial evaluation of logic programs [78].

Recent work (see e.g. Muggleton [59] and De Raedt [20]) has begun to show that non trivial logic programs can be generated automatically from examples. Techniques which treat negative examples as exceptions to rules that generalise positive examples [4] seem to be especially appropriate for formulation as logic programs combining real negation with negation by failure.

12. CONCLUSION

I have argued that, to be more useful for knowledge representation and reasoning in artificial intelligence, normal logic programming needs to be extended to include such additional features as real negation, abduction, metareasoning, terminological reasoning and constraint solving. Other extensions such as temporal reasoning and uncertainty can be implemented conveniently by metalogic programming techniques. Disjunctive logic programming, in which conclusions of rules can be disjunctions, has also been developed, notably by Loveland [53] and Minker [57] and their colleagues. Characteristic applications for these systems remain to be identified.

The field of logic programming enjoys a healthy interaction between its theory and its practice. It also enjoys good connections with diverse areas of computing including database systems, formal methods and artificial intelligence, as well as with areas outside of computing including mathematics and legal reasoning. In my opinion, however, it is the links which logic programming retains with artificial intelligence and the emerging links with legal reasoning which will be most important for the development of logic programming in the future.

ACKNOWLEDGEMENTS

This research was supported by ESPRIT Basic Research Project "Compulog" and by Fujitsu. I am grateful to Phan Minh Dung and Tony Kakas for helpful comments on a draft of this paper.

REFERENCES

[1] Ait Kaci, H. and Nasr, R. [1986]: LOGIN: "A logic programming language with built-in inheritance", Journal of Logic Programming, Vol. 3, pp. 185-215.

[2] Apt, K.R. and Bezem, M. [1990]: "Acyclic programs", Proc. of the Seventh International Conference on Logic Programming, MIT Press, pp. 579-597.

[3] Apt, K., Blair, H. and Walker, A. [1987]: "Towards a theory of declarative knowledge". In J. Minker, editor, Foundations of Deductive Databases and Logic Programming, Morgan Kaufmann, Los Altos, C.A. pp. 89-142.

[4] Bain, M. and Muggleton, S. [1990]: "Non-monotonic Learning" Machine Intelligence 12, Oxford University Press.

[5] Bowen, K.A. and Kowalski, R.A. [1982]: "Amalgamating Language and Metalanguage in Logic Programming", in Logic Programming (Clark, K.L. and Tärnlund, S.-Å., editors), Academic Press, pp. 153-173.

[6] Brachmann, R.J. and Levesque, H.J. [1984]: "The tractability of subsumption in frame based description languages", Proceedings of the Fourth National Conference of the AAAI, pp. 34-37.

[7] Bürckert, H.J.[1990]: "A resolution principle for clauses with constraints", Proc. 10th CADE, LNAI 449, pp. 178-192.

[8] Charniak, E. and McDermott, D. [1985]: "Introduction to Artificial Intelligence", Addison-Wesley.

[9] Clark, K.L. [1978]: "Negation by failure", in "Logic and databases", Gallaire, H. and Minker, J. [eds], Plenum Press, pp. 293-322.

[10] Clark, K.L. and Darlington, J. [1980]: "Algorithm classification through synthesis", Computer J. pp. 61-65.

[11] Clark, K.L. and Tärnlund, S.-A. [1977]: "A first-order theory of data and programs", In Proc IFIP 1977. Amsterdam: North-Holland, pp. 939-944.

[12] Colmerauer, A. [1990]: "An introduction to PROLOG III", Comm. ACM, pp. 70-90.

[13] Colmerauer, A., Kanoui, H. and Caneghem, M.V. [1983]: "Prolog, theoretical principles and current trends", Technology and Science of Informatics, Vol. 2, No. 4, pp. 255-292.

[14] Colmerauer, A., Kanoui, H., Pasero, R. and Roussel, P. [1973] "Un systéme de communication homme-machine en Français", Groupe d'Intelligence Artificielle, Univ. d'Aix Marseille II, Luminy, France.

[15] Console, L., Theseider Dupré, D. and Torasso, P. [1990]: "A completion semantics for object-level abduction", Proc. AAAI Symposium on Automated Abduction, Stanford, March 1990.

[16] Copi, I.M. [1954]: "Symbolic Logic", The MacMillan Company, New York.

[17] Cosmodopoulos,Y., Sergot, M., and Southwick, R.W. [1991]: "A general data-driven transformation of meta-interpreters", Department of Computing, Imperial College, London.

[18] Costantini, S. and Lanzarone, G. A. [1989]: "A metalogic programming language", Proc. Sixth International Conference on Logic Programming, MIT press, pp.218-233.

[19] Cox, P.T. and Pietrzykowski, T. [1986]: "Causes for Events: Their Computation and Applications", in Proceedings CADE-86, pp 608-621.

[20] De Raedt, L. [1991]: Interactive concept-learning. PhD thesis, Department of Computer Science, Katholieke Universiteit Leuven.

[21] Dincbas, M., van Hentenryck, P., Simonis, H., Aggoun, A., Graf, T. and Berthier. F. [1988] "The constraint logic programming language CHIP", In Proceedings of the International Conference on Fifth Generation Computer Systems FGCS-88, pp. 693-702.

[22] Dung, P.M. [1991]: "Negations as hypotheses: an abductive foundation for logic programming", Proc. ICLP-91, MIT Press.

[23] Eshghi, K. [1988]: "Abductive planning with event calculus", Proceedings of the 5th International Conference on Logic Programming, MIT press.

[24] Eshghi, K. and Kowalski, R.A. [1989]: "Abduction compared with negation by failure", Proceedings of the Sixth International Logic Programming Conference, MIT Press, pp. 234-255.

[25] Evans, C. [1989]: "Negation-as-failure as an approach to the Hanks and McDermott problem", Proc. Second International Symposium on Artificial Intelligence, Monterrey, Mexico.

[26] Finger, J.J. and Genesereth, M.R. [1985]: "RESIDUE: A Deductive Approach to Design Synthesis", Stanford University Report No. CS-85-1035.

[27] Fitting, M. [1985]: "A Kripke-Kleene semantics for logic programs". Journal of Logic Programming, Vol. 2. No. 4. pp 295-312.

[28] Gelfond, M. [1987]: "On stratified autoepistemic theories", In Proceedings AAAI-87, American Association for Artificial Intelligence, Morgan Kaufmann, Los Altos, CA, pp. 207-211

[29] Gelfond, M. and Lifschitz, V. [1988]: "The stable model semantics for logic programs", Proceedings of the Fifth International Conference and Symposium on Logic Programming, MIT press pp. 1070-1080.

[30] Gelfond, M. and Lifschitz, V. [1990]: "Logic programs with classical negation", Proceedings of the Seventh International Conference on Logic Programming, MIT Press, pp. 579-597.

[31] Hanks, S. and McDermott, D. [1986]: "Default reasoning, non-monotonic logics, and the frame problem", Proc. AAAI, Morgan and Kaufman, pp. 328-333.

[32] Hewitt, C. [1969]: "PLANNER; A language for proving theorems in robots", In Proceedings of IJCAI-1 (Washington, D.C.), pp. 295-301.

[33] Höfeld, M. and Smolka, G. [1988]: "Definite relations over constraint languages", LILOG Report 53, IWBS, IBM Deutschland, Stuttgart, Germany. To appear in the Journal of Logic Programming.

[34] Hogger, C.J. [1981]: "Derivation of logic programs", J. Ass. Comput. Mach. Vol. 28, pp. 372-422.

[35] Hogger, C.J. [1984]: Introduction to Logic Programming, Academic Press, London.

[36] Jaffar, J., Lassez, J. and Maher, M. [1987]: "Constraint Logic Programming" in Proc. of 14th ACM Symp. POPL.

[37] Kakas, A.C. and Mancarella, P. [1990], "Generalised stable models: a semantics for abduction", Proceedings of ECAI 90, pp. 385-391.

[38] Kakas, A.C. and Mancarella, P. [1990], "Database updates through abduction", Proceedings of VLDB 90.

[39] Kakas, A.C. and Mancarella, P. [1990]: "Knowledge Assimilation and Abduction", Proceedings of the ECAI-1990 Workshop on Truth Maintenance Systems, Springer-Verlag, 1990.

[40] Kleene, S.C. [1952]: "Introduction to Metamathematics", D. van Nostrand Co., Princeton.

[41] Konolige, K. [1986]: "A Deduction Model of Belief", Pitman Research Notes in Artificial Intelligence.

[42] Kowalski, R.A. [1974]: "Predicate logic as programming language", In Proceedings of IFIP 1974 (Stockholm, Sweden). North-Holland, Amsterdam, pp. 569-574).

[43] Kowalski, R.A. [1979]: Logic for problem solving. New York: Elsevier

[44] Kowalski, R.A. [1989]: "The treatment of negation in logic programs for representing legislation", Proceedings of the Second International Conference on Artificial Intelligence and Law, pp. 11-15.

[45] Kowalski, R.A. [1991]: "Legislation as logic programs", Department of Computing, Imperial College, London.

[46] Kowalski, R.A. and Kim, J.S. [1991]: "A metalogic programming approach to multi-agent knowledge and belief", to appear in Artificial Intelligence and Mathematical Theory of Computation (V. Lifschitz, ed.) Academic Press.

[47] Kowalski, R.A. and Kuehner, D. [1971] "Linear resolution with selection function". Artif. Intell. Vol. 2, pp. 227-260.

[48] Kowalski, R.A. and Sadri, F. [1990]: "Logic programs with exceptions", Proceedings of the Seventh International Conference on Logic Programming, MIT Press, pp. 598-613.

[49] Kowalski, R A., Sergot, M.J. [1990]: "The use of logical models in legal problem solving", Ratio Juris, Vol. 3, No. 2, pp. 201-218.

[50] Kunen, K. [1987]: "Negation in logic programming" Journal of Logic Programming, Vol. 4, No. 4, pp. 289-308.

[51] Lloyd, J.W. and Topor, R.W. [1984]: "Making Prolog more expressive", Journal of Logic Programming, Vol. 3, No. 1, pp. 225-240.

[52] Lloyd J.W. [1987]: "Foundations of logic programming", second extended edition, Springer-Verlag.

[53] Loveland, D.W. [1987]: "Near-Horn Prolog" Logic Programming: Proceedings of the Fourth International Conference, MIT Press, pp 456-469.

[54] McCarthy, J. [1980]: "Circumscription - a form of nonmonotonic reasoning", Artificial Intelligence, Vol. 26, No. 3, pp. 89-116.

[55] Marek, W. and Truszczynski, M. [1989]: "Stable semantics for logic programs and default theories", Proc. NACLP-89, MIT Press.

[56] Miller, D. and Nadathur, G. [1986]: "Higher-order logic programming", Proceedings of the Third International Conference on Logic Programming, Springer-Verlag, pp. 448-462.

[57] Minker, J. [1989]: "Toward a foundation of disjunctive logic programming" Logic Programming: Proceedings of the North American Conference, MIT Press, pp. 1215-1235.

[58] Moore, R.C. [1985]: "Semantical considerations on nonmonotonic logic in artificial intelligence", Artificial Intelligence, Vol. 25, pp. 75-94.

[59] Muggleton, S. [1991]: "Inductive logic programming", New Generation Computing, Vol. 8, pp. 295-318.

[60] Perlis, D. [1988]: "Language with Self-Reference II: Knowledge, Belief and Modality", Artificial Intelligence Vol. 34, pp. 179-212.

[61] Poole, D. [1988]: "A logical framework for default reasoning", Artificial Intelligence Vol. 36, pp. 27-47.

[62] Pople, H.E., Jr. [1973]: "On the mechanization of abductive logic" Proc. Third IJCAI, Stanford, Ca. pp 147-152.

[63] Przymuszynski, T. [1987]: "On the declarative semantics of stratified deductive databases and logic programs". In J. Minker, editor, Foundations of Deductive Databases and Logic Programming, Morgan Kaufmann, Los Altos, CA., pp 193-216

[64] Przymuszynski, T. [1989]: "Non-monotonic formalisms and logic programming", Proceedings of the Sixth International Logic Progamming Conference, MIT Press, pp. 655-674.

[65] Reiter, R. [1980]: "A logic for default reasoning", Artificial Intelligence, Vol. 13, pp. 81-132.

[66] Reiter, R. [1982]: "Circumscription implies predicate completion (sometimes)", Proceedings of the National Conference on Artificial Intelligence, Pittsburgh Pa.

[67] Reiter, R. and deKleer J. [1987]: "Foundations of assumption-based truth maintenance systems: preliminary report", Proc. AAAI-87, Seattle, pp. 183-188.

[68] Robinson, J.A. [1965]: "A machine-oriented logic based on the resolution principle", J. ACM 12, Vol. 1, pp. 23-41.

[69] Sergot, M. [1982]: "A query-the-user facility for logic programming", In Proc. ECICS, Stresa, Italy (eds. P. Degano & E. Sandewall) Amsterdam: North-Holland. pp. 27-41.

[70] Sergot, M.J., Sadri, F., Kowalski, R.A., Kriwaczek, F., Hammond, P. and Cory, H.T. [1986]: "The British Nationality Act as a logic program", CACM, Vol. 29, No. 5, pp. 370-386.

[71] Shanahan, M. [1989]: "Prediction is deduction but explanation is abduction", IJCAI 89.

[72] Shapiro. E.Y. [1983]: Algorithmic Program Debugging. The MIT press.

[73] Sterling, L. and Shapiro, E.Y [1986]: "The Art of Prolog", MIT Press.

[74] Stickel, M.E. [1988]: "A Prolog-like inference system for computing minimum-cost abductive explanations in natural-language interpretation", Proc. International Computer Science Conference (Artificial Intelligence: Theory and Applications) (J.-L. Lassez and F.Y.L. Chin, editors), pp. 343-350.

[74a] Takeuchi, A. and Furukawa, K. [1986]: "Partial evaluation of Prolog programs and its application to metaprogramming", Proc, IFIP, North Holland, pp. 415-420.

[75] van Emden, M.H. and Kowalski, R.A. [1976]: "The semantics of predicate logic as a programming language", J. ACM, Vol. 23, No. 4 (Oct. 1976), pp. 733-742.

[76] van Gelder, A. [1987]: "Negation as failure using tight derivations for general logic programs". In J. Minker, editor, Foundations of Deductive Databases and Logic Programming, Morgan Kaufmann, Los Altos, C.A., pp. 149-176.

[77] van Gelder, A., Ross, K. and Schlipf. [1988]: "Unfounded sets and well-founded semantics for general logic programs". In Proceedings of the Symposium on Principles of Database Systems, ACM SIGACT-SIGMOD.

[78] van Harmelen, F. and Bundy, A. [1988]: "Explanation based generalization = partial evaluation", Artificial Intelligence, Vol. 36, pp. 401-412.

[79] van Melle, W.J. [1980]: System aids in constructing consultation programs, UMI Press, Ann Arbor, Mi.

[80] Weyhrauch, R.W. [1980]: "Prolegomena to a theory of mechanized formal reasoning", Artificial Intelligence Vol. 13, pp. 133-170.

[81] Winograd, T. [1972]: Understanding natural language, Academic Press, New York.

[82] Winston, P.H. [1984]: "Artificial Intelligence", second edition, Addison Wesley.

AUTHOR INDEX